THE SOCIAL CONSTRUCTION
OF DIFFERENCE AND INEQUALITY

THE SOCIAL CONSTRUCTION OF DIFFERENCE AND INEQUALITY
Race, Class, Gender, and Sexuality

FIFTH EDITION

Tracy E. Ore
Saint Cloud State University

Connect
Learn
Succeed™

The McGraw-Hill Companies

Connect
Learn
Succeed™

THE SOCIAL CONSTRUCTION OF DIFFERENCE AND INEQUALITY: RACE, GENDER, AND INEQUALITY, FIFTH EDITION

Published by McGraw-Hill, a business unit of The McGraw-Hill Companies, Inc., 1221 Avenue of the Americas, New York, NY 10020. Copyright © 2011 by The McGraw-Hill Companies, Inc. All rights reserved. Previous editions © 2009, 2006 and 2003. No part of this publication may be reproduced or distributed in any form or by any means, or stored in a database or retrieval system, without the prior written consent of The McGraw-Hill Companies, Inc., including, but not limited to, in any network or other electronic storage or transmission, or broadcast for distance learning.

Some ancillaries, including electronic and print components, may not be available to customers outside the United States.

This book is printed on acid-free paper.

1 2 3 4 5 6 7 8 9 0 DOC/DOC 1 0 9 8 7 6 5 4 3 2 1 0

ISBN 978-0-07-802664-5
MHID 0-07-802664-4

Vice President & Editor-in-Chief: *Michael Ryan*
Vice President EDP/Central Publishing
Services: *Kimberly Meriwether David*
Publisher: *William Glass*
Sponsoring Editor: *Gina Boedeker*
Executive Marketing Manager:
  Pamela S. Cooper
Managing Developmental Editor:
  Meghan Campbell

Senior Project Manager: *Lisa A. Bruflodt*
Design Coordinator: *Margarite Reynolds*
Cover Designer: *Mary-Presley Adams*
Cover Images: *Tracy E. Ore*
Buyer: *Susan K. Culbertson*
Media Project Manager: *Sridevi Palani*
Compositor: *Laserwords Private Limited*
Typeface: *10/12 Book Antiqua*
Printer: *R. R. Donnelley*

All credits appearing on page or at the end of the book are considered to be an extension of the copyright page.

Library of Congress Cataloging-in-Publication Data

The social construction of difference and inequality : race, class, gender, and sexuality / [selected and edited by] Tracy E. Ore. — 5th ed.
    p. cm.
  Includes bibliographical references and index.
  ISBN 978-0-07-802664-5 (alk. paper)
  1. Cultural pluralism—United States. 2. Equality—United States. 3. Minorities—United States—Social conditions. 4. Social classes—United States. 5. Women—United States—Social conditions. 6. Gays—United States—Social conditions. 7. Discrimination—United States. 8. United States—Social conditions—1980- 9. United States—Race relations. 10. United States—Ethnic relations. I. Ore, Tracy E.
HN59.2.S585 2010
305.0973—dc22

                                                                    2010038242

www.mhhe.com

*This book is dedicated to the memory of my brother Brian . . .
and to all others lost in the continuing crisis of AIDS.*

About the Author

Tracy E. Ore is a professor of Sociology and the Interim Associate Provost of Undergraduate Education and Student Support Services at Saint Cloud State University. She received her Ph.D. in sociology from the University of Michigan. Her teaching areas include race and ethnicity, social inequality, democracy and citizenship, the ethics of sociological practice, social movements, and the global politics of food. She does research in the areas of sustainable agriculture, technology and the scholarship of teaching and learning, race and ethnicity, oppression and inequality, and the development of effective teaching pedagogy. She serves as a consultant for multicultural education and curriculum to a variety of organizations, and agencies and conducts workshops and trainings related to issues of inequality. She is an active member of the American Sociological Association, the Midwest Sociological Society, and the Sociologists for Women in Society.

Contents

PART II: MAINTAINING INEQUALITIES: SYSTEMS OF OPPRESSION AND PRIVILEGE   214

Examining what elements of social structure work to maintain systems of stratification based on constructions of difference.

Social Institutions: Family   240

Social Institutions: Education   303

Social Institutions: Media   458

Language and Culture   537

Violence and Social Control   584

PART III: EXPERIENCING DIFFERENCE AND INEQUALITY IN EVERYDAY LIFE   642

Examining the impact of constructions of difference and maintaining inequalities on members of society.

PART IV: RESISTANCE AND SOCIAL CHANGE   747

Examining how people working within individual and institutional contexts transform difference from a system of inequality to a system of liberation.

 Preface

Teaching about issues of inequality in a culture that focuses on individualism can be a very daunting task. Having been raised in such a culture, students in my classes often arrive with little knowledge of the systemic nature of inequality in society. While they may be aware of their own experiences of disadvantage (and perhaps privilege), they are generally not aware of how structural arrangements in society result in systems of difference and inequality. This book, which focuses on how race, class, gender, and sexuality are socially constructed as categories of difference and are maintained as systems of inequality, is an effort to help students move toward a more systemic understanding.

WHY ANOTHER RACE, CLASS, GENDER (AND SEXUALITY) READER?

With the plethora of readers on race, class, and gender currently on the market, one may wonder why another is needed. Indeed, some excellent anthologies are available that can be quite effective in demonstrating the impact of race, class, and gender inequality on the life chances of various individuals and groups in our society. However, very few of these texts thoroughly explain how such categories of difference are created, and even fewer demonstrate how social institutions work to maintain systems of inequality. The text here is structured in a way that examines how and why the categories of race, class, gender, and sexuality are socially constructed, maintained, and experienced.

This anthology is divided into four parts. Each part begins with an introductory essay that offers a conceptual framework illustrating concepts and theories (which are highlighted by boldface type) useful for understanding the issues raised by the readings in that section. These essays are not merely introductions to the readings but rather provide material that will enable students to move beyond them. Part I provides a thorough discussion of what it means to think critically as well as an extensive overview of how and why categories of difference are socially constructed. Part II discusses in greater detail how categories of difference are transformed and maintained as systems of inequality by social institutions. Part III examines how categories of difference and systems of inequality impact the everyday experiences of individuals in our society. Finally, Part IV offers a useful look at perspectives on social change and provides examples of barriers to and opportunities for transforming systems of oppression and privilege into a systems of equal access to opportunity.

In each of these sections the readings and examples were selected to cover a variety of racial and ethnic groups as well as experiences of multiracial identity. In addition, issues of sexuality are incorporated throughout each of the parts of this reader. While a few anthologies have begun to incorporate readings that address inequality on the basis of sexuality, the majority do so on only a superficial level. With the current political and social debate regarding civil rights and sexuality, it is important that texts provide sufficient material to address this area of inequality. Overall, the readings represent myriad individuals with various perspectives and life experiences. Such diversity will aid students' ability to understand perspectives and experiences that differ from their own. Finally, the part introductions as well as many of the readings selected demonstrate the intersections of race, class, gender, and sexuality and stress the importance of viewing them as interlocking systems of oppression and privilege. By moving beyond traditional additive models of examining inequality, students will be better able to see how forms of inequality are interconnected.

A NOTE ON LANGUAGE

As discussed in Part II, language serves as a link between all of the different forms of culture in a society. Although language enables us to communicate with and understand one another, it also incorporates cultural values. Thus the words we use to describe ourselves and others with regard to race, class, gender, and sexuality reflect not only our own values but those of the dominant ideology and popular discourse.

In discussing the experiences of different groups, issues of language can become particularly problematic. For example, as discussed in Part I, categories of race and ethnicity are socially constructed. In addition, the externally created labels for these categories are not always accepted by those viewed as belonging to a particular group. For example, those of Latin American descent may not accept the term *Hispanic*. Similarly, those who are indigenous to North America may not accept the term *American Indian*. However, there is rarely agreement among all members of a particular racial or ethnic group regarding the terminology with which they would like to be identified.

Recognizing the problems and limitations of language, I have attempted to be consistent in the terminology I have used in each part introduction. For example, I use the term *Latina/o* to refer to those of Latin American descent, even though not all people in this group may identify themselves in this way. I also use the terms *black* and *African American* interchangeably, as I do *American Indian* and *Native American*. In using such terms it is not my intention to homogenize divergent experiences. Rather, it is done in an effort to allow discussion of common experiences within groups as well as across groups. The terminology used by the authors of the readings was not altered, however. It is important that readers be mindful of the limitations of my language use as well as those of the other authors within this anthology.

 ## CHANGES TO THIS EDITION

With this fifth edition, I have continued to cover a variety of racial and ethnic groups and to incorporate sexuality throughout. In addition, I have maintained the focus on the intersections of race, class, gender and sexuality as interlocking systems of oppression. To keep the text current with regard to economic conditions, issues of gender and sexuality, the political and social discourse on race, as well as recent events in our country and world, I have updated all relevant statistics and changed many readings, adding a total of fourteen new readings. These include a recent report of the Southern Poverty Law Center illustrating the systemic violence directed at immigrants in the United States, updated discussions of the growing racial wealth gap in the country, demonstrated in Thomas Shapiro's article "Race, Homeownership and Wealth," and continued evidence of racial segregation in education over fifty years after *Brown v. Board of Education* as explained in Richard Kahlenberg's article "The Return of 'Separate But Equal.'" As with the fourth edition, I have selected readings that are engaging for students and that reflect a variety of experiences. I welcome any feedback that instructors and students may have.

 ## INSTRUCTOR'S MANUAL

I have prepared a written an instructor's manual to accompany this text that contains guidelines for discussion for each reading, short-answer and essay questions, suggestions for classroom activities, and recommendations for films/videos. These items were compiled to help instructors further student comprehension of the issues addressed in this volume.

 ## RACE/CLASS/GENDER/SEXUALITY SUPERSITE

This companion Website provides information about the book, including an overview, summaries of key features and what's new in the fifth edition, and information about the author.

Non–text-specific content on this site includes an annotated list of Weblinks to useful sites; a list of professional resources (e.g., professional journals); links to Websites offering current census information; a glossary;

and a comprehensive list (annotated and listed by category) of films and videos in the areas of race, class, gender, ethnicity, and sexuality.
Visit the Website by going to www.mhhe.com/Ore5e.

 ## ACKNOWLEDGMENTS

The inception and completion of this project were made possible through the efforts of many people. Foremost among these, I would like to acknowledge the students at the University of Illinois and their efforts in lobbying for a class on multiculturalism and inequality that would incorporate students' doing service in the community. Without their perseverance and commitment, I would likely not have had the opportunity to teach a course that provided such a wonderful foundation for this book. As has been the case throughout my teaching career, my students are my best teachers. Thanks go to all of my students at the colleges and universities where I have taught. I continue to learn from each of them.

I also would like to acknowledge the work of a wonderful team of reviewers: Jodi Burmeister-May, St. Cloud State University; Denise M. Dalaimo, Mt. San Jacinto College; Sharon Elise, California State University at San Marcos; Kristin G. Esterberg, University of Massachusetts at Lowell; Susan A. Farrell, Kingsborough Community College; Lisa M. Frehill, New Mexico State University; Melinda Goldner, Union College; Kelley Hall, DePauw University; Melissa Herbert, Hamline University; Eleanor A. Hubbard, University of Colorado at Boulder; Melissa Latimer, West Virginia University; Betsy Lucal, Indiana University South Bend; Anne Roschelle, State University of New York at New Paltz; Steve Schacht, State University of New York at Plattsburgh; Susan Shaw, Oregon State University; and Brett Stockdill, California State Polytechnic University at Pomona. Their insights, comments, and suggestions served me greatly in clarifying the direction of this project. I value the contribution each of them made to its completion.

For the second edition, I would like to thank the following team of reviewers: Peter Meiksins, Cleveland State University; Jackie Hogan, Bradley University; Philip A. Broyles, Shippensburg University; Heather E. Dillaway, Michigan State University; Elizabeth J. Clifford, Towson University; Tom Gershick, Illinois State University; Susan A. Farrell, Kingsborough Community College; Kristin G. Esterberg, University of Massachusetts at Lowell; and Eleanor A. Hubbard, University of Colorado at Boulder.

For the third edition, I would like to thank the following reviewers: Kristin Esterberg, University of Massachusetts Lowell; Susan Farrell, Kingsborough Community College; Eleanor Hubbard, University of Colorado Boulder; and Peter Meiksins, Cleveland State University. Again, their suggestions and comments enabled me to continue to improve this project.

For the fourth edition, I would like to thank the following team of reviewers: Tiffany Davis, University of Minnesota; Spencer Hope Davis,

Elon University; Mary Ferguson, University of Missouri-St. Louis; Christina M. Jimenez, University of Colorado at Colorado Springs; Peter Meiksins, Cleveland State University; Chadwick L. Menning, Ball State University; and Tracy Woodard Meyers, Valdosta State University. Their suggestions and comments were incredibly helpful in continuing to produce a text that will be useful to others.

For the fifth edition, I would like to thank the following team of reviewers: Christina Accomando, Humboldt State University; Rose Brewer, University of Minnesota-Twin Cities; Edith Brotman, Towson University; Julie Raulli, Wilson College; Mark Rauls, College of Southern Nevada. Their thoughtful reviews helped to guide me in providing a text that will continue to be useful to instructors in the field.

The production of the first edition of this book and its adherence to schedule was due to the work of many people. Specifically, I would like to thank Jan Fisher, Kathryn Mikulic, and Dave Mason at Publication Services for their excellent copyediting and other support. At Mayfield Publishing I would like to thank Mary Johnson, April Wells-Hayes, Marty Granahan, and Jay Bauer. My deepest thanks go to Serina Beauparlant for believing in this project and for supporting me throughout. With her vision and perseverance, I couldn't have asked for a better editor.

The creation of the second edition is due to the work of Jill Gordon, Sally Constable, Amy Shaffer, Ruth Smith, Lori Koetters, Jenny El-Shamy, Nathan Perry, and Dan Loch at McGraw-Hill. I appreciate your patience, creative efforts, and attention to detail.

The creation of the third edition is due to the work of Sherith Pankratz, Trish Starner, Larry Goldberg, Jill Gordon, Kim Menning, Melissa Williams, and Randy Hurst at McGraw-Hill. I appreciate your work, imagination, and thoroughness.

The creation of the fourth edition is due to the work of Gina Boedeker, Amanda Peabody, Leslie Oberhuber, Rich DeVitto, and Margarite Reynolds at McGraw-Hill. I am in great appreciation of your patience and commitment. The creation of the fifth edition is due to the work of Andrea Edwards, Meghan Campbell, and at McGraw-Hill. I am grateful for your persistence and excellent work.

Completing this project was also made possible through the support and caring of a wonderful community of friends. My thanks go to Eileen Gebbie for reading earlier drafts of this work. I would also like to thank my allies on the Sociology 100 team at the University of Illinois. I could always count on them for unconditional support. Thanks also go to my fellow activists who help me to always keep one foot in reality so that I do not lose perspective. Additionally, I am thankful to my community of friends for sharing their knowledge, insight, and support. Finally, I am incredibly grateful to Kramer, a consistent and stable force in my life. Her love, support, and understanding is all I need to get by.

Tracy E. Ore

PART I
Constructing Differences

INTRODUCTION

In the United States, the Census Bureau attempts to conduct a complete accounting of all residents every 10 years. The data gathered by the Bureau are very important, because they serve to determine the distribution of federal dollars to support housing assistance, highway construction, employment services, schools, hospital services, programs for the elderly, and other funding targets. In the year 2000, persons filling out census forms were given a unique opportunity. For the first time ever, those with mixed racial heritage were permitted to select more than one racial category. As a result of new governmental policy, the category "multiracial" is now a reality in the United States.

Does this mean that people who are multiracial have never before existed in this country? Of course not. Even a superficial exploration of U.S. history will show that multiracial people have been present throughout. The recent study using DNA tests to comfirm that Thomas Jefferson was the father of at least one child by his slave Sally Hemings (Foster et al., 1998) is but one example of how the history of slavery in the United States has contributed to the existence of people of multiracial descent. However, until recently government policies in the United States have not allowed for the recognition of a multiracial identity. Rather, they have enforced policies such as the rule of **hypo-descent**—one drop of black blood makes you black—to maintain distinct racial categories.

The preceding example clearly illustrates how the categories that we use to describe ourselves and those around us are the product of social rather than biological factors. Biologically, people who are multiracial certainly exist throughout the United States. Indeed, it is unlikely that anyone is "racially pure." Nevertheless, it is the social recognition, definition, and grouping of these factors that make them culturally significant in our daily interactions. Our reliance on such distinct categories is made clear when we ask someone whose race is not immediately discernible to us, "What are you?"

These culturally defined classifications are also significant in that they are structured as categories that are fundamentally *different* from one another. Thus, we expect people to be black or white, never in between.[1] It is important to point out, however, that difference isn't necessarily a negative quality. On the contrary, the existence of categories of difference adds a great deal of

---

[1]This is most notable in public discourse about the racial identity of U.S. President Barack Obama. The child of Ann Dunham—a white woman from Kansas—and Barack Obama, Sr.—a man of Luo ethnicity from Nyanza Province, Kenya—President Obama's multiracial identity is a well-known public fact. Nevertheless, he is most predominately recognized as an African American, not a person with a multiracial identity.

1

richness to our lives. The presence of different cultural traditions, types of food, forms of music, and styles of dance serves to make society more interesting. It is not the differences that are the causes of inequality in our culture. Rather, it is the meanings and values applied to these differences that makes them harmful. For example, it is not that people of color are defined as different from whites in the United States but that whites are viewed as superior and as the cultural standard against which all others are judged that transforms categories of race *differences* into a system of racial *inequality.*

The readings in this text explore how categories of difference with regard to race/ethnicity, social class, sex/gender, and sexuality are constructed and then *transformed* into systems of inequality. We will investigate *what* creates these categories and *how* they are constructed, and consider some explanations about *why* these categories are created. It is important that we understand how the processes that construct these categories simultaneously create structures of **social stratification**—a system by which society ranks categories of people in a hierarchy—and how social stratification results in systems of inequality. The readings in this text will aid us in understanding the effects that categories of difference have on *all* members of our society and how this inequality can be addressed. By examining closely the processes that construct categories of difference, we will better understand how they impact our lives. Furthermore, by recognizing how systems of inequality are socially created, we can gain a greater understanding of how to transform such systems into ones of equality.

CRITICAL THINKING

A fundamental component in examining constructions of difference and systems of inequality is **critical thinking** about the social constructs on which systems of inequality rely. This requires us to examine how the social structure has affected our values, attitudes, and behaviors. The object of this text is not to negate your present belief system and provide you with a new one, but rather to provide the tools that will allow you to think critically about the attitudes and opinions you have been given. By thinking critically, we are better able to develop a belief system that we can claim as our own.

Many of us are unsure of what is meant by critical thinking. According to various scholars, critical thinking can involve logical reasoning, reflective judgment, exploring assumptions, creating and testing meanings, identifying contradictions in arguments, and determining the validity of empirical findings and generalized conclusions. For the purposes of this text, to think critically is to ask questions about what is assumed to be real, valued, and significant in our culture. Stephen Brookfield (1987) offers a useful framework for asking these questions. He sees critical thinking as having four primary elements.

First, we must *identify and challenge assumptions.* We should try to identify the assumptions that are at the foundation of the concepts, values, beliefs, and behaviors that we deem important in our society. Once we have identified these assumptions, we need to explore their accuracy and legitimacy, considering whether or not what we take for granted does indeed reflect the realities we experience. For example, a common assumption in the United States is that women are inherently more nurturing than men and that men are inherently more aggressive than women. When thinking critically, ask whether such assumptions reflect reality or if they shape what we observe in the behaviors of women and men. In other words, do we observe women indeed being more nurturing, or do we make note of only their nurturing behavior? In addition, we need to ask whether our expectations of women and men shape the ways in which they act. For example, do men behave in a more aggressive manner because that is what is expected of them? Through identifying and challenging assumptions, we become more aware of how uncritically examined assumptions shape our perceptions and our understanding of our environments.

Second, thinking critically involves *awareness of our place and time in our culture.* When asking questions about aspects of our culture, we need to be aware of our own **standpoint**—the position from which we are asking these questions. In other words, we need to be aware of our location at a particular intersection of culture and history; how that is influenced by our race/ ethnicity, social class, sex/gender, sexuality, ability, age, and other factors; and how these in turn influence the questions we ask and the answers we accept. For example, a millionaire examining the strengths and weaknesses of the U.S. economic system would likely see different problems and solutions to these problems than would a working-class individual. Their respective class standpoints (as well as their race/ethnicity, sex/gender, sexuality, etc.) affect the ways in which they examine the world.

One's standpoint also influences what one sees as "normal" or "ordinary" behavior. This relates to the concept of **enculturation**—immersion in our own culture to the point where we assume that our way of life is "natural" or "normal." Because we are so enculturated into our own societal standards and practices, we often assume that they are the only options and, as a result, we are unaware of alternatives. Furthermore, we often view those who have other cultural standards or practices as behaving in a strange or unnatural manner. For example, people raised in a culture with strict religious teachings based on the idea of a supreme being may be so enculturated that they view those with different notions of religion (or none at all) as strange or odd. As a consequence of the depth of our enculturation we also often possess some level of **ethnocentrism**—the practice of judging another culture using the standards of one's own. Such judging is based on the assumption that one's own group is more important than or superior to other groups (Sumner, 1959). Thus we may judge those who possess different religious beliefs than ourselves not only as strange but as *wrong.* For example, many non-Muslim Americans, fueled by media stereotypes, view the practices of those that follow Islam as inappropriate, if not "un-American."

It is important to point out, however, that ethnocentrism is not in and of itself problematic. Every social system to some degree promotes its ideas and standards. Ethnocentrism becomes a problem when such ideas are used as a basis for treating people in an unequal manner. An alternative to ethnocentrism is **cultural relativism**—judging a culture by its own cultural rules and values. By being cultural relativists we can gain a better understanding of the real meaning of another culture's ideas and standards. In thinking critically it is important that we recognize the depth of our enculturation and how it is manifested in our ethnocentrism, so that we can become aware of our own standpoint and be better able to judge other cultures by their own values and ideas.

Third, when thinking critically we need to *search for alternative ways of thinking.* This means examining the assumptions that form the basis of our ideas and ways of behaving. For example, the United States is currently a society based on the notion of **civil rights**—a system based on majority rule. When we vote, the will of the "majority" becomes the will of all. This system is designed to bring *the greatest good for the greatest number.* In addition, there is a fundamental belief that if one is a "good" citizen, one *earns* rights within society, such as liberty. In a civil rights system some people inevitably do not benefit. Implicit in the statement "the greatest good for the greatest number" is the assumption that society cannot provide for everyone. To think critically about a civil rights system, we must imagine an alternative to this reality. For example, what might it be like to live in a society that operates under a **human rights** framework? Such a system recognizes each person as an individual and as valuable. It is based on the belief that everyone has inalienable rights to housing, food, education, and health care, and that society must provide these to those unable to provide for themselves. What structural changes are necessary to bring about such a society? Furthermore, if we were to create such a society, how might our own lives be transformed? Considering alternatives to current ways of thinking can provide us with new insights about widely accepted ideas.

Fourth, to think critically one must *develop a reflective analysis.* Such an analysis requires that we be skeptical, not in the sense that we don't believe anything we see but rather that we question rigid belief systems. For example, once we become aware that it is possible to have a society that operates under a human rights framework, we come to question those who claim that a system based on civil rights is the only way to operate. A reflective analysis requires that we challenge dominant ideas and popularly held notions regarding solutions to social problems.

Thinking critically frees us from personal, environmental, and institutional forces that prevent us from seeing new directions (Habermas, 1979). Furthermore, once we become critical thinkers, we are no longer passive recipients of knowledge and products of socialization. Rather, through practicing thoughtful scrutiny and continuously asking questions we become active participants and arrive at our own ideas and commitments. As a result, we ground our ideas on a solid and informed foundation, all the while realizing that we may still be wrong. When we face challenges to our ideas, we are better prepared to provide justification and evidence in their support. The readings in this text provide us with many essential tools for becoming discerning critical thinkers.

ESSENTIALISM AND SOCIAL CONSTRUCTION

As mentioned earlier, in the United States we have a system of stratification that is based on many categories of difference, including race/ethnicity, social class, sex/gender, and sexuality. We tend to view this system as fixed because of our assumptions that these categories are unchangeable. Such assumptions are often based on a belief of **essentialism**—the tenet that human behavior is "natural," predetermined by genetic, biological, or physiological mechanisms and thus not subject to change. Human behaviors that show some similarity are assumed to be expressions of an underlying human drive or tendency. In the United States, gender and sexuality are among the last realms to have their natural or biological status called into question. For most of us, essentialism informs the way we think about such things as gender and remains the **hegemonic** or culturally dominant belief in our culture. For example, many of us attribute great importance to what we perceive as biological differences between women and men and see them as central to the organization of human society. Essentialism guides the way we order our social world and determines what we value as well as what we devalue.

This text proceeds from a different perspective, however. As you read the selections in Part I, you will note that they all begin with the premise that categories such as race/ethnicity, social class, sex/gender, and sexuality are *socially constructed*. Peter Berger and Thomas Luckmann, on whose work this premise is based, state that "social order is not part of the 'nature of things,' and it cannot be derived from the 'laws of nature.' Social order exists *only* as a product of human activity" (1966, p. 52). **Social construction theory** suggests that what we see as "real" (in this case, cultural categories of difference and systems of inequality) is the result of human interaction. Through such interaction we create aspects of our culture, objectify them, internalize them, and then take these cultural products for granted. A suitable companion to critical thinking, social construction theory encourages us to ask new questions but does not imply a particular answer. Using a critical thinking framework based on the notion of social construction requires that we be committed to asking questions and challenging assumptions that impair our ability even to imagine these questions.

Adopting a framework based on social construction theory means understanding that we are not born with a sense of what it means to be male, female, or intersexual; with a disability or not; black, Latina/o, Asian, white, or Native American; gay, straight, asexual, or bisexual; or rich, working-class, poor, or middle-class. We learn about these categories through social interaction, and we are given meanings and values for these categories by our social institutions, peers, and families. What we learn depends on the culture in which we live as well as on our place within that culture. Further, how we are defined by our culture often determines how we experience our social world. As W. I. Thomas noted, if we "define situations as real, they are real in their consequences" (1966, p. 301). For example, when we define one group as inferior to another, this does not make that group inferior, yet it may result in their being experienced as inferior. To illustrate this, consider the vicious cycle that results from the assignment of substandard resources to people who are poor. For example, low-income housing is generally located in geographic areas that lack quality resources such as good public schools and access to adequate health care. Lacking such quality resources results in further social disadvantage, which can perpetuate the poverty of this group. Thus, although reality is initially *soft* as it is constructed, it can become *hard* in its effects. We will examine these effects throughout this text.

According to Berger and Luckmann, reality is socially constructed in three stages. In the first stage, **externalization,** we create cultural products through social interaction. These cultural products may be material artifacts, social institutions, or values or beliefs concerning a particular group. When these products are created, they become "external" to those who have produced them; they become products outside ourselves. For example, as Judith Lorber describes in Reading 9, "The Social Construction of Gender," the construction of gender identity starts at birth with placement within a sex category (male or female). Through dress and adornment, others become aware of the sex of the child and they treat the child according to the gendered expectations they have for that particular sex. Children then behave and respond differently because of the different treatment they receive. A situation defined as real thus becomes real in its consequences. Girls and boys are taught to act differently from each other and thus *do* act differently. As a result, boys and girls are seen as *being* different from each other.

A second example of externalization can be found in the first reading, "Racial Formations," by Michael Omi and Howard Winant. They note that the concept of race has varied over history and is subject to a great deal of debate. Using the term **racial formation,** they describe "the process by which social, economic, and political forces determine the content and importance of racial categories, and by which they shape racial meanings." The example cited at the beginning of this essay clearly illustrates the social forces involved in determining racial categories. The recognition of a multiracial identity involves more than individuals being identified as multiracial. Rather, interaction that takes place at the social, economic, and political levels serves to construct such categories of race.

The second stage, **objectivation,** occurs when the products created in the first stage appear to take on a reality of their own, becoming independent of those who created them. People lose awareness that they themselves are the authors of their social and cultural environment and of their interpretations of reality. They feel as if the products have an objective existence, and they become another part of reality to be taken for granted. For example, most of us take race categories for granted, employing an essentialist perspective that views race categories as the result of biological or genetic factors. However, as mentioned earlier, a variety of social, economic, and political forces are involved in the construction of race categories. When we forget our part in the social construction of race, or fail to recognize the social forces that operate to construct race categories and the meanings associated with them, these categories take on objective realities. The objective realities that many of us attribute to racial categories can be seen in the findings of the 2008 American community survey conducted by the U.S. Census Bureau. Nationwide, just over 2 percent of respondents identified themselves as being of mixed race. The reasons for such a low response rate vary from lack of knowledge of the options to a strong identification with one race, regardless of one's multiracial heritage. These findings demonstrate that most respondents hold on to what they see as the objective reality of clear and mutually exclusive race categories.

In the final stage, **internalization,** we learn the supposedly "objective facts" about the cultural products that have been created. This occurs primarily through **socialization,** the process of social interaction in which one learns the ways of the society and one's specific **roles**—the sets of rules and expectations attached to a social position (or **status**) in that society. In this stage we make these "facts" part of our subjective consciousness. Because of the process of internalization, members of the same culture share an understanding of reality and rarely question the origins of their beliefs or the processes by which the beliefs arose. For example, as Gregory Mantsios discusses in Reading 6, "Media Magic: Making Class Invisible," the mass media serve as a very powerful tool for shaping the way we think. A significant part of our culture, mass media operate as a very important socialization mechanism. What we see presented in the mass media, as well as how it is presented, delivers important messages about who and what is or is not valued. Specifically, mass media help us to internalize certain constructs about class in our society, perpetuating a variety of myths. Among these myths are that poverty is not a significant problem in this country, that those who are poor have only themselves to blame, that we are a middle-class society, and that blue-collar and union workers are to blame for declining economic security. As mass media present us with these images, we develop a particular view of the class structure in our country. In addition, we internalize beliefs about members of a specific class (e.g., the poor are lazy) as if they were objective facts. The role of the media in maintaining constructions of difference and the resulting systems of inequality will be explored in Part II of this text.

It is important to note here that viewing cultural products as being produced in stages does not imply that the creation of reality occurs in a neat and overt progression. In some cases, the process of externalization in the creation of a social category is clear, as shown in Jonathan Katz's discussion in "The Invention of Heterosexuality" (Reading 13) of the creation of a "heterosexual identity." However, the construction of reality is not always such a clear process. Thinking in terms of a cultural product as produced in stages, though, provides a general understanding of how the knowledge that guides our behavior is established and how it becomes a part of culture and common sense. In addition, it is important to be aware that while categories of difference are being constructed and subsequently transformed into systems of inequality, such systems of inequality are often being *maintained* by the same social forces and practices. To clearly understand how categories of difference become systems of inequality, we begin by examining the processes that construct them. The social factors that serve to maintain these constructs and their corresponding systems of inequality will be examined in detail in Part II.

WHAT CONSTRUCTS CATEGORIES OF DIFFERENCE?

The readings in this text explore how the categories of race, class, gender, and sexuality are socially constructed and transformed into systems of inequality. The preceding in-depth explanation of social construction theory was intended to give us an understanding of *how* these categories are socially constructed. To thoroughly comprehend this process, however, it is important to understand what social factors are at work in creating these categories.

Simply put, categories of difference are the result of human activity guided by the values of our culture. When parents teach their child how to behave like a "lady" or act like a "gentleman," when one child labels another "gay" as discussed in the reading "'If You Don't Kiss Me, You're Dumped': Boys, Boyfriends and Heterosexualised Masculinities in the Primary School" (Reading 14), or when a girl decides to stop playing "rough" to avoid being labeled a "tomboy"—each is engaged in the process of creating categories of difference. We take these everyday actions for granted, but they play a fundamental role in how we view the world. The kinds of categories we create, as well as the meanings we give to them, are guided by our cultural values regarding who or what is important.

This process of creating these categories occurs in a variety of contexts that we encounter every day. Perhaps the most significant of these is the **institutional context.** An **institution** is the set of rules and relationships that govern the social activities in which we participate to meet our basic needs. The major social institutions that we will examine are:

The family:	responsible for reproducing and socializing and protecting the young, regulating sexual behavior, and providing emotional comfort and support for each of its members.
Education:	responsible for teaching members of society the knowledge, skills, and values considered most important for survival of the individual and society.

The economy:	creates, controls, and distributes the human and material resources of a society.
The state:	possesses the legal power to regulate the behavior of members of that society, as well as the relationship of that society to others.
The media:	responsible for supplying members of society with information, for reinforcing the policies of other institutions, and for socializing members of society with regard to appropriate ways of behaving and accepted cultural values.

From the policies and practices of each of these institutions, influenced by our cultural values, categories of difference are created. Thus, when parents teach their child how to behave like a "lady" or act like a "gentleman," they create categories of difference within the institutional context of the family.

Another context in which we create categories of difference is the **interpersonal context**—our daily interactions with others. In these interactions we rely on common guidelines for behavior (**norms**) to define situations and create these categories. For example, when an individual, operating on stereotypes based on race and ethnicity, labels another a "foreigner," she or he is relying on what are assumed images of what is an "American." As a result, she or he creates categories of difference within an interpersonal context.

Finally, we create categories of difference in **internal contexts** by internalizing the values and beliefs established in institutional and interpersonal contexts. When a girl decides to stop playing "rough" to avoid being labeled a "tomboy," she is internalizing the ideas of what it means to be a girl that were taught to her by her family as well as her peers.

CONSTRUCTING RACE AND ETHNICITY

The institution of the state, which determines how the census should be taken and how individuals should be counted, plays an integral role in defining race categories in an institutional context. **Race** denotes a group of people who perceive themselves *and are perceived by others* as possessing distinctive hereditary traits. **Ethnicity** denotes a group of people who perceive themselves *and are perceived by others* as sharing cultural traits such as language, religion, family customs, and food preferences. As Omi and Winant illustrate in "Racial Formations," what is important about the construction of race categories is not necessarily our perception of our own race but the recognition by social institutions of our membership in that race category. Furthermore, racial and ethnic categories are significant in that they are constructed in a hierarchy from "superior" to "inferior." Karen Brodkin explains in "How Did Jews Become White Folks?" (Reading 4) that Jewish people, as well as some other immigrants to the United States in the late 19th century, were once seen as belonging to an inferior race. The institutions of the economy and the state, as well as others, played an integral role in constructing them as inferior and in later "reconstructing" them as white and no longer an inferior race. Further, as Nguyen illustrates in "Becoming Suspects" (Reading 3), both prior to and after the events of September 11, 2001, the institution of the state constructed Pakistanis and Muslims as "other," "terrorists," and "the enemy." Both authors illustrate that such processes of construction are tied to economic and political changes in the United States.

Racial categories are also constructed in interpersonal contexts. As Waters discusses in "Optional Ethnicities" (Reading 2), many of us, but particularly whites, will ask someone whose race or ethnicity is not immediately apparent, "What are you?" We do not, however, generally ask such a question of those whom we perceive to be white. Thus, in our efforts to define others we not only attempt to construct distinct racial categories but we also create white as an "unmarked" category and as a standard against which all others are judged.

Finally, race is constructed in internal contexts, where we reinforce those categories and the meanings associated with them within ourselves. This process is particularly evident when a person of color who is light-skinned attempts or desires to "pass" as a white person. Through internalizing the idea that to be other than white is to be less valued, they participate in constructing race categories as well as the meanings associated with them.

CONSTRUCTING SOCIAL CLASS

The categories of social class are also constructed within institutional contexts. Although we may view social class as a result of how much **income** (wages and salaries from earnings and investments) and **wealth** (the total amount of valuable goods) a person possesses, it is in fact more than this. What class we belong to is determined not just by how much money we have or the material possessions we own but also by the institutions of our society, including state policies and the structuring of the economy. For example, definitions of poverty created by the government affect the access some members of our society have to certain important resources. The "Thrifty Food Plan"—the least costly of four nutritionally adequate plans designed by the Department of Agriculture, based on their 1955 Household Food Consumption Survey—demonstrates how the establishment of the **poverty line**—an annual income level below which a person or family was defined as poor and therefore entitled to certain benefits—creates who is seen as poor. The poverty line is problematic, however, in the way it is determined because it relies on material standards of the 1950s rather than contemporary standards. For example, expenses for items we consider essential today—for things such as transportation, childcare, technology—were not essential costs for families of the 1950s. As a result, while the government determined in 2009 that the poverty line for a family of four was $21,756, a more accurate calculation, employing contemporary standards, would have been over $35,000. The more accurate figure would result in doubling the number of individuals defined as poor. Additionally, it is important to note that measures such as the poverty line miss a significant aspect of what it means to be poor. Poverty is more than how much money one has, but it is also a process of social exclusion (Neal, 2004). According to the United Nations, "poverty is more than a shortage of income. It is the denial of opportunities and choices most basic to human development—to lead a long, healthy, creative life and to enjoy a decent standard of living, freedom, dignity, self-esteem, and respect of others" (Townson, 2000). When institutions establish definitions and measures, they determine a person's access to resources (i.e., the ability of people living in poverty to receive aid from the government). In this way, constructions of class provide the foundation for a system of inequitably distributed resources. The impact of such a system will be discussed in greater detail later in this text.

In addition to establishing who is poor, social institutions also function to establish who is wealthy, as illustrated by Thomas Shapiro in "Race, Home Ownership and Wealth" (Reading 5). Furthermore, as Meizhu Lui discusses in Reading 7, the state, influenced by the economy, creates a social class stratification system that is increasingly divided by a "wealth gap." Finally, the values that we place on members of social classes are further influenced by social institutions such as the media, as explained by Gregory Mantsios in "Media Magic: Making Class Invisible." According to Mantsios, those who control the media (i.e., the upper class) can use this institution to create class divisions as well as define our attitudes about members of different social classes. All of these articles clearly illustrate that the rules, practices, and policies of social institutions serve to construct categories of class differences and establish a system of class inequality.

Categories of social class are also constructed in interpersonal contexts. We define who is rich, poor, middle-class, and so forth, in our interactions with others. In addition, we attach meanings to each of these categories. For example, if we see a well-dressed, "clean-cut" individual driving an expensive car, we not only may judge this individual as belonging to the upper class but we may also admire her or him and the class position we assume she or he has achieved. On the other hand, if we observe people purchasing groceries with food stamps and then taking the bus, we not only judge them as poor but are also likely to think less of them as a result of their presumed class. In each of these instances, we rely on **stereotypes**—rigid, oversimplified, often exaggerated beliefs that are applied both to an entire category of people and to each individual in it. As a result of stereotypes, we treat individuals according to the values we attribute to these classes.

It is likely that the individuals in the preceding examples would be aware of the assumptions made about them on the basis of their social class. Mantsios illustrates that such stereotypes about class dominate our media. As these individuals internalize these messages, they impact their sense of self-worth. In addition, these individuals aid in creating categories of class and the meanings associated with them.

CONSTRUCTING SEX AND GENDER

Categories of sex and gender are also socially constructed in institutional contexts. This claim may, at first glance, seem quite strange. Whether or not a person is female or male is generally seen as a biological condition. However, as Judith Lorber in "The Social Construction of Gender" and Anne Fausto-Sterling in "The Five Sexes, Revisited" (Reading 10) discuss, the categories of male and female are not always sufficient to describe the variety of sexes that exist in reality. As Fausto-Sterling points out, individuals born **intersexual**—the physical manifestation of genital/genetic/endocrinological differentiation that is viewed as different from the norm—may constitute as much as 4 percent of live births. However, these infants are placed in a program of hormonal and surgical management almost immediately after birth so that they can become "normal" males or females in society. Thus, the institutions of science and medicine and advances in physiology and surgical technology aid in constructing a reality in which there are only two sexes.

What is significant about **sex**—the genetic (and sometimes scientific) determination of male and female—is the corresponding expectations that we place on people occupying these categories with regard to **gender**—the socially defined roles expected of males and females. As Lorber and others clearly explain, gender constructs are created and justified by a variety of institutions, including the family, the state, and the economy. Thus, gender constructs are transformed into a **gender system** in which men and masculinity are at the top of the hierarchy and women and femininity are at the bottom. Our ideas about gender therefore influence the way people are sorted into social positions. For example, our expectations of women to be feminine and our corresponding assumptions about their ability to handle certain kinds of strenuous or stressful work contribute to the underrepresentation of women as CEOs and heads of governing bodies. Similarly, our expectations that males be masculine and our corresponding assumption that they are less able to be nurturing contribute to their being less likely to pursue careers as nurses or elementary school teachers, for example. Because such a gendered division of labor is established in a society that is based on **patriarchy**—a form of social organization in which males dominate females—what results is not only a gendered division of labor but an occupational hierarchy in which the work of men is valued over that of women.

Further examples of how we construct categories of sex and gender are found in interpersonal contexts. We construct these categories by acting out the two polar sex categories and fulfilling the corresponding gendered expectations that have been constructed by the social institutions of the family, education, and others. As West and Zimmerman (1987) note, we do gender through our attempts to define others and through our expectations that others display appropriate gender identity. Similar to the ways in which we view race, we are often frustrated with ambiguities of sex and gender. If the sex/gender of another individual does not fit our expectations of opposite sex categories with corresponding gendered behavior, we often seek to define the person, again asking, "What are you?" In so doing we aid in the process of constructing a sex/gender system that allows for only two sexes and requires gender categories to be distinct and polar opposites.

Finally, gender is also created in internal contexts. As Michael Kimmel illustrates in "Masculinity as Homophobia" (Reading 12), males often insecure with their "manhood" will thus act as "bullies" to prove their manhood, not only to others but to themselves. As this reading illustrates, feelings of **alienation**—a sense of not belonging to the culture or the community (as in the case with males fearing they will be labeled "sissy" if they do not "act like men")—as well as feelings of **self-alienation**—hatred for one's own position and oneself—also play a significant role in how we create these categories within ourselves. As a result, we often perpetuate the ways in which these categories are constructed in other contexts.

CONSTRUCTING SEXUALITY

Categories of sexuality are also constructed within institutional contexts. Claims that sexuality is constructed may at first appear as strange as claims of sex being a social construct. Just as we generally recognize only two categories of sex, we often recognize sexuality as existing in only two opposing categories: gay and straight. Furthermore, we tend to see these categories as polar opposites, with each fundamentally different from the other. However, as Jonathan Katz notes in "The Invention of Heterosexuality," current notions of sexuality are but one way of imagining the social relations of the sexes. Like all of the previously discussed categories, sexuality is, in fact, a very complex yet culturally defined construct. **Sexuality** can involve attraction on a physical, emotional, and social level as well as fantasies, sexual behaviors, and self-identity (Klein, 1978). However, just as we may be required to distill our variations in racial and ethnic heritage into one of a few categories, we are often required to place all of the varying aspects of our sexuality into one of two categories. Thus, a complex part of who we are becomes socially defined within rigid and limiting constructs.

As Katz illustrates through his exploration of changes in the institutions of the economy and of work, religion, and science and medicine, social institutions influence the ways in which we construct categories of sexuality. Again, what is significant about categories of sexuality is that they are transformed into systems of inequality, where one form of sexuality is valued and viewed as more appropriate than others. In the United States the policies and practices of the federal government recognize some forms of sexuality and not others. For example, the Defense of Marriage Act allows some states to exclude same-sex couples from the right to marry. Despite the existence of such an act, 26 states have recently passed constitutional amendments that ban civil unions, marriage equality, and, in a few instances, any and all legal protection for lesbian and gay families. In 2007, 11 states proposed amendments that would limit marriage and other forms of relationship recognition. Most recently, in 2008 the voters of California passed Proposition 8, The California Marriage Protection Act, which provides that only marriage between a man and a woman is valid or recognized in California. Such actions serve to grant access to resources to heterosexuals but to deny them to lesbians and gays, thus creating systems of inequality.

We also create different sexuality categories in interpersonal contexts. As Emma Renold notes in "'If You Don't Kiss Me, You're Dumped': Boys, Boyfriends and Heterosexualised Masculinities in the Primary School" (Reading 14), in addition to Kate Bornstein's discussion in "Naming All the Parts" (Reading 16), constructions of sexuality are culturally linked to constructions of gender. Each of these readings illustrates not only how constructions of difference in institutional contexts are reflected in interpersonal interactions, but also how the social construction of one category of difference is generally dependent on the social construction of another. The interrelatedness of various constructions of difference will be addressed later.

We also create categories of sexuality in internal contexts. Again, this is generally done in response to the ways sexuality is defined in the larger society. As Paula Rust illustrates in "Sexual Identity and Bisexual Identities" (Reading 15), our descriptions of sexuality divisions and our own membership in them are determined by the "sexual landscape" of the culture and what are viewed as appropriate or available categories. As we define ourselves, we perpetuate the ways in which these categories are created in other contexts.

In summary, the construction of categories of difference occurs within a variety of contexts. The readings in Part I illustrate this process. In addition, they demonstrate how the meanings we attach to these categories result in structures of inequality.

WHY CATEGORIES OF DIFFERENCE?

Often the most difficult aspect of understanding the construction of categories of difference is not the how or what but the *why*. We have difficulty understanding why such categories are created and transformed into systems of inequality. Many explanations regarding why categories of difference and their corresponding hierarchies are constructed have been offered from a variety of perspectives.

The readings in Part I offer a variety of explanations. For example, Omi and Winant in "Racial Formations" discuss some of the reasons European explorers created separate categories for the people who were indigenous to the lands that they "discovered." They explain that when the European explorers came upon people who looked different from them, their assumptions about the origin of the human species were called into question. As a result, religious debates regarding creation and whether or not God created a single species of humanity led to questions about whether or not the natives of the New World could be "saved" as well as about how they should be treated. By deeming the European settlers as children of God and indigenous people "other," the European settlers not only were able to maintain their world view but were also able to justify systems of mistreatment, including slavery, coercive labor, and extermination.

Social theorists also offer explanations regarding why elements of social structure work to create systems of stratification. For example, Kingsley Davis and Wilbert Moore (1945) assert, in what has come to be known as the **Davis-Moore thesis,** that social stratification is a universal pattern because it has beneficial consequences for the operation of society. This is the case, they reason, because societal inequality has important functions for social organization. They note that society is a complex system of occupational positions, each of which has a particular importance. Some jobs, they argue, are easy to do (with a little instruction) and can be performed by just about anyone. Others are far more challenging and can only be accomplished by certain people who possess certain scarce talents. Functionally speaking, according to Davis and Moore, the latter positions of high day-to-day responsibility are the most important.

Other social theorists argue, however, that such a perspective is too conservative and fails to point out the inequality and exploitation of such systems of stratification. Thus, they argue that social stratification is a system by which some people gain advantages at the expense of others. Karl Marx (1959), for example, contended that systems of class stratification involve inequality and exploitation and are created so that capitalists can maximize their profits. He went on to say that the economy has primary importance as the social institution with the greatest influence on the rest of society. Other institutions also create systems of stratification but do so, in general, to support the operation of the economy.

Still other theorists, such as Marilyn Frye (1983), argue that the social construction of difference is initiated with the purpose of discrimination and **oppression**—a relationship in which the dominant group benefits from the *systematic* abuse, exploitation, and injustice directed at a subordinate group. Thus, the construction of difference is not arbitrary but systematically created and transformed into systems of inequality in an effort to advantage some at the expense of others. The roles of domination and subordination in the construction of difference and the maintenance of inequality will be addressed in greater detail in Part II.

CATEGORIES OF DIFFERENCE WITHIN A MATRIX OF DOMINATION

Candace West and Sarah Fenstermaker (1995) note that although gender, race, and class (and sexuality) involve very different attributes and effects, they are comparable devices for creating social inequality. Up to this point in our discussion we have looked at the construction of each category of difference—race/ethnicity, social class, sex/gender, and sexuality—distinctly, yet the similarities in the processes of construction serve to provide a foundation for understanding how their subsequent systems of oppression interconnect. To fully understand the process of transforming difference into inequality, it is necessary to recognize the interrelationships between these systems.

What we have discussed as distinct categories of difference and systems of inequality are, according to hooks (1989), systems of oppression that interconnect in an overarching structure of domination. She argues that oppression based on race, class, gender, and sexuality is part of an interlocking politics of domination which is "a belief in domination, and a belief in the notions of superior and inferior, which are components of all of those systems" (p. 175). Patricia Hill Collins (1991) refers to this interlocking system as a **matrix of domination.** This model provides the framework for our efforts in this text in seeking to understand how categories of difference are transformed into systems of inequality and maintained as systems of oppression. Such a framework will allow us to move beyond simply describing the similarities and differences between various systems of oppression and will help us to focus on how they interconnect. We will thereby be better able to see how each system of oppression relies on the others. The ways in which these systems of oppression rely on each other to maintain inequality will be discussed in detail in Part II.

The matrix of domination also provides a framework that permits us to avoid additive analyses of systems of oppression (e.g., a black woman being viewed as doubly oppressed as a white woman). Such analyses are problematic in that they suggest that oppression can be quantified. Attempts to do this would result in our placing ourselves in competition with one another, arguing over who is more oppressed and which form of oppression is the worst. Such debates generally divide us and prevent us from working toward equality. Viewing oppression and inequality in the form of a matrix of domination enables us to see commonalities in the sources of inequality and thus provides a clearer perspective on how these inequalities should be addressed.

Viewing constructions of difference and corresponding systems of inequality as interconnected also helps us to see how all groups experience both privilege and oppression in one socially constructed system. Each of us has had a life experience that is unique, and each of us has likely experienced both oppression and privilege. As Collins (1991) notes, a person may occupy the position of oppressor, oppressed, or both. The matrix of domination permits us to understand how we all experience both oppression and privilege.

Just as categories of difference are constructed in a variety of contexts, so too is the matrix of domination. To thoroughly understand the process of social construction, as well as to understand the matrix of domination, it is important to understand what is constructed, what does the constructing, how these constructs are created, and how their corresponding systems of inequality intersect. As you read the selections in Part I, note the explanations provided by each of the authors and be aware of your reactions to them. These readings will provide you with a framework to better understand contemporary constructions of race/ethnicity, social class, sex/gender, and sexuality in the United States. In addition, by understanding the process of social construction we can be more optimistic in working toward positive social change. If we recognize the processes by which systems of inequality are constructed as interlocking systems of oppression, we can gain a greater understanding of how to deconstruct these systems while constructing systems of equality.

A FINAL COMMENT

As stated earlier, this text will help us begin the process of understanding contemporary constructions of race/ethnicity, social class, sex/gender, and sexuality in the United States. A fundamental component to examining these constructs is to think critically. In addition, it is important to employ **empathy**—the ability to identify with the thoughts and experiences of another, even though you have not shared them. Thus it is important to remain aware of your own **standpoint**—your location in society, and how that is impacted by your race/ethnicity, social class, sex/gender, sexuality, ability, age, and other personal qualities. As you read about experiences that you have not had or are challenged by perspectives offered by the authors, try not to shut yourself off to what they have to say. Rather, use this challenge as an opportunity to better understand your own ideas. As the process of critical thinking indicates, becoming aware of alternative experiences and perspectives can result in a greater understanding of why we think what we do. Finally, you may find that you come away from this text with more questions than you had upon entering. If so, see this as a positive outcome, for it is not only a sign of success in learning to think critically, but also an indication that the process of critical thinking will continue beyond this text.

REFERENCES

Berger, Peter L., and Thomas Luckmann. 1966. *The Social Construction of Reality: A Treatise in the Sociology of Knowledge.* New York: Doubleday.

Brookfield, Stephen D. 1987. *Developing Critical Thinkers: Challenging Adults to Explore Alternative Ways of Thinking and Acting.* San Francisco: Jossey-Bass.

Collins, Patricia Hill. 1991. *Black Feminist Thought: Knowledge, Consciousness, and the Politics of Empowerment.* New York: Routledge.

Davis, Kingsley, and Wilbert Moore. 1945. "Some Principles of Stratification." *American Sociological Review,* 10(2): 242–49.

Foster, Eugene A., M. A. Jobling, P. G. Taylor, P. Donnelly, P. De Knijff, Rene Mieremet, T. Zerjal, and C. Tyler-Smith. 1998. "Jefferson Fathered Slave's Last Child." *Nature* 396: 27–28.

Frye, Marilyn. 1983. *The Politics of Reality: Essays in Feminist Theory.* Trumansburg, NY: Crossing Press.

Habermas, Jurgen. 1979. *Communication and the Evolution of Society.* Translated by Thomas McCarthy. Boston: Beacon Press.

hooks, bell. 1989. *Talking Back: Thinking Feminist, Thinking Black.* Boston: South End Press.

Klein, Fritz. 1978. *The Bisexual Option.* New York: Arbor House.

Marx, Karl. 1959 (orig. 1859). "A Contribution to the Critique of Political Economy." In Karl Marx and Friedrich Engels, *Marx and Engels: Basic Writings on Politics and Philosophy,* edited by Lewis S. Feurer, 42–46. Garden City, NY: Anchor Books.

Neal, Rusty. May, 2004. "Voices: Women, Poverty and Homelessness in Canada." The National AntiPoverty Organization, Ottawa.

Sumner, William Graham. 1959 (orig. 1906). *Folkways.* New York: Dover.

Thomas, W. I. 1966 (orig. 1931). "The Relation of Research to the Social Process." In *W. I. Thomas on Social Organization and Personality,* edited by Morris Janowitz, 289–305. Chicago: University of Chicago Press.

Townson, Monica. 2000. "A Reportcard on Women and Poverty." Canadian Centre for Policy Alternatives, Ottawa.

West, Candace, and Don H. Zimmerman. 1987. "Doing Gender." *Gender & Society,* 1(2): 125–51.

West, Candace, and Sarah Fenstermaker. 1995. "Doing Difference." *Gender & Society,* 9(1) (February): 8–37.

Reading 1

RACIAL FORMATIONS

MICHAEL OMI • HOWARD WINANT

In 1982–83, Susie Guillory Phipps unsuccessfully sued the Louisiana Bureau of Vital Records to change her racial classification from black to white. The descendant of an eighteenth-century white planter and a black slave, Phipps was designated "black" in her birth certificate in accordance with a 1970 state law which declared anyone with at least one-thirty-second "Negro blood" to be black. The legal battle raised intriguing questions about the concept of race, its meaning in contemporary society, and its use (and abuse) in public policy. Assistant Attorney General Ron Davis defended the law by pointing out that some type of racial classification was necessary to comply with federal record-keeping requirements and to facilitate programs for the prevention of genetic diseases. Phipps's attorney, Brian Begue, argued that the assignment of racial categories on birth certificates was unconstitutional and that the one-thirty-second designation was inaccurate. He called on a retired Tulane University professor who cited research indicating that most whites have one-twentieth "Negro" ancestry. In the end, Phipps lost. The court upheld a state law which quantified racial identity, and in so doing affirmed the legality of assigning individuals to specific racial groupings.[1]

The Phipps case illustrates the continuing dilemma of defining race and establishing its meaning in institutional life. Today, to assert that variations in human physiognomy are racially based is to enter a constant and intense debate. *Scientific* interpretations of race have not been alone in sparking heated controversy; *religious* perspectives have done so as well.[2] Most centrally, of course, race has been a matter of *political* contention. This has been particularly true in the United States, where the concept of race has varied enormously over time without ever leaving the center stage of US history.

 WHAT IS RACE?

Race consciousness, and its articulation in theories of race, is largely a modern phenomenon. When European explorers in the New World "discovered" people who looked different than themselves, these "natives" challenged then existing conceptions of the origins of the human species, and raised disturbing questions as to whether *all* could be considered in the same "family of man."[3] Religious debates flared over the attempt to reconcile the Bible with the existence of "racially distinct" people. Arguments took place over creation itself, as theories of polygenesis questioned whether God had made only one species of humanity ("monogenesis"). Europeans wondered if the natives of the New World were indeed human beings with redeemable souls. At stake were not only the prospects for conversion, but the types of treatment to be accorded them. The expropriation of property, the denial of political rights, the introduction of slavery and other forms of coercive labor, as well as outright extermination, all presupposed a worldview which distinguished Europeans— children of God, human beings, etc.—from "others." Such a worldview was needed to explain why some should be "free" and others enslaved, why some had rights to land and property while others did not. Race, and the interpretation of racial differences, was a central factor in that worldview.

In the colonial epoch science was no less a field of controversy than religion in attempts to comprehend the concept of race and its meaning. Spurred on by the classificatory scheme of living organisms devised by Linnaeus in *Systema Naturae,* many scholars in the eighteenth and nineteenth centuries dedicated themselves to the identification and ranking of variations in humankind. Race was thought of as a *biological* concept, yet its precise definition was the subject of debates which, as we have noted, continue to rage today. Despite efforts ranging from Dr. Samuel Morton's studies of cranial capacity[4] to contemporary attempts to base racial classification on shared gene pools,[5] the concept of race has defied biological definition. . . .

Attempts to discern the *scientific meaning* of race continue to the present day. Although most physical anthropologists and biologists have abandoned the quest for a scientific basis to determine racial categories, controversies have recently flared in the area of genetics and educational psychology. For instance, an essay by Arthur Jensen which argued that hereditary factors shape intelligence not only revived the "nature or nurture" controversy, but raised highly volatile questions about racial equality itself.[6] Clearly the attempt to establish a *biological* basis of race has not been swept into the dustbin of history, but is being resurrected in various scientific arenas. All such attempts seek to remove the concept of race from fundamental social, political, or economic determination. They suggest instead that the truth of race lies in the terrain of innate characteristics, of which skin color and other physical attributes provide only the most obvious, and in some respects most superficial, indicators.

RACE AS A SOCIAL CONCEPT

The social sciences have come to reject biologistic notions of race in favor of an approach which regards race as a *social* concept. Beginning in the eighteenth century, this trend has been slow and uneven, but its direction clear. In the nineteenth century Max Weber discounted biological explanations for racial conflict and instead highlighted the social and political factors which engendered such conflict.[7] The work of pioneering cultural anthropologist Franz Boas was crucial in refuting the scientific racism of the early twentieth century by rejecting the connection between race and culture, and the assumption of a continuum of "higher" and "lower" cultural groups. Within the contemporary social science literature, race is assumed to be a variable which is shaped by broader societal forces.

Race is indeed a pre-eminently *sociohistorical* concept. Racial categories and the meaning of race are given concrete expression by the specific social relations and historical context in which they are embedded. Racial meanings have varied tremendously over time and between different societies.

In the United States, the black/white color line has historically been rigidly defined and enforced. White is seen as a "pure" category. Any racial intermixture makes one "nonwhite." In the movie *Raintree County*, Elizabeth Taylor describes the worst of fates to befall whites as "havin' a little Negra blood in ya'—just one little teeny drop and a person's all Negra."[8] This thinking flows from what Marvin Harris has characterized as the principle of *hypo-descent:*

> By what ingenious computation is the genetic tracery of a million years of evolution unraveled and each man [sic] assigned his proper social box? In the United States, the mechanism employed is the rule of hypo-descent. This descent rule requires Americans to believe that anyone who is known to have had a Negro ancestor is a Negro. We admit nothing in between. . . . "Hypo-descent" means affiliation with the subordinate rather than the superordinate group in order to avoid the ambiguity of intermediate identity. . . . The rule of hypo-descent is, therefore, an invention, which we in the United States have made in order to keep biological facts from intruding into our collective racist fantasies.[9]

The Susie Guillory Phipps case merely represents the contemporary expression of this racial logic.

By contrast, a striking feature of race relations in the lowland areas of Latin America since the abolition of slavery has been the relative absence of sharply defined racial groupings. No such rigid descent rule characterizes racial identity in many Latin American societies. Brazil, for example, has historically had less rigid conceptions of race, and thus a variety of "intermediate" racial categories exist. Indeed, as Harris notes, "One of the most striking consequences of the Brazilian system of racial identification is that parents and children and even brothers and sisters are frequently accepted as representatives of quite opposite racial types."[10] Such a possibility is incomprehensible within the logic of racial categories in the US.

To suggest another example: the notion of "passing" takes on new meaning if we compare various American cultures' means of assigning racial identity. In the United States, individuals who are actually "black" by the logic of hypo-descent have attempted to skirt the discriminatory barriers imposed by law and custom by attempting to "pass" for white.[11] Ironically, these same individuals would not be able to pass for "black" in many Latin American societies.

Consideration of the term "black" illustrates the diversity of racial meanings which can be found among different societies and historically within a given society. In contemporary British politics the term "black" is used to refer to all nonwhites. Interestingly this designation has not arisen through the racist discourse of groups such as the National Front. Rather, in political and cultural movements, Asian as well as Afro-Caribbean youth are adopting the term as an expression of self-identity.[12] The wide-ranging meanings of "black" illustrate the manner in which racial categories are shaped politically.[13]

The meaning of race is defined and contested throughout society, in both collective action and personal practice. In the process, racial categories themselves are formed, transformed, destroyed, and re-formed. We use the term *racial formation* to refer to the process by which social, economic, and political forces determine the content and importance of racial categories, and by which they are in turn shaped by racial meanings. Crucial to this formulation is the treatment of race as a *central axis* of social relations which cannot be subsumed under or reduced to some broader category or conception.

RACIAL IDEOLOGY AND RACIAL IDENTITY

The seemingly obvious "natural" and "common sense" qualities which the existing racial order exhibits themselves testify to the effectiveness of the racial formation process in constructing racial meanings and racial identities.

One of the first things we notice about people when we meet them (along with their sex) is their race. We utilize race to provide clues about *who* a person is. This fact is made painfully obvious when we encounter someone whom we cannot conveniently racially categorize—someone who is, for example, racially "mixed" or of an ethnic/racial group with which we are not familiar. Such an encounter becomes a source of discomfort and momentarily a crisis of racial meaning. Without a racial identity, one is in danger of having no identity.

Our compass for navigating race relations depends on preconceived notions of what each specific racial group looks like. Comments such as, "Funny, you don't look black," betray an underlying image of what black should be. We also become disoriented when people do not act "black," "Latino," or indeed "white." The content of such stereotypes reveals a series of unsubstantiated beliefs about who these groups are and what "they" are like.[14]

In US society, then, a kind of "racial etiquette" exists, a set of interpretative codes and racial meanings which operate in the interactions of daily life. Rules shaped by our perception of race in a comprehensively racial society determine the "presentation of self,"[15] distinctions of status, and appropriate modes of conduct. "Etiquette" is not mere universal adherence to the dominant group's rules, but a more dynamic combination of these rules with the values and beliefs of subordinated groupings. This racial "subjection" is quintessentially ideological. Everybody learns some combination, some version, of the rules of racial classification, and of their own racial identity, often without obvious teaching or conscious inculcation. Race becomes "common sense"—a way of comprehending, explaining, and acting in the world.

Racial beliefs operate as an "amateur biology," a way of explaining the variations in "human nature."[16] Differences in skin color and other obvious physical characteristics supposedly provide visible clues to differences lurking underneath. Temperament, sexuality, intelligence, athletic ability, aesthetic preferences and so on are presumed to be fixed and discernible from the palpable mark of race. Such diverse questions as our confidence and trust in others (for example, clerks or salespeople, media figures, neighbors), our sexual preferences and romantic images, our tastes in music, films, dance, or sports, and our very ways of talking, walking, eating, and dreaming are ineluctably shaped by notions of race. Skin color "differences" are thought to explain perceived differences in intellectual, physical, and artistic temperaments, and to justify distinct treatment of racially identified individuals and groups.

The continuing persistence of racial ideology suggests that these racial myths and stereotypes cannot be exposed as such in the popular imagination. They are, we think, too essential, too integral, to the maintenance of the US social order. Of course, particular meanings, stereotypes, and myths can change, but the presence of a *system* of racial meanings and stereotypes, of racial ideology, seems to be a permanent feature of US culture.

Film and television, for example, have been notorious in disseminating images of racial minorities which establish for audiences what people from these groups look like, how they behave, and "who they are."[17] The power of the media lies not only in their ability to reflect the dominant racial ideology, but in their capacity to shape that ideology in the first place. D. W. Griffith's epic *Birth of a Nation*, a sympathetic treatment of the rise of the Ku Klux Klan during Reconstruction, helped to generate, consolidate, and "nationalize" images of blacks which had been more disparate (more regionally specific, for example) prior to the film's appearance.[18] In US television, the necessity to define characters in the briefest and most condensed manner has led to the perpetuation of racial caricatures, as racial stereotypes serve as shorthand for scriptwriters, directors and actors, in commercials, etc. Television's tendency to address the "lowest common denominator" in order to render programs "familiar" to an enormous and diverse audience leads it regularly to assign and reassign racial characteristics to particular groups, both minority and majority.

These and innumerable other examples show that we tend to view race as something fixed and immutable—something rooted in "nature." Thus we mask the historical construction of racial categories, the shifting meaning of race, and the crucial role of politics and ideology in shaping race relations. Races do not emerge full-blown. They are the results of diverse historical practices and are continually subject to challenge over their definition and meaning.

 ## RACIALIZATION: THE HISTORICAL DEVELOPMENT OF RACE

In the United States, the racial category of "black" evolved with the consolidation of racial slavery. By the end of the seventeenth century, Africans whose specific identity was Ibo, Yoruba, Fulani, etc., were rendered "black" by an ideology of exploitation based on racial logic—the establishment and maintenance of a "color line." This of course did not occur overnight. A period of indentured servitude which was not rooted in racial logic preceded the consolidation of racial slavery. With slavery, however, a racially based understanding of society was set in motion which resulted in the shaping of a specific *racial* identity not only for the slaves but for the European settlers as well. Winthrop Jordan has observed: "From the initially common term *Christian*, at mid-century there was a marked shift toward the terms *English* and *free*. After about 1680, taking the colonies as a whole, a new term of self-identification appeared—*white*."[19]

We employ the term *racialization* to signify the extension of racial meaning to a previously racially unclassified relationship, social practice, or group. Racialization is an ideological process, a historically specific one. Racial ideology is constructed from pre-existing conceptual (or, if one prefers, "discursive") elements and emerges from the struggles of competing political projects and ideas seeking to articulate similar elements differently. An account of racialization processes that avoids the pitfalls of US ethnic history[20] remains to be written.

Particularly during the nineteenth century, the category of "white" was subject to challenges brought about by the influx of diverse groups who were not of the same Anglo-Saxon stock as the founding immigrants. In the nineteenth century, political and ideological struggles emerged over the classification of Southern Europeans, the Irish, and Jews, among other "non-white" categories.[21] Nativism was only effectively curbed by the institutionalization of a racial order that drew the color line *around*, rather than *within*, Europe.

By stopping short of racializing immigrants from Europe after the Civil War, and by subsequently allowing their assimilation, the American racial order was reconsolidated in the wake of the tremendous challenge placed before it by the abolition of racial slavery.[22] With the end of Reconstruction in 1877, an effective program for limiting the emergent class struggles of the later nineteenth century was forged: the definition of the working class *in racial terms*—as "white." This was not accomplished by any legislative decree or capitalist maneuvering to divide the working class, but rather by white workers themselves. Many of them were recent immigrants, who organized on racial lines as much as on traditionally defined class lines.[23] The Irish on the West Coast, for example, engaged in vicious anti-Chinese race-baiting and committed many pogrom-type assaults on Chinese in the course of consolidating the trade union movement in California.

Thus the very political organization of the working class was in important ways a racial project. The legacy of racial conflicts and arrangements shaped the definition of interests and in turn led to the consolidation of institutional patterns (e.g., segregated unions, dual labor markets, exclusionary legislation) which perpetuated the color line *within* the working class. Selig Perlman, whose study of the development of the labor movement is fairly sympathetic to this process, notes that:

> The political issue after 1877 was racial, not financial, and the weapon was not merely the ballot, but also "direct action"— violence. The anti-Chinese agitation in California, culminating as it did in the Exclusion Law passed by Congress in 1882, was doubtless the most important single factor in the history of American labor, for without it the entire country might have been overrun by Mongolian [sic] labor and *the labor movement might have become a conflict of races instead of one of classes.*[24]

More recent economic transformations in the US have also altered interpretations of racial identities and meanings. The automation of southern agriculture and the augmented labor demand of the postwar boom transformed blacks from a largely rural, impoverished labor force to a largely urban, working-class group by 1970.[25] When boom became bust and liberal welfare statism moved rightwards, the majority of blacks came to be seen, increasingly, as part of the "underclass," as state "dependents." Thus the particularly deleterious effects on blacks of global and national economic shifts (generally rising unemployment rates, changes in the employment structure away from reliance on labor intensive work, etc.) were explained once again in the late 1970s and 1980s (as they had been in the 1940s and mid-1960s) as the result of defective black cultural norms, of familial disorganization, etc.[26] In this way new racial attributions, new racial myths, are affixed to "blacks."[27] Similar changes in racial identity are presently affecting Asians and Latinos, as such economic forces as increasing Third World impoverishment and indebtedness fuel immigration and high interest rates, Japanese competition spurs resentments, and US jobs seem to fly away to Korea and Singapore.[28]. . .

Once we understand that race overflows the boundaries of skin color, superexploitation, social stratification, discrimination and prejudice, cultural domination and cultural resistance, state policy (or of any other particular social relationship we list), once we recognize the racial dimension present to some degree in every identity, institution, and social practice in the United States—once we have done this, it becomes possible to speak of *racial formation*. This recognition is hard-won; there is a continuous temptation to think of race as an *essence*, as something fixed, concrete and objective, as (for example) one of the categories just enumerated. And there is also an opposite temptation: to see it as a mere illusion, which an ideal social order would eliminate.

In our view it is crucial to break with these habits of thought. The effort must be made to understand race as *an unstable and "decentered" complex of social meanings constantly being transformed by political struggle. . . .*

NOTES

1. *San Francisco Chronicle,* 14 September 1982, 19 May 1983. Ironically, the 1970 Louisiana law was enacted to supersede an old Jim Crow statute which relied on the idea of "common report" in determining an infant's race. Following Phipps's unsuccessful attempt to change her classification and have the law declared unconstitutional, a legislative effort arose which culminated in the repeal of the law. See *San Francisco Chronicle,* 23 June 1983.
2. The Mormon church, for example, has been heavily criticized for its doctrine of black inferiority.
3. Thomas F. Gossett notes:

   Race theory . . . had up until fairly modern times no firm hold on European thought. On the other hand, race theory and race prejudice were by no means unknown at the time when the English colonists came to North America. Undoubtedly, the age of exploration led many to speculate on race differences at a period when neither Europeans nor Englishmen were prepared to make allowances for vast cultural diversities. Even though race theories had not then secured wide acceptance or even sophisticated formulation, the first contacts of the Spanish with the Indians in the Americas can now be recognized as the beginning of a struggle between conceptions of the nature of primitive peoples which has not yet been wholly settled. (Thomas F. Gossett, *Race: The History of an Idea in America* [New York: Schocken Books, 1965], p. 16.)

   Winthrop Jordan provides a detailed account of early European colonialists' attitudes about color and race in *White Over Black: American Attitudes Toward the Negro, 1550–1812* (New York: Norton, 1977 [1968]), pp. 3–43.
4. Pro-slavery physician Samuel George Morton (1799–1851) compiled a collection of 800 crania from all parts of the world which formed the sample for his studies of race. Assuming that the larger the size of the cranium translated into greater intelligence, Morton established a relationship between race and skull capacity. Gossett reports that:

   In 1849, one of his studies included the following results: The English skulls in his collection proved to be the largest, with an average cranial capacity of 96 cubic inches. The Americans and Germans were rather poor seconds, both with cranial capacities of 90 cubic inches. At the bottom of the list were the Negroes with 83 cubic inches, the Chinese with 82, and the Indians with 79. (Ibid., p. 74.)

On Morton's methods, see Stephen J. Gould, "The Finagle Factor," *Human Nature* (July 1978).

5. Definitions of race founded upon a common pool of genes have not held up when confronted by scientific research which suggests that the differences *within* a given human population are greater than those *between* populations. See L. L. Cavalli-Sforza, "The Genetics of Human Populations," *Scientific American* (September 1974), pp. 81–89.

6. Arthur Jensen, "How Much Can We Boost IQ and Scholastic Achievement?" *Harvard Educational Review,* vol. 39 (1969), pp. 1–123.

7. Ernst Moritz Manasse, "Max Weber on Race," *Social Research,* vol. 14 (1947), pp. 191–221.

8. Quoted in Edward D. C. Campbell, Jr., *The Celluloid South: Hollywood and the Southern Myth* (Knoxville: University of Tennessee Press, 1981), pp. 168–70.

9. Marvin Harris, *Patterns of Race in the Americas* (New York: Norton, 1964), p. 56.

10. Ibid., p. 57.

11. After James Meredith had been admitted as the first black student at the University of Mississippi, Harry S. Murphy announced that he, and not Meredith, was the first black student to attend "Ole Miss." Murphy described himself as black but was able to pass for white and spent nine months at the institution without attracting any notice. (Ibid., p. 56.)

12. A. Sivanandan, "From Resistance to Rebellion: Asian and Afro-Caribbean Struggles in Britain," *Race and Class,* vol. 23, nos. 2–3 (Autumn–Winter 1981).

13. Consider the contradictions in racial status which abound in the country with the most rigidly defined racial categories—South Africa. There a race classification agency is employed to adjudicate claims for upgrading of official racial identity. This is particularly necessary for the "coloured" category. The apartheid system considers Chinese as "Asians" while the Japanese are accorded the status of "honorary whites." This logic nearly detaches race from any grounding in skin color and other physical attributes and nakedly exposes race as a juridical category subject to economic, social, and political influences. (We are indebted to Steve Talbot for clarification of some of these points.)

14. Gordon W. Allport, *The Nature of Prejudice* (Garden City, New York: Doubleday, 1958), pp. 184–200.

15. We wish to use this phrase loosely, without committing ourselves to a particular position on such social psychological approaches as symbolic interactionism, which are outside the scope of this study. An interesting study on this subject is S. M. Lyman and W. A. Douglass, "Ethnicity: Strategies of Individual and Collective Impression Management," *Social Research,* vol. 40, no. 2 (1973).

16. Michael Billig, "Patterns of Racism: Interviews with National Front Members," *Race and Class,* vol. 20, no. 2 (Autumn 1978), pp. 161–79.

17. "Miss San Antonio USA Lisa Fernandez and other Hispanics auditioning for a role in a television soap opera did not fit the Hollywood image of real Mexicans and had to darken their faces before filming." Model Aurora Garza said that their faces were bronzed with powder because they looked too white. "I'm a real Mexican [Garza said] and very dark anyway. I'm even darker right now because I have a tan. But they kept wanting me to make my face darker and darker" (*San Francisco Chronicle,* 21 September 1984). A similar dilemma faces Asian American actors

who feel that Asian character lead roles inevitably go to white actors who make themselves up to be Asian. Scores of Charlie Chan films, for example, have been made with white leads (the last one was the 1981 *Charlie Chan and the Curse of the Dragon Queen*). Roland Winters, who played in six Chan features, was asked by playwright Frank Chin to explain the logic of casting a white man in the role of Charlie Chan: "The only thing I can think of is, if you want to cast a homosexual in a show, and you get a homosexual, it'll be awful. It won't be funny . . . and maybe there's something there . . ." (Frank Chin, "Confessions of the Chinatown Cowboy," *Bulletin of Concerned Asian Scholars*, vol. 4, no. 3 [Fall 1972]).

18. Melanie Martindale-Sikes, "Nationalizing 'Nigger' Imagery Through 'Birth of a Nation'," paper prepared for the 73rd Annual Meeting of the American Sociological Association, 4–8 September 1978 in San Francisco.

19. Winthrop D. Jordan, op. cit., p. 95; emphasis added.

20. Historical focus has been placed either on particular racially defined groups or on immigration and the "incorporation" of ethnic groups. In the former case the characteristic ethnicity theory pitfalls and apologetics such as functionalism and cultural pluralism may be avoided, but only by sacrificing much of the focus on race. In the latter case, race is considered a manifestation of ethnicity.

21. The degree of antipathy for these groups should not be minimized. A northern commentator observed in the 1850s: "An Irish Catholic seldom attempts to rise to a higher condition than that in which he is placed, while the Negro often makes the attempt with success." Quoted in Gossett, op. cit., p. 288.

22. This analysis, as will perhaps be obvious, is essentially DuBoisian. Its main source will be found in the monumental (and still largely unappreciated) *Black Reconstruction in the United States 1860–1880* (New York: Atheneum, 1977 [1035]).

23. Alexander Saxton argues that:

    North Americans of European background have experienced three great racial confrontations: with the Indian, with the African, and with the Oriental. Central to each transaction has been a totally one-sided preponderance of power, exerted for the exploitation of nonwhites by the dominant white society. In each case (but especially in the two that began with systems of enforced labor), white workingmen have played a crucial, yet ambivalent role. They have been both exploited and exploiters. On the one hand, thrown into competition with nonwhites as enslaved or "cheap" labor, they suffered economically; on the other hand, being white, they benefited by that very exploitation which was compelling the nonwhites to work for low wages or for nothing. Ideologically they were drawn in opposite directions. *Racial identification cut at right angles to class consciousness.* (Alexander Saxton, *The Indispensable Enemy: Labor and the Anti-Chinese Movement in California* [Berkeley and Los Angeles: University of California Press, 1971], p. 1, emphasis added.)

24. Selig Perlman, *The History of Trade Unionism in the United States* (New York: Augustus Kelley, 1950), p. 52; emphasis added.

25. Whether Southern blacks were "peasants" or rural workers is unimportant in this context. Some time during the 1960s blacks attained a higher degree of urbanization than whites. Before World War II most blacks had been rural dwellers and nearly 80 percent lived in the South.

26. See George Gilder, *Wealth and Poverty* (New York: Basic Books, 1981); Charles Murray, *Losing Ground* (New York: Basic Books, 1984).

27. A brilliant study of the racialization process in Britain, focused on the rise of "mugging" as a popular fear in the 1970s, is Stuart Hall et al., *Policing the Crisis* (London: Macmillan, 1978).

28. The case of Vincent Chin, a Chinese American man beaten to death in 1982 by a laid-off Detroit auto worker and his stepson who mistook him for Japanese and blamed him for the loss of their jobs, has been widely publicized in Asian American communities. On immigration conflicts and pressures, see Michael Omi, "New Wave Dread: Immigration and Intra-Third World Conflict," *Socialist Review,* no. 60 (November–December 1981).

 QUESTIONS FOR CRITICAL THINKING

Reading 1

1. Does Omi and Winant's discussion of race as a social rather than biological concept help you to see issues of race in new and different ways? If so, how? If not, why not?

2. How does your membership in a particular race category influence your understanding of or level of agreement with the authors' discussion?

3. Considering the author's discussion, do you think it is possible or desirable to move beyond racial divisions?

Reading **2**

OPTIONAL ETHNICITIES
For Whites Only?

MARY C. WATERS

 ETHNIC IDENTITY FOR WHITES IN THE 1990s

What does it mean to talk about ethnicity as an option for an individual? To argue that an individual has some degree of choice in their ethnic identity flies in the face of the common sense notion of ethnicity many of us believe in—that one's ethnic identity is a fixed characteristic, reflective of blood ties and given at birth. However, social scientists who study ethnicity have long concluded that while ethnicity is based in a *belief* in a common ancestry, ethnicity is primarily a *social* phenomenon, not a biological one (Alba 1985, 1990; Barth 1969; Weber [1921] 1968, p. 389). The belief that members of an ethnic group have that they share a common ancestry may not be a fact. There is a great deal of change in ethnic identities across generations through intermarriage, changing allegiances, and changing social categories. There is also a much larger amount of change in the identities of individuals over their life than is commonly believed. While most people are aware of the phenomenon known as "passing"—people raised as one race who change at some point and claim a different race as their identity—there are similar life course changes in ethnicity that happen all the time and are not given the same degree of attention as "racial passing."

White Americans of European ancestry can be described as having a great deal of choice in terms of their ethnic identities. The two major types of options White Americans can exercise are (1) the option of whether to claim any specific ancestry, or to just be "White" or American (Lieberson [1985] called these people "unhyphenated Whites"), and (2) the choice of which of their European ancestries to choose to include in their description of their own identities. In both cases, the option of choosing how to present yourself on surveys and in everyday social interactions exists for Whites because of social changes and societal conditions that have created a great deal of social mobility, immigrant assimilation, and political and economic power for Whites in the United States. Specifically, the option of being able to not claim any ethnic identity exists for Whites of European background in the United States because they are the majority group—in terms of holding political and social power, as well as being a numerical majority. The option of choosing among different ethnicities in their family backgrounds exists because the degree of discrimination and social distance attached to specific European backgrounds has diminished over time.

The Ethnic Miracle

When European immigration to the United States was sharply curtailed in the late 1920s, a process was set in motion whereby the European ethnic groups already in the United States were for all intents and purposes cut off from any new arrivals. As a result, the composition of the ethnic groups began to age generationally. The proportion of each ethnic group made up of immigrants or the first generation began to gradually decline, and the proportion made up of the children, grandchildren, and eventually great-grandchildren began to increase. Consequently, by 1990 most European-origin ethnic groups in the United States were composed of a very small number of immigrants, and a very large proportion of people whose link to their ethnic origins in Europe was increasingly remote.

This generational change was accompanied by unprecedented social and economic changes. The very success of the assimilation process these groups experienced makes it difficult to imagine how much the question of the immigrants' eventual assimilation was an open one at the turn of the century. At the peak of immigration from southern and central Europe there was widespread discrimination and hostility against the newcomers by established Americans. Italians, Poles, Greeks, and Jews were called derogatory names, attacked by nativist mobs, and derided in the press. Intermarriage across ethnic lines was very uncommon—castelike in the words of some sociologists (Pagnini and Morgan 1990). The immigrants and their children were residentially segregated, occupationally specialized, and generally poor.

After several generations in the United States, the situation has changed a great deal. The success and social mobility of the grandchildren and great-grandchildren of that massive wave of immigrants from Europe has been called "The Ethnic Miracle" (Greeley 1976). These Whites have moved away from the inner-city ethnic ghettos to White middle-class suburban homes. They are doctors, lawyers, entertainers, academics, governors, and Supreme Court justices. But contrary to what some social science theorists and some politicians predicted or hoped for, these middle-class Americans have not completely given up ethnic identity. Instead, they have maintained some connection with their immigrant ancestors' identities—becoming Irish American doctors, Italian American Supreme Court justices, and Greek American presidential candidates. In the tradition of cultural pluralism, successful middle-class Americans in the late twentieth century maintain some degree of identity with their ethnic backgrounds. They have remained "hyphenated Americans." So while social mobility and declining discrimination have created the option of not identifying with any European ancestry, most White Americans continue to report some ethnic background.

With the growth in intermarriage among people of European ethnic origins, increasingly these people are of mixed ethnic ancestry. This gives them the option of which ethnicity to identify with. The U.S. census has asked a question on ethnic ancestry in the 1980 and 1990 censuses. In 1980, 52 percent of the American public responded with a single ethnic ancestry, 31 percent gave multiple ethnic origins (up to three were coded, but some individuals wrote in more than three), and only 6 percent said they were American only, while the remaining 11 percent gave no response. In 1990 about 90 percent of the population gave some response to the ancestry question, with only 5 percent giving American as a response and only 1.4 percent reporting an uncodeable response such as "don't know" (McKenney and Cresce 1992; U.S. Bureau of the Census 1992).

Several researchers have examined the pattern of responses of people to the census ancestry question. These analyses have shown a pattern of flux and inconsistency in ethnic ancestry reporting. For instance, Lieberson and Waters (1986, 1988, p. 93) have found that parents simplify children's ancestries when reporting them to the census. For instance, among the offspring in situations where one parent reports a specific single White ethnic origin and the other parent reports a different single White origin, about 40 percent of the children are not described as the logical combination of the parents' ancestries. For example, only about 60 percent of the children of English-German marriages are labeled as English-German or German-English. About 15 percent of the children of these parents are simplified to just English, and another 15 percent are reported as just German. The remainder of the children are either not given an ancestry or are described as American (Lieberson and Waters 1986, 1993).

In addition to these intergenerational changes, researchers have found changes in reporting ancestry that occur at the time of marriage or upon leaving home. At the ages of eighteen to twenty-two, when many young Americans leave home for the first time, the number of people reporting a single as opposed to a multiple ancestry goes up. Thus while parents simplify children's ancestries when they leave home, children themselves tend to report less complexity in their ancestries when they leave their parents' homes and begin reporting their ancestries themselves (Lieberson and Waters 1986, 1988; Waters 1990).

These individual changes are reflected in variability over time in the aggregate numbers of groups determined by the census and surveys. Fairly (1991) compared the consistency of the overall counts of different ancestry groups in the 1979 Current Population Survey, the 1980 census, and the 1986 National Content Test (a pretest for the 1990 census). He found much less consistency in the numbers for northern European ancestry groups whose immigration peaks were early in the nineteenth century—the English, Dutch, Germans, and other northern European groups. In other words each of these different surveys and the census yielded a different estimate of the number of people having this ancestry. The 1990 census also showed a great deal of flux and inconsistency in some ancestry groups. The number of people reporting English as an ancestry went down considerably from 1980, while the number reporting German ancestry went up. The number of Cajuns grew dramatically. This has led officials at the Census Bureau to assume that the examples used in the instructions strongly influence the responses people give. (Cajun was one of the examples of an ancestry given in 1990 but not in 1980, and German was the first example given. English was an example in the 1980 instructions, but not in 1990.)

All of these studies point to the socially variable nature of ethnic identity—and the lack of equivalence between ethnic ancestry and identity. If merely adding a category to the instructions to the question increases the number of people claiming that ancestry, what does that mean about the level of importance of that identity for people answering the census? Clearly identity and ancestry for Whites in the United States, who increasingly are from mixed backgrounds, involve some change and choice.

Symbolic Ethnicities for White Americans

What do these ethnic identities mean to people and why do they cling to them rather than just abandoning the tie and calling themselves American?

My own field research with suburban Whites in California and Pennsylvania found that later-generation descendants of European origin maintain what are called "symbolic ethnicities." Symbolic ethnicity is a term coined by Herbert Gans (1979) to refer to ethnicity that is individualistic in nature and without real social cost for the individual. These symbolic identifications are essentially leisure time activities, rooted in nuclear family traditions and reinforced by the voluntary enjoyable aspects of being ethnic (Waters 1990). Richard Alba (1990) also found later-generation Whites in Albany, New York, who chose to keep a tie with an ethnic identity because of the enjoyable and voluntary aspects to those identities, along with the feelings of specialness they entailed. An example of symbolic ethnicity is individuals who identify as Irish, for example, on occasions such as Saint Patrick's Day, on family holidays, or for vacations. They do not usually belong to Irish American organizations, live in Irish neighborhoods, work in Irish jobs, or marry other Irish people. The symbolic meaning of being Irish American can be constructed by individuals from mass media images, family traditions, or other intermittent social activities. In other words, for later-generation White ethnics, ethnicity is not something that influences their lives unless they want it to. In the world of work and school and neighborhood, individuals do not have to admit to being ethnic unless they choose to. And for an increasing number of European-origin individuals whose parents and grandparents have intermarried, the ethnicity they claim is largely a matter of personal choice as they sort through all of the possible combinations of groups in their genealogies.

Individuals can choose those aspects of being Italian, for instance, that appeal to them, and discard those that do not. Or a person whose father is Italian, and mother part Polish and part French, might choose among the three ethnicities and present herself as a Polish American. With just a little probing, many people will describe a variety of ancestries in their family background, but do not consider these ancestries to be a salient part of their own identities. Thus the 1990 census ancestry question, which estimated that 30 percent of the population is of mixed ancestry, most surely underestimates the degree of mixing among the population. My research, and the research of Richard Alba (1990), shows that many people have already sorted through what they know of their ethnic ancestries and simplified their responses before they ever answer a census or survey question (Waters 1990).

But note that this freedom to include or exclude ancestries in your identification to yourself and others would not be the same for those defined racially in our society. They are constrained to identify with the part of their ancestry that has been socially defined as the "essential" part. African Americans, for example, have been highly socially constrained to identify as Blacks, without other options available to them, even when they know that their forebears included many people of American Indian or European background. Up until the mid-twentieth century, many state governments had specific laws defining one as Black if as little as one-thirty-second of one's ancestors were defined as Black (Davis 1991; Dominguez 1986; Spickard 1989). Even now when the one-drop rule has been dropped from our legal codes, there are still strong societal pressures on African Americans to identify in a particular way. Certain ancestries take precedence over others in the societal rules on descent and ancestry reckoning. If one believes one is part English and part German and identifies in a survey as German, one is not in danger of being accused of trying to "pass" as non-English and of being "redefined" English by the interviewer. But if one were part African and part German, one's self-identification as German would be highly suspect and probably not accepted if one "looked" Black according to the prevailing social norms.

This is reflected in the ways the census collects race and ethnic identity. While the ethnic ancestry question used in 1980 and 1990 is given to all Americans in the sample regardless of race and allows multiple responses that combine races, the primary source of information on people defined racially in the United States is the census race question or the Hispanic question. Both of these questions require a person to make a choice about an identity. Individuals are not allowed to respond that they are both Black and White, or Japanese and Asian Indian on the race question even if they know that is their background. In fact, people who disobey the instructions to the census race question and check off two races are assigned to the first checked race in the list by the Census Bureau.

In responding to the ancestry question, the comparative latitude that White respondents have does not mean that Whites pick and choose ethnicities out of thin air. For the most part people choose an identity that corresponds with some element of their family tree. However, there are many anecdotal instances of people adopting ethnicities when they marry or move to a strongly identified neighborhood or community. For instance Micaela di Leonardo (1984) reported instances of non-Italian women who married into Italian American families and "became Italian." Karen Leonard (1992) describes a community of Mexican American women who married Punjabi immigrants in California. Some of the Punjabi immigrants and their descendants were said to have "become Mexican" when they joined their wives' kin group and social worlds. Alternatively she describes the community acknowledging that Mexican women made the best curry, as they adapted to life with Indian-origin men.

But what do these identities mean to individuals? Surely an identity that is optional in a number of ways—not legally defined on a passport or birth certificate, not socially consequential in terms of societal discrimination in terms of housing or job access, and not economically limiting in terms of blocking opportunities for social mobility—cannot be the same as an identity that results from and is nurtured by societal exclusion and rejection. The choice to have a symbolic ethnicity is an attractive and widespread one despite its lack of demonstrable content, because having a symbolic ethnicity combines individuality with feelings of community. People reported to me that they liked having an ethnic identity because it gave them a uniqueness and a feeling of being special. They often contrasted their own specialness by virtue of their ethnic identities with "bland" Americanness. Being ethnic makes people feel unique and special and not just "vanilla" as one of my respondents put it.

Because "American" is largely understood by Americans to be a political identity and allegiance and not an ethnic one, the idea of being "American" does not give people the same sense of belonging that their hyphenated American identity does. When I asked people about their dual identities—American and Irish or Italian or whatever—they usually responded in a way that showed how they conceived of the relationship between the two identities. Being an American was their primary identity; but it was so primary that they rarely, if ever, thought about it—most commonly only when they left the country. Being Irish American, on the other hand, was a way they had of differentiating themselves from others whom they interacted with from day to day—in many cases from spouses or in-laws. Certain of their traits—being emotional, having a sense of humor, talking with their hands—were understood as stemming from their ethnicity. Yet when asked about their identity as Americans, that identity was both removed from their day-to-day consciousness and understood in terms of loyalty and patriotism. Although they may not think they behave or think in a certain way because they are American, being American is something they are both proud of and committed to.

Symbolic ethnicity is the best of all worlds for these respondents. These White ethnics can claim to be unique and special, while simultaneously finding the community and conformity with others that they also crave. But that "community" is of a type that will not interfere with a person's individuality. It is not as if these people belong to ethnic voluntary organizations or gather as a group in churches or neighborhoods or union halls. They work and reside within the mainstream of American middle-class life, yet they retain the interesting benefits—the "specialness"—of ethnic allegiance, without any of its drawbacks.

It has been suggested by several researchers that this positive value attached to ethnic ancestry, which became popular in the ethnic revival of the 1970s, is the result of assimilation having proceeded to an advanced stage for descendants of White Europeans (Alba 1985; Crispino 1980; Steinberg 1981). Ironically, people celebrate and embrace their ethnic backgrounds precisely because assimilation has proceeded to the point where such identification does not have that much influence on their day-to-day life. Rather than choosing the "least ethnic" and most bland ethnicities, Whites desire the "most ethnic" ones, like the once-stigmatized "Italian," because it is perceived as bringing the most psychic benefits. For instance, when an Italian father is married to an English or a Scottish or a German mother, the likelihood is that the child will be reported to the census with the father's Italian ancestry, rather than the northern European ancestries, which would have been predicted to have a higher social status. Italian is a good ancestry to have, people told me, because they have good food and a warm family life. This change in the social meaning of being Italian American is quite dramatic, given that Italians were subject to discrimination, exclusion, and extreme negative stereotyping in the early part of the twentieth century.

RACE RELATIONS AND SYMBOLIC ETHNICITY

However much symbolic ethnicity is without cost for the individual, there is a cost associated with symbolic ethnicity for the society. That is because symbolic ethnicities of the type described here are confined to White Americans of European origin. Black Americans, Hispanic Americans, Asian Americans, and American Indians do not have the option of a symbolic ethnicity at present in the United States. For all of the ways in which ethnicity does not matter for White Americans, it does matter for non-Whites. Who your ancestors are does affect your choice of spouse, where you live, what job you have, who your friends are, and what your chances are for success in American society, if those ancestors happen not to be from Europe. The reality is that White ethnics have a lot more choice and room to maneuver than they themselves think they do. The situation is very different for members of racial minorities, whose lives are strongly influenced by their race or national origin regardless of how much they may choose not to identify themselves in terms of their ancestries.

When White Americans learn the stories of how their grandparents and great-grandparents triumphed in the United States over adversity, they are usually told in terms of their individual efforts and triumphs. The important role of labor unions and other organized political and economic actors in their social and economic successes is left out of the story in favor of a generational story of individual Americans rising up against communitarian, Old World intolerance and New World resistance. As a result, the "individualized" voluntary, cultural view of ethnicity for Whites is what is remembered.

One important implication of these identities is that they tend to be very individualistic. There is a tendency to view valuing diversity in a pluralist environment as equating all groups. The symbolic ethnic tends to think that all groups are equal; everyone has a background that is their right to celebrate and pass on to their children. This leads to the conclusion that all identities are equal and all identities in some sense are interchangeable—"I'm Italian American, you're Polish American. I'm Irish American, you're African American." The important thing is to treat people as individuals and all equally. However, this assumption ignores the very big difference between an individualistic symbolic ethnic identity and a socially enforced and imposed racial identity. When White Americans equate their own symbolic ethnicities with the socially enforced identities of non-White Americans, they obscure the fact that the experiences of Whites and non-Whites have been qualitatively different in the United States and that the current identities of individuals partly reflect that unequal history.

In the next section I describe how relations between Black and White students on college campuses reflect some of these asymmetries in the understanding of what a racial or ethnic identity means. While I focus on Black and White students in the following discussion, you should be aware that the myriad other groups in the United States—Mexican Americans,

American Indians, Japanese Americans—all have some degree of social and individual influences on their identities, which reflect the group's social and economic history and present circumstance.

Relations on College Campuses

Both Black and White students face the task of developing their race and ethnic identities. Sociologists and psychologists note that at the time people leave home and begin to live independently from their parents, often ages eighteen to twenty-two, they report a heightened sense of racial and ethnic identity as they sort through how much of their beliefs and behaviors are idiosyncratic to their families and how much are shared with other people. It is not until one comes in close contact with many people who are different from oneself that individuals realize the ways in which their backgrounds may influence their individual personality. This involves coming into contact with people who are different in terms of their ethnicity, class, religion, region, and race. For White students, the ethnicity they claim is more often than not a symbolic one—with all of the voluntary, enjoyable, and intermittent characteristics I have described above.

Black students at the university are also developing identities through interactions with others who are different from them. Their identity development is more complicated than that of Whites because of the added element of racial discrimination and racism, along with the "ethnic" developments of finding others who share their background. Thus Black students have the positive attraction of being around other Black students who share some cultural elements, as well as the need to band together with other students in a reactive and oppositional way in the face of racist incidents on campus.

Colleges and universities across the country have been increasing diversity among their student bodies in the last few decades. This had led in many cases to strained relations among students from different racial and ethnic backgrounds. The 1980s and 1990s produced a great number of racial incidents and high racial tensions on campuses. While there were a number of racial incidents that were due to bigotry, unlawful behavior, and violent or vicious attacks, much of what happens among students on campuses involves a low level of tension and awkwardness in social interactions.

Many Black students experience racism personally for the first time on campus. The upper-middle-class students from White suburbs were often isolated enough that their presence was not threatening to racists in their high schools. Also, their class background was known by their residence and this may have prevented attacks being directed at them. Often Black students at the university who begin talking with other students and recognizing racial slights will remember incidents that happened to them earlier that they might not have thought were related to race.

Black college students across the country experience a sizeable number of incidents that are clearly the result of racism. Many of the most blatant ones that occur between students are the result of drinking. Sometimes late at night, drunken groups of White students coming home from parties will yell slurs at single Black students on the street. The other types of incidents that happen include being singled out for special treatment by employees, such as being followed when shopping at the campus bookstore, or going to the art museum with your class and the guard stops you and asks for your I.D. Others involve impersonal encounters on the street—being called a nigger by a truck driver while crossing the street, or seeing old ladies clutch their pocketbooks and shake in terror as you pass them on the street. For the most part these incidents are not specific to the university environment; they are the types of incidents middle-class Blacks face everyday throughout American society, and they have been documented by sociologists (Feagin 1991).

In such a climate, however, with students experiencing these types of incidents and talking with each other about them, Black students do experience a tension and a feeling of being singled out. It is unfair that this is part of their college experience and not that of White students. Dealing with incidents like this, or the ever-present threat of such incidents, is an ongoing developmental task for Black students that takes energy, attention, and strength of character. It should be clearly understood that this is an asymmetry in the "college experience" for Black and White students. It is one of the unfair aspects of life that results from living in a society with ongoing racial prejudice and discrimination. It is also very understandable that it makes some students angry at the unfairness of it all, even if there is no one to blame specifically. It is also very troubling because, while most Whites do not create these incidents, some do, and it is never clear until you know someone well whether they are the type of person who could do something like this. So one of the reactions of Black students to these incidents is to band together.

In some sense then, as Blauner (1992) has argued, you can see Black students coming together on campus as both an "ethnic" pull of wanting to be together to share common experiences and community, and a "racial" push of banding together defensively because of perceived rejection and tension from Whites. In this way the ethnic identities of Black students are in some sense similar to, say, Korean students wanting to be together to share experiences. And it is an ethnicity that is generally much stronger than, say, Italian Americans. But for Koreans who come together there is generally a definition of themselves as "different from" Whites. For Blacks reacting to exclusion, there is a tendency for the coming together to involve both being "different from" but also "opposed to" Whites.

The anthropologist John Ogbu (1990) has documented the tendency of minorities in a variety of societies around the world, who have experienced severe blocked mobility for long periods of time, to develop such oppositional identities. An important component of having such an identity is to describe others of your group who do not join in the group solidarity as devaluing and denying their very core identity. This is why it is not common for successful Asians to be accused by others of "acting White" in the United States, but it is

quite common for such a term to be used by Blacks and Latinos. The oppositional component of a Black identity also explains how Black people can question whether others are acting "Black enough." On campus, it explains some
of the intense pressures felt by Black students who do not make their racial
identity central and who choose to hang out primarily with non-Blacks. This
pressure from the group, which is partly defining itself by not being White,
is exacerbated by the fact that race is a physical marker in American society.
No one immediately notices the Jewish students sitting together in the dining
hall, or the one Jewish student sitting surrounded by non-Jews, or the Texan
sitting with the Californians, but everyone notices the Black student who is or
is not at the "Black table" in the cafeteria.

Institutional Responses

Our society asks a lot of young people. We ask young people to do something
that no one else does as successfully on such a wide scale—that is to live
together with people from very different backgrounds, to respect one
another, to appreciate one another, and to enjoy and learn from one another.
The successes that occur every day in this endeavor are many, and they are
too often overlooked. However, the problems and tensions are also real, and
they will not vanish on their own. We tend to see pluralism working in the
United States in much the same way some people expect capitalism to work.
If you put together people with various interests and abilities and resources,
the "invisible hand" of capitalism is supposed to make all the parts work
together in an economy for the common good.

There is much to be said for such a model—the invisible hand of the
market can solve complicated problems of production and distribution
better than any "visible hand" of a state plan. However, we have learned that
unequal power relations among the actors in the capitalist marketplace, as
well as "externalities" that the market cannot account for, such as long-term
pollution, or collusion between corporations, or the exploitation of child
labor, means that state regulation is often needed. Pluralism and the relations between groups are very similar. There is a lot to be said for the idea
that bringing people who belong to different ethnic or racial groups together
in institutions with no interference will have good consequences. Students
from different backgrounds will make friends if they share a dorm room or
corridor, and there is no need for the institution to do any more than provide
the locale. But like capitalism, the invisible hand of pluralism does not do
well when power relations and externalities are ignored. When you bring
together individuals from groups that are differentially valued in the wider
society and provide no guidance, there will be problems. In these cases the
"invisible hand" of pluralist relations does not work, and tensions and disagreements can arise without any particular individual or group of individuals being "to blame." On college campuses in the 1990s some of the tensions
between students are of this sort. They arise from honest misunderstandings,

lack of a common background, and very different experiences of what race and ethnicity mean to the individual.

The implications of symbolic ethnicities for thinking about race relations are subtle but consequential. If your understanding of your own ethnicity and its relationship to society and politics is one of individual choice, it becomes harder to understand the need for programs like affirmative action, which recognize the ongoing need for group struggle and group recognition, in order to bring about social change. It also is hard for a White college student to understand the need that minority students feel to band together against discrimination. It also is easy, on the individual level, to expect everyone else to be able to turn their ethnicity on and off at will, the way you are able to, without understanding that ongoing discrimination and societal attention to minority status makes that impossible for individuals from minority groups to do. The paradox of symbolic ethnicity is that it depends upon the ultimate goal of a pluralist society, and at the same time makes it more difficult to achieve that ultimate goal. It is dependent upon the concept that all ethnicities mean the same thing, that enjoying the traditions of one's heritage is an option available to a group or an individual, but that such a heritage should not have any social costs associated with it.

There are many societal issues and involuntary ascriptions associated with non-White identities. The developments necessary for this to change are not individual but societal in nature. Social mobility and declining racial and ethnic sensitivity are closely associated. The legacy and the present reality of discrimination on the basis of race or ethnicity must be overcome before the ideal of the pluralist society, where all heritages are treated equally and are equally available for individuals to choose or discard at will, is realized.

REFERENCES

Alba, Richard D. 1985. *Italian Americans: Into the Twilight of Ethnicity.* Englewood Cliffs, NJ: Prentice-Hall.

———. 1990. *Ethnic Identity: The Transformation of White America.* New Haven, CT: Yale University Press.

Barth, Frederik. 1969. *Ethnic Groups and Boundaries.* Boston: Little, Brown.

Blauner, Robert. 1992. "Talking Past Each Other: Black and White Languages of Race." *American Prospect* (Summer):55–64

Crispino, James. 1980. *The Assimilation of Ethnic Groups: The Italian Case.* Staten Island, NY: Center for Migration Studies.

Davis, F. James. 1991. *Who Is Black. One Nation's Definition.* University Park: Pennsylvania State University Press.

di Leonardo, Micaela. 1984. *The Varieties of Ethnic Experience: Kinship, Class and Gender Among Italian Americans.* Ithaca, NY: Cornell University Press.

Dominguez, Virginia. 1986. *White by Definition: Social Classification in Creole Louisiana.* New Brunswick, NJ: Rutgers University Press.

Fairly, Reynolds. 1991. "The New Census Questions about Ancestry: What Did It Tell Us?" *Demography* 28:411–29.

Feagin, Joe R. 1991. "The Continuing Significance of Race: Antiblack Discrimination in Public Places." *Americian Sociological Review* 56:101–117.

Gans, Herbert. 1979. "Symbolic Ethnicity: The Future of Ethnic Groups and Cultures in America." *Ethnic and Racial Studies* 2:1–20.

Greeley, Andrew M. 1976. "The Ethnic Miracle." *Public Interest* 45 (Fall):20–36.

Leonard, Karen. 1992. *Making Ethnic Choices: California's Punjabi Mexican Americans.* Philadelphia: Temple University Press.

Lieberson, Stanley. 1985. "Unhyphenated Whites in the United States." *Ethnic and Racial Studies* 8:159–80.

Lieberson, Stanley, and Mary Waters, 1986. "Ethnic Groups in Flux: The Changing Ethnic Responses of American Whites." *Annals of the American Academy of Political and Social Science* 487:79–91.

———. 1988. *From Many Strands: Ethnic and Racial Groups in Contemporary America.* New York: Russell Sage.

———. 1993. "The Ethnic Responses of Whites: What Causes Their Instability, Simplification, and Inconsistency?" *Social Forces* 72(2):421–50.

McKenney, Nampeo R., and Arthur R. Cresce. 1992. "Measurement of Ethnicity in the United States: Experiences of the U.S. Census Bureau." Paper presented at the Joint Canada–United States Conference on the Measurement of Ethnicity, Ottawa, Canada, April 1–3.

Spickard, Paul R. 1989. *Mixed Blood.* Madison: University of Wisconsin Press.

Steinberg, Stephen. 1981. *The Ethnic Myth: Race, Ethnicity, and Class in America.* Boston: Beacon Press.

U.S. Bureau of the Census. 1992. *Census of Population and Housing, 1990: Detailed Ancestry Groups for States.* Supplementary Reports CP-S-1-2. Washington, D.C.: U.S. Government Printing Office.

Waters, Mary C. 1990. *Ethnic Options: Choosing Identities in America.* Berkeley and Los Angeles: University of California Press.

Weber, Max. 1921. *Economy and Society: An Outline of Interpretive Sociology,* edited by Guenther Roth and Claus Wittich, translated by Ephraim Fischoff. New York: Bedminster Press.

 QUESTIONS FOR CRITICAL THINKING

Reading 2

1. What are some of the reasons whites may choose to identify with a particular ethnicity? What purpose does belonging to a particular ethnicity serve?

2. How does the freedom to include or exclude ancestries differ for whites and people of color?

3. How do "optional ethnicities" differ from ethnicities that result from exclusion and oppression? What are some of the advantages and/or disadvantages of each?

BECOMING SUSPECTS

TRAM NGUYEN

Muhammad Rafiq Butt had a wife and five children to support back home in Pakistan, and sending them money was his biggest concern in life, according to those who knew him. His two sons were too young to help, and his three daughters were close to marrying age. So he embarked on a journey as many others had, living among other men, alone, working without papers in the teeming anonymity of New York City's immigrant economy.

"He had a lot of pressure in his mind. His wish was one day to have enough money so his daughters can be married. His responsibility was to get them married. That is very important to our culture," said his friend Rashid Ahmed. "He had a lot of burden, a lot of pressures."

During his year in New York City, after arriving on a visitor visa in September 2000, Butt had been unable to find regular work. He spoke little English and his age, fifty-five, was a disadvantage when applying for the heavy labor and odd restaurant jobs he strung together. One of these jobs was at Shaheen Sweets, a restaurant and sweetshop in the "Little India" neighborhood of Jackson Heights. There, he worked alongside Ahmed and about a half-dozen other men and women in the basement, stirring vats of cheese and milk, molding mounds of dough into balls by hand, and filling white plastic bins full of the sticky-sweet *rashogollahs* that were boxed and shipped to suppliers around the country. Unbeknownst to anyone, perhaps even himself, Butt had a congenital heart defect and had developed blockages in his coronary arteries. But this didn't keep him from working every day he had a job.

Ahmed, about the same age and also living alone and supporting his family in Pakistan, often gave Butt rides to the house in Queens that he shared with a nephew and several other roommates. Then came a day in September 2001 when Ahmed arrived at the restaurant and heard from the other workers that Butt had been taken by the FBI. That was all they knew, but it did not come as a complete surprise. Many others had also begun to disappear from the streets and homes of Jackson Heights, Astoria, Midwood, and other neighborhoods across Brooklyn and Queens, and fear was starting to spread.

"You know FBI has a big name everywhere in the world," Ahmed said. "Rafiq was a very simple person. Can you imagine a person who was working for his family, who was a very simple man, how can he do anything like World Trade Center, like plane hijacking?"

On September 19, following a tip from a local caller, FBI agents arrested Muhammad Butt at his home in the middle of the night. After being held for a day at 26 Federal Plaza, immigration headquarters in Manhattan, he was transferred to Hudson County Jail in New Jersey. Inside the drab brown building, circled by barbed wire, Butt lived for the next five weeks. Out of the thousands of men being picked up and held in detention across the Northeast at that time, no one would have ever heard of him. But on October 23, 2001, his ailing heart gave out. Muhammad Butt now had the unfortunate distinction of having died in U.S. detention following the post–September 11 roundup.[1]

A taxi driver named Bilal Mirza, whose niece was engaged to marry Butt's nephew, got the phone call from the Pakistani consulate informing him of Butt's death. Jail officials declared cardiac arrhythmia as the cause of death and closed the case, but rumors swirled in the community. A follow-up investigation by Human Rights Watch found that Butt had complained to his cellmate of chest pains and in the days leading up to his death had unsuccessfully tried to get medical attention.[2] Mirza, who prepared the body in Muslim tradition for the funeral, waved aside rumors of any beatings. "No, no, no. I wash his body with my own hands, and I see he have no rash, no bruises," he said.

Rashid Ahmed, nevertheless, refused to believe that his friend's death had been due to natural causes. "I say it was not a natural death," he said, sitting in the Shaheen restaurant nearly four years later. "A person who never went to jail in his own country. He never face a single police officer in his own country. When he was in jail, maybe he thinking every time, what is happening, what is happening?"

Butt's body was shipped back to Pakistan, along with a thousand dollars he'd asked Ahmed to keep for him. It was his last remittance to his family.

In a way, it was Muhammad Butt's death that changed life for Bobby Khan. Two years later to the day, Khan, a regular visitor at Hudson County Jail, was standing in the waiting room, remembering Butt on the anniversary of his death.

But back in 2001, Khan had not yet heard of Muhammad Butt, and he was hoping never to go near a jail again. A financial analyst living in Brooklyn's Park Slope neighborhood, he was trying to concentrate on "doing very well, focusing on making money and stuff for once." He was forty-two years old, a father of two who drove a Lexus SUV with a child's car seat in the back. His days were occupied with consulting for clients among Little Pakistan's burgeoning professional and business class. The routine of a suburban husband, father, and corporate employee, while busy, was the most peace Khan had known in his life thus far. He remembered writing to friends in Pakistan after eight months in New York: "I really like living here, and it's much, much better than the circumstances back home. So I think I'm going to live here the rest of my life."

The words later struck him as ironic: "9/11 smashed all those feelings," he said. Several years after September 11, he still had trouble sleeping. Khan has deep sunken eyes and a patient, often excruciatingly polite manner that made up for a tendency to overbook his schedule and constantly run late. His placid exterior, however, belied a tumultuous past. More than twenty years before, this son of a Lahore trade unionist had rallied thousands of students as a leader in the protest movement against Pakistan's military dictatorship. Khan, whose actual first name is Ahsanullah ("Bobby" is a family nickname), was four when his father was arrested for organizing steelworkers. He remembered soldiers coming to their house, and his father disappearing for almost a year. Khan began university in Lahore in 1977. That July, General Mohammad Zia-ul-Haq deposed Prime Minister Zulfikar Ali Bhutto and had him hanged. Zia established absolute control of the government and began instituting repressive laws. In response, university students joined huge street rallies protesting the dictatorship. Khan was arrested for the first time when he was seventeen.

"Torture was very common. Not only torture but lashing you in front of people to embarrass you. Hanging [you] upside down, electric shock on sexual organs; they had so many techniques," he remembered. "It wasn't that I was physically very strong. But I survived it because I believed that I was doing something against the injustices and oppression, and this was what I believed, and still believe, is the basic mission of life."

Pakistan's image today, after the United States' war on neighboring Afghanistan, after the declared war on terrorism, after the kidnapping and killing of American journalist Daniel Pearl in Karachi, and after revelations that the state had played a murky role in the international black market for nuclear weapons materials, is of a country teetering on the edge. Pakistan is perceived to be both a key U.S. ally in the war on terror and a breeding ground for terrorists, with Osama bin Laden believed to be hiding in its northern territory. It was because of this precarious position in the war on terror, some observers said, that Pakistani immigrants in the United States faced particular scrutiny. "The mujahideen is why Americans focus on Pakistan. Ordinary Pakistanis don't know what's going on," commented journalist M. R. Farrukh of the *Pakistani Post* in New York City. "[President] Musharraf thinks he's doing great by capturing an al-Qa'ida member once in a while. But Pakistani people living here—the American government thinks we're friends of al-Qa'ida."

The Pakistan Khan remembered was a country in the throes of a dictatorship but flush with the vibrancy of a mass democracy movement. "It was a huge resistance. Millions of people were out on the streets," he described.

Thousands were jailed, and hundreds were executed by the military regime. After he was released, Khan went right back to student organizing. Six months passed, and he landed in prison again. It became a routine throughout the years of his youth. Eventually, some of the political graffiti on university grounds began to read, "Free Bobby." Khan laughed to recount his more than twenty arrests in fifteen years. At a reunion of Pakistani political exiles in New York years later, on the anniversary of Bhutto's election, old comrades recognized him by asking, "Are you the same Free Bobby?" Khan laughed again. "Me and prison go together."

Thousands of exiles ended up leaving the country during the period between 1980 and 1990, emigrating to Europe and the United States. Khan, too, left for the U.S. in 1995, initially to work as a journalist for a Pakistani newspaper and then becoming a financial analyst. Finding relief in the "general freedom of speech and employment" of his new environment, Khan let friends persuade him to stay and get a break from his political work in Pakistan.

The day he heard about Muhammad Butt, Khan had just come home to his house in Park Slope. He felt his anxiety rising as he told the news to his wife. They knew the community would be in an uproar. "It was a big shock. Everyone was alarmed—people are being killed? The common feeling was that if anybody would talk, they would be facing dire consequences," he recalled.

In the days that followed, there was more bad news. Khan heard of one man who, while he was at work, had his apartment raided by the FBI. When he found out that the FBI was looking for him, the forty-something man suffered a fatal heart attack. In Khan's neighborhood of Park Slope, a Pakistani journalist was beaten unconscious by three men who told him he looked like Osama bin Laden.[3] Stories like these circulated rapidly, thanks to what Khan characterized as the "communal, joint living style" of the Pakistani immigrants. This mirrored the wave of hate crimes across the nation. From September 11 through February 2002, hate crimes and incidents of discrimination toward Muslims soared to 1,717, according to the Council on American-Islamic Relations.[4] The violence included murder, physical assaults, death threats, harassment, vandalism, and arson.

Within the ten to fifteen blocks of Midwood, federal agents began visiting all the businesses owned by Pakistanis, asking everyone for identification, and conducting predawn raids at homes. "You can call this the phase of midnight knocks," described journalist Mohsin Zaheer of the weekly *Sada-e-Pakistan* in Midwood. Arrests began to mount. Hundreds of new arrivals were filling up Hudson County Jail and Passaic County Jail in New Jersey, the Metropolitan Detention Center in Brooklyn, and the Varick Street detention center in Manhattan.

They were disappearing into a vast system of immigration prisons that had been detaining 150,000 people annually since the mid-1990s and now hold more than 200,000 people each year. It is a system made up of hundreds of detention centers, local jails contracted to hold detainees, and prisons run by private corporations. For some asylum seekers, noncitizens who had served criminal sentences for felonies, as well as thousands of undocumented immigrants picked up by the Border Patrol, this almost invisible system of warehousing—and "removal" or deportation—had been operating and growing quietly for years before September 11.[5] Between 1994 and 2001, the daily rate of detentions had more than tripled, according to INS records. More than 60 percent of these detainees were being held in over a thousand private prisons or local jails around the country with which the INS had contracted to make room for their charges.[6] The whole system operated on the basic premise that noncitizens had to do their waiting in jail—whether they had arrived in the country by boat or plane and were waiting for an asylum hearing, or had already served prison sentences and were waiting to be deported. What the INS termed "administrative detention" in effect equaled jail time because of the conditions under which detainees were held. Yet before September 11, public concern over the detention system was negligible, mostly confined to a specialized circle of immigration attorneys, church-based groups, and human rights activists.

"After 9/11 it was just unbelievable, the scale with which specific populations started getting targeted," said Subhash Kateel, an organizer who had been working with a group of Jesuit volunteers at the Elizabeth detention center in New Jersey just before September 11. "It went from courtrooms being relatively diverse—in New York they're incredibly diverse, Chinese, Caribbean, all people of color—to being all Pakistani, all Yemeni, all Egyptian from September until June of 2002."

It wasn't until early 2002 that Amnesty International was able to obtain information and release a report on 718 detainees, mostly from Pakistan, Egypt, Turkey, and Yemen, along with a few from Tunisia, Saudi Arabia, Morocco, and Jordan.[7] Investigations by newspapers, including the *Washington Post* and *Newsday*, also attempted to piece together a picture of the scale of detention during that period. But the Department of Justice announced on November 8, 2001, that it would no longer release a running tally of the post–September 11 detainees, and the official count remained at 1,182. However, this figure reflected only the people who were being held at any given time, and not the total of all who had been arrested or the unknown amount who had been released or deported.[8] The DOJ's Public Affairs Office stopped releasing cumulative totals because "the statistics became too confusing."[9] Of the approximately 1,200 detainees, 762 were acknowledged later to be of "special interest" to the government's terrorism investigation. Charged with immigration violations, they were jailed for periods ranging from a few months to a year, waiting to be cleared by the FBI before being deported. The FBI's sweep, known as the PENTTBOM investigation, lasted from September 11, 2001, until August 6, 2002.[10] Though launched in response to the terrorist attacks, the federal crackdown opened the door to heightened, ongoing scrutiny in targeted communities that would lead to many more arrests.

As the post-9/11 detainees were deported, more immigrants continued to take their places in jail cells in the following years. They were being nabbed during periodic raids and stings that had shifted from an antiterror roundup to what was fast becoming an immigration cleanup. Since the post–September 11 fallout, community advocates and lawyers working with detainees estimate that the total arrests and detentions in the Northeast have reached up to 10,000.[11]

. . .

Bobby Khan is a Muslim ("not a very good one" he adds, chuckling) who keeps a small prayer rug thrown over a shopping cart piled with coats and blankets in the back of his office. He seldom found time to use it, crisscrossing the boroughs to meet with clients for his day job as a realtor as well as to visit detainees' families.

In the week following Muhammad Butt's death, Khan joined a hastily organized forum put on by several human rights and community-based organizations. He became something of a community spokesman to reporters after the event and began visiting prisoners and their families in the area. Eventually, he helped form a volunteer-based organization called the Coney Island Avenue Project, after Midwood's main street, to visit detainees, arrange free legal representation for them, and mobilize community speakouts and protests.

Like Khan, others in the hot spots spread between Brooklyn and New Jersey had formed grassroots responses to the crisis unfolding around them. A community-based organization called Desis Rising Up and Moving (DRUM), led by young South Asian organizers in Jackson Heights, had been working with immigrants in prison for several years prior to 9/11 and started to notice the new arrivals when they visited the New York—New Jersey area's main detention centers. Family members of detainees reached out for help to groups like DRUM, the Islamic Circle of North America, and the Asian American Legal Defense and Education Fund, which began finding out where loved ones had been taken and what was happening to them.

"It was December 2001 when I became aware of the disappearances. And they were really disappearances at that time," recalled Adem Carroll, the coordinator of the Islamic Circle's post-9/11 relief project. "I would go to the Metropolitan Detention Center with families, and they were told their husbands weren't there. But their husbands' letters were arriving, after a two-week lag or so, saying they were inside. We'd ask the staff of the jail, and they'd say no. It took until January when they started to admit they were holding them."

. . .

On October 18, 2001, at about the same time that Muhammad Butt's body was making the final trip home, a young Pakistani man named Ali Raza parked his cab outside a friend's apartment in Jamaica, Queens. It was almost

2:00 AM, and he had just finished his shift. Raza was twenty-five, with a compact build and a goatee, a small hoop earring, and a diamond stud in his nostril. He had been living on his own in Queens since arriving in the United States alone from Pakistan at age fifteen.

Raza and his friend began cooking dinner in the basement apartment, turning on some rap music. Almost half an hour later, the front door came crashing in. "Freeze! Put your hands in the air and freeze!"

Before they could even react, the two young men had guns in their faces. There were six or seven FBI agents, according to Raza. Some of them started searching the apartment. They turned over furniture and began ripping up the carpet.

"Who lives here?" one of them asked.

Raza answered, "I'm visiting here and this is my friend's place." Still confused, he remembered wondering if the neighbors had called to complain about their loud music.

"The whole house was upside down," he recalled. "Then they left and two ladies in INS uniforms came in."

The INS agents demanded IDs, setting up a laptop at the kitchen table to run checks on the men's names. "What's your status?" they asked. Raza lied. "I got a green card, but it's at my house."

His friend also lied, saying that he was born in the United States. "He had a better accent and everything, so he thought he could pull it off," Raza explained.

The agents apologized to the friend, having found nothing on his name. To Raza, they said, "Let's go to your house to look for your green card." Knowing the game was up for him, Raza admitted that he had no green card. They took him to Federal Plaza for booking that night.

"There were five hundred, maybe six hundred other guys. Egyptians, Arabic mostly. It looked like what they did with the Japanese after Pearl Harbor," Raza said. "Guards were screaming at them, cussing, calling them bin Laden, stuff like that."

Raza was given a paper to sign his consent for voluntary deportation, but he refused. "I wasn't believing them for anything because of the way they came to the house." He said they told him if he didn't sign, he would get twenty years for terrorism. All around him, immigrants were signing the papers, some who spoke no English at all. Raza said he noticed guards covering up the papers above the line where the men marked their names. By now it was 3:45 AM and Raza was taken to a cell, where he spent the rest of the night. His mind raced as he sat upright against a wall, crammed side by side with thirty-five other men.

"I had no idea what was going on. I thought, maybe I'm going in for terrorism. Or maybe I'll be sent back home," he remembered. "My only thought was they were blaming us for the terrorism."

The hours passed, and the next thing he knew, he was being shackled again and taken to a van with a dozen other men. His next destination was

Passaic County Jail in Paterson, New Jersey. The first night there, he slept on the floor of a dorm with sixty-four other people. The dorms were built to accommodate twenty people, with three bunks to a row. Raza got a blanket, but he noticed some men were on the floor with no covering.

Later, he was assigned a bunk in a dorm with forty-five other inmates, and this was where he stayed. For the next three and a half months, Raza lived in Passaic with no outside contact. Some of his fellow immigrant detainees were old men, many who barely spoke English. Sometimes, other inmates would take advantage of their naïveté about prison, confiscating their food at mealtimes. "One guy, he wouldn't give his food and he got his arm broken," Raza recalled. Or it would be the guards who turned on the fearful new prisoners. During a drug search, they were all lined up outside of their cells and ordered to face the wall and spread their legs. An older Arab man just stood there uncertainly. "I told you to face the wall!" the guard screamed into his face. Not understanding a word, the man looked back and forth in consternation. Raza said he and a few others who spoke English tried to explain, but the guard had already turned his pit bull loose. Raza later heard that the man, bitten on his leg and foot, was transferred from the jail.

The brutal treatment of detainees was later documented in numerous reports by human rights advocates and the Justice Department itself.[12] But at the time, little was known except for the stories that got out through jail-house visits and collect calls from detainees. Some Muslims began writing to the Islamic Circle for help, and over the next year, Adem Carroll's collection grew to more than a thousand harrowing letters. Many, like the following account from a detainee in the Metropolitan Detention Center, described a combination of humiliation and physical assaults that eerily presaged the abuses revealed in military prisons like Abu Ghraib several years later.

> I was brought back to MDC where Lt. Cush, De Fransisco and other three officers with two cameras asked me to take off my clothes and said that they want me to bend over for checking. They told me three times and at the fourth time I said that you have checked me three times already. They laughed at me. I said that this is physical harassment . . . I was so embarrassed for what he was ordering for. I was not able to do it again and Lt. Cush and De Fransisco picked me up and threw me against the wall and I fell on the floor. They cuffed my arms and legs and dragged me on the floor. Lt. Cush started to kick me on my back and at the same time De Fransisco started to punch me in my stomach and punched my left jaw near my ear. . . . I was all naked and bleeding while this was happening.[13]

Every afternoon, FBI agents visited Passaic. Almost four months passed before it was Raza's turn for an FBI interview, but when the day came, the much-dreaded interrogation seemed almost like a joke to him. He was taken to a separate questioning room, where a young Latino man in a suit sat at a table with two Pakistani interpreters, a man and woman. Raza thought the FBI agent looked to be the same age he was.

"I said I don't need no interpreter, but they stayed anyway," Raza said. The agent began asking questions in a professional, polite manner. He had a checklist of about twenty questions.

"The funniest question," added Raza, "was who was your Islamic teacher in high school? My Islamic teacher was eighty-five years old. I don't remember his name! But he said, give me any name. I said, okay, but I'm making it up. He was like, okay."

The agent continued doggedly down the list. How many times do you pray? Have you gone to mosque lately? Did the imams preach negative things about America? The interview lasted an hour. Once he cleared the FBI inspection, Raza got a court date for three weeks later. During his time in Passaic, he tried to get word to his roommates in Queens. None of the post-9/11 detainees were allowed a phone call, but they soon figured out a way to bribe other inmates to make calls for them. Raza bartered his food with another man, who, when he called his girlfriend, gave her the number to Raza's apartment. But when the woman called there, the phone had been disconnected.

"Nobody knew where I was. I guess they all thought I was deported, or taken to Guatemala," said Raza, meaning to say Guantánamo.

The secrecy surrounding the post-9/11 detainees rivaled that around their counterparts in the U.S. military prison in Cuba. On September 21, 2001, the chief immigration judge, Michael Creppy, issued his infamous memo ordering secret procedures and closed court hearings when dealing with "special interest" detainees. Closed hearings, combined with the Justice Department's refusal to release any names, meant that the detainees had entered a twilight zone where their families had no idea where they were, no idea of how long they would be held or what charges were being brought against them.

Despite violating constitutional guarantees of due process, the detentions had been authorized by the Department of Justice. Attorney General John Ashcroft had already announced in late September new regulations giving the government expanded power to hold noncitizens for forty-eight hours or indefinitely in a national emergency.[14] Previously, the Justice Department had a twenty-four-hour deadline to either release detainees or charge them with a crime or visa violation.

Ashcroft's policy of "preventive detention" took advantage of immigration law to hold the suspects in a system where officials had almost absolute discretion, instead of charging them in the criminal justice system, where they would have more legal rights, including access to a free lawyer. The dragnet approach, however, was causing unease even among some law enforcement agents. As early as November, several ex-FBI agents went on the record with the *Washington Post* to criticize Ashcroft's policies. "One, it is not effective," said Oliver Revell, a former FBI executive assistant director. "And two, it really guts the values of our society, which you cannot allow the terrorists to do."[15]

Yet public opinion remained mostly supportive throughout the administration's antiterrorism campaigns. In late September of 2001, Gallup polls found that a majority of Americans favored profiling Arabs.[16] A Zogby poll in 2005 found a majority of people, 54 percent, still approving of President Bush's handling of the war on terror.[17]

Meanwhile, the day of Ali Raza's court hearing arrived—more than four months after he'd been arrested without charge. The judge told him that he had been cleared of any connection to the World Trade Center attacks, but that now he had immigration charges against him.

"You want to stay here or go back?" he remembered her asking him.

"You think I look like I can go back?" he quipped.

The judge frowned. "The whole world wants to come to America. We don't have space for everybody."

"No, miss, I cannot go back," Raza replied soberly.

The judge set him a $20,000 bond.

Back in detention, Raza had got hold of a hotline number from another detainee. The man told him that there was a group called DRUM helping detainees get free legal representation. After Raza arranged for another inmate to call the organization, DRUM sent Subhash Kateel to visit Raza and he soon had a lawyer, Regis Fernandez, who attended his next court hearings and managed to get his bail reduced to $8,500. Community donations were raised to cover the bail, and by April 2002 Raza was free. He had spent a total of six months in prison.

Since he lost a deportation hearing in September of 2003, Raza was trying to prepare for an asylum appeal. "I don't have more than six months left if this appeal don't go nowhere. They can come any time to pick me up," he said. He hoped that he could convince a judge of the danger facing him in Pakistan. Pulling up his sleeve, he showed the ridged knife scars along his forearms from a kidnapping in Karachi when he was fourteen—the reason his parents sent him away to the United States.

By early 2003, most of the post-911 detainees were finally deported after the FBI had failed to find any terrorism links among them. Some of the letters in Adem Carroll's files reveal the toll on families living with separation and uncertainty over their future:

> Ali finally managed to get some anti-depressants. I know he
> was crying a lot. I also had to take anti-depressants to keep
> going. I felt out of touch with reality and in constant shock. Still,
> I sent money every week for Ali to order extra food and buy
> phone cards to call me. I also sent him letters and cards frequently

to try to keep up his spirits. There were times when he would lose all faith in the attorneys, this country, and me, and times that I was sure I was losing him. I'm still worried about losing my credit, my home, and everything we had struggled for to be together.

Since Ali's release, he has been talking through his ordeal. He said they treated him very badly in Montana during his isolation. They verbally abused him. He was not allowed a shower the entire time he was there. Ali pretended to be from Greece while on the plane so that he would not be separated as a terrorist from the rest of the detainees. In Denver, he had no reading materials or anything to do for an extremely long time. . . . He says that the food is extremely limited and that everyone is always hungry. Ali has lost approximately 15 pounds since being detained. . . . Since Ali has been released he has been constantly speaking with the detainees he came to know over the phone, wanting to visit them and help them. Leaving them behind hurts him as much as having been in there. We have started to heal but we have a long road still ahead of us.[18]

. . .

On October 21, 2001, the Makki Masjid on Coney Island Avenue held a funeral ceremony for Muhammad Butt before his body was flown back to his family in Pakistan. Hundreds of Muslims filled the prayer hall. "I wish you could have seen the faces of the people," said Mohsin Zaheer, the journalist. "It was so scary. The fear was very obvious on their faces."

Zaheer reported the story for the weekly Urdu-language newspaper *Sada-e-Pakistan,* whose offices are next door to the mosque. During the funeral, he walked up to the coffin and took a picture of Muhammad Butt—"I wanted his friends to have a final last look." The photo ran the next day on the front page of the newspaper.

"It is up to us to decide," concluded Zaheer, "was he a victim or not?"

Since the mass sweeps stopped in 2002, at least five hundred Pakistanis have been deported from the New York area, according to Khan and others. Businesses have shut down and families have relocated to Canada and other countries. About twenty thousand people have left, according to local estimates. Coney Island Avenue today is a quiet street, once the lifeline of a vibrant and growing ethnic community.

Sada-e-Pakistan, housed in one L-shaped room at the end of two narrow flights of rickety stairs, was barely surviving as a newspaper, according to Zaheer. Before the September 11 fallout, businesses were growing very fast in the thickly populated area of Midwood and Flatbush. Zaheer estimated that 40 percent of the businesses have disappeared. The community had stopped growing, and Zaheer believed, "whatever is gone is gone. It will not come back."

He added, "The misery of this community—people blame not just Bush but President Musharraf. He has helped the U.S. all he can, but he did not take a stand for Pakistanis in America. We are deprived of rights and justice from both sides. It's a very sad story."

In Bobby Khan's tiny office a few doors down, a blind man sat waiting for him. The man, Malik Shaukat, became homeless after losing his sight in a car accident. He had a deportation order under appeal and might be sent back to Pakistan before his next eye surgery at King County Hospital. If that happened, he worried that he would never get treated and, sightless, that he would be unable to support himself in his home country. After the man left, Khan sat down for a cup of sweet, milky tea. He finally said, after being pressed, that this work had worn on him. "I feel like crying all the time, but I cannot."

What lay ahead for his community? Khan, the former democracy activist, was silent a long moment before asserting a thought that sounded downright radical in the current climate: "We need to realize we have a right to be here, too."

· · ·

The end of the secret detentions did not mark the end of more post-9/11 crackdowns. Even while the detentions were in full swing, the Justice Department had begun using a database of more than three hundred thousand names to arrest immigrants with outstanding deportation orders. The program, begun in November 2001 and called the Absconder Apprehension Initiative, started out by pursuing "fugitive aliens" from countries believed to have al-Qa'ida connections. But this program went on to become one of the most wide-reaching of all post-911 policies as agents have expanded the pursuit to the entire list, which now numbers more than four hundred thousand people.[19]

At the same time as the detentions, federal agents initiated arrests at airports around the country, starting with twenty-nine Mexican workers detained in late September in Denver for using fake documents to obtain work. By December, this had become a multiagency undertaking called Operation Tarmac that eventually jailed more than one thousand mostly Latino airport workers.[20]

The official chapter on the post-911 detentions came to a close two years later when the Justice Department conducted its own investigation of what happened within the Brooklyn and New Jersey prisons. The account released by the department's inspector general in June 2003 confirmed for the mainstream public what numerous human rights reports, media accounts, and community discussions had revealed about the treatment of detainees. The 198-page report focused on the treatment of 762 "special interest" detainees and found "unduly harsh" conditions, particularly at the Metropolitan Detention Center. Although the inspector general was careful to acknowledge the "enormous challenges and difficult circumstances" the Justice Department faced at the time, the report nevertheless painted a clear picture of due process violations and human rights abuses.[21]

Though the phase of the "midnight knocks" had more or less ended, many of the government's tactics and assumptions that informed this period could be seen in different contexts and different communities around the country in the following years. The expanded rules for holding detainees without charge remained on the books and could be used again. In fact, government agencies relied on their new "automatic stay" power a year later to detain Haitian asylum-seekers in Florida.[22]

"There was 9/11. Then a post-9/11 era. And then there were the after-effects of that post-9/11 era," Mohsin Zaheer summed up wearily. Sitting at his desk, he scribbled a list on a scrap of paper to emphasize his point: "Crackdowns, deportations, people leaving the country."

He looked up from his list. "Then everybody was seen like suspects."

NOTES

1. An Algerian woman detained in Chicago reportedly killed herself in March 2004; a Korean man awaiting his deportation hearing hung himself in detention in San Pedro, California, and died three weeks later, in June 2003.
2. Human Rights Watch, *Presumption of Guilt: Human Rights Abuses of Post–September 11 Detainees,* Report, August 2002.
3. Associated Press, "Police Label Beating of Pakistani Reporter a Bias Crime," October 24, 2001.
4. Human Rights Watch, *We Are Not the Enemy: Hate Crimes against Arabs, Muslims, and Those Perceived to Be Arab or Muslim after September 11,* Report, November 2002.
5. Human Rights Watch, *Locked Away: Immigration Detainees in Jails in the United States,* Report, September 1998.
6. Ibid.
7. Amnesty International, *Amnesty International's Concerns Regarding Post September 11 Detentions in the USA,* Report, March 2002.
8. Amy Goldstein and Dan Eggen, "U.S. to Stop Issuing Detention Tallies," *Washington Post,* November 9, 2001.
9. U.S. Department of Justice, Office of the Inspector General, *The September 11 Detainees: A Review of the Treatment of Aliens Held on Immigration Charges in Connection with the Investigation of the September 11 Attacks,* Special Report, June 2003.
10. Ibid. PENTTBOM (from "Pentagon and Twin Towers bombing") was the code name for the FBI's largest investigation following the attacks of September 11, 2001.
11. This figure includes those detained from special registration and the Absconder Apprehension Initiative as well as the "persons of interest" to the 9/11 investigation.
12. In 2004, after an eighteen-month-long campaign by detainees and advocates to expose the use of dogs on prisoners in Passaic County Jail and other facilities, Immigration and Customs Enforcement ordered all U.S. jails holding immigrant detainees to stop using dogs. (New Jersey Civil Rights Defense Committee,

"Immigration Authorities End Torture by Dogs of Detainees in U.S. Jails," Press Release, December 6, 2004.)

13. Letter from Javed Iqbal, courtesy of Adem Carroll.
14. "Disposition of Cases of Aliens Arrested without Warrant," *Code of Federal Regulations,* Title 8, Pt. 287.3 (d) (1997), amended by interim rule, effective 20 September 2001.
15. Jim McGee, "Ex-FBI Officials Criticize Tactics on Terrorism," *Washington Post,* November 28, 2001.
16. *Chicago Sun-Times,* October 2, 2001.
17. Zogby International poll, February 27, 2005.
18. Letter from detainee's wife in Albany, New York (name withheld), courtesy of Adem Carroll.
19. U.S. Immigration and Customs Enforcement, "Detention and Removal Operations," home page of the Detention and Removal Office, www.ice.gov/graphics/dro (accessed March 23, 2005).
20. National Immigration Law Center, "Restoring Ground: Immigrants Post 9/11," Third National Low-Income Immigrant Rights Conference, Washington, D.C., September 2002.
21. Steve Fainaru, "Report: 9/11 Detainees Abused," *Washington Post,* June 3, 2003.
22. Human Rights First, *Assessing the New Normal: Liberty and Security for the Post-September 11 United States,* Report, September 2003.

 QUESTIONS FOR CRITICAL THINKING

Reading 3

1. Nguyen discusses how the practices of the State impacted the experiences of Muhammad Rufiq Butt and other Pakistani-Americans following the events of September 11, 2001. Other groups of color have had similar "othering" experiences. What demands have been served by othering people of color, certain ethnic groups, and other marginalized or oppressed groups throughout U.S. history?

2. What current examples can you recall of the media perpetuating stereotypes of people of color from the Middle East and Muslims? How have these stereotypes impacted your own view of the current state of U.S. international relations?

3. Considering Nguyen's discussion, do you think it is possible to change negative perceptions of people of color from the Middle East and Muslims in the United States?

Reading 4

HOW DID JEWS BECOME WHITE FOLKS?

KAREN BRODKIN

The American nation was founded and developed by the Nordic race, but if a few more million members of the Alpine, Mediterranean and Semitic races are poured among us, the result must inevitably be a hybrid race of people as worthless and futile as the good-for-nothing mongrels of Central America and Southeastern Europe.

—KENNETH ROBERTS, "WHY EUROPE LEAVES HOME"

It is clear that Kenneth Roberts did not think of my ancestors as white, like him. The late nineteenth century and early decades of the twentieth saw a steady stream of warnings by scientists, policymakers, and the popular press that "mongrelization" of the Nordic or Anglo-Saxon race—the real Americans—by inferior European races (as well as by inferior non-European ones) was destroying the fabric of the nation.

I continue to be surprised when I read books that indicate that America once regarded its immigrant European workers as something other than white, as biologically different. My parents are not surprised; they expect anti-Semitism to be part of the fabric of daily life, much as I expect racism to be part of it. They came of age in the Jewish world of the 1920s and 1930s, at the peak of anti-Semitism in America.[1] They are rightly proud of their upward mobility and think of themselves as pulling themselves up by their own boot-straps. I grew up during the 1950s in the Euro-ethnic New York suburb of Valley Stream, where Jews were simply one kind of white folks and where ethnicity meant little more to my generation than food and family heritage. Part of my ethnic heritage was the belief that Jews were smart and that our success was due to our own efforts and abilities, reinforced by a culture that valued sticking together, hard work, education, and deferred gratification.

I am willing to affirm all those abilities and ideals and their contribution to Jews' upward mobility, but I also argue that they were still far from suffi-cient to account for Jewish success. I say this because the belief in a Jewish version of Horatio Alger has become a point of entry for some mainstream Jewish organizations to adopt a racist attitude against African Americans especially and to oppose affirmative action for people of color.[2] Instead I want to suggest that Jewish success is a product not only of ability but also of the removal of powerful social barriers to its realization.

It is certainly true that the United States has a history of anti-Semitism and of beliefs that Jews are members of an inferior race. But Jews were hardly alone. American anti-Semitism was part of a broader pattern of late-nineteenth-century racism against all southern and eastern European immigrants, as well as against Asian immigrants, not to mention African Americans, Native Americans, and Mexicans. These views justified all sorts of discriminatory treatment, including closing the doors, between 1882 and 1927, to immigration from Europe and Asia. This picture changed radically after World War II. Suddenly, the same folks who had promoted nativism and xenophobia were eager to believe that the Euro-origin people whom they had deported, reviled as members of inferior races, and prevented from immigrating only a few years earlier, were now model middle-class white suburban citizens.[3]

It was not an educational epiphany that made those in power change their hearts, their minds, and our race. Instead, it was the biggest and best affirmative action program in the history of our nation, and it was for Euro-males. That is not how it was billed, but it is the way it worked out in practice. I tell this story to show the institutional nature of racism and the centrality of state policies to creating and changing races. Here, those policies reconfigured the category of whiteness to include European immigrants. There are similarities and differences in the ways each of the European immigrant groups became "whitened." I tell the story in a way that links anti-Semitism to other varieties of anti-European racism because this highlights what Jews shared with other Euro-immigrants.

 ## EURORACES

The U.S. "discovery" that Europe was divided into inferior and superior races began with the racialization of the Irish in the mid-nineteenth century and flowered in response to the great waves of immigration from southern and eastern Europe that began in the late nineteenth century. Before that time, European immigrants—including Jews—had been largely assimilated into the white population. However, the 23 million European immigrants who came to work in U.S. cities in the waves of migration after 1880 were too many and too concentrated to absorb. Since immigrants and their children made up more than 70 percent of the population of most of the country's largest cities, by the 1890s urban America had taken on a distinctly southern and eastern European immigrant flavor. Like the Irish in Boston and New York, their urban concentrations in dilapidated neighborhoods put them cheek by jowl next to the rising elites and the middle class with whom they shared public space and to whom their working-class ethnic communities were particularly visible.

The Red Scare of 1919 clearly linked anti-immigrant with anti-working-class sentiment—to the extent that the Seattle general strike by largely native-born workers was blamed on foreign agitators. The Red Scare was fueled by an economic depression, a massive postwar wave of strikes, the Russian Revolution, and another influx of postwar immigration. Strikers in the steel and garment industries in New York and New England were mainly new immigrants. "As part of a fierce counteroffensive, employers inflamed the historic identification of class conflict with immigrant radicalism." Anticommunism and anti-immigrant sentiment came together in the Palmer raids and deportation of immigrant working-class activists. There was real fear of revolution. One of President Wilson's aides feared it was "the first appearance of the soviet in this country."[4]

Not surprisingly, the belief in European races took root most deeply among the wealthy, U.S.-born Protestant elite, who feared a hostile and seemingly inassimilable working class. By the end of the nineteenth century, Senator Henry Cabot Lodge pressed Congress to cut off immigration to the United States; Theodore Roosevelt raised the alarm of "race suicide" and took Anglo-Saxon women to task for allowing "native" stock to be outbred by inferior immigrants. In the early twentieth century, these fears gained a great deal of social legitimacy thanks to the efforts of an influential network of aristocrats and scientists who developed theories of eugenics—breeding for a "better" humanity—and scientific racism.

Key to these efforts was Madison Grant's influential *The Passing of the Great Race*, published in 1916. Grant popularized notions developed by William Z. Ripley and Daniel Brinton that there existed three or four major European races, ranging from the superior Nordics of northwestern Europe to the inferior southern and eastern races of the Alpines, Mediterraneans, and worst of all, Jews, who seemed to be everywhere in his native New York City. Grant's nightmare was race-mixing among Europeans. For him, "the cross between any of the three European races and a Jew is a Jew." He didn't have good things to say about Alpine or Mediterranean "races" either. For Grant, race and class were interwoven: the upper class was racially pure Nordic; the lower classes came from the lower races.[5]

Far from being on the fringe, Grant's views were well within the popular mainstream. Here is the *New York Times* describing the Jewish Lower East Side of a century ago:

> The neighborhood where these people live is absolutely impassable
> for wheeled vehicles other than their pushcarts. If a truck driver
> tries to get through where their pushcarts are standing they apply
> to him all kinds of vile and indecent epithets. The driver is
> fortunate if he gets out of the street without being hit with a stone
> or having a putrid fish or piece of meat thrown in his face. This

neighborhood, peopled almost entirely by the people who claim to have been driven from Poland and Russia, is the eyesore of New York and perhaps the filthiest place on the western continent. It is impossible for a Christian to live there because he will be driven out, either by blows or the dirt and stench. Cleanliness is an unknown quantity to these people. They cannot be lifted up to a higher plane because they do not want to be. If the cholera should ever get among these people, they would scatter its germs as a sower does grain.[6]

Such views were well within the mainstream of the early-twentieth-century scientific community.[7] Madison Grant and eugenicist Charles B. Davenport organized the Galton Society in 1918 in order to foster research, promote eugenics, and restrict immigration.[8] Lewis Terman, Henry Goddard, and Robert Yerkes, developers of the "intelligence" test, believed firmly that southeastern European immigrants, African Americans, American Indians, and Mexicans were "feebleminded." And indeed, more than 80 percent of the immigrants whom Goddard tested at Ellis Island in 1912 turned out to be just that, as measured by his test. Racism fused with eugenics in scientific circles, and the eugenics circles overlapped with the nativism of white Protestant elites. During World War I, racism shaped the army's development of a mass intelligence test. Psychologist Robert Yerkes, who developed the test, became an even stronger advocate of eugenics after the war. Writing in the *Atlantic Monthly* in 1923, he noted:

If we may safely judge by the army measurements of intelligence, races are quite as significantly different as individuals. . . . [A]lmost as great as the intellectual difference between negro [*sic*] and white in the army are the differences between white racial groups. . . .

For the past ten years or so the intellectual status of immigrants has been disquietingly low. Perhaps this is because of the dominance of the Mediterranean races, as contrasted with the Nordic and Alpine.[9]

By the 1920s, scientific racism sanctified the notion that real Americans were white and that real whites came from northwest Europe. Racism by white workers in the West fueled laws excluding and expelling the Chinese in 1882. Widespread racism led to closing the immigration door to virtually all Asians and most Europeans between 1924 and 1927, and to deportation of Mexicans during the Great Depression.

Racism in general, and anti-Semitism in particular, flourished in higher education. Jews were the first of the Euro-immigrant groups to enter college in significant numbers, so it was not surprising that they faced the brunt of discrimination there. The Protestant elite complained that Jews were unwashed, uncouth, unrefined, loud, and pushy. Harvard University President A. Lawrence Lowell, who was also a vice president of the Immigration

Restriction League, was open about his opposition to Jews at Harvard. The Seven Sister schools had a reputation for "flagrant discrimination."

.   .   .

Columbia's quota against Jews was well known in my parents' community. My father is very proud of having beaten it and been admitted to Columbia Dental School on the basis of his skill at carving a soap ball. Although he became a teacher instead because the tuition was too high, he took me to the dentist every week of my childhood and prolonged the agony by discussing the finer points of tooth-filling and dental care. My father also almost failed the speech test required for his teaching license because he didn't speak "standard," i.e., nonimmigrant, nonaccented English. For my parents and most of their friends, English was the language they had learned when they went to school, since their home and neighborhood language was Yiddish. They saw the speech test as designed to keep all ethnics, not just Jews, out of teaching.

There is an ironic twist to this story. My mother always urged me to speak well, like her friend Ruth Saronson, who was a speech teacher. Ruth remained my model for perfect diction until I went away to college. When I talked to her on one of my visits home, I heard the New York accent of my version of "standard English," compared to the Boston academic version.

My parents believe that Jewish success, like their own, was due to hard work and a high value placed on education. They attended Brooklyn College during the Depression. My mother worked days and went to school at night; my father went during the day. Both their families encouraged them. More accurately, their families expected it. Everyone they knew was in the same boat, and their world was made up of Jews who were advancing just as they were. The picture for New York—where most Jews lived—seems to back them up. In 1920, Jews made up 80 percent of the students at New York's City College, 90 percent of Hunter College, and before World War I, 40 percent of private Columbia University. By 1934, Jews made up almost 24 percent of all law students nationally and 56 percent of those in New York City. Still, more Jews became public school teachers, like my parents and their friends, than doctors or lawyers. Indeed, Ruth Jacknow Markowitz has shown that "my daughter, the teacher" was, for parents, an aspiration equivalent to "my son, the doctor."[10]

How we interpret Jewish social mobility in this milieu depends on whom we compare them to. Compared with other immigrants, Jews were upwardly mobile. But compared with nonimmigrant whites, that mobility was very limited and circumscribed. The existence of anti-immigrant, racist, and anti-Semitic barriers kept the Jewish middle class confined to a small number of occupations. Jews were excluded from mainstream corporate management and corporately employed professions, except in the garment and movie industries, in which they were pioneers. Jews were almost totally excluded from university faculties (the few who made it had powerful patrons). Eastern European Jews were concentrated in small businesses, and in professions where they served a largely Jewish clientele.

·   ·   ·

My parents' generation believed that Jews overcame anti-Semitic barriers because Jews are special. My answer is that the Jews who were upwardly mobile were special among Jews (and were also well placed to write the story). My generation might well respond to our parents' story of pulling themselves up by their own bootstraps with "But think what you might have been without the racism and with some affirmative action!" And that is precisely what the post-World War II boom, the decline of systematic, public, anti-Euro racism and anti-Semitism, and governmental affirmative action extended to white males let us see.

 WHITENING EURO-ETHNICS

By the time I was an adolescent, Jews were just as white as the next white person. Until I was eight, I was a Jew in a world of Jews. Everyone on Avenue Z in Sheepshead Bay was Jewish. I spent my days playing and going to school on three blocks of Avenue Z, and visiting my grandparents in the nearby Jewish neighborhoods of Brighton Beach and Coney Island. There were plenty of Italians in my neighborhood, but they lived around the corner. They were a kind of Jew, but on the margins of my social horizons. Portuguese were even more distant, at the end of the bus ride, at Sheepshead Bay. The *shul,* or temple, was on Avenue Z, and I begged my father to take me like all the other fathers took their kids, but religion wasn't part of my family's Judaism. Just how Jewish my neighborhood was hit me in first grade, when I was one of two kids to go to school on Rosh Hashanah. My teacher was shocked—she was Jewish too—and I was embarrassed to tears when she sent me home. I was never again sent to school on Jewish holidays. We left that world in 1949 when we moved to Valley Stream, Long Island, which was Protestant and Republican and even had farms until Irish, Italian, and Jewish ex-urbanites like us gave it a more suburban and Democratic flavor.

Neither religion nor ethnicity separated us at school or in the neighborhood. Except temporarily. During my elementary school years, I remember a fair number of dirt-bomb (a good suburban weapon) wars on the block. Periodically, one of the Catholic boys would accuse me or my brother of killing his god, to which we'd reply, "Did not," and start lobbing dirt bombs. Sometimes he'd get his friends from Catholic school and I'd get mine from public school kids on the block, some of whom were Catholic. Hostilities didn't last for more than a couple of hours and punctuated an otherwise friendly relationship. They ended by our junior high years, when other things became more important. Jews, Catholics and Protestants, Italians, Irish, Poles, "English" (I don't remember hearing WASP as a kid), were mixed up on the block and in school. We thought of ourselves as middle class and very enlightened because our ethnic backgrounds seemed so irrelevant to high school culture. We didn't see race (we thought), and racism was not part of our peer consciousness. Nor were the immigrant or working-class histories of our families.

As with most chicken-and-egg problems, it is hard to know which came first. Did Jews and other Euro-ethnics become white because they became middle-class? That is, did money whiten? Or did being incorporated into an expanded version of whiteness open up the economic doors to middle-class status? Clearly, both tendencies were at work.

Some of the changes set in motion during the war against fascism led to a more inclusive version of whiteness. Anti-Semitism and anti-European racism lost respectability. The 1940 Census no longer distinguished native whites of native parentage from those, like my parents, of immigrant parentage, so Euro-immigrants and their children were more securely white by submersion in an expanded notion of whiteness.[11]

Theories of nurture and culture replaced theories of nature and biology. Instead of dirty and dangerous races that would destroy American democracy, immigrants became ethnic groups whose children had successfully assimilated into the mainstream and risen to the middle class. In this new myth, Euro-ethnic suburbs like mine became the measure of American democracy's victory over racism. As we shall see in chapter 5, Jewish mobility became a new Horatio Alger story. In time and with hard work, every ethnic group would get a piece of the pie, and the United States would be a nation with equal opportunity for all its people to become part of a prosperous middle-class majority. And it seemed that Euro-ethnic immigrants and their children were delighted to join middle America.

This is not to say that anti-Semitism disappeared after World War II, only that it fell from fashion and was driven underground.

. . .

Although changing views on who was white made it easier for Euro-ethnics to become middle class, economic prosperity also played a very powerful role in the whitening process. The economic mobility of Jews and other Euro-ethnics derived ultimately from America's postwar economic prosperity and its enormously expanded need for professional, technical, and managerial labor, as well as on government assistance in providing it.

The United States emerged from the war with the strongest economy in the world. Real wages rose between 1946 and 1960, increasing buying power a hefty 22 percent and giving most Americans some discretionary income. American manufacturing, banking, and business services were increasingly dominated by large corporations, and these grew into multinational corporations. Their organizational centers lay in big, new urban headquarters that demanded growing numbers of clerical, technical, and managerial workers. The postwar period was a historic moment for real class mobility and for the affluence we have erroneously come to believe was the American norm.

It was a time when the old white and the newly white masses became middle class.[12]

The GI Bill of Rights, as the 1944 Serviceman's Readjustment Act was known, is arguably the most massive affirmative action program in American history. It was created to develop needed labor force skills and to provide those who had them with a lifestyle that reflected their value to the economy. The GI benefits that were ultimately extended to 16 million GIs (of the Korean War as well) included priority in jobs—that is, preferential hiring, but no one objected to it then—financial support during the job search, small loans for starting up businesses, and most important, low-interest home loans and educational benefits, which included tuition and living expenses. This legislation was rightly regarded as one of the most revolutionary postwar programs. I call it affirmative action because it was aimed at and disproportionately helped male, Euro-origin GIs.[13]

. . .

EDUCATION AND OCCUPATION

It is important to remember that, prior to the war, a college degree was still very much a "mark of the upper class," that colleges were largely finishing schools for Protestant elites. Before the postwar boom, schools could not begin to accommodate the American masses. Even in New York City before the 1930s, neither the public schools nor City College had room for more than a tiny fraction of potential immigrant students.[14]

Not so after the war. The almost 8 million GIs who took advantage of their educational benefits under the GI Bill caused "the greatest wave of college building in American history." White male GIs were able to take advantage of their educational benefits for college and technical training, so they were particularly well positioned to seize the opportunities provided by the new demands for professional, managerial, and technical labor.

> It has been well documented that the GI educational benefits transformed American higher education and raised the educational level of that generation and generations to come. With many provisions for assistance in upgrading their educational attainments, veterans pulled ahead of nonveterans in earning capacity. In the long run it was the nonveterans who had fewer opportunities.[15]

Just how valuable a college education was for white men's occupational mobility can be seen in who benefited from the metamorphosis of California's Santa Clara Valley into Silicon Valley. Formerly an agricultural region, in the 1950s it became the scene of explosive growth in the semiconductor electronics industry. John Keller has argued that this industry epitomized the postwar economy and occupational structure. It owed its existence directly to the military and to the National Aeronautics and Space Administration (NASA), which were its major funders and market. It had an increasingly white-collar workforce. White men, who were the initial production workers in the 1950s, quickly transformed themselves into a technical and professional workforce thanks largely to GI benefits and to

> the implementation of training programs at a half-dozen junior colleges built in the valley since the mid-1950s. Indeed, a study of the local junior college system in its formative years confirmed how this institutional setup systematically facilitated the transformation of a section of the blue-collar workforce in the area into a corps of electronics technicians: 62 percent of enrollees at San Jose Junior College (later renamed San Jose City College) came from blue-collar families, and 55 percent of all job placements were as electronics technicians in the industrial and service sectors of the county economy.

As the industry expanded between 1950 and 1960 and white men left assembly work, they were replaced initially by Latinas and African American women, who were joined after 1970 by new immigrant women. Immigrating men tended to work in the better-paid unionized industries that grew up in the area.[16]

Postwar expansion made college accessible to Euromales in general and to Jews in particular. My generation's "Think what you could have been!" answer to our parents became our reality as quotas and old occupational barriers fell and new fields opened up to Jews. The most striking result was a sharp decline in Jewish small businesses and a skyrocketing increase in Jewish professionals. For example, as quotas in medical schools fell, the numbers of Jewish M.D.'s shot up. If Boston is any indication, just over 1 percent of all Jewish men before the war were doctors, but 16 percent of the postwar generation became M.D.'s. A similar Jewish mass movement took place into college and university faculties, especially in "new and expanding fields in the social and natural sciences."[17]

Although these Jewish college professors tended to be sons of businessmen and professionals, the postwar boom saw the first large-scale class mobility among Jewish men. Sons of working-class Jews now went to college and became professionals themselves—according to the Boston survey, almost two-thirds of them. This compared favorably with three-quarters of the sons of professional fathers.[18]

But if Jews' upward mobility was due to a lowering of racial barriers, then how have the children of other southern and eastern European immigrants fared? Stephen Steinberg provides one comparison—that of college faculties. Although Jews were the first group to go to college in any great numbers, the proportions of faculty comprising southern and eastern European Catholics has grown rapidly since World War II. Thus, Catholic faculty and graduate students have steadily increased, Protestants have decreased, and Jews have reached a plateau, such that Protestants are underrepresented on college faculties while Catholics were approaching parity by 1974.

Steinberg argues that the lag had less to do with values about education than with difficulties that largely rural Catholic immigrants had in translating rural skills into financial success in an urban industrial setting. Once the opportunities were provided by the GI Bill and associated programs, they too took full advantage of education as a route to upward mobility. Where the first cohorts of Jewish faculty came from small-business backgrounds, Catholic faculty came from working-class families who benefited from postwar programs.[19] Steinberg argues that class backgrounds, more specifically the occupational resources of different immigrant streams, are important for shaping their relative mobility. But we need to place his argument in the broader racial perspective of institutional whiteness. That is, Irish, Jews, and southern and eastern European Catholics were all held back until they were granted—willingly or unwillingly—the institutional privileges of socially sanctioned whiteness. This happened most dramatically after World War II (see chapter 2 for a discussion of the Irish).

Even more significantly, the postwar boom transformed America's class structure—or at least its status structure—so that the middle class expanded to encompass most of the population. Before the war, most Jews, like most other Americans, were part of the working class, defined in terms of occupation, education, and income. Already upwardly mobile before the war relative to other immigrants, Jews floated high on this rising economic tide, and most of them entered the middle class. The children of other immigrants did too. Still, even the high tide missed some Jews. As late as 1973, some 15 percent of New York's Jews were poor or near poor, and in the 1960s, almost 25 percent of employed Jewish men remained manual workers.[20]

The reason I refer to educational and occupational GI benefits as affirmative action programs for white males is because they were decidedly not extended to African Americans or to women of any race. Theoretically they were available to all veterans; in practice women and black veterans did not get anywhere near their share. Women's Army and Air Force units were initially organized as auxiliaries, hence not part of the military. When that status was changed, in July 1943, only those who reenlisted in the armed forces were eligible for veterans' benefits. Many women thought they were simply being demobilized and returned home. The majority remained and were ultimately eligible for veterans' benefits. But there was little counseling, and a social climate that discouraged women's careers and independence cut down on women's knowledge and sense of entitlement. The Veterans Administration kept no statistics on the number of women who used their GI benefits.[21]

The barriers that almost completely shut African American GIs out of their benefits were even more formidable. In Neil Wynn's portrait, black GIs anticipated starting new lives, just like their white counterparts. Over 43 percent hoped to return to school, and most expected to relocate, to find better jobs in new lines of work. The exodus from the South toward the North and West was particularly large. So it was not a question of any lack of ambition on the part of African American GIs. White male privilege was shaped against the backdrop of wartime racism and postwar sexism.

During and after the war, there was an upsurge in white racist violence against black servicemen, in public schools, and by the Ku Klux Klan. It spread to California and New York. The number of lynchings rose during the war, and in 1943 there were antiblack race riots in several large northern cities. Although there was a wartime labor shortage, black people were discriminated against when it came to well-paid defense industry jobs and housing. In 1946, white riots against African Americans occurred across the South and in Chicago and Philadelphia.

Gains made as a result of the wartime civil rights movement, especially in defense-related employment, were lost with peace-time conversion, as black workers were the first to be fired, often in violation of seniority. White women were also laid off, ostensibly to make room for jobs for demobilized servicemen, and in the long run women lost most of the gains they had made in wartime. We now know that women did not leave the labor force in any significant numbers but, instead, were forced to find inferior jobs, largely nonunion, part-time, and clerical.[22]

The military, the Veterans Administration, the U.S. Employment Service (USES), and the Federal Housing Administration effectively denied African American GIs access to their benefits and to new educational, occupational, and residential opportunities. Black GIs who served in the thoroughly segregated armed forces during World War II served under white officers. African American soldiers were given a disproportionate share of dishonorable discharges, which denied them veterans' rights under the GI Bill. Between August and November 1946, for example, 21 percent of white soldiers and 39 percent of black soldiers were dishonorably discharged. Those who did get an honorable discharge then faced the Veterans Administration and the USES. The latter, which was responsible for job placements, employed very few African Americans, especially in the South. This meant that black veterans did not receive much employment information and that the offers they did receive were for low-paid and menial jobs. "In one survey of 50 cities, the movement of blacks into peacetime employment was found to be lagging far behind that of white veterans: in Arkansas ninety-five percent of the placements made by the USES for Afro-Americans were in service or unskilled jobs."[23] African Americans were also less likely than whites, regardless of GI status, to gain new jobs commensurate with their wartime jobs. For example, in San Francisco, by 1948, black Americans "had dropped back halfway to their prewar employment status."[24]

Black GIs faced discrimination in the educational system as well. Despite the end of restrictions on Jews and other Euroethnics, African Americans were not welcome in white colleges. Black colleges were overcrowded, but the combination of segregation and prejudice made for few alternatives.

About 20,000 black veterans attended college by 1947, most in black colleges, but almost as many, 15,000, could not gain entry. Predictably, the disproportionately few African Americans who did gain access to their educational benefits were able, like their white counterparts, to become doctors and engineers, and to enter the black middle class.[25]

SUBURBANIZATION

In 1949, ensconced in Valley Stream, I watched potato farms turn into Levittown and Idlewild (later Kennedy) airport. This was the major spectator sport in our first years on Long Island. A typical weekend would bring various aunts, uncles, and cousins out from the city. After a huge meal, we'd pile into the car—itself a novelty—to look at the bulldozed acres and comment on the matchbox construction. During the week, my mother and I would look at the houses going up within walking distance.

Bill Levitt built a basic, 900–1,000 square foot, somewhat expandable house for a lower-middle-class and working-class market on Long Island, and later in Pennsylvania and New Jersey. Levittown started out as 2,000 units of rental housing at $60 a month, designed to meet the low-income housing needs of returning war vets, many of whom, like my Aunt Evie and Uncle Julie, were living in Quonset huts. By May 1947, Levitt and Sons had acquired enough land in Hempstead Township on Long Island to build 4,000 houses, and by the next February, he had built 6,000 units and named the development after himself. After 1948, federal financing for the construction of rental housing tightened, and Levitt switched to building houses for sale. By 1951, Levittown was a development of some 15,000 families.[26]

At the beginning of World War II, about one-third of all American families owned their houses. That percentage doubled in twenty years. Most Levittowners looked just like my family. They came from New York City or Long Island; about 17 percent were military, from nearby Mitchell Field; Levittown was their first house, and almost everyone was married. Three-quarters of the 1947 inhabitants were white collar, but by 1950 more blue-collar families had moved in, so that by 1951, "barely half" of the new residents were white collar, and by 1960 their occupational profile was somewhat more working class than for Nassau County as a whole. By this time too, almost one-third of Levittown's people were either foreign-born or, like my parents, first-generation U.S.-born.[27]

The Federal Housing Administration (FHA) was key to buyers and builders alike. Thanks to the FHA, suburbia was open to more than GIs. People like us would never have been in the market for houses without FHA and Veterans Administration (VA) low-down-payment, low-interest, long-term loans to young buyers.

• • •

The FHA believed in racial segregation. Throughout its history, it publicly and actively promoted restrictive covenants. Before the war, these forbade sales to Jews and Catholics as well as to African Americans. The deed to my house in Detroit had such a covenant, which theoretically prevented it from being sold to Jews or African Americans. Even after the Supreme Court outlawed restrictive covenants in 1948, the FHA continued to encourage builders to write them in against African Americans. FHA underwriting manuals openly insisted on racially homogeneous neighborhoods, and their loans were made only in white neighborhoods. I bought my Detroit house in 1972, from Jews who were leaving a largely African American neighborhood. By that time, restrictive covenants were a dead letter, but block busting by realtors was replacing it.

With the federal government behind them, virtually all developers refused to sell to African Americans. Palo Alto and Levittown, like most suburbs as late as 1960, were virtually all white. Out of 15,741 houses and 65,276 people, averaging 4.2 people per house, only 220 Levittowners, or 52 households, were "nonwhite." In 1958, Levitt announced publicly, at a press conference held to open his New Jersey development, that he would not sell to black buyers. This caused a furor because the state of New Jersey (but not the U.S. government) prohibited discrimination in federally subsidized housing. Levitt was sued and fought it. There had been a white riot in his Pennsylvania development when a black family moved in a few years earlier. In New Jersey, he was ultimately persuaded by township ministers to integrate.

· · ·

The result of these policies was that African Americans were totally shut out of the suburban boom. An article in *Harper's* described the housing available to black GIs.

> On his way to the base each morning, Sergeant Smith passes an attractive air-conditioned, FHA-financed housing project. It was built for service families. Its rents are little more than the Smiths pay for their shack. And there are half-a-dozen vacancies, but none for Negroes.[28]

Where my family felt the seductive pull of suburbia, Marshall Berman's experienced the brutal push of urban renewal. In the Bronx, in the 1950s, Robert Moses's Cross-Bronx Expressway erased "a dozen solid, settled, densely populated neighborhoods like our own. . . . [S]omething like 60,000 working- and lower-middle-class people, mostly Jews, but with many Italians, Irish, and Blacks thrown in, would be thrown out of their homes. . . . For ten years, through the late 1950s and early 1960s, the center of the Bronx was pounded and blasted and smashed."[29]

Urban renewal made postwar cities into bad places to live. At a physical level, urban renewal reshaped them, and federal programs brought private developers and public officials together to create downtown central business districts where there had formerly been a mix of manufacturing, commerce, and working-class neighborhoods. Manufacturing was scattered to the peripheries of the city, which were ringed and bisected by a national system of highways. Some working-class neighborhoods were bulldozed, but others remained. In Los Angeles, as in New York's Bronx, the postwar period saw massive freeway construction right through the heart of old working-class neighborhoods. In East Los Angeles and Santa Monica, Chicana/o and African American communities were divided in half or blasted to smithereens by the highways bringing Angelenos to the new white suburbs, or to make way for civic monuments like Dodger Stadium.[30]

Urban renewal was the other side of the process by which Jewish and other working-class Euro-immigrants became middle class. It was the push to suburbia's seductive pull. The fortunate white survivors of urban renewal headed disproportionately for suburbia, where they could partake of prosperity and the good life.

• • •

If the federal stick of urban renewal joined the FHA carrot of cheap mortgages to send masses of Euro-Americans to the suburbs, the FHA had a different kind of one-two punch for African Americans. Segregation kept them out of the suburbs, and redlining made sure they could not buy or repair their homes in the neighborhoods in which they were allowed to live. The FHA practiced systematic redlining. This was a practice developed by its predecessor, the Home Owners Loan Corporation (HOLC), which in the 1930s developed an elaborate neighborhood rating system that placed the highest (green) value on all-white, middle-class neighborhoods, and the lowest (red) on racially nonwhite or mixed and working-class neighborhoods. High ratings meant high property values. The idea was that low property values in redlined neighborhoods made them bad investments. The FHA was, after all, created by and for banks and the housing industry. Redlining warned banks not to lend there, and the FHA would not insure mortgages in such neighborhoods. Redlining created a self-fulfilling prophesy.

> With the assistance of local realtors and banks, it assigned one of the four ratings to every block in every city. The resulting information was then translated into the appropriate color [green, blue, yellow, or red] and duly recorded on secret "Residential Security Maps" in local HOLC offices. The maps themselves were placed in elaborate "City Survey Files," which consisted of reports, questionnaires, and workpapers relating to current and future values of real estate.[31]

The FHA's and VA's refusal to guarantee loans in redlined neighborhoods made it virtually impossible for African Americans to borrow money for home improvement or purchase. Because these maps and surveys were quite secret, it took the civil rights movement to make these practices and their devastating consequences public. As a result, those who fought urban renewal, or who sought to make a home in the urban ruins, found themselves locked out of the middle class. They also faced an ideological assault that labeled their neighborhoods slums and called them slumdwellers.[32]

 ## CONCLUSION

The record is very clear. Instead of seizing the opportunity to end institutionalized racism, the federal government did its level best to shut and double-seal the postwar window of opportunity in African Americans' faces. It consistently refused to combat segregation in the social institutions that were key to upward mobility in education, housing, and employment. Moreover, federal programs that were themselves designed to assist demobilized GIs and young families systematically discriminated against African Americans. Such programs reinforced white/nonwhite racial distinctions even as intrawhite racialization was falling out of fashion. This other side of the coin, that white men of northwest European ancestry and white men of southeastern European ancestry were treated equally in theory and in practice with regard to the benefits they received, was part of the larger postwar whitening of Jews and other eastern and southern Europeans.

The myth that Jews pulled themselves up by their own bootstraps ignores the fact that it took federal programs to create the conditions whereby the abilities of Jews and other European immigrants could be recognized and rewarded rather than denigrated and denied. The GI Bill and FHA and VA mortgages, even though they were advertised as open to all, functioned as a set of racial privileges. They were privileges because they were extended to white GIs but not to black GIs. Such privileges were forms of affirmative action that allowed Jews and other Euro-American men to become suburban homeowners and to get the training that allowed them—but much less so women vets or war workers—to become professionals, technicians, salesmen, and managers in a growing economy. Jews and other white ethnics' upward mobility was due to programs that allowed us to float on a rising economic tide. To African Americans, the government offered the cement boots of segregation, redlining, urban renewal, and discrimination.

Those racially skewed gains have been passed across the generations, so that racial inequality seems to maintain itself "naturally," even after legal segregation ended. Today, I own a house in Venice, California, like the one in which I grew up in Valley Stream, and my brother until recently owned a house in Palo Alto much like an Eichler house. Both of us are where we are thanks largely to the postwar benefits our parents received and passed on to us, and to the educational benefits we received in the 1960s as a result of affluence and the social agitation that developed from the black Freedom Movement. I have white, African American, and Asian American colleagues whose parents received fewer or none of America's postwar benefits and who expect never to own a house despite their considerable academic achievements. Some of these colleagues who are a few years younger than I also carry staggering debts for their education, which they expect to have to repay for the rest of their lives.

Conventional wisdom has it that the United States has always been an affluent land of opportunity. But the truth is that affluence has been the exception and that real upward mobility has required massive affirmative action programs.

· · ·

Today, in a shrinking economy, where downward mobility is the norm, the children and grandchildren of the postwar beneficiaries of the economic boom have some precious advantages. For example, having parents who own their own homes or who have decent retirement benefits can make a real difference in a young person's ability to take on huge college loans or to come up with a down payment for a house. Even this simple inheritance helps perpetuate the gap between whites and people of color. Sure, Jews needed ability, but that was never enough for more than a few to make it. The same applies today. Whatever advantages I bequeath them, my sons will never have their parents' or grandparents' experience of life on a rising economic tide.

Public policies like the anti-immigrant Proposition 187 and anti-affirmative action Proposition 209 in California, the abolition of affirmative action policies at the University of California, and media demonization of African Americans and Central American immigrants as lazy welfare cheats encourage feelings of white entitlement to middle-class privilege. But our children's and grand-children's realities are that they are downwardly mobile relative to their grandparents, not because people of color are getting the good jobs by affirmative action but because the good jobs and prosperity in general are ceasing to exist.

NOTES

1. Gerber 1986; Dinnerstein 1987, 1994.
2. On the belief in Jewish and Asian versions of Horatio Alger, see Steinberg 1989, chap. 3; Gilman 1996. On Jewish culture, see Gordon 1964; see Sowell 1981 for an updated version.
3. Not all Jews are white or unambiguously white. It has been suggested, for example, that Hasidim lack the privileges of whiteness. Rodriguez (1997, 12, 15) has begun to unpack the claims of white Jewish "amenity migrants" and the different racial meanings of Chicano claims to a crypto-Jewish identity in New Mexico. See also Thomas 1996 on African American Jews.
4. Higham 1955, 226.
5. M. Grant 1916; Ripley 1923; see also Patterson 1997; M. Grant, quoted in Higham 1955, 156.
6. *New York Times,* 30 July 1893, "East Side Street Vendors," reprinted in Schoener 1967, 57–58.

7. Gould 1981; Higham 1955; Patterson 1997, 108–115.
8. It was intended, as Davenport wrote to the president of the American Museum of Natural History, Henry Fairfield Osborne, as "an anthropological society . . . with a central governing body, self-elected and self-perpetuating, and very limited in members, and also confined to native Americans [*sic*] who are anthropologically, socially and politically sound, no Bolsheviki need apply" (Barkan 1992, 67–68).
9. Quoted in Carlson and Colburn 1972, 333–334.
10. Steinberg 1989, 137, 227; Markowitz 1993.
11. This census also explicitly changed the Mexican race to white (U.S. Bureau of the Census 1940, 2:4).
12. Nash et al. 1986, 885–886.
13. On planning for veterans, see F. J. Brown 1946; Hurd 1946; Mosch 1975; "Post-war Jobs for Veterans" 1945; Willenz 1983.
14. Willenz 1983, 165.
15. J. Nash et al. 1986, 885; Willenz 1983, 165. On mobility among veterans and non-veterans, see Havighurst et al. 1951.
16. Keller 1983, 363, 346–373.
17. Silberman 1985, 124, 121–122; Steinberg 1989, 137.
18. Silberman 1985, 121–122. None of the Jewish surveys asked what women were doing. Silberman claims that Jewish women stayed out of the labor force prior to the 1970s, but the preponderance of women among public school teachers calls this into question.
19. Steinberg 1974; 1989, chap. 5.
20. Steinberg 1989, 89–90.
21. Willenz 1983, 20–28, 94–97. I thank Nancy G. Cattell for calling my attention to the fact that women GIs were ultimately eligible for benefits.
22. Willenz 1983, 168; Dalfiume 1969, 133–134; Wynn 1976, 114–116; K. Anderson 1981; Milkman 1987.
23. Nalty and MacGregor 1981, 218, 60–61.
24. Wynn 1976, 114, 116.
25. On African Americans in the U.S. military, see Foner 1974; Dalfiume 1969; Johnson 1967; Binkin and Eitelberg 1982; Nalty and MacGregor 1981. On schooling, see Walker 1970, 4–9.
26. Hartman (1975, 141–142) cites massive abuses in the 1940s and 1950s by builders under the Section 608 program in which "the FHA granted extraordinarily liberal concessions to lackadaisically supervised private developers to induce them to produce rental housing rapidly in the postwar period." Eichler (1982) indicates that things were not that different in the subsequent FHA-funded home-building industry.
27. Dobriner 1963, 91, 100.
28. Quoted in Foner 1974, 195.
29. Berman 1982, 292.
30. On urban renewal and housing policies, see Greer 1965; Hartman 1975; Squires 1989. On Los Angeles, see Pardo 1990; Cockroft 1990.
31. Jackson 1985, 197. These ideas from the real estate industry were "codified and legitimated in 1930s work by University of Chicago sociologist Robert Park and real estate professor Homer Hoyt" (Ibid., 198–199).
32. See Gans 1962.

REFERENCES

Anderson, Karen. 1981. *Wartime Women.* Westport, Conn.: Greenwood.

Barkan, Elazar. 1992. *The Retreat of Scientific Racism: Changing Concepts of Race in Britain and the United States Between the World Wars.* New York: Cambridge University Press.

Berman, Marshall. 1982. *All That Is Solid Melts into Air: The Experience of Modernity.* New York: Simon and Schuster.

Binkin, Martin, and Mark J. Eitelberg. 1982. *Blacks and the Military.* Washington, D.C.: Brookings Institution.

Brown, Francis J. 1946. *Educational Opportunities for Veterans.* Washington, D.C.: Public Affairs Press, American Council on Public Affairs.

Cockcroft, Eva. 1990. *Signs from the Heart: California Chicano Murals.* Venice, Calif.: Social and Public Art Resource Center.

Dalfiume, Richard M. 1969. *Desegregation of the U.S. Armed Forces: Fighting on Two Fronts, 1939–1953.* Columbia: University of Missouri Press.

Dinnerstein, Leonard. 1987. *Uneasy at Home: Anti-Semitism and the American Jewish Experience.* New York: Columbia University Press.

———. 1994. *Anti-Semitism in America.* New York: Oxford University Press.

Dobriner, William. M. 1963. *Class in Suburbia.* Englewood Cliffs, N.J.: Prentice-Hall.

Eichler, Ned. 1982. *The Merchant Builders.* Cambridge, Mass.: MIT Press.

Foner, Jack. 1974. *Blacks and the Military in American History: A New Perspective.* New York: Praeger Publishers.

Gans, Herbert. 1962. *The Urban Villagers.* New York: Free Press of Glencoe.

Gerber, David, ed. 1986. *Anti-Semitism in American History.* Urbana: University of Illinois Press.

Gilman, Sander. 1996. *Smart Jews: The Construction of the Image of Jewish Superior Intelligence.* Lincoln: University of Nebraska Press.

Gordon, Milton. 1964. *Assimilation in American Life: The Role of Race, Religion and National Origins.* New York: Oxford University Press.

Gould, Stephen J. 1981. *The Mismeasure of Man.* New York: Norton.

Grant, Madison. 1916. *The Passing of the Great Race: Or the Racial Basis of European History.* New York: Charles Scribner.

Greer, Scott. 1965. *Urban Renewal and American Cities.* Indianapolis: Bobbs-Merrill.

Hartman, Chester. 1975. *Housing and Social Policy.* Englewood Cliffs, N.J.: Prentice-Hall.

Havighurst, Robert J., John W. Baughman, Walter H. Eaton, and Ernest W. Burgess. 1951. *The American Veteran Back Home: A Study of Veteran Readjustment.* New York: Longmans, Green and Co.

Higham, John. 1955. *Strangers in the Land.* New Brunswick, N.J.: Rutgers University Press.

Hurd, Charles. 1946. *The Veterans' Program: A Complete Guide to Its Benefits, Rights and Options.* New York: McGraw-Hill Book Company.

Jackson, Kenneth T. 1985. *Crabgrass Frontier: The Suburbanization of the United States.* New York: Oxford University Press.

Johnson, Jesse J. 1967. *Ebony Brass: An Autobiography of Negro Frustration Amid Aspiration.* New York: The William Frederick Press.

Markowitz, Ruth Jacknow. 1993. *My Daughter, the Teacher: Jewish Teachers in the New York City Schools.* New Brunswick, N.J.: Rutgers University Press.

Milkman, Ruth. 1987. *Gender at Work: The Dynamics of Job Segregation by Sex During World War II.* Urbana: University of Illinois Press.

Mosch, Theodre R. 1975. *The GI Bill: A Breakthrough in Educational and Social Policy in the United States.* Hicksville, N.Y.: Exposition Press.

Nalty, Bernard C., and Morris J. MacGregor, eds. 1981. *Blacks in the Military: Essential Documents.* Wilmington. Del.: Scholarly Resources, Inc.

Nash, Gary B., Julie Roy Jeffrey, John R. Howe, Allen F. Davis, Peter J. Frederick, and Allen M. Winkler. 1986. *The American People: Creating a Nation and a Society.* New York: Harper and Row.

Pardo, Mary. 1990. "Mexican-American Women Grassroots Community Activists: 'Mothers of East Los Angeles'." *Frontiers* 11, 1:1–7.

Patterson, Thomas C. 1997. *Inventing Western Civilization.* New York: Monthly Review Press.

"Postwar Jobs for Veterans." 1945. *The Annals of the American Academy of Political and Social Science* 238 (March).

Ripley, William Z. 1923. *The Races of Europe: A Sociological Study.* New York: Appleton.

Rodriguez, Sylvia. 1997. "Tourism, Whiteness, and the Vanishing Anglo." Paper presented at the conference "Seeing and Being Seen: Tourism in the American West." Center for the American West, Boulder, Colorado, 2 May.

Schoener, Allon. 1967. *Portal to America: The Lower East Side 1870–1925.* New York: Holt, Rinehart, and Winston.

Silberman, Charles E. 1985. *A Certain People: American Jews and Their Lives Today.* New York: Summit Books.

Sowell, Thomas. 1981. *Ethnic America: A History.* New York: Basic Books.

Squires, Gregory D., ed. 1989. *Unequal Partnerships: The Political Economy of Urban Redevelopment in Postwar America.* New Brunswick, N.J.: Rutgers University Press.

Steinberg, Stephen. 1974. *The Academic Melting Pot.* New York: McGraw-Hill.

Steinberg, Stephen. 1989. *The Ethnic Myth: Race, Ethnicity and Class in America.* 2d ed. Boston: Beacon Press.

Thomas, Laurence Mordekhai. 1996. "The Soul of Identity: Jews and Blacks." In *People of the Book,* ed. S. F. Fishkin and J. Rubin-Dorsky. Madison: University of Wisconsin Press, 169–186.

U.S. Bureau of the Census. 1940. *Sixteenth Census of the United States,* V.2. Washington, D.C.: U.S. Government Printing Office.

Walker, Olive. 1970. "The Windsor Hills School Story." *Integrated Education: Race and Schools* 8, 3:4–9.

Willenz, June A. 1983. *Women Veterans: America's Forgotten Heroines.* New York: Continuum.

Wynn, Neil A. 1976. *The Afro-American and the Second World War.* London: Paul Elek.

QUESTIONS FOR CRITICAL THINKING

Reading 4

1. How does Brodkin's discussion of the construction of Jews as white impact your understanding of the social construction of race and ethnicity?
2. Are there groups in our society that are currently viewed as people of color that you think will eventually be viewed as white? Which groups are these? What do you think will bring about such a change?
3. What are some of the institutional barriers that currently exist in our society that prevent changing notions of race?

SOCIAL CLASS

Reading 5

RACE, HOMEOWNERSHIP AND WEALTH

THOMAS M. SHAPIRO

 ## I. WHY WEALTH MATTERS

Wealth, as distinguished from income, offers the key to understanding racial stratification in the United States, especially the persistence of racial inequality in a post-civil rights era in which minorities have made remarkable advances. A wealth perspective provides a fresh way to examine the "playing field." It provides a concrete way of analyzing how the past connects to the present, and thus provides a mechanism to refresh our historical memory of race. Further, a wealth perspective has significant implications for our thinking about affirmative action and our conceptualization of equality. First, however, I must outline this wealth perspective and explain why it is so important.

Thomas Shapiro, "Race, Homeownership and Wealth" from *Journal of Law & Policy* 20 (2006):53–74. Copyright © 2006. Reprinted with the permission of Thomas M. Shapiro and the *Journal of Law & Policy.*

Wealth is the total value of a family's financial resources minus all debts. Income includes earnings from work or its substitutes, like pension, disability, unemployment insurance, or social assistance. Wealth is a special kind of money because it represents ownership and control of resources; income is essentially earnings or payments that replace earnings.

Most commentators and analysts are familiar and comfortable with the income comparisons that provide a window as to whether there is growing or declining racial economic inequality. However, the focus on wealth, "the net value of assets (e.g., ownership of stocks, money in the bank, real estate, business ownership, etc.) less debts," creates a different gestalt or perspective on racial inequality.[1] This gestalt has two dimensions. The first is the conceptual distinction between income and assets. While income represents the flow of resources earned in a particular time period, such as a week, month or year,[2] assets are a stock of resources that are saved or invested. Income is mainly used for day-to-day necessities, while assets are special monies—a "surplus resource available for improving life chances, providing further opportunities, securing prestige, passing status along to one's family" and securing economic security for present and future generations.[3]

The second dimension is quantitative: to what extent is there asset parity between blacks and whites? Do blacks have access to resources that they can use to plan for their future, to enable their children to obtain a quality education, to provide for the next generation's head start, and to secure their place in the political community? For these reasons, we focus on the inequality of wealth as the *sine qua non* indicator of material well-being. Without sufficient assets, it is difficult to lay claim to economic security in American society.

Income and wealth are often confused both in the public mind and in the social science literature; indeed, the social science paradigm regarding family well-being and inequality has extended to a treatment of wealth only since the mid-1990s.[4] An assets perspective that examines family financial wealth facilitates an additional lens on how advantage and disadvantage is generated and passed along in America. Unlike education, jobs, or even income, wealth allows families to secure advantages and often is the vehicle for transferring inequality across generations. Wealth data for average American families was not collected systematically until the mid-1980s. While data availability provides the capacity for an asset perspective, difficult methodological and conceptual issues remain, such as how to value a home, how to conceptualize home appreciate, how to value a business, and how to treat retirement plans.[5]

The social sciences have neglected the wealth dimension when examining the status of American families in general, and racial inequality in particular. Instead of examining a foundation of property relations, our analyses have focused on occupation, education, and income inequality. This reliance on labor market and human capital indicators began to change, however, with the collection of wealth data for typical American families in the mid-1980s, and the social science and journalistic inequality discussion turned to wealth. Indeed, the increasing wealth concentration and the mounting racial wealth gap have become topics for public conversation and public policy issues, even if at this point they are not on the imminent political agenda.[6]

The standard social science approach to examining racial inequality is to analyze how economic resources, opportunities, and power are distributed. With the focus being the economic dimension, most research has emphasized basic labor market components of jobs and wages.[7] The work of William Julius Wilson, for example, emphasizes the importance of African Americans' place in a changing occupational structure, shifts in wages, metropolitan economies, and a global economy.[8] As a result, the effects of wealth disparity and family wealth on differing opportunities and well-being for families have been neglected both by the social sciences and by policy discussions. Further, among all the other racial gaps, whites and blacks are most persistently unequal along the wealth dimension.[9]

Wealth is different from income, and, most importantly, families use wealth in very different ways than they use income. Wealth is a storehouse of a family's financial resources and, when combined with income, frames the opportunity for families to secure the "good life," however they define it, typically by human capital development, business opportunities, home ownership, community location, health, travel, comfort, or security. Wealth, then, is a special kind of money utilized to launch social mobility, create opportunities and status, or pass along advantages to one's children. Two families with similar incomes but widely disparate wealth most likely do not share similar life trajectories, and we must consider this when thinking about inequality and public policy.

The importance of wealth was borne out in the stories of the nearly 200 families interviewed for the book, *The Hidden Cost of Being African American*.[10] Families discussed about how they think about assets, how they strategize to acquire wealth, how they plan to use assets, and how they actually use them.[11] These families clearly view income and wealth very differently, so that wealth is seen as a special kind of money.[12] We asked the families if they treated wealth differently than income. The pattern of answers was resoundingly affirmative, especially among those with ample assets.[13] Wealth is seen first as a personal safety net, or an unspecified amount of money that is stored away to cushion against the unexpected health crisis, job termination, legal difficulty, or repair of the family car.[14]

Beyond serving as a personal safety net—all the more important as the social investment of the state withers—families also view financial wealth as "moving-ahead" money. One respondent succinctly summed it up by saying: "Income supplies life support, assets provide opportunities."[15] A middle class Bostonian put it this way: "My income is limited. My assets I want to hang on to for future needs."[16] One Los Angeles mother captured the thinking of many we interviewed when she said that wealth "is definitely long term. We act as if it's not even there."[17]

If income and wealth are highly correlated, such a distinction is interesting academically, but would be one without much of a difference.[18] Sociologist Lisa Keister's *Wealth in America* reviews the correlation of income and wealth, and concludes that it is weak at best.[19] According to Keister, this suggests that "studies that focus solely on income miss a large part of the story of advantage and disadvantage in America."[20]

Having the capacity to represent inequality from the past, an examination of wealth not only gauges contemporary resources differences, but also suggests a future pattern of inequalities. I suggest a paradigm shift: Wealth changes our conception of racial inequality, its nature and magnitude, origins and transmission, and whether it is increasing or narrowing. Importantly, an examination of wealth allows an analytic window into the contemporary relevance of the historical legacy of African-Americans; indeed, a wealth lens will broaden our understanding of the relationship between historical and contemporary considerations for class as well as for race.

Importantly, civil rights organizations already place the wealth gap on their agenda and have begun to build constituencies and public awareness for action.[21] While consensus is building on this agenda, how to move forward, and on which specific policies, is still a subject of debate. Thus, while homeownership is central to the discussion of closing the racial wealth gap, other mechanisms, ranging from Individual Development Accounts, to building community assets, to reparations, also offer important remedies. Framing racial inequality from a wealth perspective raises the issue of the deeply embedded racial structure of the United States.

II. THE HOMEOWNERSHIP FOUNDATION

How do families accumulate wealth? This question goes directly to the heart of the American ethos and to my argument. The leading ideological and scholarly answer is that wealth emerges from hard work, disciplined consumption, savings and wise investments, with perhaps some luck thrown in.[22] In this individual model, wealth builds slowly during one's lifetime and is life-cycle sensitive, with wealth building gradually in young families, accumulating mostly during the latter working years, and being utilized mostly during retirement.[23] This theory of wealth accumulation thus emphasizes the acquisition, accrual, and depletion of wealth within a lifetime, placing minimal weight on inheritance or on the consequences of state policies and institutional practices on subsequent wealth-accumulating opportunities.

Institutional theory and a sociology of wealth places greater value on inheritance, programs and practices. Homeownership and housing appreciation is the foundation of institutional accumulation.[24] Indeed, for most Americans, home equity represents the largest reservoir of wealth: home wealth accounts for 60% of the total wealth among America's middle class.[25] The empirically accurate American wealth narrative is not simply about individual hard work, discipline, and savings; notably it is also about structured homeownership opportunities, real estate markets, government programs encouraging homeownership, and residential segregation.[26]

America has a high homeownership rate, with 69% of Americans owning homes.[27] A series of federal policies that started in the 1930s made this high homeownership rate and subsequent middle-class wealth accumulation possible by creating a government-sponsored market. Federal policies helped create a mortgage market where homes could be purchased with long-term, low-interest loans and relatively small down payments, most particularly through the Federal Housing Administration, the Veterans Administration, and the GI Bill. In conjunction with rising wages after World War II, these policies put the American dream of home ownership within the reach of millions of families.[28] The beneficial tax treatment of home mortgages and capital gains on home sales makes home ownership more affordable. Transportation policies subsidized an infrastructure that prioritizes private automobiles and allows suburban development. While these federal policies and subsidies have been successful in anchoring America's middle class in home ownership, the same policies have traditionally reinforced residential segregation.[29]

 ## III. THE ASSET POVERTY LINE

This section examines the resource condition of typical American families by looking at wealth circumstances. The Asset Poverty Line (APL) is a tool that facilitates an examination of the wealth condition of American families. Using the conservative U.S. government policy as a standard, we asked how long can families survive at a poverty level in the absence of an income stream. In 1999, for example, the monthly poverty line for a family of four was $1392.[30] Thus, to survive at the poverty line for three months, a family needed at least $4175 in financial assets.[31] Families with less than $4175 can thus be categorized as asset poor. It is worth noting the conservative assumptions require accepting the government poverty line, at least for purposes of this exercise.[32] Adopting a three-month threshold, instead of, say, a six- or nine-month threshold, is another conservative assumption. The impact is that the actual number of families in asset poverty is underestimated. Nonetheless, the APL focuses attention on asset poverty.

Others, I hope, will push these boundaries. Nearly four households out of ten in the world's wealthiest nation do not own enough assets to live even a poverty lifestyle for three months.[33]

> If poverty is something that affects not just one in every eight, nine, or ten families [as in the income definition of poverty] but four in ten, then we need to think about poverty very differently because it is much more characteristic of American families. Over half of black American families fell below the Asset Poverty Line in 1999.[34]

Viewed in light of financial assets, America's families are far more fragile and precarious than previously thought. Moreover, both class and race features are clearly revealed.

 ## IV. THE RACIAL WEALTH GAP

Sandra McCord lives in Los Angeles with her two daughters, Kalila and Myisha.[35] Her neighborhood is poverty stricken and African-American. Sandra has worked at various low-level, poverty wage jobs, but when I talked to her, she was in school working toward her degree.[36] She has zero financial assets, owes money on some store charge cards, and manages to get by—barely—on less than poverty income.[37] Hers is not an easy life. In the midst of her daily struggles, Sandra is more troubled about her daughters' futures. She believed that the local schools were horrible and unsafe, so she navigated the system to place her daughters in better ones.[38] However, these schools are a one and a half hour public bus ride away, and Sandra must pay the bus fares. Bus fares do not cost much, unless, of course, you survive on a budget that is less than half of the poverty line. Each month this poses a cruel dilemma for Sandra: *"Sometimes, to be honest, sometimes, sometimes, when I have to wait for my check . . . sometimes my kids will have to miss a couple of days of school."*[39] Choosing between school for your children or food on the table is not an excruciatingly tragic dilemma that most of us face at month's end. This is the price Sandra and her daughters pay for living in a poor neighborhood.

The McCords are one of nearly 200 families that I interviewed for *The Hidden Cost of Being African American*. While her story and choices may sound extreme, the lack of wealth among African-Americans is a major explanation why racial inequality persists today. The typical African-American family owns just $3000 in financial wealth (excluding homes).[40]

The standard metric of racial inequality is to compare the incomes of average white and black families.[41] This measure has ranged from approximately fifty-six cents on the dollar to sixty-two cents on the dollar from the mid-1960s until now.[42] The range has been narrow, and not much movement has occurred toward more equality or toward closing the income gap. Examining wealth dramatically changes this perspective. The net worth of typical white families is $81,000, compared to $8000 for black families.[43] A typical white family's wealth is more than $73,000 greater than the typical black family's, which is a marker of the racial wealth gap expressed in dollars. The baseline racial wealth gap also shows that black families own only a dime of wealth for every dollar owned by white families. One component of this paradigm shift is the magnitude of closing a fifty-nine cent on a dollar gap, to thinking about how to close a ten cent on a dollar gap.

The prevailing explanation for this robust racial wealth gap, of course, is rooted in inequalities in contemporary class-based achievements, such as occupation, education, and income.[44] Leveling these critical differences in school achievement, jobs, and paychecks, accordingly, will eradicate the racial wealth gap. Our analysis, and that of others,[45] demonstrates the shortcomings of this class-determinist perspective on racial inequality. In the best-case scenario, comparing equally achieving white and black middle class families illustrates the significance of the historical legacy of government policies and practices, and of race and continuing contemporary institutional discrimination.

When one defines the middle class by education (college degree), an income range, or occupational status (professional, white collar), the black middle class owns about twenty-five cents of wealth for every dollar of wealth owned by the white middle class.[46] Certainly, twenty-five cents on the dollar represents advancement over ten cents on the dollar, showing that achievement matters, but a huge racial wealth gap remains when one compares equally achieving whites and blacks. At least as important, one must ask why such a dramatic racial wealth gap remains. Although beyond the scope of this essay, I already have alluded to the enduring importance of how the past continues to play out in the present and the importance of contemporary institutional arrangements in promoting differential wealth accumulating opportunities with clear racial consequences.[47]

Among the crucial issues facing families today is the effect of recent recession and jobless recovery on family economic security. My recent research argues that a widening wealth gap between minorities and whites is reversing the gains earned in schools and jobs, and is making inequality worse.[48] A report from the Pew Hispanic Center provides new data on family wealth and offers a sobering assessment of the precarious and fragile status of middle-class families—including white families, but most particularly Hispanic and African-American families.[49]

In the years prior to the 2001 recession, white, Hispanic, and African-American families generated wealth through savings, investment, and homeownership. More families acquired assets and family portfolios grew. In this context of wealth accumulation, however, the wealth gap between minority and white families was widened. The recession and its recovery brought wealth growth to an abrupt halt for millions of American families. During this period, Hispanic and African-American families lost over one-quarter of their wealth, while the wealth of white families slowly grew.[50] In 2002, a typical Hispanic family owned eleven cents of wealth for every dollar owned by a typical white family, and African-American families owned only seven cents.[51]

These net wealth losses illustrate how Hispanic and African-American families, and low-to-middle income families in general, have shouldered the burden of tightening economic times and reduced social investment during the Bush administration. Over one in four (25%) Hispanic and African-American families are asset-poor, having no liquid financial assets, compared to 13% of white families.[52] The research creates the inference that families with small or moderate amounts of wealth drew from their meager stockpile of savings to use as private safety nets.[53] In addition to making tough choices, such as giving up health insurance or spacing out medical appointments and refilling prescriptions, this is the real story of how families adapt to recession, jobless recovery, stagnating wages, outsourcing, and a dwindling federal commitment to important safety nets like unemployment benefits and the minimum wage, which has not keeping pace with inflation.

Interest-earning assets, such as savings bonds, IRA and Keogh accounts, 401(k) and thrift accounts, stocks and mutual funds, and business capital, declined precipitously among Hispanic families with assets.[54] In African-American families, stock and mutual fund investments plummeted by nearly two-thirds.[55] Surely, this reflects investment losses, but it also represents the tapping of accounts to cover insecurities about employment and income losses. These families adapt by eating the acorns they stored for their future economic mobility and security. Families will not make up these setbacks easily or in a short time span.

While the income, educational achievement, and employment gaps among Hispanics, African-Americans and whites remain steady or show some slight narrowing, the wealth gap increases. I made this argument in *The Hidden Cost of Being African American.*[56] The report and current data from the Pew Hispanic Center further corroborate that a growing wealth gap reverses the gains earned in schools, on jobs, and in paychecks. An added compounding change is that the financial portfolios of Hispanics and African-Americans have shrunk in the current economy.[57]

More than any other economic attribute, wealth represents the sedimentation of historical inequalities in the American experience, in a sense the accumulation of advantages and disadvantages for different racial, class and ethnic groups.[58] In this way, wealth provides a window to explore how our past influences the realities of today.

This is not simply a story about counting money; families think about using wealth first as a private safety net, and second as a vehicle to launch mobility into middle-class status, homeownership, business development, or a more secure retirement.[59] The recent recession and recovery—along with current public policies—are a real step backward for the self-reliance and independence of Hispanics, African-Americans, and other low-to-middle income families. These factors represent a double blow against equality and family well-being in America.

V. HOMEOWNERSHIP AND INSTITUTIONAL DISCRIMINATION

Homeownership is the largest component of the wealth portfolios of both white and black families.[60] In 2002, housing wealth accounted for 63% of all wealth in African-American families.[61] In 2004, homeownership reached historic highs, as 69% of American families lived in a home they owned.[62] In 1995, 42.2% of African-American families owned homes, increasing to a historic high of 49.5% in 2004.[63] This 7.3% increase in African-American homeownership is quite remarkable, and indicates striving, accomplishment, and success. The black-white homeownership gap stood at 28.5% in 1995 and narrowed to 26.2% in 2004.[64] Increasing black homeownership and rising home values are optimistic signs of closing the racial wealth gap. We might expect the homeownership gap to continue to close, as black homeownership starts from a considerably lower base while the higher white rate may be close to exhausting the potential of those who want to become homeowners.

However, the wealth accumulation and homeownership dynamics are marred by critical institutional factors. Nancy Denton's age-specific examination of homeownership rates for blacks and whites illustrates the importance of timing and of life course.[65] The homeownership gap is widest for the younger age groups (twenty-five to twenty-nine years old), closes incrementally with age, and reaches its narrowest point for the elderly (seventy to seventy-four years old).[66] Over the life course, the gap closes by almost half, which is very impressive. The simple conclusion is that whites can afford to buy homes earlier than can blacks. This underscores the importance of young couples needing significant parental financial support to afford homeownership.[67] In understanding this connection between homeownership and wealth accumulation, it is relevant that the earlier a family buys a home, the greater the likelihood that the home will appreciate in value and create more wealth.

As we think about closing the homeownership gap as a strategy for closing the racial wealth gap, we must attend to deeply rooted discriminatory institutional features. Three such features are apparent. First, financial institutions reject African-Americans for home mortgages at considerably higher rates—about a 60% higher rejection rate—than whites, even when white and black families are equally creditworthy.[68] As sanctioned community redlining diminishes under pressure from the civil rights movement, community organizations, the Community Reinvestment Act and other fair-lending and fair-housing laws,[69] it appears that financial institutions re-create similar results by constructing "objective" criteria of creditworthiness in such a way that individual minority families fall short far more often than white families, thereby redrawing redlines by family instead of by community.[70]

Second, blacks approved for home mortgages often pay higher interest rates on home loans. Blacks pay interest rates of approximately one third of a percent higher than whites, or about $12,000 more for the average American home over a 30-year mortgage.[71] Part of this is due to the greater ability of white families to provide larger down payments and even to pay higher service fees for lowered interest rates.[72] From interviews, discussions with bankers, and other data, it appears that many young white families can rely on significant family financial assistance with down payments and other costs.[73] Nearly one-half of all white homeowners report that they received significant financial assistance from their families.[74] In sharp contrast, seven out of eight African-American homeowners purchased homes on their own.[75] This inheritance results from the discriminatory housing markets of a previous era, marked by exclusion and residential segregation and backed by government support.[76]

African-Americans were frozen out of the greatest wealth building opportunities in American history. From the Homestead Act in the 1860s, to education and homeownership opportunities provided by the GI Bill and the Federal Housing Administration, to redlining through contemporary discrimination in housing markets, to the segregation tax on housing appreciation, major government-sponsored wealth building opportunities helped foster America's middle class and created much wealth.[77] Meanwhile, these same policies and practices left the African-American community behind at the starting gate. Inheritance of our racial past thus becomes an integral part of the wealth narrative.

One indication that this history is alive today is the fact that most young couples can purchase homes only with significant financial assistance from their parents—especially to cover down payments. For example, Briggette and Joe Barry were having a tough time coming up with the down payment for their house.[78] They traded in the kids' saving bonds, worked two jobs each around the clock, and held garage sales, but they did not make much headway. Finally, Briggette's mom said, "Well this is stupid. We've got a lot of money here," and provided significant funds to help with the down payment.[79] This transformative asset moved the Barry family into a white, suburban, middle-class community that they otherwise could not have afforded. Our history denied this possible inheritance to African-Americans, as they toiled in times and under conditions in which wealth accumulation was virtually foreclosed.

The third institutional dynamic of homeownership and home equity poses the most difficult challenges. Here, residential segregation meets housing appreciation. Homes have appreciated in value in most communities and in most areas of the country, except for in poor, minority, urban neighborhoods.[80] On average, homes owned by whites appreciate in value approximately $28,000 more than those owned by blacks.[81] Moreover, homes lose about 16% of their value when located in neighborhoods that are more than 10% black.[82] This gives a new (or old) meaning to the realtor's mantra: location, location, location. Just as home ownership creates wealth for both whites and blacks, it simultaneously widens the racial wealth gap under current conditions.

 ## VI. THE DARK SIDE OF HOMEOWNERSHIP—NEW CHALLENGES

Subprime lending is targeted to prospective homebuyers with blemished credit histories or with high levels of debt who otherwise would not qualify for conventional mortgage loans.[83] These loans bring homeownership within the grasp of millions of families, and they are essential in expanding home-ownership rates. In return for these riskier investments, financial institutions charge borrowers higher interest rates, often require higher processing and closing fees, and sometimes add special loan conditions such as prepayment penalties, balloon payments, and adjustable interest rates.[84]

The subprime market expanded greatly in the last decade as a part of new, aggressive marketing strategies by financial institutions hungrily eyeing ris-ing homeownership rates and seeing promising new markets. Moreover, the mortgage finance system in the United States became well integrated into global capital markets during this time, which offer an ever-growing array of financial products, including subprime loans. Subprime loan originations grew more than nine-fold, from $35 billion to $332 billion between 1994 and 2003.[85] Reflecting the increasing importance of subprime loans to the finan-cial industry, the subprime share of mortgage loans has seen a parallel mete-oric rise from less than 4% in 1995, to about 17% in 2004.[86]

Loan terms such as prepayment penalties and balloon payments increase the risk of mortgage foreclosure in subprime home loans, even after controlling for the borrower's credit score, loan term, and varying economic conditions.[87] For example, one study demonstrated that subprime prepay-ment penalties and balloon payments place Americans at substantially greater risk of losing their homes.[88]

A key finding is that subprime home loans with extended prepayment penalties faced 20% greater odds of entering foreclosure than loans without prepayment penalties.[89] Prepayment restrictions mean that homeowners are stuck with loan terms, unable to refinance to obtain lower rates to weather financial difficulties or take advantage of lower interest rates.[90] Another important finding demonstrates that subprime home loans with balloon payments, in which a single lump sum payment many times the regular payment amount is due at the end of the loan term, face 50% greater odds of entering foreclosure than fully amortizing loans.[91] In addition, borrow-ers whose subprime loans include fluctuating interest rates face 25% greater odds of entering foreclosure than borrowers with fixed rate subprime mortgages.[92] In the fourth quarter of 2003, 2.13% of all subprime loans across the country entered foreclosure—this was more than ten times higher than the rate for all prime loans.[93] One in five of all first-lien subprime refinance loans that originated in 1999 had entered foreclosure by December of 2003.[94]

Delinquency (falling behind in mortgage payments) and losing one's home through foreclosure hit vulnerable neighborhoods hardest.[95] Con-centrated foreclosures can negatively impact the surrounding neighbor-hoods and threaten to undo community building and revitalization efforts achieved through decades of collaborative public-private partnerships, com-munity organizing, and local policy efforts.[96]

Los Angeles is a case in point. In a short three-year period (from 2001 to 2004), over 14,000 Los Angeles families lost their homes through foreclosure.[97] The foreclosure rate was highest in the most vulnerable neighborhoods.

Predominately minority neighborhoods of Los Angeles county experienced approximately 45% of all foreclosures.[98] In the City of Los Angeles, foreclosures occur nearly twelve times more often in predominately minority communities than in areas with fewer than 20% minorities.[99]

About one in four of all Los Angeles home foreclosures occur in neighborhoods in which low-income minority families are concentrated.[100] The impact is devastating, as 7.6% of all families paying mortgages lost their homes between 2001 and 2004.[101] Los Angeles is not alone; data from Atlanta, Baltimore, Boston, Chicago, and others show that Los Angeles is part of a larger, national pattern.[102]

A study examining pricing disparities in the mortgage market provides more context, placing the Los Angeles story in a broader pattern. Of all conventional loans to blacks, nearly 30% were subprime, compared to only 10% for whites.[103] These ratios would align more closely in lending markets that operated with maximum efficiency and equity. Creditworthy criteria, like debt-to-income ratios, do not explain the greater propensity for African-Americans to receive subprime loans.[104] The report also discovered that subprime loans in minority communities increased with levels of racial segregation.[105] This suggests an alarming new form of modern redlining that targets minority neighborhoods for subprime loans.

Using a testing methodology adapted from those that explored job discrimination, the National Community Reinvestment Coalition explored how pricing disparities resulting from intensified subprime lending in minority areas occurred. Essentially, white and black testers with similar credit records and qualifications applied for pre-approval for mortgages.[106] Given similar scripts and profiles (with African-Americans actually presenting better qualifications), the testing uncovered a 45% rate of disparate treatment based on race.[107] The testing revealed practices that may have destructive effects on African-American families and communities. These include differences in interest rates quoted; differences in information about fees, rates, loan programs, and loan terms; and more frequent referrals of whites to the lender's prime lending division.[108] In *Black Wealth/White Wealth,* we wrote that differences in loan rejection rates and interest rates did not result from discriminatory lending practices, but from blacks bringing fewer financial assets to the mortgage table and, as a result, paying higher loan terms.[109] Racial pricing disparities and the targeted spread of subprime lending to minority communities, however, now persuade us that minority America is experiencing a new form of redlining organized by race and geographic space. With data like this, foreclosure, transparency, fair lending, and federal regulatory responsibility become central to public policy debates.[110]

Since homeownership results in wealth-building for most, we must consider ways to boost affordable homeownership. Similarly, we must pay more attention to protecting the assets that families already own, especially homes. The documented trends in growing credit card debt,[111] rising predatory lending, and subprime loans endanger financial assets for low-income, elderly, and minority homeowners in particular.

Addressing inequities in home mortgage applications and attending to differences in mortgage rates is conceivable using existing laws, tools, and good will, but grappling with the supposedly objective, automated credit-scoring system for credit approvals will not be easy.[112] More difficult and seemingly intractable barriers emerge when thinking through remedies for residential segregation. Because residential segregation is the lynchpin for race relations and the racial wealth gap, this must be part of the discussion.[113]

While increasing homeownership seems like an obvious strategy for closing the racial wealth gap, other cautions must be noted before becoming uncritically swept up by this strategy. Americans cashed out $333 billion worth of home equity between 2001 and 2003 when interest rates were low and refinancing was advantageous.[114] This level of refinancing and pocketing part of the appreciation was three times higher than any previous period since the data was first tracked in 1993.[115] Cashing out home equity is neither positive nor negative on its face. The real question is how families use that money. One would hope it is used for such things as new investments, improving human capital, leveraging new opportunities, and launching social mobility in other areas. Such utilization might promote better human and family development, and portend a better future. However, a majority of households used their newfound wealth in quite another fashion—to cover living expenses and repay credit card debts.[116] Cashing out home equity is particularly troublesome given the decline in homeowner's equity between 1973 and 2004. In other words, Americans own less of their homes today than they did in the 1970s and early 1980s.[117] We must be wary of this new form of "strip mining" home equity.

Another caution against going overboard on homeownership is in order. Housing should be viewed as a continuum, with affordable housing—either homeownership, rental or transitional—the goal. Not all families at all phases of their life cycles are appropriate candidates for homeownership, and policy must take this into consideration. In addition, since housing appreciation depends upon location, prescriptions for homeownership must be tempered by a realistic assessment of property valuation and the types of public, social investments that improve neighborhoods.

My discussion here has focused mostly on the exchange value of homeownership. In the larger discussion of how families employ wealth to pass along advantages and opportunities to their children, it is important to note that homes also have use value. By this I mean that homeownership (or renting) locates a family in a set of community services, contexts, and relationships, and partially defines race and class identities. For example, most children attend school according to the geographic location of their housing. Because of this selection process and because most schools are funded by local taxes, housing affordability is a large determinant of school quality, resources, and peers.[118]

Finally, more attention is needed on protecting wealth accumulation and preservation, and on the political debate and the racialized state policies embedded in our tax code. Federal asset policies cost $335 billion in 2003, the vast majority of which are in tax expenditures or credits.[119] Most of these current asset policies subsidize homeownership through the mortgage interest deduction, create incentives for retirement savings, and subsidize saving and investment for those already well off. For example, one-third of these tax benefits accrue to the wealthiest one percent.[120] Alternatively, representing the proverbial crumbs, five percent of the asset-related tax benefits go to the bottom sixty percent of the population.[121] Reversing these priorities is a good starting part for inclusive asset building policies that promote equity.

NOTES

1. Melvin L. Oliver & Thomas M. Shapiro, *Black Wealth/White Wealth: A New Perspective on Racial Inequality* 30 (1995).
2. *Id.*
3. *Id.* at 32.
4. Included in this rapidly emerging literature are: Jennifer Jellison Holme, *Buying Homes, Buying Schools: School Choice and the Social Construction of School Quality*, 72 Harv. Educ. Rev. 177 (2002); Hyungsoo Kim & Jinkook Lee, *Unequal Effects of Elders' Health Problems on Wealth Depletion Across Race and Ethnicity*, 39 J. Consumer Aff. 148 (2005); Trina Williams Shanks, *The Impacts of Household Wealth on Child Development* (Ctr. for Soc. Dev., George Warren Brown Sch. of Soc. Work, Wash. Univ., Working Paper No. 04-07, 2004), *available at* http://gwbweb.wustl.edu/csd/Publications/2004/WP04-07.pdf.

     The work of Edward Wolff anchors much of the wealth inequality field. *See* Edward N. Wolff, *Top Heavy* (2002). Many other scholars have made important contributions to understanding racial wealth inequality. These scholars include: Joseph G. Altonji et al., *Black/White Differences in Wealth*, 24 Econ. Persp. 38 (2000); Kerwin Kofi Charles & Erik Hurst, *The Transition to Home Ownership and the Black-White Wealth Gap*, 84 Rev. Econ. & Stat. 281 (2002); John Karl Scholz & Kara Levine, *U.S. Black-White Wealth Inequality, in* Social Inequality 895 (Kathryn M. Neckerman ed., 2004). The work of Mariko Chang has also made significant contributions to this literature.
5. Thomas M. Shapiro, *The Hidden Cost of Being African American: How Wealth Perpetuates Inequality* (2004); *see also* Lisa A. Keister, *Wealth in America* (2000) (discussing the conceptual and methodological issues pertaining to survey data on family wealth).
6. *See also* Wolff, *supra* note 4. This book contains a good general discussion of wealth inequality in the United States in comparative and historical contexts. The estate tax is a prime example of a political issue in which more information is available to frame the context of the political discussion.
7. Shapiro, *supra* note 5, at 33.
8. William Julius Wilson, *When Work Disappears: The World of the New Urban Poor* (1st ed. 1996).
9. Shapiro, *supra* note 5, at 33.

10. Shapiro, *supra* note 5. Much of the data for this article is taken from the author's book. The in-depth family interviews are from three cities: Los Angeles, Boston and St. Louis. In total, 183 families were interviewed for this project. The sample design called for interviewing families with young, school-age children to probe areas of community choice, homeownership, school decisions, and family financial capacity. Three quarters of the interviewed families were middle class, and one-quarter were working class or poor. Half of the families lived in urban areas, and half in surrounding suburbs. Approximately half of the families interviewed were black and the other half were white. The sample was designed to examine white and black families with similar educational, occupational, and income achievements so that the impact of wealth on critical family capacities and opportunities could be evaluated. *Id.* at 15.

11. *Id.* at 34.

12. *Id.*

13. *Id.*

14. *Id.* at 35.

15. *Id.* at 34.

16. *Id.*

17. *Id.*

18. *Id.* at 35.

19. Keister, *supra* note 5, at 10.

20. *Id.*

21. I refer to the work of many organizations, including the National Council of La Raza, the First Nations Development Institute, United for a Fair Economy, the Civil Rights Leadership Council, and others.

22. Shapiro, *supra* note 5, at 60.

23. *See* Franco Modigliani, *The Role of Intergenerational Transfers and Life Cycle Saving in the Accumulation of Wealth,* J. Econ. Persp., Spring 1988, at 15, 16.

24. Shapiro, *supra* note 5, at 107.

25. *Id.*

26. *Id.* at 107–08.

27. Joint Ctr. for Hous. Studies of Harvard Univ., The State of the Nation's Housing: 2005, at 15–19 (2005).

28. Kenneth T. Jackson, *Crabgrass Frontier: The Suburbanization of the United States* (1985).

29. *Id;* Oliver & Shapiro, *supra* note 1; Guy Stuart, *Discriminating Risk: The U.S. Mortgage Lending Industry in the Twentieth Century* (2003).

30. For a fuller discussion of this index, see Shapiro, *supra* note 5, pt. I.

31. *Id.*

32. An alternative, for example, might use data from living wage campaigns passed by several communities. The living wage figures differ by region and other factors, but the calculation is that the minimum wage needs to double to provide adequate economic resources for a family. Adopting this standard would double the Asset Poverty Line figure and pull close to two-thirds of America's families into asset poverty.

33. Shapiro, *supra* note 5, at 38.

34. *Id.*

35. *Id.* at 179.

36. *Id.*

37. *Id.*

38. *Id.*

39. *Id.* at 181 (emphasis added).

40. *Id.* at 49.

41. *Id.* at 47.

42. *Id.*

43. *Id.* at 47–49.

44. *The Black-White Test Score Gap* (Christopher Jencks & Meredith Phillips eds., 1988); James P. Smith, *Race and Ethnicity in the Labor Market: Trends over the Short and Long Term, in* 2 America Becoming 52, 52–97 (Neil J. Smelser et al. eds., 2001).

45. Keister, *supra* note 5; Oliver & Shapiro, *supra* note 1.

46. Shapiro, *supra* note 5, at 90–91 figs. 4.2–4.

47. *See supra* pages 57–58.

48. Shapiro, *supra* note 5, at 6–12.

49. Rakesh Kumar Kochhar, The Wealth of Hispanic Households: 1996 to 2002 (2004).

50. *Id.* at 11.

51. *Id.* at 5 (measuring the median net worth of white households as $88,651, that of Hispanic households as $7932, and that of black households as $5988).

52. *Id.* at 6.

53. *Id.* at 18.

54. *Id.* at 17–20.

55. *Id.* at 18 tbl. 8.

56. Shapiro, *supra* note 5, at 87–92.

57. Kochhar, *supra* note 49, at 16–22.

58. Oliver & Shapiro, *supra* note 1, at 50–52.

59. Shapiro, *supra* note 5, at 34–35.

60. Kochhar, *supra* note 49, at 36 ("Regardless of race or ethnicity, the house is the single most important asset in the portfolio of homeowners.")

61. *Id.* at 19 tbl. 19.

62. Joint Ctr. for Hous. Studies, *supra* note 27, at 36 tbl. A-8.

63. *Id.*

64. *Id.* at 36.

65. Nancy A. Denton, *Housing as a Means of Asset Accumulation: A Good Strategy for the Poor?,* in Assets for the Poor: The Benefits of Spreading Asset Ownership 232, 238–44 (Thomas M. Shapiro & Edward N. Wolff eds., 2001).

66. *Id.* at 239 tbl. 7.1. For recent data, see Joint Ctr. for Hous. Studies, *supra* note 27, at 36.

67. *See, e.g.,* Shapiro, *supra* note 5, at 60–72.

68. Oliver & Shapiro, *supra* note 1, at 141–47.

69. Joint Ctr. for Hous. Studies of Harvard Univ., The 25th Anniversary of the Community Reinvestment Act: Access to Capital in an Evolving Financial Services System (2002), *available at* http://www.jchs.harvard.edu/publications/governmentprograms/cra02-1.pdf.

70. *See* Shapiro, *supra* note 5, at 108–11.

71. *Id.* at 111.

72. *Id.* at 112.

73. *Id.* at 112–16.

74. *Id.* at 113.

75. *Id.* at 113 fig. 5.1.
76. *See* Oliver & Shapiro, *supra* note 1, at 16–18.
77. Shapiro, *supra* note 5, at 189–91 (briefly summarizing the effects of various government policies).
78. This anecdote is taken from *id.* at 73–74.
79. *Id.* at 73.
80. *Id.* at 120–21.
81. *Id.* at 121.
82. *Id.* at 122.
83. Joint Ctr. for Hous. Studies, *supra* note 27, at 17.
84. *Id.*
85. Roberto G. Quercia et al., Ctr. for Cmty. Capitalism, The Impact of Predatory Loan Terms on Subprime Foreclosures: The Special Case of Prepayment Penalties and Balloon Payments 2 (2005), http://www.kenan-flagler.unc.edu/assets/documents/foreclosurepaper.pdf.
86. *See* Joint Ctr. for Hous. Studies, *supra* note 27, at 17 fig. 20.
87. Quercia, *supra* note 85, at 27–28.
88. *Id.* at 27–30.
89. *Id.* at 27. Extended prepayment penalties are typically longer than three years. *Id.* at 23.
90. *Id.* at 8.
91. *Id.* at 25.
92. *Id.* at 24. Loans with fluctuating interest rates are known as Adjustable Rate Mortgages, and they comprised 49% of the 1999 subprime market. *Id.* at 23.
93. *Id.* at 2.
94. *Id.* at 21.
95. Mark Duda & William C. Apgar, L.A. Neighborhood Hous. Servs., Mortgage Foreclosure Trends in Los Angeles 1 (2004).
96. *Id.*
97. *Id.* at 2.
98. *Id.*
99. *Id.*
100. *Id.*
101. *Id.*
102. *Id.*
103. Nat'l Cmty. Reinvestment Coal., Preapprovals and Pricing Disparities in the Mortgage Marketplace 5 (2005).
104. *Legislative Solutions to Abusive Mortgage Lending Practices, Hearing Before the H. Subcomms. on Housing and Community Opportunity and Financial Institutions and Consumer Credit and the H. Comm. on Financial Services,* 109th Cong. 5-7 (2005) (testimony of Stella Adams).
105. *Id.* at 4.
106. *Id.* at 5.
107. *Id.* at 6.
108. *Id.*
109. Oliver & Shapiro, *supra* note 1, at 136–47.
110. *See, e.g.,* Preapprovals and Pricing Disparities in the Mortgage Marketplace, *supra* note 103, at 21–25 (recommending various legislative and regulatory actions).

111. Tamara Draut & Javier Silva, Borrowing to Make Ends Meet: The Growth of Credit Card Debt in the 90s (2003), *available at* http://www.demos-USA.org/pubs/borrowing_to_make_ends_meet.pdf.

112. John Yinger, *Closed Doors, Opportunities Lost: The Continuing Costs of Housing Discrimination, 65–70* (1995).

113. *See* Douglas S. Massey & Nancy A. Denton, *American Apartheid: Segregation and the Making of the Underclass* (1993); Yinger, *supra* note 112, at 110–14.

114. Javier Silva, *A House of Cards: Refinancing the American Dream* 1 (Dēmos, Briefing Paper No. 3, 2005), *available at* http://www.demos-USA.org/pubs/AhouseofCards.pdf.

115. *Id.*

116. *Id.* at 3.

117. *Id.* at 4.

118. Shapiro, *supra* note 5, at 138, 167–82.

119. Ctr. for Enter. Dev., Hidden in Plain Sight: A Look at the $335-Billion Asset-Building Budget 1 (2004).

120. *Id.*

121. *Id.*

 QUESTIONS FOR CRITICAL THINKING

Reading 5

1. How does Shapiro's discussion of the importance of wealth help you to understand the continuing racial economic gap in the United States?

2. How does your personal experience with regard to class influence your understanding of or level of disagreement with the author's discussion?

3. The idea of the "American dream" (if a person works hard, they will get ahead) is still common in the United States. How does this idea perpetuate misconceptions of those who are poor? Of those who are wealthy?

Reading 6

MEDIA MAGIC
Making Class Invisible

GREGORY MANTSIOS

Of the various social and cultural forces in our society, the mass media is arguably the most influential in molding public consciousness. Americans spend an average twenty-eight hours per week watching television. They also spend an undetermined number of hours reading periodicals, listening to the radio, and going to the movies. Unlike other cultural and socializing institutions, ownership and control of the mass media is highly concentrated. Twenty-three corporations own more than one-half of all the daily newspapers, magazines, movie studios, and radio and television outlets in the United States.[1] The number of media companies is shrinking and their control of the industry is expanding. And a relatively small number of media outlets is producing and packaging the majority of news and entertainment programs. For the most part, our media is national in nature and single-minded (profit-oriented) in purpose. This media plays a key role in defining our cultural tastes, helping us locate ourselves in history, establishing our national identity, and ascertaining the range of national and social possibilities. In this essay, we will examine the way the mass media shapes how people think about each other and about the nature of our society.

The United States is the most highly stratified society in the industrialized world. Class distinctions operate in virtually every aspect of our lives, determining the nature of our work, the quality of our schooling, and the health and safety of our loved ones. Yet remarkably, we, as a nation, retain illusions about living in an egalitarian society. We maintain these illusions, in large part, because the media hides gross inequities from public view. In those instances when inequities are revealed, we are provided with messages that obscure the nature of class realities and blame the victims of class-dominated society for their own plight. Let's briefly examine what the news media, in particular, tells us about class.

ABOUT THE POOR

The news media provides meager coverage of poor people and poverty. The coverage it does provide is often distorted and misleading.

The Poor Do Not Exist

For the most part, the news media ignores the poor. Unnoticed are forty million poor people in the nation—a number that equals the entire population of Maine, Vermont, New Hampshire, Connecticut, Rhode Island, New Jersey, and New York combined. Perhaps even more alarming is that the rate of poverty is increasing twice as fast as the population growth in the United States. Ordinarily, even a calamity of much smaller proportion (e.g., flooding in the Midwest) would garner a great deal of coverage and hype from a media usually eager to declare a crisis, yet less than one in five hundred articles in the *New York Times* and one in one thousand articles listed in the *Readers Guide to Periodic Literature* are on poverty. With remarkably little attention to them, the poor and their problems are hidden from most Americans.

When the media does turn its attention to the poor, it offers a series of contradictory messages and portrayals.

The Poor Are Faceless

Each year the Census Bureau releases a new report on poverty in our society and its results are duly reported in the media. At best, however, this coverage emphasizes annual fluctuations (showing how the numbers differ from previous years) and ongoing debates over the validity of the numbers (some argue the number should be lower, most that the number should be higher). Coverage like this desensitizes us to the poor by reducing poverty to a number. It ignores the human tragedy of poverty—the suffering, indignities, and misery endured by millions of children and adults. Instead, the poor become statistics rather than people.

The Poor Are Undeserving

When the media does put a face on the poor, it is not likely to be a pretty one. The media will provide us with sensational stories about welfare cheats, drug addicts, and greedy panhandlers (almost always urban and Black). Compare these images and the emotions evoked by them with the media's treatment of middle-class (usually white) "tax evaders," celebrities who have a "chemical dependency," or wealthy businesspeople who use unscrupulous means to "make a profit." While the behavior of the more affluent offenders is considered an "impropriety" and a deviation from the norm, the behavior of the poor is considered repugnant, indicative of the poor in general, and worthy of our indignation and resentment.

The Poor Are an Eyesore

When the media does cover the poor, they are often presented through the eyes of the middle class. For example, sometimes the media includes a story about community resistance to a homeless shelter or storekeeper annoyance with panhandlers. Rather than focusing on the plight of the poor, these stories are about middle-class opposition to the poor. Such stories tell us that the poor are an inconvenience and an irritation.

The Poor Have Only Themselves to Blame

In another example of media coverage, we are told that the poor live in a personal and cultural cycle of poverty that hopelessly imprisons them. They routinely center on the Black urban population and focus on perceived personality or cultural traits that doom the poor. While the women in these stories typically exhibit an "attitude" that leads to trouble or a promiscuity that leads to single motherhood, the men possess a need for immediate gratification that leads to drug abuse or an unquenchable greed that leads to the pursuit of fast money. The images that are seared into our mind are sexist, racist, and classist. Census figures reveal that most of the poor are white not Black or Hispanic, that they live in rural or suburban areas not urban centers, and hold jobs at least part of the year.[2] Yet, in a fashion that is often framed in an understanding and sympathetic tone, we are told that the poor have inflicted poverty on themselves.

The Poor Are Down on Their Luck

During the Christmas season, the news media sometimes provides us with accounts of poor individuals or families (usually white) who are down on their luck. These stories are often linked to stories about soup kitchens or other charitable activities and sometimes call for charitable contributions. These "Yule time" stories are as much about the affluent as they are about the poor: they tell us that the affluent in our society are a kind, understanding, giving people—which we are not.[*] The series of unfortunate circumstances that have led to impoverishment are presumed to be a temporary condition that will improve with time and a change in luck.

---

*American households with incomes of less than $10,000 give an average of 5.5 percent of their earning to charity or to a religious organization, while those making more than $100,000 a year give only 2.9 percent. After changes in the 1986 tax code reduced the benefits of charitable giving, taxpayers earning $500,000 or more slashed their average donation by nearly one-third. Furthermore, many of these acts of benevolence do not help the needy. Rather than provide funding to social service agencies that aid the poor, the voluntary contributions of the wealthy go to places and institutions that entertain, inspire, cure, or educate wealthy Americans—art museums, opera houses, theaters, orchestras, ballet companies, private hospitals, and elite universities. (Robert Reich, "Secession of the Successful," *New York Times Magazine,* February 17, 1991, p. 43.)

Despite appearances, the messages provided by the media are not entirely disparate. With each variation, the media informs us what poverty is not (i.e., systemic and indicative of American society) by informing us what it is. The media tells us that poverty is either an aberration of the American way of life (it doesn't exist, it's just another number, it's unfortunate but temporary) or an end product of the poor themselves (they are a nuisance, do not deserve better, and have brought their predicament upon themselves).

By suggesting that the poor have brought poverty upon themselves, the media is engaging in what William Ryan has called "blaming the victim."[3] The media identifies in what ways the poor are different as a consequence of deprivation, then defines those differences as the cause of poverty itself. Whether blatantly hostile or cloaked in sympathy, the message is that there is something fundamentally wrong with the victims—their hormones, psychological makeup, family environment, community, race, or some combination of these—that accounts for their plight and their failure to lift themselves out of poverty.

But poverty in the United States is systemic. It is a direct result of economic and political policies that deprive people of jobs, adequate wages, or legitimate support. It is neither natural nor inevitable: there is enough wealth in our nation to eliminate poverty if we chose to redistribute existing wealth or income. The plight of the poor is reason enough to make the elimination of poverty the nation's first priority. But poverty also impacts dramatically on the nonpoor. It has a dampening effect on wages in general (by maintaining a reserve army of unemployed and underemployed anxious for any job at any wage) and breeds crime and violence (by maintaining conditions that invite private gain by illegal means and rebellion-like behavior, not entirely unlike the urban riots of the 1960s). Given the extent of poverty in the nation and the impact it has on us all, the media must spin considerable magic to keep the poor and the issue of poverty and its root causes out of the public consciousness.

ABOUT EVERYONE ELSE

Both the broadcast and the print news media strive to develop a strong sense of "we-ness" in their audience. They seek to speak to and for an audience that is both affluent and like-minded. The media's solidarity with affluence, that is, with the middle and upper class, varies little from one medium to another. Benjamin DeMott points out, for example, that the *New York Times* understands affluence to be intelligence, taste, public spirit, responsibility, and a readiness to rule and "conceives itself as spokesperson for a readership awash in these qualities."[4] Of course, the flip side to creating a sense of "we," or "us," is establishing a perception of the "other." The other relates back to the faceless, amoral, undeserving, and inferior "underclass." Thus, the world according to the news media is divided between the "underclass" and everyone else. Again the messages are often contradictory.

The Wealthy Are Us

Much of the information provided to us by the news media focuses attention on the concerns of a very wealthy and privileged class of people. Although the concerns of a small fraction of the populace, they are presented as though they were the concerns of everyone. For example, while relatively few people actually own stock, the news media devotes an inordinate amount of broadcast time and print space to business news and stock market quotations. Not only do business reports cater to a particular narrow clientele, so do the fashion pages (with $2,000 dresses), wedding announcements, and the obituaries. Even weather and sports news often have a class bias. An all news radio station in New York City, for example, provides regular national ski reports. International news, trade agreements, and domestic policies issues are also reported in terms of their impact on business climate and the business community. Besides being of practical value to the wealthy, such coverage has considerable ideological value. Its message: the concerns of the wealthy are the concerns of us all.

The Wealthy (as a Class) Do Not Exist

While preoccupied with the concerns of the wealthy, the media fails to notice the way in which the rich as a class of people create and shape domestic and foreign policy. Presented as an aggregate of individuals, the wealthy appear without special interests, interconnections, or unity in purpose. Out of public view are the class interests of the wealthy, the interlocking business links, the concerted actions to preserve their class privileges and business interests (by running for public office, supporting political candidates, lobbying, etc.). Corporate lobbying is ignored, taken for granted, or assumed to be in the public interest. (Compare this with the media's portrayal of the "strong arm of labor" in attempting to defeat trade legislation that is harmful to the interests of working people.) It is estimated that two-thirds of the U.S. Senate is composed of millionaires.[5] Having such a preponderance of millionaires in the Senate, however, is perceived to be neither unusual nor anti-democratic; these millionaire senators are assumed to be serving "our" collective interests in governing.

The Wealthy Are Fascinating and Benevolent

The broadcast and print media regularly provide hype for individuals who have achieved "super" success. These stories are usually about celebrities and superstars from the sports and entertainment world. Society pages and gossip columns serve to keep the social elite informed of each others' doings, allow the rest of us to gawk at their excesses, and help to keep the American dream alive. The print media is also fond of feature stories on corporate empire builders. These stories provide an occasional "insider's" view of the private and corporate life of industrialists by suggesting a rags to riches account of corporate success. These stories tell us that corporate success is a series of smart moves, shrewd acquisitions, timely mergers, and well thought out executive suite shuffles. By painting the upper class in a positive light, innocent of any wrongdoing (labor leaders and union organizations usually get the opposite treatment), the media assures us that wealth and power are benevolent. One person's capital accumulation is presumed to be good for all. The elite, then, are portrayed as investment wizards, people of special talent and skill, whom even their victims (workers and consumers) can admire.

The Wealthy Include a Few Bad Apples

On rare occasions, the media will mock selected individuals for their personality flaws. Real estate investor Donald Trump and New York Yankees owner George Steinbrenner, for example, are admonished by the media for deliberately seeking publicity (a very un–upper class thing to do); hotel owner Leona Helmsley was caricatured for her personal cruelties; and junk bond broker Michael Milkin was condemned because he had the audacity to rob the rich. Michael Parenti points out that by treating business wrongdoings as isolated deviations from the socially beneficial system of "responsible capitalism," the media overlooks the features of the system that produce such abuses and the regularity with which they occur. Rather than portraying them as predictable and frequent outcomes of corporate power and the business system, the media treats abuses as if they were isolated and atypical. Presented as an occasional aberration, these incidents serve not to challenge, but to legitimate, the system.[6]

The Middle Class Is Us

By ignoring the poor and blurring the lines between the working people and the upper class, the news media creates a universal middle class. From this perspective, the size of one's income becomes largely irrelevant: what matters is that most of "us" share an intellectual and moral superiority over the disadvantaged. As *Time* magazine once concluded, "Middle America is a state of mind."[7] "We are all middle class," we are told, "and we all share the same concerns": job security, inflation, tax burdens, world peace, the cost of food and housing, health care, clean air and water, and the safety of our streets. While the concerns of the wealthy are quite distinct from those of the middle class (e.g., the wealthy worry about investments, not jobs), the media convinces us that "we [the affluent] are all in this together."

The Middle Class Is a Victim

For the media, "we" the affluent not only stand apart from the "other"—the poor, the working class, the minorities, and their problems—"we" are also victimized by the poor (who drive up the costs of maintaining the welfare rolls), minorities (who commit crimes against us), and by workers (who are greedy and drive companies out and prices up). Ignored are the subsidies to the rich, the crimes of corporate America, and the policies that wreak havoc on the economic well-being of middle America. Media magic convinces us to fear, more than anything else, being victimized by those less affluent than ourselves.

The Middle Class Is Not a Working Class

The news media clearly distinguishes the middle class (employees) from the working class (i.e., blue collar workers) who are portrayed, at best, as irrelevant, outmoded, and a dying breed. Furthermore, the media will tell us that the hardships faced by blue-collar workers are inevitable (due to progress), a result of bad luck (chance circumstances in a particular industry), or a product of their own doing (they priced themselves out of a job). Given the media's presentation of reality, it is hard to believe that manual, supervised, unskilled, and semiskilled workers actually represent more than 50 percent of the adult working population.[8] The working class, instead, is relegated by the media to "the other."

In short, the news media either lionizes the wealthy or treats their interests and those of the middle class as one in the same. But the upper class and the middle class do not share the same interests or worries. Members of the upper class worry about stock dividends (not employment), they profit from inflation and global militarism, their children attend exclusive private schools, they eat and live in a royal fashion, they call on (or are called upon by) personal physicians, they have few consumer problems, they can escape whenever they want from environmental pollution, and they live on streets and travel to other areas under the protection of private police forces.*[9]

The wealthy are not only a class with distinct life-styles and interests, they are a ruling class. They receive a disproportionate share of the country's yearly income, own a disproportionate amount of the country's wealth, and contribute a disproportionate number of their members to governmental bodies and decision-making groups—all traits that William Domhoff, in his classic work *Who Rules America*, defined as characteristic of a governing class.[10]

This governing class maintains and manages our political and economic structures in such a way that these structures continue to yield an amazing proportion of our wealth to a minuscule upper class. While the media is not above referring to ruling classes in other countries (we hear, for example, references to Japan's ruling elite),[11] its treatment of the news proceeds as though there were no such ruling class in the United States.

---

*The number of private security guards in the United States now exceeds the number of public police officers. (Robert Reich, "Secession of the Successful," *New York Times Magazine*, February 17, 1991, p. 42.)

Furthermore, the news media inverts reality so that those who are working class and middle class learn to fear, resent, and blame those below, rather than those above them in the class structure. We learn to resent welfare, which accounts for only two cents out of every dollar in the federal budget (approximately $10 billion) and provides financial relief for the needy,* but learn little about the $11 billion the federal government spends on individuals with incomes in excess of $1,000,000 (not needy),[12] or the $17 billion in farm subsidies, or the $214 billion (twenty times the cost of welfare) in interest payments to financial institutions.

Middle-class whites learn to fear African Americans and Latinos, but most violent crime occurs within poor and minority communities and is neither interracial† nor interclass. As horrid as such crime is, it should not mask the destruction and violence perpetrated by corporate America. In spite of the fact that 14,000 innocent people are killed on the job each year, 100,000 die prematurely, 400,000 become seriously ill, and 6 million are injured from work-related accidents and diseases, most Americans fear government regulation more than they do unsafe working conditions.

Through the media, middle-class—and even working class—Americans learn to blame blue-collar workers and their unions for declining purchasing power and economic security. But while workers who managed to keep their jobs and their unions struggled to keep up with inflation, the top 1 percent of American families saw their average incomes soar 80 percent in the last decade.[13] Much of the wealth at the top was accumulated as stockholders and corporate executives moved their companies abroad to employ cheaper labor (56 cents per hour in El Salvador) and avoid paying taxes in the United States. Corporate America is a world made up of ruthless bosses, massive layoffs, favoritism and nepotism, health and safety violations, pension plan losses, union busting, tax evasions, unfair competition, and price gouging, as well as fast buck deals, financial speculation, and corporate wheeling and dealing that serve the interests of the corporate elite, but are generally wasteful and destructive to workers and the economy in general.

It is no wonder Americans cannot think straight about class. The mass media is neither objective, balanced, independent, nor neutral. Those who own and direct the mass media are themselves part of the upper class, and neither they nor the ruling class in general have to conspire to manipulate public opinion. Their interest is in preserving the status quo, and their view

---

*A total of $20 billion is spent on welfare when you include all state funding. But the average state funding also comes to only two cents per state dollar.

†In 92 percent of the murders nationwide the assailant and the victim are of the same race (46 percent are white/white, 46 percent are black/black), 5.6 percent are black on white, and 2.4 percent are white on black. (FBI and Bureau of Justice Statistics, 1985–1986, quoted in Raymond S. Franklin, *Shadows of Race and Class,* University of Minnesota Press, Minneapolis, 1991, p. 108.)

of society as fair and equitable comes naturally to them. But their ideology dominates our society and justifies what is in reality a perverse social order—one that perpetuates unprecedented elite privilege and power on the one hand and widespread deprivation on the other. A mass media that did not have its own class interests in preserving the status quo would acknowledge that inordinate wealth and power undermines democracy and that a "free market" economy can ravage a people and their communities.

NOTES

1. Martin Lee and Norman Solomon, *Unreliable Sources,* Lyle Stuart (New York, 1990), p. 71. See also Ben Bagdikian, *The Media Monopoly,* Beacon Press (Boston, 1990).
2. Department of Commerce, Bureau of the Census, "Poverty in the United States: 1992," *Current Population Reports, Consumer Income,* Series P60–185, pp. xi, xv, 1.
3. William Ryan, *Blaming the Victim,* Vintage (New York, 1971).
4. Benjamin Demott, *The Imperial Middle,* William Morrow (New York, 1990), p. 123.
5. Fred Barnes, "The Zillionaires Club," *The New Republic,* January 29, 1990, p. 24.
6. Michael Parenti, *Inventing Reality,* St. Martin's Press (New York, 1986), p. 109.
7. *Time,* January 5, 1979, p. 10.
8. Vincent Navarro, "The Middle Class—A Useful Myth," *The Nation,* March 23, 1992, p. 1.
9. Charles Anderson, *The Political Economy of Social Class,* Prentice Hall (Englewood Cliffs, N.J., 1974), p. 137.
10. William Domhoff, *Who Rules America?,* Prentice Hall (Englewood Cliffs, N.J., 1967), p. 5.
11. Lee and Solomon, *Unreliable Sources,* p. 179.
12. *Newsweek,* August 10, 1992, p. 57.
13. *Business Week,* June 8, 1992, p. 86.

 QUESTIONS FOR CRITICAL THINKING

Reading 6

1. What assumptions do you have about members of different socioeconomic classes? Does Mantsios's discussion help you to understand the sources of these assumptions?

2. How do media representations influence our understandings of the sources of economic inequality? According to these representations, who is to blame for such inequality?

3. How do media representations of class influence policies that are created to respond to economic inequality? In your opinion, do these policies effectively address the source of the problem? Why, or why not?

Reading 7

DOUBLY DIVIDED
The Racial Wealth Gap

MEIZHU LUI

Race—constructed from a European vantage point—has always been a basis on which U.S. society metes out access to wealth and power. Both in times when the overall wealth gap has grown and in times when a rising tide has managed to lift both rich and poor boats, a pernicious wealth gap between whites and nonwhite minorities has persisted.

Let's cut the cake by race. If you lined up all African-American families by the amount of assets they owned minus their debts and then looked at the family in the middle, that median family in 2001 had a net worth of $10,700 (excluding the value of automobiles). Line up all whites, and *that* median family had a net worth of $106,400, almost 10 times more. Less than half of African-American families own their own homes, while three out of four white families do. Latinos are even less wealthy: the median Latino family in 2001 had only $3,000 in assets, and less than half own their own homes.

We do not know how much Native Americans have in assets because so little data has been collected, but their poverty rate is 26% compared to 8% for whites, even though more than half own their own homes. Nor is much information collected about Asian Americans. What we do know is that their poverty rate is 13%, and that 60% of Asian Americans own their own homes, compared to 77% of whites.

Almost 40 years after the passage of the 20th century's major civil rights legislation, huge wealth disparities persist. However, the myth that the playing field was leveled by those laws is widespread. For anyone who accepts the myth, it follows that if families of color are not on an economic par with whites today, the problem must lie with *them*.

But the racial wealth gap has nothing to do with individual behaviors or cultural deficits. Throughout U.S. history, deliberate government policies transferred wealth from nonwhites to whites—essentially, affirmative action for whites. The specific mechanisms of the transfer have varied, as have the processes by which people have been put into racial categories in the first

Meizhu Lui, "Doubly Divided: The Racial Wealth Gap" from *The Wealth Inequality Reader*, edited by Chuck Collins, Amy Gluckman, Betsy Leondar-Wright, Meizhu Lui, Amy Offner, and Adria Scharf. Copyright © 2004 by Meizhu Lui. Reprinted with the permission of The Economic Affairs Bureau, Inc.

place. But a brief review of American history, viewed through the lens of wealth, reveals a consistent pattern of race-based obstacles that have prevented Native Americans, African Americans, Latinos, and Asians from building wealth at all comparable to whites.

 ## NATIVE AMERICANS: IN THE U.S. GOVERNMENT WE "TRUST"?

When European settlers came to what would become the United States, Indian tribes in general did not consider land to be a source of individual wealth. It was a resource to be worshipped, treasured, and used to preserve all forms of life. Unfortunately for them, that concept of common ownership and the way of life they had built around it would clash mightily with the idea that parcels of land should be owned by individuals and used to generate private profit.

After the American Revolution, the official position of the new U.S. government was that Indian tribes had the same status as foreign nations and that good relations with them should be maintained. However, as European immigration increased and westward expansion continued, the settlers increasingly coveted Indian land. The federal government pressured Native Americans to sign one treaty after another giving over land: In the United States' first century, over 400 Indian treaties were signed. Indians were forcibly removed, first from the south and then from the west, sometimes into reservations.

Eventually, the Indians' last large territory, the Great Plains, was essentially handed over to whites. In one of the clearest instances of land expropriation, the 1862 Homestead Act transferred a vast amount of land from Indian tribes to white homesteaders by giving any white family 160 acres of land for free if they would farm it for five years. Of course, this massive land transfer was not accomplished without violence. General William Tecumseh Sherman, of Civil War fame, wrote: "The more [Indians] we can kill this year, the less will have to be killed the next year, for the more I see of these Indians, the more convinced I am that they all have to be killed or be maintained as a species of paupers." (Ironically, the Homestead Act is often cited as a model government program that supported asset-building.)

Out of the many treaties came the legal concept of the U.S. government's "trust responsibility" for the Native nations, similar to the relationship of a legal guardian to a child. In exchange for land, the government was to provide for the needs of the Native peoples. Money from the sale of land or natural resources was to be placed in a trust fund and managed in the best interests of the Indian tribes. The government's mismanagement of Indian assets was pervasive; yet, by law, Indian tribes could not fire the designated manager and hire a better or more honest one.

The Dawes Act of 1887 was designed to pressure Indians to assimilate into white culture: to adopt a sedentary life style and end their tradition of collective land ownership. The law broke up reservation land into individual plots and forced Indians to attempt to farm "western" style; "surplus" land was sold to whites. Under this scheme, millions more acres were transferred from Native Americans to whites.

After 1953, the U.S. government terminated the trust status of the tribes. While the stated purpose was to free Indians from government control, the new policy exacted a price: the loss of tribally held land that was still the basis of some tribes' existence. This blow reduced the remaining self-sufficient tribes to poverty and broke up tribal governments.

Thus, over a 200-year period, U.S. government policies transferred Native Americans' wealth—primarily land and natural resources—into the pockets of white individuals. This expropriation of vast tracts played a foundational role in the creation of the U.S. economy. Only in recent years, through the effective use of lawsuits to resurrect tribal rights assigned under the old treaties, have some tribes succeeded in building substantial pools of wealth, primarily from gaming businesses. This newfound casino wealth, though, cannot make up for the decimation of Native peoples or the destruction of traditional Native economies. Native Americans on average continue to suffer disproportionate poverty.

AFRICAN AMERICANS: SLAVES DON'T OWN, THEY ARE OWNED

From the earliest years of European settlement until the 1860s, African Americans were assets to be tallied in the financial records of their owners. They could be bought and sold, they created more wealth for their owners in the form of children, they had no rights even over their own bodies, and they worked without receiving any wages. Slaves and their labor became the basis of wealth creation for plantation owners, people who owned and operated slave ships, and companies that insured them. This was the most fundamental of wealth divides in American history.

At the end of the Civil War, there was an opportunity to create a new starting line. In the first few years, the Freedmen's Bureau and the occupying Union army actually began to distribute land to newly freed slaves: Freedmen's Bureau was disbanded after only seven years, and the over-whelming majority of land that freed slaves had been allotted was returned to its former white owners. Unable to get a foothold as self-employed farmers, African Americans were forced to accept sharecropping arrangements. While share-croppers kept some part of the fruits of their labor as in-kind income, the system kept them perpetually in debt and unable to accumulate any assets.

In 1883, the Supreme Court overturned the Civil Rights Act of 1875, which had given blacks the right to protect themselves and their property. By 1900, the Southern states had passed laws that kept African Americans separate and unequal, at the bottom of the economy. They began migrating to the North and West in search of opportunity.

Amazingly, some African-American families did prosper as farmers and businesspeople in the early 20th century. Some African-American communities thrived, even establishing their own banks to build savings and investment within the community. However, there was particular resentment against successful African Americans, and they were often targets of the vigilante violence common in this period. State and local governments helped vigilantes destroy their homes, run them out of town, and lynch those "uppity" enough to resist, and the federal government turned a blind eye. Sometimes entire black communities were targeted. For example, the African-American business district in north Tulsa, known as the "Black Wall Street" for its size and success, was torched on the night of June 21, 1921 by white rioters, who destroyed as many as 600 black-owned businesses.

The Depression wiped out black progress, which did not resume at all until the New Deal period. Even then, African Americans were often barred from the new asset-building programs that benefited whites. Under Social Security, workers paid into the system and were guaranteed money in retirement. However, domestic and agricultural work—two of the most significant black occupations—were excluded from the program. Unemployment insurance and the minimum wage didn't apply to domestic workers or farm workers either. Other programs were also tilted toward white people. The Home Owners' Loan Corporation was created in 1933 to help homeowners avoid foreclosure, but not a single loan went to a black homeowner.

Following World War II, a number of new programs provided a ladder into the middle class—for whites. The GI Bill of Rights and low-interest home mortgages provided tax-funded support for higher education and for homeownership, two keys to family wealth building. The GI Bill provided little benefit to black veterans, however, because a recipient had to be accepted into a college—and many colleges did not accept African-American students. Likewise, housing discrimination meant that homeownership opportunities were greater for white families; subsidized mortgages were often simply denied for home purchases in black neighborhoods.

In *The Cost of Being African American,* sociologist Thomas Shapiro shows how, because of this history, even black families whose incomes are equal to whites' generally have unequal economic standing. Whites are more likely to have parents who benefited from the land grants of the Homestead Act, who have Social Security or retirement benefits, or who own their own homes. With their far greater average assets, whites can transfer advantage from parents to children in the form of college tuition payments, down payments on homes, or simply self-sufficient parents who do not need their children to support them in old age.

These are the invisible underpinnings of the black-white wealth gap: wealth legally but inhumanely created from the unpaid labor of blacks, the use of violence—often backed up by government power—to stop black wealth-creating activities, tax-funded asset building programs closed to blacks even as they, too, paid taxes. The playing field is not level today.

For example, recent studies demonstrate that blatant race discrimination in hiring persists. But even if the playing field were level, the black/white wealth gap would still be with us.

LATINOS: IN THE UNITED STATES' BACK YARD

At the time of the American Revolution, Spain, not England, was the largest colonial landowner on the American continents. Unlike the English, the Spanish intermarried widely with the indigenous populations. In the 20th century, their descendents came to be identified as a distinct, nonwhite group. (In the 1800's Mexicans were generally considered white.) Today, Latinos come from many countries with varied histories, but the relationship of Mexicans to the United States is the longest, and people of Mexican descent are still the largest Latino group in the United States (67% in 2002).

Mexico won its independence from Spain in 1821. Three years later, the Monroe Doctrine promised the newly independent nations of Latin America "protection" from interference by European powers. However, this doctrine allowed the United States itself to intervene in the affairs of the entire hemisphere. Ever since, this paternalistic relationship (reminiscent of the "trust" relationship with Native tribes) has meant U.S. political and economic dominance in Mexico and Central and South America, causing the "push and pull" of the people of those countries into and out of the United States.

Mexicans and Anglos fought together to free Texas from Mexican rule, creating the Lone Star Republic of Texas, which was then annexed to the United States in 1845. Three years later, the United States went to war against Mexico to gain more territory and continue fulfilling its "manifest destiny"—its God-given right—to expand "from sea to shining sea." Mexico lost the war and was forced to accept the 1848 Treaty of Guadalupe Hidalgo, which gave the United States half of Mexico's land. While individual Mexican landowners were at first assured that they would maintain ownership, the United States did not keep that promise, and the treaty ushered in a huge transfer of land from Mexicans to Anglos. For the first time in these areas, racial categories were used to determine who could obtain land. The English language was also used to establish Anglo dominance; legal papers in English proving land ownership were required, and many Spanish speakers suffered as a result.

In the twentieth century, government policy continued to reinforce a wealth gap between Mexicans and whites. The first U.S.-Mexico border patrol was set up in 1924, and deportations of Mexicans became commonplace. Like African Americans, Latino workers were disproportionately represented in the occupations not covered by the Social Security Act. During World War II, when U.S. farms needed more agricultural workers, the federal government established the Bracero program, under which Mexican workers were brought into the United States to work for subminimum wages and few benefits, then kicked out when their labor was no longer needed. Even today, Mexicans continue to be used as "guest"—or really, reserve—workers to create profits for U.S. agribusiness.

The North American Free Trade Agreement, along with the proposed Central American Free Trade Agreement and Free Trade Agreement of the Americas, is the newest incarnation of the Monroe Doctrine. Trade and immigration policies are still being used to maintain U.S. control over the resources in its "back yard," and at the same time to deny those it is "protecting" the enjoyment of the benefits to be found in papa's "front yard."

 ## ASIAN AMERICANS: PERPETUAL FOREIGNERS

The first Asian immigrants, the Chinese, came to the United States at the same time and for the same reason as the Irish: to escape economic distress at home and take advantage of economic opportunity in America. Like European immigrants, the Chinese came voluntarily, paying their own passage, ready and willing to seize the opportunity to build economic success in a new land. Chinese and Irish immigrants arrived in large numbers in the same decade, but their economic trajectories later diverged.

The major reason is race. While the Irish, caricatured as apes in early cartoons, were soon able to become citizens, the Naturalization Act of 1790 limited eligibility for citizenship to "whites." Asians did not know if they were white or not—but they wanted to be! The rights and benefits of "whiteness" were obvious. Other Americans didn't know whether or not they were white, either. Lawsuits filed first by Chinese, then by Japanese, Indian (South Asian), and Filipino immigrants all claimed that they should be granted "white" status. The outcomes were confusing; for example, South Asians, classified as Caucasian, were at first deemed white. Then, in later cases, courts decided that while they were Caucasian, they were not white.

A series of laws limited the right of Asians to create wealth. Chinese immigrants were drawn into the Gold Rush; the Foreign Miners Tax, however, was designed to push them out of the mining industry. The tax provided 25% of California's annual state budget in the 1860s, but the government jobs and services the tax underwrote went exclusively to whites—one of the first tax-based racial transfers of wealth. And with the passage of the Chinese Exclusion Acts in 1882, the Chinese became the first nationality to be denied the right to join this immigrant nation; the numbers of Chinese-American citizens thus remained small until the 1960s.

The next wave of Asians came from Japan. Excellent farmers, the Japanese bought land and created successful businesses. Resentment led to the passage of the 1924 Alien Land Act, which prohibited noncitizens from owning land. Japanese Americans then found other ways to create wealth, including nurseries and the cut flower business. In 1941, they had $140 million of business wealth.

World War II would change all that. In 1942, the Roosevelt administration forced Japanese Americans, foreign-born and citizen alike, to relocate to internment camps in the inland Western states. They had a week to dispose of their assets. Most had to sell their homes and businesses to whites at fire sale prices—an enormous transfer of wealth. In 1988, a successful suit for reparations gave the survivors of the camps $20,000 each, a mere fraction of the wealth that was lost.

Today, Asians are the group that as a whole has moved closest to economic parity with whites. (There are major variations in status between different Asian nationalities, however, and grouping them masks serious problems facing some groups.) While Asian immigrants have high poverty rates, American-born Asians have moved into professional positions, and the median income of Asians is now higher than that of whites. However, glass ceilings still persist, and as Wen Ho Lee, the Chinese-American nuclear scientist who was falsely accused of espionage in 2002, found out, Asians are still defined by race and branded as perpetual foreigners.

The divergent histories of the Irish and the Chinese in the United States illustrate the powerful role of race in the long-term accumulation of wealth. Irish-Americans faced plenty of discrimination in the labor market: consider the "No Irish Need Apply" signs that were once common in Boston storefronts. But they never faced legal prohibitions on asset ownership and citizenship as Chinese immigrants did, or the expropriation of property as the Japanese did. Today, people of Irish ancestry have attained widespread material prosperity and access to political power, and some of the wealthiest and most powerful men in business and politics are of Irish descent. Meantime, the wealth and power of the Chinese are still marginal.

•   •   •

Throughout history, federal policies—from constructing racial categories, to erecting barriers to asset building by nonwhites, to overseeing transfers of wealth from nonwhites to whites—have created the basis for the current racial wealth divide. If the gap is to be closed, government policies will have to play an important role.

It's long past time to close the gap.

 QUESTIONS FOR CRITICAL THINKING

Reading 7

1. According to the author, the current racial wealth gap is the result of specific laws, policies, and court decisions that made it more difficult for people of color to build wealth. How does this argument fit with popular representations of economic differences in the United States?

2. According to the author, historical discrimination resulted in present-day inequality. How does the information presented challenge notions that economic "success" is the result of individual efforts?

3. Considering the current economic situation, do you think that there will be a shift in public policies in an effort to reduce economic inequality? Why, or why not?

Reading 8

CAPITALISM HITS THE FAN

RICK WOLFF

Let me begin by saying what I think this crisis is not. It is not a *financial* crisis. It is a systemic crisis whose first serious symptom happened to be finance. But this crisis has its economic roots and its effects in manufacturing, services, and, to be sure, finance. It grows out of the relation of wages to profits across the economy. It has profound social roots in America's households and families and political roots in government policies. The current crisis did not start with finance, and it won't end with finance.

From 1820 to around 1970, 150 years, the average productivity of American workers went up each year. Average workers produced more stuff every year than they had the year before. They were trained better, they had more machines, and they had better machines. So productivity went up every year.

And, over this period of time, the wages of American workers rose every decade. Every decade, real wages—the amount of money you get in relation to the prices you pay for the things you use your money for—were higher than the decade before. Profits also went up.

The American working class enjoyed 150 years of rising consumption, so it's not surprising that it would choose to define its own self-worth, measure its own success in life, according to the standard of consumption. Americans began to think of themselves as successful if they lived in the right neighborhood, drove the right car, wore the right outfit, went on the right vacation.

But in the 1970s, the world changed for the American working class in ways that it hasn't come to terms with—at all. Real wages stopped going up. As U.S. corporations moved operations abroad to take advantage of lower wages and higher profits and as they replaced workers with machines (and especially computers), those who lost their jobs were soon willing to work even if their wages stopped rising. So real wages trended down a little bit. The real hourly wage of a worker in the 1970s was higher than what it is today. What you get for an hour of work, in goods and services, is less now that what your parents got.

Meanwhile, productivity kept going up. If what the employer gets from each worker keeps going up, but what you give to each worker does not,

Rick Wolff, "Capitalism Hits the Fan" from *Dollars & Sense* (November/December 2008): 15–17. Reprinted with the permission of *Dollars & Sense,* the progressive economics magazine www.dollarsandsense.org.

then the difference becomes bigger, and bigger, and bigger. Employers' profits have gone wild, and all the people who get their fingers on employers' profits—the professionals who sing the songs they like to hear, the shareholders who get a piece of the action on each company's profits—have enjoyed a bonanza over the last thirty years.

The only thing more profitable than simply making the money off the worker is handling this exploding bundle of profits—packaging and repackaging it, lending it and borrowing it, and inventing new mechanisms for doing all that. That's called the finance industry, and they have stumbled all over themselves to get a hold of a piece of this immense pot of profit.

· · ·

What did the working class do? What happens to a population committed to measuring people's success by the amount of consumption they could afford when the means they had always had to achieve it, rising wages, stop? They can go through a trauma right then and there: "We can't anymore—it's over." Most people didn't do that. They found other ways.

Americans undertook more work. People took a second or third job. The number of hours per year worked by the average American worker has risen by about 20 percent since the 1970s. By comparison, in Germany, France, and Italy, the number of hours worked per year per worker has dropped 20 percent. American workers began to work to a level of exhaustion. They sent more family members—and especially women—out to work. This enlarged supply of workers meant that employers could find plenty of employees without having to offer higher pay. Yet, with more family members out working, new kinds of costs and problems hit American families. The woman who goes out to work needs new outfits. In our society, she probably needs another car. With women exhausted from jobs outside and continued work demands inside households, with families stressed by exhaustion and mounting bills, interpersonal tensions mounted and brought new costs: child care, psychotherapy, drugs. Such extra costs neutralized the extra income, so it did not solve the problem.

The American working class had to do a second thing to keep its consumption levels rising. It went on the greatest binge of borrowing in the history of any working class in any country at any time. Members of the business community began to realize that they had a fantastic double opportunity. They could get the profits from flat wages and rising productivity, and then they could turn to the working class traumatized by the inability to have rising consumption, and give them the means to consume more. So instead of paying your workers a wage, you're going to lend them the money—so they have to pay it back to you! With interest!

That solved the problem. For a while, employers could pay the workers the same or less, and instead of creating the usual problems for capitalism—workers without enough income to buy all the output their increased productivity yields—rising worker debt seemed magical. Workers could consume ever more; profits exploding in every category. Underneath the magic, however, there were workers who were completely exhausted, whose families were falling apart, and who were now ridden with anxiety because their rising debts were unsustainable. This was a system built to fail, to reach its end when the combination of physical exhaustion and emotional anxiety from the debt made people unable to continue. Those people are, by the millions, walking away from those obligations, and the house of cards comes down.

If you put together (a) the desperation of the American working class and (b) the efforts of the finance industry to scrounge out every conceivable borrower, the idea that the banks would end up lending money to people who couldn't pay it back is not a tough call. The system, however, was premised on the idea that that would not happen, and when it happened nobody was prepared.

• • •

The conservatives these days are in a tough spot. The story about how markets and private enterprise interact to produce wonderful outcomes is, even for them these days, a cause for gagging. Of course, ever resourceful, there are conservatives who will rise to the occasion, sort of like dead fish. They rattle off twenty things the government did over the last twenty years, which indeed it did, and draw a line from those things the government did to this disaster now, to reach the conclusion that the reason we have this problem now is too much government intervention. These days they get nowhere. Even the mainstream press has a hard time with this stuff.

What about the liberals and many leftists too? They seem to favor regulation. They think the problem was that the banks weren't regulated, that credit-rating companies weren't regulated, that the Federal Reserve didn't regulate better, or differently, or more, or something. Salaries should be regulated to not be so high. Greed should be regulated. I find this astonishing and depressing.

In the 1930s, the last time we had capitalism hitting the fan in this way, we produced a lot of regulation. Social Security didn't exist before then. Unemployment insurance didn't exist before then. Banks were told: you can do this, but you can't do that. Insurance companies were told: you can do that, but you can't do this. They limited what the board of directors of a corporation could do ten ways to Sunday. They taxed them. They did all sorts of things that annoyed, bothered, and troubled boards of directors because the regulations impeded the boards' efforts to grow their companies and make money for the shareholders who elected them.

You don't need to be a great genius to understand that the boards of directors encumbered by all these regulations would have a very strong incentive to evade them, to undermine them, and, if possible, to get rid of them. Indeed, the boards went to work on that project as soon as the regulations were passed. The crucial fact about the regulations imposed on business in the 1930s is that they did not take away from the boards of directors the freedom or the incentives or the opportunities to undo all the regulations and reforms. The regulations left in place an institution devoted to their undoing. But that wasn't the worst of it. They also left in place boards of directors who, as the first appropriators of all the profits, had the *resources* to undo the regulations. This peculiar system of regulation had a built-in self-destruct button.

Over the last thirty years, the boards of directors of the United States' larger corporations have used their profits to buy the president and the Congress, to buy the public media, and to wage a systematic campaign, from 1945 to 1975, to evade the regulations, and, after 1975, to get rid of them. And it worked. That's why we're here now. And if you impose another set of regulations along the lines liberals propose, not only are you going to have the same history, but you're going to have the same history faster. The right wing in America, the business community, has spent the last fifty years perfecting every technique that is known to turn the population against regulation. And they're going to go right to work to do it again, and they'll do it better, and they'll do it faster.

. . .

So what do we do? Let's regulate, by all means. Let's try to make a reasonable economic system that doesn't allow the grotesque abuses we've seen in recent decades. But let's not reproduce the self-destruct button. This time the change has to include the following: The people in every enterprise who do the work of that enterprise, will become collectively their own board of directors. For the first time in American history, the people who depend on the survival of those regulations will be in the position of receiving the profits of their own work and using them to make the regulations succeed rather than sabotaging them.

This proposal for workers to collectively become their own board of directors also democratizes the enterprise. The people who work in an enterprise, the front line of those who have to live with what it does, where it goes, how it uses its wealth, they should be the people who have influence over the decisions it makes. That's democracy.

Maybe we could even extend this argument to democracy in our political life, which leaves a little to be desired—some people call it a "formal" democracy, that isn't real. Maybe the problem all along has been that you can't have a real democracy politically if you don't have a real democracy underpinning it economically. If the workers are not in charge of their work situations, five days a week, 9 to 5, the major time of their adult lives, then how much aptitude and how much appetite are they going to have to control their political life? Maybe we need the democracy of economics, not just to prevent the regulations from being undone, but also to realize the political objectives of democracy.

⬡ QUESTIONS FOR CRITICAL THINKING

Reading 8

1. How does Wolff's discussion of the current economic crisis help you to better understand its systemic causes?

2. Wolff explains that, even though many in the United States work more hours today than they did 40 years ago, they have not experienced an improvement in their economic situation. How does this knowledge challenge the common assumption that the "American dream" is achievable by everyone?

3. The author proposes establishing more democratic business practices in order to alleviate current and future economic inequalities. Do you see his proposal as feasible? What would be the implications of adopting such practices?

SEX AND GENDER

Reading 9

THE SOCIAL CONSTRUCTION OF GENDER

JUDITH LORBER

Talking about gender for most people is the equivalent of fish talking about water. Gender is so much the routine ground of everyday activities that questioning its taken-for-granted assumptions and presuppositions is like thinking about whether the sun will come up.[1] Gender is so pervasive that in our society we assume it is bred into our genes. Most people find it hard to believe that gender is constantly created and re-created out of human interaction, out of social life, and is the texture and order of that social life. Yet gender, like culture, is a human production

Judith Lorber, "The Social Construction of Gender," and "Dismantling Noah's Ark" from *Paradoxes of Gender*. Copyright © 1994 by Judith Lorber. Reprinted with the permission of Yale University Press.

that depends on everyone constantly "doing gender" (West and Zimmerman 1987).

And everyone "does gender" without thinking about it. Today, on the subway, I saw a well-dressed man with a year-old child in a stroller. Yesterday, on a bus, I saw a man with a tiny baby in a carrier on his chest. Seeing men taking care of small children in public is increasingly common—at least in New York City. But both men were quite obviously stared at—and smiled at, approvingly. Everyone was doing gender—the men who were changing the role of fathers and the other passengers, who were applauding them silently. But there was more gendering going on that probably fewer people noticed. The baby was wearing a white crocheted cap and white clothes. You couldn't tell if it was a boy or a girl. The child in the stroller was wearing a dark blue T-shirt and dark print pants. As they started to leave the train, the father put a Yankee baseball cap on the child's head. Ah, a boy, I thought. Then I noticed the gleam of tiny earrings in the child's ears, and as they got off, I saw the little flowered sneakers and lace-trimmed socks. Not a boy after all. Gender done.

Gender is such a familiar part of daily life that it usually takes a deliberate disruption of our expectations of how women and men are supposed to act to pay attention to how it is produced. Gender signs and signals are so ubiquitous that we usually fail to note them—unless they are missing or ambiguous. Then we are uncomfortable until we have successfully placed the other person in a gender status; otherwise, we feel socially dislocated. In our society, in addition to man and woman, the status can be *transvestite* (a person who dresses in opposite-gender clothes) and *transsexual* (a person who has had sex-change surgery). Transvestites and transsexuals construct their gender status by dressing, speaking, walking, gesturing in the ways prescribed for women or men—whichever they want to be taken for—and so does any "normal" person.

For the individual, gender construction starts with assignment to a sex category on the basis of what the genitalia look like at birth.[2] Then babies are dressed or adorned in a way that displays the category because parents don't want to be constantly asked whether their baby is a girl or a boy. A sex category becomes a gender status through naming, dress, and the use of other gender markers. Once a child's gender is evident, others treat those in one gender differently from those in the other, and the children respond to the different treatment by feeling different and behaving differently. As soon as they can talk, they start to refer to themselves as members of their gender. Sex doesn't come into play again until puberty, but by that time, sexual feelings and desires and practices have been shaped by gendered norms and expectations. Adolescent boys and girls approach and avoid each other in an elaborately scripted and gendered mating dance. Parenting is gendered, with different expectations for mothers and for fathers, and people of different genders work at different kinds of jobs. The work adults do as mothers and fathers and as low-level workers and high-level bosses, shapes women's and men's life experiences, and these experiences produce different feelings, consciousness, relationships, skills—ways of being that we call feminine or masculine.[3] All of these processes constitute the social construction of gender.

Gendered roles change—today fathers are taking care of little children, girls and boys are wearing unisex clothing and getting the same education, women and men are working at the same jobs. Although many traditional social groups are quite strict about maintaining gender differences, in other social groups they seem to be blurring. Then why the one-year-old's earrings? Why is it still so important to mark a child as a girl or a boy, to make sure she is not taken for a boy or he for a girl? What would happen if they were? They would, quite literally, have changed places in their social world.

To explain why gendering is done from birth, constantly and by everyone, we have to look not only at the way individuals experience gender but at gender as a social institution. As a social institution, gender is one of the major ways that human beings organize their lives. Human society depends on a predictable division of labor, a designated allocation of scarce goods, assigned responsibility for children and others who cannot care for themselves, common values and their systematic transmission to new members, legitimate leadership, music, art, stories, games, and other symbolic productions. One way of choosing people for the different tasks of society is on the basis of their talents, motivations, and competence—their demonstrated achievements. The other way is on the basis of gender, race, ethnicity—ascribed membership in a category of people. Although societies vary in the extent to which they use one or the other of these ways of allocating people to work and to carry out other responsibilities, every society uses gender and age grades. Every society classifies people as "girl and boy children," "girls and boys ready to be married," and "fully adult women and men," constructs similarities among them and differences between them, and assigns them to different roles and responsibilities. Personality characteristics, feelings, motivations, and ambitions flow from these different life experiences so that the members of these different groups become different kinds of people. The process of gendering and its outcome are legitimated by religion, law, science, and the society's entire set of values.

GENDER AS PROCESS, STRATIFICATION, AND STRUCTURE

As a social institution, gender is a process of creating distinguishable social statuses for the assignment of rights and responsibilities. As part of a stratification system that ranks these statuses unequally, gender is a major building block in the social structures built on these unequal statuses.

As a *process,* gender creates the social differences that define "woman" and "man." In social interaction throughout their lives, individuals learn what is expected, see what is expected, act and react in expected ways, and thus simultaneously construct and maintain the gender order: "The very injunction to be given gender takes place through discursive routes: to be a good mother, to be a heterosexually desirable object, to be a fit worker, in sum, to signify a multiplicity of guarantees in response to a variety of different demands all at once" (J. Butler 1990, 145). Members of a social group neither make up gender as they go along nor exactly replicate in rote fashion what was done before. In almost every encounter, human beings produce gender, behaving in the ways they learned were appropriate for their gender status, or resisting or rebelling against these norms. Resistance and rebellion have altered gender norms, but so far they have rarely eroded the statuses.

Gendered patterns of interaction acquire additional layers of gendered sexuality, parenting, and work behaviors in childhood, adolescence, and adulthood. Gendered norms and expectations are enforced through informal sanctions of gender-inappropriate behavior by peers and by formal punishment or threat of punishment by those in authority should behavior deviate too far from socially imposed standards for women and men.

Everyday gendered interactions build gender into the family, the work process, and other organizations and institutions, which in turn reinforce gender expectations for individuals.[4] Because gender is a process, there is room not only for modification and variation by individuals and small groups but also for institutionalized change (J. W. Scott 1988, 7).

As part of a *stratification* system, gender ranks men above women of the same race and class. Women and men could be different but equal. In practice, the process of creating difference depends to a great extent on differential evaluation. As Nancy Jay (1981) says: "That which is defined, separated out, isolated from all else is A and pure. Not-A is necessarily impure, a random catchall, to which nothing is external except A and the principle of order that separates it from Not-A" (45). From the individual's point of view, whichever gender is A, the other is Not-A; gender boundaries tell the individual who is like him or her, and all the rest are unlike. From society's point of view, however, one gender is usually the touchstone, the normal, the dominant, and the other is different, deviant, and subordinate. In Western society, "man" is A, "wo-man" is Not-A. (Consider what a society would be like where woman was A and man Not-A.)

The further dichotomization by race and class constructs the gradations of a heterogeneous society's stratification scheme. Thus, in the United States, white is A, African American is Not-A; middle class is A, working class is Not-A, and "African-American women occupy a position whereby the inferior half of a series of these dichotomies converge" (P. H. Collins 1990). The dominant categories are the hegemonic ideals, taken so for granted as the way things should be that white is not ordinarily thought of as a race, middle class as a class, or men as a gender. The characteristics of these categories define the Other as that which lacks the valuable qualities the dominants exhibit.

In a gender-stratified society, what men do is usually valued more highly than what women do because men do it, even when their activities are very similar or the same. In different regions of southern India, for example, harvesting rice is men's work, shared work, or women's work: "Wherever a task is done by women it is considered easy, and where it is done by [men] it is considered difficult" (Mencher 1988, 104). A gathering and hunting society's survival usually depends on the nuts, grubs, and small animals brought in by the women's foraging trips, but when the men's hunt is successful, it is the occasion for a celebration. Conversely, because they are the superior group, white men do not have to do the "dirty work," such as housework; the most inferior group does it, usually poor women of color (Palmer 1989).

Freudian psychoanalytic theory claims that boys must reject their mothers and deny the feminine in themselves in order to become men: "For boys the major goal is the achievement of personal masculine identification with their father and sense of secure masculine self, achieved through superego formation and disparagement of women" (Chodorow 1978, 165). Masculinity may be the outcome of boys' intrapsychic struggles to separate their identity from that of their mothers, but the proofs of masculinity are culturally shaped and usually ritualistic and symbolic (Gilmore 1990).

The Marxist feminist explanation for gender inequality is that by demeaning women's abilities and keeping them from learning valuable technological skills, bosses preserve them as a cheap and exploitable reserve army of labor. Unionized men who could easily be replaced by women collude in this process because it allows them to monopolize the better-paid, more interesting, and more autonomous jobs: "Two factors emerge as helping men maintain their separation from women and their control of technological occupations. One is the active gendering of jobs and people. The second is the continual creation of sub-divisions in the work processes, and levels in work hierarchies, into which men can move in order to keep their distance from women" (Cockburn 1985, 13).

Societies vary in the extent of the inequality in social status of their women and men members, but where there is inequality, the status "woman" (and its attendant behavior and role allocations) is usually held in lesser esteem than the status "man." Since gender is also intertwined with a society's other constructed statuses of differential evaluation—race, religion, occupation, class, country of origin, and so on—men and women members of the favored groups command more power, more prestige, and more property than the members of the disfavored groups. Within many social groups, however, men are advantaged over women. The more economic resources, such as education and job opportunities, are available to a group, the more they tend to be monopolized by men. In poorer groups that have few resources (such as working-class African Americans in the United States), women and men are more nearly equal, and the women may even outstrip the men in education and occupational status (Almquist 1987).

As a *structure,* gender divides work in the home and in economic production, legitimates those in authority, and organizes sexuality and emotional life (Connell 1987, 91–142). As primary parents, women significantly influence children's psychological development and emotional attachments, in the process reproducing gender. Emergent sexuality is shaped by heterosexual, homosexual, bisexual, and sadomasochistic patterns that are gendered—different for girls and boys, and for women and men—so that sexual statuses reflect gender statuses.

When gender is a major component of structured inequality, the devalued genders have less power, prestige, and economic rewards than the valued genders. In countries that discourage gender discrimination, many major roles are still gendered; women still do most of the domestic labor and child rearing, even while doing full-time paid work; women and men are segregated on the job and each does work considered "appropriate"; women's work is usually paid less than men's work. Men dominate the positions of authority and leadership in government, the military, and the law; cultural productions, religions, and sports reflect men's interests.

In societies that create the greatest gender difference, such as Saudi Arabia, women are kept out of sight behind walls or veils, have no civil rights, and often create a cultural and emotional world of their own (Bernard 1981). But even in societies with less rigid gender boundaries, women and men spend much of their time with people of their own gender because of the way work and family are organized. This spatial separation of women and men reinforces gendered differences, identity, and ways of thinking and behaving (Coser 1986).

Gender inequality—the devaluation of "women" and the social domination of "men"—has social functions and social history. It is not the result of sex, procreation, physiology, anatomy, hormones, or genetic predispositions. It is produced and maintained by identifiable social processes and built into the general social structure and individual identities deliberately and purposefully. The social order as we know it in Western societies is organized around racial, ethnic, class, and gender inequality. I contend, therefore, that the continuing purpose of gender as a modern social institution is to construct women as a group to be the subordinates of men as a group.

THE PARADOX OF HUMAN NATURE

To say that sex, sexuality, and gender are all socially constructed is not to minimize their social power. These categorical imperatives govern our lives in the most profound and pervasive ways, through the social experiences and social practices of what Dorothy Smith calls the "everday/evernight world" (1990). The paradox of human nature is that it is *always* a manifestation of cultural meanings, social relationships, and power politics; "not biology, but culture, becomes destiny" (J. Butler 1990, 8). Gendered people emerge not from physiology or sexual orientations but from the exigencies of the social order, mostly from the need for a reliable division of the work of food production and the social (not physical) reproduction of new members. The moral imperatives of religion and cultural representations guard the boundary lines among genders and ensure that what is demanded, what is permitted, and what is tabooed for the people in each gender is well known and followed by most (C. Davies 1982). Political power, control of scarce resources, and, if necessary, violence uphold the gendered social order in the face of resistance and rebellion. Most people, however, voluntarily go along with their society's prescriptions for those of their gender status, because the norms and expectations get built into their sense of worth and identity as [the way we] think, the way we see and hear and speak, the way we fantasy, and the way we feel.

There is no core or bedrock in human nature below these endlessly looping processes of the social production of sex and gender, self and other, identity and psyche, each of which is a "complex cultural construction" (J. Butler 1990, 36). *For humans, the social is the natural.* Therefore, "in its feminist senses, gender cannot mean simply the cultural appropriation of biological sexual difference. Sexual difference is itself a fundamental—and scientifically contested—construction. Both 'sex' and 'gender' are woven of multiple, asymmetrical strands of difference, charged with multifaceted dramatic narratives of domination and struggle" (Haraway 1990, 140).

NOTES

1. Gender is, in Erving Goffman's words, an aspect of *Felicity's Condition:* "any arrangement which leads us to judge an individual's . . . acts not to be a manifestation of strangeness. Behind Felicity's Condition is our sense of what it is to be sane" (1983:27). Also see Bem 1993; Frye 1983, 17–40; Goffman 1977.
2. In cases of ambiguity in countries with modern medicine, surgery is usually performed to make the genitalia more clearly male or female.
3. See J. Butler 1990 for an analysis of how doing gender is gender identity.
4. On the "logic of practice," or how the experience of gender is embedded in the norms of everyday interaction and the structure of formal organizations, see Acker 1990; Bourdieu [1980] 1990; Connell 1987; Smith 1987.

REFERENCES

Acker, Joan. 1990. "Hierarchies, jobs, and bodies: A theory of gendered organizations," *Gender & Society* 4: 139–58.

Almquist, Elizabeth M. 1987. "Labor market gendered inequality in minority groups," *Gender & Society* 1: 400–14.

Bem, Sandara Lipsitz. 1993. *The Lenses of Gender: Transforming the Debate on Sexual Inequality.* New Haven: Yale University Press.

Bernard, Jessie. 1981. *The Female World*. New York: Free Press.

Bourdieu, Pierre. [1980] 1990. *The Logic of Practice*. Stanford, Calif.: Stanford University Press.

Butler, Judith. 1990. *Gender Trouble: Feminism and the Subversion of Identity*. New York and London: Routledge.

Chodorow, Nancy, 1978. *The Reproduction of Mothering*. Berkeley: University of California Press.

Cockburn, Cynthia. 1985. *Machinery of Dominance: Women, Men and Technical Know-how*. London: Pluto Press.

Collins, Patricia Hill. 1990. "The social construction of black feminist thought," *Signs* 14: 745–73.

Connell, R. [Robert] W. 1987. *Gender and Power: Society, the Person, and Sexual Politics*. Stanford, Calif.: Stanford University Press.

Coser, Rose Laub. 1986. "Cognitive structure and the use of social space," *Sociological Forum* 1: 1–26.

Davies, Christie. 1982. "Sexual taboos and social boundaries," *American Journal of Sociology* 87: 1032–63.

Dwyer, Daisy, and Judith Bruce (eds.). 1988. *A Home Divided: Women and Income in the Third World*. Palo Alto, Calif.: Stanford University Press.

Frye, Marilyn. 1983. *The Politics of Reality: Essays in Feminist Theory*. Trumansburg, N.Y.: Crossing Press.

Gilmore, David D. 1990. *Manhood in the Making: Cultural Concepts of Masculinity*. New Haven: Yale University Press.

Goffman, Erving. 1977. "The arrangement between the sexes," *Theory and Society* 4: 301–33.

Haraway, Donna. 1990. "Investment strategies for the evolving portfolio of primate females," in Jacobus, Keller, and Shuttleworth.

Jacobus, Mary, Evelyn Fox Keller, and Sally Shuttleworth (eds.). (1990). *Body/politics: Women and the Discourse of Science*. New York and London: Routledge.

Jay, Nancy. 1981. "Gender and dichotomy," *Feminist Studies* 7: 38–56.

Mencher, Joan. 1988. "Women's work and poverty: Women's contribution to household maintenance in South India," in Dwyer and Bruce.

Palmer, Phyllis. 1989. *Domesticity and Dirt: Housewives and Domestic Servants in the United States, 1920–1945*. Philadelphia: Temple University Press.

Scott, Joan Wallach. 1988. *Gender and the Politics of History*. New York: Columbia University Press.

Smith, Dorothy. 1987. *The Everyday World as Problematic: A Feminist Sociology*. Toronto: University of Toronto Press.

———. 1990. *The Conceptual Practices of Power: A Feminist Sociology of Knowledge*. Toronto: University of Toronto Press.

West, Candace, and Don Zimmerman. 1987. "Doing gender." *Gender & Society* 1: 125–51.

QUESTIONS FOR CRITICAL THINKING

Reading 9

1. In what ways do you see yourself "doing gender"?

2. Lorber argues that gender is a social rather than biological construct, yet the dominant notion in our society is that gender is linked to biological factors. What do you see as the reasoning behind assertions that gender is biological? What would be the implications of accepting the notion that gender is socially constructed and therefore mutable?

3. Lorber discusses many reasons why a culture maintains constructions of gender differences. What are your own ideas regarding why we maintain such constructs?

Reading **10**

THE FIVE SEXES, REVISITED

ANNE FAUSTO-STERLING

As Cheryl Chase stepped to the front of the packed meeting room in the Sheraton Boston Hotel, nervous coughs made the tension audible. Chase, an activist for intersexual rights, had been invited to address the May 2000 meeting of the Lawson Wilkins Pediatric Endocrine Society (LWPES), the largest organization in the United States for specialists in children's hormones. Her talk would be the grand finale to a four-hour symposium on the treatment of genital ambiguity in newborns, infants born with a mixture of both male and female anatomy, or genitals that appear to differ from their chromosomal sex. The topic was hardly a novel one to the assembled physicians.

Yet Chase's appearance before the group was remarkable. Three and a half years earlier, the American Academy of Pediatrics had refused her request for a chance to present the patients' viewpoint on the treatment of genital ambiguity, dismissing Chase and her supporters as "zealots." About two dozen intersex people had responded by throwing up a picket line.

Anne Fausto-Sterling, "The Five Sexes, Revisited" from *The Sciences* (July/August 2000): 19–23. Copyright © 2000 by The New York Academy of Sciences. Reprinted with the permission of *The Sciences*.

The Intersex Society of North America (ISNA) even issued a press release: "Hermaphrodites Target Kiddie Docs."

It had done my 1960s street-activist heart good. In the short run, I said to Chase at the time, the picketing would make people angry. But eventually, I assured her, the doors then closed would open. Now, as Chase began to address the physicians at their own convention, that prediction was coming true. Her talk, titled "Sexual Ambiguity: The Patient-Centered Approach," was a measured critique of the near-universal practice of performing immediate, "corrective" surgery on thousands of infants born each year with ambiguous genitalia. Chase herself lives with the consequences of such surgery. Yet her audience, the very endocrinologists and surgeons Chase was accusing of reacting with "surgery and shame," received her with respect. Even more remarkably, many of the speakers who preceded her at the session had already spoken of the need to scrap current practices in favor of treatments more centered on psychological counseling.

What led to such a dramatic reversal of fortune? Certainly, Chase's talk at the LWPES symposium was a vindication of her persistence in seeking attention for her cause. But her invitation to speak was also a watershed in the evolving discussion about how to treat children with ambiguous genitalia. And that discussion, in turn, is the tip of a biocultural iceberg—the gender iceberg—that continues to rock both medicine and our culture at large.

Chase made her first national appearance in 1993, in these very pages, announcing the formation of ISNA in a letter responding to an essay I had written for *The Sciences,* titled "The Five Sexes" [March/April 1993]. In that article I argued that the two-sex system embedded in our society is not adequate to encompass the full spectrum of human sexuality. In its place, I suggested a five-sex system. In addition to males and females, I included "herms" (named after true hermaphrodites, people born with both a testis and an ovary); "merms" (male pseudohermaphrodites, who are born with testes and some aspect of female genitalia); and "ferms" (female pseudohermaphrodites, who have ovaries combined with some aspect of male genitalia).

I had intended to be provocative, but I had also written with tongue firmly in cheek. So I was surprised by the extent of the controversy the article unleashed. Right-wing Christians were outraged, and connected my idea of five sexes with the United Nations-sponsored Fourth World Conference on Women, held in Beijing in September 1995. At the same time, the article delighted others who felt constrained by the current sex and gender system.

Clearly, I had struck a nerve. The fact that so many people could get riled up by my proposal to revamp our sex and gender system suggested that change—as well as resistance to it—might be in the offing. Indeed, a lot has changed since 1993, and I like to think that my article was an important stimulus. As if from nowhere, intersexuals are materializing before our very eyes. Like Chase, many have become political organizers, who lobby physicians and politicians to change current treatment practices. But more generally, though perhaps no less provocatively, the boundaries separating masculine and feminine seem harder than ever to define.

Some find the changes under way deeply disturbing. Others find them liberating.

Who is an intersexual—and how many intersexuals are there? The concept of intersexuality is rooted in the very ideas of male and female. In the idealized, Platonic, biological world, human beings are divided into two kinds: a perfectly dimorphic species. Males have an X and a Y chromosome, testes, a penis and all of the appropriate internal plumbing for delivering urine and semen to the outside world. They also have well-known secondary sexual characteristics, including a muscular build and facial hair. Women have two X chromosomes, ovaries, all of the internal plumbing to transport urine and ova to the outside world, a system to support pregnancy and fetal development, as well as a variety of recognizable secondary sexual characteristics.

That idealized story papers over many obvious caveats: some women have facial hair, some men have none; some women speak with deep voices, some men veritably squeak. Less well known is the fact that, on close inspection, absolute dimorphism disintegrates even at the level of basic biology. Chromosomes, hormones, the internal sex structures, the gonads and the external genitalia all vary more than most people realize. Those born outside of the Platonic dimorphic mold are called intersexuals.

In "The Five Sexes" I reported an estimate by a psychologist expert in the treatment of intersexuals, suggesting that some 4 percent of all live births are intersexual. Then, together with a group of Brown University undergraduates, I set out to conduct the first systematic assessment of the available data on intersexual birthrates. We scoured the medical literature for estimates of the frequency of various categories of intersexuality, from additional chromosomes to mixed gonads, hormones and genitalia. For some conditions we could find only anecdotal evidence; for most however, numbers exist. On the basis of that evidence, we calculated that for every 1,000 children born, seventeen are intersexual in some form. That number—1.7 percent—is a ballpark estimate, not a precise count, though we believe it is more accurate than the 4 percent I reported.

Our figure represents all chromosomal, anatomical and hormonal exceptions to the dimorphic ideal; the number of intersexuals who might, potentially, be subject to surgery as infants is smaller—probably between one in 1,000 and one in 2,000 live births. Furthermore, because some populations possess the relevant genes at high frequency, the intersexual birthrate is not uniform throughout the world.

Consider, for instance, the gene for congenital adrenal hyperplasia (CAH). When the CAH gene is inherited from both parents, it leads to a baby with masculinized external genitalia who possesses two X chromosomes and the internal reproductive organs of a potentially fertile woman. The frequency of the gene varies widely around the world: in New Zealand it occurs in only forty-three children per million; among the Yupik Eskimo of south-western Alaska, its frequency is 3,500 per million.

Intersexuality has always been to some extent a matter of definition. And in the past century physicians have been the ones who defined children as intersexual—and provided the remedies. When only the chromosomes are unusual, but the external genitalia and gonads clearly indicate either a male or a female, physicians do not advocate intervention. Indeed, it is not clear what kind of intervention could be advocated in such cases. But the story is quite different when infants are born with mixed genitalia, or with external genitals that seem at odds with the baby's gonads.

Most clinics now specializing in the treatment of intersex babies rely on case-management principles developed in the 1950s by the psychologist John Money and the psychiatrists Joan G. Hampson and John L. Hampson, all of Johns Hopkins University in Baltimore, Maryland. Money believed that gender identity is completely malleable for about eighteen months after birth. Thus, he argued, when a treatment team is presented with an infant who has ambiguous genitalia, the team could make a gender assignment solely on the basis of what made the best surgical sense. The physicians could then simply encourage the parents to raise the child according to the surgically assigned gender. Following that course, most physicians maintained, would eliminate psychological distress for both the patient and the parents. Indeed, treatment teams were never to use such words as "intersex" or "hermaphrodite"; instead, they were to tell parents that nature intended the baby to be the boy or the girl that the physicians had determined it was. Through surgery, the physicians were merely completing nature's intention.

Although Money and the Hampsons published detailed case studies of intersex children who they said had adjusted well to their gender assignments, Money thought one case in particular proved his theory. It was a dramatic example, inasmuch as it did not involve intersexuality at all: one of a pair of identical twin boys lost his penis as a result of a circumcision accident. Money recommended that "John" (as he came to be known in a later case study) be surgically turned into "Joan" and raised as a girl. In time, Joan grew to love wearing dresses and having her hair done. Money proudly proclaimed the sex reassignment a success.

But as recently chronicled by John Colapinto, in his book *As Nature Made Him,* Joan—now known to be an adult male named David Reimer—eventually rejected his female assignment. Even without a functioning penis and testes (which had been removed as part of the reassignment) John/Joan sought masculinizing medication, and married a woman with children (whom he adopted).

Since the full conclusion to the John/Joan story came to light, other individuals who were reassigned as males or females shortly after birth but who later rejected their early assignments have come forward. So, too, have cases in which the reassignment has worked—at least into the subject's midtwenties. But even then the aftermath of the surgery can be problematic. Genital surgery often leaves scars that reduce sexual sensitivity. Chase herself had a complete clitoridectomy, a procedure that is less frequently performed on intersexuals today. But the newer surgeries, which reduce the size of the clitoral shaft, still greatly reduce sensitivity.

The revelation of cases of failed reassignments and the emergence of intersex activism have led an increasing number of pediatric endocrinologists, urologists and psychologists to reexamine the wisdom of early genital surgery. For example, in a talk that preceded Chase's at the LWPES meeting, the medical ethicist Laurence B. McCullough of the Center for Medical Ethics and Health Policy at Baylor College of Medicine in Houston, Texas, introduced an ethical framework for the treatment of children with ambiguous genitalia. Because sex phenotype (the manifestation of genetically and embryologically determined sexual characteristics) and gender presentation (the sex role projected by the individual in society) are highly variable, McCullough argues, the various forms of intersexuality should be defined as normal. All of them fall within the statistically expected variability of sex and gender. Furthermore, though certain disease states may accompany some forms of intersexuality, and may require medical intervention, intersexual conditions are not themselves diseases.

McCullough also contends that in the process of assigning gender, physicians should minimize what he calls irreversible assignments: taking steps such as the surgical removal or modification of gonads or genitalia that the patient may one day want to have reversed. Finally, McCullough urges physicians to abandon their practice of treating the birth of a child with genital ambiguity as a medical or social emergency. Instead, they should take the time to perform a thorough medical workup and should disclose everything to the parents, including the uncertainties about the final outcome. The treatment mantra, in other words, should be therapy, not surgery.

I believe a new treatment protocol for intersex infants, similar to the one outlined by McCullough, is close at hand. Treatment should combine some basic medical and ethical principles with a practical but less drastic approach to the birth of a mixed-sex child. As a first step, surgery on infants should be performed only to save the child's life or to substantially improve the child's physical well-being. Physicians may assign a sex—male or female—to an intersex infant on the basis of the probability that the child's particular condition will lead to the formation of a particular gender identity. At the same time, though, practitioners ought to be humble enough to recognize that as the child grows, he or she may reject the assignment—and they should be wise enough to listen to what the child has to say. Most important, parents should have access to the full range of information and options available to them.

Sex assignments made shortly after birth are only the beginning of a long journey. Consider, for instance, the life of Max Beck: Born intersexual, Max was surgically assigned as a female and consistently raised as such. Had her medical team followed her into her early twenties, they would have deemed her assignment a success because she was married to a man. (It should be noted that success in gender assignment has traditionally been defined as living in that gender as a heterosexual.) Within a few years, however, Beck had come out as a butch lesbian; now in her mid-thirties, Beck has become a man and married his lesbian partner, who (through the miracles of modern reproductive technology) recently gave birth to a girl.

Transsexuals, people who have an emotional gender at odds with their physical sex, once described themselves in terms of dimorphic absolutes— males trapped in female bodies, or vice versa. As such, they sought psychological relief through surgery. Although many still do, some so-called transgendered people today are content to inhabit a more ambiguous zone. A male-to-female transsexual, for instance, may come out as a lesbian. Jane, born a physiological male, is now in her late thirties and living with her wife, whom she married when her name was still John. Jane takes hormones to feminize herself, but they have not yet interfered with her ability to engage in intercourse as a man. In her mind Jane has a lesbian relationship with her wife, though she views their intimate moments as a cross between lesbian and heterosexual sex.

It might seem natural to regard intersexuals and transgendered people as living midway between the poles of male and female. But male and female, masculine and feminine, cannot be parsed as some kind of continuum. Rather, sex and gender are best conceptualized as points in a multidimensional space. For some time, experts on gender development have distinguished between sex at the genetic level and at the cellular level (sex-specific gene expression, X and Y chromosomes); at the hormonal level (in the fetus, during childhood and after puberty); and at the anatomical level (genitals and secondary sexual characteristics). Gender identity presumably emerges from all of those corporeal aspects via some poorly understood interaction with environment and experience. What has become increasingly clear is that one can find levels of masculinity and femininity in almost every possible permutation. A chromosomal, hormonal and genital male (or female) may emerge with a female (or male) gender identity. Or a chromosomal female with male fetal hormones and masculinized genitalia—but with female pubertal hormones—may develop a female gender identity.

The medical and scientific communities have yet to adopt a language that is capable of describing such diversity. In her book *Hermaphrodites and the Medical Invention of Sex*, the historian and medical ethicist Alice Domurat Dreger of Michigan State University in East Lansing documents the emergence of current medical systems for classifying gender ambiguity. The current usage remains rooted in the Victorian approach to sex. The logical structure of the commonly used terms "true hermaphrodite," "male pseudo-hermaphrodite" and "female pseudohermaphrodite" indicates that only the so-called true hermaphrodite is a genuine mix of male and female. The others, no matter how confusing their body parts, are really hidden males or females. Because true hermaphrodites are rare—possibly only one in

100,000—such a classification system supports the idea that human beings are an absolutely dimorphic species.

At the dawn of the twenty-first century, when the variability of gender seems so visible, such a position is hard to maintain. And here, too, the old medical consensus has begun to crumble. Last fall the pediatric urologist Ian A. Aaronson of the Medical University of South Carolina in Charleston organized the North American Task Force on Intersexuality (NATFI) to review the clinical responses to genital ambiguity in infants. Key medical associations, such as the American Academy of Pediatrics, have endorsed NATFI. Specialists in surgery, endocrinology, psychology, ethics, psychiatry, genetics and public health, as well as intersex patient-advocate groups, have joined its ranks.

One of the goals of NATFI is to establish a new sex nomenclature. One proposal under consideration replaces the current system with emotionally neutral terminology that emphasizes developmental processes rather than preconceived gender categories. For example, Type I intersexes develop out of anomalous virilizing influences; Type II result from some interruption of virilization; and in Type III intersexes the gonads themselves may not have developed in the expected fashion.

What is clear is that since 1993, modern society has moved beyond five sexes to a recognition that gender variation is normal and, for some people, an arena for playful exploration. Discussing my "five sexes" proposal in her book *Lessons from the Intersexed,* the psychologist Suzanne J. Kessler of the State University of New York at Purchase drives this point home with great effect:

> The limitation with Fausto-Sterling's proposal is that . . . [it] still gives genitals . . . primary signifying status and ignores the fact that in the everyday world gender attributions are made without access to genital inspection. . . . What has primacy in everyday life is the gender that is performed, regardless of the flesh's configuration under the clothes.

I now agree with Kessler's assessment. It would be better for intersexuals and their supporters to turn everyone's focus away from genitals. Instead, as she suggests, one should acknowledge that people come in an even wider assortment of sexual identities and characteristics than mere genitals can distinguish. Some women may have "large clitorises or fused labia," whereas some men may have "small penises or misshapen scrota," as Kessler puts it, "phenotypes with no particular clinical or identity meaning."

As clearheaded as Kessler's program is—and despite the progress made in the 1990s—our society is still far from that ideal. The intersexual or transgendered person who projects a social gender—what Kessler calls "cultural genitals"—that conflicts with his or her physical genitals still may die for the transgression. Hence legal protection for people whose cultural and physical genitals do not match is needed during the current transition to a more gender-diverse world. One easy step would be to eliminate the category of "gender" from official documents, such as driver's licenses and passports. Surely attributes both more visible (such as height, build and eye color) and less visible (fingerprints and genetic profiles) would be more expedient.

A more far-ranging agenda is presented in the International Bill of Gender Rights, adopted in 1995 at the fourth annual International Conference on Transgender Law and Employment Policy in Houston, Texas. It lists ten "gender rights," including the right to define one's own gender, the right to change one's physical gender if one so chooses and the right to marry whomever one wishes. The legal bases for such rights are being hammered out in the courts as I write and, most recently, through the establishment, in the state of Vermont, of legal same-sex domestic partnerships.

No one could have foreseen such changes in 1993. And the idea that I played some role, however small, in reducing the pressure—from the medical community as well as from society at large—to flatten the diversity of human sexes into two diametrically opposed camps gives me pleasure.

Sometimes people suggest to me, with not a little horror, that I am arguing for a pastel world in which androgyny reigns and men and women are boringly the same. In my vision, however, strong colors coexist with pastels. There are and will continue to be highly masculine people out there; it's just that some of them are women. And some of the most feminine people I know happen to be men.

QUESTIONS FOR CRITICAL THINKING

Reading 10

1. How does viewing sex as a social construct, rather than a biological fact, impact how you view the differences you come to expect between females and males?

2. What are your theories of gender? Do you think gender is influenced more by biology, society, or interpersonal relationships?

3. How do your theories of gender affect your own actions and your interpretations of other people's attitudes and behaviors?

Reading 11

THE TRANSGENDER PARADIGM SHIFT TOWARD FREE EXPRESSION

HOLLY BOSWELL

What is transgender? What is it like to be transgendered? How many forms might this actually take? Is this paradigm shift new, and if so, how? What will it mean, not only for transgendered people, but for everyone?

Up until this decade, the emerging transgender community consisted of three recognizable components: transsexuals, cross-dressers (usually hetero-sexual), and our seldom-acknowledged cousins of gay drag. While the need to challenge culturally imposed stereotypes remains just as strong today, these three models have proven to be far too restrictive of the true range of transgender expression, ironically reinforcing the very myth that there are only two genders, as defined by most contemporary assimilationist cultures. This is changing (Boswell 1991).

In the primary cases of transsexualism and cross-dressing, notions of femininity and masculinity are thoroughly emulated—even to the point of undergoing radical surgery, or at least by challenging conformance to soci-etal expectations of gender expression. The transgenderist, as defined by Virginia Prince, is usually no different from the non-operative transsexual who expresses only one of two genders. Still, this is risky business, often involving the loss of marriages, children, parents, family, friends, and live-lihood. Such is the depth of the quest for selfhood, struggling to survive against social stigmatization and rejection.

What we are now beginning to experience is a new—yet anciently rooted—way of being that defies and transcends the absurd linkage between biological sex and gender expression. While biological sex manifests between our legs, the complexity of sexual and gender expression occurs between our ears. Even so, the concept of sex itself must be challenged as an artificial construct (Rothblatt 1995), especially in view of recurrent hermaphroditism and a host of other persistent psycho/social deviations from so-called male or female characteristics. Sex, in spite of how we have been conditioned to perceive it, is far from black or white, and is as much a state of mind—distinct from anatomy—as the outward expression we call gender. It is time to move beyond the bipolar masculine/feminine model of sex and gender based solely on anatomy. Manifesting our true humanity has much more to do with the rainbow of possibilities emanating from within our hearts, minds, and spirits.

It is important to recognize that this new paradigm of gender is coming from, and is finally being articulated by, the very people who are living it. For us, the experience comes first, then our conceptual explanation of it—unlike the academic approach of postulating a hypothesis that must then be proven. Many of us have become living proof of transgender reality. Some of us have been the willing subjects of research, but we are also recognizing the need to assert our own voices—some voices dialogue within our transgender community, and other voices remind us evermore of our rich diversity.

We are discovering how difficult it is to describe to others what it is like to be transgendered. I used to be amazed that, despite my elaborate explanations, no one could ever quite understand my experience of transgender, until I finally realized that neither have I ever understood what it is to be a man or a woman (Bornstein 1994). I seem to be neither, or maybe both, yet ultimately only myself. So, is transgender simply a result of being more honest with oneself and resistant to socialization, or is it chromosomally or hormonally induced, or better described as spirit taking precedence over form? All I know is that I could no longer live any other way, and have since found many others who share this experience.

So the word "transgender" describes much more than crossing between the poles of masculinity and femininity. It more aptly refers to the transgressing of gender norms, or being freely gendered, or transcending gender altogether in order to become more fully human. Transgender has to do with reinventing and realizing oneself more fully outside of the current systems of gender (Williams 1995). There are probably as many genders as there are people. Gender may be nothing more than a personal matrix of personality traits.

In fact, once the concept of gender is freed from various cultural and biological expectations of sex, the terms "masculine" and "feminine" become so relative that they are virtually meaningless. The Bem Sex Role Inventory lists two hundred personality characteristics such as analytical, gentle, independent, sympathetic, idealistic, and worldly. It is understood that each culture assigns different groupings of traits to each anatomical sex and leaves some in a neutral category. No trait is intrinsically masculine or feminine, though a few are more commonly attributable. As a culture evolves, it defines and re-defines which traits are appropriate for each sex through the contrived linkage of anatomy with gender. But imagine a non-polarized culture without this linkage, where each person would be free to explore and express his or her own unique set of traits. So much human potential could be unleashed that both the individual and the culture as a whole might self-actualize en masse.

Therapists today acknowledge that androgyny is a healthier gender model for self-actualization and fulfillment than either of the binary genders. This entails a process of transcending social conditioning in order to more fully become ourselves. Jung's process of individuation, with its reconciliation of animus and anima, leads to "wholeness"—a word that is related to health and holiness. If most people were more honest about it, they would probably find themselves somewhere in the middle of the bell-shaped curve of gender distribution rather than at the Rambo/bimbo extremes.

So while many people have androgynous potential, the traditions of alternative gender expression involve a minority within which these tendencies are much more pronounced. These are the profoundly transgendered, who have real difficulty conforming to the polarized codes of gender, and whose gender identities stray far beyond the normal expectations of their biological sex. This has always been so.

Despite all the new advances in hormonal and surgical procedures, many of us are choosing to customize the program to suit our individual self-definitions and expression (Mackenzie 1994). This hearkens back to the many "two-spirit" traditions throughout human history (though some of these did involve castration) and enlivens a growing awareness among transgendered people that passing is becoming passé. Only within the last few decades have transgendered people become so seduced by the ability to assimilate, made possible by recent hormonal and surgical advances (Feinberg 1992). This has relieved society of its responsibility to recognize more than two genders. All of us—transgendered and otherwise—continue to live under the constant "tyranny of passing" (Williams 1985), of questioning our sense of belonging against our self-worth. Are we living up to the societal roles and expectations that are imposed on us? Are we accepted and valued by others? How much should we care? How much societal rejection can we endure to achieve honest self-expression before we are undermined or destroyed in the process?

Diverse manifestations of transgender, however, are certainly not new. We have existed throughout history all over the planet (Williams 1986; Roscoe 1993). We are a normal, recurring expression of human nature. As a Lakota shaman explained, "To us a man is what nature, or his dreams, makes him. We accept him for what he wants to be. That's up to him." Various cultures in the past have honored our unique ability to make special contributions to society as shamans, spiritual leaders, visionaries, healers, mediators, counselors, teachers, and in other specific ways. Within these value systems, weeds don't exist. Every being has its sacred purpose, and none are to be wasted (Swifthawk 1992). Anthropologists are continually unearthing more evidence of such multifarious traditions as the *berdache* in native North America, shamans in Siberia and the Arctic, *hijiras* in India, *xanith* in the Middle East, *gallae* in the Roman Empire, certain Druid priestesses in Old Europe, the *mahu* of Polynesia, one-breasted Amazons, and many more. Ancient goddess religions, and other natural spiritual world-views, respected men and women as equals, regarded Nature as divine, revered diversity, and loved all manifestations of life. But since the replacement of Mother Nature with God the Father (about five thousand years ago), the constructs of gender have been defined more narrowly and rigidly to suit the purposes of those in control of each particular society.

So what impact does all this have on the transgender community and all of us as human beings? Because of Western civilization's emphasis on materialism and its inherently polarized value system, most transgendered people have been manifesting as their assumed opposite, either through cross-dressing or sex reassignment surgery. This is often motivated more by a need to assimilate than a quest toward truly becoming oneself, which would otherwise support the notion of gender as a many-splendored thing. Whereas cross-dressing may vicariously lead to gender insights, and trans-sexualism appropriately correct those who see their gender/anatomy variance as a problem, the newly emerging paradigm of gender will lead to a potent activation of healthy and renewable alternative gender expression.

Yes, this shift is new. Never before have we had so many options, yet chosen to manifest—despite our culture—our *true selves.* We are choosing to define ourselves outside of our cultures, and virtually outside of the very system of gender as we have known it. Transgendered people are redefining gender. This will no doubt be perceived as a radical course by the prevailing cultural consciousness for perhaps another generation or so, but it will be increasingly embraced on a personal level as the simple, honest human expression of Nature that it ultimately is. Gender liberation is a crucial key to human evolution, promoting the idea that we should strive to be *whole gendered,* cultivating all our gender traits to meet the critical challenges of our time.

Is this not a timely universal message, emanating deeply from within our collective consciousness? Are we not connected by our "continuous common humanity" (Bolin 1994), in exploring fully what it is to be ourselves—infinitely unique, yet united by the undeniable commonality of our human experience? This is the very bridge of transgender: connecting the myth of polarity into a whole, healing the illusions of our separateness, and celebrating the diversity of what it is to be fully human.

The mass media, especially cinema—after TV talk shows ad nauseam—seem to be acknowledging the revelatory human truth of transgender. This needs little documentation. Professional caregivers are gradually becoming more educated about the breadth and depth of transgender phenomena, and how they might more appropriately help their transgendered clients. This is happening at the pervasive grassroots level, and now even more extensively at this first International Congress on Gender, Cross-Dressing and Sex Issues, February 1995. There has also been an increasing influx of updated educational programming at certain annual transgender conferences, such as Southern Comfort, International Foundation for Gender Education (IFGE), and International Conference on Transgender Law and Employment Policy's (ICTLEP) law conference.

With all this newly emerging awareness comes new resolve among transgendered people to be honest, to be "out," to endeavor to educate, to be politically active, to support young people joining our ranks with new issues, to venture into the cyberspace of "virtual gender," and to gather into our own circles for the intimate, spiritual processing of who we are truly becoming (Boswell 1994).

All this is very exciting and ought to serve as a catalyst to inspire the rest of humanity. Becoming truly oneself, on any level, is a most beautiful and worthwhile process. Yet how few actually venture into this territory? Transgendered people can serve as a bridge to help others find their own way. As avid students make the best teachers, we are living advocates for the profound experience of exploring one's true humanity—nothing less. And as we are each in need of healing ourselves on this essential level, we may then be able to hope for a world that reflects the dazzling rainbow of our immense wholeness, along with our long sought harmony, and the true beauty of our natural grace.

REFERENCES

Bolin, A. 1994. Transcending and transgendering: Male-to-female transsexuals, dichotomy and diversity. In *Third sex, third gender: Beyond sexual dimorphism in culture and history,* edited by G. Herdt, 448–85. New York: Zone Books.

Bornstein, K. 1994. *Gender outlaw: On men, women and the rest of us.* New York and London: Routledge.

Boswell, H. 1991. The transgender alternative. *Chrysalis Quarterly,* 1, no. 2.

———. 1994. New berdache circling. *Tapestry,* 68.

Feinberg, L. 1992. *Transgender liberation.* New York: World View Forum.

Mackenzie, G. 1994. *Transgender nation.* Bowling Green: Bowling Green University Popular Press.

Roscoe, W. 1993. *Priests of the goddess: Gender transgression in the ancient world.* Palo Alto, Calif.: Stanford University Women's Studies.

Rothblatt, M. 1995. *The apartheid of sex.* New York: Crown.

Swifthawk, R. 1992. *We have a duty to the earth.* Houston: International Foundation for Gender Education.

Williams, C. 1985. TIGC newsletter: Albany, N.Y.

———. 1995. Why transgender? *Gender Quest* (March–April).

Williams, W. 1986. *The spirit and the flesh.* Boston: Beacon Press.

 QUESTIONS FOR CRITICAL THINKING

Reading 11

1. How does the notion of transgender challenge the ways that you view gender? Does it encourage you to see issues of gender in new and different ways? Why, or why not?

2. How does your gender identity influence your understanding of or level of agreement with the author's discussion?

3. Considering Boswell's discussion, do you think it is possible or desirable to expand or eliminate socially defined gender roles?

Reading 12

MASCULINITY AS HOMOPHOBIA
Fear, Shame, and Silence in the Construction of Gender Identity

MICHAEL S. KIMMEL

"Funny thing," [Curley's wife] said. "If I catch any one man, and he's alone, I get along fine with him. But just let two of the guys get together an' you won't talk. Jus' nothin' but mad." She dropped her fingers and put her hands on her hips. "You're all scared of each other, that's what. Ever' one of you's scared the rest is goin' to get something on you."

—JOHN STEINBECK *OF MICE AND MEN* (1937)

We think of manhood as eternal, a timeless essence that resides deep in the heart of every man. We think of manhood as a thing, a quality that one either has or doesn't have. We think of manhood as innate, residing in the particular biological composition of the human male, the result of androgens or the possession of a penis. We think of manhood as a transcendent tangible property that each man must manifest in the world, the reward presented with great ceremony to a young novice by his elders for having successfully completed an arduous initiation ritual. In the words of poet Robert Bly (1990), "the structure at the bottom of the male psyche is still as firm as it was twenty thousand years ago" (p. 230).

In this chapter, I view masculinity as a constantly changing collection of meanings that we construct through our relationships with ourselves, with each other, and with our world. Manhood is neither static nor timeless; it is historical. Manhood is not the manifestation of an inner essence; it is socially constructed. Manhood does not bubble up to consciousness from our biological makeup; it is created in culture. Manhood means different things at different times to different people. We come to know what it means to be a man in our culture by setting our definitions in opposition to a set of "others"—racial minorities, sexual minorities, and, above all, women.

Our definitions of manhood are constantly changing, being played out on the political and social terrain on which the relationships between women and men are played out. In fact, the search for the transcendent, timeless definition of manhood is itself a sociological phenomenon—we tend to search for the timeless and eternal during moments of crisis, those points of transition when old definitions no longer work and new definitions are yet to be firmly established.

This idea that manhood is socially constructed and historically shifting should not be understood as a loss, that something is being taken away from men. In fact, it gives us something extraordinarily valuable—agency, the capacity to act. It gives us a sense of historical possibilities to replace the despondent resignation that invariably attends timeless, ahistorical essentialisms. Our behaviors are not simply "just human nature," because "boys will be boys." From the materials we find around us in our culture—other people, ideas, objects—we actively create our worlds, our identities. Men, both individually and collectively, can change.

In this chapter, I explore this social and historical construction of both hegemonic masculinity and alternate masculinities, with an eye toward offering a new theoretical model of American manhood.[1] To accomplish this I first uncover some of the hidden gender meanings in classical statements of social and political philosophy, so that I can anchor the emergence of contemporary manhood in specific historical and social contexts. I then spell out the ways in which this version of masculinity emerged in the United States, by tracing both psychoanalytic developmental sequences and a historical trajectory in the development of marketplace relationships. . . .

 ## MASCULINITY AS HISTORY AND THE HISTORY OF MASCULINITY

The idea of masculinity . . . is the product of historical shifts in the grounds on which men rooted their sense of themselves as men. To argue that cultural definitions of gender identity are historically specific goes only so far; we have to specify exactly what those models were. In my historical inquiry into the development of these models for manhood.[2] I chart the fate of two models for manhood at the turn of the 19th century and the emergence of a third in the first few decades of that century.

In the late 18th and 19th centuries, two models of manhood prevailed. The *Genteel Patriarch* derived his identity from landownership. Supervising his estate, he was refined, elegant, and given to casual sensuousness. He was a doting and devoted father, who spent much of his time supervising the estate and with his family. Think of George Washington or Thomas Jefferson as examples. By contrast, the *Heroic Artisan* embodied the physical strength and republican virtue that Jefferson observed in the yeoman farmer, independent urban craftsman, or shopkeeper. Also a devoted father, the Heroic Artisan taught his son his craft, bringing him through ritual apprenticeship to status as master craftsman. Economically autonomous, the Heroic Artisan also cherished his democratic community, delighting in the participatory democracy of the town meeting. Think of Paul Revere at his pewter shop, shirtsleeves rolled up, a leather apron—a man who took pride in his work.

Heroic Artisans and Genteel Patriarchs lived in casual accord, in part because their gender ideals were complementary (both supported participatory democracy and individual autonomy, although patriarchs tended to support more powerful state machineries and also supported slavery) and because they rarely saw one another: Artisans were decidedly urban and the Genteel Patriarchs ruled their rural estates. By the 1830s, though, this casual symbiosis was shattered by the emergence of a new vision of masculinity, *Marketplace Manhood.*

Marketplace Man derived his identity entirely from his success in the capitalist marketplace, as he accumulated wealth, power, status. He was the urban entrepreneur, the businessman. Restless, agitated, and anxious, Marketplace Man was an absentee landlord at home and an absent father with his children, devoting himself to his work in an increasingly homosocial environment—a male-only world in which he pits himself against other men. His efforts at self-making transform the political and economic spheres, casting aside the Genteel Patriarch as an anachronistic feminized dandy—sweet, but ineffective and outmoded, and transforming the Heroic Artisan into a dispossessed proletarian, a wage slave.

As Tocqueville would have seen it, the coexistence of the Genteel Patriarch and the Heroic Artisan embodied the fusion of liberty and equality. Genteel Patriarchy was the manhood of the traditional aristocracy, the class that embodied the virtue of liberty. The Heroic Artisan embodied democratic community, the solidarity of the urban shopkeeper or craftsman. Liberty and democracy, the patriarch and the artisan, could, and did, coexist. But Marketplace Man is capitalist man, and he makes both freedom and equality problematic, eliminating the freedom of the artisocracy and proletarianizing the equality of the artisan. In one sense, American history has been an effort to restore, retrieve, or reconstitute the virtues of Genteel Patriarchy and Heroic Artisanate as they were being transformed in the capitalist marketplace.

Marketplace Manhood was a manhood that required proof, and that required the acquisition of tangible goods as evidence of success. It reconstituted itself by the exclusion of "others"—women, nonwhite men, nonnative-born men, homosexual men—and by terrified flight into a pristine mythic homosocial Eden where men could, at last, be real men among other men. The story of the ways in which Marketplace Man becomes American Everyman is a tragic tale, a tale of striving to live up to impossible ideals of success leading to chronic terrors of emasculation, emotional emptiness, and a gendered rage that leave a wide swath of destruction in [their] wake.

⦿ MASCULINITIES AS POWER RELATIONS

Marketplace Masculinity describes the normative definition of American masculinity. It describes his characteristics—aggression, competition, anxiety—and the arena in which those characteristics are deployed—the public sphere, the marketplace. If the marketplace is the arena in which manhood is tested and proved, it is a gendered arena, in which tensions between women and men and tensions among different groups of men are weighted with meaning. These tensions suggest that cultural definitions of gender are played out in a contested terrain and are themselves power relations.

All masculinities are not created equal; or rather, we are all *created* equal, but any hypothetical equality evaporates quickly because our definitions of masculinity are not equally valued in our society. One definition of manhood continues to remain the standard against which other forms of manhood are measured and evaluated. Within the dominant culture, the masculinity that defines white, middle class, early middle-aged, heterosexual men is the masculinity that sets the standards for other men, against which other men are measured and, more often than not, found wanting. Sociologist Erving Goffman (1963) wrote that in America, there is only "one complete, unblushing male":

> a young, married, white, urban, northern heterosexual, Protestant
> father of college education, fully employed, of good complexion,
> weight and height, and a recent record in sports. Every American
> male tends to look out upon the world from this perspective. . . .
> Any male who fails to qualify in any one of these ways is likely to
> view himself . . . as unworthy, incomplete, and inferior. (p. 128)

This is the definition that we will call "hegemonic" masculinity, the image of masculinity of those men who hold power, which has become the standard in psychological evaluations, sociological research, and self-help and advice literature for teaching young men to become "real men" (Connell, 1987). The hegemonic definition of manhood is a man *in* power, a man *with* power, and a man *of* power. We equate manhood with being strong, successful, capable, reliable, in control. The very definitions of manhood we have developed in our culture maintain the power that some men have over other men and that men have over women.

Our culture's definition of masculinity is thus several stories at once. It is about the individual man's quest to accumulate those cultural symbols that denote manhood, signs that he has in fact achieved it. It is about those standards being used against women to prevent their inclusion in public life and their consignment to a devalued private sphere. It is about the differential access that different types of men have to those cultural resources that confer manhood and about how each of these groups then develop their own modifications to preserve and claim their manhood. It is about the power of these definitions themselves to serve to maintain the real-life power that men have over women and that some men have over other men.

This definition of manhood has been summarized cleverly by psychologist Robert Brannon (1976) into four succinct phrases:

1. "No Sissy Stuff!" One may never do anything that even remotely suggests femininity. Masculinity is the relentless repudiation of the feminine.
2. "Be a Big Wheel." Masculinity is measured by power, success, wealth, and status. As the current saying goes, "He who has the most toys when he dies wins."
3. "Be a Sturdy Oak." Masculinity depends on remaining calm and reliable in a crisis, holding emotions in check. In fact, proving you're a man depends on never showing your emotions at all. Boys don't cry.
4. "Give 'em Hell." Exude an aura of manly daring and aggression. Go for it. Take risks.

These rules contain the elements of the definition against which virtually all American men are measured. Failure to embody these rules, to affirm the power of the rules and one's achievement of them is a source of men's confusion and pain. Such a model is, of course, unrealizable for any man. But we keep trying, valiantly and vainly, to measure up. American masculinity is a relentless test.[3] The chief test is contained in the first rule. Whatever the variations by race, class, age, ethnicity, or sexual orientation, being a man means "not being like women." This notion of anti-femininity lies at the heart of contemporary and historical conceptions of manhood, so that masculinity is defined more by what one is not rather than who one is.

 MASCULINITY AS THE FLIGHT FROM THE FEMININE

Historically and developmentally, masculinity has been defined as the flight from women, the repudiation of femininity. Since Freud, we have come to understand that developmentally the central task that every little boy must confront is to develop a secure identity for himself as a man. As Freud had it, the oedipal project is a process of the boy's renouncing his identification with and deep emotional attachment to his mother and then replacing her with the father as the object of identification. Notice that he reidentifies but never reattaches. This entire process, Freud argued, is set in motion by the boy's sexual desire for his mother. But the father stands in the son's path and will not yield his sexual property to his puny son. The boy's first emotional experience, then, the one that inevitably follows his experience of desire, is fear—fear of the bigger, stronger, more sexually powerful father. It is this fear, experienced symbolically as the fear of castration, Freud argues, that forces the young boy to renounce his identification with mother and seek to identify with the being who is the actual source of his fear, his father. In so doing, the boy is now symbolically capable of sexual union with a mother-like substitute, that is, a woman. The boy becomes gendered (masculine) and heterosexual at the same time.

Masculinity, in this model, is irrevocably tied to sexuality. The boy's sexuality will now come to resemble the sexuality of his father (or at least the way he imagines his father)—menacing, predatory, possessive, and possibly punitive. The boy has come to identify with his oppressor; now he can become the oppressor himself. But a terror remains, the terror that the young man will be unmasked as a fraud, as a man who has not completely and irrevocably separated from mother. It will be other men who will do the unmasking. Failure will de-sex the man, make him appear as not fully a man. He will be seen as a wimp, a Mama's boy, a sissy.

After pulling away from his mother, the boy comes to see her not as a source of nurturance and love, but as an insatiably infantilizing creature, capable of humiliating him in front of his peers. She makes him dress up in uncomfortable and itchy clothing, her kisses smear his cheeks with lipstick, staining his boyish innocence with the mark of feminine dependency. No wonder so many boys cringe from their mothers' embraces with groans of "Aw, Mom! Quit it!" Mothers represent the humiliation of infancy, helplessness, dependency. "Men act as though they were being guided by (or rebelling against) rules and prohibitions enunciated by a moral mother," writes psychohistorian Geoffrey Gorer (1964). As a result, "all the niceties of masculine behavior—modesty, politeness, neatness, cleanliness—come to be regarded as concessions to feminine demands, and not good in themselves as part of the behavior of a proper man" (pp. 56, 57).

The flight from femininity is angry and frightened, because mother can so easily emasculate the young boy by her power to render him dependent, or at least to remind him of dependency. It is relentless; manhood becomes a lifelong quest to demonstrate its achievement, as if to prove the unprovable to others, because we feel so unsure of it ourselves. Women don't often feel compelled to "prove their womanhood"—the phrase itself sounds ridiculous. Women have different kinds of gender identity crises; their anger and frustration, and their own symptoms of depression, come more from being excluded than from questioning whether they are feminine enough.[4]

The drive to repudiate the mother as the indication of the acquisition of masculine gender identity has three consequences for the young boy. First, he pushes away his real mother, and with her the traits of nurturance, compassion, and tenderness she may have embodied. Second, he suppresses those traits in himself, because they will reveal his incomplete separation from mother. His life becomes a lifelong project to demonstrate that he possesses none of his mother's traits. Masculine identity is born in the renunciation of the feminine, not in the direct affirmation of the masculine, which leaves masculine gender identity tenuous and fragile.

Third, as if to demonstrate the accomplishment of these first two tasks, the boy also learns to devalue all women in his society, as the living embodiments of those traits in himself he has learned to despise. Whether or not he was aware of it, Freud also described the origins of sexism—the systematic devaluation of women—in the desperate efforts of the boy to separate from mother. We may *want* "a girl just like the girl that married dear old Dad," as the popular song had it, but we certainly don't want to *be like* her.

This chronic uncertainty about gender identity helps us understand several obsessive behaviors. Take, for example, the continuing problem of the school-yard bully. Parents remind us that the bully is the *least* secure about his manhood, and so he is constantly trying to prove it. But he "proves" it by choosing opponents he is absolutely certain he can defeat; thus the standard taunt to a bully is to "pick on someone your own size." He can't, though, and after defeating a smaller and weaker opponent, which he was sure would prove his manhood, he is left with the empty gnawing feeling that he has not proved it after all, and he must find another opponent, again one smaller and weaker, that he can again defeat to prove it to himself.[5]

One of the more graphic illustrations of this lifelong quest to prove one's manhood occurred at the Academy Awards presentation in 1992. As aging, tough guy actor Jack Palance accepted the award for best supporting actor for his role in the cowboy comedy *City Slickers,* he commented that people, especially film producers, think that because he is 71 years old, he's all washed up, that he's no longer competent. "Can we take a risk on this guy?" he quoted them as saying, before he dropped to the floor to do a set of one-armed push-ups. It was pathetic to see such an accomplished actor still having to prove that he is virile enough to work and, as he also commented at the podium, to have sex.

When does it end? Never. To admit weakness, to admit frailty or fragility, is to be seen as a wimp, a sissy, not a real man. But seen by whom?

MASCULINITY AS A HOMOSOCIAL ENACTMENT

Other men: We are under the constant careful scrutiny of other men. Other men watch us, rank us, grant our acceptance into the realm of manhood. Manhood is demonstrated for other men's approval. It is other men who evaluate the performance. Literary critic David Leverenz (1991) argues that "ideologies of manhood have functioned primarily in relation to the gaze of male peers and male authority" (p. 769). Think of how men boast to one another of their accomplishments—from their latest sexual conquest to the size of the fish they caught—and how we constantly parade the markers of manhood—wealth, power, status, sexy women—in front of other men, desperate for their approval.

That men prove their manhood in the eyes of other men is both a consequence of sexism and one of its chief props. "Women have, in men's minds, such a low place on the social ladder of this country that it's useless to define yourself in terms of a woman," noted playwright David Mamet. "What men need is men's approval." Women become a kind of currency that men use to improve their ranking on the masculine social scale. (Even those moments of heroic conquest of women carry, I believe, a current of homosocial evaluation.) Masculinity is a *homosocial* enactment. We test ourselves, perform heroic feats, take enormous risks, all because we want other men to grant us our manhood.

Masculinity as a homosocial enactment is fraught with danger, with the risk of failure, and with intense relentless competition. "Every man you meet has a rating or an estimate of himself which he never loses or forgets," wrote Kenneth Wayne (1912) in his popular turn-of-the-century advice book. "A man has his own rating, and instantly he lays it alongside of the other man" (p. 18). Almost a century later, another man remarked to psychologist Sam Osherson (1992) that "[b]y the time you're an adult, it's easy to think you're always in competition with men, for the attention of women, in sports; at work" (p. 291).

MASCULINITY AS HOMOPHOBIA

If masculinity is a homosocial enactment, its overriding emotion is fear. In the Freudian model, the fear of the father's power terrifies the young boy to renounce his desire for his mother and identify with his father. This model links gender identity with sexual orientation: The little boy's identification with father (becoming masculine) allows him to now engage in sexual relations with women (he becomes heterosexual). This is the origin of how we can "read" one's sexual orientation through the successful performance of gender identity. Second, the fear that the little boy feels does not send him scurrying into the arms of his mother to protect him from his father. Rather, he believes he will overcome his fear by identifying with its source. We become masculine by identifying with our oppressor.

But there is a piece of the puzzle missing, a piece that Freud, himself, implied but did not follow up.[6] If the pre-oedipal boy identifies with mother, he *sees the world through mother's eyes.* Thus, when he confronts father during his great oedipal crisis, he experiences a split vision: He sees his father as his mother sees his father, with a combination of awe, wonder, terror, *and desire.* He simultaneously sees the father as he, the boy, would like to see him—as the object not of desire but of emulation. Repudiating mother and identifying with father only partially answer his dilemma. What is he to do with that homoerotic desire, the desire he felt because he saw father the way that his mother saw father?

He must suppress it. Homoerotic desire is cast as feminine desire, desire for other men. Homophobia is the effort to suppress that desire, to purify all relationships with other men, with women, with children of its taint, and to ensure that no one could possibly ever mistake one for a homosexual. Homophobic flight from intimacy with other men is the repudiation of the homosexual within—never completely successful and hence constantly reenacted in every homosocial relationship. "The lives of most American men are bounded, and their interests daily curtailed by the constant necessity to prove to their fellows, and to themselves, that they are not sissies, not homosexuals," writes psychoanalytic historian Geoffrey Gorer (1964). "An interest or pursuit which is identified as a feminine interest or pursuit becomes deeply suspect for men" (p. 129).

Even if we do not subscribe to Freudian psychoanalytic ideas, we can still observe how, in less sexualized terms, the father is the first man who evaluates the boy's masculine performance, the first pair of male eyes before whom he tries to prove himself. Those eyes will follow him for the rest of his life. Other men's eyes will join them—the eyes of role models such as teachers, coaches, bosses, or media heroes; the eyes of his peers, his friends, his workmates; and the eyes of millions of other men, living and dead, from whose constant scrutiny of his performance he will never be free. "The tradition of all the dead generations weighs like a nightmare on the brain of the living," was how Karl Marx put it over a century ago (1848/1964, p. 11). "The birthright of every American male is a chronic sense of personal inadequacy," is how two psychologists describe it today (Woolfolk & Richardson, 1978, p. 57).

That nightmare from which we never seem to awaken is that those other men will see that sense of inadequacy, they will see that in our own eyes we are not who we are pretending to be. What we call masculinity is often a hedge against being revealed as a fraud, an exaggerated set of activities that keep others from seeing through us, and a frenzied effort to keep at bay those fears within ourselves. Our real fear "is not fear of women but of being ashamed or humiliated in front of other men, or being dominated by stronger men" (Leverenz, 1986, p. 451).

This, then, is the great secret of American manhood: *We are afraid of other men.* Homophobia is a central organizing principle of our cultural definition of manhood. Homophobia is more than the irrational fear of gay men, more than the fear that we might be perceived as gay. "The word 'faggot' has nothing to do with homosexual experience or even with fears of homosexuals," writes David Leverenz (1986). "It comes out of the depths of manhood: a label of ultimate contempt for anyone who seems sissy, untough, uncool" (p. 455). Homophobia is the fear that other men will unmask us, emasculate us, reveal to us and the world that we do not measure up, that we are not real men. We are afraid to let other men see that fear. Fear makes us ashamed, because the recognition of fear in ourselves is proof to ourselves that we are not as manly as we pretend, that we are, like the young man in a poem by Yeats, "one that ruffles in a manly pose for all his timid heart." Our fear is the fear of humiliation. We are ashamed to be afraid.

Shame leads to silence—the silences that keep other people believing that we actually approve of the things that are done to women, to minorities, to gays and lesbians in our culture. The frightened silence as we scurry past a woman being hassled by men on the street. That furtive silence when men make sexist or racist jokes in a bar. That clammy-handed silence when guys in the office make gay-bashing jokes. Our fears are the sources of our silences, and men's silence is what keeps the system running. This might help to explain why women often complain that their male friends or partners are often so understanding when they are alone and yet laugh at sexist jokes or even make those jokes themselves when they are out with a group.

The fear of being seen as a sissy dominates the cultural definitions of manhood. It starts so early. "Boys among boys are ashamed to be unmanly," wrote one educator in 1871 (cited in Rotundo, 1993, p. 264). I have a standing bet with a friend that I can walk onto any playground in America where 6-year-old boys are happily playing and by asking one question, I can provoke a fight. That question is simple: "Who's a sissy around here?" Once posed, the challenge is made. One of two things is likely to happen. One boy will accuse another of being a sissy, to which that boy will respond that he is not a sissy, that the first boy is. They may have to fight it out to see who's lying. Or a whole group of boys will surround one boy and all shout "He is! He is!" That boy will either burst into tears and run home crying, disgraced, or he will have to take on several boys at once, to prove that he's not a sissy. (And what will his father or older brothers tell him if he chooses to run home crying?) It will be some time before he regains any sense of self-respect.

Violence is often the single most evident marker of manhood. Rather it is the willingness to fight, the desire to fight. The origin of our expression that one has a chip on one's shoulder lies in the practice of an adolescent boy in the country or small town at the turn of the century, who would literally walk around with a chip of wood balanced on his shoulder—a signal of his readiness to fight with anyone who would take the initiative of knocking the chip off (see Gorer, 1964, p. 38; Mead, 1965).

As adolescents, we learn that our peers are a kind of gender police, constantly threatening to unmask us as feminine, as sissies. One of the favorite tricks when I was an adolescent was to ask a boy to look at his fingernails. If he held his palm toward his face and curled his fingers back to see them, he passed the test. He'd looked at his nails "like a man." But if he held the back of his hand away from his face, and looked at his fingernails with arm outstretched, he was immediately ridiculed as a sissy.

As young men we are constantly riding those gender boundaries, checking the fences we have constructed on the perimeter, making sure that nothing even remotely feminine might show through. The possibilities of being unmasked are everywhere. Even the most seemingly insignificant thing can pose a threat or activate that haunting terror. On the day the students in my course "Sociology of Men and Masculinities" were scheduled to discuss homophobia and male-male friendships, one student provided a touching illustration. Noting that it was a beautiful day, the first day of spring after a brutal northeast winter, he decided to wear shorts to class. "I had this really nice pair of new Madras shorts," he commented. "But then I thought to myself, these shorts have lavender and pink in them. Today's class topic is homophobia. Maybe today is not the best day to wear these shorts."

Our efforts to maintain a manly front cover everything we do. What we wear. How we talk. How we walk. What we eat. Every mannerism, every movement contains a coded gender language. Think, for example, of how you would answer the question: How do you "know" if a man is homosexual? When I ask this question in classes or workshops, respondents invariably provide a pretty standard list of stereotypically effeminate behaviors. He walks a certain way, talks a certain way, acts a certain way. He's very emotional; he shows his feelings. One woman commented that she "knows" a man is gay if he really cares about her; another said she knows he's gay if he shows no interest in her, if he leaves her alone.

Now alter the question and imagine what heterosexual men do to make sure no one could possibly get the "wrong idea" about them. Responses typically refer to the original stereotypes, this time as a set of negative rules about behavior. Never dress that way. Never talk or walk that way. Never show your feelings or get emotional. Always be prepared to demonstrate sexual interest in women that you meet, so it is impossible for any woman to get the wrong idea about you. In this sense, homophobia, the fear of being perceived as gay, as not a real man, keeps men exaggerating all the traditional rules of masculinity, including sexual predation with women. Homophobia and sexism go hand in hand.

The stakes of perceived sissydom are enormous—sometimes matters of life and death. We take enormous risks to prove our manhood, exposing ourselves disproportionately to health risks, workplace hazards, and stress-related illnesses. Men commit suicide three times as often as women. Psychiatrist Willard Gaylin (1992) explains that it is "invariably because of perceived social humiliation," most often tied to failure in business:

> Men become depressed because of loss of status and power in the world of men. It is not the loss of money, or the material advantages that money could buy, which produces the despair that leads to self-destruction. It is the "shame," the "humiliation," the sense of personal "failure." . . . A man despairs when he has ceased being a man among men. (p. 32)

In one survey, women and men were asked what they were most afraid of. Women responded that they were most afraid of being raped and murdered. Men responded that they were most afraid of being laughed at (Noble, 1992, pp. 105–106).

HOMOPHOBIA AS A CAUSE OF SEXISM,
HETEROSEXISM, AND RACISM

Homophobia is intimately interwoven with both sexism and racism. The fear—sometimes conscious, sometimes not—that others might perceive us as homosexual propels men to enact all manner of exaggerated masculine behaviors and attitudes to make sure that no one could possibly get the wrong idea about us. One of the centerpieces of that exaggerated masculinity is putting women down, both by excluding them from the public sphere and by the quotidian put-downs in speech and behaviors that organize the daily life of the American man. Women and gay men become the "other" against which heterosexual men project their identities, against whom they stack the decks so as to compete in a situation in which they will always win, so that by suppressing them, men can stake a claim for their own manhood. Women threaten emasculation by representing the home, workplace, and familial responsibility, the negation of fun. Gay men have historically played the role of the consummate sissy in the American popular mind because homosexuality is seen as an inversion of normal gender development. There have been other "others." Through American history, various groups have represented the sissy, the non-men against whom American men played out their definitions of manhood, often with vicious results. In fact, these changing groups provide an interesting lesson in American historical development.

At the turn of the 19th century, it was Europeans and children who provided the contrast for American men. The "true American was vigorous, manly, and direct, not effete and corrupt like the supposed Europeans," writes Rupert Wilkinson (1986). "He was plain rather than ornamented, rugged rather than luxury seeking, a liberty loving common man or natural gentleman rather than an aristocratic oppressor or servile minion" (p. 96). The "real man" of the early 19th century was neither noble nor serf. By the middle of the century, black slaves had replaced the effete nobleman. Slaves were seen as dependent, helpless men, incapable of defending their women and children, and therefore less than manly. Native Americans were cast as foolish and naive children, so they could be infantilized as the "Red Children of the Great White Father" and therefore excluded from full manhood.

By the end of the century, new European immigrants were also added to the list of the unreal men, especially the Irish and Italians, who were seen as too passionate and emotionally volatile to remain controlled sturdy oaks, and Jews, who were seen as too bookishly effete and too physically puny to truly measure up. In the mid-20th century, it was also Asians—first the Japanese during the Second World War, and more recently, the Vietnamese during the Vietnam War—who have served as unmanly templates against which American men have hurled their gendered rage. Asian men were seen as small, soft, and effeminate—hardly men at all.

Such a list of "hyphenated" Americans—Italian-, Jewish-, Irish-, African-, Native-, Asian-, gay—composes the majority of American men. So manhood is only possible for a distinct minority, and the definition has been constructed to prevent the others from achieving it. Interestingly, this emasculation of one's enemies has a flip side—and one that is equally gendered. These very groups that have historically been cast as less than manly were also, often simultaneously, cast as hypermasculine, as sexually aggressive, violent rapacious beasts, against whom "civilized" men must take a decisive stand and thereby rescue civilization. Thus black men were depicted as rampaging sexual beasts, women as carnivorously carnal, gay men as sexually insatiable, southern European men as sexually predatory and voracious, and Asian men as vicious and cruel torturers who were immorally disinterested in life itself, willing to sacrifice their entire people for their whims. But whether one saw these groups as effeminate sissies or as brutal uncivilized savages, the terms with which they were perceived were gendered. These groups become the "others," the screens against which traditional conceptions of manhood were developed.

Being seen as unmanly is a fear that propels American men to deny manhood to others, as a way of proving the unprovable—that one is fully manly. Masculinity becomes a defense against the perceived threat of humiliation in the eyes of other men, enacted through a "sequence of postures"—things we might say, or do, or even think, that, if we thought carefully about them, would make us ashamed of ourselves (Savran, 1992, p. 16). After all, how many of us have made homophobic or sexist remarks, or told racist jokes, or made lewd comments to women on the street? How many of us have translated those ideas and those words into actions, by physically attacking gay men, or forcing or cajoling a woman to have sex even though she didn't really want to because it was important to score?

 ## POWER AND POWERLESSNESS IN THE LIVES OF MEN

I have argued that homophobia, men's fear of other men, is the animating condition of the dominant definition of masculinity in America, that the reigning definition of masculinity is a defensive effort to prevent being emasculated. In our efforts to suppress or overcome those fears, the dominant culture exacts a tremendous price from those deemed less than fully manly: women, gay men, nonnative-born men, men of color. This perspective may help clarify a paradox in men's lives, a paradox in which men have virtually all the power and yet do not feel powerful (see Kaufman, 1993).

Manhood is equated with power—over women, over other men. Everywhere we look, we see the institutional expression of that power—in state and national legislatures, on the boards of directors of every major U.S. corporation or law firm, and in every school and hospital administration. Women have long understood this, and feminist women have spent the past three decades challenging both the public and the private expressions of men's power and acknowledging their fear of men. Feminism as a set of theories both explains women's fear of men and empowers women to confront it both publicly and privately. Feminist women have theorized that masculinity is about the drive for domination, the drive for power, for conquest.

This feminist definition of masculinity as the drive for power is theorized from women's point of view. It is how women experience masculinity. But it assumes a symmetry between the public and the private that does not conform to men's experiences. Feminists observe that women, as a group, do not hold power in our society. They also observe that individually, they, as women, do not feel powerful. They feel afraid, vulnerable. Their observation of the social reality and their individual experiences are therefore symmetrical. Feminism also observes that men, as a group, *are* in power. Thus, with the same symmetry, feminism has tended to assume that individually men must feel powerful.

This is why the feminist critique of masculinity often falls on deaf ears with men. When confronted with the analysis that men have all the power, many men react incredulously. "What do you mean, men have all the power?" they ask. "What are you talking about? My wife bosses me around. My kids boss me around. My boss bosses me around. I have no power at all! I'm completely powerless!"

Men's feelings are not the feelings of the powerful, but of those who see themselves as powerless. These are the feelings that come inevitably from the discontinuity between the social and the psychological, between the aggregate analysis that reveals how men are in power as a group and the psychological fact that they do not feel powerful as individuals. They are the feelings of men who were raised to believe themselves entitled to feel that power, but do not feel it. No wonder many men are frustrated and angry.

This may explain the recent popularity of those workshops and retreats designed to help men to claim their "inner" power, their "deep manhood," or their "warrior within." Authors such as Bly (1990), Moore and Gillette (1991, 1992, 1993a, 1993b), Farrell (1986, 1993), and Keen (1991) honor and respect men's feelings of powerlessness and acknowledge those feelings to be both true and real. "They gave white men the semblance of power," notes John Lee, one of the leaders of these retreats (quoted in *Newsweek*, p. 41). "We'll let you run the country, but in the meantime, stop feeling, stop talking, and continue swallowing your pain and your hurt." (We are not told who "they" are.)

Often the purveyors of the mythopoetic men's movement, that broad umbrella that encompasses all the groups helping men to retrieve this mythic deep manhood, use the image of the chauffeur to describe modern man's position. The chauffeur appears to have the power—he's wearing the uniform, he's in the driver's seat, and he knows where he's going. So, to the observer, the chauffeur looks as though he is in command. But to the chauffeur himself, they note, he is merely taking orders. He is not at all in charge.[7]

Despite the reality that everyone knows chauffeurs do not have the power, this image remains appealing to the men who hear it at these weekend workshops. But there is a missing piece to the image, a piece concealed by the framing of the image in terms of the individual man's experience. That missing piece is that the person who is giving the orders is also a man. Now we have a relationship *between* men—between men giving orders and other men taking those orders. The man who identifies with the chauffeur is entitled to be the man giving the orders, but he is not. ("They," it turns out, are other men.)

The dimension of power is now reinserted into men's experience not only as the product of individual experience but also as the product of relations with other men. In this sense, men's experience of powerlessness is *real*—the men actually feel it and certainly act on it—but it is not *true,* that is, it does not accurately describe their condition. In contrast to women's lives, men's lives are structured around relationships of power and men's differential access to power, as well as the differential access to that power of men as a group. Our imperfect analysis of our own situation leads us to believe that we men need *more* power, rather than leading us to support feminists' efforts to rearrange power relationships along more equitable lines.

Philosopher Hannah Arendt (1970) fully understood this contradictory experience of social and individual power:

> Power corresponds to the human ability not just to act but to act
> in concert. Power is never the property of an individual; it belongs
> to a group and remains in existence only so long as the group
> keeps together. When we say of somebody that he is "in power"
> we actually refer to his being empowered by a certain number of
> people to act in their name. The moment the group, from which the
> power originated to begin with . . . disappears, "his power" also
> vanishes. (p. 44)

Why, then, do American men feel so powerless? Part of the answer is because we've constructed the rules of manhood so that only the tiniest fraction of men come to believe that they are the biggest of wheels, the sturdiest of oaks, the most virulent repudiators of femininity, the most daring and aggressive. We've managed to disempower the overwhelming majority of American men by other means—such as discriminating on the basis of race, class, ethnicity, age, or sexual preference.

Masculinist retreats to retrieve deep, wounded, masculinity are but one of the ways in which American men currently struggle with their fears and their shame. Unfortunately, at the very moment that they work to break down the isolation that governs men's lives, as they enable men to express those fears and that shame, they ignore the social power that men continue to exert over women and the privileges from which they (as the middle-aged, middle-class white men who largely make up these retreats) continue to benefit—regardless of their experiences as wounded victims of oppressive male socialization.

Others still rehearse the politics of exclusion, as if by clearing away the playing field of secure gender identity of any that we deem less than manly—women, gay men, nonnative-born men, men of color—middle-class, straight, white men can reground their sense of themselves without those haunting fears and that deep shame that they are unmanly and will be exposed by other men. This is the manhood of racism, of sexism, of homophobia. It is the manhood that is so chronically insecure that it trembles at the idea of lifting the ban on gays in the military, that is so threatened by women in the workplace that women become the targets of sexual harassment, that is so deeply frightened of equality that it must ensure that the playing field of male competition remains stacked against all newcomers to the game.

Exclusion and escape have been the dominant methods American men have used to keep their fears of humiliation at bay. The fear of emasculation by other men, of being humiliated, of being seen as a sissy, is the leitmotif in my reading of the history of American manhood. Masculinity has become a relentless test by which we prove to other men, to women, and ultimately to ourselves, that we have successfully mastered the part. The restlessness that men feel today is nothing new in American history; we have been anxious and restless for almost two centuries. Neither exclusion nor escape has ever brought us the relief we've sought, and there is no reason to think that either will solve our problems now. Peace of mind, relief from gender struggle, will come only from a politics of inclusion, not exclusion, from standing up for equality and justice, and not by running away.

NOTES

1. Of course, the phrase "American manhood" contains several simultaneous fictions. There is no single manhood that defines all American men; "America" is meant to refer to the United States proper, and there are significant ways in which this "American manhood" is the outcome of forces that transcend both gender and nation, that is, the global economic development of industrial capitalism. I use it, therefore, to describe the specific hegemonic version of masculinity in the United States, that normative constellation of attitudes, traits, and behaviors that became the standard against which all other masculinities are measured and against which individual men measure the success of their gender accomplishments.
2. Much of this work is elaborated in *Manhood: The American Quest* (in press).
3. Although I am here discussing only American masculinity, I am aware that others have located this chronic instability and efforts to prove manhood in the particular cultural and economic arrangements of Western society. Calvin, after all, inveighed against the disgrace "for men to become effeminate," and countless other theorists have described the mechanics of manly proof. (See, for example, Seidler, 1994.)
4. I do not mean to argue that women do not have anxieties about whether they are feminine enough. Ask any woman how she feels about being called aggressive; it sends a chill into her heart because her femininity is suspect. (I believe that the reason for the enormous recent popularity of sexy lingerie among women is that it enables women to remember they are still feminine underneath their corporate business suit—a suit that apes masculine styles.) But I think the stakes are not as

great for women and that women have greater latitude in defining their identities around these questions than men do. Such are the ironies of sexism: The powerful have a narrower range of options than the powerless, because the powerless can *also* imitate the powerful and get away with it. It may even enhance status, if done with charm and grace—that is, not threatening. For the powerful, any hint of behaving like the powerless is a fall from grace.

5. Such observations also led journalist Heywood Broun to argue that most of the attacks against feminism came from men who were shorter than 5 ft. 7 in. "The man who, whatever his physical size, feels secure in his own masculinity and in his own relation to life is rarely resentful of the opposite sex" (cited in Symes, 1930, p. 139).

6. Some of Freud's followers, such as Anna Freud and Alfred Adler, did follow up on these suggestions. (See especially Adler, 1980.) I am grateful to Terry Kupers for his help in thinking through Adler's ideas.

7. The image is from Warren Farrell, who spoke at a workshop I attended at the First International Men's Conference, Austin, Texas, October 1991.

REFERENCES

Adler, A. (1980). *Cooperation Between the Sexes: Writings on Women, Love and Marriage, Sexuality and Its Disorders* (H. Ansbacher & R. Ansbacher, Eds. & Trans.). New York: Jason Aronson.

Arendt, H. (1970). *On Revolution.* New York: Viking.

Bly, R. (1990). *Iron John: A Book about Men.* Reading, MA: Addison-Wesley.

Brannon, R. (1976). "The male sex role—and what it's done for us lately." In R. Brannon & D. David (Eds.), *The Forty-nine Percent Majority* (pp. 1–40). Reading, MA: Addison-Wesley.

Connell, R. W. (1987). *Gender and Power.* Stanford, CA: Stanford University Press.

Farrell, W. (1986). *Why Men Are the Way They Are.* New York: McGraw-Hill.

Farrell, W. (1993). *The Myth of Male Power: Why Men Are the Disposable Sex.* New York: Simon & Schuster.

Gaylin, W. (1992). *The Male Ego.* New York: Viking.

Goffman, E. (1963). *Stigma.* Englewood Cliffs, NJ: Prentice Hall.

Gorer, G. (1964). *The American People: A Study in National Character.* New York: Norton.

Kaufman, M. (1993). *Cracking the Armour: Power and Pain in the Lives of Men.* Toronto: Viking Canada.

Keen, S. (1991). *Fire in the Belly.* New York: Bantam.

Kimmel, M. S. (in press). *Manhood: The American Quest.* New York: HarperCollins.

Leverenz, D. (1986). "Manhood, Humiliation and Public Life: Some Stories." *Southwest Review* 71, Fall.

Leverenz, D. (1991). "The Last Real Man in America: From Natty Bumppo to Batman." *American Literary Review* 3.

Marx, K., & F. Engels. (1848/1964). "The Communist Manifesto." In R. Tucker (Ed.), *The Marx-Engels Reader.* New York: Norton.

Mead, M. (1965). *And Keep Your Powder Dry.* New York: William Morrow.

Moore, R., & Gillette, D. (1991). *King, Warrior, Magician, Lover.* New York: HarperCollins.

Moore, R., & Gillette, D. (1992). *The King Within: Accessing the King in the Male Psyche.* New York: William Morrow.

Moore, R., & Gillette, D. (1993a). *The Warrior Within: Accessing the Warrior in the Male Psyche.* New York: William Morrow.

Moore, R., & Gillette, D. (1993b). *The Magician Within: Accessing the Magician in the Male Psyche.* New York: William Morrow.

Noble, V. (1992). "A Helping Hand from the Guys." In K. L. Hagan (Ed.), *Women Respond to the Men's Movement.* San Francisco: HarperCollins.

Osherson, S. (1992). *Wrestling with Love: How Men Struggle with Intimacy, with Women, Children, Parents, and Each Other.* New York: Fawcett.

Rotundo, E. A. (1993). *American Manhood: Transformations in Masculinity from the Revolution to the Modern Era.* New York: Basic Books.

Savran, D. (1992). *Communists, Cowboys and Queers: The Politics of Masculinity in the Work of Arthur Miller and Tennessee Williams.* Minneapolis: University of Minnesota Press.

Seidler, V. J. (1994). *Unreasonable Men: Masculinity and Social Theory.* New York: Routledge.

Symes, L. (1930). "The New Masculinism." *Harper's Monthly* 161, January.

Wayne, K. (1912). *Building the Young Man.* Chicago: A. C. McClurg.

"What Men Need Is Men's Approval." (1993, January 3). *The New York Times,* p. C-11.

Wilkinson, R. (1986). *American Tough: The Tough-guy Tradition and American Character.* New York: Harper & Row.

Woolfolk, R. L., & Richardson, F. (1978). *Sanity, Stress and Survival.* New York: Signet.

 QUESTIONS FOR CRITICAL THINKING

Reading 12

1. What is your definition of manhood? What factors have influenced your definition?

2. Kimmel argues that definitions of manhood are irrevocably tied to sexuality. What would need to change in our culture so that this was no longer the case?

3. Do you think it is possible or even necessary to change dominant definitions of manhood in the United States? If so, how so? If not, why not?

Reading 13

THE INVENTION OF HETEROSEXUALITY

JONATHAN NED KATZ

eterosexuality is old as procreation, ancient as the lust of Eve and Adam. That first lady and gentleman, we assume, perceived themselves, behaved, and felt just like today's heterosexuals. We suppose that heterosexuality is unchanging, universal, essential: ahistorical.

Contrary to that common sense conjecture, the concept of heterosexuality is only one particular historical way of perceiving, categorizing, and imagining the social relations of the sexes. Not ancient at all, the idea of heterosexuality is a modern invention, dating to the late nineteenth century. The heterosexual belief, with its metaphysical claim to eternity, has a particular, pivotal place in the social universe of the late nineteenth and twentieth centuries that it did not inhabit earlier. This essay traces the historical process by which the heterosexual idea was created as ahistorical and taken-for-granted. . . .

By not studying the heterosexual idea in history, analysts of sex, gay and straight, have continued to privilege the "normal" and "natural" at the expense of the "abnormal" and "unnatural." Such privileging of the norm accedes to its domination, protecting it from questions. In making the normal the object of a thorough-going historical study we simultaneously pursue a pure truth and a sex-radical and subversive goal: we upset basic preconceptions. We discover that the heterosexual, the normal, and the natural have a history of changing definitions. Studying the history of the term challenges its power.

Contrary to our usual assumption, past Americans and other peoples named, perceived, and socially organized the bodies, lusts, and intercourse of the sexes in ways radically different from the way we do. If we care to understand this vast past sexual diversity, we need to stop promiscuously projecting our own hetero and homo arrangement. Though lip-service is often paid to the distorting, ethnocentric effect of such conceptual imperialism, the category heterosexuality continues to be applied uncritically as a

Jonathan Ned Katz, "The Invention of Heterosexuality" from *Socialist Review* (January-March 1990). Copyright © 1990 by Jonathan Ned Katz. Reprinted with the permission of the author.

universal analytical tool. Recognizing the time-bound and culturally-specific character of the heterosexual category can help us begin to work toward a thoroughly historical view of sex. . . .

 ## BEFORE HETEROSEXUALITY: EARLY VICTORIAN TRUE LOVE, 1820–1860

In the early nineteenth-century United States, from about 1820 to 1860, the heterosexual did not exist. Middle-class white Americans idealized a True Womanhood, True Manhood, and True Love, all characterized by "purity"—the freedom from sensuality.[1] Presented mainly in literary and religious texts, this True Love was a fine romance with no lascivious kisses. This ideal contrasts strikingly with late-nineteenth and twentieth century American incitements to a hetero sex.*

Early Victorian True Love was only realized within the mode of proper procreation, marriage, the legal organization for producing a new set of correctly gendered women and men. Proper womanhood, manhood, and progeny—not a normal male-female eros—was the main product of this mode of engendering and of human reproduction.

The actors in this sexual economy were identified as manly men and womanly women and as procreators, not specifically as erotic beings or heterosexuals. Eros did not constitute the core of a heterosexual identity that inhered, democratically, in both men and women. True Women were defined by their distance from lust. True Men, though thought to live closer to carnality, and in less control of it, aspired to the same freedom from concupiscence.

Legitimate natural desire was for procreation and a proper manhood or womanhood; no heteroerotic desire was thought to be directed exclusively and naturally toward the other sex; lust in men was roving. The human body was thought of as a means towards procreation and production; penis and vagina were instruments of reproduction, not of pleasure. Human energy, thought of as a closed and severely limited system, was to be used in producing children and in work, not wasted in libidinous pleasures.

The location of all this engendering and procreative labor was the sacred sanctum of early Victorian True Love, the home of the True Woman and True Man—a temple of purity threatened from within by the monster masturbator, an archetypal early Victorian cult figure of illicit lust. The home of True Love was a castle far removed from the erotic exotic ghetto inhabited most notoriously then by the prostitute, another archetypal Victorian erotic monster. . . .

---

*Some historians have recently told us to revise our idea of sexless Victorians: their experience and even their ideology, it is said, were more erotic than we previously thought. Despite the revisionists, I argue that "purity" was indeed the dominant, early Victorian, white, middle-class standard. For the debate on Victorian sexuality see John D'Emilio and Estelle Freedman, *Intimate Matters: A History of Sexuality in America* (New York: Harper & Row, 1988), p. xii.

LATE VICTORIAN SEX-LOVE: 1860–1892

"Heterosexuality" and "homosexuality" did not appear out of the blue in the 1890s. These two eroticisms were in the making from the 1860s on. In late Victorian America and in Germany, from about 1860 to 1892, our modern idea of an eroticized universe began to develop, and the experience of a heterolust began to be widely documented and named. . . .

In the late nineteenth-century United States, several social factors converged to cause the eroticizing of consciousness, behavior, emotion, and identity that became typical of the twentieth-century Western middle class. The transformation of the family from producer to consumer unit resulted in a change in family members' relation to their own bodies; from being an instrument primarily of work, the human body was integrated into a new economy, and began more commonly to be perceived as a means of consumption and pleasure. Historical work has recently begun on how the biological human body is differently integrated into changing modes of production, procreation, engendering, and pleasure so as to alter radically the identity, activity, and experience of that body.[2]

The growth of a consumer economy also fostered a new pleasure ethic. This imperative challenged the early Victorian work ethic, finally helping to usher in a major transformation of values. While the early Victorian work ethic had touted the value of economic production, that era's procreation ethic had extolled the virtues of human reproduction. In contrast, the late Victorian economic ethic hawked the pleasures of consuming, while its sex ethic praised an erotic pleasure principle for men and even for women.

In the late nineteenth century, the erotic became the raw material for a new consumer culture. Newspapers, books, plays, and films touching on sex, "normal" and "abnormal," became available for a price. Restaurants, bars, and baths opened, catering to sexual consumers with cash. Late Victorian entrepreneurs of desire incited the proliferation of a new eroticism, a commoditized culture of pleasure.

In these same years, the rise in power and prestige of medical doctors allowed these upwardly mobile professionals to prescribe a healthy new sexuality. Medical men, in the name of science, defined a new ideal of male-female relationships that included, in women as well as men, an essential, necessary, normal eroticism. Doctors, who had earlier named and judged the sex-enjoying woman a "nymphomaniac," now began to label women's *lack* of sexual pleasure a mental disturbance, speaking critically, for example, of female "frigidity" and "anesthesia."*

_____

*This reference to females reminds us that the invention of heterosexuality had vastly different impacts on the histories of women and men. It also differed in its impact on lesbians and heterosexual women, homosexual and heterosexual men, the middle class and working class, and on different religious, racial, national, and geographic groups.

By the 1880s, the rise of doctors as a professional group fostered the rise of a new medical model of Normal Love, replete with sexuality. The new Normal Woman and Man were endowed with a healthy libido. The new theory of Normal Love was the modern medical alternative to the old Cult of True Love. The doctors prescribed a new sexual ethic as if it were a morally neutral, medical description of health. The creation of the new Normal Sexual had its counterpart in the invention of the late Victorian Sexual Pervert. The attention paid the sexual abnormal created a need to name the sexual normal, the better to distinguish the average him and her from the deviant it.

HETEROSEXUALITY: THE FIRST YEARS, 1892–1900

In the periodization of heterosexual American history suggested here, the years 1892 to 1900 represent "The First Years" of the heterosexual epoch, eight key years in which the idea of the heterosexual and homosexual were initially and tentatively formulated by U.S. doctors. The earliest-known American use of the word "heterosexual" occurs in a medical journal article by Dr. James G. Kiernan of Chicago, read before the city's medical society on March 7, 1892, and published that May—portentous dates in sexual history.[3] But Dr. Kiernan's heterosexuals were definitely not exemplars of normality. Heterosexuals, said Kiernan, were defined by a mental condition, "psychical hermaphroditism." Its symptoms were "inclinations to both sexes." These heterodox sexuals also betrayed inclinations "to abnormal methods of gratification," that is, techniques to insure pleasure without procreation. Dr. Kiernan's heterogeneous sexuals did demonstrate "traces of the normal sexual appetite" (a touch of procreative desire). Kiernan's normal sexuals were implicitly defined by a monolithic other-sex inclination and procreative aim. Significantly, they still lacked a name.

Dr. Kiernan's article of 1892 also included one of the earliest-known uses of the word "homosexual" in American English. Kiernan defined "Pure homosexuals" as persons whose "general mental state is that of the opposite sex." Kiernan thus defined homosexuals by their deviance from a gender norm. His heterosexuals displayed a double deviance from both gender and procreative norms.

Though Kiernan used the new words "heterosexual" and "homosexual," an old procreative standard and a new gender norm coexisted uneasily in his thought. His word "heterosexual" defined a mixed person and compound urge, abnormal because they wantonly included procreative and nonprocreative objectives, as well as same-sex and different-sex attractions.

That same year, 1892, Dr. Krafft-Ebing's influential *Psychopathia Sexualis* was first translated and published in the United States.[4] But Kiernan and Krafft-Ebing by no means agreed on the definition of the heterosexual. In Krafft-Ebing's book, "hetero-sexual" was used unambiguously in the modern sense to refer to an erotic feeling for a different sex. "Homo-sexual" referred unambiguously to an erotic feeling for a "same sex." In Krafft-Ebing's volume, unlike Kiernan's article, heterosexual and homosexual were clearly distinguished from a third category, a "psycho-sexual hermaphroditism," defined by impulses toward both sexes.

Krafft-Ebing hypothesized an inborn "sexual instinct" for relations with the "opposite sex," the inherent "purpose" of which was to foster procreation. Krafft-Ebing's erotic drive was still a reproductive instinct. But the doctor's clear focus on a different-sex versus same-sex sexuality constituted a historic, epochal move from an absolute procreative standard of normality toward a new norm. His definition of heterosexuality as other-sex attraction provided the basis for a revolutionary, modern break with a centuries-old procreative standard.

It is difficult to overstress the importance of that new way of categorizing. The German's mode of labeling was radical in referring to the biological sex, masculinity or femininity, and the pleasure of actors (along with the procreant purpose of acts). Krafft-Ebing's heterosexual offered the modern world a new norm that came to dominate our idea of the sexual universe, helping to change it from a mode of human reproduction and engendering to a mode of pleasure. The heterosexual category provided the basis for a move from a production-oriented, procreative imperative to a consumerist pleasure principle—an institutionalized pursuit of happiness. . . .

Only gradually did doctors agree that heterosexual referred to a normal, "other-sex" eros. This new standard-model heterosex provided the pivotal term for the modern regularization of eros that paralleled similar attempts to standardize masculinity and femininity, intelligence, and manufacturing.[5] The idea of heterosexuality as the master sex from which all others deviated was (like the idea of the master race) deeply authoritarian. The doctors' normalization of a sex that was hetero proclaimed a new heterosexual separatism—an erotic apartheid that forcefully segregated the sex normals from the sex perverts. The new, strict boundaries made the emerging erotic world less polymorphous—safer for sex normals. However, the idea of such creatures as heterosexuals and homosexuals emerged from the narrow world of medicine to become a commonly accepted notion only in the early twentieth century. In 1901, in the comprehensive *Oxford English Dictionary,* "heterosexual" and "homosexual" had not yet made it.

THE DISTRIBUTION OF THE HETEROSEXUAL MYSTIQUE: 1900–1930

In the early years of this heterosexual century the tentative hetero hypothesis was stabilized, fixed, and widely distributed as the ruling sexual orthodoxy: The Heterosexual Mystique. Starting among pleasure-affirming urban working-class youths, southern blacks, and Greenwich-Village bohemians as defensive subculture, heterosex soon triumphed as dominant culture.[6]

In its earliest version, the twentieth-century heterosexual imperative usually continued to associate heterosexuality with a supposed human "need," "drive," or "instinct" for propagation, a procreant urge linked inexorably with carnal lust as it had not been earlier. In the early twentieth century, the falling birth rate, rising divorce rate, and "war of the sexes" of the middle class were matters of increasing public concern. Giving vent to heteroerotic emotions was thus praised as enhancing baby-making capacity, marital intimacy, and family stability. (Only many years later, in the mid-1960s, would heteroeroticism be distinguished completely, in practice and theory, from procreativity and male-female pleasure sex justified in its own name.)

The first part of the new sex norm—hetero—referred to a basic gender divergence. The "oppositeness" of the sexes was alleged to be the basis for a universal, normal, erotic attraction between males and females. The stress on the sexes' "oppositeness," which harked back to the early nineteenth century, by no means simply registered biological differences of females and males. The early twentieth-century focus on physiological and gender dimorphism reflected the deep anxieties of men about the shifting work, social roles, and power of men over women, and about the ideals of womanhood and manhood. That gender anxiety is documented, for example, in 1897, in *The New York Times'* publication of the Reverend Charles Parkhurst's diatribe against female "andromaniacs," the preacher's derogatory, scientific-sounding name for women who tried to "minimize distinctions by which manhood and womanhood are differentiated."[7] The stress on gender difference was a conservative response to the changing social-sexual division of activity and feeling which gave rise to the independent "New Woman" of the 1880s and eroticized "Flapper" of the 1920s.

The second part of the new hetero norm referred positively to sexuality. That novel upbeat focus on the hedonistic possibilities of male-female conjunctions also reflected a social transformation—a revaluing of pleasure and procreation, consumption and work in commercial, capitalist society. The democratic attribution of a normal lust to human females (as well as males) served to authorize women's enjoyment of their own bodies and began to undermine the early Victorian idea of the pure True Woman—a sex-affirmative action still part of women's struggle. The twentieth-century Erotic Woman also undercut nineteenth-century feminist assertion of women's moral superiority, cast suspicions of lust on women's passionate romantic friendships with women, and asserted the presence of a menacing female monster, "the lesbian."[8] . . .

In the perspective of heterosexual history, this early twentieth century struggle for the more explicit depiction of an "opposite-sex" eros appears in a curious new light. Ironically, we find sex-conservatives, the social purity advocates of censorship and repression, fighting against the depiction not just of sexual perversity but also of the new normal heterosexuality. That a more open depiction of normal sex had to be defended against forces of propriety confirms the claim that heterosexuality's predecessor, Victorian True Love, had included no legitimate eros. . . .

THE HETEROSEXUAL STEPS OUT: 1930–1945

In 1930, in *The New York Times,* heterosexuality first became a love that dared to speak its name. On April 30th of that year, the word "heterosexual" is first known to have appeared in *The New York Times Book Review.* There, a critic described the subject of André Gide's *The Immoralist* proceeding "from a heterosexual liaison to a homosexual one." The ability to slip between sexual categories was referred to casually as a rather unremarkable aspect of human possibility. This is also the first known reference by *The Times* to the new hetero/homo duo.[9]

The following month the second reference to the hetero/homo dyad appeared in *The New York Times Book Review,* in a comment on Floyd Dell's *Love in the Machine Age.* This work revealed a prominent antipuritan of the 1930s using the dire threat of homosexuality as his rationale for greater heterosexual freedom. *The Times* quoted Dell's warning that current abnormal social conditions kept the young dependent on their parents, causing "infantilism, prostitution and homosexuality." Also quoted was Dell's attack on the "inculcation of purity" that "breeds distrust of the opposite sex." Young people, Dell said, should be "permitted to develop normally to heterosexual adulthood." "But," *The Times* reviewer emphasized, "such a state already exists, here and now." And so it did. Heterosexuality, a new gender-sex category, had been distributed from the narrow, rarified realm of a few doctors to become a nationally, even internationally, cited aspect of middle-class life.[10] . . .

 HETEROSEXUAL HEGEMONY: 1945–1965

The "cult of domesticity" following World War II—the reassociation of women with the home, motherhood, and child-care; men with fatherhood and wage work outside the home—was a period in which the predominance of the hetero norm went almost unchallenged, an era of heterosexual hegemony. This was an age in which conservative mental-health professionals reasserted the old link between heterosexuality and procreation. In contrast, sex-liberals of the day strove, ultimately with success, to expand the heterosexual ideal to include within the boundaries of normality a wider-than-ever range of nonprocreative, premarital, and extra-marital behaviors. But sex-liberal reform actually helped to extend and secure the dominance of the heterosexual idea, as we shall see when we get to Kinsey.

The post-war sex-conservative tendency was illustrated in 1947, in Ferdinand Lundberg and Dr. Marnia Farnham's book, *Modern Woman: The Lost Sex.* Improper masculinity and femininity was exemplified, the authors decreed, by "engagement in heterosexual relations . . . with the complete intent to see to it that they do not eventuate in reproduction."[11] Their procreatively-defined heterosex was one expression of a postwar ideology of fecundity that, internalized and enacted dutifully by a large part of the population, gave rise to the postwar baby boom.

The idea of the feminine female and masculine male as prolific breeders was also reflected in the stress, specific to the late 1940s, on the homosexual as sad symbol of "sterility"—that particular loaded term appears incessantly in comments . . . to the fecund forties.

In 1948, in *The New York Times Book Review,* sex liberalism was in ascendancy. Dr. Howard A. Rusk declared that Alfred Kinsey's just published report on *Sexual Behavior in the Human Male* had found "wide variations in sex concepts and behavior." This raised the question: "What is 'normal' and 'abnormal'?" In particular, the report had found that "homosexual experience is much more common than previously thought," and "there is often a mixture of both homo and hetero experience."[12]

Kinsey's counting of orgasms indeed stressed the wide range of behaviors and feelings that fell within the boundaries of a quantitative, statistically accounted heterosexuality. Kinsey's liberal reform of the hetero/homo dualism widened the narrow, old hetero category to accord better with the varieties of social experience. He thereby contradicted the older idea of a monolithic, qualitatively defined, natural procreative act, experience, and person.[13]

Though Kinsey explicitly questioned "whether the terms 'normal' and 'abnormal' belong in a scientific vocabulary," his counting of climaxes was generally understood to define normal sex as majority sex. This quantified norm constituted a final, society-wide break with the old qualitatively defined reproductive standard. Though conceived of as purely scientific, the statistical definition of the normal as the-sex-most-people-are-having substituted a new, quantitative moral standard for the old, qualitative sex ethic— another triumph for the spirit of capitalism.

Kinsey also explicitly contested the idea of an absolute, either/or antithesis between hetero and homo persons. He denied that human beings "represent two discrete populations, heterosexual and homosexual." The world, he ordered, "is not to be divided into sheep and goats." The hetero/homo division was not nature's doing: "Only the human mind invents categories and tries to force facts into separated pigeon-holes. The living world is a continuum."[14]

With a wave of the taxonomist's hand, Kinsey dismissed the social and historical division of people into heteros and homos. His denial of heterosexual and homosexual personhood rejected the social reality and profound subjective force of a historically constructed tradition which, since 1892 in the United States, had cut the sexual population in two and helped to establish the social reality of a heterosexual and homosexual identity.

On the one hand, the social construction of homosexual persons has led to the development of a powerful gay liberation identity politics based on an ethnic group model. This has freed generations of women and men from a deep, painful, socially induced sense of shame, and helped to bring about a society-wide liberalization of attitudes and responses to homosexuals.[15] On the other hand, contesting the notion of homosexual and heterosexual persons was one early, partial resistance to the limits of the hetero/homo construction. Gore Vidal, rebel son of Kinsey, has for years been joyfully proclaiming:

> there is no such thing as a homosexual or a heterosexual person. There are only homo- or heterosexual acts. Most people are a mixture of impulses if not practices, and what anyone does with a willing partner is of no social or cosmic significance.
>
> So why all the fuss? In order for a ruling class to rule, there must be arbitrary prohibitions. Of all prohibitions, sexual taboo is the most useful because sex involves everyone. . . . we have allowed our governors to divide the population into two teams. One team is good, godly, straight; the other is evil, sick, vicious.[16]

•   •   •

HETEROSEXUALITY QUESTIONED: 1965–1982

By the late 1960s, anti-establishment counterculturalists, fledgling feminists, and homosexual-rights activists had begun to produce an unprecedented critique of sexual repression in general, of women's sexual repression in particular, of marriage and the family—and of some forms of heterosexuality. This critique even found its way into *The New York Times.*

In March 1968, in the theater section of that paper, freelancer Rosalyn Regelson cited a scene from a satirical review brought to New York by a San Francisco troupe:

> a heterosexual man wanders inadvertently into a homosexual bar. Before he realizes his mistake, he becomes involved with an aggressive queen who orders a drink for him. Being a broad-minded liberal and trying to play it cool until he can back out of the situation gracefully, he asks, "How do you like being a ah homosexual?" To which the queen drawls drily, "How do you like being ah whatever it is you are?"

Regelson continued:

> The Two Cultures in confrontation. The middle-class liberal, challenged today on many fronts, finds his last remaining fixed value, his heterosexuality, called into question. The theater . . . recalls the strategies he uses in dealing with this ultimate threat to his world view.[17]

•   •   •

HETEROSEXUAL HISTORY: OUT OF THE SHADOWS

Our brief survey of the heterosexual idea suggests a new hypothesis. Rather than naming a conjunction old as Eve and Adam, heterosexual designates a word and concept, a norm and role, an individual and group identity, a behavior and feeling, and a peculiar sexual-political institution particular to the late nineteenth and twentieth centuries.

Because much stress has been placed here on heterosexuality as word and concept, it seems important to affirm that heterosexuality (and homosexuality) came into existence before it was named and thought about. The formulation of the heterosexual idea did not create a heterosexual experience or behavior; to suggest otherwise would be to ascribe determining power to labels and concepts. But the titling and envisioning of heterosexuality did play an important role in consolidating the construction of the heterosexual's social existence. Before the wide use of the word heterosexual, I suggest, women and men did not mutually lust with the same profound, sure sense of normalcy that followed the distribution of "heterosexual" as universal sanctifier.

According to this proposal, women and men make their own sexual histories. But they do not produce their sex lives just as they please. They make their sexualities within a particular mode of organization given by the past and altered by their changing desire, their present power and activity, and their vision of a better world. That hypothesis suggests a number of good reasons for the immediate inauguration of research on a historically specific heterosexuality.

The study of the history of the heterosexual experience will forward a great intellectual struggle still in its early stages. This is the fight to pull heterosexuality, homosexuality, and all the sexualities out of the realm of nature and biology [and] into the realm of the social and historical. Feminists have explained to us that anatomy does not determine our gender destinies (our masculinities and femininities). But we've only recently begun to consider that *biology does not settle our erotic fates.* The common notion that biology determines the object of sexual desire, or that physiology and society together cause sexual orientation, are determinisms that deny the break existing between our bodies and situations and our desiring. Just as the biology of our hearing organs will never tell us why we take pleasure in Bach or delight in Dixieland, our female or male anatomies, hormones, and genes will never tell us why we yearn for women, men, both, other, or none. That is because desiring is a self-generated project of individuals within particular historical cultures. Heterosexual history can help us see the place of values and judgments in the construction of our own and others' pleasures, and to see how our erotic tastes—our aesthetics of the flesh—are socially institutionalized through the struggle of individuals and classes.

The study of heterosexuality in time will also help us to recognize the *vast historical diversity of sexual emotions and behaviors*—a variety that challenges the monolithic heterosexual hypothesis. John D'Emilio and Estelle Freedman's *Intimate Matters: A History of Sexuality in America* refers in passing to numerous substantial changes in sexual activity and feeling: for example, the widespread use of contraceptives in the nineteenth century, the twentieth-century incitement of the female orgasm, and the recent sexual conduct changes by gay men in response to the AIDS epidemic. It's now a commonplace of family history that people in particular classes feel and behave in substantially different ways under different historical conditions.[18] Only when we stop assuming an invariable essence of heterosexuality will we begin the research to reveal the full variety of sexual emotions and behaviors.

The historical study of the heterosexual experience can help us *understand the erotic relationships of women and men in terms of their changing modes of social organization.* Such modal analysis actually characterizes a sex history well underway.[19] This suggests that the eros-gender-procreation system (the social ordering of lust, femininity and masculinity, and baby-making) has been linked closely to a society's particular organization of power and production. To understand the subtle history of heterosexuality we need to look carefully at correlations between (1) society's organization of eros and pleasure; (2) its mode of engendering persons as feminine or masculine (its making of women and men); (3) its ordering of human reproduction; and (4) its dominant political economy. This General Theory of Sexual Relativity proposes that substantial historical changes in the social organization of eros, gender, and procreation have basically altered the activity and experience of human beings within those modes.[20]

A historical view locates heterosexuality and homosexuality in time, helping us distance ourselves from them. This distancing can help us formulate new questions that clarify our long-range sexual-political goals: What has been and is the social function of sexual categorizing? Whose interests have been served by the division of the world into heterosexual and homosexual? Do we dare not draw a line between those two erotic species? Is some sexual naming socially necessary? Would human freedom be enhanced if the sex-biology of our partners in lust was of no particular concern, and had no name? In what kind of society could we all more freely explore our desire and our flesh?

As we move toward [the year 2000], a new sense of the historical making of the heterosexual and homosexual suggests that these are ways of feeling, acting, and being with each other that we can together unmake and radically remake according to our present desire, power, and our vision of a future political-economy of pleasure.

NOTES

1. Barbara Welter, "The Cult of True Womanhood: 1820–1860," *American Quarterly*, vol. 18 (Summer 1966); Welter's analysis is extended here to include True Men and True Love.

2. See, for example, Catherine Gallagher and Thomas Laqueur, eds., "The Making of the Modern Body: Sexuality and Society in the Nineteenth Century," *Representations,* no. 14 (Spring 1986) (republished, Berkeley: University of California Press, 1987).

3. Dr. James G. Kiernan, "Responsibility in Sexual Perversion," *Chicago Medical Recorder,* vol. 3 (May 1892), pp. 185–210.

4. R. von Krafft-Ebing, *Psychopathia Sexualis, with Especial Reference to Contrary Sexual Instinct: A Medico-Legal Study,* trans. Charles Gilbert Chaddock (Philadelphia: F. A. Davis, 1892), from the 7th and revised German ed. Preface, November 1892.

5. For the standardization of gender see Lewis Terman and C. C. Miles, *Sex and Personality, Studies in Femininity and Masculinity* (New York: McGraw-Hill, 1936). For the standardization of intelligence see Lewis Terman, *Stanford-Binet Intelligence Scale* (Boston: Houghton Mifflin, 1916). For the standardization of work, see "scientific management" and "Taylorism" in Harry Braverman, *Labor and Monopoly Capital: The Degradation of Work in the Twentieth Century* (New York: Monthly Review Press, 1974).

6. See D'Emilio and Freedman, *Intimate Matters,* pp. 194–201, 231, 241, 295–96; Ellen Kay Trimberger, "Feminism, Men, and Modern Love: Greenwich Village, 1900–1925," in *Powers of Desire: The Politics of Sexuality,* eds. Ann Snitow, Christine Stansell, Sharon Thompson (New York: Monthly Review Press, 1983), pp. 131–52; Kathy Peiss, " 'Charity Girls' and City Pleasures: Historical Notes on Working Class Sexuality, 1880–1920," in *Powers of Desire,* pp. 74–87; and Mary P. Ryan, "The Sexy Saleslady: Psychology, Heterosexuality, and Consumption in the Twentieth Century," in her *Womanhood in America,* 2nd ed. (New York: Franklin Watts: 1979), pp. 151–82.

7. [Rev. Charles Parkhurst], "Woman. Calls Them Andromaniacs. Dr. Parkhurst So Characterizes Certain Women Who Passionately Ape Everything That Is Mannish. Woman Divinely Preferred. Her Supremacy Lies in Her Womanliness, and She Should Make the Most of It—Her Sphere of Best Usefulness the Home," *The New York Times,* May 23, 1897, p. 16:1.

8. See Lisa Duggan, "The Social Enforcement of Heterosexuality and Lesbian Resistance in the 1920s," in *Class, Race, and Sex: The Dynamics of Control,* ed. Amy Swerdlow and Hanah Lessinger (Boston: G. K. Hall, 1983), pp. 75–92; Rayna Rapp and Ellen Ross, "The Twenties Backlash: Compulsory Heterosexuality, the Consumer Family, and the Waning of Feminism," in Swerdlow and Lessinger; Christina Simmons, "Companionate Marriage and the Lesbian Threat," *Frontiers,* vol. 4, no. 3 (Fall 1979), pp. 54–59; and Lillian Faderman, *Surpassing the Love of Men* (New York: William Morrow, 1981).

9. Louis Kronenberger, review of André Gide, *The Immoralist, New York Times Book Review,* April 20, 1930, p. 9.

10. Henry James Forman, review of Floyd Dell, *Love in the Machine Age* (New York: Farrar & Rinehart), *New York Times Book Review,* September 14, 1930, p. 9.

11. Ferdinand Lundberg and Dr. Marnia F. Farnham, *Modern Woman the Lost Sex* (NY: Harper, 1947).

12. Dr. Howard A. Rusk, *New York Times Book Review,* January 4, 1948, p. 3.

13. Alfred Kinsey, Wardell B. Pomeroy, Clyde E. Martin, *Sexual Behavior in the Human Male* (Philadelphia: W. B. Saunders, 1948), pp. 199–200.

14. Kinsey, *Sexual Behavior,* pp. 637, 639.

15. See Steven Epstein, "Gay Politics, Ethnic Identity: The Limits of Social Construc-tionism," *Socialist Review* 93/93 (1987), pp. 9–54.

16. Gore Vidal, "Someone to Laugh at the Squares With" [Tennessee Williams], *New York Review of Books,* June 13, 1985; reprinted in his *At Home: Essays, 1982–1988* (New York: Random House, 1988), p. 48.

17. Rosalyn Regelson, "Up the Camp Staircase," *The New York Times,* March 3, 1968, Section II, p. 1:5.

18. D'Emilio and Freedman, *Intimate Matters,* pp. 57–63, 268, 356.

19. Ryan, *Womanhood;* John D'Emilio, "Capitalism and Gay Identity" in *Powers of Desire,* pp. 100–13; Jeffrey Weeks, *Coming Out: Homosexual Politics in Britain from the Nineteenth Century to the Present* (London: Quartet Books, 1977); D'Emilio and Freedman, *Intimate Matters;* Katz, "Early Colonial Exploration, Agriculture, and Commerce: The Age of Sodomitical Sin, 1607–1740," *Gay/Lesbian Almanac,* pp. 23–65.

20. This tripartite system is intended as a revision of Gayle Rubin's pioneering work on the social-historical organization of eros and gender. See "The Traffic in Women: Notes on the Political-Economy of Sex," in *Toward an Anthropology of Women,* ed. Rayna R. Reiter (New York: Monthly Review Press, 1975), pp. 157–210, and "Thinking Sex: Notes for a Radical Theory of the Politics of Sexuality," in *Pleasure and Danger: Exploring Female Sexuality,* ed. Carole S. Vance (Boston: Routledge & Kegan Paul, 1984), pp. 267–329.

 QUESTIONS FOR CRITICAL THINKING

Reading 13

1. Katz discusses the difference between sexual behavior and sexual identity. Does distinguishing between these two concepts help you to understand issues of sexuality in new and different ways? If so, how? If not, why not?

2. What reasons can you offer regarding why we maintain separate cat-egories of sexuality?

3. Do you think it is possible or desirable that we move beyond separate categories of sexuality? What would be the social implications of your answer?

Reading 14

'IF YOU DON'T KISS ME, YOU'RE DUMPED'
Boys, Boyfriends and Heterosexualised Masculinities in the Primary School

EMMA RENOLD

 ## INTRODUCTION

The sanctioning and institutionalisation of heterosexuality within school arenas has been empirically explored in a now growing volume of US, UK and
Australian research (Mahony & Jones, 1988; Thorne, 1993; Mac an Ghaill,
1994, 1996; Laskey & Beavis, 1996; Epstein, 1997a, b, Kehily & Nayak, 1997;
Epstein & Johnson, 1998; Letts & Sears, 1999; Epstein *et al.*, 2001). Schools and
schooling processes are now recognised as key social sites in the production
and reproduction of male heterosexualities and boys' sexual cultures (Kehily,
2000). Researchers have extended their understanding of 'heterosexual' practices, from sexual activity, to a wide range of discourses and performances,
through which boys (and girls) define, negotiate and essentially construct
their gendered selves. For example, Mac an Ghaill (1994) and Connell (1995)
have shown how hegemonic masculine performances are inextricably tied
to dominant notions of heterosexuality. They and others have argued that
by problematising and interrogating the 'heterosexual presumption', within
educational organisations, its 'normalisation' and subsequent 'dominance' is
made visible (Epstein & Johnson, 1994). This has led to a number of school-
based investigations into the processes by which heterosexual identities are
produced and desired and how that dominance is secured and maintained.

Overwhelmingly, these investigations have focused upon the production of older male heterosexualities (Mac an Ghaill, 1994, 1996; Epstein &
Johnson, 1994; Kehily & Nayak, 1996, 1997, 2000; Nayak & Kehily, 1997; Haywood, 1996; Redman 2000, 2001; Frosh *et al.*, 2002). Little research attention
has been paid to (hetero)sexualised pupil cultures within the primary school
(although see Wallis & VanEvery, 2000; Redman, 1996) and in particular the
diversity and ambiguities surrounding boys' heterosexual cultures within
primary/elementary school research (see Skelton 2001, pp. 149–154). This

paper hopes to offer some insight into the different ways in which Year 6 boys (aged 10/11) engage with, practice and occupy 'heterosexualities' and how integral, yet complex and contradictory heterosexual performances are to the production of 'proper' boys. It foregrounds children's own accounts and constructions of dominant notions of heterosexualised masculinities which were, for some boys, produced through the precarious and fragile subject position of 'boyfriend' but also through heterosexual fantasies/sex-play, homophobic, anti-gay and misogynistic talk and behaviour and the sexualised harassment of female classmates.

THE STUDY: RESEARCHING AND THEORISING CHILDREN'S GENDER AND SEXUAL RELATIONS

The data and analyses presented in this paper derive from doctoral research in the form of a year long ethnography exploring the construction of children's gender and sexual identities in their final year (Year 6) of primary school (Renold, 1999). The fieldwork was conducted during the academic year 1996/1996 in two primary schools, Tipton Primary and Hirstwood (both pseudonyms) situated in a small semi-rural town in the east of England [1]. Fifty-nine children, from two Year Six classes participated in the research [2]. Alongside observation, unstructured exploratory friendship group interviews was the main method used to explore children's gender and sexual relations because it maximised children's ability to create spaces (physical and discursive) from which they could freely discuss what they felt to be important and significant to them. As discussed elsewhere (Renold 2000, 2002a) I did not set out to study children's sexual cultures. However, as in many qualitative studies, the reflexivity and flexibility of the ethnographic process, combined with the longitudinal element of the research, led to a progressive focusing of ideas. From examining gender relations, I found myself increasingly witnessing a complex, interactive and daily network of heterosexual performances by both boys and girls as they negotiated their gendered selves. And from the first few weeks in the field, the interconnectedness of sexuality and gender was becoming increasingly visible and I began exploring how dominant notions of heterosexuality underscore much of children's identity work and peer relationships as they 'live out' the categories 'girl' and 'boy'.

I also began to disrupt the myth of the primary school as an 'asexual' environment and explore how young children are each subject to the pressures of 'compulsory heterosexuality' (Rich, 1980) and 'the heterosexual matrix' (Butler, 1990)—where to be a 'normal' boy and girl involves the projection of a coherent and abiding heterosexual self:

> I use the term *heterosexual matrix* . . . to designate that grid of
> cultural intelligibility through which bodies, genders, and desires

are naturalised . . . a hegemonic discursive/epistemological model of gender intelligibility that assumes that for bodies to cohere and make sense there must be a stable sex expressed through a stable gender (masculine expresses male, feminine expresses female) that is oppositionally and hierarchically defined through the compulsory practice of heterosexuality. (Butler, 1990, p. 151)

This paper seeks to examine the acting out of Butler's (1990) 'heterosexual matrix' in which the 'real' expression of masculinity and femininity is embedded within a presupposed heterosexuality. It explores how boys, multiply positioned through generational ('child') and gendered discourses ('boy'), make sense of the oppositionality of sex/gender through the often hierarchical heterosexualised economies of classroom and playground relations.

 ## THE SOCIAL WORLD OF BOYFRIENDS AND GIRLFRIENDS: A CASE OF MIXED MESSAGES

A number of studies have explored the salience of (hetero)sexualities and the discursive practices of dating, dumping and two-timing within a boyfriend/girlfriend network that permeates and structures most upper primary school children's social relations [3] (Thorne, 1993; Hatcher, 1995; Redman, 1996). This study was no exception (see Renold, 2000). For example, simple mixed-sex interactions like borrowing a pencil or helping with a class-task could be (hetero)sexualised (usually by teasing the boy/ girl involved that they 'fancy' each other). What became apparent, however, was that having a girlfriend and being a boyfriend seemed to be an increasingly *overt* 'compulsory' signifier for the public affirmation of a boy's heterosexuality, and a further performative signifier of their hegemonic masculinity [4]. The following group interview extract goes some way to highlight the pressures, pleasures and fears of the heterosexual matrix at work via a ritualised, yet diverse language of 'fancying', 'going-out', 'love' and 'embarrassment':

ER: OK, you can talk about what you like . . . .

MARTIN: Erm erm erm erm cool . . . erm Jenna fancies Michael, Michael fancies Jenna

MICHAEL: No I don't

MARTIN: Only joking

ER: How do you /feel about Jenna fancying you Michael?

MARTIN: I was only joking

MICHAEL: Not very good

ER: Why not?

MARTIN: She's a fat cow

COLIN: She put, she put on his dictionary, erm, 'good luck, I love you'

ER: Really? . . . (he nods) Have you spoke to her at all?

MICHAEL: (shakes his head to signify 'no')

MARTIN: He's shy . . . he's getting embarrassed

COLIN: I'll speak for him, 'no'

MARTIN: She's a cow

Despite the ubiquitous presence, and often highly desirable status of boy-friend, actually 'going out' [5] with a girl created conformative pressures for boys and girls. Indeed as the latter extract illustrates 'coming out' as heterosexual in this way, was often a complex and contradictory process. Despite the connection, heterosexual performances, or 'having a girlfriend', did not automatically signify hegemonic masculinity. It was usually only the boys who were good at sport (usually football), and who were deemed 'hard', 'tough', 'cool' or 'good-looking' by their peers, who were reported to be the most romantically desirable. While more gentle and non-sporting boys invested and participated in the heterosexual network of boyfriends and girlfriends, they were more often positioned as 'heterosexual failures' and subject to much teasing and ridicule, usually for pursuing or being pur-sued by 'non-desirable' girls (see Renold, 2002b). For the majority of girls in this study, the most sought after boys constituted the 'A' team (football). Heterosexual hierarchies were thus produced and the cycle of heterosexual-ity, sport and hegemonic masculinity reinforced.

I have discussed elsewhere how competing discourses surrounding the sexually innocent child and the sexual adolescent created contradictions and conflicts for many girls in ways that were not reported or observed in boys' sexual cultures (Renold, 2000). Rather, boys' contradictions lay in their ambivalent attitude towards proximity to girls. This could give rise to teasing behaviours associated with fear of the 'feminine' (often via a lan-guage of pollution, disease and contamination) or could publicly represent and confirm a boy's heterosexual masculinity. In sum, physical or emotional closeness to girls could be both masculinity confirming and masculinity denying. Indeed, teasing and ridicule, as illustrated in the extract above, predominantly occurred when boys, like Martin, rarely located themselves in heterosexual/romantic discourses and when there was a lack of boys in the group who were 'going out' or who previously had a 'girlfriend'. Furthermore, attempts to re-secure 'masculinity', often led boys to draw on alternative hegemonic discourses such as misogynist comments which usu-ally involved the objectification of girls ('she's a cow'). The fine line between romance and sexual harassment (Skelton, 2001) is discussed in more detail later in the paper.

'IT'S ALWAYS THE GIRLS THAT USE YOU':
HETEROSEXUAL/ROMANTIC DELUSIONS

With a few exceptions, most of the boys who were observed to fleetingly engage in the subject position 'boyfriend' and the heterosexualised practices of 'fancying' and 'going out' rarely felt at ease or reported any sustained pleasure. Many boys described their experiences in a less than positive light:

> MARTIN: If you have a girlfriend you have everyone saying 'oh can you come and kiss me/, can you come and kiss meee' (singsong)
>
> COLIN: Yeah it's all that/and the next day
>
> MARTIN: Will you kiss me, will you kiss me, will you kiss me?
>
> ER: And you don't want to?
>
> COLIN: NO and Harriet/is like
>
> MARTIN: Jane and Hayley, they'll be going, if you don't kiss me you're dumped

While some boys were teased for not having a girlfriend, those that did, like Martin and Colin, were often overwhelmed by girls' expectations of boys to express their commitment in a physical way ('will you kiss me', 'if you don't kiss me, you're dumped'). Indeed, Martin's concern over kissing further emphasises the ambiguity surrounding the desire for yet resistance of sexual maturity and 'older child identities' (Redman, 1996). Alternatively, other boys (below) experienced what they considered to be more than their fair share of 'dumping' (i.e. when a 'relationship' is terminated). Indeed, it seemed that a great deal of power could be exercised and experienced by being able to 'dump' relationships and girls were more ready to and more frequently changed their boyfriends than boys [6]:

> PETE: I used to be going out with Fiona but I didn't like having a relationship with her because she always used to dump me
>
> DARREN: Yeah that's what Victoria used to do—what she used to do when I was in a stress was she used to get in a bigger stress and then dump me . . . and then about five minutes later she always comes back to me and thinks its all right again, 'do you still love me' and she expects everything to be all right again
>
> ER: And what does that make you feel like?
>
> DARREN: They just use you . . . it's not fair

Indeed, the feelings of powerlessness embedded in Darren and Pete's frustration at being 'always dumped' and 'used' and the pressures of engaging in 'older' sexual activities suggest that neither one of these boys experienced the dominant subject position and power relations associated perhaps with the more traditional heterosexual discourses of patriarchy. At best, most boys experienced heterosexual relationships as fragile, ambiguous and with a mixture of unease and tension. Given these experiences, it seems difficult to understand why many boys continued to pursue girls for 'girlfriends' or subject themselves to the precarious role of 'boyfriend'. A possible explanation could be that the pressures of 'compulsory heterosexuality' (i.e. their investment at all costs to perform as heterosexual subjects), the status attached to 'older (sexually mature) identities' and the wider media/cultural discourses that bind heterosexuality with hegemonic masculinity (from TV to magazines) leave boys little discursive space for any systematic resistance without throwing into doubt their 'masculinity'.

 ## 'I'M WAITING UNTIL THE COMP': DELAYED (HETERO)SEXUALITIES AND RE(A)LATIONSHIPS

Some boys, however, did actively resist 'being a boyfriend' and avoid engaging in the heterosexualised discourses and practices of 'going-out'. As the extracts below illustrate, they either expressed a desire for a 'proper' relationship proceeding primary school, which involved intimate sexual activities. Or, they stressed that they were 'too young' or 'not ready' to have a girlfriend:

> DAVID: We don't really care about the girls in our school
>
> RYAN: Yeah
>
> ER: At other schools?
>
> DAVID: In Year Seven, but they're too old for us

•   •   •

> ER: Why's that?
>
> SEAN: Coz we don't want to/
>
> JAKE: I'm waiting until the comp/
>
> ER: You're waiting until the comp are you?
>
> RYAN: Yeah, and I'm waiting till my brother brings one home then I'll know what to do

•   •   •

> [responding to a discussion on the lack of sexual activity amongst boyfriends and girlfriends in their class]
>
> RYAN: They don't do anything, they just hold hands
>
> DAVID: Yeah, real boyfriends and girlfriends kiss properly and stuff and go around each other's houses

Drawing upon developmental discourses of childhood innocence (i.e. sexual immaturity), and exposing and positioning their peers' 'relationships' as phoney (not 'real'), Ryan, David, Jake and Sean provide a legitimate rejection to be part of the heterosexualised culture of their peers, whilst simultaneously confirming their imagined, and perhaps superior ('proper'), albeit delayed heterosexualised trajectories as older 'comprehensive' boys. It also allowed them to position boys who 'just sit and talk' with their girlfriends as subordinate and (hetero)sexually inferior [7]. However, it was not an easy position to maintain. Their 'heterosexuality' could be called into question if they failed to successfully demonstrate hegemonic forms of masculinity in other ways (usually through 'fighting' or 'football'). As I have reported in earlier papers (Renold, 1997, 2000) and as others have noted (Connolly, 1994) the two routes through which boys defined their hegemonic masculinity were usually girlfriends and sport. For example, Ryan's positioning, as successful 'sportsman', immediately follows his negative response to having a girlfriend:

> ER: So what about you three, any girlfriends, David? (shakes his head), Ryan? (shakes his head), Jake? (shakes his head) . . . so no girlfriends/
>
> RYAN: I got up to novice two in [go]carting.

However, the need to for boys to outwardly perform their heterosexualised masculinity to others could not solely be achieved by demonstrating their sporting skills. Indeed, in the pursuit of a hegemonic heterosexual masculinity, which seemed to be increasingly undermined by the refusal of girls to occupy passive sexual subject positions in 'real' boyfriend/girlfriend relationships (Renold, 2000), heterosexual identifications were displayed in ways that were not directly undermined or challenged.

 ## 'GOD, I WISH I COULD HAVE SEX': HETEROSEXUAL FANTASIES, 'SEX TALK', MISOGYNY AND SEXUALISED HARASSMENT

Boys who did not regularly 'go-out' or form heterosexual relationships with girls and even some of those who did, would define and construct their 'heterosexuality' through publicly projecting their heterosexual fantasies and desires. They located themselves firmly as (hetero)sexual subjects both within and outside classroom spaces in a variety of ways from public and private declarations for greater sexual knowledge to the sexual objectification of girls and women.

Public Desire for Sexual Knowledge   (comments follow from a sex education lesson)

PETE: We want to know more about the girls

ER: OK, so what did you want to know more about the girls? . . .
(few seconds silence and embarrassed looks)

PETE: We are interested because when you get older you've got to some-timeerer . . . coz when I'm older I won't be able to do it will I, I won't be able to/

COLIN: Yeah sometime or other you'll have to do something beginning with 's' and ending in 'x'/

ER: Sex

COLIN AND DARREN: Yeah

TIMOTHY: You wouldn't know how to would you/

.   .   .

PETE: What's the point of having sex education if you, if it's not really showing it and it's just showing your genitals and all that stuff

.   .   .

PETE: Yeah it hasn't got enough detail, it hasn't got enough details/

ER: So you want more detail

PETE AND TIMOTHY: Yeah

PETE: We want to know we want to have a man and a lady, real, having it off/

.   .   .

TIMOTHY: Today when that bloke was shaving naked they had him on for a bout three minutes and had the girl on/

DARREN: For three seconds bathing this other girl

PETE: All it shows was their boobies

ER: So you wanted to see more?

DARREN: More breast stroke (they all laugh)

Sexualising Lyric

The bell rings, signalling the end of break-time. Adrian walks across the playground singing out loud his version of Michael Jackson's *Earth Song* which has a number of lines beginning 'what about . . .'. He changes the end of the line with 'what about erections?', 'what about sex?', 'what about masturbation?'

Sexualising Classroom Talk

Mrs Fryer tries to quieten the class down. She asks them to put their lips together. Adrian shouts out 'oo err, I'm not kissing everyone in this class'. Many of the boys and girls start laughing. Mrs Fryer looks at me, smiles, rolls her eyes and gives Adrian a long look (of disapproval?).

Sexual Objectification of Girls and Women

David and Sean prepare the tables for group artwork by covering them in old newspapers. As they spread the newspapers around David comes across a picture of three top-less women posed in an intimate embrace. 'Cor—look at this—I wouldn't mind a bit of that' and he shows up the picture to Sean and a number of boys crowd round. The boys start giggling and Mrs Fryer walks over, saying 'what's the fuss, they're just naked, haven't you seen naked ladies before?'. She takes the paper from them and goes back to her marking.

Sexualisation of Body Parts

TIMOTHY: Stuart gets erections

COLIN: Yeah (they all laugh) he was talking when the video was on and goes 'I've got a stiffy' (more laughter)

Positioning themselves as dominant sexual subjects was achieved in a number of ways. David's public declaration of his sexual desires for super-models (in this case, topless models) and Darren's sexualisation of the girl in the sex education video through his call for more 'breast stroke' illustrates how some boys overtly located themselves as heterosexual using dominant discourses in which 'women are represented as passive objects of male sexual urges, needs and desires' (Mac an Ghaill, 1994, p. 92). Other (hetero)sexualised performances were maintained through more light-hearted engagements, such as altering song lyrics to sexualise the content or introducing sexual innuendo to everyday pedagogic relations. Moreover, the first extract highlights how some boys' thirst for hetero/sexual knowledge far exceeded official sex education programmes. Like Mac an Ghaill's (1994, p. 92) findings amongst older teenage boys, the boys' 'sex-talk' seemed 'publicly to validate their masculinity to their male friends'. All the extracts to some extent reveal boys' experimentation with sex and sexuality as a means of regulating their hetero/sexualities, transcending 'official' (school) sexual discourses and releasing sexual tension through humour (last extract). Pete's fear of being caught-out, not knowing what to do (when the time comes) in future sexual relationships, however, does suggest that some boys could communicate their private insecurities.

Positioning themselves as dominant sexual subjects was also achieved, however, through overt and covert forms of sexualised harassment to their female classmates and peers.

Symbolic Sexual Gestures

The class have been told they can go out—it is now break-time. Neil gets up and as he is walking out, he stops at Carrie's table. Carrie is still sitting down. Neil bends over in front of her so that his face is parallel with hers and wags his tongue up and down directly in front of her face, then walks off. Carrie looks confused and unsettled for a moment and then continues to chat with her friends.

Sexual Swear Words

ER: So what about you Darren?

PETE: Well he's been out with Mandy, I mean, not Mandy, I mean er er Victoria about three times in the past three months init? or something like that and once he went out with her for about a month didn't ya?

DARREN: Mmm

ER: What happened, why aren't you seeing her anymore?

PETE: Because she, because he called her a fucking bitch

Physical Sexual Harassment

ER: Do boys pick on you like they do the their friends?

TRUDY: They punch you in the boobs

ANABEL: Yeah they punch you in the boobs sometimes and pull your bra and that really kills/

TRUDY: Yeah, they go like that (shows me)

ER: Who does that?

ALL: Stu

ANABEL: And Ryan and that

ER: So what do you do to that/

ANABEL: Nothing, we just walk away going like this (hugging chest), 'don't touch me'

Heterosexualised harassment usually took the form of denigrating girls through sexually abusive and aggressive language, gestures or behaviours and in most cases were not reported to teaching (or non-teaching) staff (see Renold, 2002b, for a fuller discussion of sexualised bullying and harassment). On two occasions, a group of boys also took to positioning their class teacher as sexually subordinate (see Walkerdine, 1981) by calling her a 'slag' and a 'bitch' (in an interview): first, when football was banned on the playground and second, when they felt they were receiving unnecessary disciplinary treatment in the classroom. These forms of sexualised harassment/offensive sexualised behaviours were often engaged in by boys who were located lower down the heterosexual hierarchies (Darren for example was continuously 'dumped' in a string of relationships).

What I hope these extracts go some way to illustrate are the overt ways in which boys 'perform' their heterosexuality in a need to confirm their hegemonic heterosexual masculinity and how such performances, particularly the sexual objectification of women and the sexualised harassment (verbal and physical) of their female classmates, re-instated boys' heterosexual dominance, often undermined and denied through conventional and 'real' boyfriend/girlfriend relationships, as Mac an Ghaill explains:

> Externally and internally males attempt to re-produce themselves
> as powerful within social circumstances which remain out of their
> control. (1996, p. 200)

With many boys coupling heterosexual activity with maturity and 'older boys', these sexualised performances could also be interpreted as a direct challenge to the perceived 'asexuality' of the primary school environment and discourses of 'childhood innocence'. They could also be one of the ways in which boys 'collectively explore(d) the newly available forms of authority and autonomy conferred by their position at the 'top of the school' (Redman, 1996, p. 178). Indeed, their entry into heterosexuality and heterosexual discourses/practices could have thus been further reinforced by their chronological positioning within the school.

 ## ANTI-GAY TALK AND 'HOMOPHOBIC' [8] NARRATIVES

As many secondary school-based studies have illustrated, 'homophobic' discourses and anti-gay/lesbian talk and behaviours saturate boys' peer-group cultures, social relations and masculinity-making activities. However, as some primary school-based research (Letts & Sears, 1999) is beginning to uncover, younger children are *also* drawing upon the term 'gay' either as a general form of abuse, where the intention is to unsettle or upset their (usually male) peers, or to target particular boys who fail or choose not to access hegemonic masculine discourses or practices. I would argue, from my own research, that towards the end of children's primary school years, boys outwardly demonstrate a fear and loathing of homosexualities and are highly aware of how anti-gay talk/behaviours (labelling and teasing other boys as 'gay') can police and produce acceptable heterosexual masculinities. I stress 'also' because some authors (Redman, 1996) suggest that 'homosexual anxieties' are not employed as a means of defining and constituting 'normal' heterosexualities until boys are at least 12 to 13 years of age. The following extracts provide a rare discussion of how 'homosexuality' was perceived negatively, with a mixture of fear and disgust:

> RYAN: There was a programme on the other day [it is AIDS week]
>   I turned it off after a while, it was disgusting/
> ER: Why?

RYAN: Because it showed these er two men who dressed up as women and they were er they were having sex and it was really horrible

ER: And you didn't like it, so you turned it off?

RYAN: Yeah

ER: OK . . . why do you think you didn't like it?

RYAN: Well like if you see a women and a man doing it I don't really care and er/

DAVID: Coz everyone does it, every night

RYAN: You see you see people doing it that way then you don't really mind coz that's what most people do and then you see like two men doing it and you know that's horrible, disgusting

. . .

ER: When you say gay Jake what do you mean by that?

JAKE: You know, like/really sad

SEAN: A bender (Sean, Ryan and Jake laugh)/

RYAN: And you can sound gay can't you/

DAVID: Simon/he sounds gay

RYAN: Our next door neighbour/

. . .

JAKE: You know that 'supermarket sweep' (game show)?

ER: Yeah

JAKE: Well there was this man on there/

DAVID: And he (host of show) goes, 'you're really pretty aren't you'

JAKE: Yeah and he won it right, about 2000 pounds and he goes up to him and he can't stop kissing him (laughing) he kisses him about 2000 times/

RYAN: Yeah that's like Michael Barrymore/

JAKE: Yeah and/he smacked Michael Barrymore in the other day/Sean and Ryan: Yeah (they all cheer and clap)/

DAVID: Who did?

ER: Why is that good?

SEAN: Coz he's gay

Anti-gay talk and homophobic performances were expressed more often by boys who did not engage in overt heterosexual boyfriend/girlfriend relationships and more frequently than boys who *did* 'have girlfriends' and who *were* 'going out'. Indeed, the powerlessness experienced by many boys participating in the boyfriend/girlfriend cultures (i.e. being dumped or being used), the precarious position of 'boyfriend' and indeed the ambiguity of initiating physical or emotional intimacies with girls at all, produced some very confusing messages and some rather contradictory heterosexual identities.

Processes of differentiation (from 'homosexualities') and subordination (of alternative masculinities) were all ways in which these boys asserted and attempted to make coherent their heterosexual identities, which Mac an Ghaill and others (Kehily & Nayak, 1997; Redman, 2000) suggest involve external (social) and internal (psychic) processes:

> Heterosexual male students were involved in a double
> relationship of traducing the Other, including women and gays
> (external relations), at the same time as expelling femininity and
> homosexuality from within themselves (internal relations). (Mac an
> Ghaill, 1994, p. 90)

However, the differences in attitudes and homophobic behaviours in my study, seemed not to be based not on 'class' (as in Mac an Ghaill's research) but on their success at being 'tough', 'sporty' and 'cool', and in particular their sustained participation in heterosexual relationships. Unfortunately, what this study does lack, is a detailed discussion of boys' views towards homosexuality. Because of the sensitivity of discussing non-heterosexualities with primary school children, only the boys' perspectives who instigated discussions on homosexuality were recorded. This is surely an area which would benefit from further investigation.

 ## CONCLUSIONS

> Young children, according to commensense understandings, are
> innocent. They neither do, nor should they, know anything about
> sexuality. The fear is that contemporary children 'grow up too
> soon' or are 'not yet ready' for sexual knowledge. (Epstein *et al.*,
> 2001, p. 134)

This paper is situated within a growing recognition that primary schools are far from asexual environments and primary school children cannot be presumed (sexually) innocent (Thorne & Luria, 1986; Davies, 1993; Thorne, 1993; Redman, 1996; Connolly, 1998; Hatcher, 1998; Wallis & VanEvery, 2000; Skelton, 2001). Rather, as Wallis and VanEvery argue, 'sexuality (especially heterosexuality) is not only present but crucial to the organisation of primary schools, both explicitly and implicitly' (2000, p. 411) and thus in ways similar to secondary and further education sectors, a key social and cultural site for the production of children's sexual relations and identities. Primarily, the purpose of this paper has been to make visible and thus break the silence around young children's (het-ero)sexual cultures and shed some analytic light on a specific aspect of the organisational heteronormativity of the primary school—boys' sex-ual cultures and in particular how hegemonic masculinities involve the 'heterosexual presumption'. That is, how being a 'proper boy' involves establishing or at least investing in and projecting a recognisable (and hegemonic) heterosexual identity.

Throughout the paper I have highlighted how all boys are to some extent subject to the pressures of 'compulsory heterosexuality' (most evi-dent in the boyfriend/girlfriend cultures of the school, which even if they were not directly engaged in, were forever positioned in relation to it). I have also shown how boys can feel confused, anxious, and powerless because of the contradictions involved in constructing heterosexualised masculinities through boyfriend/girlfriend discourses (i.e. that intimacy with girls could be simultaneously contaminating *and* masculinity confirm-ing). In an attempt to make coherent ultimately fragile masculinities I argue that the majority of boys come to define and produce their heterosexualities through various public projections of (hetero)sexual fantasies, imagined (hetero)sexual futures, misogynistic objectifications of girls and women and homophobic/anti-gay performances towards boys and sexualised forms of harassment towards girls. Furthermore, all of these 'performances' per-meated and thus ultimately affected everyday classroom and playground interactions and as such became a significant site of learning as Kehily (2002) highlights in her discussion of gender, sexuality and pedagogy in the secondary school:

> Students develop an understanding of the meanings and implica-
> tions of sex-gender categories and also create their own meanings
> in a range of informal encounters. (2002, p. 125)

Indeed, some boys drew upon discourses of 'childhood innocence' and 'older sexualities' to legitimate delaying their active role in boyfriend/girlfriend networks, where others (see Renold, 2002) readily took up the subject position 'boyfriend' to maintain close friendships with female classmates.

Most disturbing, however, was how the regulation of hegemonic het-erosexualities through the policing and shaming of gender (Butler, 1993) which usually occurred when investment in overt heterosexual practices (girlfriends) did not automatically signify hegemonic masculinity. In these cases, such performances have real social and emotional consequences which are damaging for both boys and girls. For example, homophobic/anti-gay performances not only had the effect of subordinating alternative masculinities and non-hegemonic sexualities, but implicitly subordinates femininities and all things 'feminine' (i.e. majority of girls/'girl's activities'). However, in a moral and political climate where children's sexuality and moreover sex/uality education is a contested and contentious space (see the numerous and competing struggles in the UK over the repeal of Section 28 [9]), schools are 'legitimately anxious about the reactions of some parents and worse, the popular press if they stray into territory considered to be too risky' (Epstein *et al.,* 2001, p. 136). Headteachers and teachers are thus placed in a difficult position to openly discuss children's emerging gender and sexual identities and knowledges in ways that can challenge the more prevailing heteronormativity of boys' (and girls') peer group cultures and indeed draw upon the services or formulate the policies needed to support children's more painful and oppressive practices of gender-based and sexualised forms of harassment.

On a more positive note, primary headteachers and teachers committed to creating an anti-oppressive environment that strives for gender equity and celebrates and supports diversity within gender/sexual relations can be encouraged in a number of ways:

- First, there has been a shift in UK education policy under the Local Government Act 2000 (Section 104) stating that teachers must take steps to 'prevent any form of bullying', including 'homophobic bullying' (Social Inclusion: Pupil Support Circular 10/99). This circular also includes a specific reference to peer bullying as a result of 'or related to sexual orientation' (1.32) and includes strategies to address sexual and racial harassment (4.47). Furthermore, the government's anti-bullying pack for schools (DfEE, 2000) also offers detailed advice and guidance to prevent bullying because of perceived or actual sexual orientation. The phrasing, 'related to their sexual orientation' is an important one in relation to the findings of this study insofar as much of the homophobic/anti-gay insults directed at boys are more often related to their gender deviance (from recognisable 'masculine' traits) than their perceived or actual sexual orientation [10]. For those primary headteachers and governers wary of incorporating the term 'sexuality' into their bullying policies, conceptualising and including gender-based harassment as a form of 'bullying' will go some way to raising awareness and challenge the heteronormative status quo (because of the ways in which gender is mediated by and embedded within sexuality).

- While governing bodies have no legal obligation to provide sex education for primary school pupils, the vagueness of primary sex education guidelines create gaps which any school can harness to tackle the more oppressive forms of gendered and sexualised harassment and bullying and develop a broader understanding of sex/uality education (Redman, 1994). For example, Brown (1997) suggests that the National Curriculum Council's (NCC) recommendations on primary sex education which stress *positivity, self-image, bodies, sexuality and relationships* and most importantly, in relation to children, *agency* and *responsibility* can be effectively deployed to construct a more comprehensive and inclusive sex/uality education policy.

- Third, as this research and other studies illustrate, many boys (and girls) are aware of the contradictions and difficulties of securing a hegemonic heterosexual masculinity and respond to 'gentle challenges about the effects of narrowly constructed masculinities' (see Frosh *et al.*, 2002, p. 262). Indeed, group discussions provide a forum for some boys to openly, and sometimes critically, discuss the constraining nature of hegemonic masculinities and can thus be deployed by teachers as one way to explore the 'knock-on effect' of 'doing boy' in hegemonic ways (see MacNaughton, 2002). Group-based activities, if sensitively handled, can also be useful 'starting points' (see Kenway *et al.*, 1997) for those teachers creating policies that are grounded in children's own experiences. This is especially important given the increasing recognition that pupils be more involved and active in the policy making process (Alderson, 2000). As Skelton (2001) notes, however, any specific strategy (whether it be to tackle homophobic bullying or sexualised harassment more widely) must be integrated within a whole-school approach to gender equity and one that focuses on gender relations—girls *and* boys, masculinities *and* femininities and the power relations at play in their often oppositional construction.

While there are obviously no quick-fix solutions there are opportunities and developments (and gaps) in both policy and practice for committed teachers to support pupil's emerging gender and sexual identities and combat the damaging consequences of negotiating a heteronormative world.

NOTES

1. Tipton Primary's catchment area served white 'working' and 'middle' class families, while Hirstwood served predominantly white 'middle' class families.
2. Each child participated in a series of group interviews/discussions (six times in total) over the period of a year. Indeed, I visited each school for 2/3 days every fortnight during that year.
3. Other studies have highlighted how even 4- and 5-year-olds 'practice heterosexuality' through dating games and kiss chase (Epstein, 1997a; Connolly, 1998; Skelton, 2001).
4. The subject positions of 'boyfriend' and 'girlfriend' were discursively reproduced and maintained daily via 'messengers' (usually female) who mediated and relayed love letters, dumping letters and requests to be X's boyfriend or girlfriend.

5. Despite the active connotation of the phrase 'going out', couples rarely went anywhere. 'Going out' was a particular discourse which signified and made available the subject position 'boyfriend' or 'girlfriend' and could range from a 'couple' spending time together in their lunch break (holding hands, chatting, kissing) to simply *saying* you were 'going out' with someone.

6. I have argued elsewhere how some girls reported experiencing a great deal of power from being able to terminate relationships. For some, it seemed the only domain in which they could 'get one over the boys'.

7. Indeed, I argue in another paper how some boys draw upon the discourses and engage in the practices of the boyfriend/girlfriend culture to maintain close friendships with girls and avoid the macho-making activities associated with fighting and football free (almost) from ridicule and speculation over their gender/sexual identities (Renold, 2002).

8. I am using the term 'homophobic' to define those behaviours and practices which signify a fear of 'homosexuality' and the term 'anti-gay' to define talk and behaviour that signifies any negative sentiment regarding same-sex identities, practices or relationships. While there is obviously some overlap, differentiating 'homophobia' from 'anti-gay' sentiment offers a way of situating the realm of the unconscious within wider social and cultural relations (see Redman, 2000, for a fuller discussion of the usefulness of the term 'homophobia' as an analytic tool).

9. Section 28 of the 1988 Local Government Act prohibits local education authorities from 'promoting' the teaching of 'homosexuality as a pretended family relationship'. While Section 28 has been repealed in Scotland it has undergone two defeated repeals in England and Wales (see Redman, 1994; Epstein, 2000, and Moran, 2001, for a wider discussion of Section 28).

10. However, advice and guidance to date has centred on older children and teenagers.

REFERENCES

Butler, J. (1990) *Gender Trouble: Feminism and the Subversion of Identity* (London, Routledge).

Butler, J. (1993) *Bodies That Matter: On the Discursive Limits of Sex* (London, Routledge).

Brown, T. (1997) Sex Education, in: M. Cole, D. Hill & S. Shan (Eds) *Promoting Equality in Primary Schools* (London, Routledge).

Connell, R. W. (1995) *Masculinities: Knowledge, Power and Social Change* (Cambridge, Polity Press).

Connolly, P. (1994) Boys will be boys? Racism, sexuality and the construction of masculine identities amongst infant boys, in: J. Holland & M. Blair (Eds) *Debates and Issues in Feminist Research and Pedagogy* (Clevedon, Multilingual Matters).

Connolly, P. (1998) *Racisms, Gendered Identities and Young Children: Social Relations in a Multi-ethnic, Inner-city Primary School* (London, Routledge).

Davies, B. (1993) *Shards of Glass: Children Reading and Writing Beyond Gendered Identities* (New Jersey, Hampton Press).

Epstein, D. (1997a) Cultures of schooling/cultures of sexuality, *International Journal of Inclusive Education*, 1, pp. 37–53.

Epstein, D. (1997b) Boyz' own stories: masculinities and sexualities in schools, *Gender and Education,* 9, pp. 105–117.

Epstein, D. (2000) 'Promoting homophobia: Section 28, schools and young people', *ChildRight,* 164, pp. 14–15.

Epstein, D. & Johnson, R. (1994) On the straight and narrow: the heterosexual presumption, homophobias and schools, in: D. Epstein (Ed.) *Challenging Lesbian and Gay Inequalities in Education* (Buckingham, Open University Press).

Epstein, D. & Johnson, R. (1998) *Schooling Sexualities* (Buckingham, Open University Press).

Epstein, D., O'Flynn, S. & Telford, D. (2001) 'Othering' education: sexualities, silences and schooling, *Review of Research in Education,* 25, pp. 127–179.

Frosh, S., Phoenix, A. & Pattman, R. (2002) *Young Masculinities* (Hampshire, Palgrave).

Hatcher, R. (1995) Boyfriends, girlfriends: gender and 'race' in children's cultures, *International Play Journal,* 3, pp. 187–197.

Haywood, C. (1996) Out of the curriculum: sex talking, talking sex, *Curriculum Studies,* 4, pp. 229–251.

Kehily, M.J. (2001) Bodies in school: young men, embodiment and heterosexual masculinities, *Men and Masculinities,* 4, pp. 178–186.

Kehily, M.J. (2001) Issues of gender and sexuality in schools, in: B. Francis & C. Skelton (Eds) *Investigating Gender: Contemporary Perspectives in Education* (Buckingham, Open University Press).

Kehily, M.J. & Nayak, A. (1996) Playing it straight: masculinities, homophobias and schooling, *Journal of Gender Studies,* 5, pp. 211–229.

Kehily, M.J. & Nayak, A. (1997) Lads and laughter: humour and the production of heterosexual hierarchies, *Gender and Education,* 9, pp. 69–87.

Kenway, J. & Willis, S. with Blackmore, J. & Rennie, L. (1997) Are boys victims of feminism in schools?: Some answers from Australia, *International Journal of Inclusive Education,* 1, pp. 19–35.

Laskey, L. & Beavis, C. (1996) *Schooling and Sexualities: Teaching for a Positive Sexuality* (Geelong, Victoria, Deakin University Centre for Change).

Letts IV, W. & Sears, J.T. (Eds) (1999) *Queering Elementary Education: Advancing the Dialogue About Sexualities and Schooling* (New York, Rowman and Littlefield).

Mac An Ghaill, M. (1994) *The Making of Men: Masculinities, Sexualities and Schooling* (Open University Press, Buckingham).

Mac An Ghaill, M. (1996) Deconstructing heterosexualities within school arenas, *Curriculum Studies,* 4, pp. 191–207.

MacNaughton, G. (2000) *Rethinking Gender in Early Childhood Education* (London, Paul Chapman).

Mahony, P. & Jones, C. (Eds) (1989) *Learning Our Lines: Sexuality and Social Control in Education* (London, Women's Press).

Moran, S. (2001) Childhood sexuality and education: the case of Section 28, *Sexualities,* 4, pp. 73–89.

Nayak, A. & Kehily, M.J. (1997) Masculinities and schooling: why are young men so homophobic?, in: D.L. Steinberg, D. Epstein & R. Johnson (Eds) *Border Patrols: Policing the Boundaries of Heterosexuality* (Cassel, London).

Redman, P. (1994) Shifting ground: rethinking sexuality education, in: D. Epstein (Ed.) *Challenging Lesbian and Gay Inequalities in Education* (Buckingham, Open University Press).

Redman, P. (1996) Curtis loves Ranjit: heterosexual masculinities, schooling, and pupils' sexual cultures, *Educational Review,* 48, pp. 175–182.

Redman, P. (2000) Tarred with the same brush: homophobia and the unconscious in school-based cultures of masculinity, *Sexualities,* 3, pp. 483–499.

Redman, P. (2001) The discipline of love: negotiation and regulation in boys' performance of a romance-based heterosexual masculinity, *Men and Masculinities,* 4, pp. 186–200.

Renold, E. (1997) All they've got on their brains is football: sport, masculinity and the gendered practices of playground relations, *Sport, Education and Society,* 2, pp. 5–23.

Renold, E. (2002) *Primary school studs: (de)constructing heterosexual masculinities in the primary school,* paper presented at British Association Annual Conference, 25–27 March 2002, University of Leicester.

Renold, E. (2002a) 'Tales of the Unexpected': researching sexuality in the primary school, in: L. Pugsley & T. Welland (Eds) *Ethical Dilemmas in Qualitative Research* (Aldershot, Ashgate).

Renold, E. (2002b) 'Presumed innocence': (hetero)sexual, homophobic and heterosexist harassment amongst children in the primary school, *Childhood,* 9, pp. 415–433.

Renold, E. (2001) Learning the 'hard' way: boys, hegemonic masculinity and the negotiation of learner identities in the primary school, *British Journal of Sociology of Education,* 22, pp. 39–385.

Renold, E. (2000) 'Coming out': gender (hetero)sexuality and the primary school, *Gender and Education,* 12, pp. 309–327.

Renold, E. (1999) Presumed innocence: an ethnographic investigation into the construction of children's gender and sexual identities in the primary school (Unpublished Doctoral Dissertation, Cardiff University).

Rich, A. (1983) Compulsory heterosexuality and lesbian existence, *Signs,* 5, pp. 631–660.

Skelton, C. (2001) *Schooling the Boys: Masculinities and Primary Education* (Buckingham, Open University Press).

Thorne, B. (1993) *Gender Play: Boys and Girls in School* (Buckingham, Open University Press).

Thorne, B. & Luria, Z. (1986) Sexuality and gender in children's daily worlds, *Social Problems,* 33, pp. 176–190.

Wallis, A. & Vanevery, J. (2000) Sexuality in the primary school, *Sexualities,* 3, pp. 409–423.

QUESTIONS FOR CRITICAL THINKING

Reading 14

1. Renold discusses the ways in which children in primary schools construct heterosexual identities, even at very early ages. What are some of
   the ways that you have witnessed the gendered behaviors of girls and
   boys that later influence the construction of their sexuality as women
   and men?

2. The experiences of the children in this article indicate that heterosexual
   behavior doesn't necessarily come "naturally" to girls and boys but is
   constructed. In your opinion, how does this challenge everyday representations of heterosexuality as the norm?

3. Do you think it is possible that we can "deconstruct" sexuality? What
   would be the implications for society if we were to be successful in
   doing so?

Reading 15

SEXUAL IDENTITY AND BISEXUAL IDENTITIES
The Struggle for Self-Description in a Changing Sexual Landscape

PAULA C. RUST

As we look back over our lives, we construct them as stories. A story
has a conclusion, and the story line leads inexorably to the conclusion;
events and details that are irrelevant to the conclusion are irrelevant
to the story and distract the listener from the "real" story. When we construct
our life stories, we tend to forget the irrelevant details of our pasts. We identify the relevant experiences and interpret them as the building blocks that
made us into the people we are today, and we understand our past changes
as the twists and turns in the road we took to reach our current selves. Even
if we recognize that we have not yet completed our personal journeys and
that we will continue to rewrite our stories until we reach the final draft at

Paula C. Rust, "Sexual Identity and Bisexual Identities: The Struggle for Self-
Description in a Changing Sexual Landscape" from *Queer Studies: A Lesbian, Gay,
Bisexual, and Transgender Anthology,* edited by Brett Beeyman and Mickey Eliason.
Reprinted with the permission of New York University Press.

death, we still perceive our pasts as the paths by which we arrived at our present selves. Most of us who identify our present selves as gay, lesbian, or bisexual have constructed "coming out stories" that explain—to ourselves and to others—how we arrived at our sexual self-definitions.

Social scientists in the 1970s, seeking to redress the scientific sins that had been committed against lesbian and gay people in the past, sought to understand the lives of lesbian and gay people as they (we) understood their (our) own lives. Taking the cue from their lesbian and gay subjects, many sociologists and psychologists set out to study the process of coming out, i.e., the process of lesbian or gay identity formation. Researchers soon discovered "milestone events," or life events that lesbian and gay people had identified as relevant to their development and incorporated into their coming out stories. Typical milestone events were the first experience of a feeling of sexual attraction for someone of the same sex, the first sexual experience with someone of the same sex, the first labeling of one's self as homosexual, the first public expression of one's homosexual identity to significant others, the symbolic switch from a homosexual to a lesbian or gay identity as one's self-acceptance increased and, eventually, the integration of one's private and public identities as one came out of the closet.

Based on these observations, scientists elaborated developmental models of coming out that construct it as a linear process of self-discovery in which a false, socially imposed heterosexual identity is replaced with a lesbian or gay identity that accurately reflects the essence of the individual. These models rarely account for bisexual identity as an authentic identity; when they acknowledge bisexual identity at all, they usually cast it as a phase one might pass through on the way to adopting a lesbian or gay identity.[1] Researchers operating within these linear developmental models of coming out asked respondents for the ages at which they experienced each milestone, and then, reporting the average ages, described coming out as an ordered sequence of events. From this research, we learned that lesbians first experience sexual attraction to other women at an average age of twelve or thirteen, but do not become aware of these sexual feelings until late adolescence. They begin suspecting that they are lesbian at an average age of eighteen, but do not adopt lesbian identities until their early twenties. We learned that gay men experience these events at younger ages and in more rapid sequence than lesbians, and—from the few studies that treated bisexual identity as authentic—we learned that bisexuals come out later and more slowly than gays and lesbians.[2] Based on these findings, researchers began theorizing about why men come out more quickly than women and why bisexuals come out more slowly than monosexuals.

The portrait of sexual identity formation that is painted by these average ages is not only grossly simplified but factually inaccurate. Based on research with lesbian-identified and bisexual-identified women.[3] I have shown that average ages conceal a great deal of variation in the coming out process, both among and between lesbian and bisexual women.[4] In contrast to the linear portrait painted by average ages, lesbian and bisexual women experience each milestone event at a wide range of ages; many women do not experience all of the so-called milestone events; women who do experience these events experience them in various orders, and some women experience some events repeatedly.

Moreover, I discovered that the "finding" that bisexual women come out more slowly than lesbians is an artifact of the statistical methods used in studies based on linear models of coming out. When I calculated average ages for the over 400 women in my first study, the results confirmed earlier findings that bisexual women come out at later ages and more slowly than lesbian women. Bisexual women first felt attracted to women at an average age of 18.1, compared to 15.4 for lesbian women. Bisexual women first questioned their heterosexual identity 1.9 years later, at an average of 20.0 years, whereas lesbians first questioned their heterosexual identity 1.6 years later, at an average age of 17.0. But a closer look at the data revealed that lesbian women were twice as likely as bisexual women to have questioned their heterosexual identity before they felt attracted to women (28% vs. 14%), probably because some women were encouraged by lesbian feminist arguments about the political nature of lesbianism to identify themselves as lesbian even in the absence of sexual feelings toward women. Among women who questioned their heterosexual identities only after feeling attracted to other women, bisexual women actually did so sooner—not later—than lesbian women. In other words, the original finding that bisexual women come out more slowly than lesbian women was an artifact resulting from a failure to recognize variations in the coming out process as equally authentic patterns, rather than as deviations from an underlying linear course.

I also discovered that bisexual women had changed sexual identities more frequently in the past than lesbian women, often alternating repeatedly between lesbian and bisexual identities. Under linear developmental models, this finding would be taken as an indication of the instability of bisexual identity and the sociopsychological immaturity of bisexual-identified individuals.[5] Under more sophisticated, but still linear, social interactionist understandings of the creation of identity, this finding would be taken as evidence of the difficulty of constructing a bisexual identity in a social world that offers only two authenticated categories, heterosexual and homosexual.[6] But I also discovered that, at any given moment, a bisexual woman was as likely to be satisfied with her current sexual identity as a lesbian was with hers. This finding disproves the hypothesis that bisexual women are engaged in a constant struggle to establish a satisfactory sexual identity and suggests instead that bisexual women find different sexual identities satisfactory at different times and under different circumstances. Bisexual women's frequent identity changes do not indicate a state of searching immaturity, but a mature state of mutability.

Previous researchers have attempted to modify the linear model of coming out by introducing feedback loops, alternate routes, and contingencies.[7]

Although these modifications produce models with ample room for deviation, they do not effectively describe the formation of sexual identity. They are unable to account for the findings that bisexual women incorporate their same-sex feelings into sexual identities more quickly than lesbians and that bisexual women are as satisfied with their sexual identities as lesbians are. This inability highlights the need to develop a new model of the identity formation process.

To accommodate the empirical reality of identity change processes, linear developmental models of coming out must be abandoned in favor of a social constructionist view of identity as a description of the location of the self in relation to other individuals, groups, and institutions. The individuals, groups, and institutions to which we relate are landmarks on a sexual landscape that is itself socially constructed. From this perspective, identity change would be understood as a process of modifying one's self-description in response to changes in either the location of the self or the socially constructed landscape on which one is located. Identity change would be a necessary outcome of one's efforts to maintain an accurate self-description, not an indication that one has not yet achieved an accurate self-description. "Coming out" would not be a process of essential discovery leading to a mature and stable identity, but merely one story constructed around one of the myriad identity changes we all go through as mature adults attempting to maintain accurate self-descriptions in a changing social environment. Research on the so-called "coming out process" would be reconceptualized as research on the social contexts of identity changes that take place throughout life, and the goal of this research would be to discover the types of contextual changes that motivate individual identity change.

In the spring of 1993, I began a second study guided by the concept of sexual identity as a description of the self in relation to other individuals, groups, and institutions.[8] The overall goal of the study is to document the development of bisexual identity, community, and politics in the United States, the United Kingdom, and other, primarily English-speaking, countries. A specific goal of the study is to explore the types of contextual changes that lead individuals to change their sexual identities, with an eye toward understanding why currently bisexual-identified individuals tend to have changed their sexual identities frequently in the past. The study includes people of all gender and sexual identities, including transsexuals and transgenderists.

CHANGES IN ONE'S LOCATION ON THE SEXUAL LANDSCAPE

The most common type of change reported by individuals is change in their own locations on the sexual landscape. Change is relative, and can only be defined in relation to objects other than the self; these objects might be other individuals, social groups, or social and political institutions. Many respondents recalled that they changed their sexual identities when they developed new relationships with particular people, usually romantic or sexual relationships with people whose genders were different from the genders of the people with whom they had expected to become intimately involved. For example, a White American[9] woman who used to identify herself as a Lesbian[10] explained why she began to identify herself as Bisexual:

> About two years ago, I had been in a sexual relationship with a wonderful woman for one year, and I was identifying as lesbian at the time. I found myself attracted to a man who was interested in me. I had a sense of being at a crossroads: lesbian or "something else." She wanted a monogamous relationship and . . . I didn't want that conservatism. We broke up and I began a sexual relationship with the man.[11]

Her previous Lesbian identity represented her sexual relationship with a woman. It also represented her lack of relationship with a man, as evidenced by the fact that it had to change when she began to feel attracted to a man. The conflict between her Lesbian identity and her attraction to a man created, for her, a crossroads, i.e., the moment of change. When this attraction led to a sexual relationship with the man, she adopted a Bisexual identity that apparently represents both her (ex-)relationship to a woman and her current relationship to a man. The new identity represents her new location on the sexual landscape, a location that is described in relation to two other individuals, a woman and a man.

Sometimes the new relationship is not an actual sexual or physical one but merely a feeling of attraction toward another person, as was the case with an Irish woman who identified herself as Bisexual when she "[r]ealiz[ed] I was experiencing a sexual fantasy about a female friend." Or the relationships represented by an identity might be potential relationships. For example, a White man explained that he began identifying as a Gay Bisexual when he "recognized the reality of my past (and potential future) relationships."

For some respondents, a single relationship with an individual—whether actual, desired, or potential—is not enough to motivate a complete identity change. These respondents' identities represent their relationships to entire social groups, and they do not change their sexual identities until their relationships with individuals lead them to perceive changes in their relationships to entire social groups. For example, a Jewish Lesbian said that she fell in love with "a woman," but it was not until she realized she "was sexually attracted to women" that she "suddenly saw the possibility and even inevitability of a different (i.e., lesbian) erotic self-definition." In other words, noting that the individual with whom she had developed a relationship belonged to the social group "women," she generalized her feelings to the entire social group by "realizing" that she could potentially be attracted to any member of that group. She then adopted a Lesbian identity to represent her new relationship to this social group. Another woman explained that she did not begin to call herself Bi until her relationship to an individual man led to the realization that she was attracted to men as a social group. She wrote,

> I had been involved with a man for about two years, during which time I identified as "a lesbian who happens to be seeing a man until something else comes along." After a while I realized that I was really deeply committed to my other-sex relationship. . . . Also I became aware that I was starting to feel more generalized attraction to men other than just my lover. So "bi" seemed more accurate.

Lesbian-identified, gay-identified, and heterosexual-identified respondents often described their identities as representing a single relationship to either an individual, a group, or an institution, whereas bisexual-identified respondents usually said that their identities represent multiple relationships to various individuals, social groups, and institutions. The larger number of relationships needed to anchor bisexual identity is a function of two facts. First, landmarks in the mainstream Euro-American sexual landscape are gendered. For example, individuals are recognized as either female or male, woman or man. Social groups include "men," "women," and "lesbians," and institutions include "gay male society," "legally recognized marriage," and "the feminist movement." Second, Euro-American sexual categories are defined in reference to gender; heterosexuality is defined in terms of relationships between persons of different gender, and homosexuality is defined in terms of relationships between persons of same gender. Thus, on the gendered sexual landscape, a minimum of one landmark is necessary to anchor a monosexual identity such as lesbian, gay, or heterosexual. But in this system of dichotomous sexuality based on dichotomous gender, bisexuality can only be understood as a hybrid combination of heterosexuality and homosexuality. Thus to maintain a *bi*sexual self-description on the gendered landscape, one needs to locate oneself with respect to both female and male, or lesbian/gay and heterosexual, landmarks.

For example, a bisexual identity might represent relationships to two individuals of different genders, as it does to the White man who explained that he adopted his Bisexual identity because he "dated a man and woman at the same time." Or, it might represent relationships to two social groups, men and women, as it does to the Asian-American/Caucasian individual who wrote, "I realized I have always loved men. . . . At the same time I did not cease to love or feel attracted to women, so I discovered I was bisexual." Many bisexuals' identities represent an attraction to one gender as a social group and an actual physical or emotional relationship with a particular individual of the other gender. As one man explained, the incident that led him to adopt a Bisexual identity was "My first same-sex experience, but I realized I was still attracted to women." Although the particular landmarks varied, most bisexual-identified respondents were able to support their bisexual identities only by maintaining relationships to multiple landmarks of both genders.

CHANGES IN THE SEXUAL LANDSCAPE

Whether or not an individual changes co's[12] location on the sexual land-scape, the sexual landscape itself might change, creating new opportunities for self-description while transforming or eliminating existing possibili-ties. The types of landscape change reported by respondents included the appearance of previously invisible landmarks on the sexual landscape and historical changes in the sexual landscape.

Newly visible landmarks might consist of a single individual. For exam-ple, one Heterosexual-identified, Bisexual American woman wrote that she "had to sharpen up my own fuzzy feeling about my own bisexuality" when her daughter came out to her as bisexual. The appearance of a bisexual per-son in her life forced her to consider her relationship to this person, and in the process, to clarify her thoughts about her own sexuality. Conversely, the disappearance of an individual can eliminate the need for an identity that represents one's relationship to that individual, as it did for this Australian woman:

> I really craved to be a "lesbian" or "bisexual"—but somehow I
> couldn't take this label unless I had sexual encounters with
> women. . . . My period of confusion and questioning my
> heterosexuality passed away [when] the woman I was attracted
> to left—so I told myself I was hetero again.

Historical changes, such as the development of social and political movements, create new social groups and institutions and modify or destroy others. As these historical forces transform the sexual landscape, individuals whose identities located them on the old landscape find that they have to relate themselves to their new environment. For example, in the very early days of the second wave of the (predominantly white) feminist movement, lesbianism was labeled a "lavender herring," and feminist lesbians were encouraged to demonstrate their commitment to the feminist movement by remaining in the closet.[13] But the reconstruction of the relationship between lesbianism and feminism in the early 1970s resulted in the creation of the category of the "political lesbian" and led many women to adopt lesbian identities as an expression of commitment to the newly reconstituted femi-nist movement.[14] One respondent wrote that in 1977 she adopted her Les-bian identity because "Thru feminist politics I began to understand that my primary emotional/energetic commitment was with women." Several years earlier, a lesbian identity would not have served to express her feminist "emotional/energetic commitment" to women.

More recently, the development of a small but growing bisexual culture and social structure has created new social and political landmarks with which individuals can anchor bisexual identities. For example, an American woman mentioned that she had realized that she was bisexual since 1976, but that she only adopted a Bisexual identity "in the last five years since there was a movement." Another woman said that she "had previously identified as a Lesbian," but she "became aware of the Bi option" because "there was a growing, visible Bi community." As the number of bisexual social and political institutions continues to increase, more and more people will identify themselves as bisexual, abandoning the identities that they had considered satisfactory only a few years earlier—identities that became unsatisfactory because the landmarks to which they referred changed and new landmarks arose.

Individuals often experience changes in their personal social contexts. It is only later, when individuals look back over their lives and the lives of others, that they will see the changes they experienced as part of more global, historical contexts that had similar effects on other people. Therefore, few respondents referred to the effect of history on their sexual identities, but this lack of reference to historical change was complemented by an abundance of references to changes in respondents' individual social contexts. These alterations in social context were usually significant because they brought with them changes in the language available for self-description.

 ## CHANGES IN THE LANGUAGE AVAILABLE FOR SELF-DESCRIPTION

The distinction between changes in the sexual landscape—whether historical or personal—and changes in language is largely theoretical; in practice, they are usually interdependent and virtually indistinguishable. The relevant distinction between different constructions of the sexual landscape is in the language available for self-description, and the relevant distinctions between various languages are the different landmarks and the different relationships to these landmarks that are created by each language, i.e., in the various ways that they construct the sexual landscape.

Some people intentionally put themselves in new social contexts in the hope of finding a new language for self-description. For example, a White American woman said that she went to Coming Out Day in 1990 because she was unsure about her sexuality, but by the time she left, she was a Dyke. Several respondents mentioned that they had read the book *Bi Any Other Name: Bisexual People Speak Out,* and that this book had helped them develop bisexual identities. A Latino-American man explained that he was able to come out as Bisexual after he joined a therapy group in which a bisexual identity was available.

> I joined a bisexual men's therapy group (while still with my female partner). I had always heard the term but never really claimed it until I joined this group. I think I knew that that's what I was but when you're living in a straight environment, you don't talk about it.

Other people, through no conscious intent of their own, find themselves in social contexts where they become involved in new relationships or encounter new identities, and then discover that they can use these identities to describe themselves. For example, a Native American/Caucasian man reexamined his own "repressed bisexuality" when he observed culturally approved intimacy among men while working in the Middle East. A Caucasian man became a "punk" while serving time in a U.S. jail; he explained that he "got used to it and they treated me well so I got emotionally involved with them and dependent on them for security. There was no other term for that role." An Indian woman living in the U.S. was introduced to the Kinsey scale during a seminar on religion and sexuality. She learned that everyone "existed somewhere on this continuum" and scored herself right in the middle. Reflecting on the experience, she stated: "From that moment on, I have thought of myself continuously as someone who is what I would call today 'bisexual.'" An English man explained that he "never really 'began' to think of myself as bisexual, any more than I guess most straights begin to think of themselves as straight." He had begun to use the word "bisexual" after seeing it appear more and more frequently on electronic mail postings.

Because the terms "lesbian" and "gay" are now nearly household words, they are available as self-descriptors even outside lesbian and gay social contexts. In contrast, the concept of an authentic bisexual identity is still limited to particular social contexts, and many bisexual-identified respondents reported that they had adopted their current sexual identities only after encountering the term "bisexual" for the first time when they joined a bisexual support group, therapy group, or political group. Before they encountered the concept of bisexuality, the only terms that were available to them were synonyms for heterosexual and homosexual. Most had chosen one of these two available identities based on their conceptions of the types of relationships that could be represented by each. For example, one man called himself heterosexual, although he had a male sexual partner, because he preferred his wife as a sexual partner. For him, a heterosexual identity was an accurate description of his location on the sexual landscape because it did not deny his relationship to his male lover; it merely indicated that his relationship to his female lover was stronger. When his male partner introduced him to the term "bisexual," he discovered that bisexual identity could also describe his location by representing both of his relationships, and he changed his identity accordingly.

Language also changes when familiar terms take on new meanings or change in meaning. Many respondents reported that they had been familiar with the term "bisexual" for some time but had understood it as a temporary phase that one passed through when coming out as lesbian or gay or as an identity used by those who wish to deny their homosexuality. Once they encountered the term as a reference to a stable set of relationships involving both female and male landmarks, they became comfortable describing themselves as bisexual. For example, one woman encountered a new meaning for "bisexual" when she began associating with a new group of people:

> [I] went to a bisexual convention. Though I'd known that I liked women and I like men, meeting a group of people who had chosen this as a viable identity—not just a resting place between gay and straight—gave me a word to use with myself and a sense of legitimacy.

In contrast, another woman felt that the meaning of the word had changed over time, eventually enabling her to adopt it as an identity:

> For a long time, I was afraid to say I was bisexual, because it was largely regarded as a term for a lesbian who didn't want to "fess up" and I knew women who were like this and who used the term this way. I've only started calling myself "bisexual" in the last five years, because the term seems to have lost the "closeted lesbian" connotation.

For some individuals, a change in the meaning of a term allowed them to maintain an identity that might otherwise have had to change or forced them to change an identity that they might otherwise have been able to keep. An Anglo-American man explained that his concept of "gay" had recently broadened; previously, if he had had a heterosexual encounter, he would have given up his gay identity, but now he says, "If I were to have an occasional heterosexual encounter, I'd still call myself gay, not bisexual." Conversely, a woman who used to identify herself "solely as a Lesbian" was "distressed at the trend of women who used the word "Lesbian" to be femme, hetero-appearing career women with closet politics." Because of this trend, she no longer feels that the word "lesbian" adequately describes herself; she now calls herself a Dyke, among other things, and is "still sad over the loss of the label Lesbian."

CHANGES IN SOCIAL CONTEXT

The fact that different relationships and languages for self-description are available in different social contexts means that individuals who live their lives in multiple social contexts—which most people do, particularly those who identify as sexual minorities and/or as members of racial or ethnic minorities—have to describe themselves differently in different social contexts. The act of moving from one context to another entails a change in sexual identity simply to maintain an accurate description of one's location on the sexual landscape. At the very least, an individual might have to use different terms to describe coself in a heterosexual context than co uses in a sexual minority context and different terms in a Euro-American cultural context than in other racial and ethnic contexts.

For example, a Jewish-American man explained that he often describes himself as "queer" in gay circles because "it expresses my political identity," but that he "generally use[s] 'bi' in straight circles, since 'queer' is generally considered pejorative." In heterosexual contexts, the term "queer" does not accurately convey his sexual location because the political institution to which it refers—a radical sexual movement—is largely unknown. In contrast to Euro-American sexual culture, which emphasizes the genders of one's sexual partners, the Chicano cultures described by Joseph Carrier incorporate the Mexican cultural emphasis on the role one plays in the sex act over the gender of one's partner.[15] Thus, for Chicanos, the development of a gay identity requires a measure of assimilation to Euro-American culture, and this identity is only viable in contexts in which Euro-American concepts of sexuality operate. A Chicano, therefore, would have to describe his sexuality differently depending on the particular ethnic context he is in.

Even within LesBiGayTrans communities, there are contextual variations that necessitate identity changes as one moves from one part of a community to another. Some women identify themselves as bisexual only among other bisexuals and avoid identifying themselves as bisexual among lesbians, because a positive bisexual identity is often not available in lesbian contexts. Among lesbians, they might identify themselves as "lesbians," or they might call themselves "queer," because they feel that this is the most accurate identity available in that context. An Asian-American woman explained that she calls herself "bi" proudly—but only in certain contexts, because in other contexts her bi identity would be misunderstood and, hence, not accurately describe her location on the sexual landscape:

> [I]n a college environment, there are a few "fakes"—bi women who really do embody lots of bad bi stereotypes. In order not to be lumped in with them, I avoid that term here. However, when I go somewhere more Bi-aware . . . more aware of the diversity of us Bi women, I proudly use the term. . . . I think context is very important.

CHANGES IN THE ACCURACY OF SELF-DESCRIPTION

Individuals do not always describe their locations accurately, and identity changes occur as individuals become more accurate or more honest about describing their locations on the sexual landscape. There are many reasons that individuals might intentionally misrepresent their locations, but the most common reason is a belief that other people would disapprove of their true location. Lesbians and gay men often misrepresent their sexual locations when in heterosexual contexts, and bisexual women often misrepresent their location when in lesbian contexts. For example, a White American woman reported that she thinks of herself as a "bi dyke," but until recently, she called herself "queer," because she was afraid "bi dyke" would offend lesbians. She explained that "queer" was a word that she could "use among gay men and lesbians without them knowing I'm bisexual." Unlike the Asian-American woman quoted above, this White woman avoided identify-ing herself as bisexual in gay and lesbian contexts, not because she thought the term would be misunderstood and hence not accurately represent her, but because she wanted to mislead gay men and lesbians who would disap-prove of her true bisexual identity. She also reported that she "just recently felt justified in calling [her]self a 'bi dyke'" among lesbians. In other words, she recently changed the identity she uses in lesbian contexts; this change represented, not a change in her location on the sexual landscape, but a change in her honesty about that location.

Although the politics surrounding bisexual identities are not as intense in gay male communities as they are in lesbian communities, men are also sometimes reluctant to identify themselves as bisexual rather than gay. A Latino man reported that he had known he was bisexual since childhood, but for eleven years he dated women secretly and called himself gay, because he didn't want to lose his friends in the gay community.

It is common for individuals to feel that their previous sexual identities were the result of their own lack of honesty with themselves, even if they did not experience these identities as dishonest at the time. Because "coming out" is traditionally conceptualized as a developmental process of discover-ing and coming to terms with one's essential sexuality, many people perceive their changes in identity as processes of becoming honest with themselves about their sexuality. For example, a Caucasian man wrote, "I began to ques-tion my sexuality and finally admitted that I was in denial about my feelings towards men." Whether the identity changes that these individuals expe-rienced were the result of growing self-honesty, or whether they were the result of actual changes in their relationships or in the languages available to describe their relationships, which in hindsight they interpreted in terms of honesty, is a question that involves a discussion of essential existence that is outside the scope of this article.

Any attempt to create stable bisexual identities or bisexual communities will eventually encounter the same problems that lesbian and gay identities and communities now face. As David Bell points out, despite the theoretical attractiveness and exciting revolutionary potential of conceptualizing bisex-uality as something that exists outside fixed categories, individuals seek-ing a "home" attempt to create positively defined bisexual identities and communities.[16] Indeed, success within current modes of political discourse might necessitate the creation of a bisexual "ethnicity."[17] Creating a bisexual "home" or "ethnicity" is difficult, and during the formative stage these diffi-culties are easily attributed to the adverse conditions afforded by the current gendered, monosexual construction of sexual identity. But, if some people eventually succeed in convincing themselves that they have managed to give a specific and definable form to bisexual identity and bisexual community, they will discover that bisexual identity and community, like their mono-sexual counterparts, need constant defense. At that point, in accordance with the principles of dialectic change, a new antagonist will arise, and the defenders of bisexual identities and communities will be able to attribute their difficulties to the new antagonist, who will be constructed as a threat. But the new antagonist will no more be the real threat to bisexual identities and communities than a bisexual identity is the real threat to monosexual identities and communities. The real threat to all identity-based communities is the dynamic nature of identity itself; the appearance of a new antagonist will merely be the symptom of the tension inherent in attempting to build stable identities and communities on dynamic self-descriptions. The revolutionary potential of a bisexual identity is the potential to expose the dynamic nature of sexuality, and it has this potential only insofar as the current landscape is predominantly monosexual and gendered. If we succeed in reconstructing the sexual landscape to support a bisexual identity, we will have destroyed its revolutionary potential. We will have, in effect, created a new aristocracy and postponed the revolutionization of sexual identity until the arrival of the next antagonist.

Fortunately, bisexual political ideology is not yet moving toward the solidification of a definition of bisexuality. On the contrary, the current tendency is to resist efforts to agree on a definition.[18] If we continue on this path and refuse to follow in the footsteps of lesbian and gay movements toward the creation of a bisexual ethnicity, then we will preserve the revolutionary potential of bisexuality.

 ## ACKNOWLEDGMENTS

This research was supported in part by a grant from the Horace H. Rackham School of Graduate Studies of the University of Michigan in Ann Arbor, by research funding from Hamilton College in Clinton, New York, and by a grant from the Society for the Psychological Study of Social Issues. I am grateful to Jackie Vargas, Ana Morel, Sandy Siemoens, and Michael Peluse for their help in tabulating the data. I am solely responsible for the content of this paper.

NOTES

1. For example, Beata E. Chapman and JoAnn C. Brannock, "Proposed Model of Lesbian Identity Development: An Empirical Examination," *Journal of Homosexuality* 14, nos. 3/4 (1987): 69–80.

2. Alan P. Bell, Martin S. Weinberg, and Sue Kiefer Hammersmith, *Sexual Preference: Its Development in Men and Women* (Bloomington: Indiana University Press, 1981); Pat Califia, "Lesbian Sexuality," *Journal of Homosexuality* 4, no. 3 (Spring 1979): 255–66; Denise M. Cronin, "Coming Out among Lesbians," in *Sexual Deviance and Sexual Deviants,* ed. Erich Goode and Richard R. Troiden (New York: Morrow, 1974), 268–77; Karla Jay and Allen Young, eds., *The Gay Report: Lesbians and Gay Men Speak Out about Sexual Experiences and Lifestyles* (New York: Simon and Schuster, 1979); Harold D. Kooden, Stephen F. Morin, Dorothy I. Riddle, Martin

Rogers, Barbara E. Sang, and Fred Strassburger, *Removing the Stigma: Final Report of the Board of Social and Ethical Responsibility for Psychology's Task Force on the Status of Lesbian and Gay Male Psychologists* (Washington, D.C.: American Psychological Association, 1979); Gary J. McDonald, "Individual Differences in the Coming Out Process for Gay Men: Implications for Theoretical Models," *Journal of Homosexuality* 8, no. 1 (Fall 1982): 47–60; Carmen de Monteflores and Stephen J. Schultz, "Coming Out: Similarities and Differences for Lesbians and Gay Men," *Journal of Social Issues* 34, no. 3 (1978): 59–72; Dorothy Riddle and Stephen Morin, "Removing the Stigma: Data from Institutions," *APA Monitor* (November 1977): 16–28; Siegrid Schäfer, "Sexual and Social Problems of Lesbians," *Journal of Sex Research* 12, no. 1 (February 1976): 50–69; Richard R. Troiden, *Gay and Lesbian Identity: A Sociological Analysis* (Dix Hills, NY: General Hall, 1988).

3. Henceforth, I will use the terms "bisexual" and "lesbian" to refer to women who were, respectively, self-identified as bisexual and as lesbian at the time of this earlier study.

4. Paula C. Rust, " 'Coming Out' in the Age of Social Constructionism: Sexual Identity Formation among Lesbian and Bisexual Women," *Gender and Society* 7, no. 1 (March 1993): 50–77.

5. For example, Chapman and Brannock, "Proposed Model of Lesbian Identity Development."

6. For example, Philip Blumstein and Pepper Schwartz, "Intimate Relationships and the Creation of Sexuality," in *Homosexuality/Heterosexuality: Concepts of Sexual Orientation,* ed. David P. McWhirter, Stephanie A. Sanders, and June M. Reinisch (New York: Oxford University Press, 1990), 307–20; and Kenneth Plummer, *Sexual Stigma: An Interactionist Account* (London: Routledge and Kegan Paul, 1975).

7. For example, Vivienne C. Cass, "Homosexual Identity Formation: A Theoretical Model," *Journal of Homosexuality* 4, no. 3 (Spring 1979): 219–35; Vivienne C. Cass, "The Implications of Homosexual Identity Formation for the Kinsey Model and Scale of Sexual Preference," in *Homosexuality/Heterosexuality,* 239–66; Eli Coleman, "Developmental Stages of the Coming Out Process," *Journal of Homosexuality* 7, nos. 2/3 (Winter 1981/Spring 1982): 31–43; McDonald, "Individual Differences in the Coming Out Process for Gay Men."

8. I am collecting data via an anonymous self-administered questionnaire containing a postage-paid return envelope inside the U.S. or postal coupons outside the U.S. The cover of the questionnaire tells potential respondents that

> You can fill out this questionnaire if you are bisexual or if you call yourself bisexual, if you are coming out or questioning your sexuality, if you prefer not to label your sexual orientation, if you used to identify as bisexual, if you are lesbian or gay but have felt attracted to or had a sexual or romantic relationship with someone of the other sex at any time in your life, or if you are heterosexual but have felt attracted to or had a sexual or romantic relationship with someone of your own sex at any time in your life.

The cover of the questionnaire encouraged non-eligible individuals to give the questionnaire to an eligible friend. Respondents are, therefore, self-selected. The questionnaire is being distributed through bisexual and bisexual-inclusive social and political organizations; community centers and counseling services for gay, lesbian, and bisexual people and people exploring their sexuality; institutions dedicated to sexuality education and information dissemination; advertisements in bisexual newsletters and alternative community newspapers; fliers in alternative bookstores; conferences on topics related to sexuality and/or gender; electronic mail networks; and friendship networks. More detailed information about the methodology will be forthcoming in later publications.

Distribution began in the United States in April 1993 and in the United Kingdom in September 1993. To date, questionnaires have been completed and returned by over 450 individuals in the United States, 46 in the United Kingdom, and 22 in Australia and New Zealand. Men and women are equally represented in all countries, except the United States, where women constitute 63% of the sample. Slightly under 4% of respondents are transgendered, including postoperative male-to-female transsexuals, non-transsexual transgenderists, and crossdressers. The age distribution is broader among respondents in the United States than the U.K. The ages of U.S. respondents range from eighteen to eighty-two, with 39% in their twenties, 30% in their thirties, 19% in their forties, and 10% fifty years or older. The oldest respondent from the U.K. is fifty-nine years old, and 67% of respondents from the U.K. are in their twenties. The incomes of respondents in both countries follow normal distribution curves. In the U.S., the median income is in the range of $20–29,999 with 18% earning less than $10,000 and 21% earning $50,000 or more. In the U.K., the mean income is £14,000, with 20% earning under £5,000 and 20% earning over £25,000. Eleven percent of respondents from the United States are people of color, including African-Americans, Asian-Americans, Indigenous Peoples, and Latinas/os.

9. The terms used to describe respondents' racial and ethnic identities are the terms used by respondents themselves when they were asked, "What is your race and/or ethnicity?" Throughout this chapter, capitalization of identity terms indicates that these are the terms used by respondents themselves. Some respondents belong to small racial or ethnic groups with only a few representatives in this study; more general terms are used to describe their racial/ethnic identity in order to protect their anonymity. For example, respondents descended from indigenous tribes of North America are referred to collectively as Native Americans.

   This is an international study, and respondents are occasionally described in terms of their citizenship or country of residence as well as their racial or ethnic identities. For example, "Irish" indicates that a respondent resides in Ireland, "English" indicates that a respondent resides in England, "Australian" indicates that a respondent resides in Australia, and "American" indicates that a respondent resides in the United States. This usage of "American" to describe residents of the United States is consistent with usage by citizens of other North, Central, and South American countries, who refer to citizens of the United States as "Americans" or "Americanos/as," and is not intended to imply that citizens of these other American countries are not also Americans in the continental, rather than the national, sense of the term.

10. Terms representing particular individuals' sexual identities are capitalized. However, when these terms are used to refer to sexual identities in general rather than to the identities of specific individuals, or when they are used as identity descriptors, even if in reference to particular individuals, they are not capitalized. In respondent quotes, respondents' choices regarding capitalization are retained.

11. Quotes from respondents have been edited for space. Identifying personal details have been omitted and obvious spelling errors have been corrected.

12. "Co" is a generic pronoun that refers to a person who might be female, male, or intersexed, and woman, man, or transgendered. It is used in some alternative communities in the United States whose members believe that gendered language, including the use of the masculine pronoun "he" as a generic pronoun, reinforces gender hierarchies. I use it here because it seems particularly appropriate in a paper that discusses the difficulties that gendered language poses for bisexual-identified people. "Co" is less disruptive to the appearance of written language than slashed formations like "s/he" and "his/hers" and avoids the problems of numerical agreement that arise when "they" is used as a generic pronoun for referring to a single individual.

I invite the reader to use this chapter as an exercise in non-gendered language. Observe your emotional reactions to the non-gendered pronoun "co," and notice how it changes your understanding of the written word. In this paper, I discuss the importation of non-gendered concepts from one social context to another; the paper itself is an example of this process.

13. Toby Marotta attributed "lavender herring" to Susan Brownmiller, who referred to lesbians as "a lavender herring, perhaps, but surely no clear and present danger." See Toby Marotta, *The Politics of Homosexuality* (Boston: Houghton Mifflin, 1981), 236; and Susan Brownmiller, "Sisterhood Is Powerful!" *New York Times Magazine* (15 March 1970): 140.

14. Paula C. Rust, *Bisexuality and the Challenge to Lesbian Politics: Sex, Loyalty, and Revolution* (New York: New York University Press, 1995).

15. Joseph M. Carrier, "'Sex-Role Preference' as an Explanatory Variable in Homosexual Behavior," *Archives of Sexual Behavior* 6, no. 1 (January 1977): 53–65; Joseph M. Carrier, "Miguel: Sexual Life History of a Gay Mexican American," in *Gay Culture in America: Essays from the Field,* ed. Gilbert Herdt (Boston: Beacon Press, 1992), 202–24; J. R. Magaña and J. M. Carrier, "Mexican and Mexican American Male Sexual Behavior and Spread of AIDS in California," *Journal of Sex Research* 28, no. 3 (August 1991): 425–41.

16. David Bell, "The Trouble with Bisexuality," paper presented at the IBG, Nottingham, U.K., 1994.

17. Paula C. Rust, "Who Are We and Where Do We Go from Here? Conceptualizing Bisexuality," in *Closer to Home,* 281–310.

The term bisexual "ethnicity" refers to the notion of bisexuality as a group identity analogous to racial or ethnic group identities. It involves, for example, the concepts of group heritage and group pride. The concept of sexual ethnicity is drawn from Steven Epstein, "Gay Politics, Ethnic Identity: The Limits of Social Constructionism," *Socialist Review* 93, no. 4 (1987): 9–53, and Richard K. Herrell, "The Symbolic Strategies of Chicago's Gay and Lesbian Pride Day Parade," in *Gay Culture in America,* 225–52. Epstein and Herrell argue that the gay and lesbian movement, which is modeled after earlier racial and ethnic movements, is based on the notion of gayness as an ethnicity.

18. Rust, *Bisexuality and the Challenge to Lesbian Politics.*

REFERENCES

Baker, Karin. "Bisexual Feminist Politics: Because Bisexuality Is Not Enough." *Closer to Home: Bisexuality and Feminism.* Ed. Elizabeth Reba Weise. Seattle, WA: Seal Press, 1992. 255–67.

Bell, Alan P., Martin S. Weinberg, and Sue Kiefer Hammersmith. *Sexual Preference: Its Development in Men and Women.* Bloomington: Indiana University Press, 1981.

Bell, David. "The Trouble with Bisexuality." Paper presented at the IBG, Nottingham, U.K., 1994.

Bennett, Kathleen. "Feminist Bisexuality: A Both/And Option for an Either/Or World." *Closer to Home: Bisexuality and Feminism.* Ed. Elizabeth Reba Weise. Seattle, WA: Seal Press, 1992. 205–31.

Blumstein, Philip, and Pepper Schwartz. "Intimate Relationships and the Creation of Sexuality." *Homosexuality/Heterosexuality: Concepts of Sexual Orientation.* Ed. David P. McWhirter, Stephanie A. Sanders, and June M. Reinisch. New York: Oxford University Press, 1990. 307–20.

Califia, Pat. "Lesbian Sexuality." *Journal of Homosexuality* 4, no. 3 (Spring 1979): 255–66.

Carrier, Joseph M. " 'Sex-Role Preference' as an Explanatory Variable in Homosexual Behavior." *Archives of Sexual Behavior* 6, no. 1 (January 1977): 53–65.

———. "Miguel: Sexual Life History of a Gay Mexican American." *Gay Culture in America: Essays from the Field.* Ed. Gilbert Herdt. Boston: Beacon Press, 1992. 202–24.

Cass, Vivienne C. "Homosexual Identity Formation: A Theoretical Model." *Journal of Homosexuality* 4, no. 3 (Spring 1979): 219–35.

———. "The Implications of Homosexual Identity Formation for the Kinsey Model and Scale of Sexual Preference." *Homosexuality/Heterosexuality: Concepts of Sexual Orientation.* Ed. David P. McWhirter, Stephanie A. Sanders, and June M. Reinisch. New York: Oxford University Press, 1990. 239–66.

Chapman, Beata E., and JoAnn C. Brannock. "Proposed Model of Lesbian Identity Development: An Empirical Examination." *Journal of Homosexuality* 14, nos. 3/4 (1987): 69–80.

Coleman, Eli: "Developmental Stages of the Coming Out Process." *Journal of Homosexuality* 7, nos. 2/3 (Winter 1981/Spring 1982): 31–43.

Cronin, Denise M. "Coming Out among Lesbians." *Sexual Deviance and Sexual Deviants.* Ed. Erich Good and Richard R. Troiden. New York: William Morrow, 1974. 268–77.

de Monteflores, Carmen, and Stephen J. Schultz. "Coming Out: Similarities and Differences for Lesbians and Gay Men." *Journal of Social Issues* 34, no. 3 (1978): 59–72.

Eadie, Jo. "Activating Bisexuality: Towards a Bi/Sexual Politics." *Activating Theory: Lesbian, Gay, Bisexual Politics.* Ed. Joseph Bristow and Angelia R. Wilson. London: Lawrence and Wishart, 1993. 139–70.

Epstein, Steven. "Gay Politics, Ethnic Identity: The Limits of Social Constructionism." *Socialist Review* 93, no. 4 (1987): 9–53.

Freimuth, Marilyn J., and Gail A. Hornstein. "A Critical Examination of the Concept of Gender." *Sex Roles* 8, no. 5 (May 1982): 515–32.

Gibian, Ruth. "Refusing Certainty: Toward a Bisexuality of Wholeness." *Closer to Home: Bisexuality and Feminism.* Ed. Elizabeth Reba Weise. Seattle, WA: Seal Press, 1992. 3–16.

Hedblom, Jack H. "Dimensions of Lesbian Sexual Experience." *Archives of Sexual Behavior* 2, no. 4 (December 1973): 329–41.

Hemmings, Clare. "Resituating the Bisexual Body: From Identity to Difference." *Activating Theory: Lesbian, Gay, Bisexual Politics.* Ed. Joseph Bristow and Angelia R. Wilson. London: Lawrence and Wishart, 1993. 118–38.

Herrell, Richard K. "The Symbolic Strategies of Chicago's Gay and Lesbian Pride Day Parade." *Gay Culture in America: Essays from the Field.* Ed. Gilbert Herdt. Boston: Beacon Press, 1992. 225–52.

Hoffman, Richard J. "Vices, Gods, and Virtues: Cosmology as a Mediating Factor in Attitudes toward Male Homosexuality." *Journal of Homosexuality* 9, nos. 2/3 (Winter 1983/Spring 1984): 27–44.

Hutchins, Loraine, and Lani Kaahumanu, eds. *Bi Any Other Name: Bisexual People Speak Out.* Boston, MA: Alyson, 1991.

Jay, Karla, and Allen Young, eds. *The Gay Report: Lesbians and Gay Men Speak Out about Sexual Experiences and Lifestyles.* New York: Simon and Schuster, 1979.

Kooden, Harold D., Stephen F. Morin, Dorothy I. Riddle, Martin Rogers, Barbara E. Sang, and Fred Strassburger. *Removing the Stigma: Final Report of the Board of Social and Ethical Responsibility for Psychology's Task Force on the Status of Lesbian and Gay Male Psychologists.* Washington, DC: American Psychological Association, 1979.

Lavender, Abraham D., and Lauren C. Bressler. "Nondualists as Deviants: Female Bisexuals Compared to Female Heterosexuals-Homosexuals." *Deviant Behavior: An Interdisciplinary Journal* 2, no. 2 (January–March 1981): 155–65.

Magaña, J. R., and J. M. Carrier. "Mexican and Mexican American Male Sexual Behavior and Spread of AIDS in California." *Journal of Sex Research* 28, no. 3 (August 1991): 425–41.

Marotta, Toby. *The Politics of Homosexuality.* Boston: Houghton Mifflin, 1981.

McDonald, Gary J. "Individual Differences in the Coming Out Process for Gay Men: Implications for Theoretical Models." *Journal of Homosexuality* 8, no. 1 (Fall 1982): 47–60.

Plummer, Kenneth. *Sexual Stigma: An Interactionist Account.* London: Routledge and Kegan Paul, 1975.

Riddle, Dorothy, and Stephen Morin. "Removing the Stigma: Data from Institutions." *APA Monitor* (November 1977): 16–28.

Rust, Paula C. "The Politics of Sexual Identity: Sexual Attraction and Behavior among Lesbian and Bisexual Women." *Social Problems* 39, no. 4 (November 1992): 366–86.

———. "Who Are We and Where Do We Go from Here? Conceptualizing Bisexuality." *Closer to Home: Bisexuality and Feminism.* Ed. Elizabeth Reba Weise. Seattle, WA: Seal Press, 1992. 281–310.

———. "'Coming Out' in the Age of Social Constructionism: Sexual Identity Formation among Lesbian and Bisexual Women." *Gender and Society* 7, no. 1 (March 1993): 50–77.

———. *Bisexuality and the Challenge to Lesbian Politics: Sex, Loyalty, and Revolution.* New York: New York University Press, 1995.

Saghir, Marcel T., and Eli Robins. *Male and Female Homosexuality: A Comprehensive Investigation.* Baltimore, MD: Williams and Wilkins, 1973.

Schäfer, Siegrid. "Sexual and Social Problems of Lesbians." *Journal of Sex Research* 12, no. 1 (February 1976): 50–69.

Troiden, Richard R. *Gay and Lesbian Identity: A Sociological Analysis.* Dix Hills, NY: General Hall, 1988.

Udis-Kessler, Amanda. "Present Tense: Biphobia as a Crisis of Meaning." *Bi Any Other Name: Bisexual People Speak Out.* Ed. Loraine Hutchins and Lani Kaahumanu. Boston, MA: Alyson, 1991. 350–58.

QUESTIONS FOR CRITICAL THINKING

Reading 15

1. How does Rust's discussion of a bisexual identity challenge or expand your own perceptions of sexuality and sexual identity development?

2. How does Rust's discussion of sexual identity development illustrate how sexuality and gender identity are intertwined? Is it possible or desirable to separate these?

3. Does the existence of a bisexual identity challenge monosexual (heterosexual, lesbian, gay) identities? If so, how? If not, why not?

Reading 16

NAMING ALL THE PARTS

KATE BORNSTEIN

For the first thirty-or-so years of my life, I didn't listen, I didn't ask questions, I didn't talk, I didn't deal with gender—I avoided the dilemma as best I could. I lived frantically on the edge of my white male privilege, and it wasn't 'til I got into therapy around the issue of my transsexualism that I began to take apart gender and really examine it from several sides. As I looked at each facet of gender, I needed to fix it with a definition, just long enough for me to realize that each definition I came up with was entirely inadequate and needed to be abandoned in search of deeper meaning.

> Definitions have their uses in much the same way that road signs make it easy to travel: they point out the directions. But you don't get where you're going when you just stand underneath some sign, waiting for it to tell you what to do.

I took the first steps of my journey by trying to define the phenomenon I was daily becoming.

> There's a real simple way to look at gender: Once upon a time, someone drew a line in the sands of a culture and proclaimed with

---

great self-importance, "On this side, you are a man; on the other side, you are a woman." It's time for the winds of change to blow that line away. Simple.

Gender means *class.* By calling gender a system of classification, we can dismantle the system and examine its components. Suzanne Kessler and Wendy McKenna in their landmark 1978 book, *Gender: An Ethnomethodological Approach,* open the door to viewing gender as a social construct. They pinpoint various phenomena of gender, as follows:

GENDER ASSIGNMENT

Gender assignment happens when the culture says, "This is what you are." In most cultures, we're assigned a gender at birth. In our culture, once you've been assigned a gender, that's what you are; and for the most part, it's doctors who dole out the gender assignments, which shows you how emphatically gender has been medicalized. These doctors look down at a newly-born infant and say, "It has a penis; it's a boy." Or they say, "It doesn't have a penis; it's a girl." It has little or nothing to do with vaginas. It's all penises or no penises: gender assignment is both phallocentric and genital. Other cultures are not or have not been so rigid.

In the early nineteenth century, Kodiak Islanders would occasionally assign a female gender to a child with a penis: this resulted in a woman who would bring great good luck to her husband, and a larger dowry to her parents. The European umbrella term for this and any other type of Native American transgendered person is *berdache.* Walter Williams in *The Spirit and the Flesh* chronicles nearly as many types of *berdache* as there were nations.

> *Even as early as 1702, a French explorer who lived for four years among the Illinois Indians noted that berdaches were known "from their childhood, when they are seen frequently picking up the spade, the spindle, the ax [women's tools], but making no use of the bow and arrow as all the other small boys do."*
> —PIERRE LIETTE, *MEMOIR OF PIERRE LIETTE ON THE ILLINOIS COUNTRY*

When the gender of a child was in question in some Navajo tribes, they reached a decision by putting a child inside a *tipi* with a loom and a bow and arrow—female and male implements, respectively. They set fire to the *tipi,* and whatever the child grabbed as he/she ran out determined the child's gender. It was perfectly natural to these Navajo that the child had some say in determining its own gender. Compare this method with the following modern example:

> *[The Montana Educational Telecommunications Network, a computer bulletin board,] enabled students in tiny rural schools to communicate with students around the world. Cynthia Denton, until last year a teacher at the only public school in Hobson, Montana (population 200), describes the benefit of such links.*

"When we got our first messages from Japan, a wonderful little fifth-grade girl named Michelle was asked if she was a boy or a girl. She was extraordinarily indignant at that, and said, 'I'm Michelle—I'm a girl of course.' Then I pointed out the name of the person who had asked the question and said, 'Do you know if this is a boy or a girl?' She said, 'No, how am I supposed to know that?' I said, 'Oh, the rest of the world is supposed to know that Michelle is a girl, but you have no social responsibility to know if this is a boy or a girl?' She stopped and said, 'Oh.' And then she rephrased her reply considerably."

—JACQUES LESLIE, *THE CURSOR COWBOY*, 1993

Is the determination of one another's gender a "social responsibility"?

Do we have the legal or moral right to decide and assign our own genders?

Or does that right belong to the state, the church, and the medical profession?

If gender is classification, can we afford to throw away the very basic right to classify ourselves?

GENDER IDENTITY

Gender identity answers the question, "Who am I?" Am I a man or a woman or a what? It's a decision made by nearly every individual, and it's subject to any influence: peer pressure, advertising, drugs, cultural definitions of gender, whatever.

Gender identity is assumed by many to be "natural"; that is someone can feel "like a man," or "like a woman." When I first started giving talks about gender, this was the one question that would keep coming up: "Do you feel like a woman now?" "Did you ever feel like a man?" "How did you know what a woman would feel like?"

I've no idea what "a woman" feels like. I never did feel like a girl or a woman; rather, it was my unshakable conviction that I was not a boy or a man. It was the absence of a feeling, rather than its presence, that convinced me to change my gender.

What **does** a man feel like?
What does a woman feel like?
Do **you** feel "like a man?"
Do you feel "like a woman?"
I'd really like to know that from people.

Gender identity answers another question: "To which gender (class) do I want to belong?" Being and belonging are closely related concepts when it comes to gender. I felt I was a woman (being), and more importantly I felt I belonged with the other women (belonging). In this culture, the only two sanctioned gender clubs are "men" and "women." If you don't belong to one or the other, you're told in no uncertain terms to sign up fast. . . .

> . . . I remember a dream I had when I was no more than seven or eight years old—I might have been younger. In this dream, two lines of battle were drawn up facing one another on a devastated plain: I remember the earth was dry and cracked. An army of men on one side faced an army of women on the other. The soldiers on both sides were exhausted. They were all wearing skins—I remember smelling the untanned leather in my dream. I was a young boy, on the side of the men, and I was being tied down to a roughly-hewn cart. I wasn't struggling. When I was completely secured the men attached a long rope to the cart, and tossed the other end of the rope over to the women. The soldiers of the women's army slowly pulled me across the empty ground between the two armies, as the sun began to rise. I could see only the sun and the sky. When I'd been pulled over to the side of the women, they untied me, turned their backs to the men, and we all walked away. I looked back, and saw the men walking away from us. We were all silent.
>
> I wonder about reincarnation. I wonder how a child could have had a dream like that in such detail. I told this dream to the psychiatrist at the Army induction center in Boston in 1969—they'd asked if I'd ever had any strange dreams, so I told them this one. They gave me a 1-Y, deferred duty due to psychiatric instability.

 ## GENDER ROLES

Gender roles are collections of factors which answer the question, "How do I need to function so that society perceives me as belonging or not belonging to a specific gender?" Some people would include appearance, sexual orientation, and methods of communication under the term, but I think it makes more sense to think in terms of things like jobs, economic roles, chores, hobbies; in other words, positions and actions specific to a given gender as defined by a culture. Gender roles, when followed, send signals of membership in a given gender.

 ## GENDER ATTRIBUTION

Then there's gender attribution, whereby we look at somebody and say, "that's a man," or "that's a woman." And this is important because the way we perceive another's gender affects the way we relate to that person. Gender attribution is the sneaky one. It's the one we do all the time without thinking about it; kinda like driving a sixteen-wheeler down a crowded highway . . . without thinking about it.

In this culture, gender attribution, like gender assignment, is phallo-centric. That is, one is male until perceived otherwise. According to a study done by Kessler and McKenna, one can extrapolate that it would take the presence of roughly four female cues to outweigh the presence of one male cue: one is assumed male until proven otherwise. That's one reason why many women today get "sirred" whereas very few men get called "ma'am."

Gender attribution depends on cues given by the attributee, and per-ceived by the attributer. The categories of cues as I have looked at them apply to a man/woman bi-polar gender system, although they could be relevant to a more fluidly-gendered system. I found these cues to be useful in training actors in cross-gender role-playing.

Physical cues include body, hair, clothes, voice, skin, and movement.

> I'm nearly six feet tall, and I'm large-boned. Like most people born "male," my hands, feet, and forearms are proportionally larger to my body as a whole than those of people born "female." My hair pattern included coarse facial hair. My voice is naturally deep—I sang bass in a high school choir and quartet. I've had to study ways and means of either changing these physical cues, or drawing attention away from them if I want to achieve a female attribution from people.

Susan Brownmiller's book, *Femininity,* is an excellent analysis of the social impact of physical factors as gender cues.

Behavioral cues include manners, decorum, protocol, and deportment. Like physical cues, behavioral cues change with time and culture. *Dear Abby* and other advice columnists often freely dispense gender-specific manners. Most of the behavioral cues I can think of boil down to how we occupy space, both alone and with others.

Some points of manners are not taught in books of etiquette. They are, instead, signals we learn from one another, mostly signals acknowledging membership to an upper (male) or lower (female) class. But to commit some of *these* manners in writing in terms of gender-specific behavior would be an acknowledgment that gender exists as a class system.

> Here's one: As part of learning to pass as a woman, I was taught to avoid eye contact when walking down the street; that looking someone in the eye was a male cue. Nowadays, sometimes I'll look away, and sometimes I'll look someone in the eye—it's a behavior pattern that's more fun to play with than to follow rigidly.
> A femme cue (not "woman," but "femme") is to meet someone's eyes (usually a butch), glance quickly away, then slowly look back into the butch's eyes and hold that gaze: great hot fun, that one!
> In many transsexual and transvestite meetings I attended, when the subject of the discussion was "passing," a lot of emphasis was given to manners: who stands up to shake hands? who exits an

elevator first? who opens doors? who lights cigarettes? These are all cues I had to learn in order to pass as a woman in this culture. It wasn't 'til I began to read feminist literature that I began to question these cues or to see them as oppressive.

Textual cues include histories, documents, names, associates, relationships— true or false—which support a desired gender attribution. Someone trying to be taken for male in this culture might take the name Bernard, which would probably get a better male attribution than the name Brenda.

Changing my name from Al to Kate was no big deal in Pennsylvania. It was a simple matter of filing a form with the court and publishing the name change in some unobtrusive "notices" column of a court-approved newspaper. Bingo—done. The problems came with changing all my documents. The driver's license was particularly interesting. Prior to my full gender change, I'd been pulled over once already dressed as a woman, yet holding my male driver's license—it wasn't something I cared to repeat.

Any changes in licenses had to be done in person at the Department of Motor Vehicles. I was working in corporate America: Ford Aerospace. On my lunch break, I went down to the DMV and waited in line with the other folks who had changes to make to their licenses. The male officer at the desk was flirting with me, and I didn't know what to do with that, so I kept looking away. When I finally got to the desk, he asked "Well, young lady, what can we do for you?"

"I've got to make a name change on my license," I mumbled.

"Just get married?" he asked jovially.

"Uh, no," I replied.

"Oh! Divorced!" he proclaimed with just a bit of hope in his voice, "Let's see your license." I handed him my old driver's license with my male name on it. He glanced down at the card, apparently not registering what he saw. "You just go on over there, honey, and take your test. We'll have you fixed up soon. Oh," he added with a wink, "if you need anything special, you just come back here and ask old Fred."

I left old Fred and joined the line for my test. I handed the next officer both my license and my court order authorizing my name change. This time, the officer didn't give my license a cursory glance. He kept looking at me, then down at the paper, then me, then the paper. His face grim, he pointed over to the direction of the testing booths. On my way over to the booths, old Fred called out, "Honey, they treating you all right?" Before I could reply, the second officer snarled at old Fred to "get his butt over" to look at all my paperwork.

I reached the testing booths and looked back just in time to see a quite crestfallen old Fred looking at me, then the paper, then me, then the paper.

Mythic cues include cultural and sub-cultural myths which support membership in a given gender. This culture's myths include archetypes like: weaker sex, dumb blonde, strong silent type, and better half. Various waves of the women's movement have had to deal with a multitude of myths of male superiority.

Power dynamics as cue include modes of communication, communication techniques, and degrees of aggressiveness, assertiveness, persistence, and ambition.

Sexual orientation as cue highlights, in the dominant culture, the heterosexual imperative (or in the lesbian and gay culture, the homosexual imperative). For this reason, many male heterosexual transvestites who wish to pass as female will go out on a "date" with another man (who is dressed as a man)—the two seem to be a heterosexual couple. In glancing at the "woman" of the two, an inner dialogue might go, "It's wearing a dress, and it's hanging on the arm of a man, so it must be a woman." For the same man to pass as a female in a lesbian bar, he'd need to be with a woman, dressed as a woman, as a "date."

> I remember one Fourth of July evening in Philadelphia, about a year after my surgery. I was walking home arm in arm with Lisa, my lover at the time, after the fireworks display. We were leaning in to one another, walking like lovers walk. Coming towards us was a family of five: mom, dad, and three teenage boys. "Look, it's a coupla faggots," said one of the boys. "Nah, it's two girls," said another. "That's enough outa you," bellowed the father, "one of 'em's got to be a man. This is America!"

So sex (the act) and gender (the classification) are different, and depending on the qualifier one is using for gender differentiation, they may or may not be dependent on one another. There are probably as many types of gender (gender systems) as could be imagined. Gender by clothing, gender by divine right, gender by lottery—these all make as much sense as any other criteria, but in our Western civilization, we bow down to the great god Science. No other type of gender holds as much sway as:

Biological gender, which classifies a person through any combination of body type, chromosomes, hormones, genitals, reproductive organs, or some other corporal or chemical essence. Belief in biological gender is in fact a belief in the supremacy of the body in the determination of identity. It's biological gender that most folks refer to when they say *sex*. By calling something "sex," we grant it seniority over all the other types of gender—by some right of biology.

So, there are all these *types* of gender which in and of themselves are *not* gender, but criteria for systemic classification. And there's sex, which somehow winds up on top of the heap. Add to this room full of seeds the words *male, female, masculine, feminine, man, woman, boy, girl*. These words are not descriptive of any sexual act, so all these words fall under the category of gender and are highly subjective, depending on which system of gender one is following.

But none of this explains why there is such a widespread insistence upon the conflation of *sex* and *gender*. I think a larger question is why Eurocentric culture needs to see *so much* in terms of sex.

> It's not like gender is the **only** thing we confuse with sex. As a culture, we're encouraged to equate sex (the act) with money, success, and security; and with the products we're told will help us attain money, success and security. We live in a culture that succeeds in selling products (the apex of accomplishment in capitalism) by aligning those products with the attainment of one's sexual fantasies.
>
> Switching my gender knocked me for a time curiously out of the loop of ads designed for men or women, gays or straights. I got to look at sex without the hype, and ads without the allure. None of them, after all, spoke to me, although all of them beckoned.

 ## KINDS OF SEX

It's important to keep *gender* and *sex* separated as, respectively, *system* and *function*. Since function is easier to pin down than system, sex is a simpler starting place than gender.

Sex does have a primary factor to it which is germane to a discussion of gender: *sexual orientation*, which is what people call it, if they believe you're born with it, or *sexual preference*, which is what people call it if they believe you have more of a choice and more of a say in the matter.

> *[W]e do not need a sophisticated methodology or technology to confirm that the gender component of identity is the most important one articulated during sex. Nearly everyone (except for bisexuals, perhaps) regards it as the prime criterion for choosing a sex partner.*
>
> —Murray S. Davis,
> *Smut: Erotic Reality/Obscene Ideology*, 1983

The Basic Mix-Up

A gay man who lived in Khartoum
Took a lesbian up to his room.
They argued all night
Over who had the right
To do what, and with what, to whom.

—ANONYMOUS LIMERICK

Here's the tangle that I found: sexual orientation/preference is based in this culture solely on the gender of one's partner of choice. Not only do we confuse the two words, we make them dependent on one another. The only choices we're given to determine the focus of our sexual desire are these:

- *Heterosexual model:* in which a culturally-defined male is in a relationship with a culturally-defined female.
- *Gay male model:* two culturally-defined men involved with each other.
- *Lesbian model:* two culturally-defined women involved with each other.
- *Bisexual model:* culturally-defined men and women who could be involved with either culturally-defined men or women.

Variants to these gender-based relationship dynamics would include heterosexual female with gay male, gay male with lesbian woman, lesbian woman with heterosexual woman, gay male with bisexual male, and so forth. People involved in these variants know that each dynamic is different from the other. A lesbian involved with another lesbian, for example, is a very different relationship than that of a lesbian involved with a bisexual woman, and *that's* distinct from being a lesbian woman involved with a heterosexual woman. What these variants have in common is that each of these combinations forms its own clearly-recognizable dynamic, and none of these are acknowledged by the dominant cultural binary of sexual orientation: heterosexuality/homosexuality.

Despite the non-recognition of these dynamics by the broader culture, *all these models depend on the gender of the partner.* This results in minimizing, if not completely dismissing, other dynamic models of a relationship which could be more important than gender and are often more telling about the real nature of someone's desire. There are so many factors on which we *could* base sexual orientation. The point is there's more to sex (the act) than gender (one classification of identity).

> Try making a list of ways in which sexual preference or orientation could be measured, and then add to that list (or subtract from it) every day for a month, or a year (or for the rest of your life). Could be fun!

SEX WITHOUT GENDER

There are plenty of instances in which sexual attraction can have absolutely nothing to do with the gender of one's partner.

> *When Batman and Catwoman try to get it on sexually, it only works when they are both in their caped crusader outfits. Naked heterosexuality is a miserable failure between them. . . . When they encounter each other in costume however something much sexier happens and the only thing missing is a really good scene where we get to hear the delicious sound of Catwoman's latex rubbing on Batman's black rubber/leather skin. To me their flirtation in capes looked queer*

precisely because it was not heterosexual, they were not man and woman, they were bat and cat, or latex and rubber, or feminist and vigilante: gender became irrelevant and sexuality was dependent on many other factors. . . .

You could also read their sexual encounters as the kind of sex play between gay men and lesbians that we are hearing so much about recently: in other words, the sexual encounter is queer because both partners are queer and the genders of the participants are less relevant. Just because Batman is male and Catwoman is female does not make their interactions heterosexual—think about it, there is nothing straight about two people getting it on in rubber and latex costumes, wearing eyemasks and carrying whips and other accoutrements.

—JUDITH HALBERSTAM, "QUEER CREATURES,"
ON OUR BACKS, NOV./DEC., 1992

Sexual preference *could* be based on genital preference. (This is not the same as saying preference for a specific gender, unless you're basing your definition of gender on the presence or absence of some combination of genitals.) Preference could also be based on the kind of sex *acts* one prefers. But despite the many variations possible, sexual orientation/preference remains culturally linked to our gender system (and by extension to gender identity) through the fact that it's most usually based on the gender of one's partner. This link probably accounts for much of the tangle between sex and gender.

The confusion between sex and gender affects more than individuals and relationships. The conflation of sex and gender contributes to the linking together of the very different subcultures of gays, lesbians, bisexuals, leather sexers, sex-workers, and the transgendered.

> A common misconception is that male cross-dressers are both gay and prostitutes, whereas the truth of the matter is that most cross-dressers that I've met hold down more mainstream jobs, careers, or professions, are married, and are practicing heterosexuals.

A dominant culture tends to combine its subcultures into manageable units. As a result, those who practice non-traditional sex are seen by members of the dominant culture (as well as by members of sex and gender subcultures) as a whole with those who don non-traditional gender roles and identities. Any work to deconstruct the gender system needs to take into account the artificial amalgam of subcultures, which might itself collapse if the confusion of terms holding it together were to be settled.

In any case, if we buy into categories of sexual orientation based solely on gender—heterosexual, homosexual, or bisexual—we're cheating ourselves of a searching examination of our real sexual preferences. In the same fashion, by subscribing to the categories of gender based solely on the male/female binary, we cheat ourselves of a searching examination of our real gender identity. And now we can park sex off to the side for a while, and bring this essay back around to gender.

DESIRE

I was not an unattractive man. People's reactions to my gender change often included the remonstrative, "But you're such a good-looking guy!" Nowadays, as I navigate the waters between male and female, there are still people attracted to me. At first, my reaction was fear: "What kind of pervert," I thought, "would be attracted to a freak like me?" As I got over that internalized phobia of my transgender status, I began to get curious about the nature of desire, sex, and identity. When, for example, I talk about the need to do away with gender, I always get looks of horror from the audience: "What about desire and attraction!" they want to know, "How can you have desire with no gender?" They've got a good point: the concepts of sex and gender seem to overlap around the phenomenon of desire. So I began to explore my transgendered relationship to desire.

> About five months into living full-time as a woman, I woke up one morning and felt really good about the day. I got dressed for work, and checking the mirror before I left, I liked what I saw— at last! I opened the door to leave the building, only to find two workmen standing on the porch, the hand of one poised to knock on the door. This workman's face lit up when he saw me. "Well!" he said, "Don't you look beautiful today." At that moment, I realized I didn't know how to respond to that. I felt like a deer caught in the headlights of an oncoming truck. I really wasn't prepared for people to be attracted to me. To this day, I don't know how to respond to a man who's attracted to me—I never learned the rituals.

To me, desire is a wish to experience someone or something that I've never experienced, or that I'm not currently experiencing. Usually, I need an identity appropriate (or appropriately inappropriate) to the context in which I want to experience that person or thing. This context could be anything: a romantic involvement, a tennis match, or a boat trip up a canal. On a boat trip up the canal, I could appropriately be a passenger or a crew member. In a tennis match, I could be a player, an audience member, a concessionaire, a referee, a member of the grounds staff. In the context of a romantic involvement, it gets less obvious about what I need to be in order to have an appropriate identity, but I would need to have *some* identity. Given that most romantic or sexual involvements in this culture are defined by the genders of the partners, the *most* appropriate identity to have in a romantic relationship would be a gender identity, or something that passes for gender identity, like a gender role. A gender role might be butch, femme, top, and bottom—these are all methods of acting. So, even without a gender identity *per se*, some workable identity can be called up and put into motion within a relationship, and when we play with our identities, we play with desire.

Some identities stimulate desire; others diminish desire. To make ourselves attractive to someone, we modify our identity, or at least the appearance of an identity—and this includes gender identity.

I love the idea of being without an identity; it gives me a lot of room to play around; but it makes me dizzy, having nowhere to hang my hat. When I get too tired of not having an identity, I take one on: it doesn't really matter what identity I take on, as long as it's recognizable. I can be a writer, a lover, a confidante, a femme, a top, or a woman. I retreat into definition as a way of demarcating my space, a way of saying "Step back, I'm getting crowded here." By saying "I am the (fill in the blank)," I also say, "You are *not,* and so you are not in my space." Thus, I achieve privacy. Gender identity is a form of self-definition: something into which we can withdraw, from which we can glean a degree of privacy from time to time, and with which we can, to a limited degree, manipulate desire.

Our culture is obsessed with desire: it drives our economy. We come right out and say we're going to stimulate desire for goods and services, and so we're bombarded daily with ads and commercial announcements geared to make us desire things. No wonder the emphasis on desire spills over into the rest of our lives. No wonder I get panicked reactions from audiences when I suggest we eliminate gender as a system; gender defines our desire, and we don't know what to do if we don't have desire. Perhaps the more importance a culture places on desire, the more conflated become the concepts of sex and gender.

As an exercise, can you recall the last time you saw someone whose gender was ambiguous? Was this person attractive to you? And if you knew they called themselves neither a man nor a woman, what would it make you if you're attracted to that person? And if you were to kiss? Make love? What would you be?

 QUESTIONS FOR CRITICAL THINKING

Reading 16

1. Bornstein discusses how constructs of sex and gender are connected to sexuality. Do her ideas challenge the way in which you view gender and sexuality? Why, or why not?

2. How does your own gender and sexual identity influence your understanding of or level of agreement with the author's discussion?

3. To many of us, it is important that we are able to identify the sex of another individual. When there is ambiguity we often have a sense of frustration. Why do you think this is? If we were to have a greater tolerance for such ambiguity, how might that impact our level of tolerance for ambiguity with regard to sexuality?

PART II
Maintaining Inequalities: Systems of Oppression and Privilege

INTRODUCTION

On January 1, 2009, Atif Irfan, his brother, their wives, a sister and three children were headed to Orlando to meet with family and attend a religious conference. As they boarded the AirTran Airways plane, Irfan wondered aloud with his sister-in-law, Inayet Sahin, where the safest place to sit on the plane was. Some time later, while the plane was still at the gate, an FBI agent boarded the plane and asked Irfan and his wife to leave the plane. The rest of the family was removed shortly thereafter, along with a family friend, Abdul Aziz, a Library of Congress attorney and family friend. Although the FBI subsequently cleared the passengers and called the incident a "misunderstanding," AirTran refused to seat the passengers on another flight, forcing them to purchase last minute tickets on another airline that had been secured with the FBI's assistance. Although the men had traditional beards and the women headscarves, AirTran denied that their actions were based on the passengers' appearance. A spokesman for AirTran initially defended the airline's actions and said they would not reimburse the passengers for the cost of the new tickets. The following day, after the incident received widespread media coverage, AirTran reversed its position and issued a public apology, adding that it would in fact reimburse the passengers for the cost of their rebooked tickets.

On November 20, 2006, six Muslim Imams—recognized religious leaders and teachers of Islam—were removed from US Airways flight 300 from Minneapolis to Phoenix. They were returning to Phoenix after attending a conference in Minneapolis of the North American Imams Federation. Their removal was instigated by what passengers and crew identified as "suspicious behavior." The group drew attention initially because they were praying in the departure lounge prior to boarding.

On August 12, 2006, Raed Jarrar, an architect of Iraqi descent, was forced to remove a T-shirt bearing the slogan "We will not be silent" in English and Arabic before boarding a flight in New York. Passengers expressed concern over the meaning of the Arabic words, requesting that he remove his shirt. The slogan had been adopted by opponents to the Iraq war and other Middle Eastern conflicts and had derived from a group resistant to Nazi rule in Germany.

On September 21, 2004, Yusuf Islam, formerly known as the popular music star Cat Stevens, was refused entry into the United States. His flight from London to Washington, D.C., was rerouted to Bangor, Maine, where he was questioned by officials and then taken to Boston to catch a connecting flight in Washington for London. The justification for his barred entry was the charitable donations that he had made to humanitarian causes. His donations have helped to support children affected by the wars in Bosnia and Iraq, as well as victims of the September 11, 2001, attacks against America.

On September 17, 2001, Ashraf Khan, bearing a first-class ticket, boarded Delta Airlines flight 1469 to Dallas. This was to be the first part of a two-day trip to Pakistan to attend his brother's wedding. Khan, an 11-year U.S. resident, was approached by the pilot, who asked to speak with him in the gate area. There the pilot informed Mr. Khan that he and the crew did not feel safe flying with him on board. Further, the pilot questioned Khan about how he had obtained a first-class ticket.

On September 20, 2001, Kareem Alasady, a U.S. citizen, and his two companions, were denied flight on a Northwest Airlines flight from Minneapolis to Salt Lake City. A spokesperson for the airline stated that the crew took the appropriate action because the majority of the passengers felt uncomfortable flying with them.

In Tampa, Florida, Mohamed el-Sayed, a U.S. citizen of Egyptian origin, was denied boarding on a United Airlines flight to Washington on September 21, 2001. An airport manager told him apologetically that the pilot refused to fly with him on board, explaining, "We've reviewed your profile; your name is Mohamed."

Since the events of September 11, 2001, passengers who are perceived to be Arab or followers of Islam—which has included people who are South Asian, Latino, and Mexican—have been removed from airplanes due to the refusal by crew members and passengers to fly with them. Calling it "Flying While Arab," Michel Shehadeh, former West Coast regional director of the American-Arab Anti-Discrimination Committee (ADC), asserts that any Arab (or person perceived to be Arab) is thought to be a terrorist. Indeed, the legal department of the ADC has addressed over 60 occurrences of discrimination against men of Middle Eastern or South Asian origins by airline crew members across the country (Shora, 2002). This form of racial profiling is certainly nothing new.[1] Rather, it is based on a long history of U.S. government anti-Arab programs and policies. However, racial profiling of people perceived to be Arab or Muslim has increased greatly due to a September 12, 2001, directive from the FAA to the nation's airlines instructing security to immediately conduct "random identification checks," stating:

> Extremist groups, with a history of targeting civil action, are
> actively targeting U.S. interests, particularly in the Middle East.
> They retain a capability to conduct airline bombings, hijackings,
> suicide attacks, and possess surface-to-air missiles.

Such a directive is reinforced by other federal policies, such as the National Security Entry Exit Registration System (NSEERS), which requires

---

[1]The phrase "Flying While Arab" or "Flying While Muslim" was likely coined at the June 1999 meeting of the American Muslim Political Coordination Council.

the "special registration" of all male nationals over the age of 15 from 25 countries (with the exception of North Korea, all countries are Arab and Muslim). This registration obligates these males to report to the government to register and be fingerprinted, photographed, and questioned. Those failing to register are subject to detention and/or immediate deportation (American Civil Liberties Union, 2004).

Such profiling is similar to that experienced by blacks and Latinos for some time. For example, in May 1992 the Maryland State Police stopped a car in the early morning hours just outside of Cumberland, Maryland. The occupants—Washington, D.C., attorney Robert Wilkins and members of his family—were questioned, ticketed, and made to stand in the rain while a dog sniffed for drugs in their car. Mr. Wilkins sued, and the resulting litigation uncovered a memorandum instructing police to watch for "predominantly black" drug couriers.

In Illinois, a defense attorney hired a Latino private investigator to drive across certain counties to test the validity of assertions that the state police stopped Latinos and African Americans in disproportionate numbers. Peso Chavez, a 20-year veteran investigator and a former elected official from Santa Fe, New Mexico, was followed by an assistant to verify the legality of his driving. Even though the assistant saw no violation, state police officers stopped Chavez for a traffic offense. They asked him for permission to search his car and, when he asked whether he had to allow the search, a drug-sniffing dog was brought to the scene. Despite Chavez's unmistakable objection and his request that he be permitted to leave, the police used the dog on his car. The officers then told Chavez that the dog had "alerted" them to the presence of drugs. Chavez was put into the back of a patrol car and probed with questions as he watched the police search every part of his vehicle, open his luggage, and go through all of his personal possessions.

These are examples of a practice known as **pretext stops**—the use of traffic stops as an excuse to stop African Americans, Latinos, and other people of color in order to search their cars and question the occupants about possession of drugs. There is considerable evidence of the pervasiveness of this practice. For example, in Volusia County, Florida, a review of 1,100 videotaped traffic stops made during a drug interdiction effort revealed that approximately 70 percent of the drivers stopped were black. Black drivers were more likely to have their cars searched after being stopped than were whites, and their stops usually lasted twice as long (Harris, 1998). An investigation of drivers stopped by Maryland State troopers from January 1995 to December 1997 showed that 70 percent of drivers stopped on Interstate 95 were black. According to a survey by the ACLU, only 17.5 percent of the drivers (and likely traffic violators) on that road were black (Cole, 1999). More recently, a 2007 Department of Justice report found that blacks and Hispanics were approximately three times as likely to be searched during a traffic stop, with blacks being twice as likely to be arrested and nearly four times as likely to experience the threat or use of force during interactions with the police, (American Civil Liberties

Union, 2007). As a regional example, we can look to a statewide investigation in Minnesota of **racial profiling**—the practice of police and other officials targeting people of color for traffic stops because they believe that people of color are more likely to be engaged in criminal activity. This study revealed that police stopped African American, Latino, and American Indian drivers at a greater rate than white drivers. Such a pattern was particularly pronounced in suburban areas, with African Americans being stopped in some areas over 300 percent more often than expected. Once they were stopped, African Americans were subject to discretionary searches over twice as often as expected, even though only 11 percent were found in possession of illegal substances as compared to 18 percent of whites who were searched (Institute on Race and Poverty, Research, Education and Advocacy, 2003). Pretext stops are so common that members of black and Latino communities refer to them as DWB: driving while black or driving while brown (Fletcher, 1996).

These examples illustrate the way in which institutions maintain inequality based on categories of difference. Police officers and airline crew members, acting not on the basis of their own attitudes but on institutional policies (e.g., memorandums instructing to watch for "predominantly black" drug couriers, directives to conduct random checks mentioning "extremist groups . . . particularly in the Middle East"), help to maintain racial inequality.

As the 2009 *Climate of Fear* report from the Southern Poverty Law Center illustrates (Reading 43), practices of racial profiling can exacerbate anti-immigrant sentiments. In Suffolk County, New York, a largely white suburban area of Long Island, Latinos make up roughly 14 percent of the population. Yet they make up nearly half of the defendants appearing in court for traffic violations. New laws, such as Arizona's SB1070, further support these racial profiling practices. This law requires officials and agencies on the state and local levels to make "a reasonable attempt to determine the immigration status of a person" if they come into contact with someone they have "reasonable suspicion" to believe is undocumented. Such a perpetuation of a stereotype of Latino immigrants as criminals is often used as a justification for violence that is directed toward members of the Latino community.

Individuals are stopped because of their **status,** the socially defined position that they occupy in society. Note that only one status is important here. Although Mr. Wilkins occupied different statuses (lawyer, spouse, father, etc.) as did Mr. Chavez (investigator, former elected official, etc.), what mattered to the police was their presumed membership in a racial or ethnic group. Thus their **master status**—the most important status they occupied— was their race or ethnicity.

Each of us occupies a variety of statuses at any given moment in terms of our race, class, gender, sexuality, age, religion, (dis)ability, height, weight, and so on. While we may feel that one status is more important to ourselves than another, we don't always get to pick which is most important to others.

Just as Mr. Wilkins and Mr. Chavez were singled out for their race, each of us has likely been singled out by other individuals for some aspect of ourselves. In this section we will investigate how institutions—family, education, economy, the state, and media—support this practice and thus maintain inequality based on categories of difference.

CATEGORIES OF DIFFERENCE MAINTAINED AS A SYSTEM OF OPPRESSION AND PRIVILEGE

The value of the statuses that we occupy is determined by how they have been defined. When our statuses are defined as having value within the social structure, we experience **privilege**—a set of (not necessarily) earned rights or assets belonging to a certain status. If our statuses are devalued, the result is **oppression**, defined in Part I as a relationship of domination and subordination in which the dominant group benefits from the *systematic* abuse, exploitation, and injustice directed at a subordinate group. Oppression occurs in three forms: **institutionalized oppression**—that which is built into, supported by, and perpetuated by social institutions; **interpersonal oppression**—that which is manifested between individuals; and **internalized oppression**—that which is directed at oneself.

THE ROLE OF IDEOLOGY

Maintaining systems of inequality relies on a foundation constructed of several components. Central to this foundation is the presence of an **ideology**—a set of cultural values, beliefs, and attitudes that provide the basis for inequality and thus, in part, endorse and justify the interests of the dominant group. Systems of racial inequality in the United States rely on ideologies that include judgments about racial differences in order to maintain white privilege. Similarly, systems of class inequality rely on ideologies that include valuing the rich over the poor to uphold class privilege. Furthermore, ideologies based in **androcentrism**—the notion that males are superior to females—preserves systems of sex and gender inequality. Finally, an ideology that includes moral or religious judgments about what is and is not an appropriate sexual orientation is used to justify a system of inequality on the basis of sexuality.

The readings in this section demonstrate that the ideologies that maintain systems of inequality are built into the rules, policies, and practices of our social institutions. In addition, these ideologies often depend on one another, further illustrating the matrix of domination discussed in Part I. For example, as several of the readings in this section illustrate, the foundation of class inequality in the United States is an ideology based in capitalism. More than just the private ownership of goods, capitalism, according to some social theorists, involves exploitation because those who control the ownership of goods use the labor of workers to make a profit. Profit making, they argue, is based on paying workers less than the full value of what they produce. In order to justify paying one group less than another, we establish ideologies in which one group is viewed as less valuable than others. Thus, ideologies justifying inequality in terms of race/ethnicity, sex/gender, and sexuality perpetuate class inequality.

These interdependent ideologies and the resulting interlocking systems of inequality illustrate that oppression is *systematic*. According to Marilyn Frye, **oppression** involves:

> a system of interrelated barriers and forces which reduce, immobilize and mold people who belong to a certain group, and effect their subordination to another group. (1983, p. 33)

Thus, our circumstances are shaped not by accidental or avoidable events but by systematically related forces. To illustrate how pervasive and institutionalized oppression is, Frye offers the following analogy:

> Consider a birdcage. If you look very closely at just one wire in the cage, you cannot see the other wires. If your conception of what is before you is determined by this myopic focus, you could look at that one wire, up and down the length of it and be unable to see why a bird would not just fly around the wire any time it wanted to go somewhere. . . . There is no physical property of any one wire, *nothing* that the closest scrutiny could discover, that will reveal how a bird could be inhibited or harmed by it except in the most accidental way. It is only when you step back, stop looking at the wires one by one, microscopically, and take a macroscopic view of the whole cage, that you see why the bird doesn't go anywhere; and then you will see it in a moment. . . . It is perfectly *obvious* that the bird is surrounded by a network of systematically related barriers, no one of which could be the least hindrance to its flight, but which, by their relations to each other, are as confining as the walls of a dungeon. (Frye 1983:35)

As this analogy illustrates, comprehensive systems of oppression maintain the inequality that many experience in our culture. To fully comprehend this system, we need to employ a macro- rather than microscopic perspective, using a systemic frame of analysis to understand how each form of oppression is interrelated and maintained by our social institutions.

DEFINING FORMS OF OPPRESSION

Employing a systemic frame of analysis requires that we redefine the ways we categorize issues of discrimination. To label unjust ideas and actions, many of us usually think in terms of **prejudice**—a negative attitude toward members of a group or social category—and **discrimination**—the unequal treatment of people determined by their membership in a group. However, these concepts do not acknowledge the ways in which inequality is institutionalized. The definitions of forms of oppression that follow incorporate a more systematic perspective.

To understand issues of racial oppression within the United States, we must examine **institutional racism.** This refers to the systematic and institutionalized policy or practice by which people of color are exploited or controlled because of their perceived physical characteristics. Racism is part of our institutional structure, not simply the product of individual actions. In the previous examples, racism does not simply consist of the actions of the individual officers. Rather, it is the fact that these actions are supported by police *policy* that defines them as racist behaviors.

Furthermore, to fully understand racism we need to see how white people in the United States benefit from institutionalized racism regardless of their own individual actions. For example, as Stanley Eitzen discusses in "Names, Logos, Mascots, and Flags: The Contradictory Uses of Sports Symbols" (Reading 42), some institutions of higher education make use of Native American images and symbols in creating "mascots" for their sport teams. Despite the protest of a substantial number of American Indian individuals and organizations, places such as the University of Illinois, the home of the "Fighting Illini," institutionalize racist notions of American Indians by continuing to use these images.[2] White students at that university benefited from this practice, regardless of their participation in it, by *not* having their race objectified and dehumanized at each sporting event and on numerous university souvenirs.

Similar to racism, oppression based on social class also relies on the rules, policies, and practices of social institutions. As discussed in Part I, social class is a great deal more than individual characteristics. Rather, it is determined by a variety of factors in our social structure. Social institutions, including the state and the economy, relying on a capitalist system, create class structures that benefit some at the expense of others. The result is a heavily skewed distribution of income and wealth. According to the U.S. Census Bureau's *Current Population Survey* the median household income in 2008 was $50,303. The 20 percent of households with the highest earnings (with mean earnings of about $171,057) received 50 percent of all income, while the bottom 20 percent (with mean earnings of $11,656) received only about 3.4 percent. The distribution of income is illustrated in Figure 1. The distribution of wealth is even more concentrated than income. According to economist Edward Wolff (2010), in 2007 the top 10 percent ofthe population of the United States owned 85 percent of the wealth. As Figure 2 illustrates,

---

[2]Due to pressure from the National Collegiate Athletic Association (NCAA) officials at the University of Illinois decided to end the "Chief Illiniwek" tradition. The "Chief" made its last performance on February 21, 2007.

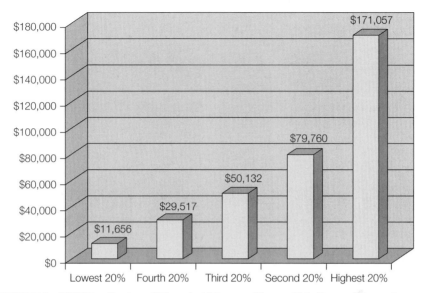

FIGURE 1   2008 Distribution of Household Income (*Source:* U.S. Census Bureau *Income, Poverty, and Health Insurance Coverage in the United States: 2008.* http://www.census.gov/prod/2009oubs/p.60-236.pdf)

1 percent of the United States owned 35 percent of the wealth (with their average net worth topping $10 million) while the bottom 80 percent possessed just 15 percent of the nation's wealth. What makes this unequal distribution even more significant is the difference in kind of wealth at various places in the social class system. For example, the majority of the net worth of the

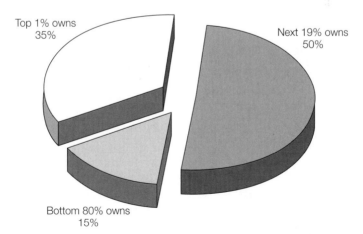

FIGURE 2   Distribution of Wealth, 2007: Share of Total Net Worth (*Source:* Reprinted by permission of the Levy Economics Institute.)

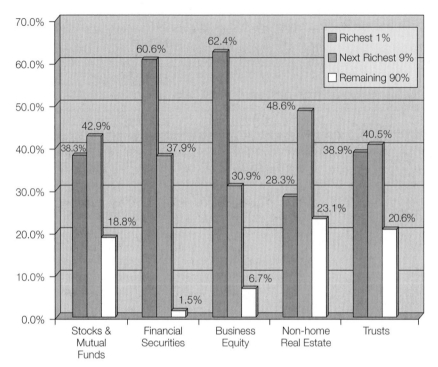

FIGURE 3   Distribution of Assets (*Source:* Reprinted by permission of the Levy Economics Institute.)

bottom 90 percent consists of assets tied up in the family home, while the distribution of stocks and bonds, financial securities, and business equity is concentrated in the richest 10 percent of the population (see Figure 3). Government policies that disproportionately tax workers while granting tax breaks to the wealthy perpetuate a skewed distribution of income and wealth. As can be seen in Figure 4, the wealthy receive a disproportionate amount of tax breaks from the federal government, with the wealthiest one percent of the country receiving 53 percent. Meanwhile, payroll taxes have significantly increased since 1980, disproportionately affecting workers. The overall impact of such a shift can be seen in the sources of federal revenues, with individual taxes accounting for 83 percent in 2006, while they only accounted for 77 percent in 1962 (see Figure 5). According to Collins, et al. (2004) such a shift of the tax burden from investment to wage income means that a wealthy person relying on earnings from dividends paid a marginal tax rate of approximately 15 percent in 2003, while a person such as a school teacher earning $28,400 paid a payroll tax of 15.3 percent *as well as* a marginal tax rate of 25 percent, for a *total* tax rate of over 40 percent.

Such systematic class inequality is defined as **classism**—a system of beliefs rooted in the institutions of society where the wealthy are privileged

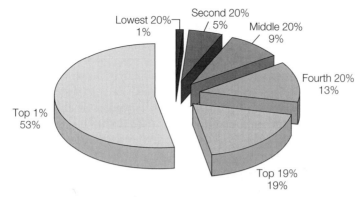

FIGURE 4   Distribution of Bush-Era Tax Cuts in 2010 (*Source*: From Bob McIntyre, "President Bush Has Made Tax Day Easier for the Rich—at the Expense of Everyone Else" (Citizens for Tax Justice, April 14, 2008), *www.ctj.org/pdf/taxday2008.pdf.* Used by permission.)

with a higher status at the expense of the oppression of the poor. The ways in which this system is maintained, as well as how issues of class intersect with race/ethnicity and sex/gender, will be discussed later.

Using a systemic analysis to understand issues of sex/gender oppression and privilege requires that we incorporate the role of institutions in definitions of sexism. Thus, for the purposes of this discussion, **sexism** is a systematic

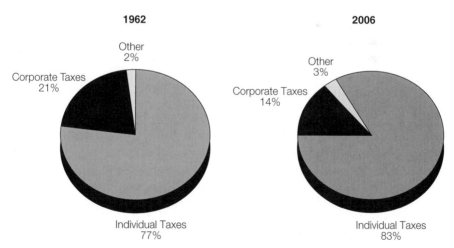

FIGURE 5   Sources of Federal Revenues, 1962 and 2006 (*Source:* Congressional Budget Office, "The Budget and Economic Outlook: Fiscal Years 2008 to 2017," January 2007, Tables E-3 and 4-1. "Individual Taxes" includes income, social insurance (payroll), excise, and estate taxes. "Other" includes customs duties and miscellaneous receipts. *http://www.cbo.gov/ftpdocs/77xx/doc7731/01-24-BudgetQutlook.pdf*)

and institutionalized policy or practice in which women are exploited or controlled due to perceptions that their sex or gender characteristics are inferior. Again, in recognizing that sexism is systematic we acknowledge that it is a product of our institutional structure, not necessarily individual actions. As a result, men do not need to individually behave in a sexist manner in order to benefit from a sexist system. For example, many physical requirements for occupations (such as height) advantage men while they disadvantage women, even though they may have little to do with the actual requirements for the job. Additional ways in which sex and gender inequality is reinforced by social institutions will be discussed later.

Finally, inequality with regard to sexuality is also institutionalized. Thus, privilege experienced by heterosexuals and the oppression experienced by those who are or are perceived to be lesbian, gay, bisexual, or transgender is perpetuated through the practices and policies of social institutions. For example, the rejection of the **Employment Non-Discrimination Act** (ENDA)—a bill to prohibit employment discrimination on the basis of sexual orientation—perpetuates the advantage experienced by heterosexuals and the stigma experienced by lesbian, gay, bisexual, and transgender individuals. Additionally, as mentioned in Part I, the passage of state constitutional amendments—and the campaign by President George W. Bush for a nationwide constitutional amendment—that ban civil unions, marriage equality, and legal protections for lesbian and gay families continue to deny access to resources for lesbian, gay, bisexual, and transgender families.[3] **Heterosexism,** as defined by Cherríe Moraga, applies directly to this example:

> The view that heterosexuality is the "norm" for all social/sexual
> relationships and as such the heterosexist imposes the model on
> all individuals through homophobia (fear of homosexuality). S/he
> supports and/or advocates this continued institutionalization of
> heterosexuality in all aspects of society—including legal and social
> discrimination against homosexuals and the denial of homosexual
> rights as a political concern. (1983:105)

Moraga indicates here that a person who is heterosexist is an active participant in oppressing those who are or are perceived to be lesbian, gay, bisexual, or transgender. However, as with all other forms of oppression it is not necessary to actively participate in discrimination against others in order to benefit from their systematic exploitation. For example, as Thomas Linneman illustrates in "How Do You Solve a Problem Like Will Truman? The Feminization of Gay Masculinities on Will & Grace" (Reading 37),

---

[3]This denial of resources was recently recognized through the finding of a federal judge in Massachusetts. On July 8, 2010 the judge ruled that the Defense of Marriage Act, a law barring the federal government from recognizing same-sex marriage, is unconstitutional, ruling that gay and lesbian couples deserve the same federal benefits as heterosexual couples.

mainstream media continue to perpetuate stereotypes of gay men. According to the Gay and Lesbian Alliance Against Defamation (GLAAD), representation of lesbian, gay, bisexual, and transgender (LGBT) individuals account for 3 percent of all scripted series regular characters in the 2009–2010 broadcast television schedule. This figure is up from 2.6 percent in 2008 and 1.1 percent in 2007. While such characters may be more present on cable programs and on more widely accessible network programs, (although these numbers have declined in recent years) lesbian, gay, bisexual, and transgender people and families are nearly invisible (Macias, 2004). Additionally, efforts to present messages inclusive and accepting of lesbian, gay, bisexual, and transgender persons are often excluded by broadcast networks. For example, a 2004 advertisement by the United Church of Christ portrayed a gay couple (along with other members of marginalized groups) being kept out of a church by two bouncers. The message was "Jesus didn't turn people away, neither do we." Major broadcasting networks, including CBS and NBC, rejected this advertisement. As a result, a heterosexual seeking to find images in the media of someone who represents her or his own sexuality is likely to find numerous examples. This ability to find representations of self is a benefit that is not only often overlooked by those who are privileged but also does not require any direct discrimination on the part of the individual who benefits.

As each of these examples illustrates, oppression on the basis of race, class, gender, and sexuality does not require the overt discrimination of bigots that we often think of when examining issues of inequality. Acts of oppression in interpersonal contexts maintain systems of inequality by engaging in oppressive practices that are a reflection of oppressive social institutions.

In summary, our experiences of oppression and privilege occur within a comprehensive system of interconnected social institutions. Thus, issues of prejudice and discrimination are transformed into experiences of institutionalized *oppression*. The remainder of this section will explore the ways in which the social institutions of family, education, work and the economy, the state, and media, along with the social forces of language and social control, maintain systems of inequality. As you consider the following, remember to keep in mind how the ideologies depend on one another, forming interlocking systems of oppression.

SOCIAL INSTITUTIONS: MAINTAINING SYSTEMS OF OPPRESSION AND PRIVILEGE

As an intangible aspect of the social structure, the role of social institutions in maintaining inequality often goes largely unnoticed. Rather, we tend to view institutionalized oppression or privilege as "the way things are." For example, when we hear of racist acts on the part of individuals, such as in the brutal killing of James Byrd in Jasper, Texas,[4] we are often rightfully outraged and horrified. At the same time, however, few of us are likely to notice the residential segregation that systematically excludes blacks from certain neighborhoods. Although the federal government eliminated overtly racially biased housing, tax, and transportation policies in the 1960s, as a recent *New York Times* article documented, a high level of racial segregation nevertheless continues to exist (Schmitt, 2001). Feagin and Sikes (1994) note that practices such as redlining (the systematic refusal on the part of some lenders to make loans in certain areas due to racial composition), racial steering, animosity on the part of whites, and discriminatory practices by mortgage lenders help maintain this segregation. The impact of such segregation influences not only wealth, but also access to important resources, such as education, employment, and good health. In this section we will examine the practices and policies of institutions in order to understand the ways in which they maintain systems of oppression.

As discussed in Part I, social institutions play a significant role in creating inequality. They define race, class, gender, and sexuality not only in terms of what does and does not exist, but also in terms of the values that we associate with each category. Thus, they confer privilege on some while oppressing others. This is done through the establishment and enforcement of policies constructed by these institutions.

The readings in this section illustrate how social institutions maintain systems of oppression and privilege and how they in turn impact access to resources. Ranging from money and property to medical care and education, **resources** are anything that is valued in society. Resources are generally considered scarce due to their unequal distribution among different groups. For example, the unequal distribution of income and wealth, as illustrated earlier, results in the perception that resources such as money and property are scarce.

The ways in which resources are distributed greatly impact an individual's **life chances**—the material advantages or disadvantages that a particular member of a social category can expect to receive based on his or her status (Weber 1946; Dahrendorf 1979). One of the most significant of life chances is the distribution of health care and the resulting impact on one's quality of life. For example, according to a recent article in the *New York Times* by Erica Goode (1999), social class is one of the most powerful

---

[4]James Byrd, 49, was beaten unconscious, then dragged by a chain from the back of a pickup truck to his death after accepting a ride from three white men in Jasper, Texas, in June 1998. One of the men, John William King, was found guilty and given the death penalty for his role in the killing. Another man, Lawrence Brewer, was also found guilty and sentenced to death. The third suspect, Shawn Berry, was sentenced to life in prison. Byrd's body was dismembered in the assault, and many of his body parts were found about a mile from his torso. When he was found, his body was so badly disfigured that Byrd had to be identified by fingerprints.

predictors of health—more powerful than genetics and even more than smoking. As a result of an unequal distribution of resources, the higher one's rung on the socioeconomic ladder, as Alejandro Reuss illustrates in "Cause of Death: Inequality" (Reading 29), the lower the risk of poor health. Furthermore, experiences of being marginalized, residing in racially segregated areas, and other forms of institutionalized racism were also found to magnify the impact of social class on health.

This example illustrates that social institutions, with their unequal distribution of valuable resources, perpetuate a cycle of disparate life chances. Obviously, if someone experiences poor health due to occupying a lower social class or living in a racially segregated neighborhood, she or he is going to be less able to fully participate in the social system, and less able to develop skills and achieve career goals than is someone who belongs to a higher social class with correspondingly better health.

Family

As a primary social institution, the family is central to maintaining systems of oppression and privilege based on race, class, gender, and sexuality. In addition, because it is so closely connected with other social institutions, such as the state and the economy, the structure of the family significantly influences and is influenced by the structure and actions of these institutions. While many of the ways systems of inequality are maintained are interconnected, perhaps the strongest connection is the relationship of family to the social structure.

For example, Lillian Rubin in "Families on the Fault Line" (Reading 18) illustrates how changes in our economic system resulted in a "crisis" in the family. Out of economic necessity, many women in white working-class families are now participating more fully in the paid workforce. When both parents attempt to work full-time, they need to find ways to pay for their child care. However, these families lack the economic resources that middle- and upper-class families have to seek quality child care. Rubin illustrates that social institutions such as the economy and the state have not responded in ways that support working-class families. As a result, they maintain systems of class inequality.

Our notions regarding what constitutes a family also maintains systems of oppression in a variety of ways. As Judith Stacey explains in "Gay and Lesbian Families Are Here" (Reading 20), "legitimizing gay and lesbian marriages would promote a democratic, pluralistic expansion of the meaning, practice, and politics of family life in the United States." However, institutional structures that determine who gets to be considered a family and whose "family values" are used as the standard against which all others are judged maintains inequality. As Stacey illustrates, these debates have significant impact on the amount of social equality or inequality experienced by various family structures.

Education

The institution of education also maintains systems of oppression and privilege. This institution reproduces the existing race, class, and gender structure through a variety of mechanisms, including the distribution of cultural capital and the existence of a hidden curriculum. In "The Return of 'Separate But Equal'" (Reading 21) Richard Kahlenberg clearly illustrates how the institution of education, over 50 years after *Brown v. Board of Education*, perpetuates race and class inequalities through the way it is structured. As his article notes, whether a student attends a resource-rich or a resource-poor educational system will impact their amount of access to **cultural capital**—social assets that include beliefs, values, attitudes, and competencies in language and culture. A concept proposed by Bordieu and Paseron (1977), cultural capital consists of ideas and knowledge people draw upon as they participate in social life, including "proper" attitudes toward education; socially approved dress and manners; and knowledge about books, music, and other forms of high and popular culture. Because cultural capital is essential for succeeding, children with less cultural capital often have fewer opportunities. In addition, the dominance of white, patriarchal, affluent class notions of what *counts* as cultural capital generally excludes the ideas and beliefs of the poor and people of color. Schools with fewer economic resources, which are often disproportionately attended by African-American, Latina/o, or Native American students, are less able to provide students with what is viewed by the dominant culture as important cultural capital, thus affecting their opportunities in the future. On the other hand, as Peter Cookson and Caroline Persell illustrate in "Preparing for Power" (Reading 22), children of higher social class have better access to this valued cultural capital and are thus better able to maintain their privilege. As a result, the educational system with its unequal distribution of cultural capital perpetuates a system of stratification based not only on race but also on class.

The institution of education also maintains race and class inequality through the existence of a **hidden curriculum**—the transmission of cultural values and attitudes, such as conformity and obedience to authority, through implied demands found in rules, routines, and regulations of schools. Because of the existence of a hidden curriculum, the values and attitudes that are reinforced in one school are not necessarily those that are promoted at another. For example, curriculum directed toward working-class students often focuses on rote memorization without much decision making, choice, or explanation of why something is done. Curriculum directed at middle-class students, however, emphasizes figuring and decision making in getting the right answer. The curriculum directed at affluent students often stresses the expression of ideas and creative activities, while that directed at elite students stresses critical thinking skills and developing analytical powers to apply abstract principles to problem solving. The readings of Cookson and Persell and Kahlenberg provide clear contrasts of the extremes of the hidden curriculum and how they maintain systems of oppression. As each of these readings illustrates, our education system is largely segregated on the basis of class. In addition, there is also significant evidence of *de facto* racial segregation. As a result, the hidden curriculum maintains class as well as racial inequality.

Mary Crow Dog and Richard Erdoes further illustrate in "Civilize Them with a Stick" (Reading 23) the ways policies in the institution of education perpetuate racial inequality. In combination with policies of the state, Native American children were forced to leave their reservations and attend boarding or day schools. These efforts to assimilate members of this group are but one example of how the institution of education maintains racial inequality.

The institution of education also constructs and perpetuates categories of difference on the basis of sex and gender. Various studies have shown how teachers pay more attention to boys in the classroom than to girls, and the ramifications of this differential treatment are numerous. For example, in "Missing in Interaction" (Reading 24), Myra and David Sadker examine a variety of ways the elementary classroom setting maintains sex and gender inequality. For example, teachers often force boys to work out problems that they don't understand but tell girls what to do, go easier on girls when disciplining their students, and reward girls for non-academic achievements such as neat penmanship or getting along with others. These and other behaviors on the part of teachers and students maintain clear sex and gender divisions that contribute to differential ways of viewing and valuing males and females in our culture as well as the inequalities that females experience in our society.

Finally, the policies and practices of the institution of education can also maintain a system of stratification in which students who are perceived to be heterosexual are deemed more important and are thus more embraced by the institution than those that are perceived to be lesbian, gay, bisexual, or transgender. As Melinda Miceli illustrates in "Schools and the Social Control of Sexuality" (Reading 25), examples of heterosexism can even be found in what may be viewed as harmless school traditions (e.g., proms and other social events), but it can also be seen in more overt and meaningful ways. For example, in recent years the U.S. Congress has voted on proposals to eliminate federal aid to schools that "promote" homosexuality. In addition, a policy enacted by the Merrimack, New Hampshire, School Board stated:

> The Merrimack School District shall neither implement nor carry out any program or activity that has either the purpose or effect of encouraging or supporting homosexuality as a positive lifestyle alternative. A program or activity, for purposes of this item, includes the distribution of instructional materials, instruction, counseling, or other services on school grounds, or referral of a pupil to an organization that affirms a homosexual lifestyle.

Although this policy was later repealed, similar policies have been passed in other school districts. Some of the policies are phrased more bluntly than the one above and simply forbid any discussion of homosexuality at all—be it positive or negative. Regardless, the ramifications of official policies such as these, as well as implicit practices based on heterosexism, are severe.

Such overt and covert ways of valuing heterosexuality result in **heteronormativity**—the ways in which the practices of social institutions prescribe heterosexuality as the norm. This can have a profound effect on those who do not fit into such a norm. As a result of heterosexist school traditions and policies like those described above, lesbian, gay, bisexual, transgender, or questioning students are likely to experience feelings of alienation and self-alienation. For example, a 1989 U.S. Department of Health and Human Services report on youth suicide indicated that over 30 percent of all completed youth suicides each year are by gay and lesbian youth, and that gay youth are two to three times more likely to have attempted or seriously considered suicide than their heterosexual peers. Lesbian, gay, and bisexual youth, as well as students who are questioning their sexuality, often need counseling that is only available in the schools. Official and unofficial policies and practices based on heterosexism ignore these concerns and maintain inequality based on sexuality.

Work and the Economy

The institution of work and the economy is perhaps the most fundamental in maintaining systems of inequality. As already noted, changes in the structure of the economy significantly impact other institutions. At times, these changes offer new opportunities and privilege to some, and at others these changes foster continued oppression. In "Jobless Ghettos" (Reading 26), William Julius Wilson illustrates that the poor conditions in some segregated neighborhoods are made worse when places of employment no longer exist. Indeed, increases in the jobless rate disproportionately affect those who are on the low end of the economic spectrum as they are less likely to have other sources of support (e.g., savings, social networks leading to new jobs, etc.).

Devah Pager, Bruce Western, and Bart Bonikowski in "Discrimination in a Low-Wage Labor Market: A Field Experiment" (Reading 27) offer additional examples of how policies within the institution of work and the economy maintain a system of inequality. Through selective recruitment and biased hiring strategies, employers favor white applicants at the expense of others. As Figure 6 indicates, there is a significant wage gap with regard to race in the United States. Policies such as those discussed by Pager et al. maintain this gap. Finally, policies of the social institution of work and the economy also perpetuate inequality with regard to sex and gender. As Christine Williams discusses in "The Glass Escalator" (Reading 28), sex segregation continues to exist within the U.S. labor force. She also reveals policies and practices with regard to hiring and supervising. These maintain a gap in the incomes of women and men, as illustrated in Table 1, and as a result, they maintain a system of inequality.

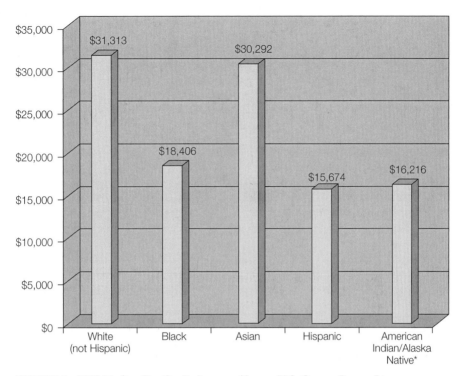

FIGURE 6   2008 Median Per-Capita Income. (*Source*: U.S. Census *Bureau Income, Poverty, and Health Insurance Coverage in the United States: 2008.* http://www.census.gov/prod/2009oubs/p.60-236.pdf)
Note: Current per-capita income data is not available for the American Indian/Alaska Native population. The amount indicated here is from the 2006 U.S. Census Bureau American Community Survey.

TABLE 1   Median Weekly Earnings of Full-Time Workers by Sex and Age, 2009

Age	Males	Females	Female Income as Percentage of Male Income
All workers, 16 years and older	$819	$657	80.2%
16–24	$458	$424	92.6%
25–34	$715	$634	88.7%
35–44	$916	$709	77.4%
45–54	$967	$712	73.6%
55–64	$965	$727	75.3%
65 years and older	$791	$602	76.1%

(*Source:* U.S. Department of Labor, U.S. Bureau of Labor Statistics, *Economic News Release,* January 22, 2010, *http://www.bls.gov/news.release/union2.t02.htm*)

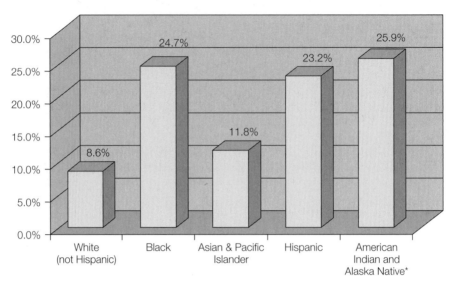

FIGURE 7   Poverty Rates by Race, 2008. (*Source*: U.S. Census Bureau *Income, Poverty, and Health Insurance Coverage in the United States: 2008.* http://www.census.gov/prod/2009oubs/p.60-236.pdf)

Note: Current poverty data is not available for the American Indian and Alaska Native population. The amount indicated here denotes 2003–2005 average poverty rate. The average is used because the American Indian and Alaska Native population is relatively small, and multiyear averages provide more reliable estimates.

The State and Public Policy

The state and public policy is another social institution that contributes to inequality. Often confused with the government, the state acts as a blueprint for how various procedures of the government should be carried out. In maintaining inequality, it acts in the interest of the dominant group or groups in society, reinforcing policies that work in their favor.

Currently, social policies regarding welfare "reform" have been the subject of much debate. As a result of the myths and stereotypes regarding people who receive aid within the welfare system, U.S. policies regarding Aid to Families with Dependent Children (AFDC) and similar entitlement programs have undergone considerable change in recent years. State policies often ignore how issues of race and class intersect. As Figure 7 illustrates, poverty is unequally distributed according to race, with people of color disproportionately representing those who are poor. Issues of poverty are exacerbated by stratification on the basis of sex, with women being more likely to be poor than men (13 percent as compared to 9.6 percent according to 2008 census data). In addition, female-headed households are also disproportionately poor, with 37.2 percent living in poverty. As Linda Burnham explains in "Welfare Reform, Family Hardship, and Women of Color"

(Reading 30), recent changes in welfare reform only maintain these economic inequalities.

The criminal justice system, also ruled by state policies, reinforces inequality, particularly with regard to race and class. As David Cole illustrates in "No Equal Justice" (Reading 32), the criminal justice system depends on unequal racial and class patterns in prosecution and incarceration. The evidence of such continuing institutionalized racism can serve as a justification for the need of corrective programs such as affirmative action. While such programs have often been accused of discriminating against those in the majority, as Barbara Reskin discusses in "The Effects of Affirmative Action on Other Stakeholders" (Reading 33), such policies rarely do this. Rather, they tend to enhance productivity and encourage improved employment practices.

Finally, as stated earlier, public policies established by the state maintain the interest of the majority. For example, state policies prohibiting concepts of multiraciality were established during the colonial period in an effort to sustain the distinction between master and slave. George Lipsitz illustrates this notion in his discussion in "The Possessive Investment in Whiteness" (Reading 34). These and other public policies were created, he argues, to maintain the control of whites over others. This motivation is reflected in contemporary policies as well, and whites continue to benefit from such a system in the United States.

Media

Like other social institutions, the media convey dominant ideologies about systems of inequality. Often the images reflected in the media represent the policies, practices, and prevailing attitudes of other social institutions. We can see policies of inclusion and exclusion regarding lesbian, gay, bisexual, and transgender individuals reflected in our television media. For example, when the Employment Non-Discrimination Act (ENDA) was rejected, denying lesbian, gay, bisexual, and transgender individuals the right to be free from employment discrimination on the basis of sexual orientation, *Ellen,* the first prime-time series to feature an out lesbian as the main character, was canceled. As illustrated in "How Do You Solve a Problem Like Will Trumen?" (Reading 37), television has failed to accurately reflect the diversity of sexuality in the United States.

Television is perhaps the most influential form of media today—viewers in the U.S. watch approximately 3 hours each day, which is equivalent to 45 days per year. As a result, this form of media possesses the power not only to influence but also to maintain our perceptions of reality. Richard Butsch, in "Five Decades and Three Hundred Sitcoms about Class and Gender" (Reading 35), discusses the inaccurate image of the "white male working-class buffoon." Such distorted images perpetuate not only our stereotypes of these groups but also their continued oppression. Further, as Kathleen Tierney, Christine Bevc, and Erica Kuligowski illustrate through discussing portrayals of the events surrounding Hurricane

Katrina ("Metaphors Matter," Reading 38), the media engage in practices of **media framing**—the process by which information and entertainment are put together by the media in order to convey a particular message to an audience. Thus, we are less able to distinguish between the realities of class in the U.S. and the ways in which it is portrayed in the mass media.

The institution of the media also maintains systems of oppression on the basis of sex and gender. For example, images in music, movies, television, and advertising degrade women. One of the ways this is accomplished is through the process of **objectification,** which Catharine MacKinnon defines as:

> the primary process of subjugation of women. It unites act with word, construction with expression, perception with enforcement, myth with reality (1982, p. 541).

Through such a process, the media support the privileges of men and the oppression of women.

As the preceding discussion illustrates, social institutions, often acting in tandem, play a significant role in maintaining inequality. As you read the selections in this section, keep in mind the earlier discussions of the matrix of domination and look closely to see the ways in which these social institutions work together to maintain interlocking systems of oppression and privilege.

LANGUAGE AND MAINTAINING INEQUALITY

One significant, yet often unexplored mechanism for maintaining inequality is language. Functioning in a manner similar to a social institution, the ways in which we use language can maintain the values, roles, norms, and ideologies of the dominant culture. The readings on language in this section demonstrate that it is a powerful tool of culture, determining how members of a society interpret their environment. According to social construction theory, our social world has no inherent meaning. Rather, the meaning of the social world is constructed, in part, through language. Language serves as the link between all of the different elements of culture and maintains a system of inequality.

There are those who feel that examining the role of language in the maintenance of inequality is trivial or misplaced. However, as Gloria Anzaldúa explains in "How to Tame a Wild Tongue" (Reading 41), issues of language are particularly significant, especially when one doesn't speak the language of the dominant culture. In addition, one of the significant functions of language is to serve the purpose of **cultural transmission**—the passing of culture (values, beliefs, symbols, behaviors) from one generation to the next. Through language, children learn about their cultural heritage and develop a sense of personal identity in relation to their group. In addition, language also helps them learn about socially constructed categories of difference and the meanings associated with them.

Language consists of words that are symbols with meaning and serves as a tool for interpreting our environment. The power of words lies in the fact that the members of a culture share their meanings and valuations. It is our common language that allows us to communicate and understand one another, and this makes for order in society. Philosopher Ernst Cassirer (1978) identified several different functions of the ability of humans to use symbols, explaining that they help to define, organize, and evaluate experiences of people. Julia Wood (1997) uses the assertions of Cassirer to illustrate the ways in which we use language to indicate cultural values and views of women and men, thereby maintaining inequality.

First, Wood argues that language *defines sex and gender*. It serves to define women and men as well as what can and cannot exist. For example, "generic" language (e.g., using the pronoun *he* to refer to both women and men or using words like *fireman, mankind, man-hour,* etc.) excludes women and dismisses their importance. As a result, men and their experiences are presented as the norm while women and their experiences are seen as deviant. In addition to establishing *who* exists, Wood argues that language defines *what* exists. For example, since we use the masculine word as the base to make compounds in the English language, it might appear that women's ability to rule or own may seem impossible in that we can have a kingdom but not a *queendom*. Does this mean that only men can have land over which they rule? Certainly not. Rather, it illustrates that we attend to what we name and tend not to recognize that which we don't name. For example, words like *sexual harassment* or *date rape* are rather recent creations. That does not mean that these are new phenomena; rather, they are phenomena that we have only recently attended to and been willing to acknowledge.

Additional ways that language is used to define our perceptions of women and men can be seen in how women are defined by their relationships. Consider, for example, the commonly used titles of respect for men and women in our society. Men are addressed as Mr., which reveals nothing about their relationship to women. But how are women typically addressed? The titles Miss and Mrs. define women in terms of their relationship to men. Even when a woman has earned a higher status title, such as Dr., she is still likely to be addressed as Miss or Mrs. On an interesting note, many states in the United States have required women to take their husband's name on marrying. It was only in 1975 that a Hawaiian statute requiring women to give up their birth names on marriage was ruled unconstitutional.

The second way that language illustrates our perceptions of women and men, according to Wood, is that it *organizes our perceptions of sex and gender*. The ability of language to organize our experiences and perceptions enables us to express cultural views of sex and gender by stereotyping men and women. In addition, the ways in which we talk about women and men in the English language encourage dualistic notions of sex and gender. For example, when we stereotype women as emotional and men as rational, we limit our abilities to recognize rationality in women and men's abilities to express emotion. Furthermore, due to the heavy emphasis that the English language places on polarity (good-bad, wrong-right, male-female), it is often difficult for us to think of things such as gender as existing along a continuum. In reality, very few of us fit on the polar ends of what a male or female is supposed to be like. Rather, most of us are somewhere in the middle. Yet we are all expected to conform to the two polar ends or suffer the consequences for not being seen as "gender appropriate."

Third, Wood argues that language *evaluates our perceptions of women and men.* Language is ideological, reflecting the values that are important in our culture. In the case of our use of the English language, we can find a great deal of evidence of linguistic sexism—the ways in which a language devalues members of one sex, almost invariably women. To illustrate this concept, consider the following word pairs: *brothers* and *sisters, husband* and *wife, men* and *women, hostess* and *host, madam* and *sir, Eve* and *Adam.* As you read these word pairs, it is likely that those in which the female term preceded the male term sounded awkward or incorrect. This is not coincidental; rather, it is a practice based on a long tradition. As Baron (1986) notes, 18th-century grammarians established the rule precisely to assert that "the supreme Being . . . is in all languages Masculine, in as much as the masculine sex is the superior and more excellent" (p. 3). According to these grammarians, to place women before men was to violate the "natural" order.

In addition, the English language often trivializes or diminishes women and things defined as feminine. As Eitzen notes in Reading 42, there is a debate in college athletic associations regarding whether the names generally applied to female sports teams trivialize or diminish the role of women in sport. While male teams are generally set as the standard, being assigned team names with little or no gender meaning (e.g., the Polar Cats, the Volunteers), female teams generally receive "feminized" team names (e.g., the Polar Kittens, the Lady Volunteers). Many argue that such a practice devalues the role of women in sport and thus in society.

An additional example of how language trivializes things that are feminine is in the use of diminutive suffixes for occupations held by women (e.g., actress, waitress, stewardess) and through the use of terms like *girls* for adult females. Furthermore, when we consider word pairs like *governor* and *governess, master* and *mistress,* or *bachelor* and *spinster,* it becomes clear that the words associated with men have very different implied meanings than those associated with women, with the latter consistently negative or demeaning. The male words suggest power or positively valued status, whereas the female words have negative connotations. Although many of these words originally had neutral connotations, over time these words declined in value, a process known as **semantic derogation.** Smith notes that "once a word or term becomes associated with women, it often acquires semantic characteristics that are congruent with social stereotypes and evaluations of women as a group" (1985, p. 48). Because such values about women are reflected in our language, our perception that women have less value than men is perpetuated. According to the **Sapir-Whorf hypothesis,** "people perceive the world through the cultural lens of language" (Sapir, 1949, p. 162). Thus, language shapes our reality.

As the preceding discussion illustrates, language plays a significant role in maintaining inequality. The readings in this section expand upon this illustration. For example, Robert Moore in "Racism in the English Language" (Reading 39) discusses the symbolism of white as positive and black as negative in the English language. As a result, language maintains racial inequality. In addition, Irving Kenneth Zola argues in "Self, Identity, and the Naming Question" (Reading 40) that those who occupy marginalized groups are not often given the opportunity to name themselves. Rather, names are generally imposed upon them by those with social power, maintaining a system in which the marginalized group is oppressed. Finally, Stanley Eitzen discusses in "Names, Logos, Mascots, and Flags: The Contradictory Uses of Sports Symbols" (Reading 42) the use of American Indian names and images in sports. Their discussion explains that such a practice maintains a system of stratification in which Native Americans are not only seen as less valuable than whites but are often objectified and seen as less than human. Each of the readings demonstrates that language is a pervasive tool of culture. In maintaining cultural values, roles, norms, and ideologies, language maintains inequality.

VIOLENCE AND SOCIAL CONTROL

Increasing violence in the United States—particularly evident in the school shootings most recently in Red Lake, Minnesota; Atlanta, Georgia; Cold Spring, Minnesota; Fort Gibson, Oklahoma; Deming, New Mexico; Conyers, Georgia; Littleton, Colorado; Pearl, Mississippi; West Paducah, Kentucky; Jonesboro, Arkansas; and Springfield, Oregon—has resulted in considerable discussion regarding the causes of and solutions to this problem. While some have been quick to blame the media or lax gun-control laws, focusing on violence as an act of individuals, it is important that we understand violence as a pervasive form of **social control**—the regulation of human behavior in any social group. As the findings of a May 1999 Gallup Poll linking antigay and racist attitudes with student-on-student violence illustrates, violence used as a mechanism for social control maintains inequality.

Several of the readings in this section illustrate how violence is used as a means of social control. For example, the Southern Poverty Law Center's report *Climate of Fear* (Reading 43) exposes the practice of "beaner hopping," a practice where youth in suburban areas go out looking for a Hispanic to beat up. This practice has resulted in most Latino immigrant families living in fear. The role of violence in controlling women is further demonstrated in the article "Sexual Assault on Campus" (Reading 44). In their discussion,

Elizabeth Armstrong, Laura Hamilton, and Brian Sweeney illustrate the factors that contribute to the existence of a **rape culture**—a set of values and beliefs that create an environment conducive to rape—in perpetuating violence against women. Furthermore, connections between homophobia, sexism, and heterosexism are evident in Suzanne Pharr's discussion of "Homophobia as a Weapon of Sexism" (Reading 46). Each of these examples illustrates that violence is used as a mechanism of social control to reinforce interlocking systems of oppression.

Michael Kaufman, in "The Construction of Masculinity and the Triad of Men's Violence" (Reading 45), explains how members of dominant groups, in this case men, are taught to be violent so that they may participate in the oppression of others. As this reading demonstrates, the impact of all forms of violence has a severe impact on an individual's ability to participate fully in society. As a result, violence perpetuates inequality.

Examining violence and social control further illustrates the interconnectedness of race, class, gender, and sexuality oppression. In working to understand the escalating violence within the United States and the world, it is important also to understand how systems of oppression interconnect. In so doing we will gain a better understanding of how violence is used to maintain interlocking systems of inequality.

CONCLUSION

As discussed in this section, constructions of difference regarding race, class, gender, and sexuality are transformed into interlocking systems of oppression and privilege. As a result, it is important that we understand how one system relies on another. The readings in this section examine the ways in which the social institutions of family, education, the economy, the state, and the media work together with language and violence and social control to maintain inequality. Once we are aware of this process, we will have a greater understanding of how to transform systems of inequality.

REFERENCES

American Civil Liberties Union. April 29, 2007. "Department of Justice Statistics Show Clear Pattern of Racial Profiling." New York. http://www.aclu.org/racialjustice/racialprofiling/29532prs20070429.html.

American Civil Liberties Union. February, 2004. "Sanctioned Bias: Racial Profiling Since 9/11." New York.

Baron, Dennis E. 1986. *Grammar and Gender.* New Haven, CT: Yale University Press.

Bordieu, Pierre, and Jean-Claude Paseron. 1977. *Society, Culture, and Education.* Beverly Hills, CA: Sage Publications.

Cassirer, Ernst. 1978. *An Essay on Man.* New Haven, CT: Yale University Press.

Cole, David. 1999. *No Equal Justice: Race and Class in the American Criminal Justice System*. New York: The New Press.

Collins, Chuck, Chris Hartman, Karen Kraut, and Gloribell Mota. April 20, 2004. "Shifty Tax Cuts: How They Move the Tax Burden off the Rich and onto Everyone Else." United for a Fair Economy, Boston, Massachusetts.

Dahrendorf, Ralf. 1979. *Life Chances*. London: Weidenfeld & Nicolson.

Feagin, Joe R., and Melvin P. Sikes. 1994. *Living with Racism: The Black Middle-Class Experience*. Boston: Beacon Press.

Fletcher, Michael A. 1996. "Driven to Extremes: Black Men Take Steps to Avoid Police Stops," *Washington Post,* March 29: A1.

Frye, Marilyn. 1983. *The Politics of Reality: Essays in Feminist Theory*. Trumansburg, New York: The Crossing Press.

Gay and Lesbian Alliance Against Defamation (GLAAD). 2009. "Where We Are on TV: GLAAD's 14th Annual Diversity Study Previews the 2009–2010 Primetime Television Season." New York. http://www.glaad.org/document.doc?id=92.

Gibson, Paul. 1989. "Gay Male and Lesbian Youth Suicide," in Marcia R. Feinleib (ed.), *Report of the Secretary's Task Force on Youth Suicide*. Washington, D.C.: U.S. Department of Health and Human Services.

Goode, Erica. 1999, "For Good Health, It Helps to Be Rich and Important." *New York Times,* June 1: D-1; D-9.

Harris, David A. 1998. "The Use of Traffic Stops against African Americans: What Can Be Done?" American Civil Liberties Freedom Network. http://www.aclu. org/ issues/policepractices/harris_statement.html.

Institute on Race and Poverty, Research, Education and Advocacy. September 22, 2003. "Minnesota Statewide Racial Profiling Report." Saint Paul, MN.

Macias, Stephen. 2004. "Reality Check: GLAAD Examines the 2004–2005 Primetime Television Season." Gay and Lesbian Alliance Against Defamation, New York.

MacKinnon, Catharine A. 1982. "Feminism, Marxism, Method, and the State: An Agenda for Theory." *Signs* 7(3): 515–44.

Moraga, Cherríe. 1983. *Loving in the War Years*. Boston: South End Press.

Sapir, Edward. 1949. *Selected Writings of Edward Sapir in Language, Culture, and Personality,* edited by David G. Mandelbaum. Berkeley: University of California Press.

Schmitt, Eric. 2001. "Analysis of Census Finds Segregation along with Diversity." *New York Times,* Wednesday, April 4.

Shora, Kareem. 2002. "Guilty of Flying While Brown." *Air and Space Lawyer* 17.

Smith, Philip M. 1985. *Language, the Sexes, and Society*. NY: Blackwell.

Weber, Max. 1946. From *Max Weber: Essays in Sociology*. Edited and translated by Hans Gerth and C. Wright Mills. New York: Oxford University Press.

Wolff, Edward N. *Recent Trends in Household Wealth in the United States: Rising Debt and the Middle-Class Squeeze—An Update to 2007* Unpublished Working Paper No. 589, The Levy Economics Institute, March 2010. http://www.levyinstitute.org/ pubs/wp_589.pdf.

Wood, Julia T. 1997. *Gendered Lives: Communication, Gender, and Culture*. 2nd ed. Belmont, CA: Wadsworth.

Reading 17

FICTIVE KIN, PAPER SONS, AND *COMPADRAZGO*
Women of Color and the Struggle for Family
Survival

BONNIE THORNTON DILL

R ace has been fundamental to the construction of families in the United States since the country was settled. People of color were incorporated into the country and used to meet the need for cheap and exploitable labor. Little attention was given to their family and community life except as it related to their economic productivity. Upon their founding, the various colonies that ultimately formed the United States initiated legal, economic, political, and social practices designed to promote the growth of family life among European colonists. As the primary laborers in the reproduction and maintenance of families, White[1] women settlers were accorded the privileges and protection considered socially appropriate to their family roles. The structure of family life during this era was strongly patriarchal: denying women many rights, constraining their personal autonomy, and making them subject to the almost unfetered will of the male head of the household. Nevertheless, women were rewarded and protected within patriarchal families because their labor was recognized as essential to the maintenance and sustenance of family life.[2] In addition, families were seen as the cornerstone of an incipient nation, and thus their existence was a matter of national interest.

In contrast, women of color experienced the oppression of a patriarchal society but were denied the protection and buffering of a patriarchal family. Although the presence of women of color was equally important to the growth of the nation, their value was based on their potential as workers, breeders, and entertainers of workers, not as family members. In the eighteenth and nineteenth centuries, labor, and not the existence or maintenance of families, was the critical aspect of their role in building the nation. Thus they were denied the societal supports necessary to make their families a vital element in the social order. For women of color, family membership was not a key means of access to participation in the wider society. In some instances, racial-ethnic families were seen as a threat to the efficiency and exploitability of the work force and were actively prohibited. In other cases, they were tolerated when it was felt they might help solidify or expand the work force. The lack of social, legal, and economic support for the family life of people of color intensified and extended women's work, created tensions and strains in family relationships, and set the stage for a variety of creative and adaptive forms of resistance.

AFRICAN AMERICAN SLAVES

Among students of slavery, there has been considerable debate over the relative "harshness" of American slavery, and the degree to which slaves were permitted or encouraged to form families. It is generally acknowledged that many slave owners found it economically advantageous to encourage family formation as a way of reproducing and perpetuating the slave labor force. This became increasingly true after 1807, when the importation of African slaves was explicitly prohibited. The existence of these families and many aspects of their functioning, however, were directly controlled by the master. Slaves married and formed families, but these groupings were completely subject to the master's decision to let them remain intact. One study has estimated that about 32 percent of all recorded slave marriages were disrupted by sale, about 45 percent by death of a spouse, about 10 percent by choice, and only 13 percent were not disrupted (Blassingame 1972). African slaves thus quickly learned that they had a limited degree of control over the formation and maintenance of their marriages and could not be assured of keeping their children with them. The threat of disruption was one of the most direct and pervasive assaults on families that slaves encountered. Yet there were a number of other aspects of the slave system that reinforced the precariousness of slave family life.

In contrast to some African traditions and the Euro-American patterns of the period, slave men were not the main providers or authority figures in the family. The mother-child tie was basic and of greatest interest to the slave owner because it was essential to the reproduction of the labor force.

In addition to the lack of authority and economic autonomy experienced by the husband-father in the slave family, use of rape of women slaves as a weapon of terror and control further undermined the integrity of the slave family.

> It would be a mistake to regard the institutionalized pattern of
> rape during slavery as an expression of white men's sexual urges,
> otherwise stifled by the specter of the white womanhood's chastity. ...
> Rape was a weapon of domination, a weapon of repression, whose

covert goal was to extinguish slave women's will to resist, and in the process, to demoralize their men. (Davis 1981: 23–24)

The slave family, therefore, was at the heart of a peculiar tension in the master-slave relationship. On the one hand, slave owners sought to encourage familiarities among slaves because, as Julie Matthaei (1982:81) states, "These provided the basis of the development of the slave into a self-conscious socialized human being." They also hoped and believed that this socialization process would help children learn to accept their place in society as slaves. Yet the master's need to control and intervene in the family life of the slaves is indicative of the other side of this tension. Family ties had the potential to become a competing and more potent source of allegiance than the master. Also, kin were as likely to socialize children in forms of resistance as in acts of compliance.

It was within this context of surveillance, assault, and ambivalence that slave women's reproductive labor[3] took place. They and their menfolk had the task of preserving the human and family ties that could ultimately give them a reason for living. They had to socialize their children to believe in the possibility of a life in which they were not enslaved. The slave woman's labor on behalf of the family was, as Angela Davis (1971) has pointed out, the only labor in which the slave engaged that could not be directly used by the slave owner for his own profit. Yet, it was crucial to the reproduction of the slave owner's labor force, and thus a source of strong ambivalence for many slave women. Whereas some mothers murdered their babies to keep them from being slaves, many sought within the family the autonomy and creativity that were denied them in other realms of the society. The maintenance of a distinct African American culture is testimony to the ways in which slaves maintained a degree of cultural autonomy and resisted the creation of a slave family that only served the needs of the master.

Herbert Gutman (1976) gives evidence of the ways in which slaves expressed a unique African American culture through their family practices. He provides data on naming patterns and kinship ties among slaves that fly in the face of the dominant ideology of the period, which argued that slaves were immoral and had little concern for or appreciation of family life. Yet Gutman demonstrates that, within a system that denied the father authority over his family, slave boys were frequently named after their fathers, and many children were named after blood relatives as a way of maintaining family ties. Gutman also suggests that after emancipation a number of slaves took the names of former owners in order to reestablish family ties that had been disrupted earlier. On plantation after plantation, Gutman found considerable evidence of the building and maintenance of extensive kinship ties among slaves. In instances where slave families had been disrupted, slaves in new communities reconstituted the kinds of family and kin ties that came to characterize Black family life throughout the South. The patterns included, but were not limited to, a belief in the importance of marriage as a long-term commitment, rules of exogamy that excluded marriage between first cousins, and acceptance of women who had children outside of marriage. Kinship networks were an important source of resistance to the organization of labor that treated the individual slave, and not the family, as the unit of labor (Caulfield 1974).

Another interesting indicator of the slaves' maintenance of some degree of cultural autonomy has been pointed out by Gwendolyn Wright (1981) in her discussion of slave housing. Until the early 1800s, slaves were often permitted to build their housing according to their own design and taste. During that period, housing built in an African style was quite common in the slave quarters. By 1830, however, slave owners had begun to control the design and arrangement of slave housing and had introduced a degree of conformity and regularity to it that left little room for the slaves' personalization of the home. Nevertheless, slaves did use some of their own techniques in construction, often hiding them from their masters.

> Even the floors, which usually consisted of only tamped earth, were evidence of a hidden African tradition: slaves cooked clay over a fire, mixing in ox blood or cow dung, and then poured it in place to make hard dirt floors almost like asphalt…. In slave houses, in contrast to other crafts, these signs of skill and tradition would then be covered over. (Wright 1981:48)

Housing is important in discussions of family because its design reflects sociocultural attitudes about family life. The housing that slave owners provided for their slaves reflected a view of Black family life consistent with the stereotypes of the period. While the existence of slave families was acknowledged, they certainly were not nurtured. Thus, cabins were crowded, often containing more than one family, and there were no provisions for privacy. Slaves had to create their own.

> Slave couples hung up old clothes or quilts to establish boundaries; others built more substantial partitions from scrap wood. Parents sought to establish sexual privacy from children. A few ex-slaves described modified trundle beds designed to hide parental lovemaking…. Even in one room cabins, sexual segregation was carefully organized. (Wright 1981:50)

Perhaps most critical in developing an understanding of slave women's reproductive labor is the gender-based division of labor in the domestic sphere. The organization of slave labor enforced considerable equality among men and women. The ways in which equality in the labor force was translated into the family sphere is somewhat speculative. Davis (1981:18), for example, suggests that egalitarianism between males and females was a direct result of slavery: "Within the confines of their family and community life, therefore, Black people managed to accomplish a magnificent feat. They transformed that negative equality which emanated from the equal oppression they suffered as slaves into a positive quality; the egalitarianism characterizing their social relations."

It is likely, however, that this transformation was far less direct than Davis implies. We know, for example, that slave women experienced what has recently been called the "double day" before most other women in this society. Slave narratives (Jones 1985; White 1985; Blassingame 1977) reveal that women had primary responsibility for their family's domestic chores. They cooked (although on some plantations meals were prepared for all the slaves), sewed, cared for their children, and cleaned house after completing a full day of labor for the master. John Blassingame (1972) and others have pointed out that slave men engaged in hunting, trapping, perhaps some gardening, and furniture making as ways of contributing to the maintenance of their families. Clearly, a gender-based division of labor did exist within the family, and it appears that women bore the larger share of the burden for housekeeping and child care.

In contrast to White families of the period, however, the division of labor in the domestic sphere was reinforced neither in the relationship of slave women to work nor in the social institutions of the slave community. The gender-based division of labor among the slaves existed within a social system that treated men and women as almost equal, independent units of labor.[4] Thus Matthaei (1982:94) is probably correct in concluding that

> whereas the white homemaker interacted with the public sphere
> through her husband, and had her work life determined by him,
> the enslaved Afro-American homemaker was directly subordinated
> to and determined by her owner.... The equal enslavement of
> husband and wife gave the slave marriage a curious kind of
> equality, an equality of oppression.

Black men were denied the male resources of a patriarchal society and therefore were unable to turn gender distinctions into female subordination, even if that had been their desire. Black women, on the other hand, were denied support and protection for their roles as mothers and wives, and thus had to modify and structure those roles around the demands of their labor. Reproductive labor for slave women was intensified in several ways: by the demands of slave labor that forced them into the double day of work; by the desire and need to maintain family ties in the face of a system that gave them only limited recognition; by the stresses of building a family with men who were denied the standard social privileges of manhood; and by the struggle to raise children who could survive in a hostile environment.

This intensification of reproductive labor made networks of kin and fictive kin important instruments in carrying out the reproductive tasks of the slave community. Given an African cultural heritage where kinship ties formed the basis of social relations, it is not at all surprising that African American slaves developed an extensive system of kinship ties and obligations (Gutman 1976; Sudarkasa 1981). Research on Black families in slavery provides considerable documentation of participation of extended kin in child rearing, childbirth, and other domestic, social, and economic activities (Gutman 1976; Blassingame 1972; Genovese and Miller 1974).

After slavery, these ties continued to be an important factor linking individual household units in a variety of domestic activities. While kinship ties were also important among native-born Whites and European immigrants, Gutman (1976:213) has suggested that these ties

> were comparatively more important to Afro-Americans than to lower-class native white and immigrant Americans, the result of their distinctive low economic status, a condition that denied them the advantages of an extensive associational life beyond the kin group and the advantages and disadvantages resulting from mobility opportunities.

His argument is reaffirmed by research on African American families after slavery (Shimkin et al. 1978; Aschenbrenner 1975; Davis 1981; Stack 1974). Niara Sudarkasa (1981:49) takes this argument one step further, linking this pattern to the African cultural heritage.

> Historical realities require that the derivation of this aspect of Black family organization be traced to its African antecedents. Such a view does not deny the adaptive significance of consanguineal networks. In fact, it helps to clarify why these networks had the flexibility they had and why they, rather than conjugal relationships, came to be the stabilizing factor in Black families.

In individual households, the gender-based division of labor experienced some important shifts during emancipation. In their first real opportunity to establish family life beyond the controls and constraints imposed by a slave master, Black sharecroppers' family life changed radically. Most women, at least those who were wives and daughters of able-bodied men, withdrew from field labor and concentrated on their domestic duties in the home. Husbands took primary responsibility for the fieldwork and for relations with the owners, such as signing contracts on behalf of the family. Black women were severely criticized by Whites for removing themselves from field labor because they were seen to be aspiring to a model of womanhood that was considered inappropriate for them. The reorganization of female labor, however, represented an attempt on the part of Blacks to protect women from some of the abuses of the slave system and to thus secure their family life. It was more likely a response to the particular set of circumstances that the newly freed slaves faced than a reaction to the lives of their former masters. Jacqueline Jones (1985) argues that these patterns were "particularly significant" because at a time when industrial development was introducing a labor system that divided male and female labor, the freed Black family was establishing a pattern of joint work and complementarity of tasks between males and females that was reminiscent of preindustrial American families. Unfortunately, these former slaves had to do this without the institutional supports given White farm families and within a sharecropping system that deprived them of economic independence.

CHINESE SOJOURNERS

An increase in the African slave population was a desired goal. Therefore, Africans were permitted and even encouraged at times to form families, as long as they were under the direct control of the slave master. By sharp contrast, Chinese people were explicitly denied the right to form families in the United States through both law and social practice. Although male laborers began coming to the United States in sizable numbers in the middle of the nineteenth century, it was more than a century before an appreciable number of children of Chinese parents were born in America. Tom, a respondent in Victor Nee and Brett de Bary Nee's book, *Longtime Californ'*, says: "One thing about Chinese men in America was you had to be either a merchant or a big gambler, have lot of side money to have a family here. A working man, an ordinary man, just can't!" (1973:80).

Working in the United States was a means of gaining support for one's family with an end of obtaining sufficient capital to return to China and purchase land. This practice of sojourning was reinforced by laws preventing Chinese laborers from becoming citizens, and by restrictions on their entry into this country. Chinese laborers who arrived before 1882 could not bring their wives and were prevented by law from marrying Whites. Thus, it is likely that the number of Chinese American families might have been negligible had it not been for two things: the San Francisco earthquake and fire in 1906, which destroyed all municipal records, and the ingenuity and persistence of the Chinese people, who used the opportunity created by the earthquake to increase their numbers in the United States. Since relatives of citizens were permitted entry, American-born Chinese (real and claimed) would visit China, report the birth of a son, and thus create an entry slot. Years later, since the records were destroyed, the slot could be used by a relative or purchased by someone outside the family. The purchasers were called "paper sons." Paper sons became a major mechanism for increasing the Chinese population, but it was a slow process and the sojourner community remained predominantly male for decades.

The high concentration of males in the Chinese community before 1920 resulted in a split household form of family. As Evelyn Nakano Glenn observes:

> In the split household family, production is separated from
> other functions and is carried out by a member living far from
> the rest of the household. The rest—consumption, reproduction
> and socialization—are carried out by the wife and other relatives
> from the home village. The split household form makes possible

maximum exploitation of the workers. The labor of prime-age male workers can be bought relatively cheaply, since the cost of reproduction and family maintenance is borne partially by unpaid subsistence work of women and old people in the home village. (1983:38–39)

The Chinese women who were in the United States during this period consisted of a small number who were wives and daughters of merchants and a larger percentage who were prostitutes. Lucia Cheng Hirata (1979) has suggested that Chinese prostitution was an important element in helping to maintain the split household family. In conjunction with laws prohibiting intermarriage, it helped men avoid long-term relationships with women in the United States and ensured that the bulk of their meager earnings would continue to support the family at home.

The reproductive labor of Chinese women, therefore, took on two dimensions primarily because of the split household family. Wives who remained in China were forced to raise children and care for in-laws on the meager remittances of their sojourning husbands. Although we know few details about their lives, it is clear that the everyday work of bearing and maintaining children and running a household fell entirely on their shoulders. Those women who immigrated and worked as prostitutes performed the more nurturant aspects of reproductive labor, that is, providing emotional and sexual companionship for men who were far from home. Yet their role as prostitutes was more likely a means of supporting their families at home in China than a chosen vocation.

The Chinese family system during the nineteenth century was a patriarchal one and girls had little value. In fact, they were considered temporary members of their father's family because when they married, they became members of their husband's family. They also had little social value; girls were sold by some poor parents to work as prostitutes, concubines, or servants. This saved the family the expense of raising them, and their earnings became a source of family income. For most girls, however, marriages were arranged and families sought useful connections through this process. With the development of a sojourning pattern in the United States, some Chinese women in those regions of China where this pattern was more prevalent would be sold to become prostitutes in the United States. Most, however, were married to men whom they saw only once or twice in the twenty- or thirty-year periods during which these men sojourned in the United States. A woman's status as wife ensured that a portion of the meager wages her husband earned would be returned to his family in China. This arrangement required considerable sacrifice and adjustment by wives who remained in China and those who joined their husbands after a long separation.

Maxine Hong Kingston tells the story of the unhappy meeting of her aunt, Moon Orchid, with her husband, from whom she had been separated for thirty years: "For thirty years she had been receiving money from him from America. But she had never told him that she wanted to come to the

United States. She waited for him to suggest it, but he never did" (1977:144). His response to her when she arrived unexpectedly was to say: " 'Look at her. She'd never fit into an American household. I have important American guests who come inside my house to eat.' He turned to Moon Orchid, 'You can't talk to them. You can barely talk to me.' Moon Orchid was so ashamed, she held her hands over her face" (1977:178).

Despite these handicaps, Chinese people collaborated to establish the opportunity to form families and settle in the United States. In some cases it took as long as three generations for a child to be born on U.S. soil.

> In one typical history, related by a 21 year old college student, great-grandfather arrived in the States in the 1890s as a "paper son" and worked for about 20 years as a laborer. He then sent for the grandfather, who worked alongside great-grandfather in a small business for several years. Great-grandfather subsequently returned to China, leaving grandfather to run the business and send remittance. In the 1940s, grandfather sent for father; up to this point, none of the wives had left China. Finally, in the late 1950s father returned to China and brought his wife back with him. Thus, after nearly 70 years, the first child was born in the United States. (Glenn 1981:14)

 ## CHICANOS

Africans were uprooted from their native lands and encouraged to have families in order to increase the slave labor force. Chinese people were immigrant laborers whose "permanent" presence in the country was denied. By contrast, Mexican Americans were colonized and their traditional family life was disrupted by war and the imposition of a new set of laws and conditions of labor. The hardships faced by Chicano families, therefore, were the results of the U.S. colonization of the indigenous Mexican population, accompanied by the beginnings of industrial development. The treaty of Guadalupe Hidalgo, signed in 1848, granted American citizenship to Mexicans living in what is now called the Southwest. The American takeover, however, resulted in the gradual displacement of Mexicans from the land and their incorporation into a colonial labor force (Barrera 1979). Mexicans who immigrated into the United States after 1848 were also absorbed into that labor force.

Whether natives of northern Mexico (which became part of the United States after 1848) or immigrants from southern Mexico, Chicanos were a largely peasant population whose lives were defined by a feudal economy and a daily struggle on the land for economic survival. Patriarchal families were important instruments of community life, and nuclear family units were linked through an elaborate system of kinship and godparenting. Traditional life was characterized by hard work and a fairly distinct pattern of sex-role segregation.

> Most Mexican women were valued for their household qualities,
> men by their ability to work and to provide for a family. Children
> were taught to get up early, to contribute to their family's labor to
> prepare themselves for adult life.... Such a life demanded disci-
> pline, authority, deference—values that cemented the working of
> a family surrounded and shaped by the requirements of Mexico's
> distinctive historical pattern of agricultural development, especially
> its pervasive debt peonage. (Saragoza 1983:8)

As the primary caretakers of hearth and home in a rural environment, a
Chicana's labor made a vital and important contribution to family survival.
A description of women's reproductive labor in the early twentieth century
may be used to gain insight into the work of the nineteenth-century rural
women.

> For country women, work was seldom a salaried job. More often
> it was the work of growing and preparing food, of making adobes
> and plastering houses with mud, or making their children's
> clothes for school and teaching them the hymns and prayers of the
> church, or delivering babies and treating sickness with herbs and
> patience. In almost every town there were one or two women who,
> in addition to working in their own homes, served other families
> in the community as *curanderas* (healers), *parteras* (midwives), and
> school-teachers. (Elasser et al. 1980:10)

Although some scholars have argued that family rituals and community life showed little change before World War I (Saragoza 1983), the
American conquest of Mexican lands, the introduction of a new system of
labor, the loss of Mexican-owned land through the inability to document
ownership, and the transient nature of most of the jobs in which Chicanos
were employed resulted in the gradual erosion of this pastoral way of life.
Families were uprooted as the economic basis for family life changed. Some
people immigrated from Mexico in search of a better standard of living and
worked in the mines and railroads. Others, who were native to the Southwest, faced a job market that no longer required their skills. They moved into
mining, railroad, and agricultural labor in search of a means of earning a
living. According to Albert Camarillo (1979), the influx of Anglo[5] capital into
the pastoral economy of Santa Barbara rendered obsolete the skills of many
Chicano males who had worked as ranch hands and farmers prior to the
urbanization of that economy. While some women and children accompanied their husbands to the railroad and mining camps, many of these camps
discouraged or prohibited family settlement.

The American period (after 1848) was characterized by considerable
transiency for the Chicano population. Its impact on families is seen in the
growth of female-headed households, reflected in the data as early as 1860.
Richard Griswold del Castillo (1979) found a sharp increase in female-headed

households in Los Angeles, from a low of 13 percent in 1844 to 31 percent in 1880. Camarillo (1979:120) documents a similar increase in Santa Barbara, from 15 percent in 1844 to 30 percent by 1880. These increases appear to be due not so much to divorce, which was infrequent in this Catholic population, as to widowhood and temporary abandonment in search of work. Given the hazardous nature of work in the mines and railroad camps, the death of a husband, father, or son who was laboring in these sites was not uncommon. Griswold del Castillo (1979) reports a higher death rate among men than women in Los Angeles. The rise in female-headed households, therefore, reflects the instabilities and insecurities introduced into women's lives as a result of the changing social organization of work.

One outcome, the increasing participation of women and children in the labor force, was primarily a response to economic factors that required the modification of traditional values. According to Louisa Vigil, who was born in 1890, "The women didn't work at that time. The man was supposed to marry that girl and take care of her.... Your grandpa never did let me work for nobody. He always had to work, and we never did have really bad times" (Elasser et al. 1980:14).

Vigil's comments are reinforced in Mario Garcia's (1980) study of El Paso. In the 393 households he examined in the 1900 census, he found 17.1 percent of the women to be employed. The majority of this group were daughters, mothers with no husbands, and single women. In Los Angeles and Santa Barbara, where there were greater work opportunities for women than in El Paso, wives who were heads of household worked in seasonal and part-time jobs, and lived from the earnings of children and relatives in an effort to maintain traditional female roles.

Slowly, entire families were encouraged to go to railroad work camps and were eventually incorporated into the agricultural labor market. This was a response both to the extremely low wages paid to Chicano laborers and to the preferences of employers, who saw family labor as a way of stabilizing the work force. For Chicanos, engaging all family members in agricultural work was a means of increasing their earnings to a level close to subsistence for the entire group and of keeping the family unit together. Camarillo provides a picture of the interplay of work, family, and migration in the Santa Barbara area in the following observation:

> The time of year when women and children were employed in
> the fruit cannery and participated in the almond and olive harvest
> coincided with the seasons when the men were most likely to be
> engaged in seasonal migratory work. There were seasons, however,
> especially in the early summer when the entire family migrated
> from the city to pick fruit. This type of family seasonal harvest
> was evident in Santa Barbara by the 1890s. As walnuts replaced
> almonds and as the fruit industry expanded, Chicano family labor
> became essential. (1979:93)

This arrangement, while bringing families together, did not decrease the hardships that Chicanas had to confront in raising their families. We may infer something about the rigors of that life from Jesse Lopez de la Cruz's description of the workday of migrant farm laborers in the 1940s. Work conditions in the 1890s were as difficult, if not worse.

> We always went to where the women and men were going to work, because if it were just the men working it wasn't worth going out there because we wouldn't earn enough to support a family.... We would start around 6:30 a.m. and work for four or five hours, then walk home and eat and rest until about three-thirty in the afternoon when it cooled off. We would go back and work until we couldn't see. Then I'd clean up the kitchen. I was doing the housework and working out in the fields and taking care of two children. (Quoted in Goldman 1981:119–120)

In the towns, women's reproductive labor was intensified by the congested and unsanitary conditions of the barrios in which they lived. Garcia described the following conditions in El Paso:

> Mexican women had to haul water for washing and cooking from the river or public water pipes. To feed their families, they had to spend time marketing, often in Ciudad Juarez across the border, as well as long, hot hours cooking meals and coping with the burden of desert sand both inside and outside their homes. Besides the problem of raising children, unsanitary living conditions forced Mexican mothers to deal with disease and illness in their families. Diphtheria, tuberculosis, typhus and influenza were never too far away. Some diseases could be directly traced to inferior city services.... As a result, Mexican mothers had to devote much energy to caring for sick children, many of whom died. (1980:320–321)

While the extended family has remained an important element of Chicano life, it was eroded in the American period in several ways. Griswold del Castillo (1979), for example, points out that in 1845 about 71 percent of Angelenos lived in extended families, whereas by 1880, fewer than half did. This decrease in extended families appears to be a response to the changed economic conditions and the instabilities generated by the new sociopolitical structure. Additionally, the imposition of American law and custom ignored, and ultimately undermined, some aspects of the extended family. The extended family in traditional Mexican life consisted of an important set of family, religious, and community obligations. Women, while valued primarily for their domesticity, had certain legal and property rights that acknowledged the importance of their work, their families of origin, and their children. In California, for example,

equal ownership of property between husband and wife had been
one of the mainstays of the Spanish and Mexican family systems.
Community-property laws were written into the civil codes with
the intention of strengthening the economic controls of the wife
and her relatives. The American government incorporated these
Mexican laws into the state constitution, but later court decisions
interpreted these statutes so as to undermine the wife's economic
rights. In 1861, the legislature passed a law that allowed the
deceased wife's property to revert to her husband. Previously it
had been inherited by her children and relatives if she died without
a will. (Griswold del Castillo 1979:69)

The impact of this and similar court rulings was to "strengthen the property rights of the husband at the expense of his wife and children" (Griswold
del Castillo 1979:69).

In the face of the legal, social, and economic changes that occurred during the American period, Chicanas were forced to cope with a series of dis-
locations in traditional life. They were caught between conflicting pressures
to maintain traditional women's roles and family customs, and the need to
participate in the economic support of their families by working outside the
home. During this period the preservation of traditional customs—such as
languages, celebrations, and healing practices—became an important element in maintaining and supporting familial ties.

According to Alex Saragoza (1983), transiency, the effects of racism and
segregation, and proximity to Mexico aided in the maintenance of traditional
family practices. Garcia has suggested that women were the guardians of
Mexican cultural traditions within the family. He cites the work of anthropologist Manuel Gamio, who identified the retention of many Mexican customs
among Chicanos in settlements around the United States in the early 1900s.

These included folklore, songs, and ballads, birthday celebrations,
saints' days, baptisms, weddings, and funerals in the traditional
style. Because of poverty, a lack of physicians in the barrios, and
adherence to traditional customs, Mexicans continued to use
medicinal herbs. Gamio also identified the maintenance of a number of oral traditions, and Mexican style cooking. (Garcia 1980:322)

Of vital importance to the integrity of traditional culture was the perpetuation of the Spanish language. Factors that aided in the maintenance
of other aspects of Mexican culture also helped in sustaining the language.
However, entry into English-language public schools introduced the children
and their families to systematic efforts to erase their native tongue. Griswold
del Castillo reports that in the early 1880s there was considerable pressure
against speakers of Spanish in the public schools. He also found that some
Chicano parents responded to this kind of discrimination by helping support
independent bilingual schools. These efforts, however, were short-lived.

Another key factor in conserving Chicano culture was the extended family network, particularly the system of *compadrazgo* (godparenting). Although the full extent of the impact of the American period on the Chicano extended family is not known, it is generally acknowledged that this family system, though lacking many legal and social sanctions, played an important role in the preservation of the Mexican community (Camarillo 1979). In Mexican society, godparents were an important way of linking family and community through respected friends or authorities. Participants in the important rites of passage in the child's life, such as baptism, first Communion, confirmation, and marriage, godparents had a moral obligation to act as guardians, to provide financial assistance in times of need, and to substitute in case of the death of a parent. Camarillo (1979) points out that in traditional society these bonds cut across class and racial lines.

The rite of baptism established kinship networks between rich and poor, between Spanish, mestizo and American Indian, and often carried with it political loyalty and economic-occupational ties. The leading California patriarchs in the pueblo played important roles in the *compadrazgo* network. They sponsored dozens of children for their workers or poorer relatives. The kindness of the *padrino* and *madrina* was repaid with respect and support from the *pobladores* (Camarillo 1979:12–13).

The extended family network, which included godparents, expanded the support groups for women who were widowed or temporarily abandoned and for those who were in seasonal, part- or full-time work. It suggests, therefore, the potential for an exchange of services among poor people whose income did not provide the basis for family subsistence. Griswold del Castillo (1979) argues that family organization influenced literacy rates and socioeconomic mobility among Chicanos in Los Angeles between 1850 and 1880. His data suggest that children in extended families (defined as those with at least one other relative living in a nuclear family household) had higher literacy rates than those in nuclear families. He also argues that those in larger families fared better economically and experienced less downward mobility. The data here are too limited to generalize to the Chicano experience as a whole, but they do reinforce the actual and potential importance of this family form to the continued cultural autonomy of the Chicano community.

 ## CONCLUSION

Reproductive labor for African American, Chinese American, and Mexican American women in the nineteenth century centered on the struggle to maintain family units in the face of a variety of assaults. Treated primarily as workers rather than as members of family groups, these women labored to maintain, sustain, stabilize, and reproduce their families while working in both the public (productive) and private (reproductive) spheres. Thus, the concept of reproductive labor, when applied to women of color, must be modified to account for the fact that labor in the productive sphere was required to achieve even minimal levels of family subsistence. Long after industrialization had begun to reshape family roles among middle-class White families, driving White women into a cult of domesticity, women of color were coping with an extended day. This day included subsistence labor outside the family and domestic labor within the family. For slaves, domestics, migrant farm laborers, seasonal factory workers, and prostitutes, the distinctions between labor that reproduced family life and labor that economically sustained it were minimized. The expanded workday was one of the primary ways in which reproductive labor increased.

Racial-ethnic families were sustained and maintained in the face of various forms of disruption. Yet the women and their families paid a high price in the process. High rates of infant mortality, a shortened life span, and the early onset of crippling and debilitating disease give some insight into the costs of survival.

The poor quality of housing and the neglect of communities further increased reproductive labor. Not only did racial-ethnic women work hard outside the home for mere subsistence, they worked very hard inside the home to achieve even minimal standards of privacy and cleanliness. They were continually faced with disease and illness that resulted directly from the absence of basic sanitation. The fact that some African women murdered their children to prevent them from becoming slaves is an indication of the emotional strain associated with bearing and raising children while participating in the colonial labor system.

We have uncovered little information about the use of birth control, the prevalence of infanticide, or the motivations that may have generated these or other behaviors. We can surmise, however, that no matter how much children were accepted, loved, or valued among any of these groups of people, their futures were precarious. Keeping children alive, helping them to understand and participate in a system that exploited them, and working to ensure a measure—no matter how small—of cultural integrity intensified women's reproductive labor.

Being a woman of color in nineteenth-century American society meant having extra work both inside and outside the home. It meant being defined as outside of or deviant from the norms and values about women that were being generated in the dominant White culture. The notion of separate spheres of male and female labor that developed in the nineteenth century had contradictory outcomes for Whites. It was the basis for the confinement of upper-middle-class White women to the household and for much of the protective legislation that subsequently developed in the workplace. At the same time, it sustained White families by providing social acknowledgment and support to women in the performance of their family roles. For racial-ethnic women, however, the notion of separate spheres served to reinforce their subordinate status and became, in effect, another assault. As they increased their work outside the home, they were forced into a productive labor sphere that was organized for men and "desperate" women who were so unfortunate or immoral that they could not confine their work to the domestic sphere. In the productive sphere, racial-ethnic women faced exploitative jobs and depressed wages. In the reproductive sphere, they were denied the opportunity to embrace the dominant ideological definition of "good" wife or mother. In essence, they were faced with a double-bind situation, one that required their participation in the labor force to sustain family life but damned them as women, wives, and mothers because they did not confine their labor to the home.

Finally, the struggle of women of color to build and maintain families provides vivid testimony to the role of race in structuring family life in the United States. As Maxine Baca Zinn points out:

> Social categories and groups subordinate in the racial hierarchy are often deprived of access to social institutions that offer supports for family life. Social categories and groups elevated in the racial hierarchy have different and better connections to institutions that can sustain families. Social location and its varied connection with social resources thus have profound consequences for family life. (1990:74)

From the founding of the United States, and throughout its history, race has been a fundamental criterion determining the kind of work people do, the wages they receive, and the kind of legal, economic, political, and social support provided for their families. Women of color have faced limited economic resources, inferior living conditions, alien cultures and languages, and overt hostility in their struggle to create a "place" for families of color in the United States. That place, however, has been a precarious one because the society has not provided supports for these families. Today we see the outcomes of that legacy in statistics showing that people of color, compared with whites, have higher rates of female-headed households, out-of-wedlock births, divorce, and other factors associated with family disruption. Yet the causes of these variations do not lie merely in the higher concentrations of poverty among people of color; they are also due to the ways race has been used as a basis for denying and providing support to families. Women of color have struggled to maintain their families against all of these odds.

NOTES

Acknowledgments: The research in this study was an outgrowth of my participation in a larger collaborative project examining family, community, and work lives of racial-ethnic women in the United States. I am deeply indebted to the scholarship and creativity of members of the group in the development of this study. Appreciation is extended to Elizabeth Higginbotham, Cheryl Townsend Gilkes, Evelyn Nakano Glenn, and Ruth Zambrana (members of the original working group), and to the Ford Foundation for a grant that supported in part the work of this study.

1. The term "White" is a global construct used to characterize peoples of European descent who migrated to and helped colonize America. In the seventeenth century, most of these immigrants were from the British Isles. However, during the time period covered by this article, European immigrants became increasingly diverse. It is a limitation of this chapter that time and space do not permit a fuller discussion of the variations in the White European immigrant experience. For the purposes of the argument being made herein and of the contrast it seeks to draw between the experiences of mainstream (European) cultural groups and those of racial-ethnic minorities, the differences among European settlers are joined and the broad similarities emphasized.
2. For a more detailed discussion of this argument and the kinds of social supports provided these families, see an earlier version of this paper: "Our Mothers' Grief: Racial-Ethnic Women and the Maintenance of Families," *Journal of Family History* 13 (4) (1988): 415–431.
3. The term "reproductive labor" is used to refer to all of the work of women in the home. This includes, but is not limited to, the buying and preparation of food and clothing, provision of emotional support and nurturance for all family members, bearing children, and planning, organizing, and carrying out a wide variety of tasks associated with socialization. All of these activities are necessary for the growth of patriarchal capitalism because they maintain, sustain, stabilize, and reproduce (both biologically and socially) the labor force.
4. Recent research suggests that there were some tasks assigned primarily to males and some others to females. Whereas some gender-role distinctions with regard to work may have existed on some plantations, it clear that slave women were not exempt from strenuous physical labor.
5. This term is used to refer to White Americans of European ancestry.

REFERENCES

Aschenbrenner, Joyce. 1975. *Lifelines: Black Families in Change.* New York: Holt, Rinehart, and Winston.

Baca Zinn, Maxine. 1990. "Family, Feminism and Race in America." *Gender and Society* 4(1) (March): 68–82.

Barrera, Mario. 1979. *Race and Class in the Southwest.* Notre Dame, Ind.: Notre Dame University Press.

Blassingame, John. 1972. *The Slave Community: Plantation Life in the Antebellum South.* New York: Oxford University Press.

_____. 1977. *Slave Testimony: Two Centuries of Letters, Speeches, Interviews, and Autobiographies.* Baton Rouge: Louisiana State University Press.

Camarillo, Albert. 1979. *Chicanos in a Changing Society.* Cambridge, Mass.: Harvard University Press.

Caulfield, Mina Davis. 1974. "Imperialism, the Family, and Cultures of Resistance." *Socialist Review* 4 (2) (October): 67–85.

Davis, Angela. 1971. "Reflections on the Black Woman's Role in the Community of Slaves." *Black Scholar* 3 (4) (December): 2–15.

_____. 1981. *Women, Race, and Class.* New York: Random House.

Degler, Carl. 1980. *At Odds.* New York: Oxford University Press.

Elasser, Nan, Kyle MacKenzie, and Yvonne Tixier Y. Vigil. 1980. *Las Mujeres.* New York: The Feminist Press.

Elasser, Nan, Kyle MacKenzie, and Yvonne Tixier Y. Vigil. 1980. *Las Mujeres.* New York: The Feminist Press.

Garcia, Mario T. 1980. "The Chicano in American History: The Mexican Women of El Paso, 1880–1920—A Case Study." *Pacific Historical Review* 49 (2) (May): 315–358.

Genovese, Eugene D., and Elinor Miller, eds. 1974. *Plantation, Town, and County: Essays on the Local History of American Slave Society.* Urbana: University of Illinois Press.

Glenn, Evelyn Nakano. 1981. "Family Strategies of Chinese-Americans: An Institutional Analysis." Paper presented at the Society for the Study of Social Problems Symposium.

_____. 1983. "Split Household, Small Producer, and Dual Earner: An Analysis of Chinese-American Family Strategies." *Journal of Marriage and the Family* 45 (1) (February): 35–46.

Goldman, Marion S. 1981. *Gold Diggers and Silver Miners.* Ann Arbor: University of Michigan Press.

Griswold del Castillo, Richard. 1979. *The Los Angeles Barrio: 1850–1890.* Los Angeles: University of California Press.

Gutman, Herbert. 1976. *The Black Family in Slavery and Freedom, 1750–1925.* New York: Pantheon.

Hirata, Lucia Cheng. 1979. "Free, Indentured, Enslaved: Chinese Prostitutes in Nineteenth Century America." *Signs* 5 (Autumn): 3–29.

Jones, Jacqueline. 1985. *Labor of Love, Labor of Sorrow.* New York: Basic Books.

_____. 1982. *Out to Work.* New York: Oxford University Press.

Kingston, Maxine Hong. 1977. *The Woman Warrior.* New York: Vintage Books.

Matthaei, Julie. 1982. *An Economic History of Women in America.* New York: Schocken Books.

Nee, Victor G., and Brett de Bary Nee. 1973. *Longtime Californ'.* New York: Pantheon Books.

Saragoza, Alex M. 1983. "The Conceptualization of the History of the Chicano Family: Work, Family, and Migration in Chicanos." In *Research Proceedings of the Symposium on Chicano Research and Public Policy.* Stanford, Calif.: Stanford University, Center for Chicano Research.

Shimkin, Demetri, E. M. Shimkin, and D. A. Frate, eds. 1978. *The Extended Family in Black Societies.* The Hague: Mouton.

Stack, Carol S. 1974. *All Our Kin: Strategies for Survival in a Black Community.* New York: Harper & Row.

Sudarkasa, Niara. 1981. "Interpreting the African Heritage in Afro-American Family Organization." In *Black Families,* Harriette Pipes McAdoo, ed. Beverly Hills, Calif.: Sage.

White, Deborah Gray. 1985. *Ar'n't I a Woman? Female Slaves in the Plantation South.* New York: W. W. Norton.

Wright, Gwendolyn. 1981. *Building the Dream: A Social History of Housing in America.* New York: Pantheon.

Zaretsky, Eli. 1978. "The Effects of the Economic Crisis on the Family." In *U.S. Capitalism in Crisis,* edited by Crisis Reader Editorial Collective. New York: Union of Radical Political Economists.

QUESTIONS FOR CRITICAL THINKING

Reading 17

1. Dill's discussion of the history of families demonstrates the importance of examining race, social class, and gender simultaneously when we examine the institution of family. Do you think that this is important? Why, or why not?

2. How do the policies of other institutions (e.g., economy, education, the state) result in additional strains on the family for women of color that white women do not experience? What policies can you think of that might alleviate some of these strains?

3. How is your own definition of family inclusive or exclusive of a diversity of race, class, or gender experiences?

Reading 18

FAMILIES ON THE FAULT LINE
America's Working Class Speaks about the Family, the Economy, Race, and Ethnicity

LILLIAN B. RUBIN

Not surprisingly, there are generational differences in what fuels the conflict around the division of labor in families. For the older couples—those who grew up in a different time, whose marriages started with another set of ground rules—the struggle is not simply around how much men do or about whether they take responsibility for the daily tasks of living without being pushed, prodded, and reminded. That's the overt manifestation of the discord, the trigger that starts the fight. But the noise of the explosion when it comes serves to conceal the more fundamental issue underlying the dissension: legitimacy. What does she have a *right* to expect? "What do I know about doing stuff around the house?" asks Frank Moreno, a forty-eight-year-old foreman in a warehouse. "I wasn't brought up like that. My pop, he never did one damn thing, and my mother never complained. It was her job; she did it and kept quiet. Besides, I work my ass off every day. Isn't that enough?"

For younger couples, those under forty, the problem is somewhat different. The men may complain about the expectation that they'll participate more fully in the care and feeding of the family, but talk to them about it quietly and they'll usually admit that it's not really unfair, given that their wives also work outside the home. In these homes, the issue between husband and wife isn't only who does what. That's there and it's a source of more or less conflict, depending upon what the men actually do and how forceful their wives are in their demands. But in most of these families there's at least a verbal consensus that men *ought* to participate in the tasks of daily life. Which raises the next and perhaps more difficult issue in contest between them: Who feels responsible for getting the tasks done? Who regards them as a duty, and for whom are they an option? On this, tradition rules.

Even in families where husbands now share many of the tasks, their wives still bear full responsibility for the organization of family life. A man may help cook the meal these days, but a woman is most likely to be the one who has planned it. He may take the children to child care, but she virtually always has had to arrange it. It's she also who is accountable for the emotional life of the family, for monitoring the emotional temperature of its members and making the necessary corrections. It's this need to be responsible for it all that often feels as burdensome as the tasks themselves. "It's not just doing all the stuff that needs doing," explains Maria Jankowicz, a white twenty-eight-year-old assembler in an electronics factory. "It's worrying all the time about everything and always having to arrange everything, you know what I mean. It's like I run the whole show. If I don't stay on top of it all, things fall apart because nobody else is going to do it. The kids can't and Nick, well, forget it," she concludes angrily.

If, regardless of age, life stage, or verbal consensus, women usually still carry the greatest share of the household burdens, why is it important to notice that younger men grant legitimacy to their wives' demands and older men generally do not? Because men who believe their wives have a right to expect their participation tend to suffer guilt and discomfort when they don't live up to those expectations. And no one lives comfortably with guilt.

It's possible, of course, that the men who speak of guilt and rights are only trying to impress me by mouthing the politically correct words. But even if true, they display a sensitivity to the issue that's missing from the men who don't speak those words. For words are more than just words. They embody ideas; they are the symbols that give meaning to our thoughts; they shape our consciousness. New ideas come to us on the wings of words. It's words that bring those ideas to life, that allow us to see possibilities unrecognized before we gave them words. Indeed, without words, there is no conscious thought, no possibility for the kind of self-reflection that lights the path of change.[1]

True, there's often a long way between word and deed. But the man who feels guilty when he disappoints his wife's expectations has a different consciousness than the one who doesn't—a difference that usually makes for at least some small change in his behavior. Although the emergence of this changing male consciousness is visible in all the racial groups in this study, there also are differences among them that are worthy of comment.

Virtually all the men do some work inside the family—tending the children, washing dishes, running the vacuum, going to the market. And they generally also remain responsible for those tasks that have always been traditionally male—mowing the lawn, shoveling the snow, fixing the car, cleaning the garage, doing repairs around the house. Among the white families in this study, 16 percent of the men share the family work relatively equally, almost always those who live in families where they and their wives work different shifts or where the men are unemployed. "What choice do I have?" asks Don Bartlett, a thirty-year-old white handyman who works days while his wife is on the swing shift. "I'm the only one here, so I do what's got to be done."

Asian and Latino men of all ages, however, tend to operate more often on the old male model, even when they work different shifts or are unemployed, a finding that puzzled me at first. Why, I wondered, did I find only two Asian men and one Latino who are real partners in the work of the family? Aren't these men subject to the same social and personal pressures others experience?

The answer is both yes and no. The pressures are there but, depending upon where they live, there's more or less support for resisting them. The Latino and Asian men who live in ethnic neighborhoods—settings where they are embedded in an intergenerational community and where the language and culture of the home country is kept alive by a steady stream of new immigrants—find strong support for clinging to the old ways. Therefore, change comes much more slowly in those families. The men who live outside the ethnic quarter are freer from the mandates and constraints of these often tight-knit communities, therefore are more responsive to the winds of change in the larger society.

These distinctions notwithstanding, it's clear that Asian and Latino men generally participate least in the work of the household and are the least likely to believe they have much responsibility there beyond bringing home a paycheck. "Taking care of the house and kids is my wife's job, that's all," says Joe Gomez flatly.

"A Chinese man mopping a floor? I've never seen it yet," says Amy Lee angrily. Her husband, Dennis, trying to make a joke of the conflict with his wife, says with a smile, "In Chinese families men don't do floors and windows. I help with the dishes sometimes if she needs me to or," he laughs, "if she screams loud enough. The rest, well, it's pretty much her job."

The commonly held stereotype about black men abandoning women and children, however, doesn't square with the families in this study. In fact, black men are the most likely to be real participants in the daily life of the family and are more intimately involved in raising their children than any of the others. True, the men's family workload doesn't always match their wives', and the women are articulate in their complaints about this.

Nevertheless, compared to their white, Asian, or Latino counterparts, the black families look like models of egalitarianism.

Nearly three-quarters of the men in the African-American families in this study do a substantial amount of the cooking, cleaning, and child care, sometimes even more than their wives. All explain it by saying one version or another of: "I just figure it's my job, too." Which simply says what is, without explaining how it came to be that way.

To understand that, we have to look at family histories that tell the story of generations of African-American women who could find work and men who could not, and to the family culture that grew from this difficult and painful reality. "My mother worked six days a week cleaning other people's houses, and my father was an ordinary laborer, when he could find work, which wasn't very often," explains thirty-two-year-old Troy Payne, a black waiter and father of two children. "So he was home a lot more than she was, and he'd do what he had to around the house. The kids all had to do their share, too. It seemed only fair, I guess."

Difficult as the conflict around the division of labor is, it's only one of the many issues that have become flash points in family life since mother went to work. Most important, perhaps, is the question: Who will care for the children? For the lack of decent, affordable facilities for the care of the children creates unbearable problems and tensions for these working-class families.

It's hardly news that child care is an enormous headache and expense for all two-job families. In many professional middle-class families, where the child-care bill can be $1,500–2,000 a month, it competes with the mortgage payment as the biggest single monthly expenditure. Problematic as this may be, however, these families are the lucky ones when compared to working-class families, many of whom don't earn much more than the cost of child care in these upper middle-class families. Even the families in this study at the highest end of the earnings scale, those who earn $42,000 a year, can't dream of such costly arrangements.

For most working-class families, therefore, child care often is patched together in ways that leave parents anxious and children in jeopardy. "Care for the little ones, that's a real big problem," says Beverly Waldov, a thirty-year-old white mother of three children, the youngest two, products of a second marriage, under three years old. "My oldest girl is nine, so she's not such a problem. I hate the idea of her being a latchkey kid, but what can I do? We don't even have the money to put the little ones in one of those good day-care places, so I don't have any choice with her. She's just *got* to be able to take care of herself after school," she says, her words a contest between anxiety and hope.

"We have a kind of complicated arrangement for the little kids. Two days a week, my mom takes care of them. We pay her, but at least I don't have to worry when they're with her; I know it's fine. But she works the rest of the time, so the other days we take them to this woman's house. It's the best we can afford, but it's not great because she keeps too many kids, and I know they don't get good attention. Especially the little one; she's just a baby, you know." She pauses and looks away, anguished. "She's so clingy when I bring her home; she can't let go of me, like nobody's paid her any mind all day. But it's not like I have a choice. We barely make it now; if I stop working, we'd be in real trouble."

Even such makeshift solutions don't work for many families. Some speak of being unable to afford day care at all. "We couldn't pay our bills if we had to pay for somebody to take care of the kids."

Some say they're unwilling to leave the children in the care of strangers. "I just don't believe someone else should be raising our kids, that's all."

Some have tried a variety of child-care arrangements, only to have them fail in a moment of need. "We tried a whole bunch of things, and maybe they work for a little while," says Faye Ensey, a black twenty-eight-year-old office worker. "But what happens when your kid gets sick? Or when the baby sitter's kids get sick? I lost two jobs in a row because my kids kept getting sick and I couldn't go to work. Or else I couldn't take my little one to the baby sitter because her kids were sick. They finally fired me for absenteeism. I didn't really blame them, but it felt terrible anyway. It's such a hassle, I sometimes think I'd be glad to just stay home. But we can't afford for me not to work, so we had to figure out something else."

For such families, that "something else" is the decision to take jobs on different shifts—a decision made by one-fifth of the families in this study. With one working days and the other on swing or graveyard, one parent is home with the children at all times. "We were getting along okay before Daryl junior was born, because Shona, my daughter, was getting on. You know, she didn't need somebody with her all the time, so we could both work days," explains Daryl Adams, a black thirty-year-old postal clerk with a ten-year-old daughter and a nine-month-old son. "I used to work the early shift—seven to three—so I'd get home a little bit after she got here. It worked out okay. But then this here big surprise came along." He stops, smiles down fondly at his young son and runs his hand over his nearly bald head.

"Now between the two of us working, we don't make enough money to pay for child care and have anything left over, so this is the only way we can manage. Besides, both of us, Alesha and me, we think it's better for one of us to be here, not just for the baby, for my daughter, too. She's growing up and, you know, I think maybe they need even more watching than when they were younger. She's coming to the time when she could get into all kinds of trouble if we're not here to put the brakes on."

But the cost such arrangements exact on marriage can be very high. When I asked these husbands and wives when they have time to talk, more often than not I got a look of annoyance at a question that, on its face, seemed stupid to them. "Talk? How can we talk when we hardly see each other?" "Talk? What's that?" "Talk? Ha, that's a joke."

Mostly, conversation is limited to the logistics that take place at shift-changing time when children and chores are handed off from one to the other. With children dancing around underfoot, the incoming parent gets a quick summary of the day's or night's events, a list of reminders about things to be done, perhaps about what's cooking in the pot on the stove. "Sometimes when I'm coming home and it's been a hard day, I think: Wouldn't it be wonderful if I could just sit down with Leon for half an hour and we could have a quiet beer together?" thirty-one-year-old Emma Guerrero, a Latina baker, says wistfully.

But it's not to be. If the arriving spouse gets home early enough, there may be an hour when both are there together. But with the pressures of the workday fresh for one and awaiting the other, and with children clamoring for parental attention, this isn't a promising moment for any serious conversation.

Some of the luckier couples work different shifts on the same days, so they're home together on weekends. But even in these families there's so little time for normal family life that there's hardly any room for anyone or anything outside.

For those whose days off don't match, the problems of sustaining both the couple relationship and family life are magnified enormously. "The last two years have been hell for us," says thirty-five-year-old Tina Mulvaney, a white mother of two teenagers. "My son got into bad company and had some trouble, so Mike and I decided one of us had to be home. But we can't make it without my check, so I can't quit.

"Mike drives a cab and I work in a hospital, so we figured one of us could transfer to nights. We talked it over and decided it would be best if I was here during the day and he was here at night. He controls the kids, especially my son, better than I do. When he lays down the law, they listen." She interrupts her narrative to reflect on the difficulty of raising children. "You know, when they were little, I used to think about how much easier it would be when they got older. But now I see it's not true; that's when you really have to begin to worry about them. This is when they need someone to be here all the time to make sure they stay out of trouble."

She stops again, this time fighting tears, then takes up where she left off. "So now Mike works days and I work graveyard. I hate it, but it's the only answer; at least this way somebody's here all the time. I get home about 8:30 in the morning. The kids and Mike are gone. It's the best time of the day because it's the only time I have a little quiet here. I clean up the house a little, do the shopping and the laundry and whatever, then I go to sleep for a couple of hours until the kids come home from school.

"Mike gets home at five; we eat; then he takes over for the night, and I go back to sleep for another couple of hours. I try to get up by 9 so we can all have a little time together, but I'm so tired that I don't make it a lot of times. And by 10, he's sleeping because he has to be up by 6 in the morning. So if I don't get up, we hardly see each other at all. Mike's here on weekends, but I'm not. Right now I have Tuesday and Wednesday off. I keep hoping for a Monday–Friday shift, but it's what everybody wants, and I don't have the seniority yet. It's hard, very hard; there's no time to live or anything," she concludes with a listless sigh.

Even in families where wife and husband work the same shift, there's less time for leisure pursuits and social activities than ever before, not just because both parents work full-time but also because people work longer hours now than they did twenty years ago.[2] Two decades ago, weekends saw occasional family outings, Friday evening bowling, a Saturday trip to the shopping mall, a Sunday with extended family, once in a while an evening out without the children. In summer, when the children weren't in school, a week night might find the family paying a short visit to a friend, a relative, or a neighbor. Now almost everyone I speak with complains that it's hard to find time for even these occasional outings. Instead, most off-work hours are spent trying to catch up with the dozens of family and household tasks that were left undone during the regular work week. When they aren't doing chores, parents guiltily try to do in two days a week what usually takes seven—that is, to establish a sense of family life for themselves and their children.

"Leisure," snorts Peter Pittman, a twenty-eight-year-old African-American father of two, married six years. "With both of us working like we do, there's no time for anything. We got two little kids; I commute better than an hour each way to my job. Then we live here for half rent because I take care of the place for the landlord. So if somebody's got a complaint, I've got to take care of it, you know, fix it myself or get the landlord to get somebody out to do it if I can't. Most things I can do myself, but it takes time. I sometimes wonder what this life's all about, because this sure ain't what I call living. We don't go anyplace; we don't do anything; Christ, we hardly have time to go to the toilet. There's always some damn thing that's waiting that you've got to do."

Clearly, such complaints aren't unique to the working class. The pressures of time, the impoverishment of social life, the anxieties about child care, the fear that children will live in a world of increasing scarcity, the threat of divorce—all these are part of family life today, regardless of class. Nevertheless, there are important differences between those in the higher reaches of the class structure and the families of the working class. The simple fact that middle-class families have more discretionary income is enough to make a big difference in the quality of their social life. For they generally have enough money to pay for a babysitter once in a while so that parents can have some time to themselves; enough, too, for a family vacation, for tickets to a concert, a play, or a movie. At $7.50 a ticket in a New York or San Francisco movie house, a working-class couple will settle for a $3.00 rental that the whole family can watch together.

Finding time and energy for sex is also a problem, one that's obviously an issue for two-job families of any class. But it's harder to resolve in working-class families because they have so few resources with which to buy some time and privacy for themselves. Ask about their sex lives and you'll be met with an angry, "What's that?" or a wistful, "I wish." When it happens, it is, as one woman put it, "on the run"—a situation that's particularly unsatisfactory for most women. For them, the pleasure of sex is related to the whole of the interaction—to a sense of intimacy and connection, to at least a few relaxed, loving moments. When they can't have these, they're likely to avoid sex altogether—a situation the men find equally unsatisfactory.

"Sex?" asks Lisa Scranton, a white twenty-nine-year-old mother of three who feigns a puzzled frown, as if she doesn't quite know the meaning of the word. "Oh yeah, that; I remember now," she says, her lips smiling, her eyes sad. "At the beginning, when we first got together, it was WOW, real hot, great. But after a while it cools down, doesn't it? Right now, it's down the toilet. I wonder, does it happen to everybody like that?" she asks dejectedly.

"I guess the worst is when you work different shifts like we do and you get to see each other maybe six minutes a day. There's no time for sex. Sometimes we try to steal a few minutes for ourselves but, I don't know, I can't get into it that way. He can. You know how men are; they can do it any time. Give them two minutes, and they can get off. But it takes me time; I mean, I like to feel close, and you can't do that in three minutes. And there's the kids; they're right here all the time. I don't want to do it if it means being interrupted. Then he gets mad, so sometimes I do. But it's a problem, a real problem."

The men aren't content with these quick sexual exchanges either. But for them it's generally better than no sex at all, while for the women it's often the other way around. "You want to talk about sex, huh?" asks Lisa's husband, Chuck, his voice crackling with anger. "Yeah, I don't mind; it's fine, only I got nothing to talk about. Far as I'm concerned, that's one of the things I found out about marriage. You get married, you give up sex. We hardly ever do it anymore, and when we do, it's like she's doing me a favor."

"Christ, I know the way we've got to do things now isn't great," he protests, running a hand through his hair agitatedly. "We don't see each other but a few minutes a day, but I don't see why we can't take five and have a little fun in the sack. Sure, I like it better when we've got more time, too. But for her, if it can't be perfect, she gets all wound and uptight and it's like . . ." He stops, groping for words, then explodes, "It's like screwing a cold fish."

She isn't just a "cold fish," however. The problems they face are deeper than that. For once such conflicts arise, spontaneity takes flight and sex becomes a problem that needs attention rather than a time out for pleasure and renewal. Between times, therefore, he's busy calculating how much time has passed: "It's been over two weeks"; nursing his wounds: "I don't want to have to beg her"; feeling deprived and angry: "I don't know why I got married." When they finally do come together, he's disappointed. How could it be otherwise, given the mix of feelings he brings to the bed with him—the frustration and anger, the humiliation of feeling he has to beg her, the wounded sense of manhood.

Meanwhile, she, too, is preoccupied with sex, not with thoughts of pleasure but with figuring out how much time she has before, as she puts it, "he walks around with his mouth stuck out. I know I'm in real big trouble if we don't do it once a week. So I make sure we do, even if I don't want to." She doesn't say those words to him, of course. But he knows. And it's precisely this, the knowledge that she's servicing him rather than desiring him that's so hard for him to take.

The sexual arena is one of the most common places to find a "his and her" marriage—one marriage, two different sex lives.[3] Each partner has a different story to tell; each is convinced that his or her version is the real one. A husband says mournfully, "I'm lucky if we get to make love once a week." His wife reports with irritation, "It's two, sometimes three times a week." It's impossible to know whose account is closest to the reality. And it's irrelevant. If that's what they were after, they could keep tabs and get it straight. But facts and feelings are often at war in family life. And nowhere does right or wrong, true or false count for less than in their sexual interactions. It isn't that people arbitrarily distort the truth. They simply report their experience, and it's feeling, not fact, that dominates that experience; feeling, not fact, that is their truth.

But it's also true that, especially for women, the difference in frequency of sexual desire can be a response—sometimes conscious, sometimes not—to other conflicts in the marriage. It isn't that men never withhold sex as a weapon in the family wars, only that they're much more likely than women to be able to split sex from emotion, to feel their anger and still experience sexual desire. For a man, too, a sexual connection with his wife can relieve the pressures and tensions of the day, can make him feel whole again, even if they've barely spoken a word to each other.

For a woman it's different. What happens—or, more likely, what doesn't happen—in the kitchen, the living room, and the laundry room profoundly affects what's possible in the bedroom. When she feels distant, unconnected, angry; when her pressured life leaves her feeling fragmented; when she hasn't had a real conversation with her husband for a couple of days, sex is very far from either her mind or her loins. "I run around busy all the time, and he just sits there, so by the time we go to bed, I'm too tired," explains Linda Bloodworth, a white thirty-one-year-old telephone operator.

"Do you think your lack of sexual response has something to do with your anger at your husband's refusal to participate more fully in the household?" I ask.

Her eyes smoldering, her voice tight, she snaps, "No, I'm just tired, that's all." Then noticing something in my response, she adds, "I know what you're thinking; I saw that look. But really, I don't think it's *because* I'm angry; I really am tired. I have to admit, though, that I tell him if he helped more, maybe I wouldn't be so tired all the time. And," she adds defiantly, "maybe I wouldn't be."

Some couples, of course, manage their sexual relationship with greater ease. Often that's because they have less conflict in other areas of living. But whether they accommodate well or poorly, for all two-job families, sex requires a level of attention and concern that leaves most people wanting much of the time. "It's a problem, and I tell you, it has to be well planned," explains thirty-four-year-old Dan Stolman, a black construction worker. "But we manage okay; we make dates or try to slip it in when the baby's asleep and my daughter's out with a friend or something. I don't mean things are great in that department. I'm not always satisfied and neither is Lorraine. But what can you do? We try to do the best we can. Sex isn't all there is to a marriage, you know. We get along really well, so that makes up for a lot.

"What I really miss is that we don't ever make love anymore. I mean, we have sex like I said, but we don't have the kind of time you need to make love. We talk about getting away for an overnight by ourselves once in a while. Lorraine's mother would come watch the kids if we asked her; the problem is we don't have any extra cash to spare right now."

Time and money—precious commodities in short supply. These are the twin plagues of family life, the missing ingredients that combine to create families that are both frantic and fragile. Yet there's no mystery about what would alleviate the crisis that now threatens to engulf them: A job that pays a living wage, quality child-care facilities at rates people can pay, health care for all, parental leave, flexible work schedules, decent and affordable housing, a shorter work week so that parents and children have time to spend together, tax breaks for those in need rather than for those in greed, to mention just a few. These are the policies we need to put in place if we're to have any hope of making our families stable and healthy.

What we have, instead, are families in which mother goes to work to relieve financial distress, only to find that time takes its place next to money as a source of strain, tension, and conflict. Time for the children, time for the couple's relationship, time for self, time for social life—none of it easily available for anyone in two-job families, not even for the children, who are hurried along at every step of the way.[4] And money! Never enough, not for the clothes children need, not for the doctor's bill, not for a vacation, not even for the kind of child care that would allow parents to go to work in peace. But large as these problems loom in the lives of working-class families, difficult as they are to manage, they pale beside those they face when unemployment strikes, especially if it's father who loses his job.

NOTES

1. See Daniel Stern, *The Interpersonal World of the Infant* (New York: Basic Books, 1985), who argues that a child's capacity for self-reflection coincides with the development of language.
2. For an excellent analysis of the increasing amount of time Americans spend at work and the consequences to family and social life, see Juliet B. Schor, *The Overworked American* (New York: Basic Books, 1992). See also Carmen Sirianni and Andrea Walsh, "Through the Prism of Time: Temporal Structures in Postindustrial America," in Alan Wolfe, ed., *America at Century's End* (Berkeley: University of California Press, 1991), for their discussion of the "time famine."
3. For the origin of the term "his and her marriage," see Jessie Bernard, *The Future of Marriage* (New York: Bantam Books, 1973).
4. David Elkind, *The Hurried Child* (New York: Addison-Wesley, 1981).

QUESTIONS FOR CRITICAL THINKING

Reading 18

1. How do economic inequalities in our society place additional burdens on working-class and poor families?

2. How do some of the solutions developed by working-class and poor families to deal with economic difficulties reinforce traditional gender roles? How do they help to challenge these roles?

3. What policy changes in the institutions of the economy or education would aid working-class and poor families? Are such changes necessary? Why, or why not?

Reading 19

STABILITY AND CHANGE IN CHICANO MEN'S FAMILY LIVES

SCOTT COLTRANE

One of the most popular pejorative American slang terms to emerge in the 1980s was "macho," used to describe men prone to combative posturing, relentless sexual conquest, and other compulsive displays of masculinity. Macho men continually guard against imputations of being soft or feminine and thus tend to avoid domestic tasks and family activities that are considered "women's work." Macho comes from the Spanish *machismo,* and although the behaviors associated with it are clearly not limited to one ethnic group, Latino men are often stereotyped as especially prone toward macho displays.[1] This chapter uses in-depth interviews with twenty Chicano couples to explore how paid work and family work are divided. As in other contemporary American households, divisions of

Scott Coltrane, "Stability and Change in Chicano Men's Family Lives" from *Men's Lives, Fifth Edition,* edited by Michael S. Kimmel and Michael A. Messner. Copyright © 2001 by Pearson Education. Reprinted with the permission of the publisher.

labor in these Chicano families were far from balanced or egalitarian, and husbands tended to enjoy special privileges simply because they were men. Nevertheless, many couples were allocating household chores without reference to gender, and few of the Chicano men exhibited stereotypical macho behavior.

Chicanos, or Mexican-Americans, are often portrayed as living in poor farm-worker families composed of macho men, subservient women, and plentiful children. Yet these stereotypes have been changing, as diverse groups of people with Mexican and Latin-American heritage are responding to the same sorts of social and economic pressures faced by families of other ethnic backgrounds. For example, most Chicano families in the United States now live in urban centers or their suburbs rather than in traditional rural farming areas, and their patterns of marital interaction appear to be about as egalitarian as those of other American families. What's more, Chicanos will no longer be a numerical minority in the near future. Because of higher-than-average birth rates and continued in-migration, by the year 2015 Chicano children will outnumber Anglos in many southwest states, including California, Texas, Arizona, and New Mexico.[2]

When family researchers study white couples, they typically focus on middle-class suburban households, usually highlighting their strengths. Studies of ethnic minority families, in contrast, have tended to focus on the problems of poor or working-class households living in inner-city or rural settings. Because most research on Latino families in the United States has not controlled for social class, wife's employment status, or recency of immigration, a narrow and stereotyped view of these families as patriarchal and culturally backward has persisted. In addition, large-scale studies of "Hispanics" have failed to distinguish between divergent groups of people with Mexican, Central American, South American, Cuban, Puerto Rican, Spanish, or Portuguese ancestry. In contrast, contemporary scholars are beginning to look at some of the positive aspects of minority families and to focus on the economic and institutional factors that influence men's lives within these families.[3]

In 1990 and 1991, Elsa Valdez and I interviewed a group of twenty middle-class Chicano couples with young children living in Southern California. We were primarily interested in finding out if they were facing the same sorts of pressures experienced by other families, so we selected only families in which both the husband and the wife were employed outside the home—the most typical pattern among young parents in the United States today. We wanted to see who did what in these families and find out how they talked about the personal and financial pushes and pulls associated with raising a family. We interviewed wives and husbands separately in their homes, asking them a variety of questions about housework, child care, and their jobs. Elsewhere, we describe details of their time use and task performance, but here I analyze the couples' talk about work, family, and gender, exploring how feelings of entitlement and obligation are shaped by patterns of paid and unpaid labor.[4]

When we asked husbands and wives to sort sixty-four common household tasks according to who most often performed them, we found that wives in most families were responsible for housecleaning, clothes care, meal preparation, and clean-up, whereas husbands were primarily responsible for home maintenance and repair. Most routine child care was also performed by wives, though most husbands reported that they made substantial contributions to parenting. Wives saw the mundane daily housework as an ever-present burden that they had to shoulder themselves or delegate to someone else. While many wives did not expect the current division of labor to change, they did acknowledge that it was unbalanced. The men, although acknowledging that things weren't exactly fair, tended to minimize the asymmetry by seeing many of the short repetitive tasks associated with housekeeping as shared activities. Although there was tremendous diversity among the couples we talked to, we observed a general pattern of disagreement over how much family work the other spouse performed.

The sociologist Jesse Bernard provides us with a useful way to understand why this might be. Bernard suggested that every marital union contains two marriages—"his" and "hers."[5] We discovered from our interviews and observations that most of the husbands and wives were, indeed, living in separate marriages or separate worlds. Her world centered around keeping track of the countless details of housework and child care even though she was employed. His world centered around his work and his leisure activities so that he avoided noticing or anticipating the details of running a home. Husbands "helped out" when wives gave them tasks to do, and because they almost always complied with requests for help, most tended to assume that they were sharing the household labor. Because much of the work the women did was unseen or taken for granted by the men, they tended to underestimate their wives' contributions and escaped the full range of tensions and strains associated with family work.

Because wives remained in control of setting schedules, generating lists for domestic chores, and worrying about the children, they perceived their husbands as contributing relatively little. A frequent comment from wives was that their husbands "just didn't see" the domestic details, and that the men would not often take responsibility for anticipating and planning for what needed to be done. Although many of the men we interviewed maintained their favored position within the family by "not seeing" various aspects of domestic life and leaving the details and planning to their wives, other couples were in the process of ongoing negotiations and, as described below, were successful at redefining some household chores as shared endeavors.

Concerning their paid work, the families we interviewed reported that both husbands and wives had jobs because of financial necessity. The men made comments like, "we were pretty much forced into it," or "we didn't really have any choice." Although most of the husbands and wives were employed full-time, only a few accepted the wife as an equal provider or true breadwinner. Using the type of job, employment schedule, and earnings of each spouse, along with their attitudes toward providing, I categorized the couples into main-provider families and co-provider families.[6] Main-provider couples considered the husband's job to be primary and the wife's job to be secondary. Co-provider couples, in contrast, tended to accept the wife's job as permanent, and some even treated the wife's job as equally important to her husband's. Accepting the wife as an equal provider, or considering the husband to have failed as a provider, significantly shaped the couples' divisions of household labor.

MAIN-PROVIDER FAMILIES

In just under half of the families we interviewed, the men earned substantially more money than their wives and were assumed to be "natural" breadwinners, whereas the women were assumed to be innately better equipped to deal with home and children. Wives in all of these main-provider families were employed, but the wife's job was often considered temporary, and her income was treated as "extra" money and earmarked for special purposes.[7] One main-provider husband said, "I would prefer that my wife did not have to work, and could stay at home with my daughter, but finances just don't permit that." Another commented that his wife made just about enough to cover the costs of child care, suggesting that the children were still her primary responsibility, and that any wages she earned should first be allocated to cover "her" tasks.

The main-provider couples included many wives who were employed part-time, and some who worked in lower-status full-time jobs with wages much lower than their husband's. These women took pride in their homemaker role and readily accepted responsibility for managing the household, although they occasionally asked for help. One part-time bookkeeper married to a recent law-school graduate described their division of labor by saying, "It's a given that I take care of children and housework, but when I am real tired, he steps in willingly." Main-provider husbands typically remained in a helper role: in this case, the law clerk told his wife," Just tell me what to do and I'll do it." He said that if he came home and she was gone, he might clean house, but that if she was home, he would "let her do it." This reflects a typical division of labor in which the wife acts as household manager and the husband occasionally serves as her helper.[8]

This lawyer-to-be talked about early negotiations between him and his wife that seemed to set the tone for current smoldering arguments about housework:

> When we were first married, I would do something and she
> wouldn't like the way that I did it. So I would say, "OK, then, you

do it, and I won't do it again." That was like in our first few years
of marriage when we were first getting used to each other, but now
she doesn't discourage me so much. She knows that if she does,
she's going to wind up doing it herself.

His resistance and her reluctance to press for change reflect an unbalanced economy of gratitude.[9] When he occasionally contributed to housework or child care, she was indebted to him. She complimented him for
being willing to step in when she asked for help, but privately lamented the
fact that she had to negotiate for each small contribution. Firmly entrenched
in the main-provider role and somewhat oblivious to the daily rituals of
housework and child care, he felt justified in needing prodding and encouragement. When she did ask him for help, she was careful to thank him for
dressing the children or for giving her a ten-minute break from them. While
these patterns of domestic labor and inequities in the exchange of gratitude
were long-standing, tension lurked just below the surface for this couple.
He commented, "My wife gets uptight with me for agreeing to help out my
mom, when she feels she can't even ask me to go to the store for her."

Another main-provider couple reflected a similar pattern of labor allocation, but claimed that the arrangement was fair to them both. The woman,
a part-time teacher's aide, acknowledged that she loved being a wife and
mother and "naturally" took charge of managing the household. She commented, "I have the say so on the running of the house, and I also decide on
the children's activities." Although she had a college degree, she described
her current part-time job as "ideal" for her. She was able to work twenty
hours per week at a neighborhood school and was home by the time her
own children returned home from their school. While she earned only $6,000
per year, she justified the low salary because the job fit so well with "the
family's schedule." Her husband's administrative job allowed them to live
comfortably since he earned almost $50,000 annually.

This secondary-provider wife said that they divided household tasks in
a conventional manner: She did most all of the cleaning, cooking, clothes-
care, and child-care tasks, while he did the yard work, home repairs, and
finances. Her major complaints were that her husband didn't notice things,
that she had to nag him, and that he created more housework for her. "The
worst part about the housework and child care is the amount of nagging I
have to do to get him to help. Also, for example, say I just cleaned the house;
he will leave the newspaper scattered all over the place or he will leave wet
towels on the bathroom floor."

When asked whether there had been any negotiation over who would
do what chores, the husband responded, "I don't think a set decision was
made; it was a necessity." His wife's response was similar, "It just evolved
that way; we never really talked about it." His provider role was taken for
granted, but occasionally she voiced some muted resentment. For example,
she commented that it upset her when he told her that she should not be

working because their youngest child was only five years old. As an after-thought, she mentioned that she was sometimes bothered by the fact that she had not advanced her career, or worked overtime, since that would have interfered with "the family's" schedule.

In general, wives of main-providers not only performed virtually all housework and child care, but both spouses accepted this as "natural" or "normal." Main-provider husbands assumed that financial support was their "job" or their "duty." When one man was asked about how it felt to make more money than his wife, he responded by saying: "It's my job; I wouldn't feel right if I didn't make more money.... Any way that I look at it, I have to keep up my salary, or I'm not doing my job. If it costs $40,000 to live nowadays and I'm not in a $40,000-a-year job, then I'm not gonna be happy."

This same husband, a head mechanic who worked between 50 and 60 hours per week, also showed how main-provider husbands sometimes felt threatened when women begin asserting themselves in previously all-male occupational enclaves:

> As long as women mind their own business, no problem with me.... There's nothing wrong with them being in the job, but they shouldn't try to do more than that. Like, if you get a secretary that's nosy and wants to run the company, hey, well, we tell her where to stick it.... When you can't do my job, don't tell me how to do it.

The mechanic's wife, also a part-time teacher's aide, subtly resisted by "spending as little time on housework as I can get away with." Nevertheless, she still considered it her sole duty to cook, and only when her husband was away at National Guard training sessions did she feel she could "slack off" by not placing "regular meals" on the family's table each night.

 ## THE PROVIDER ROLE AND FAILED ASPIRATIONS

Wives performed most of the household labor in main-provider couples, but if main-provider husbands had failed career aspirations, more domestic work was shared. What appeared to tip the economy of gratitude away from auto-matic male privilege was the wife's sense that the husband had not fulfilled his occupational potential. For example, one main-provider husband gradu-ated from a four-year college and completed two years of post-graduate study without finishing his Master's Thesis. At the time of the interview, he was making about $30,000 a year as a self-employed house painter, and his wife was making less than half that amount as a full-time secretary. His com-ments show how her evaluation of his failed or postponed career aspirations led to more bargaining over his participation in routine housework:

> She reminds me that I'm not doing what we both think I should be doing, and sometimes that's a discouragement. I might have

worked a lot of hours, and I'll come home tired, for example, and she'll say, "You've gotta clean the house," and I'll say, "Damn I'm tired; I'd like to get a little rest in," but she says "you're only doing this because it's been your choice." She tends to not have sympathy for me in my work because it was more my choice than hers.

He acknowledged that he should be doing something more "worthwhile," and hoped that he would not be painting houses for more than another year. Still, as long as he stayed in his current job, considered beneath him by both of them, she would not allow him to use fatigue from employment as a way to get out of doing housework:

I worked about 60 hours a week the last couple of weeks. I worked yesterday [Saturday], and today—if it had been my choice—I would have drank beer and watched TV. But since she had a baby shower to go to, I babysitted my nephews. And since we had you coming, she kind of laid out the program: "You've gotta clean the floors, and wash the dishes and do the carpets. So get to it buddy!" [Laughs.]

This main-provider husband capitulated to his wife's demands, but she still had to set tasks for him and remind him to perform them. In responding to her "program," he used the strategy of claimed incompetence that other main-provider husbands also used. While he admitted that he was proficient at the "janitorial stuff," he was careful to point out that he was incapable of dusting or doing the laundry:

It's amazing what you can do when you have little time and you just get in and do it. And I'm good at that. I'm good at the big cleaning, I'm good at the janitorial stuff. I can do the carpet, do the floors, do all that stuff. But I'm no good on the details. She wants all the details just right, so she handles dusting, the laundry, and stuff like that. . . . You know, like I would have everything come out one color.

By re-categorizing some of the housework as "big cleaning," this husband rendered it accountable as men's work. He drew the line at laundry and dusting, but he had transformed some household tasks, like vacuuming and mopping, into work appropriate for men to do. He was complying, albeit reluctantly, to many of his wife's requests because they agreed that he had not fulfilled "his" job as sole provider. He still yearned to be the "real" breadwinner and shared his hope that getting a better paying job would mean that he could ignore the housework:

Sharing the house stuff is usually just a necessity. If, as we would hope in the future, she didn't have to work outside the home, then I think I would be comfortable doing less of it. Then she would be the primary house-care person and I would be the primary financial-resource person. I think roles would change then, and I would be comfortable with her doing more of the dishes and more of the cleaning, and I think she would too. In that sense, I think traditional relationships—if traditional means the guy working and the woman staying home—is a good thing. I wouldn't mind getting a taste of it myself!

A similar failed aspirations pattern was found in another main-provider household, in spite of the fact that the husband had a college degree and a job as an elementary-school teacher. While his wife earned less than a sixth of what he did, she was working on an advanced degree and coordinated a nonprofit community program. In this family, unlike most of the others, the husband performed more housework than he did child care, though both he and his wife agreed that she did more of both. Nevertheless, he performed these household chores reluctantly and only in response to prodding from his wife: "Housework is mostly her responsibility. I like to come home and kick back. Sometimes she has to complain before I do anything around the house. You know when she hits the wall, then I start doing things."

This main-provider husband talked about how his real love was art, and how he had failed to pursue his dream of being a graphic artist. The blocked occupational achievement in his case was not that he didn't make good money in a respected professional job, but that he was not fulfilling his "true" potential. His failed career goals increased her willingness to make demands on him, influenced their division of household labor, and helped shape feelings of entitlement between them: "I have talents that she doesn't have. I guess that's one of my strongest strengths, that I'm an artist. But she's very disappointed in me that I have not done enough of it . . ."

Another main-provider husband held a job as a telephone lineman, and his wife ran a family day-care center out of their home, which earned her less than a third of what he made. She talked about her regrets that he didn't do something "more important" for a living, and he talked about her frequent reminders that he was "too smart for what I'm doing." Like the other failed-aspirations husbands, he made significant contributions to domestic chores, but his resentment showed when he talked about "the wife" holding a job far from home:

> What I didn't like about it was that I used to get home before the wife, because she had to commute, and I'd have to pop something to eat. Most of the time it was just whatever I happened to find in the fridge. Then I'd have to go pick up the kids immediately from the babysitter, and sometimes I had evening things to do, so what I didn't like was that I had to figure out a way to schedule baby watch or baby sitting.

Even when main-provider husbands began to assume responsibility for domestic work in response to "necessity" or "nagging," they seemed to cling to the idea that these were still "her" chores. Coincidentally, most of the secondary-provider wives reported that they received little help unless they "constantly" reminded their husbands. What generally kept secondary-provider wives from resenting their husband's resistance was their own acceptance of the homemaker role and their recognition of his superior financial contributions. When performance of the male-provider role was deemed to be lacking in some way—i.e., failed aspirations or low occupational prestige—wives' resentment appeared closer to the surface, and they were more persistent in demanding help from their husbands.

AMBIVALENT CO-PROVIDERS

Over half of the couples we interviewed were classified as co-providers. The husbands and wives in these families had more equal earnings and placed a higher value on the wife's employment than those in main-provider families, but there was considerable variation in terms of their willingness to accept the woman as a full and equal provider. Five of the twelve husbands in the co-provider group were ambivalent about sharing the provider role and were also reluctant to share most household tasks. Compared to their wives, ambivalent co-provider husbands usually held jobs that were roughly equivalent in terms of occupational prestige and worked about the same number of hours per week, but because of gender bias in the labor market, the men earned significantly more than their wives. Compared to main-provider husbands, they considered their wives' jobs to be relatively permanent and important, but they continued to use their own job commitments as justification for doing little at home. Ambivalent co-provider husbands' family obligations rarely intruded into their work lives, whereas their wives' family obligations frequently interfered with their paid work. Such asymmetrically permeable work/family boundaries are common in single-earner and main-provider families, but must be supported with subtle ideologies and elaborate justifications when husbands and wives hold similar occupational positions.[10]

Ambivalent co-provider husbands remained in a helper role at home, perceiving their wives to be more involved parents and assuming that housework was also primarily their wives' responsibility. The men used their jobs to justify their absence from home, but most also lamented not being able to spend more time with their families. For instance, one husband who worked full time as a city planner was married to a woman who worked an equal number of hours as an office manager. In talking about the time he put in at his job, he commented, "I wish I had more time to spend with my children, and to spend with my wife too, of course, but it's a fact of life that I have to work." His wife, in contrast, indicated that her paid job, which she had held for fourteen years, did not prohibit her from adequately caring for her three children, or taking care of "her" household chores. Ambivalent co-provider husbands did not perform significantly more housework and child care than main-provider husbands, and generally did fewer household chores than main-provider husbands with failed career aspirations.

Not surprisingly, ambivalent co-provider husbands tended to be satisfied with their current divisions of labor, even though they usually admitted that things were "not quite fair." One junior-high-school teacher married to a bilingual-education program coordinator described his reactions to their division of family labor:

> To be honest, I'm totally satisfied. When I had a first-period conference, I was a little more flexible; I'd help her more with changing 'em, you know, getting them ready for school, since I didn't have to be at school right away. Then I had to switch because they had some situation out at fifth-period conference, so that now she does it a little bit more than I do, and I don't help out with the kids as much in the morning because I have to be there an hour earlier.

This ambivalent co-provider clearly saw himself as "helping" his wife with the children, yet made light of her contributions by saying she does "a little bit more than I do." He went on to reveal how his wife did not enjoy similar special privileges due to her employment, since she had to pick up the children from day care every day, as well as taking them to school in the mornings:

> She gets out a little later than I do, because she's an administrator but I have other things outside. I also work out, I run, and that sort of gives me a time away, to do that before they all come here. I have community meetings in the evenings sometimes, too. So, I mean, it might not be totally fair—maybe 60/40—but I'm thoroughly happy with the way things are.

While he was "thoroughly happy" with the current arrangements, she thought that it was decidedly unfair. She said, "I don't like the fact that it's taken for granted that I'm available. When he goes out he just assumes I'm available, but when I go out I have to consult with him to make sure he is available." For her, child care was a given; for him, it was optional. He commented, "If I don't have something else to do, then I'll take the kids."

Ambivalent co-provider husbands also tended to talk about regretting that their family involvements limited their careers or personal activities. For instance the schoolteacher discussed above lamented that he could not do what he used to before he had children:

> Having children keeps me away from thinking a lot about my work. You know, it used to be, before we had kids, I could have my mind geared to work—you know how ideas just pop in; you really get into it. But with kids it doesn't get as—you know, you can't switch. It gets more difficult; it makes it hard to get into it. I don't have that

freedom of mind, you know, and it takes away from aspects of my work, like doing a little bit more reading or research that I would like to do. Or my own activities, I mean, I still run, but not as much as I used to. I used to play basketball, I used to coach, this and that . . .

Other ambivalent co-provider husbands talked about the impact of children on their careers and personal lives with less bitterness and more appreciation for establishing a relationship with their children. Encouraged by their wives to alter their priorities, some reinterpreted the relative importance of career and family commitments:

I like the way things are going. Let's put it this way. I mean, it's just that once you become a parent, it's a never-ending thing. I coach my kid for example; this past week we had four games. . . . I just think that by having a family that your life becomes so involved after awhile with your own kids, that it's very difficult. I coached at the varsity level for one year, but I had to give it up. I would leave in the morning when they were asleep, and I would get out of coaches' meetings at ten or eleven at night. My wife said to me, "Think about your priorities, man; you leave when the kids are asleep, come back when they are asleep." So I decided to change that act. So I gave it up for one year, and I was home all the time. Now I am going to coach again, but it's at lower levels, and I'll be home every day. I have to make adjustments for my family. Your attitude changes; it's not me that counts anymore.

Whereas family labor was not shared equally in this ambivalent co-provider couple, the husband, at his wife's urging, was beginning to accept and appreciate that his children were more important than his job. He was evaluating his attachment to his children on his wife's terms, but he was agreeing with her, and he had begun to take more responsibility for them.

Many of these husbands talked about struggles over wanting to spend more time on their careers, and most did not relinquish the assumption that the home was the wife's domain. For example, some ambivalent co-provider couples attempted to alleviate stress on the wife by hiring outside help. In response to a question about whether their division of labor was fair, a self-employed male attorney said, "Do you mean fair like equal? It's probably not equal, so probably it wouldn't be fair, but that's why we have a housekeeper." His wife, a social worker earning only ten percent less than he, said that the household was still her responsibility, but that she now had fewer tasks to do: "When I did not have help, I tended to do everything, but with a housekeeper, I don't have to do so much." She went on to talk about how she wished he would do more with their five- and eight-year-old children, but speculated that he probably would as they grew older.

Another couple paid a live-in babysitter/housekeeper to watch their three children during the day while he worked full-time in construction and she worked full-time as a psychiatric social worker. While she labeled the outside help as "essential," she noted that her husband contributed more to the mess than he did to its cleanup. He saw himself as an involved father because he played with his children, and she acknowledged this, but she also complained that he competed with them in games as if he were a child himself. His participation in routine household labor was considered optional, as evidenced by his comment, "I like to cook once in a while."

 ## CO-PROVIDERS

In contrast, about a third of the couples we interviewed fully accepted the wife's long-term employment, considered her career to be just as important as his, and were in various stages of redefining household labor as men's work. Like the ambivalent couples discussed above, full co-provider spouses worked about the same number of hours as each other, but on the whole, these couples worked more total hours than their more ambivalent counterparts, though their annual incomes were a bit lower. According to both husbands and wives, the sharing of housework and child care was substantially greater for full co-providers than for ambivalent co-providers, and also much more balanced than for main-providers.

Like ambivalent co-providers, husbands in full co-provider families discussed conflicts between work and family and sometimes alluded to the ways that their occupational advancement was limited by their commitments to their children. One husband and wife spent the same number of hours on the job, earned approximately the same amount of money, and were employed as engineering technicians for the same employer. When we asked him how his family involvement had affected his job performance, he responded by saying, "It should, OK, because I really need to spend a lot more time learning my work, and I haven't really put in the time I need to advance in the profession. I would like to spend, I mean I *would* spend, more time if I didn't have kids. I'd like to be able to play with the computer or read books more often." Although he talked about conflicts between job and family, he also emphasized that lost work time was not really a sacrifice because he valued time with his children so highly. He did not use his job as an excuse to get out of doing child care or housework, and he seemed to value his wife's career at least as much as his own:

> I think her job is probably more important than mine because she's been at that kind of work a lot longer than I have. And at the level she is—it's awkward the way it is, because I get paid just a little bit more than she does; I have a higher position. But she definitely knows the work a lot more, she's been doing the same type of work for about nine years already, and I've only been doing this type of engineering work for about two-and-a-half years, so she knows a lot more. We both have to work; that's for sure.

Recognition of their roughly equivalent professional status and the need for two equal providers affected this couple's division of parenting and housework. The husband indicated that he did more child care and housework than his wife, and she gave him much credit for his efforts, but in her interview, she indicated that he still did less than half. She described her husband's relationship with their seven-year-old son as "very caring," and noted that he assists the boy with homework more than she does. She also said that her husband did most of the heavy cleaning and scrubbing, but also commented that he doesn't clean toilets and doesn't always notice when things get dirty. The husband described their allocation of housework by saying, "Maybe she does less than I do, but some of the things she does, I just will not do. I will not dust all the little things in the house. That's one of my least favorite things, but I'm more likely to do the mopping and vacuuming." This husband's comments also revealed some ongoing tension about whose housework standards should be maintained. He said, "She has high standards for cleanliness that you would have to be home to maintain. Mine tend to acknowledge that you don't always get to this stuff because you have other things to do. I think I have a better acceptance that one priority hurts something else in the background."

While this couple generally agreed about how to raise their son, standards for child care were also subject to debate. He saw himself as doing more with his son than his wife, as reflected in comments such as "I tend to think of myself as the more involved parent, and I think other people have noticed that, too." While she had only positive things to say about his parenting, he offered both praise and criticism of her parenting:

> She can be very playful. She makes up fun games. She doesn't always put enough into the educational part of it, though, like exploring or reading. . . . She cherishes tune-up time [job-related study or preparation], and sometimes I feel she should be using that time to spend with him. Like at the beach, I'll play with him, but she'll be more likely to be under the umbrella reading.

Like many of the other husbands, he went on to say that he thought their division of labor was unfair. Unlike the others, however, he indicated that he thought their current arrangements favored *her* needs, not his:

> I think I do more housework. It's probably not fair, because I do more of the dirtier tasks. . . . Also, at this point, our solution tends to favor her free time more than my free time. I think that has more to do with our personal backgrounds. She has more personal friends to do things with, so she has more outside things to do whereas I say I'm not doing anything.

In this family, comparable occupational status and earnings, coupled with a relatively egalitarian ideology, led to substantial sharing of both child care and housework. While the husband tended to take more credit for his involvement than his wife gave him, we can see a difference between their talk and that of some of the families discussed above. Other husbands sometimes complained about their wife's high standards, but they also treated housework, and even parenting, as primarily *her* duty. They usually resented being nagged to do more around the house and failed to move out of a helper role. Rarely did such men consider it *their* duty to anticipate, schedule, and take care of family and household needs. In this co-provider household, in contrast, the gendered allocation of responsibility for child care and housework was not assumed. Because of this, negotiations over housework and parenting were more frequent than in the other families. Since they both held expectations that each would fulfill both provider and caretaker roles, resentments came from both spouses—not just from the wife.

Our interviews suggest that it might be easier for couples to share both provider and homemaker roles when, like the family above, the wife's earnings and occupational prestige equal or exceed those of her husband. For instance, in one of the couples reporting the most sharing of child care and housework, the wife earned $36,000 annually as the executive director of a non-profit community organization and a consultant, and her husband earned $30,000 as a self-employed general contractor. This couple started off their marriage with fairly conventional gender-role expectations and an unbalanced division of labor. While the husband's ideology had changed somewhat, he still talked like most of the main-provider husbands:

> As far as the household is concerned, I divide a house into two categories: one is the interior and the other is the exterior. For the interior, my wife pushes me to deal with that. The exterior, I'm left to it myself. So, what I'm basically saying is that generally speaking, a woman does not deal with the exterior. The woman's main concern is with the interior, although there is a lot of deviation.

In this family, an egalitarian belief system did not precede the sharing of household labor. The wife was still responsible for setting the "interior" household agenda and had to remind her husband to help with housework and child care. When asked whether he and his wife had arguments about housework, this husband laughed and said, "All the time; doesn't everybody?"

What differentiated this couple from most others is that she made more money than he did and had no qualms about demanding help from him. While he had not yet accepted the idea that interior chores were equally his, he reluctantly performed them. She ranked his contributions to child care to be equal to hers, and rated his contributions to housework only slightly below her own. While not eagerly rushing to do the cooking, cleaning, or laundry, he complied with occasional reminders and according to his wife, was "a better cleaner" than she was.

His sharing stemmed, in part, from her higher earnings and their mutual willingness to reduce his "outside chores" by hiring outside help. Unlike the more ambivalent co-providers who hired housekeepers to do "her" chores, this couple hired a gardener to work on the yard so they could both spend more time focusing on the children and the house. Rather than complaining about their division of labor, he talked about how he has come to appreciate his situation:

> Ever since I've known my wife, she's made more money than I have. Initially—as a man—I resented it. I went through a lot of head trips about it. But as time developed, I appreciated it. Now I respect it. The way I figure it is, I'd rather have her sharing the money with me than sharing it with someone else. She has her full-time job and then she has her part-time job as a consultant. The gardener I'm paying $75 per week, and I'm paying someone else $25 per week to make my lunch, so I'm enjoying it! It's self-interest.

The power dynamic in this family, coupled with their willingness to pay for outside help to reduce his chores, and the flexibility of his self-employed work schedule, led to substantial sharing of cooking, cleaning, and child care. Because she was making more money and working more hours than he was, he could not emulate other husbands in claiming priority for his provider activities.

A similar dynamic was evident in other co-provider couples with comparable earnings and career commitments. One male IRS officer married to a school teacher now made more money than his wife, but talked about his feelings when she was the more successful provider:

> It doesn't bother me when she makes more money than me. I don't think it has anything to do with being a man. I don't have any hangups about it, I mean, I don't equate those things with manhood. It takes a pretty simple mind to think that way. First of all, she doesn't feel superior when she has made more money.

The woman in this couple commented that her husband was "better" at housework than she was, but that she still had to nag him to do it. Although only two wives in our sample of Chicano families earned more than their husbands, the reversal of symbolic provider status seemed to raise expectations for increased family work from husbands. The husbands who made less than their wives performed significantly more of the housework and child care than the other husbands.

Even when wives' earnings did not exceed the husbands', some co-providers shared the homemaker role. A male college-admissions recruiter and his executive-secretary wife shared substantial housework and child care according to mutual ratings. He made $29,000 per year working a 50-hour week, while she made $22,000 working a 40-hour week. She was willing to give him more credit than he was willing to claim for child care, reflecting her sincere appreciation for his parenting efforts, which were greater than those of other fathers she knew. He placed a high value on her mothering and seemed to downplay the possibility that they should be considered equal parents. Like most of the men in this study, the college-recruiter husband was reluctant to perform house-cleaning chores. Like many co-providers, however, he managed to redefine some routine household chores as a shared responsibility. For instance, when we asked him what he liked least about housework, he laughingly replied, "Probably those damn toilets, man, and the showers, the bathrooms, gotta scrub 'em, argghh! I wish I didn't have to do any of that, you know the vacuuming and all that. But it's just a fact of life."

Even though he did more than most husbands, he acknowledged that he did less than his wife, and admitted that he sometimes tried to use his job to get out of doing more around the house. But whereas other wives often allowed husbands to use their jobs as excuses for doing less family work, or assumed that their husbands were incapable of performing certain chores like cooking or laundry, the pattern in this family resembled that of the failed-aspirations couples. In other words, the wife did not assume that housework was "her" job, did not accept her husband's job demands as justification for his doing less housework, and sometimes challenged his interpretation of how much his job required of him. She also got her husband to assume more responsibility by refraining from performing certain tasks. He commented:

> Sometimes she just refuses to do something. . . . An example would be the ironing, you know, I never used to do the ironing, hated it. Now it's just something that happens. You need something ironed, you better iron it or you're not gonna have it in the morning. So, I think, you know, that kinda just evolved. I mean, she just gradually quit doing it so everybody just had to do their own. My son irons his own clothes, I iron my own clothes, my daughter irons her own clothes; the only one that doesn't iron is the baby, and next year she'll probably start.

The sociologist Jane Hood, whose path-breaking family research highlighted the importance of provider role definition to marital power, describes this strategy as "going on strike," and suggests that it is most effective when husbands feel the specific task *must* be done.[11] Since appearing neat and well-dressed was a priority for this husband, when his wife stopped ironing his clothes, he started doing it himself. Because he felt it was important for his children to be "presentable" in public, he also began to remind them to iron their own clothes before going visiting or attending church.

While many co-provider couples reported that sharing housework was contingent upon ongoing bargaining and negotiation, others focused on how it evolved "naturally." One co-provider husband, director of a housing agency, reported that he and his wife didn't negotiate; "we pretty much do what needs to be done." His wife, an executive secretary, confirmed his description, and echoed the ad-hoc arrangements of many of the role-sharing couples: "We have not had to negotiate. We both have our specialties. He is great with dishes, I like to clean bathrooms. He does most of the laundry. It has worked out that we each do what we like best."

Although sharing tasks sometimes increases conflict, when both spouses assume that household tasks are a shared responsibility, negotiation can also become less necessary or contentious. For example, a co-provider husband who worked as a mail carrier commented, "I get home early and start dinner, make sure the kids do their homework, feed the dogs, stuff like that." He and his wife, an executive secretary, agreed that they rarely talk about housework. She said, "When I went back to work we agreed that we both needed to share, and so we just do it." While she still reminded him to perform chores according to her standards or on her schedule, she summed up her appreciation by commenting, "At least he does it without complaining." Lack of complaint was a common feature of co-provider families. Whereas many main-provider husbands complained of having to do "her" chores, the co-providers rarely talked about harboring resentments. Main-provider husbands typically lamented not having the services of a stay-at-home wife, but co-provider husbands almost never made such comparisons.

SUMMARY AND DISCUSSION

For these dual-earner Chicano couples, we found conventional masculine privilege as well as considerable sharing in several domains. First, as in previous studies of ethnic minority families, wives were employed a substantial number of hours and made significant contributions to the household income. Second, like some who have studied Chicano families, we found that couples described their decision-making to be relatively fair and equal.[12] Third, fathers in these families were more involved in child rearing than their own fathers had been, and many were rated as sharing a majority of child care tasks. Finally, while no husband performed fully half of the housework, a few made substantial contributions in this area as well.

One of the power dynamics that appeared to undergird the household division of labor in these families was the relative earning power of each spouse, though this was modified by factors such as occupational prestige, provider role status, and personal preference. In just under half of the families, the wife earned less than a third of the family income, and in all of these families the husband performed little of the routine housework or child care. In two families, wives earned more than their husbands, and these two households reported sharing more domestic labor than others. Among the other couples who shared housework and child care, there was a preponderance of relatively balanced incomes. In the two families with large financial contributions from wives, but little household help from husbands, couples hired housekeepers to reduce the wives' household workload.

While relative income appeared to make a significant difference in marital power, we observed no simple or straightforward exchange of market resources for domestic services. Other factors like failed career aspirations or occupational status influenced marital dynamics and helped explain why some wives were willing to push a little harder for change in the division of household labor. In almost every case, husbands reluctantly responded to requests for help from wives. Only when wives explicitly took the initiative to shift some of the housework burden to husbands did the men begin to assume significant responsibility for the day-to-day operation of the household. Even when they began to share the housework and child care, men tended to do some of the less onerous tasks like playing with the children or washing the dinner dishes. When we compared these men to their own fathers, or their wives' fathers, however, we could see that they were sharing more domestic chores than the generation that preceded them.

Acceptance of wives as co-providers and wives' delegation of a portion of the homemaker role to husbands were especially important to creating more equal divisions of household labor in these families. If wives made lists for their husbands or offered them frequent reminders, they were more successful than if they waited for husbands to take the initiative. Remaining responsible for managing the home and children was cause for resentment on the part of many wives, however. Sometimes wives were effective in getting husbands to perform certain chores, like ironing, by stopping doing it altogether. For other wives, sharing evolved more "naturally," as both spouses agreed to share tasks or performed the chores that they preferred.

Economies of gratitude continually shifted as the ideology, career attachments, and feelings of entitlement of each spouse changed over time. For some main-provider families, this meant that wives were grateful for husbands' "permission" to hold a job, or that wives worked harder at home because they felt guilty for making their husbands do any of the housework. Main-provider husbands usually let their job commitments limit their family work, whereas their wives took time off from work to care for a sick child or to attend a parent-teacher conference.

Even in families where co-provider wives had advanced degrees and earned high incomes, some wives' work/family boundaries were more permeable than their husbands', like the program director married to a teacher who was a "perpetual" graduate student and attended "endless" community meetings. While she was employed more hours than he, and made about the same amount of money, she had to "schedule him" to watch the children if she wanted to leave the house alone. His stature as a "community leader" provided him with subterranean leverage in the unspoken struggle over taking responsibility for the house and children. His "gender ideology," if measured with conventional survey questions, would undoubtedly have been characterized as "egalitarian," because he spoke in broad platitudes about women's equality and was washing the dishes when we arrived for the interviews. He insisted on finishing the dishes as he answered my questions, but in the other room, his wife confided to Elsa in incredulous tones, "He *never* does that!"

In other ambivalent co-provider families, husbands gained unspoken advantage because they had more prestigious jobs than their wives, and earned more money. While these highly educated attorneys and administrators talked about how they respected their wives' careers, and expressed interest in spending more time with their children, their actions showed that they did not fully assume responsibility for sharing the homemaker or parenting role. To solve the dilemma of too little time and too many chores, two of these families hired housekeepers. Wives were grateful for this strategy, though it did not alter inequities in the distribution of housework and child care, nor in the allocation of worry.

In other families, the economy of gratitude departed dramatically from conventional notions of husband as economic provider and wife as nurturing homemaker. When wives' earnings approached or exceeded their husbands', economies of gratitude shifted toward more equal expectations, with husbands beginning to assume that they must do more around the house. Even in these families, husbands rarely began doing more chores without prodding from wives, but they usually did them "without complaining." Similarly, when wives with economic leverage began expecting more from their husbands, they were usually successful in getting them to do more.

Another type of leverage that was important, even in main-provider households, was the existence of failed aspirations. If wives expected husbands to "make more" of themselves, pursue "more important" careers, or follow "dream" occupational goals, then wives were able to get husbands to do more around the house. This perception of failed aspirations, if held by both spouses, served as a reminder that husbands had no excuse for not helping out at home. In these families, wives were not at all reluctant to demand assistance with domestic chores, and husbands were rarely able to use their jobs as excuses for getting out of housework.

The economies of gratitude in these families were not equally balanced, but many exhibited divisions of household labor that contradicted cultural stereotypes of macho men and male-dominated families. Particularly salient in these families was the lack of fit between their own class position and that of their parents. Most of the parents were Mexican immigrants with little education and low occupational mobility. The couples we interviewed, in contrast, were well-educated and relatively secure in middle-class occupations. The couples could have compared themselves to their parents, evaluating themselves to be egalitarian and financially successful. While some did just that, most compared themselves to their Anglo and Chicano friends and coworkers, many of whom shared as much or more than they did. Implicitly comparing their earnings, occupational commitments, and perceived aptitudes, husbands and wives negotiated new patterns of work/family boundaries and developed novel justifications for their emerging arrangements. These were not created anew, but emerged out of the popular culture in which they found themselves. Judith Stacey labels such developments the making of the "postmodern family," because they signal "the contested, ambivalent, and undecided character of contemporary gender and kinship arrangements."[13] Our findings confirm that families are an important site of new struggles over the meaning of gender and the rights and obligations of men and women in each other and over each other's labor.

One of the most provocative findings from our study has to do with the class position of Chicano husbands and wives who shared household labor: white-collar, working-class families shared more than upper-middle-class professionals. Contrary to findings from nationwide surveys predicting that higher levels of education for either husbands or wives will be associated with more sharing, the most highly educated of our well-educated sample of Chicano couples shared only moderate amounts of child care and little housework.[14] Contrary to other predictions, neither was it the working-class women in this study who achieved the most balanced divisions of labor.[15] It was the middle occupational group of women, the executive secretaries, clerks, technicians, teachers, and mid-level administrators who extracted the most help from husbands. The men in these families were similarly in the middle in terms of occupational status for this sample—administrative assistants, a builder, a mail carrier, a technician—and in the middle in terms of income. What this means is that the highest status wives—the program coordinators, nurses, social workers, and office managers—were not able to, or chose not to, transform their salaries or occupational status into more participation from husbands. This was probably because their husbands had even higher incomes and more prestigious occupations than they did. The lawyers, program directors, ranking bureaucrats, and "community leaders" parlayed their status into extra leisure at home, either by paying for housekeepers or ignoring the housework. Finally, Chicana wives at the lowest end of the occupational structure fared least well. The teacher's aides, entry-level secretaries, day-care providers, and part-time employees did the bulk of the work at home whether they were married to mechanics or lawyers. When wives made less than a third of what their husbands did, they were only able to get husbands to do a little more if the men were working at jobs considered "below" them—a telephone lineman, a painter, an elementary-school teacher.

Only Chicano couples were included in this study, but results are similar to findings from previous interviews with Anglo couples.[16] My interpretation is that the major processes shaping divisions of labor in middle-class Chicano couples are approximately the same as those shaping divisions of labor in other middle-class couples. This is not to say that ethnicity did not make a difference to the Chicano couples we interviewed. They grew up in recently immigrating working-class families, watched their parents work long hours for minimal wages, and understood firsthand the toll that various forms of racial discrimination can take. Probably because of some of these experiences, and their own more recent ones, our informants looked at job security, fertility decisions, and the division of household labor somewhat differently than their Anglo counterparts. In some cases, this can give

Chicano husbands in working-class or professional jobs license to ignore more of the housework, and might temper the anger of some working-class or professional Chicanas who are still called on to do most of the domestic chores. If these findings are generalizable, however, it is those in between the blue-collar working-class and the upper-middle-class professionals that might be more likely to share housework and childcare.

Assessing whether these findings apply to other dual-earner Chicano couples will require the use of larger, more representative samples. If the limited sharing observed here represents a trend—however slow or reluctant—it could have far-reaching consequences. More and more Chicana mothers are remaining full-time members of the paid labor force. With the "postindustrial" expansion of the service and information sectors of the economy, Chicanos and Chicanas will be increasingly likely to enter white-collar middle-class occupations. As more Chicano families fit the occupational profile of those we studied, we may see more assumption of housework and child care by Chicano men. Regardless of the specific changes that the economy will undergo, we can expect Chicano men and women, like their Anglo counterparts, to continue to negotiate for change in their work and family roles.

NOTES

1. For a discussion of how the term *machismo* can also reflect positive attributes of respect, loyalty, responsibility and generosity, see Alfredo Mirandé, "Chicano Fathers: Traditional Perceptions and Current Realities," pp. 93–106, in *Fatherhood Today,* P. Bronstein and C. Cowan, eds. (New York: Wiley, 1988).
2. For reviews of literature on Latin-American families and projections on their future proportionate representation in the population, see Randall Collins and Scott Coltrane, *Sociology of Marriage and the Family* (Chicago: Nelson Hall, 1994); William A. Vega, "Hispanic Families in the 1980s," *Journal of Marriage and the Family* 52(1990): 1015–1024; and Norma Williams, *The Mexican-American Family* (New York: General Hall, 1990).
3. Maxine Baca Zinn, "Family, Feminism, and Race in America," *Gender & Society* 4(1990): 68–82; Mirandé, "Chicano Fathers"; Vega, "Hispanic Families"; and Williams, *The Mexican-American Family.*
4. See Coltrane, *Family Man: Fatherhood, Housework, and Gender Equity* (New York: Oxford University Press, 1994); Coltrane and Valdez, "Reluctant Compliance: Work/Family Role Allocation in Dual-Earner Chicano Families," in *Men, Work, and Family,* Jane C. Hood, ed. (Newbury Park, CA: Sage, 1994) and Valdez and Coltrane, "Work, Family, and the Chicana: Power, Perception and Equity," in *Employed Mothers and the Family Context,* Judith Frankel, ed. (New York: Springer, 1993). I thank Hilda Cortez, a summer research intern at the University of California, for help in transcribing some of the interviews and for providing insight into some of the issues faced by these families.
5. Jessie Bernard, *The Future of Marriage* (New York: World, 1972).
6. See Jane Hood, 1986. "The Provider Role: Its Meaning and Measurement." *Journal of Marriage and the Family* 48: 349–359.
7. Hood, "The Provider Role."

8. See Coltrane, "Household Labor and the Routine Production of Gender." *Social Problems* 36: 473–490.

9. I am indebted to Arlie Hochschild, who first used this term in *The Second Shift* (New York: Viking, 1987). See also Karen Pyke and Scott Coltrane, "Entitlement, Obligation, and Gratitude in Remarriage: Toward a Gendered Understanding of Household Labor Allocation."

10. I am indebted to Joseph Pleck for his conceptualization of "asymmetrically permeable" work/family boundaries ("The Work-Family Role System." *Social Problems* 24: 417–427).

11. Jane Hood, *Becoming a Two-Job Family*, p. 131.

12. See, for example, V. Cromwell and R. Cromwell, 1978. "Perceived Dominance in Decision Making and Conflict Resolution among Anglo, Black, and Chicano Couples." *Journal of Marriage and the Family* 40: 749–760; G. Hawkes and M. Taylor, 1975, "Power Structure in Mexican and Mexican-American Farm Labor Families." *Journal of Marriage and the Family* 37: 807–811; L. Ybarra, 1982. "When Wives Work: The Impact on the Chicano Family." *Journal of Marriage and the Family* 44: 169–178.

13. Judith Stacey, 1990. *Brave New Families.* New York: Basic Books, p. 17.

14. See, for instance, Donna H. Berardo, Constance Shehan, and Gerald R. Leslie, "A Residue of Tradition: Jobs, Careers, and Spouses' Time in Housework." *Journal of Marriage and the Family* 49(1987): 381–390; Catherine E. Ross, "The Division of Labor at Home." *Social Forces* 65(1987): 816–833.

15. Patricia Zavella, 1987. *Women's Work and Chicano Families.* Ithaca, NY: Cornell University Press; Stacey, *Brave New Families.*

16. See, for example, Hochschild, *Second Shift;* Hood, *Two-Job Family;* Coltrane, *Family Man.*

 QUESTIONS FOR CRITICAL THINKING

Reading 19

1. Coltrane found that many of the families he studied generally contradicted cultural stereotypes of "macho" Chicano men and male-dominated families. What perpetuates these stereotypes? What functions do they serve?

2. What observations have you made of divisions of household labor in male and female headed household? What do you see as the likelihood of truly equal sharing becoming the norm among women and men?

3. If women and men equally shared household work, how would this impact the life chances of women? Of men?

Reading 20

GAY AND LESBIAN FAMILIES ARE HERE

JUDITH STACEY

*In 1992 in Houston, I talked about the cultural war going on for the soul of
America. And that war is still going on! We cannot worship the false god of
gay rights. To put that sort of relationship on the same level as marriage is a
moral lie.*

—PAT BUCHANAN, FEBRUARY 10, 1996

*Homosexuality is a peculiar and rare human trait that affects only a small
percentage of the population and is of little interest to the rest.*

—JONATHAN RAUCH 1994

*I came to Beijing to the Fourth World Conference of Women to speak on behalf
of lesbian families. We are part of families. We are daughters, we are sisters,
we are aunts, nieces, cousins. In addition, many of us are mothers and
grandmothers. We share concerns for our families that are the same concerns
of women around the world.*

—BONNIE TINKER, *LOVE MAKES A FAMILY*, SEPTEMBER 1995

Until but a short time ago, gay and lesbian families seemed quite a
queer concept, even preposterous, if not oxymoronic, not only to
scholars and the general public, but even to most lesbians and gay
men. The grass roots movement for gay liberation that exploded into public
visibility in 1969, when gays resisted a police raid at the Stonewall bar in
New York City, struggled along with the militant feminist movement of
that period to liberate gays and women *from* perceived evils and injustices
represented by the family, rather than *for* access to its blessings and privileges. During the early 1970s, marches for gay pride and women's liberation flaunted provocative, countercultural banners, like "Smash The Family"
and "Smash Monogamy." Their legacy is a lasting public association of gay
liberation and feminism with family subversion. Yet how "queer" such

anti-family rhetoric sounds today, when gays and lesbians are in the thick of a vigorous profamily movement of their own.

Gay and lesbian families are indisputably here. In June of 1993, police chief Tom Potter joined his lesbian, police officer daughter in a Portland, Oregon gay pride march for "family values." By the late 1980s an astonishing "gay-by boom" had swelled the ranks of children living with gay and lesbian parents to between six to fourteen million.[1] *Family Values* is the title of a popular 1993 book by and about a lesbian's successful struggle to become a legal second mother to one of these "turkey-baster" babies, the son she and his biological mother have co-parented since his birth.[2] In 1989 Denmark became the first nation in the world to legalize a form of gay marriage, termed "registered partnerships," and its Nordic neighbors, Norway and Sweden soon followed suit. In 1993, thousands of gay and lesbian couples participated in a mass wedding ceremony on the Washington Mall during the largest demonstration for gay rights in U.S. history. Three years later, on March 25, 1996, Mayor of San Francisco Willie Brown proudly presided over a civic ceremony to celebrate the domestic partnerships of nearly 200 same-sex couples. "We're leading the way here in San Francisco," the mayor declared, "for the rest of the nation to fully embrace the diversity of people in love, regardless of their gender or sexual orientation."[3] By then thousands of gay and lesbian couples across the nation were eagerly awaiting the outcome of "Baehr v. Lewin," cautiously optimistic that Hawaii's Supreme Court will soon order the state to become the first in the United States, and in the modern world, to grant full legal marriage rights to same-sex couples. As this book went to press in May 1996, the Republican party had just made gay marriage opposition a wedge issue in their presidential campaign.

Gay and lesbian families are undeniably here, yet they are not queer, if one uses the term in the sense of "odd" to signify a marginal or deviant population.[4] It is nearly impossible to define this category of families in a manner that could successfully distinguish all of their members, needs, relationships, or even their values, from those of all other families. In fact, it is almost impossible to define this category in a satisfactory, substantive way at all. What should count as a gay or lesbian family? Even if we bracket the thorny matter of how to define an individual as gay or lesbian and rely on self-identification, we still face a jesuitical challenge. Should we count only families in which every single member is gay? Clearly there are not very many, if even any, of these. Or does the presence of just one gay member color a family gay? Just as clearly, there are very many of these, including those of Ronald Reagan, Colin Powell, Phyllis Schlafly and Newt Gingrich.[5] More to the point, why would we want to designate a family type according to the sexual identity of one or more of its members? No research, as we will see, has ever shown a uniform, distinctive pattern of relationships, structure, or even of "family values," among families that include self-identified gays. Of course, most nongays restrict the term gay family to units that contain one or two gay parents and their children. However, even such families that most commonsensically qualify as gay or lesbian are as diverse as are those which do not.

Gay and lesbian families come in different sizes, shapes, ethnicities, races, religions, resources, creeds, and quirks, and even engage in diverse sexual practices. The more one attempts to arrive at a coherent, defensible sorting principle, the more evident it becomes that the category "gay and lesbian family" signals nothing so much as the consequential social fact of widespread, institutionalized homophobia.[6] The gay and lesbian family label marks the cognitive dissonance, and even emotional threat, that much of the nongay public experiences upon recognizing that gays can participate in family life at all. What unifies such families is their need to contend with the particular array of psychic, social, legal, practical, and even physical challenges to their very existence that institutionalized hostility to homosexuality produces. Paradoxically, the label "gay and lesbian family" would become irrelevant if the nongay population could only "get used to it."

In this chapter I hope to facilitate such a process of normalization, ironically, perhaps, to allow the marker "gay and lesbian" as a family category once again to seem queer—as queer, that is, as it now seems to identify a *family,* rather than an individual or a desire, as heterosexual. I conclude this book with an extensive discussion of this historically novel category of family, not only because of its inherent interest, but to suggest how it crystallizes the general processes of family diversification and change that characterize what I have been describing as the postmodern family condition.[7] Gay and lesbian families represent such a new, embattled, visible and necessarily self-conscious, genre of postmodern kinship, that they more readily expose the widening gap between the complex reality of postmodern family forms and the simplistic modern family ideology that still undergirds most public rhetoric, policy and law concerning families.[8] In short, I hope to demonstrate that, contrary to Jonathan Rauch's well-meaning claim in the second epigraph above, the experience of "homosexuals"[9] should be of immense interest to everyone else. Nongay families, family scholars and policymakers alike can learn a great deal from examining the experience, struggles, conflicts, needs, and achievements of contemporary gay and lesbian families.

· · ·

A MORE, OR LESS, PERFECT UNION?

Much nearer at hand . . . than most ever dared to imagine has come the momentous prospect of legal gay marriage. The idea of same-sex marriage used to draw nearly as many jeers from gays and lesbians as from nongays. As one lesbian couple recalls, "In 1981, we were a very, very small handful of lesbians who got married. We took a lot of flak from other lesbians, as well as heterosexuals. In 1981, we didn't know any other lesbians, not a single one, who had had a ceremony in Santa Cruz, and a lot of lesbians live in that city. Everybody was on our case about it. They said, 'What are you doing,' 'How heterosexual.' We really had to sell it."[10]

Less than a decade later, gay and lesbian couples could proudly announce their weddings and anniversaries, not only in the gay press, which now includes specialized magazines for gay and lesbian couples, like *Partners Magazine,* but even in such mainstream, Midwestern newspapers as the Minneapolis *Star Tribune*.[11] Jewish rabbis, Protestant ministers, Quaker meetings, and even some Catholic priests regularly perform gay and lesbian wedding or commitment ceremonies. This phenomenon is memorialized in cultural productions within the gay community, like "Chicks In White Satin," a documentary about a Jewish lesbian wedding which won prizes at recent gay film festivals, but it has also become a fashionable pop culture motif. In December 1995, the long-running TV sitcom program "Roseanne" featured a gay male wedding in a much-hyped episode called "December Bride." Even more provocative, however, was a prime-time lesbian wedding that aired one month later on "Friends," the highest rated sitcom of the 1995–1996 television season. Making a cameo appearance on the January 18, 1996 episode, Candice Gingrich, the lesbian half-sister of right-wing Speaker of the House Newt Gingrich, conducted a wedding ceremony which joined the characters who play a lesbian couple on the series "in holy matrimony" and pronounced them "wife and wife."

When the very first social science research collection about gay parents was published in 1987, not even one decade ago, its editor concluded that however desirable such unions might be, "it is highly unlikely that marriages between same-sex individuals will be legalized in any state in the foreseeable future."[12] Yet, almost immediately thereafter, precisely this specter began to exercise imaginations across the political spectrum. A national poll reported by the *San Francisco Examiner* in 1989 found that 86 percent of lesbians and gay men supported legalizing same-sex marriage.[13] However, it is the pending *Baehr v. Lewin* court decision concerning same-sex marriage rights in Hawaii that has thrust this issue into escalating levels of front-page and prime-time prominence. Amidst rampant rumors that thousands of mainland gay and lesbian couples were stocking their hope chests with Hawaiian excursion fares, poised to fly to tropical altars the instant the first gay matrimonial bans falter, right-wing Christian groups began actively mobilizing resistance. Militant antiabortion leader Randall Terry of Operation Rescue flew to Hawaii in February 1996 to fight "queer marriage," and right-wing Christian women's leader and radio broadcast personality Beverly LaHaye urged her "Godly" listeners to fight gay marriage in Hawaii.[14]

Meanwhile, fearing that Hawaii will become a gay marriage mecca, state legislators have rushed to introduce bills that exclude same-sex marriages performed in other states from being recognized in their own, because the "full faith and credit" clause of the U.S. Constitution obligates interstate recognition of legal marriages. While fourteen states had rejected such bills by May 1995, eight others had passed them, and contests were underway in numerous others, including California.[15] On May 8, 1996, gay marriage galloped onto the nation's center political stage when Republicans introduced the Defense of Marriage Act (DOMA) which defines marriage in exclusively heterosexual terms, as "a legal union between one man and one woman as husband and wife."[16] The last legislation that Republican presidential candidate Bob Dole co-sponsored before he resigned from the Senate to pursue his White House bid full throttle, DOMA exploits homophobia to defeat President Clinton and the Democrats in November 1996. With Clinton severely bruised by the political debacle incited by his support for gay rights in the military when he first took office, but still dependent upon the support of his gay constituency, the President indeed found himself "wedged" between a rock and a very hard place. Unsurprisingly, he tried to waffle. Naming this a "time when we need to do things to strengthen the American family," Clinton publicly opposed same-sex marriage at the same time that he tried to reaffirm support for gay rights and to expose the divisive Republican strategy.[17]

Polemics favoring and opposing gay marriage rights now proliferate in editorial pages and legislatures across the nation, and mainstream religious bodies find themselves compelled to confront the issue. In March 1996 the Vatican felt called upon not merely to condemn same-sex marriage as a "moral disorder," but also to warn Catholics that they would themselves risk "moral censure" if they were to support "the election of the candidate who has formally promised to translate into law the homosexual demand."[18] Just one day after the Vatican published this admonition, the Central Conference of American Rabbis, which represents the large, generally liberal wing of Judaism, took a momentous action in direct opposition. The Conference resoundingly endorsed a resolution to "support the right of gay and lesbian couples to share fully and equally in the rights of civil marriage." Unsurprisingly, Orthodox rabbis immediately condemned the action as prohibited in the Bible and "another breakdown in the family unit."[19] One week later, in another historic development, a lead editorial in the *New York Times* strongly endorsed gay marriage.[20]

As with child custody, the campaign for gay marriage clings to legal footholds carved by racial justice pioneers. It is startling to recall how recent it was that the Supreme Court finally struck down anti-miscegenation laws. Not until 1967, that is only two years before Stonewall, did the high court, in *Loving vs. Virginia,* find state restrictions on interracial marriages to be unconstitutional. (Twenty states still had such restrictions on the books in 1967, only one state fewer than the twenty-one which currently prohibit sodomy.) A handful of gay couples quickly sought to marry in the 1970s through appeals to this precedent, but until three lesbian and gay male couples sued Hawaii in *Baehr* v. *Lewin* for equal rights to choose marriage partners without restrictions on gender, all U.S. courts had dismissed the analogy. In a historic ruling in 1993, the Hawaiian state Supreme Court remanded this suit to the state, requiring it to demonstrate a "compelling state interest" in prohibiting same-sex marriage, a strict scrutiny standard that few believe the state will be able to meet. Significantly, the case was neither argued nor adjudicated as a gay rights issue. Rather, just as ERA opponents once had warned and advocates had denied, passage of an equal rights amendment to Hawaii's state constitution in 1972 paved the legal foundation for *Baehr*.[21]

Most gay activists and legal scholars anticipate a victory for gay marriage when *Baehr* is finally decided early in 1997, but they do not all look forward to this prospect with great delight. Although most of their constituents desire the right to marry, gay activists and theorists continue to vigorously debate the politics and effects of this campaign. Refining earlier feminist and socialist critiques of the gender and class inequities of marriage, an articulate, vocal minority seeks not to extend the right to marry, but to dismantle an institution they regard as inherently, and irredeemably, hierarchical, unequal, conservative, and repressive. Nancy Polikoff, one of the most articulate lesbian legal activist-scholars opposed to the marriage campaign, argues that

> Advocating lesbian and gay marriage will detract from, and even contradict, efforts to unhook economic benefits from marriage and make basic health care and other necessities available to all. It will also require a rhetorical strategy that emphasizes similarities between our relationships and heterosexual marriages, values long-term monogamous coupling above all other relationships, and denies the potential of lesbian and gay marriage to transform the gendered nature of marriage for all people. I fear that the very process of employing that rhetorical strategy for the years it will take to achieve its objective will lead our movement's public representatives, and the countless lesbians and gay men who hear us, to believe exactly what we say.[22]

A second perspective supports legal marriage as one long-term goal of the gay rights movement, but voices serious strategic objections to making this a priority before there is sufficient public support to sustain a favorable ruling in Hawaii or the nation. Such critics fear that a premature victory will prove pyrrhic, because efforts to defend it against the vehement backlash it has already begun to incite are apt to fail, after sapping resources and time better devoted to other urgent struggles for gay rights. Rather than risk a major setback for the gay movement, they advise an incremental approach to establishing legal family status for gay and lesbian kin ties through a multifaceted struggle for family diversity.[23]

However, the largest, and most diverse, contingent of gay activist voices now supports the marriage rights campaign, perhaps because gay marriage can be read to harmonize with virtually every hue on the gay ideological spectrum. Pro-gay marriage arguments range from profoundly conservative to liberal humanist to radical and deconstructive. Conservatives, like those radicals who still oppose marriage, view it as an institution that promotes monogamy, commitment and social stability, along with interests in private property, social conformity and mainstream values. They likewise agree that legalizing gay marriage would further marginalize sexual radicals by segregating counter-cultural gays and lesbians from the "whitebread" gay couples who could then choose to marry their way into Middle America. Radicals and conservatives, in other words, envision the same prospect, but regard it with inverse sentiments.[24]

Liberal gays support legal marriage, of course, not only to affirm the legitimacy of their relationships and help sustain them in a hostile world, but as a straightforward matter of equal civil rights. As one long-coupled gay man expresses it: "I resent the fact that married people get lower taxes. But as long as there is this institution of marriage and heterosexuals have that privilege, then gay people should be able to do it too."[25] Liberals also recognize that marriage rights provide access to the social advantages of divorce law. "I used to say, 'Why do we want to get married? It doesn't work for straight people,'" one gay lawyer comments. "But now I say we should care: They have the privilege of divorce and we don't. We're left out there to twirl around in pain."[26]

Less obvious or familiar, however, are cogent arguments in favor of gay marriage that some feminist and other critical gay legal theorists have developed in response to opposition within the gay community. Nan Hunter, for example, rejects feminist legal colleague Nancy Polikoff's belief that marriage is an unalterably sexist and heterosexist institution. Building upon critical theories that reject the notion that social institutions or categories have inherent, fixed meanings apart from their social contexts, Hunter argues that legalized same-sex marriage would have "enormous potential to destabilize the gendered definition of marriage for everyone."[27]

Evan Wolfson, director of the Marriage Project of the gay legal rights organization Lambda Legal Defense, who has submitted a brief in support of *Baehr*, pursues the logic of "anti-essentialism" even more consistently. The institution of marriage is neither inherently equal nor unequal, he argues, but depends upon an ever-changing cultural and political context.[28] (Anyone who doubts this need only consider such examples as polygamy, arranged marriages, or the same-sex unions in early Western history documented by the late Princeton historian, John Boswell.) Hoping to use marriage precisely to change its context, gay philosopher Richard Mohr argues that access to legal marriage would provide an opportunity to reconstruct its meaning by serving "as a nurturing ground for social marriage, and not (as now) as that which legally defines and creates marriage and so precludes legal examination of it." For Mohr, social marriage represents "the fused intersection of love's sanctity and necessity's demands," and does not necessarily depend upon sexual monogamy.[29]

Support for gay marriage, not long ago anathema to radicals and conservatives, gays and nongays, alike, now issues forth from ethical and political perspectives as diverse, and even incompatible, as these. The cultural and political context has changed so dramatically since Stonewall that it now seems easier to understand why marriage has come to enjoy overwhelming support in the gay community than to grasp the depth of resistance to the institution that characterized the early movement. Still, I take seriously many of the strategic concerns about the costly political risks posed by a premature campaign. Although surveys and electoral struggles suggest a gradual growth in public support for gay rights, that support is tepid, uneven and fickle, as the debacle over Clinton's attempt to combat legal exclusion of gays from the military made distressingly clear. Thus, while 52 percent of those surveyed in a 1994 *Time* magazine/ CNN poll claimed to consider gay lifestyle acceptable, 64 percent did not want to legalize gay marriages or to permit gay couples to adopt children.[30]

Gay marriage, despite its apparent compatibility with mainstream family values sentiment, raises far more threatening questions than does military service about gender relations, sexuality and family life. Few contemporary politicians, irrespective of their personal convictions, display the courage to confront this contradiction, even when urged to do so by gay conservatives. In *Virtually Normal: An Argument About Homosexuality, New Republic* editor Andrew Sullivan develops the "conservative case for gay marriage," that he earlier published as an op-ed, which stresses the contribution gay marriage could make to a conservative agenda for family and political life. A review of Sullivan's book in the *New Yorker* points out that, "here is where the advocates of gay rights can steal the conservatives' clothes."[31] The epigraph to this chapter by Jonathan Rauch about the insignificance of the homosexual minority comes from a *Wall Street Journal* op-ed he wrote to persuade Republicans that they should support legal gay marriage, not only because it is consistent with conservative values, but to guard against the possibility that gay rights advocates will exploit the party's inconsistency on this issue to political advantage.[32]

The logic behind the conservative case for gay marriage strikes me as compelling. Most importantly, gay marriage would strengthen the ranks of those endangered two-parent, "intact," married-couples families whose praises conservative, "profamily" enthusiasts never seem to tire of singing. Unsurprisingly, however, the case has won few nongay conservative converts to the cause. After all, homophobia is a matter of passion and politics, not logic. The religious right regards homosexuality as an abomination, and it has effectively consolidated its influence over the Republican Party. For example, in 1994, Republicans in the Montana state senate went so far as to pass a bill that would require anyone convicted of homosexual acts to register for life as a violent offender. They reversed their vote in response to an outpouring of public outrage.[33] It was not long afterward, however, that Republican presidential contender Robert Dole returned the thousand-dollar campaign contribution from the gay Log Cabin Republicans in the name, of course, of family values. Nor have figures prominent in the centrist, secular neo-family-values campaign or the communitarian movement, whose professed values affirm both communal support for marital commitment and for tolerance, displayed much concern for such consistency. And even when, in the 1995 fall preelection season, President Clinton sought to "shore up" his standing among gays and lesbians by announcing his administration's support of a bill to outlaw employment discrimination against gays, he specifically withheld his support from gay marriage.[34] First Lady Hillary Rodham Clinton's recent book, *It Takes a Village,* ostensibly written to challenge "false nostalgia for family values," fails even to mention gay marriage or gay families, let alone to advocate village rights and resources for children whose parents are gay.[35]

Despite my personal political baptism in the heady, anti-family crucible of early second wave feminism, I, for one, have converted to the long-term cause. A "postmodern" ideological stew of discordant convictions enticed me to this table. Like Wolfson, Mohr, and Hunter, I have come to believe that legitimizing gay and lesbian marriages would promote a democratic, pluralistic expansion of the meaning, practice, and politics of family life in the United States. This could help to supplant the destructive sanctity of *the family* with respect for diverse and vibrant *families.*

To begin with, the liberal implications of legal gay marriage are far from trivial, as the current rush by the states and Congress to nullify them should confirm. The Supreme Court is certain to have its docket flooded far into the next century with constitutional conflicts that a favorable decision in Hawaii, or elsewhere, will unleash. Under the "full faith and credit" provision of the Constitution, which requires the 50 states to recognize each other's laws, legal gay marriage in one state could begin to threaten anti-sodomy laws in all the others. Policing marital sex would be difficult to legitimate, and differential prosecution of conjugal sex among same-sex couples could violate equal protection legislation. Likewise, if gay marriages were legalized, the myriad state barriers to child custody, adoption, fertility services, inheritance, and other family rights that lesbians and gay men currently suffer could also become subject to legal challenge. Moreover, it seems hard to overestimate the profound cultural implications for the struggle against the pernicious effects of legally condoned homophobia that would ensue were lesbian and gay relationships to be admitted into the ranks of legitimate kinship. In a society that forbids most public school teachers and counselors even the merest expression of tolerance for homosexuality, while lesbian and gay youth attempt suicide at rates three to five times greater than other youth,[36] granting full recognition to even just whitebread lesbian and gay relationships could have dramatic, and salutary, consequences.

Of course, considerations truer to some of my earlier, more visionary feminist convictions also invite me to join the gay wedding procession. For while I share some of Polikoff's disbelief that same-sex marriage can in itself dismantle the patterned gender and sexual injustices of the institution, I do believe it could make a potent contribution to those projects, as the research on gay relationships I discuss below seems to indicate. Moreover, as Mohr suggests, admitting gays to the wedding banquet invites gays and nongays alike to consider the kinds of place settings that could best accommodate the diverse needs of all contemporary families.

Subjecting the conjugal institution to this sort of heightened democratic scrutiny could help it to assume varied creative forms. If we begin to value the meaning and quality of intimate bonds over their customary forms, there are few limits to the kinds of marriage and kinship patterns people might wish to devise. The "companionate marriage," a much celebrated, but less often realized, ideal of modern sociological lore, could take on new life. Two friends might decide to marry without basing their bond on erotic or romantic attachment, as Dorthe, a prominent Danish lesbian activist who had initially opposed the campaign for gay marriage, fantasized after her nation's parliament approved gay registered partnerships: "If I am going to marry it will be with one of my oldest friends in order to share pensions and things like that. But I'd never marry a lover. That is the advantage of being married to a close friend. Then, you never have to marry a lover!"[37] Or, more radical still, perhaps some might dare to question the dyadic limitations of Western marriage and seek some of the benefits of extended family life through small-group marriages arranged to share resources, nurturance and labor. After all, if it is true that "The Two-Parent Family Is Better"[38] than a single-parent family, as family-values crusaders like David Popenoe tirelessly proclaim, might not three-, four-, or more-parent families be better yet, as many utopian communards have long believed?

While conservative advocates of gay marriage surely would balk at such radical visions, they correctly realize that putative champions of committed relationships and of two-parent families who oppose gay marriage can be charged with gross hypocrisy on this score. For access to legal marriage not only would promote long-term, committed intimacy among gay couples, but also would afford invaluable protection to the children of gay parents, as well as indirect protection to closeted gay youth who reside with nongay parents. Clearly, only through a process of massive denial of the fact that millions of children living in gay and lesbian families are here, and here to stay, can anyone genuinely concerned with the best interests of children deny their parents the right to marry.

In the face of arguments for legalizing gay marriage as compelling and incongruent as these, it is hard to dispute Evan Wolfson's enthusiastic claim that, "The brilliance of our movement's taking on marriage is that marriage is, at once and truly, both conservative and transformative, easily understood in basic human terms of equality and respect, and liberating in its individual and social potential."[39]

NOTES

1. The estimate that at least six million children were living with a gay parent by 1985 appeared in Schulenberg, *Gay Parenting*, and has been accepted or revised upwards by most scholars since then. See, for example, Bozett, 39; Patterson, "Children of Lesbian and Gay Parents;" Allen and Demo, "The Families of Lesbians and Gay Men: A New Frontier in Family Research."

2. Burke, *Family Values: A Lesbian Mother's Fight for Her Son.*

3. Goldberg, "Virtual Marriages for Same-Sex Couples."

4. Many gay activist groups and scholars, however, have begun to reclaim the term "queer" as a badge of pride, in much the same way that the Black power movement of the 1960s reclaimed the formerly derogatory term for blacks.

5. Reagan and Schlafly both have gay sons, Powell has a lesbian daughter, and Gingrich has a lesbian half-sister.

6. For a sensitive discussion of the definitional difficulties involved in research on gay and lesbian families, see Allen and Demo, "Families of Lesbians and Gay Men," 112–13.

7. See the introduction and chapters one and two of this book for a direct discussion of the postmodern family condition. In Stacey, *Brave New Families,* I provide a booklength, ethnographic treatment of postmodern family life in the Silicon Valley.

8. I explain my use of the term "modern" family above in the Introduction, pp. 6–8, chapter one, pp. 18–19, and chapter two, pp. 38–43.

9. Most gay and lesbian scholars and activists reject the term "homosexual" because it originated within a medical model that classified homosexuality as a sexual perversion or disease and because the term emphasizes sexuality as at the core of the individual's identity. In this chapter, I follow the generally preferred contemporary practice of using the terms "lesbians" and "gay men," but I also occasionally employ the term "gay" generically to include both women and men. I also play with the multiple, and currently shifting, meanings of the term "queer," by specifying whether I am using the term in its older pejorative sense, in its newer sense of proudly challenging fixed notions of gender and sexuality, or in its more colloquial sense of simply "odd."

10. Quoted in Sherman, ed. *Lesbian and Gay Marriage*, 191.

11. Ibid., 173.

12. Bozett, epilogue to *Gay and Lesbian Parents*, 232.

13. Cited in Sherman, *Lesbian and Gay Marriage*, 9, fn 6. A more recent poll conducted by *The Advocate* suggests that the trend of support for gay marriage is increasing. See Wolfson, "Crossing the Threshold," 583.

14. Terry announced his plans January 24, 1996, on "Randall Terry Live," and LaHaye made her pitch the next day, January 25, 1996, on "Beverly LaHaye Live."

15. Dunlap, "Some States Trying to Stop Gay Marriages before They Start," A18; Dunlap, "Fearing a Toehold for Gay Marriage, Conservatives Rush to Bar the Door," A7. Lochhead, "GOP Bill Targets Same-Sex Marriages, *San Francisco Chronicle,* May 9, 1996, A1, 15.
16. Ibid, A1.
17. Press Briefing by Mike McCurry, White House, May 14, 1996, Office of the Press Secretary.
18. "Vatican Denounces Gay-Marriage Idea." *New York Times,* Mar 29, 1996, A8.
19. Dunlap, "Reform Rabbis Vote to Back Gay Marriage," A8.
20. "The Freedom to Marry." *New York Times,* April 7, 1996, Editorials/Letters, p. 10.
21. The decision stated that the sexual orientation of the parties was irrelevant, because same-sex spouses could be of any sexual orientation. It was the gender discrimination involved in limiting one's choice of spouse that violated the state constitution. See Wolfson, "Crossing the Threshold," 573.
22. Polikoff, "We Will Get What We Ask For: Why Legalizing Gay and Lesbian Marriage Will Not 'Dismantle the Legal Structure of Gender in Every Marriage'."
23. Law Professor, Thomas Coleman, who is executive director of the "Family Diversity Project" in California, expresses these views in Sherman, 128–9.
24. Sullivan, "The Conservative Case for Gay Marriage;" Rauch, "A Pro-Gay, Pro-Family Policy."
25. Tede Matthews in Sherman, 57.
26. Kirk Johnson quoted in Wolfson, 567.
27. Hunter, "Marriage, Law and Gender," 12.
28. Wolfson, "Crossing the Threshold."
29. Mohr, *A More Perfect Union,* 48, 41, 50.
30. "Some Progress Found in Poll on Gay Rights," *San Francisco Chronicle,* June 20, 1994.
31. Ryan, "No Easy Way Out," 90. Sullivan, "Here Comes the Groom."
32. Rauch, "Pro-Gay, Pro-Family Policy."
33. Herscher, "After Reconsidering, Montana Junks Gay Sex Bill," A2.
34. Clinton, according to his senior adviser George Stephanopoulos, "thinks the proper role for the government is to work on the fight against discrimination, but he does not believe we should support (gay) marriage." Quoted in Sandalow and Tuller, "White House Tells Gays It Backs Them," A2.
35. Clinton, *It Takes A Village,* book jacket copy.
36. Remafedi, *Death by Denial.*
37. Quoted in Miller, *Out in the World,* 350.
38. This is the title and central argument of Popenoe's *New York Times* op-ed discussed above in the Introduction, p. 8 and chapter 3, pp. 53–57.
39. Wolfson, "Crossing the Threshold," 599.

EPIGRAPH SOURCES

1. Buchanan quoted in Susan Yoachum and David Tuller, "Right Makes Might in Iowa," *San Francisco Chronicle,* February 12, 1996: A1, 11.
2. Rauch (see bibliographic entry).
3. Bonnie Tinker, "Love Makes a Family," Presentation to 1995 United Nations International Women's Conference, Beijing, September 14.

REFERENCES

Allen, Katherine R., and David H. Demo, "The Families of Lesbians and Gay Men: A New Frontier in Family Research," *Journal of Marriage and the Family* 57 (February 1995): 111–27.

Bozett, Frederick W., ed. *Gay and Lesbian Parents.* New York: Praeger, 1987.

Burke, Phyllis. *Family Values: A Lesbian Mother's Fight for Her Son.* New York: Random House, 1993.

Clinton, Hillary Rodham. *It Takes A Village: And Other Lessons Children Teach Us.* New York: Simon & Schuster, 1996.

Dunlap, David W. 1995. "Some States Trying to Stop Gay Marriages before They Start," *New York Times,* 15 March, A18.

Dunlap, David W. 1996. "Fearing a Toehold for Gay Marriages, Conservatives Rush to Bar the Door," *New York Times,* 6 March, A7.

Goldberg, Carey. 1996. "Virtual Marriages for Same-Sex Couples." *New York Times,* 26 March, A8.

Herscher, Elaine. 1995. "After Reconsidering, Montana Junks Gay Sex Bill," *San Francisco Chronicle,* March 24.

Hunter, Nan D. 1991. "Marriage, Law, and Gender: A Feminist Inquiry." *Law & Sexuality,* 1, n.1:9–30.

Lochhead, Carolyn. 1996. "GOP Bill Targets Same-Sex Marriages," *San Francisco Chronicle,* 9 May, A1, 15.

Miller. Neil. *Out in the World: Gay and Lesbian Life from Buenos Aires to Bangkok.* New York: Random House, 1992.

Mohr, Richard. *A More Perfect Union. Why Straight America Must Stand Up for Gay Rights.* Boston: Beacon, 1994.

Patterson, Charlotte J. 1992. "Children of Lesbian and Gay Parents." *Child Development* 63:1025–42.

Polikoff, Nancy. 1993 "We Will Get What We Ask For: Why Legalizing Gay and Lesbian Marriage Will Not 'Dismantle the Legal Structure of Gender in Every Marriage'," *Virginia Law Review,* vol. 79: 1549–50.

Popenoe, David. 1992. "The Controversial Truth: The Two-Parent Family is Better." *New York Times,* 26 December, 13.

Rauch, Jonathan. 1994. "A Pro-Gay, Pro-Family Policy," *Wall Street Journal,* 29 November, A22.

Remafedi, Gary. ed. *Death by Denial.* Boston: Alyson Publications, 1994.

Ryan, Alan. "No Easy Way Out," *New Yorker.* September 11, 1995, p. 90.

Sandalow, Marc and David Tuller. 1995. "White House Tells Gays It Backs Them," *San Francisco Chronicle,* 21 October, A2.

Sherman, Suzanne, ed. *Lesbian and Gay Marriage: Private Commitments, Public Ceremonies.* Philadelphia: Temple University Press, 1992.

Sullivan, Andrew. "Here Comes the Groom: A (Conservative) Case for Gay Marriage." *New Republic.* v 201, n.9. August 28, 1989, 20–21.

Wolfson, Evan. "Crossing the Threshold: Equal Marriage Rights for Lesbians and Gay Men and the Intra-Community Critique," *Review of Law & Social Change,* XXI, n.3 (1994–95).

QUESTIONS FOR CRITICAL THINKING

Reading 20

1. What do you think constitutes a family? What are its important components? What has led you to define family in the way that you do (e.g., your own family experience, media, friends, other social institutions)?

2. Many of us assert that there must be some biological connection in order for there to be a "family." As a result, when we look at lesbians and gay men we often don't associate them with the ability to have "real" families. What is your perspective?

3. What are your thoughts on the right/need for lesbian/gay couples to marry? Why do you think efforts to prevent such unions (e.g., the Defense of Marriage Act, Proposition 8 etc.) are taken? How might lesbian/gay marriages challenge traditional notions of family in the United States? How might recognizing gay and lesbian families lead to greater equality for people of all sexual orientations?

SOCIAL INSTITUTIONS: EDUCATION

Reading 21

THE RETURN OF "SEPARATE BUT EQUAL"

RICHARD D. KAHLENBERG

"SEGREGATION TODAY, segregation tomorrow, segregation forever," George Wallace declared, to a thunderous ovation from a crowd of Alabamans who had gathered to see him sworn in as governor in 1963. More than forty years later, it is hard to imagine any group of Americans applauding those words. Yet the everyday reality lived by millions of schoolchildren is not too far from Wallace's defiant vision.

No longer segregated in name, the nation's schools are once again largely segregated in fact—by race and ethnicity, and, increasingly, by class.

The new segregation enjoys the backing of a new Supreme Court. In 1954, William Rehnquist was a young Court clerk, and the author of a memo of opposition to the historic ruling—in *Brown v. Board of Education*—that made integration the law of the land; Rehnquist went on to become chief justice for almost two decades. Thurgood Marshall, elevated to the Court after brilliantly arguing the *Brown* case for the plaintiffs, was replaced by Clarence Thomas, who, like a number of his colleagues, seems to have no problem with school segregation, unless it is required by law.

In a series of early 1990s decisions, the Court ruled that desegregation plans were meant to be temporary, no matter how much de facto segregation remained. Across the country, school districts from Buffalo, New York, to Charlotte, North Carolina, were released from court orders, and the mighty process that was to be executed with "all deliberate speed" ground to a halt. Even voluntary integration efforts have been found unconstitutional where they used race in deciding which students would attend which school.

With the law in retreat, geography takes command. "Housing policy is school policy," former Albuquerque mayor David Rusk succinctly observes. In some places, geography has helped bring black and white students together, with schools becoming more integrated as neighborhoods do. But while America in general has become less segregated by race, the trend has been less pronounced among families with children. White families in particular have decamped to farther-flung suburbs and exurbs; by contrast, the whites moving in the opposite direction tend to be singles and couples without children.

Racially, the nation's schools became substantially less segregated in the three decades following *Brown*. Since the early 1980s, though, some of the gains have been lost. More than 70 percent of black children now attend mostly minority schools, up from 63 percent in the 1980–81 school year, according to the Harvard Civil Rights Project. The educational experience of Latinos, now the largest minority group in the United States, is even more isolating: about 76 percent of them attend mostly minority schools. Rusk, who has studied these patterns as closely as anyone, foresees increased economic school segregation in all but six states by 2025.

Economically, segregation has increased in housing and schools alike. Two-thirds of the nation's public-school students are middle-class (as defined by their ineligibility for subsidized lunches). Nevertheless, one-quarter of the schools have a majority of students from low-income households. Poor people of color are especially likely to wind up in schools filled with others like them. That's because while low-income whites often live in middle-class neighborhoods, low-income blacks and Latinos rarely do.

Brown was the culmination of two decades of strategizing and litigating. From the early 1930s to the late 1940s, the NAACP Legal Defense and Education Fund gathered a mountain of evidence of the harm done to black children in the segregated schools of the South. Separation by race was highly insulting and damaging in itself; in addition, the NAACP legal team showed, black schools were getting the short end of the stick materially, financially, and every other way.

Since the early 1990s, lawyers representing parents in poorly funded school districts across the land have been engaged in a similar quest. In forty states and counting, they have called on the courts to outlaw the funding mechanisms (generally based on local property taxes) that cause poorer schools to be saddled with larger class sizes, less qualified teachers drawing lower salaries, and inferior and insufficient equipment and supplies. The equity campaigners point out that although low-income students need considerably more spent on their education than middle-class students do, the balance, nationally, goes the other way: affluent districts, on average, spend a cost-adjusted $7,731 per pupil, compared to $6,383 in high-poverty districts a difference of $1,348. In some places, the gap is even more striking: Illinois, Minnesota, and New York, for example, all spend at least $2,000 more per student in the wealthiest areas.

The aim of the new litigation, like that of the lawsuits that led to *Brown*, has been to move resources, not children. But while the dollar comparisons help dramatize the problem, they do not define it. Like their forebears of half a century ago, the equity campaigners have found, in their pursuit of resources, that resources are not enough. To put it another way, classmates are a resource, too—in fact, a more crucial one than books, pencils, and laptops.

Although the *Brown* decision focused on race, America learned through its implementation that class was the crucial variable. In places like Boston, where desegregation mingled working-class whites and working-class blacks, achievement gains were insignificant. But in communities where low-income blacks attended school with more affluent whites—Hartford, Wilmington, Charlotte, St. Louis, Nashville, Louisville, and others—African American achievement did rise. This was the lesson of the seminal report authored by the sociologist James Coleman in 1966: the beneficial effect of a student body with a high proportion of white students, Coleman found, came not from their race but from their stronger educational preparation and higher educational aspirations. Subsequent experience has confirmed Coleman time and again. The fact that poor kids of all races do better in a middle-class environment is, according to Harvard's Gary Orfield, "one of the most consistent findings in research on education."

Classmates provide "a hidden curriculum," as the psychiatrist Charles Pinderhughes put it. "What the pupils are learning from one another," he explained, "is probably just as important as what they are learning from the teachers." While students of all economic backgrounds add value to schools, more-affluent classmates bring more academic knowledge, which they share with others every day, on the playground as well as in the classroom. A middle-class child has a vocabulary that is, on average, four times as big as a low-income child's, and words are infectious. On the other hand, a fourth-grade child who attends a poor urban school is likely to be surrounded by peers who "can't read [or] understand a simple children's book," according to a 1998 *Education Week* analysis. Middle-class students are far less likely to act out or engage in disruptive behavior, because their life experience has given them reason to believe that education will pay off.

Yet from the right, the left, and the center, America's thinking about education has taken on a strangely pre-*Brown* quality. There exists today a solid consensus among researchers that school segregation perpetuates failure, and an equally durable consensus among politicians and policymakers that nothing much can be done about it. The equity campaigners avoid the subject, regardless of their personal convictions. Others, whether they call for more resources, more choice, or higher standards—the three great school-reform mantras of the age—are also trying to make "separate but equal" work in the face of overwhelming evidence that it does not.

The past twenty years have seen an explosion of educational policy debate, in which the conservative message has rung very loud. While liberals, loosely speaking, tend to emphasize equity and resources, conservatives have rallied behind the concept of "choice," by which they generally mean the ability of parents to transfer children from public to private schools, taking tax money with them. Talk of choice—the kind that involves vouchers, charter schools, and privatization—is everywhere.

Meanwhile, with far less notice, a handful of cities and metropolitan areas have been trying out a different form of choice—one that operates inside the world of public schools and points explicitly toward economic integration. The results are worthy of far more attention than they have received.

During the 1990s, Wake County, North Carolina, instituted a magnet-school-based racial-integration program. In response to a U.S. Fourth Circuit Court decision striking down the use of race in student assignment in Virginia and Maryland, the Wake County School Board voted in January 2000 to drop a set of explicit racial goals in favor of a system that seeks to balance student populations by socioeconomic status and student achievement. While Wake County's racial and economic integration efforts have not erased achievement gaps between economic and racial groups, integration appears to have improved the achievement of low-income and minority students. Nearly 90 percent of students performed at or above grade level on a recent set of state tests. Wake County's system has been far more successful than that of neighboring Durham, where city schools remain poverty-concentrated and are considered low-performing. La Crosse, Wisconsin, which has the nation's longest-running economic school-integration plan, has also seen rising test scores and a low dropout rate.

Despite innumerable experiments and extensive research designed to identify the keys to educational success, no other variable can compare in importance to the economic-class composition of the student body. Peers are teachers in their own right, and economic integration, in addition to its direct benefits, helps drive a variety of other school improvements. If life were fair, the best-qualified teachers would be found in the most disadvantaged schools. In real life, the best teachers are drawn to the schools with the highest socioeconomic levels. Teachers in middle-class schools are more likely to teach in their field of expertise, more likely to have higher teacher test scores, and more likely to be experienced. Their expectations are higher. The curricula they use are richer and more demanding.

Teacher quality can have a profound effect on student achievement. Recognizing that fact, some jurisdictions have used bonuses to lure talented teachers to high-poverty schools. Not very many teachers have taken the bait, though, because of all the difficulties associated with teaching in such schools. It may well be that the *only* way for large numbers of low-income students to have consistent access to high-quality teachers is to bring them into majority middle-class schools.

When parents volunteer in the classroom and participate in school activities, student achievement improves. For example, a 1996 study using National Educational Longitudinal Study data reports that "a child's academic achievement did not depend so much on whether his or her own parents participated, but on the average level of participation of all parents at the school." And socioeconomic status has been found to be the "primary predictor" of parental involvement. Low-income parents often don't have the flexibility to take time off from work, and they are more likely to feel intimidated by educators, which makes them reluctant to get involved in school activities to begin with. Middle-class parents are four times more likely to join PTAs. They have the political savvy and pull to demand high standards and adequate resources, and the wherewithal to supplement public funds with private donations.

Schools with a core of middle-class families are marked by higher expectations, higher-quality teachers, more-motivated students, more financial resources, and greater parental involvement. In short, virtually all of the conditions that educators identify as markers of good schools are more likely to be found in middle-class than in high-poverty schools.

Conservatives often use the language of equity to justify their call for choice. The wealthy, they note, can always get their children into high-quality schools; they do so either by purchasing a home in an area with top-ranked public schools or by sending their children to private school. With unexpected egalitarian passion, the champions of vouchers and educational privatization argue that poor families should have the same right. (Of course, this represents an enormous shift from the days of racial desegregation, when conservatives stood as the defenders of the "neighborhood school" above all else. Now they are the first to point out that a neighborhood school may not be such a great deal for children stuck in a poor neighborhood.)

That emphasis is largely tactical, however. The choice crusaders know that their best chance to make headway is by forming alliances with minority parents and launching programs that make special provision for the poorest of the poor. Give them a chance to speak their minds, however, and few define their hopes so narrowly. What they are after is unlimited choice for all. No matter how these plans are promoted or constructed, in any case, experience shows that the poorest families are the least likely to take advantage of them. In any population given the liberty to choose, it is the comparatively well off who will do so; everyone else will stick with the neighborhood school. Thus the conservative brand of choice leaves schools more segregated than ever.

That is also a danger of the model of reform (associated with the Bush administration's No Child Left Behind Act) that stresses testing and accountability. No Child Left Behind was promoted in the name of equity, as a way to rescue poor children from the "soft bigotry" of social promotion and low expectations. Through rigorous testing and accountability, schools in disadvantaged neighborhoods would be forced to live up to the same standards as other schools, reducing the achievement gaps among students of differing races and incomes. In return for federal funding, states would be required to test students in reading and math for grades 3–8. If a school failed to make mandated "adequate yearly progress" for a period of consecutive years, the students in that school would be free to transfer to higher-performing schools and gain access to supplemental educational services such as private tutoring. If a school missed the mark for four consecutive years, the district would be forced to take corrective action, which could include adopting a new curriculum or replacing staff.

No Child Left Behind was passed with broad bipartisan support because, on paper, it was about resources and equity as well as testing. The Bush administration promised that if a failed school went on failing, not only would parents be empowered to move their children elsewhere, but, in the most dire cases, the school itself would be overhauled. But very few student transfers have occurred. And very few schools have been overhauled. Thus, in practice, the law has largely boiled down to a program of testing and publicizing test scores—practices that can unintentionally accelerate segregation. Parents look at the scores when they decide which school districts to live in. Since the scores reflect the socioeconomic status of a district's families rather than the value that schools are adding, people with options may increasingly gravitate toward the most affluent districts.

Even without making allowances for No Child Left Behind or the adoption of vouchers, American schools are becoming more segregated. The overwhelming weight of evidence suggests that this will be bad for kids, and bad for the ideal of equal opportunity. In some high-poverty schools today, the dropout rate—which nationally has plummeted—exceeds two-thirds. Among families in the lowest 20 percent by household income, children are more than six times as likely to drop out of high school as children from families in the highest 20 percent. Few students graduating from high-poverty inner-city high schools go on to college: nationally, the figure is just 15 percent. Among high school graduates in 1996, 78 percent of high-income students but only 49 percent of their low-income cohort enrolled in college the following fall.

Education reformers have a habit of railing against "the system." In truth, America does not have an education system. It has, to oversimplify slightly, one system for middle-class students, which is working fairly well, and one for low-income and minority students, which is working very badly. Minority twelfth-graders read at about the same level as more affluent and white eighth-graders. Students in well-off suburban jurisdictions such as Naperville, Illinois, and Montgomery County, Maryland, score near the top in international math and science exams, while students in low-income, urban districts such as Chicago and Rochester, New York, test at the level of students in developing countries such as Iran.

Although the United States may have less progressive public policies than other Western industrialized countries when it comes to housing, welfare, and health care, American schools have historically been more egalitarian. Indeed, America's high tolerance for unequal outcomes rests partly on faith in the public schools as a source of equal opportunity. The *Brown* decision represented an important national acknowledgment of the degree to which the reality fell short of the ideal. *Brown* opened the door to meaningful progress in educational experience, and, perhaps just as important, to a deeper understanding of what was needed. Race was not the answer. But integration was. Today's school reformers seem determined to forget that lesson. While they talk endlessly about fixing failed schools and doing right by the victims, they preside over a set of arrangements that make American education, far too often, an instrument of inequality rather than an answer to it.

NOTES

1. Poor people of color are especially likely: David Rusk, "Trends in School Segregation," in Century Foundation Task Force on the Common School, *Divided We Fail: Coming Together Through Public School Choice* (New York: Century Foundation Press, 2002).
2. The equity campaigners point out: Kevin Carey, "The Funding Gap 2004: Many States Still Shortchange Low-Income and Minority Students," Education Trust report, Washington, DC, fall 2004, 7, table 3.
3. This was the lesson of the seminal report: James S. Coleman et al., *Equality of Educational Opportunity* (Washington, DC: Government Printing Office, 1966).
4. The fact that poor kids of all races do better: Gary Orfield and Susan Eaton, *Dismantling Desegregation: The Quiet Reversal of* Brown v. Board of Education (New York: The New Press, 1996), 53.
5. Classmates provide "a hidden curriculum": Dr. Charles Pinderhughes, quoted in U.S. Commission on Civil Rights, *Racial Isolation in the Public Schools* (Washington, DC: Government Printing Office, 1967), 1:82.
6. A middle-class child has a vocabulary: Betty Hart and Todd R. Risley, *Meaningful Differences in the Everyday Experience of Young American Children* (Baltimore, MD: Paul H. Brookes Publishing, 1995).
7. On the other hand, a fourth-grade child: See, for example, Beatrice Birman et al., *The Current Operation of the Chapter 1 Program* (Washington, DC: U.S. Department of Education, 1987), 92–93.

8. During the 1990s, Wake County: Walter Sherlin, "N.C. Integration Story Saw Tree, Not Forest," *Education Week,* June 19, 2002, 14.

9. Teachers in middle-class schools are more likely: National Center for Education Statistics, *Teacher Quality: A Report on the Preparation and Qualifications of Public School Teachers* (Washington, DC: U.S. Department of Education, 1999), 17 (teaching out of field); John F. Kain and Kraig Singleton, "Equality of Educational Opportunity Revisited," *New England Economic Review,* May–June 1996, 87, 99, 107 (teacher test scores); and Laura Lipmann, Shelley Burns, and Edith McArthur, *Urban Schools: The Challenge of Location and Poverty* (Washington, DC: National Center for Education Statistics, 1996), 86–88, 96 (experience).

10. Teacher quality can have a profound effect: For a summary of studies, see Kati Haycock, "Good Teaching Matters," *Thinking K–16* 3, no. 2 (Summer 1998): 3–13.

11. Not very many teachers have taken the bait: Eric A. Hanushek, John F. Kain, and Steven G. Rivkin, "Why Public Schools Lose Teachers," NBER Working Paper no. W8599, National Bureau of Economic Research, Cambridge, MA, November 2001.

12. When parents volunteer in the classroom: Esther Ho Sui-Chu and J. Douglas Willms, "Effects of Parental Involvement on Eighth-Grade Achievement," *Sociology of Education* 69 (April 1996): 136.

13. And socioeconomic status has been found: Gary Orfield, *City-Suburban Desegregation: Parent and Student Perspectives in Metropolitan Boston* (Cambridge, MA: Harvard Civil Rights Project, 1997), 21.

14. Middle-class parents are four times more likely: See, for example, William J. Fowler Jr., ed., *Developments in School Finance* (Washington, DC: U.S. Department of Education, 1995).

15. In some high-poverty schools today: James McPartland and Will J. Jordan, "Older Students Also Need Major Federal Compensatory Educational Resources," in *Hard Work for Good Schools: Facts Not Fads in Title I Reform,* ed. Gary Orfield and Elizabeth DeBray (Cambridge, MA: Harvard Civil Rights Project, 1999). Doris R. Entwisle, Karl L. Alexander, and Linda Steffan Olson, *Children, Schools, and Inequality* (New York: Westview Press, 1997).

16. Minority twelfth-graders read: National Center for Education Statistics, *NEAP 1998 Reading Report Card for the Nation* (Washington, DC: U.S. Department of Education, 1999), 44, 59.

17. Students in well-off suburban jurisdictions: David J. Hoff, "World-Class Education Eludes Many in the U.S.," *Education Week,* April 11, 2001, 1, 14–15.

QUESTIONS FOR CRITICAL THINKING

Reading 21

1. How does Kahlenberg's discussion make you see your own educational experience in new and different ways?

2. In what ways has your class influenced the quality of education that you have received?

3. What do you see as some solutions to class inequality in education? What do you think is the likelihood of such solutions occurring?

Reading 22

PREPARING FOR POWER
Cultural Capital and Curricula in America's Elite Boarding Schools

PETER W. COOKSON, JR. • CAROLINE HODGES PERSELL

B orrowing from the British, early American headmasters and teachers advocated a boarding school curriculum that was classical, conservative, and disciplined. It wasn't until the latter part of the nineteenth century that such "soft" subjects as English, history, and mathematics were given a place beside Latin, Greek, rhetoric, and logic in the syllabus. It was the early schoolmasters' belief that young minds, especially boys' minds, if left to their own devices, were undisciplined, even anarchic. The only reliable antidote to mental flabbiness was a rigorous, regular regime of mental calisthenics. A boy who could not flawlessly recite long Latin passages was required to increase his mental workouts. Classical languages were to the mind what cold showers were to the body: tonics against waywardness.

Girls, with some exceptions, were not thought of as needing much mental preparation for their future roles as wives and mothers. Their heads were best left uncluttered by thought; too much book learning could give a girl ideas about independence. Besides, the great majority of them were not going on to college, where even more classical languages were required.

As an intellectual status symbol, the classical curriculum helped distinguish gentlemen from virtually everyone else and thus defined the difference between an "educated" man and an untutored one, as well as the difference between high culture and popular culture. Such a division is critical to exclude nonmembers from groups seeking status. For a long time a classical curriculum was the only path to admission to a university, as Harvard and many others required candidates to demonstrate proficiency in Latin and Greek (Levine 1980). Thus, the curriculum of boarding schools has long served both social and practical functions.

Culture, much like real estate or stocks, can be considered a form of capital. As the French scholars Pierre Bourdieu and Jean-Claude Passeron

(1977) have indicated, the accumulation of cultural capital can be used to reinforce class differences. Cultural capital is socially created: What constitutes the "best in western civilization" is not arrived at by happenstance, nor was it decided upon by public election. The more deeply embedded the values, the more likely they will be perceived as value free and universal.

Thus curriculum is the nursery of culture and the classical curriculum is the cradle of high culture. The definition of what is a classical course of study has evolved, of course, since the nineteenth century. Greek and Latin are no longer required subjects in most schools—electives abound. But the disciplined and trained mind is still the major objective of the boarding school curriculum.

> The Groton curriculum is predicated on the belief that certain qualities of mind are of major importance: precise and articulate communication; the ability to compute accurately and to reason quantitatively; a grasp of scientific approaches to problem-solving; an understanding of the cultural, social, scientific, and political background of Western civilization; and the ability to reason carefully and logically and to think imaginatively and sensitively. Consequently the School puts considerable emphasis on language, mathematics, science, history, and the arts. (*Groton School* 1981–82:15)

The contrast between the relatively lean curricula of many public schools and the abundant courses offered by boarding schools is apparent. In catalogues of the boarding school's academic requirements, courses are usually grouped by subject matter, and at the larger schools course listings and descriptions can go on for several dozen pages. Far from sounding dreary, the courses described in most catalogues are designed to whet the intellectual appetite. Elective subjects in particular have intriguing titles such as "Hemingway: The Man and His Work," "Varieties of the Poetic Experience," "Effecting Political Change," "Rendezvous with Armageddon," and for those with a scientific bent, "Vertebrate Zoology" and "Mammalian Anatomy and Physiology."

Boarding school students are urged to read deeply and widely. A term course on modern American literature may include works from as many as 10 authors, ranging from William Faulkner to Jack Kerouac. Almost all schools offer a course in Shakespeare in which six or seven plays will be read.

In history, original works are far more likely to be assigned than excerpts from a textbook. A course on the presidency at one school included the following required readings: Rossiter, *The American Presidency;* Hofstadter, *The American Political Tradition;* Hargrove, *Presidential Leadership;* Schlesinger, *A Thousand Days;* Kearns, *Lyndon Johnson and the American Dream;* and White, *Breach of Faith.* Courses often use a college-level text, such as Garraty's *The American Nation* or Palmer's *A History of the Modern World.* Economic history is taught as well—in one school we observed a discussion of the interplay between politics and the depression of 1837—and the idea that there are multiple viewpoints in history is stressed. It is little wonder that many prep school graduates find their first year of college relatively easy.

An advanced-placement English class uses a collection of *The Canterbury Tales* by Geoffrey Chaucer that includes the original middle English on the left page and a modern English translation on the right. An advanced third-year French course includes three or four novels as well as two books of grammar and readings. Even social science courses require a great deal of reading. In a course called "An Introduction to Human Behavior" students are assigned 11 texts including works from B. F. Skinner, Sigmund Freud, Erich Fromm, Jean Piaget, and Rollo May.

Diploma requirements usually include: four years of English, three years of math, three years in one foreign language, two years of history or social science, two years of laboratory science, and one year of art. Many schools require a year of philosophy or religion and also may have such noncredit diploma requirements as four years of physical education, a library skills course, introduction to computers, and a seminar on human sexuality. On average, American public high school seniors take one year less English and math, and more than a year less foreign language than boarding school students (Coleman, Hoffer, and Kilgore 1982:90). Moreover, in the past two decades there has been a historical decline in the number of academic subjects taken by students in the public schools (Adleman 1983).

Because success on the Scholastic Aptitude Test is so critical for admission to a selective college, it is not uncommon for schools to offer English review classes that are specifically designed to help students prepare for the tests. Most schools also offer tutorials and remedial opportunities for students who are weak in a particular subject. For foreign students there is often a course in English as a second language.

As the arts will be part of the future roles of boarding school students, the music, art, and theater programs at many schools are enriching, with special courses such as "The Sound and Sense of Music," "Advanced Drawing," and "The Creative Eye in Film." Student art work is usually on display, and almost every school will produce several full-length plays each year, for example, *Arsenic and Old Lace, A Thurber Carnival, Dracula,* and *The Mousetrap.*

Music is a cherished tradition in many boarding schools, in keeping with their British ancestry. The long-standing "Songs" at Harrow, made famous because Winston Churchill liked to return to them for solace during World War II, are a remarkable display of school solidarity. All 750 boys participate, wearing identical morning coats with tails. Every seat is filled in the circular, sharply tiered replica of Shakespeare's Globe Theater as the boys rise in unison, their voices resonating in the rotunda.

The belief that a well-rounded education includes some "hands-on" experience and travel runs deep in the prep view of learning. Virtually every boarding school provides opportunities for its students to study and work off campus. As volunteers, Taft students, for instance, can "tutor on a one-to-one basis in inner-city schools in Waterbury, act as teachers' helpers in Waterbury Public Schools and work with retarded children at Southbury Training School." They can also work in convalescent homes, hospitals, and day-care centers, and act as "apprentices to veterinarians and help with Girl Scout troops" (*Taft* 1981–82:21). At the Ethel Walker School in Connecticut, girls can go on whale watches, trips to the theater, or work in the office of a local politician. The Madeira School in Virginia has a co-curriculum program requiring students to spend every Wednesday participating in volunteer or internship situations.

Generally speaking, the schools that take the position that manual labor and firsthand experience are good for the soul as well as the mind and body, are more progressive in orientation than other schools. At the Putney School every student has to take a tour of duty at the cow barn, starting at 5:30 A.M. In their own words, "Putney's work program is ambitious. We grow much of our own food, mill our own lumber, pick up our own trash, and have a large part in building our buildings. . . . Stoves won't heat until wood is cut and split" (*The Putney School* 1982:3).

Various styles of student-built structures dot the campus of the Colorado Rocky Mountain School, and at the tiny Midland School in California, there is no service staff, except for one cook. When the water pump breaks, faculty and students fix it, and when buildings are to be built, faculty and students pitch in. "We choose to live simply, to distinguish between our needs and our wants, to do without many of the comforts which often obscure the significant things in life" (*Midland School* 1983:1). The creed of self-reliance is reenacted every day at Midland. When a trustee offered to buy the school a swimming pool, he was turned down. Lounging around a pool is not part of the Midland philosophy.

Travel is very much part of the prep way of life and is continued right through the school year. Not only are semesters or a year abroad (usually in France or Spain) offered, but at some of the smaller schools, everyone goes on an extensive field trip. Every March at the Verde Valley School in Arizona the students travel to "Hopi, Navajo and Zuni reservations, to small villages in northern Mexico, to isolated Spanish-American communities in northern New Mexico and to ethnic neighborhoods of Southwestern cities. They live with native families, attend and teach in schools, work on ranches, and participate in the lives of the host families and their communities" (*Verde Valley School* 1982–83:9). Not all boarding schools, of course, place such a high value on rubbing shoulders with the outside world. At most of the academies, entrepreneurial, and girls' schools the emphasis is on service rather than sharing.

While boarding schools may vary in their general philosophy, the actual curricula do not widely differ. The pressures exerted on prep schools to get their students into good colleges means that virtually all students must study the same core subjects. Although not quick to embrace educational innovation, many boarding schools have added computers to their curricula. This has no doubt been encouraged by announcements by a number of Ivy League and other elite colleges that they want their future applicants to be "computer literate." While people at most boarding schools, or anywhere else for that matter, are not quite sure what is meant by computer literate, they are trying to provide well-equipped computer rooms and teachers who can move their students toward computer proficiency.

For students who have particular interests that cannot be met by the formal curriculum, almost all schools offer independent study, which gives students and teachers at boarding schools a great deal of intellectual flexibility. At Groton, for example, independent study can cover a diverse set of topics including listening to the works of Wagner, conducting a scientific experiment, or studying a special aspect of history.

The boarding school curriculum offers students an abundant buffet of regular course work, electives, volunteer opportunities, travel, and independent study, from which to choose a course of study. By encouraging students to treat academic work as an exciting challenge rather than just a job to be done, the prep schools not only pass on culture but increase their students' competitive edge in the scramble for admission to selective colleges.

THE IMPORTANCE OF SPORTS

Even the most diligent student cannot sit in classrooms all day, and because the prep philosophy emphasizes the whole person, boarding schools offer an impressive array of extracurricular activities, the most important of which is athletics. At progressive schools, the competitive nature of sport is deemphasized. The "afternoon out-of-door program" at Putney, for example, allows for a wide variety of outdoor activities that are noncompetitive; in fact, "skiing is the ideal sport for Putney as one may ski chiefly to enjoy himself, the air, the snow" (*The Putney School*, 1982;15).

Putney's sense that sport should be part of a communion with nature is not shared by most other schools, however. At most prep schools sport is about competition, and even more important, about winning. An athletically powerful prep school will field varsity, junior varsity, and third-string teams in most major sports. A typical coed or boys' school will offer football, soccer, cross-country, water polo, ice hockey, swimming, squash, basketball, wrestling, winter track, gymnastics, tennis, golf, baseball, track, and lacrosse. For the faint-hearted there are alternative activities such as modern dance, cycling, tai chi, yoga, ballet, and for the hopelessly unathletic, a "fitness" class. A truly traditional prep school will also have crew like their English forebears at Eton and Harrow. Certain schools have retained such British games as "Fives," but most stop short of the mayhem masquerading as a game called rugby.

Prep teams compete with college freshmen teams, other prep teams, and occasionally with public schools, although public school competitors are picked with care. Not only is there the possible problem of humiliation on the field, there is the even more explosive problem of fraternization in the stands when prep meets townie. Some schools, known as "jock" schools, act essentially as farm teams for Ivy League colleges, consistently providing them with athletes who have been polished by the prep experience. Many prep schools take public high school graduates for a postgraduate year, as a way of adding some size and weight to their football teams.

Prep girls also love sports; they participate as much as the boys, often in the same sports, and with as much vigor. A girls' field hockey game between Exeter and Andover is as intense as when the varsity football teams clash. Horseback riding at girls' schools is still popular; a number of the girls go on to ride in the show or hunt circuit. Unlike many of the girls in public schools, the boarding-school girl is discouraged from being a spectator. Loafing is considered to be almost as bad for girls as it is for boys.

During the school year the halls of nearly all prep schools are decorated with either bulletins of sporting outcomes or posters urging victory in some upcoming game. Pep rallies are common, as are assemblies when awards are given and competitive spirit is eulogized. Often the whole school will be bussed to an opponent's campus if the game is considered to be crucial or if the rivalry is long-standing.

Alumni return to see games, and there are frequent contests between alumni and varsity teams. Because preps retain the love of fitness and sports, it is not uncommon for the old warriors to give the young warriors a thrashing. Similarly, the prep life also invariably includes ritual competitions between, say, the girls' field hockey team and a pick-up faculty team.

Nowhere is the spirit of victory more pronounced than on the ice of the hockey rink. Few public schools can afford a hockey rink so prep schools can attract the best players without much competition. Some prep schools import a few Canadians each year to fill out the roster. Speed, strength, endurance, and fearlessness are the qualities that produce winning hockey and more than one freshman team from an Ivy League college has found itself out-skated by a prep team. Whatever else may be, in Holden Caulfield's term, "phony" about prep schools, sports are for real. This emphasis on sport is not without its critics. At the Harrow School in London, the new headmaster, who was an all-England rugby player, has begun a program to reward artistic and musical prowess as well as athletic and academic skills.

The athletic facilities at prep schools are impressive, and at the larger schools, lavish. Acres and acres of playing fields, scores of tennis courts, one or more gyms, a hockey rink, a golf course, swimming pools, squash courts, workout rooms—all can be found on many prep school campuses. Generally, the facilities are extremely well maintained. The equipment most preps use is the best, as are the uniforms. One boy described how "when your gym clothes get dirty, you simply turn them in at the locker room for a fresh set." The cost of all this, of course, is extraordinary, but considered necessary, because excellence in sport is part of the definition of a gentleman or gentlewoman.

The pressure for athletic success is intense on many campuses, and a student's, as well as a school's, social standing can ride on the narrow margin between victory and defeat. Perhaps because of this, schools generally take great pains to play schools of their own size and social eliteness. A study of who plays whom among prep schools reveals that schools will travel great distances, at considerable expense, to play other prep schools whose students and traditions are similar to their own.

EXTRACURRICULARS AND PREPARATION FOR LIFE

Not all prep school extracurricular activities require sweating, however. Like public school students, preps can work on the school newspaper or yearbook, help to organize a dance, or be part of a blood donor drive, and are much more likely than their public school counterparts to be involved in such activities. For example, one in three boarding school students is involved in student government compared to one in five public school students, and two in five are involved in the school newspaper or yearbook compared to one in five. This evidence is consistent with other research. Coleman, Hoffer, and Kilgore (1982) found that private school students participate more in extracurricular activities than do public school students. The fact that more boarding school students than public school students are involved in activities provides additional opportunities for them to practice their verbal, interpersonal, and leadership skills.

The catalogue of clubs at prep schools is nearly endless. The opportunity for students to develop special nonacademic interests is one of the qualities of life at prep schools that distinguishes them from many public schools. Special interest clubs for chess, sailing, bowling, or gun clubs are popular at boys' schools. One elite boys' school has a "war games" club. As the boys at this school are feverishly calculating their country's next strategic arms move, the girls in a Connecticut school are attending a meeting of Amnesty International. Girls, in general, tend to spend their off hours studying the gentler arts such as gourmet cooking and art history. One girls' school has a club with a permanent service mission to the governor's office.

At some schools students can learn printing, metalwork, or woodworking. The shop for the latter at Groton is amply equipped and much of the work turned out by the students is of professional quality. The less traditional schools offer clubs for vegetarian cooking, weaving, quilting, folk music, and—in subtle juxtaposition to the Connecticut girls' school—international cooking. At western schools, the horse still reigns supreme and many students spend endless hours riding, training, cleaning, and loving their own horse, or a horse they have leased from the school.

With the prep emphasis on music, choirs, glee clubs, madrigals, chamber music groups, as well as informal ensembles are all given places to practice. Most schools also have individual practice rooms, and like athletic teams, many prep musicians travel to other schools for concerts and performances.

Some schools offer a five-week "Winterim," during which students and faculty propose and organize a variety of off- and on-campus activities and studies. Such a program breaks the monotony of the usual class routine in the middle of winter, a season teachers repeatedly told us was the worst time at boarding school. It also enables students and faculty to explore new areas or interests in a safe way, that is, without grades.

In prep schools there is a perceived need for students to exercise authority as apprentice leaders early in their educational careers. The tradition of delegating real authority to students has British roots, where head boys and prefects have real power within the public schools. Head boys can discipline other boys by setting punishments and are treated by headmaster and housemasters alike as a part of the administration. In the United States, student power is generally more limited, although at the progressive schools students can be quite involved in the administrative decision-making process.

Virtually all prep schools have a student government. The formal structure of government usually includes a student body president, vice president, treasurer, secretary, class presidents, and dorm prefects, representatives, or "whips," as they are called at one school. Clubs also have presidents and there are always committees to be headed. Some schools have student-faculty senates and in schools like Wooster, in Connecticut, students are expected to play a major part in the disciplinary system. An ambitious student can obtain a great deal of experience in committee work, developing transferable skills for later leadership positions in finance, law, management, or politics.

The office of student body president or head prefect is used by the administration primarily as an extension of the official school culture, and most of the students who fill these offices are quite good at advancing the school's best public relations face. A successful student body president, like a good head, is artful in developing an easy leadership style, which is useful because he or she is in a structural political dilemma. Elected by the students but responsible to the school administration, the student politician is a classic go-between, always running the danger of being seen as "selling out" by students and as "uncooperative" by the administration. Occasionally students rebel against too much pandering to the administration and elect a rebel leader, who makes it his or her business to be a thorn in the side of the administration. A number of heads and deans of students watch elections closely, because if elections go "badly" it could mean a difficult year for them.

The actual content of real power varies by school. At some, authority is more apparent than real; at others, student power can affect important school decisions. At Putney, the "Big Committee" is composed of the school director, student leaders, and teachers. The powers of the Big Committee are laid out in the school's constitution, and students at Putney have real input into the decision-making process. At the Thacher School in California, the Student Leadership Council, which is composed of the school chairman, presidents of the three lower classes, and head prefects, is not only responsible for student activities and events, but also grants funds to groups who petition for special allocations. The power of the purse is learned early in the life of a prep school student. At the Westtown School in Pennsylvania, the student council arrives at decisions not by voting yea or nay, "but by following the Quaker custom of arriving at a 'sense of the meeting'" (*Westtown School* 1982–83:25).

Not all students, of course, participate in school politics; it may well be that many of the students most admired by their peers never run, or never would run, for a political position. The guerrilla leaders who emerge and flourish in the student underlife—or counterculture—may have far greater real power than the "superschoolies" that tend to get elected to public office.

In most coeducational schools boys tend to monopolize positions of power. The highest offices are generally held by boys; girls are found in the vice presidential and secretarial positions. Politics can be important to prep families and we suspect that a number of prep boys arrive at boarding school with a good supply of political ambition. One of the reasons advanced in support of all-girls' schools is that girls can gain important leadership experience there.

Some schools try to capture what they see as the best aspects of single-sex and coed schools. They do this by having boys and girls elect distinct school leaders, by having certain customs, places, and events that they share only with members of their own sex, and by having classes, certain other activities, and social events be coeducational. These schools, often called coordinate schools, see themselves as offering the chance to form strong single-sex bonds, to build self-confidence in adolescents, and to provide experience in working and relating to members of both sexes. Girls at coed schools more generally are likely to say they think in 10 years they will find the social skills they learned to be the most valuable part of their boarding-school experience.

 ## LEARNING BY EXAMPLE

Part of the social learning students obtain is exposure to significant public personalities. Virtually all the schools have guest speaker programs in which well-known people can be seen and heard. Some of the speakers that have appeared at Miss Porter's School in the last several years include Alex Haley, author; Russell Baker, humorist; Arthur Miller, playwright; and Dick Gregory, comedian. At the boys' schools there is a tendency to invite men who are successful in politics and journalism. Recent speakers at the Hill School include James A. Baker III, Secretary of the Treasury

(Hill class of 1948); James Reston, columnist; Frank Borman, astronaut and president of Eastern Airlines; and William Proxmire, United States senator (Hill class of 1934).

Inviting successful alumni to return for talks is one of the ways boarding schools can pass on a sense of the school's efficacy. Throughout the year panels, assemblies, and forums are organized for these occasions. Often the alumni speakers will also have informal sessions with students, visit classrooms, and stay for lunch, tea, or supper.

In keeping with cultural environments of prep schools, especially the select 16 schools, professional musicians, actors, and dancers are regularly invited to perform. Art and sculpture exhibits are common and some schools, such as Andover and Exeter, have permanent art galleries. The art at prep schools is generally either original works by artists such as Toulouse-Lautrec, Matisse, or Daumier, or the work of established contemporary artists such as Frank Stella, who graduated from Andover. At a large school there may be so much cultural activity that it is unnecessary to leave campus for any kind of high cultural event.

Those who come to elite boarding schools to talk or perform are the makers of culture. For adolescents seeking to be the best, these successful individuals give them a sense of importance and empowerment. All around them are the symbols of their special importance—in Groton's main hallway hangs a personal letter from Ronald Reagan to the headmaster, reminding the students that Groton "boasts a former President of the United States and some of America's finest statesmen." Five or six books a year will be published by a school's alumni; Exeter in particular has many alumni authors, including James Agee, Nathaniel G. Benchley, John Knowles, Dwight Macdonald, Jr., Arthur M. Schlesinger, Jr., Sloan Wilson, and Gore Vidal. Roger L. Stevens, Alan Jay Lerner, and Edward Albee are all Choate-Rosemary Hall alumni, adding luster to a theater program that trains many professional actresses and actors. A student at an elite school is part of a world where such success is expected, and celebrity and power are part of the unfolding of life. Not every school is as culturally rich as the elite eastern prep schools, but in the main, most schools work hard to develop an appreciation for high culture. At the Orme School in Arizona, a week is set aside each year in which the whole school participates in looking at art, watching art being made, and making art.

Nowhere is the drive for athletic, cultural, and academic excellence more apparent than in the awards, honors, and prizes that are given to outstanding teams or students at the end of each year. Sporting trophies are often large silver cups with the names of annual champions engraved on several sides. At some schools the triumphs have come with enough regularity to warrant building several hundred yards of glass casing to hold the dozens of medals, trophies, and other mementos that are the victors' spoils. Pictures of past winning teams, looking directly into the camera, seem frozen in time.

Academic prizes tend to be slightly less flashy but no less important. Much like British schoolmasters, American schoolmasters believe in rewarding excellence, so most schools give a number of cultural, service, and academic prizes at the end of each year. There is usually at least one prize in each academic discipline, as well as prizes for overall achievement and effort. There are service prizes for dedicated volunteers, as well as debating and creative writing prizes. Almost all schools have cum laude and other honor societies.

Sitting through a graduation ceremony at a boarding school can be an endurance test—some schools give so many prizes that one could fly from New York to Boston and back in the time it takes to go from the classics prize to the prize for the best woodworking or weaving project. But of course, the greatest prize of all is graduation, and more than a few schools chisel, paint, etch, or carve the names of the graduates into wood, stone, or metal to immortalize their passage from the total institution into the world.

REFERENCES

Adleman, Clifford. 1983. "Devaluation, Diffusion and the College Connection: A Study of High School Transcripts, 1964–1981." Washington, D.C.: National Commission on Excellence in Education.

Bourdieu, Pierre, and Jean-Claude Passeron. 1977. *Reproduction: In Education, Society, and Culture.* Beverly Hills, CA: Sage.

Coleman, James S., Thomas Hoffer, and Sally Kilgore. 1982. *High School Achievement.* New York: Basic Books, p. 90.

Levine, Steven B. 1980. "The Rise of American Boarding Schools and the Development of a National Upper Class." *Social Problems* 28:63–94.

 QUESTIONS FOR CRITICAL THINKING

Reading 22

1. How does Cookson and Persell's discussion of cultural capital challenge claims that the United States is a meritocracy (a system in which people's success depends upon their talents, abilities, and effort)?

2. What examples have you witnessed of the amount of cultural capital someone possesses impacting their ability to succeed?

3. What policy changes need to occur in the educational system in order to prevent schools (both public and private) from perpetuating inequality?

Reading 23

CIVILIZE THEM WITH A STICK

MARY CROW DOG • RICHARD ERDOES

. . . Gathered from the cabin, the wickiup, and the tepee,
partly by cajolery and partly by threats;
partly by bribery and partly by force,
they are induced to leave their kindred
to enter these schools and take upon themselves
the outward appearance of civilized life.

—ANNUAL REPORT OF THE
DEPARTMENT OF INTERIOR, 1901

It is almost impossible to explain to a sympathetic white person what a typical old Indian boarding school was like; how it affected the Indian child suddenly dumped into it like a small creature from another world, helpless, defenseless, bewildered, trying desperately and instinctively to survive and sometimes not surviving at all. I think such children were like the victims of Nazi concentration camps trying to tell average, middle-class Americans what their experience had been like. Even now, when these schools are much improved, when the buildings are new, all gleaming steel and glass, the food tolerable, the teachers well trained and well intentioned, even trained in child psychology—unfortunately the psychology of white children, which is different from ours—the shock to the child upon arrival is still tremendous. Some just seem to shrivel up, don't speak for days on end, and have an empty look in their eyes. I know of an 11-year-old on another reservation who hanged herself, and in our school, while I was there, a girl jumped out of the window, trying to kill herself to escape an unbearable situation. That first shock is always there.

Although the old tiyospaye has been destroyed, in the traditional Sioux families, especially in those where there is no drinking, the child is never left alone. It is always surrounded by relatives, carried around, enveloped in warmth. It is treated with the respect due to any human being, even a small one. It is seldom forced to do anything against its will, seldom screamed at, and never beaten. That much, at least, is left of the old family group among full-bloods. And then suddenly a bus or car arrives, full of strangers, usually white strangers, who yank the child out of the arms of those who love it, taking it screaming to the boarding school. The only word I can think of for what is done to these children is kidnapping.

Even now, in a good school, there is impersonality instead of close human contact; a sterile, cold atmosphere, an unfamiliar routine, language problems, and above all the maza-skan-skan, that damn clock—white man's time as opposed to Indian time, which is natural time. Like eating when you are hungry and sleeping when you are tired, not when that damn clock says you must. But I was not taken to one of the better, modern schools. I was taken to the old-fashioned mission school at St. Francis, run by the nuns and Catholic fathers, built sometime around the turn of the century and not improved a bit when I arrived, not improved as far as the buildings, the food, the teachers, or their methods were concerned.

In the old days, nature was our people's only school and they needed no other. Girls had their toy tipis and dolls, boys their toy bows and arrows. Both rode and swam and played the rough Indian games together. Kids watched their peers and elders and naturally grew from children into adults. Life in the tipi circle was harmonious—until the whiskey peddlers arrived with their wagons and barrels of "Injun whiskey." I often wished I could have grown up in the old, before-whiskey days.

Oddly enough, we owed our unspeakable boarding schools to the dogooders, the white Indian-lovers. The schools were intended as an alternative to the outright extermination seriously advocated by generals Sherman and Sheridan, as well as by most settlers and prospectors overrunning our land. "You don't have to kill those poor benighted heathen," the do-gooders said, "in order to solve the Indian Problem. Just give us a chance to turn them into useful farmhands, laborers, and chambermaids who will break their backs for you at low wages." In that way the boarding schools were born. The kids were taken away from their villages and pueblos, in their blankets and moccasins, kept completely isolated from their families—sometimes for as long as ten years—suddenly coming back, their short hair slick with pomade, their necks raw from stiff, high collars, their thick jackets always short in the sleeves and pinching under the arms, their tight patent leather shoes giving them corns, the girls in starched white blouses and clumsy, high-buttoned boots—caricatures of white people. When they found out— and they found out quickly—that they were neither wanted by whites nor by Indians, they got good and drunk, many of them staying drunk for the rest of their lives. I still have a poster I found among my grandfather's stuff, given to him by the missionaries to tack up on his wall. It reads:

1. Let Jesus save you.
2. Come out of your blanket, cut your hair, and dress like a white man.
3. Have a Christian family with one wife for life only.

4. Live in a house like your white brother. Work hard and wash often.
5. Learn the value of a hard-earned dollar. Do not waste your money on giveaways. Be punctual.
6. Believe that property and wealth are signs of divine approval.
7. Keep away from saloons and strong spirits.
8. Speak the language of your white brother. Send your children to school to do likewise.
9. Go to church often and regularly.
10. Do not go to Indian dances or to the medicine men.

The people who were stuck upon "solving the Indian Problem" by making us into whites retreated from this position only step by step in the wake of Indian protests.

The mission school at St. Francis was a curse for our family for generations. My grandmother went there, then my mother, then my sisters and I. At one time or other every one of us tried to run away. Grandma told me once about the bad times she had experienced at St. Francis. In those days they let students go home only for one week every year. Two days were used up for transportation, which meant spending just five days out of 365 with her family. And that was an improvement. Before grandma's time, on many reservations they did not let the students go home at all until they had finished school. Anybody who disobeyed the nuns was severely punished. The building in which my grandmother stayed had three floors, for girls only. Way up in the attic were little cells, about five by five by ten feet. One time she was in church and instead of praying she was playing jacks. As punishment they took her to one of those little cubicles where she stayed in darkness because the windows had been boarded up. They left her there for a whole week with only bread and water for nourishment. After she came out she promptly ran away, together with three other girls. They were found and brought back. The nuns stripped them naked and whipped them. They used a horse buggy whip on my grandmother. Then she was put back into the attic—for two weeks.

My mother had much the same experiences but never wanted to talk about them, and then there I was, in the same place. The school is now run by the BIA—the Bureau of Indian Affairs—but only since about 15 years ago. When I was there, during the 1960s, it was still run by the Church. The Jesuit fathers ran the boys' wing and the Sisters of the Sacred Heart ran us—with the help of the strap. Nothing had changed since my grandmother's days. I have been told recently that even in the '70s they were still beating children at that school. All I got out of school was being taught how to pray. I learned quickly that I would be beaten if I failed in my devotions or, God forbid, prayed the wrong way, especially prayed in Indian to Wakan Tanka, the Indian Creator.

The girls' wing was built like an F and was run like a penal institution. Every morning at five o'clock the sisters would come into our large dormitory to wake us up, and immediately we had to kneel down at the sides of our beds and recite the prayers. At six o'clock we were herded into the church for more of the same. I did not take kindly to the discipline and to marching by the clock, left-right, left-right. I was never one to like being forced to do something. I do something because I feel like doing it. I felt this way always, as far as I can remember, and my sister Barbara felt the same way. An old medicine man once told me: "Us Lakotas are not like dogs who can be trained, who can be beaten and keep on wagging their tails, licking the hand that whipped them. We are like cats, little cats, big cats, wildcats, bobcats, mountain lions. It doesn't matter what kind, but cats who can't be tamed, who scratch if you step on their tails." But I was only a kitten and my claws were still small.

Barbara was still in the school when I arrived and during my first year or two she could still protect me a little bit. When Barb was a seventh grader she ran away together with five other girls, early in the morning before sunrise. They brought them back in the evening. The girls had to wait for two hours in front of the mother superior's office. They were hungry and cold, frozen through. It was wintertime and they had been running the whole day without food, trying to make good their escape. The mother superior asked each girl, "Would you do this again?" She told them that as punishment they would not be allowed to visit home for a month and that she'd keep them busy on work details until the skin on their knees and elbows had worn off. At the end of her speech she told each girl, "Get up from this chair and lean over it." She then lifted the girls' skirts and pulled down their underpants. Not little girls either, but teenagers. She had a leather strap about a foot long and four inches wide fastened to a stick, and beat the girls, one after another, until they cried. Barb did not give her that satisfaction but just clenched her teeth. There was one girl, Barb told me, the nun kept on beating and beating until her arm got tired.

I did not escape my share of the strap. Once, when I was 13 years old, I refused to go to Mass. I did not want to go to church because I did not feel well. A nun grabbed me by the hair, dragged me upstairs, made me stoop over, pulled my dress up (we were not allowed at the time to wear jeans), pulled my panties down, and gave me what they called "swats"—25 swats with a board around which Scotch tape had been wound. She hurt me badly.

My classroom was right next to the principal's office and almost every day I could hear him swatting the boys. Beating was the common punishment for not doing one's homework, or for being late to school. It had such a bad effect upon me that I hated and mistrusted every white person on sight, because I met only one kind. It was not until much later that I met sincere white people I could relate to and be friends with. Racism breeds racism in reverse.

The routine at St. Francis was dreary. Six A.M., kneeling in church for an hour or so; seven o'clock, breakfast; eight o'clock, scrub the floor, peel spuds, make classes. We had to mop the dining room twice every day and scrub the tables. If you were caught taking a rest, doodling on the bench with a fingernail or knife, or just rapping, the nun would come up with a dish towel and just slap it across your face, saying, "You're not supposed to be talking; you're supposed to be working!" Monday mornings we had cornmeal mush, Tuesday oatmeal, Wednesday rice and raisins, Thursday cornflakes, and Friday all the leftovers mixed together or sometimes fish. Frequently the food had bugs or rocks in it. We were eating hot dogs that were weeks old, while the nuns were dining on ham, whipped potatoes, sweet peas, and cranberry sauce. In winter our dorm was icy cold while the nuns' rooms were always warm.

I have seen little girls arrive at the school, first graders, just fresh from home and totally unprepared for what awaited them, little girls with pretty braids, and the first thing the nuns did was chop their hair off and tie up what was left behind their ears. Next they would dump the children into tubs of alcohol, a sort of rubbing alcohol, "to get the germs off." Many of the nuns were German immigrants, some from Bavaria, so that we sometimes speculated whether Bavaria was some sort of Dracula country inhabited by monsters. For the sake of objectivity I ought to mention that two of the German fathers were great linguists and that the only Lakota-English dictionaries and grammars which are worth anything were put together by them.

At night some of the girls would huddle in bed together for comfort and reassurance. Then the nun in charge of the dorm would come in and say, "What are the two of you doing in bed together? I smell evil in this room. You girls are evil incarnate. You are sinning. You are going to hell and burn forever. You can act that way in the devil's frying pan." She would get them out of bed in the middle of the night, making them kneel and pray until morning. We had not the slightest idea what it was all about. At home we slept two and three in a bed for animal warmth and a feeling of security.

The nuns and the girls in the two top grades were constantly battling it out physically with fists, nails, and hair-pulling. I myself was growing from a kitten into an undersized cat. My claws were getting bigger and were itching for action. About 1969 or 1970 a strange young white girl appeared on the reservation. She looked about 18 or 20 years old. She was pretty and had long, blond hair down to her waist, patched jeans, boots, and a backpack. She was different from any other white person we had met before. I think her name was Wise. I do not know how she managed to overcome our reluctance and distrust, getting us into a corner, making us listen to her, asking us how we were treated. She told us that she was from New York. She was the first real hippie or Yippie we had come across. She told us of people called the Black Panthers, Young Lords, and Weathermen. She said, "Black people are getting it on. Indians are getting it on in St. Paul and California. How about you?" She also said, "Why don't you put out an underground paper, mimeograph it. It's easy. Tell it like it is. Let it all hang out." She spoke a strange lingo but we caught on fast.

Charlene Left Hand Bull and Gina One Star were two full-blood girls I used to hang out with. We did everything together. They were willing to join me in a Sioux uprising. We put together a newspaper which we called the *Red Panther.* In it we wrote how bad the school was, what kind of slop we had to eat—slimy, rotten, blackened potatoes for two weeks—the way we were beaten. I think I was the one who wrote the worst article about our principal of the moment, Father Keeler. I put all my anger and venom into it. I called him a goddam wasicun of a bitch. I wrote that he knew nothing about Indians and should go back to where he came from, teaching white children whom he could relate to. I wrote that we knew which priests slept with which nuns and that all they ever could think about was filling their bellies and buying a new car. It was the kind of writing which foamed at the mouth, but which also lifted a great deal of weight from one's soul.

On Saint Patrick's Day, when everybody was at the big powwow, we distributed our newspapers. We put them on windshields and bulletin boards, in desks and pews, in dorms and toilets. But someone saw us and snitched on us. The shit hit the fan. The three of us were taken before a board meeting. Our parents, in my case my mother, had to come. They were told that ours was a most serious matter, the worst thing that had ever happened in the school's long history. One of the nuns told my mother, "Your daughter really needs to be talked to." "What's wrong with my daughter?" my mother asked. She was given one of our *Red Panther* newspapers. The nun pointed out its name to her and then my piece, waiting for mom's reaction. After a while she asked, "Well, what have you got to say to this? What do you think?"

My mother said, "Well, when I went to school here, some years back, I was treated a lot worse than these kids are. I really can't see how they can have any complaints, because we was treated a lot stricter. We could not even wear skirts halfway up our knees. These girls have it made. But you should forgive them because they are young. And it's supposed to be a free country, free speech and all that. I don't believe what they done is wrong." So all I got out of it was scrubbing six flights of stairs on my hands and knees, every day. And no boy-side privileges.

The boys and girls were still pretty much separated. The only time one could meet a member of the opposite sex was during free time, between 4 and 5:30, in the study hall or on benches or the volleyball court outside, and that was strictly supervised. One day Charlene and I went over to the boys' side. We were on the ball team and they had to let us practice. We played three extra minutes, only three minutes more than we were supposed to. Here was the nuns' opportunity for revenge. We got 25 swats. I told Charlene, "We are getting too old to have our bare asses whipped that way. We are old enough to have babies. Enough of this shit. Next time we fight back." Charlene only said, "Hoka-hay!"

* * *

In a school like this there is always a lot of favoritism. At St. Francis it was strongly tinged with racism. Girls who were near-white, who came from what the nuns called "nice families," got preferential treatment. They waited on the faculty and got to eat ham or eggs and bacon in the morning. They got the easy jobs while the skins, who did not have the right kind of background—myself among them—always wound up in the laundry room sorting out 10-bushel baskets of dirty boys' socks every day. Or we wound up scrubbing the floors and doing all the dishes. The school therefore fostered fights and antagonism between whites and breeds, and between breeds and skins. At one time Charlene and I had to iron all the robes and vestments the priests wore when saying Mass. We had to fold them up and put them into a chest in the back of the church. In a corner, looking over our shoulders, was a statue of the crucified Savior, all bloody and beaten up. Charlene looked up and said, "Look at that poor Indian. The pigs sure worked him over." That was the closest I ever came to seeing Jesus.

I was held up as a bad example and didn't mind. I was old enough to have a boyfriend and promptly got one. At the school we had an hour and a half for ourselves. Between the boys' and the girls' wings were some benches where one could sit. My boyfriend and I used to go there just to hold hands and talk. The nuns were very uptight about any boy-girl stuff. They had an exaggerated fear of anything having even the faintest connection with sex. One day in religion class, an all-girl class, Sister Bernard singled me out for some remarks, pointing me out as a bad example, an example that should be shown. She said that I was too free with my body. That I was holding hands which meant that I was not a good example to follow. She also said that I wore unchaste dresses, skirts which were too short, too suggestive, shorter than regulations permitted, and for that I would be punished. She dressed me down before the whole class, carrying on and on about my unchastity.

• • •

We got a new priest in English. During one of his first classes he asked one of the boys a certain question. The boy was shy. He spoke poor English, but he had the right answer. The priest told him, "You did not say it right. Correct yourself. Say it over again." The boy got flustered and stammered. He could hardly get out a word. But the priest kept after him: "Didn't you hear? I told you to do the whole thing over. Get it right this time." He kept on and on.

I stood up and said, "Father, don't be doing that. If you go into an Indian's home and try to talk Indian, they might laugh at you and say, 'Do it over correctly. Get it right this time!'"

He shouted at me, "Mary, you stay after class. Sit down right now!"

I stayed after class, until after the bell. He told me, "Get over here!" He grabbed me by the arm, pushing me against the blackboard, shouting, "Why are you always mocking us? You have no reason to do this."

I said, "Sure I do. You were making fun of him. You embarrassed him. He needs strengthening, not weakening. You hurt him. I did not hurt you."

He twisted my arm and pushed real hard. I turned around and hit him in the face, giving him a bloody nose. After that I ran out of the room, slamming the door behind me. He and I went to Sister Bernard's office. I told her, "Today I quit school. I'm not taking any more of this, none of this shit anymore. None of this treatment. Better give me my diploma. I can't waste any more time on you people."

Sister Bernard looked at me for a long, long time. She said, "All right, Mary Ellen, go home today. Come back in a few days and get your diploma." And that was that. Oddly enough, that priest turned out okay. He taught a class in grammar, orthography, composition, things like that. I think he wanted more respect in class. He was still young and unsure of himself. But I was in there too long. I didn't feel like hearing it. Later he became a good friend of the Indians, a personal friend of myself and my husband. He stood up for us during Wounded Knee and after. He stood up to his superiors, stuck his neck way out, became a real people's priest. He even learned our language. He died prematurely of cancer. It is not only the good Indians who die young, but the good whites, too. It is the timid ones who know how to take care of themselves who grow old. I am still grateful to that priest for what he did for us later and for the quarrel he picked with me—or did I pick it with him?—because it ended a situation which had become unendurable for me. The day of my fight with him was my last day in school.

 QUESTIONS FOR CRITICAL THINKING

Reading 23

1. As discussed by Crow Dog and Erdoes, policies and practices of educational institutions construct Native Americans and Native American culture as deviant. What other cultures are also constructed as deviant by our educational institutions?

2. What are some of the ways that we expect marginalized groups to assimilate? How do the policies and practices of the educational institution foster this assimilation process?

3. What would our culture look like if we included the perspectives of Native Americans rather than required them to assimilate?

MISSING IN INTERACTION

MYRA SADKER • DAVID SADKER

"Candid Camera" would have a field day in elementary school. There would be no need to create embarrassing situations. Just set the camera to take a photograph every sixty seconds. Since classroom action moves so swiftly, snapshots slow down the pace and reveal subliminal gender lessons.

Snapshot #1	Tim answers a question.
Snapshot #2	The teacher reprimands Alex.
Snapshot #3	Judy and Alice sit with hands raised while Brad answers a question.
Snapshot #4	Sally answers a question.
Snapshot #5	The teacher praises Marcus for skill in spelling.
Snapshot #6	The teacher helps Sam with a spelling mistake.
Snapshot #7	The teacher compliments Alice on her neat paper.
Snapshot #8	Students are in lines for a spelling bee. Boys are on one side of the room and girls are on the other.

As the snapshots continue, the underlying gender messages become clear. The classroom consists of two worlds: one of boys in action, the other of girls' inaction. Male students control classroom conversation. They ask and answer more questions. They receive more praise for the intellectual quality of their ideas. They get criticized. They get help when they are confused. They are the heart and center of interaction. Watch how boys dominate the discussion in this upper elementary class about presidents.

The fifth-grade class is almost out of control. "Just a minute," the teacher admonishes. "There are too many of us here to all shout out at once. I want you to raise your hands, and then I'll call on you. If you shout out, I'll pick somebody else."

Order is restored. Then Stephen, enthusiastic to make his point, calls out.

STEPHEN: I think Lincoln was the best president. He held the country together during the war.

TEACHER: A lot of historians would agree with you.

MIKE: (seeing that nothing happened to Stephen, calls out):   I don't. Lincoln was okay, but my Dad liked Reagan. He always said Reagan was a great president.

DAVID: (calling out):   Reagan? Are you kidding?

TEACHER: Who do you think our best president was, Dave?

DAVID: FDR. He saved us from the depression.

MAX: (calling out):   I don't think it's right to pick one best president. There were a lot of good ones.

TEACHER: That's interesting.

KIMBERLY: (calling out):   I don't think the presidents today are as good as the ones we used to have.

TEACHER: Okay, Kimberly. But you forgot the rule. You're supposed to raise your hand.

The classroom is the only place in society where so many different, young, and restless individuals are crowded into close quarters for an extended period of time day after day. Teachers sense the undertow of raw energy and restlessness that threatens to engulf the classroom. To preserve order, most teachers use established classroom conventions such as raising your hand if you want to talk.

Intellectually, teachers know they should apply this rule consistently, but when the discussion becomes fast-paced and furious, the rule is often swept aside. When this happens and shouting out begins, it is an open invitation for male dominance. Our research shows that boys call out significantly more often than girls. Sometimes what they say has little or nothing to do with the teacher's questions. Whether male comments are insightful or irrelevant, teachers respond to them. However, when girls call out, there is a fascinating occurrence: Suddenly the teacher remembers the rule about raising your hand before you talk. And then the girl, who is usually not as assertive as the male students, is deftly and swiftly put back in her place.

Not being allowed to call out like her male classmates during the brief conversation about presidents will not psychologically scar Kimberly; however, the system of silencing operates covertly and repeatedly. It occurs several times a day during each school week for twelve years, and even longer if Kimberly goes to college, and, most insidious of all, it happens subliminally. This micro-inequity eventually has a powerful cumulative impact.

On the surface, girls appear to be doing well. They get better grades and receive fewer punishments than boys. Quieter and more conforming, they are the elementary school's ideal students. "If it ain't broke, don't fix it" is the school's operating principle as girls' good behavior frees the teacher to work with the more difficult-to-manage boys. The result is that girls receive less time, less help, and fewer challenges. Reinforced for passivity, their independence and self-esteem suffer. As victims of benign neglect, girls are penalized for doing what they should and lose ground as they go through school. In contrast, boys get reinforced for breaking the rules; they are rewarded for grabbing more than their fair share of the teacher's time and attention.

Even when teachers remember to apply the rules consistently, boys are still the ones who get noticed. When girls raise their hands, it is often at a right angle, arm bent at the elbow, a cautious, tentative, almost insecure gesture. At other times they raise their arms straight and high, but they signal silently. In contrast, when boys raise their hands, they fling them wildly in the air, up and down, up and down, again and again. Sometimes these hand signals are accompanied by strange noises, "Ooh! Ooh! Me! Me! Ooooh!" Occasionally they even stand beside or on top of their seats and wave one or both arms to get attention. "Ooh! Me! Mrs. Smith, call on me." In the social studies class about presidents, we saw boys as a group grabbing attention while girls as a group were left out of the action.

When we videotape classrooms and play back the tapes, most teachers are stunned to see themselves teaching subtle gender lessons along with math and spelling. The teacher in the social studies class about presidents was completely unaware that she gave male students more attention. Only after several viewings of the videotape did she notice how she let boys call out answers but reprimanded girls for similar behavior. Low-achieving boys also get plenty of attention, but more often it's negative. No surprise there. In general, girls receive less attention, but there's another surprise: Unlike the smart boy who flourishes in the classroom, the smart girl is the student who is least likely to be recognized.

When we analyzed the computer printouts for information about gender and race, an intriguing trend emerged. The students most likely to receive teacher attention were white males; the second most likely were minority males; the third, white females; and the least likely, minority females. In elementary school, receiving attention from the teacher is enormously important for a student's achievement and self-esteem. Later in life, in the working world, the salary received is important, and the salary levels parallel the classroom: white males at the top and minority females at the bottom. In her classroom interaction studies, Jacqueline Jordan Irvine found that black girls were active, assertive, and salient in the primary grades, but as they moved up through elementary school, they became the most invisible members of classrooms.

THE "OKAY" CLASSROOM IS NOT

In our studies of sexism in classroom interaction, we have been particularly fascinated by the ways teachers react to student work and comments because this feedback is crucially important to achievement and self-esteem. We found that teachers typically give students four types of responses.

> TEACHER   *praises:* "Good job." "That was an excellent paper." "I like the way you're thinking."

TEACHER   *remediates,* encouraging a student to correct a wrong answer or expand and enhance thinking: "Check your addition." "Think about what you've just said and try again."

TEACHER   *criticizes,* giving an explicit statement that something is not correct: "No, you've missed number four." This category also includes statements that are much harsher: "This is a terrible report."

TEACHER   *accepts,* offering a brief acknowledgement that an answer is accurate: "Uh-huh." "Okay."

Teachers praise students only 10 percent of the time. Criticism is even rarer—only 5 percent of comments. In many classrooms teachers do not use any praise or criticism at all. About one-third of teacher interactions are comprised of remediation, a dynamic and beneficial form of feedback.

More than half the time, however, teachers slip into the routine of giving the quickest, easiest, and least helpful feedback—a brief nonverbal nod, a quick "Okay." They rely more on acceptance than on praise, remediation, and criticism combined. The bland and neutral "Okay" is so pervasive that we doubt the "Okay Classroom" is, in fact, okay.

In our research in more than one hundred classrooms, we found that while boys received more of all four reactions, the gender gap was greatest in the most precise and valuable feedback. Boys were more likely to be praised, corrected, helped, and criticized—all reactions that foster student achievement. Girls received the more superficial "Okay" reaction, one that packs far less educational punch. In her research, Jacqueline Jordan Irvine found that black females were least likely to receive clear academic feedback.

At first teachers are surprised to see videotapes where girls are "Okay'd" and boys gain clear feedback. Then it begins to make sense. "I don't like to tell a girl anything is wrong because I don't want to upset her," many say. This vision of females as fragile is held most often by male teachers." What if she cries? I wouldn't know how to handle it."

The "Okay" response is well meaning, but it kills with kindness. If girls don't know when they are wrong, if they don't learn strategies to get it right, then they never will correct their mistakes. And if they rarely receive negative feedback in school, they will be shocked when they are confronted by it in the workplace.

PRETTY IS—HANDSOME DOES

Ashley Reiter, National Winner of the 1991 Westinghouse Talent Competition for her sophisticated project on math modeling, remembers winning her first math contest. It happened at the same time that she first wore her contact lenses. Triumphant, Ashley showed up at school the next day without glasses and with a new medal. "Everybody talked about how pretty I looked," Ashley remembers. "Nobody said a word about the math competition."

The one area where girls are recognized more than boys is appearance. Teachers compliment their outfits and hairstyles. We hear it over and over again—not during large academic discussions but in more private moments, in small groups, when a student comes up to the teacher's desk, at recess, in hallways, at lunchtime, when children enter and exit the classroom: "Is that a new dress?" "You look so pretty today." "I love your new haircut. It's so cute." While these comments are most prevalent in the early grades, they continue through professional education: "That's a great outfit." "You look terrific today."

Many teachers do not want to emphasize appearance. "They pull you in," a preschool teacher says. "The little girls come up to you with their frilly dresses and hair ribbons and jewelry. 'Look what I have,' they say and wait for you to respond. What are you supposed to do? Ignore them? Insult them? They look so happy when you tell them they're pretty. It's a way of connecting. I think it's what they're used to hearing, the way they are rewarded at home."

When teachers talk with boys about appearance, the exchanges are brief—quick recognition and then on to something else. Or teachers use appearance incidents to move on to a physical skill or academic topic. In one exchange, a little boy showed the teacher his shiny new belt buckle. Her response: "Cowboys wore buckles like that. They were rough and tough and they rode horses. Did you know that?"

When teachers talk to girls about their appearance, the conversations are usually longer, and the focus stays on how pretty the girl looks. Sometimes the emphasis moves from personal appearance to papers and work. When boys are praised, it is most often for the intellectual quality of their ideas. Girls are twice as likely to be praised for following the rules of form. "I love your margins" is the message.

THE BOMBING RATE

"How long do you wait for students to answer a question?" When we ask teachers to describe what they do hundreds of times daily in the classroom, their answers are all over the map: One minute. Ten seconds. Five seconds. Twenty-five seconds. Three seconds.

Mary Budd Rowe was the first researcher to frame this question and then try to answer it. Following her lead, many others conducted wait time studies and uncovered an astonishingly hurried classroom. On average, teachers wait only nine-tenths of a second for a student to answer a question. If a student can't answer within that time, teachers call on another student or answer the question themselves.

When questions are hurled at this bombing rate, some students get lost, confused, or rattled, or just drop out of the discussion. "Would you repeat that?" "Say it again." "Give me a minute. I can get it." Requests such as these are really pleas for more time to think. Nobody has enough time in the bombing rate classroom, but boys have more time than girls.

Waiting longer for a student to answer is one of the most powerful and positive things a teacher can do. It is a vote of confidence, a way of saying, "I have high expectations for you, so I will wait a little longer. I know you can get it if I give you a chance." Since boys receive more wait time, they try harder to achieve. As girls struggle to answer under the pressure of time, they may flounder and fail. Watch how it happens:

"Okay, class, get ready for your next problem. Mr. Warren has four cash registers. Each register weighs thirteen kilograms. How many kilograms do the registers weigh altogether? Linda?"
    The teacher waits half a second. Linda looks down at her book and twists her hair. She says nothing in the half-second allotted to her.
    "Michael?"
    The teacher waits two seconds. Michael is looking down at his book. The teacher waits two more seconds. Michael says, "Fifty-two?"
    "Good. Exactly right."

Less assertive in class and more likely to think about their answers and how to respond, girls may need *more* time to think. In the real world of the classroom, they receive less. For female achievement and self-esteem, it is a case of very bad timing.

BOY BASTIONS—GIRL GHETTOS

Raphaela Best spent four years as an observer in an elementary school in one of Maryland's most affluent counties. She helped the children with schoolwork, ate lunch with them, and played games with them in class and at recess. As an anthropologist, she also took copious notes. After more than one thousand hours of living with the children, she concluded that elementary school consists of separate and unequal worlds. She watched segregation in action firsthand. Adult women remember it well.

A college student recalled, "When I was in elementary school, boys were able to play basketball and kick ball. They had the side of the playground with the basketball hoops." Another college woman remembers more formal segregation: "I went to a very small grammar school. At recess and gym the boys played football and the girls jumped rope. All except one girl and one boy—they did the opposite. One day they were pulled aside. I'm not exactly sure what they were told, but the next day the schoolyard was divided in two. The boys got the middle and the girls got the edge, and neither sex was allowed on the other's part."

A third grader described it this way: "Usually we separate ourselves, but my teacher begins recess by handing a jump rope to the girls and a ball to the boys." Like the wave of a magic wand, this gesture creates strict gender lines. "The boys always pick the biggest areas for their games," she says. "We have what's left over, what they don't want."

Every morning at recess in schoolyards across the country, boys fan out over the prime territory to play kick ball, football, or basketball. Sometimes girls join them, but more often it's an all-male ball game. In the typical schoolyard, the boys' area is ten times bigger than the girls'. Boys never ask if it is their right to take over the territory, and it is rarely questioned. Girls huddle along the sidelines, on the fringe, as if in a separate female annex. Recess becomes a spectator sport.

Teachers seldom intervene to divide space and equipment more evenly, and seldom attempt to connect the segregated worlds—not even when they are asked directly by the girls.

"The boys won't let us play," a third grader said, tugging at the arm of the teacher on recess duty. "They have an all-boys club and they won't let any girls play."

"Don't you worry, honey," the teacher said, patting the little girl's hair. "When you get bigger, those boys will pay you all the attention you want. Don't you bother about them now."

As we observed that exchange, we couldn't help but wonder how the teacher would have reacted if the recess group had announced "No Catholics" or if white children had blatantly refused to play with Asians.

Barrie Thorne, a participant observer in elementary schools in California and Michigan whose students are mainly from working-class families, captured the tiny incidents that transform integrated classes into gender-divided worlds: Second-grade girls and boys eat lunch together around a long rectangular table. A popular boy walks by and looks the scene over. "Oooh, too many girls," he says, and takes a place at another table. All the boys immediately pick up their trays and abandon the table with girls, which has now become taboo.

Although sex segregation becomes more pervasive as children get older, contact points remain. School life has its own gender rhythm as girls and boys separate, come together, and separate again. But the points of contact, the together games that girls and boys play, often serve to heighten and solidify the walls of their separate worlds.

"You can't get me!" "Slobber Monster!" With these challenges thrown out, the game begins. It may be called "Girls Chase the Boys" or "Boys Chase the Girls" or "Chase and Kiss." It usually starts out one on one, but then the individual boy and girl enlist same-sex peers. "C'mon, let's get that boy." "Help, a girl's gonna get me!"

Pollution rituals are an important part of these chases. Children treat one another as if they were germ carriers. "You've got cooties" is the cry. (Substitute other terms for different cultures or different parts of the country.) Elaborate systems are developed around the concept of cooties. Transfer occurs when one child touches another. Prepared for such attack, some protect themselves by writing C.V. (cooties vaccination) on their arms.

Sometimes boys give cooties to girls, but far more frequently girls are the polluting gender. Boys fling taunts such as "girl stain" or "girl touch" or "cootie girl." The least-liked girls, the ones who are considered fat or ugly or poor, become "cootie queens," the real untouchables of the class, the most contaminating females of all.

Chasing, polluting, and invasions, where one gender attacks the play area of the other, all function as gender intensifiers, heightening perceived differences between female and male to an extreme degree. The world of children and the world of adults is composed of *different* races, but each gender is socially constructed as so different, so alien that we use the phrase "the *opposite* sex."

It is boys who work hardest at raising the walls of sex segregation and intensifying the difference between genders. They distance themselves, sending the message that girls are not good enough to play with them. Watch which boys sit next to the girls in informally sex-segregated classrooms and lunchrooms; they are the ones most likely to be rejected by male classmates. Sometimes they are even called "girls." A student at The American University remembers his school lunchroom in Brooklyn:

> At lunch our class all sat together at one long table. All the girls
> sat on one side, and the boys sat on the other. This was our system.
> Unfortunately, there were two more boys in my class than seats
> on the boys' side. There was no greater social embarrassment for a
> boy in the very hierarchical system we had set up in our class than
> to have to sit on the girls' side at lunch. It happened to me once,
> before I moved up the class social ladder. Boys climbed the rungs
> of that ladder by beating on each other during recess. To this day,
> twenty years later, I remember that lunch. It was horrible.

Other men speak, also with horror, of school situations when they became "one of the girls." The father of a nine-year-old daughter remembered girls in elementary school as "worse than just different. We considered them a subspecies." Many teachers who were victims of sexist schooling themselves understand this system and collaborate with it; they warn noisy boys of a humiliating punishment: "If you don't behave, I'm going to make you sit with the girls."

Most little girls—five, six, seven, or eight—are much too young to truly understand and challenge their assignment as the lower-caste gender. But without challenge over the course of years, this hidden curriculum in second-class citizenship sinks in. Schools and children need help— intervention by adults who can equalize the playing field.

We have found that sex segregation in the lunchroom and schoolyard spills over into the classroom. In our three-year, multi-state study of one hundred classrooms, our raters drew "gender geography" maps of each class they visited. They found that more than half of the classes were segregated by gender. There is more communication across race than across gender in elementary schools.

We have seen how sex segregation occurs when children form self-selected groups. Sometimes the division is even clearer, and so is the impact on instruction.

The students are seated formally in rows. There are even spaces between the rows, except down the middle of the room where the students have created an aisle large enough for two people standing side by side to walk down. On one side of the aisle, the students are all female; on the other side, all male. Black, white, Hispanic, and Asian students sit all around the room, but no student has broken the gender barrier.

The teacher in the room is conducting a math game, with the right team (boys) against the left team (girls). The problems have been put on the board, and members of each team race to the front of the room to see who can write the answer first. Competition is intense, but eventually the girls fall behind. The teacher keeps score on the board, with two columns headed "Good Girls" and "Brilliant Boys."

The gender segregation was so formal in this class that we asked if the teacher had set it up. "Of course not." She looked offended. "I wouldn't think of doing such a thing. The students do it themselves." It never occurred to the well-meaning teacher to raise the issue or change the seats.

In our research we have found that gender segregation is a major contributor to female invisibility. In sex-segregated classes, teachers are pulled to the more talkative, more disruptive male sections of the classroom or pool. There they stay, teaching boys more actively and directly while the girls fade into the background.

THE CHARACTER(S) OF THE CURRICULUM

At a workshop on sexism in the curriculum, we asked participants, "Have you ever read the book *I'm Glad I'm a Boy! I'm Glad I'm a Girl!*?" Since most of the teachers, principals, and parents had not read it, we showed it to them. *I'm Glad I'm a Boy! I'm Glad I'm a Girl!* is for very young children. One page shows the jobs and activities that boys can do, and the following page shows what is appropriate for girls.

The book announces that boys can be doctors and shows a large male cartoon character with a stethoscope around his neck.

"What do girls do?" we asked the audience.

"They're nurses," the parents and educators chorused as one. They may not have read this book, but they seemed to know the plot line. A little girl nurse pushing a wheelchair is drawn on the page.

"Obviously a case of occupational stereotyping with the girl receiving less of every kind of reward including money, but do you notice anything else?" we asked. Most of the people were puzzled, but a few spotted the subtlety: "Look at how little the girl is." When we showed both pages at once, the boy doctor, a cartoon version of Doogie Howser, towered over the girl pushing the wheelchair.

The next page shows boys as pilots. "What are girls?" we asked.

"Stewardesses," the audience called back. A cartoon girl with a big smile and a short skirt carries a tray of drinks. The audience chuckled as several people remarked, "Look, her underpants are showing." "A little cheesecake for the younger set," someone joked as the next picture emerged, a boy drawn as a policeman.

"What are girls?"

This one had the group confused. "Mommies?" "Criminals?" "Crossing guards?" "Meter maids?" They found it. A tough-looking female figure is shown writing out a ticket for an obviously miserable motorist caught in a parking violation. "She looks as if she's had a steroid treatment," a teacher joked. "She's very big this time." The images continued: boys as those who eat, and girls as the ones who cook; boys as the builders of homes, and girls as the ones who clean them. The picture accompanying the caption about cleaning is that of a smiling cartoon girl pushing a vacuum cleaner. She and the cleaning machine are drawn very large because there is so much work to do. This image upset the audience. "Oh, no," several groaned. Others hissed and booed.

The next caption identified boys as the ones who fix things.

"Girls break things," the audience chorused back. But this time the author had outsmarted them. "Break" was too active. The parents and educators tried other stereotypes: "Girls clean things?" "Play with things?" "Buy things?" "Girls cry over things?"

"These are great responses, but they're all too active."

"Girls watch boys?" an astute parent suggested. She was on to something. Several studies have shown that in basal readers the activity girls are most often engaged in is watching boys in action. They look at boys play baseball, admire them as they perform magic tricks, wave good-bye from behind windows as boys leave for adventure. But in this case even "watch" was too active. The audience was stumped.

"Girls are things!" a young woman burst out. She had actually outdone the author, so we displayed the page: GIRLS NEED THINGS FIXED. The smiling stationary figure is holding the wheel of her doll carriage in her hand. She isn't doing anything with the wheel; she is just standing there beside her tipped-over vehicle, clearly in need of male help. The audience groaned, but the pictures went on with boys shown as inventing while girls are described as using things boys invent. Accompanying this description is an illustration of a girl lying in a hammock and reading, thanks to a lamp invented by a boy. "Who invented the cotton gin?" we asked. Several people from around the room answered, "Eli Whitney." Like Alexander Graham Bell and Thomas Edison, this name is one of the staples of American education. "Has anyone ever heard of Catherine Littlefield Greene?" The parents and teachers were silent.

We told the story of the woman who, after the death of her husband, Nathaniel, who had been a general in the Revolutionary War, met Eli Whitney. A Yale-educated tutor, Whitney devised a model for the gin while working at Greene's Mulberry Grove Mansion. But his design was flawed;

although seeds were pulled from the cotton, they became clogged in the rollers. It was Kitty Greene who came up with the breakthrough idea of using brushes for the seeds. The concept of the machine was so simple that copycat gins sprang up on other plantations. To pay for lawsuits during the fierce battle for patent rights, Kitty Greene sold her estate. It wasn't until seven years later that Eli Whitney won full title to the cotton gin.

"Why wasn't the patent taken out in both names?" a history teacher asked. It was an excellent question, and in the answer is an important lesson for children. At a time when it was unseemly for women to write books (many female authors took male names), it was especially unlikely for a lady to patent an invention. Textbooks tell the story of the names registered in the patent office, but they leave out how sexism and racism denied groups of people access to that registry.

The caricature of gender roles isn't over, and the picture book moves from inventions to politics, showing boys as presidents and girls as their wives.

"Is this some kind of joke?" a teacher asked. "When was it written?"

We threw the question back at the audience.

"The 1920s?" someone called out.

"No, they didn't have stewardesses then. Or meter maids. I think it was the 1950s," another teacher suggested.

Most of the group were stunned to learn that the book was published in 1970 and was in circulation in libraries and schools for years afterward. Few teachers would read a book like this to children today, and if they did, the phone lines would light up in most communities. Twenty-five years ago, books like this were commonplace, and it is a sign of progress that today they are considered outrageous.

"This book is so bad, it's good," a kindergarten teacher said. "I want to show it to my class. A lot of my kids fly on planes and see male flight attendants, and one of my children has a mom who's a doctor."

We agreed that the book with its yesteryear sexism was a good teaching tool. We have shown it to students in every grade level. They had often read it critically and identified the stereotypes, but not always.

 ## BALANCING THE BOOKS

Few things stir up more controversy than the content of the curriculum. Teachers, parents, students—all seem to be aware intuitively that schoolbooks shape what the next generation knows and how it behaves. In this case research supports intuition. When children read about people in nontraditional gender roles, they are less likely to limit themselves to stereotypes. When children read about women and minorities in history, they are more likely to feel these groups have made important contributions to the country. As one sixth grader told us, "I love to read biographies about women. When I learn about what they've done, I feel like a door is opening. If they can do great things, maybe I can, too."

DOUBLE JEOPARDY

During the spring of 1992 we visited sixteen fourth-, fifth-, and sixth-grade classes in Maryland, Virginia, and Washington, D.C., and gave students this assignment:

> In the next five minutes write down the names of as many famous women and men as you can. They can come from anywhere in the world and they can be alive or dead, but they must be real people. They can't be made up. Also—and this is very important—they can't be entertainers or athletes. See if you can name at least ten men and ten women.
>
> At first the students write furiously, but after about three minutes, most run out of names. On average, students generate eleven male names but only three women's. While the male names are drawn directly from the pages of history books, the female names represent far greater student creativity: Mrs. Fields, Aunt Jemima, Sarah Lee, Princess Di, Fergie, Mrs. Bush, Sally Ride, and children's book authors such as Beverly Cleary and Judy Blume. Few names come from the pages of history. Betsy Ross, Harriet Tubman, Eleanor Roosevelt, Amelia Earhart, Sojourner Truth, Sacajawea, Rosa Parks, Molly Pitcher, and Annie Oakley are sometimes mentioned.
>
> Several students cannot think of a single woman's name. Others have to struggle to come up with a few. In one sixth-grade class, a boy identified as the star history student is stumped by the assignment and obviously frustrated:
>
> "Have you got any girls?" he asks, turning to a classmate.
>
> "Sure. I got lots."
>
> "I have only one."
>
> "Think about the presidents."
>
> "There are no lady presidents."
>
> "Of course not. There's a law against it. But all you gotta do is take the presidents' names and put Mrs. in front of them."
>
> In a fourth-grade class, a girl is drawing a blank. She has no names under her Women column. A female classmate leans over to help.
>
> "What about Francis Scott Key? She's famous." The girl immediately writes the name down. "Thanks," she says. "I forgot about her."
>
> As we are leaving this class, one girl stops us. "I don't think we did very well on that list," she says. "It was too bad you didn't let us put in entertainers. We could've put in a lot of women then. I wrote down Madonna anyway."

Given a time line extending from the earliest days of human history to current events, and given no geographic limits whatsoever, these upper-elementary schoolchildren came up with only a handful of women. The most any single child wrote was nine. In one class the total number of women's names given didn't equal ten. We were stunned!

Something was very wrong—was it with the textbooks? We decided to look at them more closely. During the summer of 1992 we analyzed the content of fifteen math, language arts, and history textbooks used in Maryland, Virginia, and the District of Columbia. When we counted pictures of males and females, we were surprised to find that the 1989 language arts textbooks from Macmillan and D.C. Heath had twice as many boys and men as girls and women. In some readers the ratio was three to one. A 1989 upper-elementary history textbook had four times as many male pictures as females. In the 1992 D.C. Heath *Exploring Our World, Past and Present,* a text for sixth graders, only eleven female names were mentioned, and not a single American adult woman was included. In the entire 631 pages of a textbook covering the history of the world, only seven pages related to women, either as famous individuals or as a general group. Two of the seven pages were about Samantha Smith, a fifth-grade Maine student who traveled to the Soviet Union on a peace mission. While we felt that Samantha Smith's story brought an interesting message to other students, we wondered why Susan B. Anthony didn't rate a single line. No wonder students knew so little about women. Given the content of their history books, it was a tribute to their creativity that they could list any female names at all.

Every day in America little girls lose independence, achievement, and self-esteem in classes like this. Subtle and insidious, the gender-biased lessons result in quiet catastrophes and silent losses. But the casualties—tomorrow's women—are very real.

 QUESTIONS FOR CRITICAL THINKING

Reading 24

1. Reflecting on your own educational experience, in what ways were traditional gender roles reinforced in your schools? In what ways do you think you were given advantage or disadvantage due to being male or female? How do you think this has impacted you today?

2. Do you see evidence of gender bias in your college classes? If so, how do you think this impacts the ways in which women and men participate in the classroom?

3. If gender biases in the educational system were eliminated, how do you think this would impact the roles of women and men in larger society?

Reading 25

SCHOOLS AND THE SOCIAL CONTROL OF SEXUALITY

MELINDA S. MICELI

The question of whether or not schools should teach students about sexuality has been one of heated debate since the early twentieth century. The simple fact remains that schools do teach students countless lessons about sexuality, in a variety of ways, every single day. As social institutions through which every citizen passes, schools have an enormous amount of power to influence the beliefs and values of young people. In this chapter, I analyze some of the ways that public schools shape America's sexual culture by looking at their informal and formal curriculum, culture, and their sex education policies. My chief claim is that schools have tried to promote what is considered a "normal" and "respectable" sexuality, that is, heterosexuality, conventional gender sexual norms, and an ideal of marriage and family. Lately, some students have begun to challenge some of these sexual norms.

SCHOOL CULTURE AND THE SOCIAL CONTROL OF SEXUALITY

Critical theorists seek to understand all the ways in which power is exercised and resisted in educational institutions. Pierre Bourdieu argued strongly from this perspective that schools have considerable social power because they appear to be neutral transmitters of the best and most valuable knowledge. Hence, dominant groups within schools can purposefully transmit inequalities and the process will be viewed as objective and fair. Schools have promoted what Bourdieu and others (e.g. Sears 1992; Giroux and McLaren 1989) have called a hegemonic curriculum, which simultaneously legitimizes the dominant culture and marginalizes or rejects other cultures and knowledge forms. The concept of hegemonic curriculum, and the closely related concept hidden curriculum, have been well documented in research into educational institutions and practices since the 1960s.

Early studies examined the ways in which upper- and middle-class, white and male culture, history, morals, behaviors, norms and values are taught and enforced in schools through the power of a hegemonic process where they are also naturalized, neutralized, and made invisible. Over the past decade and a half several studies of school culture have included an examination of a hidden sexuality curriculum in schools (Sears 1992; Epstein 1994; Miceli 1998; Best 2000; Irvine 2002; Kehily 2002). These studies have documented that normative heterosexuality is rather explicitly enforced by the culture of most schools. In overt ways it is enforced by the immense visibility of heterosexuality within the school environment—in the halls, in the cafeteria, at after school activities and functions, etc. The ways in which students, as well as teachers and administrators, incorporate heterosexual activities, behaviors, and language into the social aspects of the school establish and enforce a culture and ideology in which heterosexuality is exclusively the norm of acceptable behavior, discussion, and even feeling.

In some ways, it seems that the explicitness of heterosexuality is so immediately obvious to anyone who has spent even a few hours in any school that it is foolish to remark about this as a sociological analysis. However, as with many things, the salience of this observation is largely dependent on an individual's perspective. Heterosexual behavior and language are integrated and normalized within school culture to such a degree that they have become the natural, and often considered the "neutral," school environment or culture. Things like male–female displays of attraction and affection, discussion of opposite-sex relationships in the halls and classroom, school dances, proms, anti-gay jokes and insults, and the harassment of gay and lesbian students are not viewed as "explicitly heterosexual." These activities are generally perceived merely as a natural school environment and youth culture. However, there is a myriad of ways in which the norm of heterosexuality and the prescriptive behaviors for males and females it enforces, are constructed and maintained through the organized and spontaneous interactions among students and between students and faculty.

This normative heterosexuality not only represses and stigmatizes same-sex interactions, but also dictates a carefully gender-scripted form of heterosexuality, what Best (2005) calls the "hetero-romantic" norm that prescribes specific behavioral norms for males and females. Fulfilling these "hetero-romantic" norms is important to proving one's masculinity or femininity and to winning acceptance into peer culture. Best (2005) sheds light on how these things are constructed by the pinnacle US high school event, the senior prom.

> An event like the prom, as it comes into being through the relations and talk of its participants, embeds normative meanings about heterosexuality and gender in school and the culture beyond. Young women (and young men) come to understand their experiences and identities in terms of these cultural meanings and in this way, sustain the culture of high school as a heterosexual one

in which heterosexuality and gender inequality are normative features. Significantly, it becomes virtually impossible for young men and young women to narrate this school event and thus, their schooling and identities, without mention of gender and heterosexual codes. . . . Understanding how events like the prom legitimate specific ideological practices through its celebration of heterosexual romance is important to understanding how identities and cultural meanings are constructed through day-to-day life in contemporary American institutions.

(BEST 2005: 210–11)

Best's ethnographic study of high school proms illustrates how completely scripted this event is by gender inequalities and romanticized ideals of heterosexuality. The significance of this event, which is one night in a person's life, is amplified through its embeddedness in the culture of the high school experience. The prom is established as one of the most defining moments of high school and the teenage years, given as much or more significance as academic achievements and graduation. The importance of this event is further constructed through the mass media—teen magazines, television shows, popular music, and a long list of films whose plots revolve around the prom. In these ways having an ideal romantic prom night is a gendered accomplishment marking an important achievement in femininity (for young women the look, the dress, and getting her date to treat her well are the most significant things) and masculinity (for young men securing an attractive date and ending the evening with sex are the markers of success) and represents acceptance into the valued world of adult heterosexual relationships.

This "hetero-romantic" discourse of the prom plays a powerful role in educating adolescents about the acceptable and expected behavior governing heterosexual relationships. This is not the only lesson about the heterosexual requirement for manhood and womanhood that students receive in school; it is more like the final exam, testing years of accumulated knowledge. Social research has documented that, throughout their school years, throughout their primary and secondary school years, students are continually socialized into traditional binary gender roles. There are countless messages sent to students by faculty, administrators, and through the curriculum about preparing themselves for their future adult role in a committed—preferably by marriage—monogamous heterosexual relationship. Central to these lessons, in both the formal and the hidden curricula, are instructions about how to be properly masculine or feminine as a means of achieving the desired relationships and displaying one's heterosexuality to others. Key to proper masculinity, of course, is refusal of anything weak, sensitive, soft, nurturing—in other words, all things feminine. Key to proper femininity, conversely, is rejection of assertiveness and strength, but most importantly the acceptance of the compulsion to strive for a standard of feminine beauty set by what heterosexual men desire in women. For both male and female students, failure to do this through the correct gender performance carries the punishment not only of rejection from the opposite sex, but also through accusations of being a fag, a dyke, gay or queer. All of the lessons about correct gender behavior and the norms of heterosexuality are intimately and constantly tied to the stigmatization of homosexuality.

 BEING LESBIAN, GAY, OR BISEXUAL
IN HIGH SCHOOL

Examining the lives of gay high school students (as well as of those students who are perceived to be gay) reveals much about the ways in which educational institutions seek to enforce cultural gender and sexual norms, and to control and shape the knowledge and meanings about sexuality available to students. I spent three years observing a community center-run support group for lesbian, gay, and bisexual teenagers, and conducting in-depth interviews with thirty of these teenagers about their school experiences (Miceli 1998, 2005). The subject of the "heterosexual culture" of schools came up frequently in these discussions. In the words of two of the students I spoke with:

> "Everything throughout the entire educational system is heterosexual—boys girls, boys girls, boys girls—heterosexuals are everywhere and we have to accept them. We don't have a choice, they're the mainstream. Then there is us. We have to accept them, but they do not have to accept us."

> "At school you have to watch a completely straight place. You have to watch girls and boys holding hands; girls and boys flirting with each other. And when you are gay you realize that everyone does it so subconsciously. Everyone's flirting with each other. Even just mannerisms, not exactly flirting, it's just their straight world. Everything. And you have to watch it, and then you realize that you are not a part of it. You are just sitting in the back of the class trying to get the hell out of there."

The underlying theme of most of these conversations was that the school environment provides "straight" students with the freedom to express themselves with a wide range of acceptable behaviors, while gay students' freedom of expression is extremely limited at best, and severely persecuted at worst.

Often a support group discussion that began with one member's expression of frustration over some behavior they felt they had to hide at school would escalate into a flooded discussion, spoken in tones of frustration and pain, often masked by sarcasm, of how the norm of heterosexuality engulfed them every day at school. The students described school culture as one in which there is almost continuous discussion and concern about heterosexual relationships and dating, talk about heterosexual sex, constant open heterosexual flirtation, and regular preparation for some social event such as a football game, a school dance, or the prom. Generally, in conversation about these things, there was an interesting mixture of mocking humor and laughter at what support group members thought to be the "silliness" or immaturity of straight students' "obsession" with these activities; resentment of heterosexual students' freedom to flaunt such conversations and behaviors; and anger over the ways in which this heterosexual culture denies, makes invisible, or makes abnormal the existence and expression of lesbian, gay, and bisexual students' feelings and relationships. Many lesbian, gay, and bisexual students experience normative heterosexuality as a central part of the beliefs, values, and skills that schools are trying to teach. This culture of heteronormativity binds heterosexual students to one another and to the school, while it excludes and punishes gay students for their failure to conform.

Gay students experience schools as places that are not only explicitly heterosexual but also explicitly intolerant of homosexuality and gender nonconformity. Experiences of harassment by lesbian, gay, bisexual, and transgender (LGBT) students were common in my own qualitative research and have been well documented on a national level in the USA by several large-scale surveys of high school students. One example of such a study is GLSEN's (gay, lesbian, straight education network) "The National School Climate Survey: The School Related Experiences of Our Nation's Lesbian, Gay, Bisexual and Transgender Youth." This survey has been conducted bi-annually since 1999 to monitor how gay students experience schools. The results of the 2003 survey of 887 LGBT students from across the USA largely highlight the persistence of wide-sweeping problems for LGBT students. Findings in the report include the following: 84 percent of LGBT students reported they have been verbally harassed; 82.9 percent stated that teachers or administrators rarely, if ever, intervened when they witnessed homophobic comments; 55 percent of transgender students reported being physically harassed because of their gender identity; 41 percent of lesbian, gay, and bisexual students said that they had been physically harassed because of their sexual orientation; and 64.3 percent of LGBT students reported that, because of their sexual orientation, they felt unsafe at school (GLSEN 2003). GLSEN grades every state based on how well they protect and meet the needs of LGBT students. In 2003, forty-two states received a failing grade.

The prevalence of this harassment provides empirical evidence for the assertion that normative heterosexuality is structured and enforced by schools. In many ways schools teach students to understand sexuality as a binary of heterosexuality and homosexuality in which heterosexuality is the natural, normal, desirable form of affection and self-expression, and homosexuality is deviant, immoral, and punishable. Most students learn through their years at school that the stigmatization of homosexuality is as normal and acceptable as heterosexuality.

The existence of gay and lesbian people is rarely if ever discussed directly anywhere in the curriculum of most schools. Without accurate information about gay and lesbian people, students, both gay and straight, are more likely to accept and internalize negative stereotypes of gay people and misinformation about homosexuality. The absence of information about homosexuality and the sexual identity of gay and lesbian historical, literary, political, artistic, etc. figures is generally regarded by school officials as taking a "neutral" stance on sexuality. However, it is in reality an example of how schools act as agents of social control over sexuality by being the gatekeepers of the knowledge about sexuality deemed appropriate or relevant to teach to students.

This assertion is further supported by an examination of the controversy that has arisen in the past twenty years as gay, lesbian, bisexual, and trans-gender students and their allies have tried to make changes to the culture and curricula of schools. Beginning in isolated locations in the northeast in the late 1980s, and expanding through the 1990s, LGBT students and their heterosexual friends began to seek safe and supportive places for themselves in schools. What came to be called gay—straight alliance clubs or GSAs were established by students with the goals of meeting with peers who were interested in discussing issues revolving around being LGBT, thought to be LGBT, or being supportive of sexual diversity in high school; to educate the school community about the negative effects of homophobia; and to work at making changes to the culture and policies of schools to make them safer and more tolerant places for all students. Since the first GSA was formed in 1989, more than 2,000 have been established across the USA, with the larg-est concentrations in California and in the northeast. In this time many law-suits have been filed and won to establish the rights of LGBT students to be protected from harassment and homophobic attacks in schools and to form officially recognized school GSA clubs.

Such efforts have been met with fear, resistance, and sometimes outrage. The reaction to efforts to make schools more inclusive of gay students and less tolerant of homophobic attitudes and anti-gay harassment exposes the entrenched normative heterosexuality of schools and demonstrates just how entrenched many people are in protecting this institutionalized means of controlling sexuality. The conflict over this issue closely mirrors the debates over sex education. At the heart of the struggle over both issues is a dis-agreement over what about sexuality should be silenced and what should be spoken. However, as Foucault instructed, what is silenced speaks volumes.

SEX EDUCATION AND THE SOCIAL CONTROL OF SEXUALITY

Michel Foucault argued persuasively that Western societies simultaneously repress and obsess over sexuality. Sexual speech is both amplified and silenced. The patterns of what about sex is spoken about and what is silenced is not random, but rather both are part of the weave of power relations and social control. According to Foucault it is a mistake to conclude that, as Western cul-tures increased the amount of sexual speech and the number of arenas where sex is discussed, the less sexuality is repressed and controlled. Conversely, it is incorrect to conclude that, in spaces where sexual speech is forbidden or regulated, it is successfully repressed or absent. Foucault argued that a concerted effort to control the sexuality of youth began in the eighteenth century, with schools being a logical target of rules and regulations. However, he argued:

> It would be less than exact to say that the pedagogical institution has imposed a ponderous silence on the sex of children and adolescents. On the contrary, since the eighteenth century it has multiplied the forms of discourse on the subject; it has established various points of implantation for sex; it has coded contents and qualified speakers. Speaking about children's sex, inducing educators, physicians, administrators, and parents to speak of it, or speaking to them about it, causing children themselves to talk about it, and enclosing them in a web of discourses which sometimes address them, sometimes speak about them, or impose canonical bits of knowledge about them, or use them as a basis for constructing a science that is beyond their grasp—all this together enables us to link an intensification of the interventions of power to a multiplication of discourse. The sex of children and adolescents has become, since the eighteenth century, an important area of contention around which innumerable institutional devices and institutional strategies have been deployed.
>
> (FOUCAULT 1976: 29–30)

Sex education classes introduce direct and purposeful sexual discourse into the regulated space of the school where it was previously confined to the hidden curriculum. Janice Irvine (2002) argues that "[s]ince the sixties, as openness about sexuality in popular culture has intensified, U.S. communities have fought over whether to allow discussions about sexual topics in the classroom. At stake is what is in the best interest of young people. The history of sex education in America is part of long-standing efforts to regulate sexual morality through the control of sexual speech" (2002: 4). In her book, *Talk About Sex: the Battle over Sex Education in the United States,* Irvine provides a detailed historical account and a sophisticated sociological analysis of these battles and how they fit into larger power struggles to control cultural norms, beliefs, and values.

The idea of formal sexual education classes in schools was first proposed in the early twentieth century by a collection of moral reformers, which included suffragists, clergy, temperance workers, and physicians dedicated to eliminating venereal disease. From the beginning there was disagreement about the specific content and aim of sex education classes, and yet agreement that accurate information about sexuality needed to be taught for the good of public health. This group also felt that the restrictive measures of the Comstock laws that sought state restriction of virtually all public discussion of sexuality, including sex education and contraception information, had to be combated (Irvine 2002). Contemporary conflicts between advocates of abstinence-only and proponents of comprehensive sex education are situated in this long-standing tension between those who feel that the public is best served by limiting children's access to information about sexuality and those groups who feel that public health problems are caused by a lack of such information.

Comprehensive sexuality education stresses abstinence for youth, and it also provides information on contraception and abortion. The Sex Information and Education Council of the United States (SIECUS) was founded in 1964, and has become the leading advocate of comprehensive sexuality education programs being integrated into schools at all levels. SIECUS and its supporters argue that students should receive age-appropriate information on subjects like human reproduction, anatomy, physiology, sexually transmitted diseases, masturbation, and homosexuality, and engage in discussion of sexual values. "Advocates of comprehensive sex education endorse what they consider to be the therapeutic potential of open and informative sexual discussion in the classroom. They believe that silence has fostered ignorance, shame and social problems like teen pregnancy and sexually transmitted diseases. They view sexuality as positive and healthy and they generally support gender equality and acceptance of sexual diversity" (Irvine 2002).

Opponents criticize SIECUS's model of sexual education as irresponsible and misinformed. These groups argue that providing students with information about sexual practices, such as the use of contraceptives, has contributed to rising levels of adolescent sexual activity, sexually transmitted diseases, and teenage pregnancy. Since the 1960s conservative Catholics and Christian fundamentalists have founded a variety of political organizations in order to fight for regulation of sex education. These groups are part of the religious right, and opposition to sex education has bolstered their social movement to restore traditional sexual and gender values and norms to American culture (Irvine 2002). One of many strategies for achieving this goal is restricting the sexual discourse young people are exposed to. Carefully controlling or eliminating sexual discussion from school, they argue, is essential to efforts to protect children and adolescents from the "dangers" of sexuality and to reinstating sexual morality to the culture (Irvine 2002).

Michelle Fine (1988) and others have argued that the struggles over sex education are not only about broadly whether "talk about sex" in schools is appropriate or not, but also, through what is said and what is unsaid, to specifically define appropriate sexuality for males and females. Fine's (1988) investigation into the content of the prevalent sex education programs in the United States concluded that "within today's standard sex education curricula and many public school classrooms, we find: (1) the authorized suppression of a discourse of female sexual desire; (2) the promotion of a discourse of female sexual victimization; and (3) the explicit privileging of married heterosexuality over other practices of sexuality" (1988: 30). The sex education programs that Fine refers to emerged in the early 1980s as a result of the Adolescent Family Life Act (AFLA), the first federal law specifically passed to fund sex education. The AFLA, which is still in use and has become increasingly funded and expanded since, was written by conservative Republican senators with the goal of ending premarital teen sex and therefore teen pregnancy and teen abortion (Levine 2002). Because it is girls who get pregnant and have abortions, they became the target of the abstinence education programs. These programs, Fine (1988) and others have argued, teach girls to fear their own sexuality, to view sex as dangerous and harmful, and to guard themselves from becoming the victims of their own or males' uncontrolled sexuality. In this discourse of abstinence education, young women are held responsible not only for controlling their own sexuality but also for preventing their own victimization.

This approach to sex education in the United States contrasts sharply with that taken by many other countries. In countries like Sweden, France, Germany, and The Netherlands the approach is to educate students about sexuality in all of its aspects so that they can develop healthy and responsible sexual attitudes and behavior. Judith Levine argues that studies of sex education in other countries prove that their more comprehensive approach has been successful.

> In many European countries, where teens have as much sex as in America, sex ed starts in the earliest grades. It is informed by a no-nonsense, even enthusiastic, attitude toward the sexual; it is explicit and doesn't teach abstinence. Rates of unwanted teen pregnancy, abortion, and AIDS in every Western European country are a fraction of our own; the average age of first intercourse is about the same as in the United States.
>
> (LEVINE 2002: 98)

Interestingly, surveys on public opinion about sex education constantly find that the majority of Americans support a more comprehensive model. "In fact, the degree of consensus reported in national surveys about sex education is striking. A 1998 national survey found that 87 percent of Americans favor sex education and of those 89 percent believe that, along with abstinence, young people should also have information about contraception and STD prevention" (Irvine 2002). Despite public opinion, the issue of expanding current sex education curricula more often than not sparks intense local controversies and makes national headlines. In addition, despite the opinion polls, the federal government has continued to increase its funding of abstinence-only programs and the religious right has continued to have a loud voice in the discourse of sexuality.

> In 1997, the U.S. Congress committed a quarter billion dollars over five years to finance more education in . . . abstinence. As part of the omnibus "welfare reform bill," the government's Maternal and Child Health Bureau extended grants to the states for programs whose exclusive purpose is teaching the social, psychological, and

health gains to be realized by abstaining from sexual activity. In a country where only one in ten school-children receives more than forty hours of sex ed in any year, the regulations prohibit funded organizations from instructing kids about contraception or condoms except in terms of their failures. In a country where 90 percent of adults have sex before marriage and as many as 10 percent are gay or lesbian, the law underwrites one message and one message only: that "a mutually faithful monogamous relationship in the context of marriage is the expected standard of human sexual activity." Nonmarital sex, educators are required to tell children, "is likely to have harmful psychological effects."

(LEVINE 2002: 91)

These debates over sex education curricula are a prime example of the efforts to regulate sexual discourse, knowledge, and behavior, and of the fact that schools are central arenas in this power struggle. The amount of energy, resources, and passion spent by all sides on efforts to control what schools teach about sexuality indicates the impact schools have on the broader social control of sexuality.

REFERENCES

Best, Amy L. 2000. *Prom Night: Youth Schools and Popular Culture.* New York: Routledge.

_____. 2005. "The Production of Heterosexuality at the High School Prom", in Chrys Ingraham (ed.), *Thinking Straight: The Power, the Promise, and the Paradox of Heterosexuality.* New York: Routledge.

Epstein, Debbie (ed.). 1994. *Challenging Lesbian and Gay Inequalities in Education.* Buckingham: Open University Press.

Fine, Michelle. 1988. "Sexuality, Schooling, and Adolescent Females: The Missing Discourse of Desire." *Harvard Educational Review* 58: 29–53.

Foucault, Michel 1990. *The History of Sexuality: An Introduction. Volume 1.* New York: Vintage Books.

Giroux, Henry A. and Peter McClaren. 1989. *Critical Pedagogy: The State and Culture Struggle.* Albany: SUNY Press.

GLSEN. 2003. *The 2003 National School Climate Survey.* New York: GLSEN.

Irvine, Janice M. 2002. *Talk About Sex: The Battles over Sex Education in the United States.* Berkeley: University of California Press.

Kehily, Mary Jane. 2002. *Sexuality, Gender and Schooling: Shifting Agendas in Social Learning.* New York: Routledge.

Levine, Judith. 2002. *Harmful to Minors.* Minneapolis: University of Minnesota Press.

Miceli, Melinda S. 1998. *Recognizing All the Differences: Gay Youth and Education in America Today.* Doctoral Dissertation. Ann Arbor, MI: University of Michigan.

_____. 2005. *Standing Out, Standing Together: The Social and Political Impact of Gay–Straight Alliances.* New York: Routledge.

Sears, James T. 1992. *Sexuality and the Curriculum: The Politics and Practices of Sex Education.* New York: Teachers College Press.

⊚ QUESTIONS FOR CRITICAL THINKING

Reading 25

1. How does Micelli's discussion of how both the formal and informal curriculum shaped U.S. sexual culture help you to see the ways in which heterosexuality was reinforced in your schools? How do you think this has impacted you today?

2. There is much debate over whether or not sexuality should be taught in school, and yet as the author demonstrates, it is already taught in both overt and covert ways. How might teaching an inclusive sexuality curriculum change the experience of all youth in the public school system?

3. If sexuality biases in the educational system were eliminated, how do you think this would impact the roles of all people in the larger society, regardless of sexuality?

SOCIAL INSTITUTIONS: WORK AND ECONOMY

Reading 26

JOBLESS GHETTOS
The Social Implications of the Disappearance of Work in Segregated Neighborhoods

WILLIAM J. WILSON

In 1950, a substantial portion of the urban black population was poor but working. Urban poverty was quite extensive, but people held jobs. However, in many inner-city ghetto neighborhoods in 1990, most adults were not working in a typical week. For example, in 1950, 69 percent of all males 14 and over held jobs in a typical week in the three neighborhoods that represent the historic core of the Black Belt in Chicago—Douglas, Grand Boulevard, and Washington Park. But by 1990, only four in ten in Douglas worked in a typical week, one in three in Washington Park, and one in four in Grand Boulevard. In all, only 37 percent of all males 16 and over held jobs in a typical week in these neighborhoods.

The disappearance of work has had devastating effects not only on individuals and families but also on the social life of neighborhoods as well. Inner-city joblessness is a severe problem that is often overlooked or obscured when the focus is mainly on poverty and its consequences. Despite increases in the concentration of poverty since 1970, inner cities have always featured high levels of poverty, but the levels of inner-city joblessness reached in 1990 were unprecedented.[1]

It should be noted that when I refer to "joblessness" I am not solely referring to official unemployment. The unemployment rate represents only the *official* labor force—that is, those who are actively looking for work. It does not include those who are outside of or have dropped out of the labor market, including the nearly 6 million males age 25–60 who appear in the census statistics but do not show up in the labor statistics.[2]

These uncounted males in the labor market are disproportionately represented in the inner-city ghettos. A more appropriate measure of joblessness that takes into account both official unemployment and non-labor force participation is the employment-to-population ratio, which corresponds to the percentage of adults 16 and older who are working. In 1990, for example, only one in three adults ages 16 and older held a job in the ghetto poverty areas of Chicago, representing roughly 425,000 men, women, and children. And in the ghetto tracts of the nation's 100 largest cities, for every ten adults who did not hold a job in a typical week in 1990, there were only six employed persons.

The consequences of high neighborhood joblessness are more devastating than those of high neighborhood poverty. A neighborhood in which people are poor, but employed, is much different from a neighborhood in which people are poor and jobless. Many of today's problems in the inner-city ghetto neighborhoods—crime, family dissolution, welfare, low levels of social organization, and so on—are fundamentally a consequence of the disappearance of work.

It should be clear that when I speak of the disappearance of work, I am referring to the declining involvement in or lack of attachment to the formal labor market. It could be argued that the general sense of the term "joblessness" does not necessarily mean "non-work." Many people who are officially jobless are nonetheless involved in informal activities, ranging from unpaid housework to income from work in the informal or illegal economies.

Housework is work; baby-sitting is work; even drug dealing is work. However, what contrasts work in the formal economy with work activity in the informal and illegal economies is that work in the formal economy has greater regularity and consistency in schedules and hours. The demands for discipline are greater. It is true that some work activities outside the formal economy also call for discipline and regular schedules. Several studies reveal that the social organization of the drug industry is driven by discipline and a work ethic, however perverse. However, as a general rule, work in the informal and illegal economies is far less governed by norms or expectations that place a premium on discipline and regularity. For all these reasons, when I speak of the disappearance of work, I mean work in the formal economy, work that provides a framework for daily behavior because of the discipline and regularity that it imposes.

Thus, a youngster who grows up in a family with a steady breadwinner and in a neighborhood in which most of the adults are employed will tend to develop some of the disciplined habits associated with stable or steady employment—habits that are reflected in the behavior of his or her parents and of other neighborhood adults. These might include attachment to a routine, a recognition of the hierarchy found in most work situations, a sense of personal efficacy attained through the routine management of financial affairs, endorsement of a system of personal and material rewards associated with dependability and responsibility, and so on. Accordingly, when this youngster enters the labor market, he or she has a distinct advantage over the youngsters who grow up in households without a steady breadwinner and in neighborhoods that are not organized around work—in other words, a milieu in which one is more exposed to the less-disciplined habits associated with casual or infrequent work.

In the absence of regular employment, a person lacks not only a place in which to work and the receipt of regular income but also a coherent organization of the present—that is, a system of concrete expectations and goals. Regular employment provides the anchor for the spatial and temporal aspects of daily life. It determines where you are going to be and when you are going to be there. In the absence of regular employment, life, including family life, becomes less coherent. Persistent unemployment and irregular employment hinder rational planning in daily life, a necessary condition of adaptation to an industrial economy.[3]

 ## EXPLANATIONS OF THE GROWTH OF JOBLESS GHETTOS

What accounts for the growing proportion of jobless adults in inner-city communities? An easy explanation would be racial segregation. However, a race-specific argument is not sufficient to explain recent changes in such neighborhoods. After all, these historical Black Belt neighborhoods were just as segregated by skin color in 1950 as they are today, yet the level of employment was much higher then. One has to account for the ways in which racial segregation interacts with other changes in society to produce the recent escalating rates of joblessness.

The disappearance of work in many inner-city neighborhoods is in part related to the nationwide decline in the fortunes of low-skilled workers. Over the past two decades, wage inequality has increased sharply and gaps in labor market outcomes between the less- and more-skilled workers have risen substantially. Research suggests that these changes are the result of "a substantial decline in the relative demand for the less-educated and those doing more routinized tasks compared to the relative supply of such workers."[4] Two factors appear to have reduced the relative demand for less-skilled workers—the computer revolution (i.e., skill-based technological change) and the internationalization of economic activity. Inner-city workers face an additional problem—the growing suburbanization of jobs. Most ghetto residents cannot afford cars and therefore rely on public transit systems that make the connection between inner-city neighborhoods and suburban job locations difficult and time consuming.

Although the relative importance of the different underlying causes of the growing jobs problems of the less-skilled, including those in the inner city, continues to be debated, there is little disagreement about the underlying trends. They are unlikely to reverse themselves.[5]

Changes in the class, racial, and demographic composition of inner-city neighborhoods have also contributed to the high percentage of jobless adults in these neighborhoods. Because of the steady outmigration of more advantaged families, the proportion of non-poor families and prime-age working adults has decreased sharply in the typical inner-city ghetto since 1970. These changes have made it increasingly difficult to sustain basic neighborhood institutions or to achieve adequate levels of social organization. The declining presence of working- and middle-class blacks has also deprived ghetto neighborhoods of key resources, including structural resources, such as residents with income to sustain neighborhood services, and cultural resources, such as conventional role models for neighborhood children.

It is not surprising therefore that our research in Chicago revealed that inner-city ghetto residents share a feeling of little informal social control of their children. A primary reason is the absence of a strong organizational capacity or an institutional resource base that would provide an extra layer of social organization in their neighborhoods. It is easier for parents to control the behavior of the children in their neighborhoods when a strong institutional resource base exists and when the links between community institutions such as churches, schools, political organizations, businesses, and civic clubs are strong or secure. The higher the density and stability of formal organizations, the less illicit activities such as drug trafficking, crime, prostitution, and the formation of gangs can take root in the neighborhood.

It is within this context that the public policy discussion on welfare reform and family values should be couched. Our Chicago research suggests that, as employment prospects recede, the foundation for stable relationships becomes weaker over time. More permanent relationships such as marriage give way to temporary liaisons that result in broken unions, out-of-wedlock pregnancies and births, and, to a lesser extent, separation and divorce. The changing norms concerning marriage in the larger society reinforce the movement toward temporary liaisons in the inner city, and therefore economic considerations in marital decisions take on even greater weight. The evolving cultural patterns are seen in the sharing of negative outlooks toward marriage and toward the relationships between males and females in the inner city, outlooks that are developed in and influenced by an environment featuring persistent joblessness. This combination of factors has increased out-of-wedlock births, weakened the family structure, expanded the welfare rolls, and, as a result, caused poor inner-city blacks to be even more disconnected from the job market and discouraged about their role in the labor force. The economic marginality of the ghetto poor is cruelly reinforced, therefore, by conditions in the neighborhoods in which they live.

In the eyes of employers in metropolitan Chicago, the social conditions in the ghetto render inner-city blacks less desirable as workers, and therefore many employers are reluctant to hire them. One of the three studies that provided the empirical foundation for *When Work Disappears* included a representative sample of employers in the greater Chicago area who provided entry-level jobs. An overwhelming majority of these employers, both white and black, expressed negative views about inner-city ghetto workers, and many stated that they were reluctant to hire them. For example, a president of an inner-city manufacturing firm expressed a concern about employing residents from certain inner-city neighborhoods:

> If somebody gave me their address, uh, Cabrini Green, I might
> unavoidably have some concerns. [*Interviewer:* What would your
> concerns be?] That the poor guy probably would be frequently
> unable to get to work and . . . I probably would watch him more
> carefully, even if it wasn't fair, than I would with somebody else.
> I know what I should do though is recognize that here's a guy that
> is trying to get out of his situation and probably will work harder
> than somebody else who's already out of there and he might be
> the best one around here. But I, I think I would have to struggle
> accepting that premise at the beginning.

In addition to qualms about the neighborhood milieu, employers frequently mentioned concerns about applicants' language skills and educational training. An employer from a computer software firm expressed the view "that in many businesses the ability to meet the public is paramount and you do not talk street talk to the buying public. Almost all your black welfare people talk street talk. And who's going to sit them down and change their speech patterns?" A Chicago real estate broker made a similar point:

> A lot of times I will interview applicants who are black, who are
> sort of lower class. . . . They'll come to me and I cannot hire them
> because their language skills are so poor. Their speaking voice
> for one thing is poor. . . . They have no verbal facility with the
> language . . . and these . . . you know, they just don't know how to
> speak and they'll say "salesmens" instead of "salesmen" and that's
> a problem. . . . They don't know punctuation, they don't know

how to use correct grammar, and they cannot spell. And I can't
hire them. And I feel bad about that and I think they're being very
disadvantaged by the Chicago public school system.

Another respondent defended his method of screening out most job
applicants on the telephone on the basis of their use of "grammar and English."

I have every right to say that that's a requirement for this job. I
don't care if you're pink, black, green, yellow, or orange, I demand
someone who speaks well. You want to tell me that I'm a bigot,
fine, call me a bigot.

Finally, an inner-city banker claimed that many blacks in the ghetto
"simply cannot read. When you're talking our type of business, that disqualifies them immediately. We don't have a job here that doesn't require that
somebody have minimum reading and writing skills."

How should we interpret the negative attitudes and actions of employers? To what extent do they represent an aversion to blacks per se and to what
degree do they reflect judgments based on the job-related skills and training of
inner-city blacks in a changing labor market? I should point out that the statements made by the African-American employers concerning the qualifications
of inner-city black workers do not differ significantly from those of the white
employers. Whereas 74 percent of all the white employers who responded to
the open-ended questions expressed negative views of the job-related traits of
inner-city blacks, 80 percent of the black employers did so as well.

This raises a question about the meaning and significance of race in
certain situations—in other words, how race intersects with other factors.
A key hypothesis in this connection is that, given the recent shifts in the
economy, employers are looking for workers with a broad range of abilities:
"hard" skills (literacy, numeracy, basic mechanical ability, and other testable
attributes) and "soft" skills (personalities suitable to the work environment,
good grooming, group-oriented work behaviors, etc.). While hard skills
are the product of education and training—benefits that are apparently in
short supply in inner-city schools—soft skills are strongly tied to culture and
are therefore shaped by the harsh environment of the inner-city ghetto. If
employers are indeed reacting to the difference in skills between white and
black applicants, it becomes increasingly difficult to discuss the motives of
employers: are they rejecting inner-city black applicants out of overt racial
discrimination or on the basis of qualifications?

Nonetheless, many of the selective recruitment practices do represent
what economists call statistical discrimination: Employers make assumptions about the inner-city black workers *in general* and reach decisions based
on those assumptions before they have had a chance to review systematically the qualifications of an individual applicant. The net effect is that many
black inner-city applicants are never given the chance to prove their qualifications on an individual level because they are systematically screened

out by the selective recruitment process. Statistical discrimination, although representing elements of class bias against poor workers in the inner city, is clearly a matter of race. The selective recruitment patterns effectively screen out far more black workers from the inner city than Hispanic or white workers from the same types of backgrounds. But race is also a factor, even in those decisions to deny employment to inner-city black workers on the basis of objective and thorough evaluations of their qualifications. The hard and soft skills among inner-city blacks that do not match the current needs of the labor market are products of racially segregated communities, communities that have historically featured widespread social constraints and restricted opportunities.

Thus, the job prospects of inner-city workers have diminished not only because of the decreasing relative demand for low-skilled labor, the suburbanization of jobs, and the social deterioration of ghetto neighborhoods, but also because of negative employer attitudes. This combination of factors presents a real challenge to policy-makers. Indeed, considering the narrow range of social policy options in the "balance-the-budget" political climate, how can we immediately alleviate the inner-city jobs problem—a problem that will undoubtedly grow when the new welfare reform bill takes full effect.

PUBLIC POLICY DILEMMAS

To what extent will the inner-city jobs problem respond to macroeconomic levers that can act to enhance growth and reduce unemployment? I include here fiscal policies that regulate government spending and taxation and monetary policies that influence interest rates and control the money supply. If jobs are plentiful even for less-skilled workers during periods of economic expansion, then labor shortages reduce the likelihood that hiring decisions will be determined by subjective negative judgments concerning a group's job-related traits.

But given the fundamental structural decline in the demand for low-skilled workers, fiscal and monetary policies designed to enhance economic growth will have their greatest impact in the higher-wage sectors of the economy. Many low-wage workers, especially those in high-jobless inner-city neighborhoods who are not in or have dropped out of the labor force and who also face the problem of negative employer attitudes, will not experience any improvement in their job prospects because of such policies.

If firms in the private sector cannot use or refuse to hire low-skilled adults who are willing to take minimum-wage jobs, then the jobs problem for inner-city workers cannot be adequately addressed without considering a policy of public-sector employment of last resort. Indeed, until current changes in the labor market are reversed or until the skills of the next generation can be upgraded before it enters the labor market, many workers, especially those who are not in the official labor force, will not be able to find jobs unless the government becomes an employer of last resort. This argument applies especially to low-skilled inner-city black workers. It is bad enough that they face the problem of shifts in labor-market demand shared by all low-skilled workers; it is even worse that they confront negative employer perceptions about their work-related skills and attitudes.

Prior to the late 1970s, there was less need for the creation of public-sector jobs. Not only was economic growth fairly rapid during periods of expansion, but "the gains from growth were widely shared." Before the late 1970s, public jobs of last resort were thought of in terms of "a counter-cyclical policy to be put in place during recessions and retired during recoveries. It is only since the late 1970s that the disadvantaged have been left behind during recoveries. The labor market changes . . . seem to have permanently reduced private-sector demand for less-skilled workers."[6]

For all these reasons, the passage of the recent welfare reform bill, which did not include a program of job creation, could have negative social consequences in the inner city. Unless something is done to enhance the employment opportunities of inner-city welfare recipients who reach the time limit for the receipt of welfare, they may flood a pool already filled with low-skilled jobless workers.

New research into urban labor markets by Harry Holzer reveals the magnitude of the problem. Surveying 3,000 employers in Atlanta, Boston, and Los Angeles, Holzer found that only 5 to 10 percent of the jobs in central-city areas for non-college graduates require very few work credentials or cognitive skills. This means that most inner-city workers today not only need to have basic reading, writing, and math skills but also need to know how to operate a computer as well. Also, most employers require a high school degree, particular kinds of previous work experience, and job references. Because of the large oversupply of low-skilled workers relative to the number of low-skilled jobs, many low-educated and poorly trained individuals have difficulty finding jobs even when the local labor market is strong.[7]

The problem is that in recent years tight labor markets have been of relatively short duration, frequently followed by a recession which either wiped out previous gains for many workers or did not allow others to fully recover from a previous period of economic stagnation. It would take sustained tight labor markets over many years to draw back those discouraged inner-city workers who have dropped out of the labor market altogether, some for very long periods of time. We are currently in one of the longest economic recoveries in the last half century, a recovery that has lasted eight years and generated more than 14 million net new jobs and the lowest official unemployment rate in twenty-four years. This sustained recovery is beginning to have some positive effect on the hard-core unemployed. The ranks of those out of work for more than six months declined by almost 150,000 over a two-month period in early 1997. And, as reported in early 1998, the unemployment rate for high school dropouts declined by five points since 1992, from 12 to 7 percent. Two-fifths of this decline has come in the last year.[8]

How long this current period of economic recovery will last is anybody's guess. Some economists feel that this period of tight labor markets will last for at least several more years. If it does it will be the best antidote for low-skilled workers whose employment and earning prospects have been diminished in the late twentieth century. For example, in the inner cities the extension of the economic recovery for several more years will significantly lower the overall jobless rate not only for the low-skilled workers who are still in the labor force but for those who have been outside the labor market for many years as well. It will also enhance the job prospects of many of the welfare recipients who reach the time limit for the receipt of welfare. But, given the decreased relative demand for low-skilled labor, what will happen to all of these groups if the economy slows down? Considering the changing nature of the economy, there is little reason to assume that their prospects will be anything but bleak. Why? Simply because the economic trend that has twisted against low-skilled workers is unlikely to reverse itself, thereby diminishing over the long term their job prospects and earnings.

Concerned about these issues, I sent President Clinton a memorandum in August 1996. I pointed out that, although he has long realized the crucial relationship between welfare reform and job creation and that his initial welfare plan emphasized job creation, the bill he signed had no such provision. I pointed out that to remedy the most glaring defects of the bill, a mechanism for state and local governments to respond to widespread joblessness in the inner cities was essential. I was aware that the president was giving some thought to tax credits and wage subsidies to encourage businesses to hire welfare recipients. I pointed out that although giving subsidies and tax credits to private employers may help, research suggests that subsidies and credits are hardly sufficient by themselves to accomplish this goal.

The track record of private employers is not especially encouraging. Past efforts to subsidize employers to hire welfare recipients and other disadvantaged individuals have generally failed to work on a large scale. For example, during the late 1960s and early 1970s, the federal government funded a program by the National Alliance of Business (NAB) in which employers received a $3,200 subsidy for each disadvantaged worker, including welfare recipients, they hired (an amount that would be much higher in inflation-adjusted terms today). That effort resulted in a very low take-up rate among employers. Why? Simply because not enough employers have been willing to hire people whom they view as troublesome or "damaged goods." Indeed, a study by the economist Gary Burtless revealed that the low-income individuals who were supposed to be aided were *less* likely to be hired as a result of a targeted wage subsidy. Employers evidently thought that if the government was willing to subsidize the hiring of these individuals so heavily, they must have serious work-related problems.[9]

Studies also show that when employers do receive a subsidy for hiring such individuals—whether a tax credit or a direct subsidy—the subsidy often rewards employers for hires they would have made anyway. When that occurs, it costs the government money but the number of jobs for this population does not increase.

Although a new study by Lawrence Katz reveals that one tax credit program, the Targeted Jobs Tax Credit, "may have modestly improved the employment rates of economically disadvantaged youth,"[10] an impressive array of other studies over the past two decades suggests that a single approach involving tax credits or wage subsidies will fail to move a significant number of welfare recipients into employment.

In my memorandum to the president, I therefore urged caution in placing too many of his "eggs" in the private-sector job-placement basket. We will need a mix of both private- and public-sector initiatives to enhance employment. In inner cities, where the number of very low-skilled individuals vastly exceeds the number of low-skilled jobs even before welfare reform adds tens of thousands more people to the low-skilled labor pool, a healthy dose of public-sector job creation will be needed. Public jobs can help people shunned by private employers initially to learn acceptable work habits and build an employment record, from which they may be able to graduate to private-sector positions. In order to really make my point clear, I pointed out to President Clinton that I am not suggesting a new federal public works program because I understand the difficulties in getting such a program approved in today's political climate. I am only recommending that he enable governors and mayors to use a mix of private- and public-sector approaches as they see fit, based on local conditions. I pointed out that he could not be criticized for a "big government" approach if he allows state and local officials, so many of whom are now Republicans, to make this choice. Indeed, Governor Tommy Thompson's welfare plan in Wisconsin includes provisions for significant public- as well as private-sector employment.

The president responded that several of my recommendations were already under consideration by his administration. And during the presidential campaign, he outlined a proposal that included both tax credits to companies that hire welfare recipients and $3 billion to create public and private work slots in localities that have high unemployment and welfare dependency.

However, in the tax bill submitted to Congress on February 6, 1997, the president's proposal to strengthen the welfare-to-work initiative did not include language that would allow governors and mayors to create private or public work slots in areas plagued by high rates of unemployment and welfare receipt. Indeed the focus, although stated in vague language, was entirely on initiatives to place recipients in private-sector jobs, including a larger tax credit for businesses that hire long-term welfare recipients. The new tax credit would allow employers to deduct 50 percent of the first $10,000 in wages paid to recipients who had been on welfare for at least eighteen months.

The conclusions I draw from the current evidence is that as the president and the Congress take future steps to address the jobs problem for welfare recipients and other disadvantaged workers, they ought not rely on a stand-alone strategy of employer subsidies—either tax credits or wage subsidies. Instead, they ought to consider a mixed strategy that combines employer subsidies with job creation in the public and non-profit private sectors.

It is especially important that this mixed strategy include a plan to make adequate monies available to localities or communities with high jobless and welfare dependency rates. At the same time that the new welfare law has generated a greater need for work opportunities, high-jobless urban and rural areas will have more difficulty placing individuals in private-sector jobs. To create work opportunities for welfare recipients, these areas will therefore have to "rely more heavily upon job creation strategies in the public and private non-profit sectors."[11] West Virginia, plagued with a severe shortage of work opportunities, has provided community service jobs to welfare recipients for several years. In Wisconsin, Governor Thompson's welfare reform plan envisions community-service jobs for many parents in the more depressed areas of the state, and the New Hope program in Milwaukee provides community-service jobs for those unable to find employment in the private sector.

Thus, we could face a real catastrophe in many urban areas if steps are not taken soon to enhance the job prospects of hundreds of thousands of inner-city youths and adults.

NOTES

1. Parts of this essay are based on my latest book, *When Work Disappears: The World of the New Urban Poor* (New York: Alfred A. Knopf, 1996), which included three research studies conducted in Chicago between 1986 and 1993. The first of these included a random survey of nearly 2,500 poor and non-poor African-American, Latino, and white residents in Chicago's poor neighborhoods; a subsample of 175 participants from this survey who were reinterviewed and answered open-ended questions; a survey of 179 employers selected to reflect the distribution of employment and firm sizes in the metropolitan area; and comprehensive ethnographic research, including participant-observation research and life-history interviews in a representative sample of inner-city neighborhoods.

    The second study included a survey of a representative sample of 546 black mothers and up to two of their adolescent children (ages 11 to 16—or 887 adolescents), in working- and middle-class neighborhoods and high-poverty neighborhoods. Finally, the third study featured a survey of a representative sample of 500 respondents from two high-joblessness neighborhoods on the South Side of Chicago and six focus-group discussions involving the residents and former residents of these neighborhoods.

2. Lester Thurow, "The Crusade That's Killing Prosperity," *American Prospect*, March–April 1995, pp. 54–59.

3. Pierre Bourdieu, *Travail et Travailleurs en Algerio* (Paris: Editions Mouton, 1965).

4. Lawrence Katz, "Wage Subsidies for the Disadvantaged," Working Paper 5679, National Bureau of Economic Research, Cambridge, MA, 1996, p. 2.

5. Ibid.

6. Sheldon Danziger and Peter Gottschalk, *America Unequal* (Cambridge: Harvard University Press, 1995), p. 174.

7. Harry Holzer, *What Employers Want: Job Prospects for Less-Educated Workers* (New York: Russell Sage Foundation, 1995).
8. Sylvia Nasar, "Jobs Juggernaut Continues Surge: 30,000 Find Work," *New York Times*, March 7, 1998, pp. 1A and 1B.
9. Gary Burtless, "Are Targeted Wage Subsidies Harmful? Evidence from a Wage Voucher Experiment," *Industrial and Labor Relations Review* 39, October 1985.
10. Katz, op. cit.
11. Center on Budget and Policy Priorities, "The Administration's $3 Billion Jobs Proposal," Washington, DC, 1996.

 QUESTIONS FOR CRITICAL THINKING

Reading 26

1. How does Wilson's discussion of joblessness impact your own understanding of common notions of unemployment?

2. How does Wilson's discussion of joblessness broaden your comprehension of the functions of regular employment (beyond a paycheck)?

3. Wilson offers some strategies for addressing the problem of joblessness. What do you think of his strategies? What strategies would you offer?

Reading 27

DISCRIMINATION IN A LOW-WAGE LABOR MARKET
A Field Experiment

DEVAH PAGER • BRUCE WESTERN • BART BONIKOWSKI

Despite legal bans on discrimination and the liberalization of racial attitudes since the 1960s, racial differences in employment remain among the most enduring forms of economic inequality. Even in the tight labor market of the late 1990s, unemployment rates for black men remained twice that for whites. Racial inequality in total joblessness—including those who exited the labor market—increased among young men during this period

Devah Pager, Bruce Western, and Bart Bonikowski, "Discrimination in a Low-Wage Labor Market: A Field Experiment" from *American Sociological Review* 74 (October 2009): 777–799. Copyright © 2009 by the American Sociological Association. Reprinted with permission.

(Holzer and Offner 2001). Against this backdrop of persistent racial inequality, the question of employment discrimination has generated renewed interest. Although there is much research on racial disparities in employment, the contemporary relevance of discrimination remains widely contested.

One line of research points to the persistence of prejudice and discrimination as a critical factor shaping contemporary racial disparities (Darity and Mason 1998; Roscigno et al. 2007). A series of studies relying on surveys and in-depth interviews finds that firms are reluctant to hire young minority men—especially blacks—because they are seen as unreliable, dishonest, or lacking in social or cognitive skills (Holzer 1996; Kirschenman and Neckerman 1991; Moss and Tilly 2001; Waldinger and Lichter 2003; Wilson 1996: chap. 5). The strong negative attitudes expressed by employers suggest that race remains highly salient in employers' evaluations of workers. At the same time, research relying on interviews with employers leaves uncertain the degree to which self-reported attitudes are influential in actual hiring decisions (Pager and Quillian 2005). Indeed, Moss and Tilly (2001:151) report the puzzling finding that "businesses where a plurality of managers complained about black motivation are more likely to hire black men." In fact, across a series of analyses controlling for firm size, starting wage, the percent black in the relevant portion of the metropolitan area, and a business's average distance from black residents in the area, Moss and Tilly find that employers who overtly criticize the hard skills or interaction skills of black workers are between two and four times more likely to hire a black worker (pp. 151–52). Hiring decisions, of course, are influenced by a complex range of factors, racial attitudes being only one. Employers' stated preferences do not provide a clear picture of the degree to which negative attitudes about blacks translate into active forms of discrimination.

Research focusing on wages rather than employment offers even less evidence of contemporary discrimination. Neal and Johnson (1996), for example, estimate wage differences between white, black, and Latino young men. They find that two thirds of the black-white gap in wages in 1990 to 1991 can be explained by race differences in cognitive test scores measured 11 years earlier, and test scores fully explain wage differences between whites and Latinos. This and similar studies trace the employment problems of young minority men primarily to skill or other individual deficiencies, rather than any direct effect of discrimination (Farkas and Vicknair 1996; Neal and Johnson 1996; O'Neill 1990). Heckman (1998:101–102) puts the point most clearly, writing that "most of the disparity in earnings between blacks and whites in the labor market of the 1990s is due to differences in skills they bring to the market, and not to discrimination within the labor market." He goes on to describe labor market discrimination as "the problem of an earlier era."

Does employer discrimination continue to affect labor market outcomes for minority workers? Clear answers are elusive because discrimination is hard to measure. Without observing actual hiring decisions, it is difficult to assess exactly how and under what conditions race shapes employer behavior. We address this issue with a field experiment that allows direct observation of employer decision making. By presenting equally qualified applicants who differ only by race or ethnicity, we can observe the degree to which racial considerations affect real hiring decisions. Furthermore, we move beyond experimental estimates of discrimination to explore the *processes* by which discrimination occurs. Examining the interactions between job seekers and employers, we gain new insights into how race influences employers' perceptions of job candidate quality and desirability. Studying the multifaceted character of discrimination highlights the range of decisions that collectively reduce opportunities for minority candidates.

 CONCEPTUALIZING DISCRIMINATION

Empirical studies often portray discrimination as a single decision. Research on employment disparities, for example, considers the role of discrimination at the point of initial hire; research on pay disparities considers discrimination at the point of wage-setting decisions. In reality, discrimination may occur at multiple decision points across the employment relationship. In this way, even relatively small episodes of discrimination—when experienced at multiple intervals or across multiple contexts—can have substantial effects on aggregate outcomes.

Depictions of discriminators also often portray the labor market as divided neatly between employers with a "taste for discrimination" and those who are indifferent to race (Becker 1957). Consequently, it is suggested, job seekers can avoid discrimination by sorting themselves into sectors of the labor market where discrimination is less likely to occur (Heckman 1998:103). and Levitt (2003:5) characterize employers according to a similar dichotomy, with applicants best advised to identify and avoid employers prone to discrimination, rather than wasting time pursuing job opportunities among firms unwilling to hire them: "In the face of discriminatory employers, it is actually in the interest of both employee and employers for Blacks to signal race, either via a name or other résumé information, rather than undertaking a costly interview with little hope of receiving a job offer." According to this conceptualization of labor market discrimination, racial preferences or biases are fixed and concentrated among a specific subset of employers.

Other evidence challenges this tidy distinction between employers who do and do not discriminate. Alternative formulations of labor market discrimination encourage us to view the process as more interactive, contextual, and widespread. Theories of both statistical discrimination and stereotypes view race as a heuristic employers use to evaluate job applicants about whom little is known. Here, group-based generalizations provide guidance about the expected profile of individuals from a given group and facilitate decision making when information or time are scarce (Aigner and Cain 1977;

Fiske 1998). Heuristics of this kind are pervasive (and often unconscious). Their effects may vary depending on the availability of and attention to person-specific information (such as that conveyed through application materials or in an interview) that may interact with and potentially override initial expectations.

A long line of social psychological research investigates how stereotypes give way to individualizing information, as well as the conditions under which stereotypes demonstrate a stubborn resistance to change (Bodenhausen 1988; Fiske 1998; Trope and Thomson 1997).[1] This research suggests that salient personalizing information can quickly counteract stereotyped expectations; however, in evaluating difficult-to-observe or ambiguously relevant characteristics, or when decision makers have competing demands on their attention, stereotypes often filter information in ways that preserve expectations (Darley and Gross 1983; Dovidio and Gaertner 2000; Gilbert and Hixon 1991). In these cases of decision making under uncertainty, racial preferences or biases are unlikely to be expressed in any static or uniform way, but will vary in intensity and consequence depending on other characteristics of the applicant, the employer, and the interaction between the two.

In addition to noting the varying role of race across employment interactions, some research shifts the focus from employer characteristics to the characteristics of the job for which a given worker is being considered. Previous research points to the negative consequences of the changing composition of low-wage jobs for black men, with the shift from manufacturing to services skewing the distribution of skill demands toward "soft skills," for which black men are considered lacking (Moss and Tilly 2001). Jobs involving customer service or contact with clients heighten the salience of race because of employers' concerns about the dress and demeanor of young black men (Moss and Tilly 2001). Jobs at the "back of the house" or those emphasizing manual skills are less likely to activate concerns of this kind. In this scenario, discrimination may obtain not at the employer level but at the job level, with black applicants excluded from some job types and channeled into others. In this case, we would look to variation in discrimination not among employers but among the job openings for which workers are being considered.

Rather than viewing discrimination as a single decision, or as the result of a small group of highly prejudiced employers, a growing body of research points to the variable contexts that shape how information about applicants may be filtered and interpreted along racial lines. Decision making under uncertainty and the race-typing of jobs both make discrimination more likely. To capture the contingent and cumulative effects of discrimination implied by these theories requires an examination of how experiences of discrimination may be distributed across a wide range of decision points and may vary depending on interactions among the employer, the applicant, and the job in question.

THE CHANGING LANDSCAPE OF LOW-WAGE
LABOR MARKETS

Economic theory predicts the decline of discrimination through market competition (Becker 1957), but several features of contemporary low-wage labor
markets may sustain or renew racialized decision making. Shifts in the composition of both low-wage jobs and workers have potentially created new
incentives and opportunities for employers to enact racial preferences in
hiring. First, low-wage job growth is concentrated in service industries, in
positions that place a heavy emphasis on self-presentation, interaction with
customers, and other personality-related attributes (Moss and Tilly 2001).
As discussed earlier, employers consistently express concerns over the "soft
skills" of black men, implying a potential skills mismatch between the skill
requirements of new job growth and the perceived skill profile of black male
job seekers. Furthermore, because many of the qualities valued by employers for contemporary low-wage jobs are difficult to evaluate from a written
application or brief meeting, generalized negative perceptions of minority
workers may be more difficult for individual minority applicants to discon-
firm (Biernat and Kobrynowicz 1997).

Second, low-wage labor markets today are characterized by increasing
heterogeneity of the urban minority work force, with low-skill black workers now more likely to compete with other minority groups—in particular,
low-skill Latino workers. Interviews with employers in Los Angeles and
Chicago suggest consistent preferences for Latinos over blacks, with Latino
workers viewed as more pliant, reliable, and hard-working (Kirschenman
and Neckerman 1991; Waldinger and Lichter 2003). Given these racial preferences among employers, growing competition within the low-wage labor
market may leave black men vulnerable to discrimination relative not only
to whites, but to Latinos as well.

Finally, low-wage labor markets are increasingly supplied by workers
with criminal records. Nearly a third of black men without a college degree
have prison records by their mid-30s, adding to employers' reservations
about black male job applicants (Pager 2007b; Pettit and Western 2004). The
high rate of incarceration makes a criminal record a newly important source
of stigma that is worth studying in its own right. Moreover, we can view a
criminal record as an extreme and authoritative signal of the kinds of problematic behaviors that employers ascribe to young black men. In this context, separating the effects of criminal stigma from race provides a useful
benchmark for measuring racial stigma. In the first effort in this direction,
Pager's (2003) research in a Milwaukee field experiment compared racial
and criminal stigma among matched pairs of job seekers. Fielding a pair of
black and a pair of white job applicants (in which one member of each pair
was randomly assigned a criminal record), Pager found that a black applicant with no criminal background experiences job prospects similar to those

of a white felon. That blackness confers the same disadvantage as a felony conviction helps calibrate the deeply skeptical view of young black men in the eyes of Milwaukee employers.

The growing importance of soft skills, ethnic heterogeneity, and job seekers with criminal records suggest the persistence or increasing incidence of discrimination in contemporary low-wage labor markets. Whether based on statistical generalizations or inaccurate stereotypes, preconceived notions about the characteristics or desirability of black men relative to other applicant types are likely to structure the distribution of opportunity along racial lines.

The current study updates and extends earlier research in several ways. First, we focus directly on the question of racial discrimination, in both conceptualization and design. This emphasis allows us to situate our research within ongoing debates about discrimination and to provide a rigorous design for detecting racial discrimination. Second, we move beyond standard two-race models of discrimination by including matched black, white, and Latino job seekers, reflecting the racial heterogeneity of large urban labor markets. To our knowledge, this is the first study of its kind to simultaneously examine the employment experiences of three racial/ethnic groups. Third, to help calibrate the magnitude of racial preferences, we compare applicants affected by varying forms of stigma; specifically, we compare minority applicants with white applicants just released from prison. The present analysis provides a direct test by comparing the outcomes of minority and ex-offender applicants who visit the same employers. Finally, we extend our analysis from the quantitative evidence of differential treatment to a rich set of qualitative data that allow for an exploration of the process of discrimination. Drawing from the testers' extensive field notes that describe their interactions with employers, we provide a unique window into the range of employer responses that characterize discrimination in contemporary low-wage labor markets.

RESEARCH DESIGN AND METHODS

The New York City Hiring Discrimination Study sent matched teams of testers to apply for 340 real entry-level jobs throughout New York City over nine months in 2004. The testers were well-spoken, clean-cut young men, ages 22 to 26. Most were college-educated, between 5 feet 10 inches and 6 feet in height, and recruited in and around New York City. They were matched on the basis of their verbal skills, interactional styles (level of eye contact, demeanor, and verbosity), and physical attractiveness. Testers were assigned fictitious résumés indicating identical educational attainment and comparable qualities of high school, work experience (quantity and kind), and neighborhood of residence. Résumés were prepared in different fonts and formats and randomly varied across testers, with each résumé used by testers from each race group. Testers presented themselves as high school graduates with steady work experience in entry-level jobs. Finally, the testers passed a common training program to ensure uniform behavior in job interviews. While in the field, the testers dressed similarly and communicated with teammates by cell phone to anticipate unusual interview situations.

We fielded two teams that each included a white, Latino, and black tester. To help ensure comparability, the Latino testers spoke in unaccented English, were U.S. citizens of Puerto Rican descent, and, like the other testers, claimed no Spanish language ability. The first team tests a standard racial hierarchy, with the white tester serving as a benchmark against which to measure variation in racial and ethnic discrimination. To calibrate the magnitude of racial stigma, the second team compares black and Latino testers with a white tester with a criminal record. The criminal record was typically disclosed in answer to the standard question on employment applications, "Have you ever been convicted of a crime? If yes, please explain." We instructed testers to reveal, when asked, that they had recently been released from prison after serving 18 months for a drug felony (possession with intent to distribute, cocaine). In addition, following Pager (2003), the white tester's criminal record was also signaled on the résumé by listing work experience at a state prison and by listing a parole officer as a reference.[2]

For both teams, we sampled employers from job listings for entry-level positions, defined as jobs requiring little previous experience and no more than a high school degree. Job titles included restaurant jobs, retail sales, warehouse workers, couriers, telemarketers, customer service positions, clerical workers, stockers, movers, delivery drivers, and a wide range of other low-wage positions. Each week, we randomly drew job listings from the classified sections of the *New York Times, Daily News, New York Post, Village Voice,* and the online service Craigslist. The broad range of job listings allowed for extensive coverage of the entry-level labor market in New York. From the available population of job listings, we took a simple random sample of advertisements each week. Testers in each team applied to each job within a 24-hour period, randomly varying the order of the applicants.

 EXPERIMENTAL RESULTS

The primary results from the field experiment focus on the proportion of applications submitted by testers that elicited either a callback or a job offer from employers, by race of the applicant. Our first team assesses the effects of race discrimination by comparing the outcomes of equally qualified white, Latino, and black applicants. Figure 1a reports positive response rates for each racial/ethnic group. In applications to 171 employers, the white tester received a callback or job offer 31.0 percent of the time, compared with a positive response rate of 25.2 percent for Latinos and 15.2 percent for blacks.

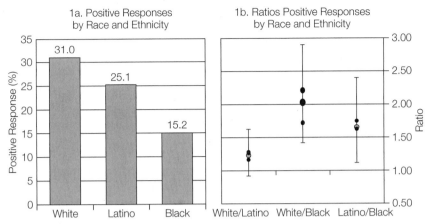

FIGURE 1 Positive Response Rates and Paired Comparisons by Race and Ethnicity.
Notes: Positive responses refer to callbacks or job offers. Hollow circles in Figure 1b
indicate point estimates of the ratio. Solid circles indicate ratios obtained by sequentially
dropping testers from the analysis. We estimated 95 percent confidence intervals from
a hierarchical logistic regression with employer and tester random effects. Number of
employers = 171.

These results show a clear racial hierarchy, with whites in the lead, followed
by Latinos, and blacks trailing behind.

Figure 1b shows the contrasts between the three race groups. Once we
adjust for employer and tester effects, the confidence interval for the white-
Latino ratio of 1.23 includes one.[3] By contrast, the white-black ratio of 2.04
is substantively large and statistically significant. The positive response rate
for blacks is also significantly lower than the rate for Latinos. The points in
the figure show the cross-validation results obtained by sequentially dropping cases associated with each individual tester. All ratios remain consistently greater than one, indicating that employers treat blacks less positively
regardless of which testers are applying for jobs. Overall, these results indicate that, relative to equally qualified blacks, employers significantly prefer
white and Latino job applicants. The findings suggest that a black applicant
has to search twice as long as an equally qualified white applicant before
receiving a callback or job offer from an employer.

The results from this first comparison indicate employers' strong
racial preferences, but the magnitude of this preference remains somewhat abstract. To calibrate the effects of race against another stigmatized
category, the ex-offender, we repeated the experiment, this time assigning a criminal record to the white tester. Figure 2a shows the percentage
of positive responses—job offers or callbacks—received by each tester. In
this experiment, whites with criminal records obtained positive responses
in 17.2 percent of 169 job applications, compared with 15.4 percent for Latinos and 13.0 percent for blacks.[4] The white testers' racial advantage narrows

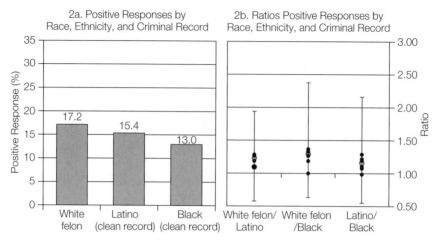

FIGURE 2   Positive Response Rates and Paired Comparisons by Race, Ethnicity, and Criminal Background.

Notes: Positive responses refer to callbacks or job offers. Hollow circles in Figure 2b indicate point estimates of the ratio. Solid circles indicate ratios obtained by sequentially dropping testers from the analysis. We estimated 95 percent confidence intervals from a hierarchical logistic regression with employer and tester random effects. Number of employers = 169.

substantially in this comparison; yet the white applicant with a criminal record still does just as well, if not better, than his minority counterparts with no criminal background.

Figure 2b shows that the white-Latino ratio is close to one and the confidence interval overlaps one by a large margin. The white-black ratio is now a statistically insignificant 1.32, compared with a significant ratio of 2.04 when the white tester had a clean record. As in the previous experiment, Latinos were preferred to blacks, but here the difference is not significant. As before, the cross-validation treatment effects, obtained by dropping employers associated with one particular tester, are all close to one. These results indicate that, regardless of which testers were sent into the field, employers differentiated little among the three applicant groups.

The comparison of a white felon with black and Latino applicants with clean backgrounds provides a vivid calibration of the effects of race on hiring decisions. While ex-offenders are disadvantaged in the labor market relative to applicants with no criminal background, the stigma of a felony conviction appears to be no greater than that of minority status. Replicating earlier results from Milwaukee (Pager 2003), these findings suggest that New York employers view minority applicants as essentially equivalent to whites just out of prison.

Theories of statistical discrimination point to the very high incarceration rates among young black men as a key explanation for employers' indifference between white felons and blacks with potentially unobserved criminal histories. Current estimates suggest that roughly 18 percent of young black men with high school degrees will experience incarceration by their early 30s (Pettit and Western 2004), and a larger fraction surely have lower level convictions and arrests. Still, the fact that known information about a white applicant's serious criminal conviction is viewed with no more concern than the assumed characteristics of a young black man points to the strength and intensity of contemporary racial attitudes. Overcoming these negative expectations, even for a candidate with otherwise appealing characteristics, requires the negotiation of a number of significant hurdles not present for white job seekers.

Race at Work: An Examination of Interactions between Applicants and Employers

The strong evidence of hiring discrimination from the field experiment provides a clear measure of the continuing significance of race in employer decision making. These numbers, however, tell us little about the process by which race comes to matter. Fortunately, the in-person design of the experiment allows us to further supplement the experimental findings with qualitative evidence from testers' field notes that report their interactions in job interviews. These detailed narratives describe employers' deliberations and suggest some of the ways race comes into play during employment interactions.

Our analysis examines cases in which testers had sufficient interaction with employers for content coding. Consistent with the notion that contemporary forms of discrimination are largely subtle and covert, many cases contain little that would lead us to anticipate the differential treatment that followed. Of those that do, however, we observe several consistent patterns in employers' responses. In particular, three categories of behavior stand out, which we refer to here as: categorical exclusion, shifting standards, and race-coded job channeling. The first type of behavior, categorical exclusion, is characterized by an immediate or automatic rejection of the black (or minority) candidate in favor of a white applicant. Occurring early in the application process, these decisions involve little negotiated interaction but appear to reflect a fairly rigid application of employers' racial preferences or beliefs. A second category of behavior, shifting standards, reflects a more dynamic process of decision making. Here we observe cases in which employers' evaluations of applicants appear actively shaped or constructed through a racial lens, with similar qualifications or deficits taking on varying relevance depending on an applicant's race. Finally, a third category of behavior moves beyond the hiring decision to a focus on job placement. Race-based job channeling represents a process by which minority applicants are steered toward particular job types, often those characterized by greater physical demands and reduced customer contact.

By observing the interactions that characterize each of these behavior types, we gain a rare glimpse into the processes by which discrimination takes place. At the same time, we emphasize that this discussion is intended as a descriptive exercise rather than a formal causal analysis. Indeed, the categories we identify are not mutually exclusive; some of the same processes may be operating simultaneously, with employers' shifting evaluations of applicant skills leading to different patterns of job channeling, or assumptions about the appropriate race of the incumbent of a particular position leading to forms of categorical exclusion. Likewise, this typology cannot account for all of the differential treatment we observe—at least half of the employer decisions were made on the basis of little or no personal contact between applicant and employer, leaving the nature of the decision entirely unobserved. With these caveats in mind, we nevertheless view the analysis as providing a unique contribution to the study of racial discrimination, revealing mechanisms at work that observational research can rarely identify.

Categorical Exclusion

Few interactions between our testers and employers revealed signs of racial animus or hostility toward minority applicants. At the same time, a close comparison of test partners' experiences shows a number of cases in which race appears to be the sole or primary criterion for an employer's decision. With little negotiation or deliberation over the selection decision, these employers' decisions seem to reflect a preexisting judgment regarding the adequacy or desirability of a minority candidate. The uncompromising nature of the employer's decision can be characterized as a form of categorical exclusion.

A clear-cut case of categorical exclusion was provided when all three testers applied for a warehouse worker position and received a perfunctory decision. Zuri, one of our black testers, reported: "The original woman who had herded us in told us that when we finished filling out the application we could leave because 'there's no interview today, guys!'... When I made it across the street to the bus stop... the woman who had collected our completed applications pointed in the direction of Simon, Josue, and myself [the three test partners] motioning for us to return. All three of us went over.... She looked at me and told me she 'needed to speak to these two' and that I could go back." Zuri returned to the bus stop, while his white and Latino test partners were both asked to come back at 5 p.m. that day to start work. Simon, the white tester, reported, "She said she told the other people that we needed to sign something—that that's why she called us over—so as not to let them know she was hiring us. She seemed pretty concerned with not letting anyone else know."

In this context, with no interview and virtually no direct contact with the employer, we observe a decision that appears to be based on little other than race. The job is a manual position for which Zuri is at least as able, yet he is readily passed over in favor of his white and Latino counterparts.

This case is unusual in that three testers were rarely present at a given location at the same time. More often, we found evidence of differential treatment only after comparing the testers' reports side by side. Here again, we observed several hiring decisions in which race appeared to be the sole or primary source of differentiation. In one example, the three testers inquired about a sales position at a retail clothing store. Joe, one of our black testers, reported that, "[the employer] said the position was just filled and that she would be calling people in for an interview if the person doesn't work out." Josue, his Latino test partner, was told something very similar: "She informed me that the position was already filled, but did not know if the hired employee would work out. She told me to leave my résumé with her." By contrast, Simon, their white test partner, who applied last, had a notably different experience: "I asked what the hiring process was—if they're taking applications now, interviewing, etc. She looked at my application. 'You can start immediately?' Yes. 'Can you start tomorrow?' Yes. '10 a.m.' She was very friendly and introduced me to another woman (white, 28) at the cash register who will be training me."

A similar case arose a few weeks later at an electronics store. Joe, the black tester, was allowed to complete an application but was told that his references would have to be checked before he could be interviewed. Meanwhile, Simon and Josue, his white and Latino partners, applied shortly afterward and were interviewed on the spot. Joe's references were never called, while Simon received a callback two days later offering him the job.

When evaluated individually, these interactions do not indicate racial prejudice or discrimination. Side by side, however, we see that minority applicants encounter barriers not present for the white applicant, with employers citing excuses for putting off the black or minority candidate (e.g., "the job has already been filled" or "we'd have to check your references before we can proceed") that appear not to apply for the white applicant. To be sure, certain cases may capture random error—perhaps a position became available between the testers' visits, or an employer was otherwise preoccupied when one applicant arrived but not another, leading to the employer's differential response. Still, the consistency of the pattern in these data suggests that random error is unlikely to be a dominant factor. Indeed, of the 171 tests conducted by the first team (no criminal background), white testers were singled out for callbacks or job offers 15 times, whereas there was only a single case in which a black tester received a positive response when his white or Latino partner did not.[5]

These cases of categorical exclusion, although directly observed in only a small number of audits (5 of the 47 cases of differential treatment across the two teams), reveal one form of discrimination in which racial considerations appear relatively fixed and unyielding.[6] Before black (or minority) candidates have the chance to demonstrate their qualifications, they are weeded out on the basis of a single categorical distinction.

Categorical exclusion represents one important form of discrimination. While these rather abrupt interactions reveal little about the underlying motivation that drives employers' decisions, they do demonstrate the sometimes rigid barriers facing minority job seekers. In these cases, black (or minority) applicants are discouraged or dismissed at the outset of the employment process, leaving little opportunity for a more nuanced review.

Shifting Standards

Making it past the initial point of contact was not the only hurdle facing minority applicants. Indeed, among those who recorded more extensive interaction with employers, we observe a complex set of racial dynamics at work. On the one hand, personal contact with employers was associated with significantly improved outcomes for all testers and a narrowing of the racial gap. The testers' interpersonal skills seemed to reduce the influence of racial bias, or at least did not exacerbate it. Yet, even in the context of this more personalized review, we see evidence of subtle bias in the evaluation of applicant qualifications. In particular, a number of cases reveal how testers' "objective" qualifications appear to be reinterpreted through the lens of race. Although testers' résumés were matched on education and work experience, some employers seemed to weigh qualifications differently depending on the applicant's race. In the following interactions, we see evidence that the same deficiencies of skill or experience appear to be more disqualifying for the minority job seekers (N = 11).

In one case, Joe, a black tester, was not allowed to apply for a sales position due to his lack of direct experience. He reported, "[The employer] handed me back my résumé and told me they didn't have any positions to offer me . . . that I needed a couple years of experience." The employer voiced similar concerns with Josue and Kevin, Joe's Latino and white partners. Josue wrote, "After a few minutes of waiting . . . I met with [the employer] who looked over my résumé. He said that he was a little worried that I would not be able to do the work." Kevin reported an even stronger reaction: "[The employer] looked at my résumé and said, 'There is absolutely nothing here that qualifies you for this position.'" Yet, despite their evident lack of qualifications, Kevin and Josue were offered the sales job and asked to come back the next morning. In interactions with all three testers, the employer clearly expressed his concern over the applicants' lack of relevant work experience. This lack of experience was not grounds for disqualification for the white and Latino candidates, whereas the black applicant was readily dismissed.

When applying for a job as a line cook at a midlevel Manhattan restaurant, the three testers encountered similar concerns about their lack of relevant experience. Josue, the Latino tester, reported, "[The employer] then asked me if I had any prior kitchen or cooking experience. I told him that I did not really have any, but that I worked alongside cooks at [my prior job as a server]. He then asked me if I had any 'knife' experience and I told him no. . . . He told me he would give me a try and wanted to know if I was available this coming Sunday at 2 p.m." Simon, his white test partner, was also invited to come back for a trial period. By contrast, Joe, the black tester, found that "they are only looking for experienced line cooks." Joe wrote, "I started to try and convince him to give me a chance but he cut me off and said I didn't qualify." None of the testers had direct experience with kitchen work, but the white and Latino applicants were viewed as viable prospects while the black applicant was rejected because he lacked experience.

In other cases, employers perceived real skill or experience differences among applicants despite the fact that the testers' résumés were designed to convey identical qualifications. In one example, the testers applied for a job at a moving company. Joe, the black applicant, spoke with the employer about his prior experience as a stockperson at a moving truck company, but "[the employer] told me that he couldn't use me because he is looking for someone with moving experience." Josue, his Latino partner, presented his experience as a stocker at a delivery company and reported a similar reaction, "He then told me that since I have no experience . . . there is nothing he could do for me." Simon, their white test partner, presented identical qualifications, but the employer responded more favorably: "'To be honest, we're looking for someone with specific moving experience. But because you've worked for [a storage company], that has a little to do with moving.' He wanted me to come in tomorrow between 10 and 11." The employer is consistent in his preference for workers with relevant prior experience, but he is willing to apply a more flexible, inclusive standard in evaluating the experience of the white candidate than in the case of the minority applicants. Employers' shifting standards, offering more latitude to marginally skilled white applicants than to similarly qualified minorities, suggest that even the evaluation of "objective" information can be affected by underlying racial considerations.

Even in cases where the white tester presented as a felon, we see some evidence that this applicant was afforded the benefit of the doubt in ways that his minority counterparts were not. In applying at an auto dealership, for example, the three testers met with very different reactions. Joe, the black tester, was informed at the outset that the only available positions were for people with direct auto sales experience. When Josue, his Latino partner, applied, the lack of direct auto sales experience was less of a problem. Josue reported, "He asked me if I had any customer service experience and I said not really. . . . He then told me that he wanted to get rid of a few bad apples who were not performing well. He asked me when I could start." Josue was told to wait for a callback on Monday. When the employer interviewed Keith, their white exfelon test partner, he gave him a stern lecture regarding his criminal background. The employer warned, "I have no problem with your conviction, it doesn't bother me. But if I find out money is missing or you're not clean or not showing up on time I have no problem ending the relationship." Despite the employer's concerns, Keith was offered the job on the spot. The benefit of the doubt conferred by whiteness persists here, even in the context of a white applicant just released from prison.

A pattern in these interactions, when compared side by side, is the use of double standards—seeking higher qualifications from blacks than non-blacks, or viewing whites as more qualified than minorities who present equivalent résumés. Recent research emphasizes employers' use of race as a proxy for difficult-to-observe productivity characteristics (Moss and Tilly 2001; Waldinger and Lichter 2003). Where we have detailed field notes on job interviews, the interactions we observe suggest that employers also use race in interpreting and weighing observable skill characteristics. Standards appear to shift as employers evaluate various applicants' qualifications differently depending on their race or ethnicity (see also Biernat and Kobrynowicz 1997; Yarkin, Town, and Wallston 1982).

Race-Coded Job Channeling

The first two categories of differential treatment focus on the decision to hire. Beyond this binary decision, employers also face decisions about where to place a worker within the organizational hierarchy. Here, at the point of job placement, we observe a third category of differential treatment. In our review of the testers' experiences, we noticed that applicants were sometimes encouraged to apply for different jobs than the ones initially advertised or about which they had inquired. In many cases, these instances of channeling suggest a race-coding of job types, whereby employers prefer whites for certain positions and minorities for others. In one case, Zuri, a black tester, applied for a sales position at a lighting store that had a sign in the front window stating "Salesperson Wanted." Zuri described the following interaction: "When she asked what position I was looking for I said I was open, but that since they were looking for a salesperson I would be interested in that. She smiled, put her head in her hand and her elbow on the table and said, 'I need a stock boy. Can you do stock boy?'" Zuri's white and Latino test partners, by contrast, were each able to apply for the advertised sales position.

Another black tester, Joe, was similarly channeled out of a customer service position in his application to a Japanese restaurant. Joe reported, "I told her I was there to apply for the waiter position and she told me that there were no server positions. I told her it was advertised in the paper, and she said there must have been a mistake. She said all she had available was a busboy position. I told her since there was no waiter position, I would apply for the busboy." Later that day, Kevin, his white test partner, was hired for the server position on the spot.

We also observed channeling of the Latino testers. Josue's fieldnotes of an audit at a clothing retailer begin by describing the "young white 20-something women running the place." One of the women interviewed him, asked about past work experience, and asked which job he was applying for. "I told her 'sales associate,'" Josue reported, and he presented a résumé on which the most recent job listed was as a sales assistant at a sporting goods store. "She then told me that there was a stock position and asked if I would be interested in that." Josue was offered the stocker job and asked to start the next day.

In many cases, these instances of channeling are coded as "positive responses" in the initial analyses. While our key concern is about access to employment of any kind, this general focus masks another form of racial bias at work. A closer analysis of the testers' experiences suggests that decisions about job placement, like hiring more generally, often follow a racial logic. We coded all instances of job channeling across both our teams and counted 53 cases (compared with 172 positive responses). By comparing the original job title to the suggested job type, we then categorized these cases as downward channeling, upward channeling, lateral channeling, or unknown. We define downward channeling as (1) a move from a job involving contact with customers to a job without (e.g., from server to busboy), (2) a move from a white-collar position to a manual position (e.g., from sales to stocker), or (3) a move in which hierarchy is clear (e.g., from supervisor to line worker). We define upward channeling as a move in the opposite direction. We focus on these two types of channeling for our current analysis. After eliminating cases in which all testers within a team were similarly channeled, we have 23 additional cases of differential treatment that were not recorded by our initial measurement of job offers and callbacks.

Like hiring criteria, job placement is also patterned by race (see Table 1). Black applicants were channeled into lower positions in nine cases, Latinos were channeled down in five cases, and whites experienced downward channeling in only one case. Many of these cases were restaurant jobs in which the tester applied for a position as a server but was steered to a job as a busboy or dishwasher. In almost all cases, the original position required extensive customer contact while the suggested position did not (e.g., salesperson to stocker). Testers were sometimes guided into lower positions because their résumés indicated limited work experience, but racial differences in channeling suggest that insufficient work experience was more penalizing for minorities than for whites. The one case of downward channeling among white applicants involved a tester presenting with a criminal background.

In fact, whites were more often channeled up than down. In at least six cases, white testers were encouraged to apply for jobs that were of a higher level or required more customer contact than the initial position they inquired about. In one case, the white tester was even encouraged to apply for a supervisory position, despite limited work experience. Kevin reported: "[The employer] then asked me if I had any experience in construction. I told him I did not. He asked if I would be okay working with people that have thick accents like his. I told him that was fine. He then told me that he wanted me to be his new company supervisor."

TABLE 1   Job Channeling by Race

Original Job Title	Suggested Job
Blacks Channeled Down	
Server	Busser
Counter person	Dishwasher/porter
Server	Busboy
Assistant manager	Entry fast-food position
Server	Busboy/runner
Retail sales	Maintenance
Counter person	Delivery
Sales	Stockboy
Sales	Not specified[a]
Latinos Channeled Down	
Server	Runner
Sales	Stock
Steam cleaning	Exterminator
Counter person	Delivery
Sales	Stock person
Whites Channeled Down	
Server	Busboy
Latinos Channeled Up	
Carwash attendant	Manager
Warehouse worker	Computer/office
Whites Channeled Up	
Line cook	Waitstaff
Mover	Office/telesales
Dishwasher	Waitstaff
Driver	Auto detailing
Kitchen job	"Front of the house" job
Receptionist	Company supervisor

Note: This table includes all cases of upward and downward channeling, except when all testers on a team were channeled similarly.
[a]Employer told tester that "sales might not be right for you."

Employers appear to have strong views about what kind of person is appropriate for what kind of job, based either on their own assumptions of worker competence or assumptions about what their clients expect or prefer in the appearance of those serving them. Consistent with the testers' field notes, employers appear to apply more stringent hiring criteria to minority workers, preferring whites for jobs that require greater skill or responsibility. In addition, minorities are disproportionately channeled out of customer service positions, consistent with other research in which employers view minority applicants as lacking communication skills or as otherwise discomfiting for customers. Although our testers presented highly effective

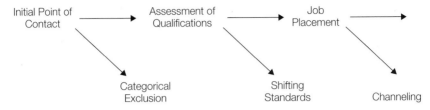

FIGURE 3 Discrimination at Three Decision Points.

styles of interpersonal communication, the cursory review process for these jobs often leaves group membership more salient than any individuating characteristics.

The three types of differential treatment we observe illustrate how employers enact their racial preferences in the hiring process. Rather than outward hostility or racial animus, we see more subtle forms of discouragement or rejection. At multiple points in the hiring process, black (or Latino) applicants face additional hurdles or barriers that reduce their chances of employment and affect the quality of jobs for which they are considered. Figure 3 illustrates the processess identified in the preceding discussion. At each of the three decision points, we see pathways deflected by various forms of racial bias. Subtle differences in employers' responses—often imperceptible to the applicants themselves—produce a pattern of outcomes systematically affected by race.

Complementing the quantitative indicators of differential treatment, these qualitative observations provide a rare window into the processes by which discrimination occurs. The three categories of differential treatment observed in these data point to the range of experiences that constitute discrimination in the employment process.[7] In a small number of cases, minority testers were disqualified early on in decisions that appear to reflect employers' fairly rigid preferences. These instances of categorical exclusion represent one of the most extreme forms of discrimination, wherein minority applicants have little opportunity to overcome employers' potential concerns. By contrast, a larger number of interactions suggest a more complicated set of negotiations at play. In evaluating applicant qualifications, minority applicants, and black men in particular, appear to be held to a higher standard than their white counterparts. Black men are disqualified more readily, or hired more reluctantly, than their white partners with identical skills and experience. Furthermore, racialized assessments of applicant quality and "fit" affect not only the decision to hire, but also decisions about job placement, with minority applicants more often channeled into positions involving less skill or customer contact. Together, these experiences illustrate how racial disadvantage is dynamically constructed and reinforced, with the assessment of applicant qualifications and suitability subject to interpretation and bias. While not an exhaustive catalogue of discrimination experiences, the fact that these dynamics are observed in natural settings' (with little prompting) attests to their relative frequency and regularity. Our testers' experiences suggest how race shapes employers' evaluations in subtle but systematic ways, with important implications for structuring opportunity along racial lines.

DISCUSSION

Sending trained testers with equivalent résumés to apply for entry-level jobs reveals clear evidence of discrimination among low-wage employers in New York City. Blacks were only half as likely to receive a callback or job offer relative to equally qualified whites; moreover, black and Latino applicants with clean backgrounds fared no better than a white applicant just released from prison. The magnitude of these racial disparities provides vivid evidence of the continuing significance of race in contemporary low-wage labor markets. There is a racial hierarchy among young men favoring whites, then Latinos, and finally blacks as the candidates of last resort.

The episodes of discrimination recorded in this study were seldom characterized by overt racism or hostility. In fact, our testers rarely perceived any signs of clear prejudice. It was only through side-by-side comparisons of our testers' experiences that patterns of subtle but consistent differential treatment were revealed. Minority applicants were disqualified more readily and hired more reluctantly than their white partners with identical skills and experience. Additionally, black and Latino applicants were routinely channeled into positions requiring less customer contact and more manual work than their white counterparts. In interactions between applicants and employers, we see a small number of cases that reflect employers' seemingly rigid racial preferences. More often, differential treatment emerged in the social interaction of the job interview. Employers appeared to see more potential in the stated qualifications of white applicants, and they more commonly viewed white applicants as a better fit for more desirable jobs.

Our findings of discrimination are particularly striking because the testers in this study represent a best-case scenario for low-wage job seekers. The testers were college-educated young men with effective styles of self-presentation. Although posing as high school graduates with more limited skills, these young men stood well above the typical applicant for these low-wage jobs. The effects of race among individuals with fewer hard and soft skill advantages may well be larger than those estimated here.

At the same time, while we find robust evidence of racial discrimination, we should be careful not to interpret these results as showing the level of discrimination actively experienced by minority job seekers in the New York labor market. Our sampling design, based on employers, not workers, over-represents small firms relative to their share of employment. The sample includes many restaurants and independent retailers for whom hiring is less bureaucratic, and who lack the human resource departments that manage the equal employment opportunity obligations of large firms (Dobbin et al. 1993). Nevertheless, our sampled employers well represent the kinds of low-skill service work that dominate low-wage urban labor markets.

A second limitation on the generalizability of our findings results from our sampling procedures based on classified advertisements. Surveys of job seekers suggest that 25 to 30 percent of low skill jobs are filled by classified ads; the remainder are filled through some combination of network referrals, walk-in applications, and employment agencies (Holzer 1987). These search strategies may generate a different distribution of employers from that reported here. Some argue that the focus on jobs advertised through metropolitan newspapers understates the extent of discrimination. Firms that wish to discriminate, it is argued, are more likely to advertise job openings through more restrictive channels, such as networks of existing employees, employment agencies, or more selective publications (Elliott 2000; Fix and Struyk 1993; Petersen, Saporta, and Seidel 2000). Others, by contrast, argue that any random sample of employers will overstate the extent of discrimination actually experienced by job seekers. If minority applicants can identify and avoid firms that discriminate, the actual incidence of labor market discrimination will be correspondingly reduced (Becker 1957; Heckman 1998).

Of course, minority workers' ability to avoid the effects of discrimination by self-selecting into nondiscriminatory firms requires that a sufficient number of nondiscriminatory employers exist; that there are no differences in the quality of jobs offered by employers who are more and less likely to discriminate; and that the search costs necessary to locate nondiscriminatory employers are trivial. Future research using microdata to track the search patterns and outcomes of black and white job seekers could better address these issues. From our data, we can safely conclude that job searches across a wide range of employers represented by the classified ads of five New York newspapers reveal substantial discrimination. Understanding how job seekers adapt to this reality remains a challenge for future research.

Our findings for the New York City labor market add to evidence of racial discrimination in employment reported from recent field experiments in Milwaukee, Boston, and Chicago (Bertrand and Mullainathan 2004; Pager 2003). The significant evidence of discrimination found in these studies contrasts sharply with recent survey research showing small racial differences in wages (Farkas and Vicknair 1996; Neal and Johnson 1996). How might these disparate findings be reconciled? First, as noted above, the presence of discrimination in the labor market may lead workers to differentially sort across employers, such that minority job seekers queue for jobs offered by employers who are less likely to discriminate.

These dynamics can lead to longer search or wait times for minority job seekers, which might not be reflected in ultimate wage offers. Indeed, data from the late 1990s show that the unemployment spells of black men (3.1 months) are about twice as long as those for whites (1.6 months) (Gottschalck 2003:2). This suggests that the primary effects of discrimination on labor market outcomes may be reflected in employment differentials rather than wages.[8]

Second, the experience of discrimination may add to the psychic costs of the job search process, prompting some to opt out altogether. If discrimination discourages all but the most motivated and able black job seekers, black wage earners would represent an increasingly select group. Since the 1990s, increasing numbers of young black men have dropped out of the formal labor market, contributing to an artificial convergence of black and white wages (Western and Pettit 2005). Without effectively accounting for the processes that precede labor force participation—including the discouraging effects of discrimination—wage estimates can account for only one incomplete picture of the larger employment process.

Our findings add to a large research program demonstrating the continuing contribution of discrimination to racial inequality in the postcivil rights era. Still, significant questions remain unanswered. The audit experiment necessarily focuses on employers' hiring behaviors but does not examine the skills, preferences, and networks of job seekers. We do not know, and few research designs have been devised to test, the relative magnitude of the effects of discrimination compared with the effects of human and social capital. Such an analysis would need to study both employers as they screen job applicants and workers as they search for jobs.

The effects of discrimination, relative to human and social capital, should also be defined broadly. As evidence of discrimination in the post-civil rights era accumulates, new research should go beyond determining whether discrimination is present to consider how the effects of discrimination unfold over the life cycle and across social space. Episodes of discrimination may not only cause unemployment at one point in time, but may have long-term effects that weaken minority workers' attachment to the labor market and reduce labor force participation. Discrimination may produce broad cultural effects in which work itself is de-legitimated as a fair source of opportunity. The effects of discrimination may also vary across the population, concentrating perhaps among the young men whose employment rates are lowest. Tracing these larger and more varied effects of discrimination show both the advantages and limits of the experimental method used here. The experiment allows us to infer discrimination with great certainty, but the effects of discrimination are narrowly defined. The broader effects of discrimination— on the cultural dimensions of economic life and over the life course—are harder to pinpoint but may indicate more fundamental and intractable inequalities. A research agenda that includes these wider consequences would be less skeptical that discrimination exists and more curious about its continuing effects on not just employment inequality, but on American race relations more broadly.

NOTES

1. Theories of statistical discrimination also predict employer responsiveness to individual characteristics (e.g., Altonji and Pierret 2001; Oettinger 1996; cf. Pager and Karafin 2009).
2. Results from Pager (2003) suggest that providing information about a criminal record to employers who do not request the information does little to affect hiring decisions.
3. In a model pooling cases from the two teams, with main effects for team and criminal background, the white-Latino gap becomes statistically significant. The generality of this result certainly deserves more study. The Puerto Ricans of New York that our Latino testers represent are a longstanding community of U.S. citizens. In other local labor markets, where markers of citizenship and accent are more prominent sources of difference, evidence of ethnic discrimination may be stronger.
4. The overall rate of positive responses is lower for all testers relative to the results presented in Figure 1. This is likely due to the staggered fielding of teams and resulting differences in the composition of employers audited across the two time periods.
5. In an additional 13 cases, both white and Latino testers received positive responses; in seven cases, the Latino tester alone was selected.
6. The denominator of 47 represents the total number of cases of black-white differential treatment from the first (N = 28) and second (N = 19) teams. In calculating the numerator, we do not include a number of additional cases of differential treatment resulting from applications in which there was little or no personal contact between testers and the employer (rates of personal contact were similar by race of tester). In such cases, differential treatment may reflect categorical exclusion (based on a visual assessment of the candidate), shifting standards (based on a review of the completed applications), random error, or something else.
7. To be sure, our study captures only a few of the many pathways in the employment process that are potentially affected by racial bias. Beyond our window of observation, the pathways of this diagram would presumably continue along later points in the employment process, including wage-setting decisions, training opportunities, promotion, and termination decisions. This research represents one incremental contribution to understanding—and documenting—the varied decision points that may be affected by race.
8. Johnson and Neal (1998), for example, find that after controlling for cognitive ability and other human capital characteristics, black-white differences in employment among young men remain large and statistically significant. The importance of employment over wages for racial inequality in economic status is likely to be especially great for young non-college-educated men, for whom the overall level of wage dispersion is low. Later in the life course, as wage dispersion increases and labor force experience accumulates, the racial wage gap becomes more pronounced (Tomaskovic-Devey, Thomas, and Johnson 2005). For a historical example, see Whatley (1990), who shows that despite the substantial racial barriers to employment that existed among Northern firms after World War I, blacks and whites experienced remarkably similar wage rates.

REFERENCES

Aigner, Dennis J. and Glen G. Cain. 1977. "Statistical Theories of Discrimination in Labor Market." *Industrial and Labor Relations Review* 30:749–76.

Altonji, Joseph G. and Charles R. Pierret. 2001. "Employer Learning and Statistical Discrimination." *Journal of Economics* 116:313–50.

Becker, Gary S. 1957. *The Economics of Discrimination.* Chicago, IL: University of Chicago Press.

Bertrand, Marianne and Sendhil Mullainathan. 2004. "Are Emily and Greg More Employable than Lakisha and Jamal? A Field Experiment on Labor Market Discrimination." *American Economic Review* 94:991–1013.

Biernat, Monica and Diane D. Kobrynowicz. 1997. "Gender and Race-Based Standards of Competence: Lower Minimum Standards but Higher Ability Standards for Devalued Groups." *Journal of Personality and Social Psychology* 72:544–57.

Bodenhausen, Galen. 1988. "Stereotypic Biases in Social Decision Making and Memory: Testing Process Models of Stereotype Use." *Journal of Personality and Social Psychology* 55(5):726–37.

Darity, William, Jr. and Patrick A. Mason. 1998. "Evidence on Discrimination in Employment: Codes of Color, Codes of Gender." *The Journal of Economic Perspectives* 12:63–90.

Darley, John M. and Paget H. Gross. 1983. "A Hypothesis-Confirming Bias in Labeling Effects." *Journal of Personality and Social Psychology* 44:20–33.

Dobbin, Frank, J. Sutton, J. Meyer, and W. R. Scott. 1993. "Equal Opportunity Law and the Construction of Internal Labor Markets." *American Journal of Sociology* 99:396–427.

Dovidio, John F. and Samuel L. Gaertner. 2000. "Aversive Racism and Selection Decisions." *Psychological Science* 11:315–19.

Elliott, James R. 2000. "Class, Race, and Job Matching in Contemporary Urban Labor Markets." *Social Science Quarterly* 81:1036–52.

Farkas, George and Keven Vicknair. 1996. "Appropriate Tests of Racial Wage Discrimination Require Controls for Cognitive Skill: Comment on Cancio, Evans, and Maume." *American Sociological Review* 61:557–60.

Fiske, Susan. 1998. "Stereotyping, Prejudice, and Discrimination." Pp. 357–411 in *The Handbook of Social Psychology,* edited by D. Gilbert, S. Fiske, and G. Lindzey. Boston, MA: McGraw Hill.

Fix, Michael and Raymond J. Struyk, eds. 1993. *Clear and Convincing Evidence: Measurement of Discrimination in America.* Washington, DC: Urban Institute Press.

Gilbert, Daniel T. and J. Gregory Hixon. 1991. "The Trouble of Thinking: Activation and Application of Stereotypical Beliefs." *Journal of Personality and Social Psychology* 60(4):509–17.

Gottschalck, Alfred O. 2003. "Dynamics of Economic Well-Being: Spells of Unemployment, 1996–1999." *Current Population Reports.* Washington, DC: US Census Bureau.

Heckman, James J. 1998. "Detecting Discrimination." *The Journal of Economic Perspectives* 12:101–116.

Holzer, Harry J. 1987. "Informal Job Search and Black Youth Unemployment." *American Economic Review* 77:446–52.

_____. 1996. *What Employers Want: Job Prospects of Less-Educated Workers.* New York: Russell Sage Foundation.

Holzer, Harry J. and Paul Offner. 2001. "Trends in Employment Outcomes of Young Black Men." Georgetown University, Washington, DC. Unpublished manuscript.

Johnson, William and Derek Neal. 1998. "Basic Skills and the Black-White Earnings Gap." Pp. 480–500 in *Black-White Test Score Differences,* edited by C. Jencks and M. Phillips. Washington, DC: Brookings Institution.

Kirschenman, Joleen and Katherine Neckerman. 1991. "'We'd Love to Hire Them, but…': The Meaning of Race for Employers." Pp. 203–234 in *The Urban Underclass,* edited by C. Jencks and P. Peterson. Washington, DC: Brookings Institute.

Moss, Philip and Chris Tilly. 2001. *Stories Employers Tell: Race, Skill, and Hiring in America.* New York: Russell Sage.

Neal, Derek and William Johnson. 1996. "The Role of Premarket Factors in Black-White Wage Differences." *Journal of Political Economy* 104:869–95.

Oettinger, Gerald S. 1996. "Statistical Discrimination and the Early Career Evolution of the Black-White Wage Gap." *Journal of Labor Economics* 14:52–78.

O'Neill, June. 1990. "The Role of Human Capital in Earnings Differences between White and Black Men." *The Journal of Economic Perspectives* 4(4):25–45.

Pager, Devah. 2003. "The Mark of a Criminal Record." *American Journal of Sociology* 108:937–75.

_____. 2007b. *Marked: Race, Crime, and Finding Work in an Era of Mass Incarceration.* Chicago, IL: University of Chicago Press.

Pager, Devah and Diana Karafin. 2009. "Bayesian Bigot? Statistical Discrimination, Stereotypes, and Employer Decision-Making." *Annals of the American Academy of Political and Social Science* 621(1):70–93.

Pager, Devah and Lincoln Quillian. 2005. "Walking the Talk: What Employers Say Versus What They Do." *American Sociological Review* 70(3):355–80.

Petersen, Trond, Ishak Saporta, and Marc-David L. Seidel. 2000. "Offering a Job: Meritocracy and Social Networks." *American Journal of Sociology* 106:763–816.

Pettit, Becky and Bruce Western. 2004. "Mass Imprisonment and the Life Course: Race and Class Inequality in U.S. Incarceration." *American Sociological Review* 59:151–69.

Roscigno, Vincent J., Lisette Garcia, Sherry Mong, and Reginald Byron. 2007. "Racial Discrimination at Work: Its Occurrence, Dimensions, and Consequences." *The New Black: Alternative Paradigms and Strategies for the 21st Century Research in Race and Ethnic Relations* 14:131–55.

Tomaskovic-Devey, Donald, Melvin Thomas, and Kecia Johnson. 2005. "Race and the Accumulation of Human Capital across the Career. A Theoretical Model and Fixed-Effects Application." *American Journal of Sociology* 111(1):58–89.

Trope, Yaacov and Erik P. Thomson. 1997. "Looking for Truth in All the Wrong Places? Asymmetric Search of Individuating Information about Stereotyped Group Members." *Journal of Personality and Social Psychology* 73(2):229–41.

Waldinger, Roger and Michael I. Lichter. 2003. *How the Other Half Works: Immigration and the Social Organization of Labor.* Berkeley, CA: University of California Press.

Western, Bruce and Becky Pettit. 2005. "Black-White Wage Inequality, Employment Rates, and Incarceration." *American Journal of Sociology* 111:553–78.

Whatley, Warren C. 1990. "Getting a Foot in the Door. 'Learning,' State Dependence, and the Racial Integration of Firms." *The Journal of Economic History* 50(1):43–66.

Wilson, William Julius. 1996. *When Work Disappears: The World of the New Urban Poor.* New York: Vintage Books.

Yarkin, K. L., J. P. Town, and B. S. Wallston. 1982. "Blacks and Women Must Try Harder. Stimulus Person's Race and Sex Attributions of Causality." *Personality and Social Psychology Bulletin* 8:21–24.

 QUESTIONS FOR CRITICAL THINKING

Reading 27

1. The authors of this article illustrate that persons in charge of hiring perpetuate racial inequality, despite beliefs that racial discrimination in the workplace has all but disappeared. How does this study demonstrate the continued need for programs like affirmative action?

2. As discussed in the introduction to this section, there remains a significant wage gap with regard to race in the United States. How do the hiring practices revealed in this study maintain this gap?

3. What are some ways of correcting race-biased hiring practices in the workplace? What do you see as the likelihood of such corrective policies being enacted?

Reading 28

THE GLASS ESCALATOR
Hidden Advantages for Men in the "Female" Professions

CHRISTINE L. WILLIAMS

The sex segregation of the U.S. labor force is one of the most perplexing and tenacious problems in our society. Even though the proportion of men and women in the labor force is approaching parity (particularly for younger cohorts of workers) (U.S. Department of Labor 1991:18), men and women are still generally confined to predominantly single-sex occupations. Forty percent of men or women would have to change major occupational categories to achieve equal representation of men and women in all jobs (Reskin and Roos 1990:6), but even this figure underestimates the true degree of sex segregation. It is extremely rare to find specific jobs where equal numbers of men and women are engaged in the same activities in the same industries (Bielby and Baron 1984).

Most studies of sex segregation in the workforce have focused on women's experiences in male-dominated occupations. Both researchers and advocates for social change have focused on the barriers faced by women who try to integrate predominantly male fields. Few have looked at the "flip-side" of occupational sex segregation: the exclusion of men from predominantly female occupations (exceptions include Schreiber 1979; Williams 1989; Zimmer 1988). But the fact is that men are less likely to enter female sex-typed occupations than women are to enter male-dominated jobs (Jacobs 1989). Reskin and Roos, for example, were able to identify 33 occupations in which female representation increased by more than nine percentage points between 1970 and 1980, but only three occupations in which the proportion of men increased as radically (1990: 20–21).

In this paper, I examine men's underrepresentation in four predominantly female occupations—nursing, librarianship, elementary school teaching, and social work. Throughout the twentieth century, these occupations have been identified with "women's work"—even though prior to the Civil War, men were more likely to be employed in these areas. These four occupations, often called the female "semi-professions" (Hodson and Sullivan 1990),

Christine L. Williams, "The Glass Escalator: Hidden Advantages for Men in the 'Female' Professions" from *Social Problems* 39, no. 3 (August 1992). Reprinted with the permission of the author and the University of California Press.

today range from 5.5 percent male (in nursing) to 32 percent male (in social work). These percentages have not changed substantially in decades. In fact, two of these professions—librarianship and social work—have experienced declines in the proportions of men since 1975. Nursing is the only one of the four experiencing noticeable changes in sex composition, with the proportion of men increasing 80 percent between 1975 and 1990. Even so, men continue to be a tiny minority of all nurses.

. . .

METHODS

I conducted in-depth interviews with 76 men and 23 women in four occupations from 1985 to 1991. Interviews were conducted in four metropolitan areas: San Francisco/Oakland, California; Austin, Texas; Boston, Massachusetts; and Phoenix, Arizona. These four areas were selected because they show considerable variation in the proportions of men in the four professions. For example, Austin has one of the highest percentages of men in nursing (7.7 percent), whereas Phoenix's percentage is one of the lowest (2.7 percent) (U.S. Bureau of the Census 1980). The sample was generated using "snowballing" techniques. Women were included in the sample to gauge their feelings and responses to men who enter "their" professions.

. . .

DISCRIMINATION IN HIRING

Contrary to the experience of many women in the male-dominated professions, many of the men and women I spoke to indicated that there is a *preference* for hiring men in these occupations. A Texas librarian at a junior high school said that his school district "would hire a male over a female."

I: Why do you think that is?

R: Because there are so few, and the . . . ones that they do have, the library directors seem to really . . . think they're doing great jobs. I don't know, maybe they just feel they're being progressive or something, [but] I have had a real sense that they really appreciate having a male, particularly at the junior high. . . . As I said, when seven of us lost our jobs from the high schools and were redistributed, there were only four positions at junior high, and I got one of them. Three of the librarians, some who had been here longer than I had with the school district, were put down in elementary schools as librarians. And I definitely think that being male made a difference in my being moved to the junior high rather than an elementary school.

Many of the men perceived their token status as males in predominantly female occupations as an *advantage* in hiring and promotions. I asked an Arizona teacher whether his specialty (elementary special education) was an unusual area for men compared to other areas within education. He said,

> Much more so. I am extremely marketable in special education. That's not why I got into the field. But I am extremely marketable because I am a man.

In several cases, the more female-dominated the specialty, the greater the apparent preference for men. For example, when asked if he encountered any problem getting a job in pediatrics, a Massachusetts nurse said,

> No, no, none. . . . I've heard this from managers and supervisory-type people with men in pediatrics: "It's nice to have a man because it's such a female-dominated profession."

However, there were some exceptions to this preference for men in the most female-dominated specialties. In some cases, formal policies actually barred men from certain jobs. This was the case in some rural Texas school districts, which refused to hire men in the youngest grades (K–3). Some nurses also reported being excluded from positions in obstetrics and gynecology wards, a policy encountered more frequently in private Catholic hospitals.

But often the pressures keeping men out of certain specialties were more subtle than this. Some men described being "tracked" into practice areas within their professions which were considered more legitimate for men. For example, one Texas man described how he was pushed into administration and planning in social work, even though "I'm not interested in writing policy; I'm much more interested in research and clinical stuff." A nurse who is interested in pursuing graduate study in family and child health in Boston said he was dissuaded from entering the program specialty in favor of a concentration in "adult nursing." A kindergarten teacher described the difficulty of finding a job in his specialty after graduation: "I was recruited immediately to start getting into a track to become an administrator. And it was men who recruited me. It was men that ran the system at that time, especially in Los Angeles."

This tracking may bar men from the most female-identified specialties within these professions. But men are effectively being "kicked upstairs" in the process. Those specialties considered more legitimate practice areas for men also tend to be the most prestigious, better paying ones. A distinguished kindergarten teacher, who had been voted citywide "Teacher of the Year," told me that even though people were pleased to see him in the classroom, "there's been some encouragement to think about administration, and there's been some encouragement to think about teaching at the university level or something like that, or supervisory-type position." That is, despite his aptitude and interest in staying in the classroom, he felt pushed in the direction of administration.

The effect of this "tracking" is the opposite of that experienced by women in male-dominated occupations. Researchers have reported that many women encounter a "glass ceiling" in their efforts to scale organizational and professional hierarchies. That is, they are constrained by invisible barriers to promotion in their careers, caused mainly by sexist attitudes of men in the highest positions (Freeman 1990). In contrast to the "glass ceiling," many of the men I interviewed seem to encounter a "glass escalator." Often, despite their intentions, they face invisible pressures to move up in their professions. As if on a moving escalator, they must work to stay in place.

A public librarian specializing in children's collections (a heavily female-dominated concentration) described an encounter with this "escalator" in his very first job out of library school. In his first six-months' evaluation, his supervisors commended him for his good work in storytelling and related activities, but they criticized him for "not shooting high enough."

> Seriously. That's literally what they were telling me. They assumed that because I was a male—and they told me this—and that I was being hired right out of graduate school, that somehow I wasn't doing the kind of management-oriented work that they thought I should be doing. And as a result, really they had a lot of bad marks, as it were, against me on my evaluation. And I said I couldn't believe this!

Throughout his 10-year career, he had had to struggle to remain in children's collections.

The glass escalator does not operate at all levels. In particular, men in academia reported some gender-based discrimination in the highest positions due to their universities' commitment to affirmative action. Two nursing professors reported that they felt their own chances of promotion to deanships were nil because their universities viewed the position of nursing dean as a guaranteed female appointment in an otherwise heavily male-dominated administration. One California social work professor reported his university canceled its search for a dean because no minority male or female candidates had been placed on their short list. It was rumored that other schools on campus were permitted to go forward with their searches—even though they also failed to put forward names of minority candidates—because the higher administration perceived it to be "easier" to fulfill affirmative action goals in the social work school. The interviews provide greater evidence of the "glass escalator" at work in the lower levels of these professions.

Of course, men's motivations also play a role in their advancement to higher professional positions. I do not mean to suggest that the men I talked to all resented the informal tracking they experienced. For many men, leaving the most female-identified areas of their professions helped them resolve internal conflicts involving their masculinity. One man left his job as a school social worker to work in a methadone drug treatment program, not because he was encouraged to leave by his colleagues, but because "I think there was some macho shit there, to tell you the truth, because I remember feeling a little uncomfortable there . . .; it didn't feel right to me." Another social worker, employed in the mental health services department of a large urban area in California, reflected on his move into administration:

> The more I think about it, through our discussion, I'm sure that's a large part of why I wound up in administration. It's okay for a man to do the administration. In fact, I don't know if I fully answered a question that you asked a little while ago about how did being male contribute to my advancing in the field. I was saying it wasn't because I got any special favoritism as a man, but . . . I think . . . because I'm a man, I felt a need to get into this kind of position. I may have worked harder toward it, may have competed harder for it, than most women would do, even women who think about doing administrative work.

Elsewhere I have speculated on the origins of men's tendency to define masculinity through single-sex work environments (Williams 1989). Clearly, personal ambition does play a role in accounting for men's movement into more "male-defined" arenas within these professions. But these occupations also structure opportunities for males independent of their individual desires or motives.

The interviews suggest that men's underrepresentation in these professions cannot be attributed to discrimination in hiring or promotions. Many of the men indicated that they received preferential treatment because they were men. Although men mentioned gender discrimination in the hiring process, for the most part they were channeled into the more "masculine" specialties within these professions, which ironically meant being "tracked" into better-paying and more prestigious specialties.

SUPERVISORS AND COLLEAGUES: THE WORKING ENVIRONMENT

Researchers claim that subtle forms of workplace discrimination push women out of male-dominated occupations (Jacobs 1989; Reskin and Hartmann 1986). In particular, women report feeling excluded from informal leadership and decision-making networks, and they sense hostility from their male co-workers, which makes them feel uncomfortable and unwanted (Carothers and Crull 1984). Respondents in this study were asked about their relationships with supervisors and female colleagues to ascertain whether men also experienced "poisoned" work environments when entering gender atypical occupations.

A major difference in the experience of men and women in nontraditional occupations is that men in these situations are far more likely to be supervised by a member of their own sex. In each of the four professions I studied, men are overrepresented in administrative and managerial capacities, or, as is the case of nursing, their positions in the organizational hierarchy are governed by men (Grimm and Stern 1974; Phenix 1987; Schmuck 1987; Williams 1989; York, Henley and Gamble 1987). Thus, unlike women who enter "male fields," the men in these professions often work under the direct supervision of other men.

Many of the men interviewed reported that they had good rapport with their male supervisors. Even in professional school, some men reported extremely close relationships with their male professors. For example, a Texas librarian described an unusually intimate association with two male professors in graduate school:

> I can remember a lot of times in the classroom there would be discussions about a particular topic or issue, and the conversation would spill over into their office hours, after the class was over. And even though there were . . . a couple of the other women that had been in on the discussion, they weren't there. And I don't know if that was preferential or not . . . it certainly carried over into personal life as well. Not just at the school and that sort of thing. I mean, we would get together for dinner. . . .

• • •

Other men reported similar closeness with their professors. A Texas psychotherapist recalled his relationships with his male professors in social work school:

> I made it a point to make a golfing buddy with one of the guys that was in administration. He and I played golf a lot. He was the guy who kind of ran the research training, the research part of the master's program. Then there was a sociologist who ran the other part of the research program. He and I developed a good friendship.

This close mentoring by male professors contrasts with the reported experience of women in nontraditional occupations. Others have noted a lack of solidarity among women in nontraditional occupations. Writing about military academies, for example, Yoder describes the failure of token women to mentor succeeding generations of female cadets. She argues that women attempt to play down their gender difference from men because it is the source of scorn and derision.

> Because women felt unaccepted by their male colleagues, one of the last things they wanted to do was to emphasize their gender. Some women thought that, if they kept company with other women, this would highlight their gender and would further isolate them from

male cadets. These women desperately wanted to be accepted as cadets, not as *women* cadets. Therefore, they did everything from not wearing skirts as an option with their uniforms to avoiding being a part of a group of women. (Yoder 1989:532)

Men in nontraditional occupations face a different scenario—their gender is construed as a *positive* difference. Therefore, they have an incentive to bond together and emphasize their distinctiveness from the female majority.

• • •

Openly gay men may encounter less favorable treatment at the hands of their supervisors. For example, a nurse in Texas stated that one of the physicians he worked with preferred to staff the operating room with male nurses exclusively—as long as they weren't gay. Stigma associated with homosexuality leads some men to enhance, or even exaggerate their "masculine" qualities, and may be another factor pushing men into more "acceptable" specialties for men.

Not all men who work in these occupations are supervised by men. Many of the men interviewed who had female bosses also reported high levels of acceptance—although levels of intimacy with women seemed lower than with other men. In some cases, however, men reported feeling shut out from decision making when the higher administration was constituted entirely by women. I asked an Arizona librarian whether men in the library profession were discriminated against in hiring because of their sex:

Professionally speaking, people go to considerable lengths to keep that kind of thing out of their [hiring] deliberations. Personally, is another matter. It's pretty common around here to talk about the "old girl network." This is one of the few libraries that I've had any intimate knowledge of which is actually controlled by women. . . . Most of the department heads and upper-level administrators are women. And there's an "old girl network" that works just like the "old boy network," except that the important conferences take place in the women's room rather than on the golf course. But the political mechanism is the same, the exclusion of the other sex from decision making is the same. The reasons are the same. It's somewhat discouraging. . . .

Although I did not interview many supervisors, I did include 23 women in my sample to ascertain their perspectives about the presence of men in their professions. All of the women I interviewed claimed to be supportive of their male colleagues, but some conveyed ambivalence. For example, a social work professor said she would like to see more men enter the social work profession, particularly in the clinical specialty (where they are underrepresented). Indeed, she favored affirmative action hiring guidelines for men in the profession. Yet, she resented the fact that her department hired "another white male" during a recent search.

· · ·

Even outside work, most of the men interviewed said they felt fully accepted by their female colleagues. They were usually included in informal socialization occasions with the women—even though this frequently meant attending baby showers or Tupperware parties. Many said that they declined offers to attend these events because they were not interested in "women's things," although several others claimed to attend everything: The minority men I interviewed seemed to feel the least comfortable in these informal contexts. One social worker in Arizona was asked about socializing with his female colleagues:

> I: So in general, for example, if all the employees were going to get together to have a party, or celebrate a bridal shower or whatever, would you be invited along with the rest of the group?
>
> R: They would invite me, I would say, somewhat reluctantly. Being a black male, working with all white females, it did cause some outside problems. So I didn't go to a lot of functions with them. . . .
>
> I: You felt that there was some tension there on the level of your acceptance . . . ?
>
> R: Yeah. It was OK working, but on the outside, personally, there was some tension there. It never came out, that they said, "Because of who you are we can't invite you" (laughs), and I wouldn't have done anything anyway. I would have probably respected them more for saying what was on their minds. But I never felt completely in with the group.

Some single men also said they felt uncomfortable socializing with married female colleagues because it gave the "wrong impression." But in general, the men said that they felt very comfortable around their colleagues and described their work places as very congenial for men. It appears unlikely, therefore, that men's underrepresentation in these professions is due to hostility toward men on the part of supervisors or women workers.

 ## DISCRIMINATION FROM "OUTSIDERS"

The most compelling evidence of discrimination against men in these professions is related to their dealings with the public. Men often encounter negative stereotypes when they come into contact with clients or "outsiders"—people they meet outside of work. For instance, it is popularly assumed that male nurses are gay. Librarians encounter images of themselves as "wimpy" and asexual. Male social workers describe being typecast as "feminine" and "passive." Elementary school teachers are often confronted by suspicions that they are pedophiles. One kindergarten teacher described an experience that occurred early in his career, which was related to him years afterward by his principal:

> He indicated to me that parents had come to him and indicated to him that they had a problem with the fact that I was a male. . . . I recall almost exactly what he said. There were three specific concerns that the parents had: One parent said, "How can he love my child; he's a man." The second thing that I recall, he said the parent said, "He has a beard." And the third thing was, "Aren't you concerned about homosexuality?"

Such suspicions often cause men in all four professions to alter their work behavior to guard against sexual abuse charges, particularly in those specialties requiring intimate contact with women and children.

Men are very distressed by these negative stereotypes, which tend to undermine their self-esteem and to cause them to second-guess their motivations for entering these fields. A California teacher said,

> If I tell men that I don't know, that I'm meeting for the first time, that that's what I do, . . . sometimes there's a look on their faces that, you know, "Oh, couldn't get a real job?"

When asked if his wife, who is also an elementary school teacher, encounters the same kind of prejudice, he said,

> No, it's accepted because she's a woman. . . . I think people would see that as a . . . step up, you know. "Oh you're not a housewife; you've got a career. That's great . . . that you're out there working. And you have a daughter, but you're still out there working. You decided not to stay home, and you went out there and got a job." Whereas for me, it's more like I'm supposed to be out working anyway, even though I'd rather be home with [my daughter].

Unlike women who enter traditionally male professions, men's movement into these jobs is perceived by the "outside world" as a step down in status. This particular form of discrimination may be most significant in explaining why men are underrepresented in these professions. Men who otherwise might show interest in and aptitudes for such careers are probably discouraged from pursuing them because of the negative popular stereotypes associated with the men who work in them. This is a crucial difference from the experience of women in nontraditional professions: "My daughter, the physician," resonates far more favorably in most people's ears than "my son, the nurse."

Many of the men in my sample identified the stigma of working in a female-identified occupation as the major barrier to more men entering their professions. However, for the most part, they claimed that these negative stereotypes were not a factor in their own decisions to join these occupations. Most respondents didn't consider entering these fields until well into adulthood, after working in some related occupation. Several social workers and librarians even claimed they were not aware that men were a minority in their chosen professions. Either they had no well-defined image or stereotype, or their contacts and mentors were predominantly men. For example, prior to entering library school, many librarians held part-time jobs in university libraries, where there are proportionally more men than in the profession generally. Nurses and elementary school teachers were more aware that mostly women worked in these jobs, and this was often a matter of some concern to them. However, their choices were ultimately legitimized by mentors, or by encouraging friends or family members who implicitly reassured them that entering these occupations would not typecast them as feminine. In some cases, men were told by recruiters there were special advancement opportunities for men in these fields, and they entered them expecting rapid promotion to administrative positions.

> I: Did it ever concern you when you were making the decision to enter nursing school, the fact that it is a female-dominated profession?
>
> R: Not really. I never saw myself working on the floor. I saw myself pretty much going into administration, just getting the background and then getting a job someplace as a supervisor and then working, getting up into administration.

Because of the unique circumstances of their recruitment, many of the respondents did not view their occupational choices as inconsistent with a male gender role, and they generally avoided the negative stereotypes directed against men in these fields.

Indeed, many of the men I interviewed claimed that they did not encounter negative professional stereotypes until they had worked in these fields for several years. Popular prejudices can be damaging to self-esteem and probably push some men out of these professions altogether. Yet, ironically, they sometimes contribute to the "glass escalator" effect I have been describing. Men seem to encounter the most vituperative criticism from the public when they are in the most female-identified specialties. Public concerns sometimes result in their being shunted into more "legitimate" positions for men. A librarian formerly in charge of a branch library's children's collection, who now works in the reference department of the city's main library, describes his experience:

> R: Some of the people [who frequented the branch library] complained that they didn't want to have a man doing the storytelling scenario. And I got transferred here to the central library in an equivalent job. . . . I thought that I did a good job. And I had been told by my supervisor that I was doing a good job.

I: Have you ever considered filing some sort of lawsuit to get that other job back?

R: Well, actually, the job I've gotten now . . . well, it's a reference librarian; it's what I wanted in the first place. I've got a whole lot more authority here. I'm also in charge of the circulation desk. And I've recently been promoted because of my new stature, so . . . no, I'm not considering trying to get that other job back.

The negative stereotypes about men who do "women's work" can push men out of specific jobs. However, to the extent that they channel men into more "legitimate" practice areas, their effects can actually be positive. Instead of being a source of discrimination, these prejudices can add to the "glass escalator effect" by pressuring men to move *out* of the most female-identified areas, and *up* to those regarded more legitimate and prestigious for men.

REFERENCES

Bielby, William T., and James N. Baron. 1984. "A Woman's Place Is with Other Women: Sex Segregation within Organizations." Pp. 27–55 in *Sex Segregation in the Workplace: Trends, Explanations, Remedies,* edited by Barbara Reskin. Washington, D.C.: National Academy Press.

Carothers, Suzanne C., and Peggy Crull. 1984. "Contrasting Sexual Harassment in Female-Dominated and Male-Dominated Occupations." Pp. 220–27 in *My Troubles Are Going to Have Trouble with Me: Everyday Trials and Triumphs of Women Workers,* edited by Karen B. Sacks and Dorothy Remy. New Brunswick, NJ: Rutgers University Press.

Freeman, Sue J. M. 1990. *Managing Lives: Corporate Women and Social Change.* Amherst, MA: University of Massachusetts Press.

Grimm, James W., and Robert N. Stern. 1974. "Sex Roles and Internal Labor Market Structures: The Female Semi-Professions." *Social Problems* 21:690–705.

Hodson, Randy, and Teresa Sullivan. 1990. *The Social Organization of Work.* Belmont, CA: Wadsworth Publishing Co.

Jacobs, Jerry. 1989. *Revolving Doors: Sex Segregation and Women's Careers.* Stanford, CA: Stanford University Press.

Phenix, Katherine. 1987. "The Status of Women Librarians." *Frontiers* 9:36–40.

Reskin, Barbara, and Heidi Hartmann. 1986. *Women's Work, Men's Work: Sex Segregation on the Job.* Washington, D.C.: National Academy Press.

Reskin, Barbara, and Patricia Roos. 1990. *Job Queues, Gender Queues: Explaining Women's Inroads into Male Occupations.* Philadelphia: Temple University Press.

Schmuck, Patricia A. 1987. "Women School Employees in the United States." Pp. 75–97 in *Women Educators: Employees of Schools in Western Counties,* edited by Patricia A. Schmuck. Albany: State University of New York Press.

Schrieber, Carol. 1979. *Men and Women in Transitional Occupations.* Cambridge, MA: MIT Press.

U.S. Bureau of the Census. 1980. *Detailed Population Characteristics,* vol. 1, Ch. D. Washington, D.C.: Government Printing Office.

U.S. Department of Labor. Bureau of Labor Statistics. 1991. *Employment and Earnings.* Washington, D.C.: Government Printing Office.

Williams, Christine L. 1989. *Gender Differences at Work: Women and Men in Non-traditional Occupations.* Berkeley: University of California Press.

Yoder, Janice D. 1989. "Women at West Point: Lessons for Token Women in Male-Dominated Occupations." Pp. 523–37 in *Women: A Feminist Perspective,* edited by Jo Freeman, Mountain View, CA: Mayfield Publishing Company.

York, Reginald O., H. Carl Henley, and Dorothy N. Gamble. 1987. "Sexual Discrimination in Social Work: Is It Salary or Advancement?" *Social Work* 32:336–40.

Zimmer, Lynn. 1988. "Tokenism and Women in the Workplace." *Social Problems* 35: 64–77.

 QUESTIONS FOR CRITICAL THINKING

Reading 28

1. Williams discusses how sex segregation continues to exist within the U.S. labor force. How do the policies and practices she reveals maintain a gap in the incomes of women and men?

2. What are some ways of correcting gender-biased hiring practices in the workplace? What do you see as the likelihood of such corrective policies being enacted?

3. How does Williams's discussion impact your own expectations for your career?

Reading 29

CAUSE OF DEATH: INEQUALITY

ALEJANDRO REUSS

 INEQUALITY KILLS

You won't see inequality on a medical chart or a coroner's report under "cause of death." You won't see it listed among the top killers in the United States each year. All too often, however, it is social inequality that lurks behind a more immediate cause of death, be it heart disease or diabetes, accidental injury or homicide. Few of the top causes of death are "equal opportunity killers." Instead, they tend to strike poor people more than rich people, the less educated more than the highly educated, people lower on the occupational ladder more than those higher up, or people of color more than white people.

Statistics on mortality and life expectancy do not provide a perfect map of social inequality. For example, the life expectancy for women in the United States is about six years longer than the life expectancy for men, despite the many ways in which women are subordinated to men. Take most indicators of socioeconomic status, however, and most causes of death, and it's a strong bet that you'll find illness and injury (or "morbidity") and mortality increasing as status decreases.

Men with less than 12 years of education are more than twice as likely to die of chronic diseases (e.g., heart disease), more than three times as likely to die as a result of injury, and nearly twice as likely to die of communicable diseases, compared to those with 13 or more years of education. Women with family incomes below $10,000 are more than three times as likely to die of heart disease and nearly three times as likely to die of diabetes, compared to those with family incomes above $25,000. African Americans are more likely than whites to die of heart disease; stroke; lung, colon, prostate, and breast cancer, as well as all cancers combined; liver disease; diabetes; AIDS; accidental injury; and homicide. In all, the lower you are in a social hierarchy, the worse your health and the shorter your life are likely to be.

Alejandro Reuss, "Cause of Death: Inequality" from *Dollars and Sense* (May/June 2001). Reprinted with the permission of *Dollars & Sense*, the progressive economics magazine www.dollarsandsense.org.

THE WORSE OFF IN THE UNITED STATES ARE NOT
WELL OFF BY WORLD STANDARDS

You often hear it said that even poor people in rich countries like the United States are rich compared to ordinary people in poor countries. While that may be true when it comes to consumer goods like televisions or telephones, which are widely available even to poor people in the United States, it's completely wrong when it comes to health.

In a 1996 study published in the *New England Journal of Medicine*, University of Michigan researchers found that African-American females living to age 15 in Harlem had a 65% chance of surviving to age 65, about the same as women in India. Meanwhile, Harlem's African-American males had only a 37% chance of surviving to age 65, about the same as men in Angola or the Democratic Republic of Congo. Among both African-American men and women, infectious diseases and diseases of the circulatory system were the prime causes of high mortality.

It takes more income to achieve a given life expectancy in a rich country like the United States than it does to achieve the same life expectancy in a less affluent country. So the higher money income of a low-income person in the United States, compared to a middle-income person in a poor country, does not necessarily translate into a longer life span. The average income per person in African-American families, for example, is more than five times the per capita income of El Salvador. The life expectancy for African-American men in the United States, however, is only about 67 years, the same as the average life expectancy for men in El Salvador.

 HEALTH INEQUALITIES IN THE UNITED STATES ARE
NOT JUST ABOUT ACCESS TO HEALTH CARE

Nearly one sixth of the U.S. population lacks health insurance, including about 44% of poor people. A poor adult with a health problem is only half as likely to see a doctor as a high-income adult. Adults living in low-income areas are more than twice as likely to be hospitalized for a health problem that could have been effectively treated with timely outpatient care, compared with adults living in high-income areas. Obviously, lack of access to health care is a major health problem.

But so are environmental and occupational hazards; communicable diseases; homicide and firearm-related injuries; and smoking, alcohol consumption, lack of exercise, and other risk factors. These dangers all tend to affect lower-income people more than higher-income, less-educated people more than more-educated, and people of color more than whites. African-American children are more than twice as likely as white children to be hospitalized for asthma, which is linked to air pollution. Poor men are nearly six times as likely as high-income men to have elevated blood-lead levels, which reflect both residential and workplace environmental hazards. African-American men are more than seven times as likely to fall victim to homicide as white men; African-American women, more than four times as likely as white women. The less education someone has, the more likely they are to smoke or to drink heavily. The lower someone's income, the less likely they are to get regular exercise.

Michael Marmot, a pioneer in the study of social inequality and health, notes that so-called diseases of affluence—disorders, like heart disease, associated with high-calorie and high-fat diets, lack of physical activity, etc.—are most prevalent among the *least affluent* people in rich societies. While recognizing the role of such "behavioral" risk factors as smoking in producing poor health, he argues, "It is not sufficient . . . to ask what contribution smoking makes to generating the social gradient in ill health, but we must ask, why is there a social gradient in smoking?" What appear to be individual "lifestyle" decisions often reflect a broader *social* epidemiology.

GREATER INCOME INEQUALITY GOES HAND IN HAND WITH POORER HEALTH

Numerous studies suggest that the more unequal the income distribution in a country, state, or city, the lower the life expectancies for people at all income levels. One study published in the *American Journal of Public Health*, for example, shows that U.S. metropolitan areas with low per capita incomes and low levels of income inequality have lower mortality rates than areas with high median incomes and high levels of income inequality. Meanwhile, for a given per capita income range, mortality rates always decline as inequality declines.

R. G. Wilkinson, perhaps the researcher most responsible for relating health outcomes to overall levels of inequality (rather than individual income levels), argues that greater income inequality causes worse health outcomes independent of its effects on poverty. Wilkinson and his associates suggest several explanations for this relationship. First, the bigger the income gap between rich and poor, the less inclined the well off are to pay taxes for public services they either do not use or use in low proportion to the taxes they pay. Lower spending on public hospitals, schools, and other basic services does not affect wealthy people's life expectancies very much, but it affects poor people's life expectancies a great deal. Second, the bigger the income gap, the lower the overall level of social cohesion. High levels of social cohesion are associated with good health outcomes for several reasons. For example, people in highly cohesive societies are more likely to be active in their communities, reducing social isolation, a known health risk factor. (See Thad Williamson, "Social Movements Are Good for Your Health," p. 7.)

Numerous researchers have criticized Wilkinson's conclusions, arguing that the real reason income inequality tends to be associated with worse
health outcomes is that it is associated with higher rates of poverty. But even
if they are right and income inequality causes worse health *simply by bringing
about greater poverty*, that hardly makes for a defense of inequality. Poverty
and inequality are like partners in crime. "[W]hether public policy focuses
primarily on the elimination of poverty or on reduction in income disparity," argue Wilkinson critics Kevin Fiscella and Peter Franks, "neither goal is
likely to be achieved in the absence of the other."

 ## DIFFERENCES IN STATUS MAY BE JUST AS IMPORTANT AS INCOME LEVELS

Even after accounting for differences in income, education, and other factors, the life expectancy for African Americans is less than that for whites.
U.S. researchers are beginning to explore the relationship between high
blood pressure among African Americans and the racism of the surrounding society. African Americans tend to suffer from high blood pressure, a
risk factor for circulatory disease, more often than whites. Moreover, studies have found that, when confronted with racism, African Americans suffer
larger and longer-lasting increases in blood pressure than when faced with
other stressful situations. Broader surveys relating blood pressure in African
Americans to perceived instances of racial discrimination have yielded complex results, depending on social class, gender, and other factors.

Stresses cascade down social hierarchies and accumulate among the
least empowered. Even researchers focusing on social inequality and
health, however, have been surprised by the large effects on mortality. Over
30 years ago, Michael Marmot and his associates undertook a landmark
study, known as Whitehall I, of health among British civil servants. Since the
civil servants shared many characteristics regardless of job classification—an
office work environment, a high degree of job security, etc.—the researchers expected to find only modest health differences among them. To their
surprise, the study revealed a sharp increase in mortality with each step
down the job hierarchy—even from the highest grade to the second highest.
Over ten years, employees in the lowest grade were three times as likely to
die as those in the highest grade. One factor was that people in lower grades
showed a higher incidence of many "lifestyle" risk factors, like smoking,
poor diet, and lack of exercise. Even when the researchers controlled for
such factors, however, more than half the mortality gap remained.

Marmot noted that people in the lower job grades were less likely to
describe themselves as having "control over their working lives" or being
"satisfied with their work situation," compared to those higher up. While
people in higher job grades were more likely to report "having to work at
a fast pace," lower-level civil servants were more likely to report feelings of

hostility, the main stress-related risk factor for heart disease. Marmot concluded that "psycho-social" factors—the psychological costs of being lower in the hierarchy—played an important role in the unexplained mortality gap. Many of us have probably said to ourselves, after a trying day on the job, "They're killing me." Turns out it's not just a figure of speech. Inequality kills—and it starts at the bottom.

REFERENCES

Berkman, Lisa, "Social Inequalities and Health: Five Key Points for Policy Makers to Know," February 5, 2001, Kennedy School of Government, Harvard University; *Health, United States, 1998, with Socioeconomic Status and Health Chartbook,* National Center for Health Statistics <www.cdc.gov/nchs>.

Geronimus, Arline T., et al., "Excess Mortality Among Blacks and Whites in the United States," *The New England Journal of Medicine* 335 (21), November 21, 1996.

Kawachi, Ichiro, Bruce P. Kennedy, and Richard G. Wilkison, eds., *The Society and Population Health Reader, Volume I: Income Inequality and Health,* 1999.

Krieger, Nancy, Ph.D., and Stephen Sidney, M.D., "Racial Discrimination and Blood Pressure: The CARDIA Study of Young Black and White Adults," *American Journal of Public Health* 86(10), October 1996.

Marmot, Michael, "Social Differences in Mortality: The Whitehall Studies," *Adult Mortality in Developed Countries: From Description to Explanation,* Alan D. Lopez, Graziella Caselli, and Tapani Valkonen, eds., 1995.

Marmot, Michael, "The Social Pattern of Health and Disease," *Health and Social Organization: Towards a Health Policy for the Twenty-First Century,* David Blane, Eric Brunner, and Richard Wilkinson, eds., 1996.

UN Development Programme, *Human Development Report 2000, World Development Indicators 2000,* World Bank.

 QUESTIONS FOR CRITICAL THINKING

Reading 29

1. How does the author's discussion impact your understanding of the impact of socioeconomic status on a person's access to resources like health care?

2. In this article the author, when discussing issues of tobacco use, states "what appear to be individual 'lifestyle' decisions often reflect a broader *social* epidemiology." What does he mean by this?

3. Some argue that policies like universal health care would address some of the problems caused by social inequality. Do you think this would be a sufficient solution? What solutions would you offer?

Reading 30

WELFARE REFORM, FAMILY HARDSHIP, AND WOMEN OF COLOR

LINDA BURNHAM

Tens of thousands of women's and human rights activists gathered in September 1995 at the United Nations Fourth World Conference on Women, held in Beijing, China, to focus their attention on improving the condition and status of women worldwide. Working through cultural, religious, political, economic, and regional differences, women from the nations of the world produced a comprehensive document, the Beijing Platform for Action, that detailed actions to be taken by governments, nongovernmental organizations, and multilateral financial and development institutions to improve women's conditions. The platform for action called on governments to take action to relieve "the persistent and increasing burden of poverty on women" and address gender "inequality in economic structures and policies, in all forms of productive activities and in access to resources" (United Nations 1995).

Yet in the seven years since Beijing, in a time of unparalleled national prosperity, policies contradictory to the spirit and intent of the platform for action were promulgated in the United States, targeting the most vulnerable citizens and, rather than assisting women onto the path of economic security, driving many deeper into poverty. While U.S. officials pledged in international forums to uphold women's human rights, those rights were substantially undermined by the 1996 passage of the Personal Responsibility and Work Opportunities Reconciliation Act (PRWORA).

 INCREASING FAMILY HARDSHIP

There are many studies that document how much worse off women are due to welfare reform. Those who remain in the welfare system, those who leave for employment, and those who might have used Aid to Families with

Based on Linda Burnham and Kaaryn Gustafson, *Working Hard, Staying Poor: Women and Children in the Wake of Welfare Reform* (Women of Color Resource Center, June 2000). Full report at www.coloredgirls.org.

Dependent Children (AFDC) are in worse shape, with less support than the woefully inadequate earlier system provided. Only a few examples of the growing grief will be highlighted here before I turn to the particular problems facing immigrants and women of color in the context of international human rights.

The stated intent of welfare reform was at least twofold: to reduce the welfare rolls and to move women toward economic self-sufficiency. The first objective has been achieved: welfare rolls have declined dramatically since 1996. Welfare reform has stripped single mothers of any sense that they are entitled to government support during the years when they are raising their children.

Despite the "success" of welfare reform, research has repeatedly found that many women who move from welfare to work do not achieve economic independence. Instead, most find only low-paid, insecure jobs that do not lift their families above the poverty line. They end up worse off economically than they were on welfare: they work hard and remain poor. Others are pushed off welfare and find no employment. They have no reported source of income.

Women in transition from welfare to work—or to no work—face particular difficulties and crises related to housing insecurity and homelessness and food insecurity and hunger.

Low-income people in the United States faced a housing crisis long before the passage of the PRWORA. In most states, the median fair-market cost of housing for a family of three is considerably higher than total income from a Temporary Aid to Needy Families (TANF) grant (Dolbeare 1999). Further, as a consequence of two decades of declining federal support for public and subsidized housing, the great majority of both current and former TANF recipients are at the mercy of an unforgiving private housing market.

The withdrawal of the federal government's commitment to need-based income support adds a powerful destabilizing element to already tenuous conditions. The evidence that welfare reform is contributing to rising levels of housing insecurity and homelessness is piling up. The author of one recent study noted: "Young children are without homes in the largest numbers since the Great Depression. Welfare reform has made things much worse. Shelters are overflowing and gridlocked" (Griffin 1999, 4A).

Utility payment problems are another important indicator of housing insecurity because they reveal that many families, while they may have a roof over them, spend at least some time without heat and light. And utility problems are often a prelude to inability to pay the rent. A 1998 survey of social service clients who had left welfare within the previous six months found that 25 percent had had their heat cut off (Sherman et al. 1998, 13). A recent Illinois study found that 61 percent of TANF recipients who were not working could not pay their utility bills. But former recipients who were working were also struggling with their budgets, and 48 percent were unable to meet their utility payments (Work, Welfare and Families 2000, 25).

Confronting the absurd and agonizing decision of whether to feed their children or house them, most mothers will use the rent money to buy food and then struggle to deal with the consequences. In one national study, 23 percent of former welfare recipients moved because they could not pay the rent (Sherman et al. 1998, 13). A New Jersey survey found that 15.8 percent of respondents who had had their benefits reduced or terminated in the previous 12 months had lost their housing (Work, Poverty and Welfare Evaluation Project 1999, 53). Furthermore, in Illinois, 12 percent of former recipients who were not working and 5 percent of former recipients who were working experienced an eviction (Work, Welfare and Families 2000, 25).

Welfare reform has also put severe pressures on an already strained shelter system. The U.S. Conference of Mayors reported that requests for emergency shelter increased by 12 percent between 1998 and 1999 in the 26 cities surveyed and were at their highest levels since 1994 (U.S. Conference of Mayors 1999, 94). "When I started here three years ago, we had plenty of family space. Since welfare reform, I don't have a bed," said a social service worker in a Salvation Army Shelter in New Orleans (Cobb 1999, 1).

According to a survey conducted by social service agencies in six states, 8 percent of the single parents who had stopped getting welfare in the previous six months had to turn to homeless shelters to house their families (Sherman et al. 1998, 16). In an Illinois study, 7 percent of former recipients who were not working and 5 percent who were became homeless (Work, Welfare and Families 2000, 25).

Although the PRWORA was trumpeted as a step toward strengthening families, increased housing insecurity and homelessness have led to families being split apart. Most family shelters do not take men, so the fathers of two-parent families that become homeless must either go to a single men's shelter or make other housing arrangements. Many shelters also do not accommodate adolescent boys or older male teens. Family breakup may be required for a shelter stay.

The housing instability of poor women and their children has profound consequences, both for them and for society as a whole. Homelessness compromises the emotional and physical health of women and children, disrupts schooling, and creates a substantial barrier to employment. It widens the chasm between those who are prospering in a strong economy and those who fall ever farther behind. In the six years since the United States made its Beijing commitments to improving women's lives, welfare policy, rather than widening poor women's access to safe and affordable housing, has created higher levels of housing instability and homelessness.

Like homelessness, the problems of food insecurity predate welfare reform. Low-income workers and welfare recipients alike have struggled for years to provide adequate food for themselves and their families. The robust economy of the late 1990s did not fundamentally alter this reality. Of families headed by single women, one in three experiences food insecurity and one in ten experiences hunger (Work, Welfare and Families 2000, 25).

Welfare reform has made women's struggles to obtain food for them-selves and their families more difficult. Several studies document that former recipients cannot pay for sufficient food and that their families skip meals, go hungry, and/or use food pantries or other emergency food assistance.

The figures are astoundingly high. In New Jersey, 50.3 percent of former recipients who were not working reported an inability to sufficiently feed themselves or their children. Former recipients who were working were no better off: Almost 50 percent reported the very same problem (Work, Pov-erty and Welfare Evaluation Project 1999, 58). The situation conveyed by an Illinois study is even more disturbing. Here, the population reporting the most difficulty with food insecurity was former recipients who were par-ticipating in the labor force. Sixty-three percent of them said that there was a time when they could not buy the food they needed, a significantly higher proportion than either former recipients who were not working or current recipients (Work, Welfare and Families 2000, 25). In other words, the higher costs associated with participating in the labor force, combined with reduc-tion or elimination of the food stamp allotment, meant women's access to adequate food became more precarious rather than less so as they moved from welfare to work. Entering the workforce came at a very high price.

The Food Stamp Program is intended to ensure that no family goes hun-gry, but many families do not receive the food stamps to which they are entitled. Even before welfare reform, the rate of participation in the Food Stamp Program was declining more rapidly than the poverty rate. The number of people receiving food stamps dropped even more steeply later, from 25.5 million average monthly recipients in 1996 to 18.5 million in the first half of 1999 (U.S. General Accounting Office 1999, 46). The rate of partic-ipation is the lowest it has been in two decades, with a growing gap between the need for food assistance and families' use of food stamps.

Welfare reform has itself contributed to the underutilization of food stamps. Many families that leave the welfare system do not know that as long as their income remains below a certain level, they are still eligible for food stamps. Believing that termination of TANF benefits disqualifies them from receiving food stamps as well, they fail to apply or to reconfirm eligibility. Confusion and misinformation on the part of eligibility workers, or their withholding of information, are also factors in the low participation of former recipients. Additional contributing factors include the lack of bilin-gual staff and burdensome application and recertification processes (Venner, Sullivan, and Seavey 2000, 17). Among families who had left welfare, only 42 percent of those who were eligible for food stamps were receiving them (Zedlewski and Brauner 1999, 1–6).

Not surprisingly, demands for food from other sources are increasing. As the welfare rolls shrink, requests for food from charities rise. Catholic Charities reported a 38 percent rise in demand for emergency food assis-tance in 1998. "For many low-income people, the 'emergency' need for food assistance has become 'chronic'—a basic component of their efforts to survive," according to the U.S. Conference of Mayors 1999 study (20). The same study showed that 85 percent of the cities surveyed experienced increased demand for emergency food and that requests for emergency food assistance increased by an average of 18 percent between 1998 and 1999 (94). In many cases, the demand for food goes unmet. As one report states, "The bottom line is that . . . for millions of households, workforce participation has been accompanied by hunger" (Venner, Sullivan, and Seavey 2000, 16).

 WOMEN OF COLOR AND IMMIGRANT WOMEN

Welfare reform is a nominally race-neutral policy suffused with racial bias, both in the politics surrounding its promulgation and in its impact. It may not have been the intent to racially target women of color for particular punishment, yet women of color and immigrant women have nonetheless been particularly hard hit in ways that were highly predictable.

Feminist theory has for some time recognized that the social and economic circumstances women of color must negotiate are shaped by the intersection of distinct axes of power—in this case primarily race, class, and gender. The relationships of subordination and privilege that define these axes generate multiple social dynamics that influence, shape, and transform each other, creating, for women of color, multiple vulnerabilities and intensified experiences of discrimination.

Welfare reform might legitimately be regarded as a class-based policy intended to radically transform the social contract with the poor. Poverty in the United States, however, is powerfully structured by racial and gender inequities. It is not possible, therefore, to institute poverty policy of any depth that does not also reconfigure other relations, either augmenting or diminishing race and gender inequalities. By weakening the social safety net for the poor, PRWORA necessarily has its greatest effect on those communities that are disproportionately represented among the poor. Communities of color and immigrant communities, already characterized by significantly higher levels of minimum-wage work, homelessness, hunger, and poor health, are further jeopardized by the discriminatory impact of welfare reform.

As a consequence of the historical legacy and current practices of, among other things, educational inequity and labor market disadvantage, patterns of income and wealth in the United States are strongly skewed along racial lines, for example, the disproportionate burden of poverty carried by people of color. While the white non-Hispanic population constituted 72.3 percent of the total population in 1998, it made up only 45.8 percent of the population living below the poverty line. In stark contrast, blacks made up just over 12 percent of the general population but 26.4 percent of the U.S. population in poverty. People of Hispanic origin, of all races, constitute 23.4 percent of the people below the poverty line, while making up 11.2 percent of the total

TABLE 1   TANF Recipients by Race, 1998 (In percentages)

White	32.7
Black	39.0
Hispanic	22.2
Native	1.5
Asian	3.4
Other	0.6
Unknown	0.7

Source: U.S. Department of Health and Human Services, 1999.

population. While 8.2 percent of the white non-Hispanic population lives in poverty, 12.5 percent of Asian and Pacific Islanders do (U.S. Census Bureau 1999, 2000).[1]

Economic vulnerabilities due to race and ethnicity may be further compounded by disadvantages based on gender and immigration/citizenship status. Thus, for households headed by single women, the poverty rates are also stark. Over 21 percent of such white non-Hispanic households were below the poverty line in 1998, as compared to over 46 percent of black and 48 percent of Hispanic female-headed households (U.S. Census Bureau 1999). Immigrants, too, are disproportionately poor, with 18 percent below the poverty line as compared to 12 percent of the native born (U.S. Census Bureau 1999). Given the disproportionate share of poverty experienced by people of color, and the significant poverty of single-mother households, it is no surprise that the welfare rolls are racially unbalanced, with women of color substantially overrepresented (see Table 1).

This racial imbalance has been cynically used for decades in the ideological campaign to undermine support for welfare—a crude but ultimately effective interweaving of race, class, gender, and anti-immigrant biases that prepared the consensus to "end welfare as we know it." Having been maligned as lazy welfare cheats and something-for-nothing immigrants, Latinas, African American women, and Asian women of particular nationality groups are now absorbing a punishing share of welfare reform's negative impacts.

Much of the data on welfare reform are not disaggregated by race. We will not know the full impact of welfare reform on women of color until we have county, statewide, and national studies of women transitioning from welfare to work that consistently include race as a variable. However, to the extent that communities of color experience some of the most devastating effects of poverty at exceptionally high rates, and to the extent that welfare reform has rendered these communities more, rather than less, vulnerable, we may expect that the policy will deepen already entrenched inequalities.

For example, African American women are massively overrepresented in the urban homeless population. Their particular vulnerability to homelessness has been shaped by, among many factors, high rates of reliance on welfare in a period in which the value of the welfare grant plummeted and housing costs climbed steeply; low marriage rates and, therefore, lack of access to a male wage; overconcentration on the bottom rungs of the wage ladder; and high unemployment rates, especially for young women with less than a high school education.

Beyond intensified impact due to disproportionate representation in the affected population, additional factors compound the disadvantages of women of color and immigrant women. One Virginia study found noteworthy differences in how caseworkers interact with black and white welfare recipients. A substantial 41 percent of white recipients were encouraged to go to school to earn their high school diplomas, while no black recipients were. A much higher proportion of whites than blacks found their caseworkers to be helpful in providing information about potential jobs (Gooden 1997). Other studies showed that blacks were removed from welfare for noncompliance with program rules at considerably higher rates than white recipients, while a higher proportion of the cases of white recipients were closed because they earned too much to qualify for welfare (Savner 2000).

Further, while welfare use is declining among all races, white recipients are leaving the welfare rolls at a much more rapid rate than blacks or Latinos. In New York City, for example, the number of whites on welfare declined by 57 percent between 1995 and 1998, while the rate of decline for blacks was 30 percent and that of Latinos 7 percent. White recipients have also been leaving the rolls at faster rates than minorities in states such as Illinois, Pennsylvania, Michigan, and Ohio. And nationally, the decline has been 25 percent for whites but only 17 percent for African Americans and 9 percent for Latinos (DeParle 1998, A1).

The causes of this phenomenon have been insufficiently studied, but some of the factors may include higher average educational levels among white recipients, greater concentrations of recipients of color in job-poor inner cities, racial discrimination in employment and housing, and discriminatory referral policies on the part of welfare-to-work case-workers. Whatever the combination of contributing factors, it appears that white recipients are making a more rapid transition into the labor force.

Some of the most punitive provisions of PRWORA are directed at immigrants. The 1996 legislation banned certain categories of legal immigrants from a wide array of federal assistance programs, including TANF, food stamps, Supplementary Security Income, and Medicaid. In the year following passage, 940,000 legal immigrants lost their food stamp eligibility. Strong advocacy reversed some of the cuts and removed some restrictions, but legal immigrants arriving in the United States after the passage of the legislation are ineligible for benefits for five years. States have the right to bar pre-enactment legal immigrants from TANF and nonemergency Medicaid as well (National Immigration Law Center 1999).

These restrictions have had profound effects on immigrant communities. First of all, many immigrant women who are on welfare face significant barriers to meeting TANF work requirements. Perhaps the most formidable obstacles are limited English proficiency and low educational levels. A study of immigrant recipients in California found that 87 percent of the Vietnamese women and 48 percent of the Mexican American women had limited or no proficiency in English. Many of these women were also not literate in their native languages, with the Mexican Americans averaging 6.5 years in school and the Vietnamese 8.7 years (Equal Rights Advocates 1999, 7). A study of Hmong women found 90 percent with little or no English proficiency, 70 percent with no literacy in the Hmong language, and 62 percent with no formal education whatsoever (Moore and Selkowe 1999).

Limited English, lack of education, and limited job skills severely restrict immigrant women's options in the job market, making it very difficult for them to comply with welfare-to-work requirements. Language problems also impede their ability to negotiate the welfare bureaucracy, which provides very limited or no translation services. These women lack information about programs to which they are entitled, and they worry about notices that come to them in English. When immigrant women recipients are able to find work, it is most often in minimum-wage or low-wage jobs without stability or benefits (Center for Urban Research and Learning 1999, 5; Equal Rights Advocates 1999, 31).

It should come as no surprise that immigrant women report high levels of hardship. In a study of Santa Clara County, California, 50 percent of the Mexican American recipients had experienced food shortages, as had 26 percent of the Vietnamese women (Equal Rights Advocates 1999, 32). One out of three Hmong women recipients in Wisconsin reported running out of food in the six months prior to the survey, and 51.8 percent said they had less food on the state's W-2 program than they had had on AFDC (Moore and Selkowe 1999, 4). Of 630 Latino and Asian households surveyed in California, Texas, and Illinois, 79 percent faced food insecurity and 8.5 percent reported experiencing severe hunger. A study of Los Angeles and San Francisco immigrant households whose food stamps had been cut found that 33 percent of the children in the San Francisco households were experiencing moderate to severe hunger (Venner, Sullivan, and Seavey 2000, 21).

Immigrant women recipients are also likely to experience severe overcrowding and to devote a huge portion of their income to housing. They share housing with relatives or with unrelated adults; live in garages or other makeshift, substandard dwellings; and worry constantly about paying the rent.

A more hidden, but still pernicious, impact of welfare reform has been the decline in applications for aid from immigrants who are eligible to receive it. One report documents PRWORA's "chilling effect on immigrants" who mistakenly believe they are no longer eligible for any benefits. Reporting on the numbers of TANF applications approved each month, this study showed a huge drop—71 percent—in the number of legal immigrant applicants approved for TANF and MediCal between January 1996 and January 1998. That number fell from 1,545 applicants in January 1996 to only 450 in January 1998 (Zimmerman and Fix 1998, 5). The intensive anti-immigrant propaganda that accompanied the passage of PRWORA and statewide anti-immigrant initiatives appears to have discouraged those who need and are entitled to aid from applying for it, surely undermining the health and welfare of immigrant women and their families.

 ## WELFARE REFORM IS INCOMPATIBLE WITH WOMEN'S HUMAN RIGHTS

One of the chief accomplishments of the Beijing conference and the Platform for Action was to position women's issues squarely within the context of human rights. Building on the foundational work of activists worldwide, Beijing became the first U.N. women's conference in which "women's rights are human rights" was articulated not as a platitude but as a strategic assertion. Indeed, the phrase was taken up by former First Lady Hillary Rodham Clinton, who, in her September 5, 1995, speech to the conference, asserted that "women will never gain full dignity until their human rights are respected and protected."

PRWORA is wholly incompatible with the strategic objectives of the Beijing Platform for Action and profoundly compromises the exercise of women's human rights. Rather than improving the status of poor women, the legislation has deepened the misery of tens of thousands of women and their children. By undermining women's access to a stable livelihood, welfare reform constructs barriers to their exercise of political, civil, cultural, and social rights.

Undoing the damage of welfare reform—and bringing U.S. policy in line with its stated commitments to the world community—will require the promulgation and implementation of policies that restore and strengthen the social safety net for women and children while funding programs that support women along the path to economic self-sufficiency. In the absence of the political will for such a comprehensive reworking of U.S. social welfare policy, advocates for poor women and families face an extended, defensive battle to ameliorate the cruelest and most discriminatory effects of this radically regressive policy.

NOTE

1. In citing Census Bureau statistics, I use their terminology. Elsewhere, I use the term "Latino" to refer to immigrants from Mexico, Central and South America, and the Spanish-speaking Caribbean and their descendants in the United States.

REFERENCES

Center for Urban Research and Learning. 1999. *Cracks in the System: Conversations with People Surviving Welfare Reform.* Chicago: Center for Urban Research and Learning, Loyola University, Howard Area Community Center, Organization of the NorthEast.

Clinton, Hillary. 1995. Remarks by First Lady Hillary Rodham Clinton for the United Nations Fourth World Conference on Women, 5 Sept.

Cobb, Kim. 1999. "Homeless Kids Problem Worst in Louisiana; Welfare Reform, Housing Crunch Are Among Reasons." *Houston Chronicle*, 15 Aug.

DeParle, Jason. 1998. "Shrinking Welfare Roll Leave Record High Share of Minorities." *New York Times*, 24 July.

Dolbeare, Cushing. 1999. *Out of Reach: The Gap Between Housing Costs and Income of Poor People in the United States*, Washington, DC: National Low-Income Housing Coalition.

Equal Rights Advocates. 1999. *From War on Poverty to War on Welfare: The Impact of Welfare Reform on the Lives of Immigrant Women.* San Francisco.

Griffin, Laura. 1999. "Welfare Cuts Leaving More Families Homeless, Study Finds." *Dallas Morning News*, 1 July.

Gooden, Susan. 1997. Examining Racial Differences in Employment Status Among Welfare Recipients. In *Race and Welfare Report.* Oakland, CA: Grass Roots Innovative Policy Program.

Moore, Thomas and Vicky Selkowe. 1999. *The Impact of Welfare Reform on Wisconsin's Hmong Aid Recipients.* Milwaukee: Institute for Wisconsin's Future.

National Immigration Law Center. 1999. *Immigrant Eligibility for Public Benefits.* Washington, DC.

Savner, Steve. 2000. Welfare Reform and Racial/Ethnic Minorities: The Questions to Ask. *Poverty & Race* 9(4):3–5.

Sherman, Arloc, Cheryl Amey, Barbara Duffield, Nancy Ebb, and Deborah Weinstein. 1998. *Welfare to What: Early Findings on Family Hardship and Well-Being.* Washington, DC: Children's Defense Fund and National Coalition for the Homeless.

United Nations. 1995. *Fourth World Conference on Women Platform for Action.* Geneva, Switzerland.

U.S. Census Bureau. 1999. *Poverty Thresholds in 1998 by Size of Family and Number of Related Children Under 18 Years.* Washington, DC.

_____. 2000. *Resident Population Estimates of the United States by Sex, Race, and Hispanic Origin.* Washington, DC.

U.S. Conference of Mayors. 1999. *A Status Report on Hunger and Homelessness in America's Cities.* Washington, DC.

U.S. Department of Health and Human Services, Administration for Children and Families. 1999. *Characteristics and Financial Circumstances of TANF Recipients.* Washington, DC.

U.S. General Accounting Office. 1999. *Food Stamp Program: Various Factors Have Led to Declining Participation.* Washington, DC.

Venner, Sandra H., Ashley F. Sullivan, and Dorie Seavey. 2000. *Paradox of Our Times: Hunger in a Strong Economy.* Medford, MA: Tufts University, Center on Hunger and Poverty.

Work, Poverty and Welfare Evaluation Project. 1999. Assessing Work First: What Happens After Welfare? Report for the Study Group on Work, Poverty and Welfare. Legal Services of New Jersey, New Jersey Poverty Research Institute, Edison, NJ.

Work, Welfare and Families. 2000. *Living with Welfare Reform: A Survey of Low Income Families in Illinois.* Chicago: Chicago Urban League and UIC Center for Urban Economic Development.

Zedlewski, Sheila R. and Sarah Brauner. 1999. *Are the Steep Declines in Food Stamp Participation Linked to Falling Welfare Caseloads?* Washington, DC: Urban Institute.

Zimmerman, Wendy and Michael Fix. 1998. *Declining Immigrant Applications for MediCal and Welfare Benefits in Los Angeles County.* Washington, DC: Urban Institute.

 QUESTIONS FOR CRITICAL THINKING

Reading 30

1. The author discusses the ways in which welfare reform has particularly affected women of color and immigrant women. How does her explanation help you to see that this is the result of institutional practices rather than individual or cultural characteristics?

2. Reflecting on this reading, what do you see needs to change with regard to policy and institutional practices in order to better aid recipients of welfare? What do you see as the likelihood of implementing such changes? What barriers exist that may prevent their implementation?

3. What solutions do you see to poverty in our country? How are these solutions informed by your own class experience?

Reading 31

BEYOND CRIME AND PUNISHMENT: PRISONS AND INEQUALITY

BRUCE WESTERN • BECKY PETTIT

E
ven during the economic boom of the 1990s, more young black men who had dropped out of school were in prison than on the job. Despite rapid growth in employment throughout the economy, released prisoners in the 1990s earned little and were often unemployed. In these two ways—high imprisonment rates among disadvantaged men and poor economic prospects for ex-inmates—the penal system affects inequality in the American society.

Inequality is disguised because data on employment often do not include the mostly poor men who are locked away behind bars. When we count prisoners among the unemployed, we find that racial inequality in employment and earnings is much greater than when we ignore them. Taking prisoners into account substantially alters our understanding of how young black men are faring, dramatically so when we focus on young black men with little education. In addition, the penal system fuels inequality by reducing the wages and employment prospects of released prisoners. The low-wage, unstable employment they experience when they return to society deepens the divisions of race and class.

For most of the 20th century, imprisonment policies had little effect on social inequality. Prison was reserved for the most violent or incorrigible offenders, and the inmate population was consequently small. This began to change in the early 1970s when stricter law enforcement enlarged the prison population. While incarceration once used to flag dangerousness or persistent deviance, by 2000 it had become a common event for poor minority males.

THE EXPANSION OF THE PENAL SYSTEM

Between 1920 and 1970, about one-tenth of one percent of Americans were confined in prisons. The prison population increased sixfold in the three decades after 1970. By June 2000, about 1.3 million people were held in

Bruce Western and Becky Pettit, "Beyond Crime and Punishment: Prisons and Inequality" from *Contexts* 1, No. 3 (2002): 37–43. Copyright © 2002 by the American Sociological Association. Reprinted with the permission of the University of California Press.

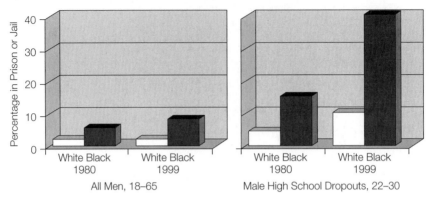

FIGURE 1   Percentage of Incarcerated Men, 1980 & 1999, by Race and Education.

state and federal prisons, and 620,000 inmates were in local jails. This translates into a total incarceration rate of seven-tenths of one percent of the U.S. population. The current incarceration rate is five times the historical average of the 1925–70 period and six to eight times the incarceration rates in Western Europe. With the important exception of homicide, however, American levels of crime are similar to those in Western Europe.

These numbers mask the concentration of imprisonment among young black men with little schooling. Although there are no official statistics, we've calculated the proportion of penal inmates among black and white men at different ages and levels of education by combining data from labor force and correctional surveys. Incarceration rates doubled among working-age men between 1980 and 1999 but increased threefold for high school dropouts in their twenties. By 1999, fewer than one percent of working-age white men were behind bars, compared to 7.5 percent of working-age black men (Figure 1). Figures for young black unskilled men are especially striking: 41 percent of all black male high school dropouts aged 22–30 were in prison or jail at midyear in 1999.

Although 9 out of 10 inmates are male (92 percent), women represent the fastest-growing segment of the inmate population. During the recent penal expansion, the female inmate population has grown more than 60 percent faster than the male inmate population. African-American women have experienced the greatest increase in criminal justice supervision.

Racial disparities in incarceration are even more stark when one counts the men who have ever been incarcerated rather than just those in prison on a given day. In 1989, about 2 percent of white men in their early thirties had ever been to prison compared to 13 percent of black men of the same age (Figure 2). Ten years later, these rates had increased by 50 percent. The risks of going to prison are about three times higher for high school dropouts. At the end of the 1990s, 14 percent of white and 59 percent of black male high school dropouts in their early thirties had prison records.

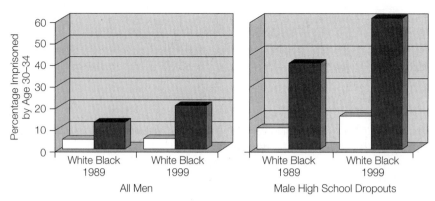

FIGURE 2   Percentage of 30 to 34 year-old Men Ever Incarcerated, 1989 & 1999, by Race and Education.

The high rate of imprisonment among black men is often explained by differences in patterns of arrest and criminal behavior. Blacks are eight times more likely to be incarcerated than whites. With the important exception of drug offenses, blacks are overrepresented among prison inmates due to race differences in crime and arrest statistics. In 1991, for instance, black men accounted for 55 percent of all homicide arrests and 47 percent of homicide offenders in prison. Drug offenses aside, about three-quarters of the racial disparity in imprisonment can be linked to racial differences in arrests and in criminal offending as reported in surveys of crime victims. Although age and educational differences in incarceration have not been studied as closely as race, crime rates are also known to be high among young, poorly educated men. In short, young, black, male high school dropouts are overrepresented in prison mainly because they commit a disproportionate number of crimes (or, at least, street crimes) and are arrested for them. But that is not the whole story.

The explosion of the penal population after 1970 does not reflect increasing crime rates. The prison population has grown steadily every year since 1974, but crime rates have fluctuated up and down with no clear trend. For example 13.4 million crimes were reported to the police in 1980. In that year 182,000 people were admitted to state and federal prisons. In 1998, 12.4 million crimes were reported, and 615,000 people were sent to prison. Crime had gone down (see "Crime Decline in Context," *Contexts*, Spring 2002), but the number of people going to prison had tripled.

To explain the prison boom, we need to look beyond trends in crime. The exceptional pattern of incarceration among drug offenders provides an important clue. Drug offenders account for a rapidly increasing share of the prison population and the surge in drug-related imprisonment coincides with shifts in drug policy. Beginning in the 1970s, state and federal governments increased criminal penalties and intensified law enforcement in an attempt to reduce the supply, distribution and use of illegal narcotics.

Drug arrests escalated sharply throughout the 1980s and 1990s, and drug offenders were widely sentenced to mandatory prison terms. While the total state prison population grew at about 8 percent annually between 1980 and 1996, the population of drug offenders in state prisons grew twice as quickly.

The war on drugs was just one part of a broad trend in criminal justice policy that also toughened punishment for violent and repeat offenders. For example, between 1980 and 1996, the average time served in state prison for murder increased from five to more than 10 years. Habitual offender provisions, such as California's three-strikes law, mandated long sentences for second and third felony convictions. Rates of parole revocation have also increased, contributing to more than a third of all prison admissions by the late 1990s.

Why did the punitive turn in criminal justice policy affect young male dropouts so dramatically? Consider two explanations. First, as we have seen, socially marginal men are the most likely to commit crimes and be arrested for them, so simply lowering the threshold for imprisonment—jailing offenders who in an earlier era would have just been reprimanded—will have the biggest impact on this group. Second, some legal scholars claim that policy was redrawn in a way that disproportionately affected young minority males with little schooling. Michael Tonry makes this argument in a prominent indictment of recent anti-drug policy. Street sweeps of drug dealers, mass arrests in inner cities and harsh penalties for crack cocaine were all important elements of the war on drugs. These measures spotlighted drug use among disadvantaged minorities but neglected the trade and consumption of illicit drugs in the suburbs by middle-class whites. From this perspective the drug war did not simply lower the threshold for imprisonment, it also targeted poor minority men.

Although the relative merits of these two explanations have not yet been closely studied, it is clear that going to prison is now extremely common for young black men and pervasive among young black men who have dropped out of school. Imprisonment adds to the baggage carried by poorly educated and minority men, making it harder for them to catch up economically and further widening the economic gap between these men and the rest of society.

 INCARCERATION CONCEALS INEQUALITY

Regardless of its precise causes, the effects of high incarceration rates on inequality are now substantial. Although the 1990s was a period of economic prosperity, improved job opportunities for many young black men were strongly outweighed by this factor. The stalled economic progress of black youth is invisible in conventional labor force statistics because prison and jail inmates are excluded from standard counts of joblessness.

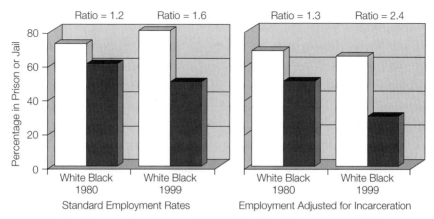

FIGURE 3 Employment Percentages of Male High School Dropouts, Aged 22 to 30, 1980 & 1999, by Race and Incarceration History.

Employment rates that count the penal population among the jobless paint a bleak picture of trends for unskilled black men in the 1990s. Standard labor force data show that nearly two-thirds of young black male high school dropouts had jobs in 1980 compared to just half in 1999 (Figure 3). When inmates are counted in the population, however, the decline in employment is even more dramatic. In 1980, 55 percent of all young black dropouts had jobs. By the end of the 1990s fewer than 30 percent had jobs, despite historically low unemployment in the labor market as a whole. Incarceration now accounts for most of the joblessness among young black dropouts, and its rapid growth drove down employment rates during the 1990s economic boom.

Because black men are overrepresented in prison and jail, incarceration also affects estimates of racial inequality. A simple measure of inequality is the ratio of white to black employment rates. In 1999, standard labor force data (which do not count convicts) show that young white dropouts were about one and a half times more likely to hold a job than their black counterparts. Once prison and jail inmates are counted among the jobless, the employment rate for young white dropouts is about two and a half times larger than for blacks. If we relied just on the usual labor force surveys, we would underestimate employment inequality for this marginal group by 50 percent.

Isolating many of the disadvantaged in prisons and jails also masks inequality in wages. When low earners go to prison and are no longer counted in the wage statistics, it appears that the average wage of workers has increased. This seeming rise in average wages doesn't represent a real improvement in living standards, however. We estimate that the wage gap between young black and white men would be 20 percent wider if all those not working, including those in prison and jail, were counted.

INCARCERATION INCREASES INEQUALITY

The penal system not only conceals inequality, it confers stigma on ex-prisoners and reduces their readiness for the job market. Consequently, ex-convicts often live at the margins of the labor market, precariously employed in low-wage jobs. Ethnographic research paints a vivid picture. For example, in Mercer Sullivan's *Getting Paid,* delinquent youth in New York City cycled through many jobs, each held for just weeks or months at a time. One subject, after entering an ex-offender employment program at age 20, briefly held a factory job, but "he was fired for being absent and then went through three different jobs in the next four months: he tried delivering groceries, being a messenger, and doing maintenance in a nursing home." His experience was typical of Sullivan's subjects.

James Austin and John Irwin's interviews with current and former inmates in *It's About Time* reveal some of the difficulties ex-convicts have finding jobs. Released prisoners may have to disclose their criminal history or risk its discovery in a background check, or jobs may require special licenses or membership unavailable to most ex-convicts. Both may serve as substantial obstacles to employment. For example, a 38-year-old ex-convict living in the San Francisco Bay Area recalls, "I was supposed to get this light industrial job. They kept putting obstacles in front of me and I talked my way over them every time, till she brought up my being on parole and then she went sour on me. If they catch me lying on the application about being in prison or being on parole, they will [report a violation] and give me four months [in prison]." He also was unable to get a job in dry cleaning because he lacked certification: "I had dry-cleaning training a long time ago, but this time I wasn't in long enough to go through the program. It takes several years. You have to have the paper to get a job. I could jump in and clean anything—silks, wools—remove any spot, use all the chemicals, but I don't got any paper. They won't let you start without the paper."

Statistical studies have tried to estimate the toll incarceration takes on earnings after release. Ideally, to measure the effect of prison time, we would compare the pay of groups who were the same in all respects except for their prison records. However, criminal offenders are unusual in ways that are hard to observe. They may be more impulsive or aggressive, and these sorts of characteristics aren't consistently measured by our usual surveys. Thus different studies yield different estimates.

With these caveats in mind, statistical studies suggest that serving time in prison, by itself and with other characteristics of workers accounted for, reduces wages by between 10 and 30 percent. However, this is a simplified picture of how imprisonment affects job opportunities. Research also shows that incarceration affects the growth—and not just the level—of wages. While pay usually increases as men get older, this is not so true for ex-convicts. This suggests that men with prison records find it hard to get jobs with career ladders or seniority pay. Instead, they are more likely to work in day labor or other casual jobs.

Because young black men with little education are imprisoned in such large numbers, the economic effects of incarceration on individual ex-convicts can add up to large economic disadvantages for minority communities. Neighborhoods with many people going to prison develop bad reputations that smear even the law abiding. In *When Work Disappears,* William Julius Wilson reports on interviews with Chicago employers which show how the stigma of criminality can attach to entire minority communities. Considering job candidates from the West Side, one employer observed, "Our black management people [would] say 'No, stay away from that area. That's a bad area . . . ' And then it came out, too, that sooner or later we did terminate everybody from that area for stealing . . . [or] drinking." National statistics also show how imprisonment widens the inequality between groups. Estimates for 1998 show that the reduced earnings of ex-convicts contribute about 10 percent to the wage gap between black and white men. About 10 percent of the pay gap between all male college graduates and all high school dropouts is due to the reduced wages that inmates earn after they are released.

THE PRICE OF SAFETY

The inequalities produced by the penal system are new. The state and federal governments have never imprisoned so many people, and this increase is the result not of more crime but of new policies toward crime. This expansion of imprisonment represents a more massive intrusion of government into the lives of the poor than any employment or welfare program. Young black men's sustained contact with official authority now sets them apart from mainstream America in a novel way.

The inegalitarian effects of criminal justice policy may be justified by gains in public safety. We have in this article treated the penal population primarily as disadvantaged and not as dangerous people, but a large proportion of prisoners are violent offenders. Many commit crimes again and again. Criminals may be poor men, but they also perpetrate crime in poor neighborhoods. From this viewpoint, the proliferation of prisons represents a massive investment in the public safety of disadvantaged urban areas.

But can enduring public safety be achieved by policies that deepen social inequality? A great deal of research indicates that effective crime control depends on reducing economic divisions, not increasing them. There is a strong link between criminal behavior and economic disadvantage. To the extent that prison undermines economic opportunities, the penal boom may be doing little to discourage crime in communities where most men have prison records. If high incarceration rates add to the stigma of residence in high-crime neighborhoods, the economic penalties of imprisonment may affect ex-convicts and law-abiding citizens alike. The criminal justice system is now a newly significant part of a uniquely American system of social inequality. Under these conditions, the punitive trend in criminal justice policy may be even tougher on the poor than it is on crime.

 QUESTIONS FOR CRITICAL THINKING

Reading 31

1. The authors explain how government policy on crime has resulted in an increase in poor men of color in prison. How does their explanation counter common media portrayals that poor men of color are more likely to be criminals?

2. The authors illustrate how the growth of the criminal justice system has contributed to greater inequality in the U.S. Whose interests are served by such an expansion?

3. As the authors state, "effective crime control depends on reducing economic divisions," not expanding the prison system. What ideas do you have for reducing economic inequality in a way that may lead to a reduction in crime?

Reading 32

NO EQUAL JUSTICE
Race and Class in the American Criminal Justice System

DAVID COLE

In April 1992, federal and state agents on a joint drug crime task force raided Room 203 of La Mirage, a seedy motel in Los Angeles, and arrested Christopher Lee Armstrong and four of his companions. That month, a federal grand jury in Los Angeles indicted the men for conspiracy to distribute more than fifty grams of crack cocaine. All five were black. To the public defenders who were assigned to represent the men, the pattern was all too familiar. Of the twenty-four crack cocaine cases the public defender office closed in the prior year, all the defendants were black. And of the fifty-three crack cases the office completed over the prior three years, forty-eight defendants were black, five Hispanic, and none white. At the same time, they knew that many whites used crack, and that white defendants had been tried for crack cocaine charges in California's state court system, where the penalties are much less harsh. Armstrong's lawyers suspected that the authorities might be routing black defendants through the federal system, while directing white defendants into the more lenient state court system. If prosecutors were treating defendants differently based on their race, they reasoned, that conduct would violate equal protection and should require dismissal of the cases. However, the best evidence of what the prosecutors were doing and why they were doing it was in the prosecutors' control. So the defense lawyers submitted to the court the evidence of racial disparity that they had, and asked for the right to conduct "discovery" of the prosecution's files to determine whether their suspicions were in fact well-founded.

SELECTIVE PROSECUTION

In making their charge of "selective prosecution," Armstrong's lawyers were not advancing a new theory. The Supreme Court had recognized long before that selective enforcement of the laws based on race violates equal protection. In *Yick Wo v. Hopkins,*[1] the Court in 1886 unanimously overturned convictions of two Chinese men for operating laundries without a license. San Francisco authorities had arrested about 150 persons for operating laundries without a license—every one of them Chinese. They had denied licenses to all Chinese applicants. And they had granted licenses to all but one of the eighty or so non-Chinese laundry operators who applied. In a unanimous decision invalidating Yick Wo's conviction, the Supreme Court stated, "Though the law itself be fair on its face, and impartial in appearance, yet, if it is applied and administered by public authority with an evil eye and an unequal hand, so as practically to make unjust and illegal discriminations, between persons in similar circumstances, material to their rights, the denial of equal justice is still within the prohibition of the constitution."[2]

The principle the Court established in *Yick Wo* is straightforward: where the government discriminates based on race in its enforcement of the criminal law, it denies equal protection of the laws. Yet at the time Christopher Armstrong's lawyers made their selective prosecution claim, there had been no reported federal or state cases since 1886 that had dismissed a criminal prosecution on the ground that the prosecutor acted for racial reasons. It seems unlikely that this is because no federal or state prosecutor in over 100 years had engaged in racial discrimination. The more likely explanation is that it is virtually impossible to prove such a claim in court.

Criminal defendants making selective prosecution claims face a classic catch-22. To establish selective prosecution, a defendant must prove that the prosecutor singled him out for prosecution because of his race, and did not prosecute others engaged in the same conduct. The best—and usually the only—evidence on these issues is in the prosecutor's control. But the courts have ruled that defendants have no right to see the prosecutor's files until they first make a "colorable showing" of selective prosecution. Thus, a defendant must provide evidence of selective prosecution *before* he gets any access to the documents and other evidence necessary to establish the claim. In the vast majority of cases, this is an insurmountable hurdle. Absent a public admission from the prosecutor of racial animus, or a remarkable racial pattern of prosecutions, defendants are not likely even to obtain discovery, much less dismissal of their claims.

The pattern Armstrong's lawyers presented to the court was quite remarkable: no white crack defendants prosecuted in federal court over a three-year period. In addition, defendants submitted two sworn statements. The first related a halfway house intake coordinator's observation that in his experience treating crack cocaine addicts, whites and blacks dealt and used the drug in equal proportions. (The United States Sentencing Commission subsequently reported in 1995 that 65 percent of those who have used crack are white.) Another, from a defense attorney experienced in state prosecutions, stated that many nonblack defendants were prosecuted for crack cocaine offenses in state court. The government's own evidence seemed to support the defendants' suspicions: it submitted a list of some 2,400 persons charged with federal crack cocaine violations over a three-year period, of which all but eleven were black, and none were white.

The trial court deemed this evidence enough to justify discovery, to determine whether the allegations of racial selectivity were in fact well-founded. But the prosecutors refused to submit to the discovery, and appealed. In May 1996, the Supreme Court reversed.[3] It stated that Armstrong's evidence was insufficient because he had failed to identify any similarly situated white defendants who had been prosecuted in state court. The Court seemed to go out of its way to ensure that Armstrong's claims of race discrimination would not see the light of day. It dismissed the criminal defense attorney's affidavit, which presented precisely the information the Court said was missing, as "hearsay" that "reported personal conclusions based on anecdotal evidence." Yet the prosecutors had never objected to the evidence in the trial court, and the general rule—which the Supreme Court enforces rigorously against criminal defendants—is that if one fails to object when evidence is introduced, the objection is waived. Only a single Justice, John Paul Stevens, dissented.

As the *Armstrong* decision suggests, and as the absence of any successful claims over more than a century confirms, the selective-prosecution defense is available in theory, but unattainable in practice. Much like the guarantee of effective assistance of counsel, the nominal availability of the selective-prosecution defense does more to legitimate the status quo as non-discriminatory than it does to protect defendants from discrimination. The Court's tactic for dealing with the issue—effectively blocking at the threshold the very investigation necessary to establish the claim—ensures that the courts will rarely if ever be forced to confront evidence of race discrimination in criminal prosecutions.

 ## STANDING TO CHALLENGE RACIAL DISCRIMINATION IN CRIMINAL LAW ENFORCEMENT

The tactic of burying race discrimination claims before they can be made is not limited to selective prosecution; it is a consistent theme throughout virtually all of the Supreme Court's doctrine governing legal challenges to discrimination in the administration of criminal justice. The Court has imposed nearly insurmountable barriers to persons challenging race discrimination at all stages of the criminal justice system, from policing to judging to sentencing. With the exception of jury discrimination, the barriers are so high that few claims are even filed, notwithstanding shocking racial disparities and widespread belief among minority groups that criminal justice is enforced in a discriminatory manner. The few suits involving claims of criminal justice abuses along racial lines that have reached the Supreme Court have almost all been dismissed on technical grounds before the issue of discrimination could even be aired. This frees the Court from having to address the messy and troubling reality of racial inequality in criminal justice, but it is also likely to breed distrust and cynicism among those who feel that the system is unfairly administered.

Adolph Lyons, a twenty-four-year-old black man, filed such a suit, and his experience is illustrative. While driving his car in Los Angeles early in the morning of October 6, 1976, Lyons was pulled over by four police officers for a burnt-out taillight. Drawing their guns, the police ordered Lyons out of his car. He complied. They told him to face the car and spread his legs. He did so. They told him to put his hands on his head. Again, he followed their orders. After they subjected him to a patdown search, Lyons dropped his hands, at which point an officer slammed Lyons's hands back on his head. When Lyons complained of pain from the car keys he was holding, the officer applied a chokehold. Lyons lost consciousness and fell to the ground. When he came to, he was spitting up blood and dirt, had urinated and defecated, and had suffered permanent damage to his larynx. The officers issued a traffic ticket for the burnt-out taillight and sent him on his way.

Lyons sued to challenge the use of the chokehold in such circumstances. Between 1975 and 1980, the LAPD had applied the chokehold on 975 occasions. By the time Lyons's case reached the Supreme Court, sixteen persons had been killed by police use of the chokehold; twelve of the victims were black men. The Supreme Court, however, dismissed the case, ruling that Lyons lacked "standing" to seek an injunction against this practice.

The "standing" doctrine holds that courts may provide relief only where they are presented with a specific and concrete dispute. At a minimum, an individual must identify some injury caused by the defendant that will be remedied through the lawsuit. Lyons sought a court order limiting the LAPD's use of chokeholds in the future. The Supreme Court said he had no right to bring such a suit, because he could not show that he would encounter another chokehold again. That Lyons had been victimized by a chokehold in the past did not mean that he faced a threat of being subjected to one in the future. In the absence of a threat of future harm, the Court concluded, there was no concrete dispute between the parties justifying judicial intervention. In essence, the Court deemed the case too abstract to decide.

The matter was hardly abstract to Lyons. He argued that, as a black man, he could not drive his car in Los Angeles without fearing that he would be pulled over again and subjected to another chokehold. Because the police had applied the chokehold even though Lyons had cooperated fully, there was nothing short of a lawsuit he could do to protect himself. Yet the Court held that in order to have standing,

> Lyons would have had not only to allege that he would have
> another encounter with the police but also to make the incredible
> assertion either (1) that *all* police officers in Los Angeles *always*
> choke any citizen with whom they happen to have an encounter,
> whether for the purpose of arrest, issuing a citation or for
> questioning, or (2) that the City ordered or authorized police
> officers to act in such manner.[4]

Lyons did not explicitly allege race discrimination, although the statistics on chokehold deaths suggest that black men had particular reason to fear its application. But the Court's holding makes it difficult to challenge any discriminatory applications of criminal law authority. Because criminal law is by its nature enforced selectively and intermittently, individuals will rarely be able to satisfy the Court's requirement that they show that an encounter with the police, a prosecutor, or judge, is sufficiently likely to recur to them in the future.

Two racially charged precursors to *Lyons* illustrate the point. *O'Shea v. Littleton*[5] arose out of the civil rights struggle in Cairo, Illinois, in the early 1970s. The plaintiffs were seventeen blacks and two whites who had been engaged in peaceful demonstrations and boycotts against racially discriminatory stores. They alleged that Cairo's criminal justice authorities were conducting a race war in retaliation for their political activities. They specifically charged that the state prosecutor, investigator, and police commissioner sought harsher penalties against black criminal defendants, and impeded black citizens' ability to have the law enforced against whites who harmed them. They also charged the local judges with setting bail rates higher for black than for white defendants. Several plaintiffs had been subject to the practices they complained of, which they claimed were motivated both by their race and by their continuing involvement in civil rights activities.

As in *Lyons,* the Supreme Court ruled that the case should be dismissed for lack of a "case or controversy." Although some of the plaintiffs had been victimized in the past, the Court stated, "past exposure to illegal conduct does not in itself show a present case or controversy regarding injunctive relief . . . if unaccompanied by any continuing, present adverse effects."[6]

Two years later, the Court reaffirmed its resistance to judicial oversight of criminal law enforcement. *Rizzo v. Goode*[7] involved the notorious Philadelphia police department, and the equally notorious Frank Rizzo, who was police chief when the case began and mayor when it ended. Rizzo prided himself on being tough on crime. During his mayoral campaign he vowed, "I'm gonna make Attila the Hun look like a faggot after this election's over," and stated that "the way to treat criminals is *spacco il capa*"—to bust their heads.[8] During his eight years as mayor, fatal shootings by Philadelphia police officers increased by about 20 percent *per year.*[9] The *Rizzo* case involved two consolidated class action lawsuits, both of which charged that the Philadelphia police force had engaged in a pattern and practice of police misconduct, and had adopted a civilian complaint procedure that was more effective at deterring civilians from filing complaints than at controlling or punishing police abuse. The district court heard 250 witnesses over the course of twenty-one days, and made detailed factual findings on approximately forty incidents of alleged police abuse. The district court found that "it is impossible to avoid the conclusion that, in the absence of probable cause for arrest, at least two classes of individuals are particularly likely to be subjected to [abuse]: poor blacks, and individuals who question or protest the initial police action."[10] It also concluded that the constitutional violations it found "cannot be dismissed as rare isolated instances."[11] Finding that the civilian complaint procedure was grossly inadequate, the court ordered the police department to implement an improved complaint procedure.

The Supreme Court reversed. Citing *O'Shea,* it expressed serious doubts as to whether the case presented a case or controversy, again because there was insufficient likelihood that the plaintiffs would be subjected to police misconduct in the future. After the Supreme Court issued its decision in *Rizzo,* the Civil Rights Division of the Justice Department launched an eight-month federal investigation into allegations of police brutality in Philadelphia. At the close of that investigation, the Justice Department itself sued the City of Philadelphia, claiming that it had discovered an extensive pattern of constitutional violations, that the police department exercised inadequate supervision, and that the misconduct was disproportionately directed at black and Hispanic citizens.[12] Backed by resources not available to private plaintiffs, the Justice Department was armed with evidence of hundreds of incidents of misconduct and abuse. It found that blacks and Hispanics comprised about a third of Philadelphia's population, but accounted for about 60 to 70 percent of the complaints of physical abuse, illegal searches and seizures, and unlawful detentions.[13] Nonetheless, the district court, reading the signs from *Rizzo* and *O'Shea*, dismissed the complaint on its own initiative.[14] The court of appeals affirmed. If the Justice Department itself could not prevail in such a suit, there is little hope for anyone else to do so.

In *Lyons, O'Shea,* and *Rizzo,* the Supreme Court repeatedly turned back legal challenges to constitutional violations in the administration of criminal justice, each of which involved claims of racial discrimination or racially disparate impact. It did so, moreover, not on the merits, but by barring such suits at the threshold. It defined standing to sue in such narrow terms that few will ever be able to satisfy its requirements in connection with a challenge to criminal law enforcement. Much like the selective prosecution cases, these rulings have the effect of foreclosing claims of discrimination before they are even aired. Because the bars operate at the threshold of the lawsuit, cases are frequently dismissed before the allegations of discrimination can even be developed. They never see the light of day. In this way, the illusion is maintained that the system forbids discrimination; the reality is that the system for all practical purposes forbids discrimination *cases.*

 ## LIMITS ON SUITS FOR DAMAGES

The restrictions erected in *O'Shea, Rizzo,* and *Lyons* apply only to suits for injunctive relief. Thus, the Supreme Court stated that Adolph Lyons could have sued the LAPD for money damages for the injuries he suffered. But suits for monetary compensation face their own set of hurdles, in many instances more formidable even than those that apply to requests for injunctions. Consider a situation faced by many black parents: your son is stopped without cause by a state police officer, ordered out of his car, and searched illegally. You want to challenge the conduct, which appeared to be predicated on nothing more than your son's race. You can't sue for injunctive relief, because you can't show that he will be stopped again, so you want to sue for damages. Who can you sue?

Not the state and not the state police. The Supreme Court has held that the state and its offices are immune from federal suits for damages under the Eleventh Amendment to the Constitution.[15] The Eleventh Amendment literally protects states only from being sued in federal court "by citizens of another state," but the Supreme Court has interpreted it broadly to bar *any* federal suits for damages against states absent their consent. The Court has also held that states cannot be sued for damages for constitutional rights violations in state court.[16] Thus, the state, the defendant with the deepest pocket, is immune.

If the police officer were employed by a city rather than by the state, you could sue the city, but only if you could point to a city policy or custom authorizing such illegal stops and searches.[17] Because most cities do not have such policies, and "custom" is notoriously hard to prove, suing the city is often not a realistic option either.

That leaves the individual officer. But the Supreme Court has also granted government officials substantial protection from suits. Some officials are absolutely immune: judges, for example, can't be sued for damages for discrimination in the courtroom, nor can prosecutors be sued for damages for discriminatory prosecutions, no matter how strong the evidence of wrongdoing. Police officers and other government officials may be sued, but they, too, have a form of immunity: under the judicially created doctrine of "qualified immunity," they may be held liable for constitutional violations only if it was clearly established at the time the conduct occurred that their actions were illegal.[18] The idea behind this doctrine makes some sense standing alone: individual officers should not be held personally liable for their wrongdoing if they could not reasonably have known that their conduct was illegal. But the Supreme Court has interpreted this immunity so broadly that, in its own words, "all but the plainly incompetent or those who knowingly violate the law" are immune.[19] As a result, shockingly few damages actions for government misconduct succeed. For example, of some 12,000 actions filed against federal officials for constitutional violations from 1971 to 1985, only four led to a successful judgment or settlement for the plaintiff.[20] When the qualified immunity rule is combined with the bars on suits against states and cities, the result often means that *no one* can be sued for a constitutional violation. The victim is made to bear the cost of the violation himself.

In addition to these legal barriers to relief, there are numerous practical hurdles to bringing a suit for damages. In many instances the violation of constitutional rights does not lead to any tangible harm. An illegal search motivated by race, for example, may be extremely intrusive and humiliating, but as long as the police do no physical damage, it will be difficult to point to harm for which one should be compensated. In addition, many such suits reduce to a swearing match between a police officer and the individual stopped. Because those who are stopped are disproportionately poor and members of minority groups, they may find it difficult to convince a judge or jury to accept their word over a police officer's.

Finally, as the *McCleskey* case demonstrated, to establish an equal protection violation, one must prove *intentional* discrimination, and it is extremely difficult to do so. Government officials do not commonly admit that their actions were motivated by prejudice. Indeed, because there is such a strong social sanction against racial prejudice, few people are even willing to admit to themselves that they have acted for racial reasons. Yet racial stereotypes affect all of us in subtle and not-so-subtle ways. The Court's prohibition of intentional discrimination weeds out the bigots who admit they are racist, but ignores (and thereby effectively legitimates) all other discrimination.

Thus, despite the Supreme Court's assurances to Lyons that he could seek damages, the likelihood of obtaining any relief in any case challenging discriminatory law enforcement is slim. This is true whether one seeks to raise selective prosecution as a defense to a particular criminal prosecution, whether one seeks injunctive relief to forestall future violations, or whether one seeks only monetary compensation for an individual case. In each setting, the Court has constructed a set of all-but-impassable barriers. And in each area, the hurdles operate at the threshold, stopping the complaint from even being aired. In this way, the illusion of a constitutional prohibition against discrimination in criminal justice is maintained, but the avenue left open for enforcing it is so narrow and difficult that few will succeed in navigating its course. At one level, that may have the effect of legitimating the system; the courts can say that they abhor and forbid race discrimination, but that they simply do not see it. But I suggest at a deeper level this strategy eats away at the system's legitimacy. The charade cannot be maintained forever. Ultimately members of minority groups are likely to conclude that the courts and the law cannot be counted on to guarantee equal protection.

NOTES

1. 118 U.S. 356 (1886).
2. Id. at 373–74.
3. *United States v. Armstrong,* 517 U.S. 456 (1996).
4. *City of Los Angeles v. Lyons,* 461 U.S. 95, 105 (1983).
5. 414 U.S. 488 (1974).
6. 414 U.S. at 495–96.
7. *Rizzo v. Goode,* 423 U.S. 362 (1976).
8. Ralph Cipriano & Tom Infield, "You Either Loved Him or Hated Him," *Phila. Inquirer,* 17 July 1991, 1A.
9. Jerome H. Skolnick & James J. Fyfe, *Above the Law: Police and the Excessive Use of Force,* 140 (1993).
10. *COPPAR v. Rizzo,* 357 F. Supp. 1289, 1317 (E.D. Pa. 1973).
11. Id. at 1319.
12. *United States v. City of Philadelphia,* 644 F.2d 187 (3d Circ. 1980).
13. 644 F.2d at 210 (Gibbons, J., dissenting from denial of petition for rehearing).
14. Id. at 209.
15. *Quern v. Jordan,* 440 U.S. 332 (1979).
16. *Will v. Mich. Dept. of State Police,* 491 U.S. 58 (1989).
17. *Monell v. Dept. of Social Services,* 436 U.S. 658 (1978).
18. *Harlow v. Fitzgerald,* 457 U.S. 800 (1982).
19. *Malley v. Briggs,* 475 U.S. 335, 341 (1986).
20. Written Statement of John J. Farley, III, Director, Torts Branch, Civil Division, U.S. Dept. of Justice, to the Litigation Section of the Bar of the District of Columbia (May 1985); cited in Cornelia Pillard, *Taking Fiction Seriously,* manuscript on file with author.

QUESTIONS FOR CRITICAL THINKING

Reading 32

1. Cole argues that the criminal justice system depends on unequal racial and class patterns in prosecution and incarceration. How does this challenge or affirm your own perceptions of the criminal justice system?

2. What policy changes do you see as necessary in our criminal justice system? How might these changes impact inequality on the basis of race in the United States?

3. Does the continuing institutionalized racism that Cole illustrates serve as a justification for the need for corrective programs such as affirmative action? If so, how? If not, why not?

Reading 33

THE EFFECTS OF AFFIRMATIVE ACTION ON OTHER STAKEHOLDERS

BARBARA RESKIN

Affirmative action policies and practices reduce job discrimination against minorities and white women, although their effects have not been large. Some critics charge that affirmative action's positive effects have been offset by its negative effects on white men, on productivity, and on the merit system. The research examined in this chapter shows that affirmative action rarely entails reverse discrimination, and neither hampers business productivity nor unduly increases the costs of doing business. Both theoretical and empirical research suggest that it enhances productivity by encouraging employment practices that better utilize workers' skills.

REVERSE DISCRIMINATION

For many people, the most troubling aspect of affirmative action is that it may discriminate against majority-group members (Lynch 1997). According to 1994 surveys, 70 to 80 percent of whites believed that affirmative action sometimes discriminates against whites (Steeh and Krysan 1996, p. 139). Men are more likely to believe that a woman will get a job or promotion over an equally or more qualified man than they are to believe that a man will get a promotion over an equally or more qualified woman (Davis and Smith 1996). In short, many whites, especially white men, feel that they are vulnerable to reverse discrimination (Bobo and Kluegel 1993). When asked whether African Americans or whites were at greater risk of discrimination at work, respondents named whites over African Americans by a margin of two to one (Steeh and Krysan 1996, p. 140). In addition, 39 percent of respondents to a 1997 *New York Times*/CBS News poll said that whites losing out because of affirmative action was a bigger problem than African Americans losing out because of discrimination (Verhovek 1997, p. 32).

Several kinds of evidence indicate that whites' fears of reverse discrimination are exaggerated. Reverse discrimination is rare both in absolute terms and relative to conventional discrimination.[1] The most direct evidence for this conclusion comes from employment-audit studies: On every measured outcome, African-American men were much more likely than white men to experience discrimination, and Latinos were more likely than non-Hispanic men to experience discrimination (Heckman and Siegelman 1993, p. 218). Statistics on the numbers and outcomes of complaints of employment discrimination also suggest that reverse discrimination is rare.

According to national surveys, relatively few whites have experienced reverse discrimination. Only 5 to 12 percent of whites believe that their race has cost them a job or promotion, compared to 36 percent of African Americans (Steeh and Krysan 1996, pp. 139–40). Of 4,025 Los Angeles workers, 45 percent of African Americans and 16 percent of Latinos said that they had been refused a job because of their race, and 16 percent of African Americans and 8 percent of Latinos reported that they had been discriminated against in terms of pay or a promotion (Bobo and Suh 1996, table 1). In contrast, of the 863 whites surveyed, less than 3 percent had ever experienced discrimination in pay or promotion, and only one mentioned reverse discrimination. Nonetheless, two-thirds to four-fifths of whites (but just one-quarter of African Americans) surveyed in the 1990s thought it likely that less qualified African Americans won jobs or promotions over more qualified whites (Taylor 1994a; Davis and Smith 1994; Steeh and Krysan 1996, p. 139).[2]

Alfred Blumrosen's (1996, pp. 5–6) exhaustive review of discrimination complaints filed with the Equal Employment Opportunity Commission offers additional evidence that reverse discrimination is rare. Of the 451,442 discrimination complaints filed with the EEOC between 1987 and 1994, only

4 percent charged reverse discrimination (see also Norton 1996, pp. 44–5).[3] Of the 2,189 discrimination cases that Federal appellate courts decided between 1965 and 1985, less than 5 percent charged employers with reverse discrimination (Burstein 1991, p. 518).

Statistics on the more than 3,000 cases that reached district and appeals courts between 1990 and 1994 show an even lower incidence of reverse-discrimination charges: Less than 2 percent charged reverse discrimination (U.S. Department of Labor, Employment Standards Administration n.d., p. 3). The small number of reverse discrimination complaints by white men does not appear to stem from their reluctance to file complaints: They filed more than 80 percent of the age discrimination complaints that the EEOC received in 1994. Instead, as former EEOC chair Eleanor Holmes Norton (1996, p. 45) suggested, white men presumably complain most about the kind of discrimination that they experience most and least about discrimination they rarely encounter.

Allegations of reverse discrimination are less likely than conventional discrimination cases to be supported by evidence. Of the approximately 7,000 reverse-discrimination complaints filed with the EEOC in 1994, the EEOC found only 28 credible (Crosby and Herzberger 1996, p. 55). Indeed, U.S. district and appellate courts dismissed almost all the reverse-discrimination cases they heard between 1990 and 1994 as lacking merit.

Although rare, reverse discrimination does occur. District and appellate courts found seven employers guilty of reverse discrimination in the early 1990s (all involved voluntary affirmative action programs), and a few Federal contractors have engaged in reverse discrimination, according to the Office of Federal Contract Compliance Program's (OFCCP) director for Region II (Stephanopoulos and Edley 1995, section 6.3).[4]

The actions and reports of Federal contractors are inconsistent with the belief that goals are *de facto* quotas that lead inevitably to reverse discrimination. In the first place, the fact that contractors rarely meet their goals means that they do not view them as quotas (Leonard 1990, p. 56). Second, only 2 percent of 641 Federal contractors the OFCCP surveyed in 1994 complained that the agency required quotas or reverse discrimination (Stephanopoulos and Edley 1995, section 6.3).

How can we reconcile the enormous gulf between whites' perceptions that they are likely to lose jobs or promotions because of affirmative action and the small risk of this happening? The white men who brought reverse discrimination suits presumably concluded that their employers' choices of women or minorities could not have been based on merit, because men are accustomed to being selected for customarily male jobs (*New York Times,* March 31, 1995).[5] Most majority-group members who have not had a firsthand experience of competing unsuccessfully with a minority man or woman or a white woman cite media reports as the source of their impression that affirmative action prompts employers to favor minorities and women (Hochschild 1995, pp. 144, 308).[6] It seems likely that politicians' and the media's emphasis on "quotas" has distorted the public's understanding of what is required and permitted in the name of affirmative action (Entman 1997). It is also likely that the public does not distinguish affirmative action in employment from affirmative action in education which may include preferences or in the awarding of contracts which have included set-asides.

AFFIRMATIVE ACTION AND AMERICAN COMMERCE

Does affirmative action curb productivity, as some critics have charged? On the one hand, affirmative action could impede productivity if it forces employers to hire or promote marginally qualified and unqualified workers, or if the paperwork associated with affirmative action programs is burdensome. On the other hand, employers who assign workers to jobs based on their qualifications rather than their sex or race should make more efficient use of workers' abilities and hence should be more productive than those who use discriminatory employment practices (Becker 1971; Leonard 1984c; Donohue 1986). Affirmative action could also increase profitability by introducing varied points of view or helping firms broaden their markets (Cox and Blake 1991; Watson, Kumar, and Michaelsen 1993).

Effects on Productivity

There is no evidence that affirmative action reduces productivity or that workers hired under affirmative action are less qualified than other workers. In the first place, affirmative action plans that compromise valid educational and job requirements are illegal. Hiring unqualified workers or choosing a less qualified person over a more qualified one because of their race or sex is illegal and is not condoned in the name of affirmative action (U.S. Department of Labor, Employment Standards Administration n.d., p. 2). Second, to the extent that affirmative action gives women and minority men access to jobs that more fully exploit their productive capacity, their productivity and that of their employers should increase.

Although many Americans believe that affirmative action means that less qualified persons are hired and promoted (Verhovek 1997, p. 32), the evidence does not bear this out. According to a study of more than 3,000 workers hired in entry-level jobs in a cross-section of firms in Atlanta, Boston, Detroit, and Los Angeles, the performance evaluations of women and minorities hired under affirmative action did not differ from those of white men or female or minority workers for whom affirmative action played no role in hiring (Holzer and Neumark 1998). In addition, Columbus, Ohio, female and minority police officers hired under an affirmative action consent decree performed as well as white men (Kern 1996). Of nearly 300 corporate executives surveyed in 1979, 72 percent believed that minority hiring did not impair productivity (*Wall Street Journal* 1979); 41 percent of CEOs surveyed in 1995 said affirmative action improved corporate productivity (Crosby and Herzberger 1996, p. 86).[7]

Studies assessing the effect of firms' racial makeup on their profits also show no effects of affirmative action on productivity. An analysis of 100 of Chicago's largest firms over a 13-year period found no statistically significant relationship between the firms' share of minority workers and their profit margins or return on equity (McMillen 1995). This absence of an association is inconsistent with companies using lower standards when hiring African American employees. Finally, according to a study that compared the market performance of the 100 firms with best and worst records of hiring and promoting women and minorities, the former averaged an 18-percent return on investments, whereas the latter's average returns were below 8 percent (Glass Ceiling Commission 1995, pp. 14, 61).[8]

Costs to Business

Estimates of the price tag of affirmative action range from a low of hundreds of millions of dollars to a high of $26 billion (Brimelow and Spencer 1993).[9] More realistic estimates put enforcement and compliance costs at about $1.9 billion (Leonard 1994, p. 34; Conrad 1995, pp. 37–8). According to Andrew Brimmer (1995, p. 12), former Governor of the Federal Reserve Board, the inefficient use of African Americans' productive capacity (as indicated by their education, training, and experience) costs the economy 70 times this much: about $138 billion annually, which is about 2.15 percent of the gross national product. Adding the cost of sex discrimination against white women would substantially increase the estimated cost of discrimination because white women outnumber African American men and women in the labor force by about three to one. The more affirmative action reduces race and sex discrimination, the lower its costs relative to the savings it engenders.

The affirmative action that the Federal executive order requires of Federal contractors adds to their paperwork. Companies with at least $50,000 in Federal contracts that employ at least 50 employees must provide written affirmative action plans that include goals and timetables, based on an annual analysis of their utilization of their labor pool. They must also provide specified information to the OFCCP and keep detailed records on the composition of their jobs and job applicants by race and sex. In response to an OFCCP survey soliciting their criticisms of the program, about one in eight Federal contractors complained about the paperwork burden (Stephanopoulos and Edley 1995, section 6.3). Keeping the records required by the OFCCP encourages the bureaucratization of human resource practices. As noted, informal employment practices, while cheaper in the short run, are also more subject to discriminatory bias and hence cost firms efficiency. Thus, implicit in the logic of the OFCCP's requirements is the recognition that formalizing personnel practices helps to reduce discrimination.

Business Support

U.S. business has supported affirmative action for at least 15 years. The Reagan administration's efforts to curtail the contract compliance program in the early 1980s drew strong opposition from the corporate sector (Bureau of National Affairs 1986). Among the groups that went on record as opposing cutbacks in Federal affirmative action programs was the National Association of Manufacturers, a major organization of U.S. employers (*The San Diego Union-Tribune* 1995, p. AA-2). All but six of 128 heads of major corporations indicated that they would retain their affirmative action plans if the Federal government ended affirmative action (Noble 1986, p. B4). A 1996 survey showed similar levels of corporate support for affirmative action: 94 percent of CEOs surveyed said that affirmative action had improved their hiring procedures, 53 percent said it had improved marketing, and—as noted above—41 percent said it had improved productivity (Crosby and Herzberger 1996, p. 86). The business community's favorable stance toward affirmative action is also seen in the jump in stock prices for firms recognized by the OFCCP for their effective affirmative action programs (Wright et al. 1995, p. 281).

Perhaps the most telling sign of business support for affirmative action is the diffusion of affirmative action practices from Federal contractors to noncontractors. As noncontractors have recognized the efficiency or market payoffs associated with more objective employment practices and a more diverse workforce, many have voluntarily implemented some affirmative action practices (Fisher 1985).

 AFFIRMATIVE ACTION AND OTHER STAKEHOLDERS

The consequences of affirmative action reach beyond workers and employers by increasing the pools of skilled minority and female workers. When affirmative action prompts employers to hire minorities or women for positions that serve the public, it can bring services to communities that would otherwise be underserved. For example, African-American and Hispanic physicians are more likely than whites and Anglos to practice in minority communities (Komaromy et al. 1996). Graduates of the Medical School at the University of California at San Diego who were admitted under a special admissions program were more likely to serve inner-city and rural communities and saw more poor patients than those admitted under the regular procedures (Penn, Russell, and Simon 1986).

Women's and minorities' employment in nontraditional jobs also raises the aspirations of other members of excluded groups by providing role models and by signaling that jobs are open to them. Some minorities and women do not pursue jobs or promotions because they expect to encounter discrimination (Mayhew 1968, p. 313). By reducing the perception that discriminatory barriers block access to certain lines of work, affirmative action curtails this self-selection (Reskin and Roos 1990, p. 305). In addition, the economic gains provided by better jobs permit beneficiaries to invest in the education of the next generation.

 ## AFFIRMATIVE ACTION, MERITOCRACY, AND FAIRNESS

Affirmative action troubles some Americans for the same reasons discrimination does: They see it as unfair and inconsistent with meritocracy (Nacoste 1990). The evidence summarized above indicates that employers very rarely use quotas and that affirmative action does not lead to the employment of unqualified workers. We know too that many employers implement affirmative action by expanding their recruiting efforts, by providing additional training, and by formalizing human resource practices to eliminate bias. By eliminating cronyism, drawing on wider talent pools, and providing for due process, these practices are fairer to all workers than conventional business practices (*Harvard Law Review* 1989, pp. 668–70; Dobbin et al. 1993, pp. 401–6). After all, managers who judge minority and female workers by their race or sex instead of their performance may judge white workers by arbitrary standards as well (Rand 1996, p. 72).

Available research does not address how often employers take into account race and gender in choosing among equally qualified applicants. Although the courts have forbidden race- and gender-conscious practices in layoffs, they have allowed employers to take into account race or gender in selecting among qualified applicants in order to remedy the consequences of having previously excluded certain groups from some jobs. Such programs trouble some Americans, as we can see from the research evidence presented in the next section.

 ## AMERICANS' VIEWS OF AFFIRMATIVE ACTION

The passage of the 1996 California Civil Rights Initiative, which barred this state from engaging in affirmative action, has been interpreted as signaling mounting public opposition to affirmative action. In reality, whites' and African Americans' views of affirmative action are both more nuanced and more positive than the California election result suggests. People's responses to opinion polls depend largely on how pollsters characterize affirmative action (Kravitz et al. 1997).[10] About 70 percent of Americans support affirmative action programs that pollsters describe as not involving "quotas" or "preferences" (Steeh and Krysan 1996, pp. 132, 134; Entman 1997, p. 37). Like a red flag, the term "quota" also triggers strong negative reactions. This happens because people view quotas as inconsistent with merit-based hiring and because quotas provoke fear of unfairly losing a job or promotion by members of groups that are not covered by affirmative action. As a result, most whites and African Americans oppose quotas (Bobo and Kluegel, 1993; Steeh and Krysan 1996, pp. 132–3, 148).

A casual reading of newspaper reports indicates considerable instability in Americans' attitudes toward affirmative action and a fair amount of opposition to affirmative action. For example, fewer than one in eight Americans surveyed in a 1995 Gallup poll approved of affirmative action programs that involve hiring quotas, and only 40 to 50 percent of Americans endorsed affirmative action programs designed to give African Americans or women preferential treatment (Moore 1995). However, polls that show low levels of support for affirmative action in the workplace typically ask about practices that are illegal and hence rare in actual affirmative action programs (Kravitz et al. 1997, p. xi). When pollsters ask about affirmative action in general or about the practices that actual affirmative action programs include, the majority of whites and African Americans are supportive.

In national polls conducted in the mid-1990s, about 70 percent of respondents endorsed affirmative action either as currently practiced or with reforms (Entman 1997, p. 37). For example, almost three-quarters of the respondents to a 1995 Gallup poll approved of employers using outreach efforts to recruit qualified minorities and women (Steeh and Krysan 1996, pp. 132, 134). Most whites and African Americans support such practices as targeted recruitment, open advertising, monitoring diversity, job training, and educational assistance designed to allow minorities to compete as individuals (e.g., training programs). More than three out of four white respondents and 85 percent of African-American respondents to a 1991 Harris survey agreed that "as long as there are no rigid quotas, it makes sense to give special training and advice to women and minorities so that they can perform better on the job" (Bobo and Kluegel 1993; Bruno 1995, p. 24).

In sum, the polls reveal that the majority of whites and African Americans have supported affirmative action since the early 1970s. Most Americans support the affirmative action procedures that employers actually use, such as taking extra efforts to find and recruit minorities and women. The broadest support is for practices that expand the applicant pool, but ignore race or gender in the selection process. Thus, Americans' first choice is enhancing equal opportunity without using race- or gender-conscious mechanisms. What most Americans oppose is quotas, an employment remedy that courts impose only under exceptional circumstances. Thus, the kinds of affirmative action practices most Americans support are in synch with what most affirmative action employers do.

 CONCLUSION

Some critics charge that any positive effects of affirmative action come at too high a price. However, the evidence suggests that the predominant effects of affirmative action on American enterprise are neutral, and some are positive. Contrary to popular opinion, reverse discrimination is rare. Workers for whom affirmative action was a hiring consideration are no less productive than other workers. There is no evidence that affirmative action impairs productivity, and there is some evidence that, when properly implemented, affirmative action increases firms' efficiency by rationalizing their business practices. These neutral to positive effects of affirmative action contribute to the broad support it enjoys in corporate America. The affirmative action practices that appear to be most common—such as special training programs or efforts to expand recruitment pools (Bureau of National Affairs 1986)—have the support of the majority of whites and people of color.

Although most affirmative action practices are neutral with respect to race and gender (e.g., eliminating subjectivity from evaluation systems), some employers take into account race and sex as "plus factors" in choosing among qualified candidates in order to reduce imbalances stemming from their past employment practices. Race- and gender-conscious practices are legal if they are part of court-ordered or voluntary affirmative action programs designed to correct a serious imbalance resulting from past exclusionary practices and as long as they are properly structured so that they do not unnecessarily or permanently limit the opportunities of groups not protected under affirmative action. At least one in four Americans opposes such race- and gender-conscious practices. More generally, any departure from strict reliance on merit troubles some Americans. Others favor taking into account group membership in order to eradicate America's occupational caste system, enhance equal opportunity, and strengthen the U.S. democracy (Steinberg 1995).

The tension between affirmative action and merit is the inevitable result of the conflict between our national values and what actually occurs in the nation's workplaces. As long as discrimination is more pervasive than affirmative action, it is the real threat to meritocracy. But because no one will join the debate on behalf of discrimination, we end up with the illusion of a struggle between affirmative action and merit.

NOTES

1. Lynch's (1989, p. 53) search for white male Southern Californians who saw themselves as victims of reverse discrimination turned up only 32 men.
2. Younger whites, those from more privileged backgrounds, and those from areas with larger black populations—especially black populations who were relatively well off—were most likely to believe that blacks benefited from preferential treatment (Taylor 1994b).
3. Two percent were by white men charging sex, race, or national origin discrimination (three-quarters of these charged sex discrimination), and 1.8 percent were by white women charging race discrimination (Blumrosen 1996, p. 5).
4. In the early years of affirmative action, some federal contractors implemented quotas; since then the OFCCP has made considerable effort to ensure that contractors understand that quotas are illegal.

5. Occupational segregation by sex, race, and ethnicity no doubt contributes to this perception by reinforcing the notion that one's sex, color, or ethnicity is naturally related to the ability to perform a particular job.
6. The disproportionate number of court-ordered interventions to curtail race and sex discrimination in cities' police and fire departments (Martin 1991) and the large number of court challenges by white men (Bureau of National Affairs 1995, pp. 5–12) probably contributed to the public's impression that hiring quotas are common.
7. No data were provided on the proportion who believed that affirmative action hampered productivity.
8. Although firms' stock prices fall after the media report a discrimination suit, they rebound within a few days (Hersch 1991; Wright et al. 1995).
9. The $26 billion estimate includes the budgets of the OFCCP, the EEOC, other federal agencies' affirmative action–related activities, and private firms' compliance costs estimated at $20 million for each million of public funds budgeted for enforcement (Brimelow and Spencer 1993). Arguably, the EEOC's budget—indeed all enforcement costs—should be chalked up to the cost of discrimination, not the cost of affirmative action.
10. Several factors affect Americans' response to surveys about affirmative action in the workplace: whether their employer practices affirmative action (Taylor 1995), their own conception of what affirmative action means (one-third of white respondents to a 1995 CBS/*New York Times* poll acknowledged that they were not sure what affirmative action is; Steeh and Krysan 1996, p. 129), whether the question also asks about affirmative action in education, whether the question asks about race- or sex-based affirmative action (although contractors are also obliged to provide affirmative action for Vietnam-era veterans and disabled persons, these groups are invisible in opinion polls), the respondents' own race and sex, the reasons respondents think racial inequality exists, and their level of racial prejudice (Bobo and Kluegel 1993). For full reviews, see Steeh and Krysan (1996) and Kravitz et al. (1997).

REFERENCES

Becker, Gary S. 1971. *A Theory of Discrimination.* 2d ed. Chicago, IL: University of Chicago Press.

Blumrosen, Alfred W. 1996. *Declaration.* Statement submitted to the Supreme Court of California in Response to Proposition 209, September 26.

Bobo, Larry and Susan A. Suh. 1996. "Surveying Racial Discrimination: Analyses from a Multi-Ethnic Labor Market." Working Paper No. 75, Russell Sage Foundation, New York.

Bobo, Lawrence and James R. Kluegel. 1993. "Opposition to Race Targeting." *American Sociological Review* 58:443–64.

Brimelow, Peter and Leslie Spencer. 1993. "When Quotas Replace Merit, Everybody Suffers." *Forbes,* February 15, pp. 80–102.

Brimmer, Andrew F. 1995. "The Economic Cost of Discrimination against Black Americans." Pp. 11–29 in *Economic Perspectives on Affirmative Action,* edited by M. C. Simms. Washington, D.C.: Joint Center for Political and Economic Studies.

Bruno, Andorra, 1995. *Affirmative Action in Employment.* CRS Report for Congress. Washington, D.C.: Congressional Research Service.

Bureau of National Affairs. 1986. *Affirmative Action Today: A Legal and Political Analysis. A BNA Special Report.* Washington, D.C.: The Bureau of National Affairs.

_____. 1995. *Affirmative Action after Adarand: A Legal, Regulatory, Legislative Outlook.* Washington, D.C.: The Bureau of National Affairs.

Burnstein, Paul. 1991. "'Reverse Discrimination' Cases in the Federal Courts: Mobilization by a Countermovement." *Sociological Quarterly* 32:511–28.

Conrad, Cecilia. 1995. "The Economic Cost of Affirmative Action." Pp. 33–53 in *Economic Perspectives on Affirmative Action,* edited by M. C. Simms. Washington, D.C.: Joint Center for Political and Economic Studies.

Cox, Taylor H. and Stacy Blake. 1991. "Managing Cultural Diversity: Implications for Organizational Competitiveness." *Academy of Management Executive* 5:45–56.

Crosby, Faye J. and Sharon D. Herzberger. 1996. "For Affirmative Action." Pp. 3–109 in *Affirmative Action: Pros and Cons of Policy and Practice,* edited by R. J. Simon. Washington, D.C.: American University Press.

Davis, James A. and Tom W. Smith. 1994. *General Social Survey* [MRDF]. Chicago IL: National Opinion Research Center [producer, distributor].

_____. 1996. *General Social Survey* [MRDF]. Chicago IL: National Opinion Research Center [producer, distributor].

Dobbin, Frank, John Sutton, John Meyer, and W. Richard Scott. 1993. "Equal Opportunity Law and the Construction of Internal Labor Markets." *American Journal of Sociology* 99:396–427.

Donohue, John J. 1986. "Is Title VII Efficient?" *University of Pennsylvania Law Review* 134:1411–31.

Entman, Robert M. 1997. "Manufacturing Discord: Media in the Affirmative Action Debate." *Press/Politics* 2:32–51.

Fisher, Ann B. 1985. "Businessmen Like to Hire by the Numbers." *Fortune Magazine,* September 16, pp. 26, 28–30.

Glass Ceiling Commission. See U.S. Department of Labor, Office of Federal Contract Compliance Programs, Glass Ceiling Commission.

Harvard Law Review. 1989. "Rethinking Weber: The Business Response to Affirmative Action." *Harvard Law Review* 102:658–71.

Heckman, James J. and Peter Siegelman. 1993. "The Urban Institute Audit Studies: Their Methods and Findings." Pp. 187–229 in *Clear and Convincing Evidence: Measurement of Discrimination in America,* edited by M. Fix and R. J. Struyk. Washington, D.C.: The Urban Institute.

Hellerstein, Judith K., David Neumark, and Kenneth R. Troske. 1998. "Market Forces and Sex Discrimination." Department of Sociology, University of Maryland, College Park. Unpublished manuscript.

Hersch, Joni. 1991. "Equal Employment Opportunity Law and Firm Profitability." *Journal of Human Resources* 26:139–53.

Hochschild, Jennifer. 1995. *Facing Up to the American Dream.* Princeton, NJ: Princeton University Press.

Holzer, Harry J. and David Neumark. Forthcoming 1998. "Are Affirmative Action Hires Less Qualified? Evidence from Employer-Employee Data on New Hires." *Journal of Labor Economics.*

Kern, Leesa. 1996. "Hiring and Seniority: Issues in Policing the Post-Judicial Intervention Period." Department of Sociology, Ohio State University, Columbus, OH: Unpublished manuscript.

Komaromy, Miriam, Kevin Grumbach, Michael Drake, Karen Vranizan, Nicole Lurie, Dennis Keane, and Andrew Bindman. 1996. "The Role of Black and Hispanic Physicians in Providing Health Care in Underserved Populations." *New England Journal of Medicine* 334:1305–10.

Kravitz, David A., David A. Harrison, Marlene E. Turner, Edward L. Levine, Wanda Chaves, Michael T. Brannick, Donna L. Denning, Craig J. Russell, and Maureen A. Conrad. 1997. *Affirmative Action: A Review of Psychological and Behavioral Research.* Bowling Green, OH: Society for Industrial and Organizational Psychology.

Leonard, Jonathan S. 1984c. "Anti-Discrimination or Reverse Discrimination: The Impact of Changing Demographics, Title VII, and Affirmative Action on Productivity" *Journal of Human Resources* 19:145–74.

———. 1990. "The Impact of Affirmative Action Regulation and Equal Employment Law on Black Employment." *Journal of Economic Perspectives* 4:47–63.

———. 1994. "Use of Enforcement Techniques in Eliminating Glass Ceiling Barriers." Report to the Glass Ceiling Commission, April, U.S. Department of Labor, Washington, D.C.

Lovrich, Nicholas P., Brent S. Steel, and David Hood. 1986. "Equity versus Productivity: Affirmative Action and Municipal Police Services." *Public Productivity Review* 39:61–72.

Lynch, Frederick R. 1989. *Invisible Victims: White Males and the Crisis of Affirmative Action.* New York: Greenwood.

———. 1997. *The Diversity Machine: The Drive to Change the White Male Workplace.* New York: Free Press.

Martin, Susan E. 1991. "The Effectiveness of Affirmative Action: The Case of Women in Policing." *Justice Quarterly* 8:489–504.

Mayhew, Leon. 1968. *Law and Equal Opportunity: A Study of Massachusetts Commission against Discrimination.* Cambridge, MA: Harvard University Press.

McMillen, Liz. 1995. "[Affirmative Action] Policies Said to Help Companies Hire Qualified Workers at No Extra Cost." *Chronicle of Higher Education,* November 17, p. A7.

Moore, David W. 1995. "Americans Today Are Dubious about Affirmative Action." *The Gallup Poll Monthly,* March, pp. 36–8.

Nacoste, Rupert Barnes. 1990. "Sources of Stigma: Analyzing the Psychology of Affirmative Action." *Law & Policy* 12:175–95.

New York Times. 1995. "Reverse Discrimination Complaints Rare, Labor Study Reports." *New York Times,* March 31, p. A23.

Noble, Kenneth. 1986. "Employers Are Split on Affirmative Goals." *New York Times,* March 3, p. B4.

Norton, Eleanor Holmes. 1996. "Affirmative Action in the Workplace." Pp. 39–48 in *The Affirmative Action Debate,* edited by G. Curry. Reading, MA: Addison-Wesley.

Penn, Nolan E., Percy J. Russell, and Harold J. Simon. 1986. "Affirmative Action at Work: A Survey of Graduates of the University of California at San Diego Medical School." *American Journal of Public Health* 76:1144–46.

Rand, A. Barry. 1996. "Diversity in Corporate America." Pp. 65–76 in *The Affirmative Action Debate,* edited by G. Curry. Reading, MA: Addison-Wesley.

Reskin, Barbara F. and Patricia Roos. 1990. *Job Queues, Gender Queues.* Philadelphia, PA: Temple University Press.

Roper Center for Public Opinion. 1995. *Poll Database:* Question ID USGALLUP.95MRW1.R32[MRDF]. Storrs, CT: Roper Center for Public Opinion [producer, distributor].

San Diego Union-Tribune. 1995. "Groups at Odds Over Affirmative Action Revisions." *San Diego Union-Tribune,* September 13, p. AA-2.

Steeh, Charlotte, and Maria Krysan. 1996. "The Polls—Trends: Affirmative Action and the Public, 1970–1995." *Public Opinion Quarterly* 60:128–58.

Steel, Brent S. and Nicholas P. Lovrich. 1987. "Equality and Efficiency Tradeoffs in Affirmative Action—Real or Imagined? The Case of Women in Policing." *Social Science Journal* 24:53–70.

Steinberg, Steven. 1995. *Turning Back: Retreat from Racial Justice in American Thought.* Boston, MA: Beacon.

Stephanopoulos, George and Christopher Edley, Jr. 1995. "Affirmative Action Review." Report to the President, Washington, D.C.

Taylor, Marylee C. 1994a. "Beliefs about the Preferential Hiring of Black Applicants: Sure It Happens, But I've Never Seen It." Pennsylvania State University, University Park, PA. Unpublished manuscript.

_____. 1994b. "Impact of Affirmative Action on Beneficiary Groups: Evidence from the 1990 General Social Survey." *Basic and Applied Social Psychology* 15:143–78.

_____. 1995. "White Backlash to Workplace Affirmative Action: Peril or Myth?" *Social Forces* 73:1385–1414.

U.S. Department of Labor, Employment Standards Administration, Office of Federal Contract Compliance Programs [cited as OFCCP]. n.d. "The Rhetoric and the Reality about Federal Affirmative Action at the OFCCP." Washington, D.C.: U.S. Department of Labor.

U.S. Department of Labor, Office of Federal Contract Compliance Programs, Glass Ceiling Commission. 1995. *Good for Business: Making Full Use of the Nation's Human Capital/The Environmental Scar.* Washington, D.C.: U.S. Government Printing Office.

Verhovek, Sam Howe. 1997. "In Poll, Americans Reject Means but Not Ends of Racial Diversity." *New York Times,* December 14, pp. 1, 32.

Wall Street Journal. 1979. "Labor Letter: A Special News Report on People and Their Jobs in Offices, Fields, and Factories: Affirmative Action Is Accepted by Most Corporate Chiefs." *Wall Street Journal,* April 3, p. 1.

Watson, Warren E., Kamalesh Kumar, and Larry K. Michaelsen. 1993. "Cultural Diversity's Impact on Interaction Process and Performance: Comparing Homogeneous and Diverse Task Groups." *Academy of Management Journal* 36:590–602.

Wright, Peter, Stephen P. Ferris, Janine S. Hiller, and Mark Kroll. 1995. "Competitiveness through Management of Diversity: Effects on Stock Price Valuation." *Academy of Management Journal* 38:272–87.

QUESTIONS FOR CRITICAL THINKING

Reading 33

1. Affirmative action programs have often been accused of being discriminatory towards those in the majority. However, as Reskin discusses, such policies rarely do this. What perpetuates the myth of affirmative action as "reverse discrimination"?

2. How might affirmative action policies enhance productivity and encourage improved employment practices?

3. What societal changes are necessary to eliminate the need for affirmative action? Are affirmative action programs still necessary? Why, or why not?

Reading 34

THE POSSESSIVE INVESTMENT IN WHITENESS
Racialized Social Democracy and the "White" Problem in American Studies

GEORGE LIPSITZ

Shortly after World War II, a French reporter asked expatriate Richard Wright his opinion about the "Negro problem" in the United States. The author replied "There isn't any Negro problem; there is only a white problem."[1] By inverting the reporter's question, Wright called attention to its hidden assumptions—that racial polarization comes from the existence of blacks rather than from the behavior of whites, that black people are a "problem" for whites rather than fellow citizens entitled to justice, and that unless otherwise specified, "Americans" means whites.[2] But Wright's formulation also placed political mobilization by African Americans in context, attributing it to the systemic practices of aversion, exploitation, denigration, and discrimination practiced by people who think of themselves as "white."

George Lipsitz, "The Possessive Investment in Whiteness: Racialized Social Democracy and the 'White' Problem in American Studies" from *American Quarterly* (September 1995). Copyright © 1995 by The American Studies Association. Reprinted with the permission of The Johns Hopkins University Press.

Whiteness is everywhere in American culture, but it is very hard to see. As Richard Dyer argues, "white power secures its dominance by seeming not to be anything in particular."[3] As the unmarked category against which difference is constructed, whiteness never has to speak its name, never has to acknowledge its role as an organizing principle in social and cultural relations.[4]

To identify, analyze, and oppose the destructive consequences of whiteness, we need what Walter Benjamin called "presence of mind." Benjamin wrote that people visit fortune-tellers not so much out of a desire to know the future but rather out of a fear of not noticing some important aspect of the present. "Presence of mind," he argued, "is an abstract of the future, and precise awareness of the present moment more decisive than foreknowledge of the most distant events."[5] In our society at this time, precise awareness of the present moment requires an understanding of the existence and the destructive consequences of "white" identity.

In recent years, an important body of American studies scholarship has started to explore the role played by cultural practices in creating "whiteness" in the United States. More than the product of private prejudices, whiteness emerged as a relevant category in American life largely because of realities created by slavery and segregation, by immigration restriction and Indian policy, by conquest and colonialism. A fictive identity of "whiteness" appeared in law as an abstraction, and it became actualized in everyday life in many ways. American economic and political life gave different racial groups unequal access to citizenship and property, while cultural practices including wild west shows, minstrel shows, racist images in advertising, and Hollywood films institutionalized racism by uniting ethnically diverse European-American audiences into an imagined community—one called into being through inscribed appeals to the solidarity of white supremacy.[6] Although cross-ethnic identification and pan-ethnic antiracism in culture, politics, and economics have often interrupted and resisted racialized white supremacist notions of American identity, from colonial days to the present, successful political coalitions serving dominant interests have often relied on exclusionary concepts of whiteness to fuse unity among otherwise antagonistic individuals and groups.[7]

Yet, while cultural expressions have played an important role in the construction of white supremacist political alliances, the reverse is also true (i.e., political activity has also played a constitutive role in racializing U.S. culture). Race is a cultural construct, but one with sinister structural causes and consequences. Conscious and deliberate actions have institutionalized group identity in the United States, not just through the dissemination of cultural stories but also through systematic efforts from colonial times to the present to create a possessive investment in whiteness for European Americans. Studies of culture too far removed from studies of social structure leave us with inadequate explanations for understanding racism and inadequate remedies for combatting it.

From the start, European settlers in North America established structures encouraging possessive investment in whiteness. The colonial and early-national legal systems authorized attacks on Native Americans and encouraged the appropriation of their lands. They legitimated racialized chattel slavery, restricted naturalized citizenship to "white" immigrants, and provided pretexts for exploiting labor, seizing property, and denying the franchise to Asian Americans, Mexican Americans, Native Americans, and African Americans. Slavery and "Jim Crow" segregation institutionalized possessive identification with whiteness visibly and openly, but an elaborate interaction of largely *covert* public and private decisions during and after the days of slavery and segregation also produced a powerful legacy with enduring effects on the racialization of experience, opportunities, and rewards in the United States possessive investment in whiteness pervades public policy in the United States past and present—not just long ago during slavery and segregation but in the recent past and present as well—through the covert but no less systematic racism inscribed within U.S. social democracy.

Even though there has always been racism in American history, it has not always been the same racism. Political and cultural struggles over power shape the contours and dimensions of racism in any era. Mass mobilizations against racism during the Civil War and civil rights eras meaningfully curtailed the reach and scope of white supremacy, but in each case reactionary forces then engineered a renewal of racism, albeit in new forms, during successive decades. Racism changes over time, taking on different forms and serving different social purposes in different eras.

Contemporary racism is not just a residual consequence of slavery and *de jure* segregation but rather something that has been created anew in our own time by many factors including the putatively race-neutral liberal social democratic reforms of the past five decades. Despite hard-fought battles for change that secured important concessions during the 1960s in the form of civil rights legislation, the racialized nature of social democratic policies in the United States since the Great Depression has, in my judgment, actually increased the possessive investment in whiteness among European Americans over the past half-century.

The possessive investment in whiteness is not a simple matter of black and white; all racialized minority groups have suffered from it, albeit to different degrees and in different ways. Most of my argument here addresses relations between European Americans and African Americans because they contain many of the most vivid oppositions and contrasts, but the possessive investment in whiteness always emerges from a fused sensibility drawing on many sources at once—on antiblack racism to be sure, but also on the legacies of racialization left by federal, state, and local policies toward Native Americans, Asian Americans, Mexican Americans, and other groups designated by whites as "racially other."

During the New Deal, both the Wagner Act and the Social Security Act excluded farm workers and domestics from coverage, effectively denying those disproportionately minority sectors of the work force protections and benefits routinely channeled to whites. The Federal Housing Act of 1934 brought home ownership within reach of millions of citizens by placing the credit of the federal government behind private lending to home buyers, but overtly racist categories in the Federal Housing Administration's (FHA's) "confidential" city surveys and appraisers' manuals channeled almost all of the loan money toward whites and away from communities of color.[8] In the post–World War II era, trade unions negotiated contract provisions giving private medical insurance, pensions, and job security largely to the mostly white workers in unionized mass-production industries rather than fighting for full employment, universal medical care, and old age pensions for all or for an end to discriminatory hiring and promotion practices by employers.[9]

Each of these policies widened the gap between the resources available to whites and those available to aggrieved racial communities, but the most damaging long-term effects may well have come from the impact of the racial discrimination codified by the policies of the FHA. By channeling loans away from older inner-city neighborhoods and toward white home buyers moving into segregated suburbs, the FHA and private lenders after World War II aided and abetted the growth and development of increased segregation in U.S. residential neighborhoods. For example, FHA appraisers denied federally supported loans to prospective home buyers in the racially mixed Boyle Heights neighborhood of Los Angeles because it was a "'melting pot' area literally honeycombed with diverse and subversive racial elements."[10] Similarly, mostly white St. Louis County secured five times as many FHA mortgages as the more racially mixed city of St. Louis between 1943 and 1960. Home buyers in the county received six times as much loan money and enjoyed per capita mortgage spending 6.3 times greater than those in the city.[11]

In concert with FHA support for segregation in the suburbs, federal and state tax monies routinely provided water supplies and sewage facilities for racially exclusive suburban communities in the 1940s and 1950s. By the 1960s, these areas often incorporated themselves as independent municipalities in order to gain greater access to federal funds allocated for "urban aid."[12] At the same time that FHA loans and federal highway building projects subsidized the growth of segregated suburbs, urban renewal programs in cities throughout the country devastated minority neighborhoods.

During the 1950s and 1960s, federally assisted urban renewal projects destroyed 20 percent of the central city housing units occupied by blacks, as opposed to only 10 percent of those inhabited by whites.[13] Even after most major urban renewal programs had been completed in the 1970s, black central city residents continued to lose housing units at a rate equal to 80 percent of what had been lost in the 1960s. Yet white displacement declined back to the relatively low levels of the 1950s.[14] In addition, the refusal first to pass, then to enforce, fair housing laws, has enabled realtors, buyers, and sellers to profit from racist collusion against minorities without fear of legal retribution.

During the decades following World War II, urban renewal helped construct a new "white" identity in the suburbs by helping destroy ethnically specific European-American urban inner-city neighborhoods. Wrecking balls and bulldozers eliminated some of these sites, while others became transformed by an influx of minority residents desperately competing for a declining number of affordable housing units. As increasing numbers of racial minorities moved into cities, increasing numbers of European-American ethnics moved out. Consequently, ethnic differences among whites became a less important dividing line in American culture, while race became more important. The suburbs helped turn European Americans into "whites" who could live near each other and intermarry with relatively little difficulty. But this "white" unity rested on residential segregation and on shared access to housing and life chances largely unavailable to communities of color.[15]

Federally funded highways designed to connect suburban commuters with downtown places of employment destroyed already scarce housing in minority communities and often disrupted neighborhood life as well. Construction of the Harbor Freeway in Los Angeles, the Gulf Freeway in Houston, and the Mark Twain Freeway in St. Louis displaced thousands of residents and bisected previously connected neighborhoods, shopping districts, and political precincts. The process of urban renewal and highway construction set in motion a vicious cycle: population loss led to decreased political power, which made minority neighborhoods more likely to be victimized by further urban renewal and freeway construction, not to mention more susceptible to the placement of prisons, waste dumps, and other projects that further depopulated these areas.

In Houston, Texas—where blacks make up slightly more than one-quarter of the local population—more than 75 percent of municipal garbage incinerators and 100 percent of the city-owned garbage dumps are located in black neighborhoods.[16] A 1992 study by staff writers for the *National Law Journal* examined the Environmental Protection Agency's response to 1,177 toxic waste cases and found that polluters of sites near the greatest white population received penalties 500 percent higher than penalties imposed on polluters in minority areas—an average of $335,566 for white areas contrasted with $55,318 for minority areas. Income did not account for these differences—penalties for low-income areas on average actually exceeded those for areas with the highest median incomes by about 3 percent. The penalties for violating all federal environmental laws about air, water, and waste pollution in minority communities were 46 percent lower than in white communities. In addition, Superfund remedies left minority communities with longer waiting times for being placed on the national priority list, cleanups that begin from 12 to 42 percent later than at white sites, and a 7 percent greater likelihood of "containment" (walling off a hazardous site) than cleanup, while white sites experienced treatment and cleanup 22 percent more often than containment.[17]

When housing prices doubled during the 1970s, white homeowners who had been able to take advantage of discriminatory FHA financing policies received increased equity in their homes, while those excluded from the housing market by earlier policies found themselves facing higher costs of entry into the market in addition to the traditional obstacles presented by the discriminatory practices of sellers, realtors, and lenders. The contrast between European Americans and African Americans is instructive in this regard. Because whites have access to broader housing choices than blacks, whites pay 15 percent less than blacks for similar housing in the same neighborhood. White neighborhoods typically experience housing costs 25 percent less expensive than would be the case if the residents were black.[18]

A recent Federal Reserve Bank of Boston study showed that minority applicants had a 60 percent greater chance of being denied home loans than white applicants with the same credit-worthiness. Boston bankers made 2.9 times as many mortgage loans per one thousand housing units in neighborhoods inhabited by low-income whites than they did to neighborhoods populated by low-income blacks.[19] In addition, loan officers were far more likely to overlook flaws in the credit records of white applicants or to arrange creative financing for them than they were with black applicants.[20]

A Los Angeles study found that loan officers more frequently used dividend income and underlying assets as criteria for judging black applicants than they did for whites.[21] In Houston, the NCNB Bank of Texas disqualified 13 percent of middle-income white loan applicants but disqualified 36 percent of middle-income black applicants.[22] Atlanta's home loan institutions gave five times as many home loans to whites as to blacks in the late 1980s. An analysis of sixteen Atlanta neighborhoods found that home buyers in white neighborhoods received conventional financing four times as often as those in black sections of the city.[23] Nationwide, financial institutions get more money in deposits from black neighborhoods than they invest in them in the form of home mortgage loans, making home lending a vehicle for the transfer of capital away from black savers and toward white investors.[24] In many locations, high-income blacks were denied loans more often than low-income whites.[25]

Federal home loan policies have placed the power of the federal government behind private discrimination. Urban renewal and highway construction programs have enhanced the possessive investment in whiteness directly through government initiatives. In addition, decisions about the location of federal jobs have also systematically supported the subsidy for whiteness. Federal civilian employment dropped by 41,419 in central cities between 1966 and 1973, but total federal employment in metropolitan areas grew by 26,558.[26] While one might naturally expect the location of government buildings that serve the public to follow population trends, the federal government's policies in locating offices and records centers in suburbs helped aggravate the flight of jobs to suburban locations less accessible to inner-city residents. Since racial discrimination in the private sector forces minority workers to seek government positions disproportionate to their numbers, these moves exact particular hardships on them. In addition, minorities who follow their jobs to the suburbs generally encounter increased commuter costs because housing discrimination makes it harder and more expensive for them to relocate than for whites.

The racialized aspects of fifty years of these social democratic policies became greatly exacerbated by the anti–social democratic policies of neoconservatives in the Reagan and Bush administrations during the 1980s and 1990s. They clearly contributed to the reinforcement of possessive investments in whiteness through their regressive policies in respect to federal aid to education and their refusal to challenge segregated education, housing, and hiring, as well as their cynical cultivation of an antiblack, countersubversive consensus through attacks on affirmative action and voting rights legislation. In the U.S. economy, where 86 percent of available jobs do not appear in classified advertisements and where personal connections provide the most important factor in securing employment, attacks on affirmative action guarantee that whites will be rewarded for their historical advantages in the labor market rather than for their individual abilities or efforts.[27]

Yet even seemingly race-neutral policies supported by both neoconservatives and social democrats in the 1980s and 1990s have also increased the absolute value of being white. In the 1980s, changes in federal tax laws decreased the value of wage income and increased the value of investment income—a move harmful to minorities who suffer from an even greater gap between their total wealth and that of whites than in the disparity between their income and white income. Failure to raise the minimum wage between 1981 and 1989 and the more than one-third decline in value of Aid for Families with Dependent Children payments hurt all poor people, but they exacted special costs on nonwhites facing even more constricted markets for employment, housing, and education than poor whites.[28]

Because they are ignorant of even the recent history of the possessive investment in whiteness—generated by slavery and segregation but augmented by social democratic reform—Americans produce largely cultural explanations for structural social problems. The increased possessive investment in whiteness generated by dis-investment in American's cities, factories, and schools since the 1970s disguises the general problems posed to our society by deindustrialization, economic restructuring, and neoconservative attacks on the welfare state as *racial* problems. It fuels a discourse that demonizes people of color for being victimized by these changes, while hiding the privileges of whiteness by attributing them to family values, fatherhood, and foresight—rather than to favoritism.

Many recent popular and scholarly studies have explained clearly the causes for black economic decline over the past two decades.[29] Deindustrialization has decimated the industrial infrastructure that formerly provided high-wage jobs and chances for upward mobility to black workers. Neoconservative attacks on government spending for public housing, health, education, and transportation have deprived African Americans of needed services and opportunities for jobs in the public sector. A massive retreat from responsibility to enforce antidiscrimination laws at the highest levels of government has sanctioned pervasive overt and covert racial discrimination by bankers, realtors, and employers.

Yet public opinion polls conducted among white Americans display little recognition of these devastating changes. Seventy percent of whites in one poll said that African Americans "have the same opportunities to live a middle-class life as whites."[30] Nearly three-fourths of white respondents to a 1989 poll believed that opportunities for blacks had improved during the Reagan presidency.[31]

It is my contention that the stark contrast between black experiences and white opinions during the past two decades cannot be attributed solely to ignorance or intolerance on the part of individuals but stems instead from the overdetermined inadequacy of the language of liberal individualism to describe collective experience.[32] As long as we define social life as the sum total of conscious and deliberate individual activities, then only *individual* manifestations of personal prejudice and hostility will be seen as racist. Systemic, collective, and coordinated behavior disappears from sight. Collective exercises of group power relentlessly channeling rewards, resources, and opportunities from one group to another will not appear to be "racist" from this perspective because they rarely announce their intention to discriminate against individuals. But they work to construct racial identities by giving people of different races vastly different life chances.

The gap between white perceptions and minority experiences can have explosive consequences. Little more than a year after the 1992 Los Angeles rebellion, a sixteen-year-old high school junior shared her opinions with a reporter from the *Los Angeles Times*. "I don't think white people owe anything to black people," she explained. "We didn't sell them into slavery; it was our ancestors. What they did was wrong, but we've done our best to make up for it."[33] A seventeen-year-old senior echoed those comments, telling the reporter:

> I feel we spend more time in my history class talking about what
> whites owe blacks than just about anything else when the issue of
> slavery comes up. I often received dirty looks. This seems strange
> given that I wasn't even alive then. And the few members of my
> family from that time didn't have the luxury of owning much, let
> alone slaves. So why, I ask you, am I constantly made to feel guilty?[34]

More ominously, after pleading guilty to bombing two homes and one car, to vandalizing a synagogue, and attempting to start a race war by murdering Rodney King and bombing Los Angeles's First African Methodist Episcopal Church, twenty-year-old Christopher David Fisher explained that "sometimes whites were picked on because of the color of their skin. . . . Maybe we're blamed for slavery."[35] Fisher's actions were certainly extreme, but his justification of them drew knowingly and precisely on a broadly shared narrative about the victimization of innocent whites by irrational and ungrateful minorities.

The comments and questions raised about the legacy of slavery by these young whites illumine broader currents in our culture that have enormous implications for understanding the enduring significance of race in our country. These young people associate black grievances solely with slavery, and they express irritation at what they perceive as efforts to make them feel guilty or unduly privileged in the present because of things that happened in the distant past. Because their own ancestors may not have been slave owners or because "we've done our best to make up for it," they feel that it is unreasonable for anyone to view them as people who owe "anything" to blacks. On the contrary, Fisher felt that his discomfort with being "picked on" and "blamed" for slavery gave him good reason to bomb homes, deface synagogues, and plot to kill black people.

Unfortunately for our society, these young whites accurately reflect the logic of the language of liberal individualism and its ideological predispositions in discussions of race. They seem to have no knowledge of the disciplined, systemic, and collective *group* activity that has structured white identities in American history. They are not alone in their ignorance; in a 1979 law journal article, future Supreme Court Justice Antonin Scalia argued that affirmative action "is based upon concepts of racial indebtedness and racial entitlement rather than individual worth and individual need" and is thus "racist."[36]

Group interests are not monolithic, and aggregate figures can obscure serious differences within racial groups. All whites do not benefit from the possessive investment in whiteness in precisely the same way; the experiences of members of minority groups are not interchangeable. But the possessive investment in whiteness always affects individual and group life chances and opportunities. Even in cases where minority groups secure political and economic power through collective mobilization, the terms and conditions of their collectivity and the logic of group solidarity are always influenced and intensified by the absolute value of whiteness in American politics, economics, and culture.[37]

In the 1960s, members of the Black Panther Party used to say that "if you're not part of the solution, you're part of the problem." But those of us who are "white" can only become part of the solution if we recognize the degree to which we are already part of the problem—not because of our race, but because of our possessive investment in it. Neither conservative "free market" policies nor liberal social democratic reforms can solve the "white problem" in America because both of them reinforce the possessive investment in whiteness. But an explicitly antiracist pan-ethnic movement that acknowledges the existence and power of whiteness might make some important changes. Pan-ethnic, antiracist coalitions have a long history in the United States—in the political activism of John Brown, Sojourner Truth, and the Magon brothers, among others—but we also have a rich cultural tradition of pan-ethnic antiracism connected to civil rights activism of the kind detailed so brilliantly in rhythm and blues musician Johnny Otis's recent book, *Upside Your Head! Rhythm and Blues on Central Avenue.*[38] These efforts by whites to fight racism, not out of sympathy for someone else but out of a sense of self-respect and simple justice, have never completely disappeared; they remain available as models for the present.[39]

Walter Benjamin's praise for "presence of mind" came from his understanding of how difficult it may be to see the present. But more important, he called for presence of mind as the means for implementing what he called "the only true telepathic miracle"—turning the forbidding future into the fulfilled present.[40] Failure to acknowledge our society's possessive investment in whiteness prevents us from facing the present openly and honestly. It hides from us the devastating costs of disinvestment in America's infrastructure over the past two decades and keeps us from facing our responsibilities to reinvest in human capital by channeling resources toward education, health, and housing—and away from subsidies for speculation and luxury. After two decades of disinvestment, the only further disinvestment we need is to disinvest in the ruinous pathology of whiteness that has always undermined our own best instincts and interests. In a society suffering so badly from an absence of mutuality, an absence of responsibility, and an absence of simple justice, presence of mind might be just what we need.

NOTES

1. Raphael Tardon, "Richard Wright Tells Us: The White Problem in the United States," *Action,* 24 Oct. 1946. Reprinted in Kenneth Kinnamon and Michet Fabre, *Conversations with Richard Wright* (Jackson, Miss., 1993), 99. Malcolm X and others used this same formulation in the 1960s, but I believe that it originated with Wright, or at least that is the earliest citation I have found so far.

2. This is also Toni Morrison's point in *Playing in the Dark: Whiteness in the Literary Imagination* (Cambridge, Mass., 1992).

3. Richard Dyer, "White," *Screen* 29 (fall 1988): 44.

4. I thank Michael Schudson for pointing out to me that since the passage of civil rights legislation in the 1960s whiteness dares not speak its name, cannot speak in its own behalf, but rather advances through a color-blind language radically at odds with the distinctly racialized distribution of resources and life chances in American society.

5. Walter Benjamin, "Madame Ariane: Second Courtyard on the Left," from *One-Way Street* (London, 1969), 98–99.

6. Richard Slotkin, *Gunfighter Nation: The Myth of the Frontier in Twentieth Century America* (New York, 1992); Eric Lott, *Love and Theft* (New York, 1993); David Roediger, *Wages of Whiteness* (New York, 1992); Michael Rogin, "Blackface White Noise: The Jewish Jazz Singer Finds His Voice," *Critical Inquiry* 18 (Spring 1992).

7. Robin Kelley, *Hammer and Hoe* (Chapel Hill, N.C., 1990); Lizabeth Cohen, *Making a New Deal* (Cambridge, 1991); George Sanchez, *Becoming Mexican American* (New York, 1993); Edmund Morgan, *American Slavery, American Freedom* (New York, 1975); John Hope Franklin, *The Color Line: Legacy for the Twenty-First Century* (Columbia, Mo., 1993).

8. See Kenneth Jackson. *Crabgrass Frontier: The Suburbanization of the United States,* (New York, 1985); and Douglas S. Massey and Nancy A. Denton, *American Apartheid: Segregation and the Making of the Underclass* (Cambridge, Mass., 1993).

9. I thank Phil Ethington for pointing out to me that these aspects of New Deal policies emerged out of political negotiations between the segregationist Dixiecrats and liberals from the north and west. My perspective is that white supremacy was not a gnawing aberration within the New Deal coalition but rather an essential point of unity between southern whites and northern white ethnics.

10. Records of the Federal Home Loan Bank Board of the Home Owners Loan Corporation. City Survey File, Los Angeles, 1939, Neighborhood D-53, National Archives, Washington, D.C., box 74, records group 195.

11. Massey and Denton, *American Apartheid,* 54.

12. John R. Logan and Harvey Molotch, *Urban Fortunes: The Political Economy of Place* (Berkeley, 1987), 182.

13. Ibid., 114.

14. Ibid., 130.

15. See Gary Gerstle, "Working-Class Racism: Broaden the Focus," *International Labor and Working Class History,* 44 (Fall 1993): 36.

16. Logan and Molotch, *Urban Fortunes,* 113.

17. Robert D. Bullard, "Environmental Justice for All," in *Unequal Protection: Environmental Justice and Communities of Color,* ed. Robert Bullard (San Francisco, 1994), 9–10.

18. Logan and Molotch, *Urban Fortunes,* 116.

19. Jim Campen, "Lending Insights: Hard Proof That Banks Discriminate," *Dollars and Sense* 191 (Jan.–Feb. 1991): 17.

20. Mitchell Zuckoff, "Study Shows Racial Bias in Lending," *The Boston Globe,* 9 October 1992, 1, 77, 78.

21. Paul Ong and J. Eugene Grisby III, "Race and Late Cycle Effects on Home Ownership in Los Angeles, 1970 to 1980," *Urban Affairs Quarterly* 23 (June 1998), 605.

22. Massey and Denton, *American Apartheid,* 108.

23. Gary Orfield and Carol Ashkinaze, *The Closing Door: Conservative Policy and Black Opportunity* (Chicago, 1991), 58, 78.

24. Logan and Molotch, *Urban Fortunes.*

25. Campen, "Lending Insights," 18.

26. Gregory Squires, "'Runaway Plants.' Capital Mobility, and Black Economic Rights," in *Community and Capital in Conflict: Plant Closings and Job Loss,* ed. John C. Raines, Lenora E. Berson, and David Mel Gracie (Philadelphia, 1982), 70.

27. Gertrude Ezorsky, *Racism and Justice: The Case for Affirmative Action* (Ithaca, N.Y., 1991), 15.

28. Orfield and Ashkinaze, *The Closing Door,* 225–26.

29. Melvin Oliver and James Johnson, "Economic Restructuring and Black Male Joblessness in United States Metropolitan Areas," *Urban Geography* 12 (Nov.–Dec. 1991); Gerald David Jaynes and Robin M. Williams, Jr., eds., *A Common Destiny: Blacks and American Society* (Washington, D.C., 1989); Reynolds Farley and Walter R. Allen, *The Color Line and the Quality of Life in America* (New York, 1987); Melvin Oliver and Tom Shapiro, "Wealth of a Nation: A Reassessment of Asset Inequality in America Shows at Least 1/3 of Households Are Asset Poor," *Journal of Economics and Sociology,* 49 (Apr. 1990); Jonathan Kozol, *Savage Inequalities: Children in America's Schools* (New York, 1991); Cornell West, *Race Matters* (Boston, 1993).

30. Orfield and Ashkinaze, *Closing Door,* 46.

31. Ibid., 206.

32. I borrow the term "overdetermination" here from Louis Althusser, who uses it to show how dominant ideologies become credible to people in part because various institutions and agencies independently replicate them and reinforce their social power.

33. Rogena Schuyler, "Youth: We Didn't Sell Them into Slavery," *Los Angeles Times,* 21 June 1993, B4.

34. Ibid.

35. Jim Newton, "Skinhead Leader Pleads Guilty to Violence, Plot," *Los Angeles Times,* 20 Oct. 1993, A1, A15.

36. Antonin Scalia, Quoted in Cheryl I. Harris, "Whiteness as Property," *Harvard Law Review* 106 (June 1993): 1767.

37. The rise of a black middle class and the setbacks suffered by white workers during deindustrialization may seem to subvert the analysis presented here. Yet the black middle class remains fragile, far less able than other middle-class groups to translate advances in income into advances in wealth and power. Similarly, the success of neoconservatism since the 1970s has rested on securing support from white workers for economic policies that do them objective harm by mobilizing counter-subversive electoral coalitions against busing and affirmative action, while carrying out attacks on public institutions and resources by representing "public" space and black space. See Oliver and Shapiro, "Wealth of a Nation." See also Logan and Harvey, *Urban Fortunes.*

38. Johnny Otis, *Upside Your Head: Rhythm and Blues on Central Avenue* (Hanover, N.H., 1993).

39. Mobilizations against plant shutdowns, for environmental protection, against cutbacks in education spending, and for reproductive rights all contain the potential for pan-ethnic antiracist organizing, but, too often, neglect of race as a central modality for how issues of employment, pollution, education, or reproductive rights are experienced isolates these social movements from their broadest possible base.

40. Walter Benjamin, "Madame Ariane: Second Courtyard on the Left," from *One-Way Street* (London, 1969), 98, 99.

QUESTIONS FOR CRITICAL THINKING

Reading 34

1. Lipsitz argues that the establishment of public policies prohibiting concepts of multiraciality were established to maintain the control of whites over others. Is this reflected in contemporary policies as well?

2. Do whites in the United States continue to benefit from historical racial policies?

3. How can an awareness that current policies and practices are informed by past racially biased policies help us to better understand racism today?

Reading 35

FIVE DECADES AND THREE HUNDRED SITCOMS ABOUT CLASS AND GENDER

RICHARD BUTSCH

Since *I Love Lucy* situation comedy has been the mainstay, the bread and butter of prime time television. It has been the most durable of genres: at least 400 sitcoms have appeared during prime time. Three hundred were domestic sitcoms depicting families; many of the rest were constructed as artificial families of friends or co-workers. Many lasted only a few weeks, some lasted for years. But each year they were key to network profits. Overall they reliably provided good ratings, and they were cheaper to produce than drama and far more sellable as reruns than any other form.

Situation comedy is built around a humorous "situation" in which tension develops and is resolved during the half hour. In episode after episode the situation is recreated. In many sitcoms, particularly those featuring a well known comic, the comic situations are embodied in a character who is always getting himself into trouble. David Grote said comic characters are traditionally of three types, the Innocent, the Fool, and the Scoundrel. The Scoundrel is rare in TV sitcoms, Sergeant Bilko being the most famous exception. Many domestic sitcoms feature children, Innocents, as the comic character. This was typical of idyllic middle-class families depicted in sitcoms such as *The Brady Bunch, The Cosby Show, Seventh Heaven.*[1] The parents are cast as wise to the children's innocence. These shows evoke a warm glow more than a loud laugh.

However, the most memorable sitcoms have been built around a Fool, such as Lucy, Archie, or Homer. Sometimes the fool is a supporting character, such as Raymond's father in *Everybody Loves Raymond.* The buffoon or fool is a classic type in comic drama, traditionally cast as someone of inferior status, a slave or servant, women, peasants and lower classes, subordinate races, etc. The fool has been used in ancient Greek and Roman drama, in

Renaissance drama, in nineteenth century minstrelsy, in ethnic humor of vaudeville. The ground has been well tread long before the creation of situation comedy.[2]

Inferior statuses are represented using negative stereotypes of women, blacks and other minorities, the old and the young, and other low statuses. Already embedded in the larger culture, these stereotypes are useful for their familiarity. Over time, stereotypes are merged into character types that recur time and again and have a special importance in the culture as stock images—the country bumpkin, the dizzy blonde—used to construct a culture's tales and even to type each other in everyday life. They become code that audiences can be expected to know and that writers can use to advance dramatic goals without having to explain. This is especially useful in a short form of drama like the 22-minute sitcom. The foolishness in sitcoms is almost always attached to a character's lower status, by representing well known stereotypes of this status group.

A higher status can be denied by representing a person as having opposite characteristics. Men are devalued by characterizing them as feminine. Adults have been devalued by characterizing them as child-like. When a person has two contradictory status positions, such as rich woman, black middle class, working-class man, the higher status can be undercut to resolve the contradiction in favor of the lower status. De-masculinizing working-class men—i.e., applying descriptors that contradict the culturally accepted definition of masculine—devalues them not only as men but also uses gender to affirm their subordinate class status.[3]

Television sitcoms have continued the tradition of representing lower status groups as inferior. They also have valuated one status by manipulating other status traits. One of the most striking patterns in the fifty years of television situation comedy is the consistency in devaluing working-class men's masculinity and thus confirming working class as a deserved lower status. This dramatic mechanism has been a central part of television sitcoms throughout the form's history. Working-class men have been persistently represented as fools, middle-class men seldom so.

There have been times before television when working-class men were not represented as fools. The Depression and World War II is the most recent era when public discourse acknowledged the positive contribution of manual labor. Muscle was depicted as heroic and patriotic—not the sculpted muscle of the gym, but muscles for work. These were the muscles that the nation depended upon to rebuild itself during the Depression and to defend itself during the war. The Roosevelt Administration celebrated these working men as strong and vital through WPA arts and building projects.

By the time television arrived, something had changed America's cultural discourse. From the 1950s on, the admiration of physical labor steadily declined. No longer were construction workers, steelworkers, miners, and manual crafts represented positively. Manual labor instead came to represent stupidity and failure, the only alternative of those men who were not smart enough to be educated to achieve mental work occupations. The mental worker, the middle class, was ascendant in cultural discourse. Since the 1950s manual workers, especially white working-class men, have been characterized as uncouth beer-bellied loudmouths, couch potatoes, wife beaters, the silent majority, racists, supporters of right wing causes.

Nowhere has this been so consistently represented to so large an audience than in television domestic sitcoms. For generations, television has presented this message, so long that few people have any memory of sympathetic, let alone heroic images of manual labor working men. White working-class men have been reduced to Homer, Archie, Fred, Ralph. Every American is familiar with these characters. They are the representatives of working-class men. They are not positive images. They confirm other discourses about America's working class that demean these people and, in doing so, resign them to their fate of low income and little respect.

Sitcom predominance on prime time television throughout its history and their consequent share of the television audience over this history means that they are pre-eminent examples of dominant culture, steadily presented to the largest population over the longest time. Pervasive and persistent images crystallize as cultural types. Alternative and oppositional images and readings appear within this context and typically refer to it. Character types, which recur across series and across time, and contrasts between types, which may only be evident when we look at the panorama of series taken together, are of especial importance.

What does this half-century of dominant culture say? While there can be many readings of these hundreds of sitcoms, there are also patterns of consistency that are a powerful means to reproduce and naturalize certain views. A wealth of studies document television images of women and of African-Americans. Some have documented images of men. An older research tradition has tabulated occupational frequencies. A handful have studied class or the intersection of gender and class.[4] Almost all of these have looked at a specific point in time. Innumerable studies have focused on the text of a single television show. Almost none have examined the pattern of images across many series and over several seasons, what we might call the historical tapestry of television culture.

Analysis across many shows and many years can reveal persistent and pervasive images. It also enables us to discover important contrasts not otherwise noticeable. For example, when we observe the treatment of men and women across shows of different classes, we discover contrasts in the representations of men and women depending on class. Such analyses add depth to our understanding of the traditional types in our culture's tales.

Richard Butsch and Lynda Glennon surveyed three decades of prime-time network domestic situation comedies from the beginning of network television in 1946 to 1980 and found persistent patterns throughout. In previous publications I extended this work to 1989.[5] This chapter extends the earlier work through the 2003–04 season. This research is based upon lists of all domestic situation comedy series compiled from Tim Brooks and Earl Marsh's 1999 edition of *The Complete Directory to Prime Time Network Shows,* the annual *TV Guide Fall Preview* issues, and the *epguides.com* website (http://epguides.com) that provides situation and episode summaries for hundreds of shows. It includes all domestic sitcoms appearing on the six broadcast networks; it does not include series appearing on cable networks or solely in syndication.[6]

I concentrate here on successful series, which had five or more first-run seasons, the determinant of successful sale on the syndication market, or ranked in the top twenty of the annual Nielsen ratings. These are the series and characters that cemented in the national culture and conversation, shows that most Americans know something about even if they haven't seen them. I will contrast working-class to middle-class series over the five decades.

Most sitcoms featured upper middle-class families of professionals and business people. But the vast majority were not successful series. Working-class family sitcoms were relatively scarce through most of the nearly six decades of broadcast network television. They were more common during transitional times for network television, seeming to be chosen only when network executives were desperate. Once on television, however, a remarkable percentage became television classics (*The Honeymooners, The Flintstones, All in the Family, The Simpsons*) and created a vivid cultural type of the working-class man. Also illustrating their exceptional success, only three prime-time animated series have aired over 100 episodes: *The Flintstones, The Simpsons,* and *King of the Hill.*[7] All three depict working-class families.

 SIMPLER TIMES: THE 1950S AND 1960S

The sitcom began as a radio genre where it gained success in the 1940s due in part to its lower costs compared to comedy-variety shows with big name stars and orchestras. Even on radio the most common situation was a family. Many of the 1950s radio sitcoms became the first television sitcoms. Even *I Love Lucy* was copied from the radio show *My Favorite Husband* in which Lucille Ball had starred. J. Fred MacDonald summed up, "Radio situation comedies were middle-class morality tales. The American family was portrayed as a vital institution in which love, trust, and self-confidence were best developed."[8]

Television production costs were many times that of radio, which affected the form of sitcom adapted to television. Advertisers were less willing to pay such costs. The networks moved to a magazine format of programming in which they owned and produced or controlled production of the programs, selling commercial time in between programs. Networks benefited from efficiencies of scale since they were producing many more programs than any advertiser or ad agency could expect to do. The breakthrough was the use of film that allowed the rerun and syndication of programs, spreading the costs over repeated use and sales.

To sustain a mass audience, the networks preferred blandness in sitcoms. Each network had a censorship office, called standards and practices, to weed out anything controversial.[9] No threatening world impinged on these early TV families, not the bomb or cold war; not 1960s Vietnam, riots, protests; not sex nor drugs. These families seldom struggle. All problems were simple and internal to the family. Almost everyone was content about their place in the family and in the world. With this reassuring formula, the characters were inevitably oversimplified stereotypes that were rather consistent from series to series.

Working-Class Stereotypes

In working-class sitcoms of the period, the man is more or less a buffoon, dumb, incompetent, irresponsible, immature, lacking good sense. His saving grace, for audiences to like and continue to watch him, is that he has a good heart and cares about his family. He is simply not capable of fulfilling his role as father and husband. Humor was built around some variant of his inadequacy as a man. The man was typically caught in a situation often of his own making.

The characterization is accentuated by contrasts to the wives and children in these working-class series, as well as by contrasts to the middle-class men in other series. Typically working-class wives and sometimes the children were portrayed as more intelligent, rational, sensible, responsible, mature than the man. Mother, not father, typically knew best. Often she had to help him out of situations. The children were often smarter than their fathers and their successes contrasted to their father's failures. At best father was benign but inferior, at worst an embarrassment.

This formula was the core of the successful 1950s series of *The Honeymooners, The Life of Riley,* and *I Remember Mama.* Chester, the father on *The Life of Riley,* was continually concocting schemes to help his family. He attempted to fix a school election so his daughter would win, but succeeded only in embarrassing her. His incessant failures were expressed in his closing line for each episode, "What a revoltin' development this is!" His wife, Peg was tolerant of Chester's fiascoes and helped him, sometimes enlisting the children, to save face. The children were Chester's intellectual superiors. While Chester tripped over the English language, Junior headed for college.

The Honeymooners lived in a bare Brooklyn apartment with few amenities. Consequently, husband Ralph was obsessed with success and modest affluence, at which he constantly schemed but invariably failed. He wanted to afford simple comforts such as a television for his wife, Alice. He tried get-rich-quick schemes, such as marketing what he thought was Alice's homemade sauce, only to learn it was dog food. Alice always quipped "I told you so." He occasionally tried more conventional means such as applying for a promotion, or a self-improvement program—means Alice approved of, but which also got nowhere. Alice's logic and sarcasm invariably bested Ralph in arguments that typically ended by him saying, in angry frustration "Just you wait Alice, one of these days, pow, right in the kisser." She recognized the foolishness of his schemes, and sometimes got him out of the messes he'd gotten them into.

I Remember Mama was one of the few working-class series in which a working-class family was taken seriously. It was a sentimental reminiscence of family life in the 1910s. No one was the butt of humor. Yet Lars the father in this Norwegian immigrant family was an "earnest bumbler" in the words of the show's scriptwriter.[10] Frequently Mama had to conspire to help him save face. The children went to Mama for advice.

Only one working-class domestic situation comedy was aired through the entire decade of the 1960s. *The Flintstones* was a cartoon version of *The Life of Riley* and *The Honeymooners*. Fred Flintstone's loudmouth brashness was like Ralph Kramden, but he was more amiable like Chester Riley. Fred's wife, Wilma exhibited motherly tolerance of Fred's shenanigans as Peg did of Chester Riley's. Typically Wilma was aware of Fred's surreptitious schemes from the beginning and provided both a safety net for him when he failed as well as a punishment, much as a mother would for a child. When Fred persuaded Barney to play hooky from work to attend a ball game, Wilma and Barney's wife Betty caught them and for their punishment the "boys" had to take the wives to the opera.

All four of these successful working-class series presented a very consistent picture of working-class men as bumblers who were inadequate to fulfill their manly role of supporting and leading their families. Failing as men confirmed the appropriateness of their lower class status, especially when compared to the middle-class TV husbands of the time.

Middle-Class Stereotypes

In most middle-class series both parents were intelligent, sensible, and mature. They were calm and affable, in stark contrast to the hysteria that typified the slapstick comedy of the working-class series. In these series the situation was typically a problem involving one of the children. The parents, seldom perplexed, guide the child through a solution, providing a moral lesson along the way. They were what Glennon and Butsch (1982) called super-parents.

Moreover, the fathers tended to be more than usually affluent and successful, further accenting the difference from working-class men. Glamorous, prestigious professions predominated over more mundane ones, e.g., stars over struggling actors, doctors over nurses, lawyers over accountants; and within a given profession, characters were very successful or young with much promise. Occupational success like this affirmed their manhood that, in turn, buttressed their class status.

The successful middle-class series of the 1950s included *The George Burns and Gracie Allen Show, The Stu Erwin Show, I Love Lucy, The Adventures of Ozzie and Harriet, Make Room for Daddy, Father Knows Best, Leave It to Beaver,* and *December Bride. Father Knows Best* is of course the prototype of its title, the completely self-assured and successful father, admired by his wife and children, the ideal of 1950s middle-class masculinity. Jim Anderson was always calm, reasonable, and ready with the answers. When the children forgot his birthday, his wife Margaret got upset. Jim, unphased, admonished her for getting angry. Ozzie Nelson wrote the scripts for *Ozzie and Harriet* to express his view of childrearing as relaxed but moral guidance (Joslyn and Pendleton, 1973). The title, *Make Room for Daddy,* made clear who was important in that family, in contrast to *I Remember Mama.*

Occasionally a middle-class series was built around a fool as the source of humor. In these cases however, the fool was almost always the wife, some variant of the movies' stock character, the "dizzy blonde." This stereotype confirmed the lower status of women while it avoided undercutting the middle-class status of the family by preserving the reputation of the husband and head of house. Gracie Allen of *The Burns and Allen Show* was the prototype of the dizzy blonde, interjecting inane statements in her husband George's conversation. In *December Bride* the mother-in-law played the scatterbrain. *I Love Lucy*—and her various reincarnations, *Here's Lucy,* etc.—was the singular example of the woman as buffoon, with the husband as the mature and sensible, though occasionally driven to distraction by his wife's antics. Lucy reversed the gender roles of *Riley* and *The Honeymooners.*

The Stu Erwin Show was the one exception to the rule, reflected in the show's other title, *Trouble with Father.* Comic actor Stu Erwin played a middle-class version of the bumbling father, a high school principal out of his depths at home, based on his stock character from movies since the 1930s.

In the working-class vacuum of the 1960s middle-class super-parents reigned with *The Donna Reed Show, The Dick Van Dyke Show, Petticoat Junction, Bewitched, Green Acres, My Three Sons,* and *Family Affair. The Donna Reed Show, My Three Sons,* and *Family Affair* were classic super-parent series. In each the parents were calm and rational. Donna Reed was nicknamed "Mother Knows Best," but the father, a pediatrician, was not ineffectual; his wife merely filled the traditional role of primary childcare. The same traditional division of labor was a continuing theme in *My Three Sons,* the difficulty an all-male household had with domestic matters. The widowed father, an engineer, however is more than adequate in helping his sons grow up, despite minor mishaps at home. His success as a man is further attested by a continual stream of women attracted to him while he is engrossed in his fatherly role. *Family Affair* revived the *Bachelor Father* formula, a prosperous bachelor who inherits children and becomes a devoted father. *The Dick Van Dyke Show* also reinforced traditional gender roles: the wife Laura typically asked the questions or posed the problem and husband Dick provided the answer. The stumbling physical humor that was Van Dyke's signature as a stand-up comic was excluded from the show.

Petticoat Junction and *Green Acres* were part of a rural nostalgia period of 1960s television. *Petticoat Junction* featured a widow with three beautiful daughters. Its principal theme was centered on how to be feminine and attract a husband. Its spinoff, *Green Acres,* featured a stereotypic "dumb blonde" wife, a la Gracie Allen, opposite a successful husband who gave up his Manhattan law practice life to be a gentleman farmer. In *Bewitched,* Samantha, the wife, was a clever witch often tempted to use her powers to get her way or help her husband's career, but also wanted to abandon witchcraft to please her husband, Darrin. Darrin was sometimes befuddled by the supernatural shenanigans, but otherwise depicted as sensible and a competent advertising executive. The 1960s domestic sitcoms uniformly continued the theme of confident, mature, and successful middle-class men posed against the caricature, Fred Flintstone, the only representative of working-class men.

 ## CHANGING TIMES: THE 1970S AND 1980S

CBS had been the dominant network of the 1960s, but many of its top shows were aging badly. Several had begun in the 1950s and their audiences were similarly aging and shrinking. Rather than seeking to please everyone, advertisers and networks began to target specific demographic groups, particularly younger audiences of 18–49. CBS brass decided it was necessary to take some risk, dropping old standbys like comic Red Skelton and introducing new shows that might attract a younger, more savvy viewership. They bought *All in the Family* and began broadcasting it in January 1971.

Norman Lear and MTM Productions began to modify situation comedy in the 1970s.[11] Life was less idyllic and characters were less one-dimensional than during the 1950s and more mediating themes appeared. Norman Lear, who produced *All in the Family, Sanford and Son,* and *Good Times,* introduced real-life problems such as racism, poverty, and abortion that were nonexistent in 1950s and 1960s sitcoms.

While introducing many controversial topics, Lear built this new style upon the old and familiar stereotype of the blustery and none too bright working-class man. Archie of *All in the Family* and Fred Sanford of *Sanford and Son* were reminiscent of Ralph Kramden and Chester Riley; James of *Good Times* was like Lars of *I Remember Mama.* In *All in the Family* producer Norman Lear intentionally made Archie a ridiculous character whose prejudices were illogical and senseless. Archie's malapropisms made him the butt of humor, just as Chester Riley's did in the 1950s. Archie also engaged in hair-brained schemes like Ralph Kramden's and Chester Riley's.

Edith was not as evidently superior to Archie as the earlier wives were. She was much more hesitant in her criticism of Archie, but she tried timidly to advise him against his hair-brained schemes. The foil for Archie was college-graduate Mike, his son-in-law, the spokesperson for Lear's upper-middle-class viewpoint. He was the liberal to Archie's silent majority; the high-brow to Archie's low-brow. In one episode Archie changed the television channel from a Beethoven concert, which Mike was watching, to midget wrestling.

Sanford and Son was a black version of *All in the Family.* Widower Fred Sanford was as bigoted and ignorant as Archie. His son, Lamont, like Mike, was oriented to improvement and middle-class manners. He was embarrassed by his father's behavior. George, the father in *The Jeffersons,* although a businessman, fit the same mold as Archie and Fred, loud and bigoted. The theme song, "Movin on Up to the East Side," expressed the fact that Jefferson was not born and bred middle class. His misbehavior in other words did not reflect on the middle class, but on his working-class roots. Like Lamont, his wife and family are embarrassed at the things he says. He and Fred, despite differences in their class, were devalued in the same way white working-class men were. Race worked as the equivalent of class, illustrating that lower statuses were interchangeable for the purpose of creating a dramatic fool.

Good Times was a black version of *I Remember Mama.* The mother Florida was the mainstay of the family. James, like Lars of *I Remember Mama,* was not a buffoon but nevertheless unable to fulfill his role as breadwinner and father-figure. He was often unemployed and hot-tempered as well. The role of fool fell to teenage J. J., the oldest son, who was the one with endless get-rich-quick schemes. Rather than a fool however, he was an irreverent jokester, with a quick wit, in contrast to his father's inadequacies. His irreverence appealed to audiences, so producers enlarged his role. Thelma and Michael were model children and ambitious: she attended college; he was very bright and talked about as a future president.

The 1980s continued the tradition of stereotyping working-class men in *Alice* (1976–1985). The show blended work and family. The surrogate father was Mel, the owner and cook of a greasy spoon Arizona diner, who was a loudmouth like Archie. Alice was the wise and calm surrogate wife, like her namesake in *The Honeymooners,* and the mother of a 12-year-old son who respected her. In *Gimme a Break,* a widowed police captain—a managerial occupation with working-class ties and traditions—is an ineffective father; his black maid bails him out when he gets himself into a domestic jam.

Middle Class in the 1970s and 1980s

Through the 1970s and 1980s TV's middle-class parents became fallible, made mistakes, got upset. But they soon gained control of the situation and resolved the problem, like the mothers and unlike the fathers of working-class series. They allowed their children to speak to them much more as equals than those in the earlier series. Yet they remained unflappable and ultimately retained their roles as guides and models to their children. They co-opted the high ground by admitting their mistakes and summarizing the moral lesson for their children, and the audience.

Of the successful middle-class sitcoms of the 1970s, *The Brady Bunch* maintained the 1950s tradition of *Father Knows Best*. The parents had the answers to all of their children's questions. When vacationing at the Grand Canyon they explained the canyon and the traditions of the local Hopi tribe as if they were trained guides. They consistently approached problems calmly and rationally, even in an episode in which one of the children is lost. The mother in *Happy Days* was a bit of a dizzy woman, a tamer version of Lucy. The father, Howard Cunningham, was the reasonable and sensible father. Fonzie, a young working-class friend of the family whom the kids admired and women found irresistible, typically supported the father's moral authority.

But other shows diverged from the earlier formula, as situation comedy expressed a new irreverence toward professionals and experts. *The Bob Newhart Show* featured a psychologist who hesitated, had self-doubts, and often was caught in his own words. His office mate, a dentist, was a schemer; and his neighbor, Howard, a divorced airplane pilot and a buffoon. *Maude* was an outspoken feminist woman whose demands continually exasperated her husband Walter. While Walter was a match for Maude, his friend Arthur, an MD, was a buffoon. As just discussed, George Jefferson, the husband in *The Jeffersons* who owned a dry-cleaning chain, was an uncouth loudmouth. Notably, none of these series that deviated from the calm, competent middle-class man, included young children to witness their limitations, as in most working-class series.

Through the early 1980s shows continued questioning of upper-middle-class professionals and authority in *Benson*, *Newhart* (a new show), and *Who's the Boss*. Bob Newhart continued to play the stuttering flummoxed character from his old show, but now as the owner/operator of a Vermont bed and breakfast. *Benson* featured a white widowed upper middle-class man who was a klutz as a governor and a father. His black butler, Benson, regularly rescues his white male boss. Confirming his ability, Benson was successively promoted from butler to budget director, lieutenant governor, and in the last episode was a candidate for governor, an unusually positive portrayal of a black male character.

The mid-1980s returned to the super-parent tradition. The classic middle-class father appeared in *The Cosby Show, Hogan Family, Family Ties,* and *Growing Pains*. *Full House* was most like the saccharine 1950s shows, with a calm, understanding widowed sportscaster father skillfully shepherding three cute daughters. In *The Cosby Show*, the father joked around with his children but also made it clear who's the boss. *Growing Pains, Family Ties,* and to a lesser degree, *The Hogan Family* featured slightly more fallible parents. In one episode of *Growing Pains* the parents insist that their daughter plead guilty to a charge of resisting arrest to avoid a trial. The daughter refuses to lie; the judge respects this and lets her off. The parents however regain the high ground by approving her behavior and summarizing the lesson. The teen son of *Family Ties* was a bit too bright for his parents, yet still held in check and respecting of them. While the fathers and mothers exhibited foibles and flaws absent in 1950s series, they were nonetheless parents who knew best.

Who's the Boss complicates the trend with its gender reversal between Angela, the quintessential upper-middle-class professional in her career and the ethnic working-class Tony as the housekeeper. But, as the title suggests, Angela is not such a success at home. Tony is a wiser parent and better housekeeper than the advertising executive, Angela. This class reversal however is veiled by the gender reversal that is the heart of the situation. Both are succeeding at what their gender is *not* supposed to do, and the woman fails in what she *is* supposed to do.

POST-MODERN TIMES: THE LATE 1980S AND THE 1990S

VCRs and communication satellites changed the television industry through the 1980s and 1990s. Satellites made it economically feasible for smaller networks to distribute programming. This in turn created a large supply of programming that made cable television attractive and multiplied the number of channels for viewers. VCRs were a second alternative to broadcast, once movies were released and rental began.[12] These changes were complemented by the growth of independent television stations and the beginning of Fox, the first new broadcast network since Dumont in the 1940s. The three networks that dominated network and radio for fifty years and that accounted for 90% of the prime-time TV audience for thirty years, watched their ratings erode steadily. In this climate networks were willing to try things they would not consider in good times. The Reagan FCC enabled this experimentation by relaxing rules on language and subject matter for TV. By the late 1980s all these pieces were in place and a new era of sitcom blossomed.

The shift began perhaps with two developments, *Roseanne* (1988) in which the Carsey-Werner production company spread their wings in ways they could not with Cosby, and the arrival of Fox with programming that pushed the envelope, like *Married with Children* (1987) and *The Simpsons* (1990) and several shows featuring black performers. Fox was ready to use sassier scripts as a wedge to gain a foothold against its established competitors.[13] These new shows were noted for regular use of irreverence, sarcasm, irony, and even insult in the dialog, forms uncommon in earlier sitcoms. They were more likely to include risqué lines about sex than introduce social issues as Lear did in the 1970s. Sitcoms in general shifted away from the morality tale typical since radio to programs about flawed families.

Working-Class Shows of the Late 1980s and 1990s

Yet, for all the talk about postmodernism at the time, sitcom scripts were not as postmodern as one might expect. All these changes were still built upon decades-old character types. While *The Simpsons* and *Married with Children* were ruder, even gross, at the same time they used the old stereotypes of working-class men as inadequate breadwinners and models for their children.

The Simpsons begins its sixteenth season in the fall of 2004. In its earlier years, Homer Simpson barely brought home the bacon. The children's "college fund" was $88.50. They couldn't afford a new TV until Homer received double his money back for guaranteed family therapy that failed. He caused a nuclear accident while waving to his son touring the nuclear power plant where he works. Repeating the tradition's negative contrasts between father and mother, Marge, like Edith Bunker, is somewhat more levelheaded than Homer. The kids are embarrassingly smarter than Homer. Second-grader Lisa bettered her dad at Scrabble; Bart consistently beat him in a boxing video game. Both better him in arguments, with him resorting to shouting.

One episode of *The Simpsons* even encapsulated the continuing tradition of working-class sitcoms. Lisa Simpson realized she has the same genes as her dad and got depressed. Then she realized all the male relatives are jerks like her dad. By contrast she discovered the females are all successes, surgeons, professors, scientists.

Married with Children portrayed a family of uniformly unlikable people. The show was a spoof of the goody-goody TV family. The contrast was not between family members but to the wholesomeness of other TV families. The father Al Bundy, a shoe salesman, was dumb, but not lovable as in the traditional working-class type. He lied and smelled bad. The show was an endless stream of put-downs. Al's wife, Peg, regularly complained of his lack of money and sexual inadequacy. Peg's friend described him as having no skills and no brain. Peg and her daughter Kelly were also depicted as dumb. Peg couldn't remember what channel her favorite TV show was on; Kelly did not know what simpleton means. The son, Bud, was the only one with any intelligence and he was an oversexed adolescent.[14]

A more conventional sitcom, *Family Matters* moderated the traditional working-class stereotype father. At first the father, a black policeman bungled his efforts. He got lost taking a shortcut, gave the wrong directions to rescuers, said the wrong things trying to impress his boss. But soon the role of fool shifted to neighbor boy Steve Urkel who became an unexpected hit with audiences. The father began to fade as the featured fool, and the role of Urkel was expanded, much as had occurred with the role of J. J. in *Good Times* in the 1970s. Yet consistent with the tradition of working-class wives, Harriet the wife was the more sensible person in the family.

Somewhat an exception to the traditional stereotype was the father, Dan Conners of *Roseanne*, who, while a bit wild, was also sensible about the kids.

In one episode Dan was the voice of wisdom when he advised Roseanne not to engage in a power struggle with teenage Becky. More striking about *Roseanne* was its refusal to apologize for their working-class ways and accept middle-class manners as superior. Dan and Roseanne were content with their working-class tastes. They could use more money, but they were not conflicted about behaving "properly" and didn't aspire to cultural upward mobility.

The Bundys also were unapologetic for not being upper middle class, but rather metaphorically thumbed their noses at those expectations. For the first time working-class characters were allowed to be themselves, instead of inferior copies of middle-class characters.

Of 53 new domestic sitcoms from 1990 to 1999, 16 featured working-class families. Eleven series featured black families, indicating another trend toward more representation of subordinate groups. Yet several notable series that did not survive five seasons reproduced the working-class stereotype. *The Dinosaurs'* father was a Jurassic Archie Bunker. The father in *Joe's Life* was an unemployed househusband while the mom supported the family. *Bless This House* featured a macho postal worker with a feisty wife and sassy daughter, and also was described as *The Honeymooners* with kids.[15] In 1991 *Roc* featured a not-too-bright black garbage man with a stereotypic macho attitude and a more educated nurse as wife. In the new *Cosby* show, the husband was an unemployed airport worker while his wife co-owns a flower shop and his daughter is a lawyer. *Costello* was criticized for its crude stereotypes of working-class men. Strong, working wives and mothers ran their families and in some shows, overshadowed their husbands. *Jesse* and *Thea,* among others, were single mothers who exhibited strength and good character that put their men to shame. Many 1990s shows featured dysfunctional families, but the more serious dysfunctions were blue collar. Alcoholism, spousal abuse, child abandonment, or children being put up for adoption appeared in working-class shows like *Grace under Fire.* Divorce and quirky personalities were more typical of middle-class shows.[16]

In *Grace under Fire,* the working-class father was an unreliable drunken "good for nothing" who abandoned the family. Grace held a traditionally male job in an oil refinery and did better than most of the men. Two of her male friends were relaxed and comfortable, a middle-class pharmacist and a local TV reporter. She dates a series of stable, apparently middle-class men.

In the late 1990s *King of the Hill,* Hank, a Texas propane gas salesman, wears white t-shirts and jeans and drinks beer from cans with his buddies, and is often clueless to questions from his son. His son and wife are also not too bright. His live-in niece-in-law Luanne Platter is frustrated and embarrassed by them. Hank's friends are a divorced military barber, a paranoid with an obsession for government conspiracy theories and a man who just mumbles. All the males are of limited intellect. Unlike older working-class series, however, so is everyone else.

The *King of Queens* is Doug, a UPS driver, with a wife, Carrie, who works in a law firm and is a little too bright for him. He is a couch potato who loves to watch sports with his buddies on his 70-inch television. Husband and wife are young, fun-loving, and not quite ready to become parents. But she is interested in self-improvement for both of them, for example by going to high-brow events. She tries to reform his bad habits, such as too much eating and TV. It's a bit like a 1990s version of Fred and Wilma's relationship.

So, while there were more shows featuring working-class people in the 1990s, the men continued to be stereotyped as not too bright, immature, and contrasted to their more capable and responsible wives or adult female relatives. With few exceptions the working-class male leads were inadequate in their masculine roles. Undercutting their status as men in turn confirmed their lower status as working class, and resolved the contradictory statuses of adult white male on the one hand and working class on the other.

Middle Class of the Late 1980s and 1990s

Unlike working-class characters of the 1990s who continued to be true to stereotype, middle-class series came in all forms and sizes. One show briefly featured a fired soap opera actor ex-husband, another a con-artist who moves in with his successful lawyer sister, another a hyperactive party planner on her third husband, and another a suspended professional athlete moves in with his professor brother. There were four black middle-class families and one mixed-race couple. Jack, the father in *Wonder Years*, is a businessman who wears a suit and tie to work. He is singularly uninvolved in his family. When asked, he advises the kids "do what your mother said."

But there continued to be plenty of warm and fuzzy middle-class families, including some with slightly offbeat parents. Most were short-lived. *Something So Right* was called *The Brady Bunch* with taboos; *Cleghorne* was called a dysfunctional *Family Ties*; and *Parenthood* was likened to *thirtysomething*. *Harts of the West, Something Wilder, The Tony Danza Show,* and *The Gregory Hines Show* featured wholesome families. While quirky or even a bit dysfunctional, these families were still warm and comforting with competent parents.

More long lasting were two conventional shows. *Step by Step* was called *The Brady Bunch* for the 1990s. Frank, the father, owned a contracting company who carries a lunch box to work, but bought pro-basketball game tickets for a "client." His wife, Carol, owned a beauty salon, although she also graduated from college. He was an outdoorsy type who was permissive with the kids while Carol was more compulsive. The children were the focus of situations.

Seventh Heaven is another saccharine *Brady Bunch* look-alike that has survived a decade. A minister and a stay-at-home mom are perfect parents to five children whose trials of growing up are the subject of the show. Issues have included dating crises, teen suicide, sibling rivalry, gang violence, hate crimes, violence in schools, drug use, vandalism, drinking and driving, teen pregnancy, and homelessness. It has thrived presenting old-fashioned moral lessons in the security of an old-fashioned ideal middle-class family.

More written and talked about were *Home Improvement, Mad About You,* and *Everybody Loves Raymond.* Many have commented on how these fathers/ husbands were portrayed less positively than in the old days. Some attributed this to women becoming the majority on writing teams for several sitcoms and holding important executive positions at the networks.[17] But, while these men are not fathers who know best, nor are they buffoons like those of working-class series.

Tim, the father in *Home Improvement,* is star of his own TV show. At home, the focus is on the antics of the father rather than the children. But his antics involve his asserting his own independence and macho masculinity, rather than making a fool of himself. He reaffirms his manhood rather than undermines it, the masculine answer to feminism, a role model for the contemporary man. *Mad About You* explored the little annoyances and knots of relationships. In doing so it also revealed the flaws and insecurities of both the man and the woman. At the same time, both were professionals with promising careers; both worked together to sort out their differences; both were mature and intelligent adults.

The social class of *Everybody Loves Raymond* is anomalous, and the character does not conform to the stereotypes of the middle-class man. Raymond is a sportswriter and joins a private golf club, but in other ways the show is similar to the working-class form. His brother is a policeman, and his parents' were stereotypic ethnic New Yorkers. His father in particular is the classic working-class television type, modeled on Ralph and Archie: loud, gruff, overbearing. Moreover Raymond appears several times on *King of Queens* as a friend of Doug, the UPS driver. Raymond is cowed by his wife and his parents. He lies and concocts schemes to avoid confronting them. Yet he is professionally successful and his children are toddlers too young to outsmart or disrespect him, as is the tradition in working-class series.

While the 1990s continued the trend to show middle-class people as imperfect, the variety of representations itself avoided the stereotyping in working-class series. Like the characters of urban sitcoms described by Michael Tueth, these middle-class men are well-educated professionals, successful, intellectually superior and emotionally intense, while also being emotionally confused and childish to a degree.[18]

THE NEW MILLENNIUM

In the new millennium, a bounty of new black and working-class sitcoms were scheduled for prime time by the six broadcast networks. Joining *King of the Hill* and *King of Queens* that began in the 1990s were two more successful white working-class shows, *Grounded for Life* and *Still Standing*, as well as three unsuccessful shows, *Fighting Fitzgeralds, Mullets,* and *My Big Fat Greek Life.* Ten new black family sitcoms appeared, including *My Wife and Kids, One on One,* and *Bernie Mac.* Only two of the ten black families are working class; the rest are very successful, most of them entertainers. Five of the ten appeared on UPN and WB where they represented half the minor networks' new sitcoms. Two Hispanic families and two gay shows set in families also appeared. Networks were clearly looking for the unconventional more than ever.

Sean of *Grounded for Life* is a grown-up kid, but he's also an echo of the old stereotype. He's continually screwing up, like Ralph and Fred. He tries to help his daughter Lily (who has been given detention for wearing too short a skirt to school) by taking pictures of the other girls, all of whom have short skirts. The principal gives them all detention and tells them it's Lily's fault. His son wants to go home to work on a science project but he insists on staying at a fair to listen to the Ramones. Sean writes a note to school explaining why his son did not finish the project. His son gets in trouble and Sean feels guilty. When he gets $1500 from his mothers' inheritance, Sean buys a guitar, then returns it out of guilt to pay for a ski trip for his daughter.

Still Standing is about a working-class Chicago couple who came of age in the 1970s and still love rock 'n' roll but now have three kids. Wife Judy is supposed to be smarter than husband Bill who always screws up. He tries to make Judy feel better by telling her the husband of a woman she envies is cheating on her. This backfires when Judy tells everyone. The difference is the wife also screws up. These two shows present couples similar to the one in *King of Queens.*

The Fitzgeralds was a rather positive portrayal of a retired fire captain, a managerial position, but one rooted in working-class culture. Unfortunately, the show was cancelled after only ten episodes. *The Mullets* is about two brothers described as "dumb and dumber." It's a classic case of laughing at white trash.[19] These new shows again portray working-class men as irresponsible and immature. The difference is that some middle-class men are now being portrayed in this way, whereas this was rarely the case before the 1990s.

Malcolm in the Middle and *According to Jim* continue the unashamedly irresponsible middle-class men of the 1990s. Malcolm's father Hal works in an unspecified office, but finds plenty of time for all kinds of fun and trouble. He hijacks the kids from school to take them to car races. He has a chance to drive a steamroller and gets a hankering to crush things. Hal has a wealthy father and one might explain the character as an eccentric who never learned to worry about practical matters like money. The mother, Lois, has the bigger part of the job of civilizing their four exceptionally rowdy boys.

Jim of *According to Jim* is a contractor in partnership with his architect brother-in-law. Jim can't give up his motorcycle. He's also in a hurry to go to a Bears game, sticking his wife's dead cat in the freezer instead of burying it. He has his sister-in-law pick out presents for his wife rather than doing it himself.

One on One and *Two and a Half Men* feature bachelors with child-raising responsibilities suddenly thrust upon them. These shows are a new version of the old formula of the affluent bachelor father, such as the 1960s *Family Affair,* which was revived in 2002 but soon cancelled. In the past the bachelors experienced a strain between their former unencumbered single life and their new obligations, and attempted to live up to those obligations. The father in *One on One* is a black version of the bachelor father. While he enjoys sports, his buddies and women, he's concerned about protecting and bringing up his daughter, Breanna, properly.

Charlie of *Two and a Half Men* is another adolescent man. He's prosperous, a bachelor, with a Malibu beach house, a Jaguar, and success with women. But when his brother's marriage falls apart, he takes him in and his fourth-grade son, creating the situational conflict between his social life and the boy. To resolve the conflict, Charlie sometimes includes the boy in his activities such as shopping for women and playing poker.

These programs depicting grown men behaving as adolescents are surrounded by shows that settle for a quirky twist on the old formula. *Even Stevens* is a show about a perfect family that focuses on a seventh grade boy. The parents, a successful attorney and a state senator, are in the background, while the boy stumbles through life, which the parent and older kids help him put back together. *My Wife and Kids* features a successful businessman who becomes a househusband so his wife can pursue her career. While he trips up, he also creates a warm and fuzzy feeling at home. Similarly *Bernie Mac,* featuring a successful comedian whose wife is a corporate executive, welcomes in and takes care of his sister's kids. Bernie is blustery but well meaning. These are slightly jazzier versions of *The Cosby Show.* Even the two shows featuring a gay character are rather tame. In both *The Ellen Show* and *Normal, Ohio,* the gay character returns to a family and hometown who by and large accept them.

CONCLUSION

The five decades can be summed up in the French phrase, *plus ca change, plus c'est la meme chose* (the more things change, the more they stay the same). While there have been variations and exceptions across five decades of television sitcoms, the stock character of the ineffectual, even buffoonish working-class man has persisted as the dominant image. In the prime-time tapestry he is contrasted with consistently competent working-class wives and children and manly middle-class fathers—a composite image in which working-class men are de-masculinized and their class status justified.

The persistence of the working-class male stereotype contrasts with the changes in representations of middle-class families. While they were stereotypically perfect in the 1950s and 1960s, from the 1970s on the depictions of the middle class progressively broadened to include a wide range of character types and situations. Nevertheless, the super parent continued to be a common representation of the middle class; and middle-class men, while sometimes represented as irresponsible, were not de-masculinized and continued to be unusually successful in their careers.

Major upheavals in American society and culture during the 1960s and 1970s and major changes in television industry and television technology in the 1980s and 1990s, brought innovations to TV's domestic sitcoms and broadened and deepened their characterizations. But they have not dislodged the pattern of class representations that are at the core of over three hundred domestic sitcoms that have been consumed nightly by the American people. If there has been any change in the class representations, it has been to leaven the starchy image of a perfect middle class. There is no sign of a return to the more positive representations of working men that were more common in 1930s and 1940s popular culture, and slowly passed away with the appearance of the television.

NOTES

1. David Grote, *The End of Comedy* (Hamden, CT: Shoestring Press, 1983), 39–41, 87–88. For alternate definitions of sitcom see Jane Feuer, "Genre Study and Television," in *Channels of Discourse*, Robert C. Allen, ed. (Chapel Hill: University of North Carolina Press, 1987), 113–133; and Susan Horowitz, "Sitcom Domesticus: A Species Endangered by Social Change," in H. Newcomb (ed.), *Television: A Critical View* (4th ed.), Horace Newcomb, ed. (New York: Oxford University Press, 1987), 106–111.

2. Grote, *The End of Comedy*, 41–43; Stuart Hall and Paddy Whannel, *The Popular Arts* (Boston, Beacon Press, 1967); Orrin Klapp, *Heroes, Villains, and Fools: The Changing American Character* (Englewood Cliffs, NJ: Prentice-Hall, 1962).

3. Joan Scott, *Gender and the Politics of History* (New York: Columbia University Press, 1988); Ava Baron, "Questions of Gender: Deskilling and De-masculinizing in the U.S. Printing Industry, 1830–1915," *Gender and History* 1 (Summer 1989), 178–199.

4. Beth Olson and William Douglas, "The Family on Television: Evaluation of Gender Roles in Situation Comedy," *Sex Roles* 36.5–6 (March 1997), 409–427; Sally Steenland, "Content Analysis of the Image of Women on Television," in *Women and Media: Content, Careers and Criticism*, Cindy M. Lont, ed. (Belmont, CA: Wadsworth, 1995); Steve Craig, ed., *Mediated Males: Men, Masculinity and the Media* (Beverly Hills: Sage, 1992); Herman Gray, "Television and the New Black Man: Black Male Images in Prime Time Situation Comedy," *Media, Culture and Society* 8 (April 1986), 223–242; Dallas Smythe, "Reality as Presented by Television," *Public Opinion Quarterly* 18 (Summer 1954), 143–156; Mark Crispin Miller, "Deride and conquer," in *Watching Television*, Todd Gitlin, ed. (New York: Pantheon, 1986), 183–228; Sari Thomas and Brian Callahan, "Allocating Happiness:

TV Families and Social Class," *Journal of Communication* 32.3 (1982), 184–190; H. Leslie Steeves and Marilyn Crafton Smith, "Class and Gender in Prime-Time Television," *Journal of Communication* 11:1 (Winter 1987), 43–63; and Marjorie Ferguson, "Images of Power and Feminine Fallacy," *Critical Studies in Mass Communication* 7 (September 1990), 215–230.

5. Richard Butsch, "Class and Gender in Four Decades of Television Situation Comedy," *Critical Studies in Mass Communication* 9:4 (December 1992), 387–99; Richard Butsch and Lynda Glennon, "Families on TV: Where Was the Working Class?" *Television* 7.2/3 (1980), 11–12; Richard Butsch and Lynda Glennon, "Social Class: Frequency Trends in Domestic Situation Comedy, 1946–1978," *Journal of Broadcasting* 27 (Winter 1983), 77–81; Lynda Glennon and Richard Butsch, "The Family as Portrayed on Television, 1946–1978," in *Television and Behavior: Ten Years of Scientific Progress and Implications for the Eighties,* Volume II, Technical Reviews, David Pearl, Lorraine Bouthilet, and Joyce Lazar, eds. (Washington, DC: U.S. Department of Health and Human Services, 1982), 264–271.

6. The occupation of the head of household was used to distinguish the class represented in the sitcom. For consistency I continue to use the same guidelines as when I began this research three decades ago, following Harry Braverman, *Labor and Monopoly Capital* (New York: Monthly Review Press, 1974), 377–380.

7. John Consoli, "Network TV," *MediaWeek* 11.9 (26 February 2001), 9.

8. J. Fred MacDonald, *Don't Touch That Dial* (Chicago: Nelson-Hall, 1979), 132–145, 141 for quote; Jess Oppenheimer, *Laughs, Luck and Lucy* (Syracuse, NY: Syracuse University Press, 1996), Chapters 10–11.

9. Robert Pekurny, "Broadcast Self-Regulation," Ph.D. Dissertation, University of Minnesota, 1977; Alfred R. Schneider, *The Gatekeeper: My 30 Years as a TV Censor* (Syracuse, NY: Syracuse University Press, 2001).

10. "From the Old Country," *Time,* 26 February 1951, 86.

11. Jane Feuer, "Genre Study and Television," in *Channels of Discourse,* 113–133; Ella Taylor, *Prime-Time Families* (Berkeley: University of California Press, 1989).

12. Richard Butsch, *The Making of American Audiences* (Cambridge: Cambridge University Press, 2000), Chapter 18; FCC Network Inquiry Special Staff, Preliminary Reports, FCC, 1980.

13. Kristal Brent Zook, *Color by Fox: The Fox Network and the Revolution in Black Television* (New York: Oxford University Press, 1999).

14. Rick Marin, "Nuking the Nuclear Family," *Newsweek* 29 April 1996, 70.

15. David Hiltbrand, "Tube," *People* 18 September 1995, 21; Helen Arthur, "Love in the Time of AIDS," *The Nation,* 25 September 1995, 327.

16. Caryn James, "Dysfunction Wears Out Its Welcome," *New York Times,* 3 December 1995, H1, H37.

17. Erica Scharrer, "From Wise to Foolish: The Portrayal of the Sitcom Father, 1950s–1990s," *Journal of Broadcasting and Electronic Media* 45:1 (Winter 2001), 23–41; Hilary De Vries, "In Comedies, Signs of a New Women's Movement," *New York Times,* 25 February 2001, AR19, AR36.

18. Michael Tueth, "Fun City: The Urban Sitcom of the 1990s," *Journal of Popular Film and Television* 28:3 (Fall 2000), 98–108.

19. On representations of white trash see Dwight Billings, Gurney Norman, and Katherine Ledford, eds., *Confronting Appalachian Stereotypes* (Lexington, KY: University Press of Kentucky, 1999); Matthew Wray and Annalee Newitz, eds., *White Trash* (New York: Routledge, 1996).

QUESTIONS FOR CRITICAL THINKING

Reading 35

1. As Butsch discusses, television images have historically represented the middle class as better than the working class. How does this help to maintain the status quo?

2. What are the ways that television images perpetuate class inequality? Have you seen examples that challenge class inequality? If so, what did these examples look like? If not, what do you think accounts for the lack of such images?

3. What are some ways that television can be used to foster greater economic equality? What might such programming look like?

Reading 36

WINNEBAGOS, CHEROKEES, APACHES, AND DAKOTAS:
The Persistence of Stereotyping of American Indians in American Advertising Brands

DEBRA MERSKIN

From early childhood on, we have all learned about "Indianness" from textbooks, movies, television programs, cartoons, songs, commercials, fanciful paintings, and product logos.[1] Since the turn of the century, American Indian images, music, and names have been incorporated into many American advertising campaigns and product images. Whereas patent medicines of the past featured "coppery, feather-topped visage of the Indian" (Larson, 1937, p. 338), butter boxes of the present show the doe-eyed, buckskin-clad Indian "princess." These stereotypes are pervasive, but not necessarily consistent—varying over time and place from the "artificially idealistic" (noble savage) to present-day images of "mystical environmentalists or uneducated, alcoholic bingo-players confined to reservations"

Debra Merskin, "Winnebagos, Cherokees, Apaches, and Dakotas: The Persistence of Stereotyping of American Indians in American Advertising Brands" from *The Howard Journal of Communications* 12 (2001): 159–169. Copyright © 2001 by Taylor & Francis. Reprinted with permission.

(Mihesuah, 1996, p. 9). Yet today a trip down the grocery store aisle still reveals ice cream bars, beef jerky, corn meal, baking powder, malt liquor, butter, honey, sour cream, and chewing tobacco packages emblazoned with images of American Indians. Companies that use these images of Indians do so to build an association with an idealized and romanticized notion of the past through the process of branding (Aaker & Biel, 1993). Because these representations are so commonplace (Land O' Lakes maiden, Jeep Cherokee, Washington Redskins logo), we often fail to notice them, yet they reinforce long-held stereotypical beliefs about Native Americans.

Trade characters such as Aunt Jemima (pancake mix), Uncle Rastus (Cream of Wheat), and Uncle Ben (rice) are visual reminders of the subservient occupational positions to which Blacks often have been relegated (Kern-Foxworth, 1994). Similarly, Crazy Horse Malt Liquor, Red Chief Sugar, and Sue Bee Honey similarly remind us of an oppressive past. How pictorial metaphors on product labels create and perpetuate stereotypes of American Indians is the focus of this study. McCracken's (1993) Meaning Transfer Model and Barthes's (1972) semiotic analysis of brand images serve as the framework for the analysis of four national brands. The following sections discuss how stereotypes are constructed and how they are articulated in, and perpetuated through, advertising.

 BACKGROUND

To understand how labels on products and brand names reinforce long-held stereotypical beliefs, we must consider beliefs already in place that facilitated this process. Goings (1994), in his study of African American stereotypes, points out that, "Racism was not a byproduct of the Civil War; it had clearly been around since the founding of the nation" (p. 7). Similarly, anti-Indian sentiments did not begin with the subjugation and dislocation efforts of the 1800s. Racial and ethnic images, part of American advertising for more than a century, were created in "less enlightened times" but have become a part of American popular culture and thought (Graham, 1993, p. 35) and persist today. The system of representation thereby becomes a "stable cultural convention that is taught and learned by members of a society" (Kates & Shaw-Garlock, 1999, p. 34).

Part of the explanation for the persistent use of these images can be found in the power and persuasiveness of popular culture representations. Goings's (1994) analysis of Black collectibles and memorabilia from the 1880s to the 1950s is a useful analogy for understanding the construction of Native American stereotypes in popular culture. He suggests that "collectible" items such as salt and pepper shakers, trade cards, and sheet music with images of happy Sambos, plump mammies, or wide-eyed pickaninnies served as nonverbal articulations of racism made manifest in everyday goods. By exaggerating the physical features of African

American men and women, and making them laughable and useable in everyday items, these household objects reinforced beliefs about the place of Blacks in American society. Aunt Jemima, the roly-poly mammy; and Uncle Rastus, the happy slave chef (ironically both remain with us today) helped make Whites feel more comfortable with, and less guilty about, maintenance of distinctions on the basis of race well after Reconstruction. These items were meant for daily use, hence constantly and subtly reinforcing stereotypical beliefs.

Similarly, Berkhofer (1979) suggests that "the essence of the white image of the Indian has been the definition of American Indians in fact and in fancy as a separate and single other. Whether evaluated as noble or ignoble, whether seen as exotic or downgraded, the Indian as image was always alien to white." (p. xv) White images of Native Americans were similarly constructed through children's games, toys, tales, art, and theater of the 1800s. Whereas "Little Black Sambo" tales reinforced the construction of racist beliefs about Blacks, songs such as "Ten Little Indians" or "cowboy and Indian" games similarly framed Indian otherness in the White mind. Goings (1994) makes an important point about the source of the construction of objects that represent this way of thinking:

> It is important to note that Black memorabilia are figures from white American history. White Americans developed the stereotypes; white Americans produced the collectibles; and white American manufacturers and advertisers disseminated both the images and the objects to a white audience. (p. xix)

The maintenance of these kinds of beliefs satisfies the human need for psychological equilibrium and order, finding support and reinforcement in ideology. Defined as "typical properties of the 'social mind' of a group" (van Dijk, 1996, p. 56), ideologies provide a frame of reference for understanding the world. *Racist* ideologies serve several social functions operating to reproduce racism by legitimating social inequalities, thereby justifying racially or ethnically constructed differences. Racist ideology is used to (1) organize specific social attitudes into an evaluative framework for perceiving otherness, (2) provide the basis for "coordinated action and solidarity among whites," and (3) define racial and ethnic identity of the dominant group (van Dijk, 25–27). These beliefs and practices are thereby articulated in the production and distribution of racist discourse.

THEORETICAL FOUNDATION

To every ad they see or hear, people bring a shared set of beliefs that serve as frames of reference for understanding the world around them. Beyond its obvious selling function, advertising images are about making meaning. Ads must "take into account not only the inherent qualities and attributes of the products they are trying to sell, but also the way in which they can make those properties mean something to us" (Williamson, 1978, p. 12).

Barthes (1972) describes these articulations as myth, that is, "a type of speech" or mode of signification that is conveyed by discourse that consists of many possible modes of representation including, but not limited to, writing, photography, publicity, and advertising. Myth is best described by the process of semiology (Barthes, 1972). Semiology "postulates a relation between two terms, a signifier and a signified" (Barthes, 1972, p. 112). The correlation of the terms *signifier, signified,* and *sign* is where associative meaning is made. What we see in an advertisement or product label, at first glance, are basic elements composed of linguistic signs (words) and iconic signs (visuals). Barthes (1972) uses a rose, for example, as a symbol of passion. Roses are not passion per se, but rather the roses (signifier) + concept of passion (signified) = roses (sign). He states that "the signifier is empty, the sign is full, it is a meaning" (Barthes, 1972, p. 113). Another example that involves race is the use of Aunt Jemima for maple syrup. We see the representation of a bandana-clad Black woman who suggests the mammy of the Deep South (signified). When placed on the bottle of syrup (sign), meaning is transferred to the otherwise ambiguous product—care giving, home cooking, and food sharing. The sign is formed at the intersection between a brand name and a meaning system that is articulated in a particular image. Quite simply, a sign, whether "object, word, or picture," has a "particular meaning to a person or group of people. It is neither the thing nor the meaning alone, but the two together" (Williamson, 1978, p. 17).

McCracken (1993, p. 125), who defines a brand as a "bundle or container of meaning," expanded on the Barthesian analysis and developed a framework for understanding the cultural relationship that brands have within society. His anthropological model (Figure 1) illustrates the meanings of brands. McCracken shows how brands assume meaning through advertising, combined with consumption behavior, and the nature of common knowledge that consumers bring to this system. The present study expands on this process by adding a reinforcement loop from consumer back to the culture where stereotypes are experienced and recirculated through the system.

A brand can have gendered meaning (maleness/femaleness), social standing (status), nationality (country meaning), and ethnicity/race (multicultural meaning). A brand can also stand for notions of tradition, trustworthiness,

FIGURE 1   Meaning Model of Brand. (*Source:* Revised from McCracken, 1993, p. 125.)

purity, family, nature, and so on. McCracken (1993) uses the Marlboro man as an example of these components with which a simple red and white box came to signify freedom, satisfaction, competence, maleness, and a quintessentially American, Western character. The product becomes part of the constellation of meanings that surrounds it and thereby "soaks up" meanings. When the rugged Marlboro man is situated on his horse, on the open plain, almost always alone, the meanings of the constellation become clear—freedom, love of the outdoors, release from the confines of industrialized society—he is a "real man," self-sufficient and individualistic. These meanings become part of a theme made up of prototypical content while simultaneously being "idealizations and not reality itself" (Schmitt & Simonson, 1997, p. 124).

Advertisements are created in such a way as to boost the commodity value of brand names by connecting them to images that resonate with the social and cultural values of a society. These images are loaded with established ideological assumptions that, when attached to a commodity, create the commodity sign. Tools of branding are thereby used to create a particular image in the mind of the consumer. According to van Dijk (1996), this pattern often serves to present an US versus THEM dichotomy, with US being White, "positive, tolerant, modern," and THEM being minorities who are "problematic, deviant and threatening" (pp. 26–27). Hence, attitudes, beliefs, and behavior that are racist serve to support a dominant ideology that focuses on difference and separatism.

These ideas and values are articulated through the construction, maintenance, and perpetuation of stereotypes. Stereotypes are overgeneralized beliefs that

> get hold of the few simple, vivid, memorable, easily grasped,
> and widely recognized characteristics about a person, reduce
> everything about the person to those traits, exaggerate and simplify
> them, and fix them without change or development to eternity.
> (Hall, 1997, p. 258)

An example is the way the "Indian problem" of the 1800s has been shown in "cowboy and Indian" films. In his analysis of the representation of Indians in film, Strickland (1998, p. 10) asks, "What would we think the American Indian was like if we had only the celluloid Indian from which to reconstruct history?" (Strickland, 1998, p. 10). The cinematic representation includes the Indian as a

> bloodthirsty and lawless savage; the Indian as enemy of progress;
> the Indian as tragic, but inevitable, victim; the Indian as a lazy, fat,
> shiftless drunk; the Indian as oil-rich illiterate; the Indian as edu-
> cated half-breed unable to live in either a white or Indian world;
> the Indian as nymphomaniac; the Indian as noble hero; the Indian
> as stoic and unemotional; the Indian as the first conservationist.
> (Strickland, 1998, p. 10)

Champagne's (1994) analysis of Indians in films and theater suggests that the longevity of James Fenimore Cooper's *Last of the Mohicans,* evidenced by its many film treatments, demonstrates that "Hollywood prefers to isolate its Indians safely within the romantic past, rather than take a close look at Native American issues in the contemporary world" (p. 719).

Natty Bumpo, in James Fenimore Cooper's *Deerslayer,* is a literary example of the male who goes from a state of "uncultured animality" to a state of "civilization and culture" (Green, 1993, p. 327). Larson (1937) describes how this stereotype was translated into a tool for marketing patent medicines:

> No sooner had James Fenimore Cooper romanticized the Indian in the American imagination in his novels than patent-medicine manufacturers, quick to sense and take advantage of this new enthusiasm, used the red man as symbol and token for a great variety of ware. How the heart of the purchaser—filled, like as not, with the heroic exploits of Cooper's Indians—must have warmed as he gazed at the effigy, symbolic of "Nature's Own Remedy." (p. 338)

The female savage becomes an Indian princess who "renounces her own family, marries someone from the dominate culture and assimilates into it." (Green, 1993, p. 327), for example, Pocahontas. From this perspective, Indians are thought of as childlike and innocent, requiring the paternalistic care of Whites; that is, they are tamable. In her study of Indian imagery in *Dr. Quinn, Medicine Woman,* Bird (1996, p. 258) suggests that what viewers see is a White fantasy filled with White concerns around "guilt and retrospective outrage." Green's (1993) analysis of the use of male Indian images in ads posits that Natives continue to be portrayed according to stereotypical images: (1) noble savage (the stoic, innocent, child of nature), (2) civilizable savage (redeemable, teachable), and (3) bloodthirsty savage (fierce, predatory, cultureless, animalistic). Taken together, these studies suggest that historically constructed images and beliefs about American Indians are at the essence of stereotypical thinking that are easily translated into product images.

METHOD

To study the articulation of racist ideology in brand images, four currently available national products (Land O' Lakes butter, Sue Bee Honey, Big Chief [Monitor] Sugar, and Crazy Horse Malt Liquor) were analyzed according to Barthes's (1972) semiotic analysis. First, the material object was identified (signifier); second, the associative elements were identified (signified); and, third, these were brought together in what we as consumers recognize as the sign. Company websites, press releases, and product packages were used for visual and textual information. Several attempts to communicate directly with the companies yielded no response. Through this method of analysis we can see how these meanings are transferred to the different products on the basis of both race and gender.

 RESULTS

The following section presents a descriptive analysis of Land O' Lakes, Sue Bee Honey, Big Chief (Monitor) Sugar, and Crazy Horse Malt Liquor brand images.

Land O' Lakes

Although not the first national manufacturer to draw on the mystique of Indianness (that honor goes to Red Man Tobacco in 1904), Land O' Lakes is certainly one of the more prominent. In 1921, the Minnesota Cooperative Creameries Association opened for business in Arden Hills, Minnesota. This company served as the central shipping agent for a small group of small, farmer-owned dairy cooperatives (Morgan, 1986, p. 63). In 1924, the group wanted a different name and solicited ideas from farmers. Mrs. E. B. Foss and Mr. George L. Swift came up with the winning name—Land O' Lakes, "a tribute to Minnesota's thousands of sparkling lakes" (p. 63). The corporate website opens with a photograph of a quiet lake amid pine trees and blue sky. The copy under the photograph reads:

> Welcome to Land O' Lakes. A land unlike anywhere else on earth.
> A special place filled with clear, spring-fed lakes. Rivers and streams
> that dance to their own rhythms through rich, fertile fields. It's the
> land we call home. And from it has flowed the bounty and goodness
> we bring to you, our neighbors and friends. (Land O' Lakes, 2000)

In addition, "The now famous Indian maiden was also created during the search for a brand name and trademark. Because the regions of Minnesota and Wisconsin were the legendary lands of Hiawatha and Minnehaha, the idea of an Indian maiden took form" (Land O' Lakes, 2000). A painting was sent to the company of an Indian maiden facing the viewer, holding a butter carton with a background filled with lakes, pines, flowers, and grazing cows.

At the Land O' Lakes corporate website, the director of communications includes a statement about the maiden image, where he agrees that the logo, the "Indian Maiden," has powerful connotations (Land O' Lakes). Hardly changed since its introduction in the 1920s, he says that Land O' Lakes has built on the "symbolism of the purity of the products" (Burnham, 1992). The company "thought the Indian maiden would be a good image. She represents Hiawatha and the Land of Gitchgoomee and the names of Midwest towns and streets that have their roots in the American Indian population" (Burnham, 1992).

The signifier is thereby the product, be it butter, sour cream, or other Land O' Lakes products. The Indian woman on the package is associated with youth, innocence, nature, and purity. The result is the generic "Indian maiden." Subsequently, the qualities stereotypically associated with this beaded, buckskinned, doe-eyed young woman are transferred to the company's products. Green's "noble savage" image is extended to include the female stereotype.

Sue Bee Honey

The Sioux Honey Association, based in Sioux City, Iowa, is a cooperative of honey producers, yielding 40 million pounds of honey annually (Sioux Honey Association, 2000). Corporate communications describe a change of the product name in 1964 from Sioux Bee to Sue Bee, "to reflect the correct pronunciation of the name" (Sioux Honey Association, 2000). The brand name and image are reinforced on trucks (both real and toys), on the bottles and jars in which the honey is sold, and through collectibles such as coffee mugs and recipe books.

Sue Bee Honey also draws upon the child-of-nature imagery in an attempt to imbue qualities of purity into their products. If we were to view Sue Bee in her full form (as she is shown on many specialty items such as mugs, glasses, and jars) we would see that she is an Indian maiden on top, with braided hair and headband, and a bee below the waist. Changing the spelling of her name from "Sioux Bee" to "Sue Bee" could be interpreted in a variety of ways—possibly simply as a matter of pronunciation, as the company asserts, or as an effort to draw attention away from the savage imagery stereotypically attributed to members of this tribe and more toward the little girlishness of the image. In this case, the product is honey, traditionally associated with trees and forests and natural places. This association works well with the girl—child Indian stereotype. By placing the girl bee on the package of honey, consumers can associate the innocence, purity, and naturalness attributed to Native American females with the quality of the product.

In the tradition of Pocahontas, both the Land O' Lakes and the Sue Bee maidens symbolize innocence, purity, and virginity—children of nature. The maiden image signifies a female "Indianness." She is childlike, as she happily offers up perhaps honey or butter (or herself) that "is as pure and healthy as she is" (Dotz & Morton, 1996, p. 11). The maiden's image is used to represent attempts to get back to nature, and the association is that this can be accomplished through the healthy, wholesome products of Land O' Lakes. Both images are encoded with socially constructed meanings about female Indian sexuality, purity, and nature.

Monitor Sugar Company

Founded in 1901, the Monitor Sugar Company processes approximately 4% of U.S. beet production into sugar (granulated, powdered, brown, and icing; Monitor Sugar Company, 2000). For 60 years the company has been producing sugar from beets, relying on the image of an American Indian in full headdress to sell the sugar goods. The products are available on grocery store shelves and in bulk for institutions, delivered by trucks with the Big Chief logo emblazoned on the sides.

So, who is this Chief said to represent? Is he a bona fide tribal leader or a composite Indian designed to communicate naturalistic characteristics associated with Indians with the sugar? Green's (1993) savage typology suggests that this individual is a combination of the noble savage (natural) and the bloodthirsty savage (ferocious). He is proud, noble, and natural and yet he is wearing a ceremonial headdress that communicates strength and stoicism.

Crazy Horse Malt Liquor

A 40-ounce beverage that is sold in approximately 40 states (Metz & Thee, 1994), Crazy Horse Malt Liquor is brewed by the Heilman Brewing Company of Brooklyn, New York. Crazy Horse Malt Liquor employs the image of Tasunke Witko (Crazy Horse) on the label of its malt liquor. On the front of the bottle is an American Indian male wearing a headdress that appears to be an eagle feather bonnet, and there is a symbol representing a medicine wheel—both sacred images in Lakota and other Native cultures (1994).

Image analysis shows that the sign is that of an actual Indian chief. Signified, however, are beliefs about Indians as warriors, westward expansion, how mighty the consumer might be by drinking this brand, and wildness of the American Western frontier.

This brand, perhaps more than any other, has come under public scrutiny because it is the image of a particular person. A revered forefather of the Oglala Sioux tribe of South Dakota, Crazy Horse died in 1877 (Blalock, 1992). The labels feature the prominent image of Chief Crazy Horse, who has long been the subject of stories, literature, and movies. Larger than life, he has played a role in American mythology.

Signifying Green's (1993) bloodthirsty savage image, Crazy Horse Malt Liquor makes use of American myths through image and association. Ironically, Crazy Horse objected to alcohol and warned his nation about the destructive effects of liquor (Specktor, 1995). As a sign, Crazy Horse represents a real symbol of early American life and westward expansionism. He was, according to the vice president of the Oglala Sioux Tribe, a "warrior, a spiritual leader, a traditional leader, a hero who has always been and is still revered by our people" (Hill, 1992; Metz & Thee, 1994, p. 50). This particular image brings together some interesting aspects of branding. Not only is the noble and bloodthirsty savage stereotype brought together in a proud, but ultimately defeated, Indian chief, but also this is an image of a real human being. The association of alcohol with that image, as well as targeting the Indian population, draws on assumptions of alcohol abuse.[2]

DISCUSSION AND CONCLUSIONS

Although there are dozens of possible examples of Native images on product labels, ranging from cigarette packages to sports utility vehicles, the examples discussed above illustrate the principles behind semiotics. The four presented here are significant examples of national brands employing stereotypical representations. When people are made aware of these products, they see how these images are consistently found in many products that employ Indian stereotypes either in product names or in their logos.

Many of these signs and symbols have been with us so long we no longer question them. Product images on packages, in advertisements, on television, and in films are nearly the only images non-Indians ever see of Native Americans. The covers of romance novels routinely feature Indian men sweeping beautiful non-Indian women off their feet as their bodices are torn away. These stereotypical representations of American Indians denies that they are human beings, and presents them as existing only in the past and as single, monolithic Indians (Merskin, 1998).

American Indians are certainly not the only racial or ethnic group to be discriminated against, overtly or covertly. Aunt Jemima and Rastus certainly have their origins in dehumanizing, one-dimensional images based on a tragic past. Yet, like Betty Crocker, these images have been updated. Aunt Jemima has lost weight and the bandana, and the Frito Bandito has disappeared (Burnham, 1992). But the Indian image persists in corporate marketing and product labeling.

These are highly visible and perhaps more openly discussed than images that appear on the products we see in grocery store aisles. An Absolut Vodka ad shows an Eskimo pulling a sled of vodka and a Grey Owl Wild Rice package features an Indian with braids, wearing a single feather, surrounded by a circle that represents (according to Grey Owl's distribution manager) the "oneness of nature" (Burnham, 1992). A partial list of others includes Apache helicopter, Jeep Cherokee, Apache rib doormats, Red Man Tobacco, Kleek-O the Eskimo (Cliquot Club ginger ale), Dodge Dakota, Pontiac, the Cleveland Indians, Mutual of Omaha, Calumet Baking Powder, Mohawk Carpet Mills, American Spirit cigarettes, Eskimo pies, Tomahawk mulcher, Winnebago Motor Homes, Indian Motorcycles, Tomahawk missiles, many high school sports teams, and the music behind the Hamm's beer commercials that begins "From the land of sky blue waters." And the list goes on.

Change is coming, but it is slow. For one thing, American Indians do not represent a significant target audience to advertisers. Representing less than 1% of the population, and the most economically destitute of all ethnic minority populations, American Indians are not particularly useful to marketers. Nearly 30% live below the official poverty line, in contrast with 13% of the general U.S. population (Cortese, 1999, p. 117). Without the population numbers or legal resources, it is nearly impossible for the voices of Natives to be heard, unlike other groups who have made some representational inroads. According to Westerman (1989), when minority groups speak, businesses are beginning to listen: "That's why Li'l Black Sambo and the Frito Bandito are dead. They were killed by the very ethnic groups they portrayed" (p. 28).

Not only does stereotyping communicate inaccurate beliefs about Natives to Whites, but also to Indians. Children, all children, are perhaps the most important recipients of this information for it is during childhood that difference is first learned. If, during the transition of adolescence, Native children internalize these representations that suggest that Indians are lazy, alcoholic by nature, and violent, this misinformation can have a life-long impact on perceptions of self and others. As Lippmann (1922/1961) wrote,

> The subtlest and most pervasive of all influences are those which create and maintain the repertory of stereotypes. We are told about the world before we see it. We imagine most things before we experience them. (p. 89)

By playing a game of substitution, by inserting other ethnic groups or races into the same situation, it becomes clear that there is a problem. Stereotypical images do not reside only in the past, because the social control mechanisms that helped to create them remain with us today.

Future research should continue to examine how the advertising and marketing practice of branding contributes to the persistent use of racist images on product labels. This study adds to the sparse literature on media representations of Native Americans in general and adds to Green's (1993) typology by including female counterparts to the male savage stereotypes. Future research could explore more images of Native Americans in ads and on products. Qualitative research with members of different tribes would add depth to this area of study.

NOTES

1. Many people have preferences about terms used to describe America's indigenous peoples. "American Indian" is commonly used, as is "Native American, Native, and Indian." These terms are used interchangeably in recognition of individual preferences, without disregarding the weight each word carries.
2. Lawsuits are currently underway to limit Heilman Breweries use of the name Crazy Horse Malt Liquor (Specktor, 1995). Several states have outlawed the sale of this beverage (Specktor, 1995). Also under review are important legal issues such as a tribe's sovereign power to exercise civil jurisdiction and the Witko family's right to protect the image of their ancestor.

REFERENCES

Aaker, D., & A. L. Biel. (1993). *Advertising's role in building strong brands.* Mahwah, NJ: Lawrence Erlbaum.

Barthes, R. (1972). *Mythologies* New York: The Noonday Press.

Berkhofer, R., Jr. (1979). *The white man's Indian: Images of the American Indian from Columbus to the present.* New York: Vintage Books.

Bird, S. E. (1996). Not my fantasy: The persistence of Indian imagery in *Dr. Quinn, Medicine Woman.* In S. E. Bird (Ed.), *Dressing in feathers: The construction of the Indian in American popular culture* (pp. 245–262). Boulder, CO: Westview Press.

Blalock, C. (1992). Crazy Horse controversy riles Congress: Controversies over Crazy Horse Malt Liquor and Black Death vodka. *Beverage Industry, 83*(9), 1–3.

Burnham, P. (1992, 27 May). Indians can't shake label as guides to good buys. *The Washington Times,* p. El.

Champagne, D. (1994). *Native America: Portrait of the peoples.* Detroit: Visible Ink.

Cortese, A. J. (1999). *Provocateur: Images of women and minorities in advertising.* New York: Rowman & Littlefield Publishers, Inc.

Dotz, W., & Morton, J. (1996). *What a character! 20th century American advertising icons.* San Francisco: Chronicle Books.

Goings, K. W. (1994). *Mammy and Uncle Mose: Black collectibles and American stereotyping.* Bloomington, IN: Indiana University Press.

Graham, R. (1993, 6 January). Symbol or stereotype One consumer's tradition is another's racial slur. *The Boston Globe,* p. 35.

Green, M. K. (1993). Images of American Indians in advertising: Some moral issues. *Journal of Business Ethics, 12,* 323–330.

Hall, S. (1997). *Representation: Cultural representations and signifying practices.* London: Sage.

Hill, R. (1992). The non-vanishing American Indian: Are the modern images any closer to the truth? *Quill* (May), 35–37.

Kates, S. M., & Shaw-Garlock, G. (1999). The ever-entangling web: A study of ideologies and discourses in advertising to women. *Journal of Advertising 28*(2), 33–49.

Kern-Foxworth, M. (1994). *Aunt Jemima, Unde Ben, and Rastus: Blacks in advertising yesterday, today, and tomorrow.* Westport, CT: Praeger.

Land O' Lakes. (2000). [On-line]. Available: http://www.landolakes.com.

Larson, C. (1937). Patent-medicine advertising and the early American press. *Journalism Quarterly, 14*(4), 333–339.

Lippmann, W. (1922/1961). *Public opinion.* New York: McMillan & Company.

McCracken, G. (1993). The value of the brand: An anthropological perspective. In D. Aaker & A. L. Biel (Eds.), *Brand equity in advertising: Advertising's role in building strong brands.* Matwah, NJ: Lawrence Erlbaum.

Merskin, D. (1998). Sending up signals: A survey of American Indian media use and representation in the mass media. *The Howard Journal of Communications, 9,* 333–345.

Metz, S., & Thee, M. (1994). Brewers intoxicated with racist imagery. *Business and Society Review, 89,* 50–51.

Mihesuah, D. A. (1996). *American Indians: Stereotypes and realities.* Atlanta, GA: Clarity Press.

Monitor Sugar Company. (2000). [On-line]. Available: http://members.aol.com/asga/mon.htm.

Morgan, H. (1986). *Symbols of America.* New York: Penguin Books.

Schmitt, B., & Simonson, A. (1997). *Marketing aesthetics: The strategic management of brands, identity, and image.* New York: The Free Press.

Sioux Honey Association. (2000). [On-line]. Available: http://www.suebeehoney.com.

Specktor, M. (1995, January 6). Crazy Horse exploited to peddle liquor. *National Catholic Reporter, 31*(10), 3.

Strickland, R. (1998). The celluloid Indian. *Oregon Quarterly* (Summer), 9–10.

van Dijk, T. A. (1996). *Discourse, racism, and ideology.* La Laguna: RCEI Ediciones.

Westerman, M. (1989, March). Death of the Frito bandito: Marketing to ethnic groups. *American Demographics, 11,* 28–32.

Williamson, J. (1978). Decoding advertisements: Ideology and meaning in advertising. New York: Marion Boyars.

 QUESTIONS FOR CRITICAL THINKING

Reading 36

1. Merskin offers numerous examples of the continued misrepresentation of American Indians in advertising brands. Why do you think such distorted images continue?

2. Do you think that the stereotypes that Merskin discusses maintain the continued oppression of American Indians in the United States? Why or why not?

3. What will bring about more positive images of American Indians in advertising and other media? What obstacles prevent such positive portrayals?

Reading 37

HOW DO YOU SOLVE A PROBLEM LIKE WILL TRUMAN?
The Feminization of Gay Masculinities
on *Will & Grace*

THOMAS J. LINNEMAN

W hile hegemonic masculinity remains the idealized form of masculinity within American culture, recent changes in gay masculinities have challenged this form. In his volume on gay masculinities,
Nardi (2000) observes, "Although rejecting hypermasculinity and effeminacy, many gay men embrace a 'very straight gay' style by enacting both
hegemonic masculinity and gay masculinity in their daily lives" (p. 6). If
many gay men are "as conventionally masculine in their dress and demeanor
as most heterosexual men" (Lorber 1994, 62), the boundaries between the
forms of masculinity may become blurred, causing significant cultural angst
(Colman 2005). By engaging in some of the behaviors of hegemonic masculinity, gay men are able to contest it (Anderson 2002). As Connell (1995)
suggests, "The 'very straight gay' is a contradictory position in the politics of
gender" (pp. 162–63). If gay men do their gender in hegemonic ways, does
this destabilize the gender order as we know it (West and Zimmerman 1987)?

Hardly. The gender order remains stable, with hegemonic masculinities firmly ensconced at the top, because American culture does a thorough
job of connecting gay masculinities to a more broadly subordinated gender
form: femininities. While many gay men may no longer act effeminately,
they remain feminized. This distinction between effeminacy and feminization has been overlooked, since much of the research on gay men has concentrated on their behavior (Green 1987; Kleinberg 1987; Levine 1998). In
speaking of the effeminacy of gay men, one implicitly lends agency to the
actor: An effeminate gay man is one who does his gender in feminine ways.
While a gay man's personal comportment is an important aspect of his gender identity, he is not the only one who constructs this identity. Indeed, the
social construction of gender implies a process of interaction (Hollander
and Howard 1996). Gender may be *done to him* by others. Even if a gay

man does not engage in effeminate behavior, he still may be feminized by others. Regardless of a gay man's comportment, his sexual object choice is not heterosexual and is therefore subordinated. Often, this subordination is manifested by feminization. Some of this feminizing is accomplished by heterosexual men who, as arbiters of hegemonic masculinity, hold an interest in clarifying this gender divide. However, feminizing can also occur through interactions among gay men themselves or interactions among gay men and women. Studying such feminization provides an opportunity to address an important question posed by Chen (1999):

> Two themes in particular have received substantial attention: how subaltern men are exploited and how subaltern men resist their exploitation. But comparatively less is known about how subaltern men . . . can contribute to their own oppression and the oppression of women. The subaltern has been understood as a victim and a resistor, but how fully has he been understood as an accomplice or even a perpetrator? (P. 587)

The meaning behind these feminizing instances may vary. Feminization could be read as praise for the gay man for embracing femininity and denying aspects of hegemonic masculinity, many of which involve harmful behavior (Kimmel and Messner 2000). Feminization also could be considered an element of camp. Definitions of camp abound and include a wide-ranging set of behaviors that many consider a potent source of power for oppressed groups (Meyer 1994; Ross 1989). Using this lens, feminization among gay men could be considered a form of political parody: Rigid gender roles are deserving of ridicule. When hegemonic masculinity puts gay men down, they are able to fight back by camping it up and in a sense taking ownership of their oppression.

However, feminization may also serve to castigate the gay man, stigmatizing him as "no better than a woman." These latter moments simultaneously oppress women and gay men. In his classic essay "It's Being So Camp as Keeps Us Going," Richard Dyer (2002) captures the conflict inherent in camp feminization:

> . . . [T]here is something rather suspect about this habit [of camping]. Isn't it tantamount to saying gay men are inferior to straight men, just as women are? Isn't it really a put down of gay men, and of women? It's hard to decide and in the end I think I'll go on doing it because I'd rather gay men identified with straight women than with straight men, since most of the values associated with masculinity in this society (aggressiveness, competitiveness, being "above" tenderness and emotion) I reject. Yet the whole practice, like so much of camp, is deeply ambiguous. So much depends on what you feel about men and women, about sex, about being gay. (Pp. 50–51)

In this ambiguity simultaneously rests potential political power as well as the possibility of a harmful cycle of self-oppression.

The feminization of gay men attests to the links between homophobia and sexism, especially among heterosexual men. Heterosexual men are markedly more homophobic than heterosexual women (Fone 2000; Kite and Whitley 1998). Fulfilling the demand to be seen as neither feminine nor gay sharply affects male behavior:

> Homophobia is intimately interwoven with both sexism and racism. The fear—sometimes conscious, sometimes not—that others might perceive us as homosexual propels men to enact all manner of exaggerated masculine behaviors and attitudes to make sure that no one could possibly get the wrong idea about us. (Kimmel 1994, 133)

The role of gender becomes even clearer when one realizes that heterosexual men's attitudes toward gay men are significantly more negative than they are toward lesbians (Herek 2002). It is not only the same-sex sexual acts that repulse some heterosexual men but also the various gender transgressions that are assumed to accompany gay identity.

This article examines how this feminization plays out within an element of American popular culture. Most of the data on gay masculinities come from in-depth interviews or life histories focusing on the individual as a site of gender construction (Anderson 2002; Connell 1992; Nardi 2000). However, it is important not to overlook other sites where gender is constructed. American media products offer the public many examples of gay masculinities. For many Americans, this may be their only exposure to the lives of gay men. Historically, these images tended toward representations of effeminate gay men (Capsuto 2000; Russo 1987). Dyer (2002) warns of the danger in allowing mainstream media to engage in camp, arguing that the media "pick up the undertow of self-oppression without ever latching on to the elements of criticism and defiance of straightness" (p. 51). As the number of gay characters in the media flourished in the last years of the twentieth century, images of gay men did become more varied. Studying these images in a systematic way remained difficult, though, since the gay characters were minor and/or fleeting. However, in the fall of 1998, a mainstream network show debuted and became a mainstay of American popular culture. That show is *Will & Grace*. The show is notable not only for its success but also because it features multiple representations of gay masculinities. As I will show below, *Will & Grace* raises an interesting question: When a corporate media product engages in camp feminization, does it effect political progress or simply reinscribe long-standing oppressions?

In its first year, *Will & Grace* immediately received accolades and found a steady audience. In its second year, it won several Emmy Awards, including Best Comedy Series. In its third season, its network moved the show to a coveted time slot, dramatically increasing its ratings. The show ranked twelfth for this season, having experienced a 44 percent increase in viewership from the previous season, with an average of 17.3 million viewers each week (Snierson 2001). Since this zenith, the show has decreased in ratings popularity, drowning in a sea of reality television. For the 2004–2005 season, the show ranked forty-first, pulling in an average of 10.2 million viewers (*Entertainment Weekly,* 2005). However, this still makes it the third most popular sitcom, and it was renewed for an eighth and final season. The show has also achieved the holy grail of sitcoms: rerun syndication. It provides the American viewing public with the most constant current stream of media images of gay men (at least upper-middle-class, white, urban gay men). It is also politically relevant, since analyses of the 2004 elections sometimes referred to the blue states as *Will & Grace* states.

The show is also important because it provides millions of viewers with multiple representations of gay masculinities. The title character fits the description of Connell's (1992) "very straight gay" or Seidman's (2005) "normal gay." Will Truman—note the last name—appears to be a poster boy for hegemonic masculinity. He is a corporate attorney, a profession occupied disproportionately by men. For most of the time he is on-screen, he is wearing a suit and tie. He is often portrayed as emotionally reserved but with a tendency for lashing out, the emotional traits characteristic of straight masculinity described by Dyer (2002) above. Shugart (2003) has argued that Will even functions as a father figure for his friend Grace, constantly serving as a source of logical advice or as a way out of a predicament. His friend and sidekick Jack McFarland embodies Connell's (1987) "emphasized femininity": he in several ways complies with his subordination and accommodates the desires of men. He proudly and continually declares his financial dependence on Will. He is obsessed with body image and skin tone. He worships celebrity divas who are iconic images of female beauty. *Will & Grace* is mainstream American media's first real and long-standing attempt at depicting multiple gay identities. The formula seems clear: Take one effeminate gay man, one very straight gay, and add two of their female friends (Grace Adler and Karen Walker).

On closer examination, though, the gendering of the two gay characters is not so distinct. I show that the very straight gay is verbally feminized more often than the effeminate gay character. While the show does have diversity in the gay characters it has developed, it ultimately reemphasizes the divide between hegemonic masculinity and the masculinities embodied by gay men. *Will & Grace* eases tensions in the gender order by pushing its gay characters again and again into the realm of femininity. On the surface, Will Truman may embody hegemonic masculinity, but he is gay and therefore feminized. Other research on *Will & Grace* (Cooper 2003; Battles and Hilton-Morrow 2002) has commented on this but only in passing. In contrast, I have conducted a content analysis of the 162 episodes from the first seven seasons of the show.

While analyzing these messages elicits important findings about the feminization of gay men, it is also paramount to understand how audiences interpret these moments. I take seriously one of the mantras of media studies: Audiences are active viewers who bring to their watching different sets of experiences and beliefs that affect how they interpret cultural products (Gamson 1998; Gamson et al. 1992). With this in mind, I also conducted a set of focus groups with both heterosexual and gay and lesbian audiences of a variety of ages to assess how audiences grapple with these representations.

METHOD

Content analysis is useful for identifying patterns in various media (Weber 1990). For this project, my research assistants and I analyzed the 162 episodes from the first seven seasons of *Will & Grace*. The source material comes from videotapes of the episodes as well as verbatim scripts from a fan's Web site (Durfee 2005). I first located every instance in which a male character was the subject of a feminine reference. Two research assistants and I then coded these instances for object (who is being talked about), source (who says it), type of reference, context, and provoking behavior.

The codes for type of reference concerned the specific substance of the reference. The codes, developed inductively, are as follows: basic (reference uses a basic term that a female is called, such as *she, girl, woman, lady,* and so on); classic (reference was one of five words that have been used since the earlier part of the twentieth century to feminize gay men: *sissy, fairy, Nancy, Mary,* and *queen*); bitch (a word used frequently enough to merit its own category); body (reference implied that the object had female body parts or desired to be of the female sex); family (reference was related to mothers or other family members); celebrity (reference compares the object to a real-life celebrity); pop culture (references to popular culture, such as movies, books, plays, operas, and other television shows); clothing (reference concerns the object wearing female clothing, makeup, or accessories); and other (reference did not fit into the above categories).

Context refers to the tone in which the reference was delivered. The codes for context are as follows: banter (reference delivered in the course of playful banter or as a joke); conflict (reference delivered in a moment of conflict, a fight, or an attempt to express disdain for the object); love (reference delivered during a loving moment or if the source was paying the object a compliment); hello/goodbye (reference was part of a greeting); and other (reference did not fit any of the above categories).

For provoking behavior, we coded whether the reference was made in response to feminine behavior on the part of the object. For example, in an episode in the third season, a frightened Will screams in a high-pitched voice in an effort to scare away a burglar. After doing so, he asks Grace, "Did I just scream like a woman?" to which she replies, "Don't flatter yourself; you scream like a girl." We coded these references as being in response to feminine behavior because the object, Will, was indeed engaging in behavior that most would find feminine.[1] In another example, Karen calls Jack "Miss Fire Island" after Jack puts on her tiara and earrings and pretends to be a beauty pageant winner. A final component of the content analysis involved using stopwatches to assess the screen time allotted to Will and Jack.

We also conducted seven focus groups—one pretest focus group and six real ones—to assess audience interpretations of both the show and the results of the content analysis. We conducted these groups near the end of the third season of the show. The six real groups were as follows: (1) gay and lesbian youth group members, (2) heterosexual high school students, (3) gay and lesbian college students, (4) heterosexual college students, (5) gay and lesbian adults, and (6) heterosexual adults. The six groups involved thirty-nine participants recruited through a variety of channels: introductory sociology classes, gay and lesbian support groups, and personal contacts. All were familiar with the show, but not all were ardent fans. Nineteen were female; twenty were male. Twenty identified as gay or lesbian; nineteen identified as heterosexual. Eleven were nonwhite; twenty-eight were white. Although the participants were a diverse group, they in no way are statistically representative of any larger population. Focus groups are not meant to elicit generalizable results (Hollander 2000, Morgan 1988). The results, then, should be viewed as descriptive and suggestive.

The focus groups lasted from one hour to two-and-a-half hours. To protect the identities of the participants and to facilitate transcription, we gave each participant a letter of the alphabet to place in front of himself or herself and asked each to choose a pseudonym that started with that letter. Prior to the discussion, the participants filled out a sheet that included questions about their viewing habits, what they like and don't like about the show, whether they consider the show to be important, how they describe the two gay characters, and whether they consider Will and Jack to be accurate portrayals of gay men. After we discussed their answers, we told the group that the first question on the second sheet was "What did all of these scenes have in common?"

The group then watched a thirteen-minute tape with twenty-five clips from the show, each having a feminine reference in it. These clips were arranged chronologically, and I developed a random sampling method that produced a representative sample of moments, stratified by object, source, context, and type of reference. After watching the clips, the participants filled out a second sheet that asked them what the scenes had in common, whether they had noticed these moments before, how frequently they thought these moments occurred, how they felt about these moments, and who (Will or Jack) they thought was the object of such references more often. Unexpectedly, members of some focus groups had difficulty with the first question. In these instances, I described what the clips had in common, and they finished filling out the sheet.[2] We then discussed these questions as a group.

Next, I presented the group with eight graphs from the content analysis. These graphs contained data from all of seasons 1 and 2 and the first two-thirds of season 3. We looked at each graph together, and I addressed any questions they had. The group then filled out a final sheet, which asked them about their reactions to the results. Finally, the group discussed these reactions.

I transcribed all the tape-recorded conversations. For analysis, I coded a few answers from the sheets they filled out, but I concentrated primarily on the discussions. To code the discussions, I gave each prominent theme (e.g., "it's just a sitcom" and "variety of gay portrayals") a separate sheet and then listed instances of each theme on the sheet, keeping track of which types of participants were more likely to discuss certain themes.

 ## RESULTS: CONTENT ANALYSIS

Some argue that *Will & Grace* offers positive depictions of the lives of gay men. Indeed, the show has been a recipient of numerous honors from the Gay & Lesbian Alliance Against Defamation, a media watchdog organization. However, as the content analysis illustrates in several ways, *Will & Grace* consistently feminizes the gay men on the show, often in potentially harmful ways. In the first seven seasons of the show, male characters were referenced in the feminine 625 times. Of these references, 605 were directed at gay men on the show. At an average of 3.5 times per episode,[3] the show equates gay men with women. There is a fair amount of variation in the number of references per episode: Twelve episodes contain no references, while three episodes contain 10 or more references. There is also some variation on a season-by-season basis, with each of the seven seasons having the following number of feminizing references: 94, 90, 103, 78, 86, 97, and 57.

One might expect that the majority of these references would be toward Jack, the more effeminate character. However, this expectation is not confirmed by the data. Will has been the object of feminine references 282 times; Jack has been the object 249 times. There have been 94 references to other people (74 of these to other gay men). This is the first instance of an important message sent by the show: Regardless of comportment, there is something immanently feminine about gay men. Despite other aspects of Will's life that are representative of hegemonic masculinity, he is gay and thus feminized.

One possibility is that Will is referenced more frequently simply because he is a primary character. In early seasons of the show, Will had significantly more screen time than Jack (in season 1, for example, Will was on screen for 323 minutes compared to Jack's 153 minutes). Later seasons are more equal, although Will still gets more screen time. Taking this into account, an interesting trend develops. In season 1, based on time between references, Jack was referenced more frequently (every 3 minutes) compared to Will (every 8 minutes). This difference held for the next three seasons. Since season 4, Will has been referenced more frequently.

Now I move on to the substance of these references,[4] providing examples to illustrate their varied nature. A large proportion of the references

(22 percent of the references to Will and 28 percent of the references to Jack) are basic: The characters are referred to as women in the course of interaction. For example, after Will suddenly leaves the country at the end of season 2, Jack explains to Grace, "Yeah, she's exhausted. Her life, like her hair, had become unmanageable." On Will's return at the beginning of season 3, the first thing he says to Jack when he sees him is, "Hey, lady!" Some of the references in this category are subtle, such as when Karen's Latina housekeeper Rosario refers to Jack as *chica* or *amiga.* The subtle nature of these references arises in the discussion of the focus group data.

Classic references account for 9 percent of the references to Will and 13 percent of the references to Jack. These references are either single names (e.g., "Bring it on, Nancy" and "What about you, Mary?") or more elaborate combinations (e.g., "blouse-wearing fairy" and "the book of Genesissy"). After Will beats Grace in poker, he jokes, "In this house, a queen beats a straight every time." These classic references link a current cultural product to a historical feminization.

The body category arose only twenty-two times (ten for Will and twelve for Jack). However, it is an important category, because it implies what some assume about gay men: They desire to be women. In the very first episode of the series, Will says to Jack, "It must be hard for you, trapped in a man's body like that." In the middle of season 2, he exclaims, "Congratulations, Jack! I wish you a long, happy life as a woman." There are several references to female physical processes that are impossible for men to go through. Twice, Will makes reference to himself being pregnant. When Jack is asked how his grieving process over the death of his father is proceeding, he obtusely replies, "I have light days and heavy days. I can ride a horse now."

Somewhat similar to the body references are the clothing references, which imply that gay men dress or at least want to dress in women's clothes. Will complains to Jack about his slovenliness thus: "You put on a maid's uniform, but you never clean." Jack campily compliments Will's attire as follows: "Nice shirt. Somewhere a ballerina is shivering." In season 4, Grace feminizes Will's lack of a boyfriend as: "You're an old maid in a threadbare caftan." Such references are quite frequent, making up 13 percent of the references to Will and 12 percent of the references to Jack.

Mother-oriented or family-oriented references make up 6 percent of the references to Will but only 3 percent of the references to Jack. This difference is most likely because Will is portrayed as responsible and Jack is not. For example, Will responds to Jack's beeper message, "What's with the page 'Baby Bear needs Mama Bear'?" Sometimes, he is considered annoyingly responsible. When Karen is talking on the phone at Grace's office, and Will and Grace enter, she says, "Oh crap, I gotta go. Mom and Mom are home." Will aspires to have a family. However, these references imply that he will be a mother, not a father. In one moment in a car when Will is questioning his ability to someday parent, Jack comforts him by saying, "You just did the soccer mom arm save!" There are also several references to Will's similarities to his mother, such as "I'm two highballs and a tight dress away from being Mom." Seldom does he compare himself to his father.

The celebrity category favors Jack. Ten percent of the references to Jack are about celebrities, whereas this category makes up only 6 percent of the references to Will. In the episode in which Karen sets up a surprise meeting between Jack and the man she thinks is Jack's father and Jack subsequently makes the moves on him, Jack exclaims in disgust, "I hit on my father! I'm Soon-Yi!" When Karen does not cooperate with Jack's production of an award acceptance video, Jack warns her, "Don't make me get all Whitney on your ass." The feminizing message is conveyed also through the dearth of masculinizing references, since Jack infrequently compares himself to male celebrities.

The next category is similar to the last, but these references deal with fictional characters rather than real-life celebrities. They constitute a large proportion of the overall number, representing 19 percent of the references to Will and 14 percent of the references to Jack. More so than the other categories, many of these references are subtle and difficult to catch in the midst of a single viewing of the show. Also, one must know a fair amount about both popular and high culture to understand them. For example, at the end of season 2, when Jack moves in with Will, Will tells him to ". . . take your bags and your menagerie, Laura . . ." If one did not know Tennessee Williams's play, one might not figure out this reference. This reference also illustrates another commonality among some of the references in this category: They make allusions to gay history and culture. Here is another example of this: Kidding Will about his temporary celibacy, Jack says, "Stuck inside the nunnery while all the other girls run around in their miniskirts and take the pill. How *do* you solve a problem like Will Truman?" making reference to *The Sound of Music,* a favorite musical among some gay men. Such subtle references reward viewers who have high levels of (gay) cultural capital.

Some references, though, are easier to catch, such as the twenty-two times (eleven each) that Will and Jack are referred to as bitches. Although it represents a small proportion of the overall number of references, the use of this term is important when considering the context during which the reference is uttered, as I discuss below.

There were a number of references that didn't fit these categories: twenty-seven to Jack (making up 11 percent of his references) and forty-six to Will (making up 16 percent of his references). Some are references to random women's names ("Wrong-o, Mary Lou") or made-up names ("Betty McUseless" and "Arrogancia"). Others are feminized adjectives, such as when Will tells Jack to "just sit there and look pretty."

Which characters are responsible for all this feminizing? It is seldom heterosexual males, who have played a secondary role on the show. There are two findings of note: First is the proportion of the references that are self-references: 21 percent for Will and 33 percent for Jack. These self-references illustrate an acceptance of femininity and a level of comfort with being thought of as a woman. Second, a significant proportion for each character comes from the other gay major character on the show: Twenty-five percent of Will's references come from Jack; 33 percent of Jack's references come from Will. The message is that this is a common way gay men interact: They do femininity to one another.

It is also critical to know the context in which the characters deliver these references. A large proportion of the references are delivered with levity as part of a moment of banter between characters. This only makes sense, since it is a sitcom. Banter makes up 37 percent of the references toward Will and 47 percent of the references toward Jack. For example, when Jack asks Will how his new glasses look, Will responds, "Guys don't make passes at girls who wear glasses," a line merely meant to provide a laugh. When Will seems surprised that Grace is doing something with a woman friend, she responds with a smile, "I have girlfriends besides you."

A key finding of the content analysis is that over a quarter of the references occur in a moment of conflict or in an effort to show disdain toward the object. Twenty-six percent of the references toward Will and 25 percent of the references toward Jack are at such moments. The overall percentage rises to 32 percent when I remove the self-references (for which only 8 percent were conflict oriented). This shows that such references are a common way to make the gay characters feel bad: I am currently mad at you, so I am going to put you down by calling you a woman. An exemplary series of these references comes from an episode in which Will and Jack are giving a sensitivity seminar to a group of police officers. When Jack ruins their presentation, Will angrily attacks him:

WILL: I just asked you to abandon that queer voice.

JACK: Queer? Who you callin' queer, you blouse-wearin' fairy?

WILL: This from the homo who minces around the gym in a Lycra onesie!

JACK: Grace wears one!

WILL: She's a woman, you girl!

JACK: Don't call me a girl! Eyebrow-plucker!

WILL: Leg-waxer!

JACK: Lady!

WILL: Tramp!

Other references are not quite as dramatic in nature, but they still are meant to express anger at the object. For example, when Grace is trying to give Jack clues while playing a game and Jack won't stop yelling possible answers, she shouts with an angry look on her face, "Let me give you a clue, woman!" When Grace is upset with Will for demanding that she pay for things, she scowls at him, "Petticoat petty, peppermint petty." When Karen isn't happy with Will's performance in the courtroom, she demands, "Get your ass out there and litigate, bitch!" As might be expected, the word *bitch* is often used to put down: Seventeen of the twenty-one times it is used to describe a gay man, it is used disparagingly. On a regular basis, the feminizing references are meant to castigate, thus doing harm to both gay men and to women. This is made all the more egregious by the fact that many of these castigating references come from the women on the show (33 percent of the references from Grace and Karen are conflict oriented).

Sometimes, these appellations are more celebratory in nature and are used to express love or at least a compliment. However, only 15 percent of the references to Will and 9 percent of the references to Jack are of this type. On a day when Karen is feeling better about Will's legal abilities, she declares, "I've got the best lawyer in town in my corner, one Miss Wilma Truman!" In an attempt to cheer him up, Will asks Jack, "Who's the prettiest lady in this room?" Overall, though, few of the references celebrate the gay characters' femininity. It is much more likely to be viewed as a weakness.

The final element of coding regarded provoking behavior. Were the references made in response to the objects acting in a feminine manner? For the vast majority of these moments, the answer is no. Only 12 percent of the references to Will and 14 percent of the references to Jack are responding to the character acting like a woman. This implies again that there is something about gay men that is inseparably feminine regardless of their comportment. One does not need to wait for feminine behavior to call a gay man *woman* or *she*.

With regard to trends over time, besides the shifting of references toward Will and away from Jack, there is one more trend of note: the referencing of heterosexual men in the feminine. This occurred four times in season 6 and fifteen times in season 7, making up 21 percent of the references in that season. Nine of these references in season 7 were part of a running joke. Jack, now an executive at a gay television network, consistently feminizes his heterosexual male assistant:

JACK: Thank you, Elizabeth. Just show her in, please.

DAVE: Uh, you know my name's Dave, right?

JACK: Listen, it's bad enough I'm the only one here with a straight assistant. Do not make me call you that ridiculous name.

DAVE: Yeah, but . . .

JACK: That will be all, Elizabeth!

Because Dave works in a queer space but does not practice queer sexuality, Jack decides that he will queer Dave's gender instead. Although these references make up a small proportion of the total, they are important because they segue nicely with developments in popular culture, such as the rise of the metrosexual and the increasing tendency to put down straight men by referring to them as bitches (Heffernan 2005).

While the findings from the content analysis may be intriguing, it is important to understand how these references are interpreted by various audiences. One of the potential pitfalls of content analysis occurs when the researcher imbues findings with too much subjective meaning. Therefore I now turn the interpretation over to the audience by presenting some of the focus group results.

RESULTS: FOCUS GROUPS

The focus group data reveal that audiences often consume the show in ways that prevent the problematizing of the feminization of gay men. While sometimes angry over these references, this anger often fails to identify the simultaneous oppression of women and gay men. That is, many focus group participants did not see the misogynistic impulse underlying some of these feminine references. Often, rather than anger, focus group participants offered enthusiastic acceptance of this feminization of gay men, arguing that the feminine references should be included in the show. Perhaps most surprising, though, is the extent to which the focus group participants were oblivious to these references.

Obliviousness   I first deal with an unexpected finding: the inability on the part of some of the participants to notice these references, even when presented with twenty-five of them back-to-back. Although I warned all groups that they would be asked, "What did all these scenes have in common?" before showing them the clips, just over 40 percent (sixteen out of thirty-nine) of the participants answered this question with the desired response ("men referenced as women," "female references," and so on). Another ten participants were on the right track, mentioning stereotypes or clichés but not mentioning the specific feminine nature of them. Another five were only slightly close, mentioning "gay jokes" or "references to homosexuality." Eight participants were completely off. While this may be considered a methodological problem, given that audiences interpret media in a wide variety of ways and thus should not be expected to be able to find this single element, I argue that it can also be considered a finding, since the obliviousness was patterned. The gay and lesbian participants were more likely than their heterosexual counterparts to notice the feminizing. Half of them completely got it, compared to 32 percent of the heterosexual participants. Another 30 percent of the gay and lesbian participants were on the right track, compared to 21 percent of the heterosexual participants. Of the six heterosexual participants who were completely on track, five of them were from the college student group. In this group before I showed the clips, one of the participants explained what he didn't like about the show:

> Another thing, they go too far with the jokes, like Karen, for example, always has the same type of jokes. It's like, get some new material or whatever. Like, it was funny the first time she called Will "Wilma," but, you know, after she does it all the time, you know, it's not so funny anymore. (group 2)

Because this type of reference was brought to this group's attention prior to the clips, this may have biased their perceptions toward such references.

During the discussion of the clips and the data, a number of participants from both the gay and straight groups admitted that they had never noticed these references before. A gay male student commented:

> She (another participant) pointed out that the thing that helped her notice it was that the clips were so repetitive, and it took me, like I said, a long time to realize what was happening, and actually when I really noticed it was when we got to the series of very short, quick clips—*that's* when I found it. And I think that says something about this too, I mean, we're talking about something that, I always laugh at it, I think it's funny, but I've never noticed, like, they're doing this all the time. And so it's subtle, and I think that makes a difference. (group 1)

Because these references are parsed out, they simply slip through some people's consciousness as they lounge on their couches enjoying the show. As one heterosexual participant said, "I really don't go into too much thought. There's not too much analysis going on" (group 2). After viewing the data, some said they wouldn't watch the show the same way now that this had been brought to their attention.

Anger   So what are the participants' interpretations of these references once they do realize they exist? Some were angry or at least concerned about the possibility that these references could reinforce stereotypes. The participants were not concerned that the stereotypes could affect their own attitudes. Rather, they expressed dismay that less sophisticated people might get the wrong idea. Those with limited exposure to openly gay men might base their perceptions only on what they see on television, and the participants saw this as a dangerous prospect. Many concerns of this type were voiced, but a typical example of this comes from an older female heterosexual participant:

> Well, it's reinforcing for people who are homophobic, the female aspect of gay guys, and from that point of view, I don't, it's meant to be funny, but it also could be not so funny . . . For some part of the audience, I think it's reinforcing perhaps what they like to think about gay men. (group 5)

One of the heterosexual high school males was upset about the frequency of the references, implying that they may be connected to antigay speech he hears at school:

> . . . [I]t's an easy way to get a laugh from the audience; it's like a cheap way. I guess it's good that it makes the show funny, but it's really inconsiderate for the writers to do that, if they're not thinking about how it could really affect, you know, people who go to school the next day and try and be funny. (group 6)

Both the gay and heterosexual groups raised this theme, mostly concerned with the possibility that antigay people would use this to perpetuate the stereotypes they held. However, many discounted the probability of this occurring, positing that such people probably would not watch the show at all.

Only one group—the gay and lesbian adult group—went beyond these notions of stereotype reinforcement and exposed the multiple oppressions implicit in many of these references. A gay man voiced, "Using feminine terms to put down men is degrading to both sexes. I love verbal volleyball, but I just don't like the use of feminine names to put down a man. I just think it's rude. It means that they're trying to put you down. I think it's just rude to both sexes" (group 3). One of the lesbian participants was the only one in this group who did not notice that all of the references were feminizing. This disturbed her fiercely:

LESBIAN 1:   But in retrospect thinking back on it, it's like, oh yeah, and it's kind of interesting, feeling like I'm a very feminist person, but missing all of these comments that *were* degrading to women and it's like, ew, that's not a good feeling missing that, but I guess I was just trying to enjoy it.

LESBIAN 2:   It's disguised.

LESBIAN 1:   Yes, it's very much disguised, but that in itself is kind of dangerous.

GAY MAN: Well, and we're immune to it too, I think.

LESBIAN 1:   Yeah. I'm feeling so desensitized. (group 3)

This theme was completely absent from the other focus groups, illustrating an apparent inability to make critical links between the oppressions that various groups face.

Acceptance   More common than anger was acceptance. There are several ways in which the participants justified the inclusion of the feminine references. First, some participants considered the source of the feminine references. They used the fact that a disproportionate number of the references came from the gay characters, either referencing themselves or targeting the other gay character. Because it is an in-joke, it is acceptable. But some still realize the danger in this, since people not in the in-joke group may not realize that it is unacceptable behavior for them. A gay youth explains,

I totally think, as a gay audience, it's OK, and I'm sorry I *do* have a double standard here because as gay people, like, I feel comfortable, like, I will call, I'll be like, "Oh, you're such a fag," and I feel it's OK for *me* to say that. However, a lot of people probably, of course they have contact with gay people, but if they're not out, they don't know this. I think when you examine it like that, it's a very dangerous presentation of what most, a lot of people will accept as the truth about the whole gay community, you know, through this TV show, like, that they don't understand, since they're not in the subculture, they don't understand where it comes from. (group 4)

Many participants brought up the fact that some of the show's writers are gay themselves. This too makes it more acceptable, as a heterosexual college student explains:

That's key. Because if it was all straight writers, I could see how, like, NBC could come under fire, you know, straight writers are making fun of, you know, this is their outlet, you know, what better way to express your inhibitions than, you know, make it a TV show. You could say, oh, I'm just using my creative license or whatever, but I think it's better that if they do actually have people who are homosexual writing the show and making the jokes. Then people in the gay community who do have a problem with it, saying it's disrespectful, then that can always be their show's backup. You know, "Well, the writers are gay, and they obviously don't have a problem with it, so . . ." I think if nobody associated with the show was gay, I would have a little more problem with the show. (group 2)

Many participants made the connection between the differential acceptability of these references and the similar way African Americans can say things about themselves that whites cannot. However, few pointed out that on *Will & Grace,* a good proportion of the references are made by heterosexual characters, which suggests a flaw in this analogy.

Another way the participants justified the references was by claiming that they accurately reflect reality. This strategy was used disproportionately by gay men and lesbians, especially the younger participants. Gay men do talk like this,[5] so why not make it a part of the show? Some gay participants, such as this college student, felt very strongly about these references:

These were like moments where the producers, the writers were reaching out to the gay audience. That's what I thought. I thought OK, these were moments where, because most of the audience is going to be composed of gays and lesbians, so these are moments where they're reaching out to them and saying, "OK, this is for you, this is where you will relate to the characters." And I think like he (another participant) said that he enjoyed them, and I do too, because these were instances where I could put myself in their shoes and I could understand what they were going through. (group 1)

Later on in the same focus group, a lesbian participant stated that she was in the process of developing a more positive attitude toward these references, because she was realizing (based on the discussion) that they do happen in reality. Another lesbian, this time from the gay youth group, commented on the relationships she has with her gay friends. She was the first to speak after being presented with the content analysis data:

> LESBIAN:　I was surprised by, like, the actual breakdown, like, of the number, the actual number, but if I really think about it, like, the times I refer to my gay male friends as actually being males are few and far between. Like, I probably call them *girl*, or, you know, refer to them in the feminine way, *way* more than they do on *Will & Grace*.

> TL:　So if someone kept track of your life like we have done here, it would be off the charts?

> LESBIAN:　Oh, most definitely. In fact, I don't think, I can't remember any time recently where I *have* referred to them as being male (laugh). It's always, like, "Hey, girl!" or "What's up, girl!" (group 4)

The heterosexual participants who spoke of having gay friends also appreciated these references, because it made them feel closer to their friends and because they knew their friends liked such references. One of the women from the heterosexual adult group stated, "If you're in the know, or you're in the lives of homosexuals, then you will really find this funny, because it's referring to something that is clearly a part of their lives and their culture, and so it's kind of the hidden community" (group 5). Another woman from the same group posited that the gay community would be upset if these references were not present, since it then would not accurately reflect their lives.

 ## DISCUSSION

On leaving the focus groups, a few participants suggested that I might be taking television a bit too seriously. When it comes right down to it, they said, *Will & Grace* is just a sitcom. However, the show's uniqueness and popularity make it worthy of careful scrutiny to see what it offers to our understanding of gender and sexuality in American popular culture. Gamson (1998) suggests that any mainstream media depiction of gay men and lesbians is likely to be a double-edged sword, with positive and negative aspects intertwined. Walters (2001) argues that old stereotypes sometimes morph into new forms that elicit different although not necessarily less damaging forms of homophobia. This article contributes to our understanding of the importance of the show and the sharp edges and morphed stereotypes hiding in it.

At first glance, the show seems to offer a very important positive component: the depiction of a character that does not resemble the typical stereotype of the effeminate gay man. However, the content analysis shows that *Will & Grace* reaffirms the close relationship between femininity and gay masculinity. Will—a gay man who in key ways accomplishes hegemonic masculinity—is perpetually feminized. The feminizing of this very straight gay archetype, combined with the finding that very few of the references are in reaction to feminine behavior, alters the connection between identities and behavior. Historically, gay characters achieved a feminized identity by doing gender in stereotypically effeminate ways. Will, regardless of how he enacts his gender, is ascribed a feminized identity because of his sexual identity. In fact, a number of the focus group participants pointed out that the audience knows Will is gay, not because of his engagement in gay sexual behavior (one of the major criticisms of the show is that Will is essentially celibate), but because he is the object of these feminizing references. These moments imply again and again that gay men are women, and feminized men are gay.

Not all of these references are merely part of playful camp exchanges. A significant proportion happen in a moment of conflict and are meant to hurt gay men by calling them women, a slap in the face to all involved. This is complicated all the more by the fact that many of these conflict references come from the women on the show. When an irate woman screams "Woman!" to a gay man's face, such an interaction encapsulates much of what keeps the current gender order stable. In a way, such moments elevate hegemonic masculinity further above its subordinates, with the work here done by the subordinated groups themselves, as Chen (1999) suggests. The large number of references in humorous contexts could be considered to be in the fine tradition of camp, breaking down rigid gender lines and ultimately making political progress. I argue, however, that these many conflict-oriented references do not lend themselves to a camp interpretation. Camp's meanings are many, but most involve self-conscious parody. Reviewing these conflict moments, I find little parody and much authentic anger among the characters. Keeping in mind that many straight audiences may not watch the show with a camp sensibility only complicates this picture.

This is one reason why it is critical to go the next step and see how the content is interpreted by its various audiences. Researchers immersed in their data may not even consider the possibility that the cultural trend they have identified goes unnoticed by the audience. Some of the references we identified in the content analysis are subtly delivered, and even when faced with a thirteen-minute stream of them, a number of focus group participants, many of them heterosexual, didn't catch on. For many, it is just a sitcom, unworthy of their close scrutiny. Researchers who engage in content analyses should at least be cognizant of such a possibility.

Even when forced to confront this characteristic of the show, many focus group participants remained unmoved. While some of them saw potential harm in the references' ability to perpetuate the feminized stereotype, others justified their inclusion by arguing that the majority of them are in-group jokes that happen in real life. Why should they be concerned about a show representing an aspect of gay culture that is real? Gay men do camp it up sometimes. More problematic, they argue, would be the exclusion of such references. Few questioned why real gay men engage in such behavior, and few saw the misogynist implications of many of the references. This research suggests how stereotypes are perpetuated through feedback mechanisms between media products and real life: The show reflects real behavior, and real people (especially youth) learn from the show that such behavior is acceptable and even expected. Camp feminization is primarily a learned cultural practice, and this may be one of the ways this cultural transmission occurs.

In what direction should research on the media and gay masculinities proceed? First, with regard to *Will & Grace,* work remains to be done. An expanded content analysis of the show could code the gay characters' every behavior and even the female characters' behavior, recording aspects both feminine and masculine. Also, creating codes that somehow measure the camp quality of these moments might elicit interesting results, but such a task is a formidable one given the extent to which camp is subject to interpretation and does not easily lend itself to objective research (Meyer 1994).

A limitation of the focus group component of this research was that it targeted only people who were audiences of *Will & Grace.* It is likely that they had more liberal attitudes toward homosexuality than the typical American. As a number of them mentioned, they were unaffected by the portrayals because they had firsthand experience with gay men. Further research on the show should include those who claim no contact. As Larry Gross (1994) posits, "The contributions of the mass media are likely to be especially powerful in cultivating images of groups and phenomena about which there is little firsthand opportunity for learning, particularly when such images are not contradicted by other established beliefs and ideologies" (p. 144). In addition, it is possibly more important to understand the construction of the feminized homosexual in antigay cultures, because this is where the stereotype will most likely produce negative behavioral effects (that is, discrimination or hate crimes).

Besides *Will & Grace,* there have been other recent shows that offer multiple representations of gay masculinities (such as *Six Feet Under* and *Queer as Folk*). Will the presence of these characters, several of whom embody hegemonic masculinities, challenge the gender order? Only time and careful study will tell.

NOTES

1. This begs the question of what behavior is feminine. We were careful to include only behaviors that we agreed most people would call stereotypically feminine: using high-pitched voices, wearing dresses or makeup, and so forth. The reliability for this variable was .93 (using the percentage agreement method discussed in Neuendorf [2002]). The reliability for the context variable was .87. References with disagreements were watched several times and discussed by the coders until resolution was reached. Season 7 was coded only by me without the aid of the assistants (who, unfortunately, had since graduated).

2. I discuss this problem or finding in depth in the results section.

3. This mean is based on a total count of 173 episodes. Through season 7, there were 162 episodes, but a number of these were hour-long episodes (which I counted as two episodes) and some were "supersize" forty-minute episodes (which I counted as 1.33 episodes). The median number of references per episode is three.

4. I concentrate on the references to Will and Jack, leaving the seventy-four references made to other gay characters behind. Of these seventy-four references, the most common categories were basic (eighteen references) and classic (sixteen references).

5. In fact, two gay participants in two separate focus groups chose female names (Antigone and Betty) as their pseudonyms.

REFERENCES

Anderson, Eric. 2002. Openly gay athletes: Contesting hegemonic masculinity in a homophobic environment. *Gender & Society* 16:860–77.

Battles, Kathleen, and Wendy Hilton-Morrow. 2002. Gay characters in conventional spaces: *Will and Grace* and the situation comedy genre. *Critical Studies in Media Communication* 19:87–105.

Capsuto, Steven. 2000. *Alternative channels: The uncensored story of gay and lesbian images on radio and television, 1930s to the present.* New York: Ballantine.

Chen, Anthony S. 1999. Lives at the center of the periphery, lives at the periphery of the center: Chinese American masculinities and bargaining with hegemony. *Gender & Society* 13:584–607.

Colman, David. 2005. Gay or straight? Hard to tell. *New York Times,* June 19, Section 9, pp. 1, 6.

Connell, Robert W. 1987. *Gender and power: Society, the person and sexual politics.* Palo Alto, CA: Stanford University Press.

_____. 1992. A very straight gay: Masculinity, homosexual experience, and the dynamics of gender. *American Sociological Review* 57:735–51.

_____. 1995. *Masculinities.* Berkeley: University of California Press.

Cooper, Evan. 2003. Decoding *Will and Grace:* Mass audience reception of a popular network situation comedy. *Sociological Perspectives* 46:513–33.

Durfee, Rob. 2005. Rob Durfee's *Will & Grace,* www.durfee.net/will (accessed June 19, 2005).

Dyer, Richard. 2002. *The culture of queers.* New York: Routledge.

Entertainment Weekly. 2005. Viewing Pleasures, June 10, 97.

Fone, Byrne. 2000. *Homophobia: A history.* New York: Metropolitan Books.

Gamson, Joshua. 1998. *Freaks talk back: Tabloid talk shows and sexual nonconformity.* Chicago: University of Chicago Press.

Gamson, William A., David Croteau, William Hoynes, and Theodore Sasson. 1992. Media images and the social construction of reality. *Annual Review of Sociology* 18:373–93.

Green, Richard. 1987. *The "sissy boy syndrome" and the development of homosexuality.* New Haven, CT: Yale University Press.

Gross, Larry. 1994. What is wrong with this picture? Lesbian women and gay men on television. In *Queer words, queer images: Communication and the construction of homosexuality,* edited by R. Jeffrey Ringer, 143–56. New York: New York University Press.

Heffernan, Virginia. 2005. Epithet morphs from bad girl to weak boy. *New York Times* March 22, E8.

Herek, Gregory M. 2002. Gender gaps in public opinion about lesbians and gay men. *Public Opinion Quarterly* 66:40–66.

Hollander, Jocelyn A. 2000. Vulnerability and dangerousness: The construction of gender through conversation about violence. *Gender & Society* 15:83–109.

Hollander, Jocelyn A., and Judith A. Howard. 1996. *Gendered situations, gendered selves: A gender lens on social psychology.* Lanham, MD: AltaMira.

Kimmel, Michael. 1994. Masculinity as homophobia: Fear, shame, and silence in the construction of gender identity. In *Theorizing masculinities,* edited by Harry Brod and Michael Kaufman, 119–41. Thousand Oaks, CA: Sage.

Kimmel, Michael, and Michael Messner. 2000. *Men's lives.* Boston: Allyn & Bacon.

Kite, Mary E., and Bernard E. Whitley, Jr. 1998. Do heterosexual women and men differ in their attitudes toward homosexuality? A conceptual and methodological analysis. In *Stigma and sexual orientation: Understanding prejudice against lesbians, gay men, and bisexuals,* edited by Gregory M. Herek, 39–61. Thousand Oaks, CA: Sage.

Kleinberg, Seymour. 1987. The new masculinity of gay men, and beyond. In *Beyond patriarchy: Essays by men on pleasure, power, and change,* edited by Michael Kaufman, 120–38. New York: Oxford University Press.

Levine, Martin P. 1998. *Gay macho: The life and death of the homosexual clone.* New York: New York University Press.

Lorber, Judith. 1994. *Paradoxes of gender.* New Haven, CT: Yale University Press.

Meyer, Moe. 1994. *The politics and poetics of camp.* New York: Routledge.

Morgan, David L. 1988. *Focus groups as qualitative research.* Newbury Park, CA: Sage.

Nardi, Peter M. 2000. *Gay masculinities.* Thousand Oaks, CA: Sage.

Neuendorf, Kimberly A. 2002. *The content analysis guidebook.* Thousand Oaks, CA: Sage.

Ross, Andrew 1989. *No respect: Intellectuals and popular culture.* New York: Routledge.

Russo, Vito. 1987. *The celluloid closet: Homosexuality in the movies.* New York: HarperCollins.

Seidman, Steven. 2005. From the polluted homosexual to the normal gay: Changing patterns of sexual regulation in America. In *Thinking straight: The power, the promise, and the paradox of heterosexuality,* edited by Chrys Ingraham, 39–61. New York: Routledge.

Shugart, Helene A. 2003. Reinventing privilege: The new (gay) man in contemporary popular media. *Critical Studies in Media Communication* 20:67–91.

Snierson, Dan. 2001. The mean season. *Entertainment Weekly,* June 1.

Walters, Suzanna D. 2001. *All the rage: The story of gay visibility in America.* Chicago: University of Chicago Press.

Weber, Robert. P. 1990. *Basic content analysis.* Thousand Oaks, CA: Sage.

West, Candace, and Don H. Zimmerman. 1987. Doing gender. *Gender & Society* 1:125–51.

QUESTIONS FOR CRITICAL THINKING

Reading 37

1. This study illustrates how the popular show *Will & Grace,* often cited as a positive representation of gay men, in actuality perpetuates stereotypes of them as effeminate. How does the author's discussion help you to see media representations of gay men in new and different ways?

2. What stereotypes of lesbians and gay men have you gotten from the media? How do you think these representations impact your own levels of heterosexism and homophobia?

3. Do you think societal changes are necessary before we see changes in the portrayals of lesbians and gay men in the media? Or, do you think that more accurate and complete portrayals will bring about change in societal attitudes?

Reading 38

METAPHORS MATTER: DISASTER MYTHS, MEDIA FRAMES, AND THEIR CONSEQUENCES IN HURRICANE KATRINA

KATHLEEN TIERNEY • CHRISTINE BEVC • ERICA KULIGOWSKI

Since the inception of the field of social science disaster research in the United States, research has focused on public responses under disaster conditions. Initiated in the late 1940s and early 1950s, disaster research in the United States was strongly associated with cold war concerns regarding how the general public might react in the event of a nuclear attack. Federal funding agencies believed that social science research on group behavior following disasters might shed light on such questions as whether

Kathleen Tierney, Christine Bevc, and Erica Kuligowski, "Metaphors Matter: Disaster Myths, Media Frames, and Their Consequences in Hurricane Katrina" from *The Annals of the American Academy of Political and Social Science* 604, No. 1 (2006): 57–81. Copyright © 2006 by the American Academy of Political and Social Science. Reprinted with the permission of Sage Publications, Inc.

people would panic and whether mass demoralization and social break-down would occur following a nuclear weapons attack (Quarantelli 1987). As studies on public responses in disasters continued, it became increasingly evident to researchers that endangered publics and disaster victims respond and adapt well during and following disasters.

By the 1960s, a body of work had accumulated indicating that panic is not a problem in disasters; that rather than helplessly awaiting outside aid, members of the public behave proactively and prosocially to assist one another; that community residents themselves perform many critical disaster tasks, such as searching for and rescuing victims; and that both social cohesiveness and informal mechanisms of social control increase during disasters, resulting in a lower incidence of deviant behavior than during nondisaster times. Early research on disasters discussed such common patterns as the "expansion of the citizenship role" and "social leveling" to explain public responses to disasters. This literature identified strong situationally induced influences, such as emergent prosocial norms, as factors leading to greater community cohesiveness during disasters. Research indicated that during the emergency period following disasters, earlier community conflicts are suspended as communities unite under conditions of extreme stress. Earlier research also documented the emergence of "therapeutic communities" within disaster-stricken populations, involving victims coming together to provide mutual support to one another (for discussions on these points, see Fritz 1961; Barton 1969; Dynes 1970; Drabek 1986).

Classic research in the disaster field also highlighted contrasts that exist between the realities associated with disaster responses and myths concerning disaster behavior—myths that persist despite empirical evidence to the contrary. The first major article discussing common disaster myths was written by pioneering disaster researchers E. L. Quarantelli and Russell Dynes. That article, titled "When Disaster Strikes (It Isn't Much Like What You've Heard and Read About)," was published in *Psychology Today* in February 1972.

Since the prevalence of disaster myths was first documented, more research has been conducted focusing on such topics as the extent to which the public believes disaster myths (Wenger et al. 1975); the manner in which popular culture—specifically the disaster film genre—both reflects and perpetuates erroneous beliefs about disaster-related behavior (Quarantelli 1985; Mitchell et al. 2000); and the incidence of media accounts featuring disaster myths, relative to other themes (Goltz 1984). Some of this research has focused on how the belief in myths influences individual and organizational decision making in disasters (see Fischer 1998). Other research has pointed to the manner in which media reports can affect public perceptions by amplifying and distorting risk-related information (Kasperson and Kasperson 2005). Outside the field of disaster research, media scholars have also analyzed patterns of reporting in disasters (Smith 1992), as well as how media accounts help to shape public opinion (Walters, Wilkins, and Walters 1989).

More recent analyses document how mythological beliefs have experienced a resurgence in the aftermath of the September 11, 2001, terrorist attacks (Tierney 2003). Focusing, for example, on the panic myth, the assumption that the public will panic in the event of another terrorist attack, especially one involving weapons of mass destruction, has been taken for granted in media and public policy discourses and is now even reflected in discussions among public health, homeland security, and emergency management professionals. These discourses often conflate the concept of panic with entirely normal and understandable public responses to risk and uncertainty, such as the upsurge of public information seeking in the 2001 anthrax attack. Intensified information seeking under conditions of threat or actual disaster impact, which can give rise to rumors of all types, has long been recognized as an extension of everyday interpersonal communicative practices and is readily explained by theories of collective behavior (Turner 1994). Although such behavior does create challenges for those who must respond to public inquiries, it does not indicate panic.

Similarly, it is well understood that under impending threats, many people who are not directly at risk will try to move out of harm's way, either because they are risk averse or because they do not fully understand or trust the warning information they have received. This sort of behavior, which researchers term the "evacuation shadow" effect, is quite common in threat situations of all types. First documented following the nuclear accident at Three Mile Island (Ziegler, Brunn, and Johnson 1981; Lindell and Perry 1992), the evacuation shadow phenomenon was seen most recently immediately prior to Hurricane Rita. Despite the fact that they are common, and despite the fact that why they occur is well understood, "inappropriate" efforts to seek safety on the part of people whom authorities do not consider at risk have also been seen as indicative of panic.

The panic myth has been consistently reinforced in various ways in the aftermath of 9/11. For example, the American Red Cross is widely viewed as a trusted source of information on disaster preparedness. Yet in 2005, the Red Cross took many researchers and disaster management professionals by surprise by launching a print and electronic media campaign whose theme was "I can't stop a [tornado, flood, fire, hurricane, terrorist attack, etc.] but I can stop panic." The campaign, which was intended to promote household preparedness for extreme events, erred in two ways. First, it conveyed the notion that there is nothing people can do to prevent disasters, which is patently false; and second, it sent a message that panic will invariably break out during disasters and other extreme events and that avoiding panic should be a top priority for the public when disasters strike. (For further discussions in inappropriate uses of the panic concept, see Clarke 2002; Tierney 2003, 2004.)

As the panic example shows, messages contained in the mass media and even in official discourse continue to promote ideas that have long been shown to be false in actual empirical research on disasters. Moreover, since the terrorist attacks of September 11, 2001, these types of messages, which continue to be vigorously challenged by experts, now seem to ring true to many audiences, in part because of the unsubstantiated and arguable but still widely accepted assumption that terrorism-related extreme events are qualitatively different from other types of emergencies and, thus, generate qualitatively different sociobehavioral responses.

Researchers have long pointed out that the belief in myths concerning disaster behavior is not problematic merely because such beliefs are untrue. Rather, these erroneous ideas are harmful because of their potential for influencing organizational, governmental, and public responses during disasters. It has been noted, for example, that incorrect assumptions about the potential for looting and social breakdown can lead to misallocations of public safety resources that could be put to better use in providing direct assistance to victims. Concerns with public panic can also lead officials to avoid issuing timely warnings and to keep needed risk-related information from the public (Fischer 1998). Such actions only serve to make matters worse when threats actually materialize.

We turn next to the substance of this article, which concerns the promulgation of disaster myths by the media during and following Hurricane Katrina. Because analyses on data collected in Katrina's aftermath are still ongoing, the article contains only preliminary observations, presented primarily in the form of examples from major press outlets that illustrate key points. We note also that at this time the media, the research community, and the nation as a whole still do not know with any degree of certainty what actually did happen during the hurricane and in the terrible days that followed. However, we emphasize that even though many questions still remain unanswered, and indeed may never be definitively answered, the images conveyed by the media during that turbulent period left indelible impressions on the public and also provided the justification for official actions that were undertaken to manage the disaster. Moreover, the media vigorously promoted those images even though media organizations themselves had little ability to verify what was actually happening in many parts of the impact region. As the sections that follow show, initial media coverage of Katrina's devastating impacts was quickly replaced by reporting that characterized disaster victims as opportunistic looters and violent criminals and that presented individual and group behavior following the Katrina disaster through the lens of civil unrest. Later, narratives shifted again and began to metaphorically represent the disaster-stricken city of New Orleans as a war zone and to draw parallels between the conditions in that city and urban insurgency in Iraq. These media frames helped guide and justify actions undertaken by military and law enforcement entities that were assigned responsibility for the postdisaster emergency response. The overall effect of media coverage was to further bolster arguments that only the military is capable of effective action during disasters.

WHAT INFLUENCES MEDIA REPORTING
ON DISASTERS?

Discussions on why media portrayals of disasters and their victims so often deviate from what is actually known about behavior during emergencies highlight a number of factors. Some explanations center on reporting conventions that lead media organizations, particularly the electronic media, to focus on dramatic, unusual, and exceptional behavior, which can lead audiences to believe such behavior is common and typical. Other explanations focus on the widespread use of standard frames that strongly shape the content of media messages. Although based on myths about disaster behavior, one such frame, the "looting frame," appears almost invariably in disaster-related reporting. As Fischer (1998) noted in his book on disaster myths,

> Looting is perhaps the most expected behavioral response to disaster. Both print and broadcast media personnel report on the alleged looting incidents, on steps being taken to prevent it, and, alternatively, on how unusual it was for the community in question not to be preyed on by looters. (p. 15)

It is common for both print and electronic media covering disasters to include content indicating that "the National Guard has been brought into (name of community) to prevent looting"—implying that looting would otherwise have been a serious problem without the use of strong external social control. Following circular reasoning, the fact that looting does not occur during a particular disaster event is then attributed to the presence of the National Guard and public safety agencies, even though it is highly likely that looting would never have been a problem in the first place. These types of frames, themes, and content make such a strong impression on audiences in part because they reflect and are consistent with other popular media portrayals of disaster behavior, such as those that appear in disaster films and made-for-TV movies.

In the question-and-answer period following her testimony before the Research Subcommittee of the House Science Committee in November 2005, University of New Orleans sociologist Shirley Laska pointed to another important factor shaping disaster reporting. She noted that while many media outlets often do have science reporters, the media almost universally lack specialists in disaster-related phenomena, particularly those involving individual, group, and organizational behavior. In her comments, Laska recounted the many hours she spent on the telephone with reporters following Hurricane Katrina—interviews that were particularly lengthy because the vast majority of the reporters with whom she spoke lacked even the most basic understanding of societal response and emergency management issues (U.S. Congress 2005). Perhaps this lack of understanding of the fundamentals of disaster-related behavior is one reason why disaster myths and their associated frames have had such a strong influence on media disaster reporting.

Disaster reporting is also linked to what is judged to be newsworthy about particular events. Decisions about what and how much to cover with respect to specific disaster events are often rooted in judgments about the social value of disaster victims and on conceptions of social distance and difference. Thus, the vast outpouring of generosity following the Indian Ocean earthquake and tsunami of December 2004 was driven both by the catastrophic nature of the disaster and by the fact that so many Western tourists happened to be in the impact region when the disaster struck. There was no comparable compassionate response from the West for the victims of the 2005 Pakistan-Kashmir earthquake, despite the fact that the death toll has now exceeded eighty-six thousand and many more victims are expected to die of starvation or freeze to death when winter grips the impact region. Hurricane Wilma battered Cancun for two days and caused widespread devastation, but most U.S. reporting focused on American tourists who were stranded in the region, rather than on the challenges faced by Cancun's residents, and reporting on the tragedy in Cancun and its catastrophic aftermath dropped off within a few days after the event, when the tourists had come home safely.

Since the media have a long record of portraying nonmainstream groups, especially minority group members, in stereotypical ways, it should come as no surprise that these same framing conventions would influence reporting on disaster victims in New Orleans following Hurricane Katrina. Indeed, in Katrina's aftermath, among the most widely circulated media images was a set of photographs in which African Americans were consistently described as "looting" goods, while whites engaging in exactly the same behaviors were labeled as "finding" supplies.

Media practices and judgments regarding newsworthiness, as well as media stereotyping, are undeniably important factors in the production of disaster news. At a more macro level, however, media treatments of disasters both reflect and reinforce broader societal and cultural trends, socially constructed metanarratives, and hegemonic discourse practices that support the status quo and the interests of elites. Thus, myths concerning the panicky public, the dangers presented by looters, and the threat disaster victims pose to the social order serve to justify policy stances adopted by law enforcement entities and other institutions concerned with social control (Tierney 2003).

We argue here that media reporting surrounding the Katrina disaster can best be understood from this last-mentioned perspective. In addition to reflecting both standard media reporting conventions and long-standing media biases regarding people of color, disaster reporting also serves broader political purposes. In the following sections, we will provide illustrative materials supporting this point. More specifically, we will argue that post-Katrina reporting led directly to the social construction of negative images of residents of the impact area, particularly African American victims and the very poor. Later shown to be inaccurate, slanted by sources that were themselves biased, and based more on rumor than on direct observation, reports constructed disaster victims as lawless, violent, exploitative, and almost less than human in the days following Katrina. Images of lawlessness and civil unrest were later replaced by media discourse characterizing New Orleans as a "war zone" and framing the challenges faced by emergency responders as not unlike those facing troops battling insurgents in Iraq.

Both reflecting and further embellishing myths concerning behavior during disasters, media stories influenced officials to adopt unproductive and outright harmful response strategies during the emergency. The stories also served to further bolster claims regarding the need for strong command-and-control procedures and for greater involvement on the part of the military in extreme events ranging from homeland security emergencies to disasters of all types. Set in a broader societal context, media depictions of events as they unfolded during the disaster provided strong evidence for arguments that strict social control should be the first priority during disaster events and that the military is the only institution capable of managing disasters.

 MEDIA REPORTING AND THE SOCIAL
CONSTRUCTION OF LOOTING AND
VIOLENCE IN HURRICANE KATRINA

The preliminary analyses presented here are based on a variety of media sources. News stories focusing specifically on the behavior of victims and the official response to the hurricane were collected from three newspapers: *The New York Times, The Washington Post,* and the New Orleans *Times-Picayune.* The period covered spanned the impact period itself and the two weeks following the disaster, from August 29, 2005, to September 11, 2005. In extracting frames and themes from these reports, we used qualitative analytic techniques, rather than quantitatively oriented analytic approaches (see Altheide 1996). We do not argue that the "civil unrest" and "war zone" frames were the only ones employed by the media. Rather, we argue that these frames and their associated discourses were among the most prominent and that they achieved prominence because they were congruent with post-9/11 official discourses regarding how disasters and other extreme events—including in particular those associated with terrorist attacks—should be managed in the United States.

Disaster Myths and the Social Construction
of Disorder in New Orleans

Rampant Looting   As noted in the sections above, the notion that U.S. disasters are followed by looting activity has long been contradicted by empirical evidence. Nonetheless, the media continue to assume that looting and lawlessness are significant elements in the public response to disasters. Media coverage of the behaviors of disaster victims following the hurricane mirrored this assumption. Moreover, particularly in the early days after the hurricane, reports referred to disaster looting behavior in ways that would usually be reserved for describing behavior during episodes of civil unrest.

The distinction between disasters and urban unrest is an important one. A substantial social science literature points to the marked distinction that exists between how individuals and groups behave during periods of civil unrest and how they behave following disasters. When civil disorders occur, looting does break out; indeed, the taking of consumer goods and the destruction of property are hallmarks of modern U.S. "commodity riots," such as the urban riots of the 1960s and the 1992 Los Angeles civil unrest. Such looting is typically carried out by groups from within the riot area (including family groups) and in full view of the media, local residents, and even law enforcement agencies. Riot-related looting behavior develops under the influence of emergent norms that not only permit but actually encourage the taking and destruction of property (Dynes and Quarantelli 1968; Quarantelli and Dynes 1970). However, research also indicates that even during riot situations, looting is selective and usually confined to particular types of stores, such as those carrying retail goods, liquor, and groceries (Tierney 1994). Moreover, studies show that individuals who loot and engage in property violence during episodes of civil unrest do so sporadically, mixing their unlawful behavior with other routine social behavior such as gathering with friends and going home for meals. Looters may or may not share common grievances or reasons for looting; some may see looting as an act of protest or retaliation, while others may view unrest as simply an opportunity to obtain goods for free (Feagin and Hahn 1973; McPhail and Wohlstein 1983; McPhail 1991).

In contrast, research has shown repeatedly that looting is highly unusual in U. S. disasters. When it does occur, it tends to be transient, to be carried out in secret, and to involve isolated groups rather than large numbers of people. Unlike looting during civil disorders, actual and potential disaster-related looting behavior is widely condemned by the residents of affected communities. Signs bearing messages such as "you loot, we shoot," which are often shown in the media following disasters, are not so much indicative of the actual occurrence of looting as they are of strong community norms against looting (Fischer 1998). Community residents also believe looting myths and act accordingly, arming themselves in an effort to prevent looting, even if such behavior has not been reported or verified by official sources. After disasters, individuals returning to their damaged homes and businesses to retrieve items may be mistakenly labeled as looters, as may those who go to others' homes to check to see whether occupants are safe. Overconcern with the possibility of looting often leads community residents to ignore evacuation warnings and remain in their homes to ward off looters—another example of how the belief in myths may actually increase the risk of death and injury in disasters (Fischer 1998; Tierney, Lindell, and Perry 2001).

This is not to say that there have never been instances of large-scale collective looting in U. S. disasters. While vanishingly rare, such episodes have occurred. Perhaps the most notable recent example is the looting that occurred on the island of St. Croix following Hurricane Hugo in 1989. Hugo was a huge storm that caused serious damage and social disruption in many parts of the Caribbean and the southeast, including parts of Puerto Rico and North and South Carolina. However, looting only emerged on St. Croix, not in other hard-hit areas. Because this was such an unusual case, disaster scholar E. L. Quarantelli spent considerable time investigating why looting was a problem on St. Croix but nowhere else Hugo had affected. Based on his fieldwork and interviews, Quarantelli attributed the looting to several factors. First, the hurricane devastated the island, completely destroying the vast bulk of the built environment. Second, government institutions, including public safety agencies, were rendered almost entirely ineffective by the hurricane's severity, so the victims essentially had no expectation that their needs would be addressed by those institutions. Third, victims had no information on when they could expect help to arrive. Equally important, according to Quarantelli, was that the lawlessness that followed Hugo was in many ways consistent with the high rates of predisaster crime on the island and also a consequence of preexisting social inequalities and class and racial resentments, which had long been exacerbated by the sharp class distinctions that characterized the tourist economy on St. Croix (see Quarantelli 2006; Rodríguez, Trainor, and Quarantelli 2006 . . .).

It can be argued that the post-Katrina conditions in New Orleans in many ways paralleled the situation on St. Croix following Hugo. Those who were unable to escape the city or find refuge after Katrina struck may well have reached the same conclusions as those who were trapped on St. Croix after Hugo. With homes, property, and livelihoods gone, with no evidence of a functioning governmental system, facing severe danger and hardship, and without having any idea of when help would arrive, many residents might have understandably concluded that they were on their own and that they had best fend for themselves.

Given the utterly miserable conditions the hurricane produced, looting might well have been collectively defined as justifiable by some of those who were forced to remain and await help in New Orleans. Many news reports featured images of desperate residents fanning out through neighborhoods in search of basic necessities such as food, water, diapers, and clothing (Barringer and Longman 2005; Coates and Eggen 2005a). However, as of this writing, no solid empirical data exist regarding how widespread (or rare) looting actually was, who took part in the episodes of looting that did occur, why they were motivated to take part, whether the goods people took could have been salvaged, or how much damage and loss looting actually caused, relative to other losses the hurricane produced. Equally important, whatever lawless behavior may have occurred has not yet been systematically analyzed in the context of "normal" rates of lawbreaking in New Orleans. What do exist are volumes of information on what the media and public officials *believed and communicated* about looting in New Orleans. As discussed below, these reports characterized post-Katrina looting as very widespread, wanton, irrational, and accompanied by violence—in short, as resembling media characterizations of riot behavior. Moreover, the media confined their reporting to the putative lawless behavior of certain categories and types of people—specifically young black males—to the exclusion of other behaviors in which these disaster victims may have engaged during the disaster, producing a profile of looters and looting groups that overlooked whatever prosocial, altruistic behaviors such groups may have undertaken.

More systematic analyses of media looting reports will come later. In this article, we offer a series of representative reports that appeared in *The New York Times, The Washington Post,* and the New Orleans *Times-Picayune* as well as from the Department of Defense's American Forces Information Service. We stress that these are typical comments that were made in these media outlets, not unusual ones. The material presented below focuses mainly on the first few days after the hurricane.

From *The New York Times:*

August 31: "These are not individuals looting. These are large groups of armed individuals." . . . "Looting broke out as opportunistic thieves cleaned out abandoned stores for a second night. In one incident, officials said a police officer was shot and critically wounded." (Treaster and Kleinfield 2005)

September 1: "Chaos gripped New Orleans on Wednesday as looters ran wild . . . looters brazenly ripped open gates and ransacked stores for food, clothing, television sets, computers, jewelry, and guns." (McFadden and Blumenthal 2005)

From *The Washington Post:*

August 31: "Even as the floodwaters rose, looters roamed the city, sacking department stores and grocery stories and floating their spoils away in plastic garbage cans. . . . Looting began on Canal Street, in the morning, as people carrying plastic garbage pails waded through waist-deep water to break into department stores. In drier areas, looters raced into smashed stores and pharmacies and by nightfall the pillage was widespread." (Gugliotta and Whoriskey 2005)

September 2: "What could be going through the minds of people who survive an almost biblical tragedy, find themselves in a hellscape of the dead and the dispossessed, and promptly decide to go looting? Obviously not much: Stealing a rack of fancy clothes when there's no place to wear them or a television when there's no electricity does not suggest a lot of deep thought." (Robinson 2005)

From the New Orleans *Times-Picayune:*

August 30: In the midst of the rising water, two men "were planning to head out to the levee to retrieve a stash of beer, champagne, and hard liquor they found washed onto the levee." (MacCash and O'Byrne 2005)

August 30: "Midafternoon Monday, a parade of looters streamed from Coleman's retail store. . . . The looters, men and women who appeared to be in their early teens to mid-40s, braved a steady rain . . . to take away boxes of clothing and shoes from the store." (Philbin 2005)

August 31: "Officials watched helplessly as looters around the city ransacked stores for food, clothing, appliances, and guns." " 'The looting is out of control. The French Quarter has been attacked,' Councilwoman Jackie Clarkson said." (McGill 2005)

Beyond Property Crime Not only were the crowds engaging in the collective theft of all types of goods, but their behavior was also violent and even deadly. Media accounts made it seem as if all of New Orleans was caught up in a turmoil of lawlessness.

From *The New York Times:*

September 2: "Chaos and gunfire hampered efforts to evacuate the Superdome, and, the New Orleans police superintendent said, armed thugs have taken control of the secondary makeshift shelter in the convention center. The thugs repelled eight squads of eleven officers each he sent to secure the place . . . rapes and assaults were occurring unimpeded in the neighborhood streets. . . . Looters set ablaze a shopping center and firefighters, facing guns, abandoned their efforts to extinguish the fires, local radio said." (Treaster and Sontag 2005)

September 3: "America is once more plunged into a snake pit of anarchy, death, looting, raping, marauding thugs, suffering infrastructure, a gutted police force, insufficient troop levels and criminally negligent government planning." (Dowd 2005)

From *The Washington Post:*

September 1: "Things have spiraled so out of control [in New Orleans] that the city's mayor ordered police officers to focus on looters and give up the search and rescue efforts." (Coates and Eggen 2005b)

September 3: A firefighter from Long Beach is quoted as saying, "People are taking clothing, liquor, things that aren't life-surviving, material items. I don't have a problem if someone is trying to get food and water, but beyond that, we're bustn' em. . . . What we're getting worried about is people are starting to shoot at us now. . . . That's the lowest form of human being haunting the earth." (Vedantam and Klein 2005)

From the New Orleans *Times-Picayune:*

August 31: According to the New Orleans homeland security chief, "There are gangs of armed men in the city, moving around the city." *(Times-Picayune* 2005a)

September 2: "Governor Kathleen Blanco called the looters 'hoodlums' and issued a warning to lawbreakers: Hundreds of National Guard hardened on the battlefield in Iraq have landed in New Orleans. 'They have M-16s, and they're locked and loaded,' she said." (Breed 2005)

Another graphic *Times-Picayune* story, published on September 1, spoke of gangs looting houses and businesses, robbing people in the street, looting gun stores, stealing guns from Wal-Mart, and assaulting disaster victims (Anderson, Perlstein, and Scott 2005). These media stories, along with stories passed through rumor networks, clearly influenced disaster management decision making. Immediately following the New Orleans levee breach, for example, Louisiana Governor Kathleen Blanco emphasized that search and rescue should take priority over all other emergency activities. However, as the September 1 story above in *The Washington Post* indicates, within three days of the hurricane's impact, she and the mayor of New Orleans ordered public safety officers to pursue lawbreakers, rather than concentrating on lifesaving activities (Coates and Eggen 2005b). This decision directly influenced the survival chances of stranded and dying disaster victims.

The material presented above comes from print media. While we have not attempted to undertake the Herculean task of analyzing electronic media, the Internet, or postings that appeared in the blogosphere, anyone who watched or read these media in the aftermath of Katrina can only conclude that the images of looting and looters these media conveyed were even more extreme. While television news did report extensively on the suffering of Katrina's victims, the intergovernmental disaster response debacle, and other topics, it also featured numerous stories of looting, rape, and lawlessness, continuously "looping" video of the activities of groups that had already become "armed, marauding thugs" in the minds of viewers. Video images also conveyed more powerfully than print media could that the "thugs" who had taken over New Orleans were young black men.

As the emergency continued, all manner of rumors were reported by the media as truth. Readers and viewers were told, for example, of multiple murders, child rape, and people dying of gunshot wounds in the Superdome. These reports were later found to be groundless, but they were accepted as accurate by both media organizations and consumers of news because they were consistent with the emerging media frame that characterized New Orleans as a "snakepit of anarchy," a violent place where armed gangs of black men took advantage of the disaster not only to loot but also to commit capital crimes.

More thoughtful analyses of looting and other forms of disaster-related collective behavior would later emerge in the media (see, for example, an article titled "Up for Grabs; Sociologists Question How Much Looting and Mayhem Really Took Place in New Orleans," which ran in the *Boston Globe* on September 11, 2005; see Shea 2005). But before these kinds of balanced reports appeared, the "armed thug" frame was already well established. Reports seemed to clearly show that the activities of armed thugs, "the lowest form of human being haunting the earth," had gone well beyond looting for necessities and had spilled over into murder, rape, and acts of random violence (Vedantam and Klein 2005). This frame provided part of the justification for the subsequent governmental response to the Katrina disaster.

 ## METAPHORS MATTER: FROM CIVIL UNREST
TO URBAN WARFARE

The inability of federal, state, and local authorities to respond rapidly and effectively to Hurricane Katrina quickly became a major scandal both in the United States and around the world. In the days immediately following the disaster, the press, the U.S. populace, and Washington officialdom all sought to understand what had gone so terribly wrong with the intergovernmental response to Hurricane Katrina. Within a few days, a broad consensus developed that Michael Brown, the director of the Federal Emergency Management Agency (FEMA), was the individual most responsible for the Katrina debacle. Brown resigned under heavy criticism on September 12, 2005. In the weeks and months following Katrina, the media have continued to report both on Brown's lack of qualifications for his position and on his lack of basic situation awareness during the Katrina disaster. Most recently, stories have focused on e-mails that Brown exchanged with colleagues at the height of the crisis, purportedly showing that he was drastically out of touch with what was actually happening in New Orleans and other areas affected by the hurricane. In the meantime, broader management system failures during Hurricane Katrina became the subject of a congressional investigation.

Even before Brown's resignation, administration officials had likely already concluded that civil authorities were incapable of responding to Katrina and that the military would have to play a significantly larger role than it has traditionally played in U.S. disasters. The president attempted to federalize and militarize the response immediately after the hurricane, but he was rebuffed by Governor Blanco (Roig-Franzia and Hsu 2005). Although the initial federal response to Katrina had been shockingly incompetent, the federal government ultimately did mobilize, and a large component of that mobilization involved military and security resources. Just two days after Hurricane Katrina made landfall in Louisiana and ten days before Brown's resignation, the president had already ordered General Russell Honore, as commander of Joint Task Force Katrina, to coordinate the military's role in rescue and relief activities throughout the Gulf Coast. Within a week (and in some cases, within days), along with first responders from around the United States, military, law enforcement, and private security companies began to converge on the region to provide all forms of assistance and to reinforce overwhelmed state and local public safety forces. They would help restore public order, joining what Governor Blanco had earlier referred to as battle-seasoned Louisiana National Guard forces, "locked and loaded," to put down looting and violence (Breed 2005). When beleaguered FEMA chief Michael Brown was finally recalled to Washington, he was replaced as chief coordinating official in the disaster region not by another civilian official but by Admiral Thad Allen.

By the fifth day after the hurricane's landfall in the Gulf region, the number of National Guard and active military deployed in Hurricane Katrina had tripled the number deployed within that same time period following Hurricane Andrew in 1992 (American Forces Information Service 2005a). With the arrival of so many command-and-control-oriented entities into the impact region, the response to Hurricane Katrina, particularly in New Orleans, began to take on a tone not seen in other U.S. disasters. Badges, uniforms, and arms—including assault weapons—were seen on the streets in large numbers. Search and rescue missions in the flooded neighborhoods of New Orleans began to resemble military search and destroy missions, as armed soldiers broke down doors and entered homes in search of stranded victims. In a city already under a strict dawn-to-dusk curfew, the movements of New Orleans residents—described as "holdouts" for their refusal to follow orders to leave their own homes and evacuate the city—were further curtailed, as sheriff's deputies were ordered to "handcuff and 'forcefully remove' holdouts" (Nolan 2005). The militarization of the response now affected even media reporters, as response personnel attempted to limit their access to sites within the city.

Once the looting and civil unrest were perceived to have exceeded the capabilities of local law enforcement, the National Guard were described as having been brought into disaster-stricken areas to help "restore and maintain law and order" to affected areas (Haskell 2005). As more military and law enforcement personnel streamed into Louisiana, and as media reporting continued to emphasize civil disorder and lawlessness, a new "war zone" metaphor began to emerge. First employed by the media, the "war zone" metaphor was quickly reflected in the discourse of both public officials and military personnel who were deployed in the impact region. With so many military and other security personnel on the ground, comparisons to wartime experiences became increasingly common. "I'd thought we'd just entered a war zone" and "the region looks like a war zone" became familiar statements (Alvarez 2005a, 2005b). In interviews, National Guard personnel likened the destruction in the Gulf region to their experiences in the Gulf War. Referring to the extensive building damage, one Guardsman noted that "some of the things you see out here you see in Iraq" (Alvarez 2005a). The extent of the devastation was characterized as shocking even to the "most seasoned veterans of past wars" (American Forces Information Service 2005c).

Within a few days after the hurricane, President Bush and other government officials described themselves as determined to regain control and protect the people from the criminal element through the presence of military forces. For example, on September 3, a *Times-Picayune* story emphasized Mr. Bush's strong law and order stance:

> "What is not working right, we're going to make it right." Referring to rampant looting and crime in New Orleans, Bush said, "We are going to restore order in the city of New Orleans. The people of this country expect there to be law and order, and we're going to work hard to get it. In order to make sure there's less violence, we've got to get food to people. We'll get on top of this situation, and we're going to help the people that need help." (Times-Picayune 2005b)

A few days later, the *New York Times* described the warlike conditions in New Orleans in this manner:

> September 11: "Partly because of the shortage of troops, violence raged inside the New Orleans convention center, which interviews show was even worse than previously described. Police SWAT team members found themselves plunging into the darkness, guided by the muzzle flashes of thugs' handguns." (Lipton et al. 2005)

Media also reported that in response to civil unrest at the convention center, one thousand National Guard military police "stormed" the convention center "to thwart a looming potentially dangerous situation" (R. Williams 2005). A National Guard officer explained that "had the Guardsmen gone in with less force, they may have been challenged and innocent people may have been caught in a fight between the Guard military police and those who didn't want to be processed or apprehended" (R. Williams 2005). After military police regained "control" of the convention center, hundreds of disaster evacuees were searched like criminal suspects for guns, illicit drugs, alcohol, contraband, and other items that had been designated as "undesirable" and then sent back into the center to await buses that would take them out of the city (R. Williams 2005).

The increasing threat and the use of military force were presented as key factors in restoring order throughout the Gulf Coast region. On September 3, for example, a news report quoted an Army major general as stating that "once you put soldiers on the streets with M-16s, things tend to settle down" (Alvarez 2005a). On September 4, the *New York Times* reported that "the mere sight of troops in camouflage battle gear and with assault rifles gave a sense of relief to many of the thousands of stranded survivors who had endured days of appalling terror and suffering." In the same article, Louisiana Governor Kathleen Blanco was quoted as stating that

> they [the military] brought a sense of order and peace, and it was a beautiful sight to see that we're ramping up. We are seeing a show of force. It's putting confidence back in our hearts and in the minds of our people. We're going to make it through. (McFadden 2005)

By September 13, the deployment of military personnel in response to Hurricane Katrina, totaling more than seventy-two thousand troops, was the largest for any natural disaster in U.S. history (American Forces Information Service 2005b). According to the media and the military press, military missions included deploying guards at street intersections (Hynes 2005), searching damaged buildings, and reinforcing social control through the use of "security" and "safety" measures.

To media, governmental, and military sources, operations in Louisiana, Alabama, Mississippi, and the rest of the impact region had come to resemble a second Iraq War. Indeed, one military official, presumably equating the disaster impact region with Iraq, was quoted as saying that "we are now fighting on two fronts" (*Times-Picayune* 2005c). A Loudon County, Virginia, sheriff mused upon sending county officers to Jefferson parish near New Orleans, stating, "I almost feel like a father sending his kids off to war or something. Things are becoming more and more violent as people become more desperate" (Laris 2005).

The media emphasized the "war zone" metaphor in multiple articles discussing the response of the people of New Orleans. For example, the *New York Times* described the thoughts of a man who had volunteered his fishing boat to rescue New Orleans residents:

> A shotgun rested in the boat next to Mr. Lovett, who said shots had been fired near him on occasion during the past week. "I don't feel like I'm in the U. S. I feel like I'm in a war. All the guns, the chaos." (Longman 2005)

New Orleans Police Superintendent Eddie Compass spoke with the *Times-Picayune* about the New Orleans Police Department's successful attempts to operate under wartime conditions:

> "In the annals of history, no police department in the history of the world was asked to do what we were asked," Compass said Monday, at the Emergency Operations Center in Baton Rouge. "We won. We did not lose one officer in battle." (Filosa 2005)

Ironically, with the increased presence of the military, the media itself began facing restrictions and threats over its coverage of the hurricane response. The National Guard and law enforcement agencies initiated various strategies to limit journalists' access to places where disaster operations were being carried out. One strategy centered on controlling the movement of journalists within the city of New Orleans (B. Williams 2005). Response agencies also began refusing media access to the Convention Center and Superdome (B. Williams 2005). When reporters protested, they were faced down by military personnel carrying loaded weapons (B. Williams 2005). As the recovery of bodies began, reporters were told, "No photos. No stories." In an article in the *San Francisco Chronicle,* a soldier was quoted as telling reporters that "the Army had a policy that requires media to be 300 meters—more than three football fields in length—away from the scene of body recoveries" (Vega 2005).

As the quote above indicates, the military's response and reaction to coverage of the deaths from Hurricane Katrina came to eerily resemble the administration's policy in Iraq, which prohibits the media from showing images of dead American soldiers. Reporters were told they would "face consequences" if they took pictures (Vega 2005). In an effort to further contain media coverage, on September 10, 2005, General Honore and Colonel Terry Ebbert announced that the media would have "zero access" to the recovery operations (CNN.com 2005b). The media were granted access to gather information and report on body recovery only after a temporary restraining order was issued at the request of CNN (CNN.com 2005a).

 ## CONCLUSIONS AND IMPLICATIONS

Myths and Their Consequences

As the foregoing discussion shows, both media reporting and official discourse following Hurricane Katrina upheld the mythical notion that disasters result in lawlessness and social breakdown. This is not to say that media coverage following Katrina provided nothing helpful or useful to victims, the American public, and audiences around the world. That was certainly not the case. The media devoted enormous resources to covering Katrina and also to performing such services as helping to locate and reunite disaster-stricken households. Reporters worked tirelessly to provide up-to-date information on all aspects of the hurricane.

However, even while engaging extensively in both reporting and public service, the media also presented highly oversimplified and distorted characterizations of the human response to the Katrina catastrophe. Ignoring the diversity and complexity of human responses to disastrous events, media accounts constructed only two images of those trapped in the disaster impact area: victims were seen either as "marauding thugs" out to attack both fellow victims and emergency responders or as helpless refugees from the storm, unable to cope and deserving of charity. These contrasting constructions are reflected in a story that appeared in the *Times-Picayune* on August 30, which discussed Louisiana Governor Blanco's reflection on displaced New Orleans disaster victims:

> Part of the population in the Dome are people "who do not have any regard for others." But many "good people" are also living in the Dome, she said, including mothers with babies. (Scott 2005)

Even as media and official discourses acknowledged that "good people"—mainly women and children—were among those victimized by Katrina, the terms used to describe the behavior of disaster victims in New Orleans, the majority of whom were people of color, were identical to those used to describe individuals and groups that engage in rioting in the context of episodes of civil unrest. Those trapped in New Orleans were characterized as irrational (because they engaged in "senseless" theft, rather than stealing for survival) and as gangs of out-of-control young males who presented a lethal threat to fellow victims and emergency responders. Officials increasingly responded to the debacle in New Orleans—a debacle that was in large measure of their own making—as if the United States were facing an armed urban insurgency rather than a catastrophic disaster. As the situation in New Orleans was increasingly equated with conditions of a "war zone," strict military and law enforcement controls, including controls on media access to response activities such as body recovery, were seen as necessary to replace social breakdown with the rule of law and order.

Once the initial media frenzy finally died down, journalists themselves were among the harshest critics of Katrina reporting. For example, in a September 29 segment that aired on the *NewsHour with Jim Lehrer,* media analysts, a journalist who had covered the Katrina disaster, and a military official were unanimous in their condemnation of how the media promoted myths of looting and violence in stories that were based almost entirely on rumor and hearsay. Noting that media reporters had by and large never actually witnessed lawlessness and violence in New Orleans, *NewsHour* guests gave numerous examples of the ways in which the media fell short of its duty to report facts, as opposed to rumors. One commentator noted that

> The central part of this story, what went wrong at the convention center and the Superdome, was wrong. American media threw everything they had at this story . . . and yet they could not get inside the convention center, they could not get inside the Superdome to dispel the lurid, the hysterical, the salaciousness of the reporting. . . . I have in mind especially the throat-slashed seven-year-old girl who had been gang-raped at the convention center—didn't happen. In fact there were no rapes at the

convention center or the Superdome that have yet been corrobo-
rated in anyway. . . . There weren't stacks of bodies in the freezer.
But America was riveted by this reporting, wholesale collapse of
the media's own levees as they let in all the rumors, and all the
innuendo, all the first-person story, because they were caught up
in their own emotionalism . . . [this was] one of the worst weeks of
reporting in the history of the American media. (Online NewsHour
2005, 5)

Ways of telling are also ways of not telling, and this same commentator
went on to say,

I think that some of the journalists involved, especially the anchors,
became so caught up in their own persona and their own celebrity
that they missed important and obvious stories. They failed to
report on the basic issues surrounding who deploys the National
Guard; they failed to report on why the Salvation Army and
the Red Cross were forbidden by state officials to deliver supplies to the Superdome and the convention center. They failed
to report what happened to the buses [that were supposed to be
used to evacuate residents of New Orleans] . . . they reported
panic-inducing, fear-inducing, hysteria-inducing events: looting,
pillaging, murder sprees, sort of the most squalid journalism you
could imagine. (Online NewsHour 2005, 7)

Outcomes and Consequences of Media Myths

Despite these and other efforts to criticize the media's performance following Katrina, initial evidence suggests that the media's relentless adherence
to disaster myths and to frames emphasizing civil unrest and urban insurgency, along with the strategic response measures these reports justified,
had a number of immediate negative consequences. For example, by calling
for curfews and viewing all victim movements around the city as suspect,
authorities likely interfered with ability of neighborhood residents and family groups to assist one another. Because they focused on combating what
the media had constructed as out-of-control looting and widespread violence, officials may have failed to take full advantage of the goodwill and
altruistic spirit of community residents and community resources, such as
churches and community-based organizations. By reassigning emergency
responders from lifesaving activities to law enforcement functions, those in
charge of the response placed law and order above the lives of hurricane
survivors. By treating disaster victims as thugs engaging in capital crimes
at worst and as troublesome "holdouts" at best, responding agencies created conflicts between themselves and disaster victims that might not have
developed otherwise and that likely destroyed the potential for the kinds of
collaborative partnership activities that major disasters require. Anecdotal

reports, not yet verified, also suggest that images of looting and lawlessness may have caused individuals and organizations from outside the affected region to hesitate before mobilizing to disaster sites in the immediate aftermath of Katrina (Laris 2005).

The treatment of disaster victims in New Orleans and other areas affected by Katrina has also reinforced the nation's racial divide. Public opinion polls conducted in the aftermath of Hurricane Katrina reveal stark differences between white and African American perceptions of the governmental response to the disaster. A survey conducted by the Pew Center for the People and the Press in early September found that a majority of those polled disapproved of the government's handling of the Katrina disaster. However, comparisons of black and white responses to the poll revealed very significant opinion differences. For example, 71 percent of blacks thought that the disaster showed that racial inequality is still a major problem in the United States, but 56 percent of white respondents said that was not the case. Two-thirds of black respondents believed that the governmental response would have been swifter had the disaster victims been white, while only 17 percent of whites thought the race of the victims made a difference. The opinions of blacks and whites differed dramatically along other dimensions as well: blacks were much more likely to report feeling angry and depressed after the hurricane; to feel sympathy for those who had been unable to evacuate; and to believe that those who may have looted did so because they needed to survive, not because they were criminals seeking to take advantage of the disaster (although 37 percent of whites expressed the latter view) (Pew Center 2005).

These disparate reactions to the government's handling of Hurricane Katrina have broader implications for other extreme events. If people of color now have such low regard for national leaders and crisis response agencies, and if their faith in mainstream institutions has been so badly shaken by the Katrina disaster, what will be their likely response in future national emergencies, such as an avian flu epidemic? If government leaders, the media, and members of the white majority see African Americans and other people of color as lawless elements who are ready to take advantage of disaster- or terrorism-related social disruption, what extreme measures are they likely to advocate to ensure the maintenance of public security during future emergencies?

Militarism and Disasters

Hurricane Katrina showed once again that the potential for catastrophe is present wherever extreme events—natural, technological, or willful—intersect with vulnerable built environments and vulnerable populations. Those left behind in the hurricane's wake were the most vulnerable groups in the impact region—individuals and households that lacked the resources to evacuate or that stayed behind for a variety of other reasons.

It was widely understood well before Katrina that New Orleans could not be successfully evacuated in the face of a major hurricane, but few concrete actions had been taken to address the needs of these most vulnerable residents.

Reflecting on the fate of these stranded victims, it is important to note that many of the nation's large urban agglomerations, and their populations, are at risk from future extreme events. These large urban centers include New York City, Los Angeles, the Bay Area of Northern California, and Miami. Highly vulnerable urban places are also home to highly diverse populations, including many who are forced to live in poverty. Will other low-income inner-city communities be seen as potential hotbeds of urban unrest and potential "war zones" in future disasters? Will the same images of violence and criminality that emerged following Katrina be applied, perhaps preemptively, to other large cities affected by extreme events?

Predictably, the failed governmental response to Hurricane Katrina has led to new calls for stronger military involvement in disaster response activities. In Katrina's wake, disasters are now being characterized as best managed not by civil authorities but by entities capable of using force—deadly force, if necessary—to put down civil unrest and restore order in the aftermath of disasters. Military institutions are widely viewed as possessing the resources, logistics capability, and strategic insights required to "get things done" when disasters strike. This militaristic approach stands in sharp contrast with foundational assumptions concerning how disasters should be managed, which emphasize the need for strengthening community resilience, building public-private partnerships, reaching out to marginalized community residents and their trusted institutions, and developing consensus-based coordinating mechanisms at the interorganizational, community, and intergovernmental levels (see Waugh 2000; Haddow and Bullock 2003).

Calls for military control following disasters are not new. Many of the same arguments for greater military involvement were made following Hurricane Andrew, which struck in 1992, and which was followed by failures on the part of the intergovernmental emergency response system that resembled those following Katrina, but on a smaller scale. However, a study later conducted to analyze the response to Andrew and recommend improvements saw no justification for giving broader authority to the military during disasters (National Academy of Public Administration 1993). Even after Katrina, opposition to greater military involvement is widespread. For example, a *USA Today* poll of thirty-eight governors found that only two governors supported the president's proposal that the military take a greater role in responding to disasters (Disaster preparedness 2005). In an Associated Press report on November 4, 2005, Montana governor Brian Schweitzer was quoted as saying that at the upcoming meeting of the Western Governors Association,

> I'm going to stand up among a bunch of elected governors and say, "Are we going to allow the military without a shot being fired to effectively do an end-run coup on civilian government? Are we going to allow that?" We're going to have a little civics lesson for some leaders who are apparently out of touch in the military.

Despite such protests, the concept of military control during disasters continues to gain traction in the aftermath of Hurricane Katrina. Distorted images disseminated by the media and public officials served to justify calls for greater military involvement in disasters. At a broader level, images of disaster victims as criminals and insurgents and of military personnel as the saviors of New Orleans are consistent with the growing prominence of militarism as a national ideology. We do not speak here of the military as an institution or of its role in national defense. Instead, following Chalmers Johnson (2004), we distinguish between the military and *militarism*—the latter referring to an ideology that places ultimate faith in the ability of the military and armed force to solve problems in both the international and domestic spheres. Johnson noted that "one sign of the advent of militarism is the assumption by the nation's armed forces of numerous tasks that should be reserved for civilians" (p. 24) and also that "certainly one of the clearest signs of militarism in America, is the willingness of some senior officers and civilian militarists to meddle in domestic policing" (p. 119). This is exactly what occurred during Hurricane Katrina—and what may become standard procedure in future extreme events.

It is now common knowledge that in the aftermath of the 2001 terrorist attacks, the Bush administration and some military officials began a reassessment of the *Posse Comitatus* act, which forbids the military to perform policing functions within the United States. This reassessment accompanied the creation in 2002 of the U.S. Northern Command (NORTHCOM), a military force whose purpose is to engage in "homeland defense." A number of analysts, including writers representing conservative think tanks like the Cato Institute, have called attention to the continual expansion of the role of the military in domestic emergency and security operations (Healey 2003). One of the most profound domestic impacts of the so-called war on terrorism is a growing acceptance of the military's involvement in a wide variety of domestic missions, including providing security at the Salt Lake City Olympics, searching for the Washington-area sniper, and now the policing and management of disaster victims.

Disasters can become "focusing events" that bring about changes in laws, policies, and institutional arrangements (Birkland 1997; Rubin and Renda-Tenali 2000). Hurricane Katrina may well prove to be the focusing event that moves the nation to place more faith in military solutions for a wider range of social problems than ever before. If this does turn out to be the case, the media will have helped that process along through its promulgation of myths of lawlessness, disorder, and urban insurgency.

REFERENCES

Altheide, David L. 1996. *Qualitative media analysis.* Thousand Oaks, CA: Sage.

Alvarez, Steve. 2005a. Alabama guard provides critical disaster response. American Forces Information Service. September 3. http://www.defenselink.mil/news/Sep2005/20050903_2612.html.

_____. 2005b. Engineers clear way in Gulf. American Forces Information Service. September 5. http://www.defenselink.mil/news/Sep2005/20050905_2618.html.

American Forces Information Service. 2005a. Day five comparison of troop numbers for Hurricanes Andrew and Katrina. September 5. http://www.defenselink.mil/news/Sep2005/050906-D-6570C-001.jpg.

_____. 2005b. Military continues Hurricane Katrina support. September 13. http://www.defenselink.mil/news/Sep2005/20050913_2723.html.

_____. 2005c. 139th Airlift Wind aids children and families after Katrina devastation. September 27. http://www.ngb.army.mil/news/story.asp?id=1934.

Anderson, Ed, Michael Perlstein, and Robert Travis Scott. 2005. We'll do what it takes to restore order. *Times-Picayune,* September 1. http://www.nola.com/newslogs/breakingtp/index.ssf?/mtlogs/nola_Times-Picayune/archives/2005_09.html.

Associated Press. 2005. States oppose greater role for military in disasters. November 4. http://www.FoxNews.com.

Barringer, Felicity, and Jere Longman. 2005. Owners take up arms as looters press their advantage. *New York Times,* September 1, sec. A.

Barton, Allen H. 1969. *Communities in disaster: A sociological analysis of collective stress situations.* Garden City, NY: Doubleday.

Birkland, Thomas. 1997. *After disaster: Agenda setting, public policy, and focusing events.* Washington, DC: Georgetown University Press.

Breed, Allen. 2005. National Guardsmen pour into New Orleans. *Times-Picayune,* September 2. http://www.nola.com/newslogs/breakingtp/index.ssf?/mtlogs/nola_Times-Picayune/archives/2005_09.html.

Clarke, Lee. 2002. Panic: Myth or reality? *Contexts* 1 (3): 21–26.

CNN.com. 2005a. Transcript of court proceedings for CNN v. Michael Brown. September 11. http://www.cnn.com/2005/LAW/09/11/katrina.mediaaccess.transcript.

_____. 2005b. U.S. won't ban media from New Orleans searches. September 10. http://www.cnn.com/2005/LAW/09/10/katrina.media.

Coates, Sam, and Dan Eggen. 2005a. A city of despair and lawlessness. *The Washington Post,* September 2, sec. A.

_____. 2005b. In New Orleans, a desperate exodus; looting persists; mayor fears huge death toll. *The Washington Post,* September 1, sec. A.

Disaster preparedness: Is the U.S. ready for another major disaster? 2005. *CQ Researcher* 15:981–1004.

Dowd, Maureen. 2005. United States of shame. *The New York Times,* September 3, sec. A.

Drabek, Thomas E. 1986. *Human system responses to disaster: An inventory of sociological findings.* New York: Springer-Verlag.

Dynes, Russell R. 1970. *Organized behavior in disaster.* Lexington, MA: Heath Lexington.

Dynes, Russell R., and E. L. Quarantelli. 1968. What looting in civil disturbances really means. *Transaction Magazine* 5 (6): 9–14.

Feagin, Joseph R., and Harlan Hahn. 1973. *Ghetto revolts: The politics of violence in American cities.* New York: Macmillan.

Filosa, Gwen. 2005. New Orleans police chief defends force. *Times-Picayune.* September 5. http://www.nola.com/newslogs/breakingtp/index.ssf?/mtlogs/nola_Times-Picayune/archives/2005_09.html.

Fischer, Henry W., III. 1998. *Response to disaster: Fact versus fiction and its perpetuation: The sociology of disaster.* 2nd ed. New York, University Press of America.

Fritz, Charles E. 1961. Disasters. In *Contemporary social problems,* ed. Robert K. Merton and Robert A. Nisbet, 651–94. New York: Harcourt.

Goltz, James D. 1984. Are the media responsible for the disaster myths? A content analysis of emergency response imagery. *International Journal of Mass Emergencies and Disasters* 2:345–68.

Gugliotta, Guy, and Peter Whoriskey. 2005. Floods ravage New Orleans; two levees give way. *The Washington Post,* August 31, sec. A.

Haddow, George D., and Jane A. Bullock. 2003. *Introduction to emergency management.* New York: Butterworth Heinemann.

Haskell, Bob. 2005. Guard troops put lives on hold to respond to Katrina. American Forces Information Service. September 4. http://www.defenselink.mil/news/Sep2005/20050904_2626.html.

Healey, Gene. 2003. *Deployed in the USA: The creeping militarization of the home front.* Policy Analysis no. 303. Washington, DC: Cato Institute.

Hynes, Kevin. 2005. Security cops patrol devastated Mississippi coast. The National Guard. September 26. http://www.ngb.army.mil/news/story.asp?id=1922.

Johnson, Chalmers. 2004. *The sorrows of empire: Militarism, secrecy, and the end of the republic.* New York: Metropolitan Books.

Kasperson, Jeanne X., and Roger E. Kasperson, eds. 2005. *Social contours of risk.* Vol. 1, *Publics, risk communication and the social amplification of risk.* London: Earthscan.

Laris, Michael. 2005. Responding with money and ammo; as donations pour in, deputies and equipment set out for stricken Gulf Coast. *The Washington Post,* September 2, sec. A.

Lindell, Michael K., and Ronald W. Perry. 1992. *Behavioral foundations of community emergency management.* Washington, DC: Hemisphere.

Lipton Eric, Christopher Drew, Scott Shane, and David Rohde. 2005. Breakdowns marked path from hurricane to anarchy. *The New York Times,* September 11, sec. 1.

Longman, Jere. 2005. Rescuers, going door to door, find stubbornness and silence. *The New York Times,* September 5, sec. A.

MacCash, Doug, and James O'Byrne. 2005. Levee breech floods Lakeview, Mid-City, Carrollton, Gentilly, City Park. *Times-Picayune,* August 30. http://www.nola.com/newslogs/breakingtp/index.ssf?/mtlogs/nola_Times-Picayune/archives/2005_08.html.

McFadden, Robert. 2005. Bush pledges more troops as the evacuation grows. *The New York Times,* September 4, sec. 1.

McFadden, Robert, and Ralph Blumenthal. 2005. Bush sees long recovery for New Orleans; 30,000 troops in largest U.S. relief effort; higher toll seen; evacuation of stadium—Police ordered to stop looters. *The New York Times,* September 1, sec. A.

McGill, Kevin. 2005. Officials throw up hands as looters ransack city. *Times-Picayune*, August 31. http://www.nola.com/newslogs/breakingtp/index.ssf?/mtlogs/nola_Times-Picayune/archives/2005_08.html.

McPhail, Clark. 1991. *The myth of the maddening crowd.* New York: Aldine de Gruyter.

McPhail, Clark, and Ronald Wohlstein. 1983. Individual and collective behavior within gatherings, demonstrations, and riots. *Annual Review of Sociology* 9:579–600.

Mitchell, Jerry T., Deborah S. K. Thomas, Arleen A. Hill, and Susan L. Cutter. 2000. Catastrophe in reel life versus real life: Perpetuating disaster myth through Hollywood films. *International Journal of Mass Emergencies and Disasters* 18:383–402.

National Academy of Public Administration. 1993. *Coping with catastrophe: Building an emergency management system to meet people's needs in natural and manmade disasters.* Washington, DC: National Academy of Public Administration.

Nolan, Bruce. 2005. Coming home; thousands return to Jefferson; more rescued in St. Bernard. *Times-Picayune*, September 6. http://www.nola.com/newslogs/breakingtp/index.ssf?/mtlogs/nola_Times-Picayune/archives/2005_09.html.

Online NewsHour. 2005. Katrina media coverage. September 29. http://www.pbs.org/newshour.

Pew Center. 2005. Two-in-three critical of Bush's relief efforts: Huge racial divide over Katrina and its consequences. September 8. Washington, DC: Pew Center for the People and the Press.

Philbin, Walt. 2005. Widespread looting hits abandoned businesses. *Times-Picayune*, August 30. http://www.nola.com/newslogs/breakingtp/index.ssf?/mtlogs/nola_Times-Picayune/archives/2005_08.html.

Quarantelli, E. L. 1985. Realities and mythologies in disaster films. *Communications: The European Journal of Communication,* 11:31–44.

_____. 1987. Disaster studies: An analysis of the social historical factors affecting the development of research in the area. *International Journal of Mass Emergencies and Disasters* 5 (3): 285–310.

_____. 2006. Looting and other criminal behavior in Hurricane Katrina: Atypical and complex but seen before in other catastrophes. Preliminary paper, University of Delaware, Disaster Research Center, Newark. http://www.udel.edu/DRC.

Quarantelli, E. L., and Russell R. Dynes. 1970. Property norms and looting: Their patterns in community crises. *Phylon* 31:168–82.

_____. 1972. When disaster strikes (it isn't much like what you've heard and read about). *Psychology Today* 5:66–70.

Robinson, Eugene. 2005. Where the good times haven't rolled. Editorial. *The Washington Post,* September 2, sec. A.

Rodríguez, Havidán, Joseph Trainor, and Enrico L. Quarantelli. 2006. Rising to the challenges of a catastrophe: The emergent and prosocial behavior following Hurricane Katrina. *Annals of the American Academy of Political and Social Science* 604:82–101.

Roig-Franzia, Manuel, and Spencer Hsu. 2005. Many evacuated, but thousands still waiting. *The Washington Post,* September 4, A01.

Rubin, Claire, and Irmak Renda-Tenali. 2000. *Disaster timeline: Selected events and outcomes (1965–2000).* Arlington, VA: Claire B. Rubin and Associates.

Scott, Robert Travis. 2005. Late Blanco statement. *Times-Picayune,* August 30. http://www.nola.com/newslogs/breakingtp/index.ssf?/mtlogs/nola_Times-Picayune/archives/2005_08.html.

Shea, Christopher. 2005. Up for grabs; sociologists question how much looting and mayhem really took place in New Orleans. *Boston Globe,* September 11, sec. E.

Smith, Conrad. 1992. *Media and apocalypse: News coverage of the Yellowstone forest fires, the Exxon Valdez oil spill, and Loma Prieta earthquake.* Westport, CT: Greenwood.

Tierney, Kathleen J. 1994. Property damage and violence: A collective behavior analysis. In *The Los Angels Riots: Lessons for the urban future,* ed. Mark Baldessare, 149–73. Boulder, CO: Westview.

_____. 2003. Disaster beliefs and institutional interests: Recycling disaster myths in the aftermath of 9–11. In *Research in social problems and public policy,* vol. 11, *Terrorism and disaster: New threats, new ideas,* ed. Lee Clarke, 33–51. New York: Elsevier Science.

_____. 2004. Collective behavior in times of crisis. Commissioned paper presented at the National Research Council Roundtable on Social and Behavioral Sciences and Terrorism, Meeting 4, "Risk Communication for Terrorism," Washington, DC, National Academies, January 30.

Tierney, Kathleen J., Michael K. Lindell, and Ronald W. Perry. 2001. *Facing the unexpected: Disaster preparedness and response in the Unites States,* Washington, DC: Joseph Henry Press.

Times-Picayune. 2005a. Blanco says evacuation buses on the way to N.O. August 31. http://www.nola.com/newslogs/breakingtp/index.ssf?/mtlogs/nola_Times-Picayune/archives/2005_08.html.

_____. 2005b. Bush stunned by conditions in New Orleans. September 3, sec. A.

_____. 2005c. No fatalities reported. September 24. http://www.nola.com/newslogs/breakingtp/index.ssf?/mtlogs/nola_Times-Picayune/archives/2005_09.html.

Treaster, Joseph, and N. R. Kleinfield. 2005. New Orleans is inundated as 2 levees fail; much of Gulf Coast is crippled; toll rises. *The New York Times,* August 31, sec. A.

Treaster, Joseph, and Deborah Sontag. 2005. Despair and lawlessness grip New Orleans as thousands remain stranded in squalor. *The New York Times,* September 2, sec. A.

Turner, Ralph H. 1994. Rumor as intensified information seeking: Earthquake rumors in China and the United States. In *Disasters, collective behavior, and social organization,* ed. Russell R. Dynes and Kathleen J. Tierney, 244–56. Newark: University of Delaware Press.

U.S. Congress. House Science Committee, Subcommittee on Research. 2005. *The role of social science research in disaster preparedness and response.* Testimony by Shirley Laska, Ph.D. November 10.

Vedantam, Shankar, and Allison Klein. 2005. You wonder why it didn't kill a million; officials upbeat in view of what might have been as survivors recount horror of what is. *The Washington Post,* September 3, sec. A.

Vega, Cecilia M. 2005. As bodies recovered, reporters are told "no photos, no stories." *San Francisco Chronicle,* September 13. http://www.sfgate.com/cgi-bin/article.cgo?file=/c/a/2005/09/13/MNG3HEMQHG1.DTL.

Walters, Lynne M., Lee Wilkins, and Tim Walters, eds. 1989. *Bad tidings: Communication and catastrophe.* Hillsdale, NJ: Lawrence Erlbaum.

Waugh, William L. 2000. *Living with hazards, dealing with disasters: An introduction to emergency management.* New York: M. E. Sharpe.

Wenger, Dennis, James D. Sykes, Thomas D. Sebok, and Joan L. Neff. 1975. It's a matter of myths: An empirical examination of individual insight into disaster response. *Mass Emergencies* 1:33–46.

Williams, Brian. 2005. Making the Quarter rounds. MSN.com, September 7. http://www.msnbc.msn.com/id/9216831/.

Williams, Rudi. 2005. Guard chief describes Katrina response operations. American Forces Information Service. September 4. http://www.defenselink.mil/news/Sep2005/20050904_2613html.

Ziegler, Donald J., Stanley D. Brunn, and James H. Johnson. 1981. Evacuation from a nuclear technological disaster. *Geographical Review* 71:1–16.

 QUESTIONS FOR CRITICAL THINKING

Reading 38

1. The disastrous events of Hurricane Katrina were heavily represented in the media, which covered not only the impact of "natural" events but also the impact of human reaction and response. How does the authors' discussion of media framing help you to understand these events in new and different ways?

2. Many of the ideas discussed by the authors can be applied to the ways in which the media frames a variety of issues. How does this reading help you to understand the ways in which the media frames issues you hear about everyday?

3. Understanding the role of the media in framing issues helps us to become more media literate. How is this useful in understanding how to address problems of social inequality?

Reading 39

RACISM IN THE ENGLISH LANGUAGE

ROBERT B. MOORE

 ## LANGUAGE AND CULTURE

An integral part of any culture is its language. Language not only develops in conjunction with a society's historical, economic and political evolution; it also reflects that society's attitudes and thinking. Language not only *expresses* ideas and concepts but actually *shapes* thought.[1] If one accepts that our dominant white culture is racist, then one would expect our language—an indispensable transmitter of culture—to be racist as well. Whites, as the dominant group, are not subjected to the same abusive characterization by our language that people of color receive. Aspects of racism in the English language that will be discussed in this essay include terminology, symbolism, politics, ethnocentrism, and context.

Before beginning our analysis of racism in language we would like to quote part of a TV film review which shows the connection between language and culture.[2]

> Depending on one's culture, one interacts with time in a very distinct fashion. One example which gives some cross-cultural insights into the concept of time is language. In Spanish, a watch is said to "walk." In English, the watch "runs." In German, the watch "functions." And in French, the watch "marches." In the Indian culture of the Southwest, people do not refer to time in this way. The value of the watch is displaced with the value of "what time it's getting to be." Viewing these five cultural perspectives of time, one can see some definite emphasis and values that each culture places on time. For example, a cultural perspective may provide a clue to why the negative stereotype of the slow and lazy Mexican who lives in the "Land of Manana" exists in the Anglo value system, where time "flies," the watch "runs" and "time is money."

A SHORT PLAY ON "BLACK" AND "WHITE" WORDS

Some may blackly (angrily) accuse me of trying to blacken (defame) the English language, to give it a black eye (a mark of shame) by writing such black words (hostile). They may denigrate (to cast aspersions; to darken) me by accusing me of being blackhearted (malevolent), of having a black outlook (pessimistic, dismal) on life, of being a blackguard (scoundrel)—which would certainly be a black mark (detrimental fact) against me. Some may black-brow (scowl at) me and hope that a black cat crosses in front of me because of this black deed. I may become a black sheep (one who causes shame or embarrassment because of deviation from the accepted standards), who will be blackballed (ostracized) by being placed on a blacklist (list of undesirables) in an attempt to blackmail (to force or coerce into a particular action) me to retract my words. But attempts to blackjack (to compel by threat) me will have a Chinaman's chance of success, for I am not a yellow-bellied Indian-giver of words, who will whitewash (cover up or gloss over vices or crimes) a black lie (harmful, inexcusable). I challenge the purity and innocence (white) of the English language. I don't see things in black and white (entirely bad or entirely good) terms, for I am a white man (marked by upright firmness) if there ever was one. However, it would be a black day when I would not "call a spade a spade," even though some will suggest a white man calling the English language racist is like the pot calling the kettle black. While many may be niggardly (grudging, scanty) in their support, others will be honest and decent—and to them I say, that's very white of you (honest, decent).

The preceding is of course a white lie (not intended to cause harm), meant only to illustrate some examples of racist terminology in the English language.

 OBVIOUS BIGOTRY

Perhaps the most obvious aspect of racism in language would be terms like "nigger," "spook," "chink," "spic," etc. While they may be facing increasing social disdain, they certainly are not dead. Large numbers of white Americans continue to utilize these terms. "Chink," "gook," and "slant-eyes" were in common usage among U.S. troops in Vietnam. An NBC nightly news broadcast, in February 1972, reported that the basketball team in Pekin, Illinois, was called the "Pekin Chinks" and noted that even though this had been protested by Chinese Americans, the term continued to be used because it was easy, and meant no harm. Spiro Agnew's widely reported "fat Jap" remark and the "little Jap" comment of lawyer John Wilson during the Watergate hearings, are surface indicators of a deep-rooted Archie Bunkerism.

Many white people continue to refer to Black people as "colored," as for instance in a July 30, 1975, *Boston Globe* article on a racist attack by whites on a group of Black people using a public beach in Boston. One white person was quoted as follows:

> We've always welcomed good colored people in South Boston but we will not tolerate radical blacks or Communists. . . . Good colored people are welcome in South Boston; black militants are not.

Many white people may still be unaware of the disdain many African Americans have for the term "colored," but it often appears that whether used intentionally or unintentionally, "colored" people are "good" and "know their place," while "Black" people are perceived as "uppity" and "threatening" to many whites. Similarly, the term "boy" to refer to African American men is now acknowledged to be a demeaning term, though still in common use. Other terms such as "the pot calling the kettle black" and "calling a spade a spade" have negative racial connotations but are still frequently used, as for example when President Ford was quoted in February 1976 saying that even though Daniel Moynihan had left the U.N., the U.S. would continue "calling a spade a spade."

 COLOR SYMBOLISM

The symbolism of white as positive and black as negative is pervasive in our culture, with the black/white words used in the beginning of this essay only one of many aspects. "Good guys" wear white hats and ride white horses; "bad guys" wear black hats and ride black horses. Angels are white, and devils are black. The definition of *black* includes "without any moral light or goodness, evil, wicked, indicating disgrace, sinful," while that of *white* includes "morally pure, spotless, innocent, free from evil intent."

A children's TV cartoon program, *Captain Scarlet*, is about an organization called Spectrum, whose purpose is to save the world from an evil extraterrestrial force called the Mysterons. Everyone in Spectrum has a color name—Captain Scarlet, Captain Blue, etc. The one Spectrum agent who has been mysteriously taken over by the Mysterons and works to advance their evil aims is Captain Black. The person who heads Spectrum, the good organization out to defend the world, is Colonel White.

Three of the dictionary definitions of white are "fairness of complexion, purity, innocence." These definitions affect the standards of beauty in our culture, in which whiteness represents the norm. "Blondes have more fun" and "Wouldn't you really rather be a blonde" are sexist in their attitudes toward women generally, but are racist white standards when applied to third world women. A 1971 *Mademoiselle* advertisement pictured a curly-headed, ivory-skinned woman over the caption, "When you go blonde go all the way," and asked: "Isn't this how, in the back of your mind, you always wanted to look? All wide-eyed and silky blonde down to there, and innocent?" Whatever the advertising people meant by this particular woman's innocence, one must remember that "innocent" is one of the definitions of the word white. This standard of beauty when preached to all women is racist. The statement "Isn't this how, in the back of your mind, you always wanted to look?" either ignores third world women or assumes they long to be white.

Time magazine in its coverage of the Wimbledon tennis competition between the black Australian Evonne Goolagong and the white American Chris Evert described Ms. Goolagong as "the dusky daughter of an Australian sheepshearer," while Ms. Evert was "a fair young girl from the middle-class groves of Florida." *Dusky* is a synonym of "black" and is defined as "having dark skin; of a dark color; gloomy; dark; swarthy." Its antonyms are "fair" and "blonde." *Fair* is defined in part as "free from blemish, imperfection, or anything that impairs the appearance, quality, or character; pleasing in appearance, attractive; clean; pretty; comely." By defining Evonne Goolagong as "dusky," *Time* technically defined her as the opposite of "pleasing in appearance; attractive; clean; pretty; comely."

The studies of Kenneth B. Clark, Mary Ellen Goodman, Judith Porter and others indicate that this persuasive "rightness of whiteness" in U.S. culture affects children before the age of four, providing white youngsters with a false sense of superiority and encouraging self-hatred among third world youngsters.

ETHNOCENTRISM OR FROM A WHITE PERSPECTIVE

Some words and phrases that are commonly used represent particular perspectives and frames of reference, and these often distort the understanding of the reader or listener. David R. Burgest[3] has written about the effect of using the terms "slave" or "master." He argues that the psychological impact of the statement referring to "the master raped his slave" is different from the impact of the same statement substituting the words: "the white captor raped an African woman held in captivity."

> Implicit in the English usage of the "master-slave" concept is
> ownership of the "slave" by the "master"; therefore, the "master" is
> merely abusing his property (slave). In reality, the captives (slave)
> were African individuals with human worth, right and dignity and
> the term "slave" denounces that human quality thereby making
> the mass rape of African women by white captors more acceptable
> in the minds of people and setting a mental frame of reference for
> legitimizing the atrocities perpetuated against African people.

The term "slave" connotes a less than human quality and turns the captive person into a thing. For example, two McGraw-Hill Far Eastern Publishers textbooks (1970) stated, "At first it was the slaves who worked the cane and they got only food for it. Now men work cane and get money." Next time you write about slavery or read about it, try transposing all "slaves" into "African people held in captivity," "Black people forced to work for no pay" or "African people stolen from their families and societies." While it is more cumbersome, such phrasing conveys a different meaning.

PASSIVE TENSE

Another means by which language shapes our perspective has been noted by Thomas Greenfield,[4] who writes that the achievements of Black people—and Black people themselves—have been hidden in

> the linguistic ghetto of the passive voice, the subordinate clause, and the "understood" subject. The seemingly innocuous distinction (between active/passive voice) holds enormous implications for writers and speakers. When it is effectively applied, the rhetorical impact of the passive voice—the art of making the creator or instigator of action totally disappear from a reader's perception—can be devastating.

For instance, some history texts will discuss how European immigrants came to the United States seeking a better life and expanded opportunities, but will note that "slaves *were brought* to America." Not only does this omit the destruction of African societies and families, but it ignores the role of northern merchants and southern slaveholders in the profitable trade in human beings. Other books will state that "the continental railroad *was built*," conveniently omitting information about the Chinese laborers who built much of it or the oppression they suffered.

Another example. While touring Monticello, Greenfield noted that the tour guide

> made all the black people at Monticello disappear through her use of the passive voice. While speaking of the architectural achievement of Jefferson in the active voice, she unfailingly shifted to passive when speaking of the work performed by Negro slaves and skilled servants.

Noting a type of door that after 166 years continued to operate without need for repair, Greenfield remarks that the design aspect of the door was much simpler than the actual skill and work involved in building and installing it. Yet his guide stated: "Mr. Jefferson designed these doors . . ." while "the doors **were installed** in 1809." The workers who installed those doors were African people whom Jefferson held in bondage. The guide's use of the passive tense enabled her to dismiss the reality of Jefferson's slaveholding. It also meant that she did not have to make any mention of the skills of those people held in bondage.

POLITICS AND TERMINOLOGY

"Culturally deprived," "economically disadvantaged" and "underdeveloped" are other terms which mislead and distort our awareness of reality. The application of the term "culturally deprived" and third world children in this society reflects a value judgment. It assumes that the dominant whites are cultured and all others without culture. In fact, third world children generally are bicultural, and many are bilingual, having grown up in their own culture as well as absorbing the dominant culture. In many ways, they are equipped with skills and experiences which white youth have been deprived of, since most white youth develop in a monocultural, monolingual environment. Burgest[5] suggests that the term "culturally deprived" be replaced by "culturally dispossessed," and that the term "economically disadvantaged" be replaced by "economically exploited." Both these terms present a perspective and implication that provide an entirely different frame of reference as to the reality of the third world experience in U.S. society.

Similarly, many nations of the third world are described as "underdeveloped." These less wealthy nations are generally those that suffered under colonialism and neocolonialism. The "developed" nations are those that exploited their resources and wealth. Therefore, rather than referring to these countries as "underdeveloped," a more appropriate and meaningful designation might be "over exploited." Again, transpose this term next time you read about "underdeveloped nations" and note the different meaning that results.

Terms such as "culturally deprived," "economically disadvantaged" and "underdeveloped" place the responsibility for their own conditions on those being so described. This is known as "Blaming the Victim."[6] It places responsibility for poverty on the victims of poverty. It removes the blame from those in power who benefit from, and continue to permit, poverty.

Still another example involves the use of "nonwhite," "minority" or "third world." While people of color are a minority in the U.S., they are part of the vast majority of the world's population, in which white people are a distinct minority. Thus, by utilizing the term "minority" to describe people of color in the U.S., we can lose sight of the global majority/minority reality—a fact of some importance in the increasing and interconnected struggles of people of color inside and outside the U.S.

To describe people of color as "nonwhite" is to use whiteness as the standard and norm against which to measure all others. Use of the term "third world" to describe all people of color overcomes the inherent bias of "minority" and "nonwhite." Moreover, it connects the struggles of third world people in the U.S. with the freedom struggles around the globe.

The term "third world" gained increasing usage after the 1955 Bandung Conference of "non-aligned" nations, which represented a third force outside of the two world superpowers. The "first world" represents the United States, Western Europe and their sphere of influence. The "second world" represents the Soviet Union and its sphere. The "third world" represents, for the most part, nations that were, or are, controlled by the "first world" or West. For the most part, these are nations of Africa, Asia and Latin America.

"LOADED" WORDS AND NATIVE AMERICANS

Many words lead to a demeaning characterization of groups of people. For instance, Columbus, it is said, "discovered" America. The word *discover* is defined as "to gain sight or knowledge of something previously unseen or unknown; to discover may be to find some existent thing that was previously unknown." Thus, a continent inhabited by millions of human beings cannot be "discovered." For history books to continue this usage represents a Eurocentric (white European) perspective on world history and ignores the existence of, and the perspective of, Native Americans. "Discovery," as used in the Euro-American context, implies the right to take what one finds, ignoring the rights of those who already inhabit or own the "discovered" thing.

Eurocentrism is also apparent in the usage of "victory" and "massacre" to describe the battles between Native Americans and whites. *Victory* is defined in the dictionary as "a success or triumph over an enemy in battle or war; the decisive defeat of an opponent." *Conquest* denotes the "taking over of control by the victor, and the obedience of the conquered." *Massacre* is defined as "the unnecessary, indiscriminate killing of a number of human beings, as in barbarous warfare or persecution, or for revenge or plunder." *Defend* is described as "to ward off attack from; guard against assault or injury; to strive to keep safe by resisting attack."

Eurocentrism turns these definitions around to serve the purpose of distorting history and justifying Euro-American conquest of the Native American homelands. Euro-Americans are not described in history books as invading Native American lands, but rather as defending *their* homes against "Indian" attacks. Since European communities were constantly encroaching on land already occupied, then a more honest interpretation would state that it was the Native Americans who were "warding off," "guarding" and "defending" their homelands.

Native American victories are invariably defined as "massacres," while the indiscriminate killing, extermination and plunder of Native American nations by Euro-Americans is defined as "victory." Distortion of history by the choice of "loaded" words used to describe historical events is a common racist practice. Rather than portraying Native Americans as human beings in highly defined and complex societies, cultures and civilizations, history books use such adjectives as "savages," "beasts," "primitive," and "backward." Native people are referred to as "squaw," "brave," or "papoose" instead of "woman," "man," or "baby."

Another term that has questionable connotations is *tribe*. The Oxford English Dictionary defines this noun as "a race of people; now applied especially to a primary aggregate of people in a primitive or barbarous condition, under a headman or chief." Morton Fried,[7] discussing "The Myth of Tribe," states that the word "did not become a general term of reference to American Indian society until the nineteenth century. Previously, the words commonly used for Indian populations were 'nation' and 'people.'" Since "tribe" has assumed a connotation of primitiveness or backwardness, it is suggested that the use of "nation" or "people" replace the term whenever possible in referring to Native American peoples.

The term *tribe* invokes even more negative implications when used in reference to American peoples. As Evelyn Jones Rich[8] has noted, the term is "almost always used to refer to third world people and it implies a stage of development which is, in short, a put-down."

"LOADED" WORDS AND AFRICANS

Conflicts among diverse peoples within African nations are often referred to as "tribal warfare," while conflicts among the diverse peoples within European countries are never described in such terms. If the rivalries between the Ibo and the Hausa and Yoruba in Nigeria are described as "tribal," why not the rivalries between Serbs and Slavs in Yugoslavia, or Scots and English in Great Britain, Protestants and Catholics in Ireland, or the Basques and the Southern Spaniards in Spain? Conflicts among African peoples in a particular nation have religious, cultural, economic and/or political roots. If we can analyze the roots of conflicts among European peoples in terms other than "tribal warfare," certainly we can do the same with African peoples, including correct reference to the ethnic groups or nations involved. For example, the terms "Kaffirs," "Hottentot" or "Bushmen" are names imposed by white Europeans. The correct names are always those by which a people refer to themselves. (In these instances Xhosa, Khoi-Khoin and San are correct.[9])

The generalized application of "tribal" in reference to Africans—as well as the failure to acknowledge the religious, cultural and social diversity of African peoples—is a decidedly racist dynamic. It is part of the process whereby Euro-Americans justify, or avoid confronting, their oppression of third world peoples. Africa has been particularly insulted by this dynamic, as witness the pervasive "darkest Africa" image. This image, widespread in Western culture, evokes an Africa covered by jungles and inhabited by "uncivilized," "cannibalistic," "pagan," "savage" peoples. This "darkest Africa" image avoids the geographical reality. Less than 20 percent of the African continent is wooded savanna, for example. The image also ignores the history of African cultures and civilizations. Ample evidence suggests this distortion of reality was developed as a convenient rationale for the European and American slave trade. The Western powers, rather than exploiting, were civilizing and christianizing "uncivilized" and "pagan savages" (so the rationalization went). This dynamic also served to justify

Western colonialism. From Tarzan movies to racist children's books like *Doctor Dolittle* and *Charlie and the Chocolate Factory,* the image of "savage" Africa and the myth of "the white man's burden" has been perpetuated in Western culture.

A 1972 *Time* magazine editorial lamenting the demise of *Life* magazine, stated that the "lavishness" of *Life's* enterprises included "organizing safaris into darkest Africa." The same year, the *New York Times'* C. L. Sulzberger wrote that "Africa has a history as dark as the skins of many of its people." Terms such as "darkest Africa," "primitive," "tribe" ("tribal") or "jungle," in reference to Africa, perpetuate myths and are especially inexcusable in such large circulation publications.

Ethnocentrism is similarly reflected in the term "pagan" to describe traditional religions. A February 1973 *Time* magazine article on Uganda stated, "Moslems account for only 500,000 of Uganda's 10 million people. Of the remainder, 5,000,000 are Christians and the rest pagan." *Pagan* is defined as "Heathen, a follower of a polytheistic religion; one that has little or no religion and that is marked by a frank delight in and uninhibited seeking after sensual pleasures and material goods." *Heathen* is defined as "Unenlightened; an unconverted member of a people or nation that does not acknowledge the God of the Bible. A person whose culture or enlightenment is of an inferior grade, especially an irreligious person." Now, the people of Uganda, like almost all Africans, have serious religious beliefs and practices. As used by Westerners, "pagan" connotes something wild, primitive and inferior—another term to watch out for.

The variety of traditional structures that African people live in are their "houses," not "huts." A *hut* is "an often small and temporary dwelling of simple construction." And to describe Africans as "natives" (noun) is derogatory terminology—as in, "the natives are restless." The dictionary definition of *native* includes: "one of a people inhabiting a territorial area at the time of its discovery or becoming familiar to a foreigner; one belonging to a people having a less complex civilization." Therefore, use of "native," like use of "pagan" often implies a value judgment of white superiority.

QUALIFYING ADJECTIVES

Words that would normally have positive connotations can have entirely different meanings when used in a racial context. For example, C. L. Sulzberger, the columnist of the *New York Times,* wrote in January 1975, about conversations he had with two people in Namibia. One was the white South African administrator of the country and the other a member of SWAPO, the Namibian liberation movement. The first is described as "Dirk Mudge, who as senior elected member of the administration is a kind of acting Prime Minister. . . ." But the second person is introduced as "Daniel Tijongarero, an intelligent Herero tribesman who is a member of SWAPO. . . ." What need was there for Sulzberger to state that Daniel Tijongarero is "intelligent"? Why not also state that Dirk Mudge was "intelligent"—or do we assume he wasn't?

A similar example from a 1968 *New York Times* article reporting on an address by Lyndon Johnson stated, "The President spoke to the well-dressed Negro officials and their wives." In what similar circumstances can one imagine a reporter finding it necessary to note that an audience of white government officials was "well-dressed"?

Still another word often used in a racist context is "qualified." In the 1960s white Americans often questioned whether Black people were "qualified" to hold public office, a question that was never raised (until too late) about white officials like Wallace, Maddox, Nixon, Agnew, Mitchell, et al. The question of qualifications has been raised even more frequently in recent years as white people question whether Black people are "qualified" to be hired for positions in industry and educational institutions. "We're looking for a qualified Black" has been heard again and again as institutions are confronted with affirmative action goals. Why stipulate that Blacks must be "qualified," when for others it is taken for granted that applicants must be "qualified"?

SPEAKING ENGLISH

Finally, the depiction in movies and children's books of third world people speaking English is often itself racist. Children's books about Puerto Ricans or Chicanos often connect poverty with a failure to speak English or to speak it well, thus blaming the victim and ignoring the racism which affects third world people regardless of their proficiency in English. Asian characters speak a stilted English ("Honorable so and so" or "Confucius say") or have a speech impediment ("rots or ruck," "very solly," "flied lice"). Native American characters speak another variation of stilted English ("Boy not hide. Indian take boy."), repeat certain Hollywood-Indian phrases ("Heap big" and "Many moons") or simply grunt out "Ugh" or "How." The repeated use of these language characterizations functions to make third world people seem less intelligent and less capable than the English-speaking white characters.

WRAP UP

A *Saturday Review* editorial[10] on "The Environment of Language" stated that language

> . . . has as much to do with the philosophical and political conditioning of a society as geography or climate . . . people in Western cultures do not realize the extent to which their racial attitudes have been conditioned since early childhood by the

power of words to ennoble or condemn, augment or detract, glorify or demean. Negative language infects the subconscious of most Western people from the time they first learn to speak. Prejudice is not merely imparted or superimposed. It is metabolized in the bloodstream of society. What is needed is not so much a change in language as an awareness of the power of words to condition attitudes. If we can at least recognize the underpinnings of prejudice, we may be in a position to deal with the effects.

To recognize the racism in language is an important first step. Consciousness of the influence of language on our perceptions can help to negate much of that influence. But it is not enough to simply become aware of the effects of racism in conditioning attitudes. While we may not be able to change the language, we can definitely change our usage of the language. We can avoid using words that degrade people. We can make a conscious effort to use terminology that reflects a progressive perspective, as opposed to a distorting perspective. It is important for educators to provide students with opportunities to explore racism in language and to increase their awareness of it, as well as learning terminology that is positive and does not perpetuate negative human values.

NOTES

1. Simon Podair, "How Bigotry Builds Through Language," *Negro Digest,* March 1967.
2. Jose Armas, "Antonio and the Mayor: A Cultural Review of the Film," *The Journal of Ethnic Studies,* Fall 1975.
3. David R. Burgest, "The Racist Use of the English Language," *Black Scholar,* Sept. 1973.
4. Thomas Greenfield, "Race and Passive Voice at Monticello," *Crisis,* April 1975.
5. David R. Burgest, "Racism in Everyday Speech and Social Work Jargon," *Social Work,* July 1973.
6. William Ryan, *Blaming the Victim.* Pantheon Books, 1971.
7. Morton Fried, "The Myth of Tribe," *National History,* April 1975.
8. Evelyn Jones Rich, "Mind Your Language," *Africa Report,* Sept./Oct. 1974.
9. Steve Wolf, "Catalogers in Revolt Against LC's Racist, Sexist Headings," *Bulletin of Interracial Books for Children,* Vol. 6, Nos. 3 & 4, 1975.
10. "The Environment of Language," *Saturday Review,* April 8, 1967.

REFERENCES

Roger Bastide, "Color, Racism and Christianity," *Daedalus,* Spring 1967.

Kenneth J. Gergen, "The Significance of Skin Color in Human Relations," *Daedalus,* Spring 1967.

UNESCO, "Recommendations Concerning Terminology in Education on Race Questions," June 1968.

Lloyd Yabura, "Towards a Language of Humanism," *Rhythm,* Summer 1971.

QUESTIONS FOR CRITICAL THINKING

Reading 39

1. Moore argues that the English language maintains racial inequality through symbolism of white as positive and black as negative. What do you think of his argument?

2. How does your membership in a particular race category influence your understanding of or level of agreement with the author's discussion?

3. Considering the author's discussion, do you think it is possible to reduce or eliminate racial stereotypes in our language?

Reading 40

SELF, IDENTITY, AND THE NAMING QUESTION
Reflections on the Language of Disability

IRVING KENNETH ZOLA

"When I use the word, it means just what I choose it to mean—neither more nor less"

—HUMPTY DUMPTY

1. THE POWER OF NAMING

Language . . . has as much to do with the philosophical and political conditioning of a society as geography or climate . . . people do not realize the extent to which their attitudes have been conditioned to ennoble or condemn, augment or detract, glorify or demean. Negative language inflicts the subconscious of most . . . people from the time they first learn to speak. Prejudice is not merely imparted or superimposed. It is metabolized in the bloodstream of

Irving Kenneth Zola, "Self, Identity, and the Naming Question: Reflections on the Language of Disability" from *Perspectives on Disability,* edited by Mark Nagler (Palo Alto, Calif.: Health Markets Research, 1993). Reprinted with the permission of the author.

society. What is needed is not so much a change in language as an awareness of the power of words to condition attitudes. [1]

A step in this awareness is the recognition of how deep is the power of naming in Western culture. According to the Old Testament, God's first act after saying "Let there be light" was to call the light "Day" and the darkness "Night." Moreover, God's first act after the creation of Adam was to bring in every beast of the field so that Adam could give them names; and "whatsoever Adam called every living creature, that was the name thereof" (Genesis 2:20). Thus what one is called tends "to stick" and any unnaming process is not without its difficulties and consequences [2]. While a name has always connoted some aspect of one's status (e.g., job, location, gender, social class, ethnicity, kinship), the mid-twentieth century seems to be a time when the issue of naming has assumed a certain primacy [3,4]. In the post–World War II era Erik Erikson [5] and Alan Wheelis [6] noted that "Who am I" or the issue of identity had become a major psychological concern of the U.S. population. The writings of C. Wright Mills [7] as well as the Women's Movement [8], however, called attention to the danger of individualizing any issue as only a "personal problem."

The power of naming was thus recognized not only as a personal issue but a political one as well. While social scientists focused more on the general "labeling" process [9–13] and the measurement of attitudes toward people with various chronic diseases and disabilities [14,15], a number of "liberation" or "rights" movements focused on the practical implications. They claimed that language was one of the mechanisms by which dominant groups kept others 'in place' [16,17]. Thus, as minority groups sought to gain more control over their lives, the issue of naming—what they are called—was one of the first battlegrounds. The resolution of this was not always clear-cut. For some, the original stigmas became the banner: Negroes and coloreds become Blacks. For others, only a completely new designation would suffice—a "Ms" has caught on as a form of address but "womyn," "wimmin" have not been so successful in severing the vocabulary connection to "men."

People with disabilities are in the midst of a similar struggle. The struggle is confounded by some special circumstances which mitigate against the easy development of either a disability pride or culture [18,19]. While most minority group members grow up in a recognized subculture and thus develop certain norms and expectations, people with chronic diseases and disabilities are not similarly prepared. The nature of their experience has been toward isolation. The vast majority of people who are born with or acquire such conditions do so within families who neither have these conditions nor associate with others who do. They are socialized into the world of the "normal" with all its values, prejudices, and vocabulary. As one generally attempts to rise out of one's status, there is always an attempt to put this status in some perspective. The statements that one is more than just a Black or a woman, etc., are commonplace. On the other hand, where chronic illness and disability are concerned, this negation is almost total and is tantamount to denial. Proof of successful integration is embodied in such statements as "I *never* think of myself as handicapped" or the supreme compliment, "I *never* think of you as handicapped."

What then of the institutions where too many spend too much of their time—the long-term hospitals, sanitoria, convalescent and nursing homes? These are aptly labeled "total institutions" [20], but "total" refers to their control over our lives, not to the potential fullness they offer. The subcultures formed within such places are largely defensive and designed to make life viable within the institution. Often this viability is achieved at such a cost that it cannot be transferred to the non-institutional world.

For most of their history, organizations of people with disabilities were not much more successful in their efforts to produce a viable subculture. Their memberships have been small in comparison to the potential disabled population, and they have been regarded more as social groups rather than serious places to gain technical knowledge or emotional support. And though there are some self-help groups which are becoming increasingly visible, militant and independent of medical influence, the movement is still in its infancy [21]. Long ago, Talcott Parsons articulated the basic dilemma facing such groups:

> The sick role is . . . a mechanism which . . . channels deviance
> so that the two most dangerous potentialities, namely group
> formation and successful establishment of the claim of legitimacy,
> are avoided. The sick are tied up, not with other deviants to form
> a "subculture" of the sick but each with a group of nonsick, his
> personal circle, and, above all, physicians. The sick thus become
> a statistical status and are deprived of the possibility of forming a
> solidary collectivity. Furthermore, to be sick is by definition to be
> in an undesirable state, so that it simply does not "make sense" to
> assert a claim that the way to deal with the frustrating aspects of
> the social system is for everyone to get sick [22, p. 477].

A mundane but dramatic way of characterizing this phenomenon can be seen in the rallying cries of current liberation movements. As the "melting pot" theory of America was finally buried, people could once again say, even though they were three generations removed from the immigrants, that they were proud to be Greek, Italian, Hungarian, or Polish. With the rise of black power, a derogatory label became a rallying cry, "Black is beautiful." And when women saw their strength in numbers, they shouted "Sisterhood is powerful." But what about those with a chronic illness or disability? Could they yell, "Long live cancer," "Up with multiple sclerosis," "I'm glad I had polio!"? "Don't you wish you were blind!" Thus, the tradition reversing of the stigma will not so easily provide a basis for a common positive identity.

2. SOME NEGATIVE FUNCTIONS OF LABELING

The struggle over labels often follows a pattern. It is far easier to agree on terms that should *not* be used than the designations that should replace them [23–25]. As with the racial, ethnic [26] and gender groups [27,28] before them, many had begun to note the negative qualities of certain "disability references" [29,30]. Others created quite useful glossaries [31].

Since, as Phillips [32] notes, the names one calls oneself reflect differing political strategies, we must go beyond a list of "do's" and "don'ts" to an analysis of the functions of such labeling [33–36]. As long ago as 1651, Thomas Hobbes—in setting his own social agenda—saw the importance of such clarifications, "seeing then that truth consists in the right ordering of names in our affirmations, a man that seeks precise truth has need to remember what every name he uses stands for; and to place it accordingly; or else he will find himself entangled in words as a bird in lime twigs; the more he struggles the more belimed" [37, p. 26].

There are at least two separate implications of such naming which have practical and political consequences. The first is connotational and associational. As Kenneth Burke [38, p. 4] wrote, "Call a man a villain and you have the choice of either attacking or avenging. Call him mistaken and you invite yourself to attempt to set him right." I would add, "Call a person sick or crazy and all their behavior becomes dismissable." Because someone has been labeled ill, all their activity and beliefs—past, present, and future—become related to and explainable in terms of their illness [20,39]. Once this occurs, society can deny the validity of anything which they might say, do, or stand for. Being seen as the object of medical treatment evokes the image of many ascribed traits, such as weakness, helplessness, dependency, regressiveness, abnormality of appearance and depreciation of every mode of physical and mental functioning [17,40,41]. In the case of a person with a chronic illness and/or a permanent disability, these traits, once perceived to be temporary accompaniments of an illness, become indelible characteristics. "The individual is trapped in a state of suspended animation socially, is perpetually a patient, is chronically viewed as helpless and dependent, in need of cure but incurable" [17, p. 420].

A second function of labeling is its potential for spread, pervasiveness, generalization. An example of such inappropriate generalizing was provided in a study by Conant and Budoff [42]. They found that a group of sighted children and adults interpreted the labels "blind" and "legally blind" as meaning that the person was totally without vision—something which is true for only a small segment of people with that designation. What was problematic became a given. Another example of this process occurs when disability and person are equated. While it is commonplace to hear of doctors referring to people as "the appendicitis in Room 306" or "the amputee down the hall," such labeling is more common in popular culture than one might believe. My own analysis of the crime-mystery genre [43] noted that after an introductory description of characters with a disability, they are often referred to by their disability—e.g., "the dwarf," "the blind man," "the one armed," the "one-legged." This is usually done by some third person observer or where the person with the disability is the speaker. The disability is emphasized—e.g., "said the blind man." No other physical or social descriptor appears with such frequency.

Perhaps not unexpectedly, such stand-in appellations are most commonly applied to villains. They were commonplace during the heyday of the pulp magazines, where the disability was incorporated into their names—"One-Eyed Joe," "Scarface Kelly"—a tradition enshrined in the Dick Tracy comic strips. It is a tradition that continues, though with more subtlety. Today we may no longer have "Clubfoot the Avenger," a mad German master-criminal who crossed swords for 25 years with the British Secret Service [44–51], but we do have "The Deaf Man," the recurring thorn in the side of Ed McBain's long-running (over 30 years) 87th Precinct novels [52–54]. All such instances can reinforce an association between disability, evil, and abnormality [55].

A very old joke illustrates the pervasiveness of such labeling:

> A man is changing a flat tyre (sic) outside a mental hospital when the bolts from his wheel roll down a nearby sewer. Distraught, he is confronted by a patient watching him who suggests, "Why don't you take one bolt off each of the other wheels, and place it on the spare?" Surprised when it works, the driver says, "How come you of all people would think of that?" Replies the patient, "I may be crazy, but I'm not stupid."

This anecdote demonstrates the flaw in thinking that a person who is mad is therefore stupid or incapable of being insightful. As the social psychological literature has long noted, this is how stigma comes about—from a process of generalizing from a single experience, people are treated categorically rather than individually and are devalued in the process [56–58]. As Longmore so eloquently concludes, a "spoiling process" [59] results whereby "they obscure all other characteristics behind that one and swallow up the social identity of the individual within that restrictive category" [17, p. 419]. Peters puts it most concretely: "The label that's used to describe us is often far more important in shaping our view of ourselves—and the way others view us—than whether we sign, use a cane, sit in a wheelchair, or use a communication board" [23, p. 25].

While many have offered vocabulary suggestions to combat the above problems of connotation and pervasiveness, few have analytically delineated what is at stake in such name changes [17,60,61]. The most provocative and historically rooted analysis is an unpublished paper by Phillips [32] who delineates four distinct strategies which underlie the renaming. While she carefully notes that further investigation may change or expand her categorization, the very idea of her schema and the historical data describing the genesis of each "recoding" remain timely.

"Cripple" and "handicapped," as nouns or adjectives, she sees as primarily "names of acquiescence and accommodation," reflecting an acceptance of society's oppressive institutions. Terms such as "physically challenged" by so personalizing the disability run the risk of fostering a "blaming the victim" stance [62]. Such terms, as well as "physically different," "physically inconvenienced," not only may be so euphemistic that they confound the public as to who is being discussed but also contribute strongly to the denial of existing realities [33]. Two other strategies represent a more activist philosophy. "Handicapper" and "differently-abled" are "names of reaction and reflection" whose purpose is to emphasize "the can-do" aspects of having a disability. To the group of Michigan advocates who coined the term [63], a "Handicapper" determines the degree to which one's own physical or mental characteristics direct life's activities. Anger, says Phillips, is basic to "names of renegotiation and inversion" where the context sets the meaning. Perhaps the best examples occur when disability activists, in the privacy of their own circles, "talk dirty," referring to themselves as "blinks," "gimps," or telling "crip" jokes and expounding on the intricacies of "crip" time. More controversy arises, however, when people publicly proclaim such terms as a matter of pride. Recently, for example, many have written about the positive aspects of "being deaf" [64,65] or, even more dramatically of being a "cripple" [66]. Kriegel [60,61] says that "cripple" describes "an essential reality," a way of keeping what needs to be dealt with socially and politically in full view. Nancy Mairs [67], a prize-winning poet who has multiple sclerosis, clearly agrees; and in the opening remarks of her essay, "On Being a Cripple," states it most vividly:

> The other day I was thinking of writing an essay on being a cripple. I was thinking hard in one of the stalls of the women's room in my office building, as I was shoving my shirt into my jeans and tugging up my zipper. Preoccupied, I flushed, picked up my book bag, took my cane down from the hook, and unlatched the door. So many movements unbalanced me, and as I pulled the door open, I fell over backwards, landing fully clothed on the toilet seat with legs splayed in front of me: the old beetle-on-its-back routine. Saturday afternoon, the building deserted, I was free to laugh aloud as I wriggled back to my feet, my voice bouncing off the yellowish tiles from all directions. Had anyone been there with me, I'd have been still and faint and hot with chagrin.
>
> I decided that it was high time to write the essay. First, the matter of semantics. I am a cripple. I choose this word to name me. I choose from among several possibilities, the most common of which are handicapped and disabled. I made the choice a number of years ago, without thinking, unaware of my motives for doing

so. Even now, I'm not sure what those motives are, but I recognize that they are complex and not entirely flattering. People—crippled or not—wince at the word cripple, as they do not at handicapped or disabled. Perhaps I want them to wince. I want them to see me as a tough customer, one to whom the fates/gods/viruses have not been kind, but who can face the brutal truth of her existence squarely. As a cripple, I swagger [67, p. 9].

When Phillips' very titles may imply an evaluation of the particular strategies, it is clear from her own caveats that while many may try to impose their terminology as "the correct language," "None feel really right" [23, p. 25].

 ## 3. RECONTEXTUALIZING NAMES

The ultimate question, of course, is whether any of these renaming procedures, singly and alone, can deal with the connotational and generalization issues discussed previously. I would argue that the context of usage may be every bit as important (as Phillips implies) as the specific terminology. Thus one of the reasons for all the negative associations to many terms is a result of such contexts. Here social scientists, researchers and clinicians are particularly at fault in the medicalizing of disability [55,68,69]. In their writings and in the transmission of these writings by the popular press and media, people with varying diseases and disabilities are inevitably referred to as "patients," a term which describes a role, a relationship and a location (i.e., an institution or hospital) from which many connotations, as previously noted, flow. For the 43 million people now designated as having a physical, mental or biological disability, only a tiny proportion are continually resident in and under medical supervision and are thus truly patients. Similarly, the terms "suffering from," "afflicted with" are projections and evaluations of an outside world. No person with a disability is automatically "suffering" or "afflicted" except in specific situations where they do indeed "hurt," are "in pain," or "feel victimized."

I am not arguing, however, for the complete elimination of medical or physical terminology. As DeFelice cautions, "The disabled movement has purchased political visibility at the price of physical invisibility. The crippled and lame had bodies, but the handicapped, or so the social workers say, are just a little late at the starting gate. I don't like that: it's banal. When we speak in metaphorical terms, we deny physical reality. The farther we get from our bodies, the more removed we are from the body politic . . ." [70].

One meaning I derive from his caution is that we must seek a change in the connotations and the pervasiveness of our names without denying the essential reality of our conditions. Thus biology may not determine our destiny, but, as with women, our physical, mental and biological differences are certainly part of that destiny [71,72].

A way of contextualizing our relationship to our bodies and our disabilities may not be in changing terms but in changing grammars. Our continual use of nouns and adjectives can only perpetuate the equation of the individual equaling the disability. No matter what noun we use, it substitutes one categorical definition for another. An adjective colors and thus connotes the essential quality of the noun it modifies. Such adjectives as "misshapen," "deformed," "defective," "invalid"—far from connoting a specific quality of the individual—tend to taint the whole person.

The same is true with less charged terms. Thus "a disabled car" is one which has totally broken down. Could "a disabled person" be perceived as anything less? Prepositions, on the other hand, imply both "a relationship to" and "a separation from." At this historical juncture the awkwardness in phrasing that often results may be all to the good, for it makes both user and hearer stop and think about what is meant, as in the phrases "people *of* color" and "persons *with* disabilities."

Distance and relationship are also at the heart of some very common verb usages. The first is between the active and passive tense. Note the two dictionary meanings:

Active   asserting that the person or thing represented by the grammatical subjects performs the action represented by the verb [73, p. 12].

Passive asserting that the grammatical subject to a verb is subjected to or affected by the action represented by that verb [73, p. 838].

Thus in describing an individual's relationship to an assistive device such as a wheelchair, the difference between "being confined to a wheelchair" and "using" one is a difference not only of terminology but of control. Medical language has long perpetuated this "disabled passivity" by its emphasis on what medicine continually *does* to its "patients" rather than *with* them [74,75].

Similarly the issues of "connotation" and "pervasiveness" may be perpetuated by the differential use of the verbs "be" and "have." The French language makes careful distinctions between when to use "etre" (be) and when to use "avoir" (have). English daily usage is blurry, but another look at Webster's does show the possibilities:

be   to equal in meaning; to have same connotation as; to have identity with; to constitute the same class as [73, p. 96].

have   to hold in possession; to hold in one's use; to consist of; to stand in relationship to; to be marked or characterized by; to experience; SYN—to keep, control, retain, or experience [73, p. 526].

Like the issue of nouns versus prepositions, verbs can also code people in terms of categories (e.g., X is a redhead) instead of specific attributes (e.g., X has red hair), allowing people to feel that the stigmatized persons are fundamentally different and establishing greater psychological and social distance [76]. Thus, as between the active and passive tense, so it is between "I am . . ." Both specify a difference in distance and control in relation to whatever it is one "is" or "has." And since renaming relates to alternative images of distance and control, grammar, which tends to be normative, concise, shared and long-lasting, may serve us better than sheer name change. Though I personally may have a generic preference (e.g., for "disability" over "handicap"), I am not arguing for any "politically correct" usage but rather examining the political advantages and disadvantages of each [36].

For example, there may be stages in the coping with a particular condition or in the perceived efficacy of a particular "therapy" (e.g., the 12 steps in Alcoholics Anonymous) when "ownership" and thus the use of "I am" is deemed essential. Those old enough to remember President Kennedy's words at the Berlin Wall, *"Ich bin ein Berliner"* (I am a Berliner), will recall the power of its message of kinship. Similarly, when we politically strategize as a minority group [77] and seek a kinship across disease and disability groups [78], the political coming-out may require a personal ownership best conveyed in terms of "I am . . ."

On the other hand, there are times when the political goals involve groups for whom disease and disability is not a permanent or central issue. On my university campus, for a myriad of reasons, people with mobility impairments are virtually non-existent. Yet we are gradually retrofitting old buildings and guaranteeing accessibility in new ones. The alliance here is among women who are or may become pregnant, parents with small children, people with injuries or time-limited diseases, and others who perceive themselves at risk, such as aging staff or faculty. They rarely see themselves as disabled but often admit to having a temporary disability or sharing a part of "the disabled experience" (e.g., "Now I know what it's like to try to climb all those stairs"). Thus where coalition politics is needed, the concept of "having" versus "being" may be a more effective way of acknowledging multiple identities and kinship, as in our use of hyphenated personal and social lineages—e.g., Afro-American.

4. A FINAL CAVEAT

One of the sad findings in Phillips' study [32] is how divisive this struggle over names has become. People thus begin to chastise "non true-believers" and emphasize to others "politically correct" usage. In so doing, we may not only damage the unity so necessary to the cause of disability rights but also fail to see the forest for the trees. Our struggle is necessary because we live in a society which devalues, discriminates against and disparages people with disabilities [77,79]. It is not our task to prove that we are worthy of the full resources and integration of our society. The fault is not in us, not in our diseases and disabilities [41,62,80,81] but in mythical denials, social arrangement, political priorities and prejudices [82].

Here too, a renaming can be of service not of us but of our oppressors [83]. As Hughes and Hughes [84] note, when we turn the tables and create epithets for our oppressors, this may be a sign of a beginning cohesiveness. Thus the growing popularity of terms like TABs and MABs (temporarily or momentarily able-bodied) to describe the general population breaks down the separateness of "us" and "them" and emphasizes the continuity and inevitability of "the disability experience." Thus, too, those who have created the terms "handicappism" [85] and "healthism" [68,86,87] equate these with all the structural "-isms" in a society which operates to continue segregation and discrimination. To return finally to the issue of naming, the words of Philip Dunne reflect well the choices and consequences of language:

> If we hope to survive in this terrifying age, we must choose our words as we choose our actions. We should think how what we say might sound to other ears as well as to our own. Above all, we should strive for clarity . . . if clarity [is] the essence of style, it is also the heart and soul of truth, and it is for want of truth that human freedom could perish [88, p. 14].

NOTES

1. *Saturday Review,* Editorial, April 8, 1967.
2. LeGuin, U. K. She unnames them. *New Yorker,* January 21, p. 27, 1985.
3. Friedrich, O. What's in a name? *Time,* p. 16, August 18, 1986.
4. Vickery, H. Finding the right name for brand X. *Insight,* pp. 54–55, January 27, 1986.
5. Erikson, H. *Childhood and Society.* New York: Norton, 1950.
6. Wheelis, A. *The Quest for Identity.* New York: Norton, 1958.
7. Mills, C. W. *The Sociological Imagination.* Oxford: Oxford University Press, 1959.
8. Boston Women's Health Book Collective. *Women and Our Bodies* (In later revised versions, *Our Bodies Ourselves*). Boston: New England Free Press, 1970.
9. Becker, H. *Outsiders.* Glencoe, IL: The Free Press, 1963.
10. Becker, H. (Ed.) *The Other Side—Perspectives on Deviance.* Glencoe, IL: The Free Press, 1964.
11. Erikson, K. Notes on the sociology of deviance. *Social Problems* 9, 307–314, 1962.
12. Erikson, K. *Wayward Puritans: A Study in the Sociology of Deviance.* New York: Wiley, 1966.
13. Schur, E. *Crimes Without Victims.* Englewood Cliffs, N.J.: Prentice-Hall, 1965.
14. Siller, J. The measurement of attitudes toward physically disabled persons. In *Physical Appearance, Stigma, and Social Behavior: The Ontario Symposium* (Edited by Herman, P. D.; Zanna M. P.; and Higgins E. T.), Vol. 3, pp. 245–288. Lawrence Hillsdale, NJ: Enbaum Associates, 1986.
15. Yuker, H.; Block, J. Z., and Young, J. H. *The Measurement of Attitudes Toward Disabled Persons.* Albertson, NY: Human Resources Center, 1966.
16. Gumperz, J. J. (Ed.) *Language and Social Identity.* Cambridge: Cambridge University Press, 1982.
17. Longmore, P. K. A Note on language and the social identity of disabled people. *America Behavior Scientific* 28, (3), 419–423, 1985.

18. Johnson, M. Emotion and pride: the search for a disability culture. *Disability Rag,* January/February, pp. 1, 4–10, 1987.

19. Zola, I. K. Whose voice is this anyway? A commentary on recent collections about the experience of disability. *Medical Human Revision* 2 (1), 6–15, 1988.

20. Goffman, E. *Asylums,* New York: Anchor, 1961.

21. Crew, N., and Zola, I. K. et al. *Independent Living for Physically Disabled People.* San Francisco: Jossey-Bass, 1983.

22. Parsons, T. *The Social System.* Glencoe: The Free Press, 1951.

23. Peters, A. Developing a language. *Disability Rag.* March/April, 1986, p. 25.

24. Peters, A. The problem with 'Gimp'. *Disability Rag.* July/August, 1986, p. 22.

25. Peters, A. Do we have to be named? *Disability Rag,* November/December, 1986, pp. 31, 35.

26. Moore, R. B. *Racism in the English Language—A Lesson Plan and Study Essay.* The Council of Interracial Books for Children, New York, 1976.

27. Shear, M. Equal writes. *Womens Revision Book 1* (11), 12–13, 1984.

28. Shear, M. Solving the great pronoun debate. *Ms.* pp. 106, 108–109, 1985.

29. Biklen, D., and Bogdan, R. Disabled—yes; handicapped—no: The language of disability, p. 5, insert in "Media Portrayals of Disabled People: A Study in Stereotypes." *Interracial Books Children Bull* 8 (3, 6, 7), 4–9, 1977.

30. Corcoran, P. J. Pejorative terms and attitudinal barriers—editorial. *Architectural Physics Medical Rehabilitation,* 58, 500, 1977.

31. Shear, M. No more supercrip. *New Directions for Women,* p. 10, November–December 1986.

32. Phillips, M. J. What we call ourselves: Self-referential naming among the disabled. *Seventh Annual Ethnography in Research Forum.* University of Pennsylvania. Philadelphia. 4–6, April 1986.

33. Chaffee, N. L. Disabled . . . handicapped . . . and in the image of God?—Our language reflects societal attitudes and influences theological perception. Unpublished paper, 1987.

34. Gill, C. J. The disability name game. *New World for Persons with Disabilities* 13 (8), 2, 1987.

35. Gillet, P. The power of words—can they make you feel better or worse? *Accent on Living,* pp. 38–39, 1987.

36. Lindsey, K. The pitfalls of politically correct language. *Sojourner,* p. 16, 1985.

37. Hobbes, T. *Leviathan.* New York: Dutton, 1950.

38. Burke, K. *Attitudes Toward History,* revised ed. Hermes, Oakland, CA, 1959.

39. Ling, B. G., Cullen, F. T., Frank, J. and Wozniak, J. F. The social rejection of former mental patients: Understanding why labels matter. *American Journal Sociology* 1987, 92 (6), 1,461–1,500, 1987.

40. Goodwin, D. Language: Perpetualizing the myths. *Impact, Inc.* (Newsletter of Center for Independent Living, Alton, IL.). Vol. 1, No. 2, pp. 1–2, 1986.

41. Zola, I. K. *Missing Pieces: A Chronicle of Living with a Disability.* Philadelphia: Temple University Press, 1982.

42. Conant, S. and Budoff, M. The development of sighted people's understanding of blindness. *Journal Visual Impairment Blindness* 76, 86–96, 1982.

43. Zola, I. K. Any distinguishing features: Portrayal of disability in the crime-mystery genre. *Policy Studying Journal* 15 (3), 485–513, 1987.

44. Williams, V. *The Man with the Clubfoot.* London: Jenkins, 1918.

45. Williams, V. *The Secret Hand.* London: Jenkins, 1918.

46. Williams, V. *Return of Clubfoot.* London: Jenkins, 1918.
47. Williams, V. *Clubfoot the Avenger.* London: Jenkins, 1924.
48. Williams, V. *The Crouching Beast.* London: Hodder & Stoughton, 1928.
49. Williams, V. *The Gold Comfit Box.* London: Hodder & Stoughton, 1932.
50. Williams, V. *The Spider's Touch.* London: Hodder & Stoughton, 1936.
51. Williams, V. *Courier to Marrakesh.* London: Hodder & Stoughton, 1944.
52. McBain, E. *Fuzz.* New York: Doubleday, 1968.
53. McBain, E. *Let's Hear It for the Deaf Man.* New York: Random House, 1973.
54. McBain, E. *Eight Black Horses.* New York: Avon, 1985.
55. Conrad, P. and Schneider, J. W. *Deviance and Medicalization: From Badness to Sickness.* C. V. St. Louis: Mosby, 1980.
56. Ainlay, S. C., Becker, G., and Coleman, L. M. (Eds). *The Dilemma of Difference: A Multidisciplinary View of Stigma.* New York: Plenum, 1986.
57. Jones, E. E.; Farina, A.; Hastorf, A. H.; Markus, H.; Miller, D.; and Scott R. *Social Stigma: The Psychology of Marked Relationships.* New York: W. H. Freeman, 1984.
58. Katz, I. *Stigma: A Social Psychological Analysis.* Hillsdale, NJ: Lawrence Erlbaum Associates, 1981.
59. Goffman, E. *Stigma: Notes on the Management of Spoiled Identity.* Prentice-Hall, NJ: Englewood Cliffs, 1963.
60. Kriegel, L. Uncle Tom and Tiny Tim: Reflection on the cripple as Negro. *American Scholar* 38, 412–430, 1969.
61. Kriegel L. Coming through manhood, disease and the authentic self. In: *Rudely Stamp'd: Imaginal Disability and Prejudice* (edited by Bicklen, D. and Bailey, L.), pp. 49–63. Washington, D.C.: University Press of America, 1981.
62. Ryan, W. *Blaming the Victim.* New York: Pantheon, 1970.
63. Gentile, E., and Taylor, J. K. Images, words and identity. Handicapper Programs. Michigan State University, East Lansing, MI, 1976.
64. *Disability Rag.* Cochlear implants: The final put-down. March/April, pp. 1, 4–8, 1987.
65. Innerst, C. A. Will to preserve deaf culture. *Insight.* November 24, pp. 50–51, 1986.
66. Milam, L. *The Crippled Liberation Front Marching Band Blues.* San Diego: MHO and MHO Works, 1984.
67. Mairs, N. On being a cripple. In *Plaintest: Essays,* pp. 9–20. Tucson, AZ: University of Arizona Press, 1986.
68. Zola, I. K. Medicine as an institution of social control. *Social Revenue.* 20, 487–504, 1972.
69. Illich, I. *Medical Nemesis: The Expropriation of Health.* London: Calder & Boyars, 1975.
70. DeFelice, R. J. A crippled child grows up. *Newsweek,* November 3, p. 13, 1986.
71. Fine, M., and Asch, A. Disabled women: Sexism without the pedestal. *Journal Social Society Welfare* 8(2), 233–248, 1981.
72. Fine, M., and Asch, A. (Eds). *Women with Disabilities—Essays in Psychology, Culture, and Politics.* Philadelphia: Temple University Press, 1988.
73. *Webster's New Collegiate Dictionary.* Springfield, MA: Merriam, 1973.
74. Edelman, M. The political language of the helping professions. In *Political Language,* pp. 59–68. New York: Academic, 1977.
75. Szasz, T. S., and Hollender, M. H. A contribution to the philosophy of medicine: The basic models of the doctor-patient relationship. *AMA Arch. Internal Media* 97, 585–592, 1956.

76. Crocker, J. and Lutsky, N. Stigma and the dynamics of social cognition. In *The Dilemma of Difference: A Multidisciplinary View of Stigma* (Edited by Ainlay, S. C.), pp. 95–121. New York: Plenum, 1986.

77. Hahn, H. Disability policy and the problem of discrimination. *American Behaviour Scientist* 28, 293–318, 1985.

78. Harris, L. et al. *Disabled Americans' Self Perceptions: Bringing Disabled Americans into the Mainstream.* Study No. 854009. New York: International Center for the Disabled, 1986.

79. Scotch, R. K. *From Goodwill to Civil Rights: Transforming Federal Disability Policy.* Philadelphia: Temple University Press, 1984.

80. Crawford, R. You are dangerous to your health: the ideology of politics of victim blaming. *International Journal of Health Services* 7, 663–680, 1977.

81. Crawford, R. Individual responsibility and health politics. In *Health Care in America: Essays in Social History* (Edited by Reverby, S. and Rosner, D.), pp. 247–268. Philadelphia: Temple University Press, 1979.

82. Gleidman, J. and Roth, W. *The Unexpected Minority: Handicapped Children in America.* New York: Harcourt, Brace, Jovanovich, 1980.

83. Saxton, M. A. Peer counseling training program for disabled women. *Journal of Social Society Welfare* 8, 334–346, 1981.

84. Hughes, E. and Hughes, H. M. "What's in a name." In *Where People Meet—Racial and Ethnic Frontiers,* pp. 130–144. Glencoe, IL: The Free Press, 1952.

85. Bogdan, R. and Biklen, D. "Handicappism." *Social Policy,* pp. 14–19, March/April, 1977.

86. Crawford, R. Healthism and the medicalization of everyday life. *International Journal of Health Services,* 10, 365–388, 1980.

87. Zola, I. K. Healthism and disabling medicalization. In *Disabling Professions* (Edited by Illich, I.; Zola, I. K.; McKnight, J.; Caplan, J.; and Shaiken, H.), pp. 41–69. London, Marion Boyars, 1977.

88. Dunne, P. Faith, hope, and clarity. *Harvard Magazine* 88 (4), 10–14, 1986.

QUESTIONS FOR CRITICAL THINKING

Reading 40

1. Zola argues that those who occupy marginalized groups are not often given the opportunity to name themselves. How do you think this helps to maintain the oppression of marginalized groups?

2. Have you experienced names being imposed upon you by others with greater social power? How does this impact your sense of self?

3. What resistance have you seen to efforts of members of marginalized groups (e.g., women, people of color, people with disabilities, etc.) to name themselves? What are some ways that we can reduce such resistance?

Reading 41

HOW TO TAME A WILD TONGUE

GLORIA ANZALDÚA

We're going to have to control your tongue," the dentist says, pulling out all the metal from my mouth. Silver bits plop and tinkle into the basin. My mouth is a motherlode.

The dentist is cleaning out my roots. I get a whiff of the stench when I gasp. "I can't cap that tooth yet; you're still draining," he says.

"We're going to have to do something about your tongue," I hear the anger rising in his voice. My tongue keeps pushing out the wads of cotton, pushing back the drills, the long thin needles. "I've never seen anything as strong or as stubborn," he says. And I think, how do you tame a wild tongue, train it to be quiet, how do you bridle and saddle it? How do you make it lie down?

"Who is to say that robbing a people of its language is less violent than war?"
—RAY QWYN SMITH[1]

I remember being caught speaking Spanish at recess—that was good for three licks on the knuckles with a sharp ruler. I remember being sent to the corner of the classroom for "talking back" to the Anglo teacher when all I was trying to do was tell her how to pronounce my name. "If you want to be American, speak 'American.' If you don't like it, go back to Mexico where you belong."

"I want you to speak English. *Pa' hallar buen trabajo tienes que saber hablar el inglés bien. Qué vale toda in educación si todavía hablas inglés con un* 'accent,'" my mother would say, mortified that I spoke English like a Mexican. At Pan American University, I, and all Chicano students were required to take two speech classes. Their purpose: to get rid of our accents.

Attacks on one's form of expression with the intent to censor are a violation of the First Amendment. *El Anglo con cara de inocente nos arrancó la lengua.* Wild tongues can't be tamed; they can only be cut out.

OVERCOMING THE TRADITION OF SILENCE

Abogadas, escupimos el oscuro.
Peleando con nuestra propia sombra
el silencio nos sepulta.

En boca cerrada no entran moscas. "Flies don't enter a closed mouth" is a saying I kept hearing when I was a child. *Ser habladora* was to be a gossip and a liar, to talk too much. *Muchachitas bien criadas,* well-bred girls don't answer back. *Es una falta de respeto* to talk back to one's mother or father. I remember one of the sins I'd recite to the priest in the confession box the few times I went to confession: talking back to my mother, *hablar pa' 'tras, repelar. Hocicona, repelona, chismosa,* having a big mouth, questioning, carrying tales are all signs of being *mal criada.* In my culture they are all words that are derogatory if applied to women—I've never heard them applied to men.

The first time I heard two women, a Puerto Rican and a Cuban, say the word "*nosotras,*" I was shocked. I had not known the word existed. Chicanas use *nosotros* whether we're male or female. We are robbed of our female being by the masculine plural. Language is a male discourse.

And our tongues have become
dry the wilderness has
dried out our tongues and
we have forgotten speech.

—Irena Klepfisz[2]

Even our own people, other Spanish speakers *nos quieren poner candados en la boca.* They would hold us back with their bag of *reglas de academia.*

OYÉ COMO LADRA: EL LENGUAJE DE LA FRONTERA

Quien tiene boca se equivoca.

—Mexican Saying

"*Pocho,* cultural traitor, you're speaking the oppressor's language by speaking English; you're ruining the Spanish language," I have been accused by various Latinos and Latinas. Chicano Spanish is considered by the purist and by most Latinos deficient, a mutilation of Spanish.

But Chicano Spanish is a border tongue which developed naturally. Change, *evolución, enriquecimiento de palabras nuevas por invención o adopción* have created variants of Chicano Spanish, *un nuevo lenguaje. Un lenguaje que corresponde a un modo de vivir.* Chicano Spanish is not incorrect; it is a living language.

For a people who are neither Spanish nor live in a country in which Spanish is the first language; for a people who live in a country in which English is the reigning tongue but who are not Anglo; for a people who cannot entirely identify with either standard (formal, Castillian) Spanish nor standard English, what recourse is left to them but to create their own language? A language which they can connect their identity to, one capable of communicating the realities and values true to themselves—a language with terms that are neither *español ni inglés,* but both. We speak a patois, a forked tongue, a variation of two languages.

Chicano Spanish sprang out of the Chicanos' need to identify ourselves as a distinct people. We needed a language with which we could communicate with ourselves, a secret language. For some of us, language is a homeland closer than the Southwest—for many Chicanos today live in the Midwest and the East. And because we are a complex, heterogeneous people, we speak many languages. Some of the languages we speak are:

1. Standard English
2. Working class and slang English
3. Standard Spanish
4. Standard Mexican Spanish
5. North Mexican Spanish dialect
6. Chicano Spanish (Texas, New Mexico, Arizona and California have regional variations)
7. Tex-Mex
8. *Pachuco* (called *caló*)

My "home" tongues are the languages I speak with my sister and brothers, with my friends. They are the last five listed, with 6 and 7 being closest to my heart. From school, the media and job situations, I've picked up standard and working class English. From Mamagrande Locha and from reading Spanish and Mexican literature, I've picked up Standard Spanish and Standard Mexican Spanish. From *los recién llegados,* Mexican immigrants, and *braceros,* I learned the North Mexican dialect. With Mexicans I'll try to speak either Standard Mexican Spanish or the North Mexican dialect. From my parents and Chicanos living in the Valley, I picked up Chicano Texas Spanish, and I speak it with my mom, younger brother (who married a Mexican and who rarely mixes Spanish with English), aunts and older relatives.

With Chicanas from *Nuevo México* or *Arizona* I will speak Chicano Spanish a little, but often they don't understand what I'm saying. With most California Chicanas I speak entirely in English (unless I forget). When I first moved to San Francisco, I'd rattle off something in Spanish, unintentionally embarrassing them. Often it is only with another Chicana *tejana* that I can talk freely.

Words distorted by English are known as anglicisms or *pochismos.* The *pocho* is an anglicized Mexican or American of Mexican origin who speaks Spanish with an accent characteristic of North Americans and who distorts and reconstructs the language according to the influence of English.[3]

Tex-Mex, or Spang-lish, comes most naturally to me. I may switch back and forth from English to Spanish in the same sentence or in the same word. With my sister and my brother Nune and with Chicano *tejano* contemporaries I speak in Tex-Mex.

From kids and people my own age I picked up *Pachuco*. *Pachuco* (the language of the zoot suiters) is a language of rebellion, both against Standard Spanish and Standard English. It is a secret language. Adults of the culture and outsiders cannot understand it. It is made up of slang words from both English and Spanish. *Ruca* means girl or woman, *vato* means guy or dude, *chale* means no, *simón* means yes, *churro* is sure, talk is *periquiar*, *pigionear* means petting, *que gacho* means how nerdy, *ponte águila* means watch out, death is called *la pelona*. Through lack of practice and not having others who can speak it, I've lost most of the *Pachuco* tongue.

CHICANO SPANISH

Chicanos, after 250 years of Spanish/Anglo colonization have developed significant differences in the Spanish we speak. We collapse two adjacent vowels into a single syllable and sometimes shift the stress in certain words such as *maíz/maiz, cohete/cuete*. We leave out certain consonants when they appear between vowels: *lado/lao, mojado/mojao*. Chicanos from South Texas pronounce *f* as *j* as in *jue (fue)*. Chicanos use "archaisms," words that are no longer in the Spanish language, words that have been evolved out. We say *semos, truje, haiga, ansina,* and *naiden*. We retain the "archaic" *j,* as in *jalar,* that derives from an earlier *h* (the French *halar* or the Germanic *halon* which was lost to standard Spanish in the 16th century), but which is still found in several regional dialects such as the one spoken in South Texas. (Due to geography, Chicanos from the Valley of South Texas were cut off linguistically from other Spanish speakers. We tend to use words that the Spaniards brought over from Medieval Spain. The majority of the Spanish colonizers in Mexico and the Southwest came from Extremadura—Hernán Cortés was one of them—and Andalucía. Andalucians pronounce *ll* like a *y,* and their *d*'s tend to be absorbed by adjacent vowels: *tirado* becomes *tirao*. They brought *et lenguaje popular, dialectos y regionalismos.*[4])

Chicanos and other Spanish speakers also shift *ll* to *y* and *z* to *s*.[5] We leave out initial syllables, saying *tar* for *estar, toy* for *estoy, hora* for *ahora* (*cubanos* and *puertorriqueños* also leave out initial letters of some words). We also leave out the final syllable such as *pa* for *para*. The intervocalic *y,* the *ll* as in *tortilla, ella, bottella,* gets replaced by *tortia* or *tortiya, ea, botea*. We add an additional syllable at the beginning of certain words: *atocar* for *tocar, agastar* for *gastar*. Sometimes we'll say *lavaste las vacijas,* other times *lavates* (substituting the *ates* verb endings for the *aste*).

We use anglicisms, words borrowed from English: *bola* from ball, *carpeta* from carpet, *máchina de lavar* (instead of *lavadora*) from washing machine.

Tex-Mex argot, created by adding a Spanish sound at the beginning or end of an English word such as *cookiar* for cook, *watchar* for watch, *parkiar* for park, and *rapiar* for rape, is the result of the pressures on Spanish speakers to adapt to English.

We don't use the word *vosotros/as* or its accompanying verb form. We don't say *claro* (to mean yes), *imagínate,* or *me emociona,* unless we picked up Spanish from Latinas, out of a book, or in a classroom. Other Spanish-speaking groups are going through the same, or similar, development in their Spanish.

 ## LINGUISTIC TERRORISM

> *Deslenguadas. Somos los del español deficiente.* We are your linguistic nightmare, your linguistic aberration, your linguistic *mestisaje,* the subject of your *burla.* Because we speak with tongues of fire we are culturally crucified. Racially, culturally and linguistically *somos huérfanos*—we speak an orphan tongue.

Chicanas who grew up speaking Chicano Spanish have internalized the belief that we speak poor Spanish. It is illegitimate, a bastard language. And because we internalize how our language has been used against us by the dominant culture, we use our language differences against each other.

Chicana feminists often skirt around each other with suspicion and hesitation. For the longest time I couldn't figure it out. Then it dawned on me. To be close to another Chicana is like looking into the mirror. We are afraid of what we'll see there. *Pena.* Shame. Low estimation of self. In childhood we are told that our language is wrong. Repeated attacks on our native tongue diminish our sense of self. The attacks continue throughout our lives.

Chicanas feel uncomfortable talking in Spanish to Latinas, afraid of their censure. Their language was not outlawed in their countries. They had a whole lifetime of being immersed in their native tongue; generations, centuries in which Spanish was a first language, taught in school, heard on radio and TV, and read in the newspaper.

If a person, Chicana or Latina, has a low estimation of my native tongue, she also has a low estimation of me. Often with *mexicanas y latinas* we'll speak English as a neutral language. Even among Chicanas we tend to speak English at parties or conferences. Yet, at the same time, we're afraid the other will think we're *agringadas* because we don't speak Chicano Spanish. We oppress each other trying to out-Chicano each other, vying to be the "real" Chicanas, to speak like Chicanos. There is no one Chicano language just as there is no one Chicano experience. A monolingual Chicana whose first language is English or Spanish is just as much a Chicana as one who speaks several variants of Spanish. A Chicana from Michigan or Chicago or Detroit is just as much a Chicana as one from the Southwest. Chicano Spanish is as diverse linguistically as it is regionally.

By the end of this century, Spanish speakers will comprise the biggest minority group in the U.S., a country where students in high schools and colleges are encouraged to take French classes because French is considered more "cultured." But for a language to remain alive it must be used.[6] By the end of this century English, and not Spanish, will be the mother tongue of most Chicanos and Latinos.

So, if you want to really hurt me, talk badly about my language. Ethnic identity is twin skin to linguistic identity—I am my language. Until I can take pride in my language, I cannot take pride in myself. Until I can accept as legitimate Chicano Texas Spanish, Tex-Mex and all the other languages I speak, I cannot accept the legitimacy of myself. Until I am free to write bilingually and to switch codes without having always to translate, while I still have to speak English or Spanish when I would rather speak Spanglish, and as long as I have to accommodate the English speakers rather than having them accommodate me, my tongue will be illegitimate.

I will no longer be made to feel ashamed of existing. I will have my voice: Indian, Spanish, white. I will have my serpent's tongue—my woman's voice, my sexual voice, my poet's voice. I will overcome the tradition of silence.

> My fingers
> Move sly against your palm
> Like women everywhere, we speak in code . . .
>   —MELANIE KAYE/KANTROWITZ[7]

 ## "VISTAS," CORRIDOS, Y COMIDA: MY NATIVE TONGUE

In the 1960s, I read my first Chicano novel. It was *City of Night* by John Rechy, a gay Texan, son of a Scottish father and a Mexican mother. For days I walked around in stunned amazement that a Chicano could write and could get published. When I read *I Am Joaquín*.[8] I was surprised to see a bilingual book by a Chicano in print. When I saw poetry written in Tex-Mex for the first time, a feeling of pure joy flashed through me. I felt like we really existed as a people. In 1971, when I started teaching High School English to Chicano students, I tried to supplement the required texts with works by Chicanos, only to be reprimanded and forbidden to do so by the principal. He claimed that I was supposed to teach "American" and English literature. At the risk of being fired, I swore my students to secrecy and slipped in Chicano short stories, poems, a play. In graduate school, while working toward a Ph.D., I had to "argue" with one advisor after the other, semester after semester, before I was allowed to make Chicano literature an area of focus.

Even before I read books by Chicanos or Mexicans, it was the Mexican movies I saw at the drive-in—the Thursday night special of $1.00 a carload— that gave me a sense of belonging. "*Vámonos a las vistas,*" my mother would call out and we'd all—grandmother, brothers, sister and cousins—squeeze into the car. We'd wolf down cheese and bologna white bread sandwiches while watching Pedro Infante in melodramatic tear-jerkers like *Nosotros los pobres,* the first "real" Mexican movie (that was not an imitation of European movies). I remember seeing *Cuando los hijos se van* and surmising that all Mexican movies played up the love a mother has for her children and what ungrateful sons and daughters suffer when they are not devoted to their mothers. I remember the singing-type "westerns" of Jorge Negrete and Miquel Aceves Mejía. When watching Mexican movies, I felt a sense of homecoming as well as alienation. People who were to amount to something didn't go to Mexican movies, or *bailes* or tune the radios to *bolero, rancherita,* and *corrído* music.

The whole time I was growing up, there was *norteño* music sometimes called North Mexican border music, or Tex-Mex music, or Chicano music, or *cantina* (bar) music. I grew up listening to *conjuntos,* three- or four-piece bands made up of folk musicians playing guitar, *bajo sexto,* drums and button accordion, which Chicanos had borrowed from the German immigrants who had come to Central Texas and Mexico to farm and build breweries. In the Rio Grande Valley, Steve Jordan and Little Joe Hernández were popular, and Flaco Jiménez was the accordion king. The rhythms of Tex-Mex music are those of the polka, also adapted from the Germans, who in turn had borrowed the polka from the Czechs and Bohemians.

I remember the hot, sultry evenings when *corridos*—songs of love and death on the Texas-Mexican borderlands—reverberated out of cheap amplifiers from the local *cantinas* and wafted in through my bedroom window.

Corridos first became widely used along the South Texas/Mexican border during the early conflict between Chicanos and Anglos. The *corridos* are usually about Mexican heroes who do valiant deeds against the Anglo oppressors. Pancho Villa's song, "*La cucaracha,*" is the most famous one. *Corridos* of John F. Kennedy and his death are still very popular in the Valley. Older Chicanos remember Lydia Mendoza, one of the great border *corrido* singers who was called *la Gloria de Tejas.* Her "*El tango negro,*" sung during the Great Depression, made her a singer of the people. The everpresent *corridos* narrated one hundred years of border history, bringing news of events as well as entertaining. These folk musicians and folk songs are our chief cultural mythmakers, and they made our hard lives seem bearable.

I grew up feeling ambivalent about our music. Country-western and rock-and-roll had more status. In the 50s and 60s, for the slightly educated and *agringado* Chicanos, there existed a sense of shame at being caught listening to our music. Yet I couldn't stop my feet from thumping to the music, could not stop humming the words, nor hide from myself the exhilaration I felt when I heard it.

There are more subtle ways that we internalize identification, especially in the forms of images and emotions. For me food and certain smells are tied to my identity, to my homeland. Wood smoke curling up to an immense blue sky; wood smoke perfuming my grandmother's clothes, her skin. The stench of cow manure and the yellow patches on the ground; the crack of a .22 rifle and the reek of cordite. Homemade white cheese sizzling in a pan, melting inside a folded *tortilla*. My sister Hilda's hot, spicy *menudo, chile colorado* making it deep red, pieces of *panza* and hominy floating on top. My brother Carito barbequing *fajitas* in the backyard. Even now and 3,000 miles away, I can see my mother spicing the ground beef, pork and venison with *chile*. My mouth salivates at the thought of the hot steaming *tamales* I would be eating if I were home.

SI LE PREGUNTAS A MI MAMÁ, "¿QUÉ ERES?"

> *"Identity is the essential core of who*
> *we are as individuals, the conscious*
> *experience of the self inside."*
>
> —KAUFMAN[9]

Nosotros los Chicanos straddle the borderlands. On one side of us, we are constantly exposed to the Spanish of the Mexicans, on the other side we hear the Anglos' incessant clamoring so that we forget our language. Among ourselves we don't say *nosotros los americanos, o nosotros los españoles, o nosotros los hispanos.* We say *nosotros los mexicanos* (by *mexicanos* we do not mean citizens of Mexico; we do not mean a national identity, but a racial one). We distinguish between *mexicanos del otro lado* and *mexicanos de este lado.* Deep in our hearts we believe that being Mexican has nothing to do with which country one lives in. Being Mexican is a state of soul—not one of mind, not one of citizenship. Neither eagle nor serpent, but both. And like the ocean, neither animal respects borders.

> *Dime con quien andas y te diré quien eres.*
> (Tell me who your friends are and I'll tell you who you are.)
> —MEXICAN SAYING

Si le preguntas a mi mamá, "¿Qué eres?" te dirá, "Soy mexicana," My brothers and sister say the same. I sometimes will answer *"soy mexicana"* and at others will say *"soy Chicana" o "soy tejana."* But I identified as *"Raza"* before I ever identified as *"mexicana"* or *"Chicana."*

As a culture, we call ourselves Spanish when referring to ourselves as a linguistic group and when copping out. It is then that we forget our predominant Indian genes. We are 70–80 percent Indian.[10] We call ourselves Hispanic[11] or Spanish-American or Latin American or Latin when linking ourselves to other Spanish-speaking peoples of the Western hemisphere and when copping out. We call ourselves Mexican-American[12] to signify we are neither Mexican nor American, but more the noun "American" than the adjective "Mexican" (and when copping out).

Chicanos and other people of color suffer economically for not acculturating. This voluntary (yet forced) alienation makes for psychological conflict, a kind of dual identity—we don't identify with the Anglo-American cultural values and we don't totally identify with the Mexican cultural values. We are a synergy of two cultures with various degrees of Mexicanness or Angloness. I have so internalized the borderland conflict that sometimes I feel like one cancels out the other and we are zero, nothing, no one. *A veces no soy nada ni nadis. Pero hasta cuando no lo soy, lo soy.*

When not copping out, when we know we are more than nothing, we call ourselves Mexican, referring to race and ancestry; *mestizo* when affirming both our Indian and Spanish (but we hardly ever own our Black ancestry); Chicano when referring to a politically aware people born and/ or raised in the U.S.; *Raza* when referring to Chicanos; *tejanos* when we are Chicanos from Texas.

Chicanos did not know we were a people until 1965 when Cesar Chavez and the farmworkers united and *I Am Joaquín* was published and *la Raza Unida* party was formed in Texas. With that recognition, we became a distinct people. Something momentous happened to the Chicano soul—we became aware of our reality and acquired a name and a language (Chicano Spanish) that reflected that reality. Now that we had a name, some of the fragmented pieces began to fall together—who we were, what we were, how we had evolved. We began to get glimpses of what we might eventually become.

Yet the struggle of identities continues, the struggle of borders is our reality still. One day the inner struggle will cease and a true integration take place. In the meantime, *tenémos que hacer la lucha. ¿Quién está protegiendo los ranchos de mi gente? ¿Quién está tratando de cerrar la fisura entre la india y el blanco en nuestra sangre? El Chicano, si, el Chicano que anda como un ladrón en su propia casa.*

Los Chicanos, how patient we seem, how very patient. There is the quiet of the Indian about us.[13] We know how to survive. When other races have given up their tongue, we've kept ours. We know what it is to live under the hammer blow of the dominant *norteamericano* culture. But more than we count the blows, we count the days the weeks the years the centuries the eons until the white laws and commerce and customs will rot in the deserts they've created, lie bleached. *Humildes* yet proud, *quietos* yet wild, *nosotros los mexicanos-Chicanos* will walk by the crumbling ashes as we go about our business. Stubborn, persevering, impenetrable as stone, yet possessing a malleability that renders us unbreakable, we, the *mestizas* and *mestizos,* will remain.

NOTES

1. Ray Gwyn Smith, *Moorland Is Cold Country,* unpublished book.
2. Irena Klepfisz, "Di rayze aheymi/The Journey Home," in *The Tribe of Dina: A Jewish Women's Anthology,* Melanie Kaye/Kantrowitz and Irena Klepfisz, eds. (Montpelier, VT. Sinister Wisdom Books, 1986), 49.

3. R. C. Ortega, *Dialectología Del Barrio,* trans. Horrencia S. Alwan (Los Angeles, CA: R. C. Ortega Publisher & Bookseller, 1977), 132.
4. Eduardo Hernandéz-Chávez, Andrew D. Cohen, and Anthony F. Beltramo, *El Lenguaje de los Chicanos: Regional and Social Characteristics of Language Used by Mexican Americans* (Arlington, VA: Center for Applied Linguistics, 1975), 39.
5. Hernandéz-Chávez, xvii.
6. Irena Klepfisz, "Secular Jewish Identity: Yidishkayt in America," in *The Tribe of Dina,* Kaye/Kantrowitz and Klepfisz, eds., 43.
7. Melanie Kaye/Kantrowitz, "Sign," in *We Speak In Code: Poems and Other Writings* (Pittsburgh, PA: Motherroot Publications, Inc., 1980), 85.
8. Rodolfo Gonzales, *I Am Joaquin/Yo Soy Joaquín* (New York, NY: Bantam Books, 1972). It was first published in 1967.
9. Kaufman, 68.
10. Chávez, 88–90.
11. "Hispanic" is derived from *Hispanis* (*España,* a name given to the Iberian Peninsula in ancient times when it was a part of the Roman Empire) and is a term designated by the U.S. government to make it easier to handle us on paper.
12. The Treaty of Guadalupe Hidalgo created the Mexican-American border in 1848.
13. Anglos, in order to alleviate their guilt for dispossessing the Chicano, stressed the Spanish part of us and perpetrated the myth of the Spanish Southwest. We have accepted the fiction that we are Hispanic, that is Spanish, in order to accommodate ourselves to the dominant culture and its abhorrence of Indians. Chávez, 88–91.

 QUESTIONS FOR CRITICAL THINKING

Reading 41

1. Much of what Anzaldúa discusses illustrates the importance of language to identity and having a sense of culture. If the United States encouraged bilingualism/multilingualism, how might this foster greater equality of some marginalized groups?

2. Many people are opposed to immigrants who don't speak English maintaining their native language and argue that the United States should make English the "official" language. What problems do you think bilingualism/multilingualism would create in our country? Aside from expecting everyone to speak English, how might these problems be avoided or alleviated?

3. Do you believe that there are double standards regarding specific languages and cultures in the United States? Are some cultures and languages considered to be more acceptable? For instance, is the reaction the same when one hears French being spoken in public, as opposed to hearing Mexican Spanish? Why, or why not?

Reading 42

NAMES, LOGOS, MASCOTS, AND FLAGS
The Contradictory Uses of Sports Symbols

STANLEY D. EITZEN

What's in a name?

—WILLIAM SHAKESPEARE

Words are tools of thought. We can use words to maintain the status quo or to think in new ways—which in turn creates the possibility of a new reality.

—SHERRYL KLEINMAN, SOCIOLOGIST

The two teams that played in the 1995 World Series were the Atlanta Braves and the Cleveland Indians. Inside the stadium, the fans of the Braves did the "tomahawk chop" and enthusiastically shouted "Indian" chants. Similarly, the fans of the Indians united behind their symbol, Chief Wahoo, waved foam tomahawks, and wore war paint and other pseudo-Native American symbols. Outside the stadium, Native American activists carried signs in protest of the inappropriate use of their symbols by Anglos. Symbols have the power to both unite followers and divide groups into "us" and "them." They also can be interpreted as symbolic of past and continued oppression.

 SYMBOLS AND SPORTS

A symbol is anything (word, gesture, or object) that carries a particular meaning for the members of a group. A raised finger (which one is important!), a green light, a whistle, a handshake, and a raised fist are all symbols with meaning. Some symbols, such as a wink, are trivial; others, such as the American flag, are vitally important.

A group's symbols serve two fundamental purposes—they bind together the individual members of a group, and they separate one group from another. Each of the thousands of street gangs in the United States, for example, has a group identity that is displayed in its name, code words, gestures,

D. Stanley Eitzen, "Names, Logos, Mascots, and Flags: The Contradictory Uses of Sports Symbols" from *Fair and Foul: Beyond the Myths and Paradoxes of Sports.* Copyright © 2009. Reprinted with permission.

distinctive clothing, and colors. The symbols of these gangs promote solidarity and set them apart from rivals. These symbols are so important that the members may risk their lives in their defense.[1]

Using symbols to achieve solidarity and community is a common group practice, as the French sociologist Émile Durkheim showed in his classic analysis of primitive religions.[2] Durkheim noted that preliterate people in a locality believed that they were related to some totem, which was usually an animal but could be some other natural object as well. All members of a common group were identified by their shared symbol, which they displayed as the emblem of their totem. This identification with an animal, a bird, or another object is common in U.S. schools. Students, former students, faculty members, and others who identify with the school adopt nicknames for the school's teams, display the school colors, wave the school banner, wear special clothing and jewelry, and engage in ritual chants and songs. These behaviors usually center around athletic contests. Sociologist Janet Lever connects these activities with Durkheim's notion of totemism: "Team worship, like animal worship, makes all participants intensely aware of their own group membership. By accepting that a particular team represents them symbolically, people enjoy ritual kinship based on a common bond. Their emblem, be it an insignia or a lapel pin or a scarf with team colors, distinguishes fellow fans from both strangers and enemies."[3]

A school's nickname is much more than a tag or a label. It conveys symbolically, as Durkheim suggests, the characteristics and attributes that define the institution. In an important way, the school's symbols represent the institution's self-concept. Schools may have names that signify the school's ethnic heritage (e.g., the Bethany College Swedes), state history (University of Oklahoma Sooners), religion (Oklahoma Baptist College Prophets), or founder (Whittier College Poets). Most schools, however, use symbols of aggression and ferocity for their athletic teams (birds, such as hawks; animals, such as bulldogs; human categories, such as pirates; and even the otherworldly, such as devils).[4] Although school names and other symbols evoke strong emotions of solidarity among followers, there is also a potential dark side to their use. The names, mascots, logos, and flags chosen by some schools may be derogatory to some groups. The symbols may dismiss, differentiate, demean, and trivialize marginalized groups, such as African Americans, Native Americans, and women. Thus they serve to maintain the dominant status of powerful groups and subordinate those groups categorized as "others." That may not have been the intent of those who decided on the particular names and mascots for a particular school, but their use diminishes these "others," thus retaining the racial and gender inequities found in the larger society.[5] School symbols in sports, then, have power not only to maintain in-group solidarity but also to separate the in-group from the out-group and perpetuate the hierarchy between them. Three conspicuous examples of this phenomenon are the use of the Confederate flag at the University of Mississippi, the use of Native American names (Redskins,

Scalpers) and other racial symbols (war paint, tomahawks, Native American dances), and the sexist names given to women's athletic teams.

Symbols of the Confederacy

At Nathan Bedford Forrest High School in Jacksonville, Florida, young African American athletes wear the Confederate army's colors on their uniforms. They call themselves the Rebels. And the school they play for is named after the slave-trading Confederate general who became the original grand wizard of the Ku Klux Klan.[6]

There is a neo-Confederate culture in much of the South.[7] There are organizations dedicated to promoting the heritage of the Confederate States of America. They fight to retain Confederate symbols, such as the Rebel battle flag, that have had a prominent place in many Southern states, most notably Alabama, Georgia, South Carolina, and Mississippi. The neo-Confederate culture and its symbols have two distinct meanings. One promotes the South's heritage. In this regard, Bob Chance of Selma, Alabama, says:

> I strongly oppose efforts to ban or to at least discourage the use
> of the Confederate battle flag. We southerners have as much right
> to our heritage as anyone else has to theirs. The flag in question
> was a battle flag which led Confederate soldiers into battle. Now
> it leads the Ole Miss Rebels into battle. That should be all there is
> to it. The so-called Rebel flag is the flag of the South—the symbol
> of many good things about our culture and history that are dear to
> the hearts of Southerners. It becomes racist only in the hands of a
> racist.[8]

The opposing view is that the Confederate flag symbolizes "antebellum slavery, Old South patriarch, Jim Crow segregation, Civil Rights lynching, and numerous other forms of oppression."[9]

The Rebel battle flag, which some individuals and groups feel should still fly over state buildings, is an object of controversy. Several states have abandoned it after considerable struggle, but South Carolina continues to use the Rebel flag as its official flag.

The University of Mississippi displays the Rebel battle flag and sings "Dixie" at football games.[10] This practice began in 1948 after the Dixiecrats, rebelling against a strong civil rights plank in the Democratic platform, walked out of the Democratic convention. In that year the University of Mississippi adopted the Rebel flag, designated "Dixie" the school's fight song, and introduced a mascot named "Uncle Reb," a caricature of an Old South plantation owner. These symbols proclaimed its support for racial segregation (its sports teams were officially designated the Rebels in 1936). In 1962 James Meredith, despite the strong opposition of Governor Ross Barnett and other white leaders in the state, became the first black student at the school. There were demonstrations at that time that supported the governor and demonstrations that opposed the racial integration of the school. Through it all, the Rebel flag and the singing of "Dixie" were symbols of defiance used by the supporters of segregation.

Over the ensuing years, the use of these symbols at the University of Mississippi caused considerable debate. On the one hand, they represented the state's heritage and as such were a source of pride, inspiration, and unity among citizens of the South. The opposing position was that these symbols represented a history of oppression against African Americans, noting that the Rebel flag was also a prominent symbol of the Ku Klux Klan. Since almost one-third of Mississippians are African Americans (among the states, Mississippi has the nation's largest African American population), the flagship university of that state should not use symbols that recall the degradation and demeaning of their ancestors. Is it proper, they ask, to use the key symbol of the Confederacy and African American enslavement as a rallying symbol for the University of Mississippi's sports teams—teams composed of whites and African Americans?

As a compromise, in 1983, twenty-one years after the University of Mississippi integrated, its chancellor ruled that the Rebel flag was no longer the official banner for the school. Chancellor Porter L. Fortune Jr. made it clear, however, that students would have the right to wave the flag at football games. And that they have done. Sports team names such as "Rebels," as well as songs such as "Dixie," have continued as official school symbols. The Uncle Reb mascot has been retired, however.

The debate continues, as summarized by Charles W. Eagles, a University of Mississippi history professor: "For some of us—those who believe in the University of Mississippi—the symbols prevent the university from being everything it can be. Others—those that are faithful to Ole Miss [the traditionalists]—think that if you took the symbols away, there wouldn't be anything there. The symbols are seen as a real burden for the University. But they're the backbone of Ole Miss."[11]

This debate demonstrates vividly the power of symbols, not only the power to unite or divide but also the hold these symbols have on people, as seen in their resistance to change and in the organized efforts to change those symbols interpreted as negative.

The Use of Native American Names and Ceremonial Acts

Ray Franks conducted an exhaustive study of the names of athletic teams at all U.S. community colleges, colleges, and universities. He found that names associated with Native Americans predominated in popular use.[12] It is estimated that about three thousand of the nation's high schools have Native American names. Major professional teams have also adopted Native American names—in baseball, the Atlanta Braves and the Cleveland Indians; in football, the Washington Redskins and the Kansas City Chiefs; in basketball, the Golden State Warriors; and in hockey, the Chicago Blackhawks.

Native American names used for sports teams can be generic (Bryant College Indians, Rio Grande College Redmen), tribal (Florida State Seminoles, University of Alaska at Fairbanks Nanooks, Central Michigan Chippewas, Eastern Michigan Hurons, Mississippi College Choctaws, Utah Utes), or they can focus on some attribute (Bradley Braves, Marquette Warriors, Lamar High School [Colorado] Savages) or some combination of names (University of Illinois Fighting Illini, North Dakota Fighting Sioux).[13]

Defenders of Native American names, logos, and mascots argue that their use is a tribute to the indigenous peoples. Native Americans, the argument goes, are portrayed as brave, resourceful, and strong. Native American names were chosen for sports teams precisely because they represent these positive traits.

Other defenders claim that the use of Native American names and mascots is no different from the use of names and mascots that represent other ethnic groups, such as the Irish or the Vikings or the Norse. Because members of these ethnic groups accept the use of their names, Native Americans should also be proud of this recognition of their heritage.

But Native American leaders object to their symbols being used by athletic teams. Since the early 1970s individuals and organizations, such as the American Indian Movement and the National Coalition on Racism in Sports and the Media, have sought to eliminate the use of Native American names, mascots, and logos by sports teams.[14] They use several key arguments, foremost, racist stereotyping. Names such as Indians, Braves, and Chiefs are not inherently offensive, but some names, logos, and mascots project a violent caricature of Native Americans (such as scalpers and savages). The official booster club of Florida State University, for example, is called "The Scalphunters." Teams that use Native American names commonly employ the tomahawk chop, war paint, and mascots dressed as Native Americans. This depiction of Native Americans as bloodthirsty warriors distorts history, since whites invaded Native American lands, oppressed native peoples, and even employed and justified a policy of genocide toward them.

Some mascots are especially demeaning to Native Americans. Consider Chief Wahoo, "the red-faced, big-nosed, grinning, drywall-toothed moron who graces the peak of every Cleveland Indians cap."[15] Is such a caricature appropriate? Clyde Bellecourt, national director of the American Indian Movement (AIM), summarizes the complaints:

> If you look up the word "redskin" in both the Webster's and Random House dictionaries, you'll find the word is defined as being offensive. Can you imagine if they called them the Washington Jews and the team mascot was a rabbi leading them in (the song) Hava Nagila, fans in the stands wearing yarmulkes and waving little sponge torahs? The word Indian isn't offensive. Brave isn't offensive, but it's the behavior that accompanies all of this that's offensive. The rubber tomahawks. The chicken-feather headdresses.

People wearing war paint and making these ridiculous war whoops with a tomahawk in one hand and a beer in the other. All of these things have significant meaning for us. And the psychological impact it has, especially on our youth, is devastating.[16]

Another problem is the imitation or misuse of symbols that have religious significance to some Native American peoples. Using dances, chants, drumming, and other rituals at sporting events clearly trivializes their meaning.

Also problematic is the homogenization of Native American cultures. Native Americans are portrayed uniformly, without regard for the sometimes enormous differences among tribes. Thus, through the use of Native American names of mascots, society defines who Native Americans are instead of allowing Native Americans to determine how society thinks of them.

There is a dispute concerning the degree to which Native Americans object to the use of Indian symbols for sports teams. On the one hand, a survey by *Indian Country Today* found that 81 percent of respondents "indicated use of American Indian names, symbols, and mascots are predominantly offensive and deeply disparaging to Native Americans."[17] This finding is contradicted by the survey reported in *Sports Illustrated*, which found that, while Native American activists are virtually united in their opposition to the use of Indian nicknames and mascots, some 83 percent of Native Americans said that professional teams should not stop using Indian nicknames, mascots, or symbols.[18]

Native American activists dismiss such opinion as misguided ("There are happy campers on every plantation," says Suzan Harjo, president of Morning Star Institute, an Indian-rights organization in Washington, D.C.) or as evidence that Native Americans' self-esteem has fallen so low that they don't even know when they're being insulted.[19] Similarly, Native Americans have been immersed in a society that demeans them and socializes them to accept their secondary status in society.

After more than forty years of protest, about seven hundred high schools and colleges throughout the nation have changed their former Native American names and mascots. Most notably, colleges and universities such as Dartmouth, Marquette, Stanford, Eastern Michigan, Eastern Washington, University of Massachusetts, Oklahoma City, St. Bonaventure, Siena, Miami of Ohio, and St. John's have taken these objections seriously and done so.

Similarly, a number of "Native American" mascots have been retired. For example, the Kansas City Chiefs retired their horse mascot "Warpaint"; the Atlanta Braves got rid of "Chief Noc-A-Homa," who used to come out of a teepee after an Atlanta home run and do a ceremonial dance; and after a long and very contentious debate the University of Illinois retired Chief Illiniwek, a mascot who pretended to be an Indian by dressing in a war bonnet and war paint.[20]

Yet many high schools and colleges resist changing their Native American nicknames and mascots to ones that do not demean a minority group. Ironically, they insist on retaining the Native American symbols even though their schools do not have a Native American heritage or significant Native American student representation. The members of these schools and their constituencies insist on retaining their Native American names because they are part of their collective identities. This allegiance to their school symbols seems to have higher priority than sensitivity to the negative consequences produced by inappropriate depictions of Native Americans.

Sexist Names for Women's Teams[21]

Many studies have shown the varied ways in which language acts in the defining, deprecation, and exclusion of women.[22] Names do this, too. Naming women's and men's athletic teams is not a neutral process. The names chosen are often badges of femininity and masculinity, inferiority and superiority. To the degree that this occurs, the names of women's and men's athletic teams reinforce a basic element of social structure: gender division and hierarchy. Team names reflect this division as well as the asymmetry that is associated with it. Despite advances made by women in sport since the implementation of Title IX, widespread naming practices continue to mark female athletes as unusual, aberrant, or invisible.

My colleague Maxine Baca Zinn and I examined the names and accompanying logos and mascots of sports teams for women and men at 1,185 coeducational four-year colleges and universities.[23] We identified eight gender-linked practices associated with names/logos that diminish and trivialize women.

First, physical markers. One common naming practice emphasizes the physical appearance of women, such as the Angelo State Rambelles or the Bellarmine College Belles (the men are the Knights). As Casey Miller and Kate Swift argue, this practice is sexist because the "emphasis on the physical characteristics of women is offensive in contexts where men are described in terms of achievement."[24]

Second, the terms "girl" or "gal." The use of "girl" or "gal" stresses the presumed immaturity and irresponsibility of women, such as the Elon College Golden Girls. "Just as boy can be blatantly offensive to minority men, so girl can have comparable patronizing and demeaning implications for women."[25]

Third, feminine suffixes. This is a popular form of gender differentiation found in the names of athletic, social, and women's groups. The practice not only marks women but also denotes a feminine derivative by establishing a "female negative trivial category."[26] The devaluation is accomplished by tagging words with feminine suffixes such as "ette" and "esse." At Dillard University, the men's team is the Blue Devils, and the women's team is the Devilettes; at Albany State, the men are the Golden Rams and the women are the Rammettes; at Duquesne University and James Madison University, the men are the Dukes and the women the Duchesses.

Fourth, the term "lady." This label has several meanings that demean women as athletes. "Lady" is used to "evoke a standard of propriety, correct behavior, and elegance,"[27] characteristics that are decidedly unathletic. Similarly, "lady" carries overtones recalling the age of chivalry. "This makes the term seem polite at first, but we must also remember that these implications are perilous: they suggest that a 'lady' is helpless, and cannot do things for herself."[28] The use of "lady" for women's teams is common, for example, the University of Florida Lady Gators or the University of Arkansas Lady Razorbacks. At Kenyon College the men are the Lords and the women are the Ladies, and at Washington and Jefferson College the men are Presidents and the women are First Ladies. In both of these instances, the names for the women's teams clearly mark their status as inferior to that of the men.

Fifth, male as a false generic. This practice assumes that the masculine in the language, word, or name choice is the norm while ignoring the feminine altogether. Miller and Swift define this procedure as "terms used of a class or group that are not applicable to all members."[29] The use of "mankind" to encompass both sexes has its parallel among men's and women's athletic teams that have the same name, for example, the Rams (Colorado State University), Stags (Concordia College), Norsemen (Luther College), the Tomcats (Thiel College), and the Hokies (a hokie is a castrated turkey) (Virginia Tech). Dale Spender has called the practice of treating the masculine as the norm "one of the most pervasive and pernicious rules that has been encoded."[30] Its consequence is to make women invisible as well as secondary to men, since they are robbed of a separate identity.

Sixth, male name with a female modifier. This practice applies the feminine to a name that usually denotes a male, giving females lower status.[31] Examples among sports teams are the Lady Friars of Providence College, the Lady Statesmen of William Penn College, the Lady Penmen of New Hampshire College, the Lady Centaurs of Columbia College, the Lady Gamecocks of the University of South Carolina (a gamecock is a fighting rooster), and the Lady Horsemen of St. Michaels's High School in Santa Fe. Using such oxymorons "reflects role conflict and contributes to the lack of acceptance of women's sport."[32]

Seventh, double gender marking. This occurs when the name of the women's team is a diminutive of the men's team name combined with "belle" or "lady" or other feminine modifier. For example, the men's teams at Mississippi College are the Choctaws, and the women's teams are designated as the Lady Chocs. At the University of Kentucky the men's teams are the Wildcats, and the women's teams are the Lady Kats. The men's teams at the University of Colorado are the Buffalos, and the women's teams are the Lady Buffs. At Augusta College the women are the Lady Jags, whereas the men are the Jaguars. Similarly, at both the University of Nebraska–Omaha and the University of Texas–Arlington, the men are the Mavericks and the women the Lady Mavs. Compounding the feminine intensifies women's secondary status. Double gender marking occurs "perhaps to underline the inappropriateness or rarity of the feminine noun or to emphasize its negativity."[33]

Eighth, male/female paired polarity. Women's and men's teams can be assigned names that represent a female/male opposition. When this occurs, the names of the men's teams embody competitiveness and other positive traits associated with sport, whereas the names for women's teams are lighthearted or cute. The essence of sport is competition, and physical skills largely determine outcomes. Successful athletes are believed to embody such traits as courage, bravura, boldness, self-confidence, and aggression. When the names that are given to men's teams imply these traits but the names for women's teams suggest that women are playful and cuddly, then women are trivialized and de-athleticized. For example, the men at the College of Wooster are called the Fighting Scots, and the women are the Scotties; Mercer University men's teams are the Bears, and the women the Teddy Bears; at the Albany College of Pharmacy the men are the Panthers, and the women the Pink Panthers; and at Fort Valley State College the men's teams are named the Wildcats, and the women's teams are the Wildkittens.

Another grouping occurs when names that could be included in one of the above categories also incorporate race. This occurs especially with teams using Native American symbols. The men's teams at Southeastern Oklahoma State University are the Savages and the women's teams are the Savagettes, using the diminutive feminine suffix combined with a negative stereotype for the racial category. Similarly, at Montclair State College the men are the Indians and the women are the Squaws. The word "squaw" also refers to a woman's pelvic area and means prostitute in some native languages. Vernon Bellecourt of the American Indian Movement says, "The issue itself is clear. . . . The word 'squaw' has got to go in all its forms. It's demeaning and degrading to Indian women and all women."[34]

Our survey found that approximately three-eighths of U.S. colleges and universities employ sexist names, and slightly over half have sexist names and/or logos for their athletic teams. Thus the identity symbols for athletic teams at those schools contribute to the maintenance of male dominance within college sports. Since the traditional masculine gender role matches most athletic qualities better than the traditional feminine gender role, the images and symbols are male. Women do not fit into this scheme. They are "other" even when they do participate. Their team names and logos tend to perpetuate and strengthen the image of female inferiority by making them secondary, invisible, trivial, or unathletic.

RESISTANCE TO CHANGE

It is important to note that many schools do not have team names, mascots, and logos that are racist or sexist. They use race-neutral and gender-neutral names, such as Bears, Eagles, Seagulls, Cougars, Wasps, Mustangs, Royals,

Saints, Big Green, or Blue Streaks. Schools that currently employ racist or sexist names could change to neutral ones that embody the traits desired in athletic teams such as courage, strength, and aggressiveness.[35] For some, such a change would be relatively easy—dropping the use of "lady" or "ette" as modifiers, for example. Teams with native American names or male names (stags, rams, hokies, centaurs) must adopt new names to eliminate the racism or sexism inherent in their present names. A few schools have made these changes. Most schools, however, resist changing names with passion because a name change negates the school's traditions.

The athletic teams at my school, Colorado State University, are called the Rams. Is it appropriate for the women's teams to be called Rams (rams are male sheep)? This question has been raised from time to time by the Faculty Women's Caucus and a few male professors, but strong resistance from journalists, student government leaders, and the Committee on Intercollegiate Athletics, as well as silence by the women athletes and the coaches of women's teams, have worked to maintain the status quo.

The naming issue at Colorado State University reveals a contradiction. Many students, including women student-athletes, express a lack of interest in the issue, yet it evokes strong emotions among others. These responses seem to originate in several sources at Colorado State and, by implication, elsewhere. These arguments parallel resistance to changing sexist language in general.[36]

Tradition, above all, is always a barrier to change. Students, alumni, faculty, and athletes become accustomed to a particular name for their university and its athletic teams, and it seems "natural." This is the argument made on behalf of the many teams that continue to use Native American names and symbols for their teams despite the objections of Native Americans. So too with names that are sexist. But even if a school name has the force of tradition, is it justified to continue using it if it is racist or sexist? If a sexist team name reinforces and socializes sexist thinking, however subtly, then it must be changed. If not, then the institution is publicly sexist.

Many see the naming issue as trivial. In 2005, after the California state legislature passed a bill banning the use of "Redskins" as a public school nickname, Governor Schwarzenegger vetoed it, saying it was a trivial issue. However, it is not trivial to the group being demeaned, degraded, and trivialized. Some progressives argue that there are more important issues to address than changing racist or sexist names of athletic teams. This illustrates the contradiction that the naming of teams is at once trivial and important. For African Americans, whether the University of Mississippi fans sing "Dixie" and wave Confederate flags is not as important as ending discrimination and getting good jobs. Similarly, for Native Americans, the derogatory use of their heritage surrounding athletic contests is relatively unimportant compared to raising their standard of living. For women, the sexist naming of athletic teams is not as significant as pay equity or breaking the "glass ceiling" or achieving equity with men in athletic departments in resources, scholarships, and media attention. Faced with a choice among these options, the naming issue would be secondary. But this sets up a false choice. We can work to remove all manifestations of racism and sexism on college campuses. Referring to language and relevant to the team names issue as well, the Association for Women in Psychology Ad Hoc Committee on Sexist Language has addressed and refuted the "trivial concern" argument: "The major objection, often even to discussing changing sexist language, is that it is a superficial matter compared with the real physical and economic oppression of women. And indeed, women's total oppression must end; we are not suggesting any diversion of energies from that struggle. We are, however, suggesting that this is an important part of it."[37]

The opposite point—that the naming issue is crucially important—is the third argument. Symbols are extremely compelling in the messages they convey.[38] Their importance is understood when rebellious groups demean or defame symbols of the powerful, such as the flag. Names and other symbols have the power to elevate or "put down" a group. If racist or sexist, they reinforce and therefore maintain the secondary status of African Americans, Native Americans, or women through stereotyping, oaricature, derogation, trivialization, diminution, or making them invisible. Most of us, however, fail to see the problem with symbols that demean or defame the powerless because these symbols support the existing power arrangements in society. Despite their apparent triviality, the symbols surrounding sports teams are important because they can (and often do) contribute to patterns of social dominance.

Colleges and universities, for the most part, are making major efforts to diversify their student bodies, faculties, and administrations by race, ethnicity, and gender. This laudable goal is clearly at odds with the existence of racist and sexist names and practices for their athletic teams. The leadership in these schools (boards of regents, chancellors, presidents, and faculty senates) must take a stand against racism and sexism in all its forms and take appropriate action. Removing all racist and sexist symbols such as names, mascots, flags, logos, and songs is an important beginning to this crucial project.

NOTES

1. See, for example, Martin Sanchez Jankowski, *Islands in the Street: Gangs and American Urban Society* (Berkeley: University of California Press, 1991).
2. Émile Durkheim, *The Elementary Forms of Religious Life,* trans. Joseph Ward Sivain (New York: Free Press, 1947). This classic was first published in 1915.
3. Janet Lever, *Soccer Madness* (Chicago: University of Chicago Press, 1983), 12.
4. See John R. Fuller and Elisabeth Anne Manning, "Violence and Sexism in College Mascots and Symbols: A Typology," *Free Inquiry in Creative Sociology* 15 (1987): 61–64.
5. Margaret Carlisle Duncan, "Representation and the Gun That Points Backwards," *Journal of Sport and Social Issues* 17 (April 1993): 42–46.
6. Dennis Cauchon, "A Slave-Holding Past: Search for Perspective," *USA Today,* March 9, 1998, p. 8A.

7. Brian Britt, "Neo-Confederate Culture," *Z Magazine* 9 (December 1996): 26–30.
8. Bob Chance, "Ole Miss" (October 26, 1997), online: www.zebra.net/~bchance/rebel.html.
9. Joshua I. Newman, "Old Times There Are Not Forgotten: Sport, Identity, and the Confederate Flag in the Dixie South," *Sociology of Sport Journal* 24 (September 2007): 262.
10. The following is taken from several sources: Newman, "Old Times There Are Not Forgotten," 261–82; William Nack, "Look Away, Dixie Land," *Sports Illustrated,* November 3, 1997, p. 114; Douglas S. Lederman, "Old Times Not Forgotten: A Battle over Symbols," in *Sport in Contemporary Society,* ed. D. Stanley Eitzen, 6th ed. (New York: Worth, 2001), 109–14; and Paula Edelson, "Just Whistlin' Dixie," *Z Magazine* 4 (November 1991): 72–74.
11. Lederman, "Old Times Not Forgotten," 132.
12. Ray Franks, *What's in a Nickname? Exploring the Jungle of College Athletic Mascots* (Amarillo, Tex.: Ray Franks, 1982).
13. The names and mascots for schools used in this essay are taken from Ray Franks, *What's in a Nickname?* This comprehensive compilation of information, although dated, is the most current listing. Therefore, some of the schools named in the chapter may have subsequently changed the names of their athletic teams.
14. This section is taken primarily from: Laurel Davis, "Protest against the Use of Native American Mascots: A Challenge to Traditional American Identity," *Journal of Sport and Social Issues* 17 (April 1993): 9–22; Ward Churchill, "Crimes against Humanity," *Sport in Contemporary Society,* ed. D. Stanley Eitzen, 6th ed. (New York: Worth, 2001), 115–22; C. Richard King and Charles Fruehling Springwood, "Fighting Spirits: The Racial Politics of Sports Mascots," *Journal of Sport and Social Issues* 24 (August 2000): 282–304; Carol Spindel, *Dancing at Halftime: Sports and the Controversy over American Indian Mascots* (New York: New York University Press, 2000); and a four-part series on Indian Mascots in the *Greeley Tribune* (Colorado), January 20–23, 2002.
15. Rick Telander, "These Nicknames, Symbols Should Offend All Americans," *Chicago Sun-Times,* October 20, 1995, p. 143.
16. Quoted in Bob Kravitz, "Aim of Native Americans' Protest Is True," *Rocky Mountain News,* January 21, 1992, p. 39.
17. *Indian Country Today,* August 8, 2001.
18. S. L. Price, "The Indian Wars," *Sports Illustrated,* March 4, 2002, pp. 64–72. For a critique of this *Sports Illustrated* article, see C. Richard King, Ellen J. Staurowsky, Lawrence Baca, Laurel R. Davis, and Cornel Pewewerdy, "Of Polls and Prejudice," *Journal of Sport and Social Issues* 26 (November 2002): 381–402.
19. Price, "Indian Wars," 69.
20. J. Wolburg, "The Demise of Native American Mascots: It's Time to Do the Right Thing," *The Journal of Consumer Marketing* 23.1 (2006): 4.
21. This section is based in part on D. Stanley Eitzen and Maxine Baca Zinn, "The De-athleticization of Women: The Naming and Gender Marking of Collegiate Sport Teams," *Sociology of Sport Journal* 6 (December 1989): 362–70; D. Stanley Eitzen and Maxine Baca Zinn, "The Sexist Naming of Athletic Teams and Resistance to Change," *Journal of Sport and Social Issues* 17 (April 1993): 34–41; D. Stanley Eitzen and Maxine Baca Zinn, "Never Mind the Braves; What about the Lady Rams?" *Baltimore Sun,* November 3, 1991, p. 3D; and D. Stanley Eitzen and Maxine Baca Zinn, "The Dark Side of Sports Symbols," *USA Today: The Magazine of the American Scene* 129 (January 2001), 48–51.

22. Barrie Thorne, Cheris Kramarae, and Nancy M. Henley, "Language, Gender, and Society: Opening a Second Decade of Research," in *Language, Gender, and Society,* ed. Barrie Thorne and Nancy M. Henley (Rowley, Mass.: Newbury House, 1985), 7–24; Nancy M. Henley, "This New Species That Seeks a New Language: On Sexism in Language and Language Change," in *Women and Men in Transition,* ed. Joyce Penfield (Albany: State University of New York Press, 1987), 3–27.

23. Eitzen and Baca Zinn, "Sexist Naming of Athletic Teams."

24. Casey Miller and Kate Swift, *The Handbook of Nonsexist Writing* (New York: Lippincott and Crowell, 1980), 87.

25. Miller and Swift, *Handbook of Nonsexist Writing,* 71.

26. Casey Miller and Kate Swift, *Words and Women: New Language in New Times* (Garden City, N.Y.: Doubleday-Anchor, 1977), 58.

27. Miller and Swift, *Words and Women,* 72.

28. Robin Lakoff, *Language and Woman's Place* (New York: Harper & Row, 1975), 25.

29. Miller and Swift, *Handbook of Nonsexist Writing,* 9.

30. Dale Spender, *Man Made Language* (London: Routledge and Kegan Paul, 1980), 3.

31. Dennis Baron, *Grammar and Gender* (New Haven, Conn.: Yale University Press, 1986), 112.

32. Fuller and Manning, "Violence and Sexism," 64.

33. Baron, *Grammar and Gender,* 115.

34. Quoted in Lois Tomas, "What's in a Name?" *In These Times,* October 19, 1997, p. 11.

35. Daniel P. Starr, "Unisex Nicknames One Way of Skirting Gender Problem," *NCAA News,* March 20, 1991, p. 4.

36. Maija S. Blaubergs, "An Analysis of Classic Arguments against Changing Sexist Language," *Women's Studies International Quarterly* 3 (1980): 135–47.

37. Association for Women in Psychology Ad Hoc Committee on Sexist Language, "Help Stamp Out Sexism: Change the Language!" *APA Monitor* 6.11 (1975): 16.

38. Sherryl Kleinman, "Why Sexist Language Matters," *Qualitative Sociology* 25.2 (2002): 299–304.

QUESTIONS FOR CRITICAL THINKING

Reading 42

1. How did reading this article help you to see the issue of sports symbols and "mascots" in new and different ways?

2. Do you think the use of American Indian/Native American "mascots" is problematic? Why, or why not? How do you think your own status in society impacts your opinion?

3. Why do you think caricature portrayals of African Americans (e.g., mammy and Sambo images) are no longer used but the use of similar images (e.g., Chief Wahoo) continues?

Reading 43

CLIMATE OF FEAR

SOUTHERN POVERTY LAW CENTER

SUFFOLK COUNTY, N.Y.—The night of Nov. 8, 2008, seven teenage males gathered in a park in Medford, N.Y., to drink beer and plot another round of a brutal pastime they called beaner-hopping. It consisted of randomly targeting Latino immigrants for harassment and physical attacks.

Five days earlier, three of them had gone on the hunt and beaten a Latino man unconscious, they later told police. "I don't go out and do this very often, maybe once a week," one of them said.

Two of the youths in the park had started their day just after dawn by firing a BB gun at Latino immigrant Marlon Garcia, who was standing in his driveway. Garcia was hit several times.

After leaving the park, the pack of seven drove around Medford. Unable to locate a victim, they set off for Patchogue, a nearby seaside village. Both communities are in Suffolk County, which occupies the eastern, less urban half of Long Island. In Patchogue, they caught sight of Hector Sierra walking downtown. They ran up to Sierra and began to punch him, but Sierra was able to flee.

Then, just before midnight, according to prosecutors, they spotted Ecuadorian immigrant Marcelo Lucero walking with a friend, Angel Loja. Lucero, 37, had come to the United States in 1992. He worked at a dry cleaning store and regularly wired money home to his ailing mother.

The seven teenagers jumped out of their vehicles and began taunting the two men with racial slurs. Loja fled, but the attackers surrounded Lucero and began punching him in the face. Trying to defend himself, Lucero removed his belt and swung it, striking one of the teens in the head. Enraged by that blow, 17-year-old Jeffrey Conroy, a star high school football and lacrosse player, allegedly pulled a knife, charged forward and stabbed Lucero in the chest, killing him.

Southern Poverty Law Center, "Climate of Fear" from *Climate of Fear: Latino Immigrants in Suffolk County, N.Y.* Reprinted with the permission of the Southern Poverty Law Center.

All seven attackers were arrested a short time later. Conroy was charged with second-degree murder and manslaughter as a hate crime. The other six were charged with multiple counts of gang assault and hate crimes.

The local and national media gave the murder of Lucero extensive coverage. This was in part because it occurred less than four months after the highly publicized slaying of a Mexican immigrant in Shenandoah, Pa. Luis Ramírez, 25, was beaten to death by drunken high school football players in a case that sparked a national discussion and heightened awareness of the rising tide of anti-immigrant violence.[1]

In few places is that trend more viciously evident than in Suffolk County, where anti-immigrant sentiment has long run deep, and where a fast-growing Latino immigrant population has been victimized by a continuing epidemic of anti-immigrant hate crimes since the late 1990s.

In recent months, Southern Poverty Law Center (SPLC) researchers interviewed more than 70 Latino immigrants living in Suffolk County, along with more than 30 local religious leaders, human rights activists, community organizers and small business owners. Their accounts are remarkably consistent and demonstrate that although Lucero's murder represented the apex of anti-immigrant violence in Suffolk County to date, it was hardly an isolated incident.

Latino immigrants in Suffolk County live in fear. Low-level harassment is common. They are regularly taunted, spit upon and pelted with apples, full soda cans, beer bottles and other projectiles. Their houses and apartments are egged, spray-painted with racial epithets and riddled with bullets in drive-by shootings. Violence is a constant threat. Numerous immigrants reported being shot with BB or pellet guns, or hit in the eyes with pepper spray. Others said they'd been run off the road by cars while riding bicycles, or chased into the woods by drivers while traveling on foot. The SPLC recorded abundant first-hand accounts of immigrants being punched and kicked by random attackers, beaten with baseball bats or robbed at knifepoint.

Political leaders in the county have done little to discourage the hatred, and some have actively fanned the flames. County Executive Steve Levy, Suffolk's top elected official, has made hostile policies targeting undocumented immigrants a central theme of his administration since he was first elected in 2003. Others have done worse, with public statements that all but endorsed violence. At a public hearing on immigration in August 2001, County Legislator Michael D'Andre of Smithtown said that if his own town should ever experience an influx of Latino day laborers like that of nearby communities, "We'll be up in arms; we'll be out with baseball bats." In March 2007, County Legislator Elie Mystal of Amityville said of Latino immigrants

---

[1]On May 26, 2010, Jeffrey Conroy, age 19, was sentenced to 25 years in prison for the first-degree manslaughter as a hate crime of Marcelo Lucero.

waiting for work on street corners, "If I'm living in a neighborhood and people are gathering like that, I would load my gun and start shooting, period. Nobody will say it, but I'm going to say it."

Most immigrants said they do not dare travel alone at night. Few let their children play outside unattended.

"We live with the fear that if we leave our houses, something will happen," said Luis, a Mexican who migrated to Suffolk County three years ago. "It's like we're psychologically traumatized from what happens here."

Like all but two immigrants contacted by the SPLC, Luis spoke for this report on the condition that, to avoid retaliation, he would be identified only by his first name and country of origin.

At best, the immigrants said, the police seem indifferent to their plight. At worst, the police contribute to it, in the form of racial profiling, selective enforcement and outright bullying. A detailed account provided by Agosto, a Guatemalan immigrant, was typical. Agosto said that in early 2008, he was waiting for work at *la placita* (little plaza), a day labor pick-up point in Brentwood, when a police car pulled up. The two officers inside told him he wasn't allowed to stand there and demanded to see his identification. When he replied that he didn't have his I.D. with him, the officers told him to get in the back of the squad car. "I thought they were giving me a ride home," he said. But when they arrived at his residence, the police officers got out of the car and told Agosto to find his I.D. When he unlocked the front door, he said, the officers barged in without asking permission to enter. The police ransacked his living quarters, rifling through drawers and knocking items off shelves.

"I was very nervous," Agosto said. "They kept pushing me and telling me to hurry up. I got even more nervous so it took me awhile to find my I.D. When you are undocumented, you get scared." When Agosto finally located his *cédula de identidad*, a Guatemalan government-issued I.D. card, the police looked it over then left. "I felt bad, like they were treating me like I was less than they were," he said. "It felt racist."

No immigrants reported serious physical abuse at the hands of Suffolk County law enforcement authorities. But time after time, they gave similar accounts of being pulled over for minor traffic violations and then interrogated, or being questioned harshly at nighttime checkpoints after watching Anglo drivers being waved through. A few said they'd been arrested for driving under the influence or for refusing to take a breathalyzer test even though in fact they'd submitted to the test and registered well below the legal limit.

Evidence suggesting unequal enforcement of the motor vehicle code in Suffolk County is easily observed in the local courts that handle minor offenses. Latinos account for roughly 14% of Suffolk County's population, but on a typical day in a Suffolk County justice court, they make up nearly half the defendants appearing for motor vehicle violations. A review of the police blotters printed in Suffolk County daily newspapers yields similarly suggestive demographic evidence: almost every day, around 50% of the drivers listed as having been fined for a motor vehicle violation have Latino surnames.

The most common violation that Latino immigrants are tagged with is violation 509, for unlicensed driving. It carries a $185 fine on top of a $150 vehicle impound charge and $25 a day for vehicle storage. Failure to appear in court or to pay a fine leads to arrest warrants.

Law enforcement officers in Suffolk County tend not to exhibit the same enthusiasm for investigating hate crimes against Latinos as they do writing them tickets, according to immigrants and other county residents interviewed for this report.

Immigrants in Suffolk County don't trust the police. They say there's no point in reporting bias-motivated harassment, threats or assaults, even severe beatings, because from what they can tell, the police take the report and then do nothing. They say that when the police arrive on the scene of a hate crime, they often accept the version of events given by the assailant or assailants, even to the point of arresting the true victim in response to false claims that the immigrant started a fight. And they say that officers discourage hate crime victims from making formal complaints by questioning them about their immigration status.

In the days following the murder of Marcelo Lucero, the Congregational Church of Patchogue invited immigrants to the church to speak about hate crimes. In all, more than 30 Latino immigrants in Suffolk County came forward with detailed accounts of their own victimization. In response, the Suffolk County Legislature formed a task force to investigate the sources of racial tension in the county. To date, the task force has held one of at least four planned hearings.

Prosecutors, meanwhile, have announced new indictments that accuse the defendants in the Lucero murder of assaulting or menacing a total of eight other Latino immigrants.

On June 24, 2008, according to prosecutors, the teenagers set upon Robert Zumba, kicking him and pinning his arms while Conroy, the alleged knife-wielder in the Lucero slaying, sliced Zumba with a blade. Members of the group repeatedly victimized another man, José Hernández, in December 2007, prosecutors said. During one attack, Conroy allegedly held a pipe in one hand and smacked it against his opposite palm, threatening, "We're going to kill you."

Immigrants who have been the victims of hate-crime violence in Suffolk County report that in most cases the attackers are white males in their teens or 20s. A few reported being attacked by African-American males, or being lured by a white female to a nearby "party" where assailants lay in wait. Almost always, the reported attackers were young.

All seven youths accused of participating in the attack on Lucero reside in Patchogue or Medford—predominantly middle-class towns whose strip malls and pizzerias appear in sharp contrast to the lavish wealth on display elsewhere in the county. Suffolk County has one of the steepest wealth gradients in the country. Six of its ZIP codes are among the 100 wealthiest in the United States. The village of Sagaponack, one of a group of seaside communities collectively known as the Hamptons, is the most expensive ZIP code in the nation, with a median home sale price in 2005 of $2.8 million. It's home to investment bankers and real estate tycoons.

The parents of the alleged Lucero attackers include a teacher, a butcher, a store clerk, a deli owner and a former K-Mart operations manager. Latino immigrants may find work in Suffolk County's rich seaside communities, but they live in the more affordable inland towns, alongside middle- and working-class American families who are more likely to view the brown-skinned newcomers as competitors for jobs than hired help.

Immigrant advocates say that the violence committed by high school students and their slightly older peers is fueled by the immigrant-bashing rhetoric they absorb in the hallways and classrooms at school, in the news media, or in conversations at home.

Demographic change in Suffolk County has been rapid over the previous two decades. Some towns have gone from being practically all white to having a 15% Latino population, made up mostly of immigrants from Central America and Mexico, according to the latest census statistics. In Patchogue and Medford, the Latino population is 24%.

Although this influx has slowed since the U.S. economy faltered last year, the nativist backlash continues. It began in earnest in the late 1990s, when about 1,500 Mexican workers showed up over the course of a few years in the small, majority-white, middle-class hamlet of Farmingville. The hamlet's central location made it ideal for contractors looking to hire day laborers for jobs throughout the county. That in turn made it attractive to immigrants drawn to the area by then-abundant employment opportunities in the landscaping, restaurant, and construction industries.

In 1998, a militant nativist group called Sachem Quality of Life formed in Farmingville and began disseminating propaganda that accused undocumented Latino immigrants of being inherently prone to rape, armed robbery and other violent crimes. Although Sachem Quality of Life is now defunct, the group, along with the Federation for American Immigration Reform and a smaller nativist group called American Patrol, heavily influenced the tone for public discourse on immigration in the area.

Nativist ideology now permeates many levels of society and government in Suffolk County. County Executive Levy in June 2006 mocked activists demonstrating against hate crime violence and the mass eviction of Latino immigrants based on the selective enforcement of zoning laws. "I will not back down to this one percent lunatic fringe," he said. "They evidently do not like me much because I am one of the few officials who are not intimidated by their politically correct histrionics."

That same year, a school board member in the Hamptons distributed an online petition to parents, teachers, and a school principal calling for undocumented immigrants to be prevented from receiving any "free services" in the U.S.

"Look, we need you to continue sending this around. . . . [G]et as many viable names on here so that someone hears our voices," the E-mail read. "It seems the only voices they hear are the illegal immigrants who say 'foul play,' or the agencies backing them. We need to stop this and stop it in the bud!"

Also in 2006, the same official distributed an E-mail containing a "hilarious" mock description of a doll called Brentwood Barbie. "This Spanish-speaking only Barbie comes with a 1984 Toyota with expired temporary plates & 4 baby Barbies in the backseat (no car seats)," it read. "The optional Ken doll comes with a paint bucket lunch pail & is missing 3 fingers on his left hand. Green cards are not available for Brentwood Barbie or Ken."

In a February 2007 public hearing on proposed legislation, County Legislator Jack Eddington of Brookhaven singled out two immigration advocates who were speaking from the podium in Spanish and demanded to know if they were in the country legally. Eddington also warned undocumented immigrants, "You better beware" and "Suffolk County residents will not be victimized anymore."

Later in 2007, Levy was reelected with 96% of the vote.

Over the years, immigrant advocates have built an energetic movement in Suffolk County. Earlier this year, on the six-month anniversary of Lucero's murder, the Long Island Immigrant Alliance and The Workplace Project organized a vigil at the site of the killing. The event featured speakers from an array of groups, including the Fundación Lucero de América (Lucero Foundation America), along with Marcelo Lucero's brother, Joselo.

A few months before the vigil, some residents of eastern Long Island formed Neighbors in Support of Immigrants, in part to counter what they perceived as a takeover of local town council and community meetings by anti-immigrant zealots. In Patchogue, residents formed the Unity Coalition with the help of the New York Division of Human Rights to work to ease tensions in that community. A more established grassroots organization, Farmingdale Citizens for Viable Solutions, runs La Casa Comunal, a community center that serves Latino day laborers. The group also documents hate crimes.

Immigrant advocates cheered the news earlier this year that the Department of Justice had begun a criminal investigation into hate crimes against Latinos in Suffolk County. The federal agency also launched a probe into the way the Suffolk County Police Department, the main law enforcement agency in the county, has handled such crimes.

Nevertheless, the Latino immigrants interviewed for this report expressed little optimism that attitudes will change. If anything, they said, their situation is growing more perilous by the day. The weak economy means that more residents are out of work and looking for someone to blame. And many of the jobs for immigrants have dried up, forcing day laborers to spend more time traveling to and from their residence or waiting for work on street corners, making them all the more vulnerable.

Although most of the Latino immigrants who are victimized in Suffolk County are undocumented, their attackers have no way of knowing their immigration status. "They don't know if I'm legal or not so it must be because we're [Latino]," said Orlando, a Guatemalan immigrant who came to Suffolk County in 2005. "The racist people aren't going to change just because we get papers."

 QUESTIONS FOR CRITICAL THINKING

Reading 43

1. As this article demonstrates, the actions of people in social institutions such as the criminal justice system and the government often contribute to the creation of a climate of hate directed at immigrants. What do you see as the responsibilities of these officials in creating a safe and fair environment for all persons living in our communities?

2. As illustrated in the report, economic difficulties faced by middle- and working-class individuals often result in misplacing blame on immigrants. Where do you think such blame should be more appropriately placed?

3. The United States is a country made up largely of immigrants and the descendents of immigrants, and yet recent immigrants face increasing resistance in their efforts to be included in society. What do you see as solutions to this resistance?

Reading 44

SEXUAL ASSAULT ON CAMPUS
A Multilevel, Integrative Approach to Party Rape

ELIZABETH A. ARMSTRONG • LAURA HAMILTON • BRIAN SWEENEY

A 1997 National Institute of Justice study estimated that between one-fifth and one-quarter of women are the victims of completed or attempted rape while in college (Fisher, Cullen, and Turner 2000).[1] College women "are at greater risk for rape and other forms of sexual assault than women in the general population or in a comparable age group" (Fisher et al. 2000:iii).[2] At least half and perhaps as many as three-quarters of the sexual assaults that occur on college campuses involve alcohol consumption on the part of the victim, the perpetrator, or both (Abbey et al. 1996; Sampson 2002). The tight link between alcohol and sexual assault suggests that many sexual assaults that occur on college campuses are "party rapes."[3] A recent report by the U.S. Department of Justice defines party rape as a distinct form of rape, one that "occurs at an off-campus house or on- or off-campus fraternity and involves . . . plying a woman with alcohol or targeting an intoxicated woman" (Sampson 2002:6).[4] While party rape is classified as a form of acquaintance rape, it is not uncommon for the woman to have had no prior interaction with the assailant, that is, for the assailant to be an in-network stranger (Abbey et al. 1996).

Colleges and universities have been aware of the problem of sexual assault for at least 20 years, directing resources toward prevention and providing services to students who have been sexually assaulted. Programming has included education of various kinds, support for *Take Back the Night* events, distribution of rape whistles, development and staffing of hotlines, training of police and administrators, and other efforts. Rates of sexual assault, however, have not declined over the last five decades (Adams-Curtis and Forbes 2004:95; Bachar and Koss 2001; Marine 2004; Sampson 2002:1).

Why do colleges and universities remain dangerous places for women in spite of active efforts to prevent sexual assault? While some argue that "we know what the problems are and we know how to change them" (Adams-Curtis and Forbes 2004:115), it is our contention that we do not have a complete explanation of the problem. To address this issue we use data from a

Elizabeth A. Armstrong, Laura Hamilton, and Brian Sweeney. 2006. "Sexual Assault on Campus: A Multilevel, Integrative Approach to Party Rape." *Social Problems*, Vol. 53, No. 4, pp. 483–499.

study of college life at a large midwestern university and draw on theoretical developments in the sociology of gender (Connell 1987, 1995; Lorber 1994; Martin 2004; Risman 1998, 2004). Continued high rates of sexual assault can be viewed as a case of the reproduction of gender inequality—a phenomenon of central concern in gender theory.

We demonstrate that sexual assault is a predictable outcome of a synergistic intersection of both gendered and seemingly gender neutral processes operating at individual, organizational, and interactional levels. The concentration of homogenous students with expectations of partying fosters the development of sexualized peer cultures organized around status. Residential arrangements intensify students' desires to party in male-controlled fraternities. Cultural expectations that partygoers drink heavily and trust party-mates become problematic when combined with expectations that women be nice and defer to men. Fulfilling the role of the partier produces vulnerability on the part of women, which some men exploit to extract nonconsensual sex. The party scene also produces fun, generating student investment in it. Rather than criticizing the party scene or men's behavior, students blame victims. By revealing mechanisms that lead to the persistence of sexual assault and outlining implications for policy, we hope to encourage colleges and universities to develop fresh approaches to sexual assault prevention.

APPROACHES TO COLLEGE SEXUAL ASSAULT

Explanations of high rates of sexual assault on college campuses fall into three broad categories. The first tradition, a psychological approach that we label the "individual determinants" approach, views college sexual assault as primarily a consequence of perpetrator or victim characteristics such as gender role attitudes, personality, family background, or sexual history (Flezzani and Benshoff 2003; Forbes and Adams-Curtis 2001; Rapaport and Burkhart 1984). While "situational variables" are considered, the focus is on individual characteristics (Adams-Curtis and Forbes 2004; Malamuth, Heavey, and Linz 1993). For example, Antonia Abbey and associates (2001) find that hostility toward women, acceptance of verbal pressure as a way to obtain sex, and having many consensual sexual partners distinguish men who sexually assault from men who do not. Research suggests that victims appear quite similar to other college women (Kalof 2000), except that white women, prior victims, first-year college students, and more sexually active women are more vulnerable to sexual assault (Adams-Curtis and Forbes 2004; Humphrey and White 2000).

The second perspective, the "rape culture" approach, grew out of second wave feminism (Brownmiller 1975; Buchward, Fletcher, and Roth 1993; Lottes 1997; Russell 1975; Schwartz and DeKeseredy 1997). In this perspective, sexual assault is seen as a consequence of widespread belief in "rape myths," or ideas about the nature of men, women, sexuality, and consent that create an environment conducive to rape. For example, men's disrespectful treatment of women is normalized by the idea that men are naturally sexually aggressive. Similarly, the belief that women "ask for it" shifts responsibility from predators to victims (Herman 1989; O'Sullivan 1993). This perspective initiated an important shift away from individual beliefs toward the broader context. However, rape supportive beliefs alone cannot explain the prevalence of sexual assault, which requires not only an inclination on the part of assailants but also physical proximity to victims (Adams-Curtis and Forbes 2004:103).

A third approach moves beyond rape culture by identifying particular contexts—fraternities and bars—as sexually dangerous (Humphrey and Kahn 2000; Martin and Hummer 1989; Sanday 1990, 1996; Stombler 1994). Ayres Boswell and Joan Spade (1996) suggest that sexual assault is supported not only by "a generic culture surrounding and promoting rape," but also by characteristics of the "specific settings" in which men and women interact (p. 133). Mindy Stombler and Patricia Yancey Martin (1994) illustrate that gender inequality is institutionalized on campus by "formal structure" that supports and intensifies an already "high-pressure heterosexual peer group" (p. 180). This perspective grounds sexual assault in organizations that provide opportunities and resources.

We extend this third approach by linking it to recent theoretical scholarship in the sociology of gender. Martin (2004), Barbara Risman (1998; 2004), Judith Lorber (1994) and others argue that gender is not only embedded in individual selves, but also in cultural rules, social interaction, and organizational arrangements. This integrative perspective identifies mechanisms at each level that contribute to the reproduction of gender inequality (Risman 2004). Socialization processes influence gendered selves, while cultural expectations reproduce gender inequality in interaction. At the institutional level, organizational practices, rules, resource distributions, and ideologies reproduce gender inequality. Applying this integrative perspective enabled us to identify gendered processes at individual, interactional, and organizational levels that contribute to college sexual assault.

Risman (1998) also argues that gender inequality is reproduced when the various levels are "all consistent and interdependent" (p. 35). Processes at each level depend upon processes at other levels. Below we demonstrate how interactional processes generating sexual danger depend upon organizational resources and particular kinds of selves. We show that sexual assault results from the intersection of processes at all levels.

We also find that not all of the processes contributing to sexual assault are explicitly gendered. For example, characteristics of individuals such as age, class, and concern with status play a role. Organizational practices such as residence hall assignments and alcohol regulation, both intended to be gender neutral, also contribute to sexual danger. Our findings suggest that apparently gender neutral social processes may contribute to gender inequality in other situations.

METHOD

Data are from group and individual interviews, ethnographic observation, and publicly available information collected at a large midwestern research university. Located in a small city, the school has strong academic and sports programs, a large Greek system, and is sought after by students seeking a quintessential college experience. Like other schools, this school has had legal problems as a result of deaths associated with drinking. In the last few years, students have attended a sexual assault workshop during first-year orientation. Health and sexuality educators conduct frequent workshops, student volunteers conduct rape awareness programs, and *Take Back the Night* marches occur annually.

The bulk of the data presented in this paper were collected as part of ethnographic observation during the 2004–05 academic year in a residence hall identified by students and residence hall staff as a "party dorm." While little partying actually occurs in the hall, many students view this residence hall as one of several places to live in order to participate in the party scene on campus. This made it a good place to study the social worlds of students at high risk of sexual assault—women attending fraternity parties in their first year of college. The authors and a research team were assigned to a room on a floor occupied by 55 women students (51 first-year, 2 second-year, 1 senior, and 1 resident assistant [RA]). We observed on evenings and weekends throughout the entire academic school year. We collected in-depth background information via a detailed nine-page survey that 23 women completed and conducted interviews with 42 of the women (ranging from 1 ¼ to 2 ½ hours). All but seven of the women on the floor completed either a survey or an interview.

With at least one-third of first-year students on campus residing in "party dorms" and one-quarter of all undergraduates belonging to fraternities or sororities, this social world is the most visible on campus. As the most visible scene on campus, it also attracts students living in other residence halls and those not in the Greek system. Dense pre-college ties among the many in-state students, class and race homogeneity, and a small city location also contribute to the dominance of this scene. Of course, not all students on this floor or at this university participate in the party scene. To participate, one must typically be heterosexual, at least middle class, white, American-born, unmarried, childless, traditional college age, politically and socially mainstream, and interested in drinking. Over three-quarters of the women on the floor we observed fit this description.

There were no non-white students among the first and second year students on the floor we studied. This is a result of the homogeneity of this campus and racial segregation in social and residential life. African Americans (who make up 3 to 5% of undergraduates) generally live in living-learning communities in other residence halls and typically do not participate in the white Greek party scene. We argue that the party scene's homogeneity contributes to sexual risk for white women. We lack the space and the data to compare white and African American party scenes on this campus, but in the discussion we offer ideas about what such a comparison might reveal.

We also conducted 16 group interviews (involving 24 men and 63 women) in spring 2004. These individuals had varying relationships to the white Greek party scene on campus. Groups included residents of an alternative residence hall, lesbian, gay, and bisexual students, feminists, re-entry students, academically-focused students, fundamentalist Christians, and sorority women. Eight group interviews were exclusively women, five were mixed in gender composition, and three were exclusively men. The group interviews covered a variety of topics, including discussions of social life, the transition to college, sexual assault, relationships, and the relationship between academic and social life. Participants completed a shorter version of the survey administered to the women on the residence hall floor. From these students we developed an understanding of the dominance of this party scene.

We also incorporated publicly available information about the university from informal interviews with student affairs professionals and from teaching (by all authors) courses on gender, sexuality, and introductory sociology. Classroom data were collected through discussion, student writings, e-mail correspondence, and a survey that included questions about experiences of sexual assault.

Unless stated otherwise, all descriptions and interview quotations are from ethnographic observation or interviews. Passages in quotation marks are direct quotations from interviews or field notes. Study participants served as informants about venues where we could not observe (such as fraternity parties).

EXPLAINING PARTY RAPE

We show how gendered selves, organizational arrangements, and interactional expectations contribute to sexual assault. We also detail the contributions of processes at each level that are not explicitly gendered. We focus on each level in turn, while attending to the ways in which processes at all levels depend upon and reinforce others. We show that fun is produced along with sexual assault, leading students to resist criticism of the party scene.

Selves and Peer Culture in the Transition from High School to College

Student characteristics shape not only individual participation in dangerous party scenes and sexual risk within them but the development of these party scenes.[5] We identify individual characteristics (other than gender) that generate interest in college partying and discuss the ways in which gendered sexual agendas generate a peer culture characterized by high-stakes competition over erotic status.

Non-Gendered Characteristics Motivate Participation in Party Scenes
Without individuals available for partying, the party scene would not exist. All the women on our floor were single and childless, as are the vast majority of undergraduates at this university; many, being upper-middle class, had few responsibilities other than their schoolwork. Abundant leisure time, however, is not enough to fuel the party scene. Media, siblings, peers, and parents all serve as sources of anticipatory socialization (Merton 1957). Both partiers and non-partiers agreed that one was "supposed" to party in college. This orientation was reflected in the popularity of a poster titled "What I Really Learned in School" that pictured mixed drinks with names associated with academic disciplines. As one focus group participant explained:

> You see these images of college that you're supposed to go out and have fun and drink, drink lots, party and meet guys. [You are] supposed to hook up with guys, and both men and women try to live up to that. I think a lot of it is girls want to be accepted into their groups and guys want to be accepted into their groups.

Partying is seen as a way to feel a part of college life. Many of the women we observed participated in middle and high school peer cultures organized around status, belonging, and popularity (Eder 1985; Eder, Evans, and Parker 1995; Milner 2004). Assuming that college would be similar, they told us that they wanted to fit in, be popular, and have friends. Even on move-in day, they were supposed to already have friends. When we asked one of the outsiders, Ruth, about her first impression of her roommate, she replied that she found her:

> Extremely intimidating. Bethany already knew hundreds of people here. Her cell phone was going off from day one, like all the time. And I was too shy to ask anyone to go to dinner with me or lunch with me or anything. I ate while I did homework.

Bethany complained to the RA on move-in day that she did not want to be roommates with Ruth because she was weird. A group of women on the floor—including Bethany, but not Ruth—began partying together and formed a tight friendship group. Ruth noted: "There is a group on the side of the hall that goes to dinner together, parties together, my roommate included. I have never hung out with them once . . . And, yeah, it kind of sucks." Bethany moved out of the room at the end of the semester, leaving Ruth isolated.

Peer Culture as Gendered and Sexualized Partying was also the primary way to meet men on campus.[6] The floor was locked to non-residents, and even men living in the same residence hall had to be escorted on the floor. The women found it difficult to get to know men in their classes, which were mostly mass lectures. They explained to us that people "don't talk" in class. Some complained they lacked casual friendly contact with men, particularly compared to the mixed-gender friendship groups they reported experiencing in high school.

Meeting men at parties was important to most of the women on our floor. The women found men's sexual interest at parties to be a source of self-esteem and status.[7] They enjoyed dancing and kissing at parties, explaining to us that it proved men "liked" them. This attention was not automatic but required the skillful deployment of physical and cultural assets (Stombler and Padavic 1997; Swidler 2001). Most of the party-oriented women on the floor arrived with appropriate gender presentations and the money and know-how to preserve and refine them. While some more closely resembled the "ideal" college party girl (white, even features, thin but busty, tan, long straight hair, skillfully made-up, and well-dressed in the latest youth styles), most worked hard to attain this presentation. They regularly straightened their hair, tanned, exercised, dieted, and purchased new clothes.

Women found that achieving high erotic status in the party scene required looking "hot" but not "slutty," a difficult and ongoing challenge (West and Zimmerman 1987). Mastering these distinctions allowed them to establish themselves as "classy" in contrast to other women (Handler 1995; Stombler 1994). Although women judged other women's appearance, men were the most important audience. A "hot" outfit could earn attention from desirable men in the party scene. A failed outfit, as some of our women learned, could earn scorn from men. One woman reported showing up to a party dressed in a knee length skirt and blouse only to find that she needed to show more skin. A male guest sarcastically told her "nice outfit," accompanied by a thumbs-up gesture.

The psychological benefits of admiration from men in the party scene were such that women in relationships sometimes felt deprived. One woman with a serious boyfriend noted that she dressed more conservatively at parties because of him, but this meant she was not "going to get any of the attention." She lamented that no one was "going to waste their time with me" and that, "this is taking away from my confidence." Like most women who came to college with boyfriends, she soon broke up with him.

Men also sought proof of their erotic appeal. As a woman complained, "Every man I have met here has wanted to have sex with me!" Another interviewee reported that: this guy that I was talking to for like ten/fifteen minutes says, "Could you, um, come to the bathroom with me and jerk me off?" And I'm like, "What!" I'm like, "Okay, like, I've known you for like, fifteen minutes, but no." The women found that men were more interested than they were in having sex. These clashes in sexual expectations are not surprising: men derived status from securing sex (from high-status women), while women derived status from getting attention (from high-status men).

These agendas are both complementary and adversarial: men give attention to women en route to getting sex, and women are unlikely to become interested in sex without getting attention first.

University and Greek Rules, Resources, and Procedures

Simply by congregating similar individuals, universities make possible heterosexual peer cultures. The university, the Greek system, and other related organizations structure student life through rules, distribution of resources, and procedures (Risman 2004).

Sexual danger is an unintended consequence of many university practices intended to be gender neutral. The clustering of homogeneous students intensifies the dynamics of student peer cultures and heightens motivations to party. Characteristics of residence halls and how they are regulated push student partying into bars, off-campus residences, and fraternities. While factors that increase the risk of party rape are present in varying degrees in all party venues (Boswell and Spade 1996), we focus on fraternity parties because they were the typical party venue for the women we observed and have been identified as particularly unsafe (see also Martin and Hummer 1989; Sanday 1990). Fraternities offer the most reliable and private source of alcohol for first-year students excluded from bars and house parties because of age and social networks.

University Practices as Push Factors   The university has latitude in how it enforces state drinking laws. Enforcement is particularly rigorous in residence halls. We observed RAs and police officers (including gun-carrying peer police) patrolling the halls for alcohol violations. Women on our floor were "documented" within the first week of school for infractions they felt were minor. Sanctions are severe—a $300 fine, an 8-hour alcohol class, and probation for a year. As a consequence, students engaged in only minimal, clandestine alcohol consumption in their rooms. In comparison, alcohol flows freely at fraternities.

The lack of comfortable public space for informal socializing in the residence hall also serves as a push factor. A large central bathroom divided our floor. A sterile lounge was rarely used for socializing. There was no cafeteria, only a convenience store and a snack bar in a cavernous room furnished with big-screen televisions. Residence life sponsored alternatives to the party scene such as "movie night" and special dinners, but these typically occurred early in the evening. Students defined the few activities sponsored during party hours (e.g., a midnight trip to Wal-Mart) as uncool.

Intensifying Peer Dynamics   The residence halls near athletic facilities and Greek houses are known by students to house affluent, party-oriented students. White, upper-middle class, first-year students who plan to rush request these residence halls, while others avoid them. One of our residents explained that "everyone knows what [the residence hall] is like and people are dying to get in here. People just think it's a total party or something." Students of color tend to live elsewhere on campus. As a consequence, our floor was homogenous in terms of age, race, sexual orientation, class, and appearance. Two women identified as lesbian; one moved within the first few weeks. The few women from less privileged backgrounds were socially invisible.

The homogeneity of the floor intensified social anxiety, heightening the importance of partying for making friends. Early in the year, the anxiety was palpable on weekend nights as women assessed their social options by asking where people were going, when, and with whom. One exhausted floor resident told us she felt that she "needed to" go out to protect her position in a friendship group. At the beginning of the semester, "going out" on weekends was virtually compulsory. By 11 p.m. the floor was nearly deserted.

Male Control of Fraternity Parties   The campus Greek system cannot operate without university consent. The university lists Greek organizations as student clubs, devotes professional staff to Greek-oriented programming, and disbands fraternities that violate university policy. Nonetheless, the university lacks full authority over fraternities; Greek houses are privately owned and chapters answer to national organizations and the Interfraternity Council (IFC) (i.e., a body governing the more than 20 predominantly white fraternities).

Fraternities control every aspect of parties at their houses: themes, music, transportation, admission, access to alcohol, and movement of guests. Party themes usually require women to wear scant, sexy clothing and place women in subordinate positions to men. During our observation period, women attended parties such as "Pimps and Hos," "Victoria's Secret," and "Playboy Mansion"—the last of which required fraternity members to escort two scantily-clad dates. Other recent themes included: "CEO/Secretary Ho," "School Teacher/Sexy Student," and "Golf Pro/Tennis Ho."

Some fraternities require pledges to transport first-year students, primarily women, from the residence halls to the fraternity houses. From about 9 to 11 p.m. on weekend nights early in the year, the drive in front of the residence hall resembled a rowdy taxi-stand, as dressed-to-impress women waited to be carpooled to parties in expensive late-model vehicles. By allowing party-oriented first-year women to cluster in particular residence halls, the university made them easy to find. One fraternity member told us this practice was referred to as "dorm-storming."

Transportation home was an uncertainty. Women sometimes called cabs, caught the "drunk bus," or trudged home in stilettos. Two women indignantly described a situation where fraternity men "wouldn't give us a ride home." The women said, "Well, let us call a cab." The men discouraged them from calling the cab and eventually found a designated driver. The women described the men as "just dicks" and as "rude."

Fraternities police the door of their parties, allowing in desirable guests (first-year women) and turning away others (unaffiliated men). Women told us of abandoning parties when male friends were not admitted. They explained that fraternity men also controlled the quality and quantity of alcohol. Brothers served themselves first, then personal guests, and then other women. Non-affiliated and unfamiliar men were served last, and generally had access to only the least desirable beverages. The promise of more or better alcohol was often used to lure women into private spaces of the fraternities.

Fraternities are constrained, though, by the necessity of attracting women to their parties. Fraternities with reputations for sexual disrespect have more success recruiting women to parties early in the year. One visit was enough for some of the women. A roommate duo told of a house they "liked at first" until they discovered that the men there were "really not nice."

The Production of Fun and Sexual Assault in Interaction

Peer culture and organizational arrangements set up risky partying conditions, but do not explain *how* student interactions at parties generate sexual assault. At the interactional level we see the mechanisms through which sexual assault is produced. As interactions necessarily involve individuals with particular characteristics and occur in specific organizational settings, all three levels meet when interactions take place. Here, gendered and gender neutral expectations and routines are intricately woven together to create party rape. Party rape is the result of fun situations that shift—either gradually or quite suddenly—into coercive situations. Demonstrating how the production of fun is connected with sexual assault requires describing the interactional routines and expectations that enable men to employ coercive sexual strategies with little risk of consequence.

College partying involves predictable activities in a predictable order (e.g., getting ready, pre-gaming,[8] getting to the party, getting drunk, flirtation or sexual interaction, getting home, and sharing stories). It is characterized by "shared assumptions about what constitutes good or adequate participation"—what Nina Eliasoph and Paul Lichterman (2003) call "group style" (p. 737). A fun partier throws him or herself into the event, drinks, displays an upbeat mood, and evokes revelry in others. Partiers are expected to like and trust partymates. Norms of civil interaction curtail displays of unhappiness or tension among partygoers. Michael Schwalbe and associates (2000) observed that groups engage in scripted events of this sort "to bring about an intended emotional result" (p. 438). Drinking assists people in transitioning from everyday life to a state of euphoria.

Cultural expectations of partying are gendered. Women are supposed to wear revealing outfits, while men typically are not. As guests, women cede control of turf, transportation, and liquor. Women are also expected to be grateful for men's hospitality, and as others have noted, to generally be "nice" in ways that men are not (Gilligan 1982; Martin 2003; Phillips 2000; Stombler and Martin 1994; Tolman 2002). The pressure to be deferential and gracious may be intensified by men's older age and fraternity membership.[9] The quandary for women, however, is that fulfilling the gendered role of partier makes them vulnerable to sexual assault.

Women's vulnerability produces sexual assault only if men exploit it. Too many men are willing to do so. Many college men attend parties looking for casual sex. A student in one of our classes explained that "guys are willing to do damn near anything to get a piece of ass." A male student wrote the following description of parties at his (non-fraternity) house:

> Girls are continually fed drinks of alcohol. It's mainly to party but my roomies are also aware of the inhibition-lowering effects. I've seen an old roomie block doors when girls want to leave his room; and other times I've driven women home who can't remember much of an evening yet sex did occur. Rarely if ever has a night of drinking for my roommate ended without sex. I know it isn't necessarily and assuredly sexual assault, but with the amount of liquor in the house I question the amount of consent a lot.

Another student—after deactivating—wrote about a fraternity brother "telling us all at the chapter meeting about how he took this girl home and she was obviously too drunk to function and he took her inside and had sex with her." Getting women drunk, blocking doors, and controlling transportation are common ways men try to prevent women from leaving sexual situations. Rape culture beliefs, such as the belief that men are "naturally" sexually aggressive, normalize these coercive strategies. Assigning women the role of sexual "gatekeeper" relieves men from responsibility for obtaining authentic consent, and enables them to view sex obtained by undermining women's ability to resist it as "consensual" (e.g., by getting women so drunk that they pass out).[10]

In a focus group with her sorority sisters, a junior sorority woman provided an example of a partying situation that devolved into a likely sexual assault.

ANNA: It kind of happened to me freshman year. I'm not positive about what happened, that's the worst part about it. I drank too much at a frat one night, I blacked out and I woke up the next morning with nothing on in their cold dorms, so I don't really know what happened and the guy wasn't in the bed anymore, I don't even think I could tell you who the hell he was, no I couldn't.

SARAH: Did you go to the hospital?

ANNA: No, I didn't know what happened. I was scared and wanted to get the hell out of there. I didn't know who it was, so how am I supposed to go to the hospital and say someone might've raped me? It could have been any one of the hundred guys that lived in the house.

SARAH: It happens to so many people, it would shock you. Three of my best friends in the whole world, people that you like would think it would never happen to, it happened to. It's just so hard because you don't know how to deal with it because you don't want to turn in a frat because all hundred of those brothers . . .

ANNA: I was also thinking like, you know, I just got to school, I don't want to start off on a bad note with anyone, and now it happened so long ago, it's just one of those things that I kind of have to live with.

This woman's confusion demonstrates the usefulness of alcohol as a weapon: her intoxication undermined her ability to resist sex, her clarity about what happened, and her feelings of entitlement to report it (Adams-Curtis and Forbes 2004; Martin and Hummer 1989). We collected other narratives in which sexual assault or probable sexual assault occurred when the woman was asleep, comatose, drugged, or otherwise incapacitated.

Amanda, a woman on our hall, provides insight into how men take advantage of women's niceness, gender deference, and unequal control of party resources. Amanda reported meeting a "cute" older guy, Mike, also a student, at a local student bar. She explained that, "At the bar we were kind of making out a little bit and I told him just cause I'm sitting here making out doesn't mean that I want to go home with you, you know?" After Amanda found herself stranded by friends with no cell phone or cab fare, Mike promised that a sober friend of his would drive her home. Once they got in the car Mike's friend refused to take her home and instead dropped her at Mike's place. Amanda's concerns were heightened by the driver's disrespect. "He was like, so are you into ménage à trois?" Amanda reported staying awake all night. She woke Mike early in the morning to take her home. Despite her ordeal, she argued that Mike was "a really nice guy" and exchanged telephone numbers with him.

These men took advantage of Amanda's unwillingness to make a scene. Amanda was one of the most assertive women on our floor. Indeed, her refusal to participate fully in the culture of feminine niceness led her to suffer in the social hierarchy of the floor and on campus. It is unlikely that other women we observed could have been more assertive in this situation. That she was nice to her captor in the morning suggests how much she wanted him to like her and what she was willing to tolerate in order to keep his interest.[11]

This case also shows that it is not only fraternity parties that are dangerous; men can control party resources and work together to constrain women's behavior while partying in bars and at house parties. What distinguishes fraternity parties is that male dominance of partying there is organized, resourced, and implicitly endorsed by the university. Other party venues are also organized in ways that advantage men.

We heard many stories of negative experiences in the party scene, including at least one account of a sexual assault in every focus group that included heterosexual women. Most women who partied complained about men's efforts to control their movements or pressure them to drink. Two of the women on our floor were sexually assaulted at a fraternity party in the first week of school—one was raped. Later in the semester, another woman on the floor was raped by a friend. A fourth woman on the floor suspects she was drugged; she became disoriented at a fraternity party and was very ill for the next week.

Party rape is accomplished without the use of guns, knives, or fists. It is carried out through the combination of low level forms of coercion—a lot of liquor and persuasion, manipulation of situations so that women cannot leave, and sometimes force (e.g., by blocking a door, or using body weight to make it difficult for a woman to get up). These forms of coercion are made more effective by organizational arrangements that provide men with control over how partying happens and by expectations that women let loose and trust their party-mates. This systematic and effective method of extracting non-consensual sex is largely invisible, which makes it difficult for victims to convince anyone—even themselves—that a crime occurred. Men engage in this behavior with little risk of consequences.

Student Responses and the Resiliency of the Party Scene

The frequency of women's negative experiences in the party scene poses a problem for those students most invested in it. Finding fault with the party scene potentially threatens meaningful identities and lifestyles. The vast majority of heterosexual encounters at parties are fun and consensual. Partying provides a chance to meet new people, experience and display belonging, and to enhance social position. Women on our floor told us that they loved to flirt and be admired, and they displayed pictures on walls, doors, and websites commemorating their fun nights out.

The most common way that students—both women and men—account for the harm that befalls women in the party scene is by blaming victims. By attributing bad experiences to women's "mistakes," students avoid criticizing the party scene or men's behavior within it. Such victim-blaming also allows women to feel that they can control what happens to them. The logic of victim-blaming suggests that sophisticated, smart, careful women are safe from sexual assault. Only "immature," "naïve," or "stupid" women get in trouble. When discussing the sexual assault of a friend, a floor resident explained that:

> She somehow got like sexually assaulted . . . by one of our friends' old roommates. All I know is that kid was like bad news to start off with. So, I feel sorry for her but it wasn't much of a surprise for us. He's a shady character.

Another floor resident relayed a sympathetic account of a woman raped at knife point by a stranger in the bushes, but later dismissed party rape as nothing to worry about "'cause I'm not stupid when I'm drunk." Even a feminist focus group participant explained that her friend who was raped "made every single mistake and almost all of them had to with alcohol. . . . She got ridiculed when she came out and said she was raped." These women contrast "true victims" who are deserving of support with "stupid" women who forfeit sympathy (Phillips 2000). Not only is this response devoid of empathy for other women, but it also leads women to blame themselves when they are victimized (Phillips 2000).

Sexual assault prevention strategies can perpetuate victim-blaming. Instructing women to watch their drinks, stay with friends, and limit alcohol consumption implies that it is women's responsibility to avoid "mistakes" and their fault if they fail. Emphasis on the precautions women should take— particularly if not accompanied by education about how men should change their behavior—may also suggest that it is natural for men to drug women and take advantage of them. Additionally, suggesting that women should watch what they drink, trust party-mates, or spend time alone with men asks them to forgo full engagement in the pleasures of the college party scene.

Victim-blaming also serves as a way for women to construct a sense of status within campus erotic hierarchies. As discussed earlier, women and men acquire erotic status based on how "hot" they are perceived to be. Another aspect of erotic status concerns the amount of sexual respect one receives from men (see Holland and Eisenhart 1990:101). Women can tell themselves that they are safe from sexual assault not only because they are savvy, but because men will recognize that they, unlike other women, are worthy of sexual respect. For example, a focus group of senior women explained that at a small fraternity gathering their friend Amy came out of the bathroom. She was crying and said that a guy "had her by her neck, holding her up, feeling her up from her crotch up to her neck and saying that I should rape you, you are a fucking whore." The woman's friends were appalled, saying, "no one deserves that." On other hand, they explained that: "Amy flaunts herself. She is a whore so, I mean . . ." They implied that if one is a whore, one gets treated like one.[12]

Men accord women varying levels of sexual respect, with lower status women seen as "fair game" (Holland and Eisenhart 1990; Phillips 2000). On campus the youngest and most anonymous women are most vulnerable. High-status women (i.e., girlfriends of fraternity members) may be less likely victims of party rape.[13] Sorority women explained that fraternities discourage members from approaching the girlfriends (and ex-girlfriends) of other men in the house. Partiers on our floor learned that it was safer to party with men they knew as boyfriends, friends, or brothers of friends. One roommate pair partied exclusively at a fraternity where one of the women knew many men from high school. She explained that "we usually don't party with people we don't know that well." Over the course of the year, women on the floor winnowed their party venues to those fraternity houses where they "knew the guys" and could expect to be treated respectfully.

Opting Out While many students find the party scene fun, others are more ambivalent. Some attend a few fraternity parties to feel like they have participated in this college tradition. Others opt out of it altogether. On our floor, 44 out of the 51 first-year students (almost 90%) participated in the party scene. Those on the floor who opted out worried about sexual safety and the consequences of engaging in illegal behavior. For example, an interviewee who did not drink was appalled by the fraternity party transport system. She explained that:

> All those girls would stand out there and just like, no joke, get into these big black Suburbans driven by frat guys, wearing like seriously no clothes, piled on top of each other. This could be some kidnapper taking you all away to the woods and chopping you up and leaving you there. How dumb can you be?

In her view, drinking around fraternity men was "scary" rather than "fun."

Her position was unpopular. She, like others who did not party, was an outsider on the floor. Partiers came home loudly in the middle of the night, threw up in the bathrooms, and rollerbladed around the floor. Socially, the others simply did not exist. A few of our "misfits" successfully created social lives outside the floor. The most assertive of the "misfits" figured out the dynamics of the floor in the first weeks and transferred to other residence halls.

However, most students on our floor lacked the identities or network connections necessary for entry into alternative worlds. Life on a large university campus can be overwhelming for first-year students. Those who most needed an alternative to the social world of the party dorm were often ill-equipped to actively seek it out. They either integrated themselves into partying or found themselves alone in their rooms, microwaving frozen dinners and watching television. A Christian focus group participant described life in this residence hall: "When everyone is going out on a Thursday and you are in the room by yourself and there are only two or three other people on the floor, that's not fun, it's not the college life that you want."

DISCUSSION AND IMPLICATIONS

We have demonstrated that processes at individual, organizational, and interactional levels contribute to high rates of sexual assault.[14] Some individual level characteristics that shape the likelihood of a sexually dangerous party scene developing are not explicitly gendered. Party rape occurs at high rates in places that cluster young, single, party-oriented people concerned about social status. Traditional beliefs about sexuality also make it more likely that one will participate in the party scene and increase danger within the scene. This university contributes to sexual danger by allowing these individuals to cluster.

However, congregating people is not enough, as parties cannot be produced without resources (e.g., alcohol and a viable venue) that are difficult for underage students to obtain. University policies that are explicitly gender-neutral—such as the policing of alcohol use in residence halls—have gendered consequences. This policy encourages first-year students to turn to fraternities to party. Only fraternities, not sororities, are allowed to have parties, and men structure parties in ways that control the appearance, movement, and behavior of female guests. Men also control the distribution of alcohol and use its scarcity to engineer social interactions. The enforcement of alcohol policy by both university and Greek organizations transforms alcohol from a mere beverage into an unequally distributed social resource.

Individual characteristics and institutional practices provide the actors and contexts in which interactional processes occur. We have to turn to the interactional level, however, to understand *how* sexual assault is generated. Gender neutral expectations to "have fun," lose control, and trust one's party-mates become problematic when combined with gendered interactional expectations. Women are expected to be "nice" and to defer to men in interaction. This expectation is intensified by men's position as hosts and women's as grateful guests. The heterosexual script, which directs men to pursue sex and women to play the role of gatekeeper, further disadvantages women, particularly when virtually *all* men's methods of extracting sex are defined as legitimate.

The mechanisms identified should help explain intra-campus, cross-campus, and over time variation in the prevalence of sexual assault. Campuses with similar students and social organization are predicted to have similar rates of sexual assault. We would expect to see lower rates of sexual assault on campuses characterized by more aesthetically appealing public space, lower alcohol use, and the absence of a gender-adversarial party scene. Campuses with more racial diversity and more racial integration would also be expected to have lower rates of sexual assault because of the dilution of upper-middle class white peer groups. Researchers are beginning to conduct comparative research on the impact of university organization on aggregate rates of sexual assault. For example, Meichun Mohler-Kuo and associates (2004) found that women who attended schools with medium or high levels of heavy episodic drinking were more at risk of being raped while intoxicated than women attending other schools, even while controlling for individual-level characteristics. More comparative research is needed.

This perspective may also help explain why white college women are at higher risk of sexual assault than other racial groups. Existing research suggests that African American college social scenes are more gender egalitarian (Stombler and Padavic 1997). African American fraternities typically do not have houses, depriving men of a party resource. The missions, goals, and recruitment practices of African American fraternities and sororities discourage joining for exclusively social reasons (Berkowitz and Padavic 1999), and rates of alcohol consumption are lower among African American students (Journal of Blacks in Higher Education 2000; Weschsler and Kuo 2003). The role of party rape in the lives of white college women is substantiated by recent research that found that "white women were more likely [than non-white women] to have experienced rape while intoxicated and less likely to experience other rape" (Mohler-Kuo et al. 2004:41). White women's overall higher rates of rape are accounted for by their high rates of rape while intoxicated. Studies of racial differences in the culture and organization of college partying and its consequences for sexual assault are needed.

Our analysis also provides a framework for analyzing the sources of sexual risk in non-university partying situations. Situations where men have a home turf advantage, know each other better than the women present know each other, see the women as anonymous, and control desired resources (such as alcohol or drugs) are likely to be particularly dangerous. Social pressures to "have fun," prove one's social competency, or adhere to traditional gender expectations are also predicted to increase rates of sexual assault within a social scene.

This research has implications for policy. The interdependence of levels means that it is difficult to enact change at one level when the other levels remain unchanged. Programs to combat sexual assault currently focus primarily or even exclusively on education (Bachar and Koss 2001; Leaning 2003). But as Ann Swidler (2001) argued, culture develops in response to institutional arrangements. Without change in institutional arrangements, efforts to change cultural beliefs are undermined by the cultural commonsense generated by encounters with institutions. Efforts to educate about sexual assault will not succeed if the university continues to support organizational arrangements that facilitate and even legitimate men's coercive sexual strategies. Thus; our research implies that efforts to combat sexual assault on campus should target all levels, constituencies, and processes simultaneously. Efforts to educate both men and women should indeed be intensified, but they should be reinforced by changes in the social organization of student life.

Researchers focused on problem drinking on campus have found that reduction efforts focused on the social environment are successful (Berkowitz 2003:21). Student body diversity has been found to decrease binge drinking on campus (Weschsler and Kuo 2003); it might also reduce rates of sexual assault. Existing student heterogeneity can be exploited by eliminating self-selection into age-segregated, white, upper-middle class, heterosexual enclaves and by working to make residence halls more appealing to upper-division students. Building more aesthetically appealing housing might allow students to interact outside of alcohol-fueled party scenes. Less expensive plans might involve creating more living-learning communities, coffee shops, and other student-run community spaces.

While heavy alcohol use is associated with sexual assault, not all efforts to regulate student alcohol use contribute to sexual safety. Punitive approaches sometimes heighten the symbolic significance of drinking, lead students to drink more hard liquor, and push alcohol consumption to more private and thus more dangerous spaces. Regulation inconsistently applied—e.g., heavy policing of residence halls and light policing of fraternities—increases the power of those who can secure alcohol and host parties. More consistent regulation could decrease the value of alcohol as a commodity by equalizing access to it.

Sexual assault education should shift in emphasis from educating women on preventative measures to educating both men and women about the coercive behavior of men and the sources of victim-blaming. Mohler-Kuo and associates (2004) suggest, and we endorse, a focus on the role of alcohol in sexual assault. Education should begin before students arrive on campus and continue throughout college. It may also be most effective if high-status peers are involved in disseminating knowledge and experience to younger college students.

Change requires resources and cooperation among many people. Efforts to combat sexual assault are constrained by other organizational imperatives. Student investment in the party scene makes it difficult to enlist the support of even those most harmed by the state of affairs. Student and alumni loyalty to partying (and the Greek system) mean that challenges to the party scene could potentially cost universities tuition dollars and alumni donations. Universities must contend with Greek organizations and bars, as well as the challenges of internal coordination. Fighting sexual assault on all levels is critical, though, because it is unacceptable for higher education institutions to be sites where women are predictably sexually victimized.

NOTES

1. Other studies have found similar rates of college sexual assault (Abbey et al. 1996; Adams-Curtis and Forbes 2004; Copenhaver and Grauerholz 1991; DeKeseredy and Kelly 1993; Fisher et al. 1998; Humphrey and White 2000; Koss 1988; Koss, Gidycz, and Wisniewski 1987; Mills and Granoff 1992; Muehlenhard and Linton 1987; Tjaden and Thoennes 2000; Ward et al. 1991).
2. While assaults within gender and by women occur, the vast majority involve men assaulting women.
3. Other forms of acquaintance rape include date rape, rape in a non-party/non-date situation, and rape by a former or current intimate (Sampson 2002).
4. On party rape as a distinct type of sexual assault, see also Ward and associates (1991). Ehrhart and Sandler (1987) use the term to refer to group rape. We use the term to refer to one-on-one assaults. We encountered no reports of group sexual assault.
5. Researchers often restrict their interest to characteristics that explain variation in the risk of perpetrating sexual assault or being victimized while taking for granted the existence of sexually risky social scenes.

6. This is consistent with Boswell and Spade's (1996) finding that women participate in dangerous party scenes because of a lack of "other means to initiate contact with men on campus" (p. 145).

7. See also Stombler and Martin (1994). Holland and Eisenhart (1990) discuss a "culture of romance" in which women derive status from boyfriends. Among the first-year women we observed, status revolved more around getting male attention than male commitment. Focus group interviews with junior and senior sorority women suggest that acquiring high-status fraternity men as boyfriends occurs after women are integrated into Greek life.

8. Pre-gaming involved the clandestine consumption of alcohol—often hard liquor—before arriving at the party.

9. Stombler and Martin (1994:156) found that fraternity men demanded "niceness" from women with whom they partied. They selected "little sisters" on the basis of physical beauty and "charm, friendliness, and outgoingness."

10. In ongoing research on college men and sexuality, Sweeney (2004) and Rosow and Ray (2006) have found wide variation in beliefs about acceptable ways to obtain sex even among men who belong to the same fraternities. Rosow and Ray found that fraternity men in the most elite houses view sex with intoxicated women as low status and claim to avoid it.

11. Holland and Eisenhart (1990) and Stombler (1994) found that male attention is of such high value to some women that they are willing to suffer indignities to receive it.

12. Schwalbe and associates (2000) suggest that there are several psychological mechanisms that explain this behavior. *Trading power for patronage* occurs when a subordinate group accepts their status in exchange for compensatory benefits from the dominant group. *Defensive othering* is a process by which some members of a subordinated group seek to maintain status by deflecting stigma to others. Maneuvering to protect or improve individual position within hierarchical classification systems is common; however, these responses support the subordination that makes them necessary.

13. While "knowing" one's male party-mates may offer some protection, this protection is not comprehensive. Sorority women, who typically have the closest ties with fraternity men, experience more sexual assault than other college women (Mohler-Kuo et al. 2004). Not only do sorority women typically spend more time in high-risk social situations than other women, but arriving at a high-status position on campus may require one to begin their college social career as one of the anonymous young women who are frequently victimized.

14. Our recommendations echo and extend those of Boswell and Spade (1996:145) and Stombler and Martin (1994:180).

REFERENCES

Abbey, Antonia, Pam McAuslan, Tina Zawacki, A. Monique Clinton, and Philip Buck. 2001. "Attitudinal, Experiential, and Situational Predictors of Sexual Assault Perpetration." *Journal of Interpersonal Violence* 16:784–807.

Abbey, Antonia, Lisa Thomson Ross, Donna McDuffie, and Pam McAuslan. 1996. "Alcohol and Dating Risk Factors for Sexual Assault among College Women." *Psychology of Women Quarterly* 20:147–69.

Adams-Curtis, Leah and Gordon Forbes. 2004. "College Women's Experiences of Sexual Coercion: A Review of Cultural, Perpetrator, Victim, and Situational Variables." *Trauma, Violence, and Abuse: A Review Journal* 5:91–122.

Bachar, Karen and Mary Koss. 2001. "From Prevalence to Prevention: Closing the Gap between What We Know about Rape and What We Do." pp. 117–42 in *Sourcebook on Violence against Women,* edited by C. Renzetti, J. Edleson, and R. K. Bergen. Thousand Oaks, CA: Sage.

Berkowitz, Alan. 2003. "How Should We Talk about Student Drinking—And What Should We Do about It?" *About Campus* May/June: 16–22.

Berkowitz, Alexandra and Irene Padavic. 1999. "Getting a Man or Getting Ahead: A Comparison of White and Black Sororities." *Journal of Contemporary Ethnography* 27:530–57.

Boswell, A. Ayres and Joan Z. Spade. 1996. "Fraternities and Collegiate Rape Culture: Why Are Some Fraternities More Dangerous Places for Women?" *Gender & Society* 10:133–47.

Brownmiller, Susan. 1975. *Against Our Will: Men, Women, and Rape.* New York: Bantam Books.

Buchward, Emilie, Pamela Fletcher, and Martha Roth, eds. 1993. *Transforming a Rape Culture.* Minneapolis, MN: Milkweed Editions.

Connell, R. W. 1987. *Gender and Power.* Palo Alto, CA: Stanford University Press.

———. 1995. *Masculinities.* Berkeley, CA: University of California Press.

Copenhaver, Stacey and Elizabeth Grauerholz. 1991. "Sexual Victimization among Sorority Women: Exploring the Link between Sexual Violence and Institutional Practices." *Sex Roles* 24:31–41.

DeKeseredy, Walter and Katharine Kelly. 1993. "The Incidence and Prevalence of Women Abuse in Canadian University and College Dating Relationships." *Canadian Journal of Sociology* 18:137–59.

Eder, Donna. 1985. "The Cycle of Popularity: Interpersonal Relations among Female Adolescents." *Sociology of Education* 58:154–65.

Eder, Donna, Catherine Evans, and Stephen Parker. 1995. *School Talk: Gender and Adolescent Culture.* New Brunswick, NJ: Rutgers University Press.

Ehrhart, Julie and Bernice Sandler. 1987. "Party Rape." *Response* 9:205.

Eliasoph, Nina and Paul Lichterman. 2003. "Culture in Interaction." *American Journal of Sociology* 108:735–94.

Fisher, Bonnie, Francis Cullen, and Michael Turner. 2000. "The Sexual Victimization of College Women." Washington, DC: National Institute of Justice and the Bureau of Justice Statistics.

Fisher, Bonnie, John Sloan, Francis Cullen, and Lu Chunmeng. 1998. "Crime in the Ivory Tower: The Level and Sources of Student Victimization." *Criminology* 36:671–710.

Flezzani, James and James Benshoff. 2003. "Understanding Sexual Aggression in Male College Students: The Role of Self-Monitoring and Pluralistic Ignorance." *Journal of College Counseling* 6:69–79.

Forbes, Gordon and Leah Adams-Curtis. 2001. "Experiences with Sexual Coercion in College Males and Females: Role of Family Conflict, Sexist Attitudes, Acceptance of Rape Myths, Self-Esteem, and the Big-Five Personality Factors." *Journal of Interpersonal Violence* 16:865–89.

Gilligan, Carol. 1982. *In a Different Voice: Psychological Theory and Women's Development.* Cambridge, MA: Harvard University Press.

Handler, Lisa. 1995. "In the Fraternal Sisterhood: Sororities as Gender Strategy." *Gender & Society* 9:236–55.

Herman, Diane. 1989. "The Rape Culture." pp. 20–44 in *Women: A Feminist Perspective,* edited by J. Freeman. Mountain View, CA: Mayfield.

Holland, Dorothy and Margaret Eisenhart. 1990. *Educated in Romance: Women, Achievement, and College Culture.* Chicago: University of Chicago Press.

Humphrey, John and Jacquelyn White. 2000. "Women's Vulnerability to Sexual Assault from Adolescence to Young Adulthood." *Journal of Adolescent Health* 27:419–24.

Humphrey, Stephen and Arnold Kahn. 2000. "Fraternities, Athletic Teams, and Rape: Importance of Identification with a Risky Group." *Journal of Interpersonal Violence* 15:1313–22.

Journal of Blacks in Higher Education. 2000. "News and Views: Alcohol Abuse Remains High on College Campus, But Black Students Drink to Excess Far Less Often Than Whites." *The Journal of Blacks in Higher Education.* 28:19–20.

Kalof, Linda. 2000. "Vulnerability to Sexual Coercion among College Women: A Longitudinal Study." *Gender Issues* 18:47–58.

Koss, Mary. 1988. "Hidden Rape: Incidence and Prevalence of Sexual Aggression and Victimization in a National Sample of Students in Higher Education." pp. 4–25 in *Rape and Sexual Assault,* edited by Ann W. Burgess. New York: Garland.

Koss, Mary, Christine Gidycz, and Nadine Wisniewski. 1987. "The Scope of Rape: Incidence and Prevalence of Sexual Aggression and Victimization in a National Sample of Higher Education Students." *Journal of Counseling and Clinical Psychology* 55:162–70.

Leaning, Jennifer. April 2003. "Committee to Address Sexual Assault at Harvard: Public Report." Cambridge, MA: Harvard University.

Lorber, Judith. 1994. *Paradoxes of Gender.* New Haven, CT: Yale University Press.

Lottes, Ilsa L. 1997. "Sexual Coercion among University Students: A Comparison of the United States and Sweden." *Journal of Sex Research* 34:67–76.

Malamuth, Neil, Christopher Heavey, and Daniel Linz. 1993. "Predicting Men's Anti-social Behavior against Women: The Interaction Model of Sexual Aggression." pp. 63–98 in *Sexual Aggression: Issues in Etiology, Assessment, and Treatment,* edited by G. N. Hall, R. Hirschman, J. Graham, and M. Zaragoza. Washington, D.C.: Taylor and Francis.

Marine, Susan. 2004. "Waking Up from the Nightmare of Rape." *The Chronicle of Higher Education.* November 26, p. B5.

Martin, Karin. 2003. "Giving Birth Like a Girl." *Gender & Society.* 17:54–72.

Martin, Patricia Yancey. 2004. "Gender as a Social Institution." *Social Forces* 82:1249–73.

Martin, Patricia Yancey and Robert A. Hummer. 1989. "Fraternities and Rape on Campus." *Gender & Society* 3:457–73.

Merton, Robert. 1957. *Social Theory and Social Structure.* New York: Free Press.

Mills, Crystal and Barbara Granoff. 1992. "Date and Acquaintance Rape among a Sample of College Students." *Social Work* 37:504–09.

Milner, Murray. 2004. *Freaks, Geeks, and Cool Kids: American Teenagers, Schools, and the Culture of Consumption.* New York: Routledge.

Mohler-Kuo, Meichun, George W. Dowdall, Mary P. Koss, and Henry Weschler. 2004. "Correlates of Rape While Intoxicated in a National Sample of College Women." *Journal of Studies on Alcohol* 65:37–45.

Muehlenhard, Charlene and Melaney Linton. 1987. "Date Rape and Sexual Aggression: Incidence and Risk Factors." *Journal of Counseling Psychology* 34:186–96.

O'Sullivan, Chris. 1993. "Fraternities and the Rape Culture." pp. 23–30 in *Transforming a Rape Culture,* edited by E. Buchward, P. Fletcher, and M. Roth. Minneapolis, MN: Milkweed Editions.

Phillips, Lynn. 2000. *Flirting with Danger: Young Women's Reflections on Sexuality and Domination.* New York: New York University.

Rapaport, Karen and Barry Burkhart. 1984. "Personality and Attitudinal Characteristics of Sexually Coercive College Males." *Journal of Abnormal Psychology* 93:216–21.

Risman, Barbara. 1998. *Gender Vertigo: American Families in Transition.* New Haven, CT: Yale University Press.

_____. 2004. "Gender as a Social Structure: Theory Wrestling with Activism." *Gender & Society* 18:429–50.

Rosow, Jason and Rashawn Ray. 2006. "Getting off and Showing Off: The Romantic and Sexual Lives of High-Status Black and White Status Men." Department of Sociology, Indiana University, Bloomington, IN. Unpublished manuscript.

Russell, Diana. 1975. *The Politics of Rape.* New York: Stein and Day.

Sampson, Rana. 2002. "Acquaintance Rape of College Students." Problem-Oriented Guides for Police Series, No. 17. Washington, DC: U.S. Department of Justice, Office of Community Oriented Policing Services.

Sanday, Peggy. 1990. *Fraternity Gang Rape: Sex, Brotherhood, and Privilege on Campus.* New York: New York University Press.

_____. 1996. "Rape-Prone versus Rape-Free Campus Cultures." *Violence against Women* 2:191–208.

Schwalbe, Michael, Sandra Godwin, Daphne Holden, Douglas Schrock, Shealy Thompson, and Michele Wolkomir. 2000. "Generic Processes in the Reproduction of Inequality: An Interactionist Analysis." *Social Forces* 79:419–52.

Schwartz, Martin and Walter DeKeseredy. 1997. *Sexual Assault on the College Campus: The Role of Male Peer Support.* Thousand Oaks, CA: Sage Publications.

Stombler, Mindy. 1994. " 'Buddies' or 'Slutties': The Collective Reputation of Fraternity Little Sisters." *Gender & Society* 8:297–323.

Stombler, Mindy and Patricia Yancey Martin. 1994. "Bringing Women In, Keeping Women Down: Fraternity 'Little Sister' Organizations." *Journal of Contemporary Ethnography* 23:150–84.

Stombler, Mindy and Irene Padavic. 1997. "Sister Acts: Resisting Men's Domination in Black and White Fraternity Little Sister Programs." *Social Problems* 44:257–75.

Sweeney, Brian. 2004. "Good Guy on Campus: Gender, Peer Groups, and Sexuality among College Men." Presented at the American Sociological Association Annual Meeting, August 17, Philadelphia, PA.

Swidler, Ann. 2001. *Talk of Love: How Culture Matters.* Chicago: University of Chicago Press.

Tjaden, Patricia and Nancy Thoennes. 2000. "Full Report of the Prevalence, Incidence, and Consequences of Violence against Women: Findings from the National Violence against Women Survey." Washington, DC: National Institute of Justice.

Tolman, Deborah. 2002. *Dilemmas of Desire: Teenage Girls Talk about Sexuality*. Cambridge, MA: Harvard University Press.

Ward, Sally, Kathy Chapman, Ellen Cohn, Susan White, and Kirk Williams. 1991. "Acquaintance Rape and the College Social Scene." *Family Relations* 40:65–71.

Weschsler, Henry and Meichun Kuo. 2003. "Watering Down the Drinks: The Moderating Effect of College Demographics on Alcohol Use of High-Risk Groups." *American Journal of Public Health*. 93:1929–33.

West, Candace and Don Zimmerman. 1987. "Doing Gender." *Gender & Society* 1:125–51.

QUESTIONS FOR CRITICAL THINKING

Reading 44

1. The authors of this study illustrate how gendered expectations of sexuality contribute to an environment in the college party scene that contributes to creating an environment that results in sexual assault. How might gender equality among college women and men in their sexual behavior reduce the incidence of rape?

2. Do you think some college party environments perpetuate a rape culture? If so, how? If not, why don't you think so?

3. Issues of rape and sexual assault are of particular concern on college campuses. Why do you think this is? What steps can all members of campus communities take to reduce or eliminate this concern?

Reading 45

THE CONSTRUCTION OF MASCULINITY
AND THE TRIAD OF MEN'S VIOLENCE

MICHAEL KAUFMAN

The all too familiar story: a woman raped, a wife battered, a lover abused. With a sense of immediacy and anger, the women's liberation movement has pushed the many forms of men's violence against women—from the most overt to the most subtle in form—into popular consciousness and public debate. These forms of violence are one aspect of our society's domination by men that, in outcome, if not always in design, reinforces that domination. The act of violence is many things at once. At the same instant it is the individual man acting out relations of sexual power; it is the violence of a society—a hierarchical, authoritarian, sexist, class-divided, militarist, racist, impersonal, crazy society—being focused through an individual man onto an individual woman. In the psyche of the individual man it might be his denial of social powerlessness through an act of aggression. In total these acts of violence are like a ritualized acting out of our social relations of power: the dominant and the weaker, the powerful and the powerless, the active and the passive . . . the masculine and the feminine.

For men, listening to the experience of women as the objects of men's violence is to shatter any complacency about the sex-based status quo. The power and anger of women's responses forces us to rethink the things we discovered when we were very young. When I was eleven or twelve years old a friend told me the difference between fucking and raping. It was simple: with rape you tied the woman to a tree. At the time the anatomical details were still a little vague, but in either case it was something "we" supposedly did. This knowledge was just one part of an education, started years before, about the relative power and privileges of men and women. I remember laughing when my friend explained all that to me. Now I shudder. The difference in my responses is partially that, at twelve, it was part of the posturing and pretense that accompanied my passage into adolescence. Now, of course, I have a different vantage point on the issue. It is the vantage point of an adult, but more importantly my view of the world is being reconstructed by the intervention of that majority whose voice has been suppressed: the women.

This relearning of the reality of men's violence against women evokes many deep feelings and memories for men. As memories are recalled and recast, a new connection becomes clear: violence by men against women is only one corner of a triad of men's violence. The other two corners are violence against other men and violence against oneself.

On a psychological level the pervasiveness of violence is the result of what Herbert Marcuse called the "surplus repression" of our sexual and emotional desires.[1] The substitution of violence for desire (more precisely, the transmutation of violence into a form of emotionally gratifying activity) happens unequally in men and women. The construction of masculinity involves the construction of "surplus aggressiveness." The social context of this triad of violence is the institutionalization of violence in the operation of most aspects of social, economic, and political life.

The three corners of the triad reinforce one another. The first corner—violence against women—cannot be confronted successfully without simultaneously challenging the other two corners of the triad. And all this requires a dismantling of the social feeding ground of violence: patriarchal, heterosexist, authoritarian, class societies. These three corners and the societies in which they blossom feed on each other. And together, we surmise, they will fall.

THE SOCIAL CONTEXT

In spite of proclamations from the skewed research of sociobiologists, there is no good evidence that men's violence is the inevitable and natural result of male genes or hormones. To the contrary, anthropology tells us of many early societies with little or no violence against women, against children, or among men. However, given the complexity of the issues concerning the roots of violence, the essential question for us is not whether men are predisposed to violence but what society does with this violence. Why has the linchpin of so many societies been the manifold expression of violence perpetrated disproportionately by men? Why are so many forms of violence sanctioned or even encouraged? Exactly what is the nature of violence? And how are patterns of violence and the quest for domination built up and reinforced?

In other words, the key questions having to do with men's violence are not biological but are related to gender and society—which is why I speak not of "male violence" (a biological category) but rather of "men's violence" (the gender category).

For every apparently individual act of violence there is a social context. This is not to say there are no pathological acts of violence; but even in that case the "language" of the violent act, the way the violence manifests itself can only be understood within a certain social experience. We are interested here in the manifestations of violence that are accepted as more or less normal, even if reprehensible: fighting, war, rape, assault, psychological abuse, and so forth. What is the context of men's violence in the prevalent social orders of today?

Violence has long been institutionalized as an acceptable means of solving conflicts. But now the vast apparati of policing and war making maintained by countries the world over pose a threat to the future of life itself.

"Civilized" societies have been built and shaped through the decimation, containment, and exploitation of other peoples: extermination of native populations, colonialism, and slavery. Our relationship with the natural environment has often been described with the metaphor of rape. An attitude of conquering nature, of mastering an environment waiting to be exploited for profit, has great consequences when we possess a technology capable of permanently disrupting an ecological balance shaped over hundreds of millions of years.

The daily work life of industrial class societies is one of violence. Violence poses as economic rationality as some of us are turned into extensions of machines, while others become brains detached from bodies. Our industrial process becomes the modern-day rack of torture where we are stretched out of shape and ripped limb from limb. It is violence that exposes workers to the danger of chemicals, radiation, machinery, speedup, and muscle strain.

The racism, sexism, and heterosexism that have been institutionalized in our societies are socially regulated acts of violence. Our cities, our social structure, our work life, our relation with nature, our history are more than a backdrop to the prevalence of violence. They are violence; violence in an institutionalized form encoded into physical structures and socioeconomic relations. Much of the sociological analysis of violence in our societies implies simply that violence is learned by witnessing and experiencing social violence: man kicks boy, boy kicks dog.[2] Such experiences of transmitted violence are a reality, as the analysis of wife battering indicates, for many batterers were themselves abused as children. [T]hrough [the child's] psychological development he embraces and takes into himself a set of gender-based social relations: the person that is created through the process of maturation becomes the personal embodiment of those relations. By the time the child is five or six years old, the basis for lifelong masculinity has already been established.

The basis for the individual's acquisition of gender is that the prolonged period of human childhood results in powerful attachments to parental figures. (Through a very complex process, by the time a boy is five or six he claims for himself the power and activity society associates with masculinity.) He embraces the project of controlling himself and controlling the world. He comes to personify activity. Masculinity is a reaction against passivity and powerlessness, and with it comes a repression of a vast range of human desires and possibilities: those that are associated with femininity.

Masculinity is unconsciously rooted before the age of six, is reinforced as the child develops, and then positively explodes at adolescence, obtaining its definitive shape for the individual. The masculine norm has its own particular nuances and traits dependent on class, nation, race, religion, and ethnicity. And within each group it has its own personal expression. In adolescence the pain and fear involved in repressing "femininity" and passivity start to become evident. For most of us, the response to this inner pain is to reinforce the bulwarks of masculinity. The emotional pain created by obsessive masculinity is stifled by reinforcing masculinity itself.

THE FRAGILITY OF MASCULINITY

Masculinity is power. But masculinity is terrifyingly fragile because it does not really exist in the sense we are led to think it exists; that is, as a biological reality—something real that we have inside ourselves. It exists as ideology; it exists as scripted behavior; it exists within "gendered" relationships. But in the end it is just a social institution with a tenuous relationship to that with which it is supposed to be synonymous: our maleness, our biological sex. The young child does not know that sex does not equal gender. For him to be male is to be what he perceives as being masculine. The child is father to the man. Therefore, to be unmasculine is to be desexed—"castrated."

The tension between maleness and masculinity is intense because masculinity requires a suppression of a whole range of human needs, aims, feelings, and forms of expression. Masculinity is one-half of the narrow, surplus-repressive shape of the adult human psyche. Even when we are intellectually aware of the difference between biological maleness and masculinity, the masculine ideal is so embedded within ourselves that it is hard to untangle the person we might want to become (more "fully human," less sexist, less surplus-repressed, and so on) from the person we actually are.

But as children and adolescents (and often as adults), we are not aware of the difference between maleness and masculinity. With the exception of a tiny proportion of the population born as hermaphrodites, there can be no biological struggle to be male. The presence of a penis and testicles is all it takes. Yet boys and men harbor great insecurity about their male credentials. This insecurity exists because maleness is equated with masculinity; but the latter is a figment of our collective, patriarchal, surplus-repressive imaginations.

In a patriarchal society being male is highly valued, and men value their masculinity. But everywhere there are ambivalent feelings. That the initial internalization of masculinity is at the father's knee has lasting significance. Andrew Tolson states that "to the boy, masculinity is both mysterious and attractive (in its promise of a world of work and power), and yet, at the same time, threatening (in its strangeness, and emotional distance).... It works both ways; attracts and repels in dynamic contradiction. This simultaneous distance and attraction is internalized as a permanent emotional tension that the individual must, in some way, strive to overcome."[3]

Although maleness and masculinity are highly valued, men are everywhere unsure of their sexuality, our needs and fears, our strengths and weaknesses, our selves are created—not simply learned—through our lived reality. The violence of our social order nurtures a psychology of violence, which in turn reinforces the social, economic and political structures of violence. The ever-increasing demands of civilization and the constant building upon inherited structures of violence suggest that the development of civilization has been inseparable from a continuous increase in violence against humans and our natural environment.

It would be easy, yet ultimately not very useful, to slip into a use of the term "violence" as a metaphor for all our society's antagonisms, contradictions, and ills. For now, let us leave aside the social terrain and begin to unravel the nature of so-called individual violence.

◎ THE TRIAD OF MEN'S VIOLENCE

The longevity of the oppression of women must be based on something more than conspiracy, something more complicated than biological handicap and more durable than economic exploitation (although in differing degrees all these may feature).

—Juliet Mitchell[4]

It seems impossible to believe that mere greed could hold men to such a steadfastness of purpose.

—Joseph Conrad[5]

The field in which the triad of men's violence is situated is a society, or societies, grounded in structures of domination and control. Although at times this control is symbolized and embodied in the individual father—patriarchy, by definition—it is more important to emphasize that patriarchal structures of authority, domination, and control are diffused throughout social, economic, political, and ideological activities and in our relations to the natural environment. Perhaps more than in any previous time during the long epoch of patriarchy, authority does *not* rest with the father, at least in much of the advanced capitalist and noncapitalist world. This has led more than one author to question the applicability of the term *patriarchy*.[6] But I think it still remains useful as a broad, descriptive category. In this sense Jessica Benjamin speaks of the current reign of patriarchy without the father. "The form of domination peculiar to this epoch expresses itself not directly as authority but indirectly as the transformation of all relationships and activity into objective, instrumental, depersonalized forms."[7]

The structures of domination and control form not simply the background to the triad of violence, but generate, and in turn are nurtured by, this violence. These structures refer both to our social relations and to our interaction with our natural environment. The relation between these two levels

is obviously extremely complex. It appears that violence against nature—
that is, the impossible and disastrous drive to dominate and conquer the
natural world—is integrally connected with domination among humans.
Some of these connections are quite obvious. One thinks of the bulldozing
of the planet for profit in capitalist societies, societies characterized by the
dominance of one class over others. But the link between the domination of
nature and structures of domination of humans go beyond this.

 ## THE INDIVIDUAL REPRODUCTION
OF MALE DOMINATION

No man is born a butcher.

—Bertolt Brecht[8]

In a male-dominated society men have a number of privileges. Compared
to women we are free to walk the streets at night, we have traditionally
escaped domestic labor, and on average we have higher wages, better jobs,
and more power. But these advantages in themselves cannot explain the
individual reproduction of the relations of male domination, that is, why the
individual male from a very early age embraces masculinity. The embracing
of masculinity is not only a "socialization" into a certain gender role, as if
there is a preformed human being who learns a role that he own masculinity and maleness, whether consciously or not. When men are encouraged to
be open, as in men's support and counseling groups, it becomes apparent
that there exists, often under the surface, an internal dialogue of doubt about
one's male and masculine credentials.

 ## MEN'S VIOLENCE AGAINST WOMEN

*In spite of the inferior role which men assign to them, women are the privi-
leged objects of their aggression.*

—Simone De Beauvoir[9]

Men's violence against women is the most common form of direct, personalized violence in the lives of most adults. From sexual harassment to rape,
from incest to wife battering to the sight of violent pornographic images, few
women escape some form of men's aggression.

My purpose here is not to list and evaluate the various forms of violence
against women, nor to try to assess what can be classed as violence per se.[10]
It is to understand this violence as an expression of the fragility of masculinity combined with men's power. I am interested in its place in the perpetuation of masculinity and male domination.

In the first place, men's violence against women is probably the clearest,
most straightforward expression of relative male and female power. That

the relative social, economic, and political power can be expressed in this manner is, to a large part, because of differences in physical strength and in a lifelong training (or lack of training) in fighting. But it is also expressed this way because of the active/passive split. Activity as aggression is part of the masculine gender definition. That is not to say this definition always includes rape or battering, but it is one of the possibilities within a definition of activity that is ultimately grounded in the body.

Rape is a good example of the acting out of these relations of power and of the outcome of fragile masculinity in a surplus-repressive society. In the testimonies of rapists one hears over and over again expressions of inferiority, powerlessness, anger. But who can these men feel superior to? Rape is a crime that not only demonstrates physical power, but that does so in the language of male-female sex-gender relations. The testimonies of convicted rapists collected by Douglas Jackson in the late 1970s are chilling and revealing.[11] Hal: "I feel very inferior to others. . . . I felt rotten about myself and by committing rape I took this out on someone I thought was weaker than me, someone I could control." Len: "I feel a lot of what rape is isn't so much sexual desire as a person's feelings about themselves and how that relates to sex. My fear of relating to people turned to sex because . . . it just happens to be the fullest area to let your anger out on, to let your feelings out on."

Sometimes this anger and pain are experienced in relation to women but just as often not. In either case they are addressed to women who, as the Other in a phallocentric society, are objects of mystification to men, the objects to whom men from birth have learned to express and vent their feelings, or simply objects with less social power and weaker muscles. It is the crime against women par excellence because, through it, the full weight of a sexually based differentiation among humans is played out.

Within relationships, forms of men's violence such as rape, battering, and what Meg Luxton calls the "petty tyranny" of male domination in the household[12] must be understood both "in terms of violence directed against women as women and against women as wives."[13] The family provides an arena for the expression of needs and emotions not considered legitimate elsewhere.[14] It is one of the only places where men feel safe enough to express emotions. As the dams break, the flood pours out on women and children.[15] The family also becomes the place where the violence suffered by individuals in their work lives is discharged. "At work men are powerless, so in their leisure time they want to have a feeling that they control their lives."[16]

While this violence can be discussed in terms of male aggression, it operates within the dualism of activity and passivity, masculinity and femininity. Neither can exist without the other. This is not to blame women for being beaten, nor to excuse men who beat. It is but an indication that the various forms of men's violence against women are a dynamic affirmation of a masculinity that can only exist as distinguished from femininity. It is my argument that masculinity needs constant nurturing and affirmation. This affirmation takes many different forms. The majority of men are not rapists or batterers, although it is probable that the majority of men have used superior physical strength or some sort of physical force or threat of force against a woman at least once as a teenager or an adult. But in those who harbor great personal doubts or strongly negative self-images, or who cannot cope with a daily feeling of powerlessness, violence against women can become a means of trying to affirm their personal power in the language of our sex-gender system. That these forms of violence only reconfirm the negative self-image and the feelings of powerlessness shows the fragility, artificiality, the precariousness of masculinity.

VIOLENCE AGAINST OTHER MEN

At a behavioral level, men's violence against other men is visible throughout society. Some forms, such as fighting, the ritualized display of violence of teenagers and some groups of adult men, institutionalized rape in prisons, and attacks on gays or racial minorities, are very direct expressions of this violence. In many sports, violence is incorporated into exercise and entertainment. More subtle forms are the verbal putdown or, combined with economic and other factors, the competition in the business, political, or academic world. In its most frightening form, violence has long been an acceptable and even preferred method of addressing differences and conflicts among different groups and states. In the case of war, as in many other manifestations of violence, violence against other men (and civilian women) combines with autonomous economic, ideological, and political factors.

But men's violence against other men is more than the sum of various activities and types of behavior. In this form of violence a number of things are happening at once, in addition to the autonomous factors involved. Sometimes mutual, sometimes one-sided, there is a discharge of aggression and hostility. But at the same time as discharging aggression, these acts of violence and the ever-present potential for men's violence against other men reinforce the reality that relations between men, whether at the individual or state level, are relations of power.[17]

Most men feel the presence of violence in their lives. Some of us had fathers who were domineering, rough, or even brutal. Some of us had fathers who simply were not there enough; most of us had fathers who either consciously or unconsciously were repelled by our need for touch and affection once we had passed a certain age. All of us had experiences of being beaten up or picked on when we were young. We learned to fight, or we learned to run; we learned to pick on others, or we learned how to talk or joke our way out of a confrontation. But either way these early experiences of violence caused an incredible amount of anxiety and required a huge expenditure of energy to resolve. That anxiety is crystallized in an unspoken fear (particularly among heterosexual men): all other men are my potential humiliators, my enemies, my competitors.

But this mutual hostility is not always expressed. Men have formed elaborate institutions of male bonding and buddying: clubs, gangs, teams, fishing trips, card games, bars, and gyms, not to mention that great fraternity of Man. Certainly, as many feminists have pointed out, straight male clubs are a subculture of male privilege. But they are also havens where men, by common consent, can find safety and security among other men. They are safe houses where our love and affection for other men can be expressed.

Freud suggested that great amounts of passivity are required for the establishment of social relations among men but also that this very passivity arouses a fear of losing one's power. (This fear takes the form, in a phallocentric, male-dominated society, of what Freud called "castration anxiety.") There is a constant tension of activity and passivity. Among their many functions and reasons for existence, male institutions mediate this tension between activity and passivity among men.

My thoughts take me back to grade six and the constant acting out of this drama. There was the challenge to fight and a punch in the stomach that knocked my wind out. There was our customary greeting with a slug in the shoulder. Before school, after school, during class change, at recess, whenever you saw another one of the boys whom you hadn't hit or been with in the past few minutes, you'd punch each other on the shoulder. I remember walking from class to class in terror of meeting Ed Skagle in the hall. Ed, a hefty young football player a grade ahead of me, would leave a big bruise with one of his friendly hellos. And this was the interesting thing about the whole business; most of the time it was friendly and affectionate. Long after the bruises have faded, I remember Ed's smile and the protective way he had of saying hello to me. But we couldn't express this affection without maintaining the active/passive equilibrium. More precisely, within the masculine psychology of surplus aggression, expressions of affection and of the need for other boys had to be balanced by an active assault.

But the traditional definition of masculinity is not only surplus aggression. It is also exclusive heterosexuality, for the maintenance of masculinity requires the repression of homosexuality.[18] Repression of homosexuality is one thing, but how do we explain the intense fear of homosexuality, the homophobia, that pervades so much male interaction? It isn't simply that many men may choose not to have sexual relations with other men; it is rather that they will find this possibility frightening or abhorrent.

Freud showed that the boy's renunciation of the father—and thus men—as an object of sexual love is a renunciation of what are felt to be passive sexual desires. For the boy to deviate from this norm is to experience severe anxiety, for what appears to be at stake is his ability to be active. Erotic attraction to other men is sacrificed because there is no model central to our society of active, erotic love for other males. The emotionally charged physical attachments of childhood with father and friends eventually breed feelings of passivity and danger and are sacrificed. The anxiety caused by the threat of losing power and activity is "the motive power behind the 'normal' boy's social learning of his sex and gender roles." Boys internalize "our culture's definition of 'normal' or 'real' man: the possessor of a penis, therefore loving only females and that actively; the possessor of a penis, therefore 'strong' and 'hard,' not 'soft,' 'weak,' 'yielding,' 'sentimental,' 'effeminate,' 'passive.' To deviate from this definition is not to be a real man. To deviate is to arouse [what Freud called] castration anxiety."[19]

Putting this in different terms, the young boy learns of the sexual hierarchy of society. This learning process is partly conscious and partly unconscious. For a boy, being a girl is a threat because it raises anxiety by representing a loss of power. Until real power is attained, the young boy courts power in the world of the imagination (with superheroes, guns, magic, and pretending to be grown-up). But the continued pull of passive aims, the attraction to girls and to mother, the fascination with the origin of babies ensure that a tension continues to exist. In this world, the only thing that is as bad as being a girl is being a sissy, that is, being like a girl.[20] Although the boy doesn't consciously equate being a girl or sissy with homosexual genital activity, at the time of puberty these feelings, thoughts, and anxieties are transferred onto homosexuality per se.

For the majority of men, the establishment of the masculine norm and the strong social prohibitions against homosexuality are enough to bury the erotic desire for other men. The repression of our bisexuality is not adequate, however, to keep this desire at bay. Some of the energy is transformed into derivative pleasures—muscle building, male comradeship, hero worship, religious rituals, war, sports—where our enjoyment of being with other men or admiring other men can be expressed. These forms of activity are not enough to neutralize our constitutional bisexuality, our organic fusion of passivity and activity, and our love for our fathers and our friends. The great majority of men, in addition to those men whose sexual preference is clearly homosexual, have, at some time in their childhood, adolescence, or adult life, had sexual or quasi-sexual relations with other males, or have fantasized or dreamed about such relationships. Those who don't (or don't recall that they have), invest a lot of energy in repressing and denying these thoughts and feelings. And to make things worse, all those highly charged male activities in the sports field, the meeting room, or the locker room do not dispel eroticized relations with other men. They can only reawaken those feelings. It is, as Freud would have said, the return of the repressed.

Nowhere has this been more stunningly captured than in the wrestling scene in the perhaps mistitled book, *Women in Love*, by D. H. Lawrence. It was late at night. Birkin had just come to Gerald's house after being put off following a marriage proposal. They talked of working, of loving, and fighting, and in the end stripped off their clothes and began to wrestle in front of the burning fire. As they wrestled, "they seemed to drive their white flesh deeper and deeper against each other, as if they would break into a oneness." They entwined, they wrestled, they pressed nearer and nearer. "A tense white knot of flesh [was] gripped in silence." The thin Birkin "seemed to penetrate into Gerald's more solid, more diffuse bulk, to interfuse his body through the body of the other, as if to bring it subtly into subjection, always seizing with some rapid necromantic foreknowledge every motion of the other flesh, converting and counteracting it, playing upon the limbs and trunk of Gerald like some hard wind. . . . Now and again came a sharp gasp of breath, or a sound like a sigh, then the rapid thudding of movement on the thickly-carpeted floor, then the strange sound of flesh escaping under flesh."[21]

The very institutions of male bonding and patriarchal power force men to constantly reexperience their closeness and attraction to other men, that is, the very thing so many men are afraid of. Our very attraction to ourselves, ambivalent as it may be, can only be generalized as an attraction to men in general.

A phobia is one means by which the ego tries to cope with anxiety. Homophobia is a means of trying to cope, not simply with our unsuccessfully repressed, eroticized attraction to other men, but with our whole anxiety over the unsuccessfully repressed passive sexual aims, whether directed toward males or females. Homophobia is not merely an individual phobia, although the strength of homophobia varies from individual to individual. It is a socially constructed phobia that is essential for the imposition and maintenance of masculinity. A key expression of homophobia is the obsessive denial of homosexual attraction; this denial is expressed as violence against other men. Or to put it differently, men's violence against other men is one of the chief means through which patriarchal society simultaneously expresses and discharges the attraction of men to other men.[22]

The specific ways that homophobia and men's violence toward other men are acted out varies from man to man, society to society, and class to class. The great amount of *directly expressed* violence and violent homophobia among some groups of working class youth would be well worth analyzing to give clues to the relation of class and gender.

This corner of the triad of men's violence interacts with and reinforces violence against women. This corner contains part of the logic of surplus aggression. Here we begin to explain the tendency of many men to use force as a means of simultaneously hiding and expressing their feelings. At the same time the fear of other men, in particular the fear of weakness and passivity in relation to other men, helps create our strong dependence on women for meeting our emotional needs and for emotional discharge. In a surplus-repressive patriarchal and class society, large amounts of anxiety and hostility are built up, ready to be discharged. But the fear of one's emotions and the fear of losing control mean that discharge only takes place in a safe situation. For many men that safety is provided by a relationship with a woman where the commitment of one's friend or lover creates the sense of security. What is more, because it is a relationship with a woman, it unconsciously resonates with that first great passive relation of the boy with his mother. But in this situation and in other acts of men's violence against women, there is also the security of interaction with someone who does not represent a psychic threat, who is less socially powerful, probably less physically powerful, and who is herself operating within a pattern of surplus passivity. And finally, given the fragility of masculine identity and the inner tension of what it means to be masculine, the ultimate acknowledgement of one's masculinity is in our power over women. This power can be expressed in many ways. Violence is one of them.

When I speak of a man's violence against himself, I am thinking of the very structure of the masculine ego. The formation of an ego on an edifice of what Herbert Marcuse called surplus repression and surplus aggression is the building of a precarious structure of internalized violence. The continual conscious and unconscious blocking and denial of passivity and all the emotions and feelings men associate with passivity—fear, pain, sadness, embarrassment—is a denial of part of what we are. The constant psychological and behavioral vigilance against passivity and its derivatives is a perpetual act of violence against oneself.

The denial and blocking of a whole range of human emotions and capacities are compounded by the blocking of avenues of discharge. The discharge of fear, hurt, and sadness, for example (through crying or trembling), is necessary because these painful emotions linger on even if they are not consciously felt. Men become pressure cookers. The failure to find safe avenues of emotional expression and discharge means that a whole range of emotions are transformed into anger and hostility. Part of the anger is directed at oneself in the form of guilt, self-hate, and various physiological and psychological symptoms. Part is directed at other men. Part of it is directed at women.

By the end of this process, our distance from ourselves is so great that the very symbol of maleness is turned into an object, a thing. Men's preoccupation with genital power and pleasure combines with a desensitization of the penis. As best he can, writes Emmanuel Reynaud, a man gives it "the coldness and the hardness of metal." It becomes his tool, his weapon, his thing. "What he loses in enjoyment he hopes to compensate for in power; but if he gains an undeniable power symbol, what pleasure can he really feel with a weapon between his legs?"[23]

BEYOND MEN'S VIOLENCE

Throughout Gabriel Garcia Márquez's *Autumn of the Patriarch*, the ageless dictator stalked his palace, his elephantine feet dragging forever on endless corridors that reeked of corruption. There was no escape from the world of terror, misery, and decay that he himself had created. His tragedy was that he was "condemned forever to live breathing the same air which asphyxiated him."[24] As men, are we similarly condemned; or is there a road of escape from the triad of men's violence and the precarious structures of masculinity that we ourselves recreate at our peril and that of women, children, and the world?

Prescribing a set of behavioral or legal changes to combat men's violence against women is obviously not enough. Even as more and more are convinced there is a problem, this realization does not touch the unconscious structures of masculinity. Any man who is sympathetic to feminism is aware of the painful contradiction between his conscious views and his deeper emotions and feelings.

The analysis in this article suggests that men and women must address each corner of the triad of men's violence and the socioeconomic, psychosexual orders on which they stand. Or to put it more strongly, it is impossible to deal successfully with any one corner of this triad in isolation from the others.

The social context that nurtures men's violence and the relation between socioeconomic transformation and the end of patriarchy have been major themes of socialist feminist thought. This framework, though it is not without controversy and unresolved problems, is one I accept. Patriarchy and systems of authoritarianism and class domination feed on each other. Radical socioeconomic and political change is a requirement for the end of men's violence. But organizing for macrosocial change is not enough to solve the problem of men's violence, not only because the problem is so pressing here and now, but because the continued existence of masculinity and surplus aggressiveness works against the fundamental macrosocial change we desire.

The many manifestations of violence against women have been an important focus of feminists. Women's campaigns and public education against rape, battering, sexual harassment, and more generally for control by women of their bodies are a key to challenging men's violence. Support by men, not only for the struggles waged by women, but in our own workplaces and among our friends is an important part of the struggle. There are many possible avenues for work by men among men. These include: forming counseling groups and support services for battering men (as is now happening in different cities in North America); championing the inclusion of clauses on sexual harassment in collective agreements and in the constitutions or bylaws of our trade unions, associations, schools, and political parties; raising money, campaigning for government funding, and finding other means of support for rape crisis centers and shelters for battered women; speaking out against violent and sexist pornography; building neighborhood campaigns against wife and child abuse; and personally refusing to collude with the sexism of our workmates, colleagues, and friends. The latter is perhaps the most difficult of all and requires patience, humor, and support from other men who are challenging sexism.

But because men's violence against women is inseparable from the other two corners of the triad of men's violence, solutions are very complex and difficult. Ideological changes and an awareness of problems are important but insufficient. While we can envisage changes in our child-rearing arrangements (which in turn would require radical economic changes) lasting solutions have to go far deeper. Only the development of non-surplus-repressive societies (whatever these might look like) will allow for the greater expression of human needs and, along with attacks on patriarchy per se, will reduce the split between active and passive psychological aims.[25]

The process of achieving these long-term goals contains many elements of economic, social, political, and psychological change, each of which requires a fundamental transformation of society. Such a transformation will not be created by an amalgam of changed individuals; but there *is* a relationship between personal change and our ability to construct organizational, political, and economic alternatives that will be able to mount a successful challenge to the status quo.

One avenue of personal struggle that is being engaged in by an increasing number of men has been the formation of men's support groups. Some groups focus on consciousness raising, but most groups stress the importance of men talking about their feelings, their relations with other men and with women, and any number of problems in their lives. At times these groups have been criticized by some antisexist men as yet another place for men to collude against women. The alternatives put forward are groups whose primary focus is either support for struggles led by women or the organization of direct, antisexist campaigns among men. These activities are very important, but so too is the development of new support structures among men. And these structures must go beyond the traditional form of consciousness raising.

Consciousness raising usually focuses on manifestations of the oppression of women and on the oppressive behavior of men. But as we have seen, masculinity is more than the sum total of oppressive forms of behavior. It is deeply and unconsciously embedded in the structure of our egos and superegos; it is what we have become. An awareness of oppressive behavior is important, but too often it only leads to guilt about being a man. Guilt is a profoundly conservative emotion and as such is not particularly useful for bringing about change. From a position of insecurity and guilt, people do not change or inspire others to change. After all, insecurity about one's male credentials played an important part in the individual acquisition of masculinity and men's violence in the first place.

There is a need to promote the personal strength and security necessary to allow men to make more fundamental personal changes and to confront sexism and heterosexism in our society at large. Support groups usually allow men to talk about our feelings, how we too have been hurt growing up in a surplus-repressive society, and how we, in turn, act at times in an oppressive manner. We begin to see the connections between painful and frustrating experiences in our own lives and related forms of oppressive behavior. As Sheila Rowbotham notes, "the exploration of the internal areas of consciousness is a political necessity for us."[26]

Talking among men is a major step, but it is still operating within the acceptable limits of what men like to think of as rational behavior. Deep barriers and fears remain even when we can begin to recognize them. As well as talking, men need to encourage direct expression of emotions—grief, anger, rage, hurt, love—within these groups and the physical closeness that has been blocked by the repression of passive aims, by social prohibition, and by our own superegos and sense of what is right. This discharge of emotions has many functions and outcomes: like all forms of emotional and physical discharge it lowers the tension within the human system and reduces the likelihood of a spontaneous discharge of emotions through outer- or inner-directed violence.

But the expression of emotions is not an end in itself; in this context it is a means to an end. Stifling the emotions connected with feelings of hurt and pain acts as a sort of glue that allows the original repression to remain. Emotional discharge, in a situation of support and encouragement, helps unglue the ego structures that require us to operate in patterned, phobic, oppressive, and surplus-aggressive forms. In a sense it loosens up the repressive structures and allows us fresh insight into ourselves and our past. But if this emotional discharge happens in isolation or against an unwitting victim, it only reinforces the feelings of being powerless, out of control, or a person who must obsessively control others. Only in situations that contradict these feelings—that is, with the support, affection, encouragement, and backing of other men who experience similar feelings—does the basis for change exist.[27]

The encouragement of emotional discharge and open dialogue among men also enhances the safety we begin to feel among each other and in turn helps us to tackle obsessive, even if unconscious, fear of other men. This unconscious fear and lack of safety are the experience of most heterosexual men throughout their lives. The pattern for homosexual men differs, but growing up and living in a heterosexist, patriarchal culture implants similar fears, even if one's adult reality is different.

Receiving emotional support and attention from a group of men is a major contradiction to experiences of distance, caution, fear, and neglect from other men. This contradiction is the mechanism that allows further discharge, emotional change, and more safety. Safety among even a small group of our brothers gives us greater safety and strength among men as a whole. This gives us the confidence and sense of personal power to confront sexism and homophobia in all its various manifestations. In a sense, this allows us each to be a model of a strong, powerful man who does not need to operate in an oppressive and violent fashion in relation to women, to other men, or to himself. And that, I hope, will play some small part in the challenge to the oppressive reality of patriarchal, authoritarian, and class societies. It will be changes in our own lives inseparably intertwined with changes in society as a whole that will sever the links in the triad of men's violence.

ACKNOWLEDGMENTS

My thanks to those who have given me comments on earlier drafts of this paper, in particular my father, Nathan Kaufman, and to Gad Horowitz. As well, I extend my appreciation to the men I have worked with in various counseling situations who have helped me develop insights into the individual acquisition of violence and masculinity.

NOTES

1. Herbert Marcuse, *Eros and Civilization* (Boston: Beacon Press, 1975; New York: Vintage, 1962); Gad Horowitz, *Repression* (Toronto: University of Toronto Press, 1977).
2. This is the approach, for example, of Suzanne Steinmetz. She says that macrolevel social and economic conditions (such as poverty, unemployment, inadequate housing, and the glorification and acceptance of violence) lead to high crime rates and a tolerance of violence that in turn leads to family aggression. See her *Cycle of Violence* (New York: Praeger, 1977), 30.
3. Andrew Tolson, *The Limits of Masculinity* (London: Tavistock, 1977), 25.
4. Juliet Mitchell, *Psychoanalysis and Feminism* (New York: Vintage, 1975), 362.
5. Joseph Conrad, *Lord Jim* (New York: Bantam Books, 1981), 146; first published 1900.
6. See, for example, Michele Barrett's thought-provoking book *Women's Oppression Today* (London: Verso/New Left Books, 1980), 10–19, 250–1.
7. Jessica Benjamin, "Authority and the Family Revisited: or, A World Without Fathers?" *New German Critique* (Winter 1978), 35.
8. Bertolt Brecht, *Three Penny Novel*, trans. Desmond I. Vesey (Harmondsworth: Penguin, 1965), 282.
9. Simone de Beauvoir, in the *Nouvel Observateur*, Mar. 1, 1976. Quoted in Diana E. H. Russell and Nicole Van de Ven, eds., *Crimes Against Women* (Millbrae, Calif.: Les Femmes, 1976), XIV.
10. Among the sources on male violence that are useful, even if sometimes problematic, see Leonore E. Walker, *The Battered Woman* (New York: Harper Colophon, 1980); Russell and Van de Ven, *op. cit.*; Judith Lewis Herman, *Father-Daughter Incest* (Cambridge, Mass.: Harvard University Press, 1981); Suzanne K. Steinmetz, *The Cycle of Violence* (New York: Praeger, 1977); Sylvia Levine and Joseph Koenig, *Why Men Rape* (Toronto: Macmillan, 1980); Susan Brownmiller, *op. cit.*; and Connie Guberman and Margie Wolfe, eds., *No Safe Place* (Toronto: Women's Press, 1985).
11. Levine and Koenig, *op. cit.*, pp. 28, 42, 56, 72.
12. Meg Luxton, *More Than a Labour of Love* (Toronto: Women's Press, 1980), 66.
13. Margaret M. Killoran, "The Sound of Silence Breaking: Toward a Metatheory of Wife Abuse" (M.A. thesis, McMaster University, 1981), 148.
14. Barrett and MacIntosh, *op. cit.*, 23.
15. Of course, household violence is not monopolized by men. In the United States roughly the same number of domestic homicides are committed by each sex. In 1975, 8.0% of homicides were committed by husbands against wives and 7.8% by wives against husbands. These figures, however, do not indicate the chain of violence, that is, the fact that most of these women were reacting to battering by their husbands. (See Steinmetz, *op. cit.*, p. 90.) Similarly, verbal and physical abuse of children appears to be committed by men and women equally. Only in the case of incest is there a near monopoly by men. Estimates vary greatly, but between one-fifth and one-third of all girls experience some sort of sexual contact with an adult male, in most cases with a father, stepfather, other relative, or teacher. (See Herman, *op. cit.*, 12 and *passim.*)
16. Luxton, *op. cit.*, p. 65.
17. This was pointed out by I. F. Stone in a 1972 article on the Vietnam war. At a briefing about the U.S. escalation of bombing in the North, the Pentagon official

described U.S. strategy as two boys fighting: "If one boy gets the other in an arm lock, he can probably get his adversary to say 'uncle' if he increases the pressure in sharp, painful jolts and gives every indication of willingness to break the boy's arm" ("Machismo in Washington," reprinted in Pleck and Sawyer, *op. cit.,* 131). Although women are also among the victims of war, I include war in the category of violence against men because I am here referring to the causality of war.

18. This is true both of masculinity as an institution and masculinity for the individual. Gay men keep certain parts of the self-oppressive masculine norm intact simply because they have grown up and live in a predominantly heterosexual, male-dominated society.
19. Horowitz, *op. cit.,* 99.
20. This formulation was first suggested to me by Charlie Kreiner at a men's counseling workshop in 1982.
21. D. H. Lawrence, *Women in Love* (Harmondsworth: Penguin, 1960), 304–5; first published 1921.
22. See Robin Wood's analysis of the film *Raging Bull.* M. Kaufman, ed. *Beyond Patriarchy* (Toronto: Oxford University Press, 1987).
23. Emmanuel Reynaud, *Holy Virility,* translated by Ros Schwartz (London: Plato Press, 1983), 41–2.
24. Gabriel Garcia Márquez, *Autumn of the Patriarch,* trans. Gregory Rabassa (Harmondsworth: Penguin, 1972), 111; first published 1967.
25. For a discussion on non-surplus-repressive societies, particularly in the sense of being complementary with Marx's notion of communism, see Horowitz, *op. cit.,* particularly chapter 7, and also Marcuse, *op. cit.,* especially chaps. 7, 10, and 11.
26. Rowbotham, *op. cit.,* 36.
27. As is apparent, although I have adopted a Freudian analysis of the unconscious and the mechanisms of repression, these observations on the therapeutic process—especially the importance of a supportive counseling environment, peer-counseling relations, emotional discharge, and the concept of contradiction—are those developed by forms of co-counseling, in particular, reevaluation counseling. But unlike the latter, I do not suppose that any of us can discharge all of our hurt, grief, and anger and uncover an essential self simply because our "self" is created.

QUESTIONS FOR CRITICAL THINKING

Reading 45

1. Kaufman argues that men's violence is not the result of biology but of social factors. What common examples can you think of where violence on the part of men is taught or encouraged?

2. Violence has a severe impact on a marginalized individual's ability to participate fully in society. How does our expectation that men should be violent limit their full participation in society as well?

3. Is it possible or desirable to change the ways in which men are socialized so as to eliminate violence? What would be necessary for this to occur?

Reading 46

HOMOPHOBIA AS A WEAPON OF SEXISM

SUZANNE PHARR

P atriarchy—an enforced belief in male dominance and control—is the ideology and sexism is the system that holds it in place. The catechism goes like this: Who do gender roles serve? Men and the women who seek power from them. Who suffers from gender roles? Women most completely and men in part. How are gender roles maintained? By the weapons of sexism: economics, violence, homophobia.

Why then don't we ardently pursue ways to eliminate gender roles and therefore sexism? It is my profound belief that all people have a spark in them that yearns for freedom, and the history of the world's atrocities—from the Nazi concentration camps to white dominance in South Africa to the battering of women—is the story of attempts to snuff out that spark. When that spark doesn't move forward to full flame, it is because the weapons designed to control and destroy have wrought such intense damage over time that the spark has been all but extinguished.

Sexism, that system by which women are kept subordinate to men, is kept in place by three powerful weapons designed to cause or threaten women with pain and loss. . . .

We have to look at economics not only as the root cause of sexism but also as the underlying, driving force that keeps all the oppressions in place. In the United States, our economic system is shaped like a pyramid, with a few people at the top, primarily white males, being supported by large numbers of unpaid or low-paid workers at the bottom. When we look at this pyramid, we begin to understand the major connection between sexism and racism because those groups at the bottom of the pyramid are women and people of color. We then begin to understand why there is such a fervent effort to keep those oppressive systems (racism and sexism and all the ways they are manifested) in place to maintain the unpaid and low-paid labor.

Susan DeMarco and Jim Hightower, writing for *Mother Jones*, report that *Forbes* magazine indicated that "the 400 richest families in America last year had an average net worth of $550 million each. These and less than a million other families—roughly 1 percent of our population—are at the prosperous tip of our society. . . . In 1976, the wealthiest 1 percent of America's families owned 19.2 percent of the nation's total wealth. (This sum of wealth counts all of America's cash, real estate, stocks, bonds, factories, art, personal property, and anything else of financial value.) By 1983, those at this 1 percent tip of our economy owned 34.3 percent of our wealth. . . . *Today, the top 1 percent of Americans possesses more net wealth than the bottom 90 percent."* (My italics.) (May, 1988, pp. 32–33)

In order for this top-heavy system of economic inequity to maintain itself, the 90 percent on the bottom must keep supplying cheap labor. A very complex, intricate system of institutionalized oppressions is necessary to maintain the status quo so that the vast majority will not demand its fair share of wealth and resources and bring the system down. Every institution—schools, banks, churches, government, courts, media, etc.—as well as individuals must be enlisted in the campaign to maintain such a system of gross inequity.

What would happen if women gained the earning opportunities and power that men have? What would happen if these opportunities were distributed equitably, no matter what sex one was, no matter what race one was born into, and no matter where one lived? What if educational and training opportunities were equal? Would women spend most of our youth preparing for marriage? Would marriage be based on economic survival for women? What would happen to issues of power and control? Would women stay with our batterers? If a woman had economic independence in a society where women had equal opportunities, would she still be thought of as owned by her father or husband?

Economics is the great controller in both sexism and racism. If a person can't acquire food, shelter, and clothing and provide them for children, then that person can be forced to do many things in order to survive. The major tactic, worldwide, is to provide unrecompensed or inadequately recompensed labor for the benefit of those who control wealth. Hence, we see women performing unpaid labor in the home or filling low-paid jobs, and we see people of color in the lowest-paid jobs available.

The method is complex: limit educational and training opportunities for women and for people of color and then withhold adequate paying jobs with the excuse that people of color and women are incapable of filling them. Blame the economic victim and keep the victim's self-esteem low through invisibility and distortion within the media and education. Allow a few people of color and women to succeed among the profitmakers so that blaming those who don't "make it" can be intensified. Encourage those few who succeed in gaining power now to turn against those who remain behind rather than to use their resources to make change for all. Maintain the myth of scarcity—that there are not enough jobs, resources, etc., to go around—among the middle-class so that they will not unite with laborers, immigrants, and the unemployed. The method keeps in place a system of control and profit by a few and a constant source of cheap labor to maintain it.

If anyone steps out of line, take her/his job away. Let homelessness and hunger do their work. The economic weapon works. And we end up saying, "I would do this or that—be openly who I am, speak out against injustice, work for civil rights, join a labor union, go to a political march, etc.—if I didn't have this job. I can't afford to lose it." We stay in an abusive situation because we see no other way to survive. . . .

Violence against women is directly related to the condition of women in a society that refuses us equal pay, equal access to resources, and equal status with males. From this condition comes men's confirmation of their sense of ownership of women, power over women, and assumed right to control women for their own means. Men physically and emotionally abuse women because they *can*, because they live in a world that gives them permission. Male violence is fed by their sense of their *right* to dominate and control, and their sense of superiority over a group of people who, because of gender, they consider inferior to them.

It is not just the violence but the threat of violence that controls our lives. Because the burden of responsibility has been placed so often on the potential victim, as women we have curtailed our freedom in order to protect ourselves from violence. Because of the threat of rapists, we stay on alert, being careful not to walk in isolated places, being careful where we park our cars, adding incredible security measures to our homes—massive locks, lights, alarms, if we can afford them—and we avoid places where we will appear vulnerable or unprotected while the abuser walks with freedom. Fear, often now so commonplace that it is unacknowledged, shapes our lives, reducing our freedom. . . .

Part of the way sexism stays in place is the societal promise of survival, false and unfulfilled as it is, that women will not suffer violence if we attach ourselves to a man to protect us. A woman without a man is told she is vulnerable to external violence and, worse, that there is something wrong with her. When the male abuser calls a woman a lesbian, he is not so much labeling her a women who loves women as he is warning her that by resisting him, she is choosing to be outside society's protection from male institutions and therefore from wide-ranging, unspecified, ever-present violence. When she seeks assistance from woman friends or a battered women's shelter, he recognizes the power in woman bonding and fears loss of her servitude and loyalty: the potential loss of his control. The concern is not affectional/sexual identity: the concern is disloyalty and the threat is violence.

The threat of violence against women who step out of line or who are disloyal is made all the more powerful by the fact that women do not have to do anything—they may be paragons of virtue and subservience—to receive violence against our lives: the violence still comes. It comes because of the woman-hating that exists throughout society. Chance plays a larger part than virtue in keeping women safe. Hence, with violence always a threat to us, women can never feel completely secure and confident. Our sense of safety is always fragile and tenuous.

Many women say that verbal violence causes more harm than physical violence because it damages self-esteem so deeply. Women have not wanted to hear battered women say that the verbal abuse was as hurtful as the physical abuse: to acknowledge that truth would be tantamount to acknowledging that *virtually every woman is a battered woman.* It is difficult to keep strong against accusations of being a bitch, stupid, inferior, etc., etc. It is especially difficult when these individual assaults are backed up by a society that shows women in textbooks, advertising, TV programs, movies, etc. as debased, silly, inferior, and sexually objectified, and a society that gives tacit approval to pornography. When we internalize these messages, we call the result "low self-esteem," a therapeutic individualized term. It seems to me we should use the more political expression: when we internalize these messages, we experience *internalized sexism,* and we experience it in common with all women living in a sexist world. The violence against us is supported by a society in which woman-hating is deeply imbedded.

In "Eyes on the Prize," a 1987 Public Television documentary about the Civil Rights Movement, an older white woman says about her youth in the South that it was difficult to be anything different from what was around her when there was no vision for another way to be. Our society presents images of women that say it is appropriate to commit violence against us. Violence is committed against women because we are seen as inferior in status and in worth. It has been the work of the women's movement to present a vision of another way to be.

Every time a woman gains the strength to resist and leave her abuser, we are given a model of the importance of stepping out of line, of moving toward freedom. And we all gain strength when she says to violence, "Never again!" Thousands of women in the last fifteen years have resisted their abusers to come to this country's 1,100 battered women's shelters. There they have sat down with other women to share their stories, to discover that their stories again and again are the same, to develop an analysis that shows that violence is a statement about power and control, and to understand how sexism creates the climate for male violence. Those brave women are now a part of a movement that gives hope for another way to live in equality and peace.

Homophobia works effectively as a weapon of sexism because it is joined with a powerful arm, heterosexism. Heterosexism creates the climate for homophobia with its assumption that the world is and must be heterosexual and its display of power and privilege as the norm. Heterosexism is the systemic display of homophobia in the institutions of society. Heterosexism and homophobia work together to enforce compulsory heterosexuality and that bastion of patriarchal power, the nuclear family. The central focus of the right-wing attack against women's liberation is that women's equality, women's self-determination, women's control of our own bodies and lives will damage what they see as the crucial societal institution, the nuclear family. The attack has been led by fundamentalist ministers across the country.

The two areas they have focused on most consistently are abortion and homosexuality, and their passion has led them to bomb women's clinics and to recommend deprogramming for homosexuals and establishing camps to quarantine people with AIDS. To resist marriage and/or heterosexuality is to risk severe punishment and loss.

It is not by chance that when children approach puberty and increased sexual awareness they begin to taunt each other by calling these names: "queer," "faggot," "pervert." It is at puberty that the full force of society's pressure to conform to heterosexuality and prepare for marriage is brought to bear. Children know what we have taught them, and we have given clear messages that those who deviate from standard expectations are to be made to get back in line. The best controlling tactic at puberty is to be treated as an outsider, to be ostracized at a time when it feels most vital to be accepted. Those who are different must be made to suffer loss. It is also at puberty that misogyny begins to be more apparent, and girls are pressured to conform to societal norms that do not permit them to realize their full potential. It is at this time that their academic achievements begin to decrease as they are coerced into compulsory heterosexuality and trained for dependency upon a man, that is, for economic survival.

There was a time when the two most condemning accusations against a woman meant to ostracize and disempower her were "whore" and "lesbian." The sexual revolution and changing attitudes about heterosexual behavior may have led to some lessening of the power of the word *whore*, though it still has strength as a threat to sexual property and prostitutes are stigmatized and abused. However, the word *lesbian* is still fully charged and carries with it the full threat of loss of power and privilege, the threat of being cut asunder, abandoned, and left outside society's protection.

To be a lesbian is to be *perceived* as someone who has stepped out of line, who has moved out of sexual/economic dependence on a male, who is woman-identified. A lesbian is perceived as someone who can live without a man, and who is therefore (however illogically) against men. A lesbian is perceived as being outside the acceptable, routinized order of things. She is seen as someone who has no societal institutions to protect her and who is not privileged to the protection of individual males. Many heterosexual women see her as someone who stands in contradiction to the sacrifices they have made to conform to compulsory heterosexuality. A lesbian is perceived as a threat to the nuclear family, to male dominance and control, to the very heart of sexism.

Gay men are perceived also as a threat to male dominance and control, and the homophobia expressed against them has the same roots in sexism as does homophobia against lesbians. Visible gay men are the objects of extreme hatred and fear by heterosexual men because their breaking ranks with male heterosexual solidarity is seen as a damaging rent in the very fabric of sexism. They are seen as betrayers, as traitors who must be punished and eliminated. In the beating and killing of gay men we see clear evidence of this hatred. When we see the fierce homophobia expressed toward gay men, we can begin to understand the ways sexism also affects males through imposing rigid, dehumanizing gender roles on them. The two circumstances in which it is legitimate for men to be openly physically affectionate with one another are in competitive sports and in the crisis of war. For many men, these two experiences are the highlights of their lives, and they think of them again and again with nostalgia. War and sports offer a cover of all-male safety and dominance to keep away the notion of affectionate openness being identified with homosexuality. When gay men break ranks with male roles through bonding and affection outside the arenas of war and sports, they are perceived as not being "real men," that is, as being identified with women, the weaker sex that must be dominated and that over the centuries has been the object of male hatred and abuse. Misogyny gets transferred to gay men with a vengeance and is increased by the fear that their sexual identity and behavior will bring down the entire system of male dominance and compulsory heterosexuality.

If lesbians are established as threats to the status quo, as outcasts who must be punished, homophobia can wield its power over all women through lesbian baiting. Lesbian baiting is an attempt to control women by labeling us as lesbians because our behavior is not acceptable, that is, when we are being independent, going our own way, living whole lives, fighting for our rights, demanding equal pay, saying no to violence, being self-assertive, bonding with and loving the company of women, assuming the right to our bodies, insisting upon our own authority, making changes that include us in society's decision-making; lesbian baiting occurs when women are called lesbians because we resist male dominance and control. And it has little or nothing to do with one's sexual identity.

To be named as lesbian threatens all women, not just lesbians, with great loss. And any woman who steps out of role risks being called a lesbian. To understand how this is a threat to all women, one must understand that any woman can be called a lesbian and there is no real way she can defend herself: there is no way to credential one's sexuality. ("The Children's Hour," a Lillian Hellman play, makes this point when a student asserts two teachers are lesbians and they have no way to disprove it.) She may be married or divorced, have children, dress in the most feminine manner, have sex with men, be celibate—but there are lesbians who do all those things. *Lesbians look like all women and all women look like lesbians.* There is no guaranteed method of identification, and as we all know, sexual identity can be kept hidden. (The same is true for men. There is no way to prove their sexual identity, though many go to extremes to prove heterosexuality.) Also, women are not necessarily born lesbian. Some seem to be, but others become lesbians later in life after having lived heterosexual lives. Lesbian baiting of heterosexual women would not work if there were a definitive way to identify lesbians (or heterosexuals).

We have yet to understand clearly how sexual identity develops. And this is disturbing to some people, especially those who are determined to discover how lesbian and gay identity is formed so that they will know where to start in eliminating it. (Isn't it odd that there is so little concern about discovering the causes of heterosexuality?) There are many theories: genetic makeup, hormones, socialization, environment, etc. But there is no conclusive evidence that indicates that heterosexuality comes from one process and homosexuality from another.

We do know, however, that sexual identity can be in flux, and we know that sexual identity means more than just the gender of people one is attracted to and has sex with. To be a lesbian has as many ramifications as for a woman to be heterosexual. It is more than sex, more than just the bedroom issue many would like to make it: it is a woman-centered life with all the social interconnections that entails. Some lesbians are in long-term relationships, some in short-term ones, some date, some are celibate, some are married to men, some remain as separate as possible from men, some have children by men, some by alternative insemination, some seem "feminine" by societal standards, some "masculine," some are doctors, lawyers and ministers, some laborers, housewives and writers: what all share in common is a sexual/affectional identity that focuses on women in its attractions and social relationships.

If lesbians are simply women with a particular sexual identity who look and act like all women, then the major difference in living out a lesbian sexual identity as opposed to a heterosexual identity is that as lesbians we live in a homophobic world that threatens and imposes damaging loss on us for *being who we are,* for choosing to live whole lives. Homophobic people often assert that homosexuals have the choice of not being homosexual; that is, we don't have to act out our sexual identity. In that case, I want to hear heterosexuals talk about their willingness not to act out their sexual identity, including not just sexual activity but heterosexual social interconnections and heterosexual privilege. It is a question of wholeness. It is very difficult for one to be denied the life of a sexual being, whether expressed in sex or in physical affection, and to feel complete, whole. For our loving relationships with humans feed the life of the spirit and enable us to overcome our basic isolation and to be interconnected with humankind.

If, then, any woman can be named a lesbian and be threatened with terrible losses, what is it she fears? Are these fears real? Being vulnerable to a homophobic world can lead to these losses:

- *Employment.* The loss of job leads us right back to the economic connection to sexism. This fear of job loss exists for almost every lesbian except perhaps those who are self-employed or in a business that does not require societal approval. Consider how many businesses or organizations you know that will hire and protect people who are openly gay or lesbian.

- *Family.* Their approval, acceptance, love.

- *Children.* Many lesbians and gay men have children, but very, very few gain custody in court challenges, even if the other parent is a known abuser. Other children may be kept away from us as though gays and lesbians are abusers. There are written and unwritten laws prohibiting lesbians and gays from being foster parents or from adopting children. There is an irrational fear that children in contact with lesbians and gays will become homosexual through influence or that they will be sexually abused. Despite our knowing that 95 percent of those who sexually abuse children are heterosexual men, there are no policies keeping heterosexual men from teaching or working with children, yet in almost every school system in America, visible gay men and lesbians are not hired through either written or unwritten law.

- *Heterosexual privilege and protection.* No institutions, other than those created by lesbians and gays—such as the Metropolitan Community Church, some counseling centers, political organizations such as the National Gay and Lesbian Task Force, the National Coalition of Black Lesbians and Gays, the Lambda Legal Defense and Education Fund, etc.—affirm homosexuality and offer protection. Affirmation and protection cannot be gained from the criminal justice system, mainline churches, educational institutions, the government.

- *Safety.* There is nowhere to turn for safety from physical and verbal attacks because the norm presently in this country is that it is acceptable to be overtly homophobic. Gay men are beaten on the streets; lesbians are kidnapped and "deprogrammed." The National Gay and Lesbian Task Force, in an extended study, has documented violence against lesbians and gay men and noted the inadequate response of the criminal justice system. One of the major differences between homophobia/heterosexism and racism and sexism is that because of the Civil Rights Movement and the women's movement racism and sexism are expressed more covertly (though with great harm); because there has not been a major, visible lesbian and gay movement, it is permissible to be overtly homophobic in any institution or public forum. Churches spew forth homophobia in the same way they did racism prior to the Civil Rights Movement. Few laws are in place to protect lesbians and gay men, and the criminal justice system is wracked with homophobia.

- *Mental health.* An overtly homophobic world in which there is full permission to treat lesbians and gay men with cruelty makes it difficult for lesbians and gay men to maintain a strong sense of well-being and self-esteem. Many lesbians and gay men are beaten, raped, killed, subjected to aversion therapy, or put in mental institutions. The impact of such hatred and negativity can lead one to depression and, in some cases, to suicide. The toll on the gay and lesbian community is devastating.

- *Community.* There is rejection by those who live in homophobic fear, those who are afraid of association with lesbians and gay men. For many in the gay and lesbian community, there is a loss of public acceptance, a loss of allies, a loss of place and belonging.
- *Credibility.* This fear is large for many people: the fear that they will no longer be respected, listened to, honored, believed. They fear they will be social outcasts.

The list goes on and on. But any one of these essential components of a full life is large enough to make one deeply fear its loss. A black woman once said to me in a workshop, "When I fought for Civil Rights, I always had my family and community to fall back on even when they didn't fully understand or accept what I was doing. I don't know if I could have borne losing them. And you people don't have either with you. It takes my breath away."

What does a woman have to do to get called a lesbian? Almost anything, sometimes nothing at all, but certainly anything that threatens the status quo, anything that steps out of role, anything that asserts the rights of women, anything that doesn't indicate submission and subordination. Assertiveness, standing up for oneself, asking for more pay, better working conditions, training for and accepting a non-traditional (you mean a man's?) job, enjoying the company of women, being financially independent, being in control of one's life, depending first and foremost upon oneself, thinking that one can do whatever needs to be done, but above all, working for the rights and equality of women.

In the backlash to the gains of the women's liberation movement, there has been an increased effort to keep definitions man-centered. Therefore, to work on behalf of women must mean to work against men. To love women must mean that one hates men. A very effective attack has been made against the word *feminist* to make it a derogatory word. In current backlash usage, *feminist* equals *man-hater* which equals *lesbian.* This formula is created in the hope that women will be frightened away from their work on behalf of women. Consequently, we now have women who believe in the rights of women and work for those rights while from fear deny that they are feminists, or refuse to use the word because it is so "abrasive."

So what does one do in an effort to keep from being called a lesbian? She steps back into line, into the role that is demanded of her, tries to behave in such a way that doesn't threaten the status of men, and if she works for women's rights, she begins modifying that work. When women's organizations begin doing significant social change work, they inevitably are lesbianbaited; that is, funders or institutions or community members tell us that they can't work with us because of our "man-hating attitudes" or the presence of lesbians. We are called too strident, told we are making enemies, not doing good. . . .

In my view, homophobia has been one of the major causes of the failure of the women's liberation movement to make deep and lasting change. (The other major block has been racism.) We were fierce when we set out but when threatened with the loss of heterosexual privilege, we began putting on brakes. Our best-known nationally distributed women's magazine was reluctant to print articles about lesbians, began putting a man on the cover several times a year, and writing articles about women who succeeded in a man's world. We worried about our image, our being all right, our being "real women" despite our work. Instead of talking about the elimination of sexual gender roles, we stepped back and talked about "sex role stereotyping" as the issue. Change around the edges for middle-class white women began to be talked about as successes. We accepted tokenism and integration, forgetting that equality for all women, for all people—and not just equality of white middle-class women with white men—was the goal that we could never put behind us.

But despite backlash and retreats, change is growing from within. The women's liberation movement is beginning to gain strength again because there are women who are talking about liberation for all women. We are examining sexism, racism, homophobia, classism, anti-Semitism, ageism, ableism, and imperialism, and we see everything as connected. This change in point of view represents the third wave of the women's liberation movement, a new direction that does not get mass media coverage and recognition. It has been initiated by women of color and lesbians who were marginalized or rendered invisible by the white heterosexual leaders of earlier efforts. The first wave was the 19th and early 20th century campaign for the vote; the second, beginning in the 1960s, focused on the Equal Rights Amendment and abortion rights. Consisting of predominantly white middle-class women, both failed in recognizing issues of equality and empowerment for all women. The third wave of the movement, multi-racial and multi-issued, seeks the transformation of the world for us all. We know that we won't get there until everyone gets there; that we must move forward in a great strong line, hand in hand, not just a few at a time.

We know that the arguments about homophobia originating from mental health and Biblical/religious attitudes can be settled when we look at the sexism that permeates religious and psychiatric history. The women of the third wave of the women's liberation movement know that *without the existence of sexism, there would be no homophobia.*

Finally, we know that as long as the word *lesbian* can strike fear in any woman's heart, then work on behalf of women can be stopped; the only successful work against sexism must include work against homophobia.

QUESTIONS FOR CRITICAL THINKING

Reading 46

1. Pharr draws connections between homophobia, sexism, and heterosexism. Considering her discussion, how is homophobia used to control us all, regardless of sexual orientation?

2. How is violence or the threat of violence used to maintain the status quo? For example, have you seen homophobia used to reinforce rigid gender roles?

3. What are some ways that we can work toward eliminating homophobia being used as a weapon of sexism?

PART III

Experiencing Difference and Inequality in Everyday Life

INTRODUCTION

In Part I we examined the ways in which categories of difference are constructed and then transformed into systems of inequality. We continued this discussion in Part II with an exploration of how systems of inequality are maintained as oppression and privilege through the role of social institutions, language, and violence. In this section we will gain a more thorough understanding of the construction and maintenance of these systems by examining the experiences of difference and inequality in everyday life.

THE IMPORTANCE OF HEARING PERSONAL ACCOUNTS

The readings in this section help to put a face on what we have discussed thus far. Although theoretical explanations and statistical information can help us to understand the prevalence of inequality in our society, as well as the ways in which systems of oppression and privilege interconnect, the picture that they offer is far from complete. Through the examination of lived experiences we gain a more complete awareness of how categories of difference are constructed and how systems of oppression and privilege are manifested in everyday life.

Stephanie Wildman and Adrienne Davis's discussion on the existence of systems of privilege in "Making Systems of Privilege Visible" (Reading 47)—particularly around "whiteness"—shows us the effect of **privilege** on one's **life chances.** By reading Annie Downey's experiences of receiving welfare in "I Am Your Welfare Reform" (Reading 56) and Nada El Sawy's encounters with negative stereotypes in "'Yes, I Follow Islam, But I'm Not a Terrorist'" (Reading 48), we gain a greater understanding of how attitudes about oppressed groups become internalized and are manifested in feelings of shame and embarrassment. Furthermore, the stories of living life as a member of a marginalized group and its accompanying stereotypes allow us to more fully comprehend how such **internalized oppression** results in the desire to **pass**—to deny one's membership in an oppressed group and to attempt to portray oneself as a member of a less stigmatized group. Each of the readings in this section demonstrates the daily grind of oppression and the perks of privilege and deepens our understanding of these issues.

Additional readings in this section demonstrate the impact of the structural factors that construct and maintain inequality, discussed in Parts I and II, on the everyday experiences of individuals. For example, Ellis Cose articulates

642

the effect of discrimination and stereotypes on African Americans in his article "A Dozen Demons" (Reading 49). Luis Rodriguez provides a further illustration in "Always Running" (Reading 50) as he tells of how he and his family, as Mexican Immigrants, are never viewed as having the right to belong in the United States. Further, Tram Nguyen, in "Separated by Deportation" (Reading 52) tells of the experiences of Abdullah Osman and other Somali refugees, representing the impact of equating Moslems with terrorists in the post 9-11 United States, disrupting the lives and livelihoods of people seeking refuge from their war-torn home countries. These and other readings in this section bring into graphic detail the everyday consequences of systems of inequality.

It is important to point out that although each of us experiences oppression and privilege each day, to examine the various factors of our own experiences while simultaneously living them is like a fish trying to examine the water in which it swims. To fully understand experiences of oppression and privilege we need to stand at a distance from these experiences. The accounts in this section provide us with the opportunity to stand "outside" and to look in on the experiences of others. By reading the stories in this section we will gain a greater understanding of the impact of oppression and privilege, not only on the lives of others but on our own lives as well.

PERSONAL ACCOUNTS AND "DECONSTRUCTING" STEREOTYPES

At the foundation of our prejudice regarding those whom we see as different from ourselves are **stereotypes**—rigid, oversimplified, and often exaggerated beliefs that are applied both to a category of people and to each individual in it. We learn these stereotypes through the process of socialization. They are fostered by the policies and practices of social institutions, as well as by our tendency to interact with people like ourselves, and we often have difficulty deconstructing or exposing the falsehoods in these stereotypes. Generally, it is not until we have frequent contact with those about whom we possess stereotypes that we are able to debunk them—and sometimes not even then. Through the sharing of personal experiences, the readings in this section provide a great deal of information that will serve to counter our stereotypes. As you read, be aware of the stereotypes that you possess and note your reactions when you encounter new information that challenges them.

THE LIVED EXPERIENCE OF THE MATRIX OF DOMINATION

Up to this point we have engaged in a primarily theoretical discussion of the matrix of domination. In examining the ways in which categories of difference are constructed and transformed into systems of inequality, we have noted some of the commonalities in the ways in which these categories are constructed. Further, our examination of the role of social institutions, language, and violence in maintaining systems of oppression and privilege has helped us to understand the similar foundations on which such systems rest. The readings in this section reveal the interrelationships of systems of oppression and privilege by providing us with an opportunity to witness the matrix of domination as lived experience. As you read the selections in this section, look closely to see how different systems of oppression and privilege interrelate in the stories the authors share. In addition, notice how some experience both oppression and privilege and how many experience more than one form of oppression simultaneously.

KEEP THIS IN MIND

Though reading personal accounts can serve to further our understanding of systems of oppression and privilege, it is important not to overgeneralize. The anecdotal evidence of a personal story doesn't in and of itself prove anything. Indeed, it is often anecdotal evidence that gets in the way of our fully seeing and accepting that systems of oppression and privilege exist. In addition, when we read the personal experiences of a member of a marginalized group, there is often a danger of expecting the writer to speak for the experiences of all members of that group. To avoid these pitfalls it is important to keep in mind the readings of the previous two sections. By understanding the experiences of the different groups examined in previous sections, we will better understand the experiences of the individuals discussed here. In addition, the readings here confirm the theoretical and statistical discussions elsewhere in this text.

A FINAL NOTE

As stated in Part I, a fundamental component to understanding the impact of systems of inequality is to employ our **empathy** skills—the ability to understand the experiences of others, even though you have not shared those experiences. The readings in this section are provided to aid you in honing your empathy skills. As you read these accounts, be mindful of how they increase your understanding of experiences with which you are not familiar. As you become more informed about the experiences of others, you will further your understanding of the construction, maintenance, and impact of systems of oppression and privilege.

Reading 47

MAKING SYSTEMS OF PRIVILEGE VISIBLE

STEPHANIE M. WILDMAN WITH ADRIENNE D. DAVIS

The notion of privilege, although part of the consciousness of popular culture, has not been recognized in legal language and doctrine. This failure to acknowledge privilege, to make it visible in legal doctrine, creates a serious gap in legal reasoning, rendering us unable to address issues of systemic unfairness.

The invisibility of privilege strengthens the power it creates and maintains. The invisible cannot be combated, and as a result privilege is allowed to perpetuate, regenerate, and re-create itself. Privilege is systemic, not an occasional occurrence. Privilege is invisible only until looked for, but silence in the face of privilege sustains its invisibility.

Silence is the lack of sound and voice. Silence may result from a desire for quiet; it may signify intense mental concentration; it may also arise from oppression or fear. Whatever the reason, when there is silence, no criticism is expressed. What we do not say, what we do not talk about, allows the status quo to continue. To describe these unspoken systems means we need to use language. But even when we try to talk about privilege, the language we use inhibits our ability to perceive the systems of privilege that constitute the status quo.

HOW LANGUAGE VEILS THE EXISTENCE OF SYSTEMS OF PRIVILEGE

Language contributes to the invisibility and regeneration of privilege. To begin the conversation about subordination, we sort ideas into categories such as race and gender. These words are part of a system of categorization that we use without thinking and that seems linguistically neutral. Race and gender are, after all, just words.

Yet when we learn that someone has had a child, our first question is usually "Is it a girl or a boy?" Why do we ask that, instead of something like "Are the mother and child healthy?" We ask, "Is it a girl or a boy?" according to philosopher Marilyn Frye, because we do not know how to relate to this new being without knowing its gender.[1] Imagine how long you could have a discussion with or about someone without knowing her or his gender. We place people into these categories because our world is gendered.

Similarly, our world is also raced, and it is hard for us to avoid taking mental notes as to race. We use our language to categorize by race, particularly, if we are white, when that race is other than white. Marge Shultz has written of calling on a Latino student in her class.[2] She called him Mr. Martínez, but his name was Rodríguez. The class tensed up at her error; earlier that same day another professor had called him Mr. Hernández, the name of the defendant in the criminal law case under discussion. Professor Shultz talked with her class, at its next session, about her error and how our thought processes lead us to categorize in order to think. She acknowledged how this process leads to stereotyping that causes pain to individuals. We all live in this raced and gendered world, inside these powerful categories, that make it hard to see each other as whole people.

But the problem does not stop with the general terms "race" and "gender." Each of these categories contains the images, like an entrance to a tunnel with many passages and arrows pointing down each possible path, of subcategories. Race is often defined as Black and white; sometimes it is defined as white and "of color." There are other races, and sometimes the categories are each listed, for example, as African American, Hispanic American, Asian American, Native American, and White American, if whiteness is mentioned at all. All these words, describing racial subcategories, seem neutral on their face, like equivalent titles. But however the subcategories are listed, however neutrally the words are expressed, these words mask a system of power, and that system privileges whiteness.

Gender, too, is a seemingly neutral category that leads us to imagine subcategories of male and female. A recent scientific article suggested that five genders might be a more accurate characterization of human anatomy, but there is a heavy systemic stake in our image of two genders.[3] The apparently neutral categories male and female mask the privileging of males that is part of the gender power system. Try to think of equivalent gendered titles, like king and queen, prince and princess, and you will quickly see that male and female are not equal titles in our cultural imagination.

Poet and social critic Adrienne Rich has written convincingly about the compulsory heterosexuality that is part of this gender power system.[4] Almost everywhere we look, heterosexuality is portrayed as the norm. In Olympic ice-skating and dancing, for example, a couple is defined as a man partnered with a woman.[5] Heterosexuality is privileged over any other relationship. The words we use, such as "marriage," "husband," and "wife," are not neutral, but convey this privileging of heterosexuality. What is amazing, says Rich, is that there are any lesbians or gay men at all.[6]

Our culture suppresses conversation about class privilege as well as race and gender privileges. Although we must have money or access to money to obtain human necessities such as food, clothing, and shelter, those fundamental needs are recognized only as an individual responsibility. The notion of privilege based on economic wealth is viewed as a radical, dangerous idea, or an idiosyncratic throwback to the past, conjuring up countries with monarchies, nobility, serfs, and peasants. Yet even the archaic vocabulary makes clear that no one wants to be categorized as a have-not. The economic power system is not invisible—everyone knows that money brings privilege. But the myth persists that all have access to that power through individual resourcefulness. This myth of potential economic equality supports the invisibility of the other power systems that prevent fulfillment of that ideal.

Other words we use to describe subordination also mask the operation of privilege. Increasingly, people use terms like "racism" and "sexism" to describe disparate treatment and the perpetuation of power. Yet this vocabulary of "isms" as a descriptive shorthand for undesirable, disadvantaging treatment creates several serious problems.

First, calling someone a racist individualizes the behavior and veils the fact that racism can occur only where it is culturally, socially, and legally supported. It lays the blame on the individual rather than the systemic forces that have shaped that individual and his or her society. White people know they do not want to be labeled racist; they become concerned with how to avoid that label, rather than worrying about systemic racism and how to change it.

Second, the isms language focuses on the larger category, such as race, gender, sexual preference. Isms language suggests that within these larger categories two seemingly neutral halves exist, equal parts in a mirror. Thus Black and white, male and female, heterosexual and gay/lesbian appear, through the linguistic juxtaposition, as equivalent subparts. In fact, although the category does not take note of it, Blacks and whites, men and women, heterosexuals and gays/lesbians are not equivalently situated in society. Thus the way we think and talk about the categories and subcategories that underlie the isms allows us to consider them parallel parts, and obscures the pattern of domination and subordination within each classification.

Similarly, the phrase "isms" itself gives the illusion that all patterns of domination and subordination are the same and interchangeable. The language suggests that someone subordinated under one form of oppression would be similarly situated to another person subordinated under another form. Thus, a person subordinated under one form may feel no need to view himself/herself as a possible oppressor, or beneficiary of oppression, within a different form. For example, white women, having an ism that defines their condition—sexism—may not look at the way they are privileged by racism. They have defined themselves as one of the oppressed.

Finally, the focus on individual behavior, the seemingly neutral subparts of categories, and the apparent interchangeability underlying the vocabulary of isms all obscure the existence of systems of privilege and power. It is difficult to see and talk about how oppression operates when the vocabulary

itself makes these systems of privilege invisible. "White supremacy" is associated with a lunatic fringe, not with the everyday life of well-meaning white
citizens. "Racism" is defined by whites in terms of specific, discriminatory
racist actions by others. The vocabulary allows us to talk about discrimination and oppression, but it hides the mechanism that makes that oppression possible and efficient. It also hides the existence of specific, identifiable
beneficiaries of oppression, who are not always the actual perpetrators of
discrimination. The use of isms language, or any focus on discrimination,
masks the privileging that is created by these systems of power.

Thus the very vocabulary we use to talk about discrimination obfuscates
these power systems and the privilege that is their natural companion. To
remedy discrimination effectively we must make the power systems and
the privileges they create visible and part of the discourse. To move toward
a unified theory of the dynamics of subordination, we have to find a way
to talk about privilege. When we discuss race, sex, and sexual orientation,
each needs to be described as a power system that creates privileges in some
people as well as disadvantages in others. Most of the literature has focused
on disadvantage or discrimination, ignoring the element of privilege. To
really talk about these issues, privilege must be made visible.

 ## WHAT IS PRIVILEGE?

What then is privilege? We all recognize its most blatant forms. "Men only
admitted to this club." "We will not allow African Americans into that
school." Blatant exercises of privilege certainly exist, but they are not what
most people think of as our way of life. They are only the tip of the iceberg,
however.

When we try to look at privilege we see several elements. First, the characteristics of the privileged group define the societal norm, often benefiting
those in the privileged group. Second, privileged group members can rely
on their privilege and avoid objecting to oppression. Both the conflation of
privilege with the societal norm and the implicit option to ignore oppression
mean that privilege is rarely seen by the holder of the privilege.

A. The Normalization of Privilege

The characteristics and attributes of those who are privileged group members are described as societal norms—as the way things are and as what is
normal in society.[7] This normalization of privilege means that members of
society are judged, and succeed or fail, measured against the characteristics
that are held by those privileged. The privileged characteristic is the norm;
those who stand outside are the aberrant or "alternative."

For example, a thirteen-year-old-girl who aspires to be a major-league
ballplayer can have only a low expectation of achieving that goal, no matter

how superior a batter and fielder she is. Maleness is the foremost "qualification" of major-league baseball players. Similarly, those who legally are permitted to marry are heterosexual. A gay or lesbian couple, prepared to make a life commitment, cannot cross the threshold of qualification to be married.

I had an example of being outside the norm recently when I was called to jury service. Jurors are expected to serve until 5 P.M. During that year, my family's life was set up so that I picked up my children after school at 2:40 and made sure that they got to various activities. If courtroom life were designed to privilege my needs, then there would have been an afternoon recess to honor children. But in this culture children's lives and the lives of their caretakers are the alternative or other, and we must conform to the norm.

Even as these child care needs were outside the norm, I was privileged economically to be able to meet my children's needs. What many would have described as mothering, not privilege—my ability to pick them up and be present in their after-school lives—was a benefit of my association with privilege.

Members of the privileged group gain many benefits by their affiliation with the dominant side of the power system. This affiliation with power is not identified as such; often it may be transformed into and presented as individual merit. Legacy admissions at elite colleges and professional schools are perceived to be merit-based, when this process of identification with power and transmutation into qualifications occurs. Achievements by members of the privileged group are viewed as the result of individual effort, rather than privilege. . . .

B. Choosing Whether to Struggle Against Oppression

Members of privileged groups can opt out of struggles against oppression if they choose. Often this privilege may be exercised by silence. At the same time that I was the outsider in jury service, I was also a privileged insider. During *voir dire*, each prospective juror was asked to introduce herself or himself. The plaintiff's and defendant's attorneys then asked additional questions. I watched the defense attorney, during voir dire, ask each Asian-looking male prospective juror if he spoke English. No one else was asked. The judge did nothing. The Asian American man sitting next to me smiled and flinched as he was asked the questions. I wondered how many times in his life he had been made to answer such a question. I considered beginning my own questioning by saying, "I'm Stephanie Wildman, I'm a professor of law, and yes, I speak English." I wanted to focus attention on the subordinating conduct of the attorney, but I did not. I exercised my white privilege by my silence. I exercised my privilege to opt out of engagement, even though this choice may not always be consciously made by someone with privilege.

Depending on the number of privileges someone has, she or he may experience the power of choosing the types of struggles in which to engage. Even this choice may be masked as an identification with oppression, thereby making the privilege that enables the choice invisible.

... Privilege is not visible to its holder; it is merely there, a part of the world, a way of life, simply the way things are. Others have a *lack,* an absence, a deficiency.

 ## SYSTEMS OF PRIVILEGE

Although different privileges bestow certain common characteristics (membership in the norm, the ability to choose whether to object to the power system, and the invisibility of its benefit), the form of a privilege may vary according to the power relationship that produces it. White privilege derives from the race power system of white supremacy. Male privilege[8] and heterosexual privilege result from the gender hierarchy.[9] Class privilege derives from an economic, wealth-based hierarchy.

 ## VISUALIZING PRIVILEGE

For me the struggle to visualize privilege has most often taken the form of the struggle to see my white privilege. Even as I write about this struggle, I fear that my own racism will make things worse, causing me to do more harm than good. Some readers may be shocked to see a white person contritely acknowledge that she is racist. I do not say this with pride. I simply believe that no matter how hard I work at not being racist, I still am. Because part of racism is systemic, I benefit from the privilege that I am struggling to see.

Whites do not look at the world through a filter of racial awareness, even though whites are, of course, members of a race. The power to ignore race, when white is the race, is a privilege, a societal advantage. The term "racism/ white supremacy" emphasizes the link between discriminatory racism and the privilege held by whites to ignore their own race.

As bell hooks explains, liberal whites do not see themselves as prejudiced or interested in domination through coercion, yet "they cannot recognize the ways their actions support and affirm the very structure of racist domination and oppression that they profess to wish to see eradicated."[10] The perpetuation of white supremacy is racist.

All whites are racist in this use of the term, because we benefit from systemic white privilege. Generally whites think of racism as voluntary, intentional conduct, done by horrible others. Whites spend a lot of time trying to convince ourselves and each other that we are not racist. A big step would be for whites to admit that we are racist and then to consider what to do about it.[11]

NOTES

1. See Marilyn Frye, The Politics of Reality: Essays in Feminist Theory 19–34 (1983) (discussing sex marking, sex announcing, and the necessity to determine gender).

2. Angela Harris and Marge Shultz, *"A(nother) Critique of Pure Reason": Toward Civic Virtue in Legal Education,* 45 Stan. L. Rev. 1773, 1796 (1993).

3. Anne Fausto-Sterling, *The Five Sexes: Why Male and Female Are Not Enough,* Sciences, Mar./Apr. 1993. (Thanks to Gregg Bryan for calling my attention to this article.) See also Frye, *supra* note 1, at 25.

4. Adrienne Rich, *Compulsory Heterosexuality and Lesbian Existence,* in Blood, Bread, and Poetry, Selected Prose 1979–1985 (1986).

5. See Stephanie M. Wildman and Becky Wildman-Tobriner, *Sex Roles Iced Popular Team?* S.F. Chron., Feb. 25, 1994, at A23.

6. Rich, *supra* note 4, at 57 ("Heterosexuality has been both forcibly and subliminally imposed on women").

7. Richard Delgado and Jean Stefancic, *Pornography and Harm to Women: "No Empirical Evidence?"* 53 Ohio St. L. J. 1037 (1992) (describing this "way things are." Because the norm or reality is perceived as including these benefits, the privileges are not visible.)

8. Catharine A. MacKinnon, Toward a Feminist Theory of the State 224 (1989).

9. Sylvia Law, *Homosexuality and the Social Meaning of Gender,* 1988 Wis. L. Rev. 187, 197 (1988); Marc Fajer, *Can Two Real Men Eat Quiche Together? Storytelling, Gender-Role Stereotypes, and Legal Protection for Lesbians and Gay Men,* 46 U. Miami L. Rev. 511, 617 (1992). Both articles describe heterosexism as a form of gender oppression.

10. bell hooks, *Overcoming White Supremacy: A Comment,* in Talking Back: Thinking Feminist, Thinking Black 113 (1989).

11. See also Jerome McCristal Culp Jr., *Water Buffalo and Diversity: Naming Names and Reclaiming the Racial Discourse,* 26 Conn. L. Rev. 209 (1993) (urging people to name racism as racism).

 ## QUESTIONS FOR CRITICAL THINKING

Reading 47

1. Wildman and Davis discuss the ways in which language hides systems of privilege in the United States. What are some of the ways in which you are privileged by your class, race, gender, education, etc.? What makes it difficult to recognize this privilege?

2. How is the invisibility of white privilege a privilege in and of itself?

3. How might recognizing the various ways that we are privileged help to reduce or eliminate inequality?

Reading 48

"YES, I FOLLOW ISLAM, BUT I'M NOT A TERRORIST"

NADA EL SAWY

As an Egyptian-American and a Muslim, I've always been dismayed by the way Islam has been generally misrepresented in the media and misunderstood by most Americans. Since the tragic events of Sept. 11, Islam has been in the spotlight, and though leaders such as President George W. Bush and New York Mayor Rudolph Giuliani have made a concerted effort to distinguish it from terrorism, some people still aren't getting the message.

I am a graduate student in journalism, often assigned to write articles about current events. The day after the terrorist attacks I headed out to Brooklyn to cover a story about an Islamic school that had been pelted with rocks and bloody pork chops in the hours after the World Trade Center towers collapsed. Whoever committed this act knew enough about Islam to know that pork is forbidden, but apparently little else about Islamic beliefs. "I wish people would stop calling us terrorists," one sixth grader told me.

When I read about Osama bin Laden or groups like the Egyptian Islamic Jihad, I want to tell them, "You're giving Islam a bad name!" I want to show people that the religion I know is one that calls for patience, harmony and understanding.

Islam may be the world's second largest religion, but in the United States, home to about 6 million of its followers, it remains a mystery. Americans seem to believe that backpacking through Europe or keeping up with the news gives them an understanding of everything about the cultures, religions and traditions that differ from their own. While I'm heartened by the sincere curiosity of some, like the stylist who asked me about my beliefs as he trimmed my hair, most people still have a long way to go.

I have yet to meet anyone—who isn't either especially well read, a religion major or a Muslim—who can accurately describe Islamic beliefs. Many people find it fascinating that I worship Allah without understanding that "Allah" is simply the Arabic word for God. Muslims use the word only because the universal teachings of Islam have been preserved in the Arabic language.

I can recall a Thanksgiving dinner with family friends several years ago when the host offered a small prayer.

As we all held hands, he started with the customary thanks for the food, family and friends. Then he proceeded to say, "And thank you to God—or whoever else you choose to worship, may it be Allah . . ." He meant well, but I remember flinching. He and his family had traveled to the Middle East, taken pictures of Muslims praying, read about the cultures they were visiting, but none of it had led to a clear understanding of Islam.

I'm not surprised when classmates confront me with the charge that Muslims around the world are killing in the name of religion. I'm careful not to mention the many Muslims who have been killed in places like Kosovo, Indonesia and Palestine. I don't want to respond with that kind of foolish rebuttal because I abhor the senseless murder of all human beings.

The truth is, fanaticism can spring from misguided excess in any religion, and Muslims who kill in the name of their beliefs are not true Muslims. Aggression is not a tenet of our religion, but rather something that is condemned except in self-defense. The Quran states: "Fight in the cause of Allah those who fight you, but commit no aggression; for Allah loves not transgressors" (al-Baqarah 2: 190).

If few people understand that Islam is a peaceful religion, even fewer know how beautiful it can be. When I studied in Cairo during my junior year of college, my grandmother had a religion teacher come to her house every week to teach us the Quran. Hearing him chant the verses was like listening to breathtaking music. There is also an element of poetry in a Muslim's everyday life. One says "Allah" or "ma sha'a Allah" ("as God wills") upon seeing something beautiful, like a sunset or a newborn baby. Whenever family members or friends part, one says, "La illah illa Allah" ("there is only one God") and the other responds, "Muhammad rasoul Allah" ("Muhammad is God's prophet").

To me, informing people about these wonderful aspects of Islam is a pleasure, not a burden. There are signs that Americans may be ready to learn. I was moved recently when I saw a woman on the subway reading a book about Islam to her young daughter. She explained that she was teaching herself, as well as her daughter. If more people take that approach, there will come a day when fanaticism is no longer equated with faith, and Muslims aren't seen as terrorists but as human beings.

QUESTIONS FOR CRITICAL THINKING

Reading 48

1. How does El Sawy's discussion of stereotypes of followers of Islam help you to understand the impact of stereotypes on one's sense of self?

2. What are the sources of your own perceptions of Muslims? How has this impacted your reactions to the events of September 11, 2001?

3. How does U.S. foreign policy and other practices shape perceptions of Arabs, Arab Americans, and those that follow Islam? How have these things impacted the overall reaction in the United States to the events of September 11, 2001?

Reading 49

A DOZEN DEMONS

ELLIS COSE

In the workplace, the continuing relevance of race takes on a special force, partly because so much of life, at least for middle-class Americans, is defined by work, and partly because even people who accept that they will not be treated fairly in the world often hold out hope that their work will be treated fairly—that even a society that keeps neighborhoods racially separate and often makes after-hours social relations awkward will properly reward hard labor and competence. What most African Americans discover, however, is that the racial demons that have plagued them all their lives do not recognize business hours—that the stress of coping extends to a non-work world that is chronically unwilling (or simply unable) to acknowledge the status their professions ought to confer.

The coping effort, in some cases, is relatively minor. It means accepting the fact, for instance, that it is folly to compete for a taxi on a street corner with whites. It means realizing that prudence dictates dressing up whenever you are likely to encounter strangers (including clerks, cops, and doormen) who can make your life miserable by mistaking you for a tramp, a slut, or a crook. And it means tolerating the unctuous boor whose only topic of party conversation is blacks he happens to know. But the price of this continual coping is not insignificant. In addition to creating an unhealthy level of stress, it puts many in such a wary state of mind that insults are seen where none were intended, often complicating communications even with sensitive, well-meaning whites who unwittingly stumble into the racial minefield.

What is it exactly that blacks spend so much time coping with? For lack of a better phrase, let's call them the dozen demons. This is not to say that they affect blacks only; as will become clear, members of other racial minority groups are often plagued by them as well. Nor is it to say that there are only twelve, or that all black Americans encounter every one. Still, if you're looking for a safe bet, you could not find one more certain than this: that any random gathering of black American professionals, asked what irks or troubles them, will eventually end up describing, in one guise or another, the following items.

1. *Inability to fit in.* During the mid 1980s, I had lunch in the Harvard Club in Manhattan with a newsroom recruiter from the *New York Times.* The lunch was primarily social, but my companion was also seeking help in identifying black, Hispanic, and Asian-American journalists he could lure to the *Times.* Though he had encountered plenty of people with good professional credentials, he was concerned about an attribute that was torturously difficult to gauge: the ability to fit into the often bewildering culture of the *Times.* He was desperate to hire good minority candidates, he said, yet hiring someone who could produce decent copy was not enough. He wanted people with class, people who could be "*Times* people."

As we talked, it became clear that he was focusing on such things as speech, manners, dress, and educational pedigree. He had in mind, apparently, a certain button-down sort, an intellectual, nonthreatening, quiet-spoken type—something of a cross between William F. Buckley and Bill Cosby. Someone who might be expected to have his own membership at the Harvard or Yale Club. Not surprisingly, he was not having much success. That most whites at the *Times* fit no such stereotype seemed not to have occurred to him. I suggested, rather gingerly, that perhaps he needed to expand his definition of a "*Times* person," that perhaps some of those he was eliminating for seemingly superficial reasons might have all the qualities the *Times* required.

Even as I made the argument, I knew that it was unpersuasive. Not because he disagreed—he did not offer much of a rebuttal—but because he and many similarly placed executives almost instinctively screened minority candidates according to criteria they did not apply to whites. The practice has nothing to do with malice. It stems more, I suspect, from an unexamined assumption that whites, purely because they are white, are likely to fit in, while blacks and other minority group members are not. Hence, he found it necessary to search for specific assurances that those he brought into the fold had qualities that would enable them, despite their color, to blend into the great white mass.

2. *Exclusion from the club.* Even the ability to fit in, however, does not necessarily guarantee acceptance. Many blacks who have made huge efforts to get the right education, master the right accent, and dress in the proper clothes still find that certain doors never seem to open, that there are private clubs—in both a real and a symbolic sense—they cannot join. . . .

In 1990, in testimony before the U.S. Senate Judiciary Committee, Darwin Davis, senior vice president of the Equitable Life Assurance Society, told of the frustrations he and some of his black friends had experienced in trying to join a country club. "I have openly approached fellow executives about memberships. Several times, they have said, 'My club has openings; it should be no problem. I'll get back to you.' Generally, one of two things happens. They are too embarrassed to talk to me or they come right out and tell me they were shocked when they made inquiries about bringing in a black. Some have even said they were told to get out of the club if they didn't like the situation as it is."

Davis, a white-haired, elegant, and genial raconteur who loves to play golf, told the Senate panel that his interest was not merely in the game but in the financial costs of exclusion. He was routinely reduced to entertaining golf-playing clients at a public course with poor facilities. "The best I can offer my client is a hamburger and a beer in a plastic cup. My competitor takes this client . . . where they have a great lunch and drinks, and use of the locker room and showers. Then, they get their shoes shined. I am out of the ball game with this client." Whenever he found out that a customer played golf, he became "anxious because I know I am on thin ice." It was "disheartening and demeaning," he added, "to know that it doesn't matter how hard I work, how proficient an executive I become, or how successful I become. I will be denied this one benefit that success is supposed to confer on those who have achieved."

Two years after his testimony, Davis told me his obsession with private clubs sprang in part from concerns about his children. Several years before, he had visited a club as a guest and happened to chance upon a white executive he knew. As they were talking, he noticed the man wave at someone on the practice range. It turned out that he had brought his son down to take a lesson from the club pro. Davis was suddenly struck by a depressing thought. "Damn!" he said to himself. "This is being perpetuated all over again. . . . I have a son the same age as his. And when my son grows up he's going to go through the same crap I'm going through if I don't do something about this. His son is learning how to . . . socialize, get lessons, and do business at a country club." His own son, Davis concluded, would "never ever be able to have the same advantages or even an equal footing."

3. *Low expectations.* Shortly after I arrived to take over the editorial pages of the New York *Daily News,* I was visited by a black employee who had worked at the paper for some time. More was on his mind than a simple desire to make my acquaintance. He had also come to talk about how his career was blocked, how the deck was stacked against him—how, in fact,

it was stacked against any black person who worked there. His frustration and anger I easily understood. But what struck me as well was that his expectations left him absolutely no room to grow. He believed so strongly that the white men at the *Daily News* were out to stymie black achievement that he had no option but failure, whatever the reality of the situation.

Even those who refuse to internalize the expectation of failure are often left with nagging doubts, with a feeling, as journalist Joe Boyce puts it, "that no matter what you do in life, there are very few venues in which you can really be sure that you've exhausted your potential. Your achievement is defined by your color and its limitations. And even if in reality you've met your fullest potential, there's an aggravating, lingering doubt . . . because you're never sure. And that makes you angry."

During the late 1970s, I met a Harvard student, Mark Whitaker, who was interning for a summer in *Newsweek*'s Washington bureau. Whitaker made it clear that he intended to go far. He had it in mind to become editor of *Newsweek*. I didn't know whether to be amused by his arrogance, awed by his ambition, or amazed by his naivete. I asked Whitaker—the product of a mixed (black/white) union—whether he had considered that his race might hold him back. He answered that maybe it would, but that he was not going to permit his color to smother his aspirations. He would not hold himself back. If he was to be stopped, it would be by someone else.

More than a decade later, when Whitaker had become a *Newsweek* assistant managing editor, I reminded him of our earlier conversation. He laughed his precocious comments off, attributing them to the ignorance and arrogance of youth. We both knew better, of course—just as we knew that many young blacks, for a variety of reasons, never even reach the point of believing that success was within their grasp.

Conrad Harper, former head of the Association of the Bar of the City of New York and a partner in Simpson Thacher & Barlett, said that throughout the years he had seen plenty of young associates "bitterly scarred by not being taken first as lawyers . . . but always first as African Americans." He had also seen affirmative action turned into a stigma and used as a club to beat capable people down. If someone's competency is consistently doubted, "the person begins to question his own abilities." The result, he added, is not only a terrible waste of talent, but in some cases psychological damage.

4. *Shattered hopes.* After two years toiling at an eminent law firm, the young associate walked away in disgust and became a public defender. For more than a year after leaving, he was "so filled with rage, I couldn't even talk about it much." A soft-spoken Mexican American, he bristles with emotion as he recalls those years.

He believes that he and other minority group hires simply never got a shot at the big assignments, which invariably went to white males. This sense of disappointment, he makes plain, was felt by all the nonwhites in his class. He remembers one in particular, a black woman who graduated with honors from Yale. All her peers thought she was headed for the stars.

Yet when she was rated periodically, she was never included in the first tier but at the top of the second.

If he had been alone in his frustration, he says, one could reject his complaint as no more than a case of sour grapes. "But the fact that all of us were having the same kinds of feelings" means something more systemic was at work. He acknowledges that many whites had similar feelings, that in the intensely competitive environment of a top law firm, no one is guaranteed an easy time. But the sense of abandonment, he contends, was exacerbated for nonwhites. By his count, every minority group member who entered the firm with him ended up leaving, having concluded that nonwhites—barring the spectacularly odd exception—were not destined to make it in that world.

5. *Faint praise.* For a year and a half during the early 1980s, I was a resident fellow at the National Research Council–National Academy of Sciences, an august Washington institution that evaluates scientific research. One afternoon, I mentioned to a white colleague who was also a close friend that it was a shame the NRC had so few blacks on staff. She replied, "Yes, it's too bad there aren't more blacks like you."

I was stunned enough by her comment to ask her what she meant. She answered, in effect, that there were so few really intelligent blacks around who could meet the standards of the NRC. I, of course, was a wonderful exception. Her words, I'm sure, were meant as a compliment, but they angered me, for I took her meaning to be that blacks (present company excluded) simply didn't have the intellect to hang out with the likes of her.

My colleague's attitude seemed to disallow the possibility of a better explanation for the scarcity of blacks than the supposedly low intellectual quality of the race. Perhaps there were so few blacks at the NRC—because they simply were not sought out, or because they were encouraged to believe, from childhood on, that they could never master the expertise that would land them in such a place. The ease with which she dismissed such possibilities in favor of a testimonial to my uniqueness disappointed and depressed me.

Blacks who have been singled out as exceptions often experience anger at the whites who commend them. One young woman, a Harvard-trained lawyer with a long list of "firsts" behind her name, had another reason for cringing whenever she was held up as a glistening departure from the norm for her race. "I don't like what it does to my relationships with other blacks," she said.

6. *Presumption of failure.* A year or so prior to my Harvard Club chat with the *Times* recruiter, I was visited at my office (then in Berkeley, California) by a *Times* assistant managing editor. I took him to lunch, and after a few drinks we fell into a discussion of people at the *Times,* among them a talented black editor whose career seemed to have stalled. Was he in line, I asked, for a high-level editorship that would soon be vacant? My companion agreed that the editor would probably do very well in the job, but then he pointed out that a black person had never held such a post

at the *New York Times.* The *Times* would have to think hard, he indicated, before changing that, for they could not afford to have a black journalist fail in such a visible position. I didn't know whether the man even wanted the job (he later told me he might have preferred something else); I know that he didn't get it, that (at least in the eyes of one *Times* assistant managing editor in 1985) his prior work and credentials could not offset the questions raised by his color. Failure at the highest levels of the *Times* was a privilege apparently reserved for whites.

The *Times'* executive's reasoning reminded me of an encounter with a newspaper editor in Atlanta who had contacted me several years earlier. He had an editorial writer's position to fill and was interested in giving me a crack at it. I was intrigued enough to go to Atlanta and spend an evening with the man. We discovered we shared many interests and friends and hit it off famously. Still, I wondered: Why in the world was he recruiting me? Interesting though Atlanta might be, and as well as he and I got along, there had never been much chance that I would leap at the job. In no way did it represent a career advancement, and the editor's budget would barely permit him to pay the salary I was already making. As the evening wore on, I put the question to him bluntly. Why did he not offer the job to someone in his newsroom for whom it would be a real step up? His answer I found more than a little unsettling. One black person, he said, had already come on staff and not performed very well. He could not afford another black failure, so he had gone after someone overqualified in an attempt to buy himself insurance.

I'm sure he was not surprised that I turned the job down. . . . I don't doubt . . . that similar preconceptions still exist, that before many executives even ask whether a minority person can do a job, they ask whether they are prepared to take a flyer on a probable failure.

7. *Coping fatigue.* When Armetta Parker headed for Midland, Michigan, to take a job as a public relations professional at the Dow Chemical Company, she assumed that she was on her way to big-time corporate success. A bright, energetic black woman then in her early thirties, Parker had left a good position at a public utility in Detroit to get on the Fortune 100 fast track.

"Dow was everything I expected and more, and everything I expected and less," she says. The town of nearly forty thousand had only a few hundred black families, and virtually no single black people her own age. Though she expected a certain amount of social isolation, "I didn't expect to get the opportunity to take a really hard look at me, at what was important to me and what wasn't." She had to face that fact that success, in that kind of corporate environment, meant a great deal of work and no social life, and that it also required a great deal of faith in people who found it difficult to recognize competence in blacks. . . .

Nonetheless, Parker did extremely well, at least initially. Her first year at the company, she made it into "The Book"—the roster of those who had been identified as people on the fast track. But eventually she realized that "I was never going to be vice president of public affairs for Dow Chemical." She believed that her color, her gender, and her lack of a technical degree all were working against her. Moreover, "even if they gave it to me, I didn't want it. The price was too high." Part of that price would have been accepting the fact that her race was not seen as an asset but as something she had to overcome. And her positive traits were probably attributed to white genes, she surmised, even though she is no more "white" than most American blacks. Even her way of talking drew attention. Upon meeting her, one colleague remarked with evident pleasure and astonishment, "You don't speak ghettoese." She had an overwhelming sense that what he meant was "You're almost like us, but not enough like us to be acceptable." . . . She realized that "good corporate jobs can be corporate handcuffs. You have to decide how high of a price you're willing to pay."

8. *Pigeonholing.* Near the end of his brashly brilliant tenure as executive editor of the *Washington Post*, Ben Bradlee observed how much both Washington and the *Post* had changed. Once upon a time, he told me, one would not have thought of appointing a black city editor. Now one could not think of not seriously considering—and even favoring—a black person for the assignment.

Bradlee, I realized, was making several points. One was about himself and his fellow editors, about how they had matured to the extent that they valued all managerial talent—even in blacks. He was also acknowledging that blacks had become so central to Washington's political, economic, and social life that a black city editor had definite advantages, strictly as a function of race. His third point, I'm sure, was wholly unintended but clearly implied: that it was still possible, even for the most enlightened management, to classify jobs by color. And logic dictates that if certain managerial tasks are best handled by blacks, others are best left to whites.

What this logic has meant in terms of the larger corporate world is that black executives have landed, out of all proportion to their numbers, in community relations and public affairs, or in slots where their only relevant expertise concerns blacks and other minorities. The selfsame racial assumptions that make minorities seem perfect for certain initially desirable jobs can ultimately be responsible for trapping them there as others move on.

9. *Identity troubles.* The man was on the verge of retiring from his position as personnel vice president for one of America's largest companies. He had acquired the requisite symbols of success: a huge office, a generous compensation package, a summer home away from home. But he had paid a price. He had decided along the way, he said matter-of-factly, that he could no longer afford to be black.

I was so surprised by the man's statement that I sat silent for several seconds before asking him to explain. Clearly he had done nothing to alter his dark brown complexion. What he had altered, he told me, was the way he allowed himself to be perceived. Early in his career, he had been moderately outspoken about what he saw as racism within and outside his former corporation. He had learned, however, that his modest attempts at advocacy got him typecast as an undesirable. So when he changed jobs, he decided to disassociate himself from any hint of a racial agenda. The strategy had clearly furthered his career, even though other blacks in the company labeled him an Uncle Tom. He was aware of his reputation, and pained by what the others thought, but he had seen no other way to thrive. He noted as well, with evident pride, that he had not abandoned his race, that he had quietly made it his business to cultivate a few young blacks in the corporation and bring their careers along; and could point to some who were doing very well and would have been doing considerably worse without his intervention. His achievements brought him enough pleasure to balance out the distress of not being "black."

Putting aside for the moment what it means to be "black," the fear of being forced to shed one's identity in order to prosper is not at all uncommon. Georgetown University law professor Anita Allen tells of a worried student who asked whether her diction would have to be as precise as Allen's if she was to be successful as a lawyer. She feared, it seemed, not merely having to change her accent, but being required to discard an important part of herself.

10. *Self-censorship and silence.* . . . [M]any blacks find their voices stilled when sensitive racial issues are raised. A big-city police officer once shared with me his frustration at waiting nineteen years to make detective. In those days before affirmative action, he had watched, one year after another, as less qualified whites were promoted over him. And each year he had swallowed his disappointment, twisted his face into a smile, and congratulated his white friends as he hid his rage—so determined was he to avoid being categorized as a race-obsessed troublemaker. And he had endured other affronts in silence, including a vicious beating by a group of white cops while carrying out a plainclothes assignment. As an undercover officer working within a militant black organization, he had been given a code word to whisper to a fellow officer if the need arose. When he was being brutalized, he had screamed out the word and discovered it to be worthless. His injuries had required surgery and more than thirty stitches. When he was asked by his superior to identify those who had beat him, he feigned ignorance; it seems a fellow officer had preceded his commander and bluntly passed along the message that it was safer to keep quiet.

Even though he made detective years ago, and even though, on the side, he managed to become a successful businessman and an exemplary member of the upwardly striving middle class, he says the anger still simmers within him. He worries that some day it will come pouring out, that some luckless white person will tick him off and he will explode, with tragic results. Knowing him, I don't believe he will ever reach that point.

But I accept his fear that he could blow up as a measure of the intensity of his feelings, and of the terrible cost of having to hold them in.

11. *Mendacity.* Even more damaging than self-imposed silence are the lies that seem an integral part of America's approach to race. Many of the lies are simple self-deception, as when corporate executives claim their companies are utterly color-blind. Some stem from unwillingness to acknowledge racial bias, as when people who have no intention of voting for a candidate of another race tell pollsters that they will. And many are lies of business, social, or political convenience, as was the case with Massachusetts Senator Edward Brooke in the early 1970s.

At the time, Brooke was the highest-ranking black politician in America. His name was routinely trotted out as a vice presidential possibility, though everyone involved knew the exercise was a farce. According to received wisdom, America was not ready to accept a black on the ticket, but Brooke's name seemed to appear on virtually everyone's list. During one such period of vice-presidential hype, I interviewed Brooke for a newspaper profile. After asking the standard questions, I could no longer contain my curiosity. Wasn't he tired, I asked, of the charade of having his name bandied about when no one intended to select him? He nodded wearily and said yes, he was.

To me, his response spoke volumes, probably much more than he'd intended. But I took it as his agreement that lies of political convenience are not merely a nuisance for those interested in the truth but a source of profound disgust and cynicism for those on whose behalf the lies are supposedly told.

12. *Guilt by association.* In the mid 1980s, I was unceremoniously tossed out of Cafe Royale, a restaurant that catered to yuppies in San Francisco, on the orders of a maitre d' who apparently mistook me for someone who had caused trouble on a previous occasion. I sued the restaurant and eventually collected a few thousand dollars from its insurance company. But I will never forget the fury I experienced at being haughtily dismissed by an exalted waiter who would not suffer the inconvenience of having to distinguish one black person from another.

My first real understanding of how poisonous such an attitude could be came to me at the age of twelve or thirteen, when I went to Marshall Field's department store in downtown Chicago in search of a Mother's Day gift. While wandering from one section of the store to another, I gradually became aware that someone was shadowing me. That someone, I ascertained, was a plain-clothes security guard. Apparently I fit his profile of a shoplifter. For several minutes, I roamed through the store, trying to ignore him, but he was determined not to be ignored. Little by little, he made his surveillance more obvious, until we were practically walking in lock step. His tactics unsettled me so much that I could no longer concentrate on shopping. Finally, I whirled to face him.

He said nothing, merely glared as my outrage mounted. *How dare he treat me like a criminal,* I thought, *simply because I'm black.* I screamed something at him; I don't remember what. Whatever it was, it had no effect; he continued to stare at me with a look somewhere between amusement and disdain. I stalked out of the store, conceding him the victory, burning with anger and humiliation. . . .

[Many commentators argue] that America's cities have become so dangerous, largely as a result of young black thugs, that racial discrimination is justified—and is even a necessary tool of survival when directed at young black men. . . .

This rationalization strikes me, to put it mildly, as dangerous. For it inevitably takes one beyond the street, and beyond those black males who are certifiably dangerous. It quickly takes one into society at large, where blacks in no way connected with street crime find themselves victims of street-crime stereotypes. Members of the law-abiding black middle class also have sons, as do those countless African Americans without substantial financial resources who have tried to pound into their children, from birth, that virtue has its rewards, that there is value in following a moral path and shunning the temptations of the street. . . .

Countless members of the black middle class are in fact volunteering every spare moment in an attempt to do whatever they can (working in homeless shelters, volunteering in literacy programs, serving as formal mentors) to better the lives of those in the so-called underclass. At the same time, however, many who belong to America's black privileged class are struggling with problems of their own that are largely unseen or dismissed.

 QUESTIONS FOR CRITICAL THINKING

Reading 49

1. Cose outlines many of the "demons" that African Americans experience as a result of racism. How are these demons in common to all people of color? Are there different demons some groups may face that others do not?

2. Were there any "demons" that the author discussed that surprised you or that you weren't aware of? How do you think your own status in society influences your reaction?

3. How does the author's discussion demonstrate that racism comes in a variety of forms that are, in most cases, less blatant than in the past. How does such covert racism make it difficult to bring about racial equality?

Reading 50

ALWAYS RUNNING

LUIS RODRIGUEZ

Our first exposure in America stays with me like a foul odor. It seemed a strange world, most of it spiteful to us, spitting and stepping on us, coughing us up, us immigrants, as if we were phlegm stuck in the collective throat of this country. My father was mostly out of work. When he did have a job it was in construction, in factories such as Sinclair Paints or Standard Brands Dog Food, or pushing doorbells selling insurance, Bibles, or pots and pans. My mother found work cleaning homes or in the garment industry. She knew the corner markets were ripping her off but she could only speak with her hands and in choppy English.

Once my mother gathered up the children and we walked to Will Rogers Park. There were people everywhere. Mama looked around for a place we could rest. She spotted an empty spot on a park bench. But as soon as she sat down an American woman, with three kids of her own, came by.

"Hey, get out of there—that's our seat."

My mother understood but didn't know how to answer back in English. So she tried in Spanish.

"Look spic, you can't sit there!" the American woman yelled. "You don't belong here! Understand? This is not your country!"

Mama quietly got our things and walked away, but I knew frustration and anger bristled within her because she was unable to talk, and when she did, no one would listen.

We never stopped crossing borders. The Rio Grande (or *Rio Bravo,* which is what the Mexicans call it, giving the name a power "Rio Grande" just doesn't have) was only the first of countless barriers set in our path.

We kept jumping hurdles, kept breaking from the constraints, kept evading the border guards of every new trek. It was a metaphor to fill our lives—that river, that first crossing, the mother of all crossings. The Los Angeles River, for example, became a new barrier, keeping the Mexicans in their neighborhoods over on the vast east side of the city for years, except for forays downtown. Schools provided other restrictions: don't speak Spanish, don't be Mexican—you don't belong. Railroad tracks divided us from communities where white people lived, such as South Gate and Lynwood across from Watts. We were invisible people in a city which thrived on glitter, big screens, and big names, but this glamour contained none of our names, none of our faces.

The refrain "this is not your country" echoed for a lifetime.

First day of school.

I was six years old, never having gone to kindergarten because Mama wanted me to wait until La Pata became old enough to enter school. Mama filled out some papers. A school monitor directed us to a classroom where Mama dropped me off and left to join some parents who gathered in the main hall.

The first day of school said a lot about my scholastic life to come. I was taken to a teacher who didn't know what to do with me. She complained about not having any room, about kids who didn't even speak the language. And how was she supposed to teach anything under these conditions! Although I didn't speak English, I understood a large part of what she was saying. I knew I wasn't wanted. She put me in an old creaky chair near the door. As soon as I could, I sneaked out to find my mother.

I found Rano's class with the mentally disabled children instead and decided to stay there for a while. Actually it was fun; they treated me like I was everyone's little brother. But the teacher finally told a student to take me to the main hall.

After some more paperwork, I was taken to another class. This time the teacher appeared nicer, but distracted. She got the word about my language problem.

"Okay, why don't you sit here in the back of the class," she said. "Play with some blocks until we figure out how to get you more involved."

It took her most of that year to figure this out. I just stayed in the back of the class, building blocks. It got so every morning I would put my lunch and coat away, and walk to my corner where I stayed the whole day long. It forced me to be more withdrawn. It got so bad, I didn't even tell anybody when I had to go to the bathroom. I did it in my pants. Soon I stunk back there in the corner and the rest of the kids screamed out a chorus of "P.U.!" resulting in my being sent to the office or back home.

In those days there was no way to integrate the non-English-speaking children. So they just made it a crime to speak anything but English. If a Spanish word sneaked out in the playground, kids were often sent to the office to get swatted or to get detention. Teachers complained that maybe the children were saying bad things about them. An assumption of guilt was enough to get one punished.

A day came when I finally built up the courage to tell the teacher I had to go to the bathroom. I didn't quite say all the words, but she got the message and promptly excused me so I didn't do it while I was trying to explain. I ran to the bathroom and peed and felt good about not having that wetness trickle down my pants leg. But suddenly several bells went on and off. I hesitantly stepped out of the bathroom and saw throngs of children leave their class. I had no idea what was happening. I went to my classroom and it stood empty. I looked into other classrooms and found nothing. Nobody. I didn't know what to do. I really thought everyone had gone home. I didn't bother to look at the playground where the whole school had been assembled for the fire drill. I just went home. It got to be a regular thing there for a while, me coming home early until I learned the ins and outs of school life.

Not speaking well makes for such embarrassing moments. I hardly asked questions. I just didn't want to be misunderstood. Many Spanish-speaking kids mangled things up; they would say things like "where the beer and cantaloupe roam" instead of "where the deer and antelope roam."

That's the way it was with me. I mixed up all the words. Screwed up all the songs.

"You can't be in a fire and not get burned."

This was my father's response when he heard of the trouble I was getting into at school. He was a philosopher. He didn't get angry or hit me. That he left to my mother. He had these lines, these cuts of wisdom, phrases and syllables, which swept through me, sometimes even making sense. I had to deal with him at that level, with my brains. I had to justify in words, with ideas, all my actions—no matter how insane. Most of the time I couldn't.

Mama was heat. Mama was turned-around leather belts and wailing choruses of Mary-Mother-of-Jesus. She was the penetrating emotion that came at you through her eyes, the mother-guilt, the one who birthed me, who suffered through the contractions and diaper changes and all my small hurts and fears. For her, dealing with school trouble or risking my life was nothing for discourse, nothing to debate. She went through all this hell and more to have me—I'd better do what she said!

Mama hated the *cholos.* They reminded her of the rowdies on the border who fought all the time, talked that *calo* slang, drank mescal, smoked marijuana, and left scores of women with babies bursting out of their bodies.

To see me become like them made her sick, made her cringe and cry and curse. Mama reminded us how she'd seen so much alcoholism, so much weed-madness, and she prohibited anything with alcohol in the house, even beer. I later learned this rage came from how Mama's father treated her siblings and her mother, how in drunken rages he'd hit her mom and drag her through the house by the hair.

The school informed my parents I had been wreaking havoc with a number of other young boys. I was to be part of a special class of troublemakers. We would be isolated from the rest of the school population and forced to pick up trash and clean graffiti during the rest of the school year.

"Mrs. Rodriguez, your son is too smart for this," the vice principal told Mama. "We think he's got a lot of potential. But his behavior is atrocious. There's no excuse. We're sad to inform you of our decision."

They also told her the next time I cut class or even made a feint toward trouble, I'd be expelled. After the phone call, my mom lay on her bed, shaking her head while sobbing in between bursts of how God had cursed her for some sin, how I was the devil incarnate, a plague, testing her in this brief tenure on earth.

My dad's solution was to keep me home after school. Grounded. Yeah, sure. I was thirteen years old already. Already tattooed. Already sexually involved. Already into drugs. In the middle of the night I snuck out through the window and worked my way to the Hills.

At sixteen years old, Rano turned out much better than me, much better than anyone could have envisioned during the time he was a foul-faced boy in Watts.

When we moved to South San Gabriel, a Mrs. Snelling took a liking to Rano. The teacher helped him skip grades to make up for the times he was pushed back in those classes with the retarded children.

Mrs. Snelling saw talent in Rano, a spark of actor during the school's thespian activities. She even had him play the lead in a class play. He also showed some facility with music. And he was good in sports.

He picked up the bass guitar and played for a number of garage bands. He was getting trophies in track-and-field events, in gymnastic meets, and later in karate tournaments.

So when I was at Garvey, he was in high school being the good kid, the Mexican exception, the barrio success story—my supposed model. Soon he stopped being Rano or even José. One day he became Joe.

My brother and I were moving away from each other. Our tastes, our friends, our interests were miles apart. Yet there were a few outstanding incidents I fondly remember in relationship to my brother, incidents which despite their displays of closeness failed to breach the distance which would later lie between us.

When I was nine, for example, my brother was my protector. He took on all the big dudes, the bullies on corners, the ones who believed themselves better than us. Being a good fighter transformed him overnight. He was somebody who some feared, some looked up to. Then he developed skills for racing and high-jumping. This led to running track and he did well, dusting all the competition.

I didn't own any talents. I was lousy in sports. I couldn't catch baseballs or footballs. And I constantly tripped when I ran or jumped. When kids picked players for basketball games, I was the last one they chose. The one time I inadvertently hit a home run during a game at school—I didn't mean to do it—I ended up crying while running around the bases because I didn't know how else to react to the cheers, the excitement, directed at something I did. It just couldn't be me.

But Rano had enemies too. There were two Mexican kids who were jealous of him. They were his age, three years older than me. One was named

Eddie Gambits, the other Rick Corral. One time they cornered me outside the school.

"You José's brother," Eddie said.

I didn't say anything.

"Wha's the matter? Can't talk?"

"Oh, he can talk all right," Ricky chimed in. "He acting the *pendejo* because his brother thinks he so bad. Well, he ain't shit. He can't even run."

"Yeah, José's just a *lambiche,* a kiss ass," Eddie responded. "They give him those ribbons and stuff because he cheats."

"That's not true," I finally answered. "My brother can beat anybody."

"Oh, you saying he can beat me," Eddie countered.

"Sure sounds like he said that," Ricky added.

"I'm only saying that when he wins those ribbons, *esta derecho,*" I said.

"It sounds to me like you saying he better than me," Eddie said.

"Is that what you saying, man?" Ricky demanded. "Com'on—is that what you saying?"

I turned around, and beneath my breath, mumbled something about how I didn't have time to argue with them. I shouldn't have done that.

"What'd you say?" Eddie said.

"I think he called you a punk," Ricky agitated.

"You call me a punk, man?" Eddie turned me around. I denied it.

"I heard him, dude. He say you are a punk-ass *puto,*" Ricky continued to exhort.

The fist came at me so fast, I don't even recall how Eddie looked when he threw it. I found myself on the ground. Others in the school had gathered around by then. When a few saw it was me, they knew it was going to be a slaughter.

I rose to my feet—my cheek had turned swollen and blue. I tried to hit Eddie, but he backed up real smooth and hit me again. Ricky egged him on; I could hear the excitement in his voice.

I lay on the ground, defeated. Teachers came and chased the boys out. But before Eddie and Ricky left they yelled back: "José ain't nothing, man. You ain't nothing."

Anger flowed through me, but also humiliation. It hurt so deep I didn't even feel the fracture in my jaw, the displacement which would later give me a disjointed, lopsided, and protruding chin. It became my mark.

Later when I told Rano what happened, he looked at me and shook his head.

"You didn't have to defend me to those dudes," he said. "They're assholes. They ain't worth it."

I looked at him and told him something I never, ever told him again.

"I did it because I love you."

I began high school a *loco,* with a heavy Pendleton shirt, sagging khaki pants, ironed to perfection, and shoes shined and heated like at boot camp.

Mark Keppel High School was a Depression-era structure with a brick and art-deco facade and small, army-type bungalows in back. Friction filled its hallways. The Anglo and Asian upper-class students from Monterey Park and Alhambra attended the school. They were tracked into the "A" classes; they were in the school clubs, they were the varsity team members and lettermen. They were the pep squads and cheerleaders.

But the school also took in the people from the Hills and surrounding community who somehow made it past junior high. They were mostly Mexican, in the "C" track (what were called the "stupid" classes), and who made up the rosters of the wood, print, and auto shops. Only a few of these students participated in school government, in sports, or in the various clubs.

The school had two principal languages. Two skin tones and two cultures. It revolved around class differences. The white and Asian kids (except for "barrio" whites and the handful of Hawaiians, Filipinos, and Samoans who ended up with the Mexicans) were from professional, two-car households with watered lawns and trimmed trees. The laboring class, the sons and daughters of service workers, janitors, and factory hands, lived in and around the Hills (or a section of Monterey Park called "Poor Side").

The school separated these two groups by levels of education: The professional-class kids were provided with college-preparatory classes; the blue-collar students were pushed into "industrial arts."

 QUESTIONS FOR CRITICAL THINKING

Reading 50

1. Rodriguez demonstrates some of the difficulties faced by children who are non-English speakers in our public school system. How would his experiences have been different if he had been taught in his own language?

2. How do the experiences of Rodriguez point to problems in our public education system? How might these problems be best addressed?

3. Is English-only teaching the best method of educating newcomers to the United States? What alternatives can you think of?

Reading 51

THE STORY OF MY BODY

JUDITH ORTIZ COFER

Migration is the story of my body.

—Victor Hernández Cruz

 ## SKIN

I was born a white girl in Puerto Rico but became a brown girl when I came to live in the United States. My Puerto Rican relatives call me tall; at the American school, some of my rougher classmates called me Skinny Bones, and the Shrimp because I was the smallest member of my classes all through grammar school until high school, when the midget Gladys was given the honorary post of front row center for class pictures and scorekeeper, bench warmer, in P.E. I reached my full stature of five feet in sixth grade.

I started out life as a pretty baby and learned to be a pretty girl from a pretty mother. Then at ten years of age I suffered one of the worst cases of chicken pox I have ever heard of. My entire body, including the inside of my ears and in between my toes, was covered with pustules which in a fit of panic at my appearance I scratched off my face, leaving permanent scars. A cruel school nurse told me I would always have them—tiny cuts that looked as if a mad cat had plunged its claws deep into my skin. I grew my hair long and hid behind it for the first years of my adolescence. This was when I learned to be invisible.

 ## COLOR

In the animal world it indicates danger: the most colorful creatures are often the most poisonous. Color is also a way to attract and seduce a mate. In the human world color triggers many more complex and often deadly reactions. As a Puerto Rican girl born of "white" parents, I spent the first years of my life hearing people refer to me as *blanca,* white. My mother insisted that I protect myself from the intense island sun because I was more prone to sunburn than some of my darker, *trigueño*[1] playmates. People were always commenting within my hearing about how my black hair contrasted so nicely with my "pale" skin. I did not think of the color of my skin consciously except when I heard the adults talking about complexion. It seems to me that the subject is much more common in the conversation of mixed-race peoples than in mainstream United States society, where it is a touchy and sometimes even embarrassing topic to discuss, except in a political context. In Puerto Rico I heard many conversations about skin color. A pregnant woman could say, "I hope my baby doesn't turn out *prieto*" (slang for "dark" or "black") "like my husband's grandmother, although she was a good-looking *negra*[2] in her time." I am a combination of both, being olive-skinned—lighter than my mother yet darker than my fair-skinned father. In America, I am a person of color, obviously a Latina. On the Island I have been called everything from a *paloma blanca*,[3] after the song (by a black suitor), to *la gringa*.[4]

My first experience of color prejudice occurred in a supermarket in Paterson, New Jersey. It was Christmastime, and I was eight or nine years old. There was a display of toys in the store where I went two or three times a day to buy things for my mother, who never made lists but sent for milk, cigarettes, a can of this or that, as she remembered from hour to hour. I enjoyed being trusted with money and walking half a city block to the new, modern grocery store. It was owned by three good-looking Italian brothers. I liked the younger one with the crew-cut blond hair. The two older ones watched me and the other Puerto Rican kids as if they thought we were going to steal something. The oldest one would sometimes even try to hurry me with my purchases, although part of my pleasure in these expeditions came from looking at everything in the well-stocked aisles. I was also teaching myself to read English by sounding out the labels in packages: L&M cigarettes, Borden's homogenized milk, Red Devil potted ham, Nestle's chocolate mix, Quaker oats, Bustelo coffee, Wonder bread, Colgate toothpaste, Ivory soap, and Goya (makers of products used in Puerto Rican dishes) everything—these are some of the brand names that taught me nouns. Several times this man had come up to me, wearing his blood-stained butcher's apron, and towering over me had asked in a harsh voice whether there was something he could help me find. On the way out I would glance at the younger brother who ran one of the registers and he would often smile and wink at me.

It was the mean brother who first referred to me as "colored." It was a few days before Christmas, and my parents had already told my brother and me that since we were in Los Estados[5] now, we would get our presents on December 25 instead of Los Reyes, Three Kings Day, when gifts are exchanged in Puerto Rico. We were to give them a wish list that they would take to Santa Claus, who apparently lived in the Macy's store downtown—at least that's where we had caught a glimpse of him when we went shopping. Since my parents were timid about entering the fancy store, we did not approach the huge man in the red suit. I was not interested in sitting on a stranger's lap anyway. But I did covet Susie, the talking schoolteacher doll that was displayed in the center aisle of the Italian brothers' supermarket. She talked when you pulled a string on her back. Susie had a limited repertoire of three sentences: I think she could say: "Hello, I'm Susie Schoolteacher," "Two plus two is four," and one other thing I cannot remember. The day the older brother chased me away, I was reaching to touch Susie's blond curls. I had been told many times, as most children have, not to touch anything in the store that I was not buying. But I had been looking at Susie for weeks. In my mind, she was my doll. After all, I had put her on my Christmas wish list. The moment is frozen in my mind as if there were a photograph of it on file. It was not a turning point, a disaster, or an earth-shaking revelation. It was simply the first time I considered—if naively—the meaning of skin color in human relations.

I reached to touch Susie's hair. It seems to me that I had to get on tip-toe, since the toys were stacked on a table and she sat like a princess on top of the fancy box she came in. Then I heard the booming "Hey, kid, what do you think you're doing!" spoken very loudly from the meat counter. I felt caught, although I knew I was not doing anything criminal. I remember not looking at the man, but standing there, feeling humiliated because I knew everyone in the store must have heard him yell at me. I felt him approach, and when I knew he was behind me, I turned around to face the bloody butcher's apron. His large chest was at my eye level. He blocked my way. I started to run out of the place, but even as I reached the door I heard him shout after me: "Don't come in here unless you gonna buy something. You PR kids put your dirty hands on stuff. You always look dirty. But maybe dirty brown is your natural color." I heard him laugh and someone else too in the back. Outside in the sunlight I looked at my hands. My nails needed a little cleaning as they always did, since I liked to paint with watercolors, but I took a bath every night. I thought the man was dirtier than I was in his stained apron. He was also always sweaty—it showed in big yellow circles under his shirt-sleeves. I sat on the front steps of the apartment building where we lived and looked closely at my hands, which showed the only skin I could see, since it was bitter cold and I was wearing my quilted play coat, dungarees, and a knitted navy cap of my father's. I was not light pink like my friend Charlene and her sister Kathy, who had blue eyes and light brown hair. My skin is the color of the coffee my grandmother made, which was half milk, *leche con café* rather than *café con leche*.[6] My mother is the opposite mix. She has a lot of café in her color. I could not understand how my skin looked like dirt to the supermarket man.

I went in and washed my hands thoroughly with soap and hot water, and borrowing my mother's nail file, I cleaned the crusted watercolors from underneath my nails. I was pleased with the results. My skin was the same color as before, but I knew I was clean. Clean enough to run my fingers through Susie's fine gold hair when she came home to me.

◎ SIZE

My mother is barely four feet eleven inches in height, which is average for women in her family. When I grew to five feet by age twelve, she was amazed and began to use the word tall to describe me, as in "Since you are tall, this dress will look good on you." As with the color of my skin, I didn't consciously think about my height or size until other people made an issue of it. It is around the preadolescent years that in America the games children play for fun become fierce competitions where everyone is out to "prove" they are better than others. It was in the playground and sports fields that my size-related problems began. No matter how familiar the story is, every child who is the last chosen for a team knows the torment of waiting to be called up. At the Paterson, New Jersey, public schools that I attended, the volleyball or softball game was the metaphor for the battlefield of life to the inner city kids—the black kids versus the Puerto Rican kids, the whites versus the blacks versus the Puerto Rican kids; and I was 4F,[7] skinny, short, bespectacled, and apparently impervious to the blood thirst that drove many of my classmates to play ball as if their lives depended on it. Perhaps they did. I would rather be reading a book than sweating, grunting, and running the risk of pain and injury. I simply did not see the point in competitive sports. My main form of exercise then was walking to the library, many city blocks away from my barrio.

Still, I wanted to be wanted. I wanted to be chosen for the team. Physical education was compulsory, a class where you were actually given a grade. On my mainly all A report card, the C for compassion I always received from the P.E. teachers shamed me the same as a bad grade in a real class. Invariably, my father would say: "How can you make a low grade for *playing games?*" He did not understand. Even if I had managed to make a hit (it never happened) or get the ball over that ridiculously high net, I already had a reputation as a "shrimp," a hopeless nonathlete. It was an area where the girls who didn't like me for one reason or another—mainly because I did better than they on academic subjects—could lord it over me; the playing field was the place where even the smallest girl could make me feel powerless and inferior. I instinctively understood the politics even then; how the not choosing me until the teacher forced one of the team captains to call my name was a coup of sorts—there, you little show-off, tomorrow you can beat us in spelling and geography, but this afternoon you are the loser. Or perhaps those were only my own bitter thoughts as I sat or stood in the sidelines while the big girls were grabbed like fish and I, the little brown tadpole, was ignored until Teacher looked over in my general direction and shouted, "Call Ortiz," or, worse, "Somebody's *got* to take her."

No wonder I read Wonder Woman comics and had Legion of Super Heroes daydreams. Although I wanted to think of myself as "intellectual," my body was demanding that I notice it. I saw the little swelling around my once-flat nipples, the fine hairs growing in secret places; but my knees were still bigger than my thighs, and I always wore long- or half-sleeve blouses to hide my bony upper arms. I wanted flesh on my bones—a thick layer of it. I saw a new product advertised on TV. Wate-On. They showed skinny men and women before and after taking the stuff, and it was a transformation like the ninety-seven-pound-weakling-turned-into-Charles-Atlas ads that I saw on the back covers of my comic books. The Wate-On was very expensive. I tried to explain my need for it in Spanish to my mother, but it didn't translate very well, even to my ears—and she said with a tone of finality, eat more of my good food and you'll get fat—anybody can get fat. Right. Except me. I was going to have to join a circus someday as Skinny Bones, the woman without flesh.

Wonder Woman was stacked. She had a cleavage framed by the spread wings of a golden eagle and a muscular body that has become fashionable with women only recently. But since I wanted a body that would serve me in P.E., hers was my ideal. The breasts were an indulgence I allowed myself. Perhaps the daydreams of bigger girls were more glamorous, since our ambitions are filtered through our needs, but I wanted first a powerful body. I daydreamed of leaping up above the gray landscape of the city to where the sky was clear and blue, and in anger and self-pity, I fantasized about scooping my enemies up by their hair from the playing fields and dumping them on a barren asteroid. I would put the P.E. teachers each on their own rock in space too, where they would be the loneliest people in the universe, since I knew they had no "inner resources," no imagination, and in outer space, there would be no air for them to fill their deflated volleyballs with. In my mind all P.E. teachers have blended into one large spiky-haired woman with a whistle on a string around her neck and a volleyball under one arm. My Wonder Woman fantasies of revenge were a source of comfort to me in my early career as a shrimp.

I was saved from more years of P.E. torment by the fact that in my sophomore year of high school I transferred to a school where the midget, Gladys, was the focal point of interest for the people who must rank according to size. Because her height was considered a handicap, there was an unspoken rule about mentioning size around Gladys, but of course, there was no need to say anything. Gladys knew her place: front row center in class photographs. I gladly moved to the left or to the right of her, as far as I could without leaving the picture completely.

 LOOKS

Many photographs were taken of me as a baby by my mother to send to my father, who was stationed overseas during the first two years of my life. With the Army in Panama when I was born, he later traveled often on tours of duty with the Navy. I was a healthy, pretty baby. Recently, I read that people are drawn to big-eyed round-faced creatures, like puppies, kittens, and certain other mammals and marsupials, koalas, for example, and, of course, infants. I was all eyes, since my head and body, even as I grew older, remained thin and small-boned. As a young child I got a lot of attention from my relatives and many other people we met in our barrio. My mother's beauty may have had something to do with how much attention we got from strangers in stores and on the street. I can imagine it. In the pictures I have seen of us together, she is a stunning young woman by Latino standards: long, curly black hair, and round curves in a compact frame. From her I learned how to move, smile, and talk like an attractive woman. I remember going into a bodega[8] for our groceries and being given candy by the proprietor as a reward for being *bonita*, pretty.

I can see in the photographs, and I also remember, that I was dressed in the pretty clothes, the stiff, frilly dresses, with layers of crinolines underneath, the glossy patent leather shoes, and, on special occasions, the skull-hugging little hats and the white gloves that were popular in the late fifties and early sixties. My mother was proud of my looks, although I was a bit too thin. She could dress me up like a doll and take me by the hand to visit relatives, or go to the Spanish mass at the Catholic church and show me off. How was I to know that she and the others who called me "pretty" were representatives of an aesthetic that would not apply when I went out into the mainstream world of school?

In my Paterson, New Jersey, public schools there were still quite a few white children, although the demographics of the city were changing rapidly. The original waves of Italian and Irish immigrants, silk-mill workers, and laborers in the cloth industries had been "assimilated." Their children were now the middle-class parents of my peers. Many of them moved their children to the Catholic schools that proliferated enough to have leagues of basketball teams. The names I recall hearing still ring in my ears: Don Bosco High versus St. Mary's High, St. Joseph's versus St. John's. Later I too would be transferred to the safer environment of a Catholic school. But I started school at Public School Number 11. I came there from Puerto Rico, thinking myself a pretty girl, and found that the hierarchy for popularity was as follows: pretty white girl, pretty Jewish girl, pretty Puerto Rican girl, pretty black girl. Drop the last two categories; teachers were too busy to have more than one favorite per class, and it was simply understood that if there was a big part in the school play, or any competition where the main qualification was "presentability" (such as escorting a school visitor to or from the principal's office), the classroom's public address speaker would be requesting the pretty and/or nice-looking white boy or girl. By the time I was in sixth grade, I was sometimes called by the principal to represent my class because I dressed neatly (I knew this from a progress report sent to my mother, which I translated for her) and because all the "presentable" white girls had moved to the Catholic schools (I later surmised this part). But I was still not one of the popular girls with the boys. I remember one incident where I stepped out into the playground in my baggy gym shorts and one Puerto Rican boy said to the other: "What do you think?" The other one answered: "Her face is OK, but look at the toothpick legs." The next best thing to a compliment I got was when my favorite male teacher, while handing out the class pictures, commented that with my long neck and delicate features I resembled the movie star Audrey Hepburn. But the Puerto Rican boys had learned to respond to a fuller figure: long necks and a perfect little nose were not what they looked for in a girl. That is when I decided I was a "brain." I did not settle into the role easily. I was nearly devastated by what the chicken pox episode had done to my self-image. But I looked into the mirror less often after I was told that I would always have scars on my face, and I hid behind my long black hair and my books.

After the problems at the public school got to the point where even non-confrontational little me got beaten up several times, my parents enrolled me at St. Joseph's High School. I was then a minority of one among the Italian and Irish kids. But I found several good friends there—other girls who took their studies seriously. We did our homework together and talked about the Jackies. The Jackies were two popular girls, one blonde and the other red-haired, who had women's bodies. Their curves showed even in the blue jumper uniforms with straps that we all wore. The blonde Jackie would often let one of the straps fall off her shoulder, and although she, like all of us, wore a white blouse underneath, all the boys stared at her arm. My friends and I talked about this and practiced letting our straps fall off our shoulders. But it wasn't the same without breasts or hips.

My final two and a half years of high school were spent in Augusta, Georgia, where my parents moved our family in search of a more peaceful environment. Then we became part of a little community of our Army-connected relatives and friends. School was yet another matter. I was enrolled in a huge school of nearly two thousand students that had just that year been forced to integrate. There were two black girls and there was me. I did extremely well academically. As to my social life, it was, for the most part, uneventful—yet it is in my memory blighted by one incident. In my junior year, I became wildly infatuated with a pretty white boy. I'll call him Ted. Oh, he was pretty: yellow hair that fell over his forehead, a smile to die for—and he was a great dancer. I watched him at Teen Town, the youth center at the base where all the military brats gathered on Saturday nights. My father had retired from the Navy, and we had all our base privileges—one other reason we moved to Augusta. Ted looked like an angel to me. I worked on him for a year before he asked me out. This meant maneuvering to be within the periphery of his vision at every possible occasion. I took the long way to my classes in school just to pass by his locker, I went to football games, which I detested, and I danced (I too was a good dancer) in front of him at Teen Town—this took some fancy footwork, since it involved subtly moving my partner toward the right spot on the dance floor. When Ted finally approached me, "A Million to One" was playing on the jukebox, and when he took me in his arms, the odds suddenly turned in my favor. He asked me to go to a school dance the following Saturday. I said yes, breathlessly. I said yes, but there were obstacles to surmount at home. My father did not allow me to date casually. I was allowed to go to major events like a prom or a concert with a boy who had been properly screened. There was such a boy in my life, a neighbor who wanted to be a Baptist missionary and was practicing his anthropological skills on my family. If I was desperate to go somewhere and needed a date, I'd resort to Gary. This is the type of religious nut that Gary was: when the school bus did not show up one day, he put his hands over his face and prayed to Christ to get us a way to get to school. Within minutes a mother in a station wagon, on her way to town, stopped to ask why we weren't in school. Gary informed her that the Lord had sent her just in time to find us a way to get there in time for roll call. He assumed that I was impressed. Gary was even good-looking in a bland sort of way, but he kissed me with his lips tightly pressed together. I think Gary probably ended up marrying a native woman from wherever he may have gone to preach the Gospel according to Paul. She probably believes that all white men pray to God for transportation and kiss with their mouths closed. But it was Ted's mouth, his whole beautiful self, that concerned me in those days. I knew my father would say no to our date, but planned to run away from home if necessary. I told my mother how important this date was. I cajoled and pleaded with her from Sunday to Wednesday. She listened to my arguments and must have heard the note of desperation in my voice. She said very gently to me: "You better be ready for disappointment." I did not ask what she meant. I did not want her fears for me to taint my happiness. I asked her to tell my father about my date. Thursday at breakfast my father looked at me across the table with his eyebrows together. My mother looked at him with her mouth set in a straight line. I looked down at my bowl of cereal. Nobody said anything. Friday I tried on every dress in my closet. Ted would be picking me up at six on Saturday: dinner and then the sock hop at school. Friday night I was in my room doing my nails or something else in preparation for Saturday (I know I groomed myself nonstop all week) when the telephone rang. I ran to get it. It was Ted. His voice sounded funny when he said my name, so funny that I felt compelled to ask: "Is something wrong?" Ted blurted it all out without a preamble. His father had asked who he was going out with. Ted had told him my name. "Ortiz? That's Spanish, isn't it?" the father had asked. Ted had told him yes, then shown him my picture in the yearbook. Ted's father had shaken his head. No. Ted would not be taking me out. Ted's father had known Puerto Ricans in the Army. He had lived in New York City while studying architecture and had seen how the spics lived. Like rats. Ted repeated his father's words to me as if I should understand *his* predicament when I heard why he was breaking our date. I don't remember what I said before hanging up. I do recall the darkness of my room that sleepless night and the heaviness of my blanket in which I wrapped myself like a shroud. And I remember my parents' respect for my pain and their gentleness toward me that weekend. My mother did not say "I warned you," and I was grateful for her understanding silence.

In college, I suddenly became an "exotic" woman to the men who had survived the popularity wars in high school, who were not practicing to be worldly: they had to act liberal in their politics, in their lifestyles, and in the women they went out with. I dated heavily for a while, then married young. I had discovered that I needed stability more than social life. I had brains for sure and some talent in writing. These facts were a constant in my life. My skin color, my size, and my appearance were variables—things that were judged according to my current self-image, the aesthetic values of the time, the places I was in, and the people I met. My studies, later my writing, the respect of people who saw me as an individual person they cared about, these were the criteria for my sense of self-worth that I would concentrate on in my adult life.

NOTES

1. *trigueño:* Brown-skinned.
2. *negra:* Black.
3. *paloma blanca:* White dove.
4. *la gringa:* A white, non-Latina woman.
5. *Los Estados:* "The States"—that is, the United States.
6. *leche con café . . . café con leche:* Milk with coffee (light brown) . . . coffee with milk (dark brown).
7. 4F: Draft-board classification meaning "unfit for military service"; hence, not physically fit.
8. *bodega:* Market.

 QUESTIONS FOR CRITICAL THINKING

Reading 51

1. Cofer's discussion illustrates that the way we see our bodies is influenced by dominant societal values and beliefs. How do you see your own perceptions of your body influenced by societal beliefs and values? How do these perceptions change in different situations?

2. Cofer experiences particular difficulties with regard to her body and dominant attitudes about gender. Do you think males experience similar problems? Why, or why not?

3. Are the experiences Cofer relates simply examples of childhood difficulties everyone experiences or are they examples of larger issues? What makes you think this?

Reading 52

SEPARATED BY DEPORTATION

TRAM NGUYEN

It was February 2003 in Minneapolis, and Abdullah Osman zipped his jacket as he crossed Cedar Street. His wife Sukra's brown eyes lit up as he entered their apartment, and his three-year-old daughter, Maria, in a pink sweatsuit with her braids bouncing, wrapped her limbs around his leg. Sukra asked if it was warm outside. He replied with a firm no, returning her smile with his eyes. "The sun must be lying then," she said, disappointment on her face.

Sukra, a petite woman in a patterned headscarf, grew up at the equator and was still adjusting to the Minnesota cold. After nearly a decade of separation, she and Abdullah were reunited less than five years ago in Minneapolis.

Unlike the stark exterior of their housing project, the inside of the Osmans' one-bedroom apartment burst with color and felt like an oasis. A Persian rug covered the linoleum living room floor. Throughout the tidy room lay Maria's toys—a purple and pink bike with training wheels, a large stuffed bear, other things that roll and squeak. Next to a computer desk stood an entertainment center, where a television was turned on to morning cartoons. A poster of the Kenyan city of Mombasa—a city that once provided its own refuge for Sukra and her family—hung above the doorway. The apartment's most distinguishing feature was an intricately patterned sectional foam sofa that circled the perimeter of the living room. "We have to have space for a lot of relatives," explained Sukra, her long headscarf draped over her upper body.

In 1999, Sukra, twenty-four, was able to join Abdullah in Minneapolis. She spoke and wrote Somali and Kiswahili, and became fluent in English after six months in the United States. She worked as an education specialist at a public elementary school, where she prepared lesson plans, translated materials for Somali students, and served as a liaison to Somali parents. Soft-spoken with a gentle smile, Sukra had earned respect within the school. "The Somali kids will listen to me even more than their teachers," she said proudly, "especially when it comes to discipline."

Abdullah worked in construction in 1996, until a wrist injury forced him to seek less-physical work. For several years he was a bus driver for

Minneapolis Public Schools, and supplemented his income by driving a taxi during evenings, weekends, and school holidays. "When people first came, they mostly worked at the meat factory," he recalled. "Now there are more jobs. And the state helps people here if they are in need. We love Minnesota."

The Cedar-Riverside neighborhood where they lived is the heart of the largest Somali community in the United States. It's a neighborhood where cafés and organic food stores, several independent theaters, and music venues that cater to the local college crowd sit alongside money-transfer agencies, halal grocers, and a Somali mall with fabrics, furniture, and other East African products. On a Sunday morning, the streets and cafés were filled with men drinking spicy tea and conversing in Somali. Many read the local Somali newspaper, which contained news of current events in Somalia and local job postings. Tall, handsome, and sharply dressed in a sweater, dark blue jeans, and black leather shoes, Abdullah, thirty-three, walked between the snowdrifts and ice patches that covered the sidewalks. He greeted almost every passerby with a warm smile, typically accompanied by a hug or a handshake.

Toward the end of 1991 the State Department began resettling refugees from Somalia's civil war, and chose Minneapolis–St. Paul as one of several resettlement destinations. Community organizations and social service agencies now estimate the city's Somali population at 35,000, more than 70 percent of whom entered the country through the U.S. refugee resettlement program.[1] Most others have been granted, or are seeking, asylum. With its robust local economy and liberal political culture, Minneapolis was a place where Somali refugees felt accepted and found opportunity. "If you want an education, you can get it," Abdullah marveled. His optimism was natural and infectious. "You can get money, food. You can raise your children, and you can find people to help them if you're having trouble. My child, Maria, is lucky. A lot of people don't have what I have. My brothers' children in Somalia aren't so lucky."

For Somalis, Minneapolis had been a safe haven, where they could reestablish family connections, and an economic base from which to support relatives abroad. But after September 11, the haven was becoming a more complicated place.

Abdullah walked casually into the Merkato café and restaurant on Sixth and Cedar. Brown tracks of snow covered the linoleum floor of the sparsely furnished café. Simple stackable chairs with black vinyl seats surrounded bare tables. Unframed posters of East African landscapes and handwritten Somali signs adorned the walls. One man, his jacket unzipped, scarf askew, and open mouth spewing bits of breakfast onto the floor, greeted Abdullah. They left the café and walked together down the street, where Abdullah bought him a cup of tea. "He's crazy," Abdullah said simply of the man's mental illness. Like a large family, people in the Somali community take care of each other. "You will never see a homeless Somali," Abdullah explained. "Someone will take them in. If I know them, they can sleep in my living room." Further down the street, Abdullah encountered a shorter, stocky man with a slight beard and of similar age. It was Omar, a friend he last saw in a refugee camp in Kenya.

For the past several years, encounters like this were as consistent as the cold winters. When Abdullah arrived in Minneapolis in 1996, there were 200 to 300 Somalis in the city. Now, more than twice that number live in the Osmans' building alone, and the community has spread throughout the suburbs and around the state.

"I moved into that building right away, and I've lived in the same apartment ever since," Abdullah said, signaling across the street to the Cedar-Riverside Plaza. Five concrete towers rise nearly forty stories above the Mississippi River and the campus of the University of Minnesota. From a distance they resemble the drab, institutional public housing projects built in inner cities during the 1950s and 1960s. Although the plaza's sixteen hundred units are occupied mostly by Somalis, local cab drivers refer to the complex as the United Nations towers because of the diversity of nationalities it contains. For thousands of new immigrants from all over the world, the plaza has represented the beginning of their pursuit of an American dream.

Abdullah's long-sleeved shirt hid most of the scars that covered his body, which he received during a decade of war, violence, and flight across borders and oceans. Until 1990 Abdullah lived in Mogadishu, a large industrialized Red Sea city that was Somalia's capital and a business and cultural hub for East Africa. His family was from the majority clan. "It was a lot like race and minorities in the U.S." according to Abdullah. While he and his brother, sister, and father enjoyed a middle-class lifestyle, other minority clans were more likely to be poor. Sukra was from a minority clan, and despite her feelings for Abdullah, a relationship between them was forbidden in their communities. As a teenager Abdullah helped Sukra's mother care for their family, which allowed him to spend time with her pretty daughter.

· · ·

The Osmans' twenty-seventh-story apartment window overlooked the Hubert Humphrey Institute, a brick building housing the University of Minnesota's school of public affairs departments. Abdullah and Sukra were close enough to see into the office window of Ali Galaydh, a professor of international development. In his tweed jacket, checkered shirt, and brightly colored tie, Galaydh seemed to blend in to the academy. Yet just two decades ago, Galaydh was Somalia's minister of industry and the youngest member of former dictator Mohammed Siad Barre's cabinet. Now he lived with his wife and three daughters in a Minneapolis suburb. He still felt the weight of a peaceful resolution to Somalia's crisis on his shoulders.

"Most people want to go back," said Galaydh, "especially the older people. My mom is from a nomadic clan, and before they would go to a new location, they would always send a scout. My mom was sitting on a rocking chair and looking out the window at the cold, and she said to me, who scouted this place? She has papers, but she wants to go back to our village in Somalia." While Galaydh had not abandoned hope, he was sober in his assessment of Somalia's prospects for the near future. "Some people pray for world peace," he said, "I pray to Almighty Allah that the weather in Minnesota would be more clement."

His sad eyes belied the academic detachment in his voice as he traced Somalia's route to civil war. "Because of the superpower rivalry, the U.S.S.R. wanted a foothold in the Horn of Africa. Somalia was a strategic location— the U.S. already had a presence in Ethiopia, and it was on the Red Sea. It was seen as the gateway to Africa."

The Soviet Union invested heavily in the armed forces of Somalia, and the military soon became the dominant force in the country. In 1969 the president was assassinated. The new leader, Siad Barre, dissolved the national assembly, banned political parties, and established a Supreme Revolutionary Council with the power to rule by decree.

"With Barre, Somalia fell into one-man rule," explained Galaydh. "There was disenchantment with a government that killed religious leaders, with the loss of democratic culture, and with corruption." Throughout the 1980s, discontent with Somalia's government intensified. Several armed movements formed, mostly operating from Ethiopia through hit-and-run tactics. The United States, meanwhile, continued to support Barre's regime, pouring hundreds of millions into arms in return for the use of military bases from which it could intervene in the Middle East.[2]

"I then realized what was going on," Galaydh continued. "Siad Barre would find the resistance fighters, and he would not only punish them but also their families. He would kill their next of kin and destroy their property." Galaydh and several other ministers defected in 1982. When resistance fighters captured urban areas in the north in 1988 and 1989, Siad Barre responded with extreme force—including aerial bombings of civilian neighborhoods. "That's when people really started to leave. They fled to the Gulf States, Ethiopia, Djibouti, the U.K., the U.S., and Canada. That was before the total collapse."

In January of 1991 a civil uprising forced Barre to flee the capital. Anarchy ensued. In Mogadishu, armed militias vying for power launched artillery with little regard for civilian casualties.

While Galaydh was safe in the United States, Abdullah and Sukra were still in Mogadishu. "There were tanks rolling through the streets," Abdullah remembered. "We were just trying to survive. All of us were shot—my brother, sister, and my father." Abdullah pointed to a scar on his leg where a bullet passed through as they were fleeing. "There were no doctors; no hospitals. You could get bandages, but you had to treat the wounds yourselves. You would just wrap yourself up and try to continue. We ran so we wouldn't get killed."

Abdullah's family escaped to a boat on the Red Sea and an uncertain future as refugees. "There were two to three hundred people packed onto a boat intended for a hundred and fifty. We only drank water for five days," said Abdullah.

After a seven-day journey at sea, their boat was the first to arrive at the undeveloped site of a United Nations refugee camp. It was a barren and remote location in the Kenyan desert, far from any population center. "We spent two weeks sleeping under a tree in hard rain before the UN officials arrived," Abdullah said. "When the UN came they counted us, then gave us tents and water tanks and two blankets a person." UN rations included corn, wheat, flour, and cooking oil. Occasionally they received kidney beans and a little sugar. While there were no cities nearby, neighboring farmers raised goats. "You would trade a pound of flour for a cup of goat's milk, and that's how you fed your children," Abdullah said.

Sukra's family remained in Somalia. "I can remember my dad saying, 'they just want to overthrow the government, then things will get better.' But all of your belongings could be stolen at any time. If you have girls, they get raped." Each new ruler was worse than the last, and soon Sukra's family had to flee Mogadishu. "They were bombing everything," she said. "We had to step over dead people, and sometimes we had to step on them, to get out." She raised her foot and pointed her toe down, as if she could still feel the flesh under her shoes. "There were empty houses everywhere, with only dead bodies inside."

Different armed factions occupied the roads that led out of the city. The factions were largely based on clanship, and often showed little mercy for people from other clans. "All of the clans have different dialects, and you had to try to guess which clan the men were from and try to speak in their dialect," Sukra remembered. "Maybe someone recognizes you, or maybe they don't believe you. If so, you're probably going to be dead." Still not yet a teenager, Sukra watched her brother and her sister die as they tried to escape Mogadishu.

Sukra and her family traveled overland to Chisimayu, another coastal city hundreds of miles south. The war followed them. In 1992, after three months imprisoned in their homes by militia forces, they escaped to the Red Sea and boarded a boat for the Kenyan city of Mombasa. "They packed eighty people on a forty-person boat. We had no food, no personal belongings," Sukra said. "The boat would stop every day, and then charge us another thousand Somali rupees to continue on." They arrived at a UN camp on the border between Kenya and Somalia. That camp became home for the next seven years.

By 2002, there were more than 300,000 Somali refugees living in UN camps in twelve countries around the world.[3] Refugee camps in Kenya are by far the most extensive, hosting over 140,000 Somali refugees. Many camps issued each person three kilograms of maize every fifteen days, only eight hundred calories per day per person. Maize has to be cooked, which requires firewood. People had to leave the camps to get firewood, and they were often raped or robbed. Wheat and oil, which they were supposed to receive, were scarce. There were well-stocked markets in most camps, so fortunate people relied on money sent from abroad.

Most refugee camps in Kenya were connected by the *taar,* or telegram. But Abdullah and Sukra had to rely on mail or an occasional phone call, for which Kenyan Telecom would charge a significant fee. In the early 1990s, soon after arriving in Kenya, Abdullah's older brother had been granted refugee status and passage to the United States. In 1996 he was able to sponsor Abdullah, his younger brother, his older sister, and their father to come to Minnesota through the refugee resettlement program. When Abdullah arrived, he found a temporary construction job and moved into his apartment in the Cedar-Riverside Plaza.

Abdullah soon found permanent work cleaning rental cars for Avis at the Minneapolis airport, and began sending money not only to his family, but to Sukra and her mother as well. "Abdullah told me, 'I want you to learn English because you will need it when you come to America,'" Sukra recounted. "So I took English classes in the camp from some North Americans, for a small fee."

In 1999, Sukra was able to get support from family members abroad to finance her passage to the United States. She was nineteen, and it was the first time she had ever been out of sight of her family. She had no documents. "I was too afraid to even look up during the trip. I didn't want to be found out," Sukra said. "But you know you're going there to help your family, so you hold onto that." Sukra arrived in San Diego, California, where she applied for asylum. After five months Sukra's asylum petition was accepted, and she moved to Minnesota to meet Abdullah. They were married six months later.

"This is home to us. This is where we came, this is where our community is," Sukra said. She and Abdullah continued to send money back to Kenya to other relatives in refugee camps, including Abdullah's mother. In January of 2001, Sukra gave birth to Maria.

"I was happy. I had my family, a job, money to pay rent, to buy clothes. We have families in Kenya and Somalia that need food, so we need to work," said Abdullah. "I felt like a man, like I had life, opportunity."

.   .   .

On Friday, June 16, 2001, Abdullah woke up at 10:00 AM to start his taxi shift. He found his first fare on Cedar Street, where he would drive a Somali man to a car repair shop three miles away. The man asked Abdullah to wait outside while he checked to see if the repairs were complete. While he waited, two men came to his window.

"One of them asked me to lend them twenty dollars," Abdullah recounted. "He said they would give me their address and I could come and pick up the money later. I told them my shift had just started so I didn't have any money." Abdullah had never met either of the men, but when they started knocking on his window, he decided it was time to leave.

"I thought they were just crazy," Abdullah said. "I didn't think they would attack me."

When Abdullah tried to get out of the car to get his passenger, one man slammed his door shut on him, then opened it and pulled him to the ground. The man hit him repeatedly. "He was much bigger and stronger then me. He had me pinned on my back and was punching me in the head," Abdullah said. "He hit me in the face, in my eyes and in my mouth." The man took the fifty dollars that were in Abdullah's shirt pocket to pay for the daily taxi rental. Then the assailant's keychain, attached to a razorblade, fell out of his pocket.

"We both saw it and reached for it, and I got it first. He was holding my wrist, but I shook it free and slashed at his arm," Abdullah said. When the razor cut the man's shoulder, he released Abdullah and ran down the street.

Three other men, who had been watching the attack, began to approach Abdullah. Frightened and in shock, Abdullah hurried to his cab and drove away. He realized that he should go back to the scene and contact the police. By the time he returned to the repair shop, the police were already there. "I was bleeding from my eyes, and from my arm," Abdullah remembered, displaying a six-inch scar between his elbow and wrist from when the man threw him to the ground. "But the people [at the scene] said I was the one who tried to kill somebody. The police threw me against the car and hand-cuffed me. They never asked me my side of the story."

Abdullah was held in jail for three days. He was not charged with a crime and was released. But two months later, while Abdullah was at work, the sheriff showed up at the Osmans' apartment door with a warrant for his arrest.

"I asked to see the warrant because I didn't believe it," recalled Sukra. "They said they didn't send notification because they thought he would flee. I said, from what? He didn't do anything wrong, so why would he flee? And where would he go? They searched the house, and even picked up the sofas to see if he was hiding."

After a call from the sheriff, Abdullah turned himself in that day. He remained in jail for eleven days until his family and friends were able to raise the $10,000 bail. His court date was set for April 2002. Abdullah hired a criminal-defense attorney based in downtown Minneapolis, who quickly learned that Abdullah's assailant had been found guilty of seven prior felonies, mostly for assault. "My attorney told me to sleep easy," Abdullah recalled. "I had never had any problems with the law. He told me that because I was working at the time, and it was self-defense, and that I was a family man, that the case would be easily dismissed." Abdullah went back to work, and life returned to normal for a brief month. Then came September 11.

•   •   •

On October 1, 2001, which was the start of the 2002 fiscal year, President Bush refused to sign the annual Presidential Determination that allows an allotted number of refugees to enter the United States. The virtual moratorium lasted until November 21, when Bush issued an order allowing 70,000 people to be resettled in the coming year, 10,000 less than the number set in 2001. Of this number, only 27,000 refugees were actually admitted.[4] Five thousand Somali refugees had been admitted from October 2000 to October 2001. In the following year, less than 200 Somali refugees entered the United States.[5] Asylum applications continue to face difficulty.

While identifying countries that might harbor terrorists, Secretary of State Colin Powell told the Senate Foreign Relations Committee at a 2002 hearing, "A country that immediately comes to mind is Somalia because it is quite a lawless place without much of a government. Terrorism might find fertile ground there and we do not want that to happen."[6] This focus on Somalia paralleled the restrictions on refugee acceptance and asylum. According to Craig Hope, director of the Episcopal Church's refugee resettlement office, "No one is going to say it's because of September 11, but that's the reason. They're being screened and watched carefully."

Soon after, Attorney General John Ashcroft's Justice Department launched a series of aggressive campaigns against immigrants. In Minnesota, the Somali community began to hear of arrests. Omar Jamal, a vocal Somali activist and director of the Somali Justice Advocacy Center in St. Paul, was accused of concealing his previous Canadian residency when he applied for asylum in 1997. Convicted in federal court a few years later, Jamal faced deportation. Another crucial blow to the community was the arrest of Mohamed Abshir Musse, a seventy-six-year-old former Somali general. His visa expired in September 2002 despite his application for renewal, and when he reported to the immigration office to comply with the new special registration program, officials ordered his deportation. Called by one former U.S. ambassador "the greatest living Somali," he has been credited for saving the lives of innumerable American soldiers during violent conflicts in the 1990s. Several members of Congress and former ambassadors sponsored a bill on his behalf. Despite the clout of his supporters, he may still be deported.[7]

"We will see a lot more asylum revocation cases, and we may lose," said Michele Garnett McKenzie, director of the Refugee and Immigration Program at the Minnesota Advocates for Human Rights. A young attorney and Minnesota native, McKenzie played a central role in connecting Minnesota immigrants with pro bono legal defense. "It might be because there's more money in the pipeline for enforcement. The local ICE [Immigration and Customs Enforcement, formerly INS] might be getting more federal support. They view it as a war-on-terrorism issue rather than an immigration issue. So there's more investigation into asylum cases."

In the case of Milagros Jimenez, asylum problems were combined with a new immigration enforcement policy, the Absconder Apprehension Initiative, resulting in what many local immigrants saw as a highly political arrest in 2002. Jimenez came to Minneapolis from Peru with her son in 1996, seeking asylum from the armed conflict with guerillas that had embroiled her son's father. She overcame the loneliness and fear of new-immigrant life to become involved with ISAIAH, a progressive faith-based organization in Minnesota. Eventually, she became the organization's first Latina organizer, despite the language barrier and her trepidations. "Sometimes we want to live like hiding, in the shadows. When we came to this country, we lost our self-confidence. You need to build your confidence again," she explained. "I knew it was risky, but I felt like I need to do it."

The risk became real as Jimenez began organizing statewide for banks and other institutions to accept the *matricular consular,* the Mexican ID, in lieu of a driver's license for undocumented immigrants. Three days before a rally where they were expecting up to two thousand people to participate, Jimenez left a late-night meeting to see an unmarked car and two men waiting for her. They had her name from an existing list of "absconders" with outstanding deportation orders, and handcuffed her and put her in the back seat without explaining anything. Jimenez was driven hours outside of the Twin Cities to a jail where she was detained for four weeks. After her release on bond, she joined hundreds of immigrants around the country ordered to wear ankle bracelets while they waited for their deportation hearings. Minneapolis was part of an eight-city pilot program started in the summer of 2004 as a house-arrest alternative to detention.[8] While it was accepted as "better than jail" by some immigrants and advocates, the electronic monitoring was hardly the solution that many were hoping for. As Jimenez went about her work in a hospital clinic, the heavy metal shackle on her leg was "terrible, so humiliating" and made her feel like a criminal.

"They're only trying to save a buck," said Jorge Saavedra, of Minneapolis' Centro Legal. "The number one issue for immigrants that end up in the enforcement system is a virtual lack of due process, especially since Sept. 11."[9]

•   •   •

Like other immigrants, Abdullah and Sukra Osman felt the chilling effect of September 11 on their adopted city.

"I was very afraid. As a person who has been through war, you know there is going to be isolation, and people targeted," said Sukra. "And it happened here. A community leader was killed, a girl got beaten up, someone was thrown off a bridge. We couldn't go out at night. I was afraid to go on the freeway to my job, because I thought someone would see me and harass me.

"And it's not like Somalia, where you can blend in and escape. Here you are so different from everyone else, so you can't hide. You stand out."

In a front-page article on October 14, 2001, the *Minneapolis Star Tribune* speculated that local Somalis had contributed to a charity linked to Osama bin Laden.[10] A day later, Ali Warsame Ali, a sixty-six-year-old retired Somali businessman, was punched in the head while waiting for a bus and died of his injuries.[11] Many community residents linked the newspaper article to a rise in hate crimes and to Ali's death. A demonstration organized by the Confederation of Somali Community drew more than five hundred Somalis to protest. "People had their headscarves pulled, their car windows smashed.

My brother had a symbol of Allah in his window and it was smashed," recalled Mohamud Noor, chairman of the Confederation's board. "Ali died because of a hate crime after September 11. There are issues of prejudice that have arisen since September 11, because of the generalization of Muslims." Somalis were even afraid to send money to relatives overseas. "People were worried," explained Noor. "If I send money, will I be targeted? Will I be linked to al-Qa'ida? Will I be targeted as a terrorist? People were afraid that the questioning process would be extended to them—that they might lose their refugee status and the benefits that come with it."

The fear that money transfers to relatives would result in government suspicion and retaliation was not unfounded. On September 23, 2001, just twelve days after the strike on the World Trade Center, President Bush announced "a strike on the financial foundation of the global terror network." This initiative targeted Islamic charities, banks, and financial institutions, including local hawalas, or money-transfer agencies. Over 40 percent of Somalia's GDP is from remittances from relatives living abroad, mostly in Europe and North America.[12] "I would say ninety-five percent of Somalis send money home, more than that," said Ahmed Omar, an owner of Barwaaqo Financial Services. It is one of dozens of hawalas that serve Minneapolis's Somali community. "People will send one hundred dollars a month to a family of five in Somalia, maybe two or three hundred to camps in Kenya because the expenses are higher. That will be enough to keep people fed, and put kids in school.

"We're still scared that they are going to come in, shut us down, or arrest us for something," Omar continued. Business slowed at Barwaaqo. Other hawalas, in Minneapolis–St. Paul, Seattle, and cities across the nation, were shut down completely. Al Barakaat, the largest hawala operating in Somalia, was one of them. "Millions of dollars were lost when they froze all of Al Barakaat's accounts around the world," Omar said. "Hawalas are like a bank for Somalis. They trust and know them, and will put all of their money in their accounts. I don't think people are getting their money back." Wire transfer agencies such as Western Union do not operate in Somalia. Hawalas are not only the trusted choice, they are often the only lifeline between those who made it out of war-torn Somalia to their relatives who remain behind. "A lot of people have suffered [from these closures]," Omar said.

September 11 affected the three most important things for Somalis in the United States—feeling safe in a place they can call home, being able to reunite with family members, and supporting relatives who live in poverty abroad. For Abdullah and many others, their life and liberty are also at stake.

· · ·

Just seven months after September 11, Abdullah was scheduled for trial. Suddenly his case, which had seemed like a sure victory, had turned on its head. "My lawyer told me that I would never win the case. My name is Abdullah. I am Muslim, and I used a box cutter," he said, bitterness and incredulity in his voice. "My lawyer said that no jury would ever acquit me."

In March of 2002, shortly before his April court appearance, his attorney offered him a settlement option. If he pled guilty, he could serve eight months in a work release program. "He told me I could work and be with my family during the day, or I could go to a trial that we'll definitely lose and face five years in prison," Abdullah recalled. "He said, 'You're a Somali Muslim, and you can't win because of September 11.'"

Abdullah and Sukra considered hiring another attorney. All were reluctant to take his case and would only do so for a high price. "Another lawyer wanted fourteen thousand dollars, and he said we would probably lose," Sukra said. "We were thinking, what choice do we have?"

Abdullah pled guilty. He was taken to a work release facility under the assumption that he would be able to go to work the next morning. When he arose at 4:00 AM, the officers told him they hadn't completed his paperwork, and that he wouldn't be able to work that day.

Then at 9:00 AM, two officers entered his cell. "One pushed his knee into my back while I was sleeping, grabbed my arms and pulled them back and cuffed me," said Abdullah. "He told me to collect my things, but they were up on a shelf and I had my hands cuffed behind my back. He threw my stuff on the floor and I had to squat down to pick it up."

The officers asked Abdullah if he was a citizen. When he explained that he was a refugee, they told him that he was no longer "eligible to be in society." Under a 1996 immigration law, noncitizens convicted of crimes that fell under the category of "aggravated felonies" are subject to consequences that include detention and deportation. Abdullah spent the next eight months in twenty-three-hour lockdown in the county jail, where he was allowed outside for less than three hours a week. During that time, he had no access to a doctor. His only solace was in weekend visits, through glass windows, from his wife and daughter.

"County jails are designed to house inmates for three weeks or a month before trials, not for extended stays," said Michele Garnett McKenzie of the Minnesota Advocates for Human Rights. "There are no programs for inmates, no education options, and few services."

After several weeks, Abdullah's health began to deteriorate. He had a neck injury from a recent car accident, but despite his pleas he was not allowed to see a doctor or receive any therapy. He began to lose weight. Sukra, with help from family and friends, hired an immigration lawyer to try to get him transferred to an immigration facility.

"We wanted to do anything to get him out of that jail," she recalled.

On November 20, 2002, immigration officials moved Abdullah from the county jail through various facilities until they placed him in the Sherburne county jail in Elk River, Minnesota. "I spent three days moving around with no food, water, blanket, nothing. Not even in refugee camps did I go that long without food," Abdullah said. "Everywhere we went they said, lunch is over, or dinner is over. Or, they would say, you won't eat pork, so there's no food." During his three months in Elk River, Sukra and Maria could only see him through a television screen. He was again denied medical treatment. "They said there was no budget, and blamed it on the immigration department. They would take other inmates out of prison to get care, but not immigrants."

During the period of his detention at Elk River, Abdullah was driven forty miles southwest to the state's immigration court in Bloomington, where a judge would decide whether he would be deported to Somalia. Minnesota had two full-time immigration judges, Joseph R. Dierkes and Kristin W. Olmanson, both of whom were located across from the INS building in Bloomington. Which judge a detainee sees is a matter of chance. "I had scars from war. We are in an interclan marriage, which isn't approved of. We brought a witness from the United Nations to testify about how dangerous Somalia is," Abdullah recounted. "One judge never sends people to Somalia. The other judge automatically sentences people to deportation. When she [Olmanson] was chosen as our judge, our lawyer and other people we knew said we had a one percent chance of winning. To her, the danger didn't matter."

Abdullah and Sukra found another attorney to help them appeal his deportation order to the Board of Immigration. For the next several months, Abdullah was shipped all over the nation. They took him first to Rush State Prison in Minnesota. "It was one of the best places I had been," he said. "I got some education, some treatment for my neck, and was able to get a sore tooth removed." On July 9, 2002, prison guards told Abdullah to pack his belongings. They moved him back to Elk River for one night, and the next day, at 3:00 AM, they told him to pack up again. They flew him to Jefferson City, Oklahoma, on a U.S. Marshals Service air transport. By 8:00 PM he was once again in a county jail. "They didn't even give me a toothbrush. There were flies everywhere. There were seventy-five or eighty people in one room. It was worse than any refugee camp. I saw people vomit blood," Abdullah remembered. "Even in Somalia if we get arrested, family can come visit, and bring food. Here all they served was beans and rice, every day."

The conditions became worse. "I was right next to the air-conditioning vent and I was cold, so I asked to be moved to an empty bunk nearby so I could sleep. Because of that they put me in solitary for a week," Abdullah said. "I threatened to call my lawyer and they put me back in a bunk. They wouldn't give me a doctor or let me see a nurse or anything. I understand that people get arrested, but at least they should get food and medical treatment. But that's not true in the U.S. People died in the Oklahoma jail. When I would ask for care they would say they had to contact Washington, D.C. I never saw a doctor."

Abdullah's travels between prisons were not over. After three months in Oklahoma, he was moved to a detention facility in Texas for nearly two months. "Every two days, they would give me a bologna sandwich. I never ate pork before that, but I had no choice. I had to survive," he said. "I saw a lot of things in county jail and immigration that I've never seen in other countries. There is nothing for immigrants."

Moving immigration detainees to different facilities around the country is "a tried-and-true tactic of deportation officials to deny people access to friends, family, counsel," said McKenzie. "It's an old-fashioned immigration enforcement tool, to make it harder for them to pursue their case." In Minnesota, advocates had been pushing for better conditions in detention. "We were making progress with the bar association to get a monitoring project into facilities for immigrant detainees," said McKenzie. "But since September 11 we've had no access [to the facilities]. People haven't felt able to pursue it."

· · ·

Abdullah's final appeals to the Board of Immigration were denied. On November 20, 2003, he received a letter saying he would be sent home under supervision until his final removal. He had been in county jails or state prisons for a year and eight months. When he arrived at home, Sukra was shocked at how thin he was.

"I was thrilled when he was released, I was so excited," remembered Sukra. "But he's still not free. We had written so many support letters. We had spent almost fifteen thousand dollars on lawyers. But none of it mattered."

Abdullah's deportation depended on the outcome of legal battles that were about to be fought all the way to the Supreme Court. In a case involving the deportation of Somali nationals living in Seattle, the Ninth Circuit Court of Appeals ruled in January 2003 that deportation requires acceptance by the government of the deportee's home country. Somalia is the only nation in the world that the U.S. Department of State categorizes as having no functioning government. Without official government acceptance, the court ruled that deportations would violate international law.

This ruling, however, came with a loophole. Cases already going through the courts in other jurisdictions were not affected by the Seattle ruling. Minneapolis is in the Eighth Circuit Court of Appeals, which ruled in February 2003 for the deportation of Somali immigrant Keyse Jama. Convicted of third-degree assault in 1999, Jama had been detained by immigration officials for nearly four years after serving his one-year sentence. His appeal to the U.S. Supreme Court was being watched around the nation for the precedent it would set on Somali deportations. In court papers, the Justice Department maintained that deportation to Somalia is "a vital tool to protect the security of this nation's borders."[13] Abdullah's fate and that of more than three thousand other Somalis with deportation orders hinged on the outcome of Jama's case.

· · ·

While the Osmans struggled through imprisonment and legal battles, Ali Galaydh, the professor and government minister, was mired in conflicts on a different scale. In 2000, the president of Somalia's neighbor state, Djibouti, hosted thousands of Somalis, including elders, community leaders, and the heads of warring factions, for a five-month peace and reconciliation conference. By its end they had agreed to establish a national charter (an interim constitution), and elect a national assembly. Another former minister under Barre's regime became president, and Galaydh became the first prime minister of Somalia's Transitional National Government in October 2000. It was the closest Somalia had come to a recognized central authority in more than a decade.

After fleeing Somalia, Galaydh taught at Harvard's Center for International Affairs until 1989, and at Syracuse's Maxwell School of Public Policy from 1989 until 1996. He had also started a transnational telecommunications company in Dubai to help develop industry in Somalia. Despite this experience, "there was nothing I ever learned or taught that could prepare me for what we were trying to do (with the transitional government)," Galaydh admitted. The president soon began to veer away from democratic principles, instead adopting strong-arm tactics reminiscent of Barre's government. Galaydh, who disagreed with the president's methods, was ousted while he was in the United States negotiating for antiterrorism funds in the wake of September 11.

At the end of its three-year mandate, the Transitional National Government that Galaydh and millions of Somalis had hoped would lead the nation to peace and economic recovery was in disarray. There was no central authority once again. "Unlike civil wars in other countries, there are no identifiable groups fighting," Galaydh explained. "The media talks about the warlords, most of whom are in Mogadishu. At best, they control a certain neighborhood in the city. They don't even have the force to dominate other neighborhoods, let alone stabilize the whole country. These are messy little wars with no winners."

It wasn't until 2004 when another transitional government was put together, this time brought about after talks that began in 2002 and were sponsored by the neighboring countries of Ethiopia, Ghana, and Kenya. By summer of 2004, the Somali leadership, based out of Kenya, had put together a parliament and elected a president.

"Unfortunately, the president they elected is a warlord, one of the more brutal ones. Now the issue is how to go back to Somalia," said Galaydh. "Their work will be cut out for them, because there is nothing on the ground in terms of a civil service, in terms of even a security detail for the president and his key people."

If the transitional government was afraid for its safety in Somalia, advocates in the United States believed that deportees would face a much worse situation, especially those without strong clan and family connections. In May 2002, the body of a Somali man deported from the United States was discovered near a Mogadishu factory.[14] The man had been kidnapped the previous evening. "If you come from the U.S. with blue jeans and nice sneakers you can get killed, or they will kidnap you and force relatives in the U.S. to cough up ten thousand dollars or more," Galaydh explained. "The absence of government institutions and the lawlessness are a threat to life."

On January 12, 2005, the Supreme Court ruled in a 5–4 decision in favor of Keyse Jama's deportation, ending the hopes of thousands that U.S. and international law could protect them from being sent back.

·   ·   ·

Since 1997, immigration authorities have deported 196 Somali nationals.[15] Of those people, 49 were deported for criminal charges, such as Abdullah's, and 147 were deported on visa violations or other issues related to immigration, like those of Omar Jamal or Mohammed Abshir Musse. Toward the end of 2004, there were 3,568 Somalis with deportation orders. About 4,000 more Somalis had deportation cases still tied up in the courts, bringing the estimated number of people affected by the Supreme Court ruling up to 8,000.[16]

In Minneapolis, chaos and alarm followed news of the ruling. A few weeks after the announcement, Somali lawyer Hassan Mohamud was preparing to pull together a hasty meeting to try to answer some of the community's urgent questions. Who are the people affected? Will they be deported, how will they be deported, and where will they go? An imam as well as a lawyer, Mohamud sat in his downtown Legal Aid office wondering what he could tell them.

"We contacted immigration, they are not answering and we don't know what to do," Mohamud said. "Logistically we don't have enough information—about where to ship and how to ship. They were saying, okay we can ship them by determining everyone's clan and then ship them where their clan has a majority. But there's no clan power—it's not a matter of who do you belong to, it's a matter of safety and there's no safe place in Somalia."

Abdullah and Sukra were waiting like everyone else to find out what would happen next. They had been living in limbo for more than three years. Abdullah's legal options had already run dry back in the winter of 2003. After submitting thirty-five job applications in a month, Abdullah finally found an employer who would look past his criminal record. Still, because of his conviction, he was paid much less than his coworkers. He now drove two hours each way for an eight-dollars-an-hour job without benefits. "It's all I can get, so I have to hold onto it," he said. Once a month, he checked in at the local immigration office. "They can come anytime and take me away," Abdullah said in a quiet, desperate tone. "They don't have to say anything."

Abdullah said goodbye to his family as he stepped out of his apartment. "My daughter is so beautiful," he said. Moments later Maria poked her head out of their doorway to play a game of peek-a-boo with her father as he walked away. He covered his face, pretending to hide, then raised his arms as if he were going to chase her into the apartment. She squealed with delight and ran inside, only to pop her head out later and say goodbye again. He smiled as he zipped up his jacket and entered the elevator. "She has lots of friends in the building," he said. "She knows all of their elevator buttons." Maria is a U.S. citizen, and if Abdullah is deported, she and Sukra cannot risk their lives to join him in Somalia. If he is deported, he will never be permitted to return. Having survived years apart, through war, poverty, injury, and death, they have always treasured their hours together. Now they must live with the knowledge that any one could be their last.

NOTES

1. Author interview with Saeed Fahia, executive director of Confederation of Somali Community in Minnesota, Minneapolis, January 20, 2005.
2. Stephen Zunes, "The Long and Hidden History of the U.S. in Somalia," AlterNet, posted January 17, 2002, www.alternet.org/story/12253.
3. Office of the United Nations High Commissioner for Refugees, "Somalia," *Global Appeal 2002*, www.unhcr.ch/Pubs/fedrs/ga2002/ga2002toc.htm.
4. James Ziglar, commissioner of U.S. Immigration and Naturalization Service, testimony before the Senate Committee on the Judiciary, Subcommittee on Immigration, February 12, 2002.
5. Confederation of Somali Community in Minnesota, February 2005.
6. Toby Harnden, "Powell Orders Watch on 'Lawless Country,'" *Daily Telegraph*, January 10, 2002.
7. Eric Black, "U.S. Diplomats Fighting for Somali," *Minneapolis Star-Tribune*, March 6, 2003.
8. Heron Marquez Estrada, "Federal Government to Release Some Immigration Detainees in State," *Minneapolis Star-Tribune*, June 19, 2004.
9. Ibid.
10. Greg Gordon, Joy Powell, Kimberly Hayes Taylor, "Terror Group May Have Received Local Funds," *Minneapolis Star-Tribune*, October 14, 2001.
11. Human Rights Watch, *We Are Not the Enemy: Hate Crimes against Arabs, Muslims, and Those Perceived to be Arab or Muslim after September 11*, Report, November 2002.
12. Author interview with Ali Galaydh, Minneapolis, January 21, 2005.
13. Mary Beth Sheridan, "For Somalis a Home and a Haven," *Washington Post*, December 27, 2002.
14. Author interview with Hassan Mohamud of the Legal Aid Society of Minneapolis and U.S. Committee for Refugees and Immigrants, Minneapolis, January 22, 2005.
15. INS document, January 13, 2003.
16. Florangela Davila, "Ruling Could Lead to Deportations," *Seattle Times*, January 13, 2005.

 QUESTIONS FOR CRITICAL THINKING

Reading 52

1. Nguyen discusses the impact of targeting the Somali community after the events of September 11, 2001. How does this reading help you to understand the impact of discrimination not only on individual lives but on families and communities as well?

2. How did this reading help you to understand the reasons immigrants have for coming to the United States and remaining despite their "illegal" status?

3. Considering Nguyen's discussion, do you think it is possible to change negative perceptions of immigrants to the United States?

Reading 53

"GEE, YOU DON'T SEEM LIKE AN INDIAN FROM THE RESERVATION"

BARBARA CAMERON

One of the very first words I learned in my Lakota language was *wasicu*, which designates white people. At that early age, my comprehension of wasicu was gained from observing and listening to my family discussing the wasicu. My grandmother always referred to white people as the "wasicu sica" with emphasis on *sica*, our word for terrible or bad. By the age of five I had seen one Indian man gunned down in the back by the police and was a silent witness to a gang of white teenage boys beating up an elderly Indian man. I'd hear stories of Indian ranch hands being "accidentally" shot by white ranchers. I quickly began to understand the wasicu menace my family spoke of.

My hatred for the wasicu was solidly implanted by the time I entered first grade. Unfortunately in first grade I became teacher's pet so my teacher had a fondness for hugging me, which always repulsed me. I couldn't stand the idea of a white person touching me. Eventually I realized that it wasn't the white skin that I hated, but it was their culture of deceit, greed, racism, and violence.

During my first memorable visit to a white town, I was appalled that they thought of themselves as superior to my people. Their manner of living appeared devoid of life and bordered on hostility even for one another. They were separated from each other by their perfectly, politely fenced square plots of green lawn. The only lawns on my reservation were the lawns of the BIA* officials or white Christians. The white people always seemed so loud, obnoxious, and vulgar. And the white parents were either screaming at their kids, threatening them with some form of punishment or hitting them. After spending a day around white people, I was always happy to go back to the reservation where people followed a relaxed yet respectful code of relating with each other. The easy teasing and joking that were inherent with the Lakota were a welcome relief after a day with the plastic faces.

Barbara Cameron, "Gee, You Don't Seem Like an Indian from the Reservation," from *This Bridge Called My Back: Writings By Radical Women of Color,* edited by Cherrie Moraga and Gloria Anzaldua (New York: Kitchen Table: Women of Color Press, 1983). Reprinted by permission.
*Bureau of Indian Affairs.

I vividly remember two occasions during my childhood in which I was cognizant of being an Indian. The first time was at about three years of age when my family took me to my first pow-wow. I kept asking my grand-mother, "Where are the Indians? Where are the Indians? Are they going to have bows and arrows?" I was very curious and strangely excited about the prospect of seeing real live Indians even though I myself was one. It's a memory that has remained with me through all these years because it's so full of the subtleties of my culture. There was a sweet wonderful aroma in the air from the dancers and from the traditional food booths. There were lots of grandmothers and grandfathers with young children running about. Pow-wows in the Plains usually last for three days, sometimes longer, with Indian people traveling from all parts of our country to dance, to share food and laughter, and to be with each other. I could sense the importance of our gathering times and it was the beginning of my awareness that my people are a great and different nation.

The second time in my childhood when I knew very clearly that I am Indian occurred when I was attending an all-white (except for me) elementary school. During Halloween my friends and I went trick or treating. At one of the last stops, the mother knew all of the children except for me. She asked me to remove my mask so she could see who I was. After I removed my mask, she realized I was an Indian and quite cruelly told me so, refusing to give me the treats my friends had received. It was a stingingly painful experience.

I told my mother about it the next evening after I tried to understand it. My mother was outraged and explained the realities of being an Indian in South Dakota. My mother paid a visit to the woman, which resulted in their expressing a barrage of equal hatred for one another. I remember sitting in our pick-up hearing the intensity of the anger and feeling very sad that my mother had to defend her child to someone who wasn't worthy of her presence.

I spent a part of my childhood feeling great sadness and helplessness about how it seemed that Indians were open game for the white people, to kill, maim, beat up, insult, rape, cheat, or whatever atrocity the white people wanted to play with. There was also a rage and frustration that has not died. When I look back on reservation life, it seems that I spent a great deal of time attending the funerals of my relatives or friends of my family. During one year I went to funerals of four murder victims. Most of my non-Indian friends have not seen a dead body or have not been to a funeral. Death was so com-mon on the reservation that I did not understand the implications of the high death rate until after I moved away and was surprised to learn that I've seen more dead bodies than my friends will probably ever see in their lifetime.

Because of experiencing racial violence, I sometimes panic when I'm the only non-white in a roomful of whites, even if they are my closest friends; I wonder if I'll leave the room alive. The seemingly copacetic gay world of San Francisco becomes a mere dream after the panic leaves. I think to myself that it's truly insane for me to feel the panic. I want to scream out my anger and disgust with myself for feeling distrustful of my white friends and I want to banish the society that has fostered those feelings of alienation. I wonder at the amount of assimilation which has affected me and how long my "Indianness" will allow me to remain in a city that is far removed from the lives of many Native Americans.

"Alienation" and "assimilation" are two common words used to describe contemporary Indian people. I've come to despise those two words because what leads to "alienation" and "assimilation" should not be so concisely defined. And I generally mistrust words that are used to define Native Americans and Brown People. I don't like being put under a magnifying glass and having cute liberal terms describe who I am. The "alienation" or "assimilation" that I manifest is often in how I speak. There isn't necessarily a third world language but there is an Indian way of talking that is an essential part of me. I like it, I love it, yet I deny it. I "save" it for when I'm around other Indians. It is a way of talking that involves "Indian humor" which I know for sure non-Indian people would not necessarily understand.

Articulate. Articulate. I've heard that word used many times to describe third world people. White people seem so surprised to find brown people who can speak fluent English and are even perhaps educated. We then become "articulate." I think I spend a lot of time being articulate with white people. Or as one person said to me a few years ago, "Gee, you don't seem like an Indian from the reservation."

I often read about the dilemmas of contemporary Indians caught between the white and Indian worlds. For most of us, it is an uneasy balance to maintain. Sometimes some of us are not so successful with it. Native Americans have a very high suicide rate.

> When I was about 20, I dreamt of myself at the age of 25–26, standing at a place on my reservation, looking to the North, watching a glorious, many-colored horse galloping toward me from the sky. My eyes were riveted and attracted to the beauty and overwhelming strength of the horse. The horse's eyes were staring directly into mine, hypnotizing me and holding my attention. Slowly from the East, an eagle was gliding toward the horse. My attention began to be drawn toward the calm of the eagle but I still did not want to lose sight of the horse. Finally the two met with the eagle sailing into the horse causing it to disintegrate. The eagle flew gently on.

I take this prophetic dream as an analogy of my balance between the white [horse] and Indian [eagle] worlds. Now that I am 26, I find that I've gone as far into my exploration of the white world as I want. It doesn't mean that I'm going to run off to live in a tipi. It simply means that I'm not interested in pursuing a society that uses analysis, research, and experimentation to concretize their vision of cruel destinies for those who are not bastards of the Pilgrims; a society with arrogance rising, moon in oppression, and sun in destruction.

Racism is not easy for me to write about because of my own racism toward other people of color, and because of a complex set of "racisms" within the Indian community. At times animosity exists between half-breed, full-blood, light-skinned Indians, dark-skinned Indians, and non-Indians who attempt to pass as Indians. The U.S. government has practiced for many years its divisiveness in the Indian community by instilling and perpetuating these Indian versus Indian tactics. Native Americans are the foremost group of people who continuously fight against premeditated cultural genocide.

I've grown up with misconceptions about Blacks, Chicanos, and Asians. I'm still in the process of trying to eliminate my racist pictures of other people of color. I know most of *my* images of other races come from television, books, movies, newspapers, and magazines. Who can pinpoint exactly where racism comes from? There are certain political dogmas that are excellent in their "analysis" of racism and how it feeds the capitalist system. To intellectually understand that it is wrong or politically incorrect to be racist leaves me cold. A lot of poor or working class white and brown people are just as racist as the "capitalist pig." We are *all* continually pumped with gross and inaccurate images of everyone else and we *all* pump it out. I don't think there are easy answers or formulas. My personal attempts at eliminating my racism have to start at the base level of those mindsets that inhibit my relationships with people.

Racism among third world people is an area that needs to be discussed and dealt with honestly. We form alliances loosely based on the fact that we have a common oppressor, yet we do not have a commitment to talk about our own fears and misconceptions about each other. I've noticed that liberal, consciousness-raised white people tend to be incredibly polite to third world people at parties or other social situations. It's almost as if they make a point to SHAKE YOUR HAND or to introduce themselves and then run down all the latest right-on third world or Native American books they've just read. On the other hand it's been my experience that if there are several third world gay people at a party, we make a point of avoiding each other, and spend our time talking to the whites to show how sophisticated and intelligent we are. I've always wanted to introduce myself to other third world people but wondered how I would introduce myself or what would I say. There are so many things I would want to say, except sometimes I don't want to remember I'm Third World or Native American. I don't want to remember sometimes because it means recognizing that we're outlaws.

At the Third World Gay Conference in October 1979, the Asian and Native American people in attendance felt the issues affecting us were not adequately included in the workshops. Our representation and leadership had minimal input, which resulted in a skimpy educational process about our struggles. The conference glaringly pointed out to us the narrow definition held by some people that third world means black people only. It was a depressing experience to sit in the lobby of Harambee House with other Native Americans and Asians, feeling removed from other third world groups with whom there is supposed to be this automatic solidarity and empathy. The Indian group sat in my motel room discussing and exchanging our experiences within the third world context. We didn't spend much time in workshops conducted by other third world people because of feeling unwelcomed at the conference and demoralized by having an invisible presence. What's worse than being invisible among your own kind?

It is of particular importance to us as third world gay people to begin a serious interchange of sharing and educating ourselves about each other. We not only must struggle with the racism and homophobia of straight white America, but must often struggle with the homophobia that exists within our third world communities. Being third world doesn't always connote a political awareness or activism. I've met a number of third world and Native American lesbians who've said they're just into "being themselves," and that politics has no meaning in their lives. I agree that everyone is entitled to "be themselves" but in a society that denies respect and basic rights to people because of their ethnic background, I feel that individuals cannot idly sit by and allow themselves to be co-opted by the dominant society. I don't know what moves a person to be politically active or to attempt to raise the quality of life in our world. I only know what motivates my political responsibility . . . the death of Anna Mae Aquash—Native American freedom fighter—"mysteriously" murdered by a bullet in the head; Raymond Yellow Thunder—forced to dance naked in front of a white VFW club in Nebraska— murdered; Rita Silk-Nauni—imprisoned for life for defending her child; my dear friend Mani Lucas-Papago—shot in the back of the head outside of a gay bar in Phoenix. The list could go on and on. My Native American History, recent and past, moves me to continue as a political activist.

And in the white gay community there is rampant racism which is never adequately addressed or acknowledged. My friend Chrystos from the Menominee Nation gave a poetry reading in May 1980, at a Bay Area feminist bookstore. Her reading consisted of poems and journal entries in which she wrote honestly from her heart about the many "isms" and contradictions in most of our lives. Chrystos' bluntly revealing observations on her experiences with the white-lesbian-feminist community are similar to mine and are probably echoed by other lesbians of color.

Her honesty was courageous and should be representative of the kind of forum our community needs to openly discuss mutual racism. A few days following Chrystos' reading, a friend who was in the same bookstore overheard a white lesbian denounce Chrystos' reading as anti-lesbian and racist.

A few years ago, a white lesbian telephoned me requesting an interview, explaining that she was taking Native American courses at a local university, and that she needed data for her paper on gay Native Americans. I agreed to the interview with the idea that I would be helping a "sister" and would also be able to educate her about Native American struggles. After we completed the interview, she began a diatribe on how sexist Native Americans are, followed by a questioning session in which I was to enlighten her mind about why Native Americans are so sexist. I attempted to rationally answer her inanely racist and insulting questions, although my inner response was to tell her to remove herself from my house. Later it became very clear how I had been manipulated as a sounding board for her ugly and distorted views about Native Americans. Her arrogance and disrespect were characteristic of the racist white people in South Dakota. If I tried to point it out, I'm sure she would have vehemently denied her racism.

During the Brigg's initiative scare, I was invited to speak at a rally to represent Native American solidarity against the initiative. The person who spoke prior to me expressed a pro-Bakke sentiment which the audience booed and hissed. His comments left the predominantly white audience angry and in disruption. A white lesbian stood up demanding that a third world person address the racist comments he had made. The MC, rather than taking responsibility for restoring order at the rally, realized that I was the next speaker and I was also T-H-I-R-D-W-O-R-L-D!! I refused to address the remarks of the previous speaker because of the attitudes of the MC and the white lesbian that only third world people are responsible for speaking out against racism. *It is inappropriate for progressive or liberal white people to expect warriors in brown armor to eradicate racism.* There must be co-responsibility from people of color and white people to equally work on this issue. It is not just MY responsibility to point out and educate about racist activities and beliefs.

Redman, redskin, savage, heathen, injun, american indian, first americans, indigenous peoples, natives, amerindian, native american, nigger, negro, black, wet back, greaser, mexican, spanish, latin, hispanic, chicano, chink, oriental, asian, disadvantaged, special interest group, minority, third world, fourth world, people of color, illegal aliens—oh, yes, about them, will the U.S. government recognize that the Founding Fathers (you know George Washington and all those guys) are this country's first illegal aliens.

We are named by others and we are named by ourselves.

Epilogue . . .

Following writing most of this, I went to visit my home in South Dakota. It was my first visit in eight years. I kept putting off my visit year after year because I could not tolerate the white people there and the ruralness and poverty of the reservation. And because in the eight years since I left home, I came out as a lesbian. My visit home was overwhelming. Floods and floods of locked memories broke. I rediscovered myself there in the hills, on the prairies, in the sky, on the road, in the quiet nights, among the stars, listening to the distant yelps of coyotes, walking on Lakota earth, seeing Bear Butte, looking at my grandparents' cragged faces, standing under wakiyan, smelling the Paha Sapa [Black Hills], and being with my precious circle of relatives.

My sense of time changed, my manner of speaking changed, and a certain freedom with myself returned.

I was sad to leave but recognized that a significant part of myself has never left and never will. And that part is what gives me strength—the strength of my people's enduring history and continuing belief in the sovereignty of our lives.

QUESTIONS FOR CRITICAL THINKING

Reading 53

1. Cameron discusses the hatred that she felt toward white people at a very early age. How is this hatred different from the racism that whites direct at American Indians?

2. What are some ways of eliminating the hatred that Cameron felt?

3. How does equating the contempt members of marginalized groups possess for whites with the racism that whites direct at people of color keep us from finding solutions to racism?

Reading 54

LIVING FEARLESSLY WITH AND WITHIN DIFFERENCES: MY SEARCH FOR IDENTITY BEYOND CATEGORIES AND CONTRADICTIONS

SHEFALI MILCZAREK-DESAI

People keep asking me where I come from
Says my son.
Trouble is I'm an American on the inside and oriental on the outside.
No Kai
Turn that outside in
THIS is what American looks like.

—MITSUYE YAMADA, "MIRROR MIRROR"[1]

People who live at the margins of categories provide an especially valuable starting point for exploring all the ways that identity can be deconstructed or reconstructed.

—MARY COOMBS

G rowing up in Phoenix, I did not know I was different until the girl behind me at the drinking fountain line called me a nigger. I was in the fifth grade. The eldest daughter of Indian immigrants, I was forced to think about my identity at a young age. At school I tried to be as "American" as possible: I wore western clothes and carefully monitored my pronunciation. Conversely, within the Indian community, I was not "Indian" enough: I did not stay indoors, babysit, and serve food to the *uncles* like other "good" Indian girls. The *aunties* shook their heads and whispered, "That girl will never get a good boy, her skin is too black and she is too *Americanized.*"

I have often wondered what this term, *Americanized,* means. To my white friends, it is positive—a sign that I have succeeded in "fitting into" U.S. culture. For Indians, it is an insult—to be bestowed upon brown girls who think they are white and call themselves *feminists.* The idea of being *Americanized* taught me that there was a rigid distinction between Indian and American (this view was reinforced by both the Indian immigrant community and my American peers). It also taught me to believe that I could either be Indian or American, but not both at the same time. I attributed my feminism and my disdain for the rigidly defined gender roles prescribed by Indian culture (or what I had been led to believe was "authentic" Indian culture) to being *Americanized.* On the other hand, when diversity, multiculturalism, and ethnic food fairs started becoming a fad in the early 1990s, I claimed my Indianness so that I could believe the exotic picture of myself that was being painted all around me. Although I had some sense that my identity was not singular—indeed, I always felt uneasy whenever someone asked me where I was from because I knew the expected (and legitimating) response was to name some far-off place instead of the mundane but truthful answer, "I'm from Phoenix"—I thought I had to choose to be either Indian or American and that I could not be both at the same time.

The project of integrating the brown girl who spoke a bizarre Gujarati-English language and ate with her hands, and the woman who called herself a feminist and had been raised in the Arizona desert, unconsciously began when I went to college and read Bharati Mukherjee's *Jasmine,* and *This Bridge Called My Back.* Through the pages of Mukherjee's book, which portrayed "Third World" women in their native countries and as western immigrants, I became aware that women of color were *other* in two respects: as women and as people of color. For the first time, I began to wonder if western feminism could apply to all women because the feminist discourse I had been exposed to in my women's studies classes employed the figure of a western woman as its model for all women. What was and was not considered feminism depended upon western women's notions of terms such as *oppression* and *liberation,* and women of color who chose to follow certain cultural customs and traditions were looked upon as "oppressed" and in need of western feminist "liberation." The feminism I learned did not allow for a two-way dialogue with women of color because women of color were not viewed as equals who could provide western feminists with important insights and lessons of their own.

And then it occurred to me that Mukherjee's characters weren't the only ones made invisible by western feminism because the feminist essays and icons I had studied did not prepare me to understand women like my own mother. Western feminism taught me that Indian women were weak because the great importance they placed on their roles as daughters, mothers, and wives led to their oppression by their families and their culture. And yet my mother left her homeland to find work, unmarried and alone, when she was very young. And she, in turn, was raised by a woman whose husband abandoned her with four children and one still in the belly so that my mother and her siblings were brought up by a household of strong, independent women. Thus, the feminism I knew did not seem to take the lives of women like my mother and grandmother into account when it defined "oppression" and "liberation," and this same feminism created an either/or choice for women of color such as myself: forcing us to choose between our cultures and our struggles as women in patriarchal systems.

The women I found in *Jasmine,* on the other hand, were different from the feminists in my women's studies texts because they redefined the very idea of what it meant to be a feminist, a woman of color, and an American. These Indian immigrant women accepted both their Indian identity and their newborn American selves: they were intimidated by America and they embraced America; they were altered by America and they altered America. In short, they found ways to live with and accept their many identities and, in the process, showed me that there was more than one way to be a feminist—a lesson my mother and grandmother had often tried to teach me.

Eager to find new ways of understanding feminism and my identity, I read *This Bridge Called My Back.* I felt an immediate solidarity with Nellie Wong's "long[ing] to be white," Rosario Morales's frustration with categorizations, and Cherríe Moraga's refusal to split the white from the brown. I learned that I was not alone, nor was I the first woman of color to feel the contradictory pulling and tearing created by simplistic invocations of words like *culture, tradition,* and *identity.*

And yet, there was something missing in both *Jasmine* and *Bridge.* I am an Indian woman, but not in the same way Mukherjee and her heroine are: I have no accent, I carry an American passport, and I have never lived in India for more than a few months. I am a woman of color, but not in the same way many of the authors of *This Bridge* are: my parents are immigrants from the other side of the world; I do not share a sense of history with women of color who can point to their roots in this country; I have known privilege through my upbringing in a middle-class family, my membership in one of the "model minorities," and my heterosexuality. Thus, although *Jasmine* and *Bridge* taught me that I had to redefine my notion of identity, they did not address the problems I would face in effecting this task. For instance, I felt "white" much of the time—I speak perfect English and I know how to "fit in" with the dominant, middle-class U.S. culture. Many of the voices emerging from *Bridge,* though they struggled with their "white" identities, seemed further removed from the dominant paradigm and I envied their ability to identify with their respective cultural groups. Additionally, many of the women of color represented in *This Bridge* found solidarity with other women of color both within and outside their respective cultural groups. I, on the other hand, had found it difficult if not impossible to find a community of American-born, Indian women similarly plagued by questions of identity, cultural meaning, and the adequacy of western feminism.

Realizing that I would have to embark upon my own journey and create an identity for myself, I traveled to India. I did this for many reasons: First, I knew what "American" culture was (it surrounded me) and I knew what Indian immigrant culture was, but I did not know what it meant to be "Indian" outside a western context. Second, although I knew my identity was different from both those Indian women who are immigrants and those who live in India, I wanted to know how to think of myself in relation to them. Finally, I journeyed to India to re-think the feminism with which I had been indoctrinated and, perhaps on an unconscious level, to seek forgiveness for the narrow western feminist light in which I had, until recently, viewed Indian women, including my grandmother and mother.

My first destination in India was the home of my maternal grandmother. When I was twelve, Ba (the Gujarati word for grandmother) had come to live with us in Phoenix. I vividly remember watching a small, wiry woman wrapped in a light-gray sari step off of the airplane. My siblings and I had expected a plump, gift-giving, cookie-baking grandmother like the ones we had seen on television. Instead, Ba seemed more interested in making sure we completed our chores and homework. For a long time, I resented this foreign woman who scolded us for our "American" ways. Since I didn't begin to appreciate Ba until the end of her stay in the United States, I was determined to visit her in India, and, this time, to really hear what she had to say.

When I went to see her, Ba lived in one of India's many burgeoning towns, once peaceful villages surrounded by forest now taken over by developers capitalizing on the insatiable needs of an overpopulated country. Ba lived with my uncle, his wife, and their son. Every morning I hauled water up four flights of stairs for the day's cleaning, cooking, bathing, and drinking needs since there was no running water in the building. Once a day, Ba and I ventured out to the local open-air market to buy fruits and vegetables for the evening meal, the leftovers from which constituted lunch the following day. I spent the rest of the day helping my aunt and Ba to clean the tiny flat, cook for my uncle and cousin, wash clothes and hang them to dry, napping when the hot Indian summer sun was at its brightest and relaxing after dinner by listening to Ba weave stories of people and places that had long since ceased to exist.

Through her memories, Ba took me to the small village where she was born and spent the first few years of her life—a place without cars or electricity, a place where the women would go to the river each day to bathe and wash their families' clothes. When Ba reached school-age, she and her sisters were sent to a convent school in India because her family valued education for girls as well as for boys. Ba confided in me that she had wanted to be a doctor but when she was eighteen, Ba met a young man who told her she was pretty and that he would die if she did not marry him. Despite her mother's advice that she stay in school and pursue her education, Ba, naive and unaccustomed to being flattered and wooed by a man, chose to abandon her would-be medical career and married my grandfather.

After her marriage, Ba moved to the big city of Bombay to live with her husband's parents in a joint-family home. When Ba was pregnant with her fifth and last child, my grandfather left her for his mistress. Ba's in-laws denounced their son's actions and offered to take care of Ba and her children. Although Ba remained with her husband's family for a brief time, she ultimately chose to return to her hometown. There, she raised her children with the aid of her widowed mother and her two unmarried sisters. Together, the four women worked to earn enough money to support the entire household. When Ba recounted her struggle to raise her five children, I marveled at my grandmother's courage and found, in her personal narrative, feminist acts of strength and defiance. Ba's "feminism," though, had little to do with overthrowing oppressive, patriarchal systems and more to do with survival. And yet, Ba's stories *were* about Indian women coming together, making their own choices, and collectively fighting to preserve their families and their freedom. The difference between the feminism I knew and the feminism I witnessed through Ba's stories was that the Indian women in these stories did not ultimately reject their cultures or the customs that upheld their cultural norms and values. Instead, they worked within their cultural framework as both traditionalists and revolutionaries. This point is illustrated well by my grandmother's views on marriage.

Despite Ba's unfortunate marriage and subsequent departure from the traditional joint-family structure in which she was expected to live, my grandmother had no repugnance toward the institution of marriage. In fact, Ba actively encouraged her daughter, my mother, to get married even though she simultaneously encouraged my mother to excel in her studies and be independent so that she would not have to rely on a man for her survival. Ultimately, Ba told me that my mother left India in order to avoid the pressure to marry. For me, Ba's desire to see her daughter married was a contradictory message because, while Ba had succeeded in living most of her life as a strong, single, independent woman, she wanted her daughter to assume a traditional role that had brought my grandmother much sorrow. Furthermore, Ba's contradictory message—praising her daughter's individual achievements while upholding traditional gender roles within the family—was the same contradictory message I struggled with in my relationship with my own mother.

My mother, perhaps desiring to do what her mother never could, wanted to become a doctor as well. But it was not a man who stole my mother's opportunity to fulfill her ambitions; my grandmother did not have enough money to pay for medical school and my mother earned her degree in physical therapy instead. When there was a shortage of nurses and physical therapists in North America, my mother decided to apply for work in Canada. When she was twenty-six, my mother left India to work as a therapist halfway across the world.

My mother arrived in North America in a sari with a single suitcase. She took a cab to the Toronto YWCA, where she was given a small room to sleep in and told she could use the communal kitchen. Today this story seems rather benign, but at the time it was almost unheard of for an unmarried Indian woman to leave India by herself and to live and work so far away from her family and homeland. My mother continued to trailblaze by not marrying until she was in her mid-thirties and, even then, it was a man of her own choosing, not someone chosen for her by her family. Even after she married and had three children, she continued to work full time. Like her own mother, my mother encouraged me and my sisters to pursue their dreams, to study hard, to be independent thinkers, and to stand up for what we believed. I learned those lessons well. The lessons I did not learn were the contradictory messages acted out on a daily basis: she came home after working twelve-hour days to cook large Indian meals for us, always serving my father hot rotis and waiting to eat until everyone else had finished. She covered her head and played the part of the quiet, loyal wife whenever we traveled to India and attended events within the Indian community. The most contradictory message, however, was my mother's wish that my sister and I would marry Indian men and have "Indian" families of our own.

In *Dislocating Cultures: Identities, Traditions, and Third World Feminisms,* Uma Narayan writes that "our relationships to our mothers resemble our relationships to the motherlands of the cultures in which we were raised. Both our mothers and our mother-cultures give us all sorts of contradictory messages, encouraging their daughters to be confident, impudent, and self-assertive even as they attempt to instill conformity, decorum, and silence seemingly oblivious to these contradictions" (8). I felt that my mother, by deviating from established cultural norms in her own life and supporting my independence, encouraged me to decide for myself whether or not to follow certain customs and traditions. At the same time, she warned that I would "lose" my Indian culture and identity if I refused to comply with cultural expectations. I found similar contradictions during the time I spent in India with Ba and in conversations with other Indian women who, despite their independence, intelligence, and ability to challenge existing paradigms, continued to value their roles within their families and their communities even if this "interfered" with their individual goals.

And then I began to see that the contradictions I found in Indian women (including my mother and grandmother) highlighted the very difference between western feminism and what I have come to think of as "Third World" feminism. While western feminism creates the illusion that I must either choose to be a strong, independent woman or play a role in my family and community, Third World feminism allows us to embrace and express several identities. For example, my grandmother taught me about the importance of self-reliance and individual courage while upholding traditional values of family, community, and marriage. Likewise, my mother's feminism (her independence, her determination, her ability to sidestep convention when it did not fulfill her needs) coexists with her traditional roles as Indian daughter, wife, and mother.

I should add, however, that what I am calling Third World feminism is not synonymous with Indian culture. In other words, the mixture of rebellion and conformity I found in so many Indian women's lives is not, I think, an inherent or even sanctioned component of Indian culture, which is largely defined and controlled by Indian men. In this way, Third World feminism shares common ground with western feminism because both strains of thought contain women who subvert and distort dominant discourses. The difference between the two lies in western feminist beliefs that there is only one "correct" way to do this: by denouncing marriage, rejecting communal/familial structures, and refusing all traditional roles. Third World feminism, on the other hand, seems able to balance western feminist values of individualism and independence with more "traditional" values of family and community because it recognizes that women can express both sets of values/identities and still challenge dominant discourses. Perhaps most important, Third World feminism recognizes the importance of what Chela Sandoval, in her essay "U.S. Third World Feminism: The Theory and Method of Oppositional Consciousness in the Postmodern World," terms "differential consciousness." According to Sandoval, "differential consciousness" refers to the ability to "read the current situation of power" and "to self-consciously [choose] and [adopt] the ideological form best suited to push against its configurations" (15). As Sandoval astutely points out, "differential consciousness requires grace, flexibility, and strength: enough strength to confidently commit to a well-defined structure of identity for one hour, day, week, month, year . . . if readings of power's formation require it" (15). Thus, Third World feminism gives expression to our ability—largely born out of necessity—to move/travel/flow in and among our many selves.

Coming to an understanding of Third World feminism not only expanded my definition of feminism, but also led me to expand my definition of identity. What I am calling Third World feminism is not a categorization in which I would place certain women, but a labeling of certain *actions.* The contradictions I witnessed in my mother's and grandmother's lives questioned my existing notion of identity, shattering what I had previously viewed as rigid and inevitable categories. Thus, Third World feminism not only destroyed western feminist categories separating "oppressed" women from "liberated" ones, but also blurred the distinction between my American and Indian identities: If what mattered were my actions and not the categories themselves, then I could resist certain traditional norms and still be

Indian and I could embrace certain roles as an Indian woman and still be American. By practicing Third World feminism—that is, by acknowledging that my many identities existed simultaneously and allowing each its own expression—I finally saw a way to escape my lifelong dilemma of having to choose between selves.

When it was time for me to leave India and say goodbye to my grandmother, Ba demonstrated what I would call an act of Third World feminism. Early in my visit, Ba told me that she had melted two gold bracelets she received at her wedding so she could give two smaller bracelets to each of her granddaughters at each of our weddings. Disturbed by Ba's assumption that I would one day marry, I asked her what would become of my pair of bracelets if I never married. Ba answered by reiterating that the bracelets were wedding presents and if I did not get married, there would be no reason to give them to me. On the day of my departure, my grandmother startled me by assuring me that I would receive two gold bracelets regardless of whether or not I eventually decided to marry. Clearly, Ba had thought about our initial conversation and had decided for herself that in this instance it was necessary to break with tradition. In doing so, she had not denounced all tradition, but she had decided that it need not apply in this circumstance. At that moment, I felt as if Ba and I had overcome a sixty-year age difference, thousands of miles, and the divide separating East from West.

I did not leave India with a perfect and complete understanding of what it means to be an Indian woman or how to define Indian culture. On the contrary, I returned to the United States thinking that Indian culture, just like my identity, is a composite of many different values, customs, traditions, and viewpoints. No one could prescribe certain guidelines I would have to follow in order to be Indian; indeed, my grandmother and mother explicitly rejected certain hegemonic guidelines for Indianness yet they remained Indian. Being in India and learning about Third World feminism taught me that what my parents and the Indian community in Phoenix touted as "Indian culture" was merely one narrow definition. I arrived at Los Angeles International Airport determined to simultaneously embrace my Indianness, my American upbringing, and my feminism.

Thankful that I did not have to wait in long lines for non–U.S. citizens at the port of entry, I headed toward a young-white-male Immigration and Naturalization officer at the station labeled "U.S. Citizens ONLY" in bright red letters. I braced myself for questioning—not only because of my brown skin, but because I was wearing traditional Indian clothes and my hands were decorated with intricate patterns of henna. To my surprise, the officer merely glanced at my passport, smiled, and boomed loudly, "Welcome home!" Dazed, I walked into the August sunshine wondering if America was my home and if I was an American.

My first reaction was, I don't want to be American: the word *American* doesn't convey my complexity, it doesn't embody my ability to speak fluent Gujarati or my ties to my Indian family or community and it sure as hell doesn't demonstrate that I have spent hours in hot little kitchens cooking with other Indian women until our sweat and laughter and tears became part of the spices and sauces with which we nourished our families. American translates into white, the eradication of culture, the homogenizing of identity.

But if I did not call myself American, how would I refer to myself? Did I prefer to string a long list of adjectives after my name so that I would introduce myself as an Indian-American-heterosexual-feminist? Wouldn't this also serve to reinforce categorized identities that, in reality, cannot be neatly separated from one another? And then I remembered what Bharati Mukherjee had told me about calling herself an American as a way to "sabotage the hyphen" in *Indian-American* because, she explained, each time one of us becomes American we change the very definition of that word and change everyone else who refers to themselves as American as well. Might I not, by referring to myself as American, be resisting categorization of my many identities? And wouldn't calling myself American while displaying my cultural heritage and background challenge any singular view of American culture (by challenging that America is blond-haired and blue-eyed) as well as any singular view of Indian culture (by challenging the notion that to be Indian I must renounce my American upbringing and feminism)?

I am aware that there are those who will say, have already said, that if I call myself American, I will lose my cultural identity, my Indianness. I think they are right if they view cultures as being separate and discrete entities, each in its own individual box with well-defined boundaries. As a child of two cultures, I cannot view culture in this way; Indian and American have both been spilling over into me for as long as I can remember. One might ask why, if my identity contains both Indian and American, I would choose to call myself "American" rather than "Indian." I think there is a very simple answer to this question: America is my homeland. Chandra Talpade Mohanty, in "Crafting Feminist Genealogies: On the Geography and Politics of Home, Nation, and Community," writes that "how one understands and defines home . . . is a profoundly political [question]" (487). In declaring America as my homeland, I have defined America in a way that is as multiple as my identity. In calling myself American, I re-create what it means to be American. Finally, by insisting, that all of my identities are included in the identity "American," I refuse to view the different parts of myself as contradictions. As Third World feminism has taught me, not viewing the "contradictions" as contradictions destroys the categories that would have me choose from among my many selves, which are, in reality, inseparable.

I am still learning how to live with my many identities and how to resist the categories others would place me in. This is not an easy task. I have begun to think of Tucson as my home since falling in love with the Sonoran desert: its melt-in-your-mouth, cotton candy, pink and purple mountains at sunset; clear azure skies and replenishing monsoons falling like big, wet, sloppy kisses in the summertime. I have also fallen in love with a white man who, I sometimes think, is as foreign to my feminist friends as he is to my Indian immigrant parents. The categorizations continue and I am a "straight" girl within the feminist community, and while I recognize the privilege accompanying that category, I feel its stinging connotations as well. And some days I wonder if I will ever be able to convince them that my heterosexuality does not contradict my feminism. To my parents and the Indian community I am the rebel Indian girl abandoning her roots and heritage to assimilate into what they consider to be "white" American culture. And some days I wonder if they will ever see that my marriage to a white man does not destroy my Indianness. It seems that everywhere I go I am defined singularly: I am a law student in the women's studies department, a radical feminist within the sterile corridors of the law school, an Indian in America, an American in India, a brown woman surrounded by whiteness. Some days I wonder if anyone sees that I am all of these at once, and other days it doesn't matter what anyone sees because I am comfortable being a contrary, existing at the margins of categories.

This, then, has ultimately been a story about how I have come to define myself and my home through the evolution of my understanding of feminism, the lives of my mother and grandmother, their motherland, and my Indianness. It has also been a story about how I grew up segregating my Indianness from my *Americanized* self, and how I have spent the last several years of my life trying to become whole again: it is a story about choosing identities without even knowing that I had the choice not to choose, and realizing that identity—like each and every one of us—is multitudinous, gyrating, and ever-changing.

NOTE

1. Mitsuye Yamada, *Camp Notes and Other Writings,* copyright © 1992 by Mitsuye Yamada. Reprinted by permission of Rutgers University Press.

 QUESTIONS FOR CRITICAL THINKING

Reading 54

1. The author relates her experiences of exploring identity and the challenges of what can be viewed as contradictory identities. What are some of the ways that we force people who occupy multiple identities to choose one identity over another?

2. What are some of the ways that people in the U.S. who are immigrants or children of recent immigrants maintain their culture and resist assimilation? What barriers do they face in attempting to do this?

3. How might the acceptance of the cultures of immigrants or children of recent immigrants help to reduce problems of racial inequality in society?

Reading 55

NICKEL-AND-DIMED ON (NOT) GETTING BY IN AMERICA

BARBARA EHRENREICH

At the beginning of June 1998 I leave behind everything that normally soothes the ego and sustains the body—home, career, companion, reputation, ATM card—for a plunge into the low-wage workforce. There, I become another, occupationally much diminished "Barbara Ehrenreich"—depicted on job-application forms as a divorced homemaker whose sole work experience consists of housekeeping in a few private homes. I am terrified, at the beginning, of being unmasked for what I am: a middle-class journalist setting out to explore the world that welfare mothers are entering, at the rate of approximately 50,000 a month, as welfare reform kicks in. Happily, though, my fears turn out to be entirely unwarranted: during a month of poverty and toil, my name goes unnoticed and for the most part unuttered. In this parallel universe where my father never got out of the mines and I never got through college, I am "baby," "honey," "blondie," and, most commonly, "girl."

My first task is to find a place to live. I figure that if I can earn $7 an hour—which, from the want ads, seems doable—I can afford to spend $500 on rent, or maybe, with severe economies, $600. In the Key West area, where I live, this pretty much confines me to flophouses and trailer homes—like the one, a pleasing fifteen-minute drive from town, that has no air-conditioning, no screens, no fans, no television, and, by way of diversion, only the challenge of evading the landlord's Doberman pinscher. The big problem with this place, though, is the rent, which at $675 a month is well beyond my reach. All right, Key West is expensive. But so is New York City, or the Bay Area, or Jackson Hole, or Telluride, or Boston, or any other place where tourists and the wealthy compete for living space with the people who clean their toilets and fry their hash browns.[1] Still, it is a shock to realize that "trailer trash" has become, for me, a demographic category to aspire to.

So I decide to make the common trade-off between affordability and convenience, and go for a $500-a-month efficiency thirty miles up a two-lane highway from the employment opportunities of Key West, meaning forty-five minutes if there's no road construction and I don't get caught behind some sun-dazed Canadian tourists. I hate the drive, along a roadside studded with white crosses commemorating the more effective head-on collisions, but it's a sweet little place—a cabin, more or less, set in the swampy back yard of the converted mobile home where my landlord, an affable TV repairman, lives with his bartender girlfriend. Anthropologically speaking, a bustling trailer park would be preferable, but here I have a gleaming white floor and a firm mattress, and the few resident bugs are easily vanquished.

Besides, I am not doing this for the anthropology. My aim is nothing so mistily subjective as to "experience poverty" or find out how it "really feels" to be a long-term low-wage worker. I've had enough unchosen encounters with poverty and the world of low-wage work to know it's not a place you want to visit for touristic purposes; it just smells too much like fear. And with all my real-life assets—bank account, IRA, health insurance, multiroom home—waiting indulgently in the background, I am, of course, thoroughly insulated from the terrors that afflict the genuinely poor.

No, this is a purely objective, scientific sort of mission. The humanitarian rationale for welfare reform—as opposed to the more punitive and stingy impulses that may actually have motivated it—is that work will lift poor women out of poverty while simultaneously inflating their self-esteem and hence their future value in the labor market. Thus, whatever the hassles involved in finding child care, transportation, etc., the transition from welfare to work will end happily, in greater prosperity for all. Now there are many problems with this comforting prediction, such as the fact that the economy will inevitably undergo a downturn, eliminating many jobs. Even without a downturn, the influx of a million former welfare recipients into the low-wage labor market could depress wages by as much as 11.9 percent, according to the Economic Policy Institute (EPI) in Washington, D.C.

But is it really possible to make a living on the kinds of jobs currently available to unskilled people? Mathematically, the answer is no, as can be shown by taking $6 to $7 an hour, perhaps subtracting a dollar or two an hour for child care, multiplying by 160 hours a month, and comparing the result to the prevailing rents. According to the National Coalition for the Homeless, for example, in 1998 it took, on average nationwide, an hourly wage of $8.89 to afford a one-bedroom apartment, and the Preamble Center for Public Policy estimates that the odds against a typical welfare recipient's landing a job at such a "living wage" are about 97 to 1. If these numbers are right, low-wage work is not a solution to poverty and possibly not even to homelessness.

It may seem excessive to put this proposition to an experimental test. As certain family members keep unhelpfully reminding me, the viability of low-wage work could be tested, after a fashion, without ever leaving my study. I could just pay myself $7 an hour for eight hours a day, charge myself for room and board, and total up the numbers after a month. Why leave the people and work that I love? But I am an experimental scientist by training. In that business, you don't just sit at a desk and theorize; you plunge into the everyday chaos of nature, where surprises lurk in the most mundane measurements. Maybe, when I got into it, I would discover some hidden economies in the world of the low-wage worker. After all, if 30 percent of the workforce toils for less than $8 an hour, according to the EPI, they may have found some tricks as yet unknown to me. Maybe—who knows?—I would even be able to detect in myself the bracing psychological effects of getting out of the house, as promised by the welfare wonks at places like the Heritage Foundation. Or, on the other hand, maybe there would be unexpected costs—physical, mental, or financial—to throw off all my calculations. Ideally, I should do this with two small children in tow, that being the welfare average, but mine are grown and no one is willing to lend me theirs for a month-long vacation in penury. So this is not the perfect experiment, just a test of the best possible case: an unencumbered woman, smart and even strong, attempting to live more or less off the land.

On the morning of my first full day of job searching, I take a red pen to the want ads, which are auspiciously numerous. Everyone in Key West's booming "hospitality industry" seems to be looking for someone like me— trainable, flexible, and with suitably humble expectations as to pay. . . .

Most of the big hotels run ads almost continually, just to build a supply of applicants to replace the current workers as they drift away or are fired, so finding a job is just a matter of being at the right place at the right time and flexible enough to take whatever is being offered that day. This finally happens to me at one of the big discount hotel chains, where I go, as usual, for housekeeping and am sent, instead, to try out as a waitress at the attached "family restaurant," a dismal spot with a counter and about thirty tables that looks out on a parking garage and features such tempting fare as "Polish [sic] sausage and BBQ sauce" on 95-degree days. Phillip, the dapper young West Indian who introduces himself as the manager, interviews me with about as much enthusiasm as if he were a clerk processing me for Medicare, the principal questions being what shifts can I work and when can I start. I mutter something about being woefully out of practice as a waitress, but he's already on to the uniform: I'm to show up tomorrow wearing black slacks and black shoes; he'll provide the rust-colored polo shirt with HEARTHSIDE embroidered on it, though I might want to wear my own shirt to get to work, ha ha. At the word "tomorrow," something between fear and indignation rises in my chest. I want to say, "Thank you for your time, sir, but this is just an experiment, you know, not my actual life."

So begins my career at the Hearthside, I shall call it, one small profit center within a global discount hotel chain, where for two weeks I work from 2:00 till 10:00 P.M. for $2.43 an hour plus tips.[2] In some futile bid for gentility, the management has barred employees from using the front door, so my first day I enter through the kitchen, where a red-faced man with shoulder-length blond hair is throwing frozen steaks against the wall and yelling, "Fuck this shit!" "That's just Jack," explains Gail, the wiry middle-aged waitress who is assigned to train me. "He's on the rag again"—a condition occasioned, in this instance, by the fact that the cook on the morning shift had forgotten to thaw out the steaks. For the next eight hours, I run after the agile Gail, absorbing bits of instruction along with fragments of personal tragedy. All food must be trayed, and the reason she's so tired today is that she woke up in a cold sweat thinking of her boyfriend, who killed himself recently in an upstate prison. No refills on lemonade. And the reason he was in prison is that a few DUIs caught up with him, that's all, could have happened to anyone. Carry the creamers to the table in a monkey bowl, never in your hand. And after he was gone she spent several months living in her truck, peeing in a plastic pee bottle and reading by candlelight at night, but you can't live in a truck in the summer, since you need to have the windows down, which means anything can get in, from mosquitoes on up.

At least Gail puts to rest any fears I had of appearing overqualified. From the first day on, I find that of all the things I have left behind, such as home and identity, what I miss the most is competence. Not that I have ever felt utterly competent in the writing business, in which one day's success augurs nothing at all for the next. But in my writing life, I at least have some notion of procedure: do the research, make the outline, rough out a draft, etc. As a server, though I am beset by requests like bees: more iced tea here, ketchup over there, a to-go box for table fourteen, and where are the high chairs, anyway? Of the twenty-seven tables, up to six are usually mine at any time, though on slow afternoons or if Gail is off, I sometimes have the whole place to myself. There is the touch-screen computer-ordering system to master, which is, I suppose, meant to minimize server-cook contact, but in practice requires constant verbal fine-tuning: "That's gravy on the mashed, okay? None on the meatloaf," and so forth—while the cook scowls as if I were inventing these refinements just to torment him. Plus, something I had forgotten in the years since I was eighteen: about a third of a server's job is "side work" that's invisible to customers—sweeping, scrubbing, slicing, refilling, and restocking. If it isn't all done, every little bit of it, you're going to face the 6:00 P.M. dinner rush defenseless and probably go down in flames. I screw up dozens of times at the beginning, sustained in my shame entirely by Gail's support—"It's okay, baby, everyone does that sometime"—because, to my total surprise and despite the scientific detachment I am doing my best to maintain, I care. . . .

On my first Friday at the Hearthside there is a "mandatory meeting for all restaurant employees," which I attend, eager for insight into our overall marketing strategy and the niche (your basic Ohio cuisine with a tropical twist?) we aim to inhabit. But there is no "we" at this meeting. Phillip, our top manager except for an occasional "consultant" sent out by corporate headquarters, opens it with a sneer: "The break room—it's disgusting. Butts in the ashtrays, newspapers lying around, crumbs." This windowless little room, which also houses the time clock for the entire hotel, is where we stash our bags and civilian clothes and take our half-hour meal breaks. But a break room is not a right, he tells us. It can be taken away. We should also know that the lockers in the break room and whatever is in them can be searched at any time. Then comes gossip; there has been gossip; gossip (which seems to mean employees talking among themselves) must stop. Off-duty employees are henceforth barred from eating at the restaurant, because "other servers gather around them and gossip." When Phillip has exhausted his agenda of rebukes, Joan complains about the condition of the ladies' room and I throw in my two bits about the vacuum cleaner. But I don't see any backup coming from my fellow servers, each of whom has subsided into her own personal funk; Gail, my role model, stares sorrowfully at a point six inches from her nose. The meeting ends when Andy, one of the cooks, gets up, muttering about breaking up his day off for this almighty bullshit.

Just four days later we are suddenly summoned into the kitchen at 3:30 P.M., even though there are live tables on the floor. We all—about ten of us—stand around Phillip, who announces grimly that there has been a report of some "drug activity" on the night shift and that, as a result, we are now to be a "drug-free" workplace, meaning that all new hires will be tested, as will possibly current employees on a random basis. I am glad that this part of the kitchen is so dark, because I find myself blushing as hard as if I had been caught toking up in the ladies' room myself: I haven't been treated this way—lined up in the corridor, threatened with locker searches, peppered with carelessly aimed accusations—since junior high school. Back on the floor, Joan cracks, "Next they'll be telling us we can't have sex on the job." When I ask Stu what happened to inspire the crackdown, he just mutters about "management decisions" and takes the opportunity to upbraid Gail and me for being too generous, with the rolls. From now on there's to be only one per customer, and it goes out with the dinner, not with the salad. He's also been riding the cooks, prompting Andy to come out of the kitchen and observe—with the serenity of a man whose customary implement is a butcher knife—that "Stu has a death wish today."

The other problem, in addition to the less-than-nurturing management style, is that this job shows no sign of being financially viable. You might imagine, from a comfortable distance, that people who live, year in and year out, on $6 to $10 an hour have discovered some survival stratagems unknown to the middle class. But no. It's not hard to get my co-workers to talk about their living situations, because housing, in almost every case, is the principal source of disruption in their lives, the first thing they fill you in on when they arrive for their shifts. After a week, I have compiled the following survey:

- Gail is sharing a room in a well-known down-town flophouse for which she and a roommate pay about $250 a week. Her roommate, a male friend, has begun hitting on her, driving her nuts, but the rent would be impossible alone.

- Claude, the Haitian cook, is desperate to get out of the two-room apartment he shares with his girlfriend and two other, unrelated, people. As far as I can determine, the other Haitian men (most of whom only speak Creole) live in similarly crowded situations.

- Annette, a twenty-year-old server who is six months pregnant and has been abandoned by her boyfriend, lives with her mother, a postal clerk.

- Marianne and her boyfriend are paying $170 a week for a one-person trailer.

- Jack, who is, at $10 an hour, the wealthiest of us, lives in the trailer he owns, paying only the $400-a-month lot fee.

- The other white cook, Andy, lives on his dry-docked boat, which, as far as I can tell from his loving descriptions, can't be more than twenty feet long. He offers to take me out on it, once it's repaired, but the offer comes with inquiries as to my marital status, so I do not follow up on it.

- Tina and her husband are paying $60 a night for a double room in a Days Inn. This is because they have no car and the Days Inn is within walking distance of the Hearthside. When Marianne, one of the breakfast servers, is tossed out of her trailer for subletting (which is against the trailer-park rules), she leaves her boyfriend and moves in with Tina and her husband.

- Joan, who had fooled me with her numerous and tasteful outfits (hostesses wear their own clothes), lives in a van she parks behind a shopping center at night and showers in Tina's motel room. The clothes are from thrift shops.[3]

It strikes me, in my middle-class solipsism, that there is gross improvidence in some of these arrangements. When Gail and I are wrapping silverware in napkins—the only task for which we are permitted to sit—she tells me she is thinking of escaping from her roommate by moving into the Days Inn herself. I am astounded: How can she even think of paying between $40 and $60 a day? But if I was afraid of sounding like a social worker, I come out just sounding like a fool. She squints at me in disbelief, "And where am I supposed to get a month's rent and a month's deposit for an apartment?" I'd been feeling pretty smug about my $500 efficiency, but of course it was made possible only by the $1,300 I had allotted myself for start-up costs when I began my low-wage life: $1,000 for the first month's rent and deposit, $100 for initial groceries and cash in my pocket, $200 stuffed away for emergencies. In poverty, as in certain propositions in physics, starting conditions are everything.

There are no secret economies that nourish the poor; on the contrary, there are a host of special costs. If you can't put up the two months' rent you need to secure an apartment, you end up paying through the nose for a room by the week. If you have only a room, with a hot plate at best, you can't save by cooking up huge lentil stews that can be frozen for the week ahead. You eat fast food, or the hot dogs and styrofoam cups of soup that can be microwaved in a convenience store. If you have no money for health insurance—and the Hearthside's niggardly plan kicks in only after three months—you go without routine care or prescription drugs and end up paying the price. Gail, for example, was fine until she ran out of money for estrogen pills. She is supposed to be on the company plan by now, but they claim to have lost her application form and need to begin the paperwork all over again. So she spends $9 per migraine pill to control the headaches she wouldn't have, she insists, if her estrogen supplements were covered. Similarly, Marianne's boyfriend lost his job as a roofer because he missed so much time after getting a cut on his foot for which he couldn't afford the prescribed antibiotic.

My own situation, when I sit down to assess it after two weeks of work, would not be much better if this were my actual life. The seductive thing about waitressing is that you don't have to wait for payday to feel a few bills in your pocket, and my tips usually cover meals and gas, plus something left over to stuff into the kitchen drawer I use as a bank. But as the tourist business slows in the summer heat, I sometimes leave work with only $20 in tips (the gross is higher, but servers share about 15 percent of their tips with the busboys and bartenders). With wages included, this amounts to about the minimum wage of $5.15 an hour. Although the sum in the drawer is piling up, at the present rate of accumulation it will be more than a hundred dollars short of my rent when the end of the month comes around. Nor can I see any expenses to cut. True, I haven't gone the lentil-stew route yet, but that's because I don't have a large cooking pot, pot holders, or a ladle to stir with (which cost about $30 at Kmart, less at thrift stores), not to mention onions, carrots, and the indispensable bay leaf. I do make my lunch almost every day—usually some slow-burning, high-protein combo like frozen chicken patties with melted cheese on top and canned pinto beans on the side. Dinner is at the Hearthside, which offers its employees a choice of BLT, fish sandwich, or hamburger for only $2. The burger lasts longest, especially if it's heaped with gut-puckering jalapenos, but by midnight my stomach is growling again.

So unless I want to start using my car as a residence, I have to find a second, or alternative, job. I call all the hotels where I filled out housekeeping applications weeks ago—the Hyatt, Holiday Inn, Econo Lodge, Hojo's, Best Western, plus a half dozen or so locally run guesthouses. Nothing. Then I start making the rounds again, wasting whole mornings waiting for some assistant manager to show up, even dipping into places so creepy that the front-desk clerk greets you from behind bulletproof glass and sells pints of liquor over the counter. But either someone has exposed my real-life housekeeping habits—which are, shall we say, mellow—or I am at the wrong end of some infallible ethnic equation: most, but by no means all, of the working housekeepers I see on my job searches are African Americans, Spanish-speaking, or immigrants from the Central European post-Communist world, whereas servers are almost invariably white and monolingually English-speaking. When I finally get a positive response, I have been identified once again as server material. Jerry's, which is part of a well-known national family restaurant chain and physically attached here to another budget hotel chain, is ready to use me at once. The prospect is both exciting and terrifying, because, with about the same number of tables and counter seats, Jerry's attracts three or four times the volume of customers as the gloomy old Hearthside. . . .

I start out with the beautiful, heroic idea of handling the two jobs at once, and for two days I almost do it: the breakfast/lunch shift at Jerry's, which goes till 2:00, arriving at the Hearthside at 2:10, and attempting to hold out until 10:00. In the ten minutes between jobs, I pick up a spicy chicken sandwich at the Wendy's drive-through window, gobble it down in the car, and change from khaki slacks to black, from Hawaiian to rust polo. There is a problem, though. When during the 3:00 to 4:00 P.M. dead time I finally sit down to wrap silver, my flesh seems to bond to the seat. I try to refuel with a purloined cup of soup, as I've seen Gail and Joan do dozens of times, but a manager catches me and hisses "No eating!" though there's not a customer around to be offended by the sight of food making contact with a server's lips. So I tell Gail I'm going to quit, and she hugs me and says she might just follow me to Jerry's herself.

But the chances of this are minuscule. She has left the flophouse and her annoying roommate and is back to living in her beat-up old truck. But guess what? she reports to me excitedly later that evening: Phillip has given her permission to park overnight in the hotel parking lot, as long as she keeps out of sight, and the parking lot should be totally safe, since it's patrolled by a hotel security guard! With the Hearthside offering benefits like that, how could anyone think of leaving? . . .

Management at Jerry's is generally calmer and more "professional" than at the Hearthside, with two exceptions. One is Joy, a plump, blowsy woman in her early thirties, who once kindly devoted several minutes to instructing me in the correct one-handed method of carrying trays but whose moods change disconcertingly from shift to shift and even within one. Then there's B.J., a.k.a. B.J.-the-bitch, whose contribution is to stand by the kitchen counter and yell, "Nita, your order's up, move it!" or, "Barbara, didn't you see you've got another table out there? Come on, girl!" Among other things, she is hated for having replaced the whipped-cream squirt cans with big plastic whipped-cream-filled baggies that have to be squeezed with both hands—because, reportedly, she saw or thought she saw employees trying to inhale the propellant gas from the squirt cans, in the hope that it might be nitrous oxide. On my third night, she pulls me aside abruptly and brings her face so close that it looks as if she's planning to butt me with her forehead. But instead of saying, "You're fired," she says, "You're doing fine." The only trouble is I'm spending time chatting with customers: "That's how they're getting you." Furthermore I am letting them "run me," which means harassment by sequential demands: you bring the ketchup and they decide they want extra Thousand Island; you bring that and they announce they now need a side of fries; and so on into distraction. Finally she tells me not to take her wrong. She tries to say things in a nice way, but you get into a mode, you know, because everything has to move so fast. . . .[4]

I make the decision to move closer to Key West. First, because of the drive. Second and third, also because of the drive: gas is eating up $4 to $5 a day, and although Jerry's is as high-volume as you can get, the tips average only 10 percent, and not just for a newbie like me. Between the base pay of $2.15 an hour and the obligation to share tips with the busboys and dishwashers, we're averaging only about $7.50 an hour. Then there is the $30 I had to spend on the regulation tan slacks worn by Jerry's servers—a setback it could take weeks to absorb. (I had combed the town's two down-scale department stores hoping for something cheaper but decided in the end that these marked-down Dockers, originally $49, were more likely to survive a daily washing.) Of my fellow servers, everyone who lacks a working husband or boyfriend seems to have a second job: Nita does something at a computer eight hours a day; another welds. Without the forty-five-minute commute, I can picture myself working two jobs and having the time to shower between them.

So I take the $500 deposit I have coming from my landlord, the $400 I have earned toward the next month's rent; plus the $200 reserved for emergencies, and use the $1,100 to pay the rent and deposit on trailer number 46 in the Overseas Trailer Park, a mile from the cluster of budget hotels that constitute Key West's version of an industrial park. Number 46 is about eight feet in width and shaped like a barbell inside, with a narrow region—because of the sink and the stove—separating the bedroom from what might optimistically be called the "living" area, with its two-person table and half-sized couch. The bathroom is so small my knees rub against the shower stall when I sit on the toilet, and you can't just leap out of the bed; you have to climb down to the foot of it in order to find a patch of floor space to stand on. Outside, I am within a few yards of a liquor store, a bar that advertises "free beer tomorrow," a convenience store, and a Burger King—but no supermarket or, alas, laundromat. By reputation, the Overseas park is a nest of crime and crack, and I am hoping at least for some vibrant, multicultural street life. But desolation rules night and day, except for a thin stream of pedestrian traffic heading for their jobs at the Sheraton or 7-Eleven. There are not exactly people here but what amounts to canned labor, being preserved from the heat between shifts.

In line with my reduced living conditions, a new form of ugliness arises at Jerry's. First we are confronted—via an announcement on the computers through which we input orders—with the new rule that the hotel bar is henceforth off-limits to restaurant employees. The culprit, I learn through the grapevine, is the ultra-efficient gal who trained me—another trailer-home dweller and a mother of three. Something had set her off one morning, so she slipped out for a nip and returned to the floor impaired. This mostly hurts Ellen, whose habit it is to free her hair from its rubber band

and drop by the bar for a couple of Zins before heading home at the end of the shift, but all of us feel the chill. Then the next day, when I go for straws, for the first time I find the dry-storage room locked. Ted, the portly assistant manager who opens it for me, explains that he caught one of the dishwashers attempting to steal something, and, unfortunately, the miscreant will be with us until a replacement can be found—hence the locked door. I neglect to ask what he had been trying to steal, but Ted tells me who he is—the kid with the buzz cut and the earring. You know, he's back there right now.

I wish I could say I rushed back and confronted George to get his side of the story. I wish I could say I stood up to Ted and insisted that George be given a translator and allowed to defend himself, or announced that I'd find a lawyer who'd handle the case pro bono. The mystery to me is that there's not much worth stealing in the dry-storage room, at least not in any fenceable quantity: "Is Gyorgi here, and am having 200—maybe 250—ketchup packets. What do you say?" My guess is that he had taken—if he had taken anything at all—some Saltines or a can of cherry-pie mix, and that the motive for taking it was hunger.

So why didn't I intervene? Certainly not because I was held back by the kind of moral paralysis that can pass as journalistic objectivity. On the contrary, something new—something loathsome and servile—had infected me, along with the kitchen odors that I could still sniff on my bra when I finally undressed at night. In real life I am moderately brave, but plenty of brave people shed their courage in concentration camps, and maybe something similar goes on in the infinitely more congenial milieu of the low-wage American workplace. Maybe, in a month or two more at Jerry's, I might have regained my crusading spirit. Then again, in a month or two I might have turned into a different person altogether—say, the kind of person who would have turned George in.

But this is not something I am slated to find out. When my month-long plunge into poverty is almost over, I finally land my dream job—housekeeping. I do this by walking into the personnel office of the only place I figure I might have some credibility, the hotel attached to Jerry's, and confiding urgently that I have to have a second job if I am to pay my rent and, no, it couldn't be front-desk clerk. "All right," the personnel lady fairly spits, "so it's housekeeping," and she marches me back to meet Maria, the housekeeping manager, a tiny, frenetic Hispanic woman who greets me as "babe" and hands me a pamphlet emphasizing the need for a positive attitude. The hours are nine in the morning till whenever, the pay is $6.10 an hour, and there's one week of vacation a year. I don't have to ask about health insurance once I meet Carlotta, the middle-aged African-American woman who will be training me. Carla, as she tells me to call her, is missing all of her top front teeth.

On that first day of housekeeping and last day of my entire project—although I don't yet know it's the last—Carla is in a foul mood. We have been given nineteen rooms to clean, most of them "checkouts," as opposed to "stay-overs," that require the whole enchilada of bed-stripping, vacuuming, and bathroom-scrubbing. When one of the rooms that had been listed as a stay-over turns out to be a checkout, Carla calls Maria to complain, but of course to no avail. "So make up the motherfucker," Carla orders me, and I do the beds while she sloshes around the bathroom. For four hours without a break I strip and remake beds, taking about four and a half minutes per queen-sized bed, which I could get down to three if there were any reason to. We try to avoid vacuuming by picking up the larger specks by hand, but often there is nothing to do but drag the monstrous vacuum cleaner—it weighs about thirty pounds—off our cart and try to wrestle it around the floor. Sometimes Carla hands me the squirt bottle of "BAM" (an acronym for something that begins, ominously, with "butyric"; the rest has been worn off the label) and lets me do the bathrooms. No service ethic challenges me here to new heights of performance. I just concentrate on removing the pubic hairs from the bathtubs, or at least the dark ones that I can see. . . .

When I request permission to leave at about 3:30, another housekeeper warns me that no one has so far succeeded in combining housekeeping at the hotel with serving at Jerry's: "Some kid did it once for five days, and you're no kid." With that helpful information in mind, I rush back to number 46, down four Advils (the name brand this time), shower, stooping to fit into the stall, and attempt to compose myself for the oncoming shift. So much for what Marx termed the "reproduction of labor power," meaning the things a worker has to do just so she'll be ready to work again. The only unforeseen obstacle to the smooth transition from job to job is that my tan Jerry's slacks, which had looked reasonably clean by 40-watt bulb last night when I hand-washed my Hawaiian shirt, prove by daylight to be mottled with ketchup and ranch-dressing stains. I spend most of my hour-long break between jobs attempting to remove the edible portions with a sponge and then drying the slacks over the hood of my car in the sun.

I can do this two-job thing, is my theory, if I can drink enough caffeine and avoid getting distracted by George's ever more obvious suffering.[5] The first few days after being caught he seemed not to understand the trouble he was in, and our chirpy little conversations had continued. But the last couple of shifts he's been listless and unshaven, and tonight he looks like the ghost we all know him to be, with dark half-moons hanging from his eyes. At one point, when I am briefly immobilized by the task of filling little paper cups with sour cream for baked potatoes, he comes over and looks as if he'd like to explore the limits of our shared vocabulary, but I am called to the floor for a table. I resolve to give him all my tips that night and to hell with the experiment in low-wage money management. At eight, Ellen and I grab a snack together standing at the mephitic end of the kitchen counter, but I can only manage two or three mozzarella sticks and lunch had been a mere handful of McNuggets. I am not tired at all, I assure myself, though it may be that there is simply no more "I" left to do the tiredness monitoring. What I would see, if I were more alert to the situation, is that the forces of destruction are already massing against me. There is only one cook on duty, a young man named Jesus ("Hay-Sue," that is) and he is new to the job. And there is Joy, who shows up to take over in the middle of the shift, wearing high heels and a long, clingy white dress and fuming as if she'd just been stood up in some cocktail bar.

Then it comes, the perfect storm. Four of my tables fill up at once. Four tables is nothing for me now, but only so long as they are obligingly staggered. As I bev table 27, tables 25, 28, and 24 are watching enviously. As I bev 25, 24 glowers because their bevs haven't even been ordered. Twenty-eight is four yuppyish types, meaning everything on the side and agonizing instructions as to the chicken Caesars. Twenty-five is a middle-aged black couple, who complain, with some justice, that the iced tea isn't fresh and the tabletop is sticky. But table 24 is the meteorological event of the century: ten British tourists who seem to have made the decision to absorb the American experience entirely by mouth. Here everyone has at least two drinks—iced tea and milk shake, Michelob and water (with lemon slice, please)—and a huge promiscuous orgy of breakfast specials, mozz sticks, chicken strips, quesadillas, burgers with cheese and without, sides of hash browns with cheddar, with onions, with gravy, seasoned fries, plain fries, banana splits. Poor Jesus! Poor me! Because when I arrive with their first tray of food—after three prior trips just to refill bevs—Princess Di refuses to eat her chicken strips with her pancake-and-sausage special, since, as she now reveals, the strips were meant to be an appetizer. Maybe the others would have accepted their meals, but Di, who is deep into her third Michelob, insists that everything else go back while they work on their "starters." Meanwhile, the yuppies are waving me down for more decaf and the black couple looks ready to summon the NAACP.

Much of what happened next is lost in the fog of war. Jesus starts going under. The little printer on the counter in front of him is spewing out orders faster than he can rip them off, much less produce the meals. Even the invincible Ellen is ashen from stress. I bring table 24 their reheated main courses, which they immediately reject as either too cold or fossilized by the microwave. When I return to the kitchen with their trays (three trays in three trips), Joy confronts me with arms akimbo: "What is this?" She means the food—the plates of rejected pancakes, hash browns in assorted flavors, toasts, burgers, sausages, eggs. "Uh, scrambled with cheddar," I try, "and that's . . . " "NO," she screams in my face. "Is it a traditional, a super-scramble, an eye-opener?" I pretend to study my check for a clue, but entropy has been up to its tricks, not only on the plates but in my head, and I have to admit that the original order is beyond reconstruction. "You don't know an eye-opener from a traditional?" she demands in outrage. All I know, in fact, is that my legs have lost interest in the current venture and have announced their intention to fold. I am saved by a yuppie (mercifully not one of mine) who chooses this moment to charge into the kitchen to bellow that his food is twenty-five minutes late. Joy screams at him to get the hell out of her kitchen, please, and then turns on Jesus in a fury, hurling an empty tray across the room for emphasis.

I leave. I don't walk out; I just leave. I don't finish my side work or pick up my credit-card tips, if any, at the cash register or, of course, ask Joy's permission to go. And the surprising thing is that you can walk out without permission, that the door opens, that the thick tropical night air parts to let me pass, that my car is still parked where I left it. There is no vindication in this exit, no fuck-you surge of relief, just an overwhelming, dank sense of failure pressing down on me and the entire parking lot. I had gone into this venture in the spirit of science, to test a mathematical proposition, but somewhere along the line, in the tunnel vision imposed by long shifts and relentless concentration, it became a test of myself, and clearly I have failed. Not only had I flamed out as a housekeeper/server, I had even forgotten to give George my tips, and, for reasons perhaps best known to hardworking, generous people like Gail and Ellen, this hurts. I don't cry, but I am in a position to realize, for the first time in many years, that the tear ducts are still there, and still capable of doing their job.

When I moved out of the trailer park, I gave the key to number 46 to Gail and arranged for my deposit to be transferred to her. She told me that Joan is still living in her van and that Stu had been fired from the Hearthside. I never found out what happened to George.

In one month, I had earned approximately $1,040 and spent $517 on food, gas, toiletries, laundry, phone, and utilities. If I had remained in my $500 efficiency, I would have been able to pay the rent and have $22 left over (which is $78 less than the cash I had in my pocket at the start of the month). During this time I bought no clothing except for the required slacks and no prescription drugs or medical care (I did finally buy some vitamin B to compensate for the lack of vegetables in my diet). Perhaps I could have saved a little on food if I had gotten to a supermarket more often, instead of convenience stores, but it should be noted that I lost almost four pounds in four weeks, on a diet weighted heavily toward burgers and fries.

How former welfare recipients and single mothers will (and do) survive in the low-wage workforce, I cannot imagine. Maybe they will figure out how to condense their lives—including child-raising, laundry, romance, and meals—into the couple of hours between full-time jobs. Maybe they will take up residence in their vehicles, if they have one. All I know is that I couldn't hold two jobs and I couldn't make enough money to live on with one. And I had advantages unthinkable to many of the long-term poor—health, stamina, a working car, and no children to care for and support. Certainly nothing in my experience contradicts the conclusion of Kathryn Edin and Laura Lein, in their recent book *Making Ends Meet: How Single Mothers Survive Welfare and Low-Wage Work,* that low-wage work actually involves more hardship and deprivation than life at the mercy of the welfare state. In the coming months and years, economic conditions for the working poor are bound to worsen, even without the almost inevitable recession. As mentioned earlier, the influx of former welfare recipients into the low-skilled workforce will have a depressing effect on both wages and the number of jobs available. A general economic downturn will only enhance these effects, and the working poor will of course be facing it without the slight, but nonetheless often saving, protection of welfare as a backup.

The thinking behind welfare reform was that even the humblest jobs are morally uplifting and psychologically buoying. In reality they are likely to be fraught with insult and stress. But I did discover one redeeming feature of the most abject low-wage work—the camaraderie of people who are, in almost all cases, far too smart and funny and caring for the work they do and the wages they're paid. The hope, of course, is that someday these people will come to know what they're worth, and take appropriate action.

NOTES

1. According to the Department of Housing and Urban Development, the "fair-market rent" for an efficiency is $551 here in Monroe County, Florida. A comparable rent in the five boroughs of New York City is $704; in San Francisco, $713; and in the heart of Silicon Valley, $808. The fair-market rent for an area is defined as the amount that would be needed to pay rent plus utilities for "privately owned, decent, safe, and sanitary rental housing of a modest (non-luxury) nature with suitable amenities."

2. According to the Fair Labor Standards Act, employers are not required to pay "tipped employees," such as restaurant servers, more than $2.13 an hour in direct wages. However, if the sum of tips plus $2.13 an hour falls below the minimum wage, or $5.15 an hour, the employer is required to make up the difference. This fact was not mentioned by managers or otherwise publicized at either of the restaurants where I worked.

3. I could find no statistics on the number of employed people living in cars or vans, but according to the National Coalition for the Homeless's 1997 report "Myths and Facts about Homelessness," nearly one in five homeless people (in twenty-nine cities across the nation) is employed in a full- or part-time job.

4. In *Workers in a Lean World: Unions in the International Economy* (Verso, 1997), Kim Moody cites studies finding an increase in stress-related workplace injuries and illness between the mid-1980s and the early 1990s. He argues that rising stress levels reflect a new system of "management by stress," in which workers in a variety of industries are being squeezed to extract maximum productivity, to the detriment of their health.

5. In 1996, the number of persons holding two or more jobs averaged 7.8 million, or 6.2 percent of the workforce. It was about the same rate for men and for women (6.1 versus 6.2), though the kinds of jobs differ by gender. About two thirds of multiple jobholders work one job full-time and the other part-time. Only a heroic minority—4 percent of men and 2 percent of women—work two full-time jobs simultaneously. (From John F. Stinson Jr., "New Data on Multiple Jobholding Available from the CPS," in the *Monthly Labor Review*, March 1997.)

QUESTIONS FOR CRITICAL THINKING

Reading 55

1. In this reading, the author illustrates some of the factors that perpetuate social stratification on the basis of class in the United States. How did the author's experiences broaden your understanding of these factors? What information did you already know?

2. Reflecting on what you read, how do you think factors of race influence the author's experiences? In other words, would her experiences have been similar if she were a woman of color?

3. U.S. economic policymakers rarely have had experience in trying to live on low-wage employment. Do you think their actions as policymakers would be influenced if they had the opportunity to have the experiences Ehrenreich did in this "experiment"?

Reading 56

I AM YOUR WELFARE REFORM

ANNIE DOWNEY

I am a single mother of two children, each with a different father. I am a hussy, a welfare rider—burden to everyone and everything. I am anything you want me to be—a faceless number who has no story.

My daughter's father has a job and makes over two grand a month; my son's father owns blue-chip stock in AT&T, Disney, and Campbell's. I call the welfare office, gather old bills, look for day care, write for my degree project, graduate with my son slung on my hip, breastfeeding.

At the welfare office they tell me to follow one of the caseworkers into a small room without windows. The caseworker hands me a packet and a pencil. There is an older woman with graying hair and polyester pants and the same pencil and packet. I glance at her; she looks at me; we are both

Annie Downey, "I Am Your Welfare Reform" from *Harper's Magazine* (May 1998). Reprinted with the permission of the author.

ashamed. I try hard to fill out the packet correctly, answering all the questions. I am nervous. There are so many questions that near the end I start to get careless. I just want to leave. I hand the case worker the packet in an envelope; she asks for my pencil and does not look at me. I exit unnoticed. For five years I've exited unnoticed. I can't imagine how to get a job. I ride the bus home.

After a few weeks a letter arrives assigning me to "Group 3." I don't even finish reading it. When my grandmother calls later to tell me that I confuse sex with love, I tell her that I am getting a job. She asks what kind. I say, "Any job."

It is 5:00 A.M. My alarm wakes up my kids. I try nursing my son back to sleep, but my daughter keeps him up with her questions: "What time is it? Who's going to take care of us when you leave?" I want to cry. It is still dark and I am exhausted. I've had three hours of sleep. I get ready for work, put some laundry in the washer, make breakfast, set out clothes for the kids, make lunches. I carry my son; my daughter follows. They cling to me. They cry when I leave. I see their faces pressed against the porch window and the sitter trying to get them inside.

I slice meat for $5.50 an hour for nine hours a day, five days a week. I barely feed my kids; I barely pay the bills.

I struggle against welfare. But I know that without welfare I would have nothing. On welfare I went from teen mom to woman with an education. I published two magazines, became an editor, a teacher. Welfare, along with Section 8 housing grants and Reach Up, gave my children a life. My daughter loves school and does well there. My son is round and at twenty months speaks wondrous sentences about the moon and stars. Welfare gave me what was necessary to be a mother.

Still, I cannot claim it. There is too much shame in me: the disgusted looks in the grocery lines, the angry voices of *Oprah* panelists, the unmitigated rage of the blue and white collars. I'm not what those voices say I am. I never buy expensive ice cream in pints. I don't do drugs. I don't own a hot tub.

I am one of 12 million people who account for less than 1 percent of the federal budget. I am one of the 26 percent of AFDC recipients who are mothers and the 36.6 percent who are white. I am one of the 68 percent of teen mothers who were sexually abused. I am $600 a month below the poverty level for a family of three. I am a hot political issue. I am 145-65-8563. Group 3.

I have brown hair and eyes. I write prose. My mother has been married and divorced twice. I have never been married. I love Pablo Neruda's poetry, Louise Gluck's essays. I love my stepfather but not my real father. My favorite book is *Love in the Time of Cholera* by Gabriel García Márquez; my favorite movie, *The Color Purple*. I miss my son's father. I love jazz. I've always wanted to learn how to ballroom dance. I have a story, and a life, and a face.

QUESTIONS FOR CRITICAL THINKING

Reading 56

1. Downey's discussion of her personal experiences on welfare provide a greater understanding of how attitudes about oppressed groups become internalized and manifested in feelings of shame and embarrassment. In what ways do our discussions of "welfare reform" add to this process?

2. What are some of your own assumptions about welfare recipients? How does Downey's experience affirm or challenge these assumptions? How is your reaction impacted by your own class position?

3. What are some ways that the system of welfare can be "reformed" to provide aid to those who need it without perpetuating feelings of shame or embarrassment in recipients?

Reading 57

LEARNING TO FIGHT

GEOFFREY CANADA

On Union Avenue, failure to fight would mean that you would be set upon over and over again. Sometimes for years. Later I would see what the older boys did to Butchie.

Butchie was a "manchild," very big for his age. At thirteen he was the size of a fully grown man. Butchie was a gentle giant. He loved to play with the younger boys and was not particularly athletic. Butchie had one flaw: he would not fight. Everyone picked on him. The older teenagers (fifteen and sixteen) were really hard on him. He was forever being punched in the midsection and chest by the older boys for no reason. (It was against the rules to punch in the face unless it was a "fair fight.")

I don't know what set the older boys off, or why they picked that Saturday morning, but it was decided that Butchie had to be taught a lesson. The older boys felt that Butchie was giving the block a bad reputation. Everyone had to be taught that we didn't tolerate cowards. Suddenly two of them grabbed Butchie. Knowing that something was wrong, that this was not the rough and tumble play we sometimes engaged in, Butchie broke away. Six of the older boys took off after him. Butchie zigzagged between the parked cars, trying desperately to make it to his building and the safety of his apartment. One of the boys cut him off and, kicking and yelling, Butchie was snagged.

By the time the other five boys caught up, Butchie was screaming for his mother. We knew that his mother often drank heavily on the weekends and were not surprised when her window did not open and no one came to his aid. One of the rules of the block was that you were not allowed to cry for your mother. Whatever happened you had to "take it like a man." A vicious punch to the stomach and a snarled command, "Shut the fuck up," and Butchie became quiet and stopped struggling. The boys marched him up the block, away from his apartment. Butchie, head bowed, hands held behind his back, looked like a captured prisoner.

There are about twelve of us younger boys out that morning playing football in the street. When the action started we stopped playing and prepared to escape to our individual apartment buildings. We didn't know if the older boys were after us, too—they were sometimes unpredictable—and we nervously kept one eye on them and one on a clear avenue of escape. As they marched Butchie down the block it became apparent that we were meant to learn from what was going to happen to Butchie, that they were really doing this for us.

The older boys took Butchie and "stretched" him. This was accomplished by four boys grabbing Butchie, one on each arm, one on each leg. Then they placed him on the trunk of a car (in the early 1960s the cars were all large) and pulled with all their might until Butchie was stretched out over the back of the car. When Butchie was completely, helplessly exposed, two of the boys began to punch him in his stomach and chest. The beating was savage. Butchie's cries for help seemed only to infuriate them more. I couldn't believe that a human body could take that amount of punishment. When they finished with him, Butchie just collapsed in the fetal position and cried. The older boys walked away talking, as if nothing had happened.

To those of us who watched, the lesson was brutal and unmistakable. No matter who you fought, he could never beat you *that* bad. So it was better to fight even if you couldn't win than to end up being "stretched" for being a coward. We all fought, some with more skill and determination than others, but we all fought.

The day my brother John went out to play on the block and had to fight Paul Henry there was plenty of wild swinging and a couple of blows landed, but they did no real damage. When no one got the better of the other after six or seven minutes, the fight was broken up. John and Paul Henry were made to shake hands and became best of friends in no time.

John was free. He could go outside without fear. I was still trapped. I needed help figuring out what would happen when I went outside. John was not much help to me about how the block worked. He was proud that he could go out and play while we were still stuck in the house. I mentioned something about going downstairs and having Ma come down to watch over me and John laughed at me, called me a baby. He had changed, he had accepted the rules—no getting mothers to fight your battles. His only instructions to me were to fight back, don't let the boys your age hit you without hitting back. Within a week I decided I just couldn't take it, and I went downstairs.

The moment I went outside I began to learn about the structure of the block and its codes of conduct. Each excursion taught me more. The first thing I learned was that John, even though he was just a year older than me, was in a different category than I was. John's peers had some status on the block; my peers were considered too young to have any.

At the top of the pecking order were the young adults in their late teens (seventeen, eighteen, and nineteen). They owned the block; they were the strongest and the toughest. Many of them belonged to a gang called the Disciples. Quite a few had been arrested as part of a police crackdown on gangs in the late fifties and early sixties. Several came out of jail during my first few years on Union Avenue. They often spent large amounts of time in other areas of the Bronx, so they were really absentee rulers.

At this time there were some girls involved in gang activities as well; many of the larger male gangs had female counterparts whose members fought and intimidated other girls. On Union Avenue there was a group of older girls who demanded respect, and received it, from even the toughest boys on the block. Some of these girls were skilled fighters, and boys would say "she can fight like a boy" to indicate that a girl had mastered the more sophisticated techniques of fistfighting. Girls on Union Avenue sometimes found themselves facing the same kind of violence as did boys, but this happened less often. All in all there was less pressure on girls to fight for status, although some did; for girls to fight there usually had to be a major triggering incident.

But status was a major issue for boys on the block. The next category in the pecking order was the one we all referred to as the "older boys," fifteen and sixteen years old. They belonged to a group we sometimes called the Young Disciples, and they were the real rulers of Union Avenue. This was the group that set the rules of conduct on the block and enforced law and order. They were the ones who had stretched Butchie.

Next were boys nine, ten, and eleven, just learning the rules. While they were allowed to go into the street and play, most of them were not allowed off the block without their mother's permission. My brother John belonged to this group.

The lowest group was those children who could not leave the sidewalk, children too young to have any status at all. I belonged to this group and I hated it. The sidewalk, while it provided plenty of opportunity to play with other children, seemed to me to be the sidelines. The real action happened in the street.

There were few expectations placed on us in terms of fighting, but we were not exempt. There was very little natural animosity among us. We played punchball, tag, and "red light, green light, one-two-three." It was the older boys who caused the problems. Invariably, when the older boys were sitting on the stoop and one of them had a brother, or cousin amongst us, it would be he who began the prelude to violence.

I'd been outside for more than a week and thought that I had escaped having to fight anyone because all the boys were my friends. But sure enough, Billy started in on me.

"David, can you beat Geoff?"

David looked at me, then back at Billy. "I don't know."

"What! You can't beat Geoff? I thought you was tough. You scared? I know you ain't scared. You betta not be scared."

I didn't like where this conversation was heading. David was my friend and I didn't know Billy; he was just an older boy who lived in my building. David looked at me again and this time his face changed; he looked threatening; he seemed angry.

"I ain't scared of him."

I was lost. Just ten minutes before David and I were playing, having a good time. Now he looked like I was his worst enemy. I became scared, scared of David, scared of Billy, scared of Union Avenue. I looked for help to the other boys sitting casually on the stoop. Their faces scared me more. Most of them barely noticed what was going on, the rest were looking half interested. I was most disheartened by the reaction of my brother John. Almost in a state of panic, I looked to him for help. He looked me directly in the eye, shook his head no, then barely perceptibly pointed his chin toward David as if to say, Quit stalling; you know what you have to do. Then he looked away as if this didn't concern him at all.

The other sidewalk boys were the only ones totally caught up in the drama. They knew that their day would also come, and they were trying to learn what they could about me in case they had to fight me tomorrow, or next week, or whenever.

During the time I was sizing up my situation I made a serious error. I showed on my face what was going on in my head. My fear and my confusion were obvious to anyone paying attention. This, I would later learn, was a rookie mistake and could have deadly consequences on the streets.

Billy saw my panic and called to alert the others. "Look at Geoff; he's scared. He's scared of you, David. Go kick his ass."

It was not lost on me that the questioning part of this drama was over. Billy had given David a direct command. I thought I was saved, however, because Billy had cursed. My rationale was that no big boy could use curses at a little boy. My brother would surely step in now and say, "C'mon, Billy, you can't curse at my little brother. After all, he's only seven." Then he would take me upstairs and tell Ma.

When I looked at John again I saw only that his eyes urged me to act, implored me to act. There would be no rescue coming from him. What was worse, the other older boys had become interested when Billy yelled,

"Kick his ass," and were now looking toward David and me. In their eyes this was just a little sport, not a real fight, but a momentary distraction that could prove to be slightly more interesting than talking about the Yankees, or the Giants, or their girlfriends. They smiled at my terror. Their smiles seemed to say, "I remember when I was like that. You'll see, it's not so bad."

Thinking on your feet is critical in the ghetto. There was so much to learn and so much of it was so important. It was my brother's reaction that clued me in. I knew John. He was a vicious tease at times, but he loved me. He would never allow me to be harmed and not help or at least go for help. He was telling me I had to go through this alone. I knew I could run upstairs, but what about tomorrow? Was I willing to become a prisoner in my apartment again? And what about how everyone was smiling at me? How was I ever going to play in the street with them if they thought I was such a baby? So I made the decision not to run but to fight.

I decided to maximize the benefits the situation afforded. I said, not quite with the conviction that I'd hoped for, "I'm not afraid of David. He can't beat me. C'mon, David, you wanna fight?"

There was only one problem—I didn't know how to fight. I hadn't seen Dan taking back John's coat, or John's fight with Paul Henry. But a funny thing happened after I challenged David. When I looked back at him, he didn't look quite so confident. He didn't look like he wanted to fight anymore. This gave me courage.

Billy taunted David, "You gonna let him talk to you like that? Go on, kick his ass."

Then Paul Henry chimed in, "Don't be scared, little Geoff. Go git him."

I was surprised. I didn't expect anyone to support me, especially not Paul Henry. But as I would learn later, most of these fights were viewed as sport by the bystanders. You rooted for the favorite or the underdog. Almost everyone had someone to root for them when they fought.

David put up his balled-up fists and said, "Come on." I didn't know how to fight, but I knew how to pretend fight. So I "put up my dukes" and stood like a boxer. We circled one another.

"Come on."

"No, *you* come on."

Luckily for me, David didn't know how to fight either. The older boys called out encouragement to us, but we didn't really know how to throw a punch. At one point we came close enough to one another for me to grab David, and we began to wrestle. I was good at this, having spent many an hour wrestling with my three brothers.

Wrestling wasn't allowed in a "real" fight, but they let us go at it a few moments before they broke us up. The older boys pronounced the fight a tie and made us shake hands and "be friends." They rubbed our heads and said, "You're all right," and then gave us some pointers on how to really fight. We both basked in the glory of their attention. The other sidewalk boys looked at us with envy. We had passed the first test. We were on our way to becoming respected members of Union Avenue.

David and I became good friends. Since we'd had a tie we didn't have to worry about any other older boys making us fight again. The rule was that if you fought an opponent, and could prove it by having witnesses, you didn't have to fight that person again at the command of the older boys. This was important, because everyone, and I mean everyone, had to prove he could beat other boys his age. Union Avenue, like most other inner-city neighborhoods, had a clear pecking order within the groups as well as between them when it came to violence. The order changed some as boys won or lost fights, but by and large the same boys remained at the top. New boys who came on the block had to be placed in the pecking order. If they had no credentials, no one to vouch for their ability, they had to fight different people on the block until it could be ascertained exactly where they fit in. If you refused to fight, you moved to the bottom of the order. If you fought and lost, your status still remained unclear until you'd won a fight. Then you'd be placed somewhere between the person you lost to and the person you beat.

The pecking order was important because it was used to resolve disputes that arose over games, or girls, or money, and also to maintain order and discipline on the block. Although we were not a gang, there were clear rules of conduct, and if you broke those rules there were clear consequences. The ranking system also prevented violence because it gave a way for boys to back down; if everybody knew you couldn't beat someone and you backed down, it was no big deal most of the time.

My "fight" with David placed me on top of the pecking order for boys on the sidewalk. I managed to get through the rest of the summer without having to fight anyone else. I had learned so much about how Union Avenue functioned that I figured I would soon know all I needed about how to survive on the block.

 QUESTIONS FOR CRITICAL THINKING

Reading 57

1. Canada describes the way in which he and other boys in his neighborhood were taught to be violent. How do his experiences demonstrate how violence as a masculine characteristic is a social construct?

2. What functions are served by socializing boys to fight?

3. What would men's relationships (to other men as well as to women) look like if they were not socialized to learn how to fight? Would the prevalence of social inequality be impacted in any way? If so, how? If not, why not?

Reading 58

SQUARE PEGS
Affronting Reason

CHERYL CHASE

"It seems that your parents weren't sure for a time whether you were a girl or a boy," Dr. Christen explained, as she handed me three, fuzzy, photostatted pages. I was twenty-one years old and had asked her to help me obtain records of a hospitalization that had occurred when I was a year and a half old, too young for me to recall. I was desperate to obtain the complete records, to determine who had surgically removed my clitoris, and why. I wanted to know against whom my rage should be directed. "Diagnosis: true hermaphrodite. Operation: clitorectomy." The hospital record showed Charlie admitted, age eighteen months. His typewritten name had been crudely crossed out and "Cheryl" scribbled over it.

Though I recall clearly the scene of Dr. Christen handing me the records and dismissing me from her office, I can recall nothing of my emotional reaction. How is it possible that I could be a *hermaphrodite?* The hermaphrodite is a mythological creature. I am a woman, a lesbian woman, though I lack a clitoris and inner labia. What did my genitals look like before the surgery? Was I born with a penis?

Fifteen years of emotional numbness passed before I was able to seek the answers to these and many other questions. Then, four years ago, extreme emotional turmoil and suicidal despair arrived suddenly, threatening to crush me. "It's not possible," I thought. "This cannot be anyone's story, much less mine. I don't want it." Yet it *is* mine. I mark that time as the beginning of my coming out as a political intersexual, an "avowed intersexual," to borrow the epithet that until recently adhered to homosexuals who refused to stay invisible.

The story of my childhood is a lie. I know now that after the clitorectomy my parents followed the physicians' advice and discarded every scrap of evidence that Charlie had ever existed. They replaced all of the blue baby clothing with pink and discarded photos and birthday cards. When I look at grandparents, aunts, uncles, I am aware that they must know that one day Charlie ceased to exist in my family, and Cheryl was there in his place.

The medical establishment uses the terms *hermaphrodite* and *intersexual* to refer to us. The word hermaphrodite, with its strong mythological associations, reinforces the notion that hermaphroditism is a fantasy, not your neighbor, your friend, your teacher, or—especially—your baby. And, because it falsely implies that one individual possesses two sets of genitals, it allows my clitoris to be labeled as a penis and the clitorectomy performed on me to be justified as "reconstructive surgery." For these reasons, I prefer the term intersexual. Kira Triea, one of many who has joined me in speaking openly about her intersexuality, also feels strongly about this point. "It irks me so when I am trying to explain to someone who I am, what my experience has been, and they begin to quote Ovid to me." For Triea—an intersexual assigned male at birth, raised as a boy, who began to menstruate through her penis at puberty, and who now lives as a lesbian-identified woman—hermaphroditism is a real presence in her life every day; she need not look to poetry penned in Latin two millennia ago.

At the beginning of my process of coming out as intersexual, I chose to examine again the three pages of medical records that I had set aside for fifteen years. The word "hermaphrodite" was horribly wounding; it drove me to the brink of suicide. I thought back to my earlier process of coming out as lesbian. The way out of this pain was to reclaim the stigmatized label, to manufacture a positive acceptance of it. This second coming out was far more painful and difficult. As a teenager recognizing my attraction to women, I visited the library, stealthily examined Del Martin and Phyllis Lyon's *Lesbian/Woman* (1991) and Radclyffe Hall's *The Well of Loneliness* (1990). I learned that other lesbians existed, that they somehow managed to live and to love women. Somehow I would find them; there was a community where my lesbianism would be understood and welcome. No such help was available to reclaim my intersexuality. The only images I found were absolutely pathologized case histories in medical texts and journals, closeups of genitals being poked, prodded, measured, sliced, and sutured, full body shots with the eyes blacked out.

For many months, I struggled to reclaim the label "hermaphrodite." I knew that I had been horribly mutilated by the clitorectomy, deprived of the experience of sexuality that most people, male or female, take for granted. What would my life be had I been allowed to keep my genitals intact? "No," I thought. "I don't wish to have a penis between my legs, for my body to look like a man's body. I could never relate sexually to a woman as if I were a man." The physicians who removed my clitoris considered instead performing a long series of surgeries to make my genitals look more male, to support the male sex assignment rather than changing it to female. Though I can offer little evidence to support the idea, I am convinced that, had I been kept male, I would now be a gay man.

"Never mind, just don't think about it," was the advice of the few people to whom I spoke, including two female therapists: "You look like a woman." There is a powerful resistance to thinking about intersex. Because they look at me and make a female attribution, most people find it impossible to imagine that my experience and my history are not female. The resistance to thinking about what my sexual experience might be is even more profound. Most people, including the two therapists mentioned above, are paralyzed by the general prohibition on explicit sex talk. But sex radicals and activists are little better. They assume that I am having "vaginal orgasms" or even "full-body orgasms." If I persist in asserting my sexual dysfunction, many patronize me. "I am completely confident that you will learn how to orgasm," one man told me, then continued his explanation of how male circumcision was just as damaging as clitorectomy, my experience to the contrary.

What is most infuriating is to read, nearly every day in popular media, denunciations of African female genital mutilation as barbaric abuses of human rights, which fail to mention that intersexed children's clitorises are removed every day in the United States. Such writers occasionally note that clitorectomy has been practiced in the United States but always hurry to assure the reader that the practice ended by the 1930s. Letters to these authors receive no reply. Letters to editors pointing out the inaccuracy are not published. In 1996, Congress passed H.R. 3610, prohibiting "the removal or infibulation (or both) of the whole or part of the clitoris, the labia minor, or the labia major" (p. H11829). However, the next paragraph specifically excludes from prohibition these operations if they are performed by a licensed medical practitioner who deems them necessary. As early as 1993, Brown University Professor of Medical Science Anne Fausto-Sterling had joined intersexuals to ask Congresswoman Pat Schroeder, in drafting the prohibition, not to neglect genital surgery performed on intersexed infants. Ms. Schroeder's office made no reply. Newspaper accounts in 1996 lauded the bill's passage as an end to clitorectomy in the United States.

It took months for me to obtain the rest of my medical records. I learned that I had been born, not with a penis, but with intersexed genitals: a typical vagina and outer labia, female urethra, and a very large clitoris. Mind you, "large" and "small," as applied to intersexed genitals, are judgments that exist only in the mind of the beholder. From my birth until the surgery, while I was Charlie, my parents and doctors considered my penis to be monstrously small, and with the urethra in the "wrong" position. My parents were so ashamed and traumatized by the appearance of my genitals that they allowed no one to see them—no baby-sitters, no possibility of tired parents being spelled for diaper-changing by a helpful grandmother or aunt. Then, in the moment that intersex specialist physicians pronounced that my "true sex" was female, my clitoris was suddenly monstrously large. All this occurred without any change in the objective size or appearance of the appendage between my legs.

Intersex is a humanly possible but (in our culture) socially unthinkable phenomenon. In modern industrial cultures, when a child is born, the experts present, whether midwives or physicians, assign a sex based on the appearance of the infant's genitals. They are required—both legally and by social custom—to assign the child as either male or female. Were parents to tell inquiring friends and relatives that their newborn's sex was "hermaphrodite," they would be greeted with sheer disbelief. Should the parents persist in labeling their child "hermaphrodite" rather than "male or female with a congenital deformity requiring surgical repair," their very sanity would be called into question.

Thus, intersexed children are always assigned to either male or female sex. In making these problematic sex assignments, specialist physicians are generally consulted; the assignment may not be made for several days, and it is sometimes changed, as was done with me. In fact, there are documented cases in which the sex assignment has been changed without soliciting the opinion of or even *informing* the child, as many as three times.[1]

Most people take for granted, even assume as "scientific fact," that there are two, and only two, sexes. In reality, however, about one in two thousand infants is born with an anatomy that refuses to conform to our preconceptions of "male" and "female." Few outside the medical profession are even aware of our existence. I now know that hundreds of thousands of people in the United States alone share my experience, and we are organizing ourselves through the Intersex Society of North America.[2] My ability to embrace the term hermaphrodite, at first halting and uncertain, has grown in depth, conviction, and pride, as I have met other intersexuals; we have shared our stories, our lives, and our anger.

Struggling to understand why society so utterly denies the phenomenon of intersexuality, I read widely in such diverse fields as philosophy, history, psychology, and ethnography. I was excited to discover that in recent years a number of scholars in these fields have begun to examine the ways in which sex and gender are socially constructed (Butler, 1990; Foucault, 1980b; Kessler and McKenna, 1978; Laqueur, 1990; Vance, 1991). These and related works constitute a recognition that the paradigms of previous investigators have caused them to overlook information about nonreproductive sexual conduct, practices, and categories. Data that were at odds with their culturally determined, heterosexist, dimorphic point of view were ignored because they could not be accounted for.

In many other cultures, however, the phenomenon of intersexuality is well known, and an intersexed child may be recognized and assigned as such at birth. Unfortunately, interpretations by ethnographers have been straight-jacketed by the absolute sexual dualism that has dominated Western thinking since Darwin. Recently though, ethnographers have given us examples of cultures in which intersexual assignment confers high status, low status, or even condemns an infant to death by exposure, as an evil omen (Edgerton, 1964; Furth, 1993; Herdt, 1994; Nanda, 1994; Roscoe, 1991). The Jewish Talmud discusses hermaphrodites in many locations and lays out regulations governing matrimony, priesthood, inheritance, and other matters for intersexuals (Berlin and Zevin, 1974). The Talmudic sages held variously that the hermaphrodite was: of uncertain sex, but in some essential way actually either male or female; part male and part female; definitely male, but only in respect to certain laws. And, in an eerie echo of modern medical practice, one Talmudic writer even differentiates the hermaphrodite, whose sex can never be resolved, from the *Tumtum,* whose sex is ascertainable through surgery.

Americans, though, are apt to express disbelief when confronted with evidence of intersexuality. Modern Western culture is the first to rely upon technology to *enforce* gender dichotomy: since the 1950s or so, surgical and hormonal means have been used to erase the evidence from intersexed infants' bodies. Medical literature speaks with one voice on the necessity of this practice, even when it concedes that surgical intervention may damage sexual function (Conte and Grumbach, 1989; Emans and Goldstein, 1990; Hendricks, 1993). Silence has been considered evidence of patient satisfaction.

For over forty years, some form of clitorectomy or clitoroplasty has been used to treat little girls with adrenogenital syndrome (one of dozens of reasons why an infant may be born intersexed). The only indication for performing this surgery has been to improve the body image of these children so that they feel "more normal" . . . *Not one has complained of loss of sensation even when the entire clitoris was removed. . . . The clitoris is clearly not necessary for orgasm* (Edgerton, 1993, p. 956).[3]

What are genitals for? It is my position that *my* genitals are for *my* pleasure. In a sex-repressive culture with a heavy investment in the fiction of sexual dichotomy, infant genitals are for discriminating male from female infants. It is very difficult to get parents, or even physicians, to consider the infant as a future adult and sexual being. Medical intersex specialists, however, pride themselves on being able to do just that.

For intersex specialists, male genitals are for active penetration and pleasure, while female genitals are for passive penetration and reproduction: men have sex; women have babies. Asked by a journalist why standard practice assigns 90 percent of intersexed infants as females (and surgically enforces the assignment by trimming or removing the clitoris), one prominent surgical specialist reasoned, "you can make a hole, but you can't build a pole" (Hendricks, 1993, p. 15). Notice how John Gearhart, a noted specialist in genital surgery for intersex children, evades questioning about orgasmic function following the presentation of his paper on additional surgeries for repair of vaginas surgically constructed in intersexed infants. (Dr. Frank, in attendance at the presentation, shares a professional interest in such surgery; the discussion was published in the *Journal of Urology* along with the paper.)

DR. FRANK: How do you define successful intercourse? How many of these girls actually have an orgasm, for example? How many of these had a clitorectomy, how many a clitoroplasty, and did it make any difference to orgasm?

DR. GEARHART: Interviews with the families were performed by a female pediatric surgeon who is kind and caring, and who I think got the maximum information from these patients. Adequate intercourse was defined as successful vaginal penetration. . . . (Bailez et al., 1992, p. 684)

Gearhart has since condemned outspoken intersexed adults as "zealots" (Angier, 1996, p. E14), and minimized reports by former patients of damaged sexual function after clitoral surgery because "some women who have never had surgery are anorgasmic" (Chase, 1996, p. 1140).

Intersex specialists often stress the importance of a heterosexual outcome for the intersexed children consigned to their care. For instance, Slijper and colleagues state, "parents will feel reassured when they know that their daughter can develop heterosexually just like other children" (Slijper et al., 1994, p. 15). Dr. Y, a prominent surgeon in the field of intersexuality, agreed to be interviewed by Ellen Lee only under condition of anonymity. He asserts that the ultimate measure of success for sex assignment of intersexed children is the "effectiveness of intercourse" they achieve as adults (Lee, 1994, p. 60). Intersexuals assigned female who choose women as sexual partners, and those assigned male who choose men as sexual partners, must then represent failures of treatment in the eyes of our parents and of intersex specialists. Indeed, my mother's reaction upon learning that I was sexual with women was to reveal to my siblings, but not to me, my hermaphroditism and history of sex change and to regret that she had allowed physicians to assign me female, rather than male.

My mother and father took me into their room one day to share a secret with me. I was ten years old, still utterly ignorant about sexual matters. "When you were a baby, you were sick," they explained. "Your clitoris was too big; it was *enlarged.*" The way they spoke the word *enlarged,* it was clear that it was being given some special, out of the ordinary, meaning. "You had to go into the hospital, and it was removed." "What is a 'clitoris'?" I asked. "A clitoris is a part of a girl that would have been a penis if she had been a boy. Yours was *enlarged,* so it had to be removed. Now everything is fine. But don't ever tell this to anyone else."

Who am I? I look at my body. It *looks* female. Yet I have always harbored a secret doubt. I remember myself as a withdrawn, depressed adolescent, trying to steal a glance of a woman's genitals. Do hers look like mine? I had never seen a naked woman up close. I had no idea that my genitals were missing parts. In fact, one cannot discern the difference between my genitals and those of any other woman without parting the outer labia. I do recall learning, from a book, about the phenomenon of masturbation. Try as I might, I could not locate a focus of pleasurable sensation in my genitals, couldn't accomplish the trick that I had read about. I wasn't able to associate this failure with the secret about the *enlarged* clitoris that had been removed. I simply couldn't take in that such an irreversible harm had been done to me and by adults who were responsible for my well-being. I often woke from a nightmare in which my life was in danger, my gender in question, and my genitals were somehow horribly deformed, spilling out of me like visceral organs. It wasn't until I became a young adult that I was able to make the connection between the removal of my clitoris and my feeble sexual response and inability to experience orgasm.

Who am I? I now assert both my femininity and my intersexuality, my "not female"-ness. This is not a paradox; the fact that my gender has been problematized is the source of my intersexual identity. Most people have never struggled with their gender, are at a loss to answer the question, "How do you know you are a woman (a man)?"

I have been unable to experience myself as totally female. Although my body passes for female, women's clothing does not fit me. The shoulders are too narrow, the sleeves too short. Most women's gloves won't go on my hands, nor women's shoes on my feet. For most women, that wouldn't be more than an inconvenience. But when the clothing doesn't fit, I am reminded of my history. Of course, men's clothing doesn't fit either. The straight lines leave no room for my large breasts or broad hips. Still, I experience something about the way that I work and move in the world as relatively masculine. And when a man expresses an intimate attraction to me, I often suspect that he may be wrestling with a conflicted homosexual orientation—attracted to a masculine part of me, but my feminine appearance renders his attraction safely heterosexual.

As woman, I am less than whole—I have a secret past; I lack important parts of my genitals and sexual response. When a lover puts her hand to my genitals for the first time, the lack is immediately obvious to her. Finally, I simply do not feel myself a woman (even less a man). But the hermaphrodite identity was too monstrous, too other, too freakish, for me to easily embrace—a medical anomaly, patched up as best the surgeons could manage. I had an article from a medical journal that stated that only twelve "true hermaphrodites" (the label applied to me by my medical records) had *ever* been recorded (Morris, 1957, p. 540).

For whose benefit does this mechanism of medical erasure and social silencing operate? Certainly, it does not benefit intersexed children. I have been brutally mutilated, left to wonder and to search for the truth in utter silence and isolation. When at age thirty-six, I finally confronted my mother, I asked her how she could possibly have kept her silence for all those years, left me to learn my history as Charlie and the label of hermaphroditism from medical records. Her response? "Well, you could have *asked* me." (I wonder what other improbable questions I should be certain to ask while she is alive . . .)

At first, I was horribly vexed by this issue of identity. My earlier experience of coming out as a lesbian helped me to see the solution to my predicament. The terms homosexual and lesbian, as with the term intersex, were inventions of medical discourse used to pathologize disapproved sexualities. I must proudly assert my identity and insist that the medical construction of intersexuality as disease is oppression, not science. I must find others who share my experience—others who will speak out with me. A community can provide emotional and logistical support for its members and mount a much more powerful resistance than individuals acting alone.

It wasn't easy to overcome my feelings of intense shame. I remember furtively using the printer, copier, and fax machine at the office, heart pounding with the fear that someone would see the documents that I was working with—medical records, articles from medical journals, a journal of my emotional progress. I still believed that intersexuality was so rare that I might never find another whose experience was similar to mine. Instead, I first sought out and spoke with transsexuals. Alice Walker had just published *Possessing the Secret of Joy*, a novel which focused Western attention on the African cultural rite euphemistically referred to as female circumcision. I thrilled to read the elderly midwife, whose long life had been spent performing clitorectomies, castigate her former victim for suggesting clitorectomy might be justified for hermaphrodites, if not for females. "It's all normal, as far as that goes, says M'lissa. You didn't make it, so who are you to judge?" (Walker, 1992, p. 257). I located and spoke with African women mutilated in this way, who are now organizing in the United States against the practices of their homelands. The examples of all these brave people helped me to deal with my shame.

I began to speak, at first indiscriminately, with friends and acquaintances about what had been done to me. Within a year, I had turned up half a dozen other intersexuals; most of them were also genitally mutilated; two were living with their atypical genitals intact. A woman clitorectomized during her teens, though she knew from masturbation that her clitoris was the focus of sexual pleasure, she was unable to express this or otherwise resist the pressure of parents and doctors; a child who had been clitorectomized just two years previous (in 1990); a woman who was grateful that her mother had resisted years of medical pressure to remove her daughter's large clitoris; a man who had been raised as a girl, switched to living as a man (with intact intersexed genitals) after he developed a masculine body at puberty; a man whose penis had been severely damaged by repeated surgeries to "correct" the position of his urethral meatus;[4] a man who had discovered that the childhood surgery which no one would explain to him had actually removed his uterus and single ovary. None of these people had ever spoken with another intersexual.

Surgeons assert that the reason why they fail to provide us with counseling is that they cannot locate mental health professionals with experience in dealing with intersexuality (Lee, 1994). Yet, surgeons perpetuate this situation by mutilating, traumatizing, stigmatizing, and silencing us, their intersexed patients. We grow up with so much shame that as adults we are not able to discuss our experience openly, and the phenomenon of intersexuality remains invisible. Indeed, as recently as 1996, one entrant in a medical ethics contest won a cash prize for her essay encouraging physicians to lie to their intersexed patients in order to prevent them from knowing their diagnoses (Natarajan, 1996). In adulthood, many who were treated as children by medical intersex specialists feel so betrayed that they shun all medical care.

What do I see when I look in the mirror? I see a female body, though scarred and missing some important genital parts. When I interact in daily life with others, though, I experience a strange sort of bodily dissociation—my perception of myself is as a disembodied entity, without sex or gender. I view healing this split as an important element of personal growth that will allow me to reclaim my sexuality and to be more effective as an intersex advocate. My body is not female; it is intersexed. Nonconsensual surgery cannot erase intersexuality and produce whole males and females; it produces emotionally abused and sexually dysfunctional intersexuals. If I label my postsurgical anatomy female, I ascribe to surgeons the power to create a *woman by removing* body parts; I accede to their agenda of "woman as lack"; I collaborate in the prohibition of my intersexual identity. Kessler quotes an endocrinologist who specializes in treating intersexed infants: "In the absence of maleness, you have femaleness. . . It's really the basic design" (Kessler, 1990, p. 15).

Must things be this way? In all cultures, at all times? Anthropologist Clifford Geertz contrasted the conceptualization of intersexuals by the Navajo and the Kenyan Pokot—"a product, if a somewhat unusual product, of the normal course of things"—with the American attitude. "Americans . . . regard femaleness and maleness as exhausting the natural categories in which persons can conceivably come: what falls between is a darkness, an offense against reason" (Geertz, 1984 p. 85). The time has come for intersexuals to denounce our treatment as abuse, to embrace and openly assert our identities as intersexuals, and to intentionally affront that sort of reason which requires that we be mutilated and silenced.

Even before intersexuals began to speak out, there were a few stirrings of awareness that something fishy was going on at the boundaries of the sexes. In 1980, Ruth Hubbard and Patricia Farnes pointed out that the practice of clitorectomy was not limited to the Third World but also occurs "right here in the United States, where it is used as part of a procedure to 'repair' by 'plastic surgery' so-called genital ambiguities" (Farnes and Hubbard, 1980, p. 9). Reacting to intersex specialist John Money's explanation to a three-year-old girl that clitorectomy "will make her look like all other girls," Anne Fausto-Sterling wryly noted, "If the surgery results in genitalia that look like those shown in [Money's] book, then [he is] in need of an anatomy lesson!" (Fausto-Sterling, 1985, p. 138). Five years later Suzanne Kessler, whose work has been influential in motivating the current discourse on gender as a social construction, interviewed physicians who specialize in managing intersexed children. She concluded that genital ambiguity is treated with surgery "not because it is threatening to the infant, but because it is threatening to the infant's culture" (Kessler, 1990, p. 25). Finally, Fausto-Sterling suggested that genital surgery should not be imposed on intersexed infants (Fausto-Sterling, 1993).

A letter to the editor in which I responded to Fausto-Sterling's article, announcing the formation of the Intersex Society of North America

(ISNA), brought emotional responses from other intersexuals (Chase, 1993). One, Morgan Holmes, has completed an extended analysis of the reasons why medical technology has been used to erase intersexuality in general, and from her own body in particular (Holmes, 1994). Until she contacted me, Holmes shared her experience of intersexuality with no living being. The only other intersexual in her universe was Herculine Barbin, the nineteenth-century French hermaphrodite whose journals were edited and published by Foucault (Foucault, 1980a). Barbin's life ended in suicide. By 1996, ISNA had grown to include more than 150 intersexuals throughout the United States and Canada, and several in Europe, Australia, and New Zealand.

In Britain, as well, intersexuals have begun to speak out against the extreme secrecy, shame, and freakishness surrounding their condition. The British movement was given a boost when the respected *British Medical Journal* carried an exchange that led to publication of an address for a support group.

> Mine was a dark secret kept from all outside the medical profession (family included), but this is not an option because it both increases the feelings of freakishness and reinforces the isolation. (Anonymous, 1994b)

> It's not that my gynecologist told me the truth that angers me (I'd used medical libraries to reach a diagnosis anyway), but that neither I nor my parents were offered any psychological support but were left to flounder in our separate feelings of shame and taboo. (Anonymous, 1994a)

Both writers have androgen insensitivity syndrome (AIS). During gestation, their XY sex chromosomes caused them to have testes, and their testes produced testosterone. But because their cells were incapable of responding to testosterone, they were born with genitals of typical female appearance but having a short vagina, without cervix or uterus. Raised as girls, with bodies that develop many adult female characteristics at puberty, women with AIS are often traumatized to read in medical records or texts that they are "genetic males" and "male pseudohermaphrodites." The publication of these letters led to a swell of visibility and participation in Britain's AIS Support Group, which by 1996 had chapters in the United States, Canada, the Netherlands, Germany, and Australia.

In Germany, intersexuals have formed the Workgroup on Violence in Pediatrics and Gynecology for mutual support and in opposition of medical abuse. In Japan, intersexuals have formed Hijra Nippon, with a similar agenda. In the United States, HELP and the Ambiguous Genitalia Support Network were separately founded by mothers who opposed the drastic surgical interventions and secrecy that medical specialists recommended for their intersexed children.[5] One of these women has a suit pending against physicians who removed her son's testes against her stated wishes.

Some intersexuals whose bodies resemble mine have an XX, some an XY karyotype; others have a mosaic karyotype, which differs from cell to cell. There is no possible way to discern my karyotype without sending a tissue sample to a laboratory. If the result were "XX," should this information bolster my identity as a female? As a lesbian? If "XY," should I reconceptualize myself as a heterosexual man? It is ludicrous that knowledge of the result of a laboratory test in which cell nuclei are stained and photographed under a microscope should determine the perception of anyone's sex or gender.

The International Olympic Committee has learned this the hard way. Since the IOC began to karyotype women in 1968, one in 500 female athletes tested have been rejected because of their unusual chromosomes; in some cases, the decision was made only after the event, and the woman was stripped of title and barred from future competition. To this writer's knowledge, only one person treated in this way has thus far been willing to speak openly about her experience. When meet officials presented Maria Patino with the news that she was "genetically male," they advised her to fake an injury and leave quietly (Pool, 1994).

When I first began to seek out other intersexuals, I expected, I wanted, to find people whose experience exactly matched mine. What I have discovered is that in one sense we are very different—the range of personalities, politics, and anatomies in our nascent intersexual movement is broad. Some of us live as women, some as men, some as open intersexuals. Many of us are homosexual, if that term is narrowly understood in terms of the social gender roles of the partners. Some of us have never been sexual. But, in another sense, our experiences are surprisingly coherent: those of us who have been subjected to medical intervention and societal invisibility share our experience of it as abuse.

I claim lesbian identity because women who feel desire for me experience that desire as lesbian, because I feel most female when being sexual, and because I feel desire for women as I do not for men. Many intersexuals share my sense of queer identity, even those who do not share this homosexual identity. One, assigned female at birth and lucky enough to escape genital surgery through a fluke, has said that she has enjoyed sex with both women and men but never with another intersexual. "I'm a heterosexual in the truest sense of the word" (Angier, 1996, p. E14).

Healing is a process without end. The feeling of being utterly alone may be the most damaging part of what has been done to us. My work as an activist—listening to, counseling, and connecting other intersexuals, and working to save children born every day from having to repeat our suffering—has been an important part of my own healing and of feeling less overwhelmed by grief and rage.

NOTES

1. Money describes a child who was assigned male at birth, female a few days later, male at age three weeks, and female at age four and a half. She was clitorectomized in conjunction with the final sex change. Her history of sex reassignments was kept secret from her, tabooed from family discussion, although she recalled it in dreams (Money, 1991, p. 239).
2. Intersex Society of North America, P.O. Box 31791, San Francisco, CA 94131. E-mail info@isna.org.http://www.isna.org.
3. Although this statement was written in connection with an article about "clitoroplasty without loss of sensitivity," the authors provide no evidence that this standard procedure, which removes nearly the entire clitoris and relocates the remainder, leaves sexual sensation intact. On the other hand, Morgan Holmes, who was subjected to it as a child, characterizes it as a "partial clitorectomy" (Holmes, 1994). Another woman, who had the procedure performed as an adult and is able to contrast her sexual experience before and after the surgery, calls it "incredibly desensitizing" (Chase, 1994, p. 3).
4. Approximately one in three or four hundred infants is born with a condition called hypospadias, in which the portion of the urethra that traverses the penis is partially or completely open. This condition is rarely harmful; it looks unusual, and the boy or man may have to sit to urinate. Hypospadias "correction" surgery is probably the second most common form of cosmetic genital surgery performed in the United States, following "routine" male circumcision.
5. AIS Support Group US, 4203 Genessee #103–436, San Diego, CA 92117–4950. E-mail <aissg@aol.com>. AG Gewalt in der Padiatrie and Gynecologie, Brandt-strasse·30, Bremen 28 215, Germany. E-mail <aggpg@t-online.de>. Hijra Nippon, Suita Yubinkyoku Todome, Honami cho 4–1 Suita shi, Osaka T564, Japan. HELP, PO Box 26292, Jacksonville, FL 32226. E-mail <help@jaxnet.com>. Ambiguous Genitalia Support Network, P.O. Box 313, Clements, CA 95227.

REFERENCES

Angier, Natalie. 1996. Intersexual healing: An anomaly finds a group. *The New York Times* (February 4): 14.

Anonymous. 1994a. Be open and honest with sufferers. *British Medical Journal* 308 (April 16): 1041–1042.

Anonymous. 1994b. Once a dark secret. *British Medical Journal* 308 (February 19): 542.

Bailcz, M. M., John P. Gearhart, Claude Migeon, and John Rock, 1992. Vaginal reconstruction after initial construction of the external genitalia in girls with salt-wasting adrenal hyperplasia. *Journal of Urology* 148: 680–684.

Berlin, Meyer, and Shlomo Josef Zevin. 1974. *Encyclopedia Talmudica*. Jerusalem: Phillip Feldheim, pp. 386–399.

Butler, Judith. 1990. *Gender Trouble: Feminism and the Subversion of Identity*. New York: Routledge.

Chase, Cheryl. 1993. Letters from readers. *The Sciences* (July/August): 3.

Chase, Cheryl. 1994. Winged labia: Deformity or gift? *Hermaphrodites with Attitude* (Winter): 3.

Chase, Cheryl. 1996. Re: Measurement of evoked potentials during feminizing genitoplasty: Techniques and applications (letter). *Journal of Urology* 156 (3): 1139–1140.

Conte, Felix A., and Melvin M. Grumbach. 1989. Pathogenesis, classification, diagnosis, and treatment of anomalies of sex. In *Endocrinology,* edited by L. J. De Groot. Philadelphia: Saunders, pp. 1810–1847.

Department of Defense Appropriations Act of 1996, 104th Congress, second session, H.R. 3610 Sec 645, Congressional Record: September 28, 1996 (House), p. HI 1829.

Edgerton, Milton T. 1993. Discussion: Clitoroplasty for clitoromegaly due to adrenogenital syndrome without loss of sensitivity (by Nobuyuki Sagehashi). *Plastic and Reconstructive Surgery* 91 (5): 956.

Edgerton, Robert B. 1964. Pokot intersexuality: An cast African example of the resolution of sexual incongruity. *American Anthropologist* 66 (6): 1288–1299.

Emans, S. Jean Herriot, and Donald Peter Goldstein. 1990. *Pediatric and Adolescent Gynecology,* third edition. Boston: Little, Brown, and Co.

Farnes, Patricia, and Ruth Hubbard. 1980. Letter to editor. *Ms Magazine* (April): 9–10.

Fausto-Sterling, Anne. 1985. *Myths of Gender: Biological Theories about Women and Men,* second edition. New York: Basic Books.

Fausto-Sterling, Anne. 1993. The five sexes: Why male and female are not enough. *The Sciences* (March/April): 20–25.

Foucault, Michel. 1980a. *Herculine Barbin, Being the Recently Discovered Memoirs of a Nineteenth-Century Hermaphrodite.* Translated by Richard McDougall. New York: Colophon.

Foucault, Michel. 1980b. *The History of Sexuality, Volume I: An Introduction.* Translated by Robert Hurley. New York: Viking.

Furth, Charlotte. 1993. Androgynous males and deficient females: Biology and gender boundaries in sixteenth- and seventeenth-century China. In *The Lesbian and Gay Studies Reader,* edited by Henry Abelove, Michellé Aina Barale, and David Helperin. New York: Routledge, pp. 479–497.

Geertz, Clifford. 1984. *Local Knowledge.* New York: Basic Books.

Hall, Radclyffe. 1990. *The Well of Loneliness.* New York: Anchor.

Hendricks, Melissa. 1993. Is it a boy or a girl? *Johns Hopkins Magazine* (November): 10–16.

Herdt, Gilbert. 1994. Mistaken sex: Culture, biology, and the third sex in New Guinea. In *Third Sex, Third Gender: Beyond Sexual Dimorphism in Culture and History,* edited by G. Herdt. New York: Zone Books, pp. 419–446.

Holmes, Morgan. 1994. Medical Politics and Cultural Imperatives: Intersexuality Beyond Pathology and Erasure. Master's Thesis, Interdisciplinary Studies, York University, Toronto.

Kessler, Suzanne. 1990. The medical construction of gender: Case management of intersexual infants. *Signs: Journal of Women in Culture and Society* 16 (1): 3–26.

Kessler, Suzanne J., and Wendy McKenna. 1978. *Gender: An Ethnomethodological Approach.* Chicago: The University of Chicago Press.

Laqueur, Thomas. 1990. *Making Sex: Body and Gender from the Greeks to Freud.* Cambridge: Harvard University Press.

Lee, Ellen Hyun-Ju. 1994. Producing Sex: An Interdisciplinary Perspective on Sex Assignment Decisions for Intersexuals. Senior Thesis, Human Biology: Race and Gender, Brown University, Providence.

Martin, Del, and Phyllis Lyon. 1991. *Lesbian/Woman.* Volcano, CA: Volcano Press.

Money, John. 1991. Biographies of gender and hermaphroditism in paired comparisons. In *The Handbook of Sexology,* edited by J. Money and H. Musaph. New York: Elsevier.

Morris, John McL. 1957. Intersexuality. *Journal of the American Medical Association* 163 (7): 538–542.

Nanda, Sarena. 1994. Hijras: An Alternative Sex and Gender Role in India. In *Third Sex, Third Gender: Beyond Sexual Dimorphism in Culture and History,* edited by G. Herdt. New York: Zone Books, pp. 373–418.

Natarajan, Anita. 1996. Medical ethics and truth-telling in the case of androgen insensitivity syndrome. *Canadian Medical Association Journal* 154: 568–570.

Pool, Robert E. 1994. *Eve's Rib: The Biological Roots of Sex Differences.* New York: Crown Publishers.

Roscoe, Will. 1991. *The Zuni Man-Woman.* Albuquerque: University of New Mexico Press.

Slijper, F.M.E., S.L.S. Drop, J.C. Molenaar, and R.J. Scholtmeijer. 1994. Neonates with abnormal genital development assigned the female sex: Parent counseling. *Journal of Sex Education and Therapy* 20 (1): 9–17.

Vance, Carol S. 1991. Anthropology rediscovers sexuality: A theoretical comment. *Social Science and Medicine* 33: 875–884.

Walker, Alice. 1992. *Possessing the Secret of Joy.* New York: Simon and Schuster.

 ## QUESTIONS FOR CRITICAL THINKING

Reading 58

1. Chase discusses the impact of maintaining the false notion of the existence of only two sexes on her life as well as the lives of other intersex individuals. Given the devastation she and others experience, what do you see as the responsibility of medical professionals to alter their practices with regard to sex assignment of intersex children at birth?

2. Chase's experiences challenge the notion that being male or female is a biological fact. How do you answer her question "How do you know you are a woman or a man?"

3. Currently, the medical profession has more power than parents in determining the sex of intersex children. Why do you think this is? What do you see as the likelihood of this practice changing?

PART IV
Resistance and Social Change

INTRODUCTION

Throughout this text we have explored how elements of the social structure construct categories of difference with regard to race, class, gender, and sexuality and transform them into systems of oppression and privilege. In Part I we examined why such categories are constructed as well as the social factors involved in the process of transforming them into systems of inequality. In Part II we explored the significance of social institutions in maintaining these systems of inequality as systems of oppression and privilege. The readings in Part III provided us with personal representations illustrating how such systems impact daily lives. The readings in each of the preceding sections have prepared us for the task of this one—to understand the ways in which we can work toward the transformation of systems of oppression and privilege into a system of equal access to opportunity.

Beginning the work of transforming systems of oppression and privilege is often difficult. When we first become aware of systems of inequality, many of us are overwhelmed and do not have a clear idea of where to begin to bring about positive social change. Furthermore, as we discuss later in this section, many of us are motivated to work for social change because of the pain that we or someone close to us experienced as a result of systems of oppression. Because of our proximity to the injustice we may not feel physically or emotionally capable of challenging "the system."

Starting to transform systems of oppression and privilege is also hindered by the role of social institutions in maintaining these systems. As discussed in Part II, social institutions work to maintain systems of inequality based on ideologies that endorse and justify the interests of the dominant group. As a result, they are not likely to be open to challenges. Actions to bring about positive social change are therefore met with resistance on the parts of these institutions and discredited, if not omitted from history all together. For example, in April 1989 in Beijing, China, a massive demonstration of Chinese students for democratic reform began on Tiananmen Square. Joined by workers, intellectuals, and civil servants until over one million people filled the square, the protestors demanded that the leadership of the country resign. The government responded on June 3 and 4 with troops and tanks, killing thousands to quell a "counter-revolutionary rebellion." Government reaction to these protests has been followed by silence. There is no public discussion of the incident in China, except for occasional government accounts defending the actions of the military. Editors of newspapers in China delete even vague references to the protests. Groups and individuals protesting injustice in the United States have been met with similar acts of resistance (e.g., the WTO protests in Seattle[1]; the use of the USA PATRIOT Act to limit actions of anti-war protestors[2]) and attempts to render their political activism invisible (e.g., the lack of media coverage of peace rallies and antiwar protests since September 11[3]). Faced with the possibility of opposition and, moreover, lacking an awareness of previous efforts to transform systems of oppression and privilege, those who would begin work toward positive social change face major difficulty.

Finally, beginning the work of transforming systems of oppression and privilege into systems of equal access to opportunity is often difficult because we underestimate our ability to impact these systems. In essence, we doubt that we will be able to bring about change. However, as Margaret Mead said, "Never doubt that a small group of thoughtful, committed citizens can change the world; indeed, it's the only thing that ever has." Efforts to create social equality are often begun by everyday individuals.

The readings in this section examine the various ways individuals and groups have worked to create positive social change. Those who bring about social change come from all walks of life. As you read these selections, consider the systems of oppression and privilege that you would like to see change—and the ways in which you would like to go about working for this change. Create your own image of what a system of equal access to opportunity would look like.

Before beginning this process it is important to remember that difference isn't always negative. On the contrary, the preservation of a distinct identity is often central to working toward positive social change. Differences are not problematic; rather, as stated in Part I of this text, it is when the meanings and values applied to these *differences* transform them into systems of *inequality* that such constructs become problematic. As we work to find solutions to inequality, it is important that we seek not to eliminate difference but rather to transform the ways in which difference has been established into a system where each individual is seen as valuable.

WHAT IS SOCIAL CHANGE?

In order to transform systems of oppression and privilege into systems of equality, it is important that we understand the concept of social change. **Social change**—fundamental alterations in the patterns of culture, structure, and social behavior over time—is always occurring. It can result from a variety of actions and can be inspired from a number of motivations. From

---

[1]For a discussion of the WTO protests, see Cockburn, Alexander, and Jeffrey St. Clair. 2000. *Five Days That Shook the World: Seattle and Beyond.* New York: Verso.
[2]For more information on the USA PATRIOT Act, go to http://www.aclu.org/keep-america-safe-free.
[3]*The Nation,* Volume 33(22), December 31, 2001, p. 8.

individual actions to collective behavior, efforts and movements to transform systems of oppression and privilege work toward **positive social change**—changing patterns of the social structure and social behavior in an effort to reduce oppression and increase inclusion for all members of society.

Such efforts often involve conflicts in **ideology.** As we discussed in Part II, the maintenance of systems of oppression depends on the presence of ideologies that provide the basis of inequality. The clash in ideology that results from challenging beliefs, values, and attitudes that see members of certain groups as inferior or superior is generally seen as disruptive to the social order and may result in strong reactions on the part of those interested in maintaining the power of the dominant group. For example, on November 14, 1960, Ruby Bridges became the first black child to enter an all-white school in the history of the U.S. South. Although only in first grade and six years old, she was an agent for social change—and also represented a clash in ideology with the racially segregated South. As a result, she needed to be escorted by U.S. marshals on the first day of school and spent her first year in that school in a class of one because all the parents pulled their children out of school to protest the integration. Although clashes in ideology such as this may act as deterrents for those wanting to transform systems of oppression, the reality that dominant ideologies don't always win out in the end can also serve as encouragement.

WHAT ARE THE GOALS OF SOCIAL CHANGE?

When seeking positive social change, we must have a clear idea of the goals we are working toward. Just as there are divergent approaches to positive social change, there are also many goals. The general goal in seeking to transform systems of oppression is to develop systems in which all have access to important resources and none are advantaged at the expense of others, but specific goals of positive social change are defined by those who seek it. As you read this section, consider the injustices that have come to matter to you and imagine how you would like to see these transformed.

For some, discussions of social change are centered around a goal of creating a society based on a system of **social justice**—a system in which each member of society has the opportunity and power to fully participate in the social system. As mentioned in Part I, in the United States we have a system based on a **civil rights** framework. Such a framework is based on the concept of "majority rule," where the will of the "majority" becomes the will for all, with some people inevitably losing. A *social justice* framework stands in contrast to such a system and provides the opportunity for each member of society to benefit. It relies on three principles.

The first principle is that *people have options.* These options relate to having access to resources and can include opportunity for work, adequate healthcare, access to housing, freedom from harassment or discrimination, and so on. In some ways, the United States can be seen as meeting this principle in that with our vast resources it appears that we all have the *option* of access to these resources. For example, with regard to opportunity for work and career choice, many of us who grew up in the United States were presented with the notion that anyone has the option to be president. You do not need to be of any particular race, class, gender, or sexuality in order to have this option.

The second principle of a social justice framework is that *people are aware of their options.* In such a framework we need to be made aware of our opportunities to access important resources such as attending college, applying for jobs, purchasing property, and receiving adequate healthcare. Considering again the opportunity to become president, many of us who grew up in the United States heard that this was a possibility and thus we were aware of this option. Indeed, we often heard such messages along with Horatio Alger stories and notions of achieving the "American dream." Many of these messages were rooted in the assumption that the United States is a **meritocracy**—a system in which people's success is a result of their talents, abilities, and efforts. However, the notion of a meritocracy ignores the advantages that are given to some and denied to others. In a socially just system, people are aware of their options and their opportunities and are not hindered by unfair disadvantages.

The third and final principle of a socially just system is that *people have the power to act on their options.* This is where the system of civil rights—and thus the system of the United States—departs from that of a social justice framework. As noted above, the assumption of a meritocracy sits at the core of the American dream. A system of oppression and privilege that derives from the social construction of difference results in an unequal distribution of power. Because of this unequal distribution, it is not our individual talents, abilities and efforts that lead to our ability to succeed but our access to power. Power, typically viewed as an ability to control people or things, can be defined in many ways. In the case of running for president, one's power directly relates to the amount of money one is able to raise to run a successful campaign. For example, according to the *United States Federal Elections Commission* in 2008, the two major presidential candidates for president (Obama and McCain) spent in excess of $700 million and $200 million respectively. Although many view Obama's win of the 2008 election as evidence that anyone can become president and the end of racial barriers, from our discussion in Part II of the distribution of income and wealth in the United States, it is obvious that there are very few people, particularly African Americans and other people of color, who possess or have access to the financial resources and other forms of power to be able to act on their option to become president. Considering this, it is clear that a civil rights system departs from one based on social justice.

A social justice framework is one of many possibilities in framing our efforts to transform systems of oppression and privilege. Another possible framework relies on **empowerment**—a process of defining ourselves rather than being defined by others. In a system based on empowerment, those who have experienced oppression are given the opportunity to create their own power in improving their own circumstances. Whatever the specific goal each of us sets our sights on, we need to establish our own strategies for working toward that goal. Many of the readings in this section offer insights that may be useful in establishing these strategies. These strategies include the importance of identity and empowerment, as discussed by Yen Le Espiritu in the article "Cultural Resistance" (Reading 60); efforts to resist corporate power, as illustrated through Anmol Chadda's discussion of opposing Wal-Mart in the article "Good for the 'Hood?" (Reading 61); the necessity of expanding our understanding of structural inequality, as in Robert Bullard's exploration of the impact of environmental racism in "Dismantling Environmental Racism in the USA (Reading 63); and the challenges to building inclusive movements as explained by Daisy Hernández and Pandora Leong in "Feminisms Future" (Reading 64). These examples are intended to broaden our understanding of how to build effective movements in order to bring about positive social change.

WHAT MOTIVATES WORK FOR SOCIAL CHANGE?

Much work has been done in a variety of contexts to bring about positive social change to transform systems of oppression and privilege. The factors that precipitate such work come from a variety of sources. Work for positive social change can be motivated by personal experiences; at other times it is motivated by dissatisfaction with social systems on the part of large groups of people. In order to understand how to create positive social change, it is important to understand what has motivated others to become involved in such efforts.

Motivation for working toward positive social change can come from factors related to the social system. For example, according to Neil Smelser (1962), when important aspects of a social system appear to be "out of joint," such as when standards of living are not what people expect them to be, people may experience **structural strain.** As an illustration, consider the notion that the United States is thought to be an affluent society. Whether our economy is in a state of recession or boom, poverty rates continue to be quite high. Further, as illustrated in Part I, such poverty rates are arbitrarily determined and don't necessarily reflect the experience of poverty accurately. According to Smelser, as the strain from this situation accumulates over time, individuals become motivated to use courses of action not defined by existing institutional arrangements. As people begin to see the strain as a problem in need of a solution, they develop shared ideas about how they should respond to it.

At other times, motivation for working toward positive social change requires precipitating factors, such as the recent mobilization on many campuses and in numerous cities to work for peace in response to the war in Iraq and Afghanistan. Other precipitating factors can be hearing stories of social injustice experienced on the part of individuals. For example, there has recently been increasing dialogue and organization around the need for the enactment of hate crimes legislation in the United States. Much of the motivation for working on such legislation arose from the brutal killings of James Byrd,[4] Matthew Shepard,[5] Billy Jack Gaither,[6] Juana Vega,[7] and Scotty Joe Weaver.[8] Indeed, increasing incidents of anti-gay hate crimes have been reported since the narrow passage of Proposition 8 in California, an anti-gay piece of legislation that provides that only marriage between a man and a woman is valid or recognized in California. Overall, the FBI reported a 1 percent decline in hate crimes in the United State in 2008—but a 6 percent increase in hate crimes against gay, lesbian, and transgender people. Acts of brutality such as these, motivated by hatred for someone seen as different or "other," have motivated individuals, organizations, and government

---

[4]James Byrd, 49, was beaten unconscious, then dragged by a chain from the back of a pickup truck to his death after accepting a ride from three white men in Jasper, Texas, in June, 1998. One of the men, John William King, was found guilty and given the death penalty for his role in the killing. Another man, Lawrence Brewer, was also found guilty and sentenced to death. The third suspect, Shawn Berry, was sentenced to life in prison. Byrd's body was dismembered in the assault and many of his body parts were found about a mile from his torso. When he was found, his body was so badly disfigured that Byrd had to be identified by fingerprints.

[5]Matthew Shepard, a University of Wyoming student, was lured from a bar and attacked by two men, allegedly because they presumed he was gay. He was struck 18 times in the head with a pistol and left to die on a fence outside Laramie in October, 1998. He was found unconscious 18 hours after he was kidnapped and died five days later. One of his attackers, Russell Henderson, was sentenced to two consecutive life sentences after pleading guilty. The other man accused in the murder, Aaron McKinney, was sentenced to life without parole.

[6]The body of Billy Jack Gaither, a 39-year-old textile worker, was found in rural Sylacauga, Alabama, some 40 miles southeast of Birmingham on February 20, 1999. Two men, Steven Eric Mullins and Charles Monroe Butler, Jr., confessed to the killing in early March after waiving their right to counsel. After bludgeoning Gaither with an axe handle, the men burned the victim's remains. They then drove his car to a deserted location and burned it as well.

[7]Juana Vega was murdered in November 2001 by Pablo Parrilla, the brother of her partner. Upset about his sister's relationship with a woman, he shot Vega five times and then repeatedly hit her with the gun and kicked her motionless body. Parrilla confessed to the killing and, following a seven-day trial, a jury found him guilty. He was sentenced to life imprisonment with extended supervision eligibility after forty-five years. Parrilla has appealed this decision.

[8]The severely burned and decomposed body of Scotty Joe Weaver was found in July 2004 by a man driving an all-terrain vehicle in Minnette, Alabama. Christopher Gaines, 20; Nichole Kelsay, 18; and Robert Porter, 18, were arrested on July 24 and charged with capital murder, according to the Associated Press. Police say they robbed Weaver of $65.00 to $85.00 and then beat, cut, and strangled him before setting him on fire. The district attorney argues that Weaver's identity as a gay man played a key role in the killing.

officials to work to enact legislation to reduce the likelihood that hate crimes will continue to occur.

Whether the motivation for working toward positive social change comes from witnessing inconsistencies between structural values, hearing stories of violence committed by those who hate, our own personal experiences with inequality, or some other source, taking on the challenge of working to improve our social environment does not occur unless we can imagine a reality that differs from what already exists. Returning to Part I, one of the fundamental aspects of critical thinking is the ability to imagine alternative ways of thinking. For example, if children experienced an inclusive representation of history, how might that positively impact their perceptions of their own race as well as those of others? What lasting impact might that have on constructions of race and the interactions of those who identify as belonging to different race categories? Critical thinking is a fundamental tool for those desiring to create positive social change. Imagining alternatives to the current social order can provide us not only with the motivation to work for positive social change, but also with a goal and some strategies for achieving that goal.

WHO CREATES POSITIVE SOCIAL CHANGE?

When we think of positive social change, we often think of large **social movements**—sustained, organized collective effort. In addition, we tend to think of those who work toward such change as being charismatic leaders with large groups of followers. Thus, if asked who were great makers of social justice, we may mention names such as Martin Luther King, Malcolm X, Emma Goldman, Ghandi, Cesar Chavez, and Jane Addams. Moreover, many of us may imagine activists as fitting a "radical" image that we don't see ourselves fitting into. In any event, we rarely identify ourselves when describing agents of change.

Although it is true that a great deal of the positive social change that has occurred in our society has involved the organization of movements and the participation of great leaders, the earlier example of Ruby Bridges illustrates that such social transformation has also involved the actions of a wide array of individuals coming from all walks of life. Thus, there is no "model" activist. An activist can be anyone with the motivation and ideas of how to transform a situation of inequality.

For example, in 1996 Kelli Peterson, a Salt Lake City East High School student, created a group that provided safe space for support and dialogue for lesbian, gay, and bisexual students and their allies at her school. Many studies and reports have indicated the need for such a group. For example, As Miceli explained in Part II in "Schools and the Social Control of Sexuality (Reading 25), a study conducted by the Gay, Lesbian, Straight Education Network (GLSEN) found that

84 percent of LGBT students reported that they have been verbally harassed; 82.9 percent stated that teachers or administrators rarely, if ever, intervened when they witnessed homophobic comments; 55 percent of transgender students reported being physically harassed because of their gender identity; 41 percent of lesbian, gay and bisexual students said that they had been physically harassed because of their sexual orientation; and 64.3 percent of LGBT students reported that, because of their sexual orientation, they felt unsafe at school.

When Kelli attempted to establish a gay/straight alliance, the School Board voted to ban all noncurricular clubs rather than allow the alliance to be formed. Through her commitment and motivation, however, she worked to organize students, faculty, and community members to overturn this decision. The gay/straight alliance now meets regularly at Salt Lake City East High School, offering a safer environment for lesbian, gay, bisexual, and transgender students and their allies.

Just as each of us participates in constructing categories of difference and systems of oppression and privilege, we can also participate in transforming them into systems of equality. Once we locate our source of motivation and establish a new vision of what is possible, we are well on our way toward creating this change.

WHERE DOES POSITIVE SOCIAL CHANGE OCCUR?

Just as a vast array of social activists and endless contributing factors transform categories of difference, there are also a large number of contexts within which we can enact positive social change. Further, as categories of difference are constructed and transformed into systems of inequality in a variety of contexts—institutional, interpersonal, and internal—so too can we work to transform systems of oppression in all contexts.

The first site of working toward positive social change is often the internal context—within ourselves. We are able to begin this work once we are able to transform how we view ourselves and our memberships within a system of oppression. To be effective agents for social change, we often must transform the negative perceptions we have of ourselves before we are able to effectively work at transforming systems of oppression in other contexts. This often involves a transformation of identity through the restoration of dignity and overcoming a previously stigmatized status.

Transforming systems of oppression within ourselves requires that we examine not only our own internalized oppression but also how we have internalized oppressive attitudes about others. One of the reasons systems of oppression persist is that individuals in those systems, regardless of their location in them, internalize the ideas of the dominant group. As Collins notes in "Toward a New Vision" (Reading 59), we often fail to see how our own ideas and behaviors perpetuate someone else's subjugation. She quotes Audre Lorde as saying:

> The true focus of revolutionary change is never merely the oppressive situations which we seek to escape but that piece of the oppressor which is planted deep within each of us (1984, p. 123).

As this quote illustrates, if we desire to engender positive social change, we need first to examine not only the ideas we have internalized that oppress ourselves but also those notions that perpetuate the oppression of others.

Transformations of systems of oppression and privilege can also occur in interpersonal contexts. Indeed, it is at this level that a great deal of positive social change begins. Here we can often use the dynamics of our interpersonal relationships as a source of leverage in seeking to transform inequality. Love between family members, commitment between spouses/partners, philosophical or religious alliances between members of communities, political coalitions between members of an organization, and so on, can all provide a foundation that makes challenges regarding oppressive or discriminatory behavior more likely to be heard and seen as valid.

We can also seek to transform systems of oppression and privilege within institutional contexts. This can involve seeking to transform the institution from within, with members of the institution using their power to create change in individuals and policies. For example, a teacher can use her or his position within the institution to change students through using a curriculum that is inclusive and focuses on transformation rather than perpetuation of systems of oppression. Additionally, a social scientist can use knowledge and skills as a researcher and status as a member of an academic institution to demonstrate the importance of transforming difference within other institutions. Further, institutions can establish policies and procedures that set precedents for the more inclusive treatment of marginalized groups. For example, when President Harry S. Truman officially desegregated the military in 1948, he helped to establish a precedent for future inclusion of blacks and African Americans in the United States.

Transforming systems of oppression and privilege within institutional contexts also involves individuals outside the institutions who use a variety of means to pressure it to change. The use of methods such as protests, boycotts (withdrawal of support, usually through money), and informing the public of the institution's discriminatory policies and practices have been very effective in bringing about change within these contexts.

It is important to note here, however, that institutions in the United States are generally organized around systems of oppression and privilege, as the readings in this text have made clear. As a result, we are often limited in the amount of change that can occur within these structures. For example, a woman who works in a large corporation that is dominated by males may risk loss of advancement, if not job security, if she challenges sexist hiring and operating practices of the institution. In addition, we should not expect that positive change will result merely because members of marginalized groups are present in powerful positions within these organizations. The success of marginalized *individuals* within an organization should not be assumed to reflect a positive change in institutional policies toward that *group.* We often assume that gender inequality will cease to exist in the workplace as more women get positions of prestige and authority. As illustrated in Part II, however, social policies that ignore the patriarchal structure on which they are built and assume that institutional changes will occur on the individual level will inevitably fail. These failures, in turn, will be blamed on the subordinated individual rather than on the social structure itself.

Regardless of the context within which we focus our efforts to generate positive social change, such change is possible from a variety of starting points. As you read this section, take note of the strategies and tools used and think critically about the possibilities that they reveal for you to transform systems of oppression and privilege in your own social world.

STRATEGIES: THE IMPORTANCE OF COALITION

As the previous discussion indicates, there is a variety of ways in which we can work to transform systems of oppression and privilege. However, it is difficult, and perhaps dangerous, to try to discern which is the *best* strategy. Indeed, such debates over strategies for generating positive social change have often stood in the way of creating any change at all and have generally only served to perpetuate inequality. However, it is important to note here that, regardless of the strategies we choose to use in the formation of positive social change, it is important to build coalitions and work across categories of difference.

Throughout this text the connections between forms of oppression have been made clear. Systems of oppression share similarities in how they are established and maintained as well as in their effect. Thus, if we seek to transform such systems we need to examine their foundations and the underlying aspects of the social structure that serve to perpetuate them. Such a *system*-rather than *issue*-based focus not only enables us to build coalitions but *requires* us to do so.

As Collins notes in "Toward a New Vision" (Reading 59), we often get caught up in asserting that there is one type of oppression that is most important and all others, as a result, become less important. As mentioned earlier, such a debate is not only endless, but is also likely to defeat all efforts to transform systems of oppression and privilege. Rather than focusing on ranking oppressions, Collins argues, we need to focus on how systems of stratification interconnect. As we discussed in Parts I and II, Collins sees these systems as operating within a matrix of domination. Significant problems occur when we miss these parallels and interconnections. Understanding the interconnections among various forms of oppression will help us to forge stronger alliances and coalitions. In addition, it is important that we understand the ideological foundations shared by various forms of stratification. We cannot hope to eradicate one form of inequality if others remain intact. While these alliances and coalitions may be difficult to develop and maintain, they are necessary if we are to eradicate all forms of domination.

FURTHER BARRIERS TO CREATING POSITIVE SOCIAL CHANGE

While coalition building presents an effective strategy for transforming categories of difference, it also can present a variety of barriers, institutional as well as personal, to bringing about positive social change. In addition to these barriers, we may face other obstacles in both interpersonal and institutional contexts.

Social control mechanisms, which reward conformity and punish or discourage nonconformity, are effective means of regulating the behavior of societal members. These mechanisms also create barriers to transforming systems of oppression by thwarting efforts to bring about positive social change. Anne Wilson Schaef (1981) offers an example of one such mechanism. Focusing on the social control of women, she uses the term *stoppers* to refer to anything that keeps women where the dominant group wants them to be. People seeking to create positive social change often face such stoppers regardless of the form of oppression that they may be seeking to transform. For example, heterosexual men who challenge other men on their sexism may experience challenges to their masculinity or have their heterosexuality called into question by other men. Women who speak out against sexism risk being called lesbians or facing physical violence. People of color who speak out about racism in their workplace face accusations of being "too angry" or "having an agenda." People who speak out against the war risk being called "un-American" or having their civil liberties curtailed.[9]

Stoppers also exist within institutional contexts and can have a more severe impact than those that occur on an individual level. As mentioned at the beginning of this essay, efforts to transform systems of oppression and privilege are often met with resistance on the part of institutions. For

---

[9]Armed government agents detained Nancy Oden, Green Party USA coordinating committee member, on November 1, 2001, at Bangor International Airport in Bangor, Maine, as she attempted to board an American Airlines flight to Chicago. Her name had been flagged by airport computers due to the Green Party's opposition to the war in Afghanistan.

example, the social institution of the state may enact policies seeking to repress the efforts of those working to transform systems of oppression and privilege. The experiences of political prisoners, including Angela Davis[10] and Leonard Peltier,[11] offer clear examples of the ways in which institutions may work to prevent the transformation of systems of oppression.

Again, to effectively transform systems of oppression and privilege it is important to be aware of individual as well as institutional barriers. Having this awareness will enable us to create effective strategies for moving beyond them.

CONCLUSION

Despite the barriers that we face when seeking to transform systems of oppression and privilege, opportunities for bringing about such change continually present themselves. As mentioned earlier, there is no single cause for inequality, and thus there is no single solution. Thinking critically about categories of difference and structures of inequality can present us with endless options for generating positive social change. By challenging our assumptions and being aware of our own standpoint, we can become more aware of how our own ideas perpetuate someone else's subjugation. By imagining alternative ways of constructing our social world, we are able to establish goals for our social action. Finally, by employing a reflexive analysis we are able to challenge dominant ideas and question rigid belief systems. Such questions and challenges will provide a good foundation for creating a structure where each individual is seen as valuable. As you read the selections in the final chapters of this text, take note of how your process of critical thinking helps you to become aware of your own goals for transforming systems of oppression and privilege.

---

[10]Currently a professor of history at the University of California–Santa Cruz, Davis was placed on the FBI's Ten Most Wanted list in 1970, after she was accused of planning the kidnapping of three imprisoned African American activists in San Quentin and supplying the gun that killed four people during the incident. She was incarcerated on charges of murder, kidnapping, and conspiracy, and her case was taken up by supporters across the country. In 1972, after 18 months in jail, she was tried and acquitted of all crimes.

[11]On June 26, 1975, two FBI agents and one Native American were killed in a shootout on the Pine Ridge Indian Reservation. This firefight led to what many see as the false incarceration of American Indian Movement member Leonard Peltier. Now 54 years old, Peltier is serving his 24th year of incarceration in Leavenworth Penitentiary in Kansas. He stands accused of the murders of the two FBI agents. To date, no credible evidence has been presented to suggest that he is guilty. All others who have been brought to trial regarding this incident were acquitted on the basis of self-defense.

REFERENCES

Lorde, Audre. 1984. *Sister Outsider.* Trumansberg, NY: The Crossing Press.

Schaef, Anne Wilson. 1981. *Women's Reality: An Emerging Female System in the White Male Society.* Minneapolis, MN: Winston Press.

Smelser, Neil J. 1962. *Theory of Collective Behavior.* New York: Free Press.

Reading 59

TOWARD A NEW VISION
Race, Class, and Gender as Categories of Analysis and Connection

PATRICIA HILL COLLINS

The true focus of revolutionary change is never merely the oppressive situations which we seek to escape, but that piece of the oppressor which is planted deep within each of us.

—AUDRE LORDE, SISTER OUTSIDER, 123

A udre Lorde's statement raises a troublesome issue for scholars and activists working for social change. While many of us have little difficulty assessing our own victimization within some major system of oppression, whether it be by race, social class, religion, sexual orientation, ethnicity, age or gender, we typically fail to see how our thoughts and actions uphold someone else's subordination. Thus, white feminists routinely point with confidence to their oppression as women but resist seeing how much their white skin privileges them. African-Americans who possess eloquent analyses of racism often persist in viewing poor white women as symbols of white power. The radical left fares little better. "If only people of color and women could see their true class interests," they argue, "class solidarity would eliminate racism and sexism." In essence, each group identifies the type of oppression with which it feels most comfortable as being fundamental and classifies all other types as being of lesser importance.

Oppression is full of such contradictions. Errors in political judgment that we make concerning how we teach our courses, what we tell our children, and which organizations are worthy of our time, talents and financial support flow smoothly from errors in theoretical analysis about the nature of oppression and activism. Once we realize that there are few pure victims or oppressors, and that each one of us derives varying amounts of penalty and privilege from the multiple systems of oppression that frame our lives, then we will be in a position to see the need for new ways of thought and action.

In *Race, Sex, & Class*, 1, no. 1, Fall 1993. Reprinted by permission of the author.

To get at that "piece of the oppressor which is planted deep within each of us," we need at least two things. First, we need new visions of what oppression is, new categories of analysis that are inclusive of race, class, and gender as distinctive yet interlocking structures of oppression. Adhering to a stance of comparing and ranking oppressions—the proverbial, "I'm more oppressed than you"—locks us all into a dangerous dance of competing for attention, resources, and theoretical supremacy. Instead, I suggest that we examine our different experiences within the more fundamental relationship of damnation and subordination. To focus on the particular arrangements that race or class or gender takes in our time and place without seeing these structures as sometimes parallel and sometimes interlocking dimensions of the more fundamental relationship of domination and subordination may temporarily ease our consciences. But while such thinking may lead to short-term social reforms, it is simply inadequate for the task of bringing about long-term social transformation.

While race, class and gender as categories of analysis are essential in helping us understand the structural bases of domination and subordination, new ways of thinking that are not accompanied by new ways of acting offer incomplete prospects for change. To get at that "piece of the oppressor which is planted deep within each of us," we also need to change our daily behavior. Currently, we are all enmeshed in a complex web of problematic relationships that grant our mirror images full human subjectivity while stereotyping and objectifying those most different than ourselves. We often assume that the people we work with, teach, send our children to school with, and sit next to . . . will act and feel in prescribed ways because they belong to given race, social class or gender categories. These judgments by category must be replaced with fully human relationships that transcend the legitimate differences created by race, class and gender as categories of analysis. We require new categories of connection, new visions of what our relationships with one another can be. . . .

[This discussion] addresses this need for new patterns of thought and action. I focus on two basic questions. First, how can we reconceptualize race, class and gender as categories of analysis? Second, how can we transcend the barriers created by our experiences with race, class and gender oppression in order to build the types of coalitions essential for social exchange? To address these questions I contend that we must acquire both new theories of how race, class and gender have shaped the experiences not just of women of color, but of all groups. Moreover, we must see the connections between the categories of analysis and the personal issues in our every-day lives, particularly our scholarship, our teaching and our relationships with our colleagues and students. As Audre Lorde points out, change starts with self, and relationships that we have with those around us must always be the primary site for social change.

HOW CAN WE RECONCEPTUALIZE RACE, CLASS
AND GENDER AS CATEGORIES OF *ANALYSIS*?

To me, we must shift our discourse away from additive analyses of oppression (Spelman, 1982; Collins, 1989). Such approaches are typically based on two key premises. First, they depend on either/or, dichotomous thinking. Persons, things and ideas are conceptualized in terms of their opposites. For example, Black/White, man/woman, thought/feeling, and fact/opinion are defined in oppositional terms. Thought and feeling are not seen as two different and interconnected ways of approaching truth that can coexist in scholarship and teaching. Instead, feeling is defined as antithetical to reason, as its opposite. In spite of the fact that we all have "both/and" identities (I am both a college professor and a mother—I don't stop being a mother when I drop my child off at school, or forget everything I learned while scrubbing the toilet), we persist in trying to classify each other in either/or categories. I live each day as an African-American woman—a race/gender specific experience. And I am not alone. Everyone has a race/gender/class specific identity. Either/or, dichotomous thinking is especially troublesome when applied to theories of oppression because every individual must be classified as being either oppressed or not oppressed. The both/and position of simultaneously being oppressed and oppressor becomes conceptually impossible.

A second premise of additive analyses of oppression is that these dichotomous differences must be ranked. One side of the dichotomy is typically labeled dominant and the other subordinate. Thus, Whites rule Blacks, men are deemed superior to women, and reason is seen as being preferable to emotion. Applying this premise to discussions of oppression leads to the assumption that oppression can be quantified, and that some groups are oppressed more than others. I am frequently asked, "Which has been most oppressive to you, your status as a Black person or your status as a woman?" What I am really being asked to do is divide myself into little boxes and rank my various statuses. If I experience oppression as a both/and phenomenon, why should I analyze it any differently?

Additive analyses of oppression rest squarely on the twin pillars of either/or thinking and the necessity to quantify and rank all relationships in order to know where one stands. Such approaches typically see African-American women as being more oppressed than everyone else because the majority of Black women experience the negative effects of race, class and gender oppression simultaneously. In essence, if you add together separate oppressions, you are left with a grand oppression greater than the sum of its parts.

I am not denying that specific groups experience oppression more harshly than others—lynching is certainly objectively worse than being held up as a sex object. But we must be careful not to confuse this issue of the saliency of one type of oppression in people's lives with a theoretical stance positing the interlocking nature of oppression. Race, class and gender may all structure a situation but may not be equally visible and/or important in people's self-definitions. In certain contexts, such as the antebellum American South and contemporary South America, racial oppression is more visibly salient, while in other contexts, such as Haiti, El Salvador and Nicaragua, social class oppression may be more apparent. For middle-class White women, gender may assume experiential primacy unavailable to poor Hispanic women struggling with the ongoing issues of low-paid jobs and the frustrations of the welfare bureaucracy. This recognition that one category may have salience over another for a given time and place does not minimize the theoretical importance of assuming that race, class and gender as categories of analysis structure all relationships.

In order to move toward new visions of what oppression is, I think that we need to ask new questions. How are relationships of domination and subordination structured and maintained in the American political economy? How do race, class and gender function as parallel and interlocking systems that shape this basic relationship of domination and subordination? Questions such as these promise to move us away from futile theoretical struggles concerned with ranking oppressions and towards analyses that assume race, class and gender are all present in any given setting, even if one appears more visible and salient than the others. Our task becomes redefined as one of reconceptualizing oppression by uncovering the connections among race, class and gender as categories of analysis.

1. The Institutional Dimension of Oppression

Sandra Harding's contention that gender oppression is structured along three main dimensions—the institutional, the symbolic and the individual—offers a useful model for a more comprehensive analysis encompassing race, class and gender oppression (Harding 1986). Systemic relationships of domination and subordination structured through social institutions such as schools, businesses, hospitals, the workplace and government agencies represent the institutional dimension of oppression. Racism, sexism and elitism all have concrete institutional locations. Even though the workings of the institutional dimension of oppression are often obscured with ideologies claiming equality of opportunity, in actuality, race, class and gender place Asian-American women, Native American men, White men, African-American women and other groups in distinct institutional niches with varying degrees of penalty and privilege.

Even though I realize that many . . . would not share this assumption, let us assume that the institutions of American society discriminate, whether by design or by accident. While many of us are familiar with how race, gender and class operate separately to structure inequality, I want to focus on how these three systems interlock in structuring the institutional dimension of oppression. To get at the interlocking nature of race, class and gender, I want you to think about the antebellum plantation as a guiding metaphor for a variety of American social institutions. Even though slavery is typically analyzed as a racist institution, and occasionally as a class institution, I suggest that slavery was a race, class, gender specific institution. Removing any one piece from our analysis diminishes our understanding of the true nature of relations of domination and subordination under slavery.

Slavery was a profoundly patriarchal institution. It rested on the dual tenets of White male authority and White male property, a joining of the political and the economic within the institution of the family. Heterosexism was assumed and all Whites were expected to marry. Control over affluent White women's sexuality remained key to slavery's survival because property was to be passed on to the legitimate heirs of the slave owner. Ensuring affluent White women's virginity and chastity was deeply intertwined with maintenance of property relations.

Under slavery, we see varying levels of institutional protection given to affluent White women, working class and poor White women and enslaved African women. Poor White women enjoyed few of the protections held out to their upper class sisters. Moreover, the devalued status of Black women was key in keeping all White women in their assigned places. Controlling Black women's fertility was also key to the continuation of slavery, for children born to slave mothers themselves were slaves.

African-American women shared the devalued status of chattel with their husbands, fathers and sons. Racism stripped Blacks as a group of legal rights, education and control over their own persons. African-Americans could be whipped, branded, sold, or killed, not because they were poor, or because they were women, but because they were Black. Racism ensured that Blacks would continue to serve Whites and suffer economic exploitation at the hands of all Whites.

So we have a very interesting chain of command on the plantation—the affluent White master as the reigning patriarch, his White wife helpmate to serve him, help him manage his property and bring up his heirs, his faithful servants whose production and reproduction were tied to the requirements of the capitalist political economy and largely propertyless, working class White men and women watching from afar. In essence, the foundations for the contemporary roles of elite White women, poor Black women, working class White men and a series of other groups can be seen in stark relief in this fundamental American social institution. While Blacks experienced the most harsh treatment under slavery, and thus made slavery clearly visible as a racist institution, race, class and gender interlocked in structuring slavery's systemic organization of domination and subordination.

Even today, the plantation remains a compelling metaphor for institutional oppression. Certainly the actual conditions of oppression are not as severe now as they were then. To argue, as some do, that things have not changed all that much denigrates the achievements of those who struggled for social change before us. But the basic relationships among Black men,

Black women, elite White women, elite White men, working class White men and working class White women as groups remain essentially intact.

A brief analysis of key American social institutions most controlled by elite White men should convince us of the interlocking nature of race, class and gender in structuring the institutional dimension of oppression. For example, if you are from an American college or university, is your campus a modern plantation? Who controls your university's political economy? Are elite White men overrepresented among the upper administrators and trustees controlling your university's finances and policies? Are elite White men being joined by growing numbers of elite White women helpmates? What kinds of people are in your classrooms grooming the next generation who will occupy these and other decision-making positions? Who are the support staff that produce the mass mailings, order the supplies, fix the leaky pipes? Do African-Americans, Hispanics or other people of color form the majority of the invisible workers who feed you, wash your dishes, and clean up your offices and libraries after everyone else has gone home?

If your college is anything like mine, you know the answers to these questions. You may be affiliated with an institution that has Hispanic women as vice-presidents for finance, or substantial numbers of Black men among the faculty. If so, you are fortunate. Much more typical are colleges where a modified version of the plantation as a metaphor for the institutional dimension of oppression survives.

2. The Symbolic Dimension of Oppression

Widespread, societally sanctioned ideologies used to justify relations of domination and subordination comprise the symbolic dimension of oppression. Central to this process is the use of stereotypical or controlling images of diverse race, class and gender groups. In order to assess the power of this dimension of oppression, I want you to make a list, either on paper or in your head, of "masculine" and "feminine" characteristics. If your list is anything like that compiled by most people, it reflects some variation of the following:

Masculine	*Feminine*
aggressive	passive
leader	follower
rational	emotional
strong	weak
intellectual	physical

Not only does this list reflect either/or dichotomous thinking and the need to rank both sides of the dichotomy, but ask yourself exactly which men and women you had in mind when compiling these characteristics. This list applies almost exclusively to middle class White men and women. The allegedly "masculine" qualities that you probably listed are only acceptable when exhibited by elite White men, or when used by Black and Hispanic men against each other or against women of color. Aggressive Black and Hispanic men are seen as dangerous, not powerful, and are often penalized when they exhibit any of the allegedly "masculine" characteristics. Working class and poor White men fare slightly better and are also denied the allegedly "masculine" symbols of leadership, intellectual competence, and human rationality. Women of color and working class and poor White women are also not represented on this list, for they have never had the luxury of being "ladies." What appear to be universal categories representing all men and women instead are unmasked as being applicable to only a small group.

It is important to see how the symbolic images applied to different race, class and gender groups interact in maintaining systems of domination and subordination. If I were to ask you to repeat the same assignment, only this time, by making separate lists for Black men, Black women, Hispanic women and Hispanic men, I suspect that your gender symbolism would be quite different. In comparing all of the lists, you might begin to see the interdependence of symbols applied to all groups. For example, the elevated images of White womanhood need devalued images of Black womanhood in order to maintain credibility.

While the above exercise reveals the interlocking nature of race, class and gender in structuring the symbolic dimension of oppression, part of its importance lies in demonstrating how race, class and gender pervade a wide range of what appears to be universal language. Attending to diversity in our scholarship, in our teaching, and in our daily lives provides a new angle of vision on interpretations of reality thought to be natural, normal and "true." Moreover, viewing images of masculinity and femininity as universal gender symbolism, rather than as symbolic images that are race, class and gender specific, renders the experiences of people of color and of nonprivileged White women and men invisible. One way to dehumanize an individual or group is to deny the reality of their experiences. So when we refuse to deal with race or class because they do not appear to be directly relevant to gender, we are actually becoming part of someone else's problem.

Assuming that everyone is affected differently by the same interlocking set of symbolic images allows us to move forward toward new analyses. Women of color and White women have different relations to White male authority and this difference explains the distinct gender symbolism applied to both groups. Black women encounter controlling images such as the mammy, the matriarch, the mule and the whore, that encourage others to reject us as fully human people. Ironically, the negative nature of these images simultaneously encourages us to reject them. In contrast, White women are offered seductive images, those that promise to reward them for supporting the status quo. And yet seductive images can be equally controlling. Consider, for example, the views of Nancy White, a 73-year-old Black woman, concerning images of rejection and seduction:

> My mother used to say that the black woman is the white man's
> mule and the white woman is his dog. Now, she said that to say

this: we do the heavy work and get beat whether we do it well or not. But the white woman is closer to the master and he pats them on the head and lets them sleep in the house, but he ain't gon' treat neither one like he was dealing with a person. (Gwaltney, 148)

Both sets of images stimulate particular political stances. By broadening the analysis beyond the confines of race, we can see the varying levels of rejection and seduction available to each of us due to our race, class and gender identity. Each of us lives with an allotted portion of institutional privilege and penalty, and with varying levels of rejection and seduction inherent in the symbolic images applied to us. This is the context in which we make our choices. Taken together, the institutional and symbolic dimensions of oppression create a structural backdrop against which all of us live our lives.

3. The Individual Dimension of Oppression

Whether we benefit or not, we all live within institutions that reproduce race, class and gender oppression. Even if we never have any contact with members of other race, class and gender groups, we all encounter images of these groups and are exposed to the symbolic meanings attached to those images. On this dimension of oppression, our individual biographies vary tremendously. As a result of our institutional and symbolic statuses, all of our choices become political acts.

Each of us must come to terms with the multiple ways in which race, class and gender as categories of analysis frame our individual biographies. I have lived my entire life as an African-American woman from a working class family and this basic fact has had a profound impact on my personal biography. Imagine how different your life might be if you had been born Black, or White, or poor, or of a different race/class/gender group than the one with which you are most familiar. The institutional treatment you would have received and the symbolic meanings attached to your very existence might differ dramatically from that you now consider to be natural, normal and part of everyday life. You might be the same, but your personal biography might have been quite different.

I believe that each of us carries around the cumulative effect of our lives within multiple structures of oppression. If you want to see how much you have been affected by this whole thing, I ask you one simple question—who are your close friends? Who are the people with whom you can share your hopes, dreams, vulnerabilities, fears and victories? Do they look like you? If they are all the same, circumstance may be the cause. For the first seven years of my life I saw only low income Black people. My friends from those years reflected the composition of my community. But now that I am an adult, can the defense of circumstance explain the patterns of people that I trust as my friends and colleagues? When given other alternatives, if my friends and colleagues reflect the homogeneity of one race, class and gender group, then these categories of analysis have indeed become barriers to connection.

I am not suggesting that people are doomed to follow the paths laid out for them by race, class and gender as categories of analysis. While these three structures certainly frame my opportunity structure, I as an individual always have the choice of accepting things as they are, or trying to change them. As Nikki Giovanni points out, "we've got to live in the real world. If we don't like the world we're living in, change it. And if we can't change it, we change ourselves. We can do something" (Tate 1983, 68). While a piece of the oppressor may be planted deep within each of us, we each have the choice of accepting that piece or challenging it as part of the "true focus of revolutionary change."

 HOW CAN WE TRANSCEND THE BARRIERS CREATED
BY OUR EXPERIENCES WITH RACE, CLASS AND
GENDER OPPRESSION IN ORDER TO BUILD
THE TYPES OF COALITIONS ESSENTIAL FOR
SOCIAL CHANGE?

Reconceptualizing oppression and seeing the barriers created by race, class and gender as interlocking categories of analysis is a vital first step. But we must transcend these barriers by moving toward race, class and gender as categories of connection, by building relationships and coalitions that will bring about social change. What are some of the issues involved in doing this?

1. Differences in Power and Privilege

First, we must recognize that our differing experiences with oppression create problems in the relationships among us. Each of us lives within a system that vests us with varying levels of power and privilege. These differences in power, whether structured along axes of race, class, gender, age or sexual orientation, frame our relationships. African-American writer June Jordan describes her discomfort on a Caribbean vacation with Olive, the Black woman who cleaned her room:

> . . . even though both "Olive" and "I" live inside a conflict neither
> one of us created, and even though both of us therefore hurt inside
> that conflict, I may be one of the monsters she needs to eliminate
> from her universe and, in a sense, she may be one of the monsters
> in mine (1985, 47).

Differences in power constrain our ability to connect with one another even when we think we are engaged in dialogue across differences. Let me give you an example. One year, the students in my course "Sociology of the Black Community" got into a heated discussion about the reasons for the upsurge of racial incidents on college campuses. Black students complained vehemently about the apathy and resistance they felt most White students expressed about examining their own racism. Mark, a White male student, found their comments particularly unsettling. After claiming that all the Black people he had ever known had expressed no such beliefs to him, he questioned how representative the viewpoints of his fellow students actually were. When pushed further, Mark revealed that he had participated in conversations over the years with the Black domestic worker employed by his family. Since she had never expressed such strong feelings about White racism, Mark was genuinely shocked by class discussions. Ask yourselves whether that domestic worker was in a position to speak freely. Would it have been wise for her to do so in a situation where the power between the two parties was so unequal?

In extreme cases, members of privileged groups can erase the very presence of the less privileged. When I first moved to Cincinnati, my family and I went on a picnic at a local park. Picnicking next to us was a family of White Appalachians. When I went to push my daughter on the swings, several of the children came over. They had missing, yellowed and broken teeth, they wore old clothing and their poverty was evident. I was shocked. Growing up in a large eastern city, I had never seen such awful poverty among Whites. The segregated neighborhoods in which I grew up made White poverty all but invisible. More importantly, the privileges attached to my newly acquired social class position allowed me to ignore and minimize the poverty among Whites that I did encounter. My reactions to those children made me realize how confining phrases such as "well, at least they're not Black," had become for me. In learning to grant human subjectivity to the Black victims of poverty, I had simultaneously learned to demand White victims of poverty. By applying categories of race to the objective conditions confronting me, I was quantifying and ranking oppressions and missing the very real suffering which, in fact, is the real issue.

One common pattern of relationships across differences in power is one that I label "voyeurism." From the perspective of the privileged, the lives of people of color, of the poor, and of women are interesting for their entertainment value. The privileged become voyeurs, passive onlookers who do not relate to the less powerful, but who are interested in seeing how the "different" live. Over the years, I have heard numerous African-American students complain about professors who never call on them except when a so-called Black issue is being discussed. The students' interest in discussing race or qualifications for doing so appear unimportant to the professor's efforts to use Black students' experiences as stories to make the material come alive for the White student audience. Asking Black students to perform on cue and provide a Black experience for their White classmates can be seen as voyeurism at its worst.

Members of subordinate groups do not willingly participate in such exchanges but often do so because members of dominant groups control the institutional and symbolic apparatuses of oppression. Racial/ethnic groups, women, and the poor have never had the luxury of being voyeurs of the lives of the privileged. Our ability to survive in hostile settings has hinged on our ability to learn intricate details about the behavior and world view of the powerful and adjust our behavior accordingly. I need only point to the difference in perception of those men and women in abusive relationships. Where men can view their girlfriends and wives as sex objects, helpmates and a collection of stereotypes categories of voyeurism—women must be attuned to every nuance of their partners' behavior. Are women "naturally" better in relating to people with more power than themselves, or have circumstances mandated that men and women develop different skills? . . .

Coming from a tradition where most relationships across difference are squarely rooted in relations of domination and subordination, we have much less experience relating to people as different but equal. The classroom is potentially one powerful and safe space where dialogues among individuals of unequal power relationships can occur. The relationship between Mark, the student in my class, and the domestic worker is typical of a whole series of relationships that people have when they relate across differences in power and privilege. The relationship among Mark and his classmates represents the power of the classroom to minimize those differences so that people of different levels of power can use race, class and gender as categories of analysis in order to generate meaningful dialogues. In this case, the classroom equalized racial difference so that Black students who normally felt silenced spoke out. White students like Mark, generally unaware of how they had been privileged by their whiteness, lost that privilege in the classroom and thus became open to genuine dialogue. . . .

2. Coalitions around Common Causes

A second issue in building relationships and coalitions essential for social change concerns knowing the real reasons for coalition. Just what brings people together? One powerful catalyst fostering group solidarity is the presence of a common enemy. African-American, Hispanic, Asian-American, and women's studies all share the common intellectual heritage of challenging what passes for certified knowledge in the academy. But politically expedient relationships and coalitions like these are fragile because, as June Jordan points out:

> It occurs to me that much organizational grief could be avoided if people understood that partnership in misery does not necessarily provide for partnership for change. When we get the monsters off our backs all of us may want to run in very different directions (1985, 47).

Sharing a common cause assists individuals and groups in maintaining relationships that transcend their differences. Building effective coalitions involves struggling to hear one another and developing empathy for each other's points of view. The coalitions that I have been involved in that lasted and that worked have been those where commitment to a specific issue mandated collaboration as the best strategy for addressing the issue at hand.

Several years ago, master degree in hand, I chose to teach in an inner-city parochial school in danger of closing. The money was awful, the conditions were poor, but the need was great. In my job, I had to work with a range of individuals who, on the surface, had very little in common. We had White nuns, Black middle class graduate students, Blacks from the "community," some of whom had been incarcerated and/or were affiliated with a range of federal anti-poverty programs. Parents formed another part of this community, Harvard faculty another, and a few well-meaning White liberals from Colorado were sprinkled in for good measure.

As you might imagine, tension was high. Initially, our differences seemed insurmountable. But as time passed, we found a common bond that we each brought to the school. In spite of profound differences in our personal biographies, differences that in other settings would have hampered our ability to relate to one another, we found that we were all deeply committed to the education of Black children. By learning to value each other's commitment and by recognizing that we each had different skills that were essential to actualizing that commitment, we built an effective coalition around a common cause. Our school was successful, and the children we taught benefited from the diversity we offered them.

. . . None of us alone has a comprehensive vision of how race, class and gender operate as categories of analysis or how they might be used as categories of connection. Our personal biographies offer us partial views. Few of us can manage to study race, class and gender simultaneously. Instead, we each know more about some dimensions of this larger story and less about others. . . . Just as the members of the school had special skills to offer to the task of building the school, we have areas of specialization and expertise, whether scholarly, theoretical, pedagogical or within areas of race, class or gender. We do not all have to do the same thing in the same way. Instead, we must support each other's efforts, realizing that they are all part of the larger enterprise of bringing about social change.

3. Building Empathy

A third issue involved in building the types of relationships and coalitions essential for social change concerns the issue of individual accountability. Race, class and gender oppression form the structural backdrop against which we frame our relationship—these are the forces that encourage us to substitute voyeurism . . . for fully human relationships. But while we may not have created this situation, we are each responsible for making individual, personal choices concerning which elements of race, class and gender oppression we will accept and which we will work to change.

One essential component of this accountability involves developing empathy for the experiences of individuals and groups different than ourselves. Empathy begins with taking an interest in the facts of other people's lives, both as individuals and as groups. If you care about me, you should want to know not only the details of my personal biography but a sense of how race, class and gender as categories of analysis created the institutional and symbolic backdrop for my personal biography. How can you hope to assess my character without knowing the details of the circumstances I face?

Moreover, by taking a theoretical stance that we have all been affected by race, class and gender as categories of analysis that have structured our treatment, we open up possibilities for using those same constructs as categories of connection in building empathy. For example, I have a good White woman friend with whom I share common interests and beliefs. But we know that our racial differences have provided us with different experiences. So we talk about them. We do not assume that because I am Black, race has only affected me and not her or that because I am a Black woman, race neutralizes the effect of gender in my life while accenting it in hers. We take those same categories of analysis that have created cleavages in our lives, in this case, categories of race and gender, and use them as categories of connection in building empathy for each other's experiences.

Finding common causes and building empathy is difficult, no matter which side of privilege we inhabit. Building empathy from the dominant side of privilege is difficult, simply because individuals from privileged backgrounds are not encouraged to do so. For example, in order for those of you who are White to develop empathy for the experiences of people of color, you must grapple with how your white skin has privileged you. This is difficult to do, because it not only entails the intellectual process of seeing how whiteness is elevated in institutions and symbols, but it also involves the often painful process of seeing how your whiteness has shaped your personal biography. Intellectual stances against the institutional and symbolic dimensions of racism are generally easier to maintain than sustained self-reflection about how racism has shaped all of our individual biographies. Were and are your fathers, uncles, and grandfathers really more capable than mine, or can their accomplishments be explained in part by the racism members of my family experienced? Did your mothers stand silently by and watch all this happen? More importantly, how have they passed on the benefits of their whiteness to you?

These are difficult questions, and I have tremendous respect for my colleagues and students who are trying to answer them. Since there is no compelling reason to examine the source and meaning of one's own privilege, I know that those who do so have freely chosen this stance. They are making conscious efforts to root out the piece of the oppressor planted within them. To me, they are entitled to the support of people of color in their efforts. Men who declare themselves feminists, members of the middle class who ally themselves with anti-poverty struggles, heterosexuals who support gays and lesbians, are all trying to grow, and their efforts place them far ahead of the majority who never think of engaging in such important struggles.

Building empathy from the subordinate side of privilege is also difficult, but for different reasons. Members of subordinate groups are understandably reluctant to abandon a basic mistrust of members of powerful groups because this basic mistrust has traditionally been central to their survival. As a Black woman, it would be foolish for me to assume that White women, or Black men, or White men or any other group with a history of exploiting African-American women have my best interests at heart. These groups enjoy varying amounts of privilege over me and therefore I must carefully watch them and be prepared for a relation of domination and subordination.

Like the privileged, members of subordinate groups must also work toward replacing judgments by category with new ways of thinking and acting. Refusing to do so stifles prospects for effective coalition and social change. Let me use another example from my own experiences. When I was an undergraduate, I had little time or patience for the theorizing of the privileged. My initial years at a private, elite institution were difficult, not because the coursework was challenging (it was, but that wasn't what distracted me) or because I had to work while my classmates lived on family allowances (I was used to work). The adjustment was difficult because I was surrounded by so many people who took their privilege for granted. Most of them felt entitled to their wealth. That astounded me.

I remember one incident of watching a White woman down the hall in my dormitory try to pick out which sweater to wear. The sweaters were piled up on her bed in all the colors of the rainbow, sweater after sweater. She asked my advice in a way that let me know that choosing a sweater was one of the most important decisions she had to make on a daily basis. Standing knee-deep in her sweaters, I realized how different our lives were. She did not have to worry about maintaining a solid academic average so that she could receive financial aid. Because she was in the majority, she was not treated as a representative of her race. She did not have to consider how her classroom comments or basic existence on campus contributed to the treatment her group would receive. Her allowance protected her from having to work, so she was free to spend her time studying, partying, or in her case, worrying about which sweater to wear. The degree of inequality in our lives and her unquestioned sense of entitlement concerning that inequality offended me. For a while, I categorized all affluent White women as being superficial, arrogant, overly concerned with material possessions, and part of my problem. But had I continued to classify people in this way, I would have missed out on making some very good friends whose discomfort with their inherited or acquired social class privileges pushed them to examine their position.

Since I opened with the words of Audre Lorde, it seems appropriate to close with another of her ideas. . . .

Each of us is called upon to take a stand. So in these days ahead, as we examine ourselves and each other, our works, our fears, our differences, our sisterhood and survivals, I urge you to tackle what is most difficult for us all, self-scrutiny of our complacencies, the idea that since each of us believes she is on the side of right, she need not examine her position (1985).

I urge you to examine your position.

REFERENCES

Butler, Johnella. 1989. "Difficult Dialogues." *The Women's Review of Books* 6, no. 5.

Collins, Patricia Hill. 1989. "The Social Construction of Black Feminist Thought." *Signs.* Summer 1989.

Gwaltney, John Langston. 1980. *Drylongso: A Self-Portrait of Black America.* New York: Vintage.

Harding, Sandra. 1986. *The Science Question in Feminism.* Ithaca, New York: Cornell University Press.

Jordan, June. 1985. *On Call: Political Essays.* Boston: South End Press.

Lorde, Audre. 1984. *Sister Outsider.* Trumansberg, New York: The Crossing Press.

_____. 1985. "Sisterhood and Survival." Keynote address, conference on the Black Woman Writer and the Diaspora, Michigan State University.

Spelman, Elizabeth. 1982. "Theories of Race and Gender: The Erasure of Black Women." *Quest* 5: 36–32.

Tate, Claudia, ed. 1983. *Black Women Writers at Work.* New York: Continuum.

 QUESTIONS FOR CRITICAL THINKING

Reading 59

1. Collins argues that we often fail to see how our own ideas and behaviors perpetuate someone else's oppression. What are some ideas or behaviors that you possess that perpetuate the inequality of others?

2. What makes it difficult to recognize the ways that we participate in transforming difference into inequality?

3. How can recognizing the ways we participate in perpetuating inequality move us toward a more equal society?

Reading 60

CULTURAL RESISTANCE
Reconstructing Our Own Images

YEN LE ESPIRITU

"One day/I going to write/about you," wrote Lois-Ann Yamanaka (1993) in "Empty Heart" (p. 548). And Asian Americans did write— "to inscribe our faces on the blank pages and screens of America's hegemonic culture" (Kim, 1993, p. xii). As a result, Asian Americans' objectification as the exotic aliens who are different from, and other than, Euro-Americans has never been absolute. Within the confines of race, class, and gender oppression, Asian Americans have maintained independent self-definitions, challenging controlling images and replacing them with Asian American standpoints. The civil rights and ethnic studies movements of the late 1960s were training grounds for Asian American cultural workers and the development of oppositional projects. Grounded in the U.S. black power movement and in anticolonial struggles of Third World countries, Asian American antihegemonic projects have been unified by a common goal of articulating cultural resistance. Given the historical distortions and misrepresentations of Asian Americans in mainstream media, most cultural projects produced by Asian American men and women perform the important tasks of correcting histories, shaping legacies, creating new cultures, constructing a politics of resistance, and opening spaces for the forcibly excluded (Kim, 1993, p. xiii; Fung, 1994, p. 165).

Fighting the exoticization of Asian Americans has been central in the ongoing work of cultural resistance. As discussed above, Asian Americans, however rooted in this country, are represented as recent transplants from Asia or as bearers of an exotic culture. The Chinese American playwright Frank Chin noted that New York critics of his play *Chickencoop Chinaman* complained in the early 1970s that his characters did not speak, dress, or act "like Orientals" (Kim, 1982, p. xv). Similarly, a reviewer described Maxine Hong Kingston's *The Woman Warrior* as a tale of "East meets West" and praised the book for its "myths rich and varied as Chinese brocade"—even though *The Woman Warrior* is deliberately anti-exotic and anti-nostalgic (quoted in Kim, 1982, p. xvi). In both of these examples, the qualifier *American* has been blithely excised from the term *Asian American*.

Yen Le Espiritu, "Cultural Resistance: Reconstructing Our Own Images" from *Asian American Women and Men: Labor, Laws, and Love*. Thousand Oaks, CA: Sage Publications, 1997, pp. 98–107. Reprinted by permission of the publisher.

Asian American cultural workers simply do not accept the exotic, one-dimensional caricatures of themselves in U.S. mass media. In the preface of *Aiiieeeee!*, a landmark collection of Asian American writers (in this case, Chinese, Japanese, and Filipinos), published in the mid-1970s, the editors announced that the anthology, and the title *Aiiieeeee!* itself, challenged the exoticization of Asian Americans.

> The pushers of white American culture . . . pictured the yellow
> man as something that when wounded, sad, angry, or swearing,
> or wondering whined, shouted, or screamed "aiiieeeee!" Asian
> America, so long ignored and forcibly excluded from creative
> participation in American culture, is wounded, sad, angry,
> swearing, and wondering, and this is his AIIIEEEEE!!! It is more
> than a whine, shout, or scream. It is fifty years of our whole voice.
> (Chan et al., 1974, p. xii)

The publication of *Aiiieeeee!* gave Asian American writers visibility and cred-ibility and sparked other oppositional projects. Jessica Hagedorn, a Filipina American writer, described the legacy of *Aiiieeeee!*: "We could not be ignored; suddenly, we were no longer silent. Like other writers of color in America, we were beginning to challenge the long-cherished concepts of a xenopho-bic literary canon dominated by white heterosexual males" (Hagedorn, 1993, p. xviii). Inspired by *Aiiieeeee!* and by other "irreverent and blasphemous" American writers, Hagedorn created an anthology of contemporary Asian American fiction in 1993—"a book I wanted to read but had never been available to me" (Hagedorn, 1993, p. xxx). In the tradition of *Aiiieeeee!*, the title of Hagedorn's anthology, *Charlie Chan Is Dead*, is vigorously political, defying and stamping out the vestiges of a "fake 'Asian' pop icon" (Hage-dorn, 1993, p. xxi). In the anthology's preface, Elaine Kim (1993) contested the homogenization of Asian Americans by juxtaposing the one-dimensional Charlie Chan to the many ways of being Asian American in contemporary United States:

> Charlie Chan is dead, never to be revived. Gone for good his
> yellowface asexual bulk, his fortune-cookie English, his stereo-
> typical Orientalist version of "the [Confucian] Chinese family,"
> challenged by an array of characters, some hip and articulate,
> some brooding and sexy, some insolent and others innocent, but
> all as unexpected as a Korean American who writes in French,
> a Chinese-Panamanian-German who longs too late to know her
> father, a mean Japanese American grandmother, a Chinese Ameri-
> can flam-dive, or a teenaged Filipino American male prostitute.
> Instead of "model minorities," we find human beings with rich
> and complex pasts and brave, often flamboyant dreams of the
> future. (p. xiii)

Taking up this theme, Wayne Chang's commercial film *Chan Is Missing* (1981) offers a range of Chinatown characters who indirectly convey the message that Chinese Americans, like other Americans, are heterogeneous (Chan, 1994, p. 530). Portraying Asian Americans in all our contradictions and complexities—as exiled, assimilated, rebellious, noble—Asian American cultural projects reveal heterogeneity rather than "producing regulating ideas of cultural unity or integration" (Lowe, 1994, p. 53). In so doing, these projects destabilize the dominant racist discourse that constructs Asians as a homogeneous group who are "all alike" and readily conform to "types" such as the Yellow Peril, the Oriental mastermind, and the sexy Suzie Wong (Lowe, 1991).

Asian American cultural projects also deconstruct the myth of the benevolent United States promised to women and men from Asia. Carlos Bulosan's *America Is in the Heart* (1946/1973), one of the core works of Asian American literature, challenges the narrative of the United States as the land of opportunity. Seduced by the promise of individual freedom through education, the protagonist Carlos discovers that as a Filipino immigrant in the United States, he is denied access to formal schooling. This disjunction between the promise of education and the unequal access of different racial and economic groups to that education—reinforced by Carlos's observations of the exploitation, marginality, and violence suffered by his compatriots in the United States—challenges his faith in the promise of U.S. democracy and abundance (Lowe, 1994, p. 56). John Okada's *No-No Boy* (1957) is another searing indictment of U.S. racist hysteria. In this portrayal of the aftermath of the internment of Japanese Americans during World War II, the protagonist, Ichiro, angrily refuses to adjust to his postinternment and postimprisonment circumstances, thus dramatizing the Asian American subject's refusal to accept the subordinating terms of assimilation (Lowe, 1994, p. 59). In the following excerpt from the poem by Cao Tan, "Tomorrow I Will Be Home," a Vietnamese refugee describes the emasculating effect of U.S. society:

> Tomorrow I will be home and someone will ask
> What have you learned in the States?
> If you want to give me a broom
> I'll tell you, I am a first class janitor.
> I wash dishes much faster than the best housewife
> And do a vacuum job better than any child
> Every day I run like a madman in my brand new car
> Every night I bury my head in my pillow and cry. . . .
>
> BICH (1989)

To reject the myth of a benevolent United States is also to refute ideological racism: the justification of inequalities through a set of controlling images that attribute physical and intellectual traits to racially defined groups (Hamamoto, 1994, p. 3). In the 1980 autobiographical fiction *China Men,*

Maxine Hong Kingston smashed the controlling image of the emasculated Asian man by foregrounding the legalized racism that turned immigrant Chinese "men" into "women" at the turn of the century. In his search for the Gold Mountain, the novel's male protagonist Tan Ao finds instead the Land of Women, where he is caught and transformed into an Oriental courtesan. Because Kingston reveals at the end of the legend that the Land of Women was in North America, readers familiar with Chinese American history will readily see that "the ignominy suffered by Tan Ao in a foreign land symbolizes the emasculation of Chinamen by the dominant culture" (Cheung, 1990, p. 240). Later in the novel, the father's failure as a provider—his emasculation—inverts the sexual roles in the family. His silence and impotent rage deepen as his wife takes on active power in the family and assumes the "masculine" traits of aggressiveness and authority. As a means of releasing his sense of frustration and powerlessness in racist America, the father lapses into silence, screams "wordless male screams in his sleep," and spouts furious misogynistic curses that frighten his daughter (Sledge, 1980, p. 10). The author/narrator Maxine traces her father's abusive behavior back to his feeling of emasculation in America: "We knew that it was to feed us you had to endure demons and physical labor" (cited in Goellnicht, 1992, p. 201). Similarly, in Louis Chu's 1961 novel *Eat a Bowl of Tea*, the protagonist's sexual impotence represents the social powerlessness of generations of Chinatown bachelors prevented by discriminatory laws and policies from establishing a traditional family life (Kim, 1982, p. xviii).

More recently, Steven Okazaki's film *American Sons* (1995)[1] tells the stories of four Asian American men who reveal how incidents of prejudice and bigotry shaped their identity and affected the way they perceived themselves and society. About his film, Okazaki (1995) explained, "Prejudice, bigotry, and violence twist and demean individual lives. *American Sons* looks at difficult issues, such as hate violence, in order to show this intimate and disturbing examination of the deep psychological damage that racism causes over generations" (n.p.). Asian American men's increasing involvement in hip-hop—a highly masculinized cultural form and a distinctly American phenomenon—is yet another contemporary denouncement of this stereotype of themselves as "effeminate, nerdy, asocial foreigners" (Choe, 1996). By exposing the role of the large society in the emasculation and oppression of Asian men, Kingston, Chu, and Okazaki invalidated the naturalization and normalization of Asian men's asexuality in U.S. popular culture.

Finally, Asian American cultural workers reject the narrative of salvation: the myth that Asian women (and a feminized Asia) are saved, through sexual relations with white men (and a masculinized United States), from the excesses of their own culture. Instead, they underscore the considerable potential for abuse in these inherently unequal relationships. Writing in Vietnamese, transplanted Vietnamese writer Tran Dieu Hang described the gloomy existence of Vietnamese women in sexist and racist U.S. society—an accursed land that singles out women, especially immigrant women, for oppression and violence. Her short story "Roi Ngay Van Moi" ("There Will Come New Days"; 1986) depicts the brutal rape of a young refugee woman by her American sponsor despite her tearful pleas in limited English (Tran, 1993, pp. 72–73). Marianne Villanueva's short story "Opportunity" (1991) also calls attention to the sexualization and racialization of Asian women. As the protagonist Nina, a "mail-order bride" from the Philippines, enters the hotel lobby to meet her American fiance, the bellboys snicker and whisper *puta,* whore: a reminder that U.S. economic and cultural colonization of the Philippines always forms the backdrop to any relations between Filipinos and Americans (Wong, 1993, p. 53). Characterizing Filipino American literature as "literature of exile," Oscar Campomanes (1992) underscored the legacy of U.S. colonization of the Philippines: "The signifiers 'Filipinos' and 'Philippines' evoke colonialist meanings and cultural redactions which possess inordinate power to shape the fates of the writers and of Filipino peoples everywhere" (p. 52). Theresa Hak Kyung Cha's *Dictee* (1982), a Korean American text, likewise challenges the myth of U.S. benevolence in Asia by tracing the impact of colonial and imperial damage and dislocation on the Korean subject (Lowe, 1994, p. 61). As Sau-Ling Cynthia Wong (1993) suggested, "To the extent that most typical cases of Asian immigration to the United States stem from an imbalance of resources writ large in the world economy, it holds in itself the seed of exploitation" (p. 53).

 CONTROLLING IMAGES, GENDER,
AND CULTURAL NATIONALISM

Cultural nationalism has been crucial in Asian Americans' struggles for self-determination. Emerging in the early 1970s, this unitary Asian American identity was primarily racial, male, and heterosexual. Asian American literature produced in those years highlighted Chinese and Japanese American male perspectives, obscuring gender and other intercommunity differences (Kim, 1993). Asian American male writers, concerned with recuperating their identities as men and as Americans, objectified both white and Asian women in their writings (Kim, 1990, p. 70). In a controversial essay entitled "Racist Love," Frank Chin and Jeffrey Paul Chan (1972) pointed to the stereotype of the emasculated Asian American man:

> The white stereotype of Asian is unique in that it is the only racial stereotype completely devoid of manhood. Our nobility is that of an efficient housewife. At our worst we are contemptible because we are womanly, effeminate, devoid of all the traditionally masculine qualities of originality, daring, physical courage, creativity. (p. 68)

In taking whites to task for their racist debasement of Asian American men, however, Chin and Chan succumbed to the influence of Eurocentric gender ideology, particularly its emphasis on oppositional dichotomous sex roles (Collins, 1990, p. 184). In a critique of "Racist Love," King-Kok Cheung (1990) contended that Chin and Chan buttressed patriarchy "by invoking gender stereotypes, by disparaging domestic efficiency as 'feminine,' and by slotting desirable traits such as originality, daring, physical courage, and creativity under the rubric of masculinity" (p. 237). Similarly, Wong (1993) argued that in their influential "Introduction" to *Aiiieeeee! An Anthology of Asian American Writers* (1974), Chan, Chin, Inada, and Wong operated on the premise that a true Asian American sensibility is "non-Christian, nonfeminine, and nonimmigrant" (p. 8).

Though limited and limiting, a masculine cultural nationalist agenda appealed to Asian American activists because of its potential to oppose and disrupt the logic of racial domination. In the following excerpt, Elaine Kim (1993), a pioneer in the field of Asian American literature, explained the appeal of cultural nationalism:

> Certainly it was possible for me as a Korean American female
> to accept the fixed masculinist Asian American identity posited
> in Asian American cultural nationalism, even when it rendered
> invisible or at least muted women's oppression, anger, and ways of
> loving and interpreted Korean Americans as imperfect imitations of
> Chinese Americans; because I could see in everyday life that not all
> material and psychic violence to women of color comes from men,
> and because, as my friends use to say, "No Chinese [American]
> ever called me a 'Gook.'" (p. x)

Kim's statement suggests that for Asian American women, and for other women of color, gender is only a part of a larger pattern of unequal social relations. Despite the constraints of patriarchy, racism inscribes these women's lives and binds them to Asian American men in what Collins (1991) called a "love and trouble" tradition (p. 184).

Because the racial oppression of Asian Americans involves the "feminization" of Asian men (Said, 1979), Asian American women are caught between the need to expose the problems of male privilege and the desire to unite with men to contest the overarching racial ideology that confines them both. As Cheung (1990) suggested, Asian American women may be simultaneously sympathetic and angry toward the men in their ethnic community: sensitive to the men's marginality but resentful of their sexism (p. 239). Maxine Hong Kingston's writings seem to reflect these conflicting emotions. As discussed above, in the opening legend of *China Men*, the male protagonist Tan Ao is captured in the Land of Women (North America), where he is forced to become a woman—to have his feet bound, his ears pierced, his eyebrows plucked, his cheeks and lips painted. Cheung (1990) argued that this legend is double-edged, pointing not only to the racist debasement of Chinese Americans in their adopted country but also to the subjugation of Chinese women both in China and in the United States (p. 240). Although the effeminization suffered by Tan Ao is brutal, it is the same mutilation that many Chinese women were for centuries forced to bear. According to Goellnicht's (1992) reading of Kingston's work, this opening myth suggests that the author both deplores the emasculation of her forefathers by main-stream America and critiques the Confucian patriarchal practices of her ances-tral homeland (p. 194). In *China Men,* Kingston also showed no acceptance of sexist practices by immigrant men. The father in this novel/autobiography is depicted as a broken man who attempts to reassert male authority by deni-grating those who are even more powerless—the women and children in his family (Cheung, 1990, p. 241; Goellnicht, 1992, p. 200).

Along the same lines, Maxine Hong Kingston's *The Woman Warrior* (1977) reveals the narrator's contradictory attitudes toward her childhood "home," which is simultaneously a site of "woman hatred" and an area of resistance against the racism of the dominant culture. The community that nourishes her imagination and suffuses her with warmth is the same community that relegates women to an inferior position, limiting them to the role of serving men (Rabine, 1987, pp. 477–478). In the following pas-sage, the narrator voices her mixed feelings toward the Chinese American community:

> I looked at their ink drawings of poor people snagging their neigh-bors' flotage with long flood hooks and pushing the girl babies on down the river. And I had to get out of hating range. . . . I refuse to shy my way anymore through our Chinatown, which tasks me with the old sayings and the stories. The swordswoman and I are not so dissimilar. May my people understand the resemblance so that I can return to them. (Kingston, 1977, p. 62)

Similarly, in a critique of Asian American sexual politics, Kayo Hatta's short video *Otemba* (1988) depicts a girl's-eye view of the final days of her mother's pregnancy as her father hopes and prays for the birth of a boy (see Tajima, 1991, p. 26).

Stripped of the privileges of masculinity, some Asian American men have attempted to reassert male authority by subordinating feminism to nationalist concerns. Lisa Lowe (1991) argued that this identity politics displaces gender differences into a false opposition of "nationalism" and "assimilation." From this limited perspective, Asian American feminists who expose Asian American sexism are cast as "assimilationist," as betray-ing Asian American "nationalism." Maxine Hong Kingston's *The Woman Warrior* (1977) and Amy Tan's *The Joy Luck Club* (1989) are the targets of such nationalist criticisms. Frank Chin, Ben Tong, and others have accused these and other women novelists of feminizing Asian American literature by exaggerating the community's patriarchal structure, thus undermining the power of Asian American men to combat the racist stereotypes of the dominant white culture. For example, when Kingston's *The Woman Warrior* received favorable reviews, Chin accused her of attempting to "cash in on the feminist fad" (Chan, 1994, p. 528). Another Asian American male had this to say about the movie *The Joy Luck Club*:

> The movie was powerful. But it could have been powerful *and inclusive*, if at least one of the Asian male characters was portrayed as something other than monstrously evil or simply wimpy. We are used to this message coming out of Hollywood, but it disturbed me deeply to hear the same message coming from Amy Tan and Wayne Wang—people of my own color. (Yoon, 1993)

Whereas Chin and others cast this tension in terms of nationalism and assimilationism, Lisa Lowe (1991) argued that it is more a debate between nationalist and feminist concerns in Asian American discourse. This insistence on a fixed masculinist identity, according to Lowe (1991), "can be itself a colonial figure used to displace the challenges of heterogeneity, or subalternity, by casting them as assimilationist or anti-ethnic" (pp. 33–34).

But cultural nationalism need not be patriarchal. Rejecting the ideology of oppositional dichotomous sex roles, Asian American cultural workers have also engaged in cross-gender projects. In a recent review of Asian American independent filmmaking, Renee Tajima (1991) reported that some of the best feminist films have been made by Asian American men. For example, Arthur Dong's *Lotus* (1987) exposes women's exploitation through the practice of footbinding (Tajima, 1991, p. 24). Asian American men have also made use of personal documentary, in both diary and autobiographical form—an approach known to be the realm of women filmmakers. Finally, there is no particular gender affiliation in subject matters: Just as Arthur Dong profiles his mother in *Sewing Woman*, Lori Tsang portrays her father's life in *Chinaman's Choice* (Tajima, 1991, p. 24).

 CONCLUSION

Ideological representations of gender and sexuality are central in the exercise and maintenance of racial, patriarchal, and class domination. In the Asian American case, this ideological racism has taken seemingly contrasting forms: Asian men have been cast as both hypersexual and asexual, and Asian women have been rendered both superfeminine and masculine. Although in apparent disjunction, both forms exit to define, maintain, and justify white male supremacy. The racialization of Asian American manhood and womanhood underscores the interconnections of race, gender, and class. As categories of difference, race and gender relations do not parallel but intersect and confirm each other, and it is the complicity among these categories of difference that enables U.S. elites to justify and maintain their cultural, social, and economic power. Responding to the ideological assaults on their gender identities, Asian American cultural workers have engaged in a wide range of oppositional projects to defend Asian American manhood and womanhood. In the process, some have embraced a masculinist cultural nationalism, a stance that marginalizes Asian American women and their needs. Though sensitive to the emasculation of Asian American men, Asian American feminists have pointed out that Asian American nationalism insists on a fixed masculinist identity, thus obscuring gender differences. Though divergent, both the nationalist and feminist positions advance the dichotomous stance of man or woman, gender or race or class, without recognizing the complex relationality of these categories of oppression. It is only when Asian Americans recognize the intersections of race, gender, and class that we can transform the existing hierarchical structure.

 ACKNOWLEDGMENTS

I thank Takeo Wong for calling my attention to Steven Okazaki's film *American Sons* (1995).

REFERENCES

Bich, N. N. (Ed.). (1989). *War and Exile: A Vietnamese Anthology.* Springfield, VA: Vietnam PEN Abroad.

Bulosan, C. (1973). *America Is in the Heart: A Personal History.* Seattle: Washington University Press. (Original work published 1946.)

Campomanes, O. (1992). Filipinos in the United States and Their Literature of Exile. In S. G. Lim & A. Ling (Eds.), *Reading the Literatures of Asian America* (pp. 49–78). Philadelphia: Temple University Press.

Cha, T. H. K. (1982). *Dictee.* New York: Tanam.

Chan, J. P., Chin, F., Inada, L. F., & Wong, S. (1974). *Aiiieeeee! An Anthology of Asian American Writers.* Washington, DC: Howard University Press.

Chan, S. (1994). The Asian American Movement, 1960s–1980s. In S. Chan, D. H. Daniels, M. T. Garcia, & T. P. Wilson (Eds.), *Peoples of Color in the American West* (pp. 525–533). Lexington, MA: D. C. Heath.

Cheung, K. K. (1990) The Woman Warrior versus the Chinaman Pacific: Must a Chinese American Critic Choose Between Feminism and Heroism? In M. Hirsch & E. F. Keller (Eds.), *Conflicts in Feminism* (pp. 234–251). New York: Routledge.

Chin, F., & Chan, J. P. (1972). Racist Love. In R. Kostelanetz (Ed.), *Seeing through Shuck* (pp. 65–79). New York: Ballantine.

Choe, Laura. (1996, February 10). "Versions": Asian Americans in Hip Hop. Paper presented at the California Studies Conference, Long Beach, CA.

Chu, L. (1961). *Eat a Bowl of Tea.* Seattle: University of Washington Press.

Collins, P. H. (1990). *Black Feminist Thought: Knowledge, Consciousness, and the Politics of Empowerment.* New York: Routledge.

Dong, A. (Director). (1982). *Sewing Woman* [Film]. San Francisco: Deep Focus Productions.

Fung, R. (1994). Seeing Yellow: Asian Identities in Film and Video. In K. Aguilar–San Juan (Ed.), *The State of Asian America* (pp. 161–171). Boston: South End.

Goellnicht, D. C. (1992). Tang Ao in America: Male Subject Positions in *China Men*. In S. G. Lim and A. Ling (Eds.), *Reading the Literature of Asian America* (pp. 191–212). Philadelphia: Temple University Press.

Hagedorn, J. (1993). Introduction: "Role of Dead Man Requires Very Little Acting." In J. Hagedorn (Ed.), *Charlie Chan Is Dead: An Anthology of Contemporary Asian American Fiction* (pp. xxi–xxx). New York: Penguin.

Hamamoto, D. Y. (1994). *Monitored Peril: Asian Americans and the Politics of Representation*. Minneapolis: University of Minnesota Press.

Kim, E. (1982). *Asian American Literature: An Introduction to the Writings and Their Social Context*. Philadelphia: Temple University Press.

_____. (1990). "Such Opposite Creatures." Men and Women in Asian American Literature. *Michigan Quarterly Review, 29*, 68–93.

_____. (1993). Preface. In J. Hagedorn (Ed.), *Charlie Chan Is Dead: An Anthology of Contemporary Asian American Fiction* (pp. vii–xiv). New York: Penguin.

Kingston, M. H. (1977). *The Woman Warrior*. New York: Vintage.

_____. (1980). *China Men*. New York: Knopf.

Lowe, L. (1991). Heterogeneity, Hybridity, Multiplicity: Marking Asian American Difference. *Diaspora, 1*, 24–44.

_____. (1994). Canon, Institutionalization, Identity: Contradictions for Asian American Studies. In D. Palumbo-Liu (Ed.), *The Ethnic Canon: Histories, Institutions, and Interventions* (pp. 48–68). Minneapolis: University of Minnesota Press.

Okada, J. (1957). *No-No Boy*. Rutland, VT: Charles E. Tuttle.

Okazaki, S. (1995). *American Sons*. Promotional brochure for the film of that name.

Rabine, L. W. (1987). No Lost Paradise: Social Gender and Symbolic Gender in the Writings of Maxine Hong Kingston. *Signs: Journal of Women in Culture and Society, 12*, 471–511.

Said, E. (1979). *Orientalism*. New York: Random House.

Sledge, L. C. (1980). Maxine Kingston's *China Men:* The Family Historian as Epic Poet. *Melus*, 7-3-22.

Tajima, R. (1991). Moving the Image: Asian American Independent Filmmaking 1970–1990. In R. Leong (Ed.), *Moving the Image: Independent Asian Pacific American Media Arts* (pp. 10–33). Los Angeles: University of California at Los Angeles, Asian American Studies Center, and Visual Communications, Southern California Asian American Studies Central.

Tran, Q. P. (1993). Exile and Home in Contemporary Vietnamese American Feminine Writing. *Amerasia Journal, 19*, 71–83.

Villanueva, M. (1991). *Ginseng and Other Tales from Manila*. Corvallis, OR: Calyx.

Wong, S. L. C. (1993). *Reading Asian American Literature: From Necessity to Extravagance*. Princeton, NJ: Princeton University Press.

Yamanaka, L. A. (1993). Empty Heart. In J. Hagedorn (Ed.), *Charlie Chan Is Dead: An Anthology of Contemporary Asian American Fiction* (pp. 544–550). New York: Penguin.

Yoon, D. D. (1993, November 26). Asian American Male: Wimp or What? *Asian Week*, p. 16.

QUESTIONS FOR CRITICAL THINKING

Reading 60

1. Espiritu discusses the ways that Asian Americans reconstruct their images. How is this an example of resistance? How might it help to bring about social change?
2. What are the barriers that Asian Americans and others face when trying to reconstruct representations of their groups?
3. What social institutions (e.g., media, education, family, etc.) can aid in the process of reconstructing negative images of marginalized groups?

Reading 61

GOOD FOR THE 'HOOD?

ANMOL CHADDHA

At the corner of Grand and Kilpatrick Avenues in Chicago, the Reverend Joseph Kyles addressed a rally last May. "Tomorrow morning," he said, "we need you to pray for the City Council to vote for Wal-Mart in this community." That Rev. Kyles would be preaching the virtues of a corporate retail behemoth was no fluke. It was part of a strategy by Wal-Mart executives to cultivate support among black city council members and church leaders for building two stores in Chicago—each about the size of ten football fields. It is also part of a broader strategy to bring Wal-Mart to the 'hood—touting not just lower prices but also racial equity.

Having built its base in rural areas in the 1960s and extending to suburban markets in the last two decades, Wal-Mart began approaching poor, urban neighborhoods most noticeably in 2003, when it tried to open a store in Inglewood, a poor city near Los Angeles. From there, the company moved to Chicago and New York City. Initial plans to open a store in Queens, New York, were dropped earlier this year, but Wal-Mart executives say they are determined to find another site in New York. With over $280 billion in annual sales and 3,500 stores across the United States, the company is now selling itself as a solution to urban racial inequality.

Anmol Chaddha, 2005, "Good for the 'Hood?" from *Color Lines*, Vol. 8, Issue 2, pp. 34–38.

The pitch goes like this: Wal-Mart is good for poor people of color because they get jobs and also get to buy cheap goods. What executives don't mention is that the jobs come with notoriously low wages and that the company has cracked down on union organizing. But Wal-Mart executives know that poor people of color are in no position to be picky about who brings what jobs to the community. As the largest private employer in the United States, with over 1.2 million workers, Wal-Mart is also the leading employer of African American and Latino workers.

Using race as a selling point for economic development projects in distressed urban areas is not just the handiwork of Wal-Mart. In 2001, developers promoted the Staples Center sports complex in Los Angeles as a boon for a hurting local economy, insisting that it would create jobs for people of color who lived nearby. A 450-foot-tall Marriott hotel is going up on 125th Street in Harlem, and Ikea is planning to open its biggest U.S. furniture store in Brooklyn. All make the same argument: they are helping poor people of color.

Amidst this urban gold rush for developers, communities of color are forced to choose between the very real need for jobs and having a voice in economic development.

LESSONS FROM INGLEWOOD

Willie Cole, a middle-aged black mother, knows firsthand the economic hardships that face the poor neighborhoods of Los Angeles. She was unemployed for two years until she landed a cashier job at a Wal-Mart that opened in Crenshaw in 2003. Although her position typically pays less than $20,000 annually, she stuck with it and was promoted into a management-training program a year later.

Cole represents Wal-Mart's best public relations argument for opening stores in poor urban areas. In fact, the company featured her in a television commercial promoting its contributions to these communities. "When Wal-Mart came in," she says in the ad, dressed in her store uniform and standing near Crenshaw High School, "they let us know that they cared." The spot has been broadcast nationally, and it received heavy airplay in Inglewood leading up to a special election there in April 2004. Wal-Mart had collected signatures for a local ballot initiative that would have exempted the company from the standard environmental reviews and public hearings required to open a store.

In Inglewood, where 47 percent of the residents are black and 46 percent are Latino, Wal-Mart claimed it would create several hundred much-needed jobs. That was attractive to a small city with an official unemployment rate that was approaching double digits. What the massive retail chain failed to mention was that its entrance has been blocked in over 200 so-called "site fights" in states such as Virginia, Vermont and Oregon. Critics, led forcefully by labor unions, denounce the company for paying low wages, providing inadequate health care benefits, displacing local businesses and contributing to undesirable sprawl. The average Wal-Mart salary is at the federal poverty level for a family of four. A study at the University of California, Berkeley, estimates that California pays $86 million in public benefits to Wal-Mart employees whose low incomes qualify them for food stamps, health care and subsidized housing—programs that are funded by taxpayers. Recent studies have identified Wal-Mart as the leading employer of workers receiving public health benefits in Alabama, Connecticut, Georgia, Tennessee, Washington and West Virginia.

When the company gathered the necessary signatures to force a special election in Inglewood, the Los Angeles Alliance for a New Economy (LAANE) formed the Coalition for a Better Inglewood with labor, religious and community allies. "We began organizing grocery workers and local small business owners to present the case against Wal-Mart to community leaders," says Tracy Gray-Barkan, senior research analyst at LAANE. The community-based organization already had some experience with local economic development issues. In 2001, it helped broker a deal with the Staples Center, getting the developers to sign a Community Benefits Agreement that required them to hire local residents, provide living-wage jobs and construct parks. Organizers in Inglewood walked into a tough fight with Wal-Mart. Just a month before the April 2004 election, polling showed residents supporting Wal-Mart's plan by a two-to-one margin, and one of its most prominent supporters was the town's black mayor, Roosevelt Dorn. Over the following weeks, the Coalition for a Better Inglewood reached out to community residents with information on the quality of Wal-Mart jobs and its effect on local business. In this heavily black and Latino city, the groups brought attention to allegations of racial discrimination in hiring by Wal-Mart, as well as a gender discrimination lawsuit that had been filed against the company, covering 1.6 million female Wal-Mart employees.

Although black Congresswoman Maxine Waters and the Reverend Jesse Jackson both lashed out against Wal-Mart's labor practices, many traditional civil rights groups stayed away. John Mack, president of the Los Angeles chapter of the Urban League, which received $65,000 over two years from Wal-Mart, told the *Los Angeles Times,* "I'd rather have a person on somebody's payroll—even if it isn't at the highest wage—than on the unemployment roll." Wal-Mart, by its own account, has made donations to the NAACP, National Council of La Raza, the Congressional Black Caucus, the Organization of Chinese Americans and the League of United Latin American Citizens.

Despite over $10 million spent on the initiative by Wal-Mart, including a newspaper advertisement that publicized its financial support of black and Latino organizations, Inglewood voters rejected the initiative 61 percent to 39 percent. The store would have been the first Wal-Mart Supercenter in a major urban area.

Ultimately, it may have been Wal-Mart's own brashness that helped organizers. The debate in Inglewood was not simply over whether Wal-Mart jobs are good or bad. The company was asking to skip the standard review procedures that normally require the city to consider the impacts of a development project. By bringing attention to Wal-Mart's attempt to circumvent the development process, organizers also framed the fight around the principles of how decisions in Inglewood are made about economic development. "The issue was about community control and community voice," says Gray-Barkan of LAANE.

The Inglewood initiative provided a spark for the Los Angeles City Council to consider an ordinance proposed by a coalition of labor groups, clergy and community organizations. In August 2004, the Council passed the ordinance, which requires a study of the economic impacts of any proposed superstore and allows the community to weigh the potential benefits and costs of the project. Whereas the Inglewood fight was a reaction to a plan initiated by Wal-Mart, "the Los Angles City Council ordinance is a proactive process for residents to have a say in what gets developed in their communities," says Gray-Barkan.

 ## A HARDER CHALLENGE IN CHICAGO

Last May, just two weeks after the special election in Inglewood, the Chicago City Council met to discuss proposed zoning changes that would allow the construction of a Wal-Mart Supercenter on the South Side and another on the West Side. It was a heated debate since Wal-Mart employed many of the same tactics it had used in Inglewood. "It brought the same seductive claims of jobs and low prices to black communities," explains Dorian Warren, an expert on race and organized labor who is currently a post-doctoral fellow with University of Chicago's School of Public Policy.

Just as it had done in Southern California, the company appealed to black church leaders and City Council members, "Any job is better than no job," the Reverend Ronald Wilks said at the time.

While the City Council debated, a coalition formed, led by Jobs With Justice, a national workers' rights organization. It included unions and progressive black church leaders who decided that it might not be politically feasible to ban Wal-Mart from Chicago, given how much residents needed jobs. Instead, the groups began pushing for a Community Benefits Agreement that would require Wal-Mart to pay higher wages and hire local residents.

To promote its position, Wal-Mart organized a town-hall meeting with religious leaders in the Austin neighborhood, the potential site of the South Side store, and flew out a black executive from its Arkansas headquarters. The ministers presented a demand that surprised the company: hire ex-offenders, a growing population on the West and South Sides that are excluded from employment opportunities. While Wal-Mart promoted its jobs as valuable opportunities for local residents, it made no promises to hire ex-offenders. Instead, Wes Gillespie, the black executive, presented himself to the church leaders as an example of the opportunities provided by Wal-Mart. And Alton Murphy, a black Wal-Mart district manager, quoted from the Bible when asked about the quality of Wal-Mart jobs. "Whatever you do," he recited from Colossans 3:23, "work at it with all your heart, as working for the Lord, not for men."

Despite the company's efforts to build support, not all of the ministers were sold on the plan. The 8,500-member Trinity United Church of Christ on the South Side became a center of opposition to Wal-Mart, and its leaders directly linked the store's attractive low prices to its low-paying jobs. "Whenever price means more to you than principle," wrote Trinity's pastor, the Reverend Jeremiah Wright, in the church newsletter, "you have defined yourself as a prostitute." Wright charged that Wal-Mart's backers among the City Council and the black religious community were "pimping" black residents and their economic hardships.

While Wal-Mart was reaching out to the black community, the United Food and Commercial Workers Local 881 could not easily build a coalition across race lines. According to Chicago labor expert Warren, "a few unions—particularly in the building trades—had historically excluded black men from well-paying union jobs by keeping them out of apprenticeship programs." In the minds of many black leaders, the rapid deindustrialization of the inner city combined with the racism of some building trades unions was largely responsible for the severe joblessness on the South and West Sides.

So when the union spoke of fighting Wal-Mart, it only stirred more resentment. "Some of these same unions never say a thing about the lack of African Americans in the trades," Alderman Isaac Carothers of the West Side complained at a City Council meeting.

Organizers opposing Wal-Mart also faced a more difficult challenge than in Inglewood. Where the company had asked to circumvent the standard review process in Inglewood, in Chicago the debate was over whether Wal-Mart was a good or bad option for residents. More importantly, perhaps, the two Chicago neighborhoods where Wal-Mart proposed its stores and whose residents are more than 90 percent African-American, face an employment crisis even worse than Inglewood. And organizers in Chicago did not have the benefit of taking the issue directly to local residents, since it was not an initiative to be decided by the voters. It was a City Council vote, and that made the fight over Wal-Mart vulnerable to council members who historically do not vote against an economic development proposal in another member's district if that alderman is in favor of the project (the practice is so prevalent that it's known as "aldermanic perogative").

As it did during the Inglewood fight, Wal-Mart made contributions to the local NAACP and gave a $5,000 contribution to City Council member Emma Mitts, who loudly voiced support for the construction of a Wal-Mart in her West Side district. In what was apparently an attempt to demonstrate its support of the community, the company donated 50 calculators to Austin High School in the district.

The morning after Rev. Kyles asked residents to pray for the approval of the two Wal-Mart stores, the City Council gave a split decision. It rejected the South Side location and approved the proposed store on the West Side. The approval of one store and the rejection of the other had much to do with the politics among members of the City Council, but it also reflected the tensions between the real need to create any jobs and the demand that these actually be good jobs. In what had been described as the most controversial City Council issue in two decades, all but two black aldermen supported the West Side Wal-Mart.

After the vote, a coalition of labor, religious and community groups began pushing for a local ordinance that would attach certain standards to the jobs at large stores like Wal-Mart. It would require so-called "big-box stores" to pay a $10 living wage, provide health benefits and remain neutral in efforts by its workers to form a union. The ordinance, which is still being debated by the City Council, is "a way to regulate the terms on which these stores will come in to the community," explains Chirag Mehta, a researcher at the Center for Urban Economic Development at the University of Illinois at Chicago. In response, the Reverend James Demus, director of the Chicago Southside's NAACP that received a donation from Wal-Mart, testified against the ordinance in early hearings.

 ## UNFINISHED BUSINESS

While Martin Luther King's 1963 "I Have a Dream" speech is the most familiar refrain of the civil rights movement, the full title of the rally was the "March on Washington for Jobs and Freedom." That is, King viewed the struggle for civil rights as linked to economic justice. In many ways, the enduring racial economic inequality since then is the unfinished business of the civil rights movement.

"It has been one of the weak links of racial justice organizing over the last three decades," says Warren, the University of Chicago expert on race and labor. "We have been unable to answer what our fundamental demands are around economic justice," he adds, "and how they relate to racial justice."

Since the rhetoric of race is being used strategically by developers, economic development is now the only area of urban policy that emphasizes issues of race—however hollow that talk may be. There is no similar discussion from local politicians when discussing education or health disparities.

All the economic development plans underway in New York, for example, require buy-in from poor communities of color. Developers are even going to absurd lengths to use race as a selling point. One proposal for the redevelopment of the Victoria Theater—a few doors down from the legendary Apollo Theater—includes a "Harlem-themed restaurant" with a menu that includes such items as a "Zora Neale Hurston salad . . . Miles Davis omelette and a Denzel burger."

For now, Wal-Mart has lost in New York City. Following the battles in Inglewood and Chicago, Wal-Mart's urban strategy continued east to Queens, New York. The proposed site there would have given Wal-Mart a store in nine of the ten largest U.S. urban markets. (The only city being left out is Detroit, which has been dealing with its own economic devastation.) But early reports of Wal-Mart's plans to open in Queens provoked an immediate outcry from labor groups that made a difference in a city where labor still yields power. By the end of February, the developer had dropped the Wal-Mart store from its proposal.

Recognizing that the promise of low-wage jobs is often being promoted to win the support of communities of color, New York City Councilman Charles Barron explains, "We need to distinguish between economic development and economic exploitation." In Barron's district, which includes some of the poorest sections of Brooklyn, a cinema complex recently opened with the promise of jobs for community residents. "All we got was a bunch of popcorn-selling jobs," says Barron.

Pitching proposals to poor communities who are desperate for jobs, private developers are able to exploit the failure of public policy to create jobs in these communities. "There are plenty of other ways to create jobs," says Councilman Barron, who argues for increased investment in public infrastructure such as hospitals and schools to revitalize poor areas like his Brooklyn district. "Private developers," he continues, "manipulate the race question for their financial gain."

In response to Wal-Mart and other development projects, groups in urban communities around the country are using a variety of tools to broker deals that also address other vital areas of economic development, such as housing. Some organizations are pushing for "inclusionary zoning," a regulation that requires developers to set aside residential units in a new development as affordable housing. Other community groups, including ones in New York, want to attach standards to jobs at Wal-Mart if it does open a store somewhere else in the city. Besides its low wages, the lack of adequate health care provided to workers places an unfair burden on the public health care system, many critics charge. A coalition of labor, community groups and responsible employers has sponsored a bill in the city council called the Health Care Security Act, which would require businesses in certain industries to either provide health coverage to their workers or pay fees that the city would use to provide public care to the workers. If passed, the bill would cover any Wal-Mart Superstores that would open in the city.

Organizers view Community Benefits Agreements and related tools as a critical first step in laying the groundwork for a long-term goal of redefining the terms of economic development.

"As long as private developers set the agenda and groups respond by asking for Community Benefits Agreements or inclusionary zoning," says Dorian Warren, the expert on race and labor from the University of Chicago, "we may just be trying to get a piece of the pie. We need to ask, 'What does a different pie look like?'"

 QUESTIONS FOR CRITICAL THINKING

Reading 61

1. Chaddha reviews the ways in which various groups organized against having Wal-Mart in their community. Why were they opposed to Wal-Mart? How did the policies and practices of Wal-Mart contribute to inequality?

2. How did this reading expand your ideas of what is involved in working for positive social change?

3. What lessons can movements for social justice learn from the people involved in this movement?

Reading 62

SEEING MORE THAN BLACK AND WHITE
Latinos, Racism, and the Cultural Divides

ELIZABETH MARTINEZ

A certain relish seems irresistible to this Latina as the mass media have been compelled to sit up, look south of the border, and take notice. Probably the Chiapas uprising and Mexico's recent political turmoil have won us no more than a brief day in the sun. Or even less: liberal Ted Koppel still hadn't noticed the historic assassination of presidential candidate Colosio three days afterward. But it's been sweet, anyway.

When Kissinger said years ago "nothing important ever happens in the south," he articulated a contemptuous indifference toward Latin America,

From *Roots of Justice: Stories of Organizing in Communities of Color.* Oakland, CA: Chardon Press, pp. 98–107.

its people, and their culture which has long dominated U.S. institutions and attitudes. Mexico may be great for a vacation, and some people like burritos, but the usual image of Latin America combines incompetence with absurdity in loud colors. My parents, both Spanish teachers, endured decades of being told kids were better off learning French.

U.S. political culture is not only Anglo-dominated but also embraces an exceptionally stubborn national self-centeredness, with no global vision other than relations of domination. The U.S. refuses to see itself as one nation sitting on a continent with 20 others all speaking languages other than English and having the right not to be dominated.

Such arrogant indifference extends to Latinos within the U.S. The mass media complain, "people can't relate to Hispanics"—or Asians, they say. Such arrogant indifference has played an important role in invisibilizing La Raza (except where we become a serious nuisance or a handy scapegoat). It is one reason the U.S. harbors an exclusively white-on-Black concept of racism. It is one barrier to new thinking about racism which is crucial today. There are others.

GOOD-BYE WHITE MAJORITY

In a society as thoroughly and violently racialized as the United States, white-Black relations have defined racism for centuries. Today the composition and culture of the U.S. are changing rapidly. We need to consider seriously whether we can afford to maintain an exclusively white/Black model of racism when the population will be 32 percent Latin/Asian/Pacific American and Native American—in short, neither Black nor white—by the year 2050. We are challenged to recognize that multi-colored racism is mushrooming, and then strategize how to resist it. We are challenged to move beyond a dualism comprised of two white supremacist inventions: Blackness and Whiteness.

At stake in those challenges is building a united anti-racist force strong enough to resist contemporary racist strategies of divide-and-conquer. Strong enough in the long run, to help defeat racism itself. Doesn't an exclusively Black/white model of racism discourage the perception of common interests among people of color and thus impede a solidarity that can challenge white supremacy? Doesn't it encourage the isolation of African Americans from potential allies? Doesn't it advise all people of color to spend too much energy understanding our lives in relation to Whiteness, and thus freeze us in a defensive, often self-destructive mode?

NO "OPPRESSION OLYMPICS"

For a Latina to talk about recognizing the multi-colored varieties of racism is not, and should not be, yet another round in the Oppression Olympics. We don't need more competition among different social groupings for that "Most Oppressed" gold. We don't need more comparisons of suffering between women and Blacks, the disabled and the gay, Latino teenagers and white seniors, or whatever. We don't need more surveys like the recent much publicized Harris Poll showing that different peoples of color are prejudiced toward each other—a poll patently designed to demonstrate that us coloreds are no better than white folk. (The survey never asked people about positive attitudes.)

Rather, we need greater knowledge, understanding, and openness to learning about each other's histories and present needs as a basis for working together. Nothing could seem more urgent in an era when increasing impoverishment encourages a self-imposed separatism among people of color as a desperate attempt at community survival. Nothing could seem more important as we search for new social change strategies in a time of ideological confusion.

My call to rethink concepts of racism in the U.S. today is being sounded elsewhere. Among academics, liberal foundation administrators, and activist-intellectuals, you can hear talk of the need for a new "racial paradigm" or model. But new thinking seems to proceed in fits and starts, as if dogged by a fear of stepping on toes, of feeling threatened, or of losing one's base. With a few notable exceptions, even our progressive scholars of color do not make the leap from perfunctorily saluting a vague multi-culturalism to serious analysis. We seem to have made little progress, if any, since Bob Blauner's 1972 book *Racial Oppression in America*. Recognizing the limits of the white-Black axis, Blauner critiqued White America's ignorance of and indifference to the Chicano/a experience with racism.

Real opposition to new paradigms also exists. There are academics scrambling for one flavor of ethnic studies funds versus another. There are politicians who cultivate distrust of others to keep their own communities loyal. When we hear, for example, of Black/Latino friction, dismay should be quickly followed by investigation. In cities like Los Angeles and New York, it may turn out that political figures scrapping for patronage and payola have played a narrow nationalist game, whipping up economic anxiety and generating resentment that sets communities against each other.

So the goal here, in speaking about moving beyond a bipolar concept of racism is to build stronger unity against white supremacy. The goal is to see our similarities of experience and needs. If that goal sounds naive, think about the hundreds of organizations formed by grassroots women of different colors coming together in recent years. Their growth is one of today's most energetic motions and it spans all ages. Think about the multi-cultural environmental justice movement. Think about the coalitions to save schools. Small rainbows of our own making are there, to brighten a long road through hellish times.

It is in such practice, through daily struggle together, that we are most likely to find the road to greater solidarity against a common enemy. But we also need a will to find it and ideas about where, including some new theory.

THE WEST GOES EAST

Until very recently, Latino invisibility—like that of Native Americans and Asian/Pacific Americans—has been close to absolute in U.S. seats of power, major institutions, and the non-Latino public mind. Having lived on both the East and West Coasts for long periods, I feel qualified to pronounce: an especially myopic view of Latinos prevails in the East. This, despite such data as a 24.4 percent Latino population of New York City alone in 1991, or the fact that in 1990 more Puerto Ricans were killed by New York police under suspicious circumstances than any other ethnic group. Latino populations are growing rapidly in many eastern cities and the rural South, yet remain invisible or stigmatized—usually both.

Eastern blinders persist. I've even heard that the need for a new racial paradigm is dismissed in New York as a California hangup. A black Puerto Rican friend in New York, when we talked about experiences of racism common to Black and brown, said "People here don't see Border Patrol brutality against Mexicans as a form of police repression," despite the fact that the Border Patrol is the largest and most uncontrolled police force in the U.S. It would seem that an old ignorance has combined with new immigrant bashing to sustain divisions today.

While the East (and most of the Midwest) usually remains myopic, the West Coast has barely begun to move away from its own denial. Less than two years ago in San Francisco, a city almost half Latino or Asian/Pacific American, a leading daily newspaper could publish a major series on contemporary racial issues and follow the exclusively Black-white paradigm. Although millions of TV viewers saw massive Latino participation in the April 1992 Los Angeles uprising, which included 18 out of 50 deaths and the majority of arrests, the mass media and most people labeled that event "a Black riot."

If the West Coast has more recognition of those who are neither Black nor white, it is mostly out of fear about the proximate demise of its white majority. A second, closely related reason is the relentless campaign by California Gov. Pete Wilson to scapegoat immigrants for economic problems and pass racist, unconstitutional laws attacking their health, education, and children's future. Wilson has almost single-handedly made the word "immigrant" mean Mexican or other Latino (and sometimes Asian). Who thinks of all the people coming from the former Soviet Union and other countries? The absolute racism of this has too often been successfully masked by reactionary anti-immigrant groups like FAIR blaming immigrants for the staggering African-American unemployment rate.

Wilson's immigrant bashing is likely to provide a model for other parts of the country. The five states with the highest immigration rates—California,

Florida, New York, Illinois and Texas—all have a governor up for re-election in 1994. Wilson's tactics won't appear in every campaign but some of the five states will surely see intensified awareness and stigmatization of Latinos as well as Asian/Pacific Islanders. *Editor's Note:* While the specific references are dated, the larger reality is still true: immigration remains a controversial issue in local and regional elections.

As this suggests, what has been a regional issue mostly limited to western states is becoming a national issue. If you thought Latinos were just "Messicans" down at the border, wake up—they are all over North Carolina, Pennsylvania and 8th Avenue Manhattan now. A qualitative change is taking place. With the broader geographic spread of Latinos and Asian/Pacific Islanders has come a nationalization of racist practices and attitudes that were once regional. The west goes east, we could say.

Like the monster Hydra, racism is growing some ugly new heads. We will have to look at them closely.

THE ROOTS OF RACISM AND LATINOS

A bipolar model of racism—racism as white on Black—has never really been accurate. Looking for the roots of racism in the U.S. we can begin with the genocide against American Indians which made possible the U.S. land base, crucial to white settlement and early capitalist growth. Soon came the massive enslavement of African people which facilitated that growth. As slave labor became economically critical, "blackness" became ideologically critical; it provided the very source of "whiteness" and the heart of racism. Franz Fanon would write, "colour is the most outward manifestation of race."

If Native Americans had been a crucial labor force during those same centuries, living and working in the white man's sphere, our racist ideology might have evolved differently. "The tawny," as Ben Franklin dubbed them, might have defined the opposite of what he called "the lovely white." But with Indians decimated and survivors moved to distant concentration camps, they became unlikely candidates for this function. Similarly, Mexicans were concentrated in the distant West; elsewhere Anglo fear of them or need to control was rare. They also did not provide the foundation for a definition of whiteness.

Some anti-racist left activists have put forth the idea that only African Americans experience racism as such and that the suffering of other people of color results from national minority rather than racial oppression. From this viewpoint, the exclusively white/Black model for racism is correct. Latinos, then, experience exploitation and repression for reasons of culture and nationality—not for their "race." (It should go without saying that while racism is an all-too-real social fact, race has no scientific basis.)

Does the distinction hold? This and other theoretical questions call for more analysis and more expertise than one article can offer. In the meantime, let's try on the idea that Latinos do suffer for their nationality and culture, especially language. They became part of the U.S. through the 1846–48 war on Mexico and thus a foreign population to be colonized. But as they were reduced to cheap or semi-slave labor, they quickly came to suffer for their "race"—meaning, as non-whites. In the Southwest of a super-racialized nation the broad parallelism of race and class embrace Mexicans ferociously.

The bridge here might be a definition of racism as "the reduction of the cultural to the biological," in the words of French scholar Christian Delacampagne now working in Egypt. Or: "racism exists wherever it is claimed that a given social status is explained by a given natural characteristic." We know that line: Mexicans are just naturally lazy and have too many children, so they're poor and exploited.

The discrimination, oppression and hatred experienced by Native Americans, Mexicans, Asian/Pacific Islanders, and Arab Americans are forms of racism. Speaking only of Latinos, we have seen in California and the Southwest, especially along the border, almost 150 years of relentless repression which today includes Central Americans among its targets. That history reveals hundreds of lynchings between 1847 and 1935, the use of counterinsurgency armed forces beginning with the Texas Rangers, random torture and murder by Anglo ranchers, forced labor, rape by border lawmen, and the prevailing Anglo belief that a Mexican life doesn't equal a dog's in value.

But wait. If color is so key to racial definition, as Fanon and others say, perhaps people of Mexican background experience racism less than national minority oppression because they are not dark enough as a group. For White America, shades of skin color are crucial to defining worth. The influence of those shades has also been internalized by communities of color. Many Latinos can and often want to pass for whites; therefore, White America may see them as less threatening than darker sisters and brothers.

Here we confront more of the complexity around us today, with questions like: What about the usually poor, very dark Mexican or Central American of strong Indian or African heritage? (Yes, folks, 200,000–300,000 Africans were brought to Mexico as slaves, which is far, far more than the Spaniards who came.) And what about the effects of accented speech or foreign name, characteristics that may instantly subvert "passing"?

What about those cases where a Mexican-American is never accepted, no matter how light-skinned, well-dressed or well-spoken? A Chicano lawyer friend coming home from a professional conference in suit, tie and briefcase found himself on a bus near San Diego that was suddenly stopped by the Border Patrol. An agent came on board and made a beeline through the all-white rows of passengers direct to my friend. "Your papers." The agent didn't believe Jose was coming from a U.S. conference and took him off the bus to await proof. Jose was lucky; too many Chicanos and Mexicans end up killed.

In a land where the national identity is white, having the "wrong" nationality becomes grounds for racist abuse. Who would draw a sharp line between today's national minority oppression in the form of immigrant-bashing, and racism?

None of this aims to equate the African American and Latino experiences; that isn't necessary even if it were accurate. Many reasons exist for the persistence of the white/Black paradigm of racism; they include numbers, history, and the psychology of whiteness. In particular they include centuries of slave revolts, a Civil War, and an ongoing resistance to racism that cracked this society wide open while the world watched. Nor has the misery imposed on Black people lessened in recent years. New thinking about racism can and should keep this experience at the center.

A DEADLY DUALISM

The exclusively white/Black concept of race and racism in the U.S. rests on a western, Protestant form of dualism woven into both race and gender relations from earliest times. In the dualist universe there is only black and white. A disdain, indeed fear, of mixture haunts the Yankee soul; there is no room for any kind of multi-faceted identity, any hybridism.

As a people, La Raza combines three sets of roots—indigenous, European, and African—all in widely varying degrees. In short we represent a profoundly un-American concept: *mestizaje* (pronounced mess-tee-zah-hey), the mixing of peoples and emergence of new peoples. A highly racialized society like this one cannot deal with or allow room for *mestizaje*. It has never learned to do much more than hiss "miscegenation!" Or, like that Alabama high school principal who recently denied the right of a mixed-blood pupil to attend the prom, to say: "your parents made a mistake." Apparently we, all the millions of La Raza, are just that—a mistake.

Mexicans in the U.S. also defy the either-or, dualistic mind in that, on the one hand, we are a colonized people displaced from the ancestral homeland with roots in the present-day U.S. that go back centuries. Those ancestors didn't cross the border; the border crossed them. At the same time many of us have come to the U.S. more recently as "immigrants" seeking work. The complexity of Raza baffles and frustrates most Anglos; they want to put one neat label on us. It baffles many Latinos too, who often end up categorizing themselves racially as "Other" for lack of anything better. For that matter, the term "Latino" which I use here is a monumental simplification; it refers to 20-plus nationalities and a wide range of classes.

But we need to grapple with the complexity, for there is more to come. If anything, this nation will see more *mestizaje* in the future, embracing innumerable ethnic combinations. What will be its effects? Only one thing seems certain: "white" shall cease to be the national identity.

A glimpse at the next century tells us how much we need to look beyond the white/Black model of race relations and racism. White/Black are real poles, central to the history of U.S. racism. We can neither ignore them nor stop there. But our effectiveness in fighting racism depends on seeing the changes taking place, trying to perceive the contours of the future. From the time of the Greeks to the present, racism around the world has had certain commonalties but no permanently fixed character. It is evolving again today, and we'd best labor to read the new faces of this Hydra-headed monster. Remember, for every head that Hydra lost it grew two more.

Sometimes the problem seems so clear. Last year I showed slides of Chicano history to an Oakland high school class with 47 African Americans and three Latino students. The images included lynchings and police beatings of Mexicans and other Latinos, and many years of resistance. At the end one Black student asked, "Seems like we have had a lot of experiences in common—so why can't Blacks and Mexicans get along better?" No answers, but there was the first step: asking the question.

 QUESTIONS FOR CRITICAL THINKING

Reading 62

1. Martinez offers some explanations for the difficulty the United States has with viewing issues of race beyond a black-white dichotomy. What do you think of her explanations?

2. Has the reality that whites will no longer be a majority in the United States impacted race relations positively or negatively?

3. How might expanding issues of race beyond the black-white dichotomy help us to move toward a system of equal access to opportunity with regard to race?

Reading 63

DISMANTLING ENVIRONMENTAL RACISM IN THE USA

ROBERT D. BULLARD

 INTRODUCTION

Despite significant improvements in environmental protection over the past several decades, millions of Americans continue to live in unsafe and unhealthy physical environments. Many economically impoverished communities and their inhabitants are exposed to greater health hazards in their homes, in their jobs and in their neighbourhoods when compared to their more affluent counterparts (Alston, 1992; Alston & Brown, 1993; Bryant & Mohai, 1992; US Environmental Protection Agency (EPA), 1992). This paper examines the root causes and consequences of differential exposure of some US populations to elevated environmental health risks.

 DEFINING ENVIRONMENTAL RACISM

In the real world, all communities are not created equal. All communities do not receive equal protection. Economics, political clout and race play an important part in sorting out residential amenities and disamenities. Environmental racism is as real as the racism found in housing, employment, education and voting (Bullard, 1993a). *Environmental racism refers to any environmental policy, practice or directive that differentially affects or disadvantages (whether intended or unintended) individuals, groups or communities based on race or colour.* Environmental racism is just one form of environmental injustice and is reinforced by government, legal, economic, political and military institutions. Environmental racism combines with public policies and industry practices to provide *benefits* for whites while shifting *costs* to people of colour (Godsil, 1990; Colquette & Robertson, 1991; Collin, 1992; Bullard, 1993a).

From New York to Los Angeles, grassroots community resistance has emerged in response to practices, policies and conditions that residents have

Robert D. Bullard, 1999, "Dismantling Environmental Racism in the USA" from *Local Environment*, Vol. 4, No. 1, pp. 5–19.

judged to be unjust, unfair and illegal. Some of these conditions include: (1) unequal enforcement of environmental, civil rights and public health laws; (2) differential exposure of some populations to harmful chemicals, pesticides and other toxins in the home, school, neighbourhood and work-place; (3) faulty assumptions in calculating, assessing and managing risks; (4) discriminatory zoning and land-use practices; and (5) exclusionary prac-tices that limit some individuals and groups from participation in decision making (C. Lee, 1992; Bullard, 1993b, 1994).

THE ENVIRONMENTAL JUSTICE PARADIGM

During its 28-year history, the US EPA has not always recognised that many government and industry practices (whether intended or unintended) have adverse impacts on poor people and people of colour. Growing grassroots community resistance has emerged in response to practices, policies and conditions that residents have judged to be unjust, unfair and illegal. The EPA is mandated to enforce the nation's environmental laws and regulations equally across the board. It is required to protect all Americans—not just individuals or groups who can afford lawyers, lobbyists and experts. Envi-ronmental protection is a right, not a privilege reserved for a few who can 'vote with their feet' and escape or fend off environmental stressors.

The current environmental protection apparatus is broken and needs to be fixed. The current apparatus manages, regulates and distributes risks (Bull-ard, 1996). The dominant environmental protection paradigm institutionalises unequal enforcement, trades human health for profit, places the burden of proof on the 'victims' and not the polluting industry, legitimates human expo-sure to harmful chemicals, pesticides and hazardous substances, promotes 'risky' technologies, exploits the vulnerability of economically and politi-cally disenfranchised communities, subsidises ecological destruction, creates an industry around risk assessment and risk management, delays clean-up actions and fails to develop pollution prevention as the overarching and dom-inant strategy (Beasley, 1990a, b; Austin & Schill, 1991; Bullard, 1993c).

Environmental justice is defined as the fair treatment and meaningful involvement of all people regardless of race, colour, national origin or income with respect to the development, implementation and enforcement of envi-ronmental laws, regulations and policies. Fair treatment means that no group of people, including racial, ethnic or socio-economic groups, should bear a disproportionate share of the negative environmental consequences result-ing from industrial, municipal and commercial operations or the execution of federal, state, local and tribal programmes and policies.

A growing body of evidence reveals that people of colour and low-income persons have borne greater environmental and health risks than the society at large in their neighbourhoods, workplaces and playgrounds. On the other hand, the environmental justice paradigm embraces a holistic approach to formulating environmental health policies and regulations, developing risk reduction strategies for multiple, cumulative and synergistic risks, ensuring public health, enhancing public participation in environmental decision-making, promoting community empowerment, building infrastructure for achieving environmental justice and sustainable communities, ensuring inter-agency co-operation and co-ordination, developing innovative public/private partnerships and collaboratives, enhancing community-based pollution prevention strategies, ensuring community-based sustainable economic development and developing geographically oriented community-wide programming.

The question of environmental justice is not anchored in a debate about whether or not decision makers should tinker with risk assessment and risk management. The environmental justice framework rests on an ethical analysis of strategies to eliminate unfair, unjust and inequitable conditions and decisions. The framework attempts to uncover the underlying assumptions that may contribute to and produce differential exposure and unequal protection. It also brings to the surface the *ethical* and *political* questions of 'who gets what, when, why and how much'. Some general characteristics of this framework include the following.

- The environmental justice framework adopts a public health model of prevention (i.e. elimination of the threat before harm occurs) as the preferred strategy.
- The environmental justice framework shifts the burden of proof to polluters/dischargers who do harm, who discriminate or who do not give equal protection to people of colour, low-income persons and other 'protected' classes.
- The environmental justice framework allows disparate impact and statistical weight or an 'effect' test, as opposed to 'intent', to infer discrimination.
- The environmental justice framework redresses disproportionate impact through 'targeted' action and resources. In general, this strategy would target resources where environmental and health problems are greatest (as determined by some ranking scheme but not limited to risk assessment).

ENDANGERED COMMUNITIES

Numerous studies reveal that low-income persons and people of colour have borne greater health and environmental risk burdens than the society at large (Mann, 1991; Goldman, 1991; Goldman & Fitten, 1994). Elevated public health risks have been found in some populations even when social class is held constant. For example, race has been found to be independent of class in the distribution of air pollution, contaminated fish consumption, municipal landfills and incinerators, abandoned toxic waste dumps, the clean-up of superfund sites and lead poisoning in children (Commission for Racial Justice, 1987; Agency for Toxic Substances and Disease Registry, 1988; West *et al.*, 1992; Bryant & Mohai, 1992; Lavelle & Coyle, 1992; Goldman & Fitten, 1994; Pirkle *et al.*, 1994).

Childhood lead poisoning is another preventable disease that has not been eradicated. Figures reported in the July 1994 *Journal of the American Medical Association* from the Third National Health and Nutrition Examination Survey (NHANES III) revealed that 1.7 million children (8.9% of children aged 1–5) are lead poisoned, defined as having blood levels equal to or above 10 µg/dl. The NHANES III data found African-American children to be lead poisoned at more than twice the rate of white children at every income level (Pirkle *et al.*, 1994). Over 28.4% of all low-income African-American children were lead poisoned compared to 9.8% of all low-income white children. During the time-period between 1976 and 1991, the decrease in blood lead levels for African-American and Mexican-American children lagged far behind that of white children.

In California, a coalition of environmental, social justice and civil libertarian groups joined forces to challenge the way the state carried out its lead screening of poor children. The Natural Resources Defense Council, the National Association for the Advancement of Colored People Legal Defense and Education Fund (NAACP LDF), the American Civil Liberties Union and the Legal Aid Society of Alameda County, California won an out-of-court settlement worth $15 million to $20 million for a blood lead testing programme. The lawsuit, *Matthews v. Coye,* involved the failure of the state of California to conduct the federally mandated testing for lead of some 557 000 poor children who received Medicaid (B. L. Lee, 1992). This historic agreement triggered similar lawsuits and actions in several other states that failed to live up to the mandates.

 ## IMPETUS FOR POLICY SHIFT

The impetus behind the environmental justice movement did not come from within government or academia, or from within largely white middle-class nationally based environmental and conservation groups. The impetus for change came from people of colour, grassroots activists and their 'bottom-up' leadership approach. Grassroots groups organised themselves, educated themselves and empowered themselves to make fundamental change in the way environmental protection is performed in their communities.

The environmental justice movement has come a long way since its humble beginning in rural, predominantly African-American, Warren County, North Carolina, where a polychlorinated biphenyl landfill ignited protests and where over 500 arrests were made. The Warren County protests provided the impetus for a US General Accounting Office (1983) study, *Siting of*

Hazardous Waste Landfills and their Correlation with Racial and Economic Status of Surrounding Communities. That study revealed that three out of four of the off-site, commercial hazardous waste landfills in Region 4 (which comprises eight states in the South) happened to be located in predominantly African-American communities, although African-Americans made up only 20% of the region's population.

The protests also led the Commission for Racial Justice (1987) to produce *Toxic Wastes and Race in the United States,* the first national study to correlate waste facility sites and demographic characteristics. Race was found to be the most potent variable in predicting where these facilities were located—more powerful than poverty, land values and home ownership. In 1990, *Dumping in Dixie: Race, Class, and Environmental Quality* (Bullard, 1994) chronicled the convergence of two social movements—social justice and environmental movements—into the environmental justice movement. This book highlighted African-Americans' environmental activism in the South, the same region that gave birth to the modern civil rights movement. What started out as local and often isolated community-based struggles against toxics and facility siting blossomed into a multi-issue, multi-ethnic and multi-regional movement.

The First National People of Color Environmental Leadership Summit (1991) was probably the most important single event in the movement's history. The Summit broadened the environmental justice movement beyond its anti-toxics focus to include issues of public health, worker safety, land use, transportation, housing, resource allocation and community empowerment (C. Lee, 1992). The meeting, organised by and for people of colour, demonstrated that it is possible to build a multi-racial grassroots movement around environmental and economic justice (Alston, 1992).

Held in Washington, DC, the day Summit was attended by over 650 grassroots and national leaders from around the world. Delegates came from all 50 states, including Alaska and Hawaii, Puerto Rico, Chile, Mexico and as far away as the Marshall Islands. People attended the Summit to share their action strategies, redefine the environmental movement and develop common plans for addressing environmental problems affecting people of colour in the USA and around the world.

On 27 October 1991, Summit delegates adopted 17 'principles of environmental justice' (see Box 1). These principles were developed as a guide for organising and networking, and relating to non-governmental organisations (NGOs). By June 1992, Spanish and Portuguese translations of the principles were being used and circulated by NGOs and community groups at the Earth Summit in Rio de Janeiro.

Federal, state and local policies and practices have contributed to residential segmentation and unhealthy living conditions in poor, working-class and people of colour communities (Bullard & Johnson, 1997). Several recent cases in California bring this point to life (Lee, 1995). Disparate highway siting and mitigation plans were challenged by community residents, churches

BOX 1
The First National People of Color Environmental
Justice Leadership Summit
24–27 October 1991, Washington, DC

Preamble

We, The People of Color, gathered together at this multi-national People of Color Environmental Leadership Summit, to begin to build a national and international movement of all peoples of color to fight the destruction and taking of our lands and communities, do hereby re-establish our spiritual interdependence to the sacredness of our Mother Earth, respect and celebrate each of our cultures, languages and beliefs about our natural world and our roles in healing ourselves; to insure environmental justice; to promote economic alternatives which would contribute to the development of environmentally safe livelihoods; and to secure our political, economic and cultural liberation that has been denied for over 500 years of colonization and oppression, resulting in the poisoning of our communities and land and the genocide of our peoples, do affirm and adopt these principles of Environmental Justice:

(1) *Environmental justice* affirms the sacredness of Mother Earth, ecological unity and the interdependence of all species, and the right to be free from ecological destruction.

(2) *Environmental justice* demands that public policy be based on mutual respect and justice for all peoples, free from any form of discrimination or bias.

(3) *Environmental justice* mandates the right to ethical, balanced and responsible uses of land and renewable resources in the interest of a sustainable planet for humans and other living things.

(4) *Environmental justice* calls for universal protection from nuclear testing and the extraction, production and disposal of toxic/ hazardous wastes and poisons that threaten the fundamental right to clean air, land, water, and food.

(5) *Environmental justice* affirms the fundamental right to political, economic, cultural and environmental self-determination of all peoples.

(6) *Environmental justice* demands the cessation of the production of all toxins, hazardous wastes, and radioactive materials, and that all past and current producers be held strictly accountable to the people for detoxification and the containment at the point of production.

(Continued)

(Continued)

(7) *Environmental justice* demands the right to participate as equal partners at every level of decision-making including needs assessment, planning, implementation, enforcement and evaluation.

(8) *Environmental justice* affirms the right of all workers to a safe and healthy work environment, without being forced to choose between an unsafe livelihood and unemployment. It also affirms the right to those who work at home to be free from environmental hazards.

(9) *Environmental justice* protects the right of victims of environmental injustice to receive full compensation and reparations for damages as well as quality health care.

(10) *Environmental justice* considers governmental acts of environmental injustice a violation of international law, the Universal Declaration of Human Rights, and the United Nations Convention of Genocide.

(11) *Environmental justice* must recognize a special legal and natural relationship of Native Peoples to the US government through treaties, agreements, compacts, and covenants affirming sovereignty and self-determination.

(12) *Environmental justice* affirms the need for urban and rural ecological policies to clean up and rebuild our cities and rural areas in balance with nature, honoring the cultural integrity of all our communities, and providing fair access for the full range of resources.

(13) *Environmental justice* calls for the enforcement of principles of informed consent, and a halt to the testing of experimental reproductive and medical procedures and vaccinations on people of color.

(14) *Environmental justice* opposes the destructive operations of multi-national corporations.

(15) *Environmental justice* opposes military occupation, repression and exploitation of lands, peoples and cultures, and other life forms.

(16) *Environmental justice* calls for the education of present and future generations which emphasizes social and environmental issues, based on our experience and an appreciation of our diverse cultural perspectives.

(17) *Environmental justice* requires that we, as individuals, make personal and consumer choices to consume as little of Mother Earth's resources and to produce as little waste as possible; and make the conscious decision to challenge and reprioritize our lifestyles to insure the health of the natural world for present and future generations.

Principles of environmental justice (adopted in Washington, DC on 27 October 1994).

and the NAACP LDF, in *Clear Air Alternative Coalition v. United States Department of Transportation* (ND Cal. C-93-0721-VRW), involving the reconstruction of the earthquake-damaged Cypress Freeway in West Oakland. The plaintiffs wanted the downed Cypress Freeway (which split their community in half) rebuilt further away. Although the plaintiffs were not able to get their plan implemented, they did change the course of the freeway in their out-of-court settlement.

The NAACP LDF has filed an administrative complaint, *Mothers of East Los Angeles, El Sereño Neighborhood Action Committee, El Sereño Organizing Committee et al. v. California Transportation Commission* et al. (before the US Department of Transportation and US Housing and Urban Development), challenging the construction of the 4.5 mile extension of the Long Beach Freeway in East Los Angeles through El Sereño, Pasadena and South Pasadena. The plaintiffs argue that the mitigation measures proposed by the state agencies to address noise, air and visual pollution discriminate against the mostly Latino El Sereño community. For example, all of the freeway in Pasadena and 80% of that in South Pasadena will be below ground level. On the other hand, most of the freeway in El Sereño will be above-grade. White areas were favoured over the mostly Latino El Sereño in the allocation of covered freeway, historic preservation measures and accommodation to local schools (Lee, 1995; Bullard & Johnson, 1997).

Los Angeles residents and the NAACP LDF have also challenged the inequitable funding and operation of bus transportation used primarily by low-income persons and people of colour residents. A class action lawsuit was filed on behalf of 350 000 low-income, people of colour, bus travellers represented by the Labor/Community Strategy Center, the Bus Riders Union, the Southern Christian Leadership Conference, Korean Immigrant Workers Advocates, and individual bus travellers. In *Labor/Community Strategy Center v. Los Angeles Metropolitan Transportation Authority* (Cal. CV 94–5936 TJH Mcx), the plaintiffs argued that the Los Angeles Metropolitan Transit Authority (MTA) uses federal funds to pursue a policy of raising the costs of bus travellers (who are mostly poor and people of colour) and reducing the quality of the service in order to fund rail and other projects in predominantly white, surburban areas.

In the end, the Labor/Community Strategy Center and its allies successfully challenged transit racism in Los Angeles. The group was able to win major fare and bus pass concessions from the Los Angeles MTA. They also forced the Los Angeles MTA to spend $89 million on 278 new, clean, compressed natural gas buses.

 ## MAKING GOVERNMENT MORE RESPONSIVE

Many of the nation's environmental policies distribute costs in a regressive pattern while providing disproportionate benefits for whites and individuals who fall at the upper end of the education and income scales. Lavelle

& Coyle (1992) uncovered glaring inequities in the way the federal EPA enforces its laws:

> There is a racial divide in the way the US government cleans up toxic waste sites and punishes polluters. White communities see faster action, better results and stiffer penalties than communities where blacks, Hispanics and other minorities live. This unequal protection often occurs whether the community is wealthy or poor.

This study reinforced what many grassroots activists have known for decades: all communities are not treated the same. Communities that are located on the 'wrong side of the tracks' are at greater risk from exposure to lead, pesticides (in the home and the workplace), air pollution, toxic releases, water pollution, solid and hazardous waste, raw sewage and pollution from industries (Goldman, 1992).

Government has been slow to ask the questions of who gets help and who does not, who can afford help and who can not, why some contaminated communities get studied while others get left off the research agenda, why industry poisons some communities and not others, why some contaminated communities get cleaned up while others are not, why some populations are protected and others are not protected, and why unjust, unfair and illegal policies and practices are allowed to go unpunished.

Struggles for equal environmental protection and environmental justice did not magically appear in the 1990s. Many communities of colour have been engaged in life and death struggles for more than a decade. In 1990, the Agency for Toxic Substances and Disease Registry (ATSDR) held a historic conference in Atlanta. The ATSDR National Minority Health Conference focused on contamination (Johnson *et al.,* 1992). In 1992, after meeting with community leaders, academicians and civil rights leaders, the US EPA (under the leadership of William Reilly) admitted there was a problem, and established the Office of Environmental Equity. The name was changed to the Office of Environmental Justice under the Clinton Administration.

In 1992, the US EPA produced one of the first comprehensive documents to examine the whole question of risk and environmental hazards in their equity report, *Environmental Equity: reducing risk for all communities* (US EPA, 1992. The report, and its Office of Environmental Equity, were initiated only after prodding from people of colour, environmental justice leaders, activists and a few academicians.

The EPA also established a 25-member National Environmental Justice Advisory Council (NEJAC) under the Federal Advisory Committee Act. The NEJAC divided its environmental justice work into six sub-committees: Health and Research, Waste and Facility Siting, Enforcement, Public Participation and Accountability, Native American and Indigenous Issues, and International Issues. The NEJAC is comprised of stakeholders representing grassroots community groups, environmental groups, NGOs, state, local and tribal governments, academia and industry.

In February 1994, seven federal agencies, including the ATSDR, the National Institute for Environmental Health Sciences, the EPA, the National Institute of Occupational Safety and Health, the National Institutes of Health, the Department of Energy and Centers for Disease Control and Prevention sponsored a National Health Symposium entitled 'Health and research needs to ensure environmental justice'. The conference planning committee was unique in that it included grassroots organisation leaders, affected community residents and federal agency representatives. The goal of the February conference was to bring diverse stakeholders and those most affected to the decision-making table (National Institute for Environmental Health Sciences, 1995). Some of the recommendations from that symposium included the following:

- Conduct meaningful health research in support of people of colour and low-income communities.
- Promote disease prevention and pollution prevention strategies.
- Promote inter-agency co-ordination to ensure environmental justice.
- Provide effective outreach, education and communications.
- Design legislative and legal remedies.

In response to growing public concern and mounting scientific evidence, President Clinton on 11 February 1994 (the second day of the National Health Symposium) issued Executive Order 12898, 'Federal actions to address environmental justice in minority populations and low-income populations'. This Order attempts to address environmental injustice within existing federal laws and regulations.

Executive Order 12898 reinforces the 30-year-old Civil Rights Act of 1964, Title VI, which prohibits discriminatory practices in programmes receiving federal funds. The Order also focuses the spotlight back on the National Environmental Policy Act (NEPA), a 25-year-old law that sets policy goals for the protection, maintenance and enhancement of the environment. The NEPA's goal is to ensure for all Americans a safe, healthful, productive and aesthetically and culturally pleasing environment. The NEPA requires federal agencies to prepare a detailed statement on the environmental effects of proposed federal actions that significantly affect the quality of human health.

The Executive Order calls for improved methodologies for assessing and mitigating impacts and health effects from multiple and cumulative exposures, the collection of data on low-income and minority populations who may be disproportionately at risk, and impacts on subsistence fishers and wildlife consumers. It also encourages the participation of the affected populations in the various phases of impact assessment, including scoping, data gathering, alternatives, analysis, mitigation and monitoring.

The Executive Order focuses on 'subsistence' fishers and wildlife consumers. Not everybody buys their fish at the supermarket. There are many people who are subsistence fishers, fishing for protein, who basically subsidise their budgets and their diets by fishing from rivers, streams and lakes that happen to be polluted. These sub-populations may be underprotected when basic assumptions are made using the dominant risk paradigm.

THE CASE OF CITIZENS AGAINST NUCLEAR TRASH VERSUS LOUISIANA ENERGY SERVICES

Executive Order 12898 was put to the test in rural north-west Louisiana. Since 1989, the Nuclear Regulatory Commission had under review a proposal from Louisiana Energy Services (LES) to build the nation's first privately owned uranium enrichment plant. A national search was undertaken by LES to find the 'best' site for a plant that would produce 17% of the nation's enriched uranium. LES supposedly used an objective scientific method in designing its site selection process.

The southern USA, Louisiana and Claiborne Parish ended up being the dubious 'winners' of the site selection process. Residents from Homer and the nearby communities of Forest Grove and Center Springs—two communities closest to the proposed site—disagreed with the site selection process and outcome. They organised themselves into a group called Citizens Against Nuclear Trash (CANT). CANT charged LES and the federal Nuclear Regulatory Commission (NRC) staff with practising environmental racism. CANT hired the Sierra Club Legal Defense Fund and sued LES.

The lawsuit dragged on for more than 8 years. On 1 May 1997, a three-judge panel of the NRC Atomic Safety and Licensing Board issued a final decision on the case. The judges concluded that 'racial bias played a role in the selection process' (NRC, 1997). The precedent-setting federal court ruling came some 2 years after President Clinton signed Executive Order 12898. The judges, in a 38-page written decision, also chastised the NRC staff for not addressing the provision called for under Executive Order 12898. The court decision was upheld on appeal on 4 April 1998.

A clear racial pattern emerged during the so-called national search and multi-stage screening and selection process (Bullard, 1995). For example, African-Americans comprise about 13% of the US population, 20% of the Southern states' population, 31% of Louisiana's population, 35% of the population of Louisiana's northern parishes and 46% of the population of Claiborne Parish. This progressive trend, involving the narrowing of the site selection process to areas of increasingly high poverty and African-American representation, is also evident from an evaluation of the actual sites that were considered in the 'intermediate' and 'fine' screening stages of the site selection process. The aggregate average percentage of black population for a 1-mile radius around all of the 78 sites examined (in 16 parishes) was 28.35%. When LES completed its initial site cuts, and reduced the list to 37 sites within nine parishes (i.e. the same as counties in other states), the aggregate percentage of black population rose to 36.78%. When LES then further limited its focus to six sites in Claiborne Parish, the aggregate average percentage of black population rose again, to 64.74%. The final site selected, the 'LeSage' site, has a 97.1% black population within a 1-mile radius.

The plant was proposed on Parish Road 39 between two African-American communities, just 0.25 miles from Center Springs (founded in 1910) and 1.25 miles from Forest Grove (founded in the 1860s just after slavery). The proposed site was in a Louisiana parish that has a per capita earnings average of only $5800 per year (just 45% of the national average, $12 800), and where over 58% of the African-American population is below the poverty line. The two African-American communities were rendered 'invisible' since they were not even mentioned in the NRC's draft environmental impact statement (NRC, 1993).

Only after intense public comments did the NRC staff attempt to address environmental justice and disproportionate impact implications, as required under the NEPA and called for under Environmental Justice Executive Order 12898. For example, the NEPA requires that the government consider the environmental impacts and weigh the costs and benefits of the proposed action. These include health and environmental effects, the risk of accidental but foreseeable adverse health and environmental effects and socio-economic impacts.

The NRC staff devoted less than a page to addressing the environmental justice concerns of the proposed uranium enrichment plant in its final environmental impact statement (FEIS). Overall, the FEIS and the environmental report are inadequate in the following respects: (1) they assess inaccurately the costs and benefits of the proposed plant; (2) they fail to consider the inequitable distribution of costs and benefits of the proposed plant between the white and African-American populations; (3) they fail to consider the fact that the siting of the plant in a community of colour follows a national pattern in which institutionally biased decision-making leads to the siting of hazardous facilities in communities of colour, which results in the inequitable distribution of costs and benefits to those communities.

Among the distributive costs not analysed in relationship to Forest Grove and Center Springs are the disproportionate burden of health and safety, effects on property values, fire and accidents, noise, traffic, radioactive dust in the air and water, and the dislocation from a road closure that connects the two communities. Overall, the CANT legal victory points to the utility of combining environmental and civil rights laws and the requirement of governmental agencies to consider Executive Order 12898 in their assessments.

In addition to the remarkable victory over LES, a company that had the backing of powerful US and European nuclear energy companies, CANT members and their allies won much more. They empowered themselves and embarked on a path of political empowerment and self-determination. During the long battle, CANT member Roy Madris was elected to the Claiborne Parish Jury (i.e. county commission), and CANT member Almeter Willis was elected to the Claiborne Parish School Board. The town of Homer, the nearest incorporated town to Forest Grove and Center Springs, elected its first African-American mayor, and the Homer town council now has two African-American members. In autumn 1998, LES sold the land on which the proposed uranium enrichment plant would have been located. The land is going back into timber production—as it was before LES bought it.

 ## CONVENT RESIDENTS VERSUS SHINTECH PLANT

Battle lines are now drawn in Louisiana on another national environmental justice test case. The community is Convent and the company is Shintech. The Japanese-owned Shintech, Inc. has applied for a Title V air permit to build an $800 million polyvinyl chloride (PVC) plant in Convent, Louisiana—a community that is over 70% African-American and where over 40% of the residents fall below the poverty line. The community already has a dozen polluting plants and a 60% unemployment rate. The plants are very close to residents' homes. Industries are lured into the black community with the promise of jobs. But, in reality, the jobs are not there for local residents.

The Shintech case raises environmental racism concerns similar to those found in the failed LES siting scheme. The US EPA is bound by Executive Order 12898 to ensure that "no segment of the population, regardless of race, color, national origin, or income, as a result of EPA's policies, programs, and activities, suffer disproportionately from adverse health or environmental effects, and all people live in clean and sustainable communities". The Louisiana Department of Environmental Quality is also bound by federal laws to administer and implement its programmes, mandates and policies in a non-discriminatory way.

Any environmental justice analysis of the Shintech proposal will need to examine the issues of disproportionate and adverse impact on low-income and minority populations near the proposed PVC plant. Clearly, it is African-Americans and low-income residents in Convent who live closest to existing and proposed industrial plants and who will be disproportionately affected by industrial pollution (Wright, 1998). African-Americans comprise 34% of the state's total population. The Shintech plant would be located in a parish, St James Parish, that ranks third in the state for toxic releases and transfers. Over 83% of St James Parish's 4526 residents are African-American. Over 17.7 million pounds of releases were reported in the 1996 toxic release inventory. The Shintech plant would add over 600 000 pounds of air pollutants annually. Permitting the Shintech plant in Convent would add significantly to the toxic burden borne by residents, who are mostly low-income and African-American.

After more than 18 months of intense organising and legal manoeuvering, residents of tiny Convent, Louisiana, and their allies forced Shintech to scrap plans to build the PVC plant. The decision came in September 1998, and was hailed around the country as a major victory against environmental racism. The driving force behind this victory was the relentless pressure and laser-like focus of the local Convent community.

 CONCLUSION

The environmental protection apparatus in the USA does not provide equal protection for all communities. The current paradigm institutionalises unequal enforcement, trades human health for profit, places the burden of proof on the 'victims' and not on the polluting industry, legitimates human exposure to harmful chemicals, pesticides and hazardous wastes, promotes 'risky' technologies, exploits the vulnerability of economically and politically disenfranchised communities and nations, subsidises ecological destruction, creates an industry around risk assessment and delays clean-up actions, and fails to develop pollution prevention, waste minimisation and cleaner production strategies as the overarching and dominant goal.

The environmental justice movement emerged in response to environmental inequities, threats to public health, unequal protection, differential enforcement and disparate treatment received by the poor and people of colour. This movement has redefined environmental protection as a basic right. It has also emphasised pollution prevention, waste minimisation and cleaner production techniques as strategies to achieve environmental justice for all Americans without regard to race, colour, national origin or income.

Both race and class factors place low-income and people of colour communities at special risk. Unequal political power arrangements have also allowed poisons of the rich to be offered as short-term economic remedies for poverty of the poor. However, there is little or no correlation between the proximity of industrial plants in communities of colour and the employment of nearby residents. Having industrial facilities in one's community does not automatically translate into jobs for nearby residents. More often than not, communities of colour are stuck with the polluting industries and poverty, while other people commute in for the jobs.

Governments must live up to their mandate of *protecting* all peoples and the environment. The call for environmental and economic justice does not stop at US borders but extends to all communities and nations that are threatened by hazardous wastes, toxic products and environmentally unsound technology. The environmental justice movement has set out the clear goal of eliminating the unequal enforcement of environmental, civil rights and public health laws, the differential exposure of some populations to harmful chemicals, pesticides and other toxins in the home, school, neighbourhood and workplace, faulty assumptions in calculating, assessing and managing risks, discriminatory zoning and land-use practices, and exclusionary policies and practices that limit some individuals and groups from participation in decision-making.

The solution to environmental injustice lies in the realm of equal protection for all individuals, groups and communities. Many of these problems could be eliminated if existing environmental, health, housing and civil rights laws were vigorously enforced in a non-discriminatory way. No community, rich or poor, urban or suburban, black or white, should be allowed to become a 'sacrifice zone' or dumping ground.

REFERENCES

Agency for Toxic Substances and Disease Registry (1988) *The Nature and Extent of Lead Poisoning in Children in the United States: a report to Congress* (Atlanta, GA, US Department of Health and Human Services).

Alston, D. (1992) Transforming a movement: people of color unite at summit against environmental racism, *Sojourner*, 21(1), pp. 30–31.

Alston, D. & Brown, N. (1993) Global threats to people of color, in: R. D. Bullard (Ed.) *Confronting Environmental Racism: voices from the grassroots* (Boston, MA, South End Press).

Austin, R. & Schill, M. (1991) Black, brown, poor, and poisoned: minority grassroots environmentalism and the quest for eco-justice, *The Kansas Journal of Law and Public Policy*, 1(1), pp. 69–82.

Beasley, C. (1990a) Of pollution and poverty: keeping watch in cancer alley, *Buzzworm*, 2(4), pp. 39–45.

Beasley, C. (1990b) Of poverty and pollution: deadly threat on native lands, *Buzzworm*, 2(5), pp. 39–45.

Bryant, B. & Mohai, P. (1992) *Race and the Incidence of Environmental Hazards* (Boulder, CO, Westview Press).

Bullard, R. D. (1993a) *Confronting Environmental Racism: voices from the grassroots* (Boston, MA, South End Press).

Bullard, R. D. (1993b) Race and environmental justice in the United States, *Yale Journal of International Law*, 18(1), pp. 319–335.

Bullard, R. D. (1993c) Environmental racism and land use, *Land Use Forum: a journal of law, policy & practice*, 2(1), pp. 6–11.

Bullard, R. D. (1994) *Dumping in Dixie: race, class and environmental quality* (Boulder, CO, Westview Press).

Bullard, R. D. (1995) Prefiled written testimony at the CANT vs. LES hearing, Shreveport, Louisiana.

Bullard, R. D. (1996) *Unequal Protection: environmental justice and communities of color* (San Francisco, CA, Sierra Club Books).

Bullard, R. D. & Johnson, G. S. (1997) *Just Transportation: dismantling race and class barriers* (Gabriola Island, BC, New Society Publishers).

Chase, A. (1993) Assessing and addressing problems posed by environmental racism, *Rutgers University Law Review*, 45(2), pp. 369–385.

Churchill, W. & LaDuke, W. (1983) Native America: the political economy of radioactive colonialism, *Insurgent Sociologist*, 13(1), pp. 51–63.

Collin, R. W. (1992) Environmental equity: a law and planning approach to environmental racism, *Virginia Environmental Law Journal,* 13(4), pp. 495–546.

Colquette, K. C. & Robertson, E. A. H. (1991) Environmental racism: the causes, consequences, and commendations, *Tulane Environmental Law Journal,* 5(1), pp. 153–207.

Commission for Racial Justice (1987) *Toxic Wastes and Race in the United States* (New York, United Church of Christ).

Godsil, R. D. (1990) Remedying environmental racism, *Michigan Law Review,* 90(394), pp. 394–427.

Goldman, B. (1991) *The Truth about Where You Live: an atlas for action on toxins and mortality* (New York, Random House).

Goldman, B. & Fitten, L. J. (1994) *Toxic Wastes and Race Revisited* (Washington, DC, Center for Policy Alternatives, NAACP, United Church of Christ).

Johnson, B. L, Williams, R. C. & Harris, C. M. (1992) *Proceedings of the 1990 National Minority Health Conference: focus on environmental contamination* (Princeton, NJ, Scientific Publishing).

Lavelle, M. & Coyle, M. (1992) Unequal protection, *The National Law Journal,* 21 September, pp. 1–2.

Lee, B. L. (1992) Environmental litigation on behalf of poor, minority children: Matthews v. Coye: a case study, paper presented at the Annual Meeting of the American Association for the Advancement of Science, Chicago, IL (9 February).

Lee, B. L. (1995) Civil rights remedies for environmental injustice building model partnerships, paper presented at the Transportation and Environmental Justice: Conference, Atlanta, GA (11 May).

Lee, C. (1992) *Proceedings: the First National People of Color Environmental Leadership Summit* (New York, United Church of Christ Commission for Racial Justice).

Mann, E. (1991) *LA's Lethal Air: new strategies for policy, organizing, and action* (Los Angeles, CA, Labor/Community Center).

National Institute for Environmental Health Sciences (1995) *Proceedings of the Health and Research Needs to Ensure Environmental Justice Symposium* (Research Triangle Park, NC, NIEHS).

NRC (1993) Draft Environmental Impact Statement for the Construction and Operation of Claiborne Enrichment Center, Homer, Louisiana, Docket No. 70-3070, Louisiana Energy Services, L.P. (November).

NRC (1997) Final initial decision—Louisiana Energy Services, US NRC, Atomic Safety and Licensing Board, Docket No. 70-3070-ML (1 May).

Pirkle, J. L., Brody, D. J., Gunter, E. W., Kramer, R. A., Paschal, D. C., Glegal, K. M. & Matle, T. D. (1994) The decline in blood lead levels in the United States: the National Health and Nutrition Examination Survey (NHANES III), *Journal of the American Medical Association,* 272, pp. 284–291.

Taliman, V. (1992) Stuck holding the nation's nuclear waste, *Race, Poverty & Environment Newsletter,* Fall, pp. 6–9.

US EPA (1991) *Hazardous Waste Exports by Receiving Country* (Washington, DC, US EPA) (10 June).

US EPA (1992) *Environmental Equity: reducing risk for all communities* (Washington, DC, US EPA).

US EPA (1993) *Toxic Release Inventory and Emission Reductions 1987–1990 in the Lower Mississippi River Industrial Corridor* (Washington, DC, EPA, Office of Pollution Prevention and Toxics).

US General Accounting Office (1983) *Siting of Hazardous Waste Landfills and their Correlation with Racial and Economic Status of Surrounding Communities* (Washington, DC, Government Printing Office).

Wernette, D. R. & Nieves, L. A. (1992) Breathing polluted air, *EPA Journal*, 18(1), pp. 16–17.

West, P., Fly, J. M., Larkin, F. & Marans, P. (1992) Minority anglers and toxic fish consumption: evidence of the state-wide survey of Michigan, in: B. Bryant & P. Mohai (Eds) *Race and the Incidence of Environmental Hazards* (Boulder, CO, Westview Press).

Wright, B. H. (1998) *St James Parish Field Observations* (New Orleans, LA, Deep. South Center for Environmental Justice, Xavier University).

 QUESTIONS FOR CRITICAL THINKING

Reading 63

1. In this article, Bullard discusses the important topic of environmental racism. In what ways is this structural maintenance of inequality new to you? Can you think of examples of environmental racism in places that you have lived in or visited?

2. Bullard illustrates the efforts of grassroots activists in attempting to change the way the government implements environmental, health, and civil rights laws. How do his examples inform your understanding of how to go about making structural social change?

3. What new insights does this reading give you with regard to personally being involved in making social change around issues of environmental racism?

Reading 64

FEMINISMS FUTURE
Young Feminists of Color Take the Mic

DAISY HERNÁNDEZ • PANDORA L. LEONG

W hen San Jose State University senior Erika Jackson tried to recruit fellow women of color for a new feminist group on campus, the overwhelming reply was the sneer "white women." Those words were code for another term: racist.

Many women of color, like their Anglo counterparts, eschew the term "feminism" while agreeing with its goals (the right to an abortion, equality in job hiring, girls' soccer teams). But women of color also dismiss the label because the feminist movement has largely focused on the concerns of middle-class white women. This has been a loss for people of color. Likewise, it's a loss for the movement if it expects to grow: the U.S. Census projects that the Latino and Asian-American population is expected to triple by 2050.

The "browning" of America has yet to serve as a wakeup call for feminist organizers. Attempts to address the racism of the feminist movement have largely been token efforts without lasting effects. Many young women of color still feel alienated from a mainstream feminism that doesn't explicitly address race. One woman of color, who wishes not to be identified and is working with the March for Women's Lives, put it this way: "We're more than your nannies and outreach workers. We're your future."

Progressive movements have a long history of internal debates, but for feminists of color the question of racism and feminism isn't about theories. It's about determining our place in the movement. As the daughters of both the civil rights and feminist movements, we were bred on grrl-power, identity politics, and the emotional and often financial ties to our brothers, fathers, aunties, and moms back home, back South, back in Pakistan, Mexico or other homelands. We live at the intersections of identities, the places where social movements meet, and it's here that our feminism begins.

Daisy Hernández, and Pandora Leong, "Feminism's Future: Young Feminists of Color Take the Mic" from *In These Times*, http://www.inthesetimes.com/main/article/724. April 21, 2004. Accessed July 1, 2010.

ORGANIZATIONS AS OBSTACLES

Feminism in the United States has stagnated in part because it has largely neglected a class and race analysis. Feminism can't survive by helping women climb the corporate ladder while ignoring cuts to welfare. Family and medical leave only matter if we have jobs with benefits. Feminism has to recruit beyond college campuses.

"If the message doesn't get broader, [communities of color] aren't going to open their arms," says Sang Hee Won of Family Planning Advocates in Albany, New York. "These issues don't resonate with an immigrant woman on the streets of New York City. I'm first generation. When I think of my parents, they have so many other things to think about. People are struggling with daily lives and it's especially hard to connect [traditional feminist] issues with their situation."

The priorities of national feminist organizations often are secondary to our daily struggles. Reproductive freedom has to include access to affordable healthcare and the economic opportunities to provide for the children some of us do want to have. Likewise, it's jarring to see the word "policing" on a feminist Web site and be directed to information on gender equity in police departments without mention of police brutality.

For feminists of color to identify with the mainstream movement, national organizations need to address race explicitly. Women of color always have participated but largely have remained ignored. Organizations purport to be aware but don't hire, promote, or recognize women of color as leaders. Affinity groups and special projects remain ghettoized add-ons.

"[Feminist organizations] try and are well-intentioned," says Lauren Martin, a New York activist. "They talk a lot but don't do a lot. Organizations I've worked with talk a lot about being anti-racist. [There would be] lots of trainings and in-services, but [racist] incidents that occurred would be brushed under the rug."

"Their attitude is, 'I'm going to empower you. I'm going to teach you,'" says Alma Avila-Peilchman, program manager at ACCESS, a reproductive rights organization in Oakland, California. "When the truth is we already have that power. We need to use it. We need to be listened to."

 CHANGE IN LEADERSHIP

The young feminists of color we interviewed called for the inclusion of women of color and low-income women in national campaigns—when the agenda is being set.

"Forming a real coalition means starting from the very beginning rather than the 'add and stir' approach," Martin says. "The beginning is when issues are defined. It doesn't work to tack our perspective on at the end and call it 'outreach.'"

Khadine Bennett, a board member of Third Wave Foundation, which supports the activism of young women, says that feminist organizations need to share their power. "Sometimes your organization is not the best one to carry out the work," she says. "Part of the mandate from funders should be to work with people of color organizations."

More than 30 years after the first charges of racism against the movement, these young feminists believe progressive women of color need to be the leaders of national feminist groups. That the executive directors of these organizations and senior staff still are overwhelmingly white testifies to the movement's division. The professionalization of the nonprofit world has deepened this divide by internalizing corporate expectations and marginalizing the involvement of women who can't afford to work for free. In pursuit of mainstream acceptance, organizations are losing touch with the grassroots that could revive feminism. There needs to be a commitment to leadership development among women of color and low-income women that includes mentoring and training.

 ## SEEKING COMMON CAUSE

The movement also should consider models already practiced by younger activists who actively seek out coalitions. "The people I know are working around anti-violence including sexuality and anti-war work and anti-globalization," says Mina Trudeau, of Hampshire College's Civil Liberties and Public Policy Program. "Our feminism is about social justice."

Election years are good moments to broaden an organization's agenda. Last fall, Erika Jackson's feminist campus group organized against Proposition 54, which would have eliminated racial classifications in California. They were the first student organization to tackle the issue, and they didn't debate whether it was a feminist issue.

"Like with public health, we talked about how it affects women of color," she says. A lack of racial classifications would hide the higher rate of low birth weight babies born to women of color. The measure was defeated in the November 2003 state election.

Leah Lakshmi Piepzna-Samarasinha, a Toronto-based spoken-word artist, sees race as a central part of the work she did in counseling women who have suffered from sexual abuse and racism. "You can't deal with the abuse and not the colonialism," she says of her work with Native American women. Healing, she adds, can often mean reconnecting to cultural pride.

Avila-Peilchman has talked to women of color "who've given up on working with white women." However, she doesn't fall into that category. "I don't think that all white women don't want to work with us. I can't think that. But how is it going to happen? When?"

These are questions the mainstream feminist movement must answer, and some are hopeful.

Trudeau observes, "There is new visioning. Maybe this happens at all different points but at this time, we're conscious of our history and of where we want to go. I think there's some back and forth, an internal dialogue that will hopefully take us to a better place."

 QUESTIONS FOR CRITICAL THINKING

Reading 64

1. Hernández and Leong point to the challenges in forming inclusive movements for social change in their discussion of the difficulties middle-class, white feminist movements have in fully recognizing the importance of the voices of women of color and low-income women. How do their experiences and observations impact your understanding of how to build effective social movements?

2. Hernández and Leong's article points to the importance of self-reflection in building effective social movements. What barriers do you see in your own ideas to building coalitions with those across racial, gender, class, and sexuality lines?

3. What are the conditions necessary for building effective coalitions in order to bring about positive social change?

Reading 65

VOICES OF A NEW MOVIMIENTO

ROBERTO LOVATO

Under cover of an oak tree on a tobacco farm deep in the heart of rural North Carolina, Leticia Zavala challenges the taller, older male migrant farm workers with talk of a boycott and *legalización*.

"We will not get anything without fighting for it," declares the intense 5-foot-1 organizer with the Farm Labor Organizing Committee (FLOC). Pen

Roberto Lovato, 2006, "Voices of a New Movimiento" from *The Nation*, June 19, 2006.

and notebook in hand, Zavala hacks swiftly through the fear and doubt that envelop many migrants. She speaks from a place, an experience, that most organizers in this country don't know: Her earliest childhood and adolescent memories are of migrating each year with her family between Mexico and Florida. "We have five buses and each of you has to decide for yourselves if you want to go to Washington with us," she says. After some deliberation most of the workers, many of whom have just finished the seven-day trek from Nayarit, Mexico, opt to get on another bus and join the May 1 *marcha* and boycott. They trust her, as do the more than 500 other migrant workers from across the state who heed the call from one of the new leaders of the *movimiento* that is upon us.

Asked why she thinks FLOC was so successful in mobilizing farm workers (the union made history after a stunning 2004 victory that secured representation and a contract for more than 10,000 H-2A "guest" workers who labor on strawberry, tobacco, yam, cucumber and other farms), Zavala talks about "the importance of networks" and the need to respond to the globalization of labor through the creation of a "migrating union." She and other FLOC organizers have followed migrant workers to Mexico, where the organization has an office—and then have followed them back over several months. She also points to the vision, strategies and tactics shared by her mentor, FLOC founder Baldemar Velásquez, who passed on to her the advice that Martin Luther King Jr. gave him during the Poor People's Campaign in 1967: "When you impact the rich man's ability to make money, anything is negotiable."

But when you ask her what is most important in the twenty-first-century matrix of successful organizing, the bespectacled, bright-eyed Zavala will bring you back to basics: "One of the biggest successes of the union is that it takes away loneliness."

The 26-year-old Zavala's vision, experience and learning are a telling reflection of how the leaders of the *movimiento* merge traditional labor and civil rights strategies and tactics with more global, networked—and personalized—organizing to meet the challenges of the quintessentially global issue of immigration. While it's important to situate the immigrant struggle within the context of the ongoing freedom struggles of African-Americans, women (like Zavala, an extraordinary number of *movimiento* leaders are *mujeres*) and others who have fought for social justice in the United States, labeling and framing it as a "new civil rights movement" risks erasing its roots in Latin American struggles and history.

The mainstream narrative of the movement emphasizes that single-minded immigrants want legalization—and how "angry Hispanics" and their Spanish-language radio DJ leaders mobilized in reaction to HR 4437 (better known as the Sensenbrenner immigration bill, which would criminalize the undocumented). But Zavala and other *movimiento* leaders across the country say that while it's true that the Sensenbrenner bill provided a spark, explaining this powerful movement of national and even global significance as a reaction to DJ-led calls to "*marchar!*" leaves many things—and people—out of the picture.

This time, there is no Martin Luther King or César Chávez centering and centralizing the movement. Instead, grassroots leaders like Zavala mix, scratch and dub different media (think MySpace.com and text messaging, radio and TV, butcher paper and bullhorns) while navigating the cultural, political and historical currents that yoke and inspire the diverse elements making up this young, decentralized, digital-age *movimiento*.

At the older end of the age and experience spectrum (the average Latino is 26) is 44-year-old Juan José Gutiérrez. He started organizing in the late 1970s, distributing mimeographed copies of the radical newspaper *Sin Fronteras* to immigrant workers in the face of hostility from the anti-Communist right. The director of Latino Movement USA and a key figure in the recent (and, to some, controversial) May 1 boycott, Gutiérrez has logged thousands of miles and met hundreds of leaders in his efforts to build one of many vibrant movement networks. "Since January, I've been to about thirty-five different cities and seen old and new leadership coming together to create something that has never been seen before," says Gutiérrez, who migrated to Los Angeles from Tuxpan, Jalisco, Mexico, when he was 11. "The [Spanish-language] DJs played a role, an important role, but they let us put our message in their medium. You can trace this movement all the way back to 1968."

Unlike the *movimiento* leaders who cut their teeth organizing in left-leaning Latin America, Gutiérrez traces his political roots to post-civil rights East LA; he and many of the most important Mexican and Chicano immigrant rights leaders in LA—including union leader Maria Elena Durazo, longtime activist Javier Rodriguez and LA Mayor Antonio Villaraigosa—came out of the Centro de Acción Social Autónomo (Center for Autonomous Social Action), or CASA, a seminal Chicano political organization founded by legendary leaders Bert Corona and Soledad "Chole" Alatorre in 1968. One of the central tasks of CASA, which from its inception had a strong working-class and trade union orientation, was organizing undocumented workers. Gutiérrez and others who have covered the country spiderlike for years see a direct line from the organizing around the amnesty law of 1986, which legalized 3 million undocumented workers, to immigrant rights organizing in California (home to one of every three immigrants in the United States), the fight against Proposition 187 of 1994 (which tried to deny health and education benefits to the children of the undocumented) and the historic shift of the AFL-CIO in 2000, when it decided to undertake immigrant organizing.

Having hopped back and forth among many of the more than 200 cities and towns that staged actions in April and May, Gutiérrez sees different kinds of leaders emerging from the grassroots: "There are, of course, the undocumented, who are also leading things in local communities; there are legal immigrants getting involved, because they have friends and family who are affected by the anti-immigrant policies; and there are immigrants from different countries who bring their own political, sometimes radical, experiences from places like Guatemala and El Salvador."

One of the "radical" legacies that New York immigrant rights leader Miguel Ramírez has carried with him since fleeing El Salvador is an intensely collective outlook on personal and political identity. Ramírez, who heads the Queens-based Centro Hispano Cuzcatlán, recalls how one of his US-born colleagues told him to "correct" the résumé he used to apply for his first organizing job in New York. "He [the friend] told me I had to take out the 'we,'" says 53-year-old Ramírez, whose bushy mustache often lifts to reveal a disarming smile. "I didn't know it was wrong to write, 'We organized a forum, we organized a workshop, we organized a network.'"

The experience and approach of Ramírez, who left his homeland in 1979 after many of his fellow students at the University of El Salvador were persecuted and killed, show that the US *movimiento* is as much the northernmost expression of a resurgent Latin American left as it is a new, more globalized, human rights–centered continuation of the Chicano, civil rights and other previous struggles that facilitated immigrant rights work here.

Ramírez, who estimates that since migrating he's helped organize more than 100 marches—all of them "very disciplined and without incidents"—is informed by the experience of organizing students, campesinos and others in revolutionary El Salvador, where one of every three Salvadorans adopted radicalized politics during the war. Lacking the wealth and pro-US government politics of Cuban-Americans and other, more conservative immigrant groups, Ramírez and many Salvadoran immigrants (most of whom were denied legal status and benefits granted to Cubans, Vietnamese and others) created organizations that then formed vast multi-issue, mass-based networks challenging the foreign and domestic policies of the most powerful country on earth.

This robust legacy energizes Ramírez and Centro Hispano Cuzcatlán, which organizes around worker rights, housing and immigration, as they play definitive roles in the construction of local networks like the Immigrant Communities in Action coalition. Through the coalition, Centro joined Indian, Pakistani, Korean, Filipino, Bangladeshi, Indonesian and other groups that have organized some of the country's most diverse marches.

Reflecting the historic and ongoing tensions between more election- and legislative-focused immigrant rights advocates in Washington and local and regional players, Ramírez, like the younger Zavala, calmly insists the *movimiento* must look beyond the upcoming elections and even the pending immigration bill. "In the end, it's an issue of power, one that can only be addressed by constant organizing."

US-born Latinos also feel Ramírez's urgency about organizing around immigration. Their ranks include teens and twentysomethings relatively new to politics, along with veterans like Wisconsin's Christine Neumann-Ortiz, who was influenced by several Latin American movements as well as the struggle against California's Proposition 187.

"To see those thousands of people marching against Prop 187 was an inspiration," says Ortiz, who heads Voces de la Frontera, an immigrant worker center in the belly of the anti-immigrant beast, James Sensenbrenner's Milwaukee. "I was very impressed that there was that kind of response [to Prop 187]. We used that as a lesson," says Ortiz, who was one of the main organizers of marches of 30,000 and 70,000 people, some of the largest marches ever in a state with a storied progressive past.

Ortiz was not caught off guard by the *movimiento*. "I'm happy to be alive to see this shift," she states from one of Voces's three offices in Wisconsin, "but I'm not at all surprised. We've been building up networks of people over many years."

She and other activists point to years of service and advocacy on behalf of immigrants, which built up good will and trust in the community, as being defining factors in the ability to rally people into political action.

Founded in Austin, Texas, with a mission to build solidarity between US and Mexican maquiladora workers following the signing of the NAFTA accords in nearby San Antonio in 1994, Voces de la Frontera embodies a local-global sensibility. Ortiz started the Milwaukee Voces in November 2001 in response to the growing needs of Milwaukee's fast-growing Latino immigrant population. Like the settlement houses and mutual aid societies and other organizations that supported German and other white European immigrant workers of previous, more progressive eras in Wisconsin and elsewhere, Voces provides a critical support structure for the mostly Mexican and Central American workers in the agricultural, hotel and restaurant, construction and manufacturing industries in HR 4437 country.

Sensenbrenner "wants to leave a legacy. So did McCarthy. Immigrants in Wisconsin know his hypocrisy better than anyone," says Ortiz, whose German and Mexican immigrant heritage portends the not-so-distant future of once wholly white Wisconsin. "He is encroaching on his own base. Dairy farmers in his own district are revolting because he's attacking their economic base. This can't last in the long term," she says, as if eyeing developments in post-Prop 187 California, where short-term anti-immigrant backlash led to a longer-term movement that gave Los Angeles its first Latino (and progressive) mayor—and gave the *movimiento* a vision of its potential.

Like organizers in Los Angeles, Chicago and other cities, Ortiz and Voces have built strong and deep relationships with the local Spanish-language media. But they're also keenly aware of who's leading the charge. "We had lists of more than 4,000 workers before the radio stations or Sensenbrenner came into the picture," Ortiz explains.

As they continue to organize and lobby around the immigration debate in Congress, around the inevitable backlash at the local and state levels and around a more proactive agenda, Ortiz and many of the other leaders of the immigrant rights movement are keeping their eyes on a larger prize, beyond the issue of immigration. "We're going to change this country," she says, adding, "We've gained public sympathy for immigrants. We've gained recognition and power, and we are an inspiration to the larger movement for change." She is especially motivated when she describes the effect of the *movimiento* on the generations to come. Like the "Hmong students who went to a Sensenbrenner town hall meeting in South Alice [a Milwaukee suburb] and chanted 'Si se puede, Si se puede' at him." Asked if the backlash will damage the *movimiento*, Ortiz responds, "In the long run this will make us stronger and build our movement."

 QUESTIONS FOR CRITICAL THINKING

Reading 65

1. Lovato discusses the reasons why it is important to organize for change beyond electoral politics. Why does he think this is so important?

2. As is often said, the United States is made up predominantly of immigrants and their descendants. In what ways are recent immigrants treated in similar ways to those of the past? In what ways are they treated differently? What do you think needs to occur in order to provide more access to equal opportunity for recent waves of immigrants?

3. After reading this text, what do you see as important issues of social inequality? What are you willing to do to address these issues?